# The BVR/AHLA Guide to Healthcare Valuation

## Third Edition

Mark O. Dietrich, CPA/ABV
Editor

BVR
What It's Worth
1000 SW Broadway, Suite 1200, Portland OR 97205
(503) 291-7963 • www.bvresources.com

BVR
What It's Worth


Second printing, 2012
Printed in the United States of America.



Publisher: Sarah Andersen

Managing Editor: Janice Prescott

Chair and CEO: David Foster

President: Lucretia Lyons

Vice President of Sales: Lexie Gross

Customer Service Manager: Jasmine Pearsall

ISBN: 978-1-935081-97-5

Library of Congress Control Number: 2012935628

# Table of Contents

# Introduction

The third edition of the BVR/AHLA *Guide to Healthcare Valuation* brings together again the country's top healthcare industry experts in an expansion of the second edition's comprehensive undertaking aimed at providing both preparers and users of valuation reports with an in-depth understanding of individual industry subsectors. The *Guide* has been reorganized into major knowledge segments: the healthcare marketplace, regulatory considerations in healthcare valuation, physician practices, physician services and hospital relationships, and other healthcare enterprises and includes 12 new chapters—five devoted to the first comprehensive approach to compensation valuation—and 14 revised and updated chapters.

The 2010 Federal Healthcare Reform legislation, or PPACA, contributes to the quandary faced in healthcare valuation as appraisers, attorneys, and industry members probe the plethora of new regulations implementing the reform for knowledge and speculate on what yet-to-be-issued regulations will say. Even as the PPACA seeks to impose uniform insurance regulations across an industry characterized by the uniqueness of regional and local markets, the *Guide*'s opening segment includes a detailed analysis of healthcare markets, updated to reflect the increasing recognition in the trade press and general media of the role that local market forces play.

Despite the significance of national trends and the federal Medicare program in the valuation of healthcare enterprises, these local differences in provider reimbursement by health insurers and individual state Medicaid programs lead to significant differences in operating results and value. A chapter devoted to the unique challenges that local markets present to appraisers in assessing cost of capital and forecasting cashflow is included.

Each member of the panel of valuation experts provides guidance consistent with the mandatory regulatory constraints on valuation assumptions and methodologies in the healthcare industry. Specific risks under the Stark law and anti-kickback statute are addressed in a separate chapter, along with *real* advice on how to deal with them in a valuation engagement. The import of the nonprofit hospital sector is addressed in another chapter on inurement and tax exemption issues. The risks associated with valuation engagements in a unique practice area are examined in a new chapter on the *Bradford Regional* case, including some suggestions on the choice of valuation model assumptions where the parties are in a position to refer to one another. A detailed analysis of the unwarranted abuse of the cost approach in valuing goodwill and other intangible assets written by a number of leading experts rounds out the regulatory discussion.

Notably, each of the valuation chapters provides keen insights on the significance of understanding the revenue cycle. The manner in which healthcare providers—such as physicians, hospitals, imaging, or ambulatory surgery centers—are paid or reimbursed for their services varies radically. As such, an assumption about inflation or growth in per-unit reimbursement appropriate for one of these sectors may be wholly inappropriate for another.

The most significant additions to the third edition are five chapters totaling 65,000 words representing the first comprehensive application of the general principles of business valuation to compensation valuation. With the present trend of increasing physician employment by hospitals and health systems, compensation valuation is becoming the most important focus of the valuation community. These five chapters cover the economics of physician practices along with the income, market and cost approaches to value.

The largest number of provider entities and the most frequent valuation engagement remains physician practices, and the *Guide* reflects this. In addition to a new chapter on physician buy-ins and buyouts and a revised and updated chapter on valuation methods for physicians, the *Guide* includes chapters on personal and enterprise goodwill and noncompete agreements, how to analyze current procedural technology (CPT) codes, damages, and the use of Medical Group Management Association (MGMA) data. Two chapters address the tax aspects of transactions, which can have a significant effect on the manner in which a valuation method is approached. Where a medical practice valuation is the most common form of healthcare valuation, the most common reason for that valuation is a divorce. Two chapters on the unique issues of divorce valuation are also included.

Physician business relationships with hospitals and other provider entities are perhaps the major driving force in the healthcare industry today, and the *Guide* devotes seven separate chapters to valuation engagements in this critical market segment, including a new chapter on whole-hospital co-management agreements. I am certain the heretofore unseen scale of these comprehensive works will stand as a major contribution to the healthcare community's body of knowledge.

The *Guide's* final segment contains chapters on the valuation of imaging centers, ambulatory surgery centers, dialysis centers, hospitals, home health agencies, and a new chapter on valuation issues associated with accountable care organizations.

As editor and technical editor for this third edition of the *Guide* and on behalf of the American Health Lawyers Association and Business Valuation Resources, our thanks to all of the contributors for their hard work on behalf of their colleagues, who we are certain, will find the *Guide to Healthcare Valuation* an important and valuable addition to their professional library.

Mark O. Dietrich
CPA/ABV

# About the Authors

## ABOUT THE EDITOR

**Mark O. Dietrich, CPA/ABV,** is editor, technical editor, and contributing author to the Business Valuation Resources/American Health Lawyers' Association *Guide to Healthcare Valuation 3rd Edition* (2012), editor and principal author of Business Valuation Resources' *Guide to Physician Practice Valuation* (2nd Edition, due in 2012), and co-author with Gregory Anderson, CPA, CVA, of *The Financial Professional's Guide to Healthcare Reform* to be published by John Wiley & Sons in 2012. Mark is also author of the *Medical Practice Valuation Guidebook* and co-author of PPC's *Guide to Healthcare Consulting*, along with more than 100 articles on valuation, taxation, managed care, and the healthcare regulatory environment. Mark's career experience includes serving as partner-in-charge of the annual audit of an 80 physician tax-exempt faculty group practice, representation of tax-exempt and taxable entities in Internal Revenue Service field audits, participation in the development of a 250-physician independent network and negotiation of its managed care and Medicare Advantage contracts, and more than 200 valuation engagements in the healthcare industry.

A regular speaker at national conferences on healthcare valuation and other topics, Mark also lectured in the United Kingdom during 2009 and 2011 on managed care, healthcare valuation, and valuation of medical practices to Her Majesty's Revenue and Customs and has been invited to Scotland and Northern Ireland in 2012. He is a member of the editorial board of *Financial Valuation and Litigation Expert* and the AICPA's National Healthcare Industry Conference Committee and will chair that conference in 2012. Mark has also served on the AICPA's ABV Credential Committee and ABV Exam Review Course Task Force.

## CONTRIBUTING AUTHORS

**Gregory D. Anderson, CPA/ABV, CVA,** is a partner in the Health Care Practice Group of HORNE LLP, a CPA and business advisory firm headquartered in the southeastern United States. He concentrates his practice in the design and valuation of hospital-physician employment and other compensation arrangements; income distribution plans of physician group practices; and valuation of medical practices, hospitals, and other healthcare facilities. He serves as the firm's healthcare valuation services director and writes and lectures on fair market value, physician compensation, and Stark lawmatters.

**Steven Andes, Ph.D., CPA** is the American Osteopathic Association's director of physician information and professor and research assistant at the University of Illinois at Chicago. He attended University of Illinois at Urbana-Champaign, DePaul University, and Loyola University of Chicago.

**G. Don Barbo, CPA/ABV** is a director with Deloitte Financial Advisory Services LLP in the Life Science & Health Care industry team. Don has extensive experience in healthcare valuation engagements involving mergers and acquisitions, divestitures, partnership transactions, leasing arrangements, divorces, and commercial damages. His healthcare valuation experience includes hospitals, ambulatory surgery centers, imaging centers, cardiac catheter centers, and physician practices. He has also served as the chief financial officer for a physician practice management company. Don has published numerous articles and is a frequent speaker regarding the valuation of healthcare businesses. He also serves on the Panel of Experts for the Healthcare Section of the Financial Valuation and Litigation Expert's newsletter. He holds an undergraduate degree in accounting from Texas Tech University and an MBA from the SMU Cox School of Business.

**Randy A. Biernat, CPA/ABV/CFF,** is a senior managing consultant at BKD CPAs & Advisors in Indianapolis. Randy's background includes providing business valuations, fair market value analyses, and general consulting services for a wide variety of healthcare clients. He has significant experience in performing healthcare appraisals and fair market value analyses in nearly all segments of the healthcare services industry. Randy graduated with highest distinction from the Kelley School of Business at Indiana University-Purdue University Indianapolis with a Bachelor of Science degree in finance. He also completed his Master of Professional Accountancy from the Kelley School of Business at IUPUI. Randy holds the designations of certified public accountant, accredited in business saluation, and certified in financial forensics. Randy is a member of the American Institute of Certified Public Accountants (AICPA), the Healthcare Financial Management Association, the Business Valuation, Forensic, and Litigation Support Section of the AICPA, and the Indiana CPA Society.

**Ann S. Brandt, Ph.D.**, is a partner at Healthcare Appraisers Inc. Dr. Brandt specializes in valuing compensation arrangements that may have Stark and anti-kickback implications. Working primarily with hospitals, pharmaceutical companies, and medical device companies, Dr. Brandt leads the firm's life sciences service line. She has specific expertise in valuing thought leader compensation and data acquisition arrangements as well as clinical trials and principal investigator compensation. In addition, she has extensive experience in providing valuation and consulting services related to co-management and physician management arrangements. Dr. Brandt has more than 25 years of healthcare experience as a clinician, consultant, strategist, marketer, and professor. Prior to joining HealthCare Appraisers, she served as a senior consultant specializing in healthcare information technology and process redesign at a *Fortune* 15 technology and consulting company. She has extensive experience in physician-hospital partnerships as well as in operational restructuring, information management, and clinical transformation. In addition, she has owned and operated several healthcare-related businesses.

**Mark Browne, M.D.,** is a partner and consulting principal in the healthcare consulting group of Pershing Yoakley & Associates and has 12 years of physician executive experience and expertise. He is a national speaker on topics such as quality and healthcare reform with a focus on preparing for a value-based model of healthcare delivery. Dr. Browne is clinically trained as a primary care physician in both internal medicine and pediatrics. He is a graduate of Ohio University, obtained his doctorate of medicine from Wright State University School of Medicine and holds a Master's of Medical Management from Carnegie Mellon University.

**Carol W. Carden, CPA/ABV, ASA, CFE,** is a principal with PYA and provides business valuation and related consulting services to a wide variety of business organizations, primarily in the healthcare industry. Ms. Carden's primary areas of expertise are in finance, valuation, managed care, and revenue cycle operations for healthcare organizations. She has performed appraisals of businesses and securities for a wide variety of purposes such as mergers, acquisitions, joint ventures, management service agreements, and other intangible assets. She is also a nationally recognized speaker and writer on healthcare valuation topics. She is the chair of the Business Valuation Committee for the AICPA, was chair of the 2010 National AICPA Business Valuation Conference, and was on the planning committee for the 2011 AICPA National Healthcare Conference.

**Frank Cohen, CMPA** is principal and senior analyst for The Frank Cohen Group, LLC and a certified Master Black Belt in Lean Six Sigma. As a consultant and researcher, his areas of expertise include data mining, predictive analytics, applied statistics, process improvement, and evidence-based decision support. Mr. Cohen is the author of several books, including his newest, *Lean Six Sigma for the Medical Practice: Improving Profits by Improving Processes*. He has participated in and published numerous articles and studies and trained thousands of physicians, administrators, CPAs, and other healthcare professionals in all areas of healthcare analytics. He spent eight years as a physician assistant in the Navy and as a civilian, as well as a clinic administrator and hospital CEO. His clients include hospitals, medical practices, medical associations, legal and accounting professionals, government agencies, and other healthcare professionals.

**Edward J. Dupke, CPA/ABV,** is a senior consultant at Clifton Larson Allen LLP, based in the firm's Phoenix office. He is active in the firm's business valuation and forensic services. Mr. Dupke is a former chairman of the AICPA Business Valuation Committee and a past chairman of the Michigan Association of CPAs. Ed has over 35 years of professional experience in public accounting and business valuation practice, has been qualified as an expert witness in both state and federal courts and is a regular instructor in business valuation at both the state and national level. He is a co-author of *Financial Valuation: Applications and Models* (Hitchner) John Wiley & Sons, New York, 2003. Mr. Dupke is a past member of the AICPA Board of Directors and chair of its Strategic Planning Committee. He is a past member of the AICPA Forensic and Litigation Committee and chairs the AICPA task force writing business valuation standards for CPAs.

**J. Gregory Endicott, CPA/ABV, ASA, MBA,** is the managing director of Strategic Value Group LLC, a firm that provides business valuation and related consulting services primarily in the areas of healthcare and financial reporting. Mr. Endicott's primary areas of expertise are in valuations for transactional, compliance, and financial reporting purposes. He has performed appraisals of businesses, intangible assets, compensation arrangements, and other agreements for a variety of purposes and is a nationally recognized speaker.

**David Fein, MBA,** is the CEO and president of ValuSource, which for over 20 years has been the leading provider of business valuation software, data and report writers for CPAs, mergers and acquisitions professionals, and business owners. Since 1997, Mr. Fein has partnered with the Medical Group Management Association (MGMA) to develop its interactive survey CD-ROMs, which provide data and benchmarking tools on physicians' compensation, business costs, and coding practices. ValuSource has crucial technology and data for anyone that needs to benchmark or value a medical practice.

**Gregory S. Feltenberger, MBA, CACMPE, FACHE, CPHIMS,** has over 16 years of operational health care experience. He is the chief of information project management at the Office of the Air Force Surgeon General, Air Force Medical Support Agency, Decision Support Branch, in Falls Church, Va. Greg has been a chief information officer, chief of information management, and group practice manager. In addition, Greg completed a 10-month fellowship in survey development, analysis, and performance measurement at the MGMA. He is a Ph.D. student at Old Dominion University in the health services research program. He is a fellow in the American College of Medical Practice Executives (ACMPE), the standard-setting and certification body of the MGMA; a fellow in the American College of Healthcare Executives; a certified medical practice executive in the American College of Medical Practice Executives; and a certified professional in healthcare information and management systems in the Healthcare Information and Management Systems Society. Greg is principal and co-founder of SmHart Inc. (www.SmHart.net), an education, training, and organizational improvement consulting firm. Finally, Greg co-authored a book titled, *Benchmarking Success: The Essential Guide for Medical Practices* with David N. Gans, published by the MGMA in 2008.

**Andrea M. Ferrari, JD, MPH,** is a senior associate at HealthCare Appraisers. She has experience structuring, negotiating, reviewing, and executing many types of healthcare transactions, including mergers and acquisitions, hospital-physician joint ventures, physician recruitment arrangements, compensated on-call coverage arrangements, physician employment arrangements, medical director and physician consulting arrangements, clinical trial and research sponsorship agreements, and billing and other service arrangements. Ms. Ferrari is a member of the Florida Bar and is a Florida-licensed healthcare risk manager. She received a JD with a certificate of concentration in health law from Boston University School of Law and a Master of Public Health degree with a concentration in Health Law from Boston University School of Medicine/Public Health. She received her Bachelor's degree (economics) from Smith College.

**Ronald D. Finkelstein, CPA/ABV,** is a principal in the accounting and tax services department at Morrison, Brown, Argiz & Farra LLC (MBAF), where he directs the firm's Health Care Services Group. Ron has extensive experience in assisting healthcare providers with merger and acquisition transactions. Ron has been a frequent lecturer both locally and nationally on a wide variety of healthcare accounting and practice management topics. Clients include ambulatory surgery centers, imaging centers, anatomic and clinical laboratories, health maintenance organizations, home health providers, hospitals, and physician group practices. A contributing editor to the quarterly publication *Practice Management Advisor,* Ron is a former member of the Steering Committee of the AICPA National Healthcare Industry Conference and past president of the National CPA Health Care Advisor's Association. In addition, Ron is a member of the Healthcare Financial Management Association, the MGMA, and the American Health Lawyers Association.

**David N. Gans, MSHA, FACMPE,** administers research and development at MGMA-ACMPE and its research affiliate, the MGMA Center for Research in Englewood, Col. He is an educational program speaker, author of a monthly column in *MGMA Connexion,* and he provides technical assistance to the association's staff and members on topic areas of benchmarking, use of survey data, financial management, cost-efficiency, physician compensation and productivity, managerial compensation, the resource-based relative value scale, employee staffing, cost accounting, medical group organization, and emergency preparedness. He is a retired colonel in the United States Army Reserve. He is a fellow in the American College of Medical Practice Executives and a certified medical practice executive in the American College of Medical Practice Executives.

**Lydia M. Glatz, CPA,** is a senior manager at Morrison, Brown, Argiz & Farra LLC (MBAF). She focuses on providing tax, accounting, and consulting services to clients in the healthcare industry. Her experience in the healthcare due diligence area has helped numerous buyers and sellers reach successful M&A transactions. Her clients include ambulatory surgery centers, physician practice management companies, and physician group practices in the primary care; ear, nose and throat; obstetrics and gynecology; radiology; and anesthesia specialties. Lydia has written several articles on issues affecting physicians and the healthcare industry. She is past president of the Broward chapter of the Florida Institute of Certified Public Accountants and has a B.S. in accounting from Florida Atlantic University.

**Alice G. Gosfield, Esq.,** is the principal of Alice G. Gosfield & Associates, P.C. in Philadelphia. Her legal career has been restricted to health law with an emphasis on representation of physicians and their group configurations and a focus on noninstitutional reimbursement including Medicare, managed care, fraud and abuse compliance and avoidance, medical staff issues and utilization management, and quality issues. Ms.

Gosfield served as chairman of the board of directors of the National Committee for Quality Assurance and on four committees of the Institute of Medicine of the National Academy of Sciences. She is the first chairman of the board of PROMETHEUS Payment Inc. and served as president of the American Health Lawyers Association and chaired its Physician and Physician Organizations Institute. She is a graduate of Barnard College and New York University School of Law.

**Matthew D. Jenkins, JD,** is a partner in the Richmond, Va., office of Hunton & Williams LLP and heads the firm's Health Law Group. He has worked extensively with hospitals and multihospital systems on regulatory, corporate, governance, and transactional matters. He has led a number of nonprofit entities through conversion transactions resulting in the creation of substantial community foundations. His work also involves legislative matters and practice before administrative agencies. Mr. Jenkins is a member of the American Bar Association's Health Law Section, where he serves as a vice-chair of the Transactional & Business Interest Group. He served two terms as a governor's appointee on the Special Advisory Commission on Mandated Health Insurance Benefits for the Commonwealth of Virginia. He is a past chair of the Health Law Section of the Virginia State Bar. Mr. Jenkins earned his J.D. in 1984 from the University of Virginia.

**Tracy Farryl Katz, Esq., CPA,** is a partner at Gursey Schneider LLP in the firm's Litigation Support Department, specializing in the area of forensic accounting in family law and civil litigation matters. She has performed a wide range of litigation accounting services including: business appraisals, determination of gross cash flow available for support, determination of celebrity goodwill, net spendable evaluations, pension plan allocations, stock option apportionments, characterization of assets, analysis of reimbursement claims, lifestyle analyses, and contract and royalty analyses in the film, television, and music industries. She graduated from the Southwestern School of Law in Los Angeles.

**W. James Lloyd, CPA/ABV, ASA, CBA, CFE,** is a senior member of the valuation, transaction advisory, and litigation consulting practice of Pershing Yoakley & Associates P.C. (PYA), a certified public accounting and healthcare consulting firm based in Knoxville, Tenn. Mr. Lloyd provides business valuation, fair market value compensation, economic damages analysis, and related consulting services to a wide range of business organizations, primarily in the healthcare industry. Mr. Lloyd has valued hundreds of healthcare organizations, intangible assets, and various economic relationships between hospitals and physicians. Mr. Lloyd is the chair of the AICPA's ABV Credential Committee and is a frequent speaker at various national and regional conferences.

**David McMillan, CPA,** is a principal in the healthcare consulting group of Pershing Yoakley & Associates. His areas of concentration are: feasibility studies for various healthcare entities; certificate of need preparation, support, and litigation; mergers and acquisitions support; strategic planning and forecasting; debt financings; valuations; and operational analysis. David is a 1992 honors graduate of the University of Tennessee

Knoxville with a Bachelor of Science degree in Business Administration and is licensed as a certified public accountant.

**Robert M. Mundy, CPA, ABV, CVA,** has a broad background in business valuations with extensive experience in healthcare valuation engagements involving mergers and acquisitions, financial reporting, joint ventures, divestitures, partnership transactions, leasing arrangements, and divorce settlements. His healthcare valuation experience includes general acute care and specialty hospitals, diagnostic imaging centers, ambulatory surgery centers, skilled nursing facilities, assisted living centers, cancer treatment centers, cardiac catheter labs, and a variety of physician practices. He has also held business valuation and auditing positions at a regional public accounting firm.

**Kenneth W. Patton, ASA,** works with Mercer Capital, a business valuation and investment banking firm, on a project-by-project basis, after retiring as president of the company in 2009. He provides valuation and corporate advisory services for estate and gift tax planning and compliance matters, employee stock ownership plans, profit sharing plans, limited and general partnerships, mergers and acquisitions, corporate planning and reorganizations. He has a bachelor's degree in economics from the University of Tennessee and a master's degree in finance from Rhodes College.

**James M. Pinna, Esq.,** is an attorney in the Richmond, Va., office of Hunton & Williams LLP and practices with the firm's Health Law Group. He works primarily with hospitals, multihospital systems, and other healthcare providers on regulatory, transactional, corporate governance, and compliance matters. He is a vice chair of the Business & Transactions Interest Group of the American Bar Association's Health Law Section and a member of the American Health Lawyers Association. Previously, he worked in business development for National Nephrology Associates, a privately held dialysis company based in Nashville. Mr. Pinna earned his J.D. from the University of Virginia.

**Robert F. Reilly, MBA, CPA, CMA, CFA, ASA, CBA,** is a managing director of Willamette Management Associates. Robert has been the principal analyst on over 2,000 valuations of businesses, business interests, and intellectual properties in virtually every industry and business sector. Robert holds an MBA in finance from Columbia University. He is a member of the American Economic Association, National Association of Business Economists, American Society of Appraisers, Institute of Business Appraisers, American Bankruptcy Institute, Institute of Property Taxation, and several other professional organizations. He is co-author of the following six textbooks: *Valuing a Business: The Analysis and Appraisal of Closely Held Companies, The Handbook of Advanced Business Valuation, Valuing Intangible Assets, Valuing Small Businesses and Professional Practices, Valuing Accounting Practices,* and *Valuing Professional Practices: A Practitioners Approach.*

**Jason Ruchaber, CFA, ASA,** is a partner with HealthCare Appraisers and head of business valuation services in the Colorado office. Mr. Ruchaber has more than 14 years of finance and valuation experience, the last 11 of which have been spent exclusively in business valuation and litigation consulting. Prior to joining HealthCare Appraisers, Mr. Ruchaber was a principal in Cogence Group P.C., a business valuation and litigation support firm located in Portland, Ore. Mr. Ruchaber has also worked in Standard & Poor's Corporate Value Consulting practice, where he focused on intellectual property valuation and damages calculations. Mr. Ruchaber is a member of the CFA Institute, the Denver Society of Financial Analysts, the American Society of Appraisers, and the Licensing Executives Society International. Mr. Ruchaber is a frequent speaker and author on healthcare valuation topics.

**Scott Safriet, AVA, MBA,** is a partner at HealthCare Appraisers. He has almost 20 years of broad healthcare experience, the last six of which have been focused exclusively on healthcare valuation, primarily addressing any type of agreement or compensation arrangement that may have Stark and anti-kickback implications. Mr. Safriet is a frequent speaker and writer on healthcare valuation topics.

**Alan B. Simons, CPA/ABV, CFF, CMPE, DABFA,** is the principal-in-charge of LarsonAllen's national health care valuation practice and the business valuation and litigation support practice for the Philadelphia office. He is an active member of the Healthcare Financial Management Association (HFMA), the Medical Group Management Association (MGMA), the American Health Lawyers Association (AHLA), the American Society of Appraisers (ASA candidate), the Institute of Business Appraisers (IBA), the American Institute of Certified Public Accountants (AICPA), the Pennsylvania Institute of Certified Public Accountants (PICPA), and the Forensic and Valuation Services Division of the AICPA.

**Douglas G. Smith** is managing partner, Barrington Lakes Group LLC, a consulting firm specializing in the diagnostic imaging sector. Barrington Lakes Group provides consulting services to radiology group practices, imaging centers, and hospitals and health systems. Smith is a frequent speaker on a variety of topics for the diagnostic imaging services sector.

**Timothy R. Smith, CPA/ABV,** is the president of Touchstone Valuation LLC, a valuation consulting firm specializing in the healthcare industry. Tim has over 17 years of experience in the industry, including 14 years at Hospital Corporation of America (HCA). At HCA, he performed regulatory compliance reviews on hundreds of third-party appraisals for acquisitions and divestitures, leasing agreements, service contracts, and other forms of compensation arrangements. Tim also developed HCA's requirements for the engagement and use of business and compensation valuation firms. His HCA experience included contractual negotiations and due diligence for hundreds of physician practice acquisitions and divestitures. Following his HCA tenure, Tim worked for over three years with HealthCare Appraisers Inc., where he specialized in employment agreement valuations and served as director of professional practice.

**Todd J. Sorensen, MBA, AVA,** is a partner with VMG Health. He specializes in providing valuation and transaction advisory services to the firm's healthcare clients. He has acted as financial advisor in transactions with physician groups, acute care hospitals, health maintenance organizations, preferred provider organizations, diagnostic centers, ambulatory surgery centers, home health agencies, physical and operational therapy centers, institutional pharmacies, retail pharmacies and rural health clinics. Mr. Sorensen received his MBA from Baylor University.

**Burl Stamp, FACHE,** is a principal in the healthcare consulting group of Pershing Yoakley & Associates and the president of PYA|Stamp, an affiliate company that specializes in performance improvement for hospitals, physicians, and health systems. Burl's expertise spans both strategic and operational disciplines within health care. He is the author of *The Healing Art of Communication,* a healthcare professional's guidebook to improving communication. He is a graduate of Washington University in St. Louis—Olin Business School and Southeast Missouri State University.

**Reed Tinsley, CPA, CVA, CFP, CHBC,** is the owner of Reed Tinsley, CPA. He is a certified valuation analyst and certified healthcare business consultant. Reed has published numerous articles in national and regional publications and is frequently asked to speak on a variety of health care topics, including valuation, operational management, revenue enhancement, and financial oversight. He has also written *Medical Practice Management Handbook for CPAs,* originally published by Harcourt Brace. He attended the University of Texas at Austin and the University of Texas at Austin—The Red McCombs School of Business.

**Stacey D. Udell, CPA/ABV/CFF, ASA, CVA,** a partner in the public accounting firm of Gold Gocial Gerstein LLC. Ms. Udell specializes in business valuation, forensic accounting, economic damages, and litigation support for a wide range of businesses and professional practices for purposes such as estate and gift tax planning and compliance, divorce, business succession planning, mergers and acquisitions, shareholder litigation, and bankruptcy proceedings. Ms. Udell is a contributing author to the *Family Law Services Handbook,* published by John Wiley & Sons.

**Kathie L. Wilson, CPA, CVA,** maintains a consulting practice, assisting accountants and attorneys in the areas of medical practice accounting and valuation and family law litigation in the San Francisco Bay Area. She holds a Masters in Taxation from Bentley College and a B.A. in business administration from the University of Washington.

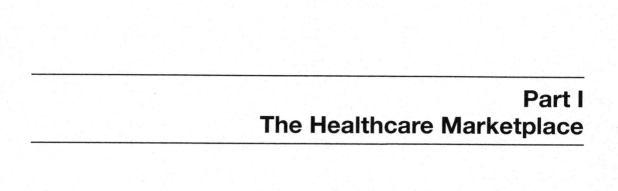

# Part I
# The Healthcare Marketplace

Chapter 1

# Is the New Healthcare Act Really a 'Reform'?

*By Mark O. Dietrich, CPA/ABV*

The extent of the "reform" included in the Patient Protection and Affordable Care Act of 2010 (PPACA) remains a matter for debate. The legislation does contain some elements of reform, particularly in terms of basic terms and benefits that a health insurance policy must contain, although in December 2011 the Department of Health and Human Services (DHHS) to a large extent ceded to the individual states the particulars of what benefits were to be included. The legislative language proposing to compensate providers, in part, on the basis of quality and *not* to compensate them for errors in care might also be seen as "reform" if it is not subsequently repealed or weakened. That said, much of the legislation reflects the traditional lobbying clout, or lack thereof, of various segments of the industry and leaves in doubt what reforms will ultimately be realized and, more importantly, what the effect of that realization will be.

From a standpoint of the valuation of healthcare enterprises, reform suggests the following financial factors:

1. Consolidation.
2. Higher volumes at lower rates.
3. Higher emphasis on payment for quality.
4. Lower volume providers will be at risk.
5. Cost shifts from older and sicker to younger and healthier.
6. Cost shifts to small business.

7. Cost shifts to the individual from his or her health insurance.

8. Increasing demand and cost for primary care and risk of severe physician shortages.

9. Expansion of midlevel providers: nurse practitioners and physician assistants.

10. Heightened uncertainty, particularly for small business and employers with 50 employees or more that are facing the play or pay penalty.

The following is a brief overview of where we were before the changes, followed by a summary of the significant elements of the legislation.

### A Brief Overview of the Healthcare Insurance Industry

Health insurance is a low-margin business when viewed over the time period known as the underwriting cycle. As in the business cycle for any industry, health insurance companies will experience periods of high profits, low profits, and outright losses. During loss periods, insurers tend to shed unprofitable lines of business, which often include the sick and dying or those businesses that employ disproportionate numbers of such individuals. During profitable periods, risk taking tends to increase, and expansion of market share is sought, often resulting in marginal new business. Exhibit 1 below illustrates the historical underwriting cycle and the periods of earnings before interest and taxes.[1] Interestingly, managed care companies tend to do well during weaker economic growth.

During the profitable period of the underwriting cycle, insurers also earn investment returns on their cash reserves, further enhancing profitability; during down periods, the lack of investment returns exacerbates losses.

### Medicare National Coverage Determinations (NCDs)

Medicare has been and will remain the most important program in the healthcare delivery system. A critical feature of both the pre-reform and post-reform healthcare system is Medicare's national coverage determinations:

> An NCD sets forth the extent to which Medicare will cover specific services, procedures, or technologies on a national basis. Medicare contractors are required to follow NCDs. If an NCD does not specifically exclude/limit an indication or circumstance

1 Data source: Health Care-Managed Care, Jan. 7, 2010, Barclays Capital.

**Exhibit 1. Historical Underwriting Cycle**

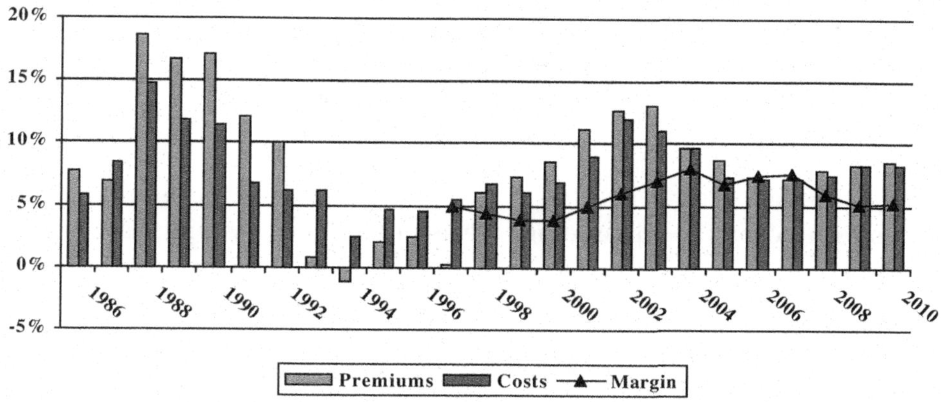


> or the item or service is not mentioned at all in an NCD or in a Medicare manual, it is up to the Medicare contractor to make the coverage decision (see LMRP). Prior to an NCD taking effect, CMS must first issue a manual transmittal, CMS ruling, or *Federal Register* notice giving specific directions to our claims-processing contractors. That issuance, which includes an effective date and implementation date, is the NCD. If appropriate, the agency must also change billing and claims processing systems and issue related instructions to allow for payment. The NCD will be published in the *Medicare National Coverage Determinations Manual.* An NCD becomes effective as of the date listed in the transmittal that announces the manual revision.[2]

In English, this means the Centers for Medicare and Medicaid Services (CMS) determines what is and is not covered by Medicare. That, of course, has a dramatic impact on what type of care and services Medicare beneficiaries can receive and, notably, what services *anyone* receives, something that is not widely understood. Some classic examples include the rapid approval by CMS (then HCFA) of drug-eluting stents for treatment of coronary artery disease, which led to the explosive growth in interventional cardiology back in the 1990s and a dispute that rages today between the cardiac surgery community and the interventional cardiology community about the efficacy of coronary artery bypass surgery versus stents.

Medicare NCDs have significant influence across all insurance and delivery venues. Absent Medicare approval, implementing a new technology is rarely financially feasible since the elderly receive a large amount of healthcare services. Many insurers peg their coverage and payment rates to Medicare as well.

2 questions.cms.hhs.gov/cgi-bin/cmshhs.cfg/php/enduser/std_adp.php?p_faqid=2652&p_created=1079978647.

Another more recent example is the type of procedures for which PET (positron emission tomography) scanners are approved. PET is used in conjunction with CT, and both are very expensive technologies and therefore represent expensive services to provide to beneficiaries. The combination of PET and CT is used primarily for cancer treatment planning and effectiveness evaluation. Not all potential usages have been approved.

There are also numerous local coverage decisions (LCDs), where the Medicare intermediary (the contractors retained by the governmental to pay Medicare claims on its behalf) for a given area may approve a service that has not been subject to a NCD.

### Reform Components

The legislation contains four basic sections listed below.

1. Tax increases.
2. Insurance market changes and expansion.
3. Medicare changes.
4. Medicaid expansion and changes.

### 1. Tax increases

Tax increases are generally outside the scope of this chapter. Most of the tax increase revenue ($210 billion) comes from expanding the Medicare payroll tax to investment income. Other smaller but significant increases are the Cadillac plan tax ("Cadillacs" and "Chevys" are discussed later), penalty taxes for failure to have health insurance coverage, a tax on tanning parlors, penalty taxes on tax-exempt hospitals for not meeting community benefit standards, and a number of reductions in the tax-favored treatment of medical expenditures.

#### *Tax-Exempt Hospitals*

Scrutiny of the tax-exempt healthcare sector has been ongoing for a number of years now, and proponents of that scrutiny used the reform legislation to expand the monitoring of tax-exempt hospitals. The community benefit standard that formed the basis of the federal tax exemption has now been codified, and hospitals are required to conduct a periodic community health needs assessment using a broad section of community members and then adopt an implementation strategy. Failure to undertake the assessment and implementation can result in a $50,000 excise tax penalty.

Exempt hospitals are also required to adopt and make available a Financial Assistance Policy for those unable to fully pay for care. For these individuals, no more than the lowest amounts charged to patients who have insurance covering such care are allowed.

Notably, the annual tax return, Form 990, which has undergone major expansions in the level of required disclosure, particularly with respect to compensation arrangements for key employees, will now be expanded once again. Now required are the community needs assessment and implementation report described above as well as a copy of the hospitals' audited financial statements. This latter provision may have significant implications in the valuation community due to the volume of physician practice acquisitions, many of which include arguably questionable amounts for goodwill and intangible assets. Under the provisions of Financial Accounting Standard 164, annual impairment testing of acquired goodwill and intangibles is required, and if there is no value found by the auditors, it must be written off. Clearly, the write-off of recently acquired intangible assets will give regulators and other users of the financial statements cause for concern.

#### *Cadillac Tax*

Perhaps the most peculiar feature of the reform in its final iteration is the nondeductible 40% excise tax on high-cost plans that is not effective until 2018; whether it survives until then is an open question. The threshold levels for what constitutes a high-cost plan in 2018 are already established: $10,200 for a single plan and $27,500 for a family plan. In high-cost areas of the country such as New England, New York, Minnesota, Indiana, and Alaska, these levels are likely to be exceeded for typical policies long before 2018. In fact, the 10% threshold for the federal government to challenge insurers' justification for annual premium increases has driven up the cost of health insurance by just under 10%, making attainment of the Cadillac tax level greater.

The chief actuary at CMS had the following comment in his April 22, 2010 "Estimated Financial Effects of the Patient Protection and Affordable Care Act," as amended:

> Because plan benefit values will generally increase faster than the threshold amounts for defining high-cost plans (which, after 2019, are indexed by the CPI), additional plans would become subject to the excise tax over time, prompting many of those employers to scale back coverage.

Thus, it seems counterintuitive that a proposal designed to expand coverage, sold in part on the basis that one would be able to keep his or her present coverage and doctor, would be expected to cause what will be significant cutbacks in coverage to Chevy plans. One interpretation is that the level of insurance enjoyed by various segments of the population will become more egalitarian. Another implication is that increasing amounts of costs will be borne out of pocket by individuals, creating a disincentive to use the healthcare system.

### Massachusetts: The Model for Reform

Given the size and diversity of the United States, it is fascinating that the model chosen for the entire nation is taken to a high degree of precision from a model developed for one of its smallest states, as shown in Exhibit 2. That state is rather unique in the way its healthcare delivery system works, particularly given the urban concentration of its population and the dominance of high-cost teaching hospitals in the provision of healthcare.

**Exhibit 2. Feature Comparison of U.S. and Massachusetts Healthcare Models**

| Massachusetts Feature | Federal Feature? |
|---|---|
| Individual mandate | Yes |
| Penalty for lack of coverage thru tax system as of 2012<br>$83 each month, $996 for year for individuals aged 18 to 26.<br>$105 each month, $1,260 for year for individuals 27 or older | Yes, but much lower |
| No lifetime limits, waiting periods, or barriers for pre-existing medical conditions | Yes |
| Subsidies based on federal poverty limit (FPL) | Yes |
| State has own "health connector" insurance exchange | Yes |
| Children eligible to age 26 | Yes |
| Employer penalty | Yes |
| Benefit tiers (platinum, gold, silver, bronze) | Yes |
| Medicaid expansion | Yes |
| Merging the individual and small group markets | Allowed |
| Targeted primary care recruitment | Yes |
| Insurance market and rating rules | Yes |
| Rating variation in the individual and the small group market and the exchanges based only on<br>age (limited to 3-to-1 ratio),<br>premium rating area,<br>family composition, and<br>tobacco use (limited to 1.5-to-1 ratio) | Yes |
| Lack of antitrust reform | Yes |

### *A Summary of Massachusetts Reform Results*

1. Highest rate of insured residents in the nation, 97.4%.
2. Among the highest premiums in nation.
3. Many mandated benefits, e.g., IVF.
4. Among the highest rate of healthcare cost increase in nation, although other states have recently caught up.
5. Antitrust issues—state attorney general now investigating.
6. Unemployment rate 50% higher than neighboring New Hampshire.
7. Self-insured employers continue to increase to avoid the merged individual and small group market premium increases.
8. Statutory ban on small employers banding together to obtain benefits of self-insured market except in rare circumstances as a result of August 2010 legislation and recent implementing regulations.
9. Premium gap and benefits gap between small group market and self-insured large group market growing.

The Massachusetts Division of Healthcare Finance & Policy maintains quarterly reports that contain extensive data about the changes in health insurance premiums and healthcare costs. Before the federal legislation contributed to the rapid increase in premiums nationwide, Massachusetts experienced a crisis commencing in late 2009 through the summer of 2010, resulting in both administrative and legislative efforts to rein in the explosion of healthcare costs wrought by its own reform legislation.

## 2. Insurance Market Changes and Expansion

Certain healthcare insurance plans are exempt from all but a few of the new insurance market requirements, although these few could be expensive to those otherwise exempt plans and their insureds. Exempt plans include grandfathered plans and government plans.

### *Grandfathering as of March 23, 2010 (Including Renewals)*

The legislation permits individual and employer-sponsored insurance plans to remain basically the same. However, the following provisions from the legislation apply to those otherwise grandfathered plans: must extend dependent coverage to age 26, must eliminate annual limits on coverage, must eliminate lifetime limits on coverage by 2014, must prohibit rescission of coverage, and must eliminate waiting periods for coverage of greater than 90 days.

Interim regulations issued June 22, 2010 made the preservation of grandfathered status questionable because a number of common changes one might expect disqualify the plan from grandfathered status.

1. Entering into a new policy, certificate, or contract of insurance after March 23, 2010 including simply changing the insurer. *This provision was eliminated in the revision to these regulations in November 2010.*

2. Eliminating all, or substantially all, benefits to diagnose or treat a particular condition.

3. Increasing the fixed-amount and percentage cost-sharing by more than specified amounts to reflect medical inflation.

4. Changes that decrease the employer contribution rate for coverage by more than 5%, such as decreasing the employer-paid share of premium from 75% to 65%.

5. Changes that impose a new or modified annual limit on benefits.

As the introduction would suggest, the insurance market is where there is arguably some real reform, although one's reaction to that reform will likely depend upon how well one understands what it means in dollars-and-cents terms to the affected populations. The reforms include:

1. Rating rules.

2. Mandatory provisions with respect to coverage and prohibitions against certain other provisions.

3. Medical loss ratio (MLR) requirements.

4. Minimum coverage requirements.

#### *Rating Rules*

Health plan premiums will be allowed to vary based on age (by a 3-to-1 ratio), geographic area, tobacco use (by a 1.5-to-1 ratio), and the number of family members. These are generally effective in 2014.

#### *Mandatory Provisions With Respect to Coverage and Prohibitions Against Certain Other Provisions*

Health insurers will be prohibited from imposing lifetime limits on coverage of the "minimum essential benefits" (see below) and will be prohibited from rescinding coverage, except in cases of fraud, which started generally in 2011. Young adults are allowed to remain on their parents' health insurance up to the year in which they attain age 26 (see IRS Notice 2010-38). Waiting periods for coverage will be limited to 90 days starting in 2014.

### *Medical Loss Ratio (MLR) Requirements*

MLR refers to the portion or percentage of the premium spent on actual healthcare costs for insured individuals, although regulations need to be issued to define MLR for purposes of the reform legislation. These provisions become effective during 2011 through 2013 and provide:

1. Large group plans must spend 85% of premium.
2. Small group and individual plans must spend 80% of premium.
3. Excess not spent on actual healthcare costs must generally be rebated through a reduction in subsequent premiums.

The final regulations did not permit insurers to exclude from administrative costs the commissions to sales agents common in the small group and individual market.

### *Minimum Coverage Requirements*

Insurance policies not subject to the grandfather rules will be required to provide the following minimum essential coverage or benefits:

1. Ambulatory patient services.
2. Emergency services.
3. Hospitalization.
4. Maternity and newborn care.
5. Mental health and substance use disorder services, including behavioral health treatment.
6. Prescription drugs.
7. Rehabilitative and habilitative services and devices.
8. Laboratory services.
9. Preventive and wellness services and chronic disease management.
10. Pediatric services, including oral and vision care.

In a bulletin dated Dec. 16, 2011, the Department of Health and Human Services stunned most observers by announcing that forthcoming regulations would to a large extent permit individual states to define minimum essential benefits by reference to one of the following policies from each state:

1. One of the three largest small group plans in the state.
2. One of the three largest state employee health plans.
3. One of the three largest federal employee health plan options.
4. The largest HMO plan offered in the state's commercial market.

In addition, the deductible in the small group market will be limited to $2,000 for an individual and $4,000 for family. "First dollar" coverage will be required for primary care, meaning there can be no cost-sharing (deductible, co-pay) for primary care services.

## Analysis

One of the most perplexing aspects of the reform debate is the lack of focus on the near-term and long-term impact on both the cost of insurance and the coverage provided by that insurance. In simple terms, annual and lifetime benefit caps on the minimum essential benefits, for example, keep the underlying expense to the insurer both lower and more predictable. Insurance premiums are in large part a function of probability adjusted by actuarial computed expected outlays, with administrative costs and profit added on, as shown in Exhibit 3.

**Exhibit 3. Division of Insurance Premiums by Cost and Percentage**

| | Annual Cost | Percent |
|---|---|---|
| MLR | $9,360 | 85% |
| Administration | 1,101 | 10% |
| Profit | 551 | 5% |
| | 11,012 | 100% |

Exhibit 4 shows what might happen to total costs included in the MLR when the limits on pre-existing conditions and annual limits are removed.

Expected cost in a large population insured for healthcare is typically a function of the statistical normal distribution as shown in the classic bell curve-type distribution, illustrated in Exhibit 5 for 50,000 insured lives, with illustrative[3] costs per member per month. The average cost per member per month (PMPM) is $780.

3 Note: This is not intended to be an actuarially valid model but rather to illustrate the concepts.

**Exhibit 4. Pre-Reform and Post-Reform Costs in the MLR**

| PRE-REFORM | Number | Cost | Total |
|---|---|---|---|
| Standard Insured | 9,000 | $2,000 | $18,000,000 |
| Pre-existing conditons | 500 | 2,000 | 1,000,000 |
| Annual Limits | 10 | 200,000 | 2,000,000 |
| Total Costs | | 9,510 | 21,000,000 |
| Cost per Insured: | | | 2,208 |
| **POST-REFORM** | **Number** | **Cost** | **Total** |
| Standard Insured | 9,000 | 2,000 | 18,000,000 |
| Pre-existing conditons | 500 | 10,000 | 5,000,000 |
| Annual Limits | 10 | 500,000 | 5,000,000 |
| Total Costs | | 9,510 | 28,000,000 |
| Cost per Insured: | | | 2,944 |
| **Percent Increase:** | | | **33.33%** |

**Exhibit 5. Expected Healthcare Cost per Member in a Large Population**

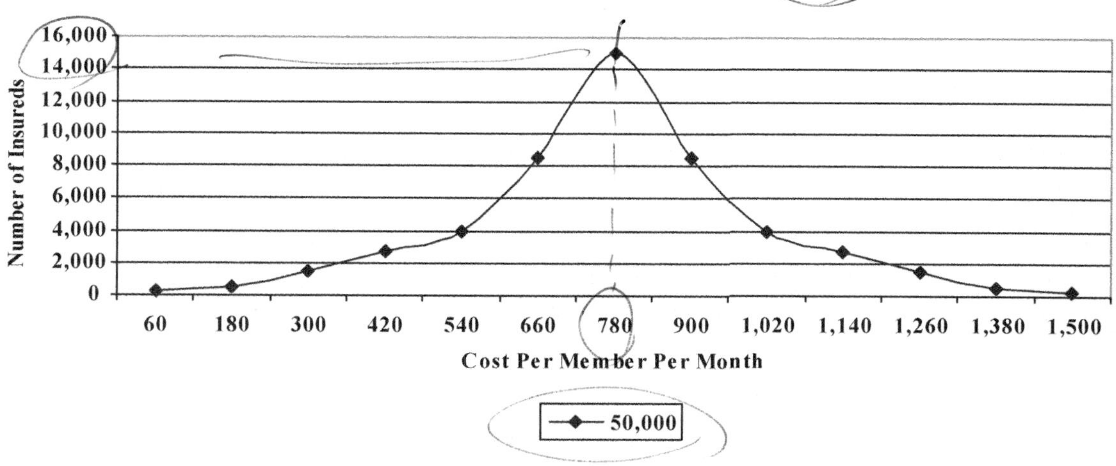


In the bell curve in Exhibit 6, high-cost individuals are shown at the extreme right, while low-cost individuals are shown at the extreme left. The clustering in the center is where most individual's cost experience will lie. Naturally, to the extent that an insurer could cause its insured to fall into the center and left of the curve, its costs would be less. If an insurer charged a premium commensurate with the entire curve, it would expect to make a considerable profit. Thus, one stated goal of the reform was to institute safeguards against this sort of cherry picking of more healthy people and to prevent dropping of unhealthy people from coverage when the cherry picking failed to work.

**Exhibit 6. Costs of Healthcare for a Smaller Population**

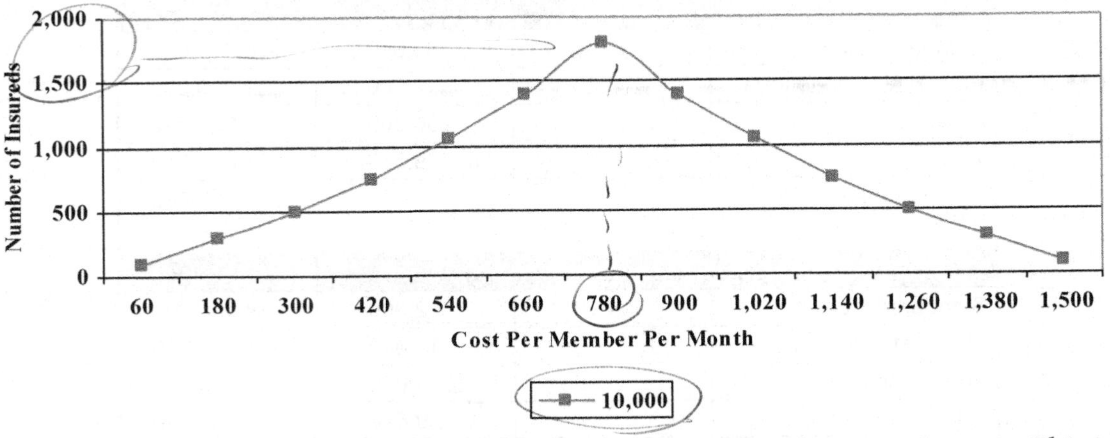


Smaller populations are more unpredictable than large populations, of course. This is summed up in the commonly used phrase "the law of large numbers," which, again, simply means that the aggregate behavior of a large population is more predictable—here in terms of the cost of healthcare—than the behavior of a small population. This could be shown as a smaller sample population of 10,000 compared to 50,000, as in Exhibit 7.

**Exhibit 7. Comparison of the Costs of Smaller and Larger Populations**

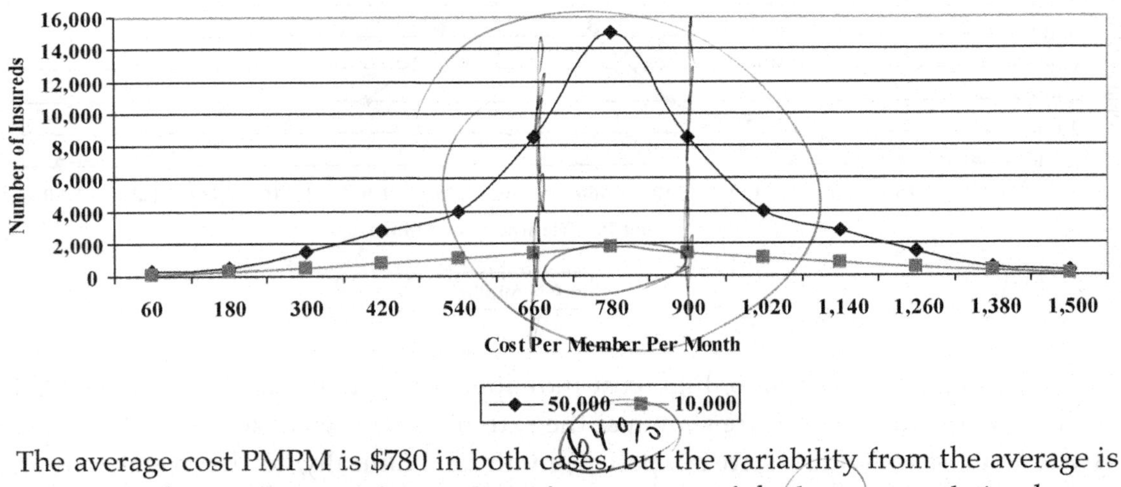


The average cost PMPM is $780 in both cases, but the variability from the average is greater in the smaller population: Sixty-four percent of the larger population has an expected cost PMPM between $660 and $900, while only 46% of the smaller population lies in that range, as shown in Exhibit 8.

Exhibit 8. Adverse Selection of Less Healthy Individuals

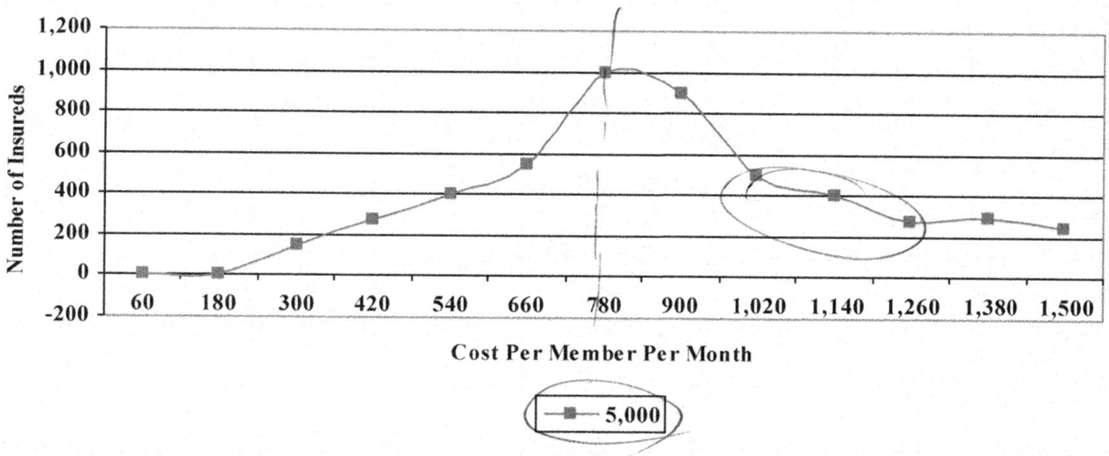


Here is an example of what we call in the industry "adverse selection" or a population of individuals that is less healthy than the "normal" aggregate population reflected in the original bell curve. The cost of providing healthcare for these individuals is much greater on a per-capita basis than in the aggregate population. Thus, the cost of providing health insurance to such a group would be higher. The average cost PMPM is $886.20, nearly 14% higher than the larger groups.

The insurance industry historically carved out the aggregate population into three distinct components with relativistic designations.

1. Large group market, *typically* more than 50 insureds.
2. Small group market, *typically* less than 50 insureds.
3. Individual market, one person, as the name suggests.

"Large" is a subjective term, of course. It can then be divided into those employers, including governmental entities, that are large enough to self-insure and those that are not.

## Self-Insured Groups

In light of the above discussion, another aspect of the reform debate that would be perplexing if not for the fact that the debate took place in the political arena is lack of discussion of how the self-insured escaped much of the cost burden of the changes in rating and coverage requirements contained in the reform legislation. This is perhaps the single largest failure of the so-called reform, because it precludes the lowest aggregate cost per capita from being realized for all individuals contained in the aggregate population, therefore shifting those costs to the small group market. Cherry picking of healthy people is still possible for the self-insured. This will be described in greater detail below.

### *How Insurance Works for a Large Group*

As described in simple terms above, insurance premiums are in large part a function of probability adjusted expected outlays, with administrative costs and profit added on. Those costs are more predictable for large populations than for small populations, and therefore, the cost of actuarial uncertainty (risk) reflected in the premium charged is also less. From an administrative standpoint, insuring, say, 200 people under a single contract is cheaper than insuring 40 groups of five people each under 40 contracts or 200 individuals.

Another key aspect for a large group desiring to self-insure is negotiating leverage. The larger an entity is, the more premium dollars it can bring to an insurer. As previously noted, the provision of health insurance is a low-margin business. A large employer contract can contribute disproportionately to the bottom line of the insurer, if appropriately priced in terms or premiums, because of the effect of spreading the insurer's relatively high fixed costs over more insureds.

To summarize, larger entities have lower premiums due to:

1. Predictability of cost.
2. Lower administrative costs.
3. Potential contribution to profitability of the insurer.

### *Self-Insured Employers*

Depending upon the makeup of the employees of a given employer in terms of demographics and healthcare status, an employer may decide to take advantage of the positive actuarial stability of a large group. In this case, the employer insures itself and is directly responsible for the dollar amount of those claims. It utilizes the health insurance company for its provider network (physicians, hospitals, etc.) and claims processing. This line of business is known as administrative services only (ASO) in the trade. The employee may carry an insurance card with the name of an insurance company on it, but the risk associated with the insurance is assumed by the employer. The employer makes monthly premium payments to the insurance company based upon the insurer's estimate of the costs associated with the insured group.

Given the importance of demographics, it frequently is advantageous for larger employers with a prevalence of young employees to self-insure. Industries attracting younger employees such as technology can realize substantial savings through self-insurance versus being insured by the insurance company.

Self-insuring is not without risk, and to guard against catastrophic losses if the costs of one or more employees fall outside the expected range, the employer purchases stop loss insurance. A combination of actuarial input and gumption are used to determine the level at which the stop loss insurance becomes effective. For example, an employer might decide to be at-risk for the first $50,000 of healthcare costs for an employee. Once the costs exceed that level, the stop loss coverage cuts in and pays a negotiated percentage of the excess cost, generally 90% with the risk-bearing employer liable for the remaining 10%.

### 3. Medicare Changes

All told, reductions in the Medicare program are supposed to pay approximately $500 million of the cost of the reform legislation, less the costs associated with closing the so-called "donut hole" in the Medicare Part D Prescription Drug program.

#### *Changes to the "Market Basket" Update for Healthcare Facilities*

The "market basket" refers to the annual healthcare inflation index that has historically been used to increase the fees paid by Medicare for acute hospital services. For both inpatient and outpatient services, acute care hospitals will be subject to reductions in the market basket update according to the following schedule:

FY 2010-2011 market basket update reduced by 0.25% (effective April 1, 2010)

FY 2012-2013 market basket update reduced by 0.10%

FY 2014 market basket update reduced by 0.30%

FY 2015-2016 market basket update reduced by 0.20%

FY 2017-2019 market basket update reduced by 0.75%

A similar reduction applies to inpatient rehabilitation facilities.

#### *Hospital Productivity Adjustment*

Hospitals will also be subject to a new productivity adjustment starting in 2012 based on economywide productivity changes and the 10-year moving average in GDP, similar to a major component in the Medicare formula for the physician fee schedule update. This provision has created a good deal of concern in the hospital community. The chief actuary at CMS had the following comment in his April 22, 2010, "Estimated Financial Effects of the Patient Protection and Affordable Care Act, as Amended":

> It is important to note that the estimated savings shown in this memorandum for one category of Medicare provisions may be unrealistic. The PPACA introduces permanent annual productivity adjustments to price updates for most providers (such as hospitals, skilled nursing facilities, and home health agencies), using a 10-year moving average of economywide private, nonfarm productivity gains. While such payment update reductions will create a strong incentive for providers to maximize efficiency, it is doubtful that many will be able to improve their own productivity to the degree achieved by the economy at large.[4] Over time, a sustained reduction in payment updates, based on productivity expectations that are difficult to attain, would cause Medicare payment rates to grow more slowly than, and in a way that was unrelated to, the providers' costs of furnishing services to beneficiaries. Thus, providers for whom Medicare constitutes a substantive portion of their business could find it difficult to remain profitable and, absent legislative intervention, might end their participation in the program (possibly jeopardizing access to care for beneficiaries). Simulations by the Office of the Actuary suggest that roughly 15% of Part A providers would become unprofitable within the 10-year projection period as a result of the productivity adjustments.[5] Although this policy could be monitored over time to avoid such an outcome, changes would likely result in smaller actual savings than shown here for these provisions.

A number of additional provisions with respect to quality also take place starting in 2013, including payment reductions for preventable hospital readmissions; a bundling pilot program that is designed to pay a single fee for physician and hospital services; and value-based purchasing (VBP), where institutions with proven positive outcomes would be preferred by the Medicare program. Ultimately, as much as 6% of the DRG (diagnosis-related group) payment to a hospital may be at risk for quality factors.

Disproportionate share hospitals (DSH) receive additional Medicare payments to compensate them for providing care to the indigent. In 2014, DSH will be subject to reductions of 15%, since many of the indigent they now treat should be eligible for Medicaid coverage as described below.

4 "The provision of most health services tends to be very labor-intensive. Economywide productivity gains reflect relatively modest improvements in the service sector together with much larger improvements in manufacturing. Except in the case of physician services, we are not aware of any empirical evidence demonstrating the medical community's ability to achieve productivity improvements equal to those of the overall economy. The Office of the Actuary's most recent analysis of hospital productivity highlights the difficulties in measurement but suggests that such productivity has been small or negligible from 1981 to 2005."

5 "The simulations were based on actual fiscal year 2007 Medicare and total facility margin distributions for hospitals, skilled nursing facilities, and home health agencies. Provider revenues and expenditures were projected using representative growth rates and the Office of the Actuary's best estimates of achievable productivity gains for each provider type, and holding all other factors constant. A sensitivity analysis suggested that the conclusions drawn from the simulations would not change significantly under different provider behavior assumptions."

### *Ambulatory Surgery Centers (ASCs)*

ASCs compete directly with hospital outpatient departments for outpatient surgical cases and will be subject to a productivity adjustment factor as well. For example, if the reform legislation had been effective in 2010, rather than receiving a 1.2% increase, ASCs would have seen a 0.1% decrease as a result of the 1.3% productivity adjustment.

### *Medicare Advantage*

Medicare Advantage is the program that privatizes Medicare coverage for beneficiaries who choose to opt out of the traditional Medicare program. It underwent major revisions in the 2003 Medicare Modernization Act aimed at halting the decline in enrollment that resulted from changes made in the 1997 Omnibus Budget Reconciliation Act (OBRA). OBRA had made major cuts in the payments in health insurers participating in what was then Medicare + Choice.

Approximately 24% of all Medicare beneficiaries are enrolled in Medicare Advantage plans, but they are most prevalent in a few states, including Florida, California, Arizona, Massachusetts, and Washington. Despite being targeted for elimination in earlier versions of the reform legislation, the cutbacks in the payments from the government to private insurers are not as draconian as might have been expected and are summarized as follows:

1. 2010 and 2011 rates will remain the same, *unadjusted for inflation.*

2. 2012 will be 96.5% of the current rate.

3. 2013 will be 98% of the current rate.

4. 2014 will be 100% of the current rate.

In effect, the inflation adjustment previously allowed is eliminated, and further cuts are then made with reference to the baseline rate from 2009.

These cuts are particularly significant to HMOs and their participating physician groups that employ risk-based payment mechanisms. These types of arrangements represent large profit streams in Florida, Massachusetts, and California, to name three.

Generically, the changes in setting the capitation rate are described in the following from the Kaiser Family Foundation:

> [The legislation] restructure[s] payments to Medicare Advantage (MA) plans by setting payments to different percentages of Medicare fee-for-service (FFS) rates, with higher payments for areas with low FFS rates and lower payments (95% of FFS) for areas

with high FFS rates. Phase-in revised payments over three years beginning in 2011, for plans in most areas, with payments phased in over longer periods (four years and six years) for plans in other areas. Provide bonuses to plans receiving four or more stars, based on the current five-star quality rating system for Medicare Advantage plans, beginning in 2012; qualifying plans in qualifying areas receive double bonuses. Modify rebate system with rebates allocated based on a plan's quality rating. Phase-in adjustments to plan payments for coding practices related to the health status of enrollees, with adjustments equaling 5.7% by 2019. Cap total payments, including bonuses, at current payment levels. Require Medicare Advantage plans to remit partial payments to the secretary if the plan has a medical loss ratio of less than 85%, beginning in 2014. Require the secretary to suspend plan enrollment for three years if the medical loss ratio is less than 85% for two consecutive years and to terminate the plan contract if the medical loss ratio is less than 85% for five consecutive years.[6]

### *Accountable Care Organizations*

The federal legislation similarly looks to physicians and hospitals to establish accountable care organizations. These structures are described in detail in Chapter 38.

### *Primary Care Physicians (PCPs)*

PCPs are one of the big winners in the reform, at least for the near term, including the increased emphasis from the ACO and medical home provisions described above. PCPs are defined as physicians specializing in family medicine, internal medicine, geriatric medicine, and pediatric medicine if at least 60% of total Medicare allowed charges are for office, skilled nursing facility (SNF), home, rest home, and other visits specified by CPT codes. From 2011 to 2015, eligible PCPs will receive a bonus equal to 10% of Medicare payments[7] for these services.

The relevant CPT codes are as follows:

1. 99201 through 99215 (the most common codes)
    a. Office—new and established patients visits
2. 99304 through 99340
    a. Nursing facility visits
3. 99341 through 99350
    a. Home visits

6 Summary of new health reform law—last modified April 8, 2010.

7 Since Medicare pays 80% of the allowed charge and the beneficiary the other 20%, this results in an 8% overall increase.

### *Other Physician Changes*

General surgeons practicing in a health provider shortage area (HPSA) will also receive a 10% bonus in their Medicare payments. Physicians will be subject to and able to participate in the bundling pilots. There will also be a physician quality incentive program.

## 4. Medicaid Expansion and Changes

Of the 34 million uninsured who are supposed to receive coverage from the reform, 20 million are the result of the expansion of Medicaid, the program for low-income individuals, the cost of which is shared between the federal and state governments.[8] Other than in a few states with very expansive benefits, Medicaid in the past did cover adults who have no children; the expansion also picks up a large category of low-income families previously ineligible. This is the single largest cost item in the reform, representing more than $450 billion over the first 10 years, most of which is picked up by the federal government through increased deficit spending, as suggested in the following quote from the aforementioned report of the CMS chief actuary:

> We assume that employers and individuals would take roughly three to five years to fully adapt to the new insurance coverage options and that the enrollment of additional individuals under the Medicaid coverage expansion would be completed by the third year of implementation. Because of these transition effects and the fact that most of the coverage provisions would be in effect for only six of the 10 years of the budget period, the cost estimates shown in this memorandum do not represent a full 10-year cost for the new legislation.

At present, those covered under Medicaid vary significantly from state to state, with states such as Massachusetts, Arizona, Delaware, Hawaii, Maine, New York, and Vermont having the richest benefits. The reform legislation establishes a minimum uniform standard for Medicaid coverage in all states—those under age 65 with income up to 133% of the federal poverty limit, with the federal government paying most of the costs. The states providing more than the minimum coverage are required to maintain it, thus missing out on the subsidies.

### *Primary Care Physicians (PCPs)*

For 2013 and 2014, PCPs treating Medicaid patients will be reimbursed at a rate equal to 100% of the Medicare rate.

8 50% to 76% is paid for by the federal government.

### *Summary*

The principal expansion of insurance coverage and the principal cost of the reform is the Medicaid program, while aside from tax increases, the principal offset of the cost are reductions in Medicare spending. Providers that lose through reduced Medicare spending hope to benefit from increased Medicaid spending.

## Conclusions

If the experience of the model state, Massachusetts, is any indicator, small group premiums will skyrocket in those states that merge the small group and individual markets. States with health insurance premiums above the median are likely to find many of the insurance policies subject to the excise tax on Cadillac plans, which will in turn lead to cutbacks in benefits designed to avoid the excise. Assuming such a plan has survived as a grandfathered plan up to the point of the benefit cuts, it will then lose grandfathered status and be subject to the entire array of reform's rules.

It is possible that businesses will increase their migration from high-cost states to low-cost states or even move operations overseas, exacerbating already difficult domestic employment opportunities. On the other hand, it is possible that some equalization of healthcare costs in existing lower-cost states may decrease their competitive advantage. To the extent the excise tax applies in high-cost states, there will be a redistribution of income from those states to lower-cost, lower-income states.

The primary care physician shortage will be exacerbated by the rise in the number of insured individuals and the mandated "first dollar" coverage for primary care services. Where the physician to fill this gap will come from remains unseen, despite the enhanced payments for primary case services and the attempt to refocus residency slots on primary care.

Perhaps the largest effects will come from Medicaid expansion. Already the leading budget buster in virtually every state in the union, when the federal government subsidies for the expansion expire, states will be confronted with a need for enormous tax increases. Whether reform-driven Medicaid expansion is ultimately added to the list of unfunded federal government mandates will have to wait until the turn of the next decade.

## Sources of Information

CMS Chief Actuary

- s3.amazonaws.com/thf_media/2010/pdf/OACT-Memo-FinImpactofPPACA-Enacted.pdf

Massachusetts Division of Healthcare Finance & Policy

- www.mass.gov/Eeohhs2/docs/dhcfp/r/pubs/10/key_indicators_feb_10.ppt
- www.mass.gov/Eeohhs2/docs/dhcfp/cost_trend_docs/presentations/2010_03_16_dianna_welch_trends.ppt

Commonwealth Fund

- "Paying the Price: How Health Insurance Premiums Are Eating Up Middle-Class Incomes"; August 2009
- www.commonwealthfund.org/Content/Publications/Data-Briefs/2009/Aug/Paying-the-Price-How-Health-Insurance-Premiums-Are-Eating-Up-Middle-Class-Incomes.aspx

Kaiser Family Foundation

- Kaiser Fast Facts. Data Source: accessed on May 8, 2010; facts.kff.org/chartbook.aspx?cb=56

Law Firm Sonnenschein Summary

- www.sonnenschein.com/docs/Health_Care_Reform_Side-by-Side.pdf

Kaiser Family Foundation on Reform

- healthreform.kff.org/ (generally)
- www.kff.org/healthreform/upload/8061.pdf

Kaiser Family Foundation Subsidy Calculator

- healthreform.kff.org/Subsidycalculator.aspx

Kaiser Family/Alliance for Health Reform Podcast on Private Insurance Changes

- www.kff.org/healthreform/ahr043010video.cfm

AHLA Tax and Finance Practice Group Members Briefing March 24, 2010 on Changes for Tax-Exempt Hospitals

McDermott, Will & Emory *Health Care Reform: Legislation Affects Ambulatory Surgery Centers* April 2, 2010

Deloitte Center for Health Solutions, Paul H. Keckley, Ph.D. Executive Director: *Accountable Care Organizations: A New Model for Sustainable Innovation*

Chapter 2

# The Healthcare Economy

*By Mark O. Dietrich, CPA/ABV*

The following material is based upon data from the Centers for Medicaid and Medicare Office of the Actuary released in September 2011. That office historically prepared annual projections of national health expenditures (NHE) released in February of each year using an established model that incorporates three separate factors: actuarial, econometric, and judgmental. The February 2010 NHE release was made in September 2010 to reflect the reform, and the most recent update was then released in September 2011. The projections go through 2020.[1]

The September 2010 projection described the impact of the Patient Protection and Affordable Care Act (Affordable Care Act):

> Growth in National Health Expenditures (NHE) in the United States over the coming decade is expected to be slightly higher as a result of the implementation of the Patient Protection and Affordable Care Act (Affordable Care Act), as well as other relevant legislative and regulatory changes since the publication of our February 2010 projections. Average annual growth in NHE for 2009 through 2019 is expected to be 6.3%, 0.2 percentage points faster than pre-reform estimates. NHE as a share of gross domestic product (GDP) is expected to be 19.6% by 2019, or 0.3 percentage points higher than projected before reform.

1 A detailed description of the methodology is located at www.cms.hhs.gov/NationalHealthExpendData/downloads/projections-methodology-2006.pdf and the data are at www.cms.hhs.gov/NationalHealthExpendData/03_NationalHealthAccountsProjected.asp.

> Many of the major Affordable Care Act's provisions go into effect in 2014, resulting in substantive differences in projected growth of NHE compared to estimates made pre-reform. An expansion of Medicaid coverage (to all persons under age 65 in households with incomes less than 138% of the federal poverty level), combined with the advent of state-level health insurance exchanges, is expected to result in NHE growth of 9.2% in 2014 (2.6 percentage points higher than projected before reform was passed).
>
> Over the latter stages of the projection period (2015 through 2019), the impact of the Affordable Care Act on health coverage is anticipated to continue as more people acquire, or shift, into new or different coverage. By 2019, 92.7% of the U.S. population is expected to have health insurance (an increase of 10 percentage points) driven, in part, by growth in Medicaid, which when combined with the Children's Health Insurance Program (CHIP), is projected to cover 82 million persons. Also by 2019, 30.6 million people are expected to be enrolled in health insurance exchange plans.
>
> [Post-reform] Principally due to the expansion of Medicaid eligibility and additional CHIP funding in 2014, Medicaid and CHIP enrollment is expected to increase by 21.8 million people, with total spending projected to grow 17.4% (11.1 percentage points faster than the pre-reform projection). The federal government is expected to finance most of the care for the new Medicaid beneficiaries through a 100% federal medical assistance percentage, which will phase down to 90% in 2020 and thereafter.
>
> Provisions of the Affordable Care Act are projected to result in a lower average annual Medicare spending growth rate for 2012 through 2019 (6.2%), 1.3 percentage points lower than pre-reform estimates. The relatively lower projected Medicare expenditure growth rate reflects reduced annual payment updates for most Medicare services, substantial reductions to managed care plan payments, and the creation of the Independent Payment Advisory Board.

The September 2011 forecast for the decade through 2020 is as follows, with healthcare spending reaching 19.6% of GDP by that time, driven in part by a large jump in the GDP-share in 2009 due to the recession, as modified by the Affordable Care Act:

> In 2010, NHE is projected to have reached $2.6 trillion and grown 3.9%, down from 4.0% in 2009. Estimated spending growth in 2010 was slow due to continuing declines in employment and private health insurance coverage associated with the recent recession. GDP growth is projected to have been 3.8% in 2010, nearly the same rate of growth as NHE. The health share of GDP is expected to have remained constant between 2009 and 2010, at 17.6%.

Between 2011 and 2013, health spending is projected to grow faster due to expected improvements in the economy, reaching a rate of 5.5% by 2013. Private health insurance and out-of-pocket spending are both projected to grow faster over this period. Private health insurance spending is projected to grow 4.8% in 2013, up from 2.6% in 2010, as employer-sponsored insurance enrollment is expected to increase with gains in employment. Out-of-pocket spending is projected to grow 3.9% in 2013, up from 1.8% in 2010, as growth in household incomes is expected to lead to more healthcare spending and as employers are anticipated to increase cost-sharing requirements in employer-sponsored insurance plans.

In 2014, health spending is projected to grow 8.3%. This projected acceleration in the growth rate, up from 5.5% in 2013, is primarily the result of the Affordable Care Act's coverage-related expansions. Medicaid eligibility is set to increase to persons under age 65 in families with income up to 138% of the federal poverty level in 2014. As a result, Medicaid enrollment is expected to increase by 19.5 million people and spending is projected to grow 20.3%. The new health insurance exchanges are expected to cover 13.9 million people in 2014 and contribute to 9.4% growth in private health insurance spending. Because people gaining coverage through the Medicaid expansion and the exchanges are expected to be younger and in better health than currently insured persons, on average, it is anticipated that a relatively higher share of their new costs would go toward physician and clinical services and prescription drugs and a lower share toward hospital and long-term care services.

Over the projection period (2010-2020), average annual health spending growth (5.8%) is anticipated to outpace average annual growth in the overall economy by 1.1 percentage points (4.7%). By 2020, national health spending is expected to reach $4.6 trillion and comprise 19.8% of GDP. The government-sponsored share of health spending is projected to increase from 45% in 2010 to about 50% by 2020, driven by expected robust Medicare enrollment growth, Medicaid coverage expansions, and exchange plan premium and cost-sharing subsidies."

Medicare spending is expected to have slowed in 2010 due to the reform's cutbacks in Medicare Advantage payments. The statement below regarding slower growth due to physician fee schedules cuts appears annually, but those cuts never take place.

Medicare spending is estimated to have been $525 billion in 2010 as growth slowed to 4.5%, down from 7.9% in 2009, due in part to an across-the-board reduction in the rate of growth for payments to Medicare's private health plans by 3.4% . Medicare is projected to grow 5.9% in 2011, but only 1.7% in 2012; the slow growth in 2012 is driven by a 29.4% reduction in physician payment rates required under the Medicare

> sustainable growth rate (SGR) formula.[2] (Under an alternative scenario where physician payment rate updates are based on growth in the Medicare Economic Index (MEI), Medicare spending growth is projected to accelerate to 6.6% in 2012.) Average annual Medicare spending growth is anticipated to be 6.3% for 2013 through 2020, reflecting increasing enrollment (as the oldest baby boomers become eligible for Medicare) that will drive up spending, and provisions of the Affordable Care Act that call for reduced fee-for-service provider payment updates and lower payments to private plans.

Hospital spending trends were described as follows. The reform legislation contemplates paying for the expansion in significant part through cutbacks in hospital spending; however, the chief actuary of CMS[3] does not believe many of those savings can be realized:

> Hospital spending growth is estimated to have slowed by half a percentage point, to 4.6% in 2010, and to reach $794.3 billion, with slower growth in spending by private health insurance plans and Medicare. For 2011 through 2013, growth in hospital spending is projected to accelerate, reaching 5.3% by 2013, as private health insurance spending growth rates increase with a rebound in enrollment and Medicare growth increases as the oldest baby boomers start to enroll. Hospital spending growth is projected to accelerate to 7.2% in 2014. This faster growth rate reflects increases in service use due to the coverage expansions under Medicaid and private insurance, partially offset by lower Medicare payment rate increases for hospitals mandated by the Affordable Care Act. Hospital spending is projected to grow 6.2% per year during the period 2015 to 2020, with Medicare spending growth generally outpacing private health insurance spending growth, reflecting the shift of baby boomers onto Medicare.

The government researchers found that physician spending growth increased only 2.4% in 2010. Although recent history suggests otherwise, the physician spending growth rate was forecast to decline in 2010 due to projected cuts under both Medicare's sustainable growth rate formula (see discussion infra) and whether that formula is suspended by Congressional action. The alternative growth calculation without those cuts is 4.5 percentage points.

> Physician and clinical services spending growth is estimated to have slowed to a historically low rate of 2.4% in 2010, with spending of $517.8 billion, driven by a reduction in visits related to the recession and a less severe flu season than in 2009. Spending growth is expected to accelerate to 4% in 2011 and then slow to 0.8% in 2012, due to

2 Such "required" cuts have been consistently overturned by Congress for many years.
3 s3.amazonaws.com/thf_media/2010/pdf/OACT-Memo-FinImpactofPPACA-Enacted.pdf.

> the 29.4% Medicare physician payment rate cut under Medicare's SGR formula. (If the payment rate update was based on the growth rate of the MEI, physician and clinical spending would be projected to grow 4.5% in 2012.) In 2014, physician and clinical services spending is projected to grow 8.9%, related to the Medicaid and exchange coverage expansions. Physician and clinical services spending is projected to grow at an average rate of 5.6% between 2015 and 2020, with Medicaid and Medicare spending growth generally outpacing private health insurance spending growth.

One of the principal drivers of the increase in health expenditures is prescription drug costs. It is important to understand the underlying components of the increase because the general growth rate in health expenditures will not serve as a valid proxy for the industry's individual subsets, which often have different rates of growth.

> Prescription drug spending is projected to have grown 3.5% in 2010, to $258.6 billion, with continued slow growth in the use of drugs and an increasing share of prescriptions being filled with generic drugs. While growth between 2011 and 2013 is projected to be faster (at an average rate of 5.7% annually), the loss of patent protection of several of the best-selling brand-name drugs in 2011 limits growth. In 2014, prescription drug spending is expected to grow faster, at a rate of 10.7%, driven by a substantial increase in the use of drugs by newly insured persons in Medicaid and the exchange plans. Prescription drug spending growth is expected to average 7.2% from 2015 through 2020, reflecting slower increases in generic drugs' share of the market and the costs of new drugs becoming available during these years.

Exhibit 1 plots the increase in total national expenditures (left axis) using projected data for the years 2006 to 2020 against those for prescription drugs (right axis). Note that there was a flattening of prescription growth commencing in 2006 followed by an upturn in the rate of increase commencing in 2009. Factors contributing to this rapid increase in prescription drug spending include consumer advertising and new product development, along with increased reliance on clinical pharmacology.

Each year, coincident with the release of the annual projections of national health expenditures, members of the CMS Office of the Actuary publish an article in the journal *Health Affairs* on the projections. The 2011 projections initially appeared in the January, 2011 edition.[4] Data contained in that article based on the NHE indicate that pharmaceutical spending increases continue to outstrip all other sectors except home health, rising

4 Anne Martin, David Lassman, Lekha Whittle, Aaron Catlin and the National Health Expenditure Accounts Team: "Recession Contributes to Slowest Annual Rate of Increase in Health Spending in Five Decades," *Health Affairs*, 30, no.1 (2011): 11-22.

**Exhibit 1. National Health Expenditures and Prescription Drugs**

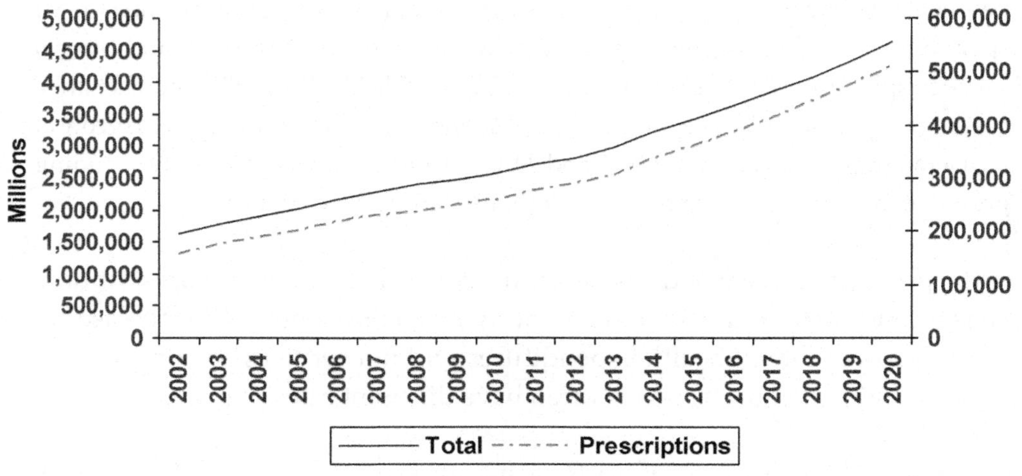

**Exhibit 2. Annual Increase by Category**

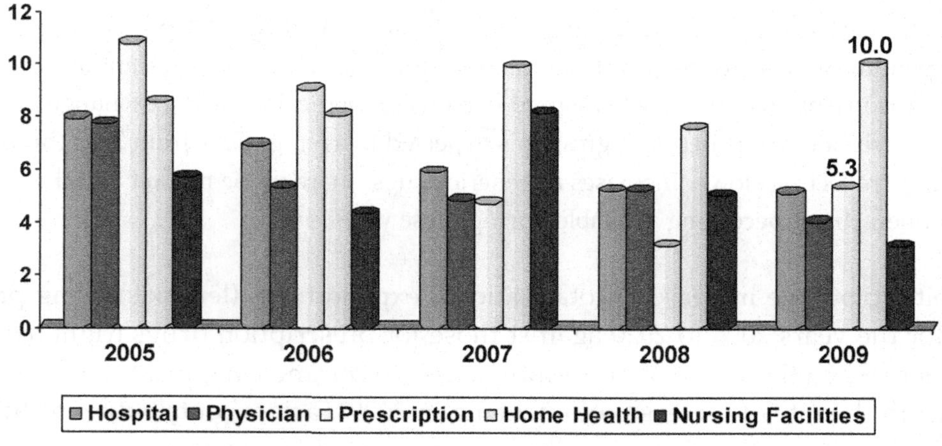


at 5.3%, compared to 4% for physician services. Home health spending is exploding due to the aging population and a push by government and private insurers to move care for the elderly out of more expensive nursing home settings, as shown in Exhibit 2.

The trend can be seen comparatively with other components in Exhibit 3 based on the 2011 Milliman Medical Index, with pharmacy spending having slowed relative to other sectors except for physicians as indicated in Exhibit 2.[5]

5 publications.milliman.com/periodicals/mmi/pdfs/milliman-medical-index-2011.pdf, May 11, 2011.

**Exhibit 3. Annual Increase by Category**

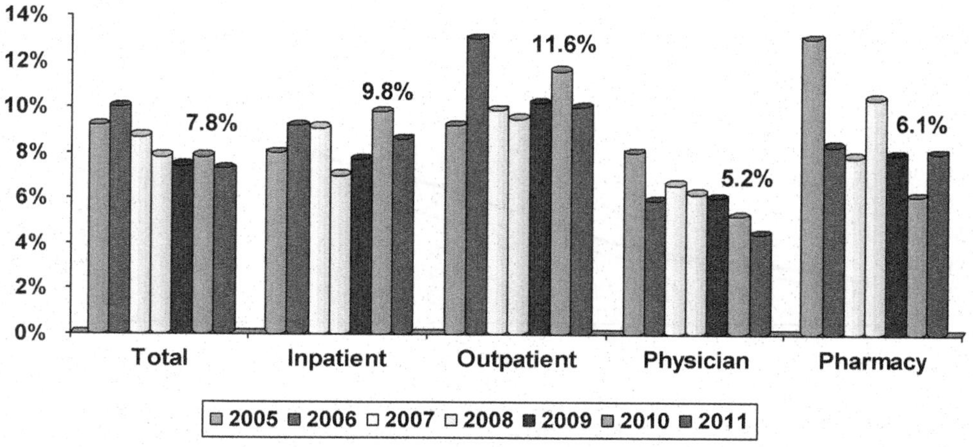


Prescription drug spending is important for a variety of reasons. Physicians and mental health professionals increasingly rely upon pharmaceuticals to treat various conditions, often as a substitute for surgery or other procedures (e.g., coronary artery disease). The new Medicare prescription drug benefit was effective in 2006.

In contrast to prescription drugs, Medicare spending (Exhibit 4, right axis, purple line) was increasing at slightly more than the overall national rate before Part D. Note the extraordinary effect that the new Medicare drug benefit has on Medicare spending by comparing the current projection to the prior projection as reflected in the red line. Shifting prescription drug spending to Medicare has caused the rate of growth in Medicare and overall spending to come close together. [The decline from 1997 to 2000 reflects the success of the Balanced Budget Act (BBA) of 1997 in slowing Medicare spending increases, which was cited by the chief actuary of CMS in his analysis of the healthcare reform legislation.] As noted above, projected Medicare spending post-reform is budgeted to grow more slowly than pre-reform, based upon a variety of factors, including limits in the annual hospital market basket updates for payments discussed infra. However, the chief actuary questions whether such changes will occur.

Medicaid (Exhibit 5) is a program shared between the federal and state government that covers the poor and, historically more significant, nursing home costs for lower-income seniors. Program spending slows in 2006 due to the advent of the Medicare prescription drug benefit as described above and then resumes growth at a higher rate. This pattern is also reflective of the aging population, slower economic growth post-Sept. 11, the continuation of the recession that began in 2008, and immigration patterns. Where Medicaid spending was expected to outstrip Medicare spending in 2005, the Medicare drug benefit had changed that, until the coming explosion in Medicaid spending as a

**Exhibit 4. National Health Expenditures and Medicare**

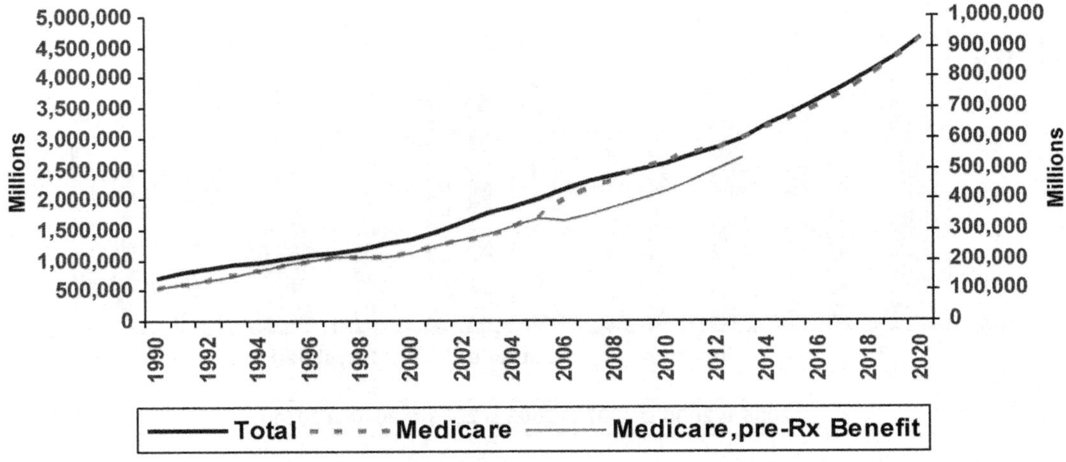


**Exhibit 5. National Health Expenditures and Medicaid**

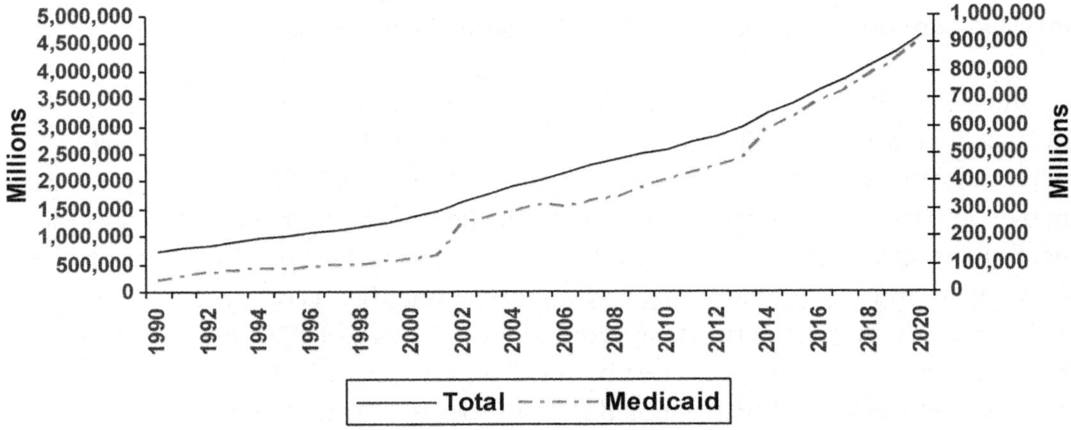


result of the reform legislation. Medicaid is one of,[6] if not the, principal deficit driver in state budgets and generally speaking is the largest line item in those budgets. Post-reform, Medicaid is expected to grow dramatically, as more than 50% of the newly insured are supposed to be covered by Medicaid.

Finally, the actual and projected trends for hospital and physician expenditures are plotted (Exhibit 6, right axis) against national health expenditures. As noted elsewhere in this report, physician expenditures are projected to grow more slowly for a variety of reasons, including present Medicare reimbursement limitations.

6 Unionized state employee pensions and benefits being the principal other one.

**Exhibit 6. National Health Expenditure, Hospital and Physician Costs**

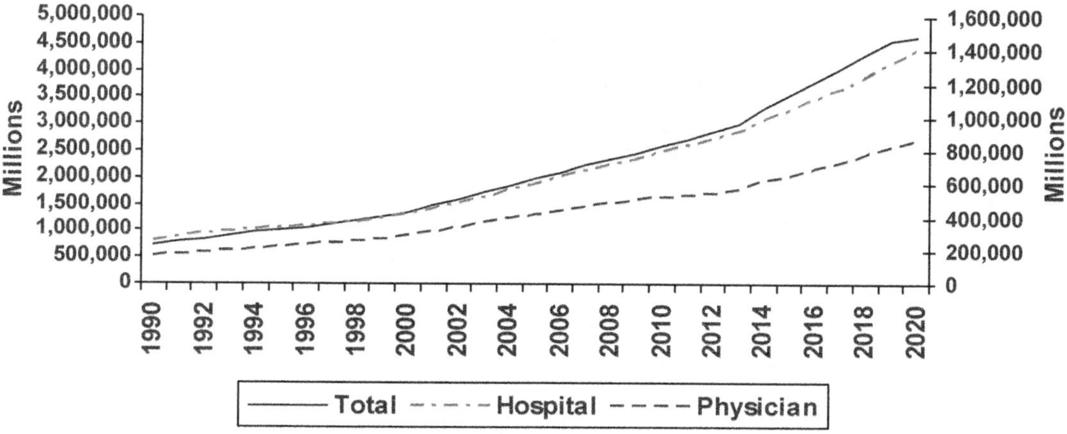


Healthcare spending is expected to continue to outstrip growth in GDP, exacerbated in the recession, as shown in Exhibit 7 from MedPAC's *2010 Report to Congress.*

**Exhibit 7. Health Care Spending Growth**

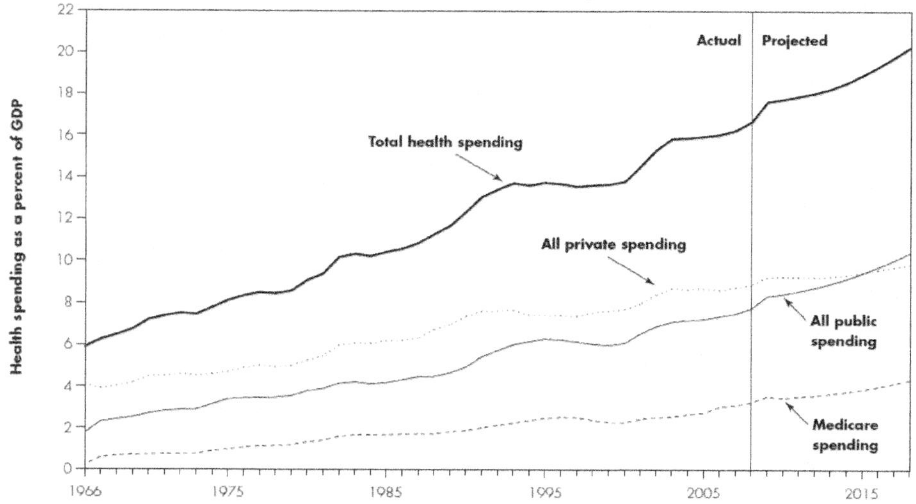


Note: GDP (gross domestic product). Total health spending is the sum of all private and public spending. Medicare spending is one component of all public spending.

Source: CMS, Office of the Actuary, National Health Expenditure Accounts, 2009.

There are five principal sponsors of sources for the payment of health expenditures, as shown in Exhibit 8.[7]

7 Ibid. "Recession Contributes to Slowest Annual Rate of Increase in Health Spending in Five Decades," *Health Affairs*, 30, no.1 (2011):11-22.

**Exhibit 8. 2009 National Health Expenditures, by Sponsor**

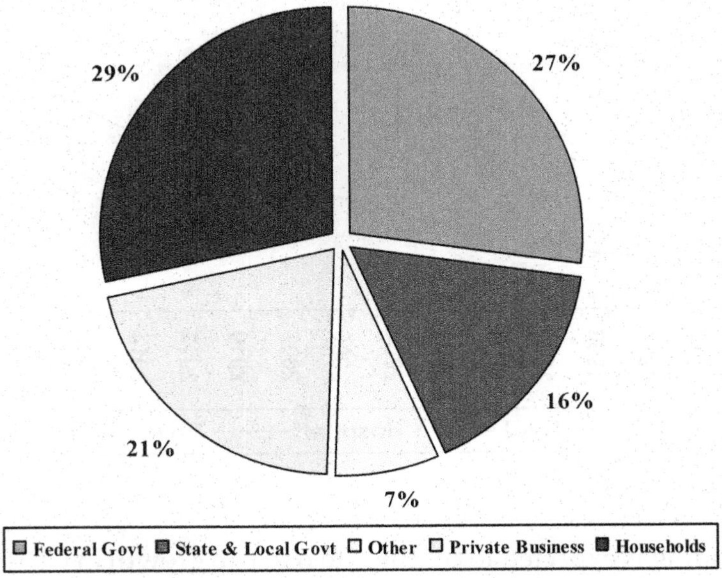


## Healthcare Indicators

### *Utilization*

Overall, inpatient admissions (or discharges) for the over-age-65 (Medicare) population continue to grow, based upon data from MedPAC's *2011 Report to Congress,* even though the *rate* of inpatient admissions per 1,000 population has grown less dramatically. (See Exhibit 9.) More services take place in the outpatient department of hospitals as well. This type of analysis is significant in valuing medical practices that have material earnings from hospital services. This would include the surgical specialties and consultative medical specialties, such as cardiology and particularly invasive cardiology. It also is connected to the trend to move surgical cases to ambulatory surgery centers, one of the most significant trends of the last decade.

A contributing factor to the loss of inpatient hospital revenue for nonsurgical physicians is the increasing presence of hospitalists, specially trained internists who typically work for a hospital and follow a patient throughout the course of their hospitalization. Many times, physicians who would prefer to follow their own patients while in-hospital are pressured into allowing the employed hospitalists to handle the care—and take the corresponding revenue stream.

**Exhibit 9. Hospital Discharge and Admissions Trend**[8]

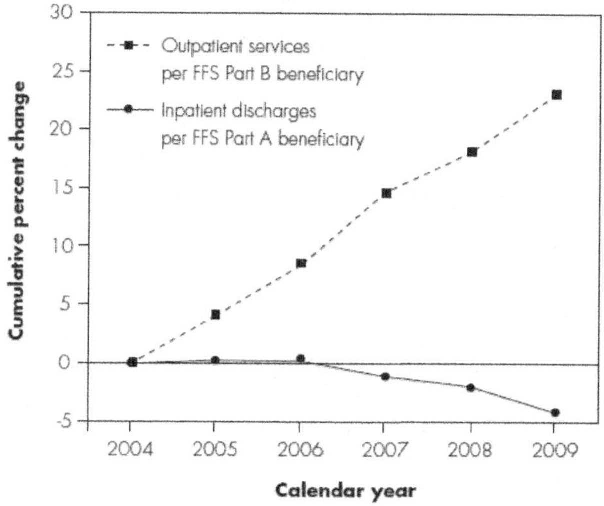


Note: FFS (fee-for-service). Data are for short-term general and surgical hospitals, including critical access and children's hospitals.

Source: MedPAC analysis of MedPAR and hospital outpatient claims data from CMS.

### *Costs*

Costs per inpatient admission had increased relatively slowly before 2001. This pattern is consistent with other data discussed herein indicating that hospitals are seeing large revenue increases after years of pricing pressure. Overall data (Exhibit 10) on hospital costs per day show a steady increase each year.

**Exhibit 10. Inpatient Cost Trend**[9]

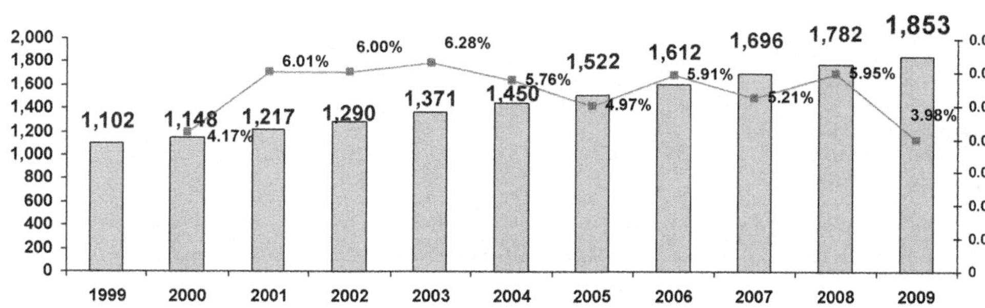


In contrast to hospital inpatient costs, outpatient visit costs have been increasing at a steadier rate as shown in Exhibits 11 and 12 from MedPac's 2011 *Report to Congress.* Hospitals have been progressively moving volume toward, and expanding the services

8 *2011 Report to Congress,* Medicare Payment Advisory Commission.

9 http://www.statehealthfacts.kff.org/comparemaptable.jsp?ind=273&cat=5, 2009 data.

of, outpatient settings where the government had historically been less successful in controlling utilization and price. Hospital inpatient services have for several decades been paid a fixed rate per *discharge* diagnosis (DRG) (known as a prospective payment system—PPS[10]) that varies principally based upon the number of admissions, rather than the number of days, in the hospital. Until comparatively recently, *outpatient* services were not paid under a PPS. This was changed by the BBA and implemented in August 2000. Such changes, of course, are very forecasting long-term growth trends.

**Exhibit 11. Cost Growth in 2009**

| | Annual cost growth | | | |
|---|---|---|---|---|
| **Cost measure** | **2006** | **2007** | **2008** | **2009** |
| Inpatient costs per discharge | 5.1% | 4.2% | 5.5% | 3.0% |
| Outpatient costs per service | 2.6 | 5.6 | 5.1 | 4.8 |
| Weighted average | 4.6 | 4.5 | 5.4 | 3.3 |
| Input price inflation | 4.2 | 3.4 | 4.3 | 2.6 |

Note: Cost growth numbers are not adjusted for reported changes in case mix. Analysis excludes critical access hospitals and Maryland hospitals. The weighted average is based on hospitals' inpatient and outpatient Medicare costs.

Source: MedPAC analysis of Medicare Cost Report and claims files from CMS.

**Exhibit 12. Medicare Growth in 2009**

| Hospital services | 2004 | 2008 | 2009 | Mean annual change 2004–2009 | Change 2008–2009 |
|---|---|---|---|---|---|
| **Inpatient services** | | | | | |
| Total FFS payments (in billions) | $100 | $110 | $114 | 2.7% | 3.7% |
| Payments per FFS enrollee | 2,831 | 3,202 | 3,337 | 3.6 | 4.2 |
| **Outpatient services** | | | | | |
| Total FFS payments (in billions) | 24 | 31 | 34 | 8.6 | 11.2 |
| Payments per FFS enrollee | 723 | 988 | 1,104 | 10.6 | 11.7 |
| **Inpatient and outpatient services** | | | | | |
| Total FFS payments (in billions) | 124 | 140 | 148 | 3.8 | 5.3 |
| Payments per FFS enrollee | 3,554 | 4,191 | 4,441 | 5.0 | 6.0 |

Note: FFS (fee-for-service). Reported hospital spending includes all hospitals covered by Medicare's inpatient prospective payment system along with critical access hospitals. Maryland hospitals are excluded. Fiscal year 2009 payments include partial imputation to account for hospitals that typically do not submit their cost reports to CMS before CMS makes the most recent year available to the public. Although the number of Medicare beneficiaries grew significantly from 2004 to 2009, the number of FFS beneficiaries declined over that time due to the shift of beneficiaries to the Medicare Advantage program. For the purposes of calculating payments per FFS beneficiary, we identified populations of FFS beneficiaries eligible for inpatient (Part A) and outpatient (Part B) coverage and excluded enrollees in Maryland. Due to rounding, totals may not equal the sum of their parts.

Source: MedPAC analysis of CMS hospital cost reports and MedPAR files.

Finally, outpatient visit growth continues to increase, while actual inpatient days per 1,000 continue to decline.[11]

10 www.cms.gov/providers/.

11 www.statehealthfacts.kff.org/comparemaptable.jsp?ind=390&cat=8, 2009 data.

**Exhibit 13. Hospital Outpatient and Inpatient Volume**

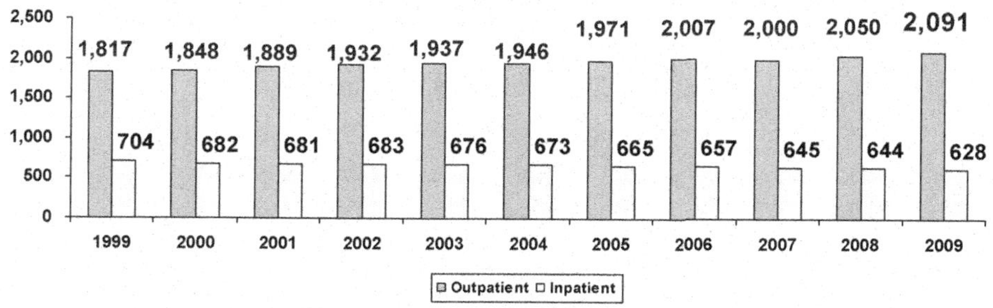


Medical expense inflation continues to outstrip the overall CPI, with hospital inflation leading the way, consistent with the inpatient costs per admission in Exhibit 13. Physician costs, in contrast, are increasing at a rate less than that of the medical CPI and significantly less than hospital costs and GDP (Exhibit 14). Hospital costs before 2000 and then again after 2008 had risen at a rate slightly less than GDP, reflecting the downward pressure on costs and utilization from HMOs and limited government payment increases. As the economy entered recession in 2008, healthcare expenditures continued to increase, even increasing during 2009, when the GDP and CPI otherwise declined, leading to concerns about deflation elsewhere in the economy. Once again, the healthcare segment proved to be more or less indifferent to the broad economy, an important factor to consider when conducting the valuation of healthcare entities because growth is rarely negative, even in a recession. [12,13]

**Exhibit 14. % Change: CPI-All, GDP and Various CPI-Healthcare**

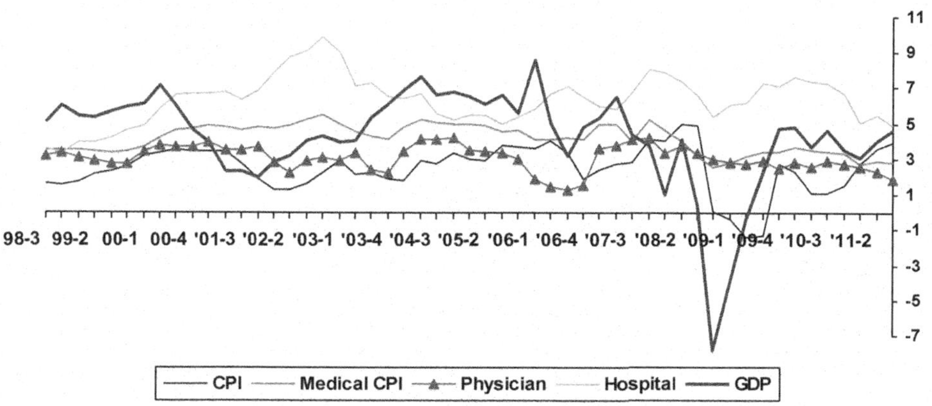


*(Rates shown in Exhibit 14 represent the percent change from same period of previous year.)*

12 www.bls.gov/cpi/#tables, Nov. 22, 2011.
13 www.bea.gov/newsreleases/national/gdp/gdpnewsrelease.htm, Table 1, Current Dollar.

A comparison of the CPI and medical care CPI with a trend line for medical care is shown in Exhibit 15. The recession has flattened the cost trend in the medical CPI.

**Exhibit 15. CPI and CPI Healthcare**

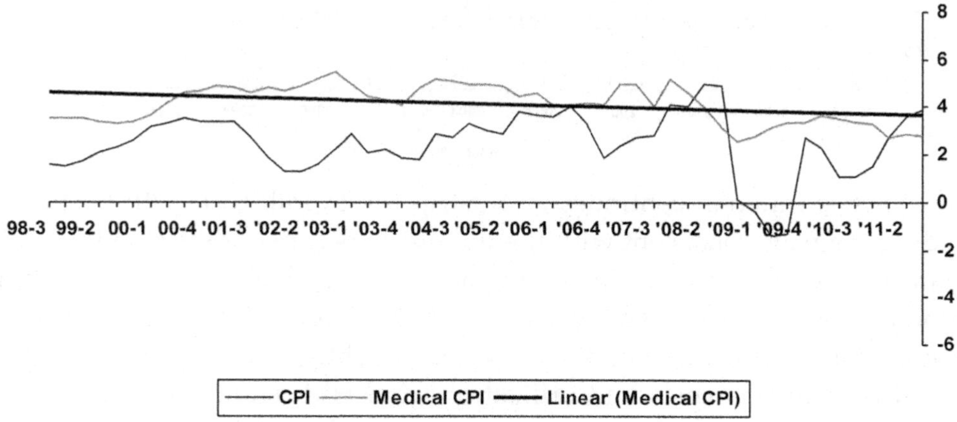


More telling, perhaps, is the CPI for medical care services (physicians and hospitals) versus that of physicians and hospitals taken alone, indicating that hospital costs are the main driver of healthcare inflation (Exhibit 16).

**Exhibit 16. CPI Healthcare[14]**

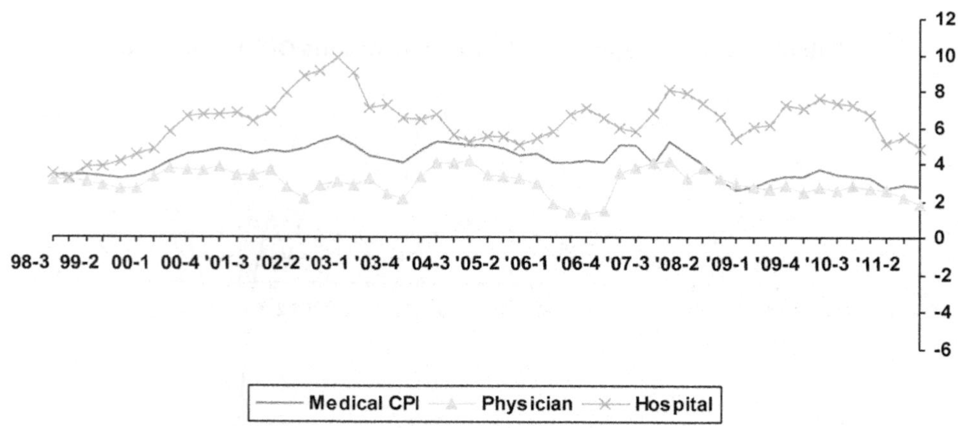


The data indicate that physician practice expenses were increasing at a higher rate than physician earnings, including fringe benefits,[15] although both are less than the medical CPI as shown in Exhibit 17. Data on physician wages and salaries are no longer

14 www.cms.hhs.gov/MedicareProgramRatesStats/03_HlthCrInds.asp#TopOfPage.

15 www.cms.hhs.gov/MedicareProgramRatesStats/04_MarketBasketData.asp.

presented, although they showed considerably lower growth then the reported earnings number through the last data point, in 2004, before subsequent revisions to the data. Benefit growth accounts for a significant part of the reported increase. Importantly, the values are also *productivity adjusted* using Bureau of Labor Statistics nonfarm multifactor productivity, a generic workforce measure that does not reflect physician practices. Historically, both reports and projections of practice expense growth being less than the rate of earnings growth do not, in fact, materialize; however, they continue to appear in the forecast! The year 2007 represents an exception due to the significant rate increases for physicians, offsetting years of accelerating costs without increases in per unit fees.

CMS forecasts of physician earnings typically reflect the threat of significant cuts due to failure to repeal the sustainable growth rate formula discussed elsewhere herein in the absence of legislative change, unless those cuts have been legislatively deferred, such as was the case in 2005 through 2011. This is a result of the artificial constraints placed upon increases in physician reimbursement by the Medicare program, which are not present for any other class of provider (e.g., hospitals or home health care), although the reform legislation imposes certain productivity targets on hospitals for the first time. However, the reform legislation imposes requirements for productivity gains on hospitals, which, notably, the chief actuary of CMS says are likely unobtainable.

**Exhibit 17. MD Earnings and Practice Expense Trend**[16, 17]

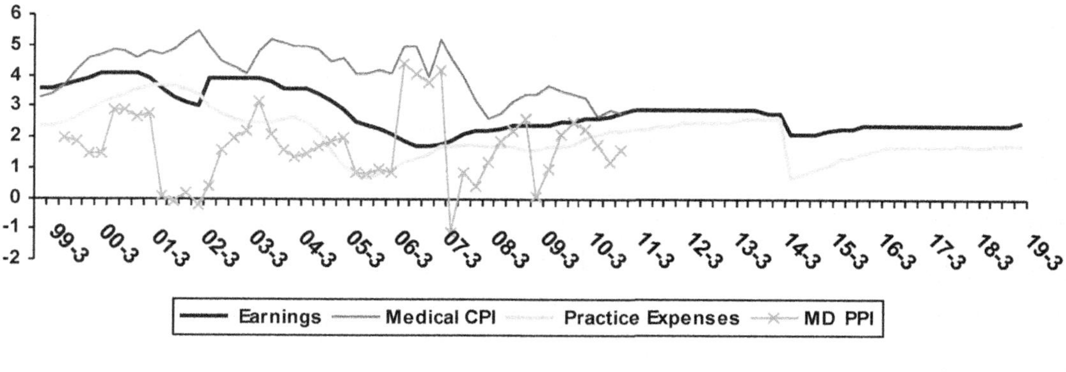


This PPI for physicians has steadily maintained a compound rate of growth of approximately 2%, although the year-to-year changes are quite volatile, particularly in 2007. In fact, the *compound* rate of growth in physician fees during this 15-year period was only 1.96% (Exhibit 18).

16 www.bls.gov/schedule/archives/ppi_nr.htm, Nov. 22, 2011.
17 www.bls.gov/cpi/#tables.

Exhibit 18. Producer Price Index, Physician Services

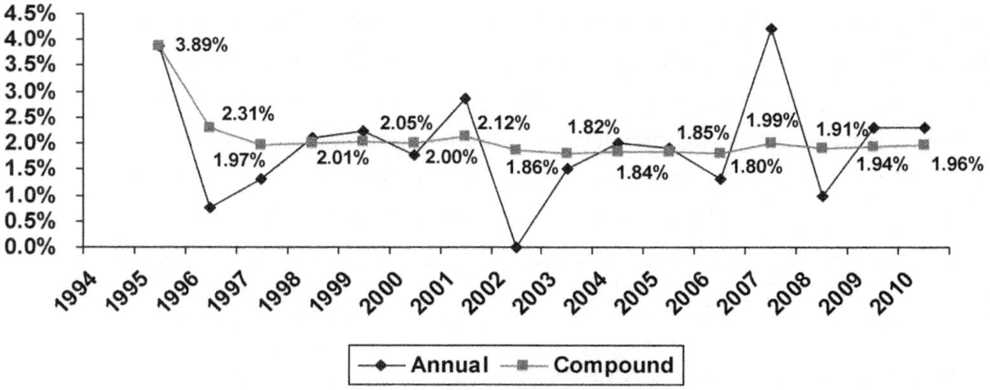


## Trends in Physician Supply and Demand and Utilization

Exhibit 19 illustrates the breakdown of patient office visits by individual physician specialties from the National Center for Health Statistics.[18] General and family practice, internal medicine, and pediatrics accounted for 50.61% of all patient office visits in 2007, down from 51% in 2006.

Exhibit 19. Patent Office Visits by Individual Physician Specialties

| Specialty | 2007 % of visits | 2006 % of visits | 2005 % of visits | 2004 % of visits | 2003 % of visits | 2002 % of visits | 2001 % of visits | 2000 % of visits |
|---|---|---|---|---|---|---|---|---|
| General practice/ family practice | 22.9% | 23.1% | 22.4% | 22.8% | 24.6% | 24.2% | 23.9% | 24.1% |
| Internal medicine | 14.5 | 13.9 | 17.4 | 16.1 | 15.6 | 17.6 | 15.3 | 15.2 |
| Pediatrics | 13.2 | 13.6 | 13.4 | 12.8 | 10.4 | 13.5 | 12.6 | 12.6 |
| All others | 10.6 | 13.0 | 12.1 | 13.5 | 13.1 | 11.7 | 11.0 | 11.7 |
| Obstetrics/gynecology | 7.4 | 7.7 | 6.7 | 7.2 | 8.8 | 7.9 | 7.9 | 7.9 |
| Ophthalmology | 5.9 | 6.4 | 6.1 | 5.2 | 5.4 | 5.6 | 6.1 | 5.2 |
| Orthopedic surgery | 5.1 | 5.3 | 4.8 | 4.8 | 4.8 | 4.3 | 5.3 | 5.6 |
| Dermatology | 4.5 | 2.8 | 3.4 | 3.7 | 3.3 | 3.6 | 4.3 | 4.2 |
| Cardiovascular | 3.3 | 2.9 | 2.8 | 2.5 | 2.8 | 2.3 | 3.2 | 2.6 |
| Psychiatry | 3.3 | 2.8 | 2.9 | 3.4 | 3.2 | 2.4 | 3.1 | 3.5 |
| General surgery | 2.0 | 1.6 | 2.5 | 2.1 | 2.2 | 1.9 | 2.2 | 2.1 |
| Otolaryngology | 2.0 | 1.9 | 2.3 | 2.2 | 2.4 | 1.9 | 2.0 | 2.0 |
| Urology | 1.9 | 2.0 | 2.0 | 2.0 | 2.0 | 1.9 | 1.9 | 2.3 |
| Neurology | 1.7 | 1.4 | 1.4 | 1.6 | 1.4 | 1.1 | 1.2 | 1.0 |

18 National Health Statistics 2007 NAMCS micro-data file documentation. Note that not all of the possible physician specialties were separately tracked in the NCHS study.

Data from the *2007 National Ambulatory Medical Care Survey*[19] show the shift from small practices to larger practices over the last 10 years in Exhibit 20.

**Exhibit 20. Shift From Larger Practices to Smaller Practices**

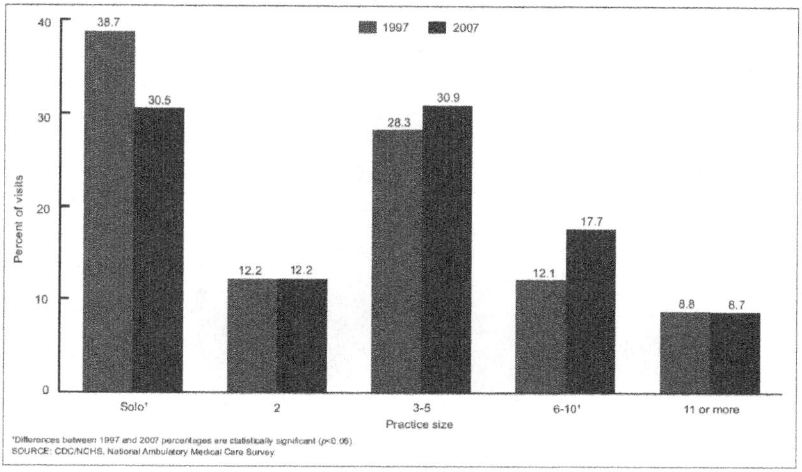


Figure 1. Percentage of office visits by practice size: United States, 1997 and 2007

Exhibit 21 shows expected office visits per patient per year from the same NCHS data[20] and is valuable for estimating patient volume in an office setting, particularly where capitation may be involved.

**Exhibit 21. Total Office Visits Per Patient Per Year for All Physician Specialties[21]**

| Age | All | Female | Male |
|---|---|---|---|
| <1 | 7.316 | | |
| 1–4 | 3.413 | | |
| 5–14 | 1.998 | | |
| <15 | 1.966 | 3.838 | 2.855 |
| 15–24 | 2.488 | 2.646 | 1.411 |
| 25–44 | 3.733 | 2.533 | 1.621 |
| 45–64 | 7.124 | 3.339 | 3.183 |
| 65–74 | 6.689 | 4.252 | 6.609 |
| >75 | 7.610 | 6.756 | 8.014 |
| Total | 7.316 | 7.347 | 2.855 |

19 *National Ambulatory Medical Care Survey: 2007 Summary*, Nov. 3, 2010 www.cdc.gov/nchs/data/nhsr/nhsr027.pdf.
20 *National Ambulatory Medical Care Survey: 2007 Summary*, Nov. 3, 2010 www.cdc.gov/nchs/data/nhsr/nhsr027.pdf.
21 *National Ambulatory Medical Care Survey: 2007 Summary*, Nov. 3, 2010 www.cdc.gov/nchs/data/nhsr/nhsr027.pdf.

Exhibit 22 takes the data from Exhibit 21 and depicts all specialties accounting for more than 4% of patient visits. It is important to note that these specialties are predominantly primary care, or specialties such as ophthalmology and ob/gyn that have primary care-like features, i.e., the need to be seen by many patients regularly. Only orthopedics and ophthalmology among the non-primary care specialties have significant patient volume.

**Exhibit 22. Concentration of Visits/Physicians by Specialty**

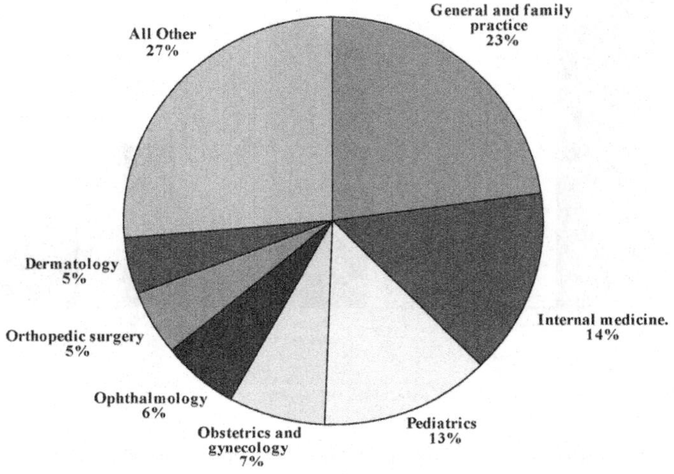


The Kaiser Family Foundation breaks down Primary Care Physicians in 2008 in Exhibit 23.

**Exhibit 23. Breakdown of Primary Care Physicians**

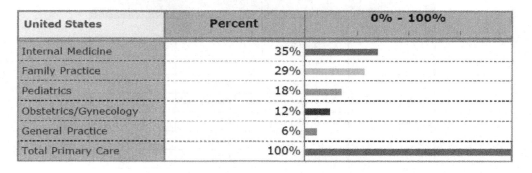

| United States | Percent | 0% - 100% |
|---|---|---|
| Internal Medicine | 35% | |
| Family Practice | 29% | |
| Pediatrics | 18% | |
| Obstetrics/Gynecology | 12% | |
| General Practice | 6% | |
| Total Primary Care | 100% | |

In interpreting the relative number of *office* visits among the various specialties illustrated, readers should bear in mind that the surgical specialties in particular perform many of their services in *hospital* settings. In addition, the medical specialties, such as cardiology and nephrology, for example, have many encounters in the hospital as well, such as for consultations requested by other physicians.[22]

22 www.cdc.gov/nchs/fastats/docvisit.htm.

The physician recruiting firm Merritt Hawkins released its annual report in May 2011. Data on annual recruiting engagements indicate that the specialties in highest demand include family medicine, internal medicine, hospitalist, orthopedic surgery, ob/gyn, and cardiology. Hospitals or existing practices looking to recruit such physicians typically find the starting salary very high and the structure of a future buy-in on the table from the outset.

Primary care physicians in internal medicine and family practice are in high demand, bucking the specialist trend, making it difficult or impossible in many markets to sell an interest in a practice at a significant price. Some speculate that the shortage of specialists is driving the demand for internists and family practitioners, who may provide higher-level adult medical care when specialists such as cardiologists are not available.

A serious shortage of physicians and particularly primary care (generalist) physicians is expected in the next several decades. This has negative implications for practice value because the ease of entry into the market for new suppliers is enhanced when demand for services is unmet and in excess.[23]

Medicare-participating physicians by specialty and region are shown in Exhibits 24 and 25 from the publication *2009 CMS Statistics*.[24] The regional data is of particular note, given the differing concentrations of physicians per 100,000 population around the country.

**Exhibit 24. Part B Practicioners/CMS Region**

| | Active practitioners | Practitioners per 100,000 population |
|---|---|---|
| All regions | 1,245,003 [1] | 413 |
| Boston | 96,484 | 676 |
| New York | 147,395 | 527 |
| Philadelphia | 133,101 | 459 |
| Atlanta | 221,727 | 374 |
| Chicago | 211,442 | 410 |
| Dallas | 118,319 | 323 |
| Kansas City | 62,890 | 469 |
| Denver | 46,248 | 444 |
| San Francisco | 151,680 | 325 |
| Seattle | 55,717 | 449 |

[1] Includes non-Federal physicians, limited licensed and non-physician practitioners. Practitioners with multi-State practices are duplicated in the enumeration for each State in which they operate.

NOTES: Physicians as of July 2007. Civilian population as of July 1, 2007. Resident population for outlying areas and the Virgin Islands are not available.

SOURCES: CMS, ORDI, and the Bureau of the Census.

23 "Will Generalist Physician Supply Meet Demands of an Increasing and Aging Population?" Jack M. Colwill, James M. Cultice, and Robin L. Kruse; *Health Affairs*, 29 April 2008.

24 www.cms.gov/ResearchGenInfo/02_CMSStatistics.asp.

**Exhibit 25. Part B Practitioners Active in Patient Care/Selected Years**

| | July 2007 | |
|---|---|---|
| | Number | Percent |
| All Part B Practitioners | 1,087,845 | 100.0 |
| | | |
| Physician Specialties | 667,340 | 61.3 |
| Primary Care | 246,314 | 22.6 |
| Medical Specialties | 108,694 | 10.0 |
| Surgical Specialties | 108,031 | 9.9 |
| Emergency Medicine | 36,644 | 3.4 |
| Anesthesiology | 38,358 | 3.5 |
| Radiology | 37,595 | 3.5 |
| Pathology | 13,984 | 1.3 |
| Obstetrics/Gynecology | 38,515 | 3.5 |
| Psychiatry | 38,921 | 3.6 |
| Other and Unknown | 284 | 0.0 |
| Limited Licensed Practitioners | 126,006 | 11.6 |
| Non-physician Practitioners | 294,499 | 27.1 |

NOTES: Specialty code is self-reported and may not correspond to actual board certification. Totals do not necessarily equal the sum of rounded components. Reflect unduplicated counts.

SOURCE: CMS Office of Research, Development, and Information

*2010 CMS Statistics*[25] suggest there are considerably fewer practitioners today than there were three years ago (see Exhibit 26).

**Exhibit 26. Medicare Participating and Nonparticipating Physicians and Practitioners**

| | Calendar Year 2010 |
|---|---|
| All Part B Practitioners | 973,299 |
| | |
| Physician Specialties | 616,749 |
| Internal Medicine[1] | 103,840 |
| Family Practice | 82,242 |
| Emergency Medicine | 40,066 |
| Anesthesiology | 38,300 |
| Radiology[2] | 36,034 |
| Obstetrics/Gynecology | 32,367 |
| Psychiatry[3] | 28,739 |
| Cardiology | 24,590 |
| Orthopedic Surgery | 22,765 |
| Other and Unknown | 207,806 |
| Limited Licensed Practitioners | 96,004 |
| Non-physician Practitioners | 260,546 |

[1] Includes the Internal Medicine, Endocrinology, and Medical Oncology.
[2] Includes Radiology, Nuclear Medicine, and Interventional Radiology.
[3] Includes Psychiatry and Neuropsychiatry.

NOTE: Top 9 specialties presented, in terms of total counts.

SOURCE: CMS, Office of Financial Management.

25 www.cms.gov/ResearchGenInfo/02_CMSStatistics.asp.

## Trends in Health Insurance Coverage

According to the Census Bureau's 2011 survey:[26] "in 2010, the percentage of people without health insurance, 16.3%, was not statistically different from the rate in 2009. The number of uninsured people increased to 49.9 million in 2010 from 49 million in 2009. The percentage of people with health insurance in 2010 was not statistically different from 2009, while the number of insured increased to 256.2 million in 2010 from 255.3 million in 2009. The percentage of people covered by private health insurance decreased in 2010, to 64%, while the number of people covered by private health insurance was not statistically different from 2009, at 195.9 million. The percentage of people covered by private health insurance has been decreasing since 2001. The percentage and number of people covered by government health insurance increased to 31% and 95 million in 2010 from 30.6% and 93.2 million in 2009. The percentage of people covered by employment-based health insurance decreased to 55.3% in 2010 from 56.1% in 2009. The number of people covered by employment-based health insurance decreased to 169.3 million from 170.8 million. The percentage and number of people covered by Medicaid in 2010, 15.9% and 48.6 million, were not statistically different from 2009 estimates (Exhibit 27). The percentage and number of people covered by Medicare increased in 2010, to 14.5% and 44.3 million."

Exhibit 27 indicates the percentages of the United States population covered by insurance during 2009 and 2010. The figures in the accompanying table add to more than 100% because some individuals were covered by more than one form of insurance during the year.

### Exhibit 27. Coverage by Type of Health Insurance: 2009 and 2010

(People as of March of the following year. For information on confidentiality protection, sampling error, nonsampling error, and definitions, see *www.census.gov/apsd/techdoc/cps/cpsmar11.pdf*)

| Coverage type | 2009 | 2010 |
|---|---|---|
| Any private plan[1] | 64.5 | *64.0 |
| Any private plan alone[2] | 53.3 | *52.7 |
| Employment-based[1] | 56.1 | *55.3 |
| Employment-based alone[2] | 46.6 | *45.8 |
| Direct-purchase[1] | 9.6 | *9.8 |
| Direct-purchase alone[2] | 3.7 | 3.7 |
| Any government plan[1] | 30.6 | *31.0 |
| Any government plan alone[2] | 19.4 | 19.7 |
| Medicare[1] | 14.3 | *14.5 |
| Medicare alone[2] | 4.5 | *4.7 |
| Medicaid[1] | 15.7 | 15.9 |
| Medicaid alone[2] | 11.2 | 11.2 |
| Military health care[1,3] | 4.1 | 4.2 |
| Military health care alone[2,3] | 1.3 | 1.3 |
| Uninsured | 16.1 | 16.3 |

*Statistically different from zero at the 90 percent confidence level.

[1]The estimates by type of coverage are *not* mutually exclusive; people can be covered by more than one type of health insurance during the year.

[2]The estimates by type of coverage are mutually exclusive; people did not have any other type of health insurance during the year.

[3]Military health care includes Tricare and CHAMPVA (Civilian Health and Medical Program of the Department of Veteran Affairs), as well as care provided by the Department of Veterans Affairs and the military.

Source: U.S. Census Bureau, Current Population Survey, 2010 and 2011 Annual Social and Economic Supplements.

26 www.census.gov/prod/2011pubs/p60-239.pdf, issued September 2011.

***Summary***

The preceding review indicates that healthcare spending is advancing at a rate in excess of that of inflation and exceeds GDP growth. The success of managed care in controlling medical costs has long since come to an end, resulting in a focus on new insurance products that are putting the consumer at increased risk for their decisions, something the reform legislation purports to reinforce. *Overall* trends in healthcare spending, however, are neither indicative nor predictive of trends in specific subsectors of the industry. Physician incomes generally are increasing at a rate less than the medical CPI, even as their operating expenses increase at a greater rate. Hospital expenses have consistently grown faster than the CPI and recently, at a rate faster than GDP, particularly in the recession. This latter trend reflects increases in both utilization and unit prices.

## Concentration of Market Share

As can be seen in Exhibit 28, based upon a Government Accountability Office study, the provision of health insurance is significantly state-specific. Most markets are dominated by a few insurance companies; many are dominated by a *single* company. This fact results in strikingly different market conditions from state to state and virtual oligopolistic or monopolistic valuation of physician services.

**Exhibit 28. Provision of Health Insurance, by State**

| | Number of Licensed Carriers | Largest Carrier | Market Share of Largest Carrier | Market Share of 5 Largest Carriers | Rank of Largest BCBS carrier | Market Share of all BCBS carriers |
|---|---|---|---|---|---|---|
| Alabama | NA | BCBS of Alabama | 78.0% | NA | 1 | NA |
| Alaska | 12 | Premera Blue Cross | 66.0 | 100.0% | 1 | 66.0% |
| Arizona | 53 | United of Arizona | 29.0 | 66.0 | 2 | 19.0 |
| Colorado | 27 | United | 24.0 | 72.0 | 3 | 13.0 |
| Connecticut | 25 | Anthem BCBS of Connecticut | NA | NA | 1 | NA |
| Delaware | 16 | BCBS of Delaware | 58.0 | 99.0 | 1 | 58.0 |
| District of Columbia | 13 | Group H&M BCBS | 43.0 | 97.0 | 1 | 65.0 |
| Florida | 29 | United of Florida | 22.0 | 78.0 | 3 | 31.0 |
| Georgia | 75 | BCBS of Georgia | 27.0 | 65.0 | 1 | 41.0 |
| Idaho | 16 | BCBS of Idaho | 45.0 | 97.0 | 1 | 87.0 |
| Illinois | 51 | NA | NA | NA | NA | NA |
| Iowa | 60 | Wellmark BCBS | 56.0 | 91.0 | 1 | 68.0 |
| Kansas | 28 | BCBS of Kansas | NA | NA | 1 | NA |
| Kentucky | 10 | Anthem BCBS | 43.0 | 93.0 | 1 | 43.0 |
| Louisiana | 35 | Louisiana BCBS | 29.0 | 85.0 | 1 | 54.0 |
| Maine | 12 | Anthem BCBS | 48.0 | 98.0 | 1 | 63.0 |
| Maryland | 16 | CareFirst | 43.0 | 90.0 | 1 | 59.0 |

continued

**Exhibit 28. Provision of Health Insurance, by State, Continued**

| | Number of Licensed Carriers | Largest Carrier | Market Share of Largest Carrier | Market Share of 5 Largest Carriers | Rank of Largest BCBS carrier | Market Share of all BCBS carriers |
|---|---|---|---|---|---|---|
| Massachusetts | 25 | BCBS of Massachusetts | 32.0 | 86.0 | 1 | 39.0 |
| Michigan | 45 | BCBS of Michigan | 62.0 | 78.0 | 1 | 69.0 |
| Minnesota | 11 | BCBSM | 45.0 | 98.0 | 1 | 45.0 |
| Missouri | 38 | Health Alliance Life | 46.0 | 87.0 | 3 | 8.0 |
| Montana | 13 | BCBS of Montana | 36.0 | 85.0 | 1 | 36.0 |
| Nevada | 35 | Health Plan of Nevada | NA | NA | NA | NA |
| New Jersey | 16 | Aetna Health | 37.0 | 86.0 | 2 | 27.0 |
| New York | 29 | Oxford | 21.0 | 63.0 | 2 | 36.0 |
| North Carolina | 32 | BCBS of North Carolina | 54.0 | 89.0 | 1 | 54.0 |
| North Dakota | 9 | Noridian/BCBS | 93.0 | 99.0 | 1 | 93.0 |
| Ohio | 63 | Community BCBS | 32.0 | 79.0 | 1 | 32.0 |
| Oklahoma | 36 | Group Health BCBS | 30.0 | 71.0 | 1 | 49.0 |
| Oregon | 12 | Lifewise (Premera) | 25.0 | 79.0 | 5 | 14.0 |
| Rhode Island | 3 | BCBS of Rhode Island | NA | NA | 1 | NA |
| South Carolina | 29 | BCBS of South Carolina | 49.0 | 87.0 | 1 | 49.0 |
| Tennessee | 41 | BCBS of Tennessee | 49.0 | 85.0 | 1 | 49.0 |
| Texas | 58 | United | 19.0 | 59.0 | 3 | 17.0 |
| Utah | 22 | Regence BCBS | 40.0 | 93.0 | 1 | 40.0 |
| Vermont | 12 | BCBS of Vermont | 73.0 | 100.0 | 1 | 84.0 |
| Virginia | 45 | Anthem BCBS | NA | NA | 1 | NA |
| Washington | 12 | Premera Blue Cross | 57.0 | 92.0 | 1 | 85.0 |
| West Virginia | 33 | BCBS | 43.0 | 77.0 | 1 | 43.0 |
| Wisconsin | 50 | United of Wisconsin | 20.0 | 49.0 | 3 | 6.0 |
| Wyoming | 15 | BCBS of Wyoming | 40.0 | 74.0 | 1 | 38.0 |
| Average | 29.05 | | 43.3 | 83.7 | 1 | 46.5 |

(Source: *GAO Private Health Insurance Study*)

Reflective of the GAO study, an independent study was conducted in January 2008 by Mark Dietrich[27] (published in the Summer 2008 edition of *Business Valuation Review*) of the distribution of for-profit and nonprofit health insurers and providers in a number of specific markets in the United States. The findings are summarized as follows.

The degree of revenue and profit for healthcare provider entities varies significantly from state to state and even within different regions of individual states. As a threshold matter, areas with high healthcare spending and particularly high Medicare[28] spending tend to offer the greatest opportunity for profit. The elderly, of course, receive the bulk of medical care. Given that high localized spending is the primary driver of profit,

27 "Healthcare Market Structure and Its Implication for Valuation of Privately Held Provider Entities: An Empirical Analysis," *Business Valuation Review*, Summer 2008.

28 Medicare spending varies considerably from region to region with states such as Florida, Texas, California, and Tennessee having high per capita and total dollar spending and many for-profit providers.

the other factors contributing to the pattern of location of larger for-profit providers include:

- The presence and market strength of Blue Cross plans,
- The degree of market strength of local nonprofit hospitals versus for-profit hospitals,
- The degree of market strength of local nonprofit health insurers versus for-profit health insurers,
- Certificate of need laws, and
- Other local demographic and economic factors including:
  - Income levels of population;
  - Health insurance coverage statistics, including coverage by Medicaid;
  - Hospital spending per capita and in total; and
  - Physician spending per capita and in total.

Healthcare markets are highly localized and use of out-of-market data because the valuation of a healthcare business requires a detailed analysis of conditions in the source market as well as the subject market. Regulatory restrictions on the use of market data in the Stark laws cannot be dismissed because there are fundamental economic reasons for those restrictions as well as professional standards that require they be respected. Markets in which larger for-profit provider entities are present will have transactions that reflect not only the local market conditions but also the revenue and earnings growth inherent in the motivation of public companies. Public healthcare providers such as AMSG are consolidators driven by acquisition growth. Even those nonprofit markets where healthcare spending and insurer concentration are otherwise similar to for-profit markets may have very different values for local entities than are indicated by consolidator-driven multiples. Thus, methods under the market approach have to be used with considerable skill and intensive analysis.[29]

Large for-profit providers of this type pay prices for healthcare businesses that reflect the actions of the stock market, as described in the following quote. Nonprofit providers that dominate healthcare delivery in Connecticut do not have an economic basis to pay multiples driven by the stock market. The following quote is also taken from the article:

> Growth potential in the form of acquisition growth is typically only available to publicly traded companies whose stock prices are in large part driven by expected

29 "Healthcare Market Structure and Its Implication for Valuation of Privately Held Provider Entities: An Empirical Analysis"; *Business Valuation Review*, Summer 2008.

> growth rates. High growth rates typically result in high valuation multiples due to low capitalization rates. Economies of scale from acquisitions that affect future "same store" profit growth also contribute to localized valuation differences. As such, all things being equal, a growth-driven public company is able to pay a higher value for a given business because the stock market rewards growth.[30]

Based on this analysis, larger for-profit providers—publicly traded or private equity funded—are primarily located south of the Mason-Dixon Line, where labor unions have historically been less prevalent. Primary locations for these large providers include Florida, Texas, Tennessee, and California. As such, transactions engaged in by these companies are not deemed relevant for valuation purposes in Connecticut since they do not do business here and therefore, would not be part of the universe of hypothetical buyers.

### The State of Managed Care

As noted elsewhere herein, one of the most significant issues affecting the healthcare economy and therefore, the forecast of future cash flow is the underwriting cycle. In part, that cycle of premium increases and decreases reflects the relationship between the costs of provider payments and the premium charged. Exhibit 29 reflects both seasonality as well as overall decreases.

**Exhibit 29. Premium and Cost Trends[31]**

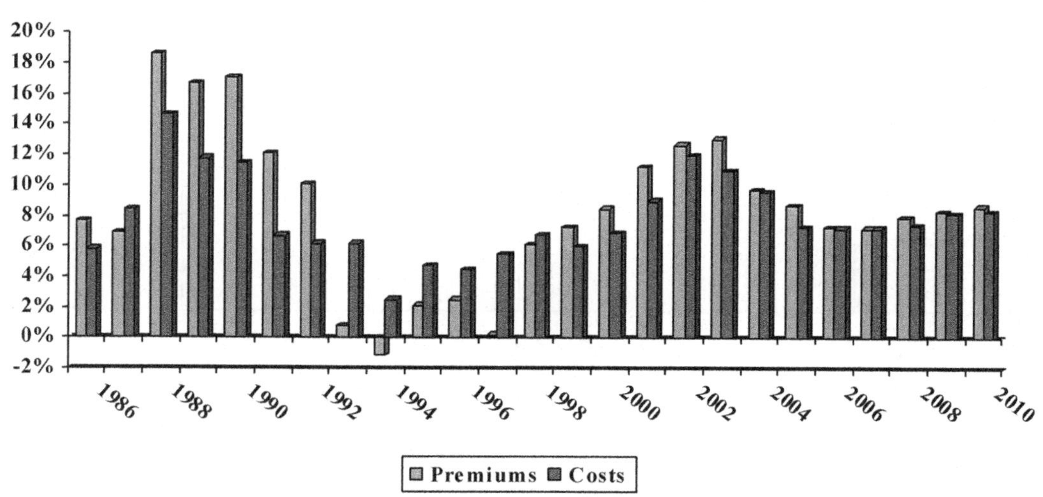


30 See also "Understanding the Difference Between Strategic Value and Fair Market Value in Consolidating Industries" *Business Valuation Review*, June 2002, by Mark O. Dietrich.

31 Based on *Health Care- Managed Care*, Jan. 7, 2010, Barclays Capital, sourced from Milliman, CMS, and company documents.

An important trend influencing health insurance premium growth is the use of so-called "buy-downs," or cost shifting to employees via cost-sharing for premiums, deductibles, and co-pays for care. To elaborate, "cost-sharing of premiums" refers to the practice of having the employer pay less than 100% of the cost of insurance. "Deductible" refers to the practice of requiring the employee to pay a certain amount, say $1,000, out-of-pocket before insurance takes over. A "co-pay" refers to the amount that an employee must pay for each medical encounter, such as $25 for an office visit or $250 per hospital visit. Another increasingly common buy-down is to charge a higher co-pay on prescriptions for name-brand drugs versus generics (referred to as a tiered formulary). Clearly, cost sharing by the consumers of their health care substantially influences the volume of consumption.

Each of these devices reduces the premium charged by the health insurer for coverage and also reduces the health insurers' medical costs. Thus, when we read that premiums are increasing by 12%, the overall cost of medical care—including that now borne by the consumer—is likely increasing at a higher rate. This is also reflected in the fact that before the recession, most health insurers were experiencing a decrease in their medical costs (the medical loss ratio—MLR). This cyclical phenomenon was a major contributor to reform's mandating minimum MLRs

The historical pattern in the aggregate MLR for various companies in the industry are shown in Exhibit 30. As the MLR declines, profits are likely to increase.

**Exhibit 30. Trend in MLR**

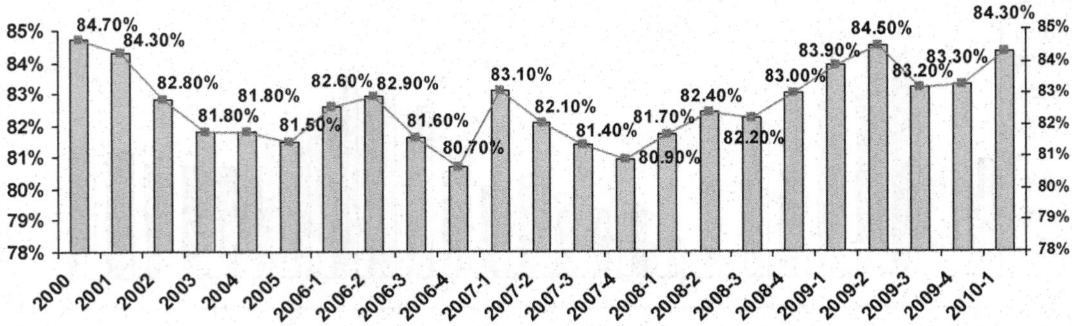


(Source: Health Care-Managed Care, Jan. 7, 2010, Barclays Capital, based on company documents)

Medical costs included in the MLR consist of four distinct components: inpatient, outpatient, physician, and pharmacy. Inpatient costs refer to hospital and other facilities, while outpatient includes ambulatory surgery, imaging, and lab work.

Managed care insurers at one time were actually engaged in taking risk for the cost of care of their insureds. Due to the catastrophic losses of the 1990s, which forced many, particularly smaller, competitors out of business, the industry has increasingly turned to providing *self-funded* or *self-insured* plans to employers. Under these arrangements, the insurer acts as the administrator[32] on behalf of the employer, and the employer (and its employees via any cost-sharing) assume the risk of their care. The insurer charges a fee for providing access to its provider network, paying claims, and providing "stop-loss," or excess limits, coverage.[33] Typical stop-loss levels vary with the size of the insured group and the resultant actuarial risk but may be as little as $10,000 or as high as $100,000 or more. Self-insured plans also escaped many of reform's more burdensome provisions, and reform is likely to accelerate the trend toward self-insuring for those employers large enough to consider it. Although newly self-insured groups will not escape reforms to the underlying benefit requirements, they will avoid the enormous cost increases associated with merging the small group and individual markets contemplated by the legislation as happened in Massachusetts, the model for reform.

#### *Premium Trend*

The increase in medical insurance premiums exploded again in 2011, in significant part due to the federal reform legislation, which exposes insurers to significant additional risk and cost from coverage of previously uninsured and likely unhealthier individuals. In addition, the legislation contains a "jawboning" provision requiring insurers to defend increases in excess of 10% to the federal Department of Health and Human Services (HHS), but not permitting HHS to do anything about it. Not surprisingly, most insurers raised premiums just under that level!

According to the Kaiser Family Foundation and Health Research and Educational Trust (HRET) *2011 Employer Health Benefits Survey* released in September 2011:

> The key findings from the 2011 survey, conducted from January 2011 through May 2011, include increases in the average single and family premiums, as well higher enrollment in high deductible health plans with savings options (HDHP/SOs). The 2011 survey includes new questions on the percentage of firms with grandfathered health plans, changes in benefits for preventive care, enrollment of adult children due to the new health reform law, and the use of stop-loss coverage by firms with self-funded plans.
>
> The average annual premiums for employer-sponsored health insurance in 2011 are $5,429 for single coverage and $15,073 for family coverage. Compared to 2010,

32 Also known as ASO or administrative services only business.
33 See the Glossary at the end of this report.

premiums for single coverage are 8% higher and premiums for family coverage are 9% higher. The 9% growth rate in family premiums for 2011 is significantly higher than the 3% growth rate in 2010. Since 2001, average premiums for family coverage have increased 113% (Exhibit 31). Average premiums for family coverage are lower for workers in small firms (those with three to 199 workers) than for workers in large firms, those with 200 workers or more ($14,098 versus $15,520), shown in Exhibit 32. Average premiums for HDHP/SOs are lower than the overall average for all plan types for both single and family coverage.

There is significant variation around the average annual premiums as a result of factors such as benefits, cost sharing, and geographic cost differences. Nineteen percent of covered workers are in plans with an annual total premium for family coverage of at least $18,087 (120% of the average family premium), while 21% of covered workers are in plans where the family premium is less than $12,058 (80% of the average premium). [34]

As suggested by the first sentence in the last quoted paragraph above, comparison of premiums without knowledge of underlying benefit and cost-sharing *is not possible.*

**Exhibit 31. Average Annual Premiums for Single and Family Coverage, 1999-2011**

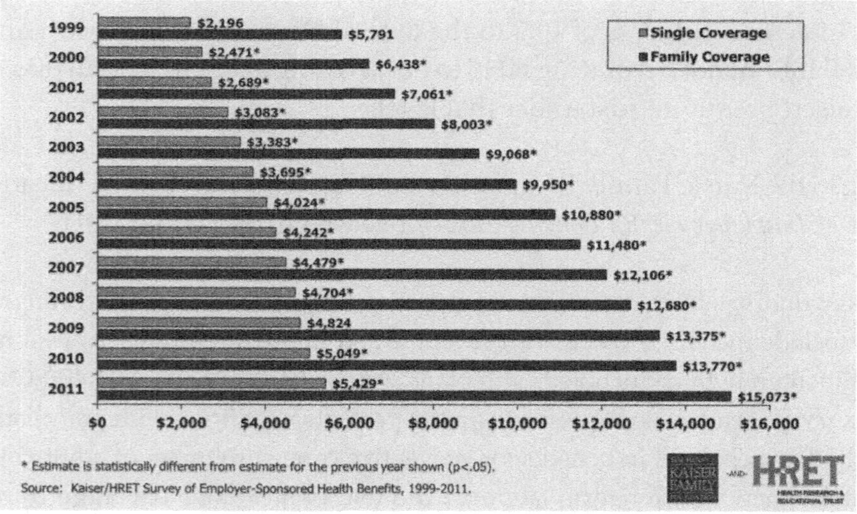


In addition to the significant increases in overall costs, the portion of that cost borne by the employee has grown significantly, especially for family plans.

34 ehbs.kff.org/ 2011 Report.

**Exhibit 32. Average Annual Worker Premium Contributions Paid by Covered Workers for Single and Family Coverage, 1999- 2011**

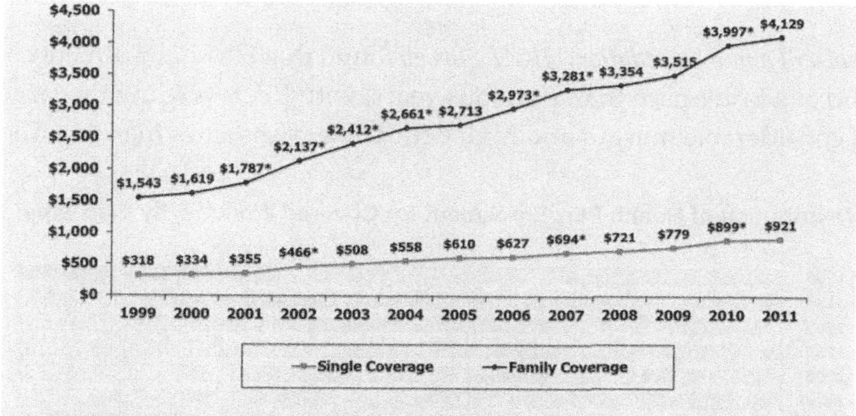


*Estimate is statistically different from estimate for the previous year shown (p<.05).
Source: Kaiser/HRET Survey of Employer-Sponsored Health Benefits, 1999-2011.

### *Product Trend*

Another significant trend is the move away from HMO (tightly restricted) products and into PPO (preferred provider organization) and POS (point of service) products. In a PPO,[35] insureds pay lower costs when seeing a provider who is "in-network," while deductibles, co-pays, and even overall benefit limits may apply when seeing out-of-network providers. A curious but critical result of the movement away from HMOs is the contribution of the *unmanaged* forms of insurance to the cost spiral! The ability of patients insured by PPOs to self-refer and the general lack of data from insurers to the provider community on those patients preclude the type of clinical management shown to improve health and reduce cost.

A POS plan is one in which the insured typically has to choose an in-network primary care physician but may be allowed to self-refer to specialists (in or out of network), again with deductibles, co-pays, and perhaps overall benefit limits. In some cases, insurers have attempted to place capitated provider groups at-risk for out-of-network care in POS plans. (This is perhaps the best analogy to the accountable care organization model that would place providers at-risk for the cost of care to unmanaged, fee-for-service Medicare beneficiaries.)

The dramatic shift away from HMO products in the managed care business in recent years is indicated in Exhibit 33. It is important to note that managed care companies referred to generically as "HMOs" may in fact offer PPO and POS products. This is

35 See the Glossary at the end of this report.

certainly true of Blue Cross/Blue Shield plans, Aetna/US Healthcare, and United Health, to name a few.

The *2011 Kaiser Family Foundation/HRET Survey* found that HMO enrollment continued to decline, and at a faster pace than previous years, with PPOs holding the largest market share by a considerable margin and high deductible plans showing a significant spike.

**Exhibit 33. Distribution of Health Play Enrollment for Covered Workers, by Plan Type, 1988-2011[36]**

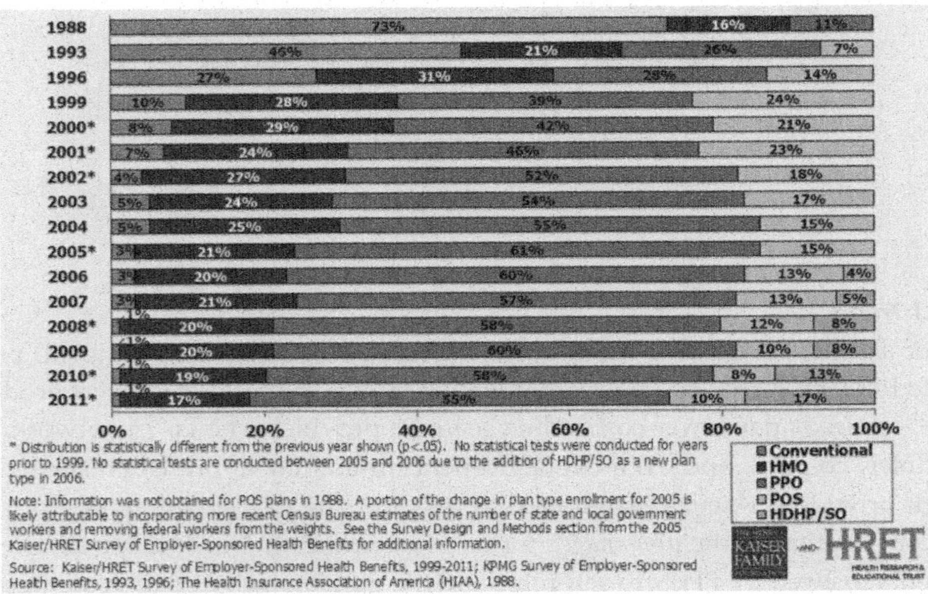


### *Regional Differences*

Exhibit 34, from the *Kaiser/HRET Survey*, indicates the substantial differences between the various regions of the country, something that apparently was completely ignored in the reform legislation and particularly the so-called Cadillac tax on health insurance plans. Plans in high-cost states such as Massachusetts in the Northeast will reach the Cadillac-plan level in 2018, while plans in lower-cost areas may never reach it.

### *Firm Size Differences*

More compelling is the significant difference in the out of pocket cost of health insurance coverage to small firm employees versus large firm employees, a critical failure of the Massachusetts reform legislation that the federal legislation is modeled on. (See Exhibits 35 and 36.)

36 PPO (preferred provider organization), POS (point of service plan), HDHP (high deductible health plan).

## Exhibit 34. Average Monthly and Annual Premiums for Covered Workers, by Plan Type and Region

| | Monthly | | Annual | |
|---|---|---|---|---|
| | *Single Coverage* | *Family Coverage* | *Single Coverage* | *Family Coverage* |
| **HMO** | | | | |
| Northeast | $486* | $1,332 | $5,826* | $15,981 |
| Midwest | 472 | 1,322 | 5,659 | 15,861 |
| South | 428 | 1,273 | 5,131 | 15,279 |
| West | 428 | 1,229 | 5,131 | 14,743 |
| **ALL REGIONS** | **$446** | **$1,274** | **$5,350** | **$15,288** |
| **PPO** | | | | |
| Northeast | $496* | $1,375* | $5,948* | $16,503* |
| Midwest | 485 | 1,337 | 5,824 | 16,042 |
| South | 426* | 1,175* | 5,118* | 14,104* |
| West | 491 | 1,350 | 5,892 | 16,200 |
| **ALL REGIONS** | **$465** | **$1,284** | **$5,584** | **$15,404** |
| **POS** | | | | |
| Northeast | $537 | $1,438 | $6,442 | $17,253 |
| Midwest | 464 | 1,229 | 5,569 | 14,746 |
| South | 450 | 1,210 | 5,403 | 14,519 |
| West | 506 | 1,268 | 6,067 | 15,211 |
| **ALL REGIONS** | **$487** | **$1,272** | **$5,841** | **$15,260** |
| **HDHP/SO** | | | | |
| Northeast | $398 | $1,139 | $4,781 | $13,673 |
| Midwest | 390 | 1,137 | 4,675 | 13,640 |
| South | 409 | 1,201 | 4,902 | 14,407 |
| West | 404 | 1,072 | 4,846 | 12,865 |
| **ALL REGIONS** | **$399** | **$1,142** | **$4,793** | **$13,704** |
| **ALL PLANS** | | | | |
| Northeast | $482* | $1,334* | $5,785* | $16,013* |
| Midwest | 458 | 1,276 | 5,497 | 15,310 |
| South | 426* | 1,194* | 5,110* | 14,329* |
| West | 460 | 1,259 | 5,514 | 15,103 |
| **ALL REGIONS** | **$452** | **$1,256** | **$5,429** | **$15,073** |

* Estimate is statistically different within plan and coverage types from estimate for all firms not in the indicated region (p<.05).

Source: Kaiser/HRET Survey of Employer-Sponsored Health Benefits, 2011.

## Exhibit 35. Percentage of Covered Workers Enrolled in a Plan With a General Annual Deductible of $1,000 or More for Single Coverage, by Firm Size

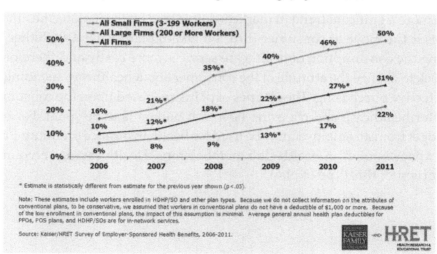

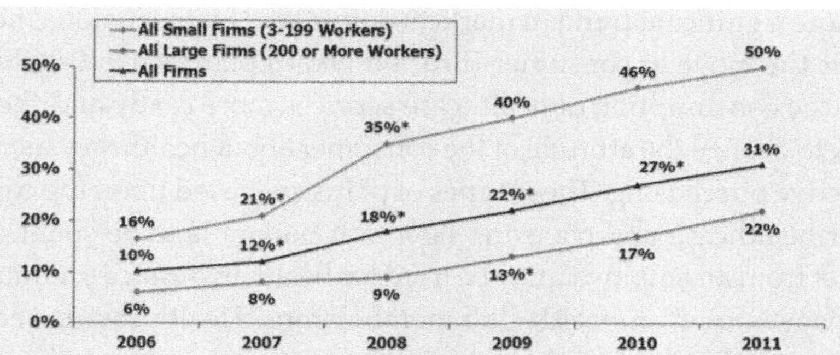


* Estimate is statistically different from estimate for the previous year shown (p<.05).

Note: These estimates include workers enrolled in HDHP/SO and other plan types. Because we do not collect information on the attributes of conventional plans, to be conservative, we assumed that workers in conventional plans do not have a deductible of $1,000 or more. Because of the low enrollment in conventional plans, the impact of this assumption is minimal. Average general annual health plan deductibles for PPOs, POS plans, and HDHP/SOs are for in-network services.

Source: Kaiser/HRET Survey of Employer-Sponsored Health Benefits, 2006-2011.

**Exhibit 36. Percentage of Covered Workers Enrolled in a Plan With a General Annual Deductible of $2,000 or More for Single Coverage, by Firm Size**

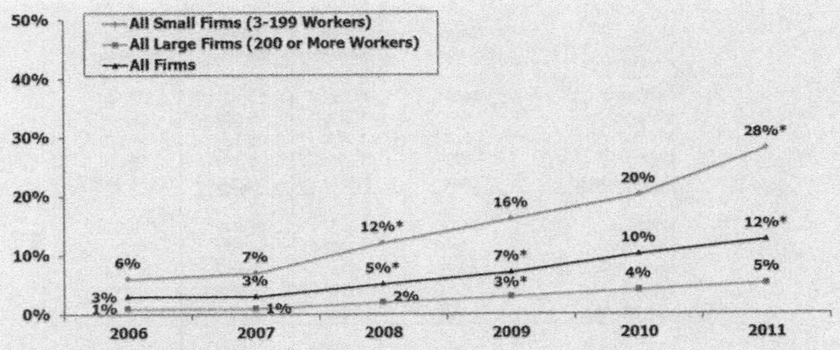


* Estimate is statistically different from estimate for the previous year shown (p<.05).

Note: These estimates include workers enrolled in HDHP/SO and other plan types. Because we do not collect information on the attributes of conventional plans, to be conservative, we assumed that workers in conventional plans do not have a deductible of $2,000 or more. Because of the low enrollment in conventional plans, the impact of this assumption is minimal.

Source: Kaiser/HRET Survey of Employer-Sponsored Health Benefits, 2006-2011.

### *Decline in HMOs*

As a result of the major financial losses of the 1990s, there has been both a reduction in the number of managed care companies and greater enrollment growth in those who survived, as insureds were forced to find solvent insurers. CMS reports that the number of HMOs has declined from a peak of 652 in 1997 to 490 in 2002, with further losses in 2003 and 2004. The Kaiser Family Foundation[37] indicates the number of HMOs in July 2008 was 577 (see Exhibit 37), down from 602 in the previous year. By July 2010, the count had declined to only 452. This has resulted in growth in enrollment and premiums for the *major* players, despite an overall *decrease* in the number of individuals covered by managed care products, as noted above in *Trends in Health Insurance Coverage*.

Perhaps a more significant trend in markets dominated by the national health insurance companies is the move to consumer-directed health plans (CDHPs). Rather than simply making the consumption of healthcare services more costly and therefore painful, CDHPs seek to change the attitude of the consumer about healthcare spending, focusing on cost-effective purchasing. These types of plans are based upon the consumer having a budget for healthcare and choosing how that budget is to be spent. For example, a $5,000 budget from an employer may be used for health insurance premiums, uninsured medical expenses, or even health club memberships. Health savings accounts (HSAs) are one variant of this type of plan.

37 www.statehealthfacts.org/.

**Exhibit 37. Number of HMOs by State**

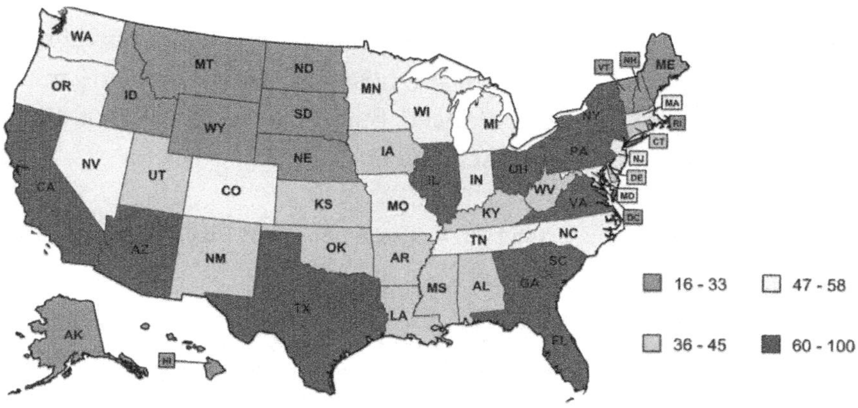


### *Summary*

Managed care plans are in a period of significant change brought about by the combined uncertainty of the recession and the reform legislation. Employers are shifting more of the costs of healthcare onto employees via benefit buy-downs. The backlash against the tightly managed care characteristic of HMOs has resulted in a rapid growth of PPO and POS plans, both of which feature higher consumer costs and drive overall costs higher as well due to the fundamental lack of clinical control over spending in those products. Current indications are that CDHPs, including HSAs, are likely to be the growth product in the foreseeable future. The federal reform legislation will exacerbate the growing disparity between the high cost of benefits in the small employer market and the lower cost in the large employer market.

## Acute Care Hospitals: Average Length of Stay

### *Medicare patients ALOS*

Average length of stay (ALOS) is a measurement of the average number of days a patient stays in the hospital for each discharge. Earlier in this report, it was noted that the number of admission and discharges is showing an uptrend. In contrast, ALOS had steadily declined from 1992 until 2004 (Exhibit 38 presents the most recent year for which data are available). The 2007 and 2008 ALOS, however, was the same, and declines appear to have bottomed out.[38]

This trend is very significant for hospitals, which, as noted earlier, are paid a *fixed amount per discharge*. Under such a payment system, there is a financial incentive to get the patient out of the hospital sooner, because *costs* tend to be correlated with days in the

38 www.cms.hhs.gov/MedicareFeeforSvcPartsAB/03_MEDPAR.asp#TopOfPage, last updated September, 2011.

hospital and revenues are *fixed* based on the admission and discharge (and its character). Therefore, the hospital is likely to lose money on a long stay, and make money on a short stay. The inability to drive length of stay down still farther accounts in part for the strong adverse reaction from the hospital industry to cuts mandated by the BBA and later mitigated by the Balanced Budget Revision Act of 1999 and the Benefits Improvement and Protection Act of 2000.

**Exhibit 38. Average Length of Stay, by Year**

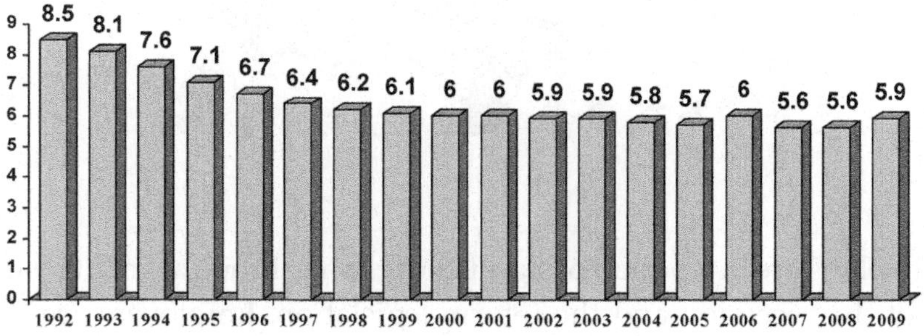


### *All patients ALOS*

ALOS is one of the key factors for evaluating the cost-adjusted clinical efficiency of hospital-based treatment. *The 2007 and 2006 Hospital Discharge Survey* from the Centers for Disease Control[39] (released in December 2010 and July 2008, respectively) found that hospitalization ALOS for the population taken as a whole was 4.8 days, identical to the 2006 survey result. Males had an average length of stay of 5.2 days, compared with 4.5 days for females, also identical to the 2006 results. ALOS per admission in 2007 was highest in the Northeast, at 5.3 days; followed by the South, at 4.9; the West, at 4.6 days; and Midwest, at 4.2, which are identical to 2006 (see Exhibits 39 and 40). This data are for all admissions, as opposed to the Medicare data, which are for Medicare patients only.

**Exhibit 39. Data by Region**

| | 2006 Rate per 10,000 | 2006 ALOS | 2006 Days/1,000 | 2007 Rate per 10,000 | 2007 ALOS | 2007 Days/1,000 |
|---|---|---|---|---|---|---|
| N. East | 1,330.7 | 5.3 | 705.3 | 1,330.7 | 5.3 | 703.2 |
| Midwest | 1,202.3 | 4.2 | 505.0 | 1,202.3 | 4.2 | 507.8 |
| South | 1,212.0 | 4.9 | 593.9 | 1,212.0 | 4.9 | 594.7 |
| West | 940.2 | 4.6 | 432.5 | 940.2 | 4.6 | 432.3 |
| Total | 1,168.7 | 4.8 | 561.0 | 1,168.7 | 4.8 | 557.8 |

39 www.cdc.gov/nchs/nhds.htm July 30, 2008; released December 2010; rates per 10,000 unchanged in report from 2006.

**Exhibit 40. Graph of Regional Data**

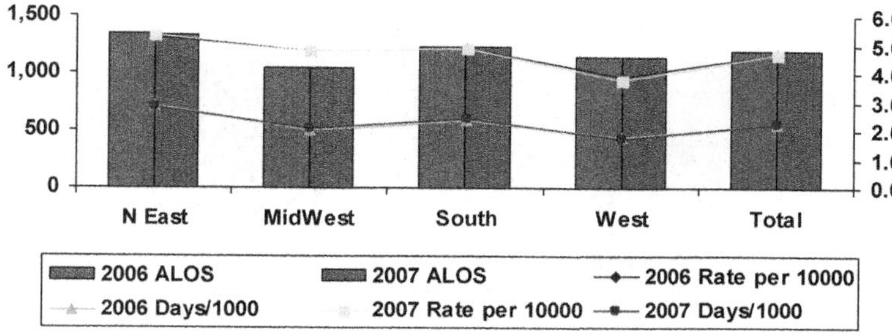


The comparison of data by age group (or cohort) for 2007 and 2006 shows virtually no change, with ALOS holding steady (see Exhibits 41 and 42).

**Exhibit 41. Data by Age Cohort**

| | 2006 Rate per 10,000 | 2006 ALOS | 2006 Days/1,000 | 2007 Rate per 10,000 | 2007 ALOS | 2007 Days/1,000 |
|---|---|---|---|---|---|---|
| <15 | 378.2 | 4.8 | 181.5 | 378.0 | 4.8 | 180.9 |
| 15-44 | 861.2 | 3.7 | 318.6 | 861.0 | 3.7 | 322.9 |
| 45-64 | 1,161.2 | 5.0 | 580.6 | 1,161.0 | 5.0 | 579.3 |
| 65 | 3,507.9 | 5.5 | 1,929.3 | 3,507.0 | 5.5 | 1,919.7 |

**Exhibit 42. Graph of Age Data**

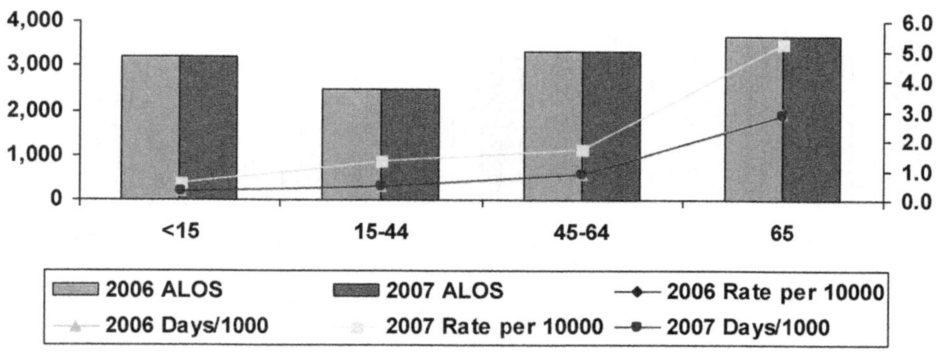


***Principal Reason for Admission***

Heart disease diagnoses represent 22% of all 18,482 admissions for males, with cardiac catheterization the most frequent procedure, and 11% of 27,482 for females. Thus, coronary artery bypass surgery, cardiac catheterization, and angioplasty are main revenue drivers in acute care hospitals, followed by digestive procedures of the type principally done by general surgeons (see Exhibit 43).

**Exhibit 43. Principal Category of Admission and Discharge**

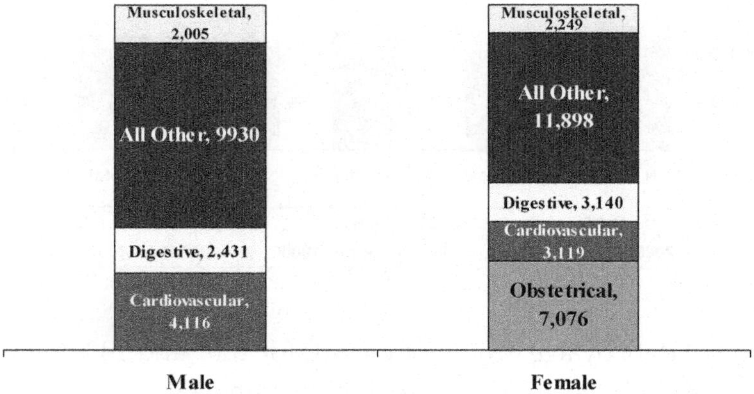


Source: Table 32. Number of all-listed procedures for discharges from short-stay hospitals, by sex and procedure category: United States, 2006

### *Costs per stay*

Hospital costs vary significantly from state to state, reflecting differences in wage scales, living costs, and real estate, to name a few. Representative data for 2008 and 2007 from the American Hospital Association find that costs are generally highest on the coasts, lowest in the mountain states, and increasing almost everywhere (see Exhibit 44); data for 50 states are shown in Exhibit 45.[40]

**Exhibit 44. Cost Per Inpatient Hospital Day**

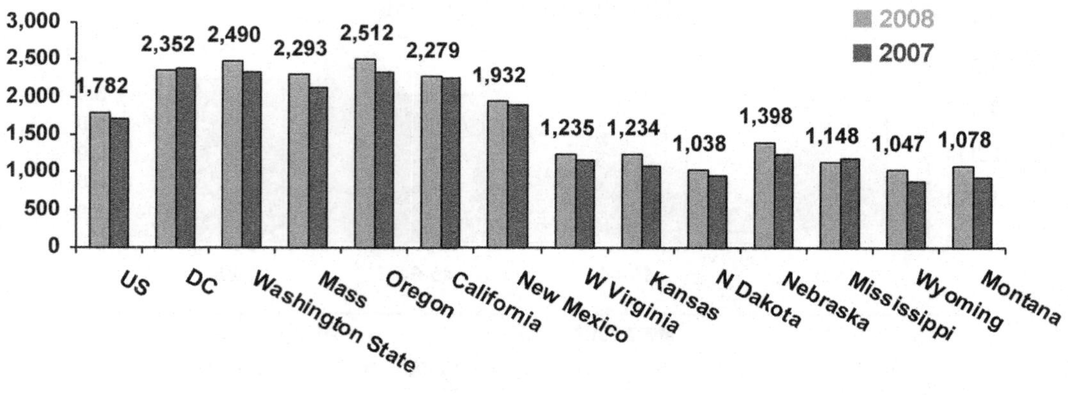


40 www.statehealthfacts.kff.org/cgi-bin/healthfacts.cgi?action=profile, 2007 data.

**Exhibit 45. Hospital Costs by State**

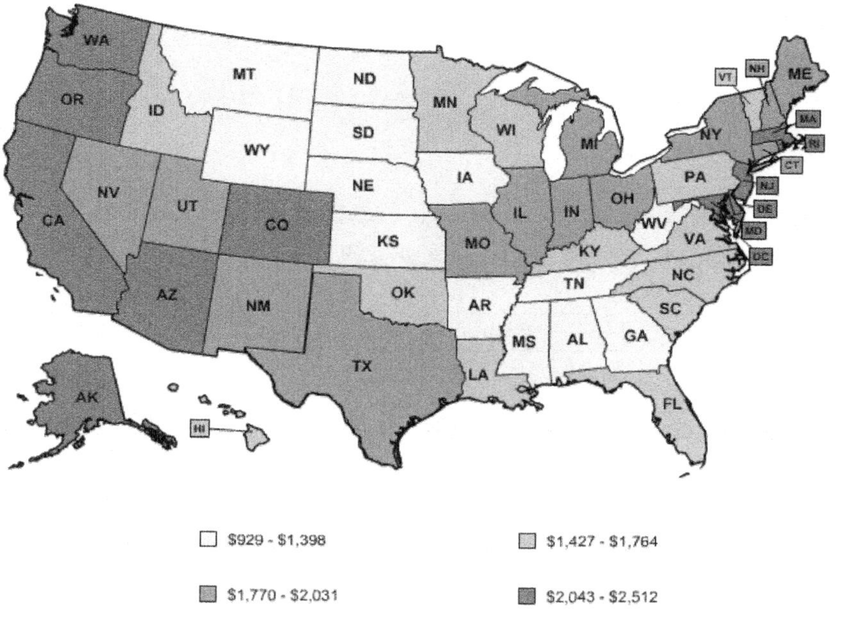


## Acute Care Hospital Payments

Medicare inpatient hospital payments from the federal government are based upon a statutory formula pegged to a "market basket" of economic inputs. The actual update is usually less than the market basket for budgetary reasons.[41] Exhibit 46 shows the history for hospitals since 1988, with the substantial declines after the Balanced Budget Act of 1997. The 2011 increase is 2.6% for those hospitals that submit quality data, reduced by the 0.25% mandated by the healthcare reform legislation, for a net of 2.35%. Hospitals not submitting quality data receive only 0.35%. There is a separate adjustment for coding intensity of 2.9%, making the true adjustment a negative (0.55%). CMS estimated the effect of the 2012 final rule at a 1% increase.[42]

The 2010 increase is described as follows:

> The Centers for Medicare & Medicaid Services (CMS) today announced that acute care hospitals will receive an inflation update in their payment rates of 2.1% in fiscal year 2010. Earlier this year, CMS had proposed to reduce payments to account for the effect of increases in aggregate payments due to changes in hospital coding practices that do not reflect increases in patient's severity of illness.[43]

41 A CMS explanation of the Medicare inpatient and other payment formulas is located at www.cms.gov/reports/hcimu/hcimu_04292002_append.pdf.
42 Medicare's FY 2012 Hospital Inpatient Prospective Payment System final rule, Fact Sheet, August 2011.
43 Ibid.

**Exhibit 46. Inpatient PPS Update—Urban**

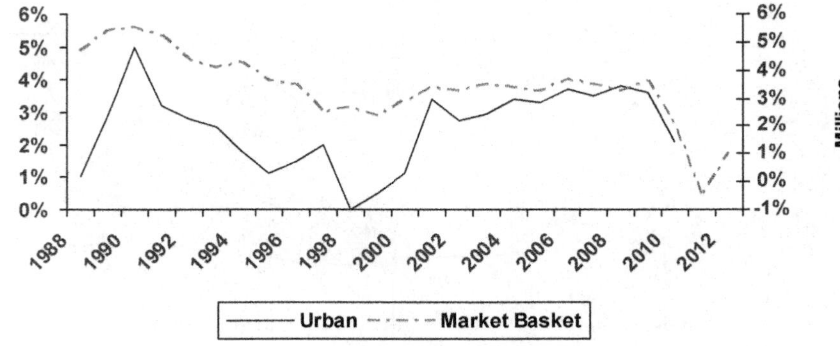


One of the key financial components of paying for the new federal healthcare reform legislation is a cutback in the market basket update, in part through required adjustments for productivity using a 10-year moving average of economywide private, nonfarm productivity gains, somewhat analogous to one element of the physician sustainable growth rate calculation discussed elsewhere herein.

The market basket update for 2009 was 3.6%. "In this final [2009] rule, CMS completes the transition so that its payment rates are 100% cost-based. In addition, CMS is making changes to hospital cost reports that will allow Medicare to distinguish between high- and low-cost supplies and devices and to further refine and improve our cost-based payments." [44]

> The final rule updates IPPS rates by a market basket of 3.6% for inflation (1.6% for hospitals that do not submit quality data). However, CMS estimates that the new MS-DRGs will result in improvements in coding and documentation that increase spending without a real change in patient severity of illness. CMS estimates that Medicare spending for inpatient hospital services in FY 2009 will increase 1.8% as a result of changes in coding and documentation. However, rather than reducing IPPS rates by 1.8% in FY 2009 for budget neutrality, the law requires CMS to reduce the IPPS rates by 0.9% for FY 2009. If based on a retrospective review of FY 2008 and FY 2009 claims, CMS determines that improvements in documentation and coding from adopting the MS-DRGs led to an increase in total Medicare spending for inpatient hospital services, the law requires CMS to apply further adjustments to Medicare's IPPS rates in FY 2010 and later years to recoup this increased spending.[45]

44 www.cms.hhs.gov/apps/media/press/factsheet.asp?Counter=3223.
45 www.cms.hhs.gov/apps/media/press/factsheet.asp?Counter=3223.

For 2008, most hospitals saw an increase of 3.5%, although changes (moving toward hospital costs rather than charges) being made gradually by CMS to the DRG system could result in some hospitals seeing actual decreases.

> Payments to all hospitals will increase by an estimated average of 3.5% for FY 2008 when all provisions of the rule are taken into account, primarily as a result of the 3.3% market basket increase. Payments to specific hospitals may increase more or less than this amount depending on the patients they serve. For instance, urban hospitals generally treat more severely ill patients and are estimated to receive a 3.8% increase in payments.[46]

Hospitals with a large percentage of Medicare admissions are confronted with revenues rising at less than operating costs, the latter reflected in the market basket. Principal areas for rising costs include prescription drugs, labor (including a severe shortage of nursing staff), and liability insurance. The principal factors driving hospital revenue, besides the Medicare market basket, include the aging population's demand for more services, increase in market share, and the success of negotiations with insurers.

## THE MEDICARE PROGRAM AND PHYSICIANS

> The Medicare program has two components. Hospital insurance (HI), or Medicare Part A, helps pay for hospital, home health, skilled nursing facility, and hospice care for the aged and disabled. Supplementary medical insurance (SMI) consists of Medicare Part B and Part D. Part B helps pay for physician, outpatient hospital, home health, and other services for the aged and disabled who have voluntarily enrolled. Part D provides subsidized access to drug insurance coverage on a voluntary basis for all beneficiaries and premium and cost-sharing subsidies for low-income enrollees. Medicare also has a Part C, which serves as an alternative to traditional Part A and Part B coverage. Under this option, beneficiaries can choose to enroll in and receive care from private Medicare Advantage and certain other health insurance plans that contract with Medicare. The costs for such beneficiaries are generally paid on a prospective, capitated basis from the HI and SMI Part B trust fund accounts.[47]

When Medicare began on July 1, 1966, approximately 19 million people enrolled. In 2009, almost 46 million people are enrolled in one or both of Parts A and B of the Medicare program, and almost 11 million of them have chosen to participate in a Medicare Advantage plan (see Exhibit 47).[48]

46 www.cms.hhs.gov/apps/media/press/release.asp?Counter=2335.

47 2010 Medicare Trustees' Report.

48 Office of the Actuary Summary as of Nov. 1, 2009, www.cms.hhs.gov/MedicareProgramRatesStats/02_SummaryMedicareMedicaid.asp.

Part A is generally provided automatically and free of premiums to persons age 65 or over who are eligible for Social Security or railroad retirement benefits, whether they have claimed these monthly cash benefits or not. Also, workers and their spouses with a sufficient period of Medicare-only coverage in federal, state, or local government employment are eligible beginning at age 65. Similarly, individuals who have been entitled to Social Security or railroad retirement disability benefits for at least 24 months and government employees with Medicare-only coverage who have been disabled for more than 29 months are entitled to Part A benefits. (As noted previously, the waiting period is waived for persons with Lou Gehrig's Disease. It should also be noted that, over the years, certain liberalizations have been made to both the waiting period requirement and the limit on earnings allowed for entitlement to Medicare coverage based on disability.) Part A coverage is also provided to insured workers with ESRD (and to insured workers' spouses and children with ESRD), as well as to some otherwise ineligible aged and disabled beneficiaries who voluntarily pay a monthly premium for their coverage. In 2008, Part A provided protection against the costs of hospital and specific other medical care to about 45 million people (37.5 million aged and 7.4 million disabled enrollees). Part A benefit payments totaled $232.3 billion in 2008.[49]

Medicare originally consisted of two parts: HI, also known as Part A, and SMI, which in the past, was also known simply as Part B. Part A helps pay for inpatient hospital, home health, skilled nursing facility, and hospice care. Part A is provided free of premiums to most eligible people; certain otherwise ineligible people may voluntarily pay a monthly premium for coverage. Part B helps pay for physician, outpatient hospital, home health, and other services. To be covered by Part B, all eligible people must pay a monthly premium."[50]

The Balanced Budget Act of 1997 (BBA) made a number of significant changes in the Medicare program, many of which are phased in over multiple years. These changes are significant to the providers affected by them and in many cases, may mean lower revenues from the Medicare program. Exceptions to this were physicians who perform primarily cognitive services rather than procedures; they actually received significantly improved reimbursement.

Subsequent modifications in the dramatic changes wrought by the BBA by the Balanced Budget Revision Act of 1999 (BBRA) and the Benefits Improvements Act of 2000 (BIPA) primarily affected hospitals, skilled nursing facilities, Medicare+ Choice Plans, and

49 Office of the Actuary Summary, ibid .
50 Office of the Actuary Summary, ibid.

other nonphysician providers. In November 2003, a comprehensive revision of the Medicare+ Choice program was legislated in the Medicare Modernization Act. After 2004, the new Medicare Advantage private plans' capitation rates grow at the same rate as fee-for-service Medicare, although the reported high rate of profits to insurers caused Congress to implement cutbacks in the Medicare Advantage Plan payments as part of the healthcare reform legislation.

**Exhibit 47. Total Medicare Private Health Enrollment[51]**

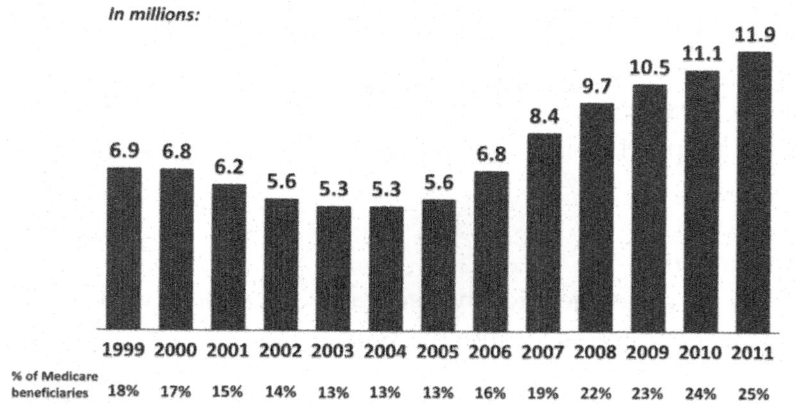


**NOTE:** Includes cost and demonstration plans, and enrollees in Special Needs Plans as well as other Medicare Advantage plans.
**SOURCE:** MPR/Kaiser Family Foundation analysis of CMS Medicare Advantage enrollment files, 2008-2011, and MPR, "Tracking Medicare Health and Prescription Drug Plans Monthly Report," 2001-2007; enrollment numbers from March of the respective year, with the exception of 2006, which is from April.

## Physician Reimbursement

Medicare pays physicians under the resource-based relative value scale (RBRVS) where each current procedural terminology code (CPT) is assigned a certain number of relative value units (RVUs). These RVUs are then multiplied by a conversion factor to set the fee Medicare pays. Prior to the BBA, there were three such conversion factors: one for surgery, one for primary care and one for other nonsurgical services. The BBA substituted a single conversion factor based upon the primary care factor for the three prior conversion factors. The effect has been a broad cutback in reimbursement for surgical services.

## Resource-Based Relative Value Scale

The number of RVUs is based upon the consumption of three types of resources in the delivery of physician services:

51 Medicare Advantage Enrollment Market Update, Kaiser Family Foundation, September 2011, www.kff.org/medicare/.

#### *Physician Work*

The principal factors comprising this component are time, technical skill and physical effort, mental effort and judgment, and the stress on the physician of certain patient risk factors.

#### *Practice Costs*

This component looks at the cost of delivering services by physician type, for example, family medicine versus cardiac surgery. Physician practice costs per dollar of revenue tend to be much higher in primary care than surgery.

#### *Malpractice Insurance Cost*

Surgical specialties, particularly obstetrics, neurosurgery, and cardiac surgery, tend to have the highest malpractice insurance. This is the least important of the three components.

#### *Geographic Adjustment*

There is an additional adjustment for the geographic location of the practice based upon various government studies, including the census, HUD data, and others.[52]

The changeover to RBRVS mandated by the BBA resulted in a substantial increase in the RVUs assigned to office-based CPT codes. A significant portion was related to the practice expenses component described above, due to the fact that office-based physicians have higher operating costs per dollar of revenue than do hospital-based physicians. In addition, HCFA (CMS) believed that the prior reimbursement system overcompensated hospital-based surgeons and similar physicians because the Medicare program paid the hospital separately for the cost of its facilities, which had been used by the surgeons.

#### *The Evaluation and Management Codes*

In the office-based specialties, primary care, and consultative medicine, RBRVS is particularly significant in how office visits and other evaluation and management services are to be coded and reimbursed. RBRVS requires that physicians code according to a three-factor test:

1. *History* of the patient and complaint;
2. *Examination* of the patient necessary, and
3. *Complexity* of medical decision making.

52 The fee schedule for each geographic area can be located at www.cms.gov/providers/pufdownload/carrcrst.asp.

Each of these three factors has four levels of intensity associated with it. For example, a Level III office examination, or CPT 99213, requires the second level of intensity in each of the history, exam, and decision making components. A Level IV exam, or CPT 99214, requires the third level of intensity in two of the three components. Under RBRVS reimbursement systems, such as Medicare, the patient's chart *must document the level of service for each component.*[53]

Exhibit 48, using the pre-BBA 1997 schedule and the 2011 National Physician Fee Schedule, demonstrates how increasing levels of service, as reflected in the CPT codes, result in increasing levels of payment under Medicare RBRVS, as well as the cumulative effect in reimbursement of the changes described herein.[54]

**Exhibit 48. Comparative Fees for Established Patient Sick Visits**

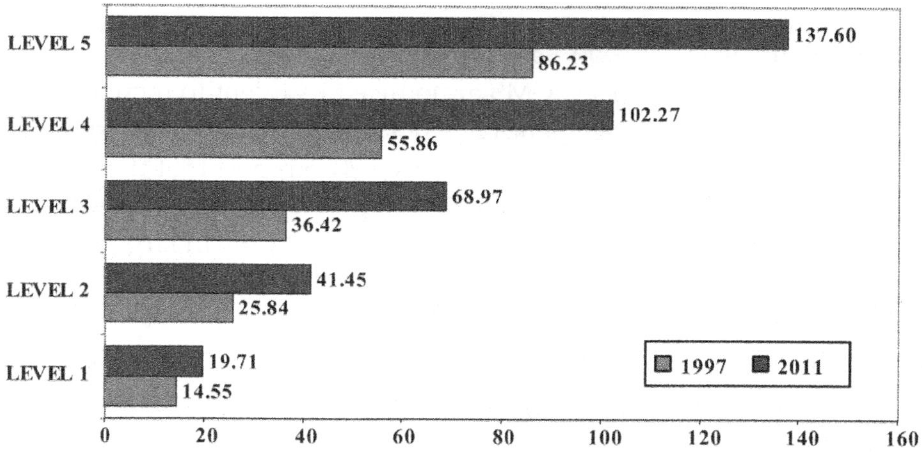


RBRVS is also typically used by HMOs, which therefore tend to pay higher rates for primary care services, since such services are key to the provision of healthcare to members.

There has been a marked shift in the use of these five codes over the last 12 years as indicated in Exhibit 49 based on data taken from CMS.[55]

53 Various versions of the documentation guidelines can be located at www.cms.gov/medlearn/emdoc.asp.
54 The National Physician Fee Schedule is at www.cms.gov/PhysicianFeeSched/PFSNPAF/list.asp?filterType=none&filterByDID=-99&sortByDID=2&sortOrder=descending&intNumPerPage=10.
55 e.g., www.cms.gov/apps/ama/license.asp?file=/MedicareFeeforSvcPartsAB/Downloads/Level1SERV07.pdf.

**Exhibit 49. Shift in the Use of Five Codes**

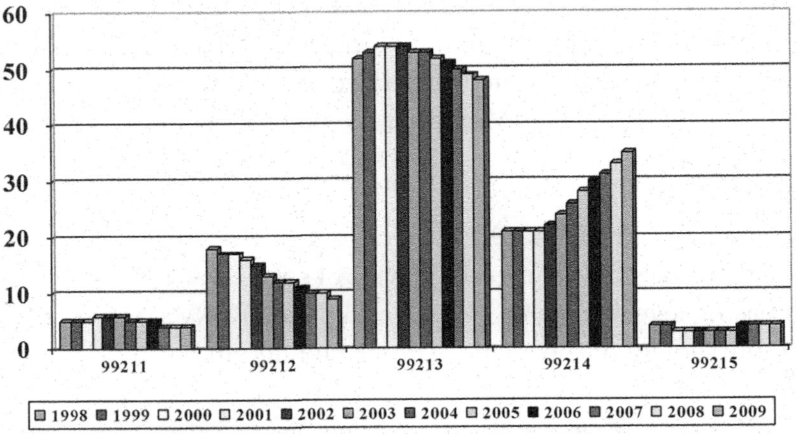


### *2007 Increases in the Value of E&M Services*

In the June 29, 2006 *Federal Register*, CMS announced its intent to increase the relative values of evaluation and management (E&M) services in 2007, following closely on the heels of a suggestion by MedPAC in its March 2006 report that these services had declined in value, in large part to the benefit of high-tech imaging services. The final rule was released Nov. 2, 2006 and adopted the proposed rule in large part.

> The work component for RVUs associated with an intermediate office visit [99213], the most commonly billed physician's service, will increase by 37%. The work component for RVUs for an office visit requiring moderately complex decision making and for a hospital visit also requiring moderately complex decision making will increase by 29% and 31%, respectively. Both of these services rank in the top 10 most frequently billed physicians' services out of more than 7,000 types of services paid under the physician fee schedule.

The 99213 code presently has a fully implemented work RVU value of 0.67. Under the final rule, the value rises to 0.92 RVUs. This represents an increase in the value of nearly 18%. Significantly, because of the budget neutrality provisions of the existing Part B system, the increased cost associated with the increased RVUs has to come from reduction in the value of other services, and CMS reduced all work RVUs by 10.1% to meet the budget neutrality provisions. CMS is also changing the practice expense component of the RVUs to be phased in over four years through 2010.

The following discussion tracks the history of changes in physician reimbursement since the enactment of the BBA and demonstrates the significant and often unpredictable changes.

## Medicare Conversion Factor

### *Overview of the Problem*

In March of each year, CMS releases its preliminary estimate (the final calculation is released in September) of the SGR and the conversion factor for the following year. For example, the annual computation *had* estimated that Medicare physician reimbursement would *drop* by 5.7% in 2003, as a result of two errors in 1998 and 1999 that affected the statutory limit on allowed expenditures for physician services. These errors carried forward to all future years, resulting in a lower overall limit on physician spending of approximately 6.4%. The compound rate of increase in the annual physician fee schedule update from 1998 through 2005 was only ***0.3%***! The Consolidated Appropriations Resolution of 2003 permitted CMS to correct the 1998 and 1999 errors, resulting in an *increase* in the fee schedule for 2003 rather than the prior decrease. Annual declines in the vicinity of 4% to 5% are generally expected under existing law. The Medicare Modernization Act of November 2003 overrode the scheduled decreases in the 2004 and 2005 conversion factors with 1.5% increases.

The pattern since 2006 has been for Congress to belatedly suspend the statutory cutbacks in the conversion factor. The 2007 conversion factor of $35.9848 initially reflected a decrease of 5% and was subsequently overturned by Congress and left equal to the 2006 factor. The 2008 factor was scheduled to drop by 10.1% until the end of December 2007, when the Medicare, Medicaid, and SCHIP Extension Act of 2007 legislation updated the conversion factor by 0.5%, to $38.0870. In July 2008, Congress extended the $38.09 conversion factor for the balance of 2008 over the president's veto and put a 1.1% increase in place for 2009. As of November 2009, Congress had not acted to repeal the scheduled cut for 2010. *Note:* See the discussion regarding the calculation of the 2010 and 2009 later herein as Exhibit 50 cannot be understood absent that discussion.

**Exhibit 50. Medicare Conversion Factor**

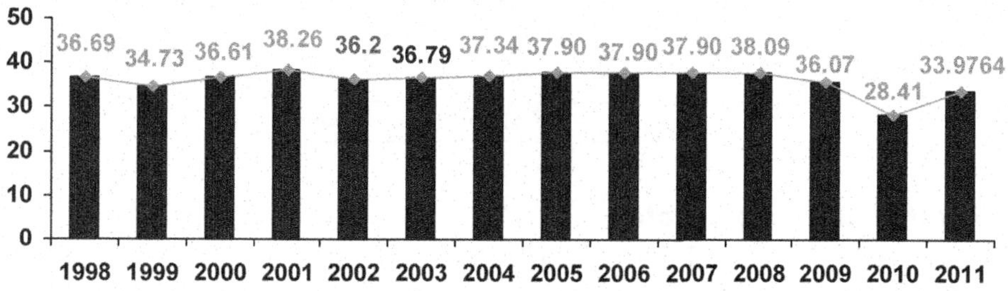


Exhibit 51 traces the growth rate in *real* GDP (in 1996 dollars) and the Medicare SGR, MEI, and the actual conversion factor update. CMS made critical mistakes in computing the 2000 and 2001 conversion factors resulting in excess payments that were being paid back prior to the February 2003 legislative change. Note that the two regain parity in 2005.[56] The red line plots what spending *would have been* based upon inflation in physician practice expenses, similar to that used to set fees for other sectors of the healthcare industry, such as hospitals.

**Exhibit 51. Percent Change in Real GDP and Physician Spending**

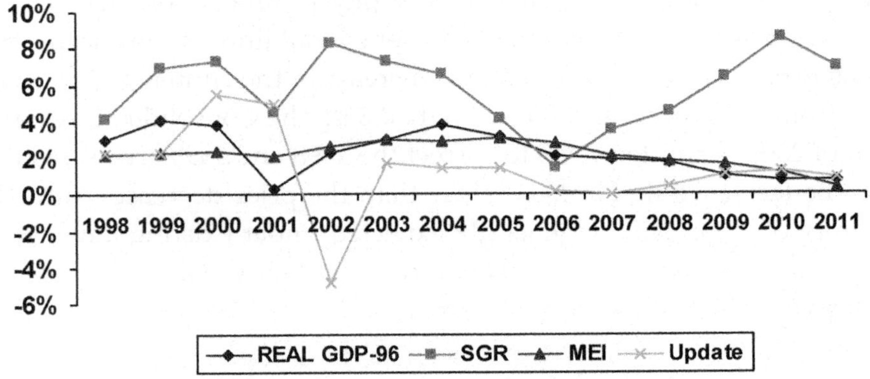


Exhibit 52 demonstrates that despite the SGR attempt to limit growth in physician spending, actual spending is considerably higher.

**Exhibit 52. Quarterly SGR "Allowed" Versus Actual Expenditures**

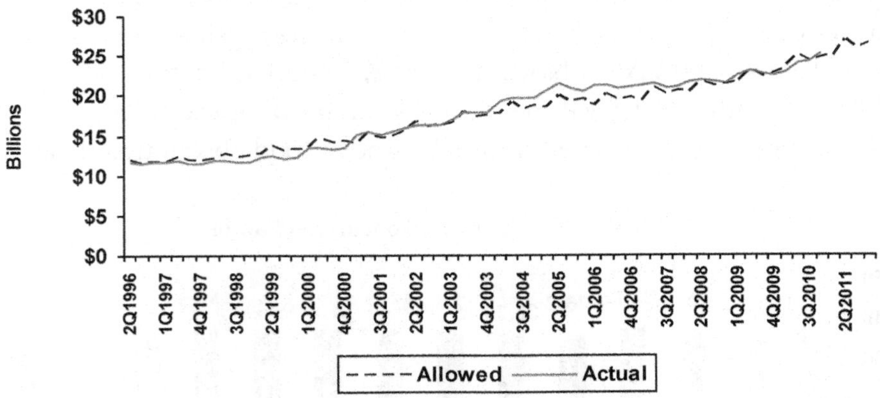


***Determining the Conversion Factor***

CMS first determines the MEI, which measures the weighted average price change for various inputs involved with producing physicians' services. The MEI is then multiplied

56 Data from www.cms.hhs.gov/NationalHealthExpendData/Downloads/proj2007.pdf and www.cms.hhs.gov/SustainableGRatesConFact/01_overview.asp.

by the update adjustment factor, which is based upon a statutory formula that limits annual expenditures for physician services (see SGR above). The MEI is similar in concept to the market basket update for hospitals described elsewhere herein.

> The MEI is a fixed-weight input price index, with an adjustment for the change in economywide labor productivity. This index, which has 1996 base weights, is comprised of two broad categories: physician's own time and physician's practice expense.[57]

A review of these factors for 2003 as a representative year illuminates in part the underlying mathematical rationale. For example, the increase in nonphysician salaries and benefits was computed at 4.2% and given a weight in the overall computation of 16.8%. In effect, the MEI is an inflation adjustment factor for the cost of delivering physician services, including the estimated effect of productivity growth based on broad factors in the economy—not in physician offices. The update is equal to the product of one plus the percentage increase in the MEI (divided by 100) and one plus the update adjustment factor.

The update adjustment factor is designed "to reflect success or failure in meeting the expenditure target that the law refers to as 'allowed expenditures.'" Allowed expenditures are equal to actual expenditures in a base period updated each year by the SGR.

The SGR is based upon the following:

1. The estimated change in fees for physicians' services.
2. The estimated change in the average number of Medicare fee-for-service beneficiaries.
3. The estimated projected growth in real GDP per capita, which CMS estimated at 2.8% for 2004. The Medicare Modernization Act changed the GDP factor to a 10-year average growth, but it had little effect on the computation of the conversion factor, and in fact, due to the rapid growth of the economy in the last two years before the 2008 recession, has actually made the situation worse rather than better!
4. The estimated change in expenditures due to changes in law or regulations.

The base period allowed expenditures to roll forward from an initial fiscal year ending March 31, 1997. The formula reduces or increases for the current and future years by

57 *Federal Register* Vol. 66, No. 212, Nov. 1, 2001.

any excess or deficient expenditure in prior years. This is the critical point that a valuator or consultant must understand: Physician expenses under the Medicare program cannot exceed a limit established by a pre-determined, statutory formula, built off of historical expenditures and real GDP.

#### *Recap of the annual computation*

To recap, the MEI is basically an inflation factor based upon physician compensation and physician office expenses; the annual allowed expenditures are based upon FY March 1997 expenditures increased by the SGR; and the update adjustment factor, which forces the projected expenditures for the upcoming year to be no more than a predetermined limit.

#### *Overview of Year-by-Year Changes in the Conversion Factor*

Commencing with the phase-in of the changes mandated by the BBA, 1998 saw substantial increases in fee-for-service revenue for physicians in office-based medical specialties such as internal medicine, family medicine, and cardiology. Much of this rise stemmed from increases in the relative value of the evaluation and management codes. Radiology and pathology also saw significant increases.

In contrast, hospital-based surgical specialties such as orthopedics and cardiac surgery saw dramatic reductions in reimbursement.

CMS continued to refine its implementation of the BBA changes. The 1999 change generally provided moderate increases for the office-based medical specialties, ranging from 2% for internal medicine to 7% for family practice. The variability in the level of increase can be explained by the different utilization of individual CPT codes among the various specialties.

Cardiac surgery and neurosurgery received significant cutbacks from the 1999 changes, and radiology suffered a cut of 10%, undoing the increase received under the 1998 changes. Similarly, pathology reimbursement was cut by 13%. Cardiology practices saw reimbursement cut by 9% as fees for invasive procedures such as cardiac catheterization and balloon angioplasty received significant cuts. The conversion factor was set at $34.73, a significant decrease (5.3%) from the 1998 factor of $36.69.

As a result of intensive lobbying by the profession, CMS undertook a major revision in the assessment of the *practice expense component* of the RBRVS in 2000. The conversion factor was set at $36.6137, an increase over 1999 of 5.4%, which basically recaptured the 1999 decrease of 5.3%. Some of the practice specialties that had previously received dramatic cuts found those cuts mitigated, while others found no such relief.

Notably, a highly successful lobbying effort by its trade association resulted in a dramatic turnaround for pathology, with reimbursement increases of 9% over three years partially offsetting the prior year's 13% decline.

The changes in the practice expenses component of services provided by the various specialties must be *revenue neutral* under the law. As such, to the extent that any specialty received more reimbursement, other specialties received less. Cardiology, cardiac surgery, and gastroenterology received reimbursement cuts, primarily due to decreases in the RVUs associated with procedures performed by these physicians, such as echocardiography.

In November 2000, CMS issued the scheduled updates to the RBRVS for 2001. The update reflected changes mandated by the BBA and subsequent legislation. The 2001 physician fee schedule conversion factor was $38.2581 per RVU, an increase of 4.5% over the 2000 factor of $36.6137.

Changes in 2002 basically followed the legislative formula, with the RVU changes of the BBA now phased in fully. The 2002 physician fee schedule conversion factor was *$36.1992, a 5.4% decrease from the 2000 factor of $38.2581 per RVU*. This reflected primarily decreased growth in per capita GDP as well as the cumulative effect of various errors made in prior computations of the SGR that resulted in it being set at too high a level.

The annual physician fee schedule update is difficult to predict with any certainty until the annual measurement date (September 1) occurs. After a cut in the 2003 conversion factor of 4.4% was announced belatedly at the end of 2002, Congress modified the conversion factor in mid-February to eliminate the cumulative effect of prior errors that had overstated earlier conversion factors.

"For CY 2002, the MEI is equal to 3% (1.030). The update adjustment factor is equal to –1.1% (0.989) … The act requires an additional 0.2% (0.998) reduction to the update for 2003. Thus, the product of the MEI (1.030), the update adjustment factor (0.989), and the statutory adjustment factor (0.998) equals the CY 2003 update of 1.0166 [1.6%]."

Applying the 1.0162 factor (adjusted for budget neutrality) to the 2002 conversion factor of $36.1992 results in the 2003 conversion factor of *$36.7856*.

Prior to yet another legislative "fix" in the Medicare Modernization Act (Act) of 2003, the 2004 update was to be equal to the following: the product of one plus the percentage increase in the MEI (divided by 100) and one plus the update adjustment factor (UAF).

For CY 2004, the MEI is equal to 2.9% (1.029). The UAF is –7% (0.930). Section 1848(d)(4)(F) of the act requires an additional 0.2% (0.998) reduction to the update for 2004. Thus, the product of the MEI (1.029), the UAF (0.930), and the statutory adjustment factor (0.998) would have resulted in a CY 2004 update of –4.5% (0.9551). The calculation for 2005 would have produced an update of approximately –3.3%. The act set the increase at 1.5% for 2004 as well as 2005. Thus, the 2004 physician fee schedule conversion factor will be *$37.3374* and the 2005 conversion factor is *$37.8975.*

As of Nov, 2, 2005, CMS announced the final rule for the conversion factor in 2006 of *$36.1770*, a decrease of 4.4%, which was subsequently revised in February 2006 by the Deficit Reduction Act to maintain the 2005 conversion factor is *$37.8975*. The 2007 conversion factor—*$37.8975*—is identical to 2006 as a result of the repeal of the scheduled decrease in the Tax Relief and Health Care Act of 2006, thus there was no increase for three years. A 10.1% cut was due to be implemented in 2008, but was (again) suspended at the last minute by Congress and an increase of 0.5% (one-half of one percent) was adopted, or *$38.09*. The 2009 Medicare physician fee schedule final rule on Oct. 30, 2008 provides for the statutorily mandated 1.1% update for calendar year 2009; *however*, the budget neutrality adjustment to the conversion factor associated with the review and reallocation of RVUs was -6.41%, resulting in a rate of *$36.07*.

***2011 Changes***

The CMS issued the 2011 Medicare physician fee schedule final rule on Nov, 2, 2010, which provided for the statutorily mandated negative update for calendar year 2011, resulting in a conversion factor of $25.5217; subsequently, Congress overturned the cut yet again, resulting in a conversion factor of $33.9764.

Exhibit 53, taken from the final rule, shows the changes in expected payments for each of the various physician specialties based upon revisions in the RVUs for the various CPT codes billed to Medicare by each of those specialties. The principal changes affecting payments to the various specialties are in the practice expense (PE) RVUs, while less significant changes are in the work (physician effort) RVUs. The "full" and "tran" refer to the phase-in of the RVU changes over four years; the "tran" represents the effect in 2011, which is the second year of the phase-in period. "Full" represents what the impact would look like in 2013.

## Exhibit 53. 2011 Summary of Changes by Principal Affected Practice Specialty

| Specialty | Allowed Charges (mil) | Impact of Work and | Impact of PE RVU and MPPR Changes | | Impact of MEI | Combined Impact | |
|---|---|---|---|---|---|---|---|
| | | | Full | Tran | | Full | Tran |
| TOTAL | $81,980 | 0% | 0% | 0% | 0% | 0% | 0% |
| ALLERGY/IMMUNOLOGY | $181 | 0% | 0% | 1% | 4% | 4% | 5% |
| ANESTHESIOLOGY | $1,793 | 0% | 4% | 2% | -3% | 2% | -1% |
| CARDIAC SURGERY | $382 | 0% | -1% | 0% | 0% | -1% | 0% |
| CARDIOLOGY | $6,951 | 0% | -5% | -2% | 1% | -5% | -2% |
| COLON AND RECTAL SURGERY | $138 | 0% | 4% | 2% | 0% | 5% | 3% |
| CRITICAL CARE | $240 | 0% | 3% | 2% | -2% | 1% | 0% |
| DERMATOLOGY | $2,749 | 0% | 2% | 2% | 3% | 5% | 4% |
| EMERGENCY MEDICINE | $2,600 | 0% | 2% | 1% | -3% | -2% | -3% |
| ENDOCRINOLOGY | $395 | 1% | 4% | 2% | 0% | 4% | 2% |
| FAMILY PRACTICE | $5,512 | 0% | 4% | 2% | 0% | 4% | 2% |
| GASTROENTEROLOGY | $1,800 | 0% | 3% | 1% | -1% | 2% | 1% |
| GENERAL PRACTICE | $728 | 0% | 3% | 1% | 0% | 3% | 1% |
| GENERAL SURGERY | $2,286 | 0% | 3% | 1% | 0% | 3% | 1% |
| GERIATRICS | $188 | 0% | 5% | 2% | -2% | 4% | 1% |
| HAND SURGERY | $103 | 0% | 4% | 2% | 2% | 6% | 4% |
| HEMATOLOGY/ONCOLOGY | $1,912 | 0% | -4% | -2% | 2% | -2% | 0% |
| INFECTIOUS DISEASE | $584 | 0% | 4% | 2% | -2% | 3% | 0% |
| INTERNAL MEDICINE | $10,696 | 0% | 3% | 2% | -1% | 3% | 1% |
| INTERVENTIONAL PAIN MGMT | $390 | -1% | 3% | 1% | 1% | 2% | 0% |
| INTERVENTIONAL RADIOLOGY | $224 | -2% | -8% | -4% | 0% | -9% | -5% |
| MULTISPECIALTY CLINIC/OTHER | $46 | 0% | -7% | -5% | 1% | -5% | -4% |
| NEPHROLOGY | $1,946 | 1% | 1% | 1% | -1% | 1% | 1% |
| NEUROLOGY | $1,457 | 0% | 5% | 2% | 0% | 5% | 2% |
| NEUROSURGERY | $642 | -2% | 1% | 0% | 1% | 0% | -1% |
| NUCLEAR MEDICINE | $59 | 0% | -7% | -4% | 0% | -6% | -4% |
| OBSTETRICS/GYNECOLOGY | $670 | 0% | 1% | 1% | 1% | 2% | 2% |
| OPHTHALMOLOGY | $5,287 | -1% | 4% | 0% | 1% | 4% | 0% |
| ORTHOPEDIC SURGERY | $3,432 | 0% | 3% | 1% | 1% | 4% | 3% |
| OTOLARNGOLOGY | $941 | 0% | 3% | 2% | 1% | 5% | 3% |
| PATHOLOGY | $1,069 | -1% | -1% | 0% | 0% | -2% | -1% |
| PEDIATRICS | $68 | 0% | 2% | 1% | 0% | 2% | 1% |
| PHYSICAL MEDICINE | $895 | 0% | 4% | 2% | -1% | 4% | 1% |
| PLASTIC SURGERY | $317 | 0% | 4% | 2% | 1% | 5% | 3% |
| PSYCHIATRY | $1,149 | 1% | 2% | 1% | -3% | 0% | -1% |
| PULMONARY DISEASE | $1,786 | -1% | 2% | 1% | -1% | 1% | -1% |
| RADIATION ONCOLOGY | $1,939 | -2% | -9% | -3% | 4% | -7% | -1% |
| RADIOLOGY | $5,052 | -2% | -12% | -7% | -1% | -14% | -10% |
| RHEUMATOLOGY | $511 | 0% | 1% | 0% | 2% | 2% | 2% |
| THORACIC SURGERY | $398 | 0% | -1% | 0% | 0% | -1% | 0% |
| UROLOGY | $1,950 | -1% | -6% | -3% | 1% | -7% | -3% |
| VASCULAR SURGERY | $708 | -1% | -3% | -2% | 0% | -4% | -2% |
| AUDIOLOGIST | $54 | 0% | -6% | -1% | 2% | -5% | 0% |
| CHIROPRACTOR | $756 | 0% | 4% | 2% | -2% | 2% | 0% |
| CLINICAL PSYCHOLOGIST | $577 | 0% | -6% | -2% | -4% | -10% | -6% |
| CLINICAL SOCIAL WORKER | $390 | 0% | -5% | -2% | -4% | -9% | -5% |
| DIAGNOSTIC TESTING FACILITY | $909 | 0% | -27% | -16% | 2% | -23% | -15% |
| INDEPENDENT LABORATORY | $1,039 | -1% | -7% | -3% | 5% | -4% | 1% |
| NURSE ANES / ANES ASST | $726 | 0% | 4% | 2% | -4% | 1% | -1% |
| NURSE PRACTITIONER | $1,212 | 0% | 4% | 2% | -1% | 4% | 1% |
| OPTOMETRY | $970 | 0% | 4% | 1% | 1% | 6% | 2% |
| ORAL/MAXILLOFACIAL SURGERY | $40 | 0% | 5% | 3% | 2% | 7% | 5% |
| PHYSICAL/OCCUPATIONAL THERA | $2,204 | 0% | 0% | -3% | -2% | -1% | -5% |
| PHYSICIAN ASSISTANT | $893 | 0% | 3% | 2% | 0% | 3% | 1% |
| PODIATRY | $1,801 | 0% | 6% | 3% | 1% | 7% | 4% |
| PORTABLE X-RAY | $94 | 0% | 2% | 0% | 6% | 7% | 6% |
| RADIATION THERAPY CENTERS | $71 | 0% | -13% | -5% | 8% | -6% | 3% |
| OTHER | $69 | 2% | 3% | 1% | 0% | 5% | 3% |

### *2010 Changes*

The CMS issued the 2010 Medicare physician fee schedule final rule on Oct. 30, 2009, which provides for the statutorily mandated -21.2% update for calendar year 2010; *however,* the budget neutrality adjustment is included in the conversion factor now where historically it was applied to a reduction of RVUs for each CPT code. This makes the apparent conversion factor lower than it might otherwise have been. As noted elsewhere herein, the cut in the conversion factor has not been implemented as of May 2010 and was in fact repealed in June 2010. Even though that cut was not implemented, the practice expense RVU changes shown in Exhibits 54 and 55 do take effect.

**Exhibit 54. 2010 Changes in Individual CPT Code Reimbursement**

| CPT[1]/ HCPCS | MOD | Description | Facility | | | Non-facility | | |
|---|---|---|---|---|---|---|---|---|
| | | | 2009 ($) | 2010 ($) | Percent Change | 2009 ($) | 2010 ($) | Percent Change |
| 11721 | | Debride nail, 6 or more | 27.77 | 20.74 | -25% | 40.39 | 31.25 | -23% |
| 17000 | | Destruct premalg lesion | 48.69 | 40.90 | -16% | 69.97 | 57.95 | -17% |
| 27130 | | Total hip arthroplasty | 1359.71 | 1082.84 | -20% | NA | NA | NA |
| 27244 | | Treat thigh fracture | 1144.39 | 917.52 | -20% | NA | NA | NA |
| 27447 | | Total knee arthroplasty | 1456.37 | 1158.40 | -20% | NA | NA | NA |
| 33533 | | CABG, arterial, single | 1892.05 | 1534.21 | -19% | NA | NA | NA |
| 35301 | | Rechanneling of artery | 1067.93 | 868.66 | -19% | NA | NA | NA |
| 43239 | | Upper GI endoscopy, biopsy | 165.55 | 134.08 | -19% | 323.16 | 257.08 | -20% |
| 66821 | | After cataract laser surgery | 251.38 | 216.45 | -14% | 266.53 | 228.67 | -14% |
| 66984 | | Cataract surg w/iol, 1 stage | 638.74 | 549.09 | -14% | NA | NA | NA |
| 67210 | | Treatment of retinal lesion | 561.56 | 478.93 | -15% | 580.67 | 493.98 | -15% |
| 71010 | | Chest x-ray | NA | NA | NA | 24.16 | 18.18 | -25% |
| 71010 | 26 | Chest x-ray | 9.02 | 7.10 | -21% | 9.02 | 7.10 | -21% |
| 77056 | | Mammogram, both breasts | NA | NA | NA | 107.48 | 82.95 | -23% |
| 77056 | 26 | Mammogram, both breasts | 44.36 | 34.66 | -22% | 44.36 | 34.66 | -22% |
| 77057 | | Mammogram, screening | NA | NA | NA | 81.15 | 61.64 | -24% |
| 77057 | 26 | Mammogram, screening | 35.71 | 27.84 | -22% | 35.71 | 27.84 | -22% |
| 77427 | | Radiation tx management, x5 | 188.27 | 153.11 | -19% | 188.27 | 153.11 | -19% |
| 78465 | 26 | Heart image (3d), multiple | 78.99 | 62.21 | -21% | 78.99 | 62.21 | -21% |
| 88305 | 26 | Tissue exam by pathologist | 37.15 | 28.97 | -22% | 37.15 | 28.97 | -22% |
| 90801 | | Psy dx interview | 128.04 | 100.27 | -22% | 152.92 | 121.01 | -21% |

continued

**Exhibit 54. 2010 Changes in Individual CPT Code Reimbursement, continued**

| CPT[1]/ HCPCS | MOD | Description | Facility | | | Non-facility | | |
|---|---|---|---|---|---|---|---|---|
| | | | 2009 ($) | 2010 ($) | Percent Change | 2009 ($) | 2010 ($) | Percent Change |
| 90862 | | Medication management | 45.08 | 35.79 | -21% | 55.18 | 44.31 | -20% |
| 90935 | | Hemodialysis, one evaluation | 66.36 | 53.12 | -20% | NA | NA | NA |
| 92012 | | Eye exam established pat | 45.80 | 38.35 | -16% | 70.69 | 58.80 | -17% |
| 92014 | | Eye exam & treatment | 70.33 | 58.80 | -16% | 103.15 | 85.79 | -17% |
| 92980 | | Insert intracoronary stent | 847.93 | 644.53 | -24% | NA | NA | NA |
| 93000 | | Electrocardiogram, complete | 20.92 | NA | NA | 20.92 | 15.62 | -25% |
| 93010 | | Electrocardiogram report | 9.02 | 7.10 | -21% | 9.02 | 7.10 | -21% |
| 93015 | | Cardiovascular stress test | 100.27 | 73.00 | -27% | 100.27 | 73.00 | -27% |
| 93307 | 26 | Echo exam of heart | 49.77 | 38.35 | -23% | 49.77 | 38.35 | -23% |
| 93510 | 26 | Left heart catheterization | 248.86 | 185.21 | -26% | 248.86 | 185.21 | -26% |
| 98941 | | Chiropractic manipulation | 30.30 | 24.15 | -20% | 33.90 | 27.27 | -20% |
| 99203 | | Office/outpatient visit, new | 68.17 | 57.38 | -16% | 91.97 | 76.98 | -16% |
| 99213 | | Office/outpatient visit, est | 44.72 | 38.06 | -15% | 61.31 | 51.70 | -16% |
| 99214 | | Office/outpatient visit, est | 69.25 | 58.80 | -15% | 92.33 | 77.55 | -16% |
| 99222 | | Initial hospital care | 122.63 | 100.27 | -18% | NA | NA | NA |
| 99223 | | Initial hospital care | 180.33 | 147.14 | -18% | NA | NA | NA |
| 99231 | | Subsequent hospital care | 37.15 | 30.11 | -19% | NA | NA | NA |
| 99232 | | Subsequent hospital care | 66.72 | 54.26 | -19% | NA | NA | NA |
| 99233 | | Subsequent hospital care | 95.58 | 77.83 | -19% | NA | NA | NA |
| 99236 | | Observ/hosp same date | 207.38 | 166.18 | -20% | NA | NA | NA |
| 99239 | | Hospital discharge day | 96.30 | 77.83 | -19% | NA | NA | NA |
| 99243 | | Office consultation | 97.38 | Discontinued | Discontinued | 124.79 | Discontinued | Discontinued |
| 99244 | | Office consultation | 154.00 | Discontinued | Discontinued | 184.30 | Discontinued | Discontinued |
| 99253 | | Inpatient consultation | 114.69 | Discontinued | Discontinued | NA | NA | NA |
| 99254 | | Inpatient consultation | 165.55 | Discontinued | Discontinued | NA | NA | NA |
| 99283 | | Emergency dept visit | 61.31 | 48.57 | -21% | NA | NA | NA |
| 99284 | | Emergency dept visit | 114.33 | 91.18 | -20% | NA | NA | NA |

## Exhibit 55. 2010 Summary of Changes by Principal Affected Practice Specialty

| | (A) | (B) | (C) | (D) | (E) | (F) | (G) | (H) |
|---|---|---|---|---|---|---|---|---|
| | Specialty | Allowed Charges (mil $) | Impact of Work RVU Changes | Impact of PE RVU Changes** | | Impact of MP RVU Changes | Combined Impact | |
| | | | | Full | Tran | | Full | Tran |
| 1 | TOTAL | 77,796 | 0% | 0% | 0% | 0% | 0% | 0% |
| 2 | ALLERGY/IMMUNOLOGY | 173 | 0% | -1% | 0% | 0% | -2% | 0% |
| 3 | ANESTHESIOLOGY | 1,744 | 0% | 4% | 1% | 0% | 3% | 0% |
| 4 | CARDIAC SURGERY | 373 | -1% | -1% | 0% | 2% | 1% | 1% |
| 5 | CARDIOLOGY | 7,158 | -1% | -10% | -5% | -1% | -13% | -8% |
| 6 | COLON AND RECTAL SURGERY | 130 | -1% | 4% | 1% | 1% | 4% | 1% |
| 7 | CRITICAL CARE | 223 | -1% | 2% | 1% | 1% | 3% | 1% |
| 8 | DERMATOLOGY | 2,520 | 1% | 1% | 1% | 1% | 3% | 3% |
| 9 | EMERGENCY MEDICINE | 2,416 | 0% | 2% | 1% | 0% | 3% | 1% |
| 10 | ENDOCRINOLOGY | 374 | -1% | 3% | 0% | 0% | 2% | 0% |
| 11 | FAMILY PRACTICE | 5,094 | 2% | 5% | 2% | 1% | 7% | 4% |
| 12 | GASTROENTEROLOGY | 1,792 | -2% | 0% | 0% | 1% | 0% | -1% |
| 13 | GENERAL PRACTICE | 727 | 1% | 4% | 1% | 0% | 6% | 3% |
| 14 | GENERAL SURGERY | 2,227 | -1% | 3% | 1% | 1% | 4% | 1% |
| 15 | GERIATRICS | 170 | 1% | 6% | 2% | 1% | 8% | 3% |
| 16 | HAND SURGERY | 89 | -1% | 3% | 1% | -1% | 2% | -1% |
| 17 | HEMATOLOGY/ONCOLOGY | 1,897 | 0% | -5% | -1% | 0% | -6% | -1% |
| 18 | INFECTIOUS DISEASE | 554 | -1% | 3% | 0% | 1% | 3% | 0% |
| 19 | INTERNAL MEDICINE | 10,133 | 1% | 4% | 1% | 1% | 5% | 2% |
| 20 | INTERVENTIONAL PAIN MANAGE. | 356 | -2% | 3% | -1% | 0% | 0% | -3% |
| 21 | INTERVENTIONAL RADIOLOGY | 225 | -1% | -9% | -2% | 0% | -10% | -3% |
| 22 | NEPHROLOGY | 1,803 | -1% | 2% | 0% | 1% | 2% | 1% |
| 23 | NEUROLOGY | 1,414 | -3% | 4% | 1% | 0% | 1% | -2% |
| 24 | NEUROSURGERY | 591 | -1% | 2% | 0% | 0% | 1% | -1% |
| 25 | NUCLEAR MEDICINE | 74 | -5% | -15% | -10% | -2% | -23% | -18% |
| 26 | OBSTETRICS/GYNECOLOGY | 624 | 0% | 0% | -1% | 0% | 0% | -1% |
| 27 | OPHTHALMOLOGY | 4,758 | 0% | 11% | 3% | 2% | 13% | 5% |
| 28 | ORTHOPEDIC SURGERY | 3,261 | 0% | 3% | 1% | -1% | 2% | 0% |
| 29 | OTOLARNGOLOGY | 933 | -1% | 1% | -1% | 0% | 0% | -2% |
| 30 | PATHOLOGY | 994 | 0% | -1% | 1% | -1% | -3% | -1% |
| 31 | PEDIATRICS | 65 | 1% | 3% | 1% | 0% | 4% | 2% |
| 32 | PHYSICAL MEDICINE | 824 | -1% | 6% | 2% | 0% | 5% | 1% |
| 33 | PLASTIC SURGERY | 284 | 0% | 4% | 1% | 1% | 5% | 2% |
| 34 | PSYCHIATRY | 1,095 | 0% | 2% | 1% | 1% | 3% | 2% |
| 35 | PULMONARY DISEASE | 1,765 | -1% | 2% | 0% | 1% | 2% | 0% |
| 36 | RADIATION ONCOLOGY | 1,809 | 0% | -3% | 0% | -2% | -5% | -1% |
| 37 | RADIOLOGY | 5,056 | 0% | -14% | -3% | -2% | -16% | -5% |
| 38 | RHEUMATOLOGY | 493 | 0% | -1% | 0% | 0% | -2% | -1% |
| 39 | THORACIC SURGERY | 389 | -1% | 0% | 0% | 2% | 1% | 1% |
| 40 | UROLOGY | 1,993 | -1% | -8% | -3% | 0% | -10% | -4% |
| 41 | VASCULAR SURGERY | 656 | -1% | -3% | -2% | 0% | -3% | -2% |
| 42 | AUDIOLOGIST | 36 | -1% | -16% | -9% | -7% | -23% | -17% |
| 43 | CHIROPRACTOR | 713 | 0% | 3% | 1% | 1% | 4% | 2% |
| 44 | CLINICAL PSYCHOLOGIST | 544 | 0% | -8% | -2% | 0% | -8% | -2% |
| 45 | CLINICAL SOCIAL WORKER | 362 | 0% | -7% | -1% | 0% | -7% | -1% |
| 46 | NURSE ANESTHETIST | 681 | 0% | 4% | 1% | 0% | 4% | 1% |
| 47 | NURSE PRACTITIONER | 1,018 | 1% | 5% | 1% | 1% | 6% | 3% |
| 48 | OPTOMETRY | 848 | 1% | 10% | 3% | 1% | 12% | 5% |
| 49 | ORAL/MAXILLOFACIAL SURGERY | 36 | -1% | 4% | 1% | 0% | 3% | 0% |
| 50 | PHYSICAL/OCCUPATIONAL THERAPY | 1,883 | 0% | 9% | 3% | -1% | 8% | 2% |
| 51 | PHYSICIAN ASSISTANT | 757 | 0% | 4% | 1% | 0% | 5% | 2% |
| 52 | PODIATRY | 1,682 | 1% | 6% | 2% | -1% | 6% | 2% |
| 53 | DIAGNOSTIC TESTING FACILITY | 923 | -1% | -29% | -7% | -4% | -34% | -12% |
| 54 | INDEPENDENT LABORATORY | 970 | 0% | -5% | 0% | -1% | -7% | -1% |
| 55 | PORTABLE X-RAY SUPPLIER | 87 | 0% | 8% | 3% | -1% | 7% | 2% |

### *2009 Changes*

The CMS issued the 2009 Medicare physician fee schedule final rule on Oct. 30, 2008, which provides for the statutorily mandated 1.1% update for calendar year 2009 (see Exhibit 56); *however,* the budget neutrality adjustment to the conversion factor associated with the review and reallocation of RVUs was -6.41%, resulting in a rate of $36.07 (last year, the budget neutrality adjustment was accomplished by applying an across-the-board reduction to work RVUs of 10%). As described below, *an additional 4% in payment incentives* for adopting electronic prescribing and reporting on certain quality measures was part of the final rule; thus, any forecast of 2009 and subsequent cash flows would have to consider the likelihood of qualifying for the incentive.

> ... the reporting period for the 2009 PQRI [Physician Quality Reporting Initiative] is defined as the entire year, or Jan. 1, 2009 through Dec. 31, 2009. Therefore, for the 2009 PQRI, eligible professionals who satisfactorily report data on quality measures for covered professional services furnished between Jan. 1, 2009 through Dec. 31, 2009 will receive an incentive payment equal to 2% of the total estimated allowed charges submitted by no later than Feb. 28, 2010 for all covered professional services furnished between Jan. 1, 2009 and Dec. 31, 2009.
>
> Specifically, for 2009, in accordance with Section 1848(m)(2) of the act, as added by Section 132(a) of the MIPPA, a "successful electronic prescriber" as defined by MIPPA and further discussed below, is eligible to receive an incentive payment equal to 2% of the total estimated allowed charges submitted not later than two months after the end of the reporting period for all covered professional services furnished during the 2009 reporting period. This new E-Prescribing Incentive Program is separate from and in addition to any incentive payment that eligible professionals may earn through the PQRI program discussed above.[58]

**Exhibit 56. Percent Change From 2008 to 2009**

| | | | Facility (e.g., HOPD) | | | Non-Facility (MD Office) | | |
|---|---|---|---|---|---|---|---|---|
| CODE | MOD | DESCRIPTION | 2008 | 2009 | Change | 2008 | 2009 | Change |
| 11721 | | Debride nail, 6 or more | $27.42 | $27.77 | 1% | $39.61 | $40.39 | 2% |
| 17000 | | Destruct premalg. lesion | 46.47 | 48.69 | 5 | 67.41 | 69.97 | 4 |
| 27130 | | Total hip arthroplasty | 1,336.09 | 1,359.71 | 2 | NA | NA | NA |
| 27244 | | Treat thigh fracture | 1,077.10 | 1,144.39 | 6 | NA | NA | NA |
| 27447 | | Total knee arthroplasty | 1,435.12 | 1,456.37 | 1 | NA | NA | NA |
| 33533 | | CABG, arterial, single | 1,854.84 | 1,892.05 | 2 | NA | NA | NA |
| 35301 | | Rechanneling of artery | 1,045.11 | 1,067.93 | 2 | NA | NA | NA |
| 43239 | | Upper GI endoscopy, biopsy | 156.92 | 165.55 | 5 | 329.07 | 323.16 | -2 |
| 66821 | | After cataract laser surgery | 253.53 | 222.81 | -12 | 270.97 | 237.80 | -12 |
| 66821 | | After cataract laser surgery | 249.47 | 251.38 | 1 | 266.23 | 266.53 | 0 |

continued

58 CMS-1403-FC

**Exhibit 56. Percent Change From 2008 to 2009, continued**

| | | | Facility (e.g., HOPD) | | | Non-Facility (MD Office) | | |
|---|---|---|---|---|---|---|---|---|
| CODE | MOD | DESCRIPTION | 2008 | 2009 | Change | 2008 | 2009 | Change |
| 66984 | | Cataract surg. w/iol, 1 stage | 626.15 | 638.74 | 2 | NA | NA | NA |
| 67210 | | Treatment of retinal lesion | 545.79 | 561.56 | 3 | 567.88 | 580.67 | 2 |
| 71010 | | Chest X-ray | NA | NA | NA | 25.52 | 24.16 | -5 |
| 71010 | 26 | Chest X-ray | $8.76 | $9.02 | 3% | $8.76 | $9.02 | 3% |
| 77056 | | Mammogram, both breasts | NA | NA | NA | 104.74 | 107.48 | 3 |
| 77056 | 26 | Mammogram, both breasts | 41.9 | 44.36 | 6 | 41.9 | 44.36 | 6 |
| 77057 | | Mammogram, screening | NA | NA | NA | 82.65 | 81.15 | -2 |
| 77057 | 26 | Mammogram, screening | 33.9 | 35.71 | 5 | 33.9 | 35.71 | 5 |
| 77427 | | Radiation tx management, x5 | 177.1 | 188.27 | 6 | 177.1 | 188.27 | 6 |
| 78465 | 26 | Heart image (3d), multiple | 74.27 | 78.99 | 6 | 74.27 | 78.99 | 6 |
| 88305 | 26 | Tissue exam by pathologist | 36.18 | 37.15 | 3 | 36.18 | 37.15 | 3 |
| 90801 | | Psy. dx interview | 125.31 | 128.04 | 2 | 147.02 | 152.92 | 4 |
| 90862 | | Medication management | 43.8 | 45.08 | 3 | 52.18 | 55.18 | 6 |
| 90935 | | Hemodialysis, one evaluation | 65.13 | 66.36 | 2 | NA | NA | NA |
| 92012 | | Eye exam established pat. | 43.04 | 45.80 | 6 | 70.08 | 70.69 | 1% |
| 92014 | | Eye exam and treatment | 66.27 | 70.33 | 6 | 101.69 | 103.15 | 1 |
| 92980 | | Insert intracoronary stent | 806.3 | 847.93 | 5 | NA | NA | NA |
| 93010 | | Electrocardiogram report | 8.38 | 9.02 | 8 | 8.38 | 9.02 | 8 |
| 93015 | | Cardiovascular stress test | 103.98 | 100.27 | -4 | 103.98 | 100.27 | -4 |
| 93307 | 26 | Echo exam of heart | 47.23 | 49.77 | 5 | 47.23 | 49.77 | 5 |
| 93510 | 26 | Left heart catheterization | 241.09 | 248.86 | 3 | 241.09 | 248.86 | 3 |
| 98941 | | Chiropractic manipulation | 28.57 | 30.30 | 6 | 33.14 | 33.9 | 2 |
| 99203 | | Office/outpatient visit, new | 65.51 | 68.17 | 4 | 91.03 | 91.97 | 1 |
| 99213 | | Office/outpatient visit, est. | 41.9 | 44.72 | 7 | 59.8 | 61.31 | 3 |
| 99214 | | Office/outpatient visit, est. | 65.51 | 69.25 | 6 | 89.89 | 92.33 | 3 |
| 99223 | | Initial hospital care | 171.77 | 180.33 | 5 | NA | NA | NA |
| 99231 | | Subsequent hospital care | 35.42 | 37.15 | 5 | NA | NA | NA |
| 99232 | | Subsequent hospital care | 63.22 | 66.72 | 6 | NA | NA | NA |
| 99233 | | Subsequent hospital care | 90.65 | 95.58 | 5 | NA | NA | NA |
| 99236 | | Observ./hosp. same date | 200.34 | 207.38 | 4 | NA | NA | NA |
| 99239 | | Hospital discharge day | 92.93 | 96.30 | 4 | NA | NA | NA |
| 99243 | | Office consultation | 92.93 | 97.38 | 5 | 122.26 | 124.79 | 2 |
| 99244 | | Office consultation | 145.49 | 154.00 | 6 | 179.01 | 184.3 | 3 |
| 99253 | | Inpatient consultation | 108.55 | 114.69 | 6 | NA | NA | NA |
| 99254 | | Inpatient consultation | 156.54 | 165.55 | 6 | NA | NA | NA |
| 99283 | | Emergency dept. visit | 59.03 | 61.31 | 4 | NA | NA | NA |
| 99284 | | Emergency dept. visit | 108.93 | 114.33 | 5 | NA | NA | NA |
| 99291 | | Critical care, first hour | 204.15 | 212.07 | 4 | 250.99 | 253.91 | 1 |
| 99292 | | Critical care, add'l 30 min. | 102.45 | 106.04 | 3 | 111.98 | 114.69 | 2% |
| 99348 | | Home visit, est. patient | NA | NA | NA | 76.17 | 79.35 | 4 |
| 99350 | | Home visit, est. patient | NA | NA | NA | 155.78 | 160.86 | 3 |
| G0008 | | Admin. influenza virus vac. | NA | NA | NA | 20.57 | 20.92 | 2 |
| G0317 | | ESRD related svs 4+mo 20+yrs | $283.09 | $245.29 | -13% | $283.09 | $245.29 | -13 |

### *2009 Changes in Individual CPT Code Reimbursement*

Despite the apparent cut in the 2009 conversion factor, the increase in RVUs for many office-based procedures results in a fairly significant increase for the two most commonly used codes, 99213 and 99214, as well as the consultation codes and hospital inpatient codes. As seen in Exhibit 57, those increases are being paid for by diagnostic imaging providers.

### *2009 Summary of Changes by Principal Affected Practice Specialty*

Exhibit 57 shows CMS's estimate of the impact on payments in **2009** from ***both*** the Work and Practice Expense RVU changes described in the previous section ***and*** the Conversion Factor. Note that imaging providers are primarily bearing the brunt of the changes in RVUs.

**Exhibit 57. Increases for 99213, 99214, Consultation Codes, and Hospital Inpatient Codes**

| Specialty | Allowed Charges -mil | RVU Changes* | Budget Neutrality | Statutory 1.1% | Total*** |
|---|---|---|---|---|---|
| Total | $81,669 | 0% | 0% | 1% | 1% |
| Allergy/immunology | 184 | 1 | -3 | 1 | -1 |
| Anesthesiology | $1,966 | -1% | 3% | 1% | 3% |
| Cardiac surgery | 400 | 0 | 1 | 1 | 2 |
| Cardiology | 7,775 | -2 | -1 | 1 | -2 |
| Colon and rectal surgery | 136 | 0 | 1 | 1 | 2 |
| Critical care | 224 | 0 | 2 | 1 | 3 |
| Dermatology | 2,557 | 2 | -2 | 1 | 1 |
| Emergency medicine | 2,451 | 0 | 3 | 1 | 4 |
| Endocrinology | 385 | 0 | 0 | 1 | 2 |
| Family practice | 5,354 | 0 | 0 | 1 | 2 |
| Gastroenterology | 1,883 | 2 | 1 | 1 | 3 |
| General practice | 842 | 0 | 0 | 1 | 2 |
| General surgery | 2,408 | 1 | 1 | 1 | 3 |
| Geriatrics | 175 | 0 | 2 | 1 | 3 |
| Hand surgery | 88 | -1 | -1 | 1 | -1 |
| Hematology/oncology | 2,019 | -1 | -2 | 1 | -1 |
| Infectious disease | 561 | 1 | 2 | 1 | 4 |
| Internal medicine | 10,662 | 0 | 1 | 1 | 2 |
| Interventional radiology | 228 | -1 | 0 | 1 | 0 |
| Nephrology | 1,840 | -1 | 1 | 1 | 2 |

continued

**Exhibit 57. Increases for 99213, 99214, Consultation Codes, and Hospital Inpatient Codes, continued**

| Specialty | Allowed Charges -mil | RVU Changes* | Budget Neutrality | Statutory 1.1% | Total*** |
|---|---|---|---|---|---|
| Neurology | 1,489 | 0 | 0 | 1 | 1 |
| Neurosurgery | 620 | -1 | 0 | 1 | 0 |
| Nuclear medicine | 79 | -1 | -2 | 1 | -1 |
| Obstetrics/gynecology | 654 | 0 | 0 | 1 | 0 |
| Ophthalmology | 5,026 | 0 | 0 | 1 | 0 |
| Orthopedic surgery | 3,454 | 0 | 0 | 1 | 0 |
| Otolarngology | 984 | -1 | -1 | 1 | -1 |
| Pathology | 1,007 | 0 | 0 | 1 | 1 |
| Pediatrics | 72 | 1 | 0 | 1 | 2 |
| Physical medicine | 850 | 0 | 1 | 1 | 1 |
| Plastic surgery | 288 | 0 | 0 | 1 | 1 |
| Psychiatry | 1,169 | 1 | 2 | 1 | 4 |
| Pulmonary disease | 1,828 | 1 | 1 | 1 | 3 |
| Radiation oncology | 1,854 | -1 | -3 | 1 | -3 |
| Radiology | 5,554 | 0 | -1 | 1 | 0 |
| Rheumatology | 521 | 0 | -1 | 1 | -1 |
| Thoracic surgery | 431 | 0 | 1 | 1 | 2 |
| Urology | 2,146 | 0 | -1 | 1 | 0 |
| Vascular surgery | 685 | 0 | -1 | 1 | 1 |
| Audiologist | 33 | -9 | -2 | 1 | -10 |
| Chiropractor | 768 | -1 | 2 | 1 | 2 |
| Clinical psychologist | 571 | -2 | 3 | 1 | 2 |
| Clinical social worker | 378 | -1 | 3 | 1 | 3 |
| Nurse anesthetist | 846 | 0 | 4 | 1 | 5 |
| Nurse practitioner | 963 | 1 | 1 | 1 | 3 |
| Optometry | 867 | 0 | -1 | 1 | 0 |
| Oral/maxillofacial surgery | 38 | 1 | -1 | 1 | 1 |
| Physical/occupational Therapy | 1,772 | 2 | 0 | 1 | 3 |
| Physician assistant | 711 | 0 | 1 | 1 | 2 |
| Podiatry | 1,727 | 1 | -1 | 1 | 1 |
| Diagnostic testing facility | 1,186 | -2 | -5 | 1 | -6 |
| Independent laboratory | 878 | 5 | -4 | 1 | 2 |
| Portable X-ray supplier | $87 | 2% | -4% | 1% | -2% |

* PE changes are CY 2009 third-year transition changes. For fully implemented CY 2010 PE changes, see CMS-1403-FC.

** Prior to the application of the OPPS imaging caps under DRA 5102.

***Components may not sum to total due to rounding.

*Note:* Exhibit 58 reflects CMS calculation of fee schedule changes[59] *before* the repeal of the 10.1% cut in the 2008 conversion factor; a revised table was not issued. You can *estimate* the changes for each code by adding 0.5% to the 2007 numbers shown in conjunction with Exhibit 58.

**Exhibit 58. 2008 Changes in Individual CPT Code Reimbursement**

| | | | Facility (e.g., HOPD) | | | Non-Facility (MD Office) | | |
|---|---|---|---|---|---|---|---|---|
| CODE | MOD | DESCRIPTION | 2007 | 2008 | Change | 2007 | 2009 | Change |
| 11721 | | Debride nail, 6 or more | $28.80 | $24.53 | -15% | $39.03 | $35.43 | -9% |
| 17000 | | Destruct premalg. lesion | 44.72 | 41.56 | -7 | 63.29 | 60.30 | -5 |
| 27130 | | Total hip arthroplasty | 1,360.52 | 1,194.77 | -12 | NA | NA | NA |
| 27244 | | Treat thigh fracture | 1,100.92 | 963.11 | -13 | NA | NA | NA |
| 27447 | | Total knee arthroplasty | 1,464.74 | 1,283.35 | -12 | NA | NA | NA |
| 33533 | | CABG, arterial, single | 1,908.52 | 1,658.44 | -13 | NA | NA | NA |
| 35301 | | Rechanneling of artery | 1,071.74 | 934.49 | -13 | NA | NA | NA |
| 43239 | | Upper GI endoscopy, biopsy | 155.00 | 140.36 | -9 | 325.16 | 294.01 | -10 |
| 66821 | | After cataract laser surgery | 253.53 | 222.81 | -12 | 270.97 | 237.80 | -12 |
| 66984 | | Cataract surg. w/iol, 1 stage | 641.98 | 560.08 | -13 | NA | NA | NA |
| 67210 | | Treatment of retinal lesion | 556.34 | 487.86 | -12 | 580.59 | 507.96 | -13 |
| 71010 | | Chest X-ray | NA | NA | NA | 26.15 | 22.83 | -13 |
| 71010 | 26 | Chest X-ray | 8.72 | 7.84 | -10 | 8.72 | 7.84 | -10 |
| 77056 | | Mammogram, both breasts | NA | NA | NA | 97.40 | 93.35 | -4 |
| 77056 | 26 | Mammogram, both breasts | 41.31 | 37.48 | -9 | 41.31 | 37.48 | -9 |
| 77057 | | Mammogram, screening | NA | NA | NA | 81.86 | 73.93 | -10 |
| 77057 | 26 | Mammogram, screening | 33.35 | 30.32 | -9 | 33.35 | 30.32 | -9 |
| 77427 | | Radiation tx management, x5 | 176.22 | 158.42 | -10 | 176.22 | 158.42 | -10 |
| 78465 | 26 | Heart image (3d), multiple | 73.14 | 66.43 | -9 | 73.14 | 66.43 | -9 |
| 88305 | 26 | Tissue exam by pathologist | 37.90 | 32.36 | -15 | 37.90 | 32.36 | -15 |
| 90801 | | Psy. dx interview | 129.99 | 112.08 | -14 | 145.15 | 131.50 | -9 |
| 90862 | | Medication management | 44.72 | 39.18 | -12 | 50.40 | 46.67 | -7 |
| 90935 | | Hemodialysis, one evaluation | 67.46 | 58.26 | -14 | NA | NA | NA |
| 92012 | | Eye exam established pat. | 34.11 | 38.50 | 13 | 61.77 | 62.69 | 1 |
| 92014 | | Eye exam and treatment | 55.71 | 59.28 | 6 | 91.33 | 90.96 | 0 |
| 92980 | | Insert intracoronary stent | 795.85 | 720.88 | -9 | NA | NA | NA |
| 93000 | | Electrocardiogram, complete | 24.63 | 20.78 | -16 | 24.63 | 20.78 | -16 |
| 93010 | | Electrocardiogram report | 8.34 | 7.50 | -10 | 8.34 | 7.50 | -10 |
| 93015 | | Cardiovascular stress test | 104.22 | 93.01 | -11 | 104.22 | 93.01 | -11 |
| 93307 | 26 | Echo exam of heart | 46.99 | 42.24 | -10 | 46.99 | 42.24 | -10 |

continued

59 CMS-1385-FC.pdf, http://www.cms.hhs.gov/PhysicianFeeSched/

**Exhibit 58. 2008 Changes in Individual CPT Code Reimbursement, continued**

| | | | Facility (e.g., HOPD) | | | Non-Facility (MD Office) | | |
|---|---|---|---|---|---|---|---|---|
| CODE | MOD | DESCRIPTION | 2007 | 2008 | Change | 2007 | 2009 | Change |
| 93510 | 26 | Left heart catheterization | 242.92 | 215.31 | -11 | 242.92 | 215.31 | -11 |
| 98941 | | Chiropractic manipulation | 28.80 | 25.55 | -11 | 33.35 | 29.64 | -11 |
| 99203 | | Office/outpatient visit, new | 67.08 | 58.60 | -13 | 91.71 | 81.42 | -11 |
| 99213 | | Office/outpatient visit, est. | 42.07 | 37.48 | -11 | 59.50 | 53.15 | -11 |
| 99214 | | Office/outpatient visit, est. | 66.32 | 58.60 | -12 | 90.20 | 80.40 | -11 |
| 99222 | | Initial hospital | 119.00 | 104.59 | -12 | NA | NA | NA |
| 99223 | | Initial hospital | 173.57 | 153.65 | -11 | NA | NA | NA |
| 99231 | | Subsequent hospital care | 35.62 | 31.68 | -11 | NA | NA | NA |
| 99232 | | Subsequent hospital care | 63.67 | 56.55 | -11 | NA | NA | NA |
| 99233 | | Subsequent hospital care | 90.95 | 81.08 | -11 | NA | NA | NA |
| 99236 | | Observ/hosp. same date | 205.40 | 179.20 | -13 | NA | NA | NA |
| 99239 | | Hospital discharge day | 94.74 | 83.13 | -12 | NA | NA | NA |
| 99243 | | Office consultation | 93.23 | 83.13 | -11 | 122.41 | 109.36 | -11 |
| 99244 | | Office consultation | 145.91 | 130.14 | -11 | 179.26 | 160.12 | -11 |
| 99253 | | Inpatient consultation | 108.77 | 97.09 | -11 | NA | NA | NA |
| 99254 | | Inpatient consultation | 156.52 | 140.02 | -11 | NA | NA | NA |
| 99283 | | Emergency dept. visit | 60.64 | 52.81 | -13 | NA | NA | NA |
| 99284 | | Emergency dept. visit | 110.28 | 97.44 | -12 | NA | NA | NA |
| 99291 | | Critical care, first hour | 208.82 | 182.61 | -13 | 256.19 | 224.17 | -12 |
| 99292 | | Critical care, add'l 30 min. | 104.60 | 91.64 | -12 | 114.45 | 100.16 | -12 |
| 99348 | | Home visit, est. patient | NA | NA | NA | 66.32 | 68.14 | 2 |
| 99350 | | Home visit, est. patient | NA | NA | NA | 150.83 | 139.34 | -8 |
| G0008 | | Admin. influenza virus vac. | NA | NA | NA | 18.95 | 18.40 | -3 |
| G0317 | | ESRD related svs 4+mo 20+yrs | 283.09 | 245.29 | -13 | 283.09 | 245.29 | -13 |

## 2008 Summary of *RVU* Changes by Principal Affected Practice Specialty

Exhibit 59 shows CMS's estimate of the impact on payments in 2008 from *only* the work and PE RVU changes described in the previous section *without* either the suspended cut in the conversion factor *or* the 0.5% increase. It should offer a rough estimate of the relative positions of the specialties for 2008. Note the winners and losers, particularly anesthesiology.

**Exhibit 59. CMS's Estimate of Impact on Payments in 2008**

| Specialty | Percent Change |
|---|---|
| Total | 0% |
| Allergy/immunology | 2 |
| Anesthesiology | 14 |
| Cardiac surgery | -2 |
| Cardiology | -2 |
| Colon and rectal surgery | 0 |
| Critical care | -1 |
| Dermatology | 2 |
| Emergency medicine | -2 |
| Endocrinology | -1 |
| Family practice | 0 |
| Gastroenterology | 0 |
| General practice | 0 |
| General surgery | -1 |
| Geriatrics | 3 |
| Hand surgery | -2 |
| Hematology/oncology | -1 |
| Infectious disease | -1 |

| Specialty | Percent Change |
|---|---|
| Internal medicine | 0 |
| Interventional radiology | -2 |
| Nephrology | -3 |
| Neurology | -1 |
| Neurosurgery | -2 |
| Nuclear medicine | 4 |
| Obstetrics/gynecology | -1 |
| Ophthalmology | 1 |
| Orthopedic surgery | -1 |
| Otolaryngology | 1 |
| Pathology | -2 |
| Pediatrics | 0 |
| Physical medicine | -1 |
| Plastic surgery | -1 |
| Psychiatry | 0 |
| Pulmonary disease | -1 |
| Radiation oncology | 0 |
| Radiology | 0 |

| Specialty | Percent Change |
|---|---|
| Rheumatology | -1 |
| Thoracic surgery | -2 |
| Urology | -1 |
| Vascular surgery | -1 |
| Audiologist | 12 |
| Chiropractor | -2 |
| Clinical psychologist | -3 |
| Clinical social worker | -3 |
| Nurse anesthetist | 22 |
| Nurse practitioner | 2 |
| Optometry | 4 |
| Oral/maxillofacial surgery | -1 |
| Physical/occupational therapy | 0 |
| Physicians assistant | 2 |
| Podiatry | 0 |
| Diagnostic testing facility | 3 |
| Independent laboratory | 2 |
| Portable X-ray supplier | 0 |

Chapter 3

# Healthcare Market Structure and Its Implication for Valuation of Privately Held Provider Entities—An Empirical Analysis

*By Mark O. Dietrich, CPA/ABV*

### Author's Note

I originally conducted this study in early 2008 to see if I could confirm my hypothesis and experience that there were underlying structural reasons that existed in local markets that would explain—and convince my colleagues of—the vast differences in reimbursement, profitability, and market participants that I had encountered in my appraisal and consulting practice and seminar presentations. As the research demonstrated, there *were* longstanding, historical reasons for these differences. The results first appeared in the Summer 2008 edition of *Business Valuation Review* and the information is reprinted with permission.

Subsequent to my research, a variety of other studies appeared, including one by the Government Accountability Office (GAO), another in the journal *Health Affairs*, one by the Center for Studying Health System Change, and one by KQED National Public Radio reporter Sarah Varney.[1] A series of annual studies titled "National Insurer Report Card" by the American Medical Association of concentration of insurer market share also bears out the findings in this article.

The GAO report *Nonprofit Hospitals: Variation in Standards and Guidance Limits Comparison of How Hospitals Meet Community Benefit Requirements* was released in September 2008. Figure 1 is taken from that report and shows a concentration of nonprofit hospitals consistent with my research.

1 www.npr.org/2010/11/18/131410569/big-hospital-chains-use-clout-to-dictate-premiums, November 2010.

The *Health Affairs* study "The Increased Concentration of Health Plan Markets Can Benefit Consumers Through Lower Hospital Prices"[2] found that markets in which insurers held the upper hand in terms of market power had lower hospital prices by approximately 12%, while most markets had high concentrations of hospital market power and this latter condition led to higher hospital prices.

Research Brief No. 16 from the Center for Studying Health System Change, "Wide Variation in Hospital and Physician Payment Rates Evidence of Provider Market Power," looked at eight specific healthcare markets—Cleveland; Indianapolis; Los Angeles; Miami; Milwaukee; Richmond, Va.; San Francisco; and rural Wisconsin—and found dramatic differences in inpatient hospital rates consistent with local market power of insurers and providers.

Finally, Greg Anderson and I documented much of my earlier work as well as our joint work elsewhere herein ("Evaluating RVU-Based Compensation Arrangements") in our 2012 book *The Financial Professional's Guide to Healthcare Reform*. Timothy Smith's work in this third edition of the *Healthcare Guide* expands on and emphasizes Greg's and my seminal work on market differences in RVU payment rates and the resultant limitations on generic market data.

**Figure 1. Geographic Distributions of Nonprofit Hospitals in 2006**

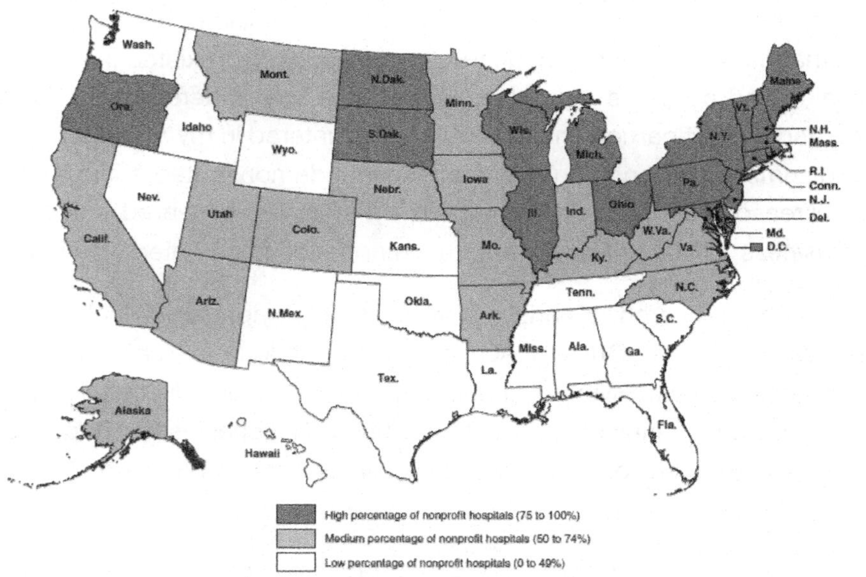


Sources: GAO analysis of 2006 CMS data; Map Resources (map).

Note: Hospitals include nonfederal, acute care, general hospitals.

2 Glenn A. Melnick, Yu-Chu Shen and Vivian Yaling Wu, *Health Affairs*, 30, no.9 (2011):1728-1733.

### Results of Original Study

The explosion in healthcare transactions after a 10-year hiatus has created a booming market for appraisal and valuation services. One of the peculiar aspects of the healthcare industry is that many if not most transactions must be supported by an independent appraisal due to governmental regulatory concerns. As such, failure of appraisers or valuation analysts to understand healthcare markets and government regulations can lead to transactions taking place at prices inconsistent with both economic reality and, as discussed later herein, regulatory parameters. These transactions can then find their way into databases relied upon by other appraisers resulting in further transactions based upon suspect opinions of value.

The degree of revenue and profit for healthcare provider entities varies significantly from state to state and even within different regions of individual states. As a threshold matter, areas with high healthcare spending and particularly high Medicare[3] spending tend to offer the greatest opportunity for profit. The elderly, of course, receive the bulk of medical care. Given that high localized spending is the primary driver of profit, what other factors contribute to the pattern of location of larger for-profit providers?

- The presence and market strength of Blue Cross plans;
- The degree of market strength of local nonprofit hospitals versus for-profit hospitals;
- The degree of market strength of local nonprofit health insurers versus for-profit health insurers;
- Certificate of need laws; and
- Other local demographic and economic factors.

As discussed later herein with respect to Blue Cross plans and nonprofit hospitals, these primary indicators reflect prevailing attitudes in different areas of the nation about the appropriateness of "profit" motivation in the provision of health care. In turn, the presence or lack thereof of these larger for-profit providers and insurers has a substantial impact on the acquisition and sales value of provider entities. This impact can be traced to at least two specific factors: the likelihood that for-profit entities will be acquirers of providers in a given area and the revenue and profit growth potential inherent in such acquisitions.

3 Medicare is a federal program primarily for the elderly and is distinct from Medicaid, a state-determined program for the poor that is funded 50% by federal funds and 50% by state funds.

Growth potential in the form of acquisition growth is typically only available to publicly traded companies whose stock prices are in large part driven by expected growth rates. High growth rates typically result in high valuation multiples due to low capitalization rates. Economies of scale from acquisitions that affect future "same store" profit growth also contribute to localized valuation differences. As such, all things being equal, a growth-driven public company is able to pay a higher value for a given business because the stock market rewards growth.[4]

The Stark laws contain restrictions on the use of "comparable" market data, much of which are pegged to local market conditions. As far back as 1994, published statements of the Internal Revenue Service focused on local factors that determined the character of a market. The factors discussed in this chapter suggest that the government agencies' views of fair market value should be seriously considered by appraisers and analysts in their own opinions of fair market value.

This study offers appraisers and valuation analysts a foundation for comparing market conditions in different areas of the country. In turn, it provides a basis for determining whether market data in the form of merged and acquired companies or guideline companies is comparable to a given subject company that is being valuated.

### Data Sources and Impact on Analysis

Sources of data utilized in this study include that maintained by The Kaiser Family Foundation (KFF). KFF maintains data on the breakdown of for-profit and not-for-profit hospitals for each of the 50 states, along with Medicare and Medicaid enrollment, spending, length of stay, and other detailed statistical data, some of which are described and utilized in this article. Detail of the market share of each state's health maintenance organization (HMO) and preferred provider organization (PPO) enrollment is available from each state's division or department of insurance or, for example, from Lehman Brothers' *Managed Care Guidebook*.[5] Often states will provide detail at the county level as well. Data on local Medicare spending from the Centers for Medicare and Medicaid (CMS) were also utilized, along with information taken directly from the Securities and Exchange Commission (SEC) filings of the public companies discussed.

Local market conditions can lead to dramatic differences in provider revenue, profitability, and related acquisition demand. This affects both the relevance of transaction

4 See "Understanding the Difference Between Strategic Value and Fair Market Value in Consolidating Industries" *Business Valuation Review*, June 2002, by the author.

5 Used in this study's market analysis.

data in determining fair market value as well as the perceived risk of provider entities in a given market area, which in turn affects the discount rate and value determined under the income approach.

As will be seen from the analysis throughout this chapter, for-profit public companies engaged in the healthcare industry tend to concentrate their activities in certain states, notably Texas and Florida, which have specific characteristics discernible from the data sources. The analysis considers presence and dominance of the following companies and certain of their competitors:

- Ambulatory surgery: AmSurg (AMSG);
- Hospitals: HCA, Tenet, HMA, Vanguard;
- Health insurers: United Healthcare (United), as well as Aetna, Cigna, Humana and Health Net, collectively referred to later as "other public"; and
- Imaging: Radnet.

### Public Healthcare Insurers

One key to understanding the strategy of provider entities such as AMSG discussed later is to examine the presence of the for-profit health insurers in a given state as well as the concentration of market power by those companies along with Blue Cross plans and local HMOs. The more concentrated a market is in terms of health insurers, the less likely a healthcare services provider will be able to negotiate favorable contracts. This is because market control over pricing is then held by those few insurers.[6] That, of course, leads to an expectation of lower profits.

A number of large publicly traded companies are engaged in providing health insurance, primarily in a managed-care format. These include United Healthcare, Aetna, Cigna, Humana, and Health Net.[7] There has been a spate of consolidation in the industry stemming back to the late 1990s, when a number of smaller entities got burned at the bottom of the so-called "underwriting cycle."[8] Aggressive setting of premiums over multiyear contracts to build market share resulted in bankruptcy or near-bankruptcy for such companies as Oxford when the costs increased more rapidly than expected. The consolidation trend continues today, driven in part by Medicare Advantage contracts as

6 The Federal Trade Commission and Department of Justice Anti-Trust Division favor insurers over providers.

7 Wellpoint is a large public company; however, it owns Blue Cross plans, including Anthem, which are otherwise addressed.

8 This is the business cycle for the insurance industry and refers generally to the annual gap between premium increases and cost increases and the medical loss ratio, that portion of the premium expended on medical costs.

reflected in the acquisition of PacifiCare—the originator of Secure Horizons, the oldest Medicare HMO in the country—by United. Given the present backlash against managed care, Medicare HMOs are the principal source of growth for these public health insurers.

For purpose of this analysis, using data from Lehman Brothers' *2007 Managed Care Guidebook*, the market shares of each of the 50 states were divided into subgroupings based upon 1) Blue Cross plans; 2) United (the largest public health insurer); 3) Aetna, Cigna, Health Net, and Humana; and 4) local HMOs with strong market presence, e.g., Harvard Pilgrim and Tufts in Massachusetts. After eliminating states[9] where for-profit insurers had small market share, where for-profit providers had little or no market presence, and rural states, 35 states were left in the sample.

The remaining states were then ranked by the concentration of market power in the hands of those insurers as well as by the number of insurers[10] operating in each market. Concentration percentages were as high as 98% in Alaska, where the Blue Cross plan had a 49% share and the named public companies collectively had a 49% share as well. Rhode Island's market consolidation ratio was 97%, with 58% in the Blue Cross plan and 26% in United. The lowest concentrations were in Wisconsin and Kansas. The latter market is highly stratified, however, as described later herein.

### Market Share

Exhibits 1, 2, and 3 summarize the analysis for eight states, divided into those where public for-profit providers are principally present (Florida, Texas, California, and Tennessee) and those where they have little or no presence (New York, North Carolina, Massachusetts, and Michigan). Market concentration is defined here as the total market share of the Blue Cross plans, public health insurers, and large local health insurers. Average is the market concentration divided by the number of insurers included in the market concentration total. Blue Cross Plans are discussed in the next section.

Exhibit 1 lists the above larger states where for profit providers are prevalent. Although market concentration varies, these states generally have smaller Blue Cross plans and a large market presence of for-profit health insurers (shown as United and other public). Tennessee is the only state in the top half of market concentration[11] where for-profit providers are prevalent—and it is the location of the headquarters of many of those companies.

9 Hawaii, Idaho, Iowa, Maine, Montana, Nebraska, Nevada, New Mexico, North Dakota, Oklahoma, South Dakota, Utah, Vermont, West Virginia.
10 For example, New York has multiple Blue Cross plans.
11 The median is 85% versus 86% for Tennessee.

**Exhibit 1. Insurance Market Concentration in States Where For-Profit Providers are Prevalent**

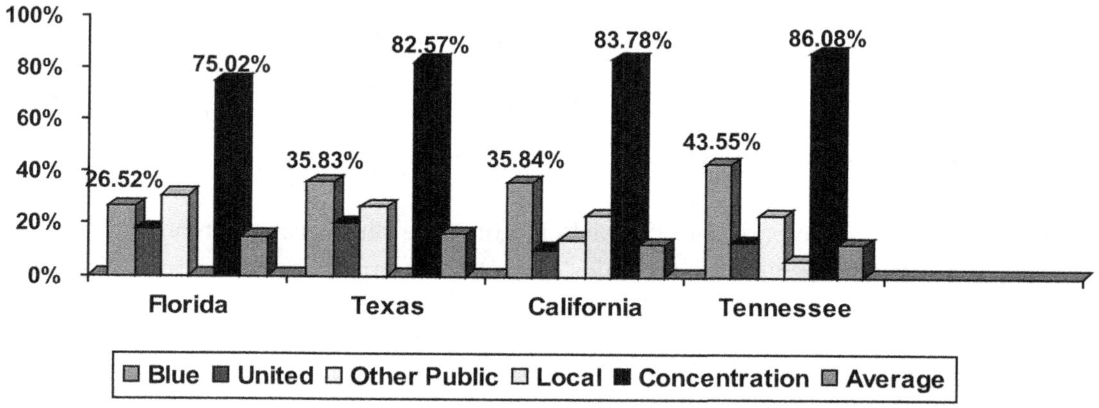


Exhibit 2 is of representative larger states where for profit providers are not prevalent. Although market concentration again varies, these states generally have very large Blue Cross plans and a small market presence of for-profit health insurers.

**Exhibit 2. Insurance Market Concentration States Where For-Profit Providers are not Prevalent**

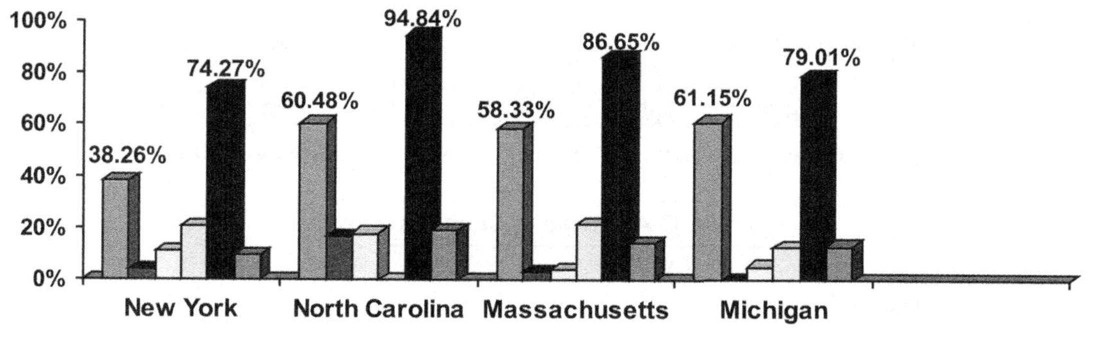


## History of Blue Cross Plans

The history of Blue Cross plans plays an important part in the structure of today's health insurance and provider markets. Blue Cross plans expanded rapidly during the Second World War's period of wage and price controls as union sought enhanced benefits to supplement their members' limited incomes. At one point, there were more than 100 Blue Cross plans, the majority of which were located in the industrialized states primarily north of the Mason-Dixon Line in what is sometimes called the Rust Belt. Certain plans refused to contract with for-profit hospitals, thus serving as an effective barrier to market entry. Blue Cross plans also enjoyed a tax-exempt status[12] for many years and protection from anti-trust action in many states.

12 Repealed in the Tax Reform Act of 1986.

As will be seen below, this type of insurance market analysis is one critical element in understanding why public healthcare companies locate in some states and not others. In turn, the acquisition transactions of those public companies are likely only relevant in such states. Further, if an analyst or appraiser is considering the guideline publicly trade company method, it is likely only relevant in those states where the purported guideline companies are active.

Exhibit 3 combines the earlier two charts to compare Blue Cross, for-profit (the combined United and other public companies' share), and market concentration. In markets where for-profit insurers are prevalent (Florida, Texas, California, and Tennessee), Blue Cross plans are less so and for-profit hospitals also tend to be more prevalent, as seen in the next section.

**Exhibit 3. Comparative Insurance Market Consolidation**

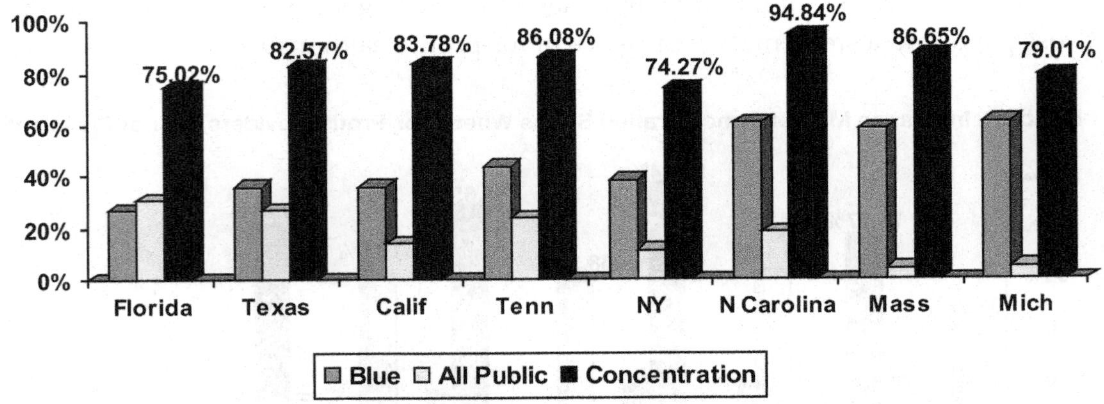


## Public Hospital Companies

As a basis for the analysis of four[13] public, for-profit hospital providers, extracts from their 2006 Form 10-Ks follow below. From these extracts, the primary state locations and the extent of concentration can be observed as well as the rationale for locating there (see Tenet and Vanguard Health below). Two other hospital chains not discussed below are LifePoint and Community Health. LifePoint,[14] based in Brentwood, Tenn., has operations primarily in the rural South and border states including Alabama, Louisiana, Kentucky, and Virginia. Community Health,[15] based in Franklin, Tenn., has many of its facilities in Texas, Alabama, Tennessee, northeastern Illinois, and southeastern Pennsylvania.

13 HCA has since been taken private in one of the largest leveraged buy outs ever.

14 LifePoint Hospitals operated 50 hospitals in 19 states as of May 2007.

15 As of Dec. 31, 2006, it owned, leased, or operated 77 hospitals, with an aggregate of 9,117 licensed beds in 22 states.

HCA (now privately held)

We operated 173 hospitals at Dec. 31, 2006, and 73 of those hospitals are located in Florida and Texas. Our Florida and Texas facilities' combined revenues represented approximately 51% of our consolidated revenues for the year ended Dec. 31, 2006. This concentration makes us particularly sensitive to regulatory, economic, environmental, and competition changes in those states.

Tenet

As of Dec. 31, 2006, the largest concentrations of licensed beds in our general hospitals were in California (23.6%), Florida (22.8%), and Texas (18.3%). Strong concentrations of hospital beds within market areas help us contract more successfully with managed care payers; reduce management, marketing and other expenses; and more efficiently utilize resources. However, such concentrations increase the risk that, should any adverse economic, regulatory, environmental, or other development occur in these areas, our business, financial condition, results of operations or cash flows could be materially adversely affected.

HMA Health Management Associates Inc.

As of Dec. 31, 2006, we operated 60 hospitals, with a total of 8,589 licensed beds. During the year ended Dec. 31, 2006, we operated facilities in Alabama, Arkansas, Florida, Georgia, Kentucky, Mississippi, Missouri, North Carolina, Oklahoma, Pennsylvania, South Carolina, Tennessee, Texas, Virginia, Washington, and West Virginia.

Our facilities are heavily concentrated in Florida and Mississippi, which makes us sensitive to regulatory, economic, and competitive changes in those states, as well as the harmful effects of hurricanes and other severe weather activity in such states. We operated 61 hospitals on Feb. 23, 2007, with 29 of those hospitals in Florida and Mississippi. Such geographic concentration of our hospitals makes us particularly sensitive to regulatory, economic, environmental, and competitive changes in those states. Any material changes therein in Florida or Mississippi could have a disproportionate effect on our business.

Vanguard Health

Our ability to negotiate favorable contracts with health maintenance organizations, insurers offering preferred provider arrangements and other managed care plans significantly affects the revenues and operating results of our hospitals. Revenues

> derived from health maintenance organizations, insurers offering preferred provider arrangements and other managed care plans, including Medicare and Medicaid managed care plans, accounted for approximately 52% of our net patient revenues for the year ended June 30, 2007. Managed care organizations offering prepaid and discounted medical services packages represent an increasing portion of our admissions, a general trend in the industry which has limited hospital revenue growth nationwide and a trend that may continue if the Medicare Modernization Act increases enrollment in Medicare managed care plans. In addition, private payers are increasingly attempting to control healthcare costs through direct contracting with hospitals to provide services on a discounted basis, increased utilization review, including the use of hospitalists, and greater enrollment in managed care programs such as health maintenance organizations and preferred provider organizations. Additionally, the trend toward consolidation among private managed care payers tends to increase their bargaining prices over fee structures.
>
> Approximately 35% of our net patient revenues for the year ended June 30, 2007 came from Medicare and Medicaid programs, excluding Medicare and Medicaid managed plans. In recent years, federal and state governments have made significant changes in the Medicare and Medicaid programs. Some of those changes adversely affect the reimbursement we receive for certain services. In addition, due to budget deficits in many states, significant decreases in state funding for Medicaid programs have occurred or are being proposed.
>
> Historically, we have concentrated our operations in markets with high population growth and median income in excess of the national average.

At first glance, Vanguard may represent a partial anomaly in the public companies discussed herein. Seventeen percent of its hospital beds are located in Massachusetts, with approximately half of those in Framingham and Natick[16] and the other half in Worcester, 20 miles west. The Framingham and Natick facilities were acquired from Tenet after that entity's difficulties stemming from a federal government investigation of its Alvaredo facility in San Diego, Calif.; Tenet had acquired them in 1999 from the predecessor of Hospital Corporation of America (HCA) after that entity encountered regulatory problems leading to a fine of nearly $1 billion. Prior to that, Columbia and HCA acquired the facilities as a result of financial difficulties experienced by the local nonprofit institutions in competing with larger nonprofit entities.

16 The author lives in Framingham and formerly resided in Natick, a bordering community located in Middlesex county, which has the 19th highest total Medicare spending in the nation.

Vanguard is a much smaller entity than either HCA or Tenet as can be seen from Exhibit 4 of the total number of beds each entity has and therefore, is less significant to the analysis. It is clear once again that Florida and Texas are primary locations for for-profit hospital providers.

**Exhibit 4. Number of Beds by State**

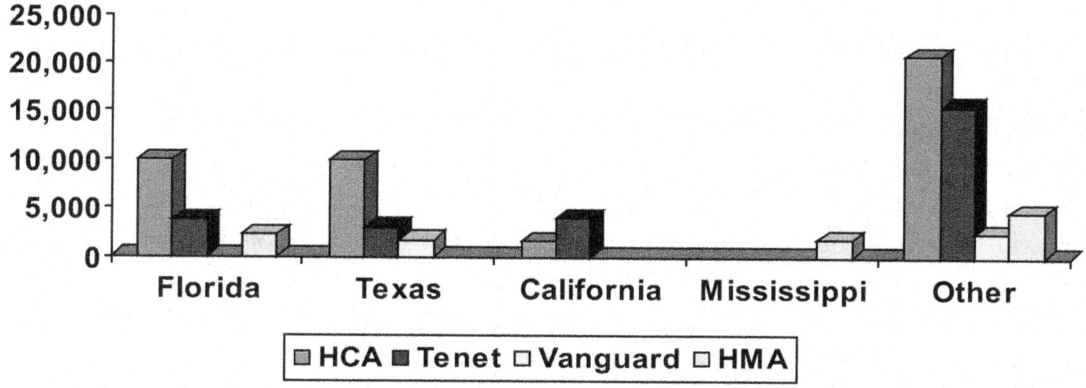


On a percentage basis, HCA and Tenet each have more than 40% of their hospital beds in Florida and Texas (see Exhibit 5).

**Exhibit 5. Percent of Beds by Company by State**

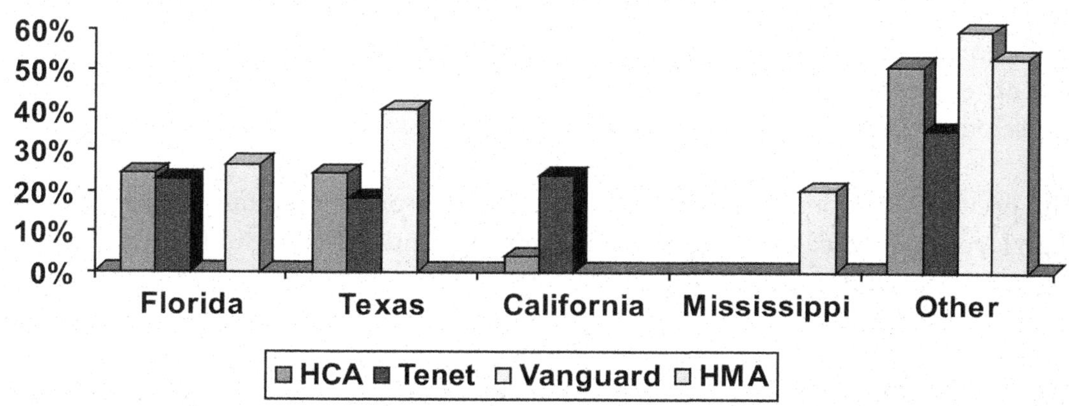


For the valuation of an individual hospital in a state other than Florida, Texas, or California, what is the relevance of transactions by one of these publicly traded entities? As the author and Reed Tinsley, CPA, CVA noted in a co-authored article in the December 2006 American Bar Association's *The Heath Lawyer*:

> What does [out of market] transaction data say or reveal about the value of a hospital with EBITDA of $1 million located in North Carolina? Does it tell a valuator that it could be worth the median [multiple] value of $5 million or the [average multiple] value

> of $7.5 million—the average being 50% greater than the median? Could it be worth [the highest multiple value of] $18.2 million? Given the Stark regulations requirement that comparable transactions be in a particular market at the time of acquisition, can any of these [out-of-market] multiples be used?

## Medicare Part A Spending

Medicare divides providers into two general groupings: Part A hospital insurance, which is paid for by the combined employer-employee 2.9% Medicare tax, and Part B physician insurance, which is paid for out of general federal revenues, after a nominal premium contribution by beneficiaries withheld from Social Security checks. Medicare Advantage, the risk-based Medicare HMO program, publishes per-capita rates county by county across the country split into Part A and Part B components. There are more than 3,200 counties, including Puerto Rico and Guam, with published rates. Because these rates are one proxy for local county Medicare spending,[17] they provide useful insight into a public healthcare provider's location strategy.

Medicare spending is driven by two principal factors: utilization or volume of service, typically expressed in per-beneficiary measures, and price or rate per unit of service. Although beyond the scope of this article, utilization data are readily available from such sources as the Medicare Payment Advisory Commission's (MedPAC) 2007 report *Assessing Alternatives to SGR*.[18] While price or rate is a function of statutory formulas and local cost of service differences, utilization is a function of medical practice styles. The differences in utilization are dramatic and warrant study by an appraiser looking to use out-of-market valuation multiples.

The previous sections discussion on location of for-profit hospitals is consistent with high levels of Medicare spending. Of the top 50 counties, five are in Florida (which has nine of the top 100), four in Texas (which has 15 of the top 100 and another 22 in the next 200) and one in California (which also has nine of the top 100). Two of the top 10 counties (Dade and Okeechobee) are in Florida. The location of individual facilities in other states, such as Louisiana, is typically driven by high localized spending as reflected in Medicare Part A or B statistics.

For total Medicare spending, both Part A and Part B, the pattern is similar but more dramatic for Florida and California as shown in Exhibits 6 and 7.

---

17 At least for the high-cost counties; low-cost counties have artificially higher rates than their fee-for-service equivalents as a means of inducing Medicare Advantage Plans to offer coverage.

18 Utilization and utilization growth is very high in Florida, for example, and low in mature managed care markets such as San Francisco and Portland, Ore.

**Exhibit 6. # of Top 200 Counties for Part A Per Capita Spending**

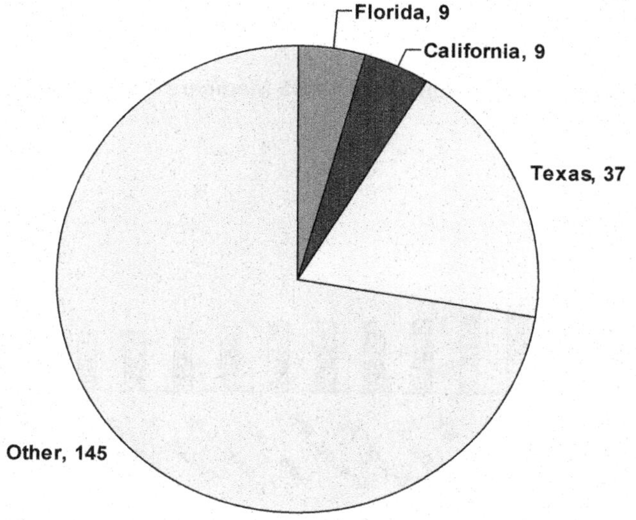


**Exhibit 7. # of Top 200 Counties for Part A & B Total Spending**

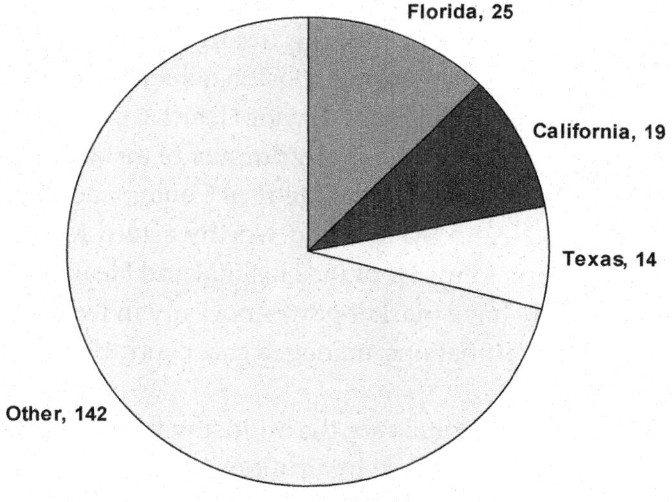


The counties shown in Exhibit 8 have the largest total dollar Medicare spending. Two counties—Maricopa County, Ariz. and Middlesex County, Mass.—which appear elsewhere in the article where the presence of public for-profit providers was not explained by other factors are clearly explained in this chart. Despite the high levels of Medicare spending, no significant for-profit hospitals are present in Cook County (Chicago) or the various boroughs of New York City,[19] for example. These are counties where unions have historically been very strong.

**Exhibit 8. 20 Largest Counties for 2005 Medicare Spending ($Billions)**

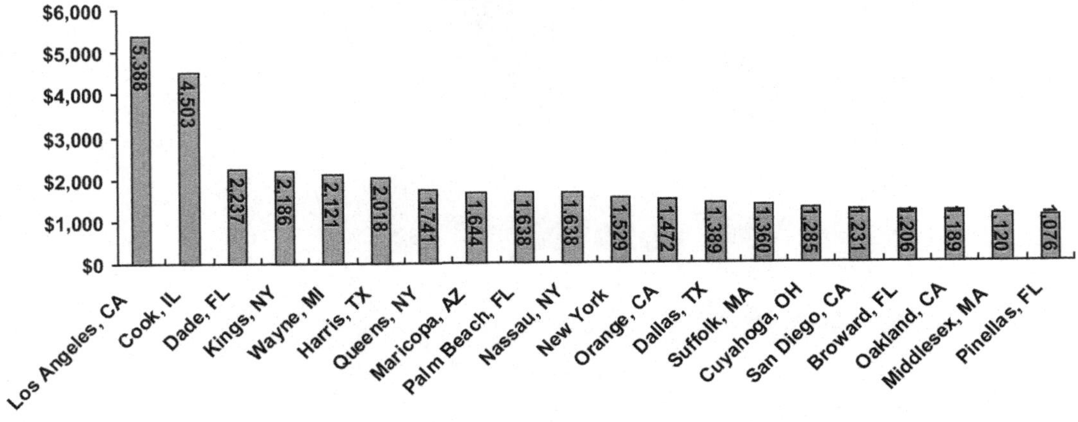


## Other Hospital Market Factors

Perhaps the most difficult factor to quantify without local market knowledge or study is the presence of not-for-profit hospitals, particularly large, wealthy teaching hospitals. These institutions tend to be present in large urban markets. Examples include the Harvard-Affiliated Partners Health System in Boston, which includes the Massachusetts General and Brigham & Women's Hospitals; Baylor Health Care System in Dallas;[20] Yale-New Haven Hospital in New Haven, Conn.; any number of institutions in New York City, including Mount Sinai Hospital, Beth Israel Medical Center, and NYU Medical Center; The University of Chicago Health System and Northwestern Memorial Hospital and Health System in Chicago; and Johns Hopkins Hospital and Health System in Baltimore. These institutions frequently have market power not only in terms of hospital volume, but also in terms of physician affiliations, managed care contracts, and political influence.

Another example of nonprofit hospitals are the multistate religious health systems, such as Ascension Health. Many times these institutions are located in underserved areas where access to healthcare is limited by income considerations. They may also be small institutions located in rural areas where providing multidiscipline and emergency care is unprofitable and requires charitable support.

19 Less than 3.2 % and 1% of hospital beds in Illinois and New York, respectively, are for-profit according to the Kaiser Family Foundation.
20 A highly competitive market with both for-profit and nonprofit hospitals.

There is nothing that precludes the reporting of acquisitions by not-for-profit hospitals of other hospitals, physician practices, surgery centers, and the like. However, there is often no requirement of reporting, and it is certainly less common than reporting by the public for-profit companies described herein.[21] Some transactions may warrant reporting under generally accepted accounting principles (GAAP) and generally accepted auditing standards (GAAS) and many states require not-for-profits to file financial statements with the state Attorney General's office; fairness opinions may also be required. Analysts and appraisers need to keep in mind that single-state or single-locale not-for-profit transactions[22] likewise reflect only that local market's considerations and are equally suspect as value indicators in other markets.

### Valuation Imperative

Appraisers and analysts should bear in mind that in addition to the Stark laws and anti-kickback statutes that apply to all healthcare providers, nonprofit and tax-exempt providers are subject to the requirements of the Internal Revenue Code, including anti-inurement and intermediate sanctions provisions.

### Example

One common business strategy that hospitals utilize in acquiring physician-owned entities such as ambulatory surgery centers and imaging centers include converting them to hospital outpatient billing or so-called "provider-based billing."[23] This typically results in a higher revenue stream for the same services as both government and nongovernment insurers frequently have different payment levels for the same service based upon the type of provider submitting the bill, i.e., higher revenue for hospital entities than physician entities. Notwithstanding the business strategy, including the enhanced revenue in a valuation where the standard is fair market value raises serious if not fatal concerns. Since physicians cannot access this billing routine when they own the entity outright, including the enhanced revenue available to a hospital owner creates issues under both the Stark law and anti-kickback statute as well as anti-inurement issues for tax-exempt entities.

21 For competitive reasons and regulatory fear, among others.

22 For example, North and South Carolina not-for-profit integrated healthcare system Novant Health's acquisition of imaging provider MQ Associates.

23 Medicare requires eligible healthcare providers to bill services in two parts: one for the facility or technical fee to the hospital or facility for owning the building and equipment and employing nonphysician staff and one for physicians for interpreting and performing the test or procedure known as the professional fee; a hospital-owned facility may be able to bill under higher hospital rates.

## Surgery Centers

After medical practice purchases, surgery center transaction are perhaps the most common form of healthcare transaction. As a result of private equity deals, AmSurg (AMSG) is one of the few remaining public companies in this line of business. Due to the importance of acquisitions to the value of this company and to the valuation of individual surgery centers, the article addresses AMSG in detail. Although the primary location of its facilities is Florida, followed by Tennessee and California, it does, in fact, have locations in many other states, which make it a particularly interesting subject for analysis. A number of these other locations are examined for consistency with the factors discussed elsewhere herein.

A review of AMSG's Dec. 31, 2006 10-K filing with the SEC revealed the following statements:

> Practice-based [ambulatory surgery centers] ASCs, such as those in which we own a majority interest, depend upon third-party reimbursement programs, including governmental and private insurance programs, to pay for services rendered to patients. We derived approximately 35%, 35%, and 37% of our revenues in the years ended Dec. 31, 2006, 2005, and 2004, respectively, from governmental healthcare programs, primarily Medicare. The Medicare program currently pays ASCs and physicians in accordance with predetermined fee schedules.
>
> At Dec. 31, 2006, 30 of the 156 surgery centers we operated were located in the state of Florida. This concentration makes us particularly sensitive to adverse weather conditions and other factors that affect the state of Florida.
>
> Ninety-two percent of our centers specialize in gastroenterology or ophthalmology procedures. These specialties have a higher concentration of older patients than other specialties, such as orthopedic or [gastro]enterology. We believe the aging demographics of the U.S. population will be a source of procedure growth for these specialties. We target these medical specialties because they generally involve a high volume of lower-risk procedures that can be performed in an outpatient setting on a safe and cost-effective basis.
>
> We begin our acquisition process with a due diligence review of the target center and its market. We use experienced teams of operations and financial personnel to conduct a thorough review of all aspects of the center's operations, including the following:
>
> - market position of the center and the physicians affiliated with the center;
> - payor and case mix;
> - growth opportunities;
> - staffing and supply review; and
> - equipment assessment.

> In presenting the advantages to physicians of developing a new practice-based ASC in partnership with us, our development staff emphasizes the proximity of a practice-based surgery center to a physician's office, the simplified administrative procedures, the ability to schedule consecutive cases without preemption by inpatient or emergency procedures, the rapid turnaround time between cases, the high technical competency of the center's clinical staff that performs only a limited number of specialized procedures and the state-of-the-art surgical equipment. We also focus on our expertise in developing and operating centers. In addition, as part of our role as the manager of our surgery center limited partnerships and limited liability companies, we market the centers to third-party payors.

The 10-K also reveals that 105 of the 156 centers are gastroenterology, four multispecialty, 40 ophthalmic, and seven orthopedic. Appraisers and analysts should consider the prospects for these service lines versus other (*non*gastroenterology—also called endoscopy—or ophthalmology) medical service lines when contemplating using AMSG acquisition multiples. It is critical to understand precisely what types of procedures a facility is performing as part of the assessment of market data's relevance.

Exhibit 9 displays AMSG's historical cumulative acquisitions of surgery centers (103, or 66% of the total), and Exhibit 10 shows its cumulative total centers (156) to emphasize the importance of acquisition growth to the value of the company.

**Exhibit 9. AMSG Cumulative Acquisitions**

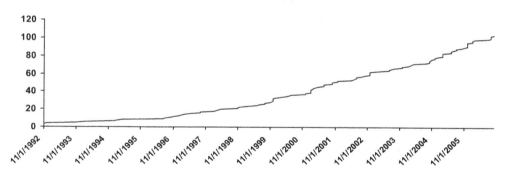

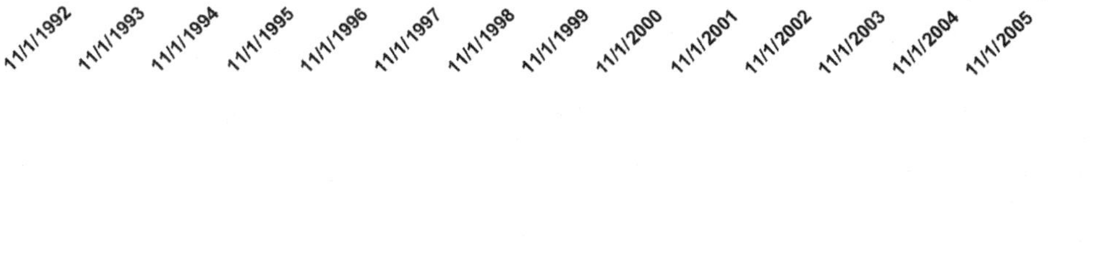

**Exhibit 10. AMSG Cumulative Centers**

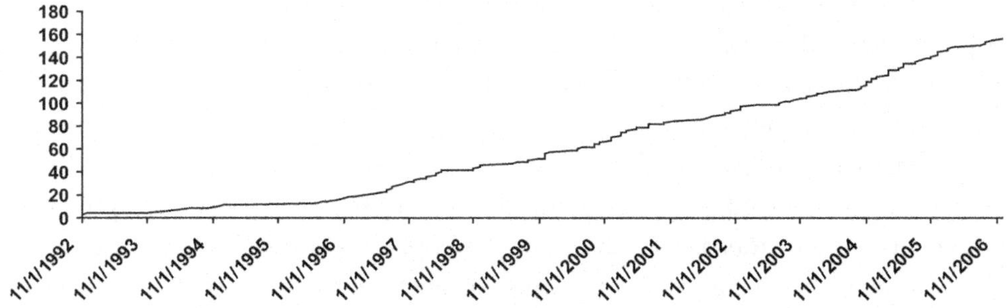


Exhibit 11 shows the location of AMSG's operating rooms (ORs) by state for purposes of the later analysis of the reason for locating in certain states and not others.

**Exhibit 11. AMSG ORs by State**

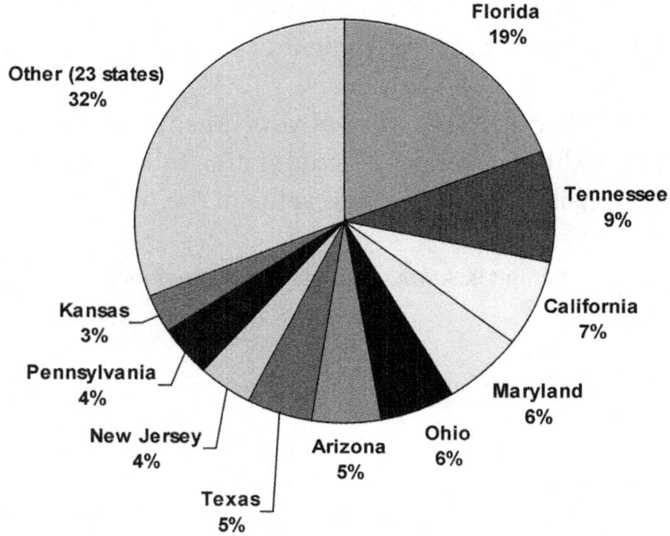


## Medicare Part B Spending

The states in which AMSG is located consistently have the highest rates for Part B physician spending—and that is where such transactions are or may be relevant depending upon further analysis. Of the 200 counties with the highest Part B Medicare Advantage rates, half (101) are located in the 10 states in which AMSG has most of its facilities. Of the top 50 counties, five are in Florida, four in Texas (which has 15 of the top 100 and another 22 in the next 200) and six in New Jersey. Two of the top 10 counties (Dade and Okeechobee) are in Florida. Only Arizona does not appear in the top 200 (see Exhibit 12).

Exhibit 12. # of Top 200 Counties for Part B Per Capita Spending

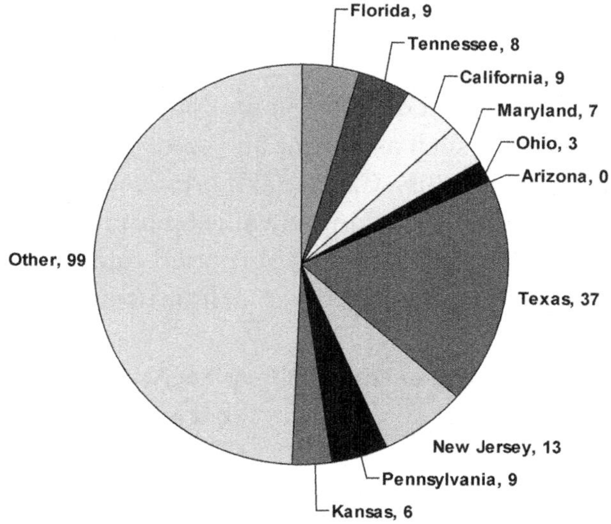


## Prevalence of For Profit Hospitals

Earlier, the presence of for-profit hospitals and health insurers was examined. Exhibit 13 shows the percentage of for-profit hospitals[24] for each of the 10 states where AMSG has the largest number of ORs, with the largest states at the left. Florida, Tennessee, and California have 35% of AMSG's capacity. Florida has the second highest percentage of for-profit hospitals in the country, with Tennessee seventh.

Exhibit 13. Prevalence of For Profit Hospitals For AMSG's Major States

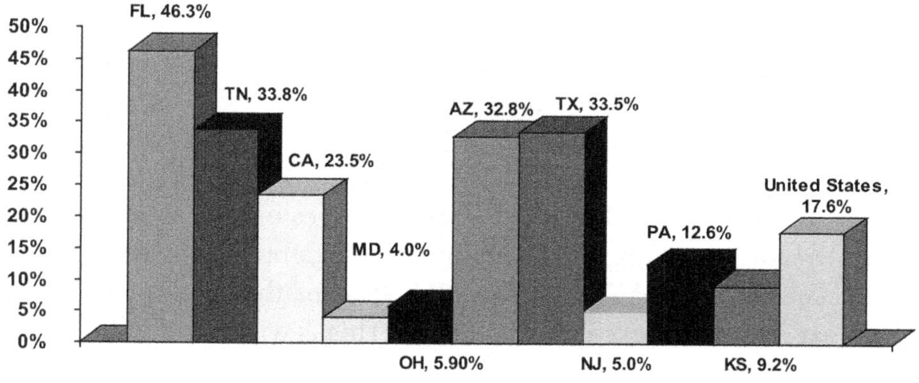


Pennsylvania is below the national average, but the activity in this state could be explained in part by a strong state government commitment to rating outpatient surgery

24 Kaiser Family Foundation State Health Facts, www.statehealthfacts.kff.org/.

facilities, including going so far as to require extensive financial disclosure[25] on top of clinical quality.

Another manner to evaluate for-profit presence is by the number of hospital beds (see Exhibit 14) as opposed to the number of hospitals. Both data sets are relevant because a number of specialty hospitals, such as cardiac and orthopedic, may have relatively few beds but extremely high profitability. Cardiac and orthopedic care is at the core of most hospitals' profitability. Appraisers seeking to value a hospital should be certain to understand the underlying case mix of both the purported comparables and the subject. A specialty orthopedic hospital transaction is likely of little use in valuing a general hospital.

**Exhibit 14. Prevalence of For Profit Beds For AMSG's Major States**

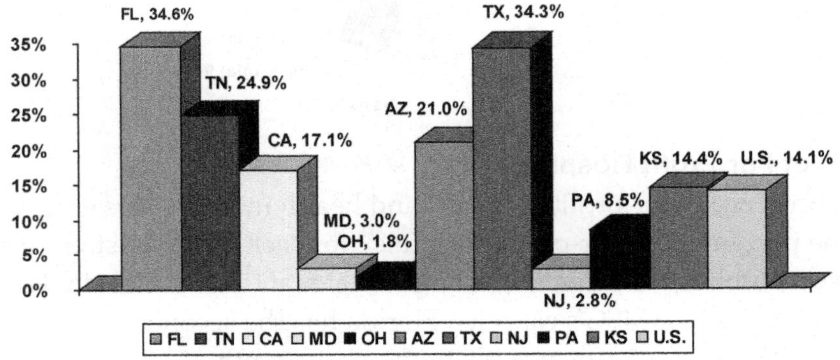


Exhibit 15 summarizes criteria that impact the desirability of locating a surgery center in a given state based upon the 10 states above. Bold items are those that appear partially determinative. For example, Florida has the third highest number of for-profit hospital beds in the country, is ranked 4th in overall healthcare spending, 6th in the concentration of population in metropolitan areas, 9th in spending on physician services, and 19th in per-capita healthcare spending. The percentage of overall spending in the state on physician services is more than 3% greater than the national average.

For certain of the principal states in which AMSG does business, the listed factors do not appear to readily explain the desirability. For example, Kansas is ranked 8th in overall physician spending as a percentage (31.5%) of healthcare expenses but otherwise does not appear attractive based on the criteria. This is where individual local market conditions become important.

Kansas is a largely rural state with population centers in larger cities. The following is the location of the AMSG facilities:

25 Pennsylvania Health Care Cost Containment Council, www.phc4.org.

- Hutchinson, Kan.
- Overland Park, Kan.
- Shawnee, Kan.
- Topeka, Kan.
- Wichita, Kan.

Overland Park and Shawnee are part of suburban Kansas City (the metropolitan area includes the larger Kansas City, Mo.), while Hutchinson is a suburb of Wichita. Thus, the ranking of Kansas as a rural state is misleading with respect to the location of the AMSG facilities.

Similarly, Arizona has only high total spending for health care as a positive criteria in the analysis. Arizona, however, has a very high percentage of Medicare-eligible retirees and as noted earlier, Medicare is a key source of revenue for AMSG. Below is a listing of AMSG's Arizona locations.

- Mesa, Ariz.
- Peoria, Ariz.
- Phoenix, Ariz.
- Sun City, Ariz.
- Yuma, Ariz.

**Exhibit 15. Criteria That Impact the Desirability of Locating a Surgery Center in a Given State**

| | | | RANKINGS | | | | |
|---|---|---|---|---|---|---|---|
| Top 10 AMSG States | For-Profit Beds % | MD Spending% | For-Profit Beds | Total Healthcare Spending | Metropolitan Pop | MD Spending | Per Capita |
| Florida | **34.6%** | 31.5% | **3** | **4** | **6** | **9** | 19 |
| Tennessee | **24.9%** | 31.4% | **10** | 15 | 26 | **10** | 21 |
| California | **17.1%** | 33.4% | 18 | **1** | **2** | **3** | 44 |
| Maryland | **3.0%** | 28.7% | 34 | 19 | **7** | 20 | 18 |
| Ohio | 1.8% | 26.8% | 39 | 7 | 25 | 35 | 15 |
| Arizona | **21.0%** | 33.0% | 15 | 21 | 14 | **5** | 50 |
| Texas | **34.3%** | 30.8% | **4** | **3** | **11** | **11** | 45 |
| New Jersey | 2.8% | 28.2% | 35 | **9** | **1** | 27 | 13 |
| Pennsylvania | 8.5% | 26.6% | 28 | **5** | 22 | 38 | 11 |
| Kansas | 14.4% | 31.5% | 22 | 31 | 35 | **8** | 24 |
| United States | 14.1% | 28.2% | NA | NA | NA | NA | |

**Explanations**
For-Profit Beds %: The percentage of all hospitals beds owned by for-profit hospitals.
MD Spending %: The portion of the state's healthcare spending that goes to physician services.
**Rankings**
For-Profit Beds: The rank based on total for-profit beds, with 1 being highest,
Total Healthcare Spending: The rank based upon total dollars spent.
Metropolitan Population: The rank based upon the percentage of the states population located in metropolitan areas (as opposed to rural).
MD Spending: The rank based upon total dollars spent.
Per Capita: The rank based upon per capita income.

Sun City, Mesa, and Peoria are part of greater Phoenix (Maricopa County, described earlier herein), one of the fastest growing metropolitan areas in the nation, with Sun City a prime locale for retirees. Maricopa County has the third highest total Medicare spending in the country at *$1.64 billion*. Yuma is near the Mexican border, and an even more localized market analysis would be in order.

New Jersey is a particularly interesting case in point where the criteria do not appear to explain the presence of AMSG. Fortunately, the Center for Studying Health System Change,[26] which tracks development in 12 markets nationally includes Northern New Jersey, where three of the faculties are located. This is an area where specialist physicians—which would include gastroenterology and ophthalmology—have been terminating provider agreements with insurers to compel higher fees as out-of-network providers. Ambulatory surgery centers are being developed as part of this strategy to shift revenue from hospitals to physicians.

## Characteristics of areas with no AMSG locations

AMSG has no facilities in Vermont, Massachusetts, Maine, New Hampshire, and Rhode Island and a single one in Connecticut. Thus, the New England area, for example, would not appear to be a target market. These states have comparatively few for-profit beds (Rhode Island and Vermont have none) and high market concentration of insurers (see Exhibit 16). Maine, New Hampshire, Connecticut, and Vermont have more than 94% market concentration as defined earlier herein, and the largest insurer in each market is a Blue Cross plan, with 67%, 38%, 33%, and 60% market share, respectively.

**Exhibit 16. For Profit Beds in AMSG's No Facility States**

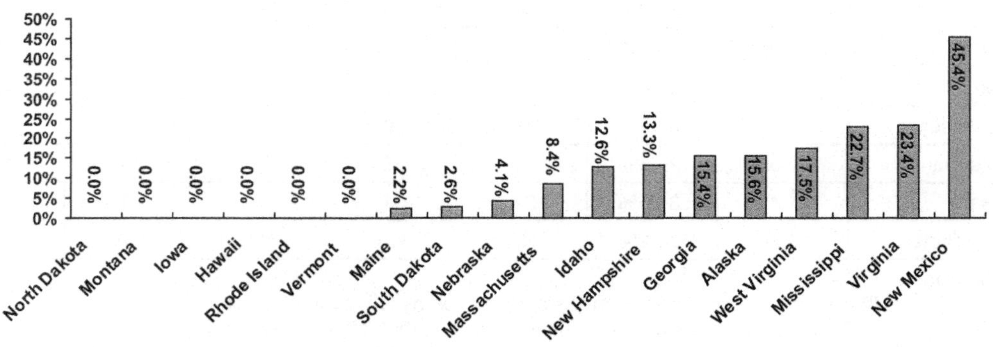


26 www.hschange.org.

## Valuation Imperative

An appraiser or analyst should also consider the requirement or lack thereof for a certificate of need (CON) in each state[27] where a purported comparable operates and in the state where the valuation subject is located. Florida, Texas, Pennsylvania, and California do not require a CON for an ASC! Lack of a CON makes it easier to establish an ASC—although actually having a difficult-to-obtain CON in a state that requires them is generally deemed to be a valuation positive, assuming the CON is transferable. Some states waive a CON for expenditures below a specified level, e.g., $1 million for an MRI in Missouri.

## Radnet

The one large publicly traded[28] provider of fixed location imaging services, Radnet—which acquired its principal competitor Radiologix in the fall of 2006—has the majority of its facilities in three of the same states (California, Maryland, and Florida) listed above, with a concentration in California.

Exhibit 17 reflects total units of equipment (e.g., MRI, CT, and so on).

**Exhibit 17. Radnet, Units by State**

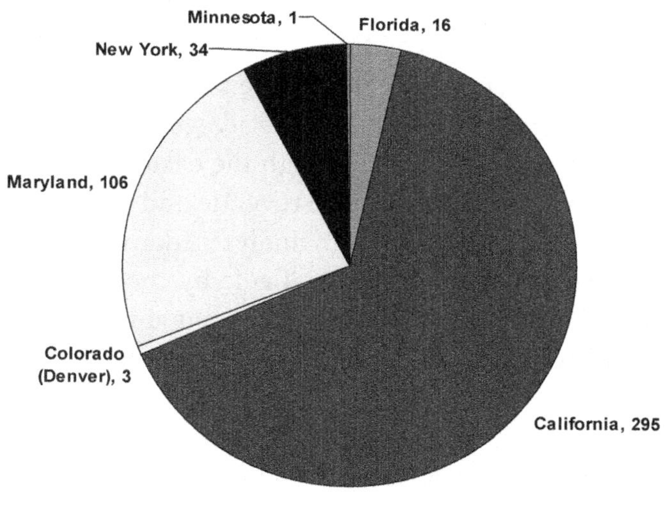


27 www.ncsl.org/programs/health/cert-need.htm, a CON is basically a form of state-issued license.

28 Alliance is the other with primarily mobile imaging and locations in many states. It has recently turned its attention to development of PET and CT. The revenue prospects for different types of imaging can vary dramatically.

**Exhibit 18. Radnet, California Units**

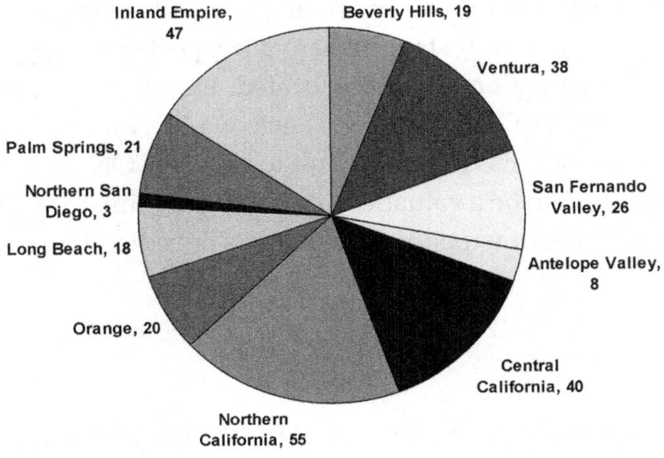


Certainly, a substantive argument could be made that the multiples paid by Radnet for imaging centers in California would be relevant to the valuation of an imaging center located in California (see Exhibit 18). It seems questionable, particularly in light of regulatory considerations, that those transactions would be relevant in New Mexico or Georgia, for example. At best, the multiples might provide some insight, especially if the effect of acquisition growth could be eliminated.

## Acquisition Versus Same Store Growth

One of the most important and fundamental differences between a single location valuation subject and a large multilocation, multimarket alleged comparable is the availability of acquisition growth to enhance value through the earnings or cash flow capitalization rate[29] or to offset a decline in same-store revenue and profit growth. Consider the following statement from Lehman Brothers analyst Adam Feinstein about AMSG in anticipation of the announcement of the final rule by the Centers for Medicare and Medicaid with respect to the adoption of a new revenue model for ASCs that would contain significant cutbacks for endoscopy:

> In regards to an LBO, AMSG has noted that it believes that the overhang created by the proposed changes in Medicare reimbursement (with a final rule expected sometime this summer [*2007*] and the changes expected to take effect on Jan. 1, 2008) reduces the likelihood that a financial sponsor would be interested in acquiring the company (due to the anticipated negative impact in 2008 and 2009). In addition, we get the sense that the company is not interested in going private since *the company has noted that it believes it needs to undertake 12 to 15 acquisitions per year in 2008 and 2009*

29 Defined as the discount rate less the long-term or perpetual growth rate.

*in order to generate the same cash flow in those years as it will in 2007 (with the anticipated negative impact from the changes in Medicare reimbursement being offset by the cash flow the company acquires).*[30] (*Emphasis added*)

### Valuation Imperative

One observation about the valuation implication of AMSG's statement regarding new acquisitions is that for those acquisitions to be accretive to earnings—a necessity if the stock price is to be maintained—acquisition multiples are likely to drop! This is a key test that the appraiser or analyst should employ as part of the reality check for an ultimate valuation conclusion if the merged and acquired company method is being used: Would the acquisition be accretive to earnings?

Another observation is that a single-location endoscopy center, for example, is unlikely to be in a position to respond to per-unit revenue cutbacks by acquiring other endoscopy centers; at best, it might hope to attract additional providers to its facility assuming it had excess capacity.

How would the plan by a public surgery center consolidator to offset per-unit revenue declines impact the transaction price for a single-location provider? Unless that provider is located in a state that the consolidator is active in or likely to become active in, there would be no impact. The universe of hypothetical buyers under the fair market value standard or even for strategic value does not include buyers who are not present in the market. Exhibit 19 presents AMSG's 35 most recent centers by state.

**Exhibit 19. New Centers: 2005-2006**

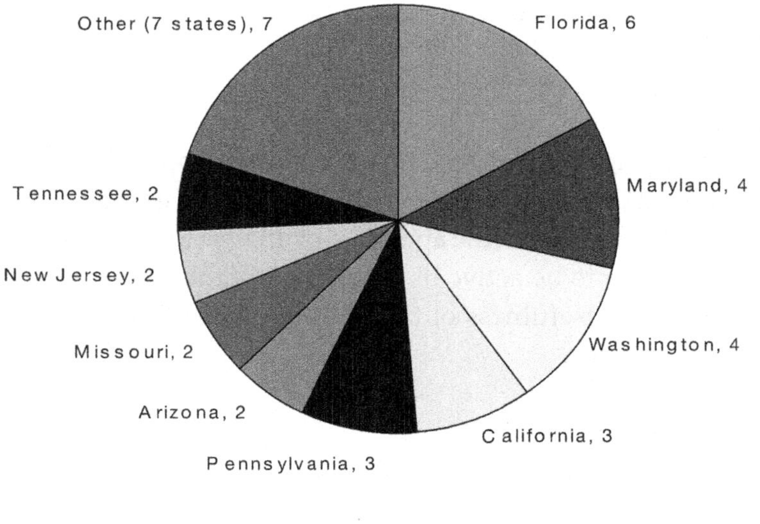


30 Lehman Brothers Health Care Facilities: March Quarter Review: "Buyouts Rule the Day", May 18, 2007.

## Implications for Valuation of Private Healthcare Providers

### *Follow the Money*

The old adage "follow the money" is employed in many professions. As the analysis in this article demonstrates, to some extent you can find large for-profit providers by looking at high local rates of healthcare spending. Or perhaps it is more accurate to say you will *not* find those providers where there is low healthcare spending. Factors in addition to total and per-capita spending play a significant role in the desirability of a particular location for larger for-profit entities and highlight the importance of understanding local market conditions, including:

- Income levels of population;
- Health insurance coverage statistics, including coverage by Medicaid;
- Hospital spending per capita and in total;
- Physician spending per capita and in total;
- Competing nonprofit providers, including whether the entities have established integrated healthcare networks;
- Identity and market share of health insurers; in large states, regional market concentration should be considered along with statewide data; HMO penetration (reported by KFF) versus indemnity and other types of health insurance should also be considered; and
- Competing for-profit local providers, e.g., Shields MRI in Massachusetts.

### *All Healthcare is Local*

Healthcare markets are highly localized. When seeking to apply comparable transactions under the merged and acquired company method or the guideline publicly traded company method, it is incumbent on the appraiser or analyst to establish that an acquirer or public company is likely to be active in the market of the valuation subject. Failure to establish that limits the usefulness of the market data and may, in fact, lead to an erroneous conclusion of value.

Other relevant local market factors:

- The concentration of the population in urban versus rural areas; urban areas provide easier access;

- In rural areas, the extent and quality of road systems enabling access to healthcare providers; barriers to access such as bridges or ferries from peninsula or island communities; and

- Age distribution of population.

Earlier, portions of public hospital company 10-Ks were cited that described the economies of scale and negotiating leverage with managed care insurers that were obtained through concentrating activities in a given state. It stands to reason that acquisition multiples in that state could properly reflect the inherent value from the economies of scale, but it is difficult to see how that acquisition multiple could be applied to a valuation subject in another state.

Another element to consider is localized supply and demand for a particular healthcare provider. Hospitals often compete to acquire physician practices, seeking to increase or defensively maintain inpatient admissions and referrals for tests. Nonetheless, there are regulatory prohibitions against considering such admissions and referrals in the purchase price and any demand-driven increase in value is limited to factors not precluded by law. Many times, it is difficult to appropriately include even factors such as reduced cost of capital or economies of scale due to the need to rely upon the fair market value standard.

### Other Uses of Market Data

There is an arbitrage effect when private company cash flows are moved into the public markets via acquisition, as described earlier with respect to evaluating whether a particular acquisition would be accretive to earnings. If possible, an appraiser or analyst might attempt to extract acquisition growth from valuation multiples to obtain an indication of market value when acquisition-driven market data are used to value a subject in a market where no such buyer is present. This would require analyzing the out-of-market acquirer's stock and EBITDA valuation multiples and extracting that portion representing acquisition-driven growth. A fundamental analysis can also be performed on the subject to derive discounts from the public company's value for size and growth, for example.[31]

31 See, e.g., Goeldner, "Adjusting Market Multiples of Public Guideline Companies for the Closely Held Business," ASA 18th Annual BV Conference, October 1999.

### Valuation Imperative

Of course, not all transaction data represents activity of publicly traded companies. However, it is reasonable to believe that privately held or nonprofit buyers of healthcare entities in markets dominated by public for-profits find acquisition prices driven by what the public for-profit is willing to pay, *even if* the nonprofit cannot match the growth rate. There are many policy and economic implications beyond the scope of this article with respect to the availability of tax-exempt bonds to lower a nonprofit's cost of capital.

### Regulatory Issues

At the outset of the article, it was stated "that the government agencies' views of 'fair market value' should be seriously considered by appraisers and analysts in their own opinions of fair market value." The core of the Stark regulations limitations on use of market data in establishing fair market value can be found in the following extract:

> Usually the fair market price is the price at which bona fide sales have been consummated for assets of like type, quality, and quantity in a particular market at the time of acquisition. . . .[32]

The presence of this statement, drafted at the Department of Health and Human Services, which operates the Medicare program, likely reflects that agency's intimate familiarity with differences in local healthcare spending and providers.

Appraisers conforming to uniform standards of professional appraisal practice (USPAP) and other standards frequently cite those standards as the basis for employing certain methods even in the face of apparent government rejection, typically in tax court or other tax-oriented proceedings. For example, USPAP Standards Rule 9-4 provides in part that

> An appraiser must, when necessary for credible assignment results, analyze the effect on value, if any, of: ... sales of capital stock or other ownership interests in similar business enterprises.

However, the Jurisdictional Exception Rule provides

> If any part of USPAP is contrary to the law or public policy of any jurisdiction, only that part shall be void and of no force or effect in that jurisdiction.

32 420 CFR 411.351.

Appraisers and analysts should not assume that government's views of fair market value are inconsistent with the usage of that term in the appraisal profession and do well to remember that the law always trumps professional standards. Improper use of market data in the face of the above regulation could result in unlawful conduct.

## Conclusion

The results of this study are important to appraisers and analysts working in the healthcare industry. Healthcare markets are highly localized and use of out-of-market data for the valuation of a healthcare business requires a detailed analysis of conditions in the source market as well as the subject market (see Exhibit 20 on next page). Regulatory restrictions on the use market data in the Stark laws cannot be dismissed because there are fundamental economic reasons for those restrictions as well as professional standards that require they be respected.

Markets in which larger for-profit provider entities are present will have transactions that reflect not only the local market conditions, but also the revenue and earnings growth inherent in the motivation of public companies. Public healthcare providers, such as AMSG, are consolidators driven by acquisition growth. Even those nonprofit markets where healthcare spending and insurer concentration are *otherwise* similar to for-profit markets may have very different values for local entities than is indicated by consolidator-driven multiples. Thus, methods under the market approach have to be used with considerable skill and intensive analysis.

There are few absolutes in valuation in general and healthcare valuation in particular. However, terms such as "north," "south," "Rust Belt," and "Mason-Dixon Line" seem to have consequential importance. Finally, there is an abundance of readily available and often free data on local healthcare markets that enable the appraiser or analyst to accomplish the tasks necessary for the appropriate application and weighting of the market approach.

*My thanks to Barry Sziklay, James Rigby, Michael Crain, Nancy Fannon, Don Barbo, Kevin Yeanoplos, and Carol Carden who contributed to the review of this paper but may or may not agree with its conclusions.*

**Exhibit 20. Factors to Consider When Evaluating Out of Market Transactions**

| Factor | Subject Market | Comparable Market | Data * Source(s) |
|---|---|---|---|
| Economic and demographic factors | | | |
| Medicare Part A spending total and per capita | | | 1, 2 |
| Medicare Part B spending total and per capita | | | 1, 2 |
| Pending or anticipated per unit revenue changes | | | 3, 4 |
| Hospital spending per capita and in total | | | 1 |
| Physician spending per capita and in total | | | 1 |
| Per capita income levels of population | | | 1 |
| Age distribution of population | | | 1 |
| The concentration of the population in urban versus rural areas | | | 1 |
| In rural areas, the extent and quality of road systems enabling access to healthcare providers; barriers to access such as bridges or ferries from peninsula or island communities | | | |
| Health insurance coverage statistics, including coverage by Medicaid | | | 1 |
| Presence of Medicare Advantage plans | | | 2 |
| Medicaid spending and crisis status (Medicaid is typically the single largest line item in a state budget) | | | 1 |
| Health insurer factors | | | |
| Identity and market share of health insurers; in large states, regional market concentration should be considered along with statewide data; HMO penetration versus indemnity and other types of health insurance should also be considered | | | 1, 5, 6, 7 |
| Whether or not insurers use network fee schedules or individually negotiated fee schedules | | | |
| Utilization factors | | | |
| Hospital length of stay | | | 1 |
| Hospital days per 1,000 | | | 1 |
| Hospital cost per day | | | 1 |
| Imaging per capita, rate of increase | | | 3 |
| Inpatient versus outpatient surgery | | | 1 |
| Market competition factors | | | |
| Presence of publicly held provider entities | | | 6 |
| Competing for-profit local providers | | | |
| Competing not-for-profit providers | | | |

continued

**Exhibit 20. Factors to Consider When Evaluating Out of Market Transactions, continued**

| Factor | Subject Market | Comparable Market | Data * Source(s) |
|---|---|---|---|
| The percentage of all hospitals beds owned by for-profit hospitals | | | 1 |
| The rank by state based on total for-profit beds | | | 1 |
| Presence of integrated hospital systems | | | |
| Presence of integrated delivery systems with physician networks | | | |
| Potential economies of scale resulting from multiple locations in terms of costs, negotiating strength, marketing, etc. | | | |
| Whether or not insurers use network fee schedules or individually negotiated fee schedules (again) | | | |
| Intensity of market competition for acquisitions | | | 6 |
| Impact of acquisition growth on stock price | | | |
| Legal factors | | | |
| For physician practices, enforceability of noncompete laws including judicial precedent | | | |
| Certificate of need laws for various provider entities | | | 8 |
| Federal regulatory status | | | 9 |
| Anti-kickback<br>Stark laws<br>False Claims Act<br>CMS administrative sanctions<br>Enforcement trends, e.g., big pharmaceutical companies are current target | | | |
| State regulatory status | | | |
| Political factors | | | |
| Lobby strength of state hospital association, medical society, imaging, ASC, chiropractic, etc. | | | |
| Board representation on provider entities, particularly exempt hospitals and teaching hospitals | | | |

*Data Sources:
1. www.statehealthfacts.org/.
2. www.cms.hhs.gov/MedicareAdvtgSpecRateStats/.
3. www.medpac.gov.
4. Centers for Medicare & Medicaid generally.
5. Lehman Brothers analysis.
6. SEC filings.
7. State Insurance Commissioner.
8. www.ncsl.org/programs/health/cert-need.htm.
9. www.cms.hhs.gov/home/regsguidance.asp.

Chapter 4

# Quality Performance and Valuation: What's the Connection?

*By Alice G. Gosfield, Esq.*

When the Institute of Medicine (IOM) published *Crossing the Quality Chasm* in 2001,[1] a new era in health care was launched. With no less a goal than the promulgation of a blueprint to drive healthcare delivery in the 21st century, the report announced and explicated those values intended to determine how care is purchased, provided, and evaluated for the foreseeable future. Later characterized as the STEEEP values, the IOM called for care to meet six explicit standards. Care should be:

- Safe—delivered in a manner that avoids injuries;
- Timely—explicitly organized to reduce waits and harmful delays;
- Effective—based on scientific knowledge avoiding underuse and overuse;
- Efficient—avoiding waste of equipment, supplies, ideas, and energies and although not articulated, economically efficient;
- Equitable—not variable in quality because of gender, ethnicity, location, and socioeconomic status; and
- Patient-centered—respectful and responsive to patient preferences, needs, and values and therefore, subject to patient choice, which itself implies a more transparent and publicly reported healthcare system.

1 Corrigan, et al., National Academy Press, Washington, D.C.

The report called for new payment models that would enhance the ability to render care in concordance with the values.

Quality problems in health care had long been identified as overuse, misuse, and underuse.[2] Overuse occurs when the patient gets too much of the proper treatment. Misuse is when the patient gets the wrong treatment. Underuse occurs when the patient does not get all the services he or she needs. All three have been found to be endemic in American healthcare. Overuse has led payors to impose blunt force control measures, such as prior authorization of provider services, post-payment review, and recoupment for medically unnecessary services. Misuse has gotten little attention in payment policy, but most of the pay-for-performance (P4P) programs, which are burgeoning throughout the country, are focused on underuse because they pay physicians to do things they have not been doing enough of,[3] in part in response to studies that have demonstrated that Americans are receiving only about 55% of the services that evidence says should be used to treat them.[4]

## Pay for Performance

With the call for better quality performance, we have seen a proliferation of P4P programs: initiatives primarily sponsored by health plans to pay mostly physicians, but sometimes hospitals as well, additional monies on top of the capitation, fee for service, or DRG payments they are already being paid, for performance as measured in enunciated metrics. The explosion of more measures themselves[5] has also been part of this changed environment with the National Quality Forum—a public-private partnership of multiple stakeholders (www.nqf.org)—providing consensus approval of measures created by others, to be applied nationally for a plethora of clinical conditions and services.

The data so far available about P4P programs, which began to appear around 2003, are neither robust nor compelling.[6] Many of these programs did not start with a threshold of performance against which to measure improved performance. There remain many

2 Chassin, Galvin and The National Roundtable for Health Care, "The Urgent Need to Improve Health Care Quality." *JAMA*, (Sept 16, 1998); 280; pp.1000-1005.

3 Gosfield, "Pay for Performance: Transitional at Best," *Managed Care* (Jan. 2005) www.managedcaremag.com/archives/0501/0501.p4p_gosfield.html.

4 McGlynn, et al., "The Quality of Health Care Delivered to Adults in the United States," 548 NEJM 2635 (Jan. 16, 2003).

5 Gosfield, "The Performance Measures Ball: Too Many Tunes, Too Many Dancers?," *Health Law Handbook* (Gosfield. ed.), 2005 Edition, WestGroup a Thomson Company, pp. 227-283, www.gosfield.com/PDF/Ch4Gosfield.pdf.

6 See Gosfield, "Physician Compensation for Quality: Behind the Group's Green Door," *Health Law Handbook* (Gosfield, ed.), 2008 edition, pp. 3-7.

questions about the extent to which they are improving the quality of health care services; yet there is a sense of inevitability about them, and they are proliferating throughout the country.

All of them have added more money on top of the already existing payment systems. Sometimes these payments are a percentage of a shared pool of money (CMS-Premier Hospital program), an enhancement to the capitation rates (the most typical model), or a fixed stipend (the Bridges to Excellence model).[7] Most of them pay for physicians to do something they were not doing before—perform more tests, prescribe more drugs—to get better scores.

While the commercial payors have led the way in the development of these programs, Medicare is squarely in this business as well, with its demonstration projects[8], reduced payment to hospitals that do not report their quality results[9], and an incipient program for physicians, which pays them merely for reporting information, not for achieving specific scores.[10] The quality-payment nexus is more tightly joined with the refusal of payors, including Medicare, to pay hospitals at all for "never events"—errors and patient safety failures that never should have occurred in the first place, such as wrong-site surgery, bed sores, and hospital-acquired pneumonia.[11]

## Efficiency

The obverse of this pay-for-performance (or no pay for no performance) phenomenon is the parallel expansion of efficiency-based measurement, primarily in the form of tiered networks that exclude more expensive providers from eligibility to render care, when the health plan deems them too expensive.[12] Highly controversial, they have been characterized as "networks of the cheapest" by some,[13] with allegations of defamatory and misguided characterization of the providers reported. Tensions have run so high that on one hand, the New York State Attorney General has investigated the operation of these programs,[14] while on the other, a voluntary agreement among health plans and providers emerged regarding how these programs will be unfurled.[15] Still, the issue of

7 www.bridgestoexcellence.org.
8 www.cms.hhs.gov/HospitalQualityInits/35_HospitalPremier.asp#TopOfPage; www.cms.hhs.gov/DemoProjectsEvalRpts/downloads/MMA646_PGP_FactSheet.pdf.
9 www.cms.hhs.gov/HospitalQualityInits/15_HospitalQualityAlliance.asp#TopOfPage.
10 www.cms.hhs.gov/PQRI.
11 Gabriel, "Medicare: Uncle Sam's New Scrutiny," *Physicians' Practice* (May 2008) www.physicianspractice.com/index/fuseaction/articles.details/articleID/1159.htm.
12 See, Shay, "Transparency and the Law," *Health Law Handbook* (Gosfield, ed.), 2008 edition, pp. 77-121.
13 uft-a.com/latest_issues/issues.htm#netcheapest.
14 www.oag.state.ny.us/press/2007/nov/nov13c_07.html.
15 healthcaredisclosure.org/docs/files/PatientCharterDisclosureRelease040108.pdf.

the efficiency of healthcare delivery is also in high relief as the quality mandates are also emphasized.

Crystallizing one side of the government's interest in performance, quality has now been cited by the Office of the Inspector General (OIG) as grounds for fraud and abuse enforcement.[16] Similarly the Department of Justice is paying attention to quality and its failures as the basis for enforcement.[17] Where providers exercise so much budgetary constraint that patients do not get appropriate care, criminal penalties have been imposed and false claims have been assessed in still other contexts.

So the extent to which quality and payment are linked and made the basis for regulatory accountability is increasing. What does this quality-payment connection have to do with a book on valuation? As the implications of these connections are emerging, placing a value on what quality is will be an increasingly important challenge in a variety of ventures going forward.

### The Legal Nexus With Valuation

Framed in terms that speak to the quality problems of overuse, misuse, and underuse, the Stark statute is about overuse. The law was enacted because of data in the early 1990s that showed that physicians will refer patients to a provider entity in which they are invested, sometimes when those services are not medically necessary. The Stark statute[18] is a strict liability statute—no intent is required to find a violation. It affects physician referrals only for a specified hit list of "designated health services" (DHS) and prohibits both the referral of Medicare patients to entities with which they have financial relationships for those services and the entity's submission of claims pursuant to a tainted referral, unless the relationship complies with an exception.[19] Violations entail $15,000 civil money penalties for each claim submitted as a result of an improper referral, as well as the payment being deemed an overpayment.

There are many exceptions, including for personal services and rental of space and equipment. Many of them are particularly important for transactions between physicians and the hospitals to which they refer, because all inpatient and outpatient hospital services are DHS. There are a number of exceptions that require that payment reflect fair

16 Co-authored with the American Health Lawyers Association, "Corporate Responsibility and Health Care Quality," oig.hhs.gov/fraud/docs/complianceguidance/CorporateResponsibilityFinal%209-4-07.pdf.

17 www.gosfield.com/newissues.htm#pptjgs.

18 42 USC 1395nn.

19 For more information on the Stark statute, see, Gosfield, Chapter 3, *Medicare and Medicaid Fraud and Abuse*, 2008 ed., WestGroup, a Thomson Company, and www.gosfield.com/publications.

market value and others that no payment directly reflects the volume or value of referrals of DHS. In addition, because of the effort to forestall improper referrals whenever they might arise, the statute establishes that some of its exceptions are only available for application by a medical group that meets specific standards, among which are standards regarding how the physicians in the group are compensated.[20]

An older, broader, but less rigid statute is often, today, included by nonlawyers under the rubric of Stark, but the anti-kickback statute (AKS) is entirely different and not even in the same title of the Social Security Act.[21] The AKS sweeps into its ambit all federal health payment programs and all parties to a violating transaction. Whoever solicits, pays, offers, or receives any remuneration, in cash or in kind, covertly or overtly, directly or indirectly, for the referral, to induce the referral, or for ordering, providing, leasing, furnishing, recommending, or arranging for the provision of any service, item, or good payable under a federal program can be found to have violated the law. Penalties are criminal—up to $25,000 fine, up to five years in jail, or both—but also can be punished by a $50,000 civil money penalty for each violation.

Unlike Stark, though, the AKS has an intent requirement. To violate it, one must knowingly and willfully engage in improper behavior. The AKS can also be said to reflect a desire to curb overuse of services that can result from a desire to realize the financial opportunities in business relationships involving patients whose care is paid for by the government. Unlike the regulations under Stark, which provide refinement to the strict prohibitions in the statute, the safe harbor regulations[22] under the AKS report only what is explicitly safe. Arrangements that do not comply do not necessarily violate the statute but will be evaluated on their facts and circumstances as reviewed with prosecutorial discretion. Like the Stark statute, the AKS also focuses heavily on the fair market value of the financial relationships involved.

While Stark targets leases of real estate and equipment for a discussion of payment for quality, the fair market value of *services* is far more relevant. The definition of "fair market value" for Stark purposes turns on "general market value."

> *Fair market value* means the value in arm's-length transactions, consistent with the general market value. "General market value" means the price an asset would bring as the result of *bona fide* bargaining between well-informed parties to the agreement

20 Gosfield, "Physician Compensation for Quality: Behind The Group's Green Door," *Health Law Handbook* (Gosfield, ed.), 2008 edition, WestGroup, a Thomson Company pp. 1-44, gosfield.com/PDF/gosfield.2008%20HLH.articlewithcoverpage.122807.pdf.
21 42 USC 1320a-7b(b)(1) and (2).
22 42 CFR §1001.952 et seq.

> who are not otherwise in a position to generate business for the other party on the date of acquisition of the asset or at the time of the service agreement. Usually the fair market price is the price at which *bona fide* sales have been consummated for assets of like type, quality, and quantity in a particular market at the time of acquisition or the compensation that has been included in *bona fide* service agreements with comparable terms at the time of the agreement, where the price or compensation has not been determined in any manner that takes into account the volume or value of anticipated or actual referrals.[23]

This definition was streamlined from an earlier version that created a safe harbor for hourly payments to physicians for services rendered. Payments for medical directorships, for example, were traditionally compensated on the basis of an hourly payment with documentation of time spent. The Stark regulations had taken this further, with a safe harbor for hourly payments reflecting an average of the 50$^{th}$ percentile of four out of six compensation surveys or the 50$^{th}$ percentile of what emergency department physicians were paid in the community as with at least three emergency departments. With the publication of the Stark III regulations, that aspect of the definition was removed, thereby enhancing the flexibility of the definition and opening the door to more creative ways of quantifying the value of physicians' personal services.

Although there is a similar definition of "fair market value" in the space and equipment lease safe harbor, there is none generally for AKS purposes or in the personal services and management contract exception, which is far more relevant to quality-based payments. The payment terms state that:

> The aggregate compensation paid ... over the term of the agreement is set in advance, is consistent with fair market value in arms-length transactions, and is not calculated in a manner that takes into account the volume or value of any referrals or business otherwise generated between the parties for which payment may be made in whole or in part under Medicare or under a state health care program.[24]

### Valuing Quality

Against this background of performance measurement, payment change, and fraud and abuse regulations, a range of initiatives is now emerging, particularly where hospitals and physicians relate to each other, that is intended to improve quality of care. Because much of what occurs in a hospital is ultimately derivative of a physician order

23 42 USC §411.351 (72 Fed Reg. 51081, Sept 5, 2007).

24 42 CFR §1001.952(d)(5).

(even though a lot of what is being scored in hospital pay-for-performance programs involves teamwork in the institution among nurses, technicians, and others), for many scores, the collaboration between hospitals and physicians is essential for hospitals to succeed.[25] To pay physicians for their help, some measure of value becomes essential, especially in light of the impact of Stark and the AKS on these relationships.

As hospitals seek to improve their quality scores, for which they are at risk of reduced Medicare payments for reporting failures, they increasingly seek to engage physicians with them.[26] Paying the physicians for their activities in support of improvement can fall under the "personal services arrangement" exception under the Stark regulations, but the payment must be based on fair market value. Some commentators now argue that lost opportunity time is a reasonable measure of fair market value when the job being performed by the physicians requires their special expertise.[27] Different specialties would be paid differently under this analysis. The types of activities for which this type of payment is relevant can include selection of clinical practice guidelines, pathways, protocols, or other approaches to standardization of care, as well as medical staff leadership and service on medical staff committees, since the whole raison d'etre of the medical staff organization is to monitor and assure the quality of care in the institution and provide recommendations to the board about privileges, credentialing, and corrective action.

Another approach to improving quality and efficiency has been through implementation of the modern versions of gainsharing that the OIG has approved. Gainsharing has been a basis for fraud enforcement against hospitals since 1983, when diagnosis-related groups (DRGs) were introduced. When gainsharing re-emerged as a potential approach to bonding with physicians and saving money for the hospital in July 1999, the OIG published a very critical statement that it would not approve programs that paid physicians to reduce services, even if they were from a baseline of overuse.[28] With six favorable opinions in 2005[29] and more in subsequent years, the OIG approved a revamped, time-limited, surgical- and procedure-focused approach to gainsharing, which turned in part on the valuation and payment methodologies. Under the gainsharing

25 Gosfield, "In Common Cause for Quality," *Health Law Handbook* (Gosfield ed.), 2006 edition, WestGroup, a Thomson Company, pp. 177-222, www.gosfield.com/PDF/commoncausequalityCh5.pdf; Reinertsen, Gosfield, Rupp and Whittington, *"Engaging Physicians in a Shared Quality Agenda."* IHI Innovation Series white paper. Cambridge, MA: Institute for Healthcare Improvement; 2007. www.gosfield.com/PDF/IHIEngagingPhysiciansWhitePaper2007.pdf; and www.uft-a.com.

26 Gosfield and Reinertsen, "Sharing The Quality Agenda with Physicians," *Trustee* (Oct. 2007) pp. 12-17.

27 Johnson, "Fair Market Value Support Required, " ALHA, *Health Law Weekly* (May 2008), www.healthlawyers.org/Template.cfm?Section=HLW_Archive&template=/ahlatestcode/google/g_articlelayout.cfm&ContentID=55890&IssueDate=2008-05-30%2000%3A00%3A00.

28 oig.hhs.gov/fraud/docs/alertsandbulletins/gainsh.htm.

29 Advisory Opinions 05-01 through 05-06, oig.hhs.gov/fraud/advisoryopinions/opinions0106.html.

programs, which are intended to save money by standardizing supplies used, those that are explicitly approved do so because they have safeguards that prevent reduction of clinical services to patients. All of them are time-limited to one year. They pay physicians half of the savings over thresholds currently achieved, so they reward actual improvement. The cost savings are calculated by subtracting the actual costs for the year of the supplies from historic costs associated with a set of recommended practices during specified procedures rendered. From these results are subtracted any inappropriate reductions that would run afoul of the prohibition on a hospital paying physicians to reduce their services.[30]

While the OIG was clear that the arrangements implicated the prohibition on payment to reduce services, the safeguards cited as supporting approval included, among the eight reasons cited: transparency and disclosure to patients; credible medical support that the arrangement wouldn't adversely affect patient care; all surgeries were included and not just those paid for by federal programs; the cost savings reflected actual costs and "not an accounting convention"; using clinical benchmarks of historical and current performance, any undue inducement to restrict care was mitigated.

Those reasons motivated the government to believe civil money penalties for reduction of services was inappropriate. In addition, addressing the compensation under the anti-kickback statute because the program was limited to surgeons already on staff, the additional payment from the program, the OIG said, would not induce others to join the staff to get the money. Because only surgeons would benefit, referrals from other physicians, such as cardiologists, would not be stimulated by the program. The payment reflected additional risk to the surgeons from changing their behaviors, which the OIG regarded as potentially not much more than "simple common sense," but a change in operating room practice based on standardized rules nonetheless. As a result of the analysis, in quality terms, the OIG postulated that the risks of underuse had been avoided by the safeguards against reduction of services, while the risks of overuse had been avoided by not encouraging additional referrals to obtain the additional, time-limited money the program would make available. While many would regard the analysis as purely financial, in fact, at its core, it reflects quality concerns.

Yet another tantalizing opportunity to improve quality was raised with the publication of the Stark III regulations. The regulators said compensation related to patient satisfaction goals or other quality measures unrelated to the volume or value of business generated by the referring physician and unrelated to reducing or limiting services

30 Advisory Opinion 07-21.

would be permitted under the personal service arrangements exception.[31] This relatively open-ended recognition of the changing environment offers the opportunity to pay physicians not on a time basis, but on a value-of-contribution basis, now that the definition of fair market value no longer drives toward hourly payments. Of course, the protection would only pertain provided that all requirements of the exception are satisfied. The regulators have cited as a legitimate example compensation to reward physicians for providing appropriate preventive care services when the arrangement is otherwise structured to satisfy the requirements of the exception.

How physicians have contributed to improved performance could be valued by looking at each quality metric with a financial impact and assessing the ratio of their contribution to their accomplishment, as distinct from the contributions of nurses, technicians, pharmacists, and others. Similarly, payments that recognize physician contributions to commercial pay-for-performance enhancements to hospital reimbursement would also be permitted under this acknowledgement.

What likely is *not* proper under the definition is looking at hospital payment on the DRG and subtracting from it the fair market value of the hospital contributions (e.g., heat, light, staff, building, and license) and paying the remainder to the physicians.

In its co-authored guidance to hospital boards regarding trustee responsibilities for quality with the American Health Lawyers Association, the OIG cited as a risk area the ways that incentive pools will be developed when otherwise independent providers seek to collaborate to achieve both improved efficiency and higher quality scores.[32] To set a value on the services rendered and results achieved, as contributed by each participant in an incentive pool, will present additional challenges to providers and those assisting them in constructing their arrangements within the boundaries of the law. Some have looked to commercial disease management companies as the analogues for valuation of the services rendered. These companies typically are paid performance bonuses for achieving specific targets or benchmarks. Given the definition of fair market value under the Stark regulations, this is one general market source of comparison to support the legitimacy of the compensation that might be earned.

Selecting targets that do not reflect a shift to reduced services to patients is also important to avoid the potential for civil money penalties. Reduced length-of-stay measures would not be a good choice. Those measures that reflect correction of underuse—use of

31 72 Federal Register 51046 (Sept 5, 2007).
32 oig.hhs.gov/fraud/docs/complianceguidance/CorporateResponsibilityFinal%209-4-07.pdf.

beta blockers after heart attack, door to balloon time in providing angioplasty, timely administration of drugs—are less problematic.

While Medicare now pays for improved hospital mortality scores, paying physicians or hospitals or giving them bonuses for killing fewer of their patients is not an ideal page one story, if characterized inappropriately. So valuation in this delicate arena may have public relations implications if the underpinnings of the financial model are made public. Worse yet are the risks from discovery requests and potential application in a lawsuit where a patient is harmed.

The likelihood that quality performance measures, particularly in combination with financial benefits to the participants, will become integral to malpractice actions is very high.[33]

## Conclusion

With the highly increased attention to quality performance in health care generally, business relationships where financial value attaches to that performance are proliferating. The law establishes significant restrictions on what is legitimate to take into account in valuations that support these new relationships, but it also offers new opportunities to connect the financial implications of improved quality of care with financial consequences.

33 Gosfield and Reinertsen, "The 100,000 Lives Campaign: Crystallizing Standards of Care for Hospitals", *Health Affairs* (Nov. 2005), pp. 1560-1570.

Chapter 5

# Factors in Forecasting Cash Flow and Estimating Cost of Capital in Healthcare

*By Carol W. Carden, CPA/ABV, ASA, CFE and Mark O. Dietrich, CPA/ABV*

It is critical when undertaking the valuation of any company to have a good understanding of the risks associated with the future cash flows. In today's environment in the healthcare industry, it has never been more important or more difficult to appropriately assess risk and correctly apply discount or capitalization rates. It is equally difficult in the uncertain healthcare environment to develop revenue forecasting assumptions that are reasonable and reflective of likely trends in the various healthcare industry sectors. This article offers some guidance on the myriad of factors that impact the cost of capital and risk assessment and cash flow forecasting for healthcare industry transactions.

## What Comprises the 'Healthcare Industry'?

Before delving into a discussion about the risk and uncertainty associated with the healthcare industry, it is important to first establish the different types of organizations included under this broad umbrella. At 17% of the U.S. economy, healthcare is the single largest segment. The treatment of "healthcare" as a single industry obscures the fact that it is really a complex set of separate subsections that are to one extent or another interrelated and may have very different prospects at different points in time.

Primary components of the industry include physicians, facilities, pharmaceutical and life sciences, medical equipment manufacturers and technology, and home health care. As a further division, facilities include acute care hospitals, long-term care hospitals, skilled nursing facilities, freestanding ambulatory surgery centers (ASCs) and senior housing. These are all dramatically different businesses. Acute care hospitals compete with ASCs for outpatient surgery, for example, but ASCs are paid only 60% of what a hospital outpatient department receives for the same case. Therefore, even two businesses that provide essentially the same service have very different risk characteristics and future revenue prospects.

In the physician sector, hospital-based physicians, such as anesthesiologists or neonatal intensive care unit (NICU) physicians favored by private equity investors, are very different from one another and from other types of practices, which typically have much greater overhead than they do.

Each of these sectors is likely to have a very different risk profile. That risk, to a large extent, is a function of the relative success or failure of industry lobbyists in winning support for their subsection from government payors, such as Medicare and Medicaid. As such, identifying trends in future government program revenue is one key to the accurate assessment of risk as well as the forecasting of future cash flow.

**Government Influence**

No other segment of the economy is so closely tied to the action of federal and state governments. Government influence flows from the executive branch through regulatory authorities such as the Office of the Inspector General, Federal Trade Commission, Anti-Trust Division of the Department of Justice (DOJ), states' attorneys general, DOJ Civil and Criminal Division, Centers for Medicare & Medicaid Services (CMS), and numerous others. Each of these agencies plays a critical role in the prospects for the various components of the healthcare industry.

The legislative branch plays a less frequent but often dramatic role in subsector prospects as discussed in greater detail later in this article. At the state level, the Medicaid program for low-income and indigent individuals is a significant factor for many individual companies within each subsector but may not be significant to others who do not service that population. Reform legislation at the state level—such as universal coverage in Massachusetts—can have a highly localized effect. It is critical in assessing the risk and cash flows associated with a healthcare company that you have a good understanding of the potential impact of government action or inaction on your particular healthcare subsector.

## Identifying Factors That Contribute to Risk

One of the great challenges of business valuation is quantification of future changes in cash flow through the forecast or the discount rate. Due to the high level of regulation and government influence in healthcare, the forecasting of revenue growth assumptions is much more difficult than a similar undertaking for a less-regulated industry. On the other hand, there are a number of sources for near-term trend analysis for the healthcare industry as well as longer-term crystal ball gazing to assist in this undertaking.

### *Near-Term Forecasting and Risk Assessment*

Each year in March, the Medicare Payment Advisory Commission (MedPAC) issues its report to Congress regarding Medicare payment policy. While the MedPAC report is not authoritative, it serves as a good indicator of potential areas of Medicare payment action as well as which sectors are likely to be targeted for significant reimbursement changes or industry restructuring. Many times, recommendations from the MedPAC report will be included in the proposed physician fee schedule as discussed below.

CMS publishes each year proposed and—after a comment period—final regulations announcing rates for the subsequent calendar year. For example, the proposed Medicare Physician Fee Schedule (MPFS) Rule is typically published in July or August and the final rule in early November. While labeled "physician fee schedule," the MPFS also contains proposed fees for outpatient, physician-based healthcare entities, such as ASCs. There is approximately three months' notice about what is likely to occur in the next calendar year. There have also been instances, such as when the ASC fee schedule was completely revamped in 2005, when fee changes are so significant that they will be phased in over a number of years, providing a reliable revenue assumption forecasting tool for the short term.

Notably, since 2003, massive cuts in the physician fee schedule have been announced in the proposed rule only to be overturned by Congress in late December before a January 1 effective date and replaced with small increases in the range of 0.5% to 1.5% due to the sustainable growth rate (SGR) formula. It is beyond the scope of this article to discuss the SGR in detail, but in summary, the premise of the SGR is that budget neutrality is related to changes in the MPFS, but has historically not been achieved. Therefore, to place the MPFS back in "balance" would require a significant single-year reduction across the board in physician fees. As such, when dealing with a valuation date that falls after the proposed rule but before the final rule is issued, application of revenue assumptions from the proposed rule must be tempered, based upon the likelihood of implementation in the analyst's professional judgment.

The proposed and final rules are closely watched by management and industry analysts, although seemingly less so by investors, given the lag in some stock's price response. For example, Alliance Imaging (AIQ) is a provider of magnetic resonance imaging (MRI), positron emission tomography and computed tomography (PET/CT) and radiation therapy, primarily on an outpatient basis. Approximately 80% of its revenue comes from contracts with hospitals and much of that is subject to the Hospital Outpatient Prospective Payment System (HOPPS). Nonetheless, it has a significant exposure to the MPFS.

Exhibit 1 plots AIQ's stock price and volume for the period from June 2009 to November 2009. As can be seen, there was some reaction to the MPFS proposed rule on July 1 that called for significant cuts in the payment rates for MRI and radiation therapy, particularly intensity-modulated radiation therapy (IMRT), an expensive form of radiation therapy. Thereafter, the stock recovered much of the loss in value following the announcement, only to plunge following the company's earnings conference call when management quantified the loss in net revenue (and effectively operating income) at more than $5.5 million. From an appraiser's standpoint in looking at a comparable company, one would have to believe that the impact of the proposed cuts (which were in large part adopted as part of the final rule on October 31) was subject to calculation and therefore reasonably knowable at the beginning of July.

**Exhibit 1. AIQ Price and Volume**

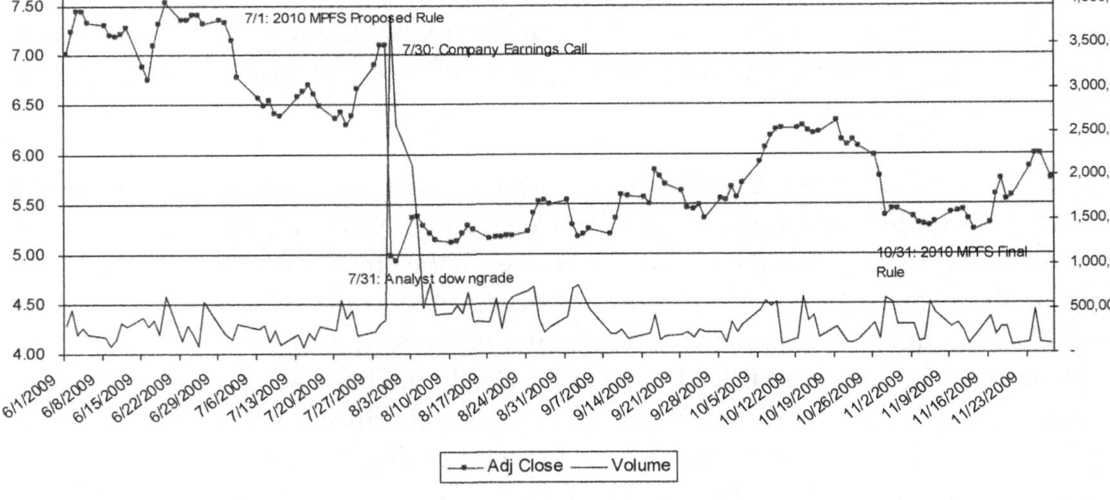


The drop of about 30% in the stock's price on July 31 is a function of three factors: 1) expected and known reduction in future cash flow; 2) increased risk of cash flows; and 3) selling pressure due to high trading volume. Note that despite the quantification of the loss in cash flow, the stock's price recovers after the downward price pressure of the sell-off is gone. When the proposed rule is finalized at the end of October, the stock's price declines again. Investor reaction appears more immediate, since the reductions under the proposed rule announced July 31 are confirmed on October 31 and "all hope is lost."

*Point: The response of public market investors as reflected in stock prices often lags knowledge of likely or pending reimbursement changes. Aside from the tendency to view bad news about one's investment in the most favorable light, the lag may be due to awaiting the assessment of professional industry analysts, e.g., Joshua Raskin & Adam Feinstein of Barclays Capital.*

### Identifying Reimbursement Trends That Are Not Sustainable

Perhaps the single largest error made in forecasting cash flows for a medical practice or other entity that relies on the MPFS is failure to evaluate the likely direction that reimbursement for that particular sector is headed using the tools just discussed. Additionally, as a general rule, no single location, market or service line healthcare entity will have reimbursement growth rate assumptions greater than 3% over the long term. Growth of this magnitude is possible in the discrete periods of the forecast, but given the complexity of the regulations just discussed, it is highly unlikely, and quite likely impossible, for any sector to grow at a rate greater than 2.5% to 3% over the long term. The key to identifying and addressing risk and future cash flows is that frequently utilized, high-cost procedures and tests will be targeted for dramatic cutbacks. It is not a matter of if, but of when, the cuts will be implemented.

#### *As an Example:*

Current procedural terminology (CPT) code 78465,[1] heart image (3rd) multiple, is a single photon emission computed tomography (SPECT) code for myocardial infusion and represented a staggering 10.3% ($2,072,176,147) of charges for cardiovascular physicians billing Medicare in 2007, the highest single code in terms of charges as well as frequency of billing.[2] CPT code 78465 also represented 10.4% ($2,017,599,660) of charges in 2006 and 10.4% ($1,863,154,763) of charges in 2005. Exhibit 2 depicts the growth in allowed charges (left axis)—those that Medicare actually approves for payment as opposed to those that are submitted—from 2003 to 2008 and billed charges (right axis)—those actually submitted by providers—from 2005 to 2007.

1 Codes are copyright, American Medical Association. This code was "cross-walked," or changed to 78452, in the period between the 2010 proposed and final rules. One more complication that emphasizes the import of understanding CPT codes.

2 Current data can be downloaded at www.cmpasupport.com/download/files/Top10Procs_2008.zip, and historical data are available at www.cms.hhs.gov/MedicareFeeforSvcPartsAB/04_MedicareUtilizationforPartB.asp#TopOfPage.

**Exhibit 2. Growth in Allowed Charges and Billed Charges**

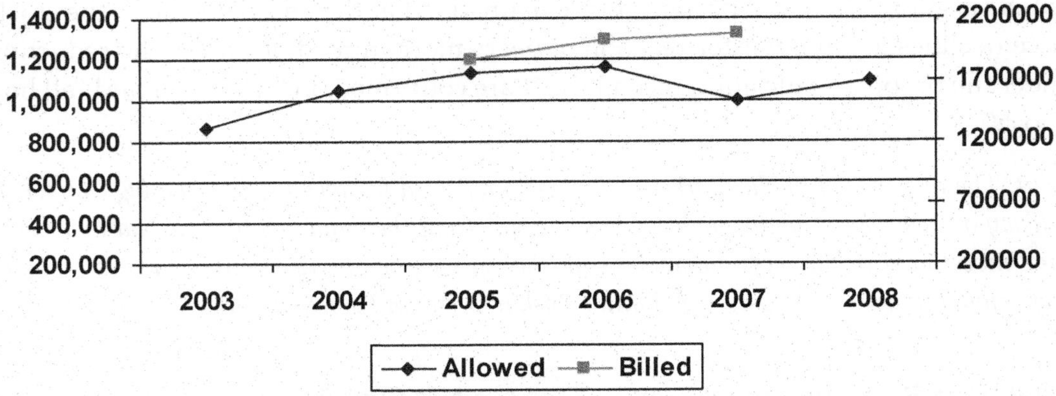


The technical component (TC) paid in connection with ownership of the equipment, employment of a technician, and provision of supplies and other overhead is approximately *85%* of the global fee for CPT code 78465. The Medicare program sets fees by assigning a value factor in terms of relative value units (RVU) to each code and multiplying that by a dollar rate, called a conversion factor.[3] Thus, the fee paid for a code is proportional to the RVU value assigned to it.

RVU values are based upon three principal factors: The cost of providing the service, known as the practice expense component; the physician work associated with providing the service or interpreting the results of a test; and the cost of malpractice insurance. Therefore, the more resources a particular service consumes in terms of physician time and effort, as well as operating costs, the higher the RVU assignment will be, and therefore, the higher the associated payment will be. The TC consists of a practice expense component and a small malpractice component.

In 2007, the TC had an RVU value of 11.51. That declined to 11.26 in 2008 and 10.73 in 2009. The final rule published in November 2009 set the RVUs for the TC at 8.32, a drop of 22%. This illustrates one of the critical insights that experienced healthcare industry appraisers possess: *expensive procedures will be targeted for dramatic cutbacks eventually. As stated previously, it is not a matter of if, but when, this will occur.*

Other notable examples of such cuts include the Deficit Reduction Act of 2005, which dramatically reduced the explosive growth in spending on high-tech imaging (e.g., MRI and CT), perhaps the most significant of the past decade, part of a continuing trend highlighted by the earlier discussion of AIQ. Another example is the Medicare Modernization

3 The concept of RVUs is analogous to billable hours while the conversion factor is analogous to a billing rate per hour. For example, if a code has an RVU value of 10 and the conversion factor is $50, it would have a fee of $500.

Act of 2003 (MMA), which changed the methodology for paying for physician office chemotherapy drugs from one based on published list prices (average wholesale price) to one based on *actual* average selling price. The scale of the cuts was such that many physicians were unable to continue in-office chemotherapy and incomes of affected specialties such as oncologists dropped dramatically. The MMA also expanded the Medicare Advantage program in a manner that proved to be highly questionable from a cost-benefit standpoint, causing MedPAC to devote an entire chapter in its 2009 *Report to Congress* on the problems therewith. This is a likely target for near-term cuts.

A final example, and one that garnered much attention due to the tax court case *Caracci*,[4] involved home health agencies and the changeover from a cost-based payment system to a prospective payment system (PPS) in the late 1990s.

Point: If a healthcare service or procedure reflects dramatic profits, it probably is going to change, change soon and change in a significant, negative fashion.

### Understanding the Impact of Payor Relationships

To this point in the article, we have focused much of our discussion on understanding the direction that governmental payors, such as Medicare and Medicaid, are headed. However, it is critical that the appraiser also gain an understanding regarding the composition and reimbursement trends for the remaining payors. Many times, commercial payors tend to follow the direction of Medicare, albeit with a lag of one or more years. Therefore, the analyst should review and be familiar with the reimbursement terms for the most significant commercial contracts held by a healthcare organization to effectively forecast cash flows.

An often overlooked but important consideration is whether or not the company has a significant amount of out-of-network business. In this situation, the company does not hold a contract with the commercial payor, but treats patients of the payor nonetheless. In the early periods of this practice, it can be a lucrative arrangement for the healthcare company because it may receive fees that are higher than would be included in a contract. However, over the long term, this tactic will generally fail, resulting in a decrease in fees, if not in the complete elimination of a portion of the company's patient base. Therefore, when determining the level of revenues to forecast as well as the associated risk, it is critical to understand whether the company has exposure in this area and to factor such risks into the assessment of the discount/capitalization rate.

4 118 T.C. No. 25, *Sta-Home Health Agency, et al. v. Commissioner*, Case No. 02-60912 (5th Cir.), July 11, 2006.

Additionally, as with any company being appraised, it is critical to assess concentration of risk when determining the appropriate discount rate/cost of capital. The tool used to assess concentration of risk for a healthcare company is the "payor mix." The payor mix is a reflection of the proportionate level of revenues attributable to the various payors, such as Medicare and Medicaid, as well as significant commercial health insurers, such as BlueCross/BlueShield or United Healthcare. If the appraiser determines that the healthcare company has a concentration with a particular payor, it would likely increase the assessment of risk related to the cash flows. Additionally, it would be imperative that the appraiser gain a very thorough understanding of the direction of reimbursement trends for that particular payor to ensure the revenue forecast is achievable.

Another important factor to analyze in terms of payor mix is the proportion of patients who are self-pay or any significant changes in the proportion of self-pay patients. A significant increase in self-pay patients can trigger the appraiser to the fact that the company has lost an important commercial insurance contract or that the geographic location of the company has been harder hit by economic changes than anticipated. Generally speaking, the collections rate on self-pay patients will be extremely low and most collections will happen very early in the process if at all.

*Point: You cannot assess the risk and discount rate or estimate future cash flow without knowledge of the underlying revenue sources. The risk of Medicare and Medicaid revenues is substantially different, and both of these may be very different from those of nongovernment payors; those individuals with insurance, co-pays, and deductibles; and uninsured individuals.*

### Using Guideline Company Data to Forecast Cash Flows and Assess Risk

To the extent that a public company's operations are representative of a given valuation subject's risk and prospects, it can provide insight into both the discount rate and forecast of cash flow. However, there are several critical limitations on the use of these data in a healthcare industry context that are often overlooked.

There have been two significant trends in the broader healthcare industry that affect the availability of guideline data and their usefulness. The first of these is consolidation within the payor industry. Consolidation of health insurers was possible due to their long-standing anti-trust waiver. This has in turn led to an ongoing and dramatic consolidation trend amongst providers. The practical outcome of these two interrelated and parallel trends has been to create a situation in many markets where providers pass increasing costs back to insurers that then pass those costs back to employers and insureds through their premiums. Consolidation has also led to a declining number of guideline companies. The remaining companies are larger, more diverse in their revenue sources, and therefore, less exposed—or risky—to changes in a given market area.

*Point: Future cash flow depends upon the relative market power of a company.*[5] *Market risk is a function of many factors, and in the healthcare industry, size and diversity—particularly diversity as to revenue sources and number of distinct geographic market areas in which the company operates—are drivers of market or negotiating power.*[6]

Additionally, the detail regarding the guideline's payor contracts will likely not be known to the appraiser. Therefore, it is impossible for the appraiser to make the necessary adjustments to make the guideline truly "comparable."

As discussed previously, commercial insurance contracts can have a dramatic impact on the risk assessment as well as the revenue forecast. Therefore, even if the guideline operates in only one industry segment that coincides with the subject company, the guideline can still have a much different revenue outlook and cost of capital due to interaction with commercial insurance payors across different geographic markets. To illustrate, if you are appraising a healthcare company that operates in the state of Alabama where BlueCross/BlueShield is by far the most dominant commercial payor, application of revenue trends from a guideline would have very little, if any, relevance to determining the revenue forecast or risk assessment of the company.

As an example, much of the consolidation of physician practices by hospital buyers is driven by the ability of a larger, integrated entity to obtain better contracts and rates from insurers. Many times, independent physician practices will be unable to obtain the higher rates available to physicians who are part of a hospital-physician entity. Certain affiliation structures leave the physician practices as freestanding entities that obtain their insurer contracts through the affiliation structure, but otherwise are independent. These practices will earn better incomes and therefore, have higher values, all things equal. The relevance of market transactions of these practices to those without such payor contracts is limited or nonexistent.

Smaller, privately held companies with one or a few locations are typically less diverse and more exposed to local market conditions. Therefore, to extrapolate reimbursement trends from a guideline to a local healthcare company is a recipe for disaster! A guideline may be able to achieve higher growth rates over a longer period of time related solely to the fact that it has a diversified revenue base that insulates it from the impact of significant changes to any one segment of its business. In contrast, the local

5 For a detailed analysis of health insurer and payor market strength, see *Competition in Health Insurance, Comprehensive Study of U.S. Markets, 2007 update*, American Medical Association.

6 For further healthcare industry risk factors, see "Healthcare Market Structure and Its Implication for Valuation of Privately Held Provider Entities: An Empirical Analysis"; *Business Valuation Review*, Summer 2008, Mark O. Dietrich, CPA/ABV.

healthcare company typically has "all its eggs in one basket" and can be significantly benefitted or harmed from changes to one industry segment. Additionally, using the cost of capital of a guideline for purposes of assessing the risk of a local healthcare company again ignores the impact of size and diversity on the assessment of risk and would likely result in an overvaluation of the local healthcare company.

*Point: You cannot assess the relevance of revenue-based market multiples to a valuation subject without knowing the underlying quality of the payor contracts of both comparable and subject.*

*Point: In healthcare, only pure-play comparable companies are typically appropriate. Even a pure play may have limits due to geographic diversity or difference in markets served, revenue sources, and localized trends.*

Because public stock prices do not react as one might "expect" them to or it might be better said "when" one expects them to, attempting to draw conclusions about cost of capital and trends using guideline companies becomes even more difficult in a healthcare industry context. This fact, combined with the limitations just discussed, makes determination of discount rates and cost of capital and revenue forecasting assumptions using a guideline company approach a virtual exercise in futility for a healthcare company. Therefore, the appraiser is better served to rely upon a buildup or capital asset pricing model for purposes of assessing risk for healthcare companies. Comparisons can be made to guideline companies benchmarks, but this approach is better suited as a pressure test rather than a primary method.

## Conclusion

It is critical in any valuation assignment to develop a cash flow projection that is reasonable and achievable and to then estimate value based on a realistic assessment of risk related to those cash flows. In the healthcare industry in particular, these tasks are complicated by the myriad of regulations that govern healthcare companies and impact their ability to achieve projected results. When you add to this complication significant potential changes in how healthcare is delivered and reimbursed in the U.S., the result is an assignment that is extremely complex and requires a substantial amount of experience to accomplish successfully. This article discussed various factors that contribute to the risk of a healthcare company as well as provided guidance regarding the means by which a business appraiser can go about doing the necessary research to appropriately forecast cash flows and assess cost of capital.

# Part II
# Regulatory Considerations in Healthcare Valuation

Chapter 6

# Valuation Standards

*By Edward J. Dupke, CPA/ABV*

Medical practice valuation, like most market segments in valuation, is impacted as to form and content by the valuation standards followed by the valuation practitioner.

The discussion of business valuation standards is distinguished from the concept of "standard of value." The standard of value for a given valuation could be fair market value, fair value—state courts, fair value—financial reporting, investment value, intrinsic value, book value, liquidation value, or others. Discussion of these standards of value will be covered elsewhere in this book.

This chapter is devoted to the valuation standards prepared and adopted by the American organizations that have issued standards. These organizations include the American Institute of Certified Public Accountants (AICPA), the Appraisal Foundation (AF), the American Society of Appraisers (ASA), and the National Association of Certified Valuation Analysts (NACVA). Omitted from this listing is the Institute of Business Appraisers (IBA), which has combined its future direction with NACVA.

Each of these organizations has addressed its standards to serve the needs of its members. For example, the AICPA is an organization of CPAs. Its standards are written from the perspective of CPA practice.

The AF has authored the Uniform Standards of Professional Appraisal Practice (USPAP) for the benefit of appraisers. This set of standards is the only one that is multidisciplinary. There are 10 USPAP standards. Standards 1 through 6 apply to real estate appraisers. Standards 7 and 8 apply to personal property (equipment) appraisers, and Standards

9 and 10 apply to business valuation appraisers. Recently, the application of Standard 3, dealing with the review of the report of another appraiser, was extended to cover business valuation and equipment valuation applications as well as real estate valuation.

The NACVA standards are written to serve the needs of its members, most of whom are CPAs.

The ASA standards are written to serve the needs of business valuation appraisers. ASA also requires that its members conform to USPAP.

The business valuation standards of each of these organizations are dynamic documents in that they are constantly being re-evaluated and changed as the valuation profession changes. The practitioner should check with the respective organization to gather the most recent information and data related to the standards of a particular organization.

**Impact of the Daubert and Kuhmo Tire decisions**

Those who choose to spend their professional life as expert witnesses in the litigation arena have been impacted by these two decisions of the U.S. Supreme Court. From the early 1920s forward, expert testimony has been governed by the *Frye* test. These criteria resulted from the *Frye v. United States* case, decided in 1923. The opinion of the *Frye* court stated that scientific expert testimony was admissible only if the scientific methodology on which it was based was generally accepted within the scientific community. This "generally accepted methodology" doctrine has governed expert testimony from the 1920s until the *Daubert* decision.

In the *Daubert v. Merrill Dow Pharmaceuticals* case, the issue centered around the scientific knowledge of the expert witnesses and their ability to assist the trier of fact in understanding the scientific nuances of the case. The *Daubert* court opined that the court had a "gatekeeping" function. This function requires that the court first determine whether the witness qualifies as an expert in the stated field identified and second decide whether the proposed testimony is, in fact, scientific knowledge that will assist the trier of fact to understand or decide a fact that is at issue. The *Daubert* court further suggested that there are four factors that must be considered in making the gate keeping decision. These factors are:

- Whether the theory can be (or has been) tested.
- Whether the theory or technique has been subjected to peer review or publication.

- The theory's potential rate of error.
- The theory's general acceptance in the scientific community, as described in *Frye*.

The *Daubert* court did not abandon the principles of *Frye* but expanded them. The *Daubert* court further opined that the inquiry into whether expert testimony was reliable should be "flexible."

In the *Kuhmo Tire* case, the Supreme Court held that the "gatekeeping" role it outlined in *Daubert* applied to all expert testimony, not just scientific testimony. The court gave a qualified "yes" to the four *Daubert* factors.

For business valuation experts, the documents that establish generally accepted valuation procedures that have been tested by the peer group are standards. The AICPA business valuation standards have undergone three exposures to the peer group, including two public exposures. The USPAP standards have a public exposure each time the standards are to be changed. The ASA and NACVA all circulate their standards among their members each time there is to be a significant change. Clearly, the standards of each of these organizations satisfy the *Daubert* test of peer review.

In healthcare valuation, a further standard is implicit in expert testimony: an understanding of the specific regulatory factors affecting the underlying assumptions used in a valuation engagement.

### AICPA Business Valuation Standard

The AICPA issued its Statement on Standards for Valuation Services No. 1, *Valuation of a Business, Business Ownership Interest, Security, or Intangible Asset* in June 2007 effective for engagements entered into after Jan. 1, 2008. This is a principle-based standard rather than a primer on how to do business valuation.

The standard endorses the concept that in performing the valuation, the valuation practitioner is to take into consideration information and data that was "known or knowable" as of the valuation date. It suggests that the practitioner is generally not to take into consideration information or data becoming "known or knowable" after the valuation date. The standard also endorses the concept that each business valuation report is restricted to the client and any others who may be identified in it and it is to be used only for the purpose specified in it. It may not be used by the client for any other purpose and may not be used by others for any purpose.

The standard applies to all AICPA members and CPAs licensed to practice in states that have adopted the AICPA standards as part of their respective state's accountancy laws. All of the AICPA ethics pronouncements apply to those who are bound by this standard.

The standard applies to all engagements to estimate value in which the valuation practitioner applies approaches and methodology and exercises professional judgment in the process. There are a number of exceptions to the standard related directly to activity of CPAs on behalf of their clients. A key focus is the maintenance of the CPA's independence to perform an attest function.

The standard adheres to existing AICPA principles of ethics that document ethical conduct for all client engagements and further document when and how audit independence is impaired. For publicly traded companies, the Sarbanes-Oxley legislation is controlling and forbids the CPA or the CPA firm from performing any valuation work on behalf of its audit clients. For closely held companies, the AICPA ethics rules are slightly more flexible. Audit independence for closely held companies is impaired if the valuation performed by the individual CPA or the CPA firm is material to the financial statements undergoing an attest function. If the valuation is not material to the financial statements, there is no audit impairment.

The exceptions to the standard come generally under the headings of audit exception, members in industry exception, economic damages litigation exception, two tax exceptions, and an exception when the valuation in question is provided to the valuation practitioner by the client or a third party. We will not discuss these in detail here because they are clearly explained in the standard.

There is also a jurisdictional exception provided in this standard that if any part of this standard differs from published governmental, judicial, or accounting authority or such authority specifies valuation development procedures or reporting procedures, then the valuation practitioner should follow the applicable published authority or stated procedures with respect to that part applicable to the valuation in which the practitioner is engaged. All other parts of the standard remain in effect. A classic example of the jurisdictional exception is the tax regulations on transfer pricing. These regulations specify exactly how the calculation of the transfer pricing adjustments are to be made and exactly how these calculations are to be reported in the tax return. These regulations supersede the business valuation standard for this type of calculation and are to be followed as prescribed in the regulations. In the healthcare area, the Stark regulations with respect to consideration of the market approach to valuation are another example of the jurisdictional exception.

*Editor's note: When the standard of value is fair market value, as it generally is for a healthcare transaction or valuation engagement, the market approach needs to be considered in the light of these definitions found in the Stark regulations.*

> Fair market value means the value in arm's-length transactions consistent with general market value. "General market value" means the price that an asset would bring as the result of bona fide bargaining between well-informed buyers and sellers who are not otherwise in a position to generate business for the other party or the compensation that would be included in a service agreement as a result of bona fide bargaining between well-informed parties to the agreement who are not otherwise in a position to generate business for the other party, on the date of acquisition or at the time of the service agreement. Usually the fair market price is the price at which bona fide sales have been consummated for assets of like type, quality, and quantity in a particular market at the time of acquisition.... (420 CFR 411.351)
>
> Moreover, the definition of fair market value in the statute and regulation is qualified in ways that do not necessarily comport with the usage of the term in standard valuation techniques and methodologies. For example, the methodology must exclude valuations where the parties to the transactions are at arm's length but in a position to refer to one another. (69 *Fed. Reg.* 16053)

*The jurisdictional exception should also be considered with respect to the types of normalization adjustments that are considered in the income approach, given the above statement that the well-informed buyers and sellers are not otherwise in a position "to generate business for the other party."*

*A simple example of this can be seen in a comparison of a generic commercial lease with a commercial lease subject to Stark. A Dunkin' Donuts store located inside a Home Depot would expect to pay rent based upon the customer traffic in the Home Depot. Typical leases provide for a percentage of revenues in such a circumstance. In stark contrast (pun intended), a lease of space for an MRI and CT scan center in a medical office building occupied by neurologists and orthopedic surgeons could not consider the fact that those two medical specialties are the highest users of such testing. The lease would have to reflect only the real estate value, not the patient referrals from the physicians, and a percentage of revenue certainly could not be charged.*

One additional exemption provided in the AICPA business valuation standard is from the reporting section of the standard for litigation or for certain controversy proceedings. As such, a valuation performed for a matter before a court, an arbitrator, a mediator, or other facilitator or a matter in a governmental or administrative proceeding is exempt from the reporting provisions of the standard. The developmental provisions of the statement still apply.

Two types of engagements are permitted under the AICPA business valuation standard. These are the valuation engagement and the calculation engagement.

Under a valuation engagement, the valuation practitioner is free to apply any valuation approaches and methods deemed appropriate in the circumstances. This engagement is said to be unrestricted. The result of the engagement is expressed as a conclusion of value and may be either a single amount or a range.

Under a calculation engagement, the valuation practitioner and the client agree on the valuation approaches and methods and the extent of the procedures the practitioner will perform in the process of calculating the value of the subject interest. The result of the calculation engagement is expressed as a calculated value and may be either a single amount or a range. It is important to note that a calculation engagement does not include all of the procedures that would be required in a valuation engagement.

The developmental provisions of the standard cover the three most common approaches to valuation, namely the income-based approach, the asset-based approach, and the market-based approach.

The reporting provisions of the standard permit flexibility in reporting. Under the valuation engagement, the provided written reports may either be a detailed report or a summary report. The detailed written report is structured to provide sufficient information to permit intended users to understand the data, the reasoning, and the analysis underlying the valuation practitioner's conclusion of value. The standard provides items that are to be included in the detailed report. A summary report is an abridged version of a detailed report. It is not intended to provide all of the detail but will still convey a description of the work done and the conclusions of value reached.

Under a calculation engagement, a calculation report is permitted. The calculation report is intended to convey an understanding of the approaches and methodology used in the calculation and to identify the calculated value.

Regardless of the type of engagement, each report is required to contain a valuation analyst's representation, a summary of assumptions and limiting conditions, and a statement of qualifications of the valuation analyst.

Oral reports are permitted for both valuation engagements and calculation engagements.

The AICPA business valuation standard also included four appendices. One appendix includes an illustrative list of assumptions and limiting conditions, a second includes the *International Glossary of Business Valuation Terms*, a third includes a supplemental glossary of business valuation terms from the CPA's perspective, and the fourth appendix includes Interpretation No. 1-01, which contains questions and answers related to practice issues dealing with the standard. The interpretation carries the same force and effect as the standard and has sections related to general areas of practice, tax engagements, personal financial planning engagements, and other engagements.

The Valuation Standards subcommittee of the AICPA Business Valuation committee monitors the standard and from time to time, issues updates and questions and answers related to the standard and practice under the standard. The standard can be downloaded from the AICPA Web Site at aicpa.org.

In a memorandum released May 13, 2008, the AICPA Valuation Standards subcommittee ruled that **statements on standards for valuation services** (SSVS) do not apply to the following valuation engagements:

- Professional or executive compensation;
- Rental rate on equipment or real estate;
- Contractual price for professional or other services; and
- Transfer price for goods and services between a for-profit entity and a not-for-profit entity.

The subcommittee made this decision on the basis that the above were not intangible assets. It is important to point out that a valuation analyst could be engaged to value a specific intangible asset, such as an employment contract or an equipment lease, as opposed to expressing an opinion on the market value of services and goods. Such valuation of intangible assets would be subject to SSVS.

## USPAP Standards

The USPAP are a product of the Appraisal Standards Board of the Appraisal Foundation. The AF was formed as part of the FIRREA Act in the late 1980s. It was part of Congress' response to the savings and loan crisis of the 1980s.

The AF has a central board and two standing boards, the Appraiser Qualifications Board and the Appraisal Standards Board. The Appraiser Qualifications Board was primarily responsible for authoring the regulations used by the states in the early 1990s in the process of registering real estate appraisers.

The Appraisal Standards Board is primarily responsible for publishing the USPAP and providing periodic updates to these standards.

There are 10 USPAP Standards and a number of published advisory opinions. Of the 10 original standards, Standards 1 to 6 relate to real estate appraisal, Standards 7 and 8 relate to development and reporting of a personal property appraisal, and Standards 9 and 10 relate to development and reporting of a business valuation. In recent years, the application of Standard 3, appraisal review development and reporting, has been extended beyond real estate appraisal to personal property appraising and to business valuation. Standard 3 contains the work to be done in evaluating the work and the report of another appraiser and issuing a report thereon.

Of the USPAP standards, Standard 9 deals with the development of a business appraisal, and Standard 10 deals with reporting the result of the business appraisal. Within each standard, USPAP utilizes what it terms "rules" to expand on the standard itself. For example, in Standard 9, the standard proper states:

> In developing an appraisal of an interest in a business enterprise or intangible asset, an appraiser must identify the problem to be solved, determine the scope of work necessary to solve the problem, and correctly complete the research and analysis necessary to produce a credible appraisal.

This generic statement is followed by rules that provide the specifics. The rules, for example, require that the appraiser "be aware of, understand, and correctly employ those recognized approaches, methods, and procedures that are necessary to produce a credible appraisal; not commit a substantial error of omission or commission that significantly affects an appraisal; and not render appraisal services in a careless or negligent manner, such as by making a series of errors that, although individually might not significantly affect the results of an appraisal, in the aggregate affect the credibility of those results."

Like the AICPA standards, the USPAP standards identify the intended user and use of the appraisal and determine the scope of the work necessary to produce a credible appraisal and then require the appraiser to perform the appraisal in conformity with the scope of work so determined.

Chapter 10 covers business appraisal reporting. Again, the standard begins with a generic paragraph describing what needs to be done:

> In reporting the results of an appraisal of an interest in a business enterprise or intangible asset, an appraiser must communicate each analysis, opinion, and conclusion in a manner that is not misleading.

The generic standard is followed by rules that provide the detail related to the standard. These rules provide for a written or oral report that must: "clearly and accurately set forth the appraisal in a manner that is not misleading; contain sufficient information to enable the intended user(s) to understand the report; and clearly and accurately disclose all assumptions, extraordinary assumptions, hypothetical conditions, and limiting conditions used in the assignment." Other rules discuss the content to be included in the appraisal report and the limitations on its use.

*Editor's note: The aforementioned Stark restrictions on the market approach often make it inapplicable. Standards Rule 10-2 requires that any exclusion of an approach be explained.*

Standard 3 covers "appraisal review, development, and reporting." The generic description used in Standard 3 is:

> In performing an appraisal review assignment, an appraiser acting as a reviewer must develop and report a credible opinion as to the quality of another appraiser's work and must clearly disclose the scope of the work performed.

The rules for Standard 3 provide the detail procedures for performing and reporting a review of another appraiser's work.

In addition to the respective rules for each standard, the Appraiser Standards Board of the Appraisal Foundation from time to time issues advisory opinions. These advisory opinions do not establish new standards or interpret standards. They illustrate specific situations and offer advice from the Appraisal Standards Board.

The USPAP standards are the only American standards that cover multiple disciplines. They contain standards for real estate appraising, personal property appraising, and business valuation. One of the criticisms leveled at these standards is that they are multidisciplinary and so real estate and personal property appraisers who are members of the Appraisal Standards Board are voting and deciding on standards for appraising that is not in their area of expertise (business valuation, for example). The USPAP standards must be followed when preparing appraisal reports for certain governmental agencies that have adopted USPAP. The Internal Revenue Service is not an agency that has adopted USPAP. The ASA is the only business valuation credentialing organization whose members are required to follow USPAP.

## American Society of Appraisers Business Valuation Standards

The ASA business valuation standards are prepared by its business valuation standards committee. The chairmanship of this committee moves on a two-year rotating basis. Although the ASA is a multidisciplinary organization, the business valuation standards are prepared by business valuation practitioners. This differs from USPAP, where preparation of the standards is the responsibility of the Appraisal Standards Board. Members of this board may be from any of the three appraisal disciplines and may vote on the standards designed for any of the other disciplines.

There are eight sections to the Introduction to the ASA business valuation standards. These include:

Section 1 – Introduction

1. Describes ASA as a multidisciplinary organization
2. Defines appraisal practice and property
   a. Appraisal practice applies to any of the following four items:
      - Determination of the value of property;
      - Forecasting of the earning power of property;
      - Estimation of the cost of:
        - Production of a new property;
        - Replacement of an existing property by purchase or production of an equivalent property;
        - Reproduction of an existing property by purchase or production of an identical property;
        - Determining nonmonetary benefits or characteristics that contribute to value.

   b. The term "property" is used to describe the rights to the future benefits of something owned or possessed to the exclusion of others.
3. Notes that the Principles of Appraisal Practice and the Code of Ethics are promulgated to:
   a. Inform those who use the services of appraisers what, in the opinion of the ASA, constitutes competent and ethical appraisal practice.

   b. Serve as a guide to ASA members in achieving competency and adhering to ethical standards.

c. To aid in accomplishing the purposes of the ASA, which include:

- Fosterage of appraisal education.
- Improvement and development of appraisal techniques.
- Encouragement of sound professional practices.
- Establishment of criteria of sound performance for use of employers of staff appraisers.
- Epitomize those appraisal practices that experience has found to be effective in protecting the public against exploitation.

Section 2 of the introduction describes the objectives of appraisal work, including:

1. The various objectives of appraisal work.
2. The objective character of the results of an appraisal engagement.

Section 2 focuses on the objectivity required of the appraiser and of the final result.

Section 3 of the introduction details the appraiser's primary duties and responsibilities generally. These include:

1. The appraiser's obligation to determine and to describe the apposite kind of value or estimated cost.
2. The appraiser's obligation to determine numerical results with whatever degree of accuracy the particular objectives of the engagement necessitate.
3. The appraiser's obligation to avoid giving a false numerical result.
4. The appraiser's obligation to attain competency and to practice ethically.
5. The professional character of appraisal practice.
6. The appraiser's fiduciary relationship to third parties.

Section 4 of the introduction section restates the appraiser's obligations to his or her client. These include:

1. The confidential character of an appraisal engagement.
2. The appraiser's obligation to provide competent service.
3. The appraiser's obligation relative to giving testimony.
4. The appraiser's obligation to document appraisal testimony.

5. Clarification of the appraiser's obligation to serving more than one client in the same matter.

6. Discussion of a written contract for appraisal services.

Section 5 of the introduction covers the appraiser's obligation to other appraisers and to the ASA. These include:

1. Protecting the professional reputation of other appraisers.
2. The appraiser's obligation relative to the ASA's disciplinary actions.

Section 6 discusses various appraisal practices and methods including:

1. Various kinds of value.
2. Selection of the appraisal method.
3. Fractional appraisals.
4. Contingent and limiting conditions affecting an appraisal.
5. Hypothetical appraisals.
6. Appraisals in which access to pertinent data is denied.
7. Ranges of value or estimated cost and reliability estimates.
8. Values or estimated costs under different hypotheses.
9. Inspection, investigation, analysis, and description of the subject property.
10. Collaboration between appraisers and utilization of the services of members of other professions.

Section 7 discusses unethical and unprofessional appraisal practices including:

1. Contingent fees deemed to be unethical.
2. Percentage fees based on the amount of the value.
3. Disinterested appraisal—the appraiser has no vested interest.
4. Responsibility connected with signatures to appraisal reports.
5. Nonadvocacy.
6. Unconsidered opinions and preliminary reports.
7. Advertising and solicitation.
8. Misuse of membership designations.
9. Causes for disciplinary action by the ASA.

Section 8 discusses the items to be included in a quality appraisal report including:

1. Description of the property that is the subject of an appraisal report.
2. Statement of the objectives of the appraisal work.
3. Statement of the contingent and limiting conditions to which the appraisal finding is subject.
4. Description and explanation of the appraisal method used.
5. Statement of the appraiser's disinterestedness.
6. Appraiser's responsibility to communicate each analysis, opinion, and conclusion in a manner that is not misleading.
7. Mandatory recertification statement.
8. Signatures to appraisal reports and the inclusion of dissenting opinions.

In the general preamble to the standards, the ASA business valuation standards take the following action:

1. The principles of appraisal practice and the code of ethics of the ASA and the USPAP standards are incorporated by reference.
2. There is an affirmative statement that these standards represent the minimum criteria to be followed by business appraisers in developing and reporting the valuation of a business, business ownership interest, and securities.
3. Deviation from the standard should not create any assumption that a legal duty has been breached.

Having put all of this information on the record, the ASA moves to the eight BVS standards, which include:

- BVS I—General requirements for developing a business valuation

    1. Preamble.
    2. Appropriate definition of the assignment.
    3. Information collection and analysis.
    4. Approaches, methods, and procedures.
    5. Documentation and retention.
    6. Reporting.

BVS I describes the general requirements for developing a business valuation and includes the items the appraiser must identify and define, the scope of the work, and the types of appraisals that are available under the ASA standards. These would include the appraisal, the limited appraisal, and calculations. The information collection and analysis section generally follows the guidelines in Revenue Ruling 59-60.

- BVS II—Financial Statement Adjustments

    1. Preamble.
    2. Conceptual framework.
    3. Documentation of adjustments.

BVS II describes the potential adjustments to the financial statements. It defines the adjustments as modifications to the financial information that are relevant and significant to the appraisal process. The standard notes that all adjustments should be fully described and supported.

- BVS III—Asset-Based Approach to Business Valuation

    1. Preamble.
    2. The asset-based approach.

BVS III generally describes the asset approach to business valuation as the value of the assets less the value of the liabilities. The standard makes the affirmative statement that the asset-based approach should not be the sole appraisal approach for an operating company unless this approach is customarily used by buyers and sellers.

- BVS IV—Income Approach to Business Valuation

    1. Preamble.
    2. The income approach.
    3. Anticipated benefits.
    4. Conversion of anticipated benefits.

BVS IV generally describes the income approach to business valuation. It notes that both the capitalization of benefits and the discounted future benefits methods are acceptable. It describes the process of converting a stream of anticipated benefits to value.

- BVS V—Market Approach to Business Valuation
    1. Preamble.
    2. The market approach.
    3. Reasonable basis for comparison.
    4. Selection of valuation ratios.
    5. Rules of thumb.

BVS V generally describes the market approach to business valuation. It notes that this method includes both the guideline public company method and the analysis of prior transactions in the ownership of the subject company method. It emphasizes that the valuation ratios should be meaningful given all of the relevant factors.

- BVS VI—Reaching a Conclusion of Value
    1. Preamble.
    2. General.
    3. Selection and weighting of methods.
    4. Additional factors to consider.

BVS VI describes the process the appraiser should use in determining a conclusion of value following completion of the appraisal work. The selection and reliance on the methods used will depend on the facts and circumstances of the case. The appraiser will use informed judgment to determine the relative weight to be accorded to each valuation method used.

- BVS VII—Valuation Discounts and Premiums
    1. Preamble.
    2. The concepts of discounts and premiums.
    3. The application of discounts and premiums.

BVS VII covers modification of the computed appraised value through the use of discounts or premiums as appropriate. It attaches significant importance to the conceptual basis underlying the application of a discount or premium. It emphasizes that discounts and premiums come into play when there is a difference between the base value and value of the subject interest. When discounts and premiums are appropriate, the rationale accompanying them should be thoroughly explained.

- BVS VIII—Comprehensive Written Business Valuation Reports

    1. Preamble.
    2. Signature and certification.
    3. Assumptions and limiting conditions.
    4. Definition of the valuation assignment.
    5. Business description.
    6. Financial analysis.
    7. Valuation methodology.
    8. Comprehensive written business valuation report format.
    9. Confidentiality of the report.

BVS VIII covers the written business valuation report. Similar to USPAP and the AICPA business valuation standards, it requires that the report contain the listing of assumptions and limiting conditions and that the certification (representation in the AICPA standards) be signed by at least one individual responsible for the valuation conclusion. The standard goes on to describe generally the items to be included in the written report, including Items 4 through 8 above. It concludes with a comment on the confidentiality of the report, which is similar to the restricted use provisions of the AICPA and USPAP standards.

- BVS IX—Intangible Asset Valuation

    1. Preamble.
    2. Principles.
    3. Valuation methodology.
    4. Factors.

BVS IX covers the methodology to be followed in all valuations of intangible assets by ASA members. "This standard applies to appraisals and may not necessarily apply to limited appraisals and calculations as defined in BVS-1…." The standard describes the valuation approaches that should be considered in valuing intangible assets including the income approach, the market approach, and the cost approach. It also defines certain factors that the appraiser should consider in the valuation of an intangible asset.

Appendix A to BVS-IX provides definitions and examples of intellectual property including patents, trade secrets, trademarks, and copyrighted works. It also provides additional factors the appraiser should consider within each category of intellectual property.

The nine standards are followed and embellished by a glossary and two statements on business valuation standards: one on the guideline company valuation method and one on the merger and acquisition market method. These two statements have the full effect of standards.

Lastly, the ASA standards have advisory opinions and procedural guidelines that supplement the information contained in the standards.

### National Association of Certified Valuation Analysts

The NACVA is an organization of certified public accountants and other valuation professionals who perform valuation services. It is based in Salt Lake City, Utah and provides business valuation and consulting technical education to its membership. Because many of its members are CPAs, the business valuation standards committee of NACVA conformed its standards to the AICPA standards when they became effective. Although structured in a slightly different manner, the underlying principles and their impact on valuation practitioners is very similar to that of the AICPA standards.

The NACVA standards consist of six standard sections and an appendix. The appendix contains the *International Glossary of Business Valuation Terms*, which was a collaborative effort among a number of business valuation credentialing organizations including the AICPA, the ASA, the NACVA, the IBA, and the Canadian Institute of Chartered Business Valuators (CICBV).

Section 1—Preamble and General and Ethical Standards

1. Preamble—All members shall comply with these standards.
2. General and ethical standards—Members shall perform their work in compliance with the code of professional conduct, which includes:

   a. Integrity and objectivity.

   b. Professional competence.

c. Due professional care.

d. Understandings and communications with clients.

e. Planning and supervision.

f. Sufficient relevant data.

g. Confidentiality.

h. No commission of acts discreditable to the profession.

i. Client interest.

j. Financial interest in the property being valued (if any).

Section 1 is the overview and identifies the general and ethical standards that NACVA members are required to observe.

Section 2—Member Services

1. Valuation services.

    a. Valuation engagement.

    b. Calculation engagement.

2. Other services.

Section 2 describes the two types of valuation services that a NACVA member may perform: a valuation engagement and a calculation engagement. It further describes that a member may perform other services including consulting, fraud, damage determinations, and other nonvaluation services.

Section 3—Development Standards

1. General.
2. Expression of value.
3. Identification of the assignment and the scope of the work.
4. Fundamental analysis.
5. Scope limitations.
6. Use of specialists.

7. Valuation approaches and methods.
8. Rules of thumb.
9. Financial statement adjustments.
10. Earnings determination.
11. Capitalization and discount rate.
12. Marketability, control, and other premiums and discounts.
13. Documentation.

Section 3 presents the development standards and represents the key developmental elements. Similar to the AICPA standards, the NACVA standards indicate that the value may be represented as a single value or as a range of values.

Section 4—Reporting Standards

1. General.
2. Form of report.
3. Contents of report.
   a. Summary reports.
   b. Detailed reports.
   c. Calculation reports.
   d. Statement that the report is in conformity with NACVA standards.
4. Litigation engagement reporting standards.

Section 4 describes the reporting standard. It specifies that the report may be given in writing or orally and should be appropriate for the circumstances of the engagement. The standard suggests that the wording used in the report should effectively communicate important thoughts, methods, and reasoning and identify supporting documentation in a simple and concise manner. This section provides an exemption from the reporting portion of the standard for certain controversy proceedings, including matters before a court, an arbitrator, a mediator, or other facilitator or a matter in a governmental or administrative proceeding.

Section 5—Other Guidelines and Requirements

1. Other organizations whose guidelines may require compliance:

   a. Department of Labor (DOL).

   b. Internal Revenue Service (IRS).

   c. Applicable court rules.

   d. Federal and state laws.

   e. The Appraisal Foundation (USPAP).

   f. Financial Accounting Standards Board (FASB).

2. International Glossary of Business Valuation Terms.

Section 5 alerts the NACVA member to other organizations whose rules and regulations may require compliance depending upon the nature of the assignment.

Section 6—Effective Date

Section 6 indicates that these standards are effective for engagements accepted on or after Jan. 1, 2008.

## Conclusion

While each of these standards contains certain idiosyncrasies, the differences relate primarily to the membership to whom they are addressed. For example, the AICPA standards are directed toward CPAs. Many of the NACVA members are also CPAs, and both of these standards are written with language and understanding common to CPAs. The business valuation section of USPAP and the ASA business valuation standards are written within the context of an appraiser. The language and the references are directed in that manner.

Overall, there may be differences in terminology, but the thrust of each of these standards is clear. They are directed toward assisting the members of each of the respective organizations in performing a credible business valuation and accurately reporting the results of their work to clients and other appropriate parties.

Chapter 7

# The Anti-Kickback Statute and Stark Law: Avoiding Valuation of Referrals

*By James M. Pinna, Esq. and Matthew D. Jenkins, JD*

The federal anti-kickback statute, 42 U.S.C. § 1320a-7b(b), sets forth the general principle that healthcare providers cannot exchange remuneration in return for referrals of federal healthcare program business. The federal physician self-referral law or Stark Law, 42 U.S.C. § 1395nn, incorporates a similar principle by prohibiting certain physician referrals to entities that physicians have compensation arrangements with unless the arrangement meets an applicable exception by, among other things, not providing compensation based on the volume or value of referrals by the physician. The fundamental prohibition on providing remuneration in return for referrals exemplified in these two statutes has important consequences in the valuation context and requires that healthcare providers and their advisors be careful to avoid ascribing value to prior or anticipated referrals when structuring transactions involving healthcare providers. This chapter explores the framework created by the anti-kickback statute and the Stark Law and some of the specific valuation contexts in which healthcare providers and their advisors should be attentive to avoiding the attribution of value to referrals.

## The Anti-Kickback Statute

The anti-kickback statute prohibits the knowing and willful offer, payment, solicitation, or receipt of "any remuneration (including any kickback, bribe, or rebate) directly or indirectly, overtly or covertly, in cash or in kind," to induce or reward referrals of items or services reimbursable by a federal healthcare program.[1] In addition to criminal penalties, violations of the anti-kickback statute can lead to the imposition of civil sanctions and administrative exclusion from participation in federal healthcare programs (which carries a lower burden of proof than that which is required to sustain a criminal conviction). To prove a violation of the anti-kickback statute, the government must show that an entity: "(a) knowingly and willfully; and (b) with the intent to induce the referral of federal healthcare program business solicited, received, offered, or paid remuneration."[2] Courts have interpreted the anti-kickback statute to prohibit arrangements if one purpose of the arrangement is the inducement of referrals of federal healthcare program patients, regardless of whether there are other appropriate purposes for the arrangement.[3]

Investment and compensation arrangements between healthcare providers should be structured in a manner that does not ascribe value to referrals of federal healthcare program business to avoid implicating the anti-kickback statute. Several courts, as well as the Office of Inspector General of the Department of health and Human Services (OIG), have indicated that certain facts and circumstances in such arrangements, such as paying greater than fair market value for services or items, can support an inference that improper remuneration is being paid to induce referrals.[4] When structuring and valuing investment and compensation arrangements, healthcare providers and their advisors should look to guidance provided by the OIG and court decisions to identify

1 42 U.S.C. § 1320a-7b(b). A "federal healthcare program" includes any plan or program that provides health benefits, whether directly, through insurance, or otherwise, which are funded directly, in whole, or in part by the federal government. 42 U.S.C. § 1320a-7b(f).

2 *Hanlester Network v. Shalala*, 51 F.3d 1390, 1397-1400 (9th Cir. 1995).

3 *United States v. Greber*, 760 F.2d 68 (3d Cir. 1985), cert. denied, 474 U.S. 988 (1985).

4 See *United States v. Lipkis*, 770 F.2d 1447 (9th Cir. 1985) (Noting that the fair market value of services provided under an arrangement was substantially less than the compensation received, and there is no question that there was payment for the referrals as well as the described services); *United States ex rel. Constantino Perales v. St. Margaret's Hospital*, 243 F. Supp. 2d 843, 851 (C.D. Ill. 2003) (Indicating that payment in excess of fair market value for a physician practice may create an inference of improper remuneration); *United States ex rel. Obert-Hong v. Advocate Health Care*, 211 F. Supp. 2d 1045, 1049 (N.D. Ill. 2002) (Indicating that payment in excess of fair market value for a physician practice may create an inference of improper remuneration); *OIG Special Fraud Alert: "Arrangements for the Provision of Clinical Laboratory Services"* (Issued October 1994), republished at 59 Fed. Reg. 65372 (Dec. 19, 1994) (Whenever a laboratory offers or gives to a source of referrals anything of value not paid for at fair market value, the inference may be made that the thing of value is offered to induce the referral of business. The same is true whenever a referral source solicits or receives anything of value from the laboratory. By "fair market value," we mean value for general commercial purposes. However, fair market value must reflect an arms-length transaction that has not been adjusted to include the additional value that one or both of the parties has attributed to the referral of business between them); Letter from D. McCarty Thornton, Associate General Counsel, OIG to T.J. Sullivan, Technical Assistant, Office of the Associate Chief Counsel, Employee Benefits and Exempt Organizations dated December 22, 1992 (available at oig.hhs.gov/fraud/docs/safeharborregulations/acquisition122292.htm) (Indicating that payment in excess of fair market value may create an inference of improper remuneration); *OIG Supplemental Compliance Program Guidance for Hospitals*, 70 Fed. Reg. 4858, 4866 (Jan. 31, 2005) (Arrangements under which hospitals (a) provide physicians with items or services for free or less than fair market value; (2) relieve physicians of financial obligations they would otherwise incur; or (3) inflate compensation paid to physicians for items or services pose significant risk. In such circumstances, an inference arises that the remuneration may be in exchange for generating business).

what could be considered improper remuneration for referrals and how to structure their arrangements to avoid problematic remuneration.

**Remuneration**. Health care providers and their advisors should first understand what could be considered improper remuneration under the anti-kickback statute. In plain English, the term "remunerate" is defined as "to pay an equivalent for."[5] Congress used the term "any remuneration" in the anti-kickback statute to more broadly capture various forms of value that may be traded in exchange for referrals to strengthen the capability of the government to detect, prosecute, and punish fraudulent activities under the Medicare and Medicaid programs.[6] The language "directly or indirectly, overtly or covertly, in cash or in kind" makes clear that the form or manner of remuneration can include indirect, covert, and in-kind transactions. Courts have held that remuneration encompasses both traditional kickback payments, where no actual service was performed, as well as payments for which some service was performed.[7] The fact that Congress included a specific exception for discounts under the anti-kickback statute demonstrates that it otherwise extends even to arrangements where there is no direct payment at all from the party receiving referrals.

Even the mere opportunity to earn profits can constitute improper remuneration to induce referrals. For instance, giving a person the opportunity to generate consulting or service fees, even if those fees are the result of actual services provided, could potentially constitute improper remuneration if coupled with an improper intent to induce referrals.[8] The ability to generate a fee could also potentially constitute

5 Merriam-Webster Online Dictionary (2011).

6 See H.R. Rep. No. 95-393, Pt. II, 95th Cong., 1st Sess. 53 *reprinted in* 1977 U.S.C.C.A.N. 3039, 3056; *Medicare and State Health Care Programs: Fraud and Abuse; OIG Anti-Kickback Provisions*, 56 Fed. Reg. 35952, 35958 (July 29, 1991) (Congress' intent in placing the term "remuneration" in the statute in 1977 was to cover the transferring of anything of value in any form or manner whatsoever. The statute's language makes clear that illegal payments are prohibited beyond merely "bribes," "kickbacks," and "rebates," which were the three terms used in the original 1972 statute); Hanlester Network, 51 F.3d at 1398 (Noting that the phrase "any remuneration" was intended to broaden the reach of the law that previously referred only to kickbacks, bribes, and rebates); Greber, 760 F.2d at 71 (Indicating that Congress included "any remuneration" to make it clear that even if the transaction was not considered to be a "kickback" for which no service had been rendered, payment could nevertheless violate the statute).

7 *Greber*, 760 F.2d at 71; *United States v. Bay State Ambulance and Hospital Rental Service, Inc.*, 874 F.2d 20, 30 (1st Cir. 1989).

8 See *Bay State Ambulance*, 874 F.2d at 29 (Court acknowledged that opportunity to earn consulting fees could constitute improper remuneration, rejecting defendant's argument that consulting fees had to be of substantially more value than services performed to constitute illegal remuneration and upholding jury instruction indicating that payments could be illegal remuneration if they were made with improper purpose); *Medicare and State Health Care Programs: Fraud and Abuse; Clarification of the Initial OIG Safe Harbor Provisions and Establishment of Additional Safe Harbor Provisions Under the Anti-Kickback Statute*, 64 Fed. Reg. 63518, 63548 (Nov. 19, 1999) (Noting that the opportunity to split a global fee may constitute something of value to a referring party apart from any payment for the referral, such as where an optometrist and ophthalmologist network refers patients for cataract surgery only to ophthalmologists who agree to split the global surgical fee by referring patients back to the optometrist for post-operative care).

improper remuneration when an existing supplier of a healthcare service (e.g., a lab company or radiation therapy center) contracts to supply those services to a provider in a position to refer business (e.g., a physician group) that can then bill and collect fees for business typically provided by the existing supplier.[9] Additionally, the OIG has taken the position that the mere opportunity to invest in a joint venture (and consequently receive profit distributions) may in certain circumstances constitute improper remuneration if offered in exchange for past or anticipated referrals.[10]

As indicated by the examples discussed above, healthcare providers should bear in mind that potentially problematic remuneration may take many forms, including: (a) payments or kickbacks for referrals where no services are performed in return; (b) payments for which some services or items was were provided in return; (c) discounts or rebates off the price of an item or service received; or (d) the opportunity to earn profits by generating fees for services or receiving distributions from an investment.

**Fair Market Value**. One of the primary means to ensure there is no remuneration for referrals in an arrangement is to make sure that the parties pay or receive fair market value in exchange for the items or services provided. Some of the most commonly cited instances of potentially improper remuneration are where a party provides items or services to another party for more or less than fair market value or provides an inappropriate discount or premium to the fair market value purchase price of an investment interest. For example, in the context of purchasing physician practices, courts have held that "to the extent that a payment exceeds the fair market value of the practice, or the value of the services, it can be inferred that the excess amount paid over fair market value is intended as payment for the referral of program-related business."[11] Conversely, it can be argued that when the amount paid for services, items, or investment interests is fair market value, there is a presumption that there is no remuneration in exchange for referrals because the amount paid is solely attributable to the service,

9 *OIG Special Advisory Bulletin on Contractual Joint Ventures*, 68 Fed. Reg. 23148 (April 30, 2003); see also OIG Advisory Opinion No. 04-17 (Dec. 10, 2004); OIG Advisory Opinion No. 08-10 (Aug. 19, 2008) (Noting that arrangement where intensity-modulated radiation therapy facility block leases time to urologists who then bill Medicare for the professional and technical components could potentially result in problematic remuneration to the urologists in the form of the difference between the fees collected and the fixed amounts to be paid to the facility under the block lease arrangement).

10 OIG Advisory Opinion No. 98-19 (Dec. 14, 1998); OIG Advisory Opinion No. 97-5 (Oct. 6, 1997).

11 *Perales*, 243 F. Supp. 2d at 849; Obert-Hong, 211 F. Supp. 2d at 1049.

item, or investment interest provided.[12] Note, however, that the OIG has not chosen to provide safe harbor protection to all arrangements that are consistent with fair market value, but rather only a small subset of such arrangements, and the OIG has taken the position that fair market value alone will not insulate an arrangement from violating the anti-kickback statute.[13]

When considering the question of fair market value in the context of healthcare transactions, traditional methods of economic valuation may not always comport with the proscriptions of the anti-kickback statute. For example, parties unfamiliar with the limitations imposed by the anti-kickback statute might normally expect the purchase price for a physician practice acquisition by a hospital to account for potential revenues from anticipated referrals by the selling physician to the hospital for nonphysician services. However, the anti-kickback statute dictates that anticipated referrals to the hospital must be excluded from the calculation of a fair market value purchase price.[14] The safe harbor regulations under the anti-kickback statute also dictate that for purposes of determining the value of space or equipment rentals, "fair market value" is specifically defined to exclude the additional value one party would attribute to the property or equipment as a result of its proximity or convenience to sources of referrals (such as the added value a hospital places on having referring physicians located in a medical building the hospital owns on its property).[15] Additionally, parties should be careful in evaluating comparable market data in healthcare transactions. Merely because another buyer is willing to pay a particular price does not mean the price is fair market value especially if the price offered attributes value to referrals expected to result from the arrangement. Thus, in a market where physician practice acquisition activity is strong, those involved in structuring a transaction should be alert to the risks posed by relying on uninformed pronouncements of the "going rate" as a reliable indication of fair market value in the context of the anti-kickback statute.

12 See Letter from D. McCarty Thornton (Noting the importance of fair market value in the context of physician practice acquisitions and stating that "it is necessary to consider the amounts paid for the practice or as compensation to determine whether they reasonably reflect the fair market value of the practice or the services rendered, to determine whether such items in reality constitute remuneration for referrals"); *United States ex rel. Goodstein v. McLaren*, 202 F. Supp. 2d 671 (E.D. Mich. 2002) (Holding that a lease for medical office space was based on fair market value and not remuneration for referrals of Medicaid patients to the defendant based on applying the statutory allowances for lessee and lessor relationships); U.S. ex rel. Obert-Hong, 211 F. Supp.2d at 1049 (Holding that "the Anti-Kickback Act does not prohibit hospitals from acquiring medical practices, nor does it preclude the seller-doctor from making future referrals to the buyer-hospital, provided there are no economic inducements for those referrals. To comply with the statute, the hospital must simply pay fair market value for the practice's assets").

13 70 Fed. Reg. at 4864 (Neither a legitimate business purpose for the arrangement, nor a fair market value payment, will legitimize a payment if there is also an illegal purpose to induce federal healthcare program business).

14 *Obert-Hong*, 211 F. Supp.2d at 1049.

15 42 C.F.R. § 1001.952(b) and (c); 56 Fed. Reg. at 35971-73.

**Investment Arrangements.** The OIG has provided guidance as to appropriate structures for investment arrangements by creating safe harbors that protect certain types of investment interests and provide that the distributions related to such investment interests will not constitute "remuneration" under the anti-kickback statute when all of the safe harbor requirements are satisfied.[16] These safe harbors contain two common requirements that are important to consider in the valuation context: (a) terms on which an investment interest is offered to an investor must not be related to previous or expected volume of referrals, and (b) payment to an investor in return for the investment interest must be directly proportional to the capital investment of that investor.[17]

The OIG has provided further guidance on investment arrangements in its Special Fraud Alerts identifying problematic features that could result in a business arrangement that violates the anti-kickback statute.[18] In the OIG's view, these improper investment arrangements are not intended "to raise investment capital legitimately to start a business, but to lock up a stream of referrals from the physician investors and to compensate them indirectly for these referrals."[19] Two of the "questionable features" identified by the OIG as potential indicators of a "suspect joint venture" are: (a) the amount of capital invested by the physician is "disproportionately small" and the returns on investment may be "disproportionately large" when compared to a typical investment in a new business enterprise; and (b) investors may be paid what the OIG terms "extraordinary returns" on the investment in comparison with the risk involved, often well over "50% to 100% per year."[20]

One of the key principles in the guidance on investment arrangements from the OIG is that the amount of payment to each investor must be directly proportional to capital invested. The OIG has issued two separate advisory opinions related to investment in surgery centers that have created some confusion as to what the OIG considers to be disproportionate returns to investors and whether valuation of intangible assets could be construed as attributing value to investor referrals.

In Advisory Opinion 07-05, the OIG took the surprising position that a hospital's purchase of ownership interests in an existing surgery center for fair market value from certain physician owners could potentially generate prohibited remuneration under the federal anti-kickback statute.[21] This result turned in part on the fact that the hospital and

16 42 C.F.R. § 1001.952(a) and (r).
17 *Id.*
18 OIG Special Fraud Alert: Joint Venture Arrangements (Issued August 1989), republished in 59 Fed. Reg. 65372 (Dec. 19, 1994).
19 *Id.*
20 *Id.*
21 OIG Advisory Opinion No. 07-05 (June 12, 2007).

the physicians would not receive investment returns directly proportional to the dollar amount of their invested capital (although returns would be directly proportional to percentage ownership interests) because the price paid for investment interests by the hospital (as a later investor) would be higher (due to appreciation in value) than price originally paid for investment interests by the physicians.

The position taken by the OIG in Advisory Opinion 07-05 stands in stark contrast to its position in Advisory Opinion 01-21, which concluded that the distribution of profit and losses in direct proportion to each investor's percentage of equity ownership in a surgery center (as opposed to original capital investment) does not increase the risk of fraud and abuse, even though it does prevent the arrangement from meeting the anti-kickback statute safe harbor for surgery centers.[22] In fact, the OIG explained in Advisory Opinion 01-21 that there was a reasonable basis for different prices paid by later investors, namely, the appreciation in value of the surgery center over time. The sale of ownership interests in an existing surgery center must occur at fair market value to avoid an inference of improper remuneration to the purchaser or seller, and the OIG could not possibly condone a later investor paying the same price as an original investor when such price is below fair market value due to subsequent appreciation in the value of the underlying security. It should also be noted that when the OIG originally established the safe harbor for investment interests, it explained that "to receive protection, dividend payments can only be tied to the number of shares owned by an investor, and not to his or her referrals," an acknowledgment that dividends are tied to shares of ownership interest held rather than the amount of capital invested.[23] Advisory Opinion 07-05 may be distinguished, however, based on the unique concerns raised by the OIG that the investment by the hospital appeared to be intended to allow specific physician investors to realize a gain on their investment, raising the possibility that the hospital's investment was intended to influence the referrals of those selected physicians.

In Advisory Opinion 09-09, the OIG took the position that the independent development of two surgery centers by a hospital and a group of physicians and the merger of those surgery centers into a joint venture could potentially generate prohibited remuneration under the anti-kickback statute because the hospital and the physicians might receive investment returns that were not directly proportional to their invested capital, but that the risk of abuse was low in part because the valuation of the surgery centers contributed to the joint venture was based on a tangible asset valuation.[24] The OIG noted, however, that under certain circumstances it might be concerned if the valuations of

22 OIG Advisory Opinion No. 01-21 (Nov. 16, 2001).

23 *Medicare and State Health Care Programs: Fraud and Abuse; OIG Anti-Kickback Provisions;* Rule, 56 Fed. Reg. 35952, 35970 (July 29, 1991).

24 OIG Advisory Opinion No. 09-09 (July 22, 2009).

the surgery centers included intangible assets by using a cash flow analysis that could potentially include the value of referrals by the parties to their respective surgery center prior to the merger.

Advisory Opinion 09-09 dealt with a unique, multistep transaction that appeared to be structured to avoid state certificate of need restrictions by developing separate single operating room surgery centers (that would not require certificate of need approval) and then merging them together to create a two operating room surgery center (which would have required certificate of need approval if developed on its own). The key distinguishing feature of this transaction was that the contribution of the surgery centers to the joint venture was agreed to ex ante ("before the event") by the parties. Absent certificate of need restrictions, one could reasonably expect that the parties would have taken the more simple approach of making initial capital contributions to the joint venture and having it develop a two operating room surgery center. As a result, it is reasonable for the OIG to view the contributions of the surgery centers as initial capital investments, rather than contributions of going concerns, and using a tangible asset valuation of the surgery centers serves to prevent either party from abusing the agreed-to arrangement by directing referrals to a particular surgery center to increase the value of their capital contribution. In contrast, if either of the surgery centers had been in operation for many years, and the proposed joint venture had not been agreed to ex ante by the parties, then the contribution of the surgery center, or the purchase of ownership interests therein, should not be viewed merely as an initial capital investment. Dictating a tangible asset valuation in such circumstances could actually lead to the very situation that the OIG wants the parties to avoid: improper remuneration that could be related to referrals. For example, if the physicians purchased ownership interests in an existing surgery center owned by the hospital based on a tangible asset valuation of $1 million when the fair market value of the surgery center was actually $5 million (based on the income approach), then the physicians could be viewed as receiving remuneration (in the form of a discounted purchase price) in exchange for referrals.

At first blush, the OIG's position in Advisory Opinion 09-09 appears to create an untenable conflict between the regulatory framework of the anti-kickback statute and business valuation standards that require a valuator to consider all appropriate valuation approaches and which indicate that the income approach may be the preferred approach for businesses with positive cash flow. However, upon further examination of the unique structure of the transaction at issue, the OIG's position proves to be a reasonable one in the specific scenario where the parties agree to contribute the surgery centers to a joint venture ex ante to their development, and these contributions are, in effect, treated as initial capital investments by parties to the joint venture rather than as contributions of going business concerns. Advisory Opinion 09-09 should not be read in any way to discredit valuations based on the income approach, and in many cases the income approach may be absolutely necessary to ensure that none of the parties to a transaction give or receive improper remuneration by transaction at other than fair market value.

**Compensation Arrangements.** The OIG has provided guidance regarding appropriate structures for compensation arrangements by creating safe harbors that protect certain types of compensation arrangements when all of the safe harbor requirements are satisfied. There is a safe harbor for employment arrangements that protects "any amount paid by an employer to an employee, who has a bona fide employment relationship with such employer, for employment in the furnishing of any item or service for which payment may be made in whole or in part under Medicare, Medicaid or other federal healthcare programs."[25] This safe harbor gives broad protection for compensation paid to employees, regardless of whether such compensation is fair market value or whether it takes into account the volume or value of referrals. However, as discussed below, the Stark Law does require that compensation to physician employees be consistent with fair market value and not take into account the volume or value of referrals.

With respect to other types of compensation arrangements, the safe harbors for space rentals, equipment rentals, and personal services and management contracts generally include the following characteristics: (a) the aggregate compensation paid over the term of the agreement is set in advance, is consistent with fair market value in arms-length transactions, and is not determined in a manner that takes into account the volume or value of any referrals or business otherwise generated between the parties for which payment may be made in whole or in part under a federal healthcare program,; and (b) the aggregate services contracted for do not exceed those that are reasonably necessary to accomplish the commercially reasonable business purpose of the services.[26] The OIG has noted that per patient, per order, per click, and percentage-based compensation arrangements are disfavored under the anti-kickback statute because they inherently vary based on the volume and value of business generated between the parties.[27]

25 42 U.S.C. § 1320a-7b(b)(3)(B); 42 C.F.R. § 1001.952(i)

26 42 C.F.R. § 1001.952(b), (c) & (d).

27 See 56 Fed. Reg. at 35973 (noting that percentage or per-unit agreements between healthcare providers in a position to refer Medicare or Medicaid business threaten to violate the statute because the payments in these arrangements are directly tied to the volume of business or amount of revenue generated, providing an improper incentive to refer); OIG Advisory Opinion 03-8 (April 3, 2003) (noting that that "per patient", "per order", "per click" and similar payment arrangements with referral sources are disfavored); OIG Advisory Opinion 06-02 (March 21, 2006) (noting that percentage-based compensation was inherently problematic from a fair market value perspective because the compensation necessarily relates to the volume and value of business generated between the parties).

## The Stark Law

The Stark Law prohibits physicians having a financial relationship with an entity from referring patients to such entity for certain "designated health services" provided to Medicare beneficiaries, unless such financial relationship meets one of the exceptions enumerated under the statute or the regulations promulgated thereunder.[28] The Stark Law also prohibits entities from billing individuals or Medicare for designated health services furnished pursuant to a prohibited referral, and any payments (including co-payments) received in violation of this prohibition must be refunded. A financial relationship under the Stark Law can take the form of a direct or indirect ownership interest or compensation arrangement. The Stark Law and the regulations promulgated thereunder define a referral as the request by a physician for, or ordering of, or the certifying or recertifying of the need for, any designated health service for which payment may be made under Medicare, but not including any designated health service personally performed by the referring physician.[29]

**Fair Market Value**. For a compensation arrangement between an entity providing designated health services and a referring physician to avoid the prohibitions on physician referrals, the exceptions under the Stark Law generally require that remuneration under such compensation arrangement be: (a) set in advance; (b) consistent with fair market value; and (c) not determined in a manner that takes into account the volume or value of referrals or other business generated.[30] Note that, unlike the employment safe harbor to the anti-kickback statute, the employment exception to the Stark Law does require that compensation paid to physician employees be consistent with fair market value and not determined in a manner that takes into account the volume or value of referrals. The Centers for Medicare and Medicaid Services (CMS) has also noted that the definition of "fair market value" under the Stark Law is qualified in ways that do not necessarily comport with the usage of the term in standard valuation methodologies. In particular, the Stark Law requires that the methodology for analyzing fair market value exclude valuations where the parties to the transactions are at arm's length but in a position to refer to one another.[31]

28 42 U.S.C. § 1395nn. Designated health services include clinical laboratory services; physical therapy, occupational therapy, and speech-language pathology services; radiology and certain other imaging services; radiation therapy services and supplies; durable medical equipment and supplies; parenteral and enteral nutrients, equipment, and supplies; prosthetics, orthotics, and prosthetic devices and supplies; home health services; outpatient prescription drugs; inpatient and outpatient hospital services. 42 U.S.C. § 1395nn(h)(6); 42 C.F.R. § 411.351.

29 42 U.S.C. § 1395nn(h)(5); 42 CFR § 411.351.

30 See 42 C.F.R. § 411.357(a) (rental of office space), (b) (rental of equipment), (c) (employment), (d) (personal services), (f) (isolated transactions), (i) (payments by physician) and (l) (fair market value).

31 *Medicare Program; Physicians' Referrals to Health Care Entities With Which They Have Financial Relationships (Phase II); Interim Final Rule*; 69 Fed. Reg. 16054, 16107 (March 26, 2004).

For purposes of the Stark Law, fair market value is defined as the value in arm's-length transactions, consistent with the "general market value," which means the price that an asset would bring as the result of bona fide bargaining between well-informed buyers and sellers who are not otherwise in a position to generate business for the other party, or the compensation that would be included in a service agreement as the result of bona fide bargaining between well-informed parties to the agreement who are not otherwise in a position to generate business for the other party, on the date of acquisition of the asset or at the time of the service agreement.[32] The Stark Law regulations also note that a "fair market price" is usually the price at which bona fide sales have been consummated for assets of like type, quality, and quantity in a particular market at the time of acquisition, or the compensation that has been included in bona fide service agreements with comparable terms at the time of the agreement, where the price or compensation has not been determined in any manner that takes into account the volume or value of anticipated or actual referrals.[33] Note that the foregoing language reflects that the particular market in which a transaction occurs is important in assessing the relevance of comparable transactions.

With respect to space and equipment rentals, the Stark Law regulations specifically define fair market value as the value of rental property for general commercial purposes (not taking into account its intended use, provided that costs incurred by the lessor in developing or upgrading the property or maintaining the property or its improvements may be considered), and in the case of a space rental, this value may not be adjusted to reflect the additional value the prospective lessee or lessor would attribute to the proximity or convenience to the lessor when the lessor is a potential source of patient referrals to the lessee.[34]

**Per-Unit and Percentage-Based Compensation**. The exceptions under the Stark Law permit per-unit and percentage-based compensation in certain limited circumstances. Unlike the safe harbors under the anti-kickback statute, per-unit or percentage-based compensation can meet the Stark Law requirement of being "set in advance" as long as the per-unit of service amount or specific formula for calculating the compensation is (a) set forth in the written agreement between the parties in sufficient detail so that it can be objectively verified; and (b) may not be changed or modified during the course of the agreement in any manner that takes into account the volume or value of referrals or other business generated by the referring physician.[35] Per-unit compensation (but not percentage-based compensation) is also deemed not to take into account "the

32 42 C.F.R. § 411.351.
33 *Id.*
34 *Id.*
35 42 C.F.R. § 411.354(d).

volume or value of referrals" under the Stark Law if the compensation is fair market value for services or items actually provided and does not vary during the course of the compensation arrangement in any manner that takes into account referrals or other business generated by the referring physician.[36]

Per-unit or percentage-based compensation may not, however, be used in space or equipment rentals if the per-unit charge reflects services provided to patients referred by the lessor to the lessee or the compensation is based on a percentage of revenue raised, earned, billed, collected or otherwise attributable to the services performed or business generated in the rented space or using the leased equipment.[37] Although CMS has not prohibited percentage-based compensation in arrangements involving nonprofessional services (such as management or billing services), it has indicated that it intends to continue to monitor these types of compensation arrangements for potential abuse.[38] CMS has also noted that it does not consider an agreement to be at fair market value if the lessee is paying a physician-owned lessor substantially more for equipment than it would have to pay a non-physician-owned lessor and has serious questions as to the commercial reasonableness of an agreement if the lessee is performing a sufficiently high volume of procedures such that it would be economically feasible to purchase the equipment rather than lease it.[39] In the view of CMS, these types of arrangements raise the question of whether the lessee is paying more than what it would have to pay another lessor (or if the lessee purchased the equipment) to avoid losing referrals from the lessor.[40] Potential issues that can arise when a lessee is paying a physician lessor more for equipment than it would have to pay a third-party lessor are illustrated in the *Bradford* case discussed below.

### Valuation Scenarios to Consider

The following examples of valuation contexts are intended to identify particular scenarios in which healthcare providers and their advisors should be attentive to avoiding the attribution of value to referrals of federal healthcare program business when structuring and valuing business arrangements. These examples also draw on lessons that can be learned from OIG advisory opinions and court cases involving healthcare providers engaged in similar business arrangements.

---

36 *Id.*; See also 69 Fed. Reg. at 16066-70 (Indicating that percentage compensation arrangements can meet the set in advance requirement, but must also meet the volume or value and other business generated requirement).

37 42 C.F.R. § 411.357(a), (b), (l) and (p).

38 See *Medicare Program; Changes to the Hospital Inpatient Prospective Payment Systems and Fiscal Year 2009 Rates;* 73 Fed. Reg. 48434, 48710 (Aug. 19, 2008). Note that in its 2009 Hospital Inpatient Prospective Payment System Proposed Rule, CMS originally proposed to limit percentage compensation arrangement only to personally performed services. *Medicare Program; Proposed Changes to the Hospital Inpatient Prospective Payment Systems and Fiscal Year 2009 Rates*, 73 Fed. Reg. 23528, 23694 (April 30, 2008).

39 See 73 Fed. Reg. at 48714.

40 *Id.*

**Compensation Arrangements With Physicians**. To avoid prohibited referrals under the Stark Law or an inference of improper remuneration for referrals under the anti-kickback statute, compensation arrangements between healthcare providers and referring physicians should be at fair market value for actual items or services furnished and should not take into account, directly or indirectly, the value or volume of any past or anticipated referrals or other business generated by the physician. When structuring compensation arrangements with physicians within the regulatory framework of the Stark Law and anti-kickback statute, it is important to consider both the amount and type of compensation provided.

Compensation that is fixed in advance may more easily fit within a Stark Law exception or safe harbor to the anti-kickback statute because there is no opportunity for compensation to vary during the term of the arrangement based upon referrals. However, healthcare providers must be attentive to make sure the fixed compensation amounts are fair market value for the actual services provided. For example, although compensation based on actual hours worked may not be considered fixed compensation, it may more accurately reflect the fair market value of services provided than a fixed monthly payment (particularly if physicians work less than the anticipated time per month). Health care providers should also be careful when resetting fixed compensation amounts under an arrangement to make sure that the compensation is not adjusted in a manner that provides incentives for increases in referrals.

An example of how fixed compensation arrangements can still pose potential problems is the case of *U.S. v. Campbell (2011)*.[41] This case was based on part-time employment contracts between the University of Medicine and Dentistry of New Jersey and local cardiologists serving as clinical assistant professors with fixed salaries ranging from $50,000 to $180,000 that were alleged to have been entered into by the hospital to ensure a sufficient number of cardiac procedures to avoid losing Level 1 Trauma Center accreditation. The hospital entered into a settlement agreement with the government for alleged violations of the False Claims Act related to these contracts and the government then sought damages from an individual cardiologist related to his contract with the hospital. This case illustrates that healthcare providers and their advisors should carefully consider the specific facts and circumstances of compensation arrangements with referring physicians and keep in mind that even fixed salaries may still pose a problem if the salary is not tied to actual services provided by the physician.

Percentage and per-unit based compensation arrangements with physicians are more prone to being viewed as tied to the volume or value of referrals and should be carefully

41 *U.S. v. Campbell*, 2011 WL 43013, No. 08-1951 (D.N.J., Jan. 4, 2011).

reviewed to ensure they meet all of the applicable requirements under a Stark Law exception and do not involve space or equipment rentals where the rental charge reflects services provided to patients referred by the lessor to the lessee. Even if a per-unit or percentage-based compensation arrangement meets a Stark Law exception, there is no safe harbor protection for such arrangements under the anti-kickback statute. Moreover, while percentage or per-unit based compensation methodologies may be common in certain business arrangements, such methodologies may be disfavored under the anti-kickback statute when they involve physicians. For instance, although management agreements often include fees based on a percentage of revenue, this type of management fee may raise concerns when the manager is owned by physicians in a position to make referrals to the business being managed.

The need for careful attention when structuring compensation arrangements with physicians is illustrated by the case of *U.S. ex rel Drakeford v. Tuomey Healthcare System, Inc. (2010)*.[42] This was a qui tam case brought by an orthopedic surgeon contending that the hospital's part-time employment of surgeons violated the Stark Law because the compensation was based on the volume or value of referrals from the physicians to the hospital. The part-time employment agreements tied physician compensation to collections for personally performed professional services, which by itself is a fairly common structure and unlikely to raise concerns under the Stark Law because personally performed services are not considered referrals. However, the agreements also had several unusual features, including 10-year terms, only applying to outpatient surgeries (but not inpatient surgeries or work done in the office), imposing significant noncompete covenants requiring all outpatient surgeries to be performed in the hospital's outpatient surgery center and providing total compensation and benefits that were approximately 30% higher than actual collections for professional services. Taken as a whole, the government characterized these part-time employment agreements as an attempt to limit competition from physician-owned surgery centers by providing compensation and benefits that were significantly higher than what the physician could reasonably expect to collect for their professional services. Although the hospital contended it had legal opinions and third-party valuations supporting the appropriateness of the arrangements, the jury found that these part-time employment agreements violated the Stark Law and the hospital had improperly billed Medicare for approximately $45 million in services tied to referrals that were prohibited under the Stark Law. The *Tuomey* case serves as a reminder that even though employment arrangements with physicians may have safe harbor protection under the anti-kickback statute, they are still susceptible to violating the Stark Law and should be evaluated as a whole to ensure that compensation is fair market value, commercially reasonable, and not tied to volume or value of referrals.

42 *U.S. ex rel. Drakeford v. Tuomey Healthcare System, Inc.*, No. 3:05-CV-02858-MJP (D.C.S.C., March 29, 2010).

**Physician Practice Acquisitions.** Hospital acquisitions of physician practices are transactions that commonly require the parties to determine the fair market value of the practice being acquired. As mentioned above, hospitals cannot attribute value to prior or anticipated referrals for hospital services by physician owners when calculating the purchase price for a physician practice. When a physician practice is valued on a going concern basis, revenues tied to referrals from physician owners to the hospital for non-physician services must be excluded because they are unrelated to the going concern value of the business being acquired. This does not mean, however, that the hospital has to disregard revenues of the physician practice attributable to (ai) professional services of the physician owners, because these services do not constitute a referral to another person or entity for reimbursable services or items; or (b) other revenue of the practice, to the extent this revenue is reflective of the going concern value of the practice's business. It is also important that the value of a physician practice on a going concern basis incorporate the post-transaction compensation paid to the physicians by the acquiring hospital. This issue was highlighted in the case of *Derby v. Commissioner (2008)*, where the tax court denied a charitable deduction for the intangible value of a medical practice claimed by the physician owners in connection with the acquisition of a health system that included a purchase price tied solely to tangible assets.[43] This case illustrates that intangible value may not exist if post-transaction compensation to physicians eliminates any potential cash flow to the acquirer of the practice.

When substantially all of the cash flows from a physician practice are allocated to physician compensation, thereby eliminating any residual going concern value, it is common for the practice to be valued on a cost approach basis. This approach determines the liquidation value of the individual assets of the practice as opposed to the going concern value of the practice as a whole. While establishing the value of tangible assets such as equipment and furniture under the cost approach may be fairly straight forward, determining what value, if any, can be attributed to other intangible assets of the practice under the cost approach requires careful consideration. Certain types of intangible assets (like goodwill) may not have any value in the absence of any going concern value for the business (i.e., in the absence of positive post-transaction cash flow net of physician compensation).

For an asset to be attributed value in a liquidation scenario, the practice must have a bona fide right of ownership to the asset that it can legally transfer to the buyer.[44] This may require valuators to consider contractual rights and relevant laws governing the right to ownership of such assets (for example, the transferability of a noncompete under an employment contract). For an asset to have quantifiable value under the cost

43 *Derby v. Commissioner*, T.C. Memo 2008-45 (2008).

44 See Shannon P. Pratt, Robert F. Reilly & Robert P. Schweihs, *Valuing a Business: The Analysis and Appraisal of Closely Held Companies*, 325 (4th Ed., 2000).

approach, it must also generate some measurable amount of economic benefit to the buyer, whether in the form of an income or cost avoidance.[45] In other words, the buyer must have a need to acquire the asset for its employment of the physicians such that it would otherwise have to go out and incur the cost of acquiring the asset independently. The value of the asset should take into consideration any functional or economic obsolescence as well as any obligations and costs associated with ownership of the asset. For example, costs of storage and retrieval should be considered in the context of placing value on medical records. Similarly, credit for prior years of service granted to nonphysician employees should be considered in analyzing the value of any trained workforce whose employment contracts are transferred to the buyer.

**Acquisitions of Physician-Owned Ancillary Businesses.** Another type of transaction that often requires careful consideration under the regulatory framework of the Stark Law and anti-kickback statute is the acquisition of physician-owned ancillary businesses. In-office ancillary businesses such as laboratory, imaging, and surgical suites that are operated as part of a physician practice will often derive substantially all of their business from referrals by the physician owners of the practice. As a result, healthcare providers acquiring these in-office ancillary businesses need to be careful to structure the acquisition in a manner that does not improperly attribute value to anticipated referrals by the physician owners of the practice.

Some of the potential pitfalls to consider when structuring acquisitions of physician-owned ancillary business are highlighted in the case of *United States ex rel. Singh v. Bradford Regional Medical Center*, involving a qui tam action brought against a hospital and local physicians relating to a nuclear camera sublease arrangement.[46] The court in this case concluded that the sublease arrangement between the parties created financial relationships that violated the Stark Law and resulted in prohibited referrals by the physicians to the hospital. Central to this conclusion was the court's determination that payments under the sublease, which included substantial amounts attributable to a noncompete agreement, were greater than what would be paid in the absence of the ability of the physicians to generate referrals to the hospital and inflated to compensate the physicians for their ability to generate such referrals. Thus, the court was able to conclude that the noncompete payments were arrived at by taking into account the volume and value of anticipated referrals by the physicians and were therefore not fair market value for purposes of the Stark Law. Although the hospital had obtained a report from an accountant analyzing the noncompete payments under the sublease using

45 *Id.*

46 *United States ex rel. Singh v. Bradford Regional Medical Center*, 752 F. Supp. 2d 602 (W.D. Pa., 2010). *Editor's Note: The* Bradford *case is also discussed in Chapter 8.*

the competitive business valuation method and concluding that they were fair market value, in reaching this conclusion, the accountant had improperly taken into account anticipated revenues to the hospital for not only nuclear imaging services but also CT/MRI, inpatient, and outpatient services based on the assumption that the physicians would likely refer this business to the hospital in the absence of a financial interest in their own facilities (although not required to do so by the noncompete).[47]

The *Bradford* case underscores the need for careful attention when structuring acquisitions of physician-owned ancillary businesses and valuing intangible assets (such as noncompetes) in these arrangements. It also emphasizes the need to consider the element of commercial reasonableness in these types of arrangements. One of the problems in the *Bradford* case was that the parties structured what would typically be a business acquisition as an equipment lease. While it is common for value to be allocated to intangible assets as a component of the larger assemblage of assets in a business acquisition, this allocation of value is rarely applicable to leasing arrangements. Moreover, paying for intangible assets over time (through monthly lease payments) increases the risk that such payments may be linked to a continued expectation of referrals. When evaluating payments for intangible assets in acquisitions of physician-owned ancillary businesses, healthcare providers and their advisors should also keep in mind the general concept of commercial reasonableness that is embodied in the regulatory framework of the Stark Law and anti-kickback statute. In essence, the parties need to ask whether it is commercially reasonable for a purchaser to pay for intangible assets associated with a physician-owned ancillary business absent any expectation of referrals from the physician sellers. Facts to consider in this analysis are (a) whether the location and services of the acquired business are well suited for integration with the purchaser; (b) whether the purchaser will have to relocate or restructure the business; and (c) whether acquiring the business is more cost-effective than the alternative of independently developing a facility, buying or leasing equipment, recruiting staff, incurring start-up losses, and competing with the physicians.

Another issue highlighted in the *Bradford* case is the importance of making sure that payments for intangible assets do not take into account the volume or value of referrals from physician sellers, particularly when the fair market value of intangible assets is determined using discounted cash flows reflecting revenues from referrals by physician sellers under the income approach. Generally accepted valuation standards require consideration of all appropriate valuation approaches, including the asset approach, income approach, and market approach, and for a business that generates positive cash flows,

47 Report of Charles T. Day (attached as Exhibit 7 to Relators' Appendix), 752 F. Supp. 2d 602.

the income approach is in many cases the preferred methodology.[48] When applying the income approach, it is extremely important that fair market value be determined using projected cash flows that reflect the ability of the business to generate cash flows in the absence of any obligation of physician sellers to continue referring to the business. The risk that physician sellers will no longer refer to the business should be accounted for by using appropriate growth assumptions and discount rates. This risk will be higher and the fair market value will be lower if physician sellers are the primary or only source of referrals to the business (which is often the case with physician-owned ancillary businesses). Assuming the income approach appropriately accounts for the risk that physician sellers will no longer refer to the business, arguably there will be no consideration tied to anticipated referrals from physician sellers. Conversely, disregarding the income approach when projected cash flows reflect referrals from physician sellers could actually lead to a purchase price that is below fair market value and may raise concerns under the anti-kickback statute. For example, if a physician-owned ancillary business is sold at below fair market value to a physician-owned hospital or surgery center in which the physician sellers are investors, the discounted purchase price could be viewed as consideration for anticipated referrals by other physician owners of the acquiring entity (which could result in higher distributions to the physicians sellers from such acquiring entity). Those involved in structuring transactions where such discounting assumptions are invoked to eliminate value attributable to future referrals from physician sellers should be alert to communications between the parties where, in pursuit of a higher valuation, selling physicians or their representatives may inappropriately attempt to argue that future referrals should be anticipated. Such communications may have a tendency to taint an otherwise appropriately structured transaction with evidence of improper intent.

**Noncompete Agreements.**[49] Like other types of intangible assets, valuation of noncompete agreements with healthcare providers requires careful consideration. Noncompete agreements may be attributed value to the extent the noncompete is an enforceable mechanism to preserve the value of an acquired business by prohibiting the detrimental effect of a seller from competing with the acquired business. Assessing the enforceability of the noncompete requires consideration of applicable state laws. The value of a noncompete is related to the avoidance of the potential negative impact on cash flows from allowing the seller to establish a competing business and should not be based on the anticipated volume or value of referrals from the seller because the

48 See National Association of Certified Valuation Analysts Professional Standards, Section 3.7; American Society of Appraisers Business Valuation Standards BSV-I, Section IV; American Institute of Certified Public Accountants Statement on Standards for Valuation Services No. 1, paragraph 31; Shannon P. Pratt, Robert F. Reilly & Robert P. Schweihs, *Valuing a Business: The Analysis and Appraisal of Closely Held Companies*, 40 (4th Ed., 2000)
49 *Editor's Note: The valuation of noncompete agreements is covered in Chapter 21.*

seller could refer business to another entity regardless of the presence of a noncompete. The value of a noncompete should also take into account the reasonable ability of the seller to engage in competitive activity. For example, a physician might be able to establish an inexpensive surgery or imaging suite in his or her office relatively easily, but establishing a separately licensed surgery or imaging center may not be a realistic scenario.

The competitive business valuation method is a commonly accepted methodology for analyzing the value of a noncompete in the context of a larger assemblage of assets. However, as illustrated by the *Bradford* case discussed above, this methodology must be appropriately applied by assessing the present value of anticipated economic damage to the buyer if the seller were allowed to compete.[50] This requires an analysis of the realistic potential loss in earnings from the specific business being acquired by allowing the seller to compete with the business (in contrast, the accountant's report in the *Bradford* case included revenues associated with CT/MRI, inpatient, and outpatient services that were unrelated to the nuclear camera business). Moreover, the result of the competitive business valuation method should conform with or fit into the context of the overall purchase price for the business. For example, if the total enterprise value of the business is $100, the logical fair market value of the noncompete would be significantly less than $100 after accounting for the value of other identifiable assets included within the enterprise value.

When the enterprise value of a business is determined on a going concern basis, the value of a noncompete would be encompassed within the overall purchase price for the business (unless the noncompete was not factored into the enterprise value). However, when a business is valued using the cost approach, the value of a noncompete, if any, would have to be determined separately from the value of other identifiable assets based on the impact to projected cash flows of the business by allowing the seller to compete with the business in the future. In such case, valuators should carefully consider the reasonable ability of the seller to compete with the business. If the business is being valued on a cost approach because the sellers are losing money, then the sellers may have little ability to successfully compete with the business and the value of a noncompete may be may be minimal or nonexistent. In the context of noncompetes from physician sellers, it is important to remember that physician sellers cannot be prohibited from making referrals to competing businesses (i.e., they can only be prohibited from owning a competing business). Therefore, the value of a noncompete from a physician seller cannot be determined based on referrals made by the physician seller to the acquired

50 See Robert F. Reilly & Robert P. Schweihs, *Valuing Intangible Assets*, 400-09 (1999); IRS Coordinated Issue All Industries Covenants Not to Compete (February 19, 1996); *Ansan Tool v. Commissioner*, T.C. Memo 1992-121.

business because they can make those referrals to a competing business regardless of the presence of a noncompete.

Noncompete agreements often arise in the context of physician practice acquisitions where the selling physicians agree not to compete with the purchaser under the terms of their employment agreements with the purchaser. In this case, the noncompete agreement is given in return for compensation provided under the employment agreement, rather than the purchase agreement. If the practice assets were valued using the cost approach, there would be no separate consideration for the noncompete as part of the purchase price.

Another situation that sometimes arises is when physicians desire to receive consideration for contributing a noncompete agreement in connection with their investment in a joint venture. If physicians are making a cash investment in a joint venture, then there is no associated business being acquired that they could adversely compete with and there would be no value to attribute to their noncompete agreement. In comparison, if physicians are contributing an existing business to a joint venture in return for investment interests in the joint venture, then the consideration for their noncompete would be encompassed within the fair market value purchase price paid for the business being contributed.

**Investment in De Novo Joint Ventures**. When valuing investment interests in de novo (new) joint ventures that include investors in a position to make referrals to the joint venture, the anti-kickback statute generally requires that anticipated referrals from such investors, which might otherwise be taken into account in a normal commercial setting, must be disregarded in determining the value of contributions to the joint venture or the value of the joint venture itself. In the context of a de novo joint venture, there is no existing business to be valued and the purchase price for investment interests should be based solely on the capital required to start up and operate the business. The purchase price for investment interests should not vary between individual investors, as such variance could give rise to an inference of improper remuneration in exchange for anticipated referrals and the OIG has indicated its concern when investors who are potential referral sources for the investment entity are permitted to obtain their investment interests at insider prices or at prices more favorable than those available to the general public.[51]

51 64 Fed. Reg. at 63522.

In contrast, if a party is contributing capital to a de novo joint venture in the form of assets related to an ongoing business, then it is important that such assets be fairly valued and that the contributing party receives fair market value investment interests in exchange. Additionally, investors may contribute capital in the form of pre-operational services or sweat equity, provided that the investment interests received in return are fair market value for actual services contributed.[52] However, it is important that the valuation of any assets or sweat equity contributed does not assign any value to anticipated referrals by the contributing party to the de novo joint venture.

**Investment in Existing Joint Ventures**. Just as with de novo joint ventures, the value of investment interests in existing joint ventures that include investors in a position to make referrals to the joint venture also should not attribute value to anticipated referrals from such investors. In contrast to a de novo joint venture, an existing joint venture typically has going concern value that may be affected by revenues stemming from referrals made by investors. Additionally, the inflow and outflow of investors actively involved in providing services in connection with a joint venture (which may actually be required to meet the anti-kickback statute safe harbor for ambulatory surgery centers) could potentially impact future revenues of the joint venture. In these circumstances, it is important that the value of investment interests is determined using projected cash flows based on the historical operations of the joint venture, as opposed to the projected future referrals by investors. When a business is valued using projected cash flows based on historical operations, the value of the business is based on the projected ability of the business to continue to operate in a profitable manner. Potential outflows of investors and losses in revenue would be reflected in the discount premium applied to the cash flows of the joint venture (reflecting a higher risk with respect to future operations), however potential inflows of investors and additional revenues attributable to potential referrals from those investors should not be reflected in the purchase price because this could be construed as attributing value to anticipated referrals.

For example, if a physician owner of a surgery center is retiring and selling his or her ownership interests to a new physician and the new physician performs procedures that receive higher reimbursement than the retiring physician, the valuation of the ownership interests in the surgery center should not reflect any anticipated increase in reimbursement from the activity of the new physician at the surgery center because it would reflect the value of anticipated referrals. In contrast, if a surgery center invests in a new piece of high-technology equipment enabling it to perform certain cutting-edge procedures that receive higher reimbursement, the valuation of the surgery center should reflect the projected revenues from this new equipment. The important distinction here

52 See 56 Fed. Reg. at 35970.

is that in the latter case, the valuation is appropriately based on the projected ability of the business to perform new procedures and is not based on projections of anticipated referrals from a new physician investor.

In valuing an existing joint venture, it is also important that an appropriate discount premium is applied so that the amount of capital invested by new investors is not disproportionately small compared to disproportionately large returns that an enforcement authority might assert to be "extraordinary returns" in comparison with the risk involved.[53] Assuming that a joint venture has a significant operating history and a relatively stable risk profile that allows for the application of an appropriate discount premium, the mere purchase of an investment interest should avoid any inference of improper remuneration to the purchaser, the seller, or other investors as long as the purchase is not targeted toward certain investors in return for their referrals and the purchase price is fair market value. The logical argument that can be made here is that if the price paid for an investment interest is fair market value, then the value of the purchase price consideration is equivalent to the value of the investment interest received and there is no additional remuneration that could be attributed to referrals.

**Investment in Existing Joint Ventures With Limited Operating History.** Sometimes investors may purchase ownership interests in an existing joint venture that has a limited operating history and minimal or no cash flow. This scenario presents unique challenges for valuators. The valuation of investment interests in an existing joint venture with a limited operating history should be careful to avoid (a) underestimating the value that has been created by the formation of the business; or (b) overestimating the value that has been created by the formation of the business by ascribing value to anticipated referrals from physician investors.

To be sure, there is some value created by the syndication of ownership interests and the formation of a joint venture. This value is likely to increase as the business reaches additional milestones such as obtaining additional financing, constructing a facility, purchasing equipment, obtaining licenses and other regulatory approvals, and commencing operations because the related risk of future cash flows declines. Until those milestones are reached, the risk that they might not be met would warrant additional discounts to the value of the business. The attainment of certain milestones means that the purchase price for ownership units in the business likely is no longer based solely

53 Note that the OIG has stated that "a reasonable return can be appropriately measured only in light of the risk of the investment. An investor would surely expect a much higher return from an investment in an expensive piece of diagnostic equipment that might soon become obsolete than from an investment in a relatively inexpensive piece of equipment that can be expected to generate a steady profit stream for the foreseeable future." 56 Fed. Reg. at 35970.

upon the equity capital required to start up the business. If, following syndication and formation of the joint venture, the fair market value of the business has increased, then it would no longer be appropriate to sell units to physician investors at the initial offering price if this price is less than the then-current fair market value of the business.

On the other hand, a joint venture with a limited operating history has significantly higher risks than an existing business with stable, continuing operations, and there is less certainty that a startup business will be able to meet projected cash flow levels. When there is no operating history upon which to base cash flow projections, valuators may be relying principally on their analysis of management's preliminary projections for future cash flows. Management's future cash flow projections, in an attempt to be more accurate, may incorporate an analysis of procedures expected to be performed by physician owners and other physicians in the community. This analysis might be particularly relevant in the context of surgery centers, where the anti-kickback statute safe harbor affirmatively requires that physician owners perform at least one-third of their procedures in the surgery center. To avoid attributing value to anticipated referrals from physician owners, the valuation of a business with a limited operating history should avoid ascribing certainty to any referrals from physician investors. Thus, a discounted cash flow analysis should include an appropriate discount rate to reflect, among the many other business risks, that physician owners are not required to make referrals to the facility (except to the extent to meet regulatory requirements under the anti-kickback statute safe harbor for surgery centers) and that there can be no assurance that the business will meet its cash flow projections.

Chapter 8

# Bradford Regional Medical Center: Lessons for the Inexperienced

*By Mark O. Dietrich, CPA/ABV*

The federal whistleblower or qui tam law allows a private citizen (plaintiff) to bring a civil action[1] on behalf of the government against an alleged violator seeking damages, of which the qui tam plaintiff (or relator) may claim 15% to 35% of the total damages ultimately paid. The government may choose to join in the action against the alleged violator, bringing the enormous prosecutorial clout of the federal government to bear against the defendant. Thus, there are significant financial incentives to bring a qui tam action. This November 2010 case involved a whistleblower on whose behalf the government had intervened.

The facts of the case include the sublease of a nuclear medicine camera[2] by two physicians on the Bradford Regional Medical Center (BRMC) staff who were threatened with loss of hospital admitting privileges for competing with BRMC in the provision of nuclear medicine scans. Nuclear medicine scans represent the highest dollar cost to the Medicare Part B program performed by cardiologists. More importantly in the context of this guide, a valuation of a "noncompete" prepared by a CPA (referred to as CPA or [name] Redacted) is at the center of the case.

The background as summarized by the court is as follows:

1 There is a segment of the litigation bar that specializes in these cases.

2 SPECT, or single photon emission computed tomography, is the technical term. The fixed units look like a small CT or MRI unit, while the mobile units have a chair in which the patient sits and the camera rotates around that chair, generating an image of the heart.

> Before entering into a final sublease, BRMC had a fair market value assessment prepared by an accountant, Redacted. (Leonhardt[3] Dep. at 54; BRMC 30(b)(6) Dep. at 146-148.) BRMC sought this report to determine whether BRMC was paying fair market value under the proposed sublease arrangement. (Leonhardt Dep. at 54-55; BRMC 30(b)(6) Dep. at 148-149.) In September 2003, the board of BRMC received Mr. Redacted's report. The report concluded that the amounts to be paid pursuant to the proposed sublease were reasonable. (BRMC 30(b)(6) Dep. Appx., at 146-149.)
>
> In performing his fair market value analysis, Mr. Redacted compared the revenues BRMC expected to generate with the sublease in place to the revenues BRMC expected to receive without the sublease in place. (Report of Redacted, C.P.A.; Leonhardt Dep. at 55-56.) The projections were based on the expectation that V&S would refer such business to the hospital if the sublease arrangement was approved. (Id.) According to defendants, the basis of Mr. Redacted's report was what benefits BRMC would have lost had it terminated the medical staff appointment and clinical privileges of Drs. Vaccaro and Saleh pursuant to BRMC's policy. BRMC advised Drs. Vaccaro and Saleh that its valuation expert indicated that he could support the fair market value of the sublease, however neither Vaccaro nor Saleh received or reviewed a copy of Mr. Redacted's written valuation.

In denying, in part, both parties' cross-motions for summary judgment, the court concluded:

> Again, the record evidence is not strongly in favor of defendants [BRMC, et al.] as it tends to show that defendants entered into the equipment sublease fully aware that the arrangement, which had at its core a noncompete payment roughly equal to the referral business BRMC would gain from the doctors and the business V&S would lose from abandoning its own camera, may not be permitted under the Stark Act and Anti-Kickback Act. However, we are unable to conclude as a matter of law that defendants acted "knowingly" for purposes of the False Claims Act.
>
> For the foregoing reasons, we will deny defendants' motions for summary judgment and grant in part and deny in part relator's motion for summary judgment.[4]

As those of us trained in tax law[5] learn, court decisions are case-fact specific. The valuation report in this case was obtained through the federal court system's PACER service[6]

3 The hospital's CEO.
4 docs.justia.com/cases/federal/district-courts/pennsylvania/pawdce/1:2004cv00186/3406/145/
5 The author has a Masters in Taxation degree.
6 Thank you to Kathie Wilson, CPA/CVA one of the guide's contributing authors.

since it was part of the public record. A review of that report indicates that it is not the typical valuation one would expect to see in a circumstance such as this; for example, the report states that the fair market value was tested against Section 482 of the Internal Revenue Code. As such, fewer risks might have been perceived from an initial reading of the court's decision in those circumstances where the parties are relying upon the fair market value exception based upon an appropriately prepared report. At the same time, even a good report is never an absolute defense against an allegation under the Stark law or anti-kickback statute. Further, it is clear that in the court's view, factors cited in the valuation report were consistent with the purchase of referrals, e.g., "these statements, however, do not counter the record evidence that the analysis in the [CPA valuation] report was based on the assumption that the physicians would likely refer this business to the hospital" and that Mr. Leonhardt's summary presentation showed an expected profit for BRMC from entering into the lease agreement that was based on receiving business from V&S."

This suggests the court believed that the valuation had as an underlying assumption that all the nuclear scans done in the physicians' office would be referred post-transaction to the acquiring hospital. This, in turn, might indicate strategic value rather than fair market value, depending on how the valuation was performed. Given the requirement of the Stark regulations defining the modifications to fair market value, a compliant fair market value analysis would have considered the risk of the hospital (and other potential competitors) *not* receiving all of the referrals, to wit:

420 CFR 411.351 states: "Fair market value means the value in arm's-length transactions consistent with general market value. 'General market value' means the price that an asset would bring as the result of bona fide bargaining between well-informed buyers and sellers *who are not otherwise in a position to generate business for the other party.*" [Emphasis added]

And from Stark II-Phase 2: "Moreover, the definition of 'fair market value' in the statute and regulation is qualified in ways that do not necessarily comport with the usage of the term in standard valuation techniques and methodologies. For example, the methodology must exclude valuations where the parties to the transactions are at arm's length but in a position to refer to one another. In addition, the definition itself differs depending on the type of transaction: Leases or rentals of space and equipment cannot take into account the intended use of the rented item, and *in cases where the lessor is in a position to refer to the lessee, the valuation cannot be adjusted or reflect the value of proximity or convenience to the lessor.*" [Emphasis added]

Thus the cash flow analysis and the discount rate developed in connection with such a valuation would have to reflect something other than the actual relationship between purchaser and seller. The court clearly believed that the actual relationship was the basis for the valuation. And, it is clear from the court's opinion that the modifications to fair market value spelled out in the above two quotes from the Stark regulations were not taken into account.

The OIG's office has long expressed concern with the sale of ancillary designated health services ancillaries (DHS) owned by physicians to a hospital or other buyer when the DHS will remain in the selling physician's office and continue to be used by the physicians. Although it involved a surgery center, similar issues in the OIG's perspective can be seen in Advisory Opinion No. 07-05. [7]

The following section illuminates key issues in the case and then what fair market value in a regulatory context (should) mean to an appraiser and how the fundamental measure of an appropriate discount rate and measure of cash flows *should* avoid much of the inherent issue of "valuing referrals."[8]

The quotation below is one of the most damning elements of the fact pattern. Although the court does not mention it, fair market value includes a criterion that neither party is under duress.

> Drs. Vaccaro and Saleh had a history of referring patients to BRMC for nuclear imaging until they invested in their own General Electric nuclear camera. With their own camera, they no longer needed to refer patients to BRMC for imaging. BRMC threatened to revoke the doctors' hospital privileges, which led to lengthy negotiations.

Equally as problematic are the contents of the valuation report:

> Mr. [CPA] explained that his table is "based on the assumption that the physicians would likely refer this business to the hospital in the absence of a financial interest in their own facilities or services, although they are not required to do so by virtue of any of the covenants contained in the agreements or otherwise."
>
> Therefore, the report itself indicates that the analysis of whether the noncompetition agreement represents a fair market value is based, in part, on anticipated referrals

7 As I and other observers noted at the time, this advisory seemed to misconstrue fair market value, while emphasizing the focus on referrals. oig.hhs.gov/fraud/docs/advisoryopinions/2007/AdvOpn07-05C.pdf.

8 Note: Chapter 7 of the *BVR/AHLA Guide to Healthcare Valuation*, "The Anti-Kickback Statute and Stark Law," looks at many of the issues discussed in this case, including noncompete agreements, and Chapters 18 and 19 look at the mechanics of actually valuing a noncompete.

from the doctors. BRMC affirmed that the report evaluated expected revenues based on the assumption that defendants would likely refer the business to BRMC.

Here is additional material along the same lines taken from the deposition of the hospital CEO and the portion of the court's opinion that followed the excerpt:

> Q. It's fair to say that the purpose of the noncompete agreement was to protect that revenue stream [referrals from Dr. Saleh and Dr. Vaccaro].
>
> A. The purpose of the noncompete, from my point of view, was to make sure that Drs. Vaccaro and Saleh didn't have a financial incentive to refer away from the hospital.
>
> Q. Because if they didn't have a financial incentive to refer away, they would refer it to you?
>
> A. We could hope that they would, yes.
>
> Q. You did more than hope. You expected they would refer to you?
>
> A. Expected they would refer a good bit of it to us, yeah.
>
> A compensation arrangement does not take into account the volume or value of referrals or other business generated between the parties if the compensation is fixed in advance and will result in fair market value compensation, and the compensation does not vary over the term of the arrangement in any manner that takes into account referrals or other business generated.
>
> While the value agreed upon by parties who are in a position to refer business to each other and who take into account anticipated referrals will be a fair value as between the parties, such an arrangement is not fair market value under the Stark Act. Here, the compensation arrangement between the parties is greater than what would be paid in the absence of the ability of Dr. Saleh and Dr. Vaccaro to provide referrals for BRMC's nuclear camera business.

As indicated above, the court concluded that the defendant hospital, et al., by their plain statements, considered the volume or value of referrals. Notwithstanding that, the court went on to say that even if that had not been the case, the defendants could not rely upon the fair market value exception because the *valuation itself* expressly considered referrals. Apparently key to this conclusion was the fact that the lease of the nuclear camera approximated $30,000 per month, of which nearly 80% was for a noncompete agreement. Further, a net present value analysis of the cost of the noncompete was compared to the revenues from inpatient and outpatient services the hospital expected to derive from the acquisition of the nuclear medicine camera.

Now, it would be foolhardy to suggest that a different valuation model might have caused the court to rule differently. However, assume for the sake of argument that none of the defendants or the valuation report was on record as stating that they considered referrals when negotiating or valuing the arrangements. What type of assumptions might an appraiser have put into a valuation model that would not take into account the volume of value of referrals from the seller to the buyer to conform to the requirement that "'general market value' means the price that an asset would bring as the result of bona fide bargaining between well-informed buyers and sellers *who are not otherwise in a position to generate business for the other party*" and "the definition itself differs depending on the type of transaction: Leases or rentals of space and equipment cannot take into account the intended use of the rented item, and *in cases where the lessor is in a position to refer to the lessee, the valuation cannot be adjusted or reflect the value of proximity or convenience to the lessor*." [Emphasis added]

Before going to the Stark modifications of fair market value, it is important to note that the use of an appropriate equity discount rate and weighted average cost of capital are designed to account for the investment risk inherent in owning a business. One of the many differences between fair market value and strategic, investment value, or value to the [existing] owner is the use of a market-based rate of return to discount future cash flows to present value. There is no discussion in the case about this at all. A value to the owner standard in the instant case might have resulted from the use of a risk-free rate, which in turn would have resulted in a much higher value than if a market-based rate of return[9] were utilized. At least from the standpoint of an appraiser undertaking an exercise of determining fair market value, the very use of a market-based rate of return will eliminate a significant portion of the value of referrals from the existing owners, because a hypothetical seller or buyer is substituted through the discount rate for the actual seller or buyer. The next part of the discussion focuses on the adjustment to the cash flows subject to discounting necessary to move from a value to the owner standard to a fair market standard that from an appraisal standpoint, does not consider referrals.

The subject nuclear medicine camera had been and remained post-transaction in the offices of the selling physicians for several years (through December 2006, about three years). During time, of course, most of the cases would come from the two selling physicians. It is not clear whether before or after the transaction, any patients came

9 The report in this case actually used an 18% discount rate.

from other physicians on the hospital staff, though that would clearly be relevant to the determination of fair market value as well as to the hindsight required in the prosecution of the litigation. To meet the requirement that "the valuation cannot be adjusted or reflect the value of proximity or convenience to the lessor," an appraisal of a nuclear medicine camera lease would merely look to what the rent on the piece of equipment might be—and that would already have been clear from the GE lease, which the hospital assumed.

An appraiser valuing a nuclear medicine business—which is where a noncompete would become relevant—as opposed to simply a lease would have to base volume assumptions and resultant cash flows on what a freestanding nuclear camera owned, say, by an independent nonphysician vendor would expect to receive in referrals from the medical community assuming that the referring physicians had no financial interest in the business. In a rural market such as that of BRMC, it is likely that before the physicians in the case acquired their nuclear camera, all of those cases had gone to the hospital and there was no competing provider. This would make the task challenging, indeed, but one would think the assumption would be two market competitors, the hospital and the independent vendor, and how that independent vendor might fare against the hospital— and not giving effect to the hospital's threat to revoke the staff privileges of physicians who did not refer to it.

A noncompete is part of the overall value of a business and represents the business that would be lost if the seller competed post-transaction, adjusted for the possibility that if allowed to compete, the seller would, in fact, do so, with the resultant cash flows discounted to present value at the discount rate used to determine the value of the business. This is referred to as the "with [the value with the noncompete in place] and without [the value without the noncompete in place] method." A noncompete is not in addition to the value of the business. In the instant case, there appears from the record to be confusion between the value of a lease, the value of a noncompete, and the value of a nuclear medicine business, among other things. Where that confusion originated is not clear.

One possible interpretation of the impact of the decision is that in circumstances such as this, the price paid for an operating business should be allocated to various component assets including the value of a noncompete to identify that portion of the value that is attributable to the sellers—assuming that noncompete value is based solely upon the sellers' DHS referrals. Such an approach would require some thinking about the traditional model of noncompete valuation. The two steps discussed above— an appropriate return to a hypothetical; buyer or seller and identifying cash flows available to a market participant not in a position to refer— need first to be considered in the noncompete analysis. Then, the appraiser also has to ask himself or herself how much business the buyer would lose if the sellers competed and what the likelihood of that competition is.

The larger question for the valuation community would seem to be whether an entire practice that owns DHS can be purchased *with* the valuation including the cash flows from DHS *and* the physicians being employed post-transaction by the purchaser. As suggested earlier, it has been clear to many for some time that purchasing DHS separately from a purchase of an entire practice and leaving the DHS physically present in the still independent practice is problematic from the government's standpoint.

It seems as well that a hospital buyer should be first guided not only by qualified legal counsel, but also by an opinion of fair market value from an appraiser with the requisite expertise to apply the regulatory standard to a valuation engagement *before* the hospital embarks on discussing price with a physician-seller in a position to refer DHS. This is a little different from retaining a neutral, subject to a confidentiality agreement, to evaluate financial terms in provider integration transactions subject to antitrust review before determining whether a memorandum of understanding is appropriate to move forward. Separately, the lack of statutory authority for the OIG to opine on fair market value is problematic and warrants extreme caution. Finally, threatening physicians in a position to refer DHS with loss of staff privileges if they compete is not a good idea.

Chapter 9

# Valuation Issues Affecting Tax-Exempt Healthcare Organizations

*By Robert F. Reilly, MBA, CPA, CMA, CFA, ASA, CBA*

This discussion focuses on the regulatory reasons why tax-exempt healthcare organizations retain valuation analysts to perform transaction valuations, reasonableness of compensation analyses, and similar fair market value analyses. This discussion will not present a "how to" explanation of valuation approaches, methods, and procedures for the valuation analyst. Such "how to" procedural explanations are presented elsewhere in this text (and in numerous principles and advanced valuation texts). Rather, this discussion will summarize the regulatory considerations that the valuation analyst (and all parties to a proposed transaction) should be aware of with respect to the valuation of a tax-exempt healthcare organization.

With regard to most tax-exempt organization transactions, the principal parties (and the valuation analyst) should be concerned with at least three potential regulatory challenges: (1) Medicare fraud and abuse challenges, (2) Internal Revenue Service private inurement issues, and (3) Stark laws compliance issues. This discussion will focus on the second potential regulatory challenge: federal income tax issues related to private inurement allegations and the related intermediate sanctions excise tax penalties. In particular, this discussion focuses on: what type of transaction price or structure may result in a private inurement, what parties are subject to the private inurement considerations, what types of transactions are encompassed in the spectrum of private inurement considerations, what the Internal Revenue Service looks for in its consideration of private inurement issues, and how the intermediate sanctions penalties work in instances of alleged private inurement.

The first half of this discussion will summarize the tax-related regulatory issues related to tax-exempt healthcare organization transactions. The valuation analyst should be generally aware of these issues in the fair market value analysis of any transaction involving (1) a tax-exempt entity and a for-profit entity or (2) a tax-exempt entity and any "disqualified person." The second half of this discussion will present a sample illustrative valuation analysis and report related as a hypothetical purchase of a tax-exempt healthcare entity by a newly formed for-profit healthcare entity. As will be presented, that hypothetical transactional valuation is prepared to provide the hypothetical transaction participants (who are created to be "disqualified persons") with professional assurance related to any private inurement aspects of the proposed transaction.

## Valuation Issues

It is noteworthy that the private inurement and excess benefit issues related to tax-exempt healthcare entities encompass two types of transactions: (1) the transfer of property and (2) the transfer for services. Both of these types of tax-exempt organization transactions involve valuation issues and fair market value valuations. Both of these types of transactions are analyzed by valuation analysts who estimate a fair market value related to a proposed or consummated transaction. And the term "fair market value" is defined the same way for both types of transactions. According to Treasury Regulation Section 53.4958-(b)(1)(i):

> Fair market value is defined as the price at which property or the right to use property would change hands between a willing buyer and a willing seller, neither being under any compulsion to buy, sell, or transfer property or the right to use property and both having reasonable knowledge of relevant facts.

Many valuation analysts are more familiar with valuations related to the transfer of property-type transactions. This type of transaction occurs when the tax-exempt entity buys or sells a business, a business ownership (equity) interest, or operating assets. Some common examples exclude when the tax-exempt healthcare entity buys or sells a hospital, clinic, physicians' practice, MRI center, urgent care center, HMO, home healthcare agency, medical equipment provider, or any other healthcare delivery organization. And these transactions encompass the purchase or sale of either assets or equity interests.

Many valuation analysts may be less familiar with valuations related to the transfer of services-type transactions. This type of transaction occurs when the tax-exempt entity hires employees or contracts for professional services. Some common examples include when the tax-exempt healthcare entity compensates a chief executive officer (CEO) or other executives, pays a medical director (or other physician professionals), hires a physician group to manage the emergency room or operating room, rents office or professional space to or from staff physicians, leases equipment to or from staff physicians, provides billing or other administrative services to staff physicians, or generally enters into any joint venture or related contractual agreement with staff physicians. To analyze such services-type transactions for concerns of private inurement, valuation analysts are often asked to opine on the fair market value of the services transfer transaction.

## Other Regulatory Considerations

In addition to Internal Revenue Service and taxation considerations, tax-exempt healthcare entities should comply with numerous other federal and state regulations regarding the transfers of property and services. This section provides a very brief summary of some of these other regulatory considerations that the valuation analyst should be aware of.

The Medicare fraud and abuse statutes make it illegal to pay, offer, or induce any remuneration in exchange for patient referrals. For example, a hospital cannot pay a staff physician in exchange for his or her patient referrals to that hospital. Accordingly, in a physician practice acquisition transaction, a hospital cannot pay any purchase price related to the physician's current or expected patient referrals. Therefore, tax-exempt acquirers (and any other healthcare industry acquirers) should not structure a transaction that appears to involve either (1) a "kickback" payment for physicians' patient referrals or (2) a "lockup" of physicians' patent referrals.

The Stark laws prohibit physicians with a financial relationship with an entity from referring patients to the entity for "designated health services" covered by either Medicare or Medicaid programs.

The Medicare anti-kickback laws prohibit the giving or receipt of anything of value to induce the referral of medical business reimbursed under the Medicare or Medicaid programs. Unlike the Stark laws, summarized next, the Medicare anti-kickback law is an "intent-based" statute. In addition, the Medicare anti-kickback law statutes make it clear that the healthcare entity payments for any property or services should be based on fair market value (and should not be variable, based on patient volume or patient referrals).

The Stark II statute became effective on Jan. 1, 1995. Like the Stark I statute, Stark II was intended to curb abuses inherent in physician self-referral arrangements. Like Stark I, Stark II prohibits physicians who have a financial relationship with a healthcare entity (whether tax-exempt or for-profit) from referring their patients to the entity for "designated health services" covered by either Medicare or Medicaid programs.

A financial relationship consists of an ownership or investment interest in the healthcare entity or a compensation arrangement with the healthcare entity. If the physician (1) does not own any portion of the healthcare entity and (2) does not pay the entity or receive any kind of payment from the entity for the referral or for anything else, then there is no financial relationship. Under the Stark legislation, a financial relationship can exist between a physician and a healthcare entity even if that relationship does not involve designated health services or the Medicare or Medicaid programs.

For example, a compensation arrangement is defined in the Stark II statute as any arrangement involving any remuneration between (1) a physician (or family member) and (2) a healthcare entity. This remuneration can involve payments for anything, such as payments for rent, payments for nonmedical services, or payments for housing or travel expenses. Accordingly, the Stark statutes would interpret the purchase of a physician's practice by a hospital (and the related payment to the selling physicians) as a financial arrangement.

Section 1877(e)(6) of the Stark II regulations provides that an isolated transaction, such as a one-time sale of a property or a practice, is not considered to be a compensation arrangement for purposes of the prohibition on patient referrals. This is true if the following conditions are met:

- The amount of remuneration for the one-time transaction sale is consistent with fair market value and is not determined, directly or indirectly, in a manner that takes into account the volume or the value of the physician's patient referrals.
- The remuneration is provided under an agreement that would be commercially reasonable even if no patient referrals are made to the acquirer healthcare entity.
- The arrangements meet any other requirements the secretary may impose by regulation as needed to protect against Medicare program or patient abuse.

It is noteworthy that the term "isolated transaction" is defined as a transaction involving a single payment between two or more persons. A transaction that involves long-term or installment payments is not considered to be an isolated transaction.

To comply with the Stark laws, a healthcare entity's property or practice purchase transaction (1) should be priced at fair market value and (2) should be structured with a purchase price that is not paid in installments.

To comply with the Stark laws related to the payment for services, the healthcare entity purchase transaction should be structured as follows:

1. There should be a written agreement signed by parties that specifies the services to be covered under the arrangement.
2. The term of the agreement should be at least one year.
3. The aggregate services contracted for should not exceed those that are reasonable and necessary for the legitimate business purpose of the subject arrangement.
4. The compensation to be paid by the healthcare entity over the term of the agreement should be:
    - defined in advance.
    - not in excess of fair market value.
    - not determined in a manner that takes into account patient volume or the value of any patient referrals or other business generated by the parties.

## Definitions

This section will summarize the definitions of certain terminology that is associated with the tax-related regulation (and valuation) of healthcare organization transactions.

### 1. Tax-exempt organization

First, a nonprofit entity is not the same as a tax-exempt organization, and a tax-exempt entity is not the same as a charitable institution. There are many types of tax-exempt organizations:

- Section 501(c)(4)—civic leagues and social welfare organizations.
- Section 501(c)(5)—labor, agricultural, and horticultural organizations.
- Section 501(c)(6)—business leagues.
- Section 501(c)(7)—social and recreational clubs.

This discussion focuses on the tax regulation with regard to Section 501(c)(3), "charitable organizations." The requirements to be a Section 501(c)(3) organization include:

- The organization is organized and operated exclusively for exempt purposes.
- The net earnings of the organization do not inure to the benefit of individuals.
- The organization is without substantial lobbying activity.
- The organization is without any political activity.
- Examples of Section 501(c)(3) organization include schools, churches, and hospitals.

Again, the focus of this discussion is on Section 501(c)(3), public charity healthcare organizations.

There are numerous advantages of Section 501(c)(3) status, including:

- exemption from most federal and state income taxes.
- exemption from most state sales taxes.
- exemption from certain payroll taxes.
- state and local property tax benefits.
- preferred U.S. postal service mailing rates.
- charitable contribution deductions allowed for its donors.
- eligibility for tax-exempt bond financing.

To maintain its Section 501 (c)(3) status, the healthcare organization is required to operate "exclusively" for exempt purposes. However, the term "exclusively" doesn't mean exclusively—it means "primarily."

**2. Disqualified person**

This term (which is also used in the private foundation tax statutes) refers to the person or persons who have a close relationship with a tax-exempt organization.

**3. Excess benefit transaction**

This is the type of property transfer or services transfer transaction that is at the heart of the intermediate sanctions rules. It is an impermissible transaction between (1) a tax-exempt organization and (2) a disqualified person.

#### 4. Excess benefit

An excess benefit is the impermissible aspect of a tax-exempt organization transaction that constitutes an excess benefit transaction. It is the amount that is used to compute one or more of the intermediate sanctions excise tax penalties.

#### 5. Revenue-sharing transaction

This is a transaction between a tax-exempt organization and a disqualified person, where the benefit flowing to the disqualified person is based, in whole or in part, on the revenue flow of the tax-exempt organization.

#### 6. Initial contract exception

This is one broad exception to the concept of the excess benefit transaction. Based on the initial contract exception, the transaction created by the initial relationship between the tax-exempt organization and the disqualified person is exempted from the intermediate sanctions excise tax penalties.

#### 7. Initial tax

This is the tax that is initially levied on an excess benefit amount. This tax is also referred to as a first-tier tax.

#### 8. Additional tax

This is the tax that can be imposed on an excess benefit amount, if the initial tax is not timely paid.

#### 9. Correction

A correction is the process that is required to undo an excess benefit transaction and return the parties to the economic position they were in before the excess benefit transaction was entered into.

### Tax-Exempt Organization Transactions—Private Inurement and Excess Benefits

Tax-exempt organizations are exempt from federal income tax as organizations described in Section 501(c)(3) only if they are organized and operated exclusively for charitable purposes within the meaning of the statute. However, such tax-exempt organizations are subject to certain restrictions with regard to acquisition, professional services, employee compensation, and other types of transactions.

The Internal Revenue Code (the Service) and many state attorneys general view tax-exempt organizations as charitable trusts for the benefit of the public. The regulatory scheme of Section 501(c)(3) is designed to:

1. ensure the furtherance of public purposes; and
2. prevent the diversion of charitable assets into private hands.

Accordingly, the tax law includes two important types of restrictions (or prohibited activities) related to tax-exempt organization transactions.

***Private Inurement***

The first type of restriction relates to private inurement. For Section 501(c)(3) tax-exempt organizations, no part of the net earnings may inure to the benefit of any private shareholder or individual. This means that an individual can't receive the tax-exempt organization's funds, except as reasonable payment for goods or services. There is no minimum threshold related to the private inurement restriction, and there is no de minimis exception.

The private inurement restriction applies only to "private shareholders or individuals," commonly referred to as "insiders" (i.e., those having a personal and private interest in or opportunity to influence the activities of the organization from the inside). It is noteworthy that the term "insider" does not appear in the Internal Revenue Code or regulations. However, it is widely used in the related legal, accounting, and valuation literature.

The intermediate sanctions provisions of Section 4958 were added to the Internal Revenue Code in 1996 and (as discussed below) used the terms "excess benefits transaction" and "disqualified person." The legislative history of Section 4958 states that "[t]he Committee intends that physicians will be considered disqualified persons only if they are in a position to exercise substantial influence over the affairs of an organization." The tax-exempt organization's payment of excessive or greater-than-reasonable compensation to an insider, such as a healthcare entity officer or director, is a prime example of prohibited private inurement.

***Private Benefit***

The second type of restriction relates to private benefit. Section 501(c)(3) tax-exempt organizations should be organized and operated to serve public rather than private interests. Unlike the private inurement transaction restrictions, the private benefit transaction restrictions are not absolute. To be a permissible transaction, a private benefit transaction should be incidental to (or a necessary concomitant of) accomplishment of the public benefits involved. Private benefit should be balanced against the public benefit. And, the Service has issued regulations that provide examples illustrating the test for serving a public rather than a private interest.

The private benefit prohibition is not limited to insiders. For example, some incidental private benefit is always present in hospital-physician relationships (e.g., when a private practice physician uses a tax-exempt hospital facilities to treat his or her paying patients).

Any private inurement or too much (i.e., other than incidental) private benefit could cause a tax-exempt hospital to lose its tax exemption. Until 1995, the revocation of the organization's tax exemption was the only sanction available to the Service. However, with regard to both private inurement and excess private benefit, the Service now relies principally on the imposition of Section 4958 intermediate sanctions excise tax penalties.

#### *Excess Benefit*

Section 4958, enacted as part of the 1996 Taxpayer Bill of Rights, allows the Service to impose penalty excise taxes on certain "excess benefits transactions" between "disqualified persons" and tax-exemption organizations described in Sections 501(c)(3) or 501(c)(4).

Excess benefit transactions include:

1. a transaction priced at other than fair market value (FMV) in which a disqualified person (a) pays less than FMV to the tax-exempt organization or (b) charges the tax-exempt organization more than FMV for a good or service;
2. an unreasonable compensation transaction, in which a disqualified person receives greater than a FMV level of compensation from the tax-exempt organization; and
3. a prohibited revenue-sharing transaction, in which a disqualified person receives payment based on the revenue of the tax-exempt organization in an arrangement specified in Section 4958 regulations that violates the inurement prohibition under current law.

### Disqualified Persons

Section 4958 defines certain people to be "disqualified persons" with respect to a tax-exempt organization, including:

1. voting members of the tax-exempt organization's governing board;
2. persons who have or share ultimate responsibility for implementing the decisions of the governing body or for supervising management, administration, or operation of the tax-exempt organization (such as president, chief executive officer, chief operating officer, treasurer, and chief financial officer unless demonstrated otherwise); and

3. persons with a material financial interest in a provider-sponsored organization.

The Section 4958 regulations clarify that this category of disqualified persons can include organizations such as management companies.

Section 4958 identifies other parties as not being a disqualified person:

1. all organizations described in Section 501(c)(3) (although the Pension Protection Act of 2006 appears to have created on exception for supporting organizations);
2. with respect to Section 501(c)(4) organizations, other Section 501(c)(4) organizations; and
3. full-time or part-time employees receiving total direct and indirect economic benefits in an amount less than the amount of compensation necessary to be highly compensated, as defined in Section 414(q)(1)(B)(i) (i.e., $100,000 in 2007), who are not substantial contributors within the meaning of Section 507(d)(2) (taking into account certain adjustments) or otherwise within the definition of "disqualified person."

In all other cases, the Section 4958 regulations indicate that a "disqualified person" is (1) any person who was, at any time during the previous five years, in a position to exercise substantial influence over the affairs of the organization, (2) certain family members (lineal descendents, brothers and sisters, whether by whole or half-blood, and spouses of any of them), or (3) an entity 35% or more of which is controlled by such persons.

The legislative history of Section 4958 recognizes that a nonemployee, such as a management company or the employee of a subsidiary (even a taxable subsidiary), could be in a position to exercise substantial influence. The Section 4958 regulations provide that, in the case of multiple organizations affiliated by common control or governing documents, the determination of whether a person does or does not have substantial influence is made separately for each applicable tax-exempt organization.

The Pension Protection Act of 2006 added several new classifications of disqualified persons. Any disqualified person with respect to a Section 509(a)(3) supporting organization is a disqualified person with respect to the supported organization. Any substantial contributor to a donor-advised fund is a disqualified person with respect to the donor-advised fund. Any investment advisor to an organization sponsoring a donor-advised fund is a disqualified person with respect to the sponsoring organization.

### The Initial Contract Rule

The Section 4958 regulations establish an "initial contract rule" to protect from intermediate sanctions liability certain "fixed" payments for the provision of services or the sale of property made under a binding written contract. The initial contract only applies to persons who were not disqualified persons immediately before entering into the initial contract. Fixed payments are defined to include an amount of cash or other property that is either (1) specified in the contract or (2) determined using a fixed formula specified in the initial contract. And payments that include a variable component (such as achieving certain levels of revenue or business activity) may qualify as a fixed payment as long as the components are calculated pursuant to a pre-established, objective formula.

### Section 4958 Penalty Excise Taxes

Under Section 4958, a disqualified person is liable for (1) an initial 25% penalty excise tax on the amount of the excess benefit and (2) an additional penalty tax of 200% on the amount of the excess benefit if the transaction is not timely corrected. A tax-exempt organization manager who knowingly, willfully, and without reasonable cause participates in an excess benefit transaction is personally liable for a 10% penalty tax (up to a maximum of $20,000) on the amount of the excess benefit.

It is noteworthy that no Section 4958 penalties are assessed on the tax-exempt organization itself. Of course, a tax exemption revocation remains an option of the Service in extreme cases.

### Intermediate Sanctions

The purpose of the intermediate sanctions tax law is to prevent wrongdoing by persons who have a special relationship with tax-exempt organizations, particularly charitable entities. Before the enactment of the intermediate sanctions laws, the Internal Revenue Service, when faced with one of these inappropriate transactions, had essentially two choices:

1. apply the private inurement doctrine or the private benefit doctrine and revoke the tax-exempt status of the subject organization, or

2. ignore the matter (and perhaps informally attempt to influence the behavior of the parties involved on a going-forward basis).

From the Service's standpoint, these two options were not sufficient. Accordingly, the Treasury and the Internal Revenue Service urged Congress to enact the intermediate sanctions legislation.

Revocation of an organization's tax-exempt status is a particularly harsh consequence. Moreover, the loss of the subject organization's tax-exempt status does not necessarily resolve the underlying problem—the party that obtained the inappropriate benefit still has it. Often, the only individuals truly punished in these situations are the beneficiaries of the tax-exempt organization's programs.

Intermediate sanctions are penalties imposed on the person or persons who engage in the inappropriate transaction with the tax-exempt organization. These sanctions are called "intermediate" because they fall between (1) the revocation of tax-exempt status and (2) inaction on the part of the Service. Also, the sanctions are not applied to the tax-exempt organization that was abused. Rather, the sanctions are imposed on the person or persons who improperly benefited from the subject property or services transfer transaction.

It is noteworthy that the intermediate sanctions law does not replace either (1) the private inurement doctrine or (2) the private benefit doctrine. Rather, the Service now has a range of taxpayer penalty options. The Service can impose the sanctions alone. The Service can impose both the sanctions and the private inurement doctrine or the Service can find the sanctions do not apply and nonetheless invoke the private benefit doctrine.

### Intermediate Sanction Taxes

The intermediate sanctions are, in fact, federal excise taxes. These federal excise taxes are applied to the amount involved in the impermissible transaction—i.e., the excess benefit. The person who pays for intermediate sanctions tax (again, not the tax-exempt organizations) is referred to as a disqualified person.

The first intermediate sanctions tax is an "initial tax." The initial tax is 25% of the amount of the excess benefit. Also, the excess benefit property or services transaction must be reversed. This reversal or refund of the excess benefit transaction is intended to put the parties in the same economic position they were in before the excess benefit transaction was entered into. This process is referred to as correction of the transaction.

If (1) the initial tax is not timely paid and (2) the offending transaction is not timely and properly corrected, then an "additional tax" may be imposed. This intermediate sanctions tax is 200% of the amount of the excess benefit. In some instances, the trustees, directors, or officers with the tax-exempt organization may also be required to pay a tax of 10% of the amount of the excess benefit.

Under certain circumstances, the intermediate sanctions tax may be abated. Generically, the Section 4958 intermediate sanctions excise taxes are referred to as "penalties."

### Intermediate Sanctions and Applicable Tax-Exempt Organizations

The Section 4958 intermediate sanctions statute and associated regulations apply with respect to public charities and tax-exempt social welfare organizations. These entities are called "applicable tax-exempt organizations" for this Section 4958 purpose.

Applicable tax-exempt organizations include any organization described in either of these two categories of tax-exempt organizations at any time during the five-year period ending on the date of the property sale or services transfer transactions. Accordingly, public charities can be:

1. churches, integrated auxiliaries of churches, and associations and conventions of churches;
2. colleges, universities, and schools;
3. hospitals, other providers of healthcare, and medical research organizations;
4. foundations supportive of governmentally operated colleges and universities;
5. units of government;
6. publicly supported charitable, educational, religious, scientific, and similar organizations; and
7. organizations that are supportive of other types of public charities.

Tax-exempt social welfare organizations include entities that are: (1) civic in nature, (2) assist a community in various ways, and (3) engage in more advocacy (usually lobbying) than is allowed for charitable organizations. Therefore, an entity qualifies as an applicable tax-exempt organization if it operated as either type of tax-exempt organization at any time in the five-year period before the excess benefit transaction occurred. This five-year period rule is referred to as the "lookback rule," and this five-year period is referred to as the "lookback period."

Section 4958 provides for no exemptions from these rules (e.g., for small organizations or religious entities). That is, all domestic public charities and all social welfare organizations are applicable tax-exempt organizations. However, a foreign organization that is tax-exempt, by determination of the Service or by treaty, as a charitable or social welfare entity is not an applicable tax-exempt organization if it receives substantially all of its support from sources outside the United States.

The Section 4958 definition of the term "applicable tax-exempt organization" encompasses the concept of recognition of the entity's tax-exempt status. Most categories of tax-exempt organizations are tax exempt because they satisfy one or more federal tax law definitions of the term. However, to be recognized as tax exempt, some organizations (1) must file notice with the Service to that effect and (2) have their exempt status recognized by the Service. This recognition is accomplished by the Service's issuing of a determination letter or private ruling.

For an organization to be a tax-exempt charitable organization, it typically files a notice with, and has its tax-exempt status recognized by, the Service. Some charitable organizations, such as churches and certain other religious organizations and small organizations, are exempt from this requirement of recognition. For a charitable organization to be recognized as an applicable tax-exempt organization, it should be in compliance with the recognition requirements.

To be tax exempt, social welfare organizations do not need to have their exempt status recognized by the Service. An organization can qualify as an applicable tax-exempt organization by reason of being an exempt social welfare organization in the following four ways:

1. The organization has applied for and received recognition from the Service as an exempt social welfare organization.
2. The organization has filed an application for recognition with the Service, seeking exempt social welfare status.
3. The organization has filed an annual information return as an exempt social welfare organization.
4. The organization has otherwise held itself out as an exempt social welfare organization.

A governmental unit or an affiliate of a governmental unit will not be recognized as an applicable tax-exempt organization if the governmental unit is (1) exempt from or not subject to taxation without regard to the general statutory basis for tax exemption or (2) relieved from the requirement of filing an annual information return. A governmental entity may be recognized as tax-exempt as an integral part of the state (1) by reason of the doctrine of intergovernmental immunity or (2) because its income is excluded from federal taxation.

An entity qualifies as a governmental unit if it is:

1. a state or local governmental unit as defined in the rules providing an exclusion from gross income for interest earned on bonds issued by these units;

2. entitled to receive deductible charitable contributions as a unit of government; or

3. an Indian tribal government or a political subdivision of this type of government.

#### Intermediate Sanctions and Individual Executives and Professionals

Under the Section 4958 intermediate sanctions law, excise taxes are imposed on excess benefit transactions that occur on or after Sept. 14, 1995. The Section 4958 excise taxes do not apply to any transaction made pursuant to a written contract that was binding on Sept. 13, 1995, and continued in force through the time of the subject transaction.

An excess benefit transaction is any transaction in which a Section 501(c)(3) or 501(c)(4) organization provides an economic benefit to a disqualified person that has a greater value than what it receives from that person. An excess benefit transaction would include: (1) providing compensation to a person in excess of the value of the services rendered or (2) selling or renting property to a person for less than the property's sale or rental value. The excess benefit is measured as the difference of the fair market value of the benefit provided to the person and the fair market value of the consideration received by the tax-exempt organization.

As summarized above, there are two types of Section 4958 excise taxes. The first type of excise tax is imposed on the disqualified person who receives an excess benefit. That tax is equal to 25% of the amount of excess benefit. There is an additional excise tax equal to 200% of the amount of the excess benefit if it is not corrected before (1) the date that the Service's deficiency notice is mailed for the 25% tax or (2) the date that the 25% tax is assessed, whichever comes first. The second type of excise tax is imposed on "organizational managers" who knowingly, willfully, and without reasonable cause or participate in the excess benefit transaction. This Section 4958 excise tax is equal to 10% of the amount of the excess benefit, but no more than $20,000.

A disqualified person is defined in Section 4958 as someone who, at any time during the five years preceding an excess benefit transaction, was in a position to exercise "substantial influence" over the affairs of the tax-exempt organization. If an individual is considered to be a disqualified person, then certain related parties are also considered disqualified persons. These related parties include: spouses; brothers or sisters; spouses of brothers or sisters; direct ancestors; direct descendants and their spouses; and corporations, partnerships, and trusts in which the disqualified person has more than a 35% interest.

Certain individuals within a tax-exempt organization are automatically identified as disqualified persons. These individuals include: (1) any individual who serves as a voting member of the governing body of the tax-exempt organization, (2) any individual who has the power or responsibilities of the president, chief executive officer, or chief operating officer of the tax-exempt organization, and (3) any individual who has the power or responsibilities of treasurer or chief financial officer of the tax-exempt organization.

An employee of a tax-exempt organization is not considered a disqualified person if he or she: (1) receives less than $100,000 of direct or indirect benefits from the tax-exempt organization for the year (adjusted for inflation), (2) is not a member of a specifically included category above, and (3) is not a substantial contributor of the organization.

The Service looks at specified facts and circumstances to indicate whether a person has "substantial influence" over the subject tax-exempt organization. In particular, the Service often considers the following factors in deciding whether an individual has "substantial influence" over the tax-exempt organization:

1. The person founded the tax-exempt organization;
2. The person is a substantial contributor;
3. The person's compensation is based on the revenue derived from the activities of the tax-exempt organization;
4. The person has authority to control or determine a significant portion of the organization's capital expenditures, operating budget, or compensation for employees; or
5. The person has managerial authority or serves as a key adviser to a person with managerial authority.

The following types of facts and circumstances would indicate to the Service that a person does not have "substantial influence" over the tax-exempt organization:

1. The person has taken a bona fide vow of poverty;
2. The person is an independent contractor (e.g., an attorney) who would not benefit from a transaction aside from the receipt of professional fees; or
3. The person is a donor who receives no more preferential treatment than other donors making comparable contributions as part of a solicitation intended to attract a substantial number of contributions.

An individual can be liable for the 10% excise tax penalty on organization managers if he or she is an officer, director, or trustee of the tax-exempt organization or is a person with powers or responsibilities similar to those of officers, directors, or trustees. Attorneys, accountants, and investment advisers acting as independent contractors are typically not considered to be organizational managers. Any person who has authority merely to recommend particular administrative or policy decisions, but not to implement them without approval of a superior, is also excluded.

A tax-exempt organization's manager will be considered to have "participated" in an excess benefit transaction not only by affirmative steps, but also by silence or inaction. That would be the case when the organization's manager does not exercise a duty to speak or take action. However, the tax-exempt organization manager will not be considered to have participated in a transaction when he or she opposed it in a manner consistent with that manager's responsibilities to the tax-exempt organization.

Tax-exempt organization managers can avoid the 10% penalty if they can show that they did not act willfully or knowingly. Tax-exempt organization managers can meet this requirement if, after disclosing all facts to an attorney, they receive a reasoned written legal opinion that a transaction does not provide an excess benefit. This procedure will protect the manager even if a transaction is later determined to be an excess benefit transaction.

Compensation to an organization's management for services rendered will not be considered an excess benefit if it is an amount that would ordinarily be paid for similar services in a similar situation. For purposes of this Section 4958 excise tax, compensation includes, but is not limited to: salary, fees, bonuses, severance payments, and all forms of deferred compensation that are earned and vested, whether paid under a tax-qualified plan or not. If deferred compensation is paid to a manager in one year for services performed by the manager in two years or more, then that compensation will be allocated to the years in which the services are performed.

Compensation also includes all benefits, whether or not included in income for federal tax purposes. For example, such benefits include: medical, dental, life insurance, disability, and both taxable and nontaxable fringe benefits (other than job-related fringe benefits and fringe benefits of inconsequential value).

An economic benefit will not be treated as reasonable compensation unless the tax-exempt organization clearly indicates its intention to treat it as compensation at the time it is provided. For example, if the tax-exempt organization fails to include compensation or other payments to disqualified persons on a Form W-2 (for employees) or Form 1099 (for board members and other nonemployees) and does not treat the payments as compensation on its Form 990, then the payments will be considered an excess benefit.

A special rule applies to arrangements that compensate a disqualified person in proportion to the revenue generated by the tax-exempt organization. Such compensation may be considered an excess benefit even if it does not exceed the fair market value of the services provided. This result can occur if, at any point, the arrangement permits a person to receive additional compensation without providing proportional benefits to the tax-exempt organization. Whether such compensation is an excess benefit will depend on the facts of the individual case. The Service will consider such factors as: (1) the relationship between the size of the benefit provided and the quality and quantity of the services provided and (2) the ability of the party receiving the compensation to control the activities that generate the revenue.

To avoid the above-mentioned 200% excise tax, the excess benefit must be undone to the extent possible. In addition, other procedures may be necessary to place the tax-exempt organization in the same position that it would have been in if the excess benefits transaction was made under the highest fiduciary standards. An excess benefit can be corrected if the disqualified person repays the tax-exempt organization an amount equal to the excess benefit plus an interest element for the period the excess benefit was outstanding. A correction may also be accomplished, in some situations, by: (1) returning the transferred property to the tax-exempt organization and (2) making any additional procedures necessary to make the tax-exempt organization whole.

### Excess Benefit Transaction Presumption of Reasonableness

There is an important "presumption of reasonableness" that every tax-exempt organization subject to the intermediate sanctions law may endeavor to take advantage of. That presumption is in favor of the tax-exempt organization that a compensation arrangement or property sale or rental is not an excess benefit. To qualify for this presumption of reasonableness, the tax-exempt organization must meet the following three requirements:

1. The compensation arrangement or property sale or rental must be approved by the tax-exempt organization's governing body or a committee of the governing body composed entirely of individuals who do not have a conflict of interest with respect to the subject transaction;

2. The governing body or its committee must have obtained and relied on "appropriate data" as to comparability prior to making its decision; and

3. The governing body or its committee must have "adequately documented" the basis for its decision at the time it was made.

These three presumption of reasonableness requirements are summarized below.

### Conflict of Interest

A member of a tax-exempt organization governing body or its committee will be treated as not having a conflict of interest if he or she:

1. is not (a) the disqualified person benefiting from the subject transaction or (b) a person related to the disqualified person;

2. is not an employee subject to the control or direction of the disqualified person;

3. does not receive compensation or other payments subject to approval of the disqualified person;

4. has no financial interest affected by the subject transaction; and

5. will not receive any economic benefit from another transaction in which the disqualified person must grant approval.

### Appropriate Data

The category of "appropriate data" includes such information and documents as: (1) the compensation levels actually paid by similarly situated organizations, both for-profit and tax-exempt, for similar positions, (2) independent compensation surveys compiled by independent consulting firms, (3) actual written offers from similar organizations competing for the services of the disqualified person, and (4) independent appraisals of the fair market value of the to-be-transferred property. There is a special "appropriate data" relief provision for tax-exempt organizations with annual gross receipts of less than $1 million. Such a tax-exempt organization will be automatically treated as satisfying the appropriate data requirement if it has data on the level of compensation actually paid by five comparable organizations in similar communities for similar services.

### Adequate Documentation

To meet the "adequate documentation" requirement, the tax-exempt organization governing body or its committee must have written or electronic records showing (1) the terms of the transaction and the date it was approved, (2) the members of the tax-exempt organization governing body or committee who were present during debate on the transaction and the names of those who voted on it, (3) the comparability data obtained, and (4) what was done about the members who had a conflict of interest. For a decision to be documented concurrently, the records must be prepared by the next meeting of the governing body or committee occurring after the final action is taken. Also, the records must be reviewed and approved by the governing body or committee as reasonable, accurate, and complete within a reasonable time period thereafter.

For purposes of this presumption of reasonableness exclusion, a tax-exempt organization governing body is: (1) a board of directors, (2) a board of trustees, or (3) an equivalent controlling body of the tax-exempt organization. A committee of the tax-exempt organization governing body (1) may be composed of any individuals permitted under state law to serve on such a committee and (2) may act on behalf of the governing body to the extent permitted by state law. The tax-exempt organization should note that if a committee member is not on the governing board and the presumption of reasonableness is relied upon, then the committee member becomes an "organization manager" for purposes of the 10% excise tax penalty. In other words, the committee member is treated like a member of the tax-exempt organization governing body if the presumption of reasonableness relied upon is rebutted by the Service. Also, a person will not be treated as a member of the governing body or its committee if he or she (1) meets with other members only to answer questions and (2) is not present during debate and voting on the transaction.

In addition, a tax-exempt organization subject to the intermediate sanctions law should note that this presumption of reasonableness is only a presumption. The Service can rebut the presumption of reasonableness if there is information indicating that (1) the compensation was not reasonable or (2) the property transfer was not at a fair market value price. However, these three requirements should go a long way toward helping a tax-exempt organization avoid the Section 4958 intermediate sanctions penalties.

## Valuation Analyst Considerations Regarding Private Inurement

This section will summarize a "top 10" list of valuation analyst considerations with regard to valuations performed for tax-exempt healthcare organizations. These valuations include both (1) fair market value appraisals of property (business interests or assets) bought and sold by the healthcare organization and (2) fair market value appraisals of the services paid for by the healthcare organization (paid as either employee compensation or vendor fees).

These considerations may not affect the valuation approaches, methods, and procedures that the valuation analyst selects and performs. And these considerations may not affect the valuation analyst's conclusions regarding the fair market value of the subject property or services. However, these are 10 factors related to the intermediate sanctions law and regulations that the valuation analyst should be aware of during the conduct of the tax-exempt healthcare organization valuation.

### *1. Tax-exempt Healthcare Organizations*

The Internal Revenue Code grants a tax exemption for nonprofit hospitals and other healthcare organizations provided that their net earnings do not inure (1) to the benefit of private shareholders or (2) to individuals with a "personal and private" interest in the healthcare entity's activities.

### *2. Criteria to be Recognized as a Tax-Exempt Organization*

To meet the statutory criteria to be recognized as a tax-exempt healthcare entity, the organization must comply with the following rules:

- Physicians cannot be "in a position to exercise substantial influence over the affairs of (the hospital)."
- The total compensation must be "reasonable" and the incentive arrangement may not be a disguised distribution of profits.
- The compensation arrangements must be negotiated or established in the context of an arm's-length relationship.
- There is a ceiling or reasonable maximum compensation level.

### *3. No Inurement*

No portion of a tax-exempt healthcare organization's income or assets may inure to the benefit of "insiders." For purposes of this consideration, the term "insiders" may be defined as someone with decision power (e.g., board members, officers, founders, selected physicians, and so on). Examples of such private inurement may include:

- excessive employee or subcontractor compensation;
- compensation based on the "net earnings" of the tax-exemption organization; and
- any transfer of property or services at less than a fair market value price.

#### *4. Penalty for Private Inurement*

There are taxation-related penalties for any violation of this no-inurement rule. The Service may apply a broad spectrum of remedies, including:

- revocation of the subject healthcare entity's tax-exempt status;
- settlement of the amount of the inurement; and
- the Section 4958 intermediate sanctions excise taxes.

#### *5. Purpose of Intermediate Sanctions*

The objective of the Section 4958 intermediate sanctions law is to curb potential abuses by penalizing participating parties (both those that benefit from the abuse and those that knowingly authorize it). The intermediate sanctions law applies if there is an "excess benefit" transaction with a "disqualified person." An excess benefit transaction occurs when the economic benefit given in a transaction is greater than the consideration received by the healthcare tax-exempt organization. A disqualified person is any person having the ability to exercise influence over the affairs of the tax-exempt organization.

#### *6. Imposition of Penalty Excise Taxes*

Section 4958 imposes excise tax penalties on:

1. the disqualified person who has to correct the excess amount (i.e., pay it back to the tax-exemption healthcare organization) plus pay a penalty tax of 25%; and
2. the organization manager who has to pay a tax equal to 10% of the excess benefit amount (not to exceed $20,000 per transaction).

#### *7. Rebuttable Presumption of Reasonableness*

There is a rebuttable presumption of reasonableness with regard to the tax-exempt healthcare organization entering into property or services transfer transactions when:

1. the transaction is approved in advance by an independent, authorized body of the tax-exempt organization;

2. the decision was based on the appropriate comparability data; and
3. the decision is adequately and timely documented (i.e., written down by the later of the next meeting or 60 days).

#### *8. Excess Benefit Transaction*

An excess benefit transaction is any transaction in which an economic benefit is provided by the tax-exempt healthcare organization directly or indirectly to or for the use of any "disqualified person" if the fair market value of the benefit exceeds the fair market value of the consideration.

#### *9. Disqualified Persons*

For purposes of the Section 4958 intermediate sanctions rules, a "disqualified person" includes:

1. a voting member of a board of the tax-exempt organization;
2. the chief executive officer, chief operating officer, treasurer, or chief financial officer;
3. any person, at any time during the previous five years, in a position to exercise substantial influence over the affairs of the organization;
4. identified family members of the above; and
5. a 35% controlled entity.

#### *10. Not Disqualified Person*

For purposes of the Section 4958 intermediate sanctions rules, the following "persons" are not disqualified persons:

1. organizations described in Section 501(c)(3); this exception was created by the Pension Protection Act of 2006;
2. other Section 501(c)(4) organizations (applicable for Section 501(c)(4) organizations only); and
3. employees receiving less than $100,000 a year in compensation.

### Reasonableness of Tax-Exempt Organization Compensation

One of the current controversy areas related to the intermediate sanctions requirements relates to the reasonableness of compensation. This is particularly true with regard to healthcare industry tax-exempt organizations. This reasonableness of compensation issue appears to be the current focus of Internal Revenue Service scrutiny with regard to tax-exempt healthcare entities. To alleviate concerns regarding intermediate sanctions, the tax-exempt healthcare entity should establish that its executives and physician employees are not paid more than a fair market value-level of compensation.

Related to this reasonableness of compensation issue, many tax-exempt healthcare entities are considering the formation of a dedicated compensation committee. Such a compensation committee would:

1. adopt a written charter;

2. be comprised of independent directors; and

3. be authorized to approve the organization's executive compensation.

And such a compensation committee would likely adopt a written compensation policy.

When considering the reasonableness of tax-exempt healthcare organization compensation, the Service looks at how the organization determined and documented the comparability of its executive compensation to other similarly situated organizations. In particular, the valuation analyst can assist the tax-exempt healthcare organization with the following:

1. compensation levels paid by similarly situated organizations, both taxable and tax-exempt;

2. independent compensation surveys compiled by independent consulting firms;

3. actual written offers from similar institutions; and

4. independent appraisals of the fair market value of the subject executive compensation.

The valuation analyst can assemble compensation data and prepare a compensation appraisal that considers the following:

1. make sure that any compensation consultant relied on is independent and has no incentive to support higher pay and benefits;

2. use data for the same or the closest functional position, and support these data in the board minutes; and

3. use data for organizations with a similar level of annual revenue, or show that the compensation data was "normalized" to fit organizations of a similar size.

In the preparation of a fair market value compensation appraisal (i.e., a reasonableness of compensation study), the valuation analyst should note the following:

1. for-profit entity compensation data are permitted, but do not rely exclusively on for-profit entity compensation data;
2. include compensation data related to prevalence and the value of significant employee benefits; and
3. make sure that every element is considered and the total compensation is assessed for reasonableness (and approved by an authored body of the tax-exempt healthcare organization).

The approving body of the tax-exempt healthcare organization is protected in relying on the valuation analyst's written reasoned analysis, if the valuation analyst certifies that he or she:

1. holds themselves out to the public as a compensation consultant;
2. performs this type of compensation valuation regularly; and
3. is qualified to perform such compensation valuations.

Such a written certification should be included in every type of compensation appraisal performed by the valuation analyst.

### Recent Developments

Effective March 28, 2008, the Treasury issued final Section 501(c)(3) regulations regarding applicable tax-exempt organizations and excess benefit transactions. These new regulations clarify the substantive requirements for tax exemption under Section 501(c)(3). These new regulations also clarify the relationship between the substantive requirements for tax exemption under Section 501(c)(3) and the imposition of Section 4958 excise taxes on excess benefit transactions.

These new regulations discuss both (1) the imposition of the Section 4958 intermediate sanctions excise taxes and (2) the possible revocation of a tax-exempt organization's exemption status. Regulation 1.501(c)(3)-1 adds a new paragraph F that includes in part:

> (ii) *Determination of whether revocation of tax-exempt status is appropriate when Section 4958 excise taxes also apply.* In determining whether to continue to recognize the tax-exempt status of an applicable tax-exempt organization (as defined in Section 4958(e)

and Section 53.4958-2) described in Section 4958(c)3 that engaged in one or more excess benefit transactions (as defined in Section 4958(c) and Section 53,4958-4) that violate the prohibition on inurement under Section 501(c)(3), the Commissioner will consider all relevant facts and circumstances, including, but not limited to, the following—

(A) The size and scope of the organization's regular and ongoing activities that further exempt purposes before and after the excess benefit transaction or transactions occurred;

(B) The size and scope of the excess benefit transaction or transactions (collectively, if more than one) in relation to the size and scope of the organization's regular and ongoing activities that further exempt purposes;

(C) Whether the organization has been involved in multiple excess benefit transactions with one or more persons;

(D) Whether the organization has implemented safeguards that are reasonably calculated to prevent excess benefit transactions; and

(E) Whether the excess benefit transaction has been corrected (within the meaning of Section 4958(f)(6) and Section 53-4958-7) or the organization has made good-faith efforts to seek correction from the disqualified person(s) who benefited from the excess benefit transaction.

(iii) All factors will be considered in combination with each other.

In addition, the new regulations provide several examples regarding private inurement and the application of the Section 4958 intermediate sanctions penalty taxes. While it is not related to a healthcare industry organization, the following example is included in the March 28, 2008 regulations and is relevant to this intermediate sanctions discussion:

*Example 1.* (i) O was created as a museum for the purpose of exhibiting art to the general public. In Years 1 and 2, O engages in fundraising and in selecting, leasing, and preparing an appropriate facility for a museum. In Year 3, a new board of trustees is elected. All of the new trustees are local art dealers. Beginning in Year 3 and continuing to the present, O uses a substantial portion of its revenue to purchase art solely from its trustees at prices that exceed fair market value. O exhibits and offers for sale all of the art it purchases. O's Form 1023, "Application for Recognition of Exemption," did not disclose the possibility that O would purchase art from its trustees.

> (ii) O's purchases of art from its trustees at more than fair market value constitute excess benefit transactions between applicable tax-exempt organizations and disqualified persons under Section 4958. Therefore, these transactions are subject to the applicable excise taxes provided in that section. In addition, O's purchase of art from its trustees at more than fair market value violate the proscription against inurement under Section 501(c)(3) and paragraph (c)(2) of this section.

The following example from the March 28, 2008 regulations is also relevant to this discussion of private inurement, excess benefits transactions, and the Section 4958 intermediate sanctions penalties:

> *Example 4.* (i) O conducts activities that further exempt purposes. O uses several buildings in the conduct of its exempt activities. In Year 1, O sold one of the buildings to Company K for an amount that was substantially below fair market value. The sale was a significant event in relation to O's other activities. C, O's chief executive officer, owns all of the voting stock of Company K. When O's board of trustees approved the transaction with Company K, the board did not perform due diligence that could have made it aware that the price paid by Company K to acquire the building was below fair market value. Subsequently, but before the IRS commences an examination of O, O's board of trustees determines that Company K paid less than the fair market value for the building. Thus, O concludes that an excess benefit transaction occurred. After the board makes this determination, it promptly removes C as chief executive officer, terminates C's employment with O, and hires legal counsel to recover the excess benefit from Company K. In addition, O promptly adopts a conflict of interest policy and new contract review procedures designed to prevent future recurrences of this problem.
>
> (ii) The sale of the building by O to Company K at less than fair market value constitutes an excess benefit transaction between an applicable tax-exempt organization and a disqualified person under Section 4958 in Year 1. Therefore, this transaction is subject to the applicable excise taxes provided in that section. In addition, this transaction violates the proscription against inurement under Section 501(c)(3) and paragraph (c)(2) of this section.

## Revocation of Tax-Exempt Status

As indicated in the recently issued Section 501(c)(3) regulations, the Service still possesses its ultimate weapon with regard to tax-exempt healthcare organizations—i.e., the revocation of the organization's tax-exempt status. With regard to healthcare industry entities and other tax-exempt organizations, the valuation analyst should be aware that the Service may seek revocation—in addition to the provision of the Section 4958 intermediate sanctions excise taxes.

The Service has made it clear that it will consider a list of facts and circumstances in determining when the level of excess benefit transactions will jeopardize a healthcare organization's tax exemption. These factors include, but are not limited to, the following:

1. the size and scope of the tax-exempt organization's regular and ongoing activities that further exempt purposes before and after the excess benefit transaction or transactions occurred;
2. the size and scope of the excess benefit transaction or transactions (collectively, if there are more than one) in relation to the size and scope of the tax-exempt organization's regular and ongoing activities that further exempt purposes;
3. whether the tax-exempt organization has been involved in repeated excess benefit transactions;
4. whether the tax-exempt organization has implemented safeguards that are reasonably calculated to prevent future violations; and
5. whether the excess benefit transaction has been corrected or the tax-exempt organization has made good-faith efforts to seek correction from the disqualified persons who benefited from it.

In other words, both the valuation analyst and the tax-exempt organization board should be aware that the imposition of the Section 4958 excise taxes are the Service's "intermediate" weapon. Revocation of the tax-exempt organization's exemption status is still the Service's ultimate weapon.

### Summary and Conclusion

The valuation analyst should be aware of the Section 4958 relationship with other federal tax laws and with other federal and state regulations. There are three general sets of federal laws that are intended to achieve the same objective: prevent persons who have a close relationship with a tax-exempt healthcare organization from manipulating the flow of income or assets to them for their private benefit. These federal laws include the Stark legislation, the Medicare fraud and abuse statutes, and the tax-exempt organization provisions of the Internal Revenue Code.

All of these federal laws (and many corresponding state laws) are directly influenced by the following three legal concepts:

1. the private inurement doctrine;
2. the private benefit doctrine; and
3. the self-dealing rules.

The valuation analyst should be aware that the private inurement doctrine directly influences the Section 4958 intermediate sanctions rules. In many ways, the Section 4958 rules are a codification of the private inurement legal doctrine. The legal concepts of private inurement and excess benefit transactions are essentially identical. The same is true with respect to the legal concepts of the insider and the disqualified person. In the case of the private inurement doctrine, the ultimate sanction is the Service's revocation of tax-exempt status. The Service can apply the private inurement doctrine either (1) in lieu of the intermediate sanctions excise tax penalties or (2) in addition to the Section 4958 excise tax penalties.

The valuation analyst should be aware that the private benefit doctrine is applicable only to charitable organizations. That is, this legal doctrine is not applicable to other types of tax-exempt organizations, including social welfare organizations. The private inurement doctrine is applicable to both public charities and private foundations. In many ways, the legal concepts of private benefit and private inurement are essentially the same. That is, every transaction that is a private inurement is also a private benefit. The ultimate sanction, too, is the same: the Service's revocation of the organization's tax-exempt status.

The two principal differences between these legal doctrines are: (1) a private benefit transaction does not require an insider and (2) the tax law recognizes the idea of incidental private benefit. Therefore, the private benefit doctrine can apply even where the private inurement doctrine and the Section 4958 intermediate sanctions tax penalties cannot apply.

The valuation analyst should be aware that the rules concerning self-dealing and the Section 4958 intermediate sanctions rules do not overlap. This is because the legal rules concerning self-dealing apply to charitable organizations only with respect to private foundations. In contrast, the Section 4958 intermediate sanctions tax rules apply only with respect to public charities. Nonetheless, the self-dealing rules are still significant within the intermediate sanctions context. This is because the Section 4958 intermediate sanctions rules are patterned largely on the private foundation rules.

The valuation analyst should be aware that most healthcare industry professional advisers consider the Section 4958 intermediate sanctions rule to be a good idea. The Section

4958 provisions place the sanction—i.e., the excise tax penalties—where it should be: on the persons who inappropriately extracted a benefit from charitable and social welfare organizations and not on the tax-exempt healthcare organization itself. The intermediate sanctions rules—based on a standard of reasonableness—are an improvement over the unnecessarily stringent private foundation rules. Those rules effectively prohibit transactions with foundations and disqualified persons with respect to them.

The valuation analyst who practices in the healthcare industry should be aware of the various regulatory requirements with regard to property transfer fair market value appraisals and compensation for services fair market value appraisals. The valuation analyst should be familiar with the regulatory environment with regard to private inurement, excess benefit transactions, intermediate sanctions excise tax penalties, and other tax-exempt organization regulatory issues. The valuation analyst should be aware of these issues to provide valuation services to tax-exempt healthcare organizations that will help them address these regulatory concerns.

Chapter 10

# Converting Physician Practices to Tax-Exempt Status: Is There an Upside to the Downturn?

*By Mark O. Dietrich, CPA/ABV*

Historically, hospitals and physician practices have integrated for a variety of non-tax-related reasons. Integrated delivery systems provide hospitals with immediate direct revenues from an expanded patient base and offer the potential for substantial indirect revenues flowing from inpatient referrals. The physicians who sell their practice may benefit from having access to an established hospital and its attendant perks, such as superior managed care contracts and the ability to offer patients a wider range of services. Another particularly significant consideration, given the long-standing opposition of the Federal Trade Commission (FTC) and Department of Justice (DOJ) to physician joint-contracting efforts, includes qualification under the *Copperweld* doctrine,[1] where common legal control permits the negotiation of nonrisk contracts in addition to risk-based and quality-based contracts.

Tax benefits play a role, however. When the acquiring hospital is tax-exempt, another benefit is the ability to operate the acquired physician practice on a tax-exempt basis. The obvious incentive is the ability to retain the practice's profits free of income tax, but this strategy presents a variety of issues.

This article is concerned with the tax aspects of a physician practice's acquisition and conversion to tax-exempt status. Basis tax principles of the transaction are discussed first. The article then explains how to reduce the tax cost of the transaction through

1 *See Copperweld v. Independence Tube*, 467 U.S. 752 (1984).

proper valuation techniques. The article concludes with a comment on how the current economic downturn may benefit acquiring hospitals and selling physicians by reducing their tax cost.

### Basic Tax Consequences

A Section 501(c)(3)[2] hospital seeking to acquire a for-profit physician practice to operate on a tax-exempt basis typically structures the acquisition through a newly formed nonprofit corporation, of which the hospital is the sole member and ultimate governing authority. The newly formed entity purchases the practice's assets or stock if the practice is in corporate form. When the physician practice is organized as a Subchapter C corporation, the selling physicians face an unavoidable "double tax" if they sell the corporation's assets to the hospital. First, the corporation pays tax on any gain realized from the sale of its assets,[3] leaving only the after-tax proceeds available for distribution to the physician shareholders. The shareholders are then individually taxed on any distributions received from the corporation.[4] Reversing the two steps does not change the result; double taxation similarly applies if the corporation first distributes its assets to its shareholders, who then sell them to the hospital. The Internal Revenue Service (IRS) illustrated these principles in the following example in its 2000 Exempt Organizations Continuing Professional Education Text (EO CPE Text):

> In 1990, 10 physicians invested $50,000 each ($500,000 in total) in a C corporation to purchase land and construct a freestanding ambulatory surgery center. The ambulatory surgery center was constructed and has thrived. In 1999, the physician-owners decided to sell the center to a local hospital. The hospital wanted to purchase the corporate assets instead of the stock because of liability concerns and to operate as a tax-exempt organization. Assume for this example that the C corporation's basis in its assets is $1 million and it has no liabilities. If it sells its assets to the hospital for $6 million, it will be taxed on its gain (35% × $5 million = $1.75 million), leaving $4.25 million for the physician-shareholders in liquidation. They will net about $2.57 million on the sale after paying individual tax (39.6% × $4.25 million = $1.68 million).[5]

The physician-shareholders can avoid double taxation, however, by instead selling their stock in the C corporation. In a taxable stock purchase, the selling shareholders are still

2 Unless otherwise specified, all section references are to the Internal Revenue Code of 1986, as amended (Code).
3 Code Section 1001.
4 Code Sections 301 and 311.
5 Charles F. Kaiser III and Thomas Miller, *IRS Exempt Organizations Continuing Professional Education Text for FY 2000*, Topic U, Treas. Reg. Section 1.337(d)-4 and Exempt Organizations (2000 EO CPE Text), at p. 3 of the PDF, *available at* www.irs.gov/pub/irs-tege/eotopicu00.pdf.

subject to one level of tax on the gain realized from the sale of their stock, but there is no corporate-level tax on the sale. The above example continues:

> In contrast, if the hospital buys the C corporation stock from the physicians, the physicians will be taxed $1.68 million on their gain on the stock, but the corporate tax, $1.75 million, will be deferred.[6]

The preceding example illustrates that the selling shareholders are theoretically able to increase their after-tax proceeds by $1.75 million by selling their stock in the C corporation rather than selling the corporation's assets. But the 2000 EO CPE Text importantly points out that corporate-level tax is not eliminated; it merely shifts to the purchaser. Although the hospital could continue to defer the corporate-level tax as long as it operates the C corporation as a for-profit subsidiary, this is not an effective use of its tax-exempt status. If the hospital wishes to operate the physician practice on a tax-exempt basis, it must either convert the subsidiary to a tax-exempt organization or distribute the subsidiary's assets to itself—both options trigger taxable gain to the hospital.[7]

A hospital engaging in an arm's-length stock purchase should adjust the purchase price to account for the corporate-level tax it would eventually incur on the built-in gain. The failure to consider the tax could constitute a private benefit to the selling shareholders and implicate the anti-inurement or intermediate sanctions provisions of the code.[8] Thus, the shareholders in the preceding example have not necessarily increased their after-tax proceeds by $1.75 million by selling stock rather than assets. An appraisal prepared in connection with such a stock transaction must consider this tax.

## Valuing Intangible Assets

An arm's-length acquisition of a physician practice requires an independent appraisal, and thus a 1996 EO CPE Text discussing the valuation of medical practices has become a staple in the healthcare appraisal community.[9] Although instructional on the use of the discounted cash-flow method under the income approach, the document importantly establishes criteria for the allocation of intangible asset value that while basic to valuation theory, are often overlooked in valuing medical practices.

6 *Id.* at p. 3 of the PDF.

7 Code Sections 311 and 337(b)(2); see Treas. Reg. Section 1.337(d)-4.

8 See 2000 EO CPE Text, supra note 5, at p. 2 of the PDF.

9 Charles F. Kaiser and Amy Henchey, *IRS Exempt Organizations Continuing Professional Education Text for FY 1996*, Topic Q, "Valuation of Medical Practices" (1996 EO CPE Text), *available at* www.irs.gov/pub/irs-tege/eotopicq96.pdf.

For example, the 1996 EO CPE Text explains that although the value of goodwill can be allocated to specific intangible assets, "the value of the latter is limited to the value of the former, as calculated under the income approach."[10] In other words, the total value of the individual intangible assets cannot exceed the total value of the medical practice net of the aggregate fair market value of the tangible assets.

The authors of the 1996 EO CPE Text also point out that intangible value is not always present in a medical practice, a fact appraisers all too frequently overlook. Rather, they mistakenly attribute value to certain intangible assets even when the discounted cash-flow method shows that the medical practice has no overall intangible value. This error often occurs with intangible assets that are typically valued using the cost method, such as medical records, assembled workforce, and trade name. Appraisers forget that using the cost method to value such intangible assets is only appropriate if the income approach first finds the presence of intangible value.

### Personal Versus Enterprise Goodwill

Well-defined tax principles, originally enunciated by the United States Tax Court in *Martin Ice Cream*[11] and *Norwalk*[12] and recently re-emphasized in *Derby*,[13] establish a framework for potentially reducing the value of corporate-level intangible assets, thus reducing the tax cost of converting a physician practice to tax-exempt status. These cases illustrate how to distinguish between personal goodwill, i.e., goodwill owned personally by the business' owners or employees, and goodwill owned by the corporation.

In *Derby*, a group of independent physicians decided to affiliate with a larger healthcare organization and sold the tangible assets of their practices to a tax-exempt medical foundation that was affiliated with multiple hospitals in an integrated delivery system. The acquiring organization, however, refused to purchase the goodwill or similar intangible assets associated with the physicians' practices, citing, in part, potential violation of the Medicare and Medicaid anti-kickback statute. Instead, the physicians donated their intangibles to the tax-exempt foundation and claimed charitable contribution deductions. The tax court, however, denied the physicians' deductions, finding that the physicians received consideration for their intangible assets in the form of future employment with the medical foundation.

---

10 *Id.* at p. 22 of the PDF.

11 *Martin Ice Cream v. Commissioner*, 110 T.C. 189 (1998).

12 *Norwalk v. Commissioner*, T.C. Memo. 1998-279; *see "Goodwill Requires Enforceable Covenant Not to Compete," CPA Expert* (Spring 1999).

13 *Derby v. Commissioner*, T.C. Memo. 2008-45.

The *Derby* court observed that the terms of employment contracts—and particularly noncompetition provisions—are a crucial factor in determining whether enterprise goodwill is present and whether a physician has assigned his or her professional goodwill to the practice, thereby making it a practice asset. However, many appraisers incorrectly believe that fair market value contemplates or requires the sellers agreeing to provide the buyers with a noncompete agreement. This assumption is often blindly included in the valuation without confirmation, as was the case in *Derby*.

Appraisers must keep in mind that noncompete agreements can be independently valued, and that such agreements do not contain standard provisions. The nature of the included (or excluded) provisions drives the value of noncompete agreements. Moreover, different states have different statutory and judicial precedents on what is and what is not enforceable in such an agreement, and these also may have a consequential effect on value. It is more accurate to state that fair market value contemplates understanding the terms of the transaction and the laws that govern it before attempting to assign value to the whole or its component parts.

*Derby* also emphasized the necessity of using negotiated post-transaction compensation in the valuation model. Reasonable compensation is a critical aspect of determining whether and to what extent any enterprise goodwill (as distinct from personal goodwill) is present and how much of that enterprise goodwill would be allocable to a noncompete agreement. A November 2005 article in the *Journal of Accountancy* articulated why an accurate valuation must incorporate compensation:

> If the selling physician(s) still will be employed by the practice after the sale, the cash flow the buyer is purchasing—the subject of the valuation—can't be known without including a realistic amount of post-sale compensation in the valuation model.[14]

The threshold question in such a valuation is relatively easy to state, if difficult to appraise or value: How much of the practice's value would be lost if the physicians competed or were able to compete with the practice following conversion. Importantly, this question applies *whether or not* the physicians have a pre-existing noncompete agreement, because it is the basis for the methodology used to value that noncompete agreements.

The valuation method's mechanics are beyond the scope of this article but can be summarized as follows:

1. Determine reasonable compensation under the fair market value standard for the physicians post-conversion;

14 *"Medical Practices: A BV Rx, J".* Accountancy (Nov. 2005).

2. Determine the value of the entity assuming that noncompete agreements are in place based on historical and forecasted entity cash-flows using the discounted cash-flow method;
3. Allocate that value first to working capital assets (cash, receivables, inventory), then to property and equipment, and finally any remainder to intangible assets in the manner contemplated by the residual method of allocation described in the regulations under Section 338;
4. Allocate that intangible value first to any readily identifiable intangible assets, such as a below-market lease on real property assumable by a purchaser, trade name, trained workforce, patient charts, or others that the buyer could retain if the sellers competed. (Trained workforce contemplates an enforceable nonsolicitation provision; patient chart valuation requires an understanding of the extent to which a patient requesting transfer of his or her personal health information to a new practice entity could be charged);
5. Any remaining value is attributable to the sellers' noncompete agreement (an ordinary income component) and personal goodwill (a capital asset component);
6. Assess and quantify the entity cash flows that would be lost if the sellers competed post-transaction;
7. Revisit any allocation in Step 3 above to identifiable intangible assets;
8. Assess and quantify the probability that the sellers would, in fact, compete post-transaction;[15]
9. The quantified probability is applied to the forecasted cash flow expected to be lost as a result of competition then discounted to present value to determine the noncompete's value. This step must consider the enforceability of a noncompete in the applicable jurisdiction; and
10. The balance is a capital asset in the nature of personal goodwill of the sellers.

### Hypothetical Sale

Appraisers are often confused by the concept of the hypothetical buyer and seller in the fair market value standard. They mistakenly believe that it requires the use of hypothetical assumptions such as an enforceable noncompete agreement, even when the interest being valued has no such agreements in place.

15 For litigation, alternative damage causation theories may be relevant such as violation of fiduciary obligations or intent to defraud via the sale, among others.

Appraisers must understand that a valuation in an actual transaction is significantly different than a valuation based upon a hypothetical sale. Valuations accompanying an estate and gift tax reporting, litigation, or a property division for marital dissolution, unlike a business acquisition, lack transactional documents and do require the appraiser to make a variety of assumptions.

An interest in the assets or equity of a private company is a specific basket of legal and contractual rights and obligations and economic risks and rewards. Each of that basket's characteristics must be evaluated to determine at what price a member of the universe of hypothetical buyers and sellers would transact. The "hypothetical" aspect of the valuation in a real transaction is what buyer and seller would pay for the specific business or business interest being transacted *as reflected in the transaction documents.*

Understanding this difference is critical in a healthcare transaction because failure to do so may implicate the anti-kickback statute, Stark law, or other civil and criminal penalty provisions. It is perhaps easier to understand within the concept of post-closing adjustments in an actual transaction. A typical post-closing adjustment in the purchase of the stock or equity of a business would be an increase or decrease in the sales price based upon the actual measure of the liabilities assumed and paid; in an asset transaction, those liabilities would typically not be assumed. Another adjustment would be for any difference in the value of accounts receivable purchased versus ultimately collected, if they are purchased at all. Certainly, a hospital purchasing a physician practice for a value that includes the accounts receivable when they are not transferred would be placed in significant jeopardy. Paying an amount that assumes a noncompete is in place without obtaining one as part of the transaction should be viewed no differently.

## Advantages of a Down Economy

The current troubled economic times may offer an unforeseen and counterintuitive benefit to hospitals and physicians seeking to integrate. Namely, the depressed economy may produce depressed valuations of physician practices. This might not sound like a reward, but lower valuations translate to reduced tax costs in converting physician practices to tax-exempt status.

One cause for lower valuations is that perceived risk is significantly higher in the current environment than at any other time in recent memory. Risk and value are inversely related. Another factor is that access to capital is significantly more difficult. Despite heretofore unforeseen low interest rates, many entities are unable to borrow money at any rate. Inability to access debt capital in turn requires increasing amounts of more-expensive equity capital. But as the stock market indicates, that well has been reduced to a trickle.

An appraiser typically captures these factors in the valuation multiple through development of the discount rate or cost of capital. Traditional methods of developing that multiple, however, do not capture the current combination of increased risk and decreased availability of capital.

In addition to lower enterprise values, increased marketability discounts—including consideration of liquidity factors—may be available for conversions taking place now. As the economic depression reduces the pool of potential buyers, it is becoming more difficult to find a suitable acquirer. A smaller market thus warrants consideration of a larger valuation discount for lack of marketability.

## Conclusion

The contractual agreements a physician practice entity has in place with its owner- and nonowner-physicians determine how much of the goodwill or intangible value is owned by the practice and how much is owned personally by the physicians. To the extent that the enforceability of a noncompete, nonsolicitation, trade secrets, or other provision is limited or barred by state law, that portion of the agreement will have less or conceivably no value. A practice owned by physicians that has no post-termination noncompete agreements does not contractually own the personal goodwill of those physicians and therefore, should not recognize a taxable gain on that personal goodwill in a conversion to tax-exempt status.

Chapter 11

# What Goes Around Comes Around: *Derby v. Commissioner*

*By Mark O. Dietrich, CPA/ABV*

Established healthcare valuation principles from the 1990s remain in full force and effect.

The tax court case *Derby, et al. v. Commissioner*[1] is important for a variety of reasons, not the least of which is its instructive value as today's consolidation in the healthcare industry mirrors that in the early and mid-1990s when the *Derby* case originated. Key factors in the case include those which this author has repeatedly cited in numerous articles over the last 10 years in *CPA Expert* and the *Journal of Accountancy,* among others. Those factors are as follows:

1. The use of expected post-transaction physician compensation in the discounted cash flow model based on the transaction documents *rather than* use of some arbitrary compensation figure, such as the median, for a given physician specialty.
2. Allocating enterprise or invested capital value among working capital, fixed assets, and intangible assets.
3. Carefully studying transaction documents to discern the character and extent of any intangibles being transferred or not being transferred.
4. The critical import of allocating between personal and professional goodwill and enterprise goodwill when valuing a medical practice for acquisition by a hospital.

1 *Charles A. and Marian L. Derby, et al.,1 Petitioners v. Commissioner,* Respondent, T.C. Memo. 2008-45, Gale, Judge.

5. The importance of any noncompete agreement in determining the value of the medical practice and the import of *Norwalk v. Commissioner.*

6. The need for "donative intent" when claiming a deduction for the value of a medical practice or other enterprise allegedly donated to a tax-exempt entity.

7. The relevance of the Friendly Hills private letter ruling and the 1994 Exempt Organizations Continuing Professional Education Technical Instruction Program manuals.

8. The citation of the anti-kickback statute (AKS).

9. The issue of the timeliness of the valuation versus the date of the transaction.

This is a well-written decision that highlights the typical issues in the valuation of a physician practice for sale or other transfer to a hospital or integrated delivery system. As such, Judge Gale's words are frequently quoted.

### Case Summary

The case arose out of a claimed charitable deduction for the intangible value of the medical practices of more than a dozen physicians who sold their medical practices to Sutter Medical Foundation (Sutter) in 1994. The purchase agreements contained payments for fixed assets, while the selling physicians retained their accounts receivable.

The transaction took place during the period of consolidation of the healthcare industry associated with the rise of managed care and capitation on the West Coast in the early 1990s, which later spread across the country. Although restrictive managed care and capitation have fallen into disfavor and lost market share over the last six or seven years, consolidation is once again the rage in healthcare. Although some markets, such as Boston, are reconsidering the use of capitation, much of the present consolidation is driven by the more typical revenue concerns associated with fee for service medicine. Major hospital and ancillary testing revenue sources, such as cardiology, orthopedics, and high-tech imaging, are driving many of today's transactions.

The key decisions for the court were whether there had, in fact, been a *donative* transfer of intangible value, what the value was, and *if* the claimed value of the donation was overstated, whether the donor-physicians were subject to understatement of overvaluation penalties. As such, the valuations submitted by the taxpayers in connection with the donation received careful scrutiny from the court.

Critical in the ultimate resolution of the donation issue was a review of the history of the transaction with Sutter, which had declined to *pay* anything for intangible value, citing the AKS and the "famous" Thornton Letter in which the then Deputy Counsel of the Office of the Inspector General stated that a sale of goodwill by a physician to a hospital was problematic. Peter Grant, legal counsel in the seminal integrated delivery system transaction of the 1990s, represented the *Derby* physicians known as the Davis Medical Group (DMG).

> Unlike Foundation, Sutter Health was unwilling to pay anything for the intangible assets, or goodwill, that might be associated with petitioners' medical practices ... first, and principally, because Sutter Health's management believed that doing so might constitute a crime under the Medicare and Medicaid antikickback statute, 42 U.S.C. Sec. 1320a-7b(b), prohibiting payments for referrals of patients eligible for Medicare or Medicaid; and second, because Sutter Health's management believed, on the basis of their projections of the financial performance of the UHMG physicians' group after acquisition, that any additional payment for intangibles would have rendered the deal financially nonviable for Sutter Health.
>
> Mr. Grant recommended that petitioners structure the transfers of the intangibles as donations because that technique had been used in connection with an acquisition of a group medical practice by a nonprofit medical foundation (*Friendly Hills Healthcare Foundation*), for which Mr. Grant had served as an adviser. Mr. Grant was familiar with the annual *Exempt Organizations Continuing Professional Education Technical Instruction Program manuals*, including the manual for 1994.... *[Emphasis added]*

### Transaction Overview

The parties retained Houlihan Lokey (Houlihan), the valuation firm in the Friendly Hills transaction, and arranged for an appraisal of the "business enterprise value" defined below. Note the emphasized items.

> The fair market value of the aggregate assets of [the Davis Medical Group] *exclusive of any benefit or element of value conferred upon Sutter* [Health] as a consequence of its current or proposed relationship with.... [Davis Medical Group], and *with consideration of proposed post-transaction compensation and benefits to the physician group.*

Houlihan also agreed to "allocate the appraised value ... to each of its physician/shareholders" using a method to be agreed upon in consultation [physician] steering committee, but the agreed-upon method "[had to] be acceptable to Houlihan." *[Emphasis added]*

SWMG (Davis Medical Group later changed its name to Sutter West Medical Group, or SWMG) entered into a professional services agreement (PSA) or employment contract with Sutter as part of the transaction.[2] The court spelled out the key economic terms of the PSA, which included a very limited noncompete—the terms of which are critical in this valuation and, for that matter, any such valuation—and a complex revenue sharing formula that included a minimum compensation guaranty. The PSA also contained what amounted to a signing bonus that the court would see as in part a payment for goodwill.

> The PSA contained a noncompete provision, under which SWMG and its physician shareholder/employees were prohibited from participating in the ownership, management, operation, or control of any business or person providing healthcare services within the service area covered by the agreement. However, specifically exempted from this prohibition was any SWMG physician who left the employment of SWMG.... Departing physician may give written notice to the departing physician's patients named in the departing physician's patient list furnished to SMF on or before the ... effective date ... announcing the departing physician's separation from ... SWMG and his or her new practice location, and offering the patient an opportunity to choose whether his or her patient records should remain with SMF or be transferred to the departing physician.
>
> To provide an incentive to SWMG to form and sustain a group, SMF will pay SWMG a physician access bonus.... The "physician access bonus" was $35,000 for each of SWMG's full-time physicians.

The transaction documents stated that the seller and buyer believed the purchase price was less than the fair market value and that the difference was being donated. Significantly, the document contained a provision requiring the appraisal be completed within 60 days—designed to avoid a "stale" valuation. Finally, a discounted cashflow model was used. All of the factors outlined in the case closely track the Friendly Hills private letter ruling and the *1994 Exempt Organizations Continuing Professional Education Technical Instruction Program* manual.

As discussed above, the donation was to be allocated among 29 physicians who formed the group practice based on the valuation. In actuality, the donation was allocated using a formula designed by one of the physicians that attributed "(i) 50% of the aggregate value on the basis of each physician's share of gross revenues generated in the year preceding the transfer to SMF; (ii) 25% on the basis of each physician's 'years in the community,' with up to a maximum of five years being counted; and (iii) 25% on the

2 This is a standard feature of purchase transactions.

basis of each physician's share of the aggregate fixed assets transferred to SMF by the SWMG physicians." Although the physicians attached a Form 8283 to their tax returns, Sutter never reflected the donation in its tax return—despite the transaction documents obligating it to do so.

### Taxpayers' Valuation for Trial

For healthcare industry appraisers and valuation analysts, the issues surrounding the appraisal submitted for trial are the most important. Perhaps the most significant feature of the appraisal prepared for the trial was the use of median compensation for the physician-sellers rather than the actual compensation negotiated in the transaction! This remains an item of ill-considered debate and frequently results in mistaken assumptions in physician practice and other professional practice valuation, despite being long-settled and in direct conflict with fair market value.[3] The question can be stated as follows: Would the hypothetical buyer pay a price for the practice based on a *lower* compensation than he or she intended to pay post-transaction, thereby paying twice to the extent of the extra compensation.[4]

> ... the national median for the "Western Region" for a weighted average of the medical specialties comprising SWMG, or 45.18%" in determining the physician compensation expense for the discounted cashflow model.[5] *However, the actual negotiated compensation negotiated in the transaction "provided for compensation to SWMG equal to 57.75% of fee-for-service revenue, 47% to 53% of capitation revenue, and at least 55% of risk pool revenue. [Emphasis added]*

The Dutcher Appraisal contained other significant weaknesses in the view of the court. There was no allocation of any intangible value to the professional goodwill of the physicians[6] as opposed to enterprise goodwill, which the court differentiated as follows:

> ... no allocation of any value to the professional goodwill of the SWMG physicians despite the fact that Mr. Dutcher distinguishes, in the case of the goodwill of a professional practice, between "practice" goodwill and "professional" goodwill, the former attributable to characteristics of the practice entity such as patient records, provider contracts, and workforce in place; and the latter attributable to the personal

3 See, e.g., "Medical Practices: A BV RX," *Journal of Accountancy*, November 2005.

4 Besides the inurement risk under the Internal Revenue Code, this error creates risk under the AKS and Stark laws.

5 The phrase "national median for the 'Western Region'" appears to be a misnomer. The data were taken from the MGMA *Physician Compensation Survey* 1994 report based on 1993 data.

6 "Identifying And Measuring Personal Goodwill in a Professional Practice," *CPA Expert*, Spring 2005 and Summer 2005.

> attributes of the individual practitioner, such as charisma, skill, and reputation and he acknowledge[d] that professional goodwill is not transferable.

Dutcher's testimony that professional goodwill is not transferable would have been one of many fatal blows to the taxpayers' position. The court went on to discuss the lack of noncompete agreements and importantly emphasized the continuing viability of *Norwalk v. Commissioner,*[7] perhaps the seminal case on the ownership and valuation of personal goodwill and noncompetes. A noncompete is the contractual basis for transferring personal or professional goodwill to an employer. The court also observed that the willing buyer would have insisted on "a significant discount" due to the lack of a noncompete!

> There is no adjustment for the fact that the SWMG physicians were not required to execute noncompete agreements. Mr. Dutcher treated each SWMG physician as transferring an allocable share of SWMG's intangibles, including goodwill, which was not treated as diminished in any way by the physicians' not having executed noncompete agreements with respect to SWMG or SMF. However, in *Norwalk v. Commissioner,* T.C. Memo. 1998-279, we found that there is no transferable or salable goodwill where a company's business depends on its employees' personal relationships with clients and the employees have not provided covenants not to compete.... We also believe that, under the willing buyer/willing seller standard of fair market value ... a willing buyer of SWMG on the transaction date would have insisted on a significant discount with respect to the value of the entity's intangible assets, precisely on account of the absence of noncompete agreements from the SWMG physicians.

Other problems cited by the court included the taxpayers' use of an intangible value allocation model developed by one of the taxpayers rather than one based upon sound appraisal techniques and failure to include in the valuation any consideration of the $35,000 signing bonus described above.

### The Donation

There is a fundamental requirement in a charitable transfer that the contributor have "donative intent" to receive a tax deduction. Donative intent contemplates a disinterested gift to a charitable organization without the donor receiving any corresponding benefit. It remains commonplace to attempt to structure physician practice transfers as part-sale, part-donation in the current environment.

7 T.C. Memo. 1998-279; See "Goodwill Requires Enforceable Covenant Not to Compete," *CPA Expert,* Spring 1999.

In its analysis of the transaction, the court found that the taxpayers received significant benefits from the transaction that belied any intent to make a disinterested donation with no consideration in return. The court cited the advantages of patient retention, negotiating leverage as part of a larger system, compensation based upon a percentage of net revenue, all of which was embodied in an employment contract with "carefully delineated terms."

## Conclusion

Consolidation trends are cyclical and the wave that collapsed 10 years ago in the healthcare industry is back yet again. *Derby* reminds us that the old adage "those who fail to learn from history are doomed to repeat it" remains in full force and effect. From the standpoint of the hypothetical buyer, the court reiterated old guidance with respect to the common sense requirement that the value of the practice be based on expected post-transaction compensation. Equally important, the court restated the principles espoused in the *Norwalk* case that contracts—in this case the purchase and sale and professional services agreement—be part of the analysis of intangible value due to the impact of (any) noncompete agreements. Thus, when valuing a medical practice for purposes of an actual transaction, the appraiser must be familiar with the terms of that transaction if the buyer and seller are to rely upon it for regulatory purposes. As the court seemed to suggest of the appraisal submitted by the taxpayers in this case, something other than that which the parties transacted was valued. Transactional valuation *requires* understanding the terms of the transaction to opine on fair market value.

Chapter 12

# Assessing Intangible Value in a Physician Practice Acquisition

*By Gregory D. Anderson, CPA/ABV, CVA; Carol W. Carden, CPA/ABV, ASA, CFE; Mark O. Dietrich, CPA/ABV; J. Gregory Endicott, CPA/ABV, ASA, MBA; W. James Lloyd, CPA/ABV, ASA, CBA, CFE; Todd J. Sorenson, MBA, AVA; Reed Tinsley, CPA, CVA, CFP, CHBC; and Kathie L. Wilson, CPA, CVA*

Due in large part to concerns over healthcare reform and declining reimbursement rates, physicians are increasingly looking for opportunities to sell their practices to hospitals and work as employees. Similarly, hospital systems are interested in acquiring key practices to solidify or expand their provider networks. These transactions are clearly subject to the regulatory restrictions of commercial reasonableness and fair market value imposed by the Stark law[1] and the anti-kickback statute (AKS),[2] as well as the Internal Revenue Code Section 501(c) (3) regulations if the hospital is a not-for-profit entity. Many practices have very low or sometimes negative projected post-transaction earnings after adjusting for the physician's anticipated post-transaction compensation. Accordingly, an income approach valuation methodology, such as the discounted cash flow (DCF) method, will generally result in zero or a very low value for the practice. In such cases, the cost approach will be utilized instead. However, the problem arises when the cost approach results in substantial values being attributed to intangible assets,[3] such as physician workforce, that are not supported by an appropriate level of net cash flow needed to provide an economic return to the hypothetical buyer.

1 42 U.S.C. Sec. 1395nn.
2 42 U.S.C. Sec. 1320a-7b.
3 There are certain specifically identifiable assets (such as a certificate of need or electronic medical record systems) that may have value even in the absence of DCF value to the existing owner.

This chapter addresses the appropriateness of assigning substantial value to intangible assets, such as physician workforce, under the fair market value standard and going-concern premise of value, without such amounts being appropriately supported by net cash flow under the income approach.

The chapter first defines the key terms used and describes typical intangible assets, then looks at the theoretical underpinning of the cost approach as described in accepted valuation texts and court cases, then examines, critiques, and ultimately dismisses the sole use of the cost approach to value physician workforce as both a violation of professional standards and the regulatory structure for fair market value.

## Key Concepts and Definitions

The following key concepts and definitions are important for understanding the analysis and conclusions expressed in this chapter.

*Commercial reasonableness:* Transactions between hospitals and physicians with the ability to refer designated health services (DHS) must be commercially reasonable. The Stark regulations explain commercial reasonableness as: "An arrangement will be considered commercially reasonable, in the absence of referrals, if the arrangement would make commercial sense if entered into by a reasonable entity of similar type and size and a reasonable physician of similar scope and specialty, even if there were no potential designated health services referrals."[4]

Accordingly, the commercial reasonableness requirement means the transaction must make good business sense *without* the potential of future referrals from either party.

*Fair market value:* The most widely used definition of fair market value is: "the price at which property or service would change hands between a willing buyer and a willing seller, neither being under a compulsion to buy or sell and both having reasonable knowledge of the relevant facts."[5]

The Stark regulations define fair market value similarly as "the value in arm's-length transactions, consistent with the general market value," and general market value is defined as "the price that an asset would bring as the result of bona fide bargaining between well-informed buyers and sellers who are not otherwise in a position to generate business for the other party or compensation that would be included in a service

4 69 *Fed. Reg.* 16093 (March 26, 2004).
5 Estate Tax Reg. 20.2031.1-1(b); Revenue Ruling 59-60, 1959-1, C.B. 237.

agreement as the result of bona fide bargaining between well-informed parties to the agreement who are not otherwise in a position to generate business for the other party on the date of the acquisition of the asset or at the time of the service agreement."[6]

*Strategic value:* In contrast to fair market value, strategic value is the value to a particular buyer rather than to a hypothetical buyer. There are a variety of strategic considerations that a specific buyer may employ in determining strategic value, some of which would likely not violate the Stark law and others of which almost certainly would. For example, a tax-exempt hospital would have access to tax-exempt bonds to acquire a practice, providing a low cost of capital and a correspondingly higher multiple of value. It would also not pay any income tax on income from the practice if the transaction were properly structured resulting in a higher cash flow and strategic value. Although they do not violate the Stark law, these two items likely violate the anti-inurement rules. When compared to a hypothetical nonhospital buyer, a hospital obtains various inpatient referrals from a physician practice, of course, but consideration of these referrals directly or indirectly is prohibited.

*Income approach valuation methodology:* The income approach is a general way of determining an indication of value based on the future income (benefits) expected to be generated by the asset. This approach is based on the fundamental valuation principle that an asset's worth is directly related to the present value of the future benefits of ownership. The most common income approach methodology is the DCF method, which discounts anticipated future net cash flow to present value by using a discount rate that reflects the time value of money and the risk associated with the asset.

The income approach is generally used to value operating companies that produce positive cash flow under the going concern premise of value.

*Cost approach valuation methodology:* The asset approach, which is also commonly referred to as the cost approach,[7] is a general way of determining an indication of value based on the entity's underlying assets and liabilities. This approach is based on the theory that an asset's worth is directly related to the amount that would be required to reproduce or replace it. The cost approach generally results in an upper limit of value for assets that can be easily replaced or reproduced, since no prudent investor would pay more for an asset than the cost to create a comparable one. Similarly, no prudent investor would pay to create an asset that would not generate an income return under the regulatory structure commensurate with the outlay that is allowed.

6 420 CFR 411.351. See also Section 1877(h)(3) of the Social Security Act.
7 The terms are used interchangeably.

**Typical Physician Practice Assets —Least Controversial to Most Controversial**

- Furniture and equipment
- Accounts receivable
- Leasehold improvements
- Trade name
- Telephone numbers
- Patient charts
- Nonphysician workforce
- Physician workforce

*Intangible asset:* Intangible assets are non-physical assets, such as trademarks, patents, securities, contracts, and goodwill that have rights and provide economic benefits to the owner.[8]

*Goodwill:* Goodwill is a type of intangible asset that is related to the entity's name, reputation, customer loyalty, and similar factors not separately identified.[9] Assembled workforce is generally considered to be an integral part of goodwill and not identifiable as a separate asset.[10]

## The Context for Valuing Physician Workforce

While the proper premises of value to apply may be debated, there is little argument that tangible assets such as furniture and equipment and accounts receivable have some value in this context. Reasonable minds may differ on the proper treatment or value of intangible assets such as trade name and telephone numbers—intangible assets that may often be differentiated because they possess the potential for being both legally protectable and separately marketable.

Other intangible assets or economic phenomena that may not meet the definition of an intangible asset are of particular concern as you move further along in the list. Some appraisers make the mistake of not only assigning value to these items in the absence of cash flows, but also in attaching value to something that may not be an asset in the first place. In their book, *Valuing Intangible Assets,* Robert Reilly and Robert Schweihs note that, for an intangible asset to exist from a valuation perspective, it must include the following:

1. It should be subject to specific identification and recognizable description.
2. It should be subject to legal existence and protection.
3. It should be subject to the right of private ownership, and the private ownership should be legally transferable.

8 Hitchner, James R., *Financial Valuation Applications and Models,* John Wiley & Sons Inc., 2003, p. 13.

9 Ibid.

10 See Statement of Financial Accounting Standards No. 164, Not-for-Profit Entities: Mergers and Acquisitions, paragraph A54; the IRS may recognize assembled workforce as a separate intangible when there is a DCF value to support it.

4. There should be some tangible evidence or manifestation of the existence of the intangible asset (e.g., a contract, a license, a registration document, a computer diskette, a listing of customers, a set of financial statements, etc.).

5. It should have been created or have come into existence at an identifiable time or as the result of an identifiable event.

6. It should be subject to being destroyed or to a termination of existence at an identifiable time or as the result of an identifiable event.[11]

It is in this area that we see some valuations incorrectly assign value to phenomena such as a workforce in place when no legal right exists, such as in the case of a physician without an employment agreement or the nonphysician workforce of a physician practice in an at-will employment state.

The disparity of treatment and the rather large magnitude in associated value, however, approaches darker shades of gray as you approach the physician workforce in place. Our attempt here is not to minimize the need to properly treat each of the tangible and intangible asset classes, but the most controversial asset in this context also happens to be the item that some appraisers are attaching the greatest magnitude of value to—the physician workforce.

When practice acquisition valuations based on the cost approach imply intangible value attributable to physician workforce in the observed range of $50,000 to more than $400,000, there is cause for concern over the validity of the valuation analysis and the intentions of the parties.

## Example

The argument for the attachment of significant value to the physician workforce in place arises out of a legitimate business consideration for hospitals in some scenarios. The scenario goes something like this:

Hospital X chief executive officer (CEO) in a two-hospital town relies almost exclusively on Heart Group, the only cardiology group of substance in the area, to generate volume (i.e., referrals) for Hospital X's cardiology line of business. Heart Group currently splits business between Hospital X and Hospital Y. Heart Group informs both Hospital X and Hospital Y that it wants to entertain the sale of its practice and employment. Faced with the potential loss of the cardiologists that generate all of the volumes in the cardiology

11 *Valuing Intangible Assets.* Reilly, Robert F. and Schweihs, Robert P. McGraw-Hill (New York, 1999), p. 5.

lines of business at his hospital, Hospital X CEO argues that if he doesn't buy Heart Group, he'll have to recruit and employ physicians to practice at Hospital X—absorbing recruiting costs and significant losses in the process. To further complicate the fact pattern, Hospital Y has retained a valuation firm that values these costs to re-create the physician workforce at $300,000 per physician despite that firm's analysis that there will be little to no cash flow from the cardiology practice after paying the cardiologists' salaries. Hospital X CEO is really left with no choice; he or she feels she or she must at least match Hospital Y's offer.

As is explained in more detail below, the sole reliance on the cost approach to value intangible assets is generally inappropriate. Whether the intangible assets are related to payments for physician workforce, noncompete agreements, or compensation, they must be viewed in the context of an even exchange between the parties with no benefit, *directly or indirectly*, ascribed to referrals. In the absence of an expectation of income from the acquired physician practice, the only source of income necessary to meet the fair market value standard is from future referrals associated with that practice.

### A Review of the Significant Issues

Among the many problems with relying solely on the cost approach to value intangible assets related to an ongoing business enterprise is that it is inconsistent with valuation theory and the valuation guidance offered by the Stark regulations. While not necessarily exhaustive, the following is a list of the significant issues that would all need to be resolved favorably to attach significant value to the physician workforce in place.

**1. Assuming a hospital can be considered the typical or likely buyer is inconsistent with both the classical and regulatory definitions of fair market value.**

One argument often cited as a reason for hospitals paying for a physician workforce is the avoidance of costs related to recruiting and employing such physicians to meet their community need. The momentum of many of the concepts associated with healthcare reform such as bundled payments and accountable care organizations (ACOs) generates additional support for the business case for hospital employment of physicians. Given that hospitals will likely need to employ physicians and provided there are strong contractual relationships in place to secure it, there is little question or argument that securing a physician workforce in place brings *strategic value* (as distinguished earlier herein from fair market value) to a hospital in that it allows a hospital to forego the costs associated with recruiting and ramping up a physician workforce. However, this is inconsistent with both the classical and regulatory definitions of fair market value in the context of the acquisition of the assets of a physician practice since those assets must be shown to generate income and that income must not be proscribed by applicable regulations. For business appraisals performed in the context of hospitals purchasing physician practices, healthcare regulations and statutes require any transaction to occur at *fair market value (FMV).*

As stated earlier, FMV is classically defined as the price at which an asset would exchange between a willing buyer and a willing seller, neither being under compulsion to buy or sell, each having reasonable knowledge of all relevant facts, and with equity to both. Based on the guidelines established by the Stark II regulations, we typically expand our definition of FMV to encompass general market value (GMV), which is the price that an asset would bring as the result of bona fide bargaining between well-informed buyers and sellers who are not otherwise in a position to generate business for the other party or the compensation that would be included in a service agreement as the result of bona fide bargaining between well-informed parties to the agreement who are not otherwise in a position to generate business for the other party, on the date of acquisition of the asset or at the time of the service agreement (42 C.F.R. 411.351) and where the compensation has not been determined in any manner that takes into account the volume or value of anticipated or actual referrals and where the arrangement would be commercially reasonable even if no referrals were made to the employer (42 C.F.R. 411.351 and 42 C.F.R. 411.357(c)).

Given the definition of fair market value, the practice of simply assuming that a hospital is avoiding a significant cost by simply paying for a physician workforce or that a hospital should be considered the most likely buyer of the physician practice appears to be somewhat inconsistent with the classical definition of FMV in that there is some compulsion for hospitals to buy physician practices. Even if one is somehow able to get comfortable with being consistent with the classical definition of FMV, the assumption that a hospital is the only typical or likely buyer of a physician practice appears to be even more directly inconsistent with the further restrictions under Stark II that the assumed buyer not be in a position to benefit from the business generated by the seller.

**2. Replication cost as a valuation methodology has significant weaknesses and its use to value the physician workforce is inconsistent with all premises of value other than going concern.**

A book looked upon as an authoritative text in the valuation profession is *Valuing a Business: The Analysis and Appraisal of Closely Held Businesses.*[12] Chapter 14 provides

12 *Valuing a Business: The Analysis and Appraisal of Closely Held Businesses*, Shannon P. Pratt, 4th Edition.

guidance to appraisers in conducting the cost approach. According to the authors, conducting the cost approach requires the appraiser to not only choose the proper standard of value, but also to choose the proper premise of value. The four premises of value delineated include:

- Value in continued use as part of a going concern;
- Value in place as part of a mass assemblage of assets;
- Value in exchange, as part of an orderly disposition; and
- Value in exchange, as part of a forced liquidation.

Based on generally accepted interpretations of the guidance provided by this authoritative text, the only of the four premises of value above that would ultimately result in any significant value for the physician workforce in place is value in continued use as part of a going concern. According to the authors, "Under this premise, it is assumed that the subject assets are sold as a mass assemblage and as part of an *income producing* (emphasis added) business enterprise."[13] The assumption that the practice is income-producing is in complete contradiction to the reasoning used to rely exclusively on the cost approach. As previously discussed, relying exclusively on the cost approach is a function of the fact that considering the proposed compensation arrangement with the physicians, there is either no income or at least not enough income to justify any value over and above the value of the tangible assets.

The weaknesses of the cost approach in differentiating what has value and what does not have value are not limited to physician workforce. Michael Crain, CPA/ABV, ASA, CFA, a well-known and highly regarded member of the appraisal community, observes:

"Some criticize the cost approach by arguing that the evidence of a relationship between cost and price is weak, and thus, the cost approach is not a reliable way to estimate the value of something. One example of weak relationships is the decline in real estate prices in the late 2000s. It is conceivable that the costs of building some homes were higher than their market prices. Further, these downward price movements were weakly correlated with the costs of building a home. *A closely related argument is that the cost approach is overly simplistic and can violate the first principle of valuation that says the value of something is the expected future benefits expected from it, discounted to the present. This principle links value to future returns, whereas the cost approach has strictly a historical perspective."* (Emphasis added)

13 Ibid., Chapter 14, page 314.

"Another argument criticizing the cost approach is that it assumes that if a firm develops something, it is valuable. We know from theory and observation that firm managers use trial and error in their operations. Simply put, some things managers do work and some do not. *The cost approach is unable to distinguish between the costs of successful and unsuccessful efforts.*"[14] (Emphasis added)

The 2008 tax court case *Derby*[15] specifically addresses the cost approach issue for tax-exempt hospitals and related entities. Although the valuation in that case was a misuse[16] of the income approach, the principle that FMV constitutes an even exchange between hypothetical buyer and seller is the same.

"The Dutcher appraisal takes no account of the $35,000 'Physician Access Bonus' payable to each SWMG physician over the initial two years of the affiliation. Ignoring these payments when computing distributable earnings that SWMG would generate results in a overstatement of those earnings and a corresponding overstatement of the value of SWMG's intangible assets (since, under Mr. Dutcher's analysis, intangible asset value equals present value of future distributable earnings, less tangible assets and implied working capital)."

The point here, of course, is not limited to the physician access bonus. Any transaction involving the purchase of a medical practice must consider all the elements of that transfer in determining whether the transaction meets the FMV standard, as modified by the Stark law. This includes post-transaction compensation in addition to the purchase price and contractual terms.

"Petitioners have not shown that the value of what they transferred to SMF exceeded the value of the benefits they received in return. As noted above, those benefits included, in the first instance, employment that was compensated with shares of revenue (47% to 57.75%) that significantly exceeded the median share of revenue (45.18%) devoted to physician compensation in petitioners' specialties; a $35,000 'physician access bonus' for each SWMG physician, including petitioners; an absence of restrictions on establishing a competing medical practice in the event of cessation of employment with SMF; and greater economic security in the managed care environment."

**3. Financial reporting, court cases, and other guidance point to *allocating* value to workforce in place *not* separately valuing it.**

14 Michael A. Crain, "Study Guide, Business Valuation for Forensic Accountants" (working paper, School of Accounting, Florida Atlantic University, 2010) used with permission.
15 T.C. Memo. 2008-45.
16 Given the court's detailed rejection of the assumptions utilized.

Similarly, it should be noted that while using replication costs to estimate the value of the workforce in place is widely accepted in valuation texts and other sources of guidance when allocating value, it is not necessarily sanctioned as proper for assigning value in the cost approach. Nowhere is this more clear than in the application of the Financial Accounting Standard Board's Statements on Financial Accounting Standards (SFAS). Citing SFAS 141, Valuation for Financial Reporting notes that "SFAS 141 specifically prohibits the recognition of assembled workforce as an intangible asset apart from goodwill." (Michael J. Mard, 2002). The Internal Revenue Service (IRS) has also offered several pieces of guidance regarding the valuation of physician practices. One of the often referenced pieces of guidance used for valuation of physician practices is *Valuing Physician Practices* (Charles F. Kaiser, 1996). It should be noted that while this article discusses at length the value of various tangible and intangible assets such as equipment, trade name, patient charts and workforce in place utilizing cost to re-create in an the cost approach, the context is clearly one *of allocating the value obtained from the income approach* (DCF method) and not one of using the cost approach in isolation.

**4. Ability to terminate without cause may limit ability to protect value.**

In the previous phase of physician practice transactions, many of the employment agreements included terms of five years or more without the ability for either party to terminate without cause. In addition, many of the employment agreements included trailing covenants not to compete that combined with inability to terminate without cause, made it not only virtually impossible for either party to terminate the agreement during the initial term, but also extremely difficult for the physicians to remain in a community following the initial term, absent employment with the hospital. One feature in the current phase of physician practice transactions that distinguishes it from the previous phase is that in many cases, the employment agreements permit either party to terminate the employment agreement without cause with only 90 to 180 days' notice, *with no restrictions on future competition*. This is certainly not always the case. However, if the subject employment agreements include the ability to terminate without cause and permit a physician to remain in the community, the potential inability to legally protect the physician workforce beyond the rolling 90-to-180-day virtual term of the employment agreements should be considered.

The tax court case *Derby* specifically addresses this issue for tax-exempt hospitals and related entities. Failure to follow these principles raises the specter of the intermediate sanctions provisions and anti-inurement provisions of the Internal Revenue Code, particularly with the post-reform emphasis on disclosure in Form 990—and the public access to those forms, including by potential qui tam plaintiffs and their attorneys.

There is no adjustment for the fact that the SWMG physicians were not required to execute noncompete agreements. Mr. Dutcher treated each SWMG physician as transferring an allocable share of SWMG's intangibles, including goodwill, which was not treated as diminished in any way by the physicians' not having executed noncompete agreements with respect to SWMG or SMF. However, in *Norwalk v. Commissioner*, T.C. Memo. 1998-279, we found that there is no transferable or salable goodwill where a company's business depends on its employees' personal relationships with clients and the employees have not provided covenants not to compete.... *We also believe that, under the willing buyer-willing seller standard of fair market value enunciated in Rev. Proc. 59-60, 1959-1 C.B. 237, to which Mr. Dutcher purportedly adhered, a willing buyer of SWMG on the transaction date would have insisted on a significant discount with respect to the value of the entity's intangible assets*, precisely on account of the absence of noncompete agreements from the SWMG physicians. Indeed, the SWMG physicians not only did not execute noncompete agreements, but they also had the benefit of the 'free to compete' provision in the PSA that facilitated their reclaiming their patients in the event they decided to cease working for SWMG/SMF. Mr. Dutcher's failure to account for the risk to his estimated five-year stream of earnings posed by SWMG physicians' departing with their patients is contrary to well-established valuation principles and common sense and results in an inflated value for the SWMG physicians' goodwill. (Emphasis added)

... and (5) rather than a noncompete agreement, the 'free to compete' provision, which secured for each petitioner the express right, upon his or her termination of employment with SWMG/SMF, to have his or her patients as of the date of affiliation with SMF notified of the departure and given the option of having the patient's medical records transferred to the departing physician. In addition, when petitioners' circumstances before the transaction are considered, a second tier of benefits they secured in the transaction with SMF becomes apparent. First, petitioners solved their core economic problem arising from the advent of managed care; namely, the risk of loss from having patients requiring extraordinary care. After the transaction, by virtue of the minimum compensation guaranties, this risk was largely transferred to SMF, which could better manage it given SMF's greater patient population and resources. Second, as a result of their affiliation with a relatively large health care organization, petitioners secured the benefits of greater leverage in negotiating contracts with HMOs and greater efficiencies in providing care, with any resulting enhancement in revenues inuring to their benefit by virtue of SWMG's compensation being determined as a percentage of net revenues. In sum, by transferring their practices to SMF in the transaction at issue, petitioners ensured for themselves the continued ability to maintain or improve their accustomed level of earnings from the practice of medicine—something they had concluded was not likely to be possible had they continued to maintain solo or small group practices.

The example described earlier of a hospital relying upon a single heart group for admissions parallels to a large extent the recent qui tam case *Bradford Regional Medical Center* in which the Federal District Court for Western Pennsylvania granted summary judgment to the qui tam plaintiffs on violations of the Stark law. That case involved the "lease" of a Nuclear Medicine Camera from two internists who were responsible for a significant share of the hospital's high-tech imaging and inpatient and outpatient referrals. There, the hospital was confronted with the loss of the nuclear medicine scans that severely restricted its ability to recruit a cardiologist. Further risk apparently existed with respect to the possibility that the physicians might acquire their own MR or CT scanner, both of which have cardiac applications.

Part of the court's analysis was that the record indicated that the defendant hospital had clearly considered the volume and value of referrals in the price paid for the nuclear medicine camera sublease, *which price included a noncompete agreement*. As such, the valuation prepared in connection with that sublease was irrelevant, since the FMV exception could only be used if the sublease did not consider referrals in the first instance. Further, the valuation also discussed loss of referrals, and there the definition of FMV was not consistent with the modifications of the Stark law.

**5. Lack of any evidence indicating hospitals could sell physician workforce back for any significant value.**

Another key to valuing physician practices is consistent treatment of controversial items, regardless of which party is on the buyer side and which is on the seller side. We believe collectively performing hundreds of valuations for both potential purchases from physicians and sales to physicians provides a balanced perspective to approaching these issues. We are not aware of a single instance, even when enforceable employment agreements and covenants exist, that hospitals have successfully sold a physician workforce to the physicians. The accepted method for establishing the value of a noncompete covenant is to use the income approach.

**6. Analyses typically include no consideration for physician age and need to amortize the asset.**

Like Number 4, another concept that may often be ignored in assigning value to physician workforce is that of inevitability—it is inevitable that eventually the physician workforce must be replenished and the employer will incur the costs associated with recruitment and ramp up. In this sense, any cost to re-create the physician workforce is simply a present value exercise. Ignoring the other five factors or even assuming an appraiser is comfortable with his or her ability to successfully navigate the mine field, this must be considered.

## Conclusion

Under the FMV standard of value, there is no basis for exclusive reliance on the cost approach in valuing intangible assets in general and physician workforce in particular when there is no expectation of income from the underlying assets of a going concern. The professional literature of valuation theory that serves as the basis for FMV provides no support. Additionally, the commercial reasonableness requirement under the Stark law that a transaction make sense in the absence of referrals would almost assuredly be violated by paying for physician workforce without such values being adequately supported by cash flows under the income approach. Given that both the economic value and the fair market value of an asset is the present value of expected future benefits of ownership, implicit in the use of the cost approach—and in our view, explicitly assumed—is income from the referrals to be received.

*This chapter was originally published as a white paper by HORNE LLP in February 2011. The statements herein represent general principles of valuation. The specific circumstances present in a given engagement may affect the extent of their application.*

Chapter 13

# What Is to Be Learned From *Caracci*?

*By Mark O. Dietrich, CPA/ABV, and Kenneth W. Patton, ASA*

The appropriate use of the market approach in healthcare industry valuation is one of the most critical issues confronting the appraisal industry today. Many healthcare industry appraisers believe that market data are often unreliable or even misleading and must be used with abundant caution. Therefore, they focus primarily on the income approach. These appraisers cite such factors as local Medicaid coverage differences, the monopsonistic market power of local health insurers, the lack of sufficient data to determine comparability, and regulatory restrictions on the use of market data contained in the Stark regulations.

Appraisers who believe that the market approach, along with the income approach, should be given significant weight focus on the importance of actual transactions and not substituting one's judgment for that of the market. Where both groups agree is that use of market data in the healthcare industry requires significant skill and in-depth analysis. In this article, two leading experts, who have contrasting views on the topic, explore those issues in depth.

To illustrate our viewpoints, we discuss these issues in the context of the Fifth Circuit's reversal of the tax court's opinion in *Caracci*,[1] which poses a number of questions to business valuation professionals. With respect to the valuation issues only, Mark Dietrich believes that the Fifth Circuit's decision was more correct than the tax court's decision, while Ken Patton believes that the tax court's decision was more correct.[2] Ken Patton brings years of healthcare industry valuation expertise (although fewer years than

1 118 TC 379 (2002), rev'd.: 456 F.3d 444, 98 AFTR2d 2006-5264: (CA-5, 2006).
2 The authors offer no opinion as to any of the legal aspects of this case.

Mark Dietrich) and more to the point, his knowledge of this specific market through his experience valuing other healthcare companies in the region during this time.[3]

### The Key Valuation Issue and Valuation Experts

In *Caracci*, the key valuation issue was the value of the assets transferred from a not-for-profit entity to a for-profit entity.

The valuation expert for the taxpayers, Sta-Home entities and the Caraccis, was Allen D. Hahn, a director in PricewaterhouseCoopers Northeast Region Corporation Valuation Consulting Group. The valuation expert for the Internal Revenue Service (IRS) was Charles A. Wilhoite, a managing director of Willamette Management Associates and the national director of its healthcare industry services. In its opinion, the tax court recognized the experience and qualifications of the experts.

### History of Sta-Home

Sta-Home was a collection of entities that provided home healthcare services primarily paid for by Medicaid to residents of Mississippi. Reimbursements were limited to the cost of providing the service, which apparently precluded the possibility of profitability. Sta-Home completed a corporate reorganization in 1995, which ultimately led to the litigation with the IRS.

Sta-Home was approximately 20 years old at the time of the reorganization. According to the courts' decisions, it:

- Had a well-established brand name;
- Had well-documented intellectual capital (manuals, procedures);
- Had a "generally good reputation";
- Had a certificate of need and accreditation by the Joint Commission on the Accreditation of Healthcare Organizations (JCAHO); and
- Was the largest provider of home healthcare services in Mississippi.

For perspective, as shown in Exhibit 1, Sta-Home's scale of operations had increased dramatically from 1991 to 1995. A question immediately comes to mind: Why would the owners grow the business to this extent if there was no chance of economic success?

3 Neither of the authors (or their firms) was involved in the case; therefore, they are relying solely on publicly available information.

**Exhibit 1. Sta-Home's Revenues and Expenses (1991–1995)**

| Year | Revenue | Expenses | Net Income |
|---|---|---|---|
| 1991 | $11,736,061 | $11,799,721 | ($63,660) |
| 1992 | $18,442,072 | $18,414,315 | $27,757 |
| 1993 | $25,162,701 | $25,208,255 | ($45,554) |
| 1994 | $36,882,957 | $37,141,686 | ($258,729) |
| 1995 | $44,101,849 | $44,535,239 | ($433,390) |

## Position of the Parties

This case involved the conversion of Mississippi's largest home health agency chain, Sta-Home, from tax-exempt to for-profit status in 1995.[4] The entity had more than $44 million in revenues and a loss of $433,390 in that year, as well as a large share of the Mississippi market. Such conversions were common at this time. They took place against the expectation[5] of a prospective payment system (PPS)[6] replacing Medicare's cost-based system for paying for home healthcare. The PPS was ultimately adopted in the Balanced Budget Act of 1997. It paid agencies in 60-day episodes of care, rather than on the basis of costs incurred. The cost-based system had led to the spending of excessive amounts on delivering care. Prior to the adoption of the PPS, home health agencies were often acquired by hospitals (and there was an active market in Mississippi). The hospitals, which were already paid by Medicare under a PPS, could therefore shift costs to the home health agency and obtain higher reimbursement for the same services.

The conversion was audited by the IRS, which found that the tax-exempt entities had approximately $18.5 million in net equity value that had been improperly transferred to the subsequent owners. The new owners maintained that the liabilities assumed exceeded the value of the assets received. The IRS asserted that the net excess benefit of $18.5 million triggered excise taxes and penalties of more then $250 million. The tax court subsequently reduced this to $46 million.

## Tax Court Opinion

According to Judge Laro's opinion, a valuation prepared contemporaneously with the transaction at the insistence of special tax counsel for Sta-Home was initially rejected

4 The entities operated under state certificates of need.

5 A virtual certainty in the view of co-author Mark Dietrich. The tax court stated in its opinion that "national expenditures for home nursing care grew from $3.8 billion in 1990 to $20.5 billion in 1997," a circumstance that guaranteed congressional action and always has.

6 A PPS pays for services on the basis of a fee set in advance.

by that counsel for failure to conform to Revenue Ruling 59-60[7] and to address the existence of intangible assets. A second appraisal found that the equity value of the entities was negative, although the tax court record indicates that special tax counsel remained concerned about the quality of the appraisal.

### The Standard of Value

A key issue in the case was the conflict between the normalization of earnings adjustments available to a hypothetical willing buyer and those available only to a specific buyer or specific class of buyers and whether the latter constituted fair market value. The following is quoted from the tax court's opinion:

> During 1995, the primary buyers of home health agencies were hospitals, nursing homes, and other home health agencies. They were able to take advantage of a mechanism known as "cost shifting."

Cost shifting was commonly used at that time by hospitals that were paid under a PPS. The PPS generated a fixed payment so that if costs could be transferred to the home health agency, additional revenue could be generated with no additional cost. The inclusion of this attribute by the tax court was critical in the determination of fair market value.

The taxpayer's expert, Hahn, valued the cost gap at $667,000 based upon his view that a buyer would have a one-year benefit from that strategy. The tax court disagreed:

> This value is too low. The cost gaps were available under the then-current reimbursement program. They would cease to exist under a PPS. Although there had been discussions of a PPS for several years, Congress had passed no such legislation at the time of the transfer, and there is no evidence that the prospect of such legislation had a negative effect upon the value of home health care agencies.

### Hahn's Valuation Approaches

The tax court reviewed and critiqued each expert's use of the market approach. Hahn also relied primarily on an adjusted balance sheet methodology (a version of the cost approach), in which he valued the trained workforce and certificate of need. Hahn placed considerably less reliance on market comparables because purported comparables were "idiosyncratic" and lacked sufficient detail.

7 1959-1 CB 237.

The tax court also noted Hahn's testimony that guideline public companies were not appropriate comparables because home health care was part of a broader service mix. In effect, there were no "pure-play" public companies.

### Wilhoite's Valuation Approaches

Wilhoite relied primarily on the market approach utilizing both guideline public companies and guideline acquisitions. The tax court appeared to indicate a clear preference for this approach. Wilhoite derived revenue pricing multiples for market value of invested capital (MVIC), the use of which was a key issue in the Fifth Circuit's decision.[8]

The tax court discussed the two comparable acquired companies deemed most like Sta-Home, according to Wilhoite. The court then went on to develop its own view of the proper multiple.

There was no discussion by the tax court of differences in payor mix between the purported comparables and Sta-Home, which was 95% Medicare-based. The court did observe that Mississippi had the largest per-capita spending on home health in the country under the Medicare program, but that speaks more to volume of services than rate per unit of service—and the latter drives profits. The court did allude to Hahn's testimony that successful home health agencies had nongovernment patients and more profitable lines of business, such as infusion therapy. These are all critical, and likely conclusive, differences as to comparability. Regardless of these concerns about the comparables, the tax court held that the taxpayers owed a crushing amount of excise taxes and penalties.

### Appellate Court Opinion

The Fifth Circuit severely criticized the IRS for its numerous errors in the assessment process, Judge Laro for engaging in valuation, and Wilhoite for his failure to understand the Mississippi marketplace. The Fifth Circuit first observed that Sta-Home had looked for a hospital buyer unsuccessfully. Where Judge Laro had been dismissive of the taxpayer's expert, Hahn, the Fifth Circuit embraced him, observing that the IRS had also attempted to retain him and that he spent eight weeks in Mississippi working on the case[9] compared to Wilhoite's two days. Wilhoite's lack of experience in the home healthcare industry in particular, as opposed to his general valuation experience, was

8 Of particular note is the IRS expert's reliance on revenue multiples from *out-of-market* transactions and public companies. This is a notoriously bad multiple in the view of many healthcare valuation experts and one specifically banned by the later-issued Stark II regulations discussed below.

9 These facts do not appear in the tax court decision.

also cited. Significantly, the Fifth Circuit noted that: "Wilhoite used market-based and income-based approaches to assign values to all Sta-Home's assets in general, *without valuing any of Sta-Home's assets in particular....*" (Italics added for emphasis).

### Synonymous Standard of Value?

*Caracci* implicitly raises an issue regarding the standard of value. Without question, all of the parties believed that fair market value was applicable. The potential for sale of Sta-Home was discussed by the tax court and even more by the Fifth Circuit. Although fair market value is generally considered to refer to hypothetical willing buyers and sellers, it is evident that the very specific circumstances of potential buyers were considered.

Wilhoite used a method known as cost shifting in his analysis. Economic profits are created by charging a portion of the expense base to another business unit. Cost shifting was in frequent use in the region as a means of creating value for Medicare home health agencies. Because cost shifting incorporates business synergies, it raises the specter that the standard of value had really morphed into investment value, which is defined in the *International Glossary of Business Valuation Terms* as "the value to a particular investor based on individual requirements and expectations."[10] If virtually every market participant has the potential to use the cost-shifting benefits, investment value might effectively become synonymous with fair market value.

The third standard of value, intrinsic value, is defined in the *International Glossary* as "the value that an investor considers, on the basis of an evaluation of available facts, to be the 'true' or 'real' value that will become the market value when other investors reach the same conclusion."

Why is intrinsic value important in this case? First, there was great debate about the future of home health care as a business due to the implementation of PPS. Market participants in the geographical area had widely different views. Market transactions occurring contemporaneously and after the valuation date indicated that Medicare-dependent home health agencies had value. Taking the opposite position with respect to Sta-Home clearly reflected a different view of the company's intrinsic prospects.

Second, the valuation of health care entities can be very volatile based on potential change in reimbursement rates. Note carefully the use of the word "potential." Medicare

10 American Society of Appraisers Business Valuation Standards, Glossary, last revised June 2005. www.appraisers.org.

changes are often first rumored, followed by proposals that may not be implemented for a year or more, and then the actual implementation. The analyst is left to make key decisions about prospective economic conditions of a business in the face of both great and unique uncertainties. Without question, actual market transactions can differ from an individual analyst's belief about the future. The circumstances of Sta-Home reflect this conundrum. While hindsight may give comfort to an analyst's position, appraisers must look at the broader market and attempt to reconcile actual market activity with their expectations and the expectations of others.

### Key Regulatory Issues in Health Care

Certain regulatory structures discussed here were not in place or well-understood at the time of the Sta-Home conversion. However, they are critical to assessing the relevance of the *Caracci* decision to appraisals in today's marketplace.

The following are excerpts from a synopsis of the anti-kickback statute extracted from an advisory opinion of the Office of the Inspector General:

> The anti-kickback statute makes it a criminal offense knowingly and willfully to offer, pay, solicit, or receive any remuneration to induce or reward referrals of items or services payable by a federal health care program. See Section 1128B(b) of the act. Where remuneration is paid purposefully to induce or reward referrals of items or services paid for by a federal health care program, the anti-kickback statute is violated. By its terms, the statute ascribes criminal liability to parties on both sides of an impermissible "kickback" transaction. For purposes of the anti-kickback statute, "remuneration" includes the transfer of anything of value, directly or indirectly, overtly or covertly, in cash or in kind.[11]

A buyer paying a seller for the profits associated with the buyer's subsequent provision of new services to the seller's patients may well be seen as paying a prohibited kickback for future referrals, particularly when the sellers remain employed by or active in the business.[12]

11 See Office of the Inspector General Advisory Opinion No. 03-12.

12 See *McLeod Regional Medical Center to Pay U.S. Over $15 Million to Resolve False Claims Act Allegations*, U.S. Department of Justice Press Release, Nov. 1, 2002.

## VALUATION QUESTIONS RAISED BY THE CASE

At this point, the authors engage in some point-counterpoint by addressing valuation questions raised by the tax court and Fifth Circuit's decisions.

*What is required for market comparability?*

*Dietrich*: Payment mechanisms are one of the most fascinating things about health care. Most health care is covered by private insurance or government programs such as Medicare (as in Sta-Home) or Medicaid. What is not widely understood is that the level of payment for those services varies radically from state to state and even market to market. Most urban markets are dominated by a few health insurers that hold significant influence over the fees paid to providers. Very few insurers have national market coverage, and those that do have significant market share in only a few states.[13] To use a guideline public company method or a guideline acquisition, the analyst would need to look at the payor mix for both the guideline and the subject and see whether they were similar. In a poor state such as Mississippi, the insurance market is unlikely to have been attractive because most patients would have had Medicaid, which pays the least. This would have made the out-of-market guideline transactions and public companies worthless.

*Patton*: The payment mechanism is clearly one of the most important factors in healthcare valuation. Reimbursement rates and sources vary by region and by state or even locality. Mississippi is a poor state that was experiencing a surge in home health visits, as compared with national activity. At the time, it shared these characteristics with the nearby states of Alabama, Louisiana, Arkansas, and portions of Tennessee and Kentucky. A market comparison to publicly traded companies or individual transactions outside the geographic region would likely be problematic. Nevertheless, there was acquisition activity in the aforementioned states in Medicare-based agencies, and demand for them was evident. Mercer Capital had observed market pricing in the range of $10 to $15 per visit for Medicare-based companies in the region.

*Can appraisers differ reasonably about the implications of a foreseeable change?*

*Dietrich*: Perhaps the most important issue raised in *Caracci* is the tax court's specific rejection of the impending change to a PPS, which was the basis of Hahn's position. Medicare had been converting various healthcare industry sectors from cost-based and other reimbursement systems to PPS to control rapidly expanding costs. There was no

13 See Government Accounting Office *Private Health Insurance: Number and Market Share of Carriers in the Small Group Health Insurance Market.*

doubt PPS was coming and, therefore, the change was reasonably foreseeable on the valuation date.

*Patton*: Although there was little doubt that the change to PPS was coming, there was apparently considerable doubt as to the precise timing and the implications of its implementation. The prevailing temporary payment system (PIP) had placed considerable strain on the financial resources of Sta-Home and other home healthcare agencies. Yet, the company continued to grow the base of visits. Does this speak to a different view on the implication of the ultimate shift to PPS? Other companies were amassing size under a general theory that a well-operated company could prosper under PPS. Notwithstanding the ultimate wisdom of that position (based on a subsequent event), companies in the region were increasing their size in the belief that customer accumulation created value.

*Does "market data" necessarily apply to the subject interest being valued?*

*Dietrich*: Another problem is the conflict between the Fifth Circuit's view that Sta-Home had pursued buyers unsuccessfully and the tax court's apparent dismissal of this. It is important to understand that strategic buyers in a market do not need to buy every player in that market. Generally, they will buy only a sufficient mass to service the market area. There are antitrust implications to owning too much market share. If the hospitals in Sta-Home's service area had already acquired home health agencies, they would be unlikely to acquire another.

*Patton*: A market for Medicare-dependent home health agencies clearly existed in the region. Yet, was there a market for this specific company based on conditions in Mississippi? As the geographical market shrinks, the analysis moves away from hypothetical buyers and sellers to a very specific list of each. In this case, Sta-Home would be the seller, and the list of buyers was thought to be very limited. At the same time, why was it appropriate to limit the list of likely buyers to Mississippi-based entities? An analyst should not substitute his or her judgment for that of the marketplace and assume his or her analysis considers every reasonable type of buyer. In many respects, courts in these types of cases began to move toward an investment value standard that might well be reasonable in an industry highly influenced by regulations and dominated by a narrow payment structure.

*When does data become "irrelevant history"?*

*Dietrich*: Historical transactions would have been increasingly irrelevant measures as the PPS loomed ever closer, at least to the extent they were based on the cost gap.

Comparability can be a function of time. If a major change in the reimbursement program occurs, comparability is lost. Therefore, one must be able to relate the reimbursement systems to the timing of the transaction.

*Patton*: My co-author should be given great credit for emphasizing this crucial point. The viability of any healthcare business is extremely exposed to the payment system. To the extent that payments are made by a government entity (Medicare, Medicaid, or local tax support), the prospects for that business can (and do) change greatly as reimbursement changes. Home health care literally exploded in the early 1990s. It was obvious that some reaction from the U.S. government would occur. Transactions that occurred during the time frame of growth may not be relevant to a specific valuation. The underlying conditions are just not comparable. Nevertheless, transactions for Medicare-based agencies continued to occur within the region for several years after 1995 at pre-1995 levels. This was apparently due to the differences in outlook for the industry and the impact of PPS. The important point is, however, that allegedly comparable transactions can become dated literally overnight as the reimbursement rules change.

*What does it mean to be reasonably informed of the relevant facts?*

*Dietrich*: Knowledge of impending legislative changes in health care, even if several years in the future, is critical to developing a realistic cash-flow forecast. Many of these changes are driven by the recommendation of the Medicare Payment Advisory Commission, established by Congress as part of the Balanced Budget Act of 1997 to advise it about needed changes. Equally important, extremely rapid growth in revenues in a particular industry subsector is compelling evidence that future growth is likely to be curtailed. For example, this happened in the summer of 2005 with respect to high-tech imaging after four years of rapid growth, when payments for diagnostic exams, such as magnetic residence imaging (MRI) and computed tomography (CT), were curtailed and positron emission tomography (PET) was brought within the purview of the Stark laws, which govern physician self-referral for Medicare and Medicaid patients.

As the present author noted in an article,[14] discussing the then-just-released tax court's decision in *Caracci*:

> Moreover, these cost-shifting strategies have been the subject of numerous civil and criminal proceedings under the Medicare fraud and abuse statute. In fact, MedPAC's current [2002] report[15] notes that:

14 "Valuation, Tax Exemption, 'Fair Market Value,' and the Tax Court (*Caracci, et al. v. Commissioner*)", Medical Management Advisor, May, 2002.

15 *Report to the Congress: Medicare Payment Policy*, March 2002; see page 93 forward.

> The new payment system's [The payment system was changed from a cost-based system to an interim system with stricter payment limits in 1997, then changed again to the prospective payment system in October 2000.] adjustments to eligibility and fraud and abuse reduction efforts were intended to reduce spending and redirect the benefit toward briefer, more intense care. Changes in spending and use between 1997 and 1999 demonstrate that these changes had some dramatic effects (*McCall, et al.* 2001): Total Medicare spending on home health fell 52%. . . .

Allowing for the inherent distortions in reporting caused by the cost-shifting strategy used by hospitals with respect to home health agencies, Exhibit 2 presents a graph that illustrates the four-year margin, from 1996–1999, on Medicare home health business for hospitals (the arguably strategic class of acquirer that was the basis for the tax court decision). This shows the decreased spending in those years, which occurred even though the PPS was not finally implemented due to delays until 2000. The bottom dropped out two years before the implementation.

**Exhibit 2. Four-Year Margin (1996–1999)**

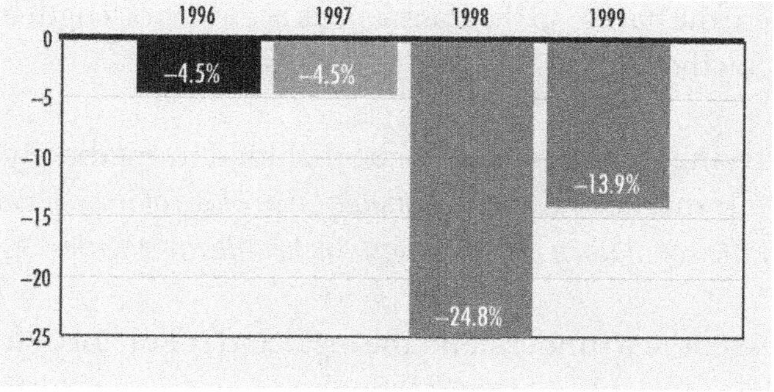


What is astounding about the tax court decision is that this information was known at the time of the trial; the court either was unaware of it or ignored it. The information very clearly demonstrates that Hahn was correct. The court's rationale seemingly cannot be that the information came after the valuation date as can be seen clearly from the following statement by the court concerning post-valuation date data.[16]

Home health agencies remained under a cost-reimbursement system until Sept. 30, 1999, when legislation passed by Congress in 1997 providing a PPS for home health agencies took full effect. The Health Care Financial Administration (HCFA) encountered problems implementing the system, and it was not finally implemented until Oct. 1, 2000. The requirement for regional market value evidence is now spelled out in the Stark laws.

16 Later in the opinion, the court stated that Hahn's inclusion of a one-year "cost gap" should have been a two-year "cost gap," apparently because the PPS was, in fact, passed in 1997, two years after the Sta-Home transaction.

Although implemented well after the Sta-Home transaction, abuses in valuing such transactions are a principal reason for the rule:

> Fair market value means the value in arm's-length transactions consistent with general market value. "General market value" means the price that an asset would bring as the result of bona fide bargaining between well-informed buyers and sellers who are not otherwise in a position to generate business for the other party or the compensation that would be included in a service agreement as a result of bona fide bargaining between well-informed parties to the agreement who are not otherwise in a position to generate business for the other party, on the date of acquisition or at the time of the service agreement. Usually the fair market price is the price at which bona fide sales have been consummated for assets of like type, quality, and quantity in a particular market at the time of acquisition.[17]
>
> Moreover, the definition of "fair market value" in the statute and regulation is qualified in ways that do not necessarily comport with the usage of the term in standard valuation techniques and methodologies. For example, the methodology must exclude valuations where the parties to the transactions are at arm's length but in a position to refer to one another.[18]

The following clarifying statement should be included immediately following the standard definition of fair market value: *Reasonable knowledge of the relevant facts contemplates an understanding of the regulatory environment for healthcare entities.*

*Patton*: It is surely essential to understand the legal and regulatory structure. Once again, however, market data from relevant transactions appear to offer a different interpretation of the specific implications of the prospective changes in the home healthcare industry. Nevertheless, the comments above are extremely important in understanding the rules of valuation in a highly regulated industry such as health care.

*How does the valuation analyst balance historical results with changes in the strategic position of the industry and varying views of the industry?*

*Dietrich*: The single most powerful tool for differentiating "strategic" value inherent in acquisition prices from fair market value is a disciplined application of the income approach on a stand-alone basis. If the value indications under the market approach

17 420 CFR 411.351 (Emphasis added).

18 "Medicare Program; Physicians' Referrals to Health Care Entities With Which They Have Financial Relationships (Phase II)"; Interim Final Rule; 69 Fed. Reg. 16053.

cannot be sustained on a stand-alone basis,[19] the analyst needs to perform an analysis to justify a crossover from strategic value to fair market value in the marketplace.[20] In other sectors of the economy, such as banking, most, if not all, buyers have "strategic" opportunities from things such as economies of scale. Because the definition of fair market value in health care is qualified by the regulatory environment, only certain types of otherwise strategic adjustments can be considered. Each category of "strategic" opportunity must be identified, evaluated for appropriateness under the statutes and regulations, and then, if appropriate, included in the valuation model (typically a discounted cash flow) to justify the value conclusion under the income approach. The value indications of the different approaches cannot be said to have been reconciled absent such an undertaking.

For example, it might be appropriate to value a subject in a sector that is being consolidated on the basis of consolidator transactions if the consolidators are active in the subject's service area. In that case, otherwise strategic adjustments such as a lower cost of capital, higher growth rates, and lower operating costs might be appropriate normalization adjustments in an income approach.[21]

At the same time, and more important, it is incumbent on the analyst to eliminate the possibility that market data may have included strategic considerations that violate the Stark laws, anti-kickback statute, or IRS regulations and rulings for exempt entities; *Caracci*, after all, was about excise taxes for an excess benefit transaction. In the two opinions, it is not clear whether there was testimony about the appropriateness from a regulatory standpoint of considering acquisition multiples based on agencies that included infusion or respiratory therapy. The tax court made it clear that Hahn, who was a leading expert in this area, eliminated them (appropriately):

> From these privately held transactions, Hahn excluded sales of privately held home health agencies that provided sophisticated "infusion or respiratory therapy" because those could attract reimbursement at a higher rate than those available to the more traditional home health care agencies such as Sta-Home.

*Patton*: An analyst must consider the regulatory structure. Once again, this is a situation in which many of the prospective buyers are likely to view acquisition targets from the perspective of investment value. Hence, fair market value and investment value begin to merge.

---

19 Damodoran describes stand-alone value in his writings on evaluating acquisitions. www.stern.nyu.edu/~adamodar/.

20 See Dietrich, "Understanding the Difference Between Strategic and Fair Market Value in Consolidating Industries," 21 *Business Valuation Review* 77 (June 2002).

21 *Ibid.*

*Can a business that appears to be losing money in perpetuity have goodwill or is there the potential for creating value even when there is no direct way to create profits?*

*Dietrich*: This question is certainly one that often confronts appraisers. I believe the prevailing view among appraisers who limit themselves to the healthcare industry is that if one cannot generate a cash return, one generally cannot have intangible value. Because the definition of fair market value is constrained by what is legally permissible (for example, a cocaine dealership has no fair market value because it is illegal), one cannot ascribe fair market value to potential exit strategies from a losing business that are inconsistent with the law.

Outside this regulatory constraint, a business that always loses money may have value to a larger entity due to economies of scale or other arguably strategic opportunities as discussed in the preceding section. A simple proscribed example would be a physician practice that earns the physician less than a reasonable salary, but generates significant revenues to a hospital through admissions and tests. The practice has a large value to the hospital, but the hospital cannot pay for that value since it violates both the Stark laws and the anti-kickback statute.

Value may exist on other than a stand-alone basis in such a circumstance as Sta-Home, but demonstrating that value to be consistent with fair market value is a required and significant burden on the appraiser and the parties to any transaction.

*Patton*: The Fifth Circuit places great reliance on a strain of thought that Sta-Home's operations could not have goodwill because the court could not identify a stream of profitability. Consider the following comment by the court:

> For Sta-Home, the overwhelming dependence on Medicare reimbursement meant that added revenue meant added reimbursement costs, which in turn, generated greater losses.

Given the growth in revenue of 276% evident in Exhibit 1 and the strategies of similar companies, why didn't Sta-Home just stop growing if the owners really believed that there was no hope of an economic return?

The tax court explained that it believed that this apparently illogical conclusion made sense: It found that Sta-Home had the potential to make a profit, which demonstrated that its assets had substantial fair market value.

There is a disconnect between the court's theory and the behavior of the owners of Sta-Home and the owners of other companies in the marketplace.

> To operate despite their perennial cash-flow problems, their lack of profitability, their increasing operating losses, and their increasing deficits.

> ... its patients—would only enable the agencies to lose money for the indefinite future.

Can a business that appears to be losing money in perpetuity have goodwill? Here again, the growth of the size of the business could indicate an alternative theory about the creation of value not linked to reported profitability. Again, there is a disconnect between the business strategy of Sta-Home (and other similar companies in the region) and the observations of the Fifth Circuit. Rational people stop amassing assets when it continually increases their losses unless they believe that there is an economic return on some basis in the future.

The Fifth Circuit posits the following argument that goodwill is derived from excess earnings; therefore, in this case, there can be no goodwill. It states:

> The tax court's mistaken belief that Sta-Home's intangible assets had substantial fair market value led it to ignore its own long-recognized position that unprofitable intangible assets do not contribute to fair market value unless those assets produce net income or earnings. Revenue Ruling 59-60 requires the IRS to assign zero value to unprofitable intangible assets. See Rev. Rule 59-60, 1959-1 C.B. 237 ("The presence of goodwill and its value, therefore, rests upon the excess of net earnings over and above a fair return on the net tangible assets.")

Putting aside the Fifth Circuit's legal position, the court's implicit economic position requires discussion. First and foremost, all value is a function of future benefits. The past may be instructive but is not determinative of value. The core question for any asset or business value is: "What benefits will it produce in the future?"

Most assets and businesses have the prospect of a visible positive return in the hands of its current owners. Value is most visible when net income is present. However, every valuation analyst has to be open to an alternative view of value creation that is not apparent until the ultimate sale of the assets. Appraisers often place virtually all of the value in a discounted cash flow analysis in the terminal value; therefore, interim profitability is not essential.

What happens, however, when profitability is never likely or even expected to occur in the hands of the current owner? Can goodwill exist? Of course it can, and it does. How could this be true? In one simple scenario, value in excess of cost can be created by accumulating a customer base. By selling the amassed base in bulk, there is value to the buyer, which is often a typical market participant. The seller realizes the value of its efforts to accumulate the customers.

*Did the tax court and Wilhoite err by basing the valuation of the assets on the market value of invested capital?*

*Patton*: The tax court and Wilhoite based the value of the assets, including the intangible assets, on the market value of invested capital. The Fifth Circuit said this was in error, and the value of the assets, including the intangible assets, should be based on a valuation of the direct value of the assets themselves. Was the tax court in error? From a valuation perspective, the answer is an emphatic "no."

The Fifth Circuit favors an approach to valuing goodwill by valuing the asset directly. Further, it seems not to accept the notion that the value of the assets must equal the value of the liabilities by referring to it as an accounting concept. This is incorrect. The value of the assets will, by definition, from a valuation perspective, be the value of the total invested capital plus other liabilities and nonoperating assets. Additionally, the concept of direct valuation of goodwill will require the use of income methods that ultimately require the determination of total invested capital.

*Dietrich*: Perhaps both courts got ahead of their knowledge in writing their opinions. The left-hand or asset side of the accounting equation must, of necessity, equal the right-hand or invested capital side. The Fifth Circuit thought a more meaningful result could be obtained from the left-hand side, while the tax court believed in the invested capital approach inherent in use of the guideline methods in which individual assets are not valued. It is a useful exercise to allocate value to the assets after making a preliminary determination of invested capital, and the present author often does so both analytically and in reports. Identifying the amount of intangible value is important in healthcare appraisal because this is where the regulatory risk is greatest.

## Looking Ahead

The opinions of the tax court and the Fifth Circuit in *Caracci* raise very interesting questions for business valuation professionals. The authors have attempted to address several of them. While they may not agree on every point, hopefully readers will find their insights helpful and that this article furthers the discussion.

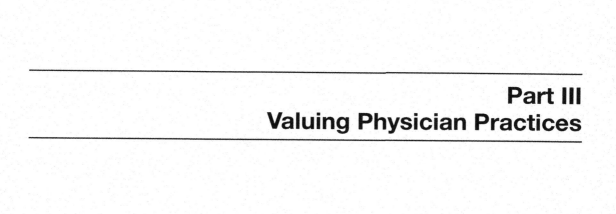

# Part III
# Valuing Physician Practices

Chapter 14

# Choosing and Using the Right Valuation Methods for Physician Practices

*By Mark O. Dietrich, CPA/ABV*

### The Market in 2011-2012

Healthcare industry transactions are in full swing, rivaling the volume of activity during the 1990s consolidation, although without the presence of significant public company players. The focus on cardiology practices common after the reductions in nuclear medicine's technical component in 2010 have been supplanted by a heavy emphasis on primary care practices as hospitals and integrated providers gear up for Medicare accountable care organizations (ACO) resulting from the reform legislation and the issuance of arguably more favorable final regulations in October 2011. Even if ACO participation proves to be small as many predict, the focus on primary care-oriented and the overall shortage of primary care physicians will drive the market.

Another notable difference between today's market and that of the 1990s is that there is recognition in most quarters, but certainly not all, of the need to carefully tie physician compensation to the forecast used to value the practice. Another is that physician compensation is typically linked to productivity—and increasingly as measured by work RVUs or wRVUs—and not fixed, the latter practice having led to low patient volumes and large operating losses. The importance of focusing on post-transaction compensation was re-emphasized in the 2008 Tax Court case *Derby,* cited in numerous places herein.

The consensus today, including that of many of the contributors to this guide, is that future physician compensation is typically a more significant element of a transaction than is the value of the practice. In many circumstances, hospitals and integrated delivery systems have superior contracts with insurers that in turn permit physicians to receive better compensation for the same amount of work, something published research in a variety of publications supports.[1] Over the course of five years or more, compensation is typically more valuable than sales proceeds to a physician, given the range of valuation multiples. Readers should note that it is not appropriate to value the practice using the buyer's better insurer contracts because that is inconsistent with fair market value although as described in the chapter on fair market compensation, those rate differences have become significant for evaluating post-transaction compensation.

As a final observation, practices with intensive investment in ancillaries are likely to be more valuable, all things being equal. Given the Stark laws restrictions or prohibition on post-transaction compensation with respect to the technical component of ancillary services in different employment and independent contractor settings, there is not the usual tradeoff between future compensation and current value.

## Introduction

Simply stated, valuation models require two major components: future cash flows and a discount or capitalization rate. All valuation results are a function of the interaction between these two factors. Once the valuation analyst has gained a sufficient knowledge of the marketplace, regulatory environment, and the subject practice as described elsewhere in this guide, the actual measuring of value can begin.

Other chapters to review in this guide are:

1. Healthcare Market Structure and Its Implication for Valuation of Privately Held Provider Entities—An Empirical Analysis
2. Stark Law and the Anti-Kickback Statute: Avoiding Valuation of Referrals
3. Factors in Forecasting Cash Flow and Estimating Cost of Capital in Healthcare
4. Critical Condition: A Coding Analysis for a Physician Practice Valuation[2]
5. Why Transaction Structure Affects Value and Other Nuances of Valuing Medical Practices
6. Understanding and Using the Technical and Professional Component of Ancillary Revenue When Valuing Medical Practices
7. Understanding Healthcare Markets

1 See Chapter 3.
2 In my view, you cannot value a physician practice without doing a coding analysis.

8. A Valuation Model for the Formation of ACOs
9. Tax-Exempt Healthcare Organization Valuation Issues Related to Excess Benefits, Private Inurement, and Intermediate Sanctions
10. The CPA's Role in Mergers and Acquisitions: Due Diligence Assistance to PPMCs and Private Equity Firms
11. Evaluating RVU-Based Compensation Arrangements

Many experienced valuation analysts new to healthcare will be familiar and (perhaps) more comfortable with the market approach based upon databases such as those maintained by the IBA or Pratt's Stats. When considering the merged and acquired company method, bear in mind that the historical data available regarding the "acquisition" of practices via management services agreements with physician practice management companies (PPMCs) are generally not relevant.[3] A PPMC transaction is fundamentally different from an outright purchase of the practice and therefore, should not be used for such a valuation without various adjustments, including those to cash-equivalent consideration and compensation. Finally, my experience is that physicians focus on cash returns in the form of additional compensation when they buy practices and regulators expect hospitals to focus on cash returns from within the practice.

This chapter is organized with a discussion of rules of thumb presented first, in the expectation that someone new to medical practice valuation will benefit from a frame of reference when studying the actual methods. Bear in mind that such rules are not methods and merely provide an oft-suspect means of a reality check.

A presentation of a discounted cash flow valuation is beyond the scope of the chapter but considerable detail about the differences in DCFs for physician practices is provided. A discussion of the build-up method for determining discount and capitalization rates then follows.

The chapter explains in detail the use of the excess earnings method and the capitalization of cash flows (CCF). The focus of this chapter is on asset purchases, not stock purchases, since the vast majority of physician practice transactions, aside from buy-ins, are assets only.

3 This guide's chapter on "The CPA's Role in Mergers and Acquisitions Due Diligence Assistance to PPMC's and Private Equity Firms" suggests there are limited circumstances such as anesthesia and pathology where these types of transactions remain relevant.

The excess earnings method is presented in its traditional physician-to-physician transaction approaches, using *pretax* excess earnings and a discount and capitalization rate applicable to *pretax* earnings for a hypothetical physician buyer.

#### *Insight and Analysis*

A notable aspect of valuing a physician practice is the need to get into the detail behind operating expenses for normalization purposes to identify discretionary expenses available to the owner of the practice in lieu of taking taxable compensation. A general ledger is a basic element of a data request—like it or not! Prior to commencing the actual quantitative valuation analysis, I review in detail the normalized operating results and compare them to statistical norms from the Medical Group Management Association (MGMA) or other sources.[4] You need to ask, "How would the practice look if operated by the typical buyer or seller?" Bear in mind that the hypothetical buyer of a physician practice is interested primarily in what the cash return of the practice will be, not what anecdotal or "market" data say the practice might be bought or sold for.

For perhaps the best analysis of the general limitations of market data in valuation, see Business Valuation Resources' *The Comprehensive Guide to the Use and Application of the Transaction Databases* by Nancy Fannon, CPA/ABV and Heidi Walker, CPA/ABV.

### Alleged Comparative Practice Sales Method

Medical practices, like most businesses, have rules of thumb for valuation. These are commonly expressed as a percentage of the practice's receipts. The most common source of such information is *The Goodwill Registry*, published annually by The Health Care Group of Plymouth Meeting, Pa. This consulting firm's figures are cited in such trade publications as *Medical Economics* and *Physicians Management*, which are widely read by physicians. The *Registry* contains information on practice sales, valuations, and divorce settlements accumulated by The Health Care Group from its own activities, as well as others who submit data to it. The data is usually (and abusedly) cited as an average percentage of revenues ostensibly paid for "goodwill."

#### *Insight and Analysis*

It is a commonplace principle of research in the scientific community that "the plural of anecdote is not data." Valuation analysts do well to remember this when using rules of thumb.

4 *The CPA's Role in Mergers and Acquisitions Due Diligence Assistance to PPMC's and Private Equity Firms* provides details and a checklist on how to approach gaining an understanding of a practice.

#### Rules of Thumb and Market Date: Understanding Comparatives

A comparative is only as useful as the underlying analysis of the subject practice. For example, if you decide to purchase a four-bedroom home, you cannot go to a realtor's office and get a standard price for a home. The price will vary with numerous factors, such as the age of the house, the size of the rooms, the number of bathrooms, the quality of the kitchen, the size of the lot, and so on. A medical practice is no different. It is not possible to value any practice by taking a percentage of its receipts. Further, just because Practice A is valued at 60% of receipts does not mean that Practice B is worth 60%. It may be worth 10%—or nothing.

#### *Insight and Analysis*

These "rules" originate from physician-to-physician transactions and have always been of limited use in a market area in which physician practice management companies operate or for purchases by hospitals or integrated delivery systems; in the latter circumstance, serious regulatory issues are raised from such use. In addition, during the buying frenzy of the mid-1990s, the market value (as reflected by actual transactions) often exceeded these levels. Like any rules of thumb, they need to be considered within the context of market conditions at the time a valuation is performed. I do not endorse use of such rules as valuation methods and caution against their use even as reality checks, especially where regulatory factors govern. Reconciliation of the results of a market approach with the income approach is critical, and the latter should be given preference. A weighting using a disparate result from a goodwill percentage with a disciplined income approach will simply dilute the meaningfulness of the income approach, not lead to a more accurate conclusion of value.

#### Use of the Goodwill Registry to Determine Intangible Value

If one were to accept the premise that the *Goodwill Registry* constitutes a valid source of market data on the intangible value of medical practices, it is necessary to understand precisely what that valuation method includes.

The *Goodwill Registry* contains the following definition of "goodwill:"

> As we see it, professional practice "goodwill" is a combination of practice intangibles varying, on a case-by-case basis, as to existence and value. That combination might include location, use of a practice's or an *individual's name*, patient information (embodied in the clinical record), a favorable leasehold, *a covenant not to compete, compensation for past (or future) management and entrepreneurial services, payments made for referral to an associate or recommendation of a successor*, patient lists, credit records, patient care and or employee contracts, as well as assignments of future income." (*Emphasis added* to

> identify those items denoting personal goodwill rather than practice goodwill and therefore not divisible property.)[5]

Thus, the reported values in the *Goodwill Registry* clearly *include*, for example, nondivisible personal goodwill via a noncompete, which is relevant in many jurisdictions for marital dissolution purposes. The entries also include *control* and *noncontrol* transactions, valuations which did not result in a transaction and final divorce settlements, which are court decisions, not transactions. For "market data" to be valid, they must represent actual transactions.

#### Valuation Community Professional Standards

Besides my own views of the limitations of rules of thumb, the broad valuation profession holds a similar view. A rule of thumb is a means of estimating what a transaction value might be, using a "deal" price rather than cash equivalents. Valuation analysts use rules of thumb to gauge or reality check the results of valuation methods under the three approaches to valuation. Rules of thumb are widely disparaged as valuation *methods* in the professional literature:

> Formula values are not substitutes for careful consideration of other appropriate valuation methods that are applicable to the business being appraised.[6]

> Sometimes called "rules of thumb," the industry method can prove to be a valuable tool but should *never* be relied upon by itself for the valuation of an appraisal subject.... If enough transactions take place using a particular method, the end result is that *there are market data that will support the use of that method*. However, if these formulas are the only methods used, *an inappropriate valuation may result*.[7] (*Emphasis added*)

> Rule of thumb—a mathematical relationship between or among variables based on experience, observation, *hearsay*, or a combination of these, usually applicable to a specific industry.[8] (*Emphasis added*)

More importantly, rules of thumb do not represent *cash-equivalent values*, which are a key requirement of the definition of fair market value. Cash-equivalent value might well include proceeds attributable to a *stock* sale, not an *asset* sale. Rules of thumb represent the value of assets, not stock. There is a substantial difference between valuing the *stock* of an entity, which is sometimes the relevant task such as in marital dissolution, and

5 *Goodwill Registry*, Explanatory Notes.
6 Glenn Desmond, *Handbook of Small Business Valuation Formulas*, as quoted in *The Lawyers' Business Valuation Handbook*, ibid, page 189.
7 *Understanding Business Valuation*, 2d Edition, Gary R. Trugman, American Institute of CPAs, 2002, page 255.
8 International Glossary of Business Valuation Terms.

valuing the *assets*. The purchaser of *assets* obtains *tax benefits* consisting of 1) the basis step-up in fixed assets (e.g., equipment and furniture) and the resultant additional depreciation deduction; and 2) the basis attributable to intangible assets and the resultant amortization deduction (IRC §197 allows the purchase price of intangibles to be written off over 15 years, generating substantial tax savings). Rules of thumb are "deal" prices representing the "value" of *assets*.

There are no data provided in the *Goodwill Registry* to determine whether or not the values reflected are cash-equivalent values, a necessary prerequisite for its use in determining fair market value.

#### Levin Associates' Health Care Acquisition Report

One source used widely during the consolidation era of the 1990s for "market" data was Irving Levin Associate's *Health Care Acquisition Report*. This report includes the following data points: location of the acquired practice, a brief description, the price paid (which may or may not represent cash-equivalent value, a prerequisite for fair market value), a brief summary of deal terms, the number of units (physicians) acquired, price paid divided by revenue and price paid divided by income. Few are actually reported, since the information is not publicly available. This report led to the questionable practice of valuing physicians based upon the number working for the acquired practice—something akin to the method during the stock market bubble of valuing software companies with large accumulated deficits based on the number of engineers and programmers.

#### Pratt's Stats[9]

*Pratt's Stats*, perhaps the most comprehensive and justifiably highly regarded of the databases, has data entry points for state, city, firm, and individual submitting the report of the transaction, 14 income statement items, 13 balance sheet items, actual transaction data based upon equity, market value of invested capital, allocation to noncompete agreement and other assets, and dozens of yes-or-no questions about the transaction as well as ratios computed from the core financial data. Often, however, not all of the data is submitted for each transaction, and there are very few medical practices. Regionalization is also critical to assessing the usefulness of this market data. For example, in November 2004, nearly 90% of 96 items identified as general dentistry were from three states: Pennsylvania, Arizona, and Oregon. Fifty of the entries were submitted by one brokerage firm and 20 by another. As the investigations of Wall Street investment bankers indicate, a few individuals' views of the market value of a business can distort the picture. Even broadly held views of market value, such as those that

9 Edited portions of this discussion appeared in "Medical Practices: A BV Rx," *Journal of Accountancy*, November 2005 by the author.

preceded the bursting of the stock market bubble in March 2000, can be based upon a *lack* of "reasonable knowledge of relevant facts."

A closer look at regional economics and the market data presents an even greater challenge. Managed care and its limitations on services and pricing are most prevalent in urban areas, where population density and employers make attractive insurance markets. Rural areas have less managed care and fewer patients per square mile. The profitability of a practice per unit of service is likely to be better in areas with less managed care. For example, an analysis of mean physician salaries from the Medical Group Management Association's (MGMA) *Physician Compensation and Production Survey* for 2011 indicates that incomes were greatest for both primary care and specialty care in the southern region, where population density is typically low (urban areas of Florida notwithstanding). The greater incomes are a function of several factors, including lower managed care, higher unit fees, and lower operating costs and in some areas, considerably higher utilization. This greatly limits the common use of goodwill percentage averages paid for all practices of a particular specialty from the *Goodwill Registry*. Valuation is, after all, a function of cash flow from profit not cash flow from revenue!

#### Guideline Publicly Traded Companies

With very rare exception, a physician practice should not be valued based upon public company multiples. It is very difficult indeed to find a public company, even in SIC 801, which is comparable to a physician practice. Pediatrix Medical Group Inc. (NYSE: PDX), Mednax (NYSE: MD), and IntegraMed America Inc. (NASDAQ: INMD) could be relevant in limited circumstances depending upon the nature of the transaction.

### *Insight and Analysis*

Always look at the underlying components of any SIC data to be certain you understand what the companies actually do. The result is often surprising.

#### Current Recruiting Data

Data on annual recruiting engagements from such firms as Merritt Hawkins[10] and Delta Medical indicate that the specialties in highest demand include internists, family medicine, orthopedic surgery, gastroenterology, dermatology, interventional and general radiology, and interventional cardiology. Hospitals or existing practices looking to recruit such physicians typically find the starting salary very high and the structure of a future buy-in on the table from the outset. It is not uncommon for a well-informed physician exiting residency to base his or her employment decision on competing buy-in opportunities—and the lower the better. For example, orthopedic surgeons are

10 www.merritthawkins.com/.

often looking for practices with ambulatory surgery centers, which offer significantly enhanced incomes and better working conditions, and the buy-in opportunity has to be affordable.

Recruiting data are another application of the market approach in that they represent market data on physician income. Income is what the investor in a physician practice is buying. There is a substantive question of whether a hypothetical buyer will pay for an asset that generates less income to that hypothetical buyer than a position as a noninvestor employee. Thus, it is important to compare the earnings available from the practice being valued to that offered in the recruiting market.

A serious shortage of physicians and particularly primary care (generalist) physicians is expected in the next several decades. This shortage will be dramatically increased as a result of the reform legislation and the attempt to bring some 40 million people or more into the primary care system. This has negative implications for practice value because new suppliers' ease of entry into the market is enhanced when there is unmet, excess demand for services.[11] It also puts a premium on midlevel providers as well as the renewed interest in so-called "minute clinics"[12] in chain pharmacies and supermarkets.

The ratio of physician to population varies quite significantly from state to state and from urban to suburban and rural areas. Medicare-participating physicians by specialty

**Exhibit 1. Number of Medicare-Participating Physicians by Specialty**

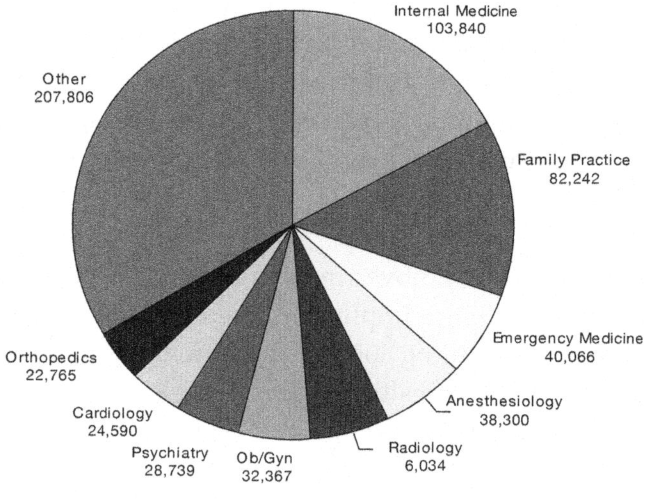


11 "Will Generalist Physician Supply Meet Demands of an Increasing and Aging Population?" Jack M. Colwill, James M. Cultice, and Robin L. Kruse; *Health Affairs*, 29 April 2008.
12 Known as walk-in medical centers, freestanding emergi-centers or "doc in the boxes" in the 1980s and 1990s.

**Exhibit 2. Number of Medicare Part B Providers by Region**

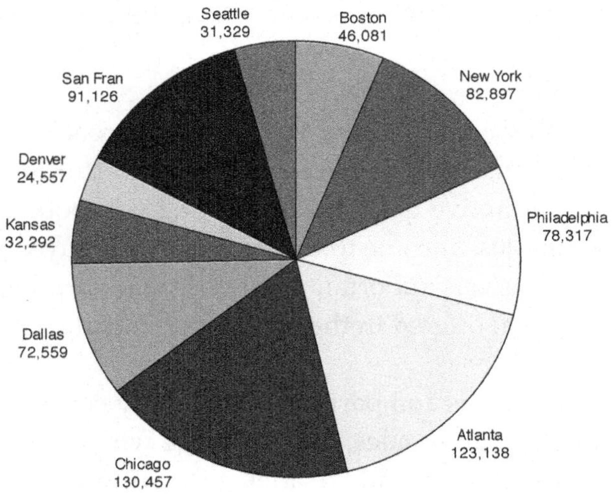


and region can be found in the publication *2010 CMS Statistics,*[13] shown in Exhibits 1 and 2. This in turn affects the value of practices as well as the incomes available in recruitment settings.

#### Value of Transactions in Another Market Area

There are regional differences in what sellers will pay for physician practices, much of which are or were driven by the presence or lack of presence of for-profit buyers, as well as such items as the enforceability of noncompetes and enhanced income opportunities. These factors, along with the Stark regulations' requirement that data in a "particular market" be used for determining fair market value, make the data for one region of questionable relevance to another in the absence of appropriate correlation. What should drive price differentials on an economic level from market to market are differences in the availability of cash profits and ease of entry of competitors.[14]

### *Insight and Analysis*

For those circumstances in which government regulations such as the Stark laws or the anti-kickback statute (AKS) are implicated, regionalized market data are further suspect. In recognition of the seeming abuses—intentional or unintentional—of market data, the Stark II regulations specifically define fair market value as "the price at which bona fide sales have been consummated for assets of like type, quality, and quantity in a particular market at the time of acquisition"[15] (emphasis added).

13 www.cms.gov/ResearchGenInfo/02_CMSStatistics.asp.
14 See Chapter 3.
15 420 CFR 411.351.

During the consolidation of the 1990s, the vast majority of purchases were in the South and Southwest, although the available market data were widely used in all regions. The Stark II regulations create a critical limitation on market data when the valuation is being undertaken for regulatory purposes, unless the valuation analyst can demonstrate that data from one region or state are somehow relevant to another.

The *IRS Exempt Organizations Continuing Professional Education Technical Instruction Program Textbook* for 1995[16] states the following in a section entitled "Establishing Comparability Under the Market Approach": "Factors affecting comparability include markets served; practice and specialty type; competitive position; profitability; growth prospects; risk perceptions; financial composition (capital structure); physician compensation; physician age, health and reputation; physician productivity; average revenues per physician; cost structure; and average revenue per visit or covered life to revenue to revenue mix (capitated versus fee for service)" citing *Financial Valuation: Businesses and Business Interests*. I know of no database with such information!

#### Empirical Study of Healthcare Markets

My chapter herein "Healthcare Market Structure and Its Implication for Valuation of Privately Held Provider Entities: An Empirical Analysis" was originally published in the Summer 2008 *Business Valuation Review*. The idea for that article came from a Government Accounting Office study of market share of health insurers in various states and my experience that pricing and profit differed significantly across the country. I reasoned that this insurer market share[17] and related market power would be one key element defining a market and set out to find out how it and other factors contributed. This, in turn, would define comparability for purposes of the market approach to valuation.

Here is a summary of my findings as to the key elements defining a market:

1. Total Medicare spending and Medicare spending per capita;
2. The presence and market strength of Blue Cross plans;
3. The degree of market strength of local nonprofit hospitals versus for-profit hospitals;
4. The degree of market strength of local nonprofit health insurers versus for-profit health insurers,
5. Certificate of need laws; and
6. Other local demographic and economic factors.

16 www.irs.gov/pub/irs-tege/.
17 I am indebted to legendary health law attorney J.D. Epstein for his insights on this topic.

These factors contribute to the fact that most (certainly not all) larger for-profit healthcare providers are primarily located in Florida, Texas, California, and Tennessee. They also confirm the underlying rationale for the Stark Laws' restrictions on the use of out-of-market data as "comparable." The "Checklist of Factors to Consider When Evaluating the Significance of Out-of-Market Transactions" included in this guide provides a means for undertaking this analysis as well as links to Web sites where the underlying data are located.

As I observed with my friend Reed Tinsley in a 2006 article for the American Bar Association's Health Law Section:

> If the acquirer is a public company, an important dynamic is in effect. Public companies' stock prices or valuation multiples are heavily based upon their earnings growth. The higher the earnings growth, the higher the valuation multiple and the higher the value of the company. Thus, that growth needs to continue or the stock's price will decline. There is an arbitrage effect when the earnings of private companies are placed in the public equity markets through acquisition that can enable a public company to afford a higher price than a private company, all other things being equal.[18] Although fair market value in a given market area may be driven by the economics of public companies, the Stark requirement that comparable transactions be in a particular market at the time of acquisition addresses this if public companies are not active acquirers in a given market area.[19]

### Other Common Pitfalls in the Market Approach

Valuation analysts frequently prefer the market approach to valuing a business. As a colleague observed, "Appraisers are market observers, not market makers."[20] Trouble is, to observe, you have to have your eyes open and understand what you are looking at. Courts tend to understand easily that if businesses of a certain type sell for three times earnings, then a given business is likely worth three times earnings. Valuation analysts tend to be comfortable for the same reason; there is less judgment[21] in the market approach than in the income approach, if a good database of transactions for a type of business exists.

18 See, e.g., "Understanding the Difference Between Strategic and Fair Market Value in Consolidating Industries," *Business Valuation Review*, May 2002, by the author.

19 "Identifying Appropriate Business Valuation Approaches Under Stark and the AKS," the author with Reed Tinsley, CPA, CVA, *The Health Lawyer*, American Bar Association, December 2006.

20 Perhaps not the first to say it, but I heard it from Steve Bravo, CPA/ABV, ASA.

21 My opinion.

Medical practices present a unique challenge for proper use of the market approach. As we will see in the analysis that follows, the market data often do not contain sufficient data to determine precisely what the multiples in a given transaction were.

#### Example

Assume that a representative transaction in a database contains the following information:

Date of Transaction: July 1, 1997
Type of Practice: Ophthalmology
Subject Revenues: $1,000,000
Owner compensation: $450,000
Earnings after taxes: $2,000
Purchase Price: $540,000
Debts assumed: $0
Working Capital Included: Yes
*Multiples*:
Owner's Discretionary Comp: 1.20
Revenues: 0.54

What does this tell us about the value of this practice or about the practice we are trying to value today? Painfully little, unfortunately.

#### *Analysis*

The year 1997 represented the last "big year" of buying by the PPMC industry, which collapsed and died following the failed merger between MedPartners and Phycor at the end of that year. We do not know if the above transaction was a purchase by a PPMC, but it likely was, since very few other transactions in medical practices were disclosed.[22]

PPMC's purchased practices were based upon a multiple of earnings contracted to the PPMC. The contracted earnings typically were 15% to 20% of the earnings of the physician. In the above sample transaction, the purchase price of $540,000 could have been based upon a multiple applied to an earnings stream between $67,500 (15% of $450,000) and $90,000 (20% of $450,000). As such, the correct valuation multiple to be garnered from this transaction could be as little as six ($540,000 divided by $90,000) or as much as eight ($540,000 divided by $67,500). Generally, such multiples ranged between four and seven, but we cannot tell what the multiple was from the transaction. The purchase

22 At least in my review of the databases, many if not most of the transactions predate 1998 and fall into the PPMC era.

price included working capital, intangibles, and fixed assets. The illustrated multiples of 1.20 times owner's discretionary cash flow and 0.54 of revenues are not meaningful if this is a PPMC transaction. The PPMC was not buying 100% of the physician's earnings, nor was it buying the revenues—it was buying a portion of the practice's earnings before physician compensation.

*If* this was a physician-to-physician transaction, of course, the valuation multiples would be more meaningful. One clue that this is *not* a physician-to-physician transaction, however, is that accounts receivable were included—that is rarely the case in a physician-to-physician deal, while it was normally the case in a PPMC transaction. This, of course, is critical to the valuation analyst attempting to use the data to develop a market conclusion of value.

#### Particular Problems for Hospital Buyers

It is critical from a regulatory standpoint that the hospital receives an accurately determined fair market value for the practice. Using market data from the 1990s to establish trends that include a class of buyers (PPMCs) no longer present for most physicians, even if normally reasonable to general business valuation analysts, is a serious mistake from a regulatory standpoint. Besides the problems with using such data outlined above, equally important is the fact that the market conditions today are no longer what they were in 1990s.

Use of the *Goodwill Registry* rule of thumb based on a percentage of collected revenues is risky from a regulatory standpoint.

> Using the *Goodwill Registry* to value a practice for purchase by a hospital would be a critical mistake as there would be no way of determining if the hospital was receiving an appropriate return on its investment without a disciplined application of the income approach described earlier. This is because an asset that has or will generate no cash flow has no value to the hypothetical buyer of the fair market value standard.[23]

When confronted with this type of valuation engagement, a valuation analyst can also consider a *replication cost* approach, looking at such intangible assets as workforce-in-place and going concern value, in addition to fixed assets, such as equipment and furniture. At a minimum, one might think the practice should be worth the cost to a physician buying it of establishing a similar practice, including the quantification of the

23 "Identifying Appropriate Business Valuation Approaches Under Stark and the AKS," the author with Reed Tinsley, CPA, CVA, *The Health Lawyer*, American Bar Association, December 2006.

reduced revenue during the start-up period. Nonetheless, there is a substantive question for a hospital as to whether replication cost is appropriate because a hypothetical investor will likely not invest in something that lacks cash return.

> The key question, of course, is whether or not the hypothetical buyer of the fair market value standard would incur a value based upon replication cost if there was no return on the investment. Most experienced healthcare appraisers would likely answer no in the absence of some additional mitigating factors. It is worth noting that, at least in this author's view, a hospital employing a physician post-transaction should evaluate the practice value differently than a physician buying a practice from another physician, where the seller retires or otherwise ceases to practice in the service area.
>
> Tax-exempt hospitals generally are subject to a standard of providing community benefit for the costs they expend. Thus, one potential mitigating factor in utilizing replication cost would be where the acquiring hospital met the community benefit standard. This might occur where the service area of the target physician was underserved and/or the physician serving that area planned to leave for a better opportunity.[24]

Note should be taken as well of any contractual relationships between the hospital and the physician in the proposed transaction documents, including a covenant not to compete held by the hospital and any guaranteed rights under an employment contract held by the physician. Valuing such contractual rights can be an important part of a proper fair market value determination when a transaction is being consummated or unwound. This was a critical issue in *Derby v. Commissioner,*[25] which involved valuation issues associated with the donation of the intangible value of a medical practice to a tax-exempt hospital.[26]

#### Conclusion

Old market data in particular are only relevant if the market conditions today are the same as when the comparable transaction took place. We cannot sell 100 shares of a NASDAQ market index future today for the same price that we would have gotten in March 2000 or November 2007. Similarly, we cannot sell a physician practice today for the same market multiple, or even to the same class of buyers, as we could have from 1990 to 1997. Care needs to be taken to understand current market conditions and transaction terms when using databases of market transactions.

24 "Regulatory Issues in Using Replication Cost for Valuing Physician Practices," *Financial Valuation and Litigation Expert*, February/March 2007 by the author.

25 *Charles A. and Marian L. Derby, et al., Petitioners v. Commissioner, Respondent*, T.C. Memo. 2008-45, GALE, Judge.

26 "What Goes Around Comes Around: *Derby v. Commissioner*"; see chapter 11 of this guide.

## Understanding Physician Practice Discount and Capitalization Rates

### *Insight and Analysis*

What is a discount rate? One of the most difficult concepts to grasp in valuation is the relationship between stock market returns and discount rates for businesses. A discount rate is the percentage of cash return an investor expects to receive for an investment of given risk. In the stock market—from where we derive discount rates used in all valuation engagements—the cash return consists of dividends plus capital appreciation on the stock. In a medical practice, the return consists of enhanced compensation and perhaps dividends, if the practice is an S corporation or limited liability company (LLC), or if the entity is an ambulatory surgery center or imaging center. There *may* also be capital appreciation at the time the practice is sold, although most physicians realize the bulk of the net present value of their investment through annual earnings, not from a business sale. When a business distributes all or most of its cash profits, it tends to have a lower rate of appreciation than a business that reinvests its cash.

The terms discount rate, expected rate of return, and cost of equity[27] all mean the same thing. It is important to note that the *actual* return in a given year is not likely to be equal to the *expected* return—that is what risk is all about! Over a long period of time, for investments in physician practices with the same risk profile, the actual return should equal the expected return—much the same way that stocks go up and down and have good years and bad years but are known to outperform bonds and money market funds over the long haul.[28]

A capitalization rate is obtained, of course, by subtracting the expected long-term (perpetual) growth rate in net cash flows from the discount rate. Growth rates are discussed in detail below.

#### Practice Risk Premium: Being Objective With the Subjective?

The actual unsystematic risk premium—$RP_u$— or the medical practice premium will depend upon whether your build-up method approach uses 1) the microcap premium or 2) the 10th decile premium.[29] For example, a portion of the unsystematic risk of the typical physician practice is accounted for in the 10th decile premium, considering that the healthcare industry is *less* risky than the broad market (S&P 500) from which the equity risk premium for large companies is derived. That said, many physician practices have dramatic additional risk, such as those that rely upon a single product and

27 As seen later herein, the same terms can apply to debt or the cost of capital.
28 At least prior to the start of the recession in 2008.
29 Or even the 10b risk premium, being the bottom half of the 10th percentile.

earn most or all their profits from a single insurer. This can be seen by examining the industry risk premium data for healthcare companies contained in the valuation edition of the *Morningstar Yearbook*, bearing in mind that excessive reliance on the industry risk premium leads to errors as well.[30] As I stated in a peer-reviewed 2007 article on the *Delaware Open MRI* case, better known for its S corporation tax-effecting scheme:

> Perhaps the most fundamental valuation mistake in the healthcare industry is failure to differentiate the risk of a small entity operating in a single state (Delaware) in a single line of business (MRI) with a few dominant health insurers from the risk of large public entities operating in multiple states in multiple lines of business with multiple health insurers paying for the cost of services. Use of the industry risk premium in the build-up method compounds this typical error.[31]

The risk premium for the medical practice being valued (i.e., unsystematic risk) is a highly subjective number and one that is heavily dependent upon the knowledge and skill of the valuation analyst. Some valuation analysts use a list of risk factors with a range of premium percentages assigned to each factor, while others use a single percentage and justify the additional premium in their written report. The following is a nonexhaustive listing of some of the factors that should be considered in developing the practice risk premium.

1. Specialty;
2. Reliance on single product and service or payor;
3. Presence or lack of a repeat patient (customer) base;
4. Reliance upon individual skills and referrals from other physicians;
5. Profitability;
6. Total receipts;
7. Payor mix and quality of contracts;
8. Coding (!);
9. Age and gender of provider;
10. Quality of staff, particularly billing staff;
11. Longevity of staff;
12. Number of active patients;

30 The single largest source of error is blindly relying on Morningstar data in any event.

31 See, e.g., "A Healthcare Appraiser Reviews a Judge-Appraiser's 'Report'" *Business Valuation Review*, Summer 2007, by the author.

13. Number of competitors;
14. Ease of entry into the market;
15. Current recruiting salaries;
16. Risk of reimbursement changes;
17. Available market strategies; and
18. Underwriting cycle for health insurance industry (see discussion below).

Additional risk factors for markets or practices with capitation are:

1. Likely transition to capitation;
2. Presence of Medicare capitation;
3. Experience with capitation;
4. Covered lives;
5. Reserves for capitated referrals or risk pools; and
6. The underwriting cycle for health insurance industry is particularly important here.

The chapter on accountable care organizations deals with the specific risk issues for those entities and participating practices.

Exhibit 3 appeared in the article "Medical Practices: A BV Rx" in the November 2005 *Journal of Accountancy.*

**Exhibit 3. Medical Practice Risk Premiums**

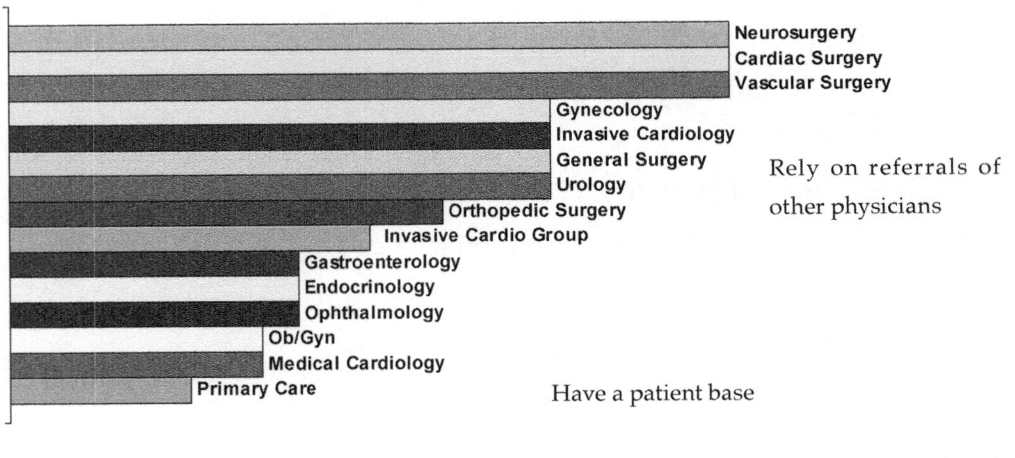

## Weighted Average Cost of Capital (WACC)

Another commonly overlooked fact of valuation is the accounting equation, something that was emphasized by the Fifth Circuit Court of Appeals when overturning the Tax Court's decision in *Caracci*.[32] If equity and long-term debt (including the current portion of long-term debt) are the *right side* of the accounting equation used in the market value of invested capital (MVIC), the *left side* of the equation includes tangible assets, such as furniture and equipment and working capital assets (such as accounts receivable and prepaid items), and intangible assets, such as personal and enterprise or practice goodwill, as well as the value of any noncompete agreement or enterprise value (EV). In computing the value of the business enterprise, working capital is reduced by accounts payable and accrued items to arrive at net working capital (NWC). Note that a valuation model that measures EV will include the entire value of the operating assets: tangible, intangible, and net working capital.

If the goal of a valuation engagement is to value MVIC/EV (the invested capital or operating assets of the practice, again, both equity and long-term debt), then use of the WACC is appropriate. If the goal of the valuation is to value a controlling interest in the practice, as is common for hospital buyers or transfers of solo practices to a new physician, the WACC can be used and the ratio of debt and equity can be based upon the optimum mix of debt and equity for any hypothetical willing buyer or seller. This is because a control buyer has the ability to alter the capital structure to the optimal ratio and debt is cheaper than equity, all things being equal. (The optimum capital structure of a specific buyer should not be used, as this is in the nature of a strategic adjustment inconsistent with fair market value.)

The discounted cash flow method when applied to an asset purchase and sale of a controlling interest should use a weighted average cost of capital, consisting of the result of the risk-adjusted equity rate above, and the after-tax cost of debt. If a control interest is being purchased, such as 100% of the practice, the percentage of debt utilized should, again, represent the optimum obtainable in the marketplace, and the cost of debt should reflect that of the hypothetical owner. If a minority interest is being valued, the percentage and cost of debt should generally be the present level in the practice since a minority owner cannot alter them—but be certain to read the discussion of excessive debt later in this chapter.

### *Insight and Analysis*

The interest rate for debt used in computing this weighted average cost of capital, as well as the percentage of debt to equity available, must also consider those circumstances

32 "What Is To Be Learned From *Caracci*?" Ken Patton, ASA and the author, Chapter 13 in this guide.

where a lender is looking to the personal guarantees of the owner(s), as well as the assets of the practice as collateral. In my view, a valuation analyst should consider adding a premium to the interest rate cost of debt for the value of the guarantees.[33]

#### Valuation Tip

The percentage of debt should be a function of the underlying assets and the normal financing pattern for medical practices. Fixed assets are often financed, accounts receivable less frequently so. Equipment intensive practices such as radiology, dentistry, ophthalmology, or sports medicine (with physical therapy) have greater percentages of debt than, for example, primary care practices or general surgery.

We know as well from the capital asset pricing model (CAPM) that, all other things being equal, the more debt a company has versus an industry norm, the higher its cost of equity will be! The implications of this are profound because they demonstrate a *dynamic relationship* between the percentage of debt in the WACC and the cost of equity, which is part of the WACC. Therefore, although mathematically a valuation analyst can lower the WACC by increasing the percentage of debt in that computation, the CAPM—and relevering of beta—tells us that the cost of equity must be simultaneously adjusted. If the percentage of debt in the capital structure goes up, the cost of equity goes up as well. If the percentage of debt in the capital structure goes down, the cost of equity goes down as well. The example in this chapter's "In-Depth Review of the Excess Earnings Method" explores the impact of excessive debt as well. Medical practices with more debt than other practices of the same size and specialty have greater risk and therefore greater equity discount rates.

#### Growth Rate

As noted earlier, the cap rate is determined by subtracting the growth rate from the discount rate. The growth rate should reflect the long-term prospects for the practice's growth. The growth can come from increases in reimbursement for services, whether fee-for-service or capitation, or addition of providers or ancillary services, such as lab and imaging. Generally, this expansion is forecasted during the first five years. It is important to remember that the terminal growth rate is a growth rate into *perpetuity*[34] and must be sustainable. Very few businesses can sustain growth rates in excess of the inflation rate forever.

33 See, e.g., "Valuing Small Businesses and Professional Practices," Chapter 27.

34 As I am fond of saying, forever is a long time.

***Insight and Analysis***

There is a great opportunity for influencing the ultimate valuation conclusion via the growth rate, either deliberately or through an error of judgment. I recall one situation in a specialty practice where the independent valuation analyst used a cap rate on after-tax earnings of 13%, without first developing a discount rate, although this discount rate must have been at least 22%, implying a long-term growth rate into perpetuity of 9%—almost inconceivable!

I generally use the current estimate of the long-term rate of inflation as a ceiling on the growth rate; a reasonable range in my view in the absence of contradictory evidence is 2% to 2.5%. You can obtain the current rate of inflation estimate at the Philadelphia Federal Reserve Bank's Web site at www.philadelphiafed.org/research-and-data/real-time-center/survey-of-professional-forecasters/2011/survq311.cfm. I should emphasize that in my view, it is wholly inappropriate to use the nominal growth rate in the gross domestic product (GDP—real growth plus inflation) as a long-term growth rate.

#### General Price Per Unit of Service

What about increases in fees per unit of service? From 1994 to 2010, or 15 years, the compound rate of increase was only 1.96%, based on data from the Bureau of Labor Statistics' Producer Price Index for Physician Services, shown in Exhibit 4.

**Exhibit 4. Medical Loss Ratio Trend**

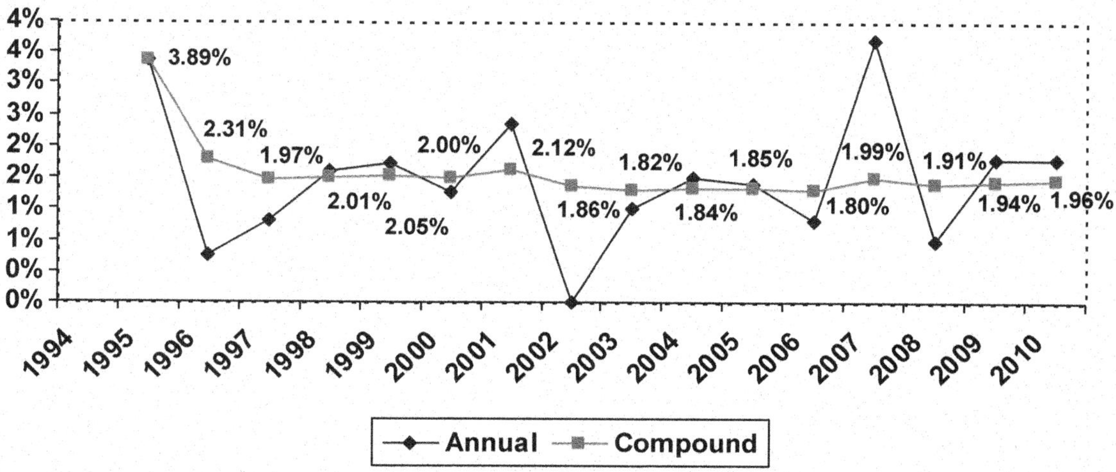


#### Medicare Price Per Unit of Service

Clearly, there is no evidence that unit reimbursement is growing at that GDP rate, and the capacity to provide units of service in a small practice is limited. Under federal law, Medicare expenditures for physician services are limited by a complex formula that considers the change in fees, the number of beneficiaries, growth in GDP per capita, and the impact of new laws. The Medicare sustainable growth rate, or SGR is then applied to the Medicare economic index (MEI), which measures the weighted average price change in physician services. The MEI[35] is a physician practice-specific measure of inflation and generally is less than 2.5%, absent recessions, when it is much lower. The Medicare Payment Advisory Commission or MedPAC Web site has the data each March (www.medpac.gov). For 2008, the scheduled increase of 0.5% (19 cents) was a result of legislation temporarily overturning the SGR methodology that would have resulted in a 10.5% decrease in the conversion factor used to set the fee schedule. The compound rate of increase from 1998 to 2009 amounted to only 0.43% and has since turned negative. (See Exhibit 5.)

**Exhibit 5. History of Medicare Conversion Factor**

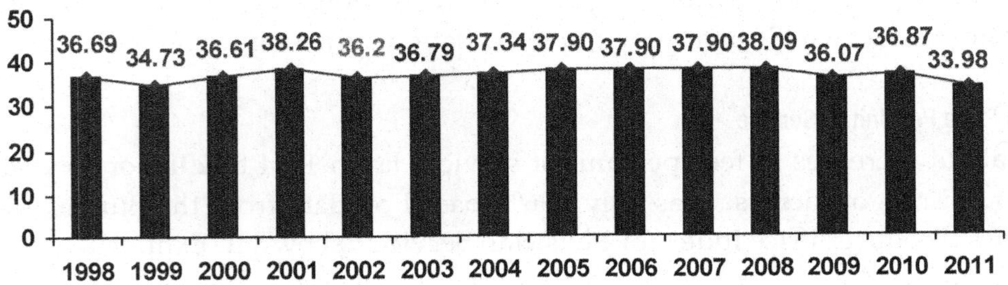


As I observed in the 2006 article for the American Bar Association's Health Law Section:

> In the valuation community, much of the potential inaccuracy in growth rates stems from a poor understanding of the impact of growth on value and of the limitations in the growth of per unit revenue under the current reimbursement system. For example, the Medicare Conversion Factor, which represents the value per Relative Value Unit (RVU), of services provided under Part B, has increased less than .5% in the last nine years; the compound rate of growth—which would be used to compare it to inflation, for example—is virtually zero, while annual inflation has been in the 3% range. What drives Part B revenue in general is utilization along with intensity of service as reflected in coding.[36]

#### Underwriting Cycle

One of the primary influences on the forecast of future cash flow is the underwriting cycle in the health insurance industry. Exhibit 6 reflects the historical cycle of premium

35 This is similar to the market basket used for hospitals described in that chapter.

36 "Identifying Appropriate Business Valuation Approaches Under Stark and the AKS," the author with Reed Tinsley, CPA, CVA, *The Health Lawyer*, American Bar Association, December 2006.

increases and cost[37] increases. Note that in recent years, the rate of increase in premiums and costs has been equal. However, you can also see that at the end of the 1990s, a period of aggressive premium cutting in the face of mounting costs when the industry tried to buy market share. This led to the failure of many smaller insurers and the consolidation that affects the ability of providers to negotiate fees today.[38]

**Exhibit 6. Premium and Cost Trends**

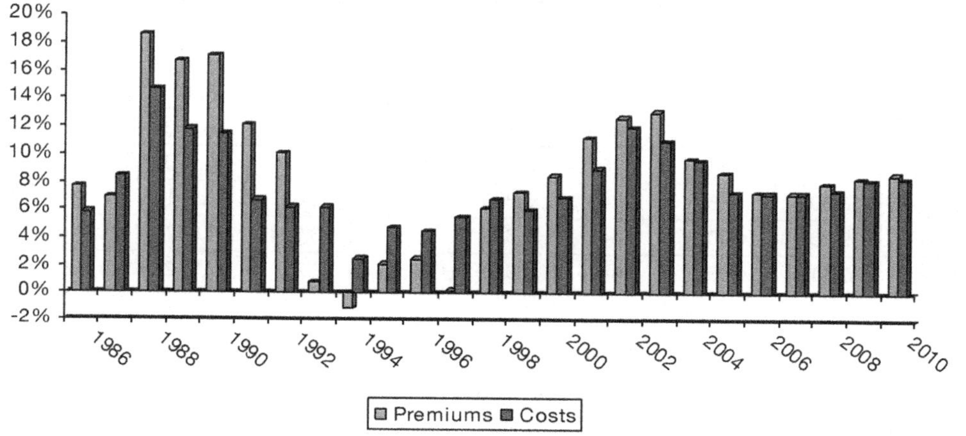


### Medical Loss Ratio

In part, that cycle of premium increases and decreases reflects the relationship between the costs of provider payments and the premium charged. Exhibit 7 reflects overall changes in the medical loss ratio (MLR), which represents the portion of the health insurance premium dollar spent on medical care on insured individuals. As the percentage goes down, less money is paid to providers of healthcare and insurance company profits increase. [39]

**Exhibit 7. Medical Loss Ratio Trend**

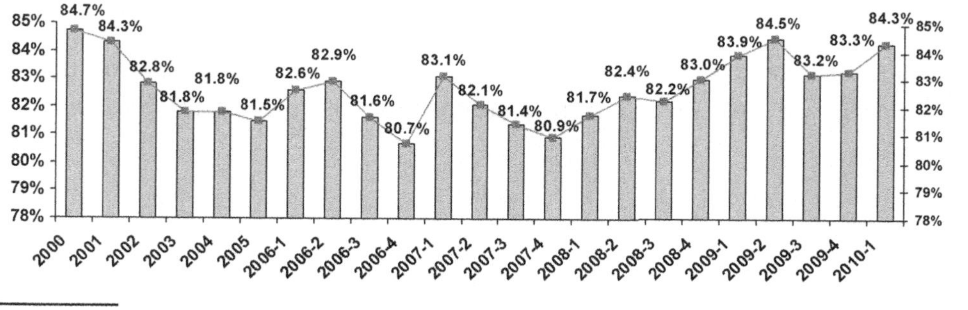


37 Cost here is the amount paid by the health insurers for the care of their insureds.

38 Based on *Health Care-Managed Care*, Jan. 7, 2010, Barclays Capital, sourced from Milliman, CMS, and company documents.

39 Based on *Health Care-Managed Care*, Jan. 7, 2010, Barclays Capital, sourced from Milliman, CMS and company documents.

### Growth in Units of Service

On a more practice-specific level, look at the impact of various units of service volume growth rates on a practice currently seeing 4,500 patients a year. (See Exhibit 8.)

**Exhibit 8. Unit Growth**

| | Base Year | 1 | 2 | 3 | 4 | 5 | 6 | 7 | 8 |
|---|---|---|---|---|---|---|---|---|---|
| Visits | 4,500 | | | | | | | | |
| Growth rate | 4.00% | 4,680 | 4,867 | 5,062 | 5,264 | 5,475 | 5,694 | 5,922 | 6,159 |
| Growth rate | 5.00 | 4,725 | 4,961 | 5,209 | 5,470 | 5,743 | 6,030 | 6,332 | 6,649 |
| Growth rate | 6.00 | 4,770 | 5,056 | 5,360 | 5,681 | 6,022 | 6,383 | 6,766 | 7,172 |
| Growth rate | 7.00 | 4,815 | 5,152 | 5,513 | 5,899 | 6,311 | 6,753 | 7,226 | 7,732 |
| Growth rate | 8.00 | 4,860 | 5,249 | 5,669 | 6,122 | 6,612 | 7,141 | 7,712 | 8,329 |
| Growth rate | 9.00 | 4,905 | 5,346 | 5,828 | 6,352 | 6,924 | 7,547 | 8,226 | 8,967 |
| Growth rate | 10.00 | 4,950 | 5,445 | 5,990 | 6,588 | 7,247 | 7,972 | 8,769 | 9,646 |

If this were a solo primary care practice, the maximum number of encounters is going to top out at between 4,500 and 5,500, depending upon whether it is adult, pediatric, or a mix of both![40]

### Conclusion of Growth Rate Discussion

External evidence of the growth rate may be obtained by reviewing government data on the healthcare segment of the economy. Historically, this segment grows by well in excess of the inflation rate. However, the growth is driven in large part by the aging population and new technology and is generally spread over more physicians, not focused on existing physicians. Therefore, the long-term growth rate for a given practice is much less than that for the industry as a whole. Only very large entities involved in a substantial cross section of the healthcare delivery system have an opportunity to match the industry growth rate.

> Perhaps the greatest risk of overestimating value and implicating Stark or the AKS stems from improper or unrealistic assumptions as to future growth in cash flow or profits.[41]

40 See, e.g., "Computing the Growth Rate in Physician Practice Revenue," *CPA Expert*, Winter 2005 by the author.
41 "Identifying Appropriate Business Valuation Approaches Under Stark and the AKS," the author with Reed Tinsley, CPA, CVA, *The Health Lawyer*, American Bar Association, December 2006.

### *Discounted Cash Flow (DCF)*

#### Development of Assumptions

Underlying the discounted cash flow method is the necessity of developing a five-year forecast of financial operations. The normalization of earnings process described above typically provides the base year for the financial forecast. Various assumptions about the increases in revenues, expenses, numbers of patients, penetration of capitation, and capitation rates then need to be made. The acquiring entity should play a crucial role in this process, as the ability to achieve the forecast will depend in large part on the actions taken by the acquirer's management after the acquisition. If the valuation is conducted by a CPA, a representation letter signed by the acquirer, and perhaps the seller, acknowledging development of the assumptions used in the model should be considered.

Where the capitalization of excess earnings methods tend to focus on normalized historical results and assumes those results will continue (often an incorrect assumption), the discounted cash flow method requires that future results be forecasted and the cash flows there from be discounted. The future results are forecasted, of course, based upon an analysis of the historical results. Future physician earnings must be forecasted as well. Note: This method is typically used in larger transactions and for regulatory purposes. It is rarely used in a buy-in or sale of a small practice.

#### Expense Growth

In addition to the discussion about growth rates in revenues in the previous section, as the number of patients and encounters increases, underlying operating costs must increase as well. Items such as nonphysician salaries and fringe benefits, supplies, and telephone will typically vary as a function of volume. Rent may be a function of the underlying lease, and depreciation will be a function of capital expenditures. The cash cost of purchases must be at least equal to the depreciation expense in the terminal period calculation— to continue to have deprecation expense, you have to continue to buy fixed assets!

An excellent source of expected increases in physician operating costs is the MedPAC Annual Report to Congress released each March. Exhibit 9 is from the 2009 report.

In its March 2011 report, MedPAC stated the following with respect to price increases in physician practices:[42]

42 The author observes that this is wholly inconsistent with his experience.

**Exhibit 9. Forecasted Input Price Increases and Weights for Physician Services for 2009**

| Input component | Price increases for 2009 | Category weight |
|---|---|---|
| **Total** | **2.6%** | **100.0%** |
| **Physician work** | **2.7** | **52.5** |
| Wages and salaries | 2.4 | 42.7 |
| Fringe benefits (nonwage compensation) | 3.5 | 9.7 |
| **Physician practice expense** | **2.4** | **47.5** |
| Nonphysician employee compensation | 2.9 | 18.7 |
| Wages and salaries | 2.9 | 13.8 |
| Fringe benefits (nonwage compensation) | 2.8 | 4.8 |
| Office expense | 2.1 | 12.2 |
| Professional liability insurance | 2.3 | 3.9 |
| Medical equipment | 0.7 | 2.1 |
| Drugs and supplies | 3.0 | 4.3 |
| Pharmaceuticals | 1.7 | 2.3 |
| Medical materials and supplies | 3.9 | 2.0 |
| Other professional expense | 2.1 | 6.4 |

> CMS's 2012 forecast of the MEI—a measure of changes in the market basket of input prices for physician and other health professional services, adjusted for productivity growth in the national economy—is revised quarterly and has ranged from 1% (most recent) to 0.7%. For these forecasts, CMS collects pricing data from various data sets and surveys.

Of course, local economic conditions have to be considered as well.

#### Cash Flow Adjustments

This is a forecast of cash flow, not earnings! Valuation analysts unfamiliar with the deep discounts experienced by physicians from their usual charges for services frequently make major mistakes if they attempt to take accrual revenues and apply a bad-debt allowance. It is not uncommon for physicians to have a 40% or greater difference between gross revenues and net revenues. (See discussion of accounts receivable infra.) The various payors, such as Medicare or HMOs, determine what physicians are paid, and the physicians have little or no control. As a general rule, the discount rate applied to earnings is higher than that applied to cash flow due to the lag between generating earnings and collecting the cash.

Only the excess earnings method typically requires a separate measure of the value of tangible personal property, while the discounted cash flow method calculation includes both the tangible and intangible value of the practice in MVIC. Nonetheless, in a practice with large amounts of equipment such as that used in MR or CT imaging, radiation oncology or a blood chemistry lab, a separate measure of fixed assets is important to determine the depreciation expense that goes into the DCF and reduces income tax expense, thereby increasing value. Bear in mind that healthcare transactions are usually of assets, not equity, and therefore the basis step-up in the hands of the acquirer is relevant. The same rationale applies to amortizing any intangible value under IRC Section 197.

MVIC includes net working capital (NWC) as well, although NWC is often backed out of the valuation model as buyers typically do not acquire it in an asset purchase. The upshot is that it is very difficult to value the operating assets of a healthcare enterprise without allocating MVIC (the right hand side of the accounting equation) to the assets on the left-hand side.

***Insight and Analysis***

The reason NWC is not acquired is the difficulty of measuring the collectible value of accounts receivable, as well as a general desire not to assume liabilities. Even when it is acquired, retroactive adjustments to the purchase price are typically made based upon the ultimate receivable collections and actual payments of liabilities.

#### Physician Compensation

This is the most critical component of the model because it is generally the single largest expense. The compensation should be based upon some reasonable measure, *such as the employment agreement expected to be entered into as part of the transaction or some other measure consistent with the standard of value in the transaction, if the sellers will continue as employees post-acquisition.*[43] For example, if the physicians will have an incentive equal to 35% of any increase in net revenues, this should be reflected as part of the model. If additional providers will be added during the forecast period, the cost of salary and fringe benefits should be added.

***Insight and Analysis***

In fact, the valuation submitted in connection with the Friendly Hills transaction in 1991, cited in *Derby* and therefore relevant today, contains a letter signed by the managing partner stating that the partners recognized they were selling a portion of their earnings and that their future incomes would be less by virtue of that sale. In relevant part he states:

> It has been clearly stated to the partners that, in the past, their compensation reflected not only the value of their medical services, but also the profits attributable to their ownership of the network; that the latter element will be replaced by a cash payment, which they can invest ... that the medical group's income will thereafter be derived from arms-length contract for medical services; and that these rates will necessarily

43 *Charles A. and Marian L. Derby, et al., Petitioners v. Commissioner, Respondent*, T.C. Memo. 2008-45, GALE, Judge

be significantly lower than the total historical income they have been receiving.... (Friendly Hills Valuation Report).

### Relative Value Units

RVU-based compensation models are increasingly common when hospitals acquire physician practices. Medicare and other payors pay physicians under the Resource-Based Relative Value Scale (RBRVS) where each current procedural terminology code is assigned a certain number of relative value units (RVUs). These RVUs are then multiplied by a dollar-value conversion factor to set the fee Medicare pays.

The number of relative value units is based upon the consumption[44] of three types of resources in the delivery of physician services:

#### Physician Work

The principal factors comprising this component are time, technical skill and physical effort, mental effort and judgment, and the stress on the physician of certain patient risk factors.

#### Practice Costs

This component looks at the cost of delivering services by physician type, for example, family medicine versus cardiac surgery. Physician practice costs per dollar of revenue tend to be much higher in primary care than surgery.

#### Malpractice Insurance Cost

Surgical specialties, and particularly obstetrics, neurosurgery and cardiac surgery, tend to have the highest malpractice insurance. This is the least important of the three components.

#### Geographic Adjustment

There is an additional adjustment for the geographic location of the practice based upon various government studies, including the census, HUD data, and others.

Physician work RVUs or wRVUs are used in RVU-based models because they measure the work effort of the physician and avoid regulatory risks inherent in using broader measures of RVUs. For example, a cardiologist interpreting the result of a stress test ordered on a patient may be allocated the wRVU from the professional component of the global fee in a productivity-based compensation system, but not the practice

44 It is worth observing that the process of allocating RVUs is highly politicized; see www.medpac.gov for the Medicare Payment Advisory Commission discussion of this and related issues.

expense RVUs associated with the technical component of the global fee. To illustrate the impact of wRVUs, CPT code 93015—cardiac stress testing—has a wRVU weight of 0.75, whereas CPT code 33206—insertion of a cardiac pacemaker—has a weight of 7.31. Obviously, the work effort involved in the more invasive insertion of a pacemaker will be rewarded with a higher level of compensation in a wRVU based compensation model.

***Insight and Analysis***

This is one of the most difficult assumptions in a forecast because the acquirer may not have any idea what the incentive portion of a physician's compensation will be or what the outcome of a wRVU-based model will be. Although not advisable for a variety of regulatory reasons, the compensation arrangement is sometimes negotiated after the purchase price determined by the valuation has been agreed to by the parties to the transaction. My standard report advises the client that it should consider revisiting the valuation if the compensation ultimately negotiated differs from that in the valuation model. (See also *Derby v. Commissioner.*)[45] Whatever the amount used, bear in mind that "the accepted interpretation of reasonable compensation under the fair market value standard is the salary necessary to hire a nonowner replacement physician of equal experience."[46]

If the client does not specify a compensation formula (subject to its meeting an overall test of reasonableness for the valuation model), I will either work with it to develop a formula that meets the fair market value criteria I am opining on or suggest retention of an independent compensation consultant. Many acquirers now use work RVUs as a basis for measuring productivity, and compensation is a function of those RVUs and a payment rate. One of the many reasons I obtain data by CPT code when valuing a practice is that they are frequently not possible for the client to determine compensation without that data.

As a final observation, because compensation and value of the practice are opposite sides of the same coin—as compensation goes up, value goes down—the question often arises about changing compensation to make the value different, while maintaining the required mathematical relationship between the two. All valuation models are *dynamic.* You cannot properly change one assumption without considering the impact on all the others. One simple example: If you were to decrease compensation payable post-transaction to generate a higher value, you would have to consider the impact on the physician's productivity, which would then effect all the revenue and variable expense assumptions!

45 *Charles A. and Marian L. Derby, et al.,1 Petitioners v. Commissioner, Respondent,* T.C. Memo. 2008-45, GALE, Judge.
46 "Medical Practices: A BV Rx," *Journal of Accountancy,* November 2005 by the author.

***Insight and Analysis***

Notwithstanding the following discussion, I want to emphasize that I regard the MGMA data as the most useful in performing valuations. The key is to use it expertly.

## Using the MGMA Compensation and Cost Data

As noted elsewhere herein, statistical data cannot be used blindly. The valuation analyst needs to understand the data to use them effectively in the valuation process. One of the most commonly used sources of data on compensation is the MGMA Compensation and Production Survey. The document contains numerous tables listing compensation, including means, medians, 75th percentile, single specialty, multispecialty, regional data, and a host of others. Which ones are relevant?

Table 1.1 in the MGMA data represents all physicians included in the survey by specialty. It is therefore the largest database, and arguably the means, medians, and other data items are the most representative: Without commenting on statistical science, the larger the population sampled, the more meaningful the data.[47]

There has been a marked shift over the last several years in the source of the MGMA data as well, with participating physicians increasingly shifting to hospital-employed and away from private practice-employed settings. Fully 47% of the physicians in the Compensation Report for 2011, based on 2010 data, were hospital employees versus 41% for physician-owned practices. In the 2009 report, based on 2008 data, the numbers were 37% and 51%, respectively. This shift of 10% of the underlying sample from private practice to hospital employment reflects the current trend in consolidation as well. (See Exhibit 10.)

**Exhibit 10. Shifting Pattern of MGMA Survey Participants**

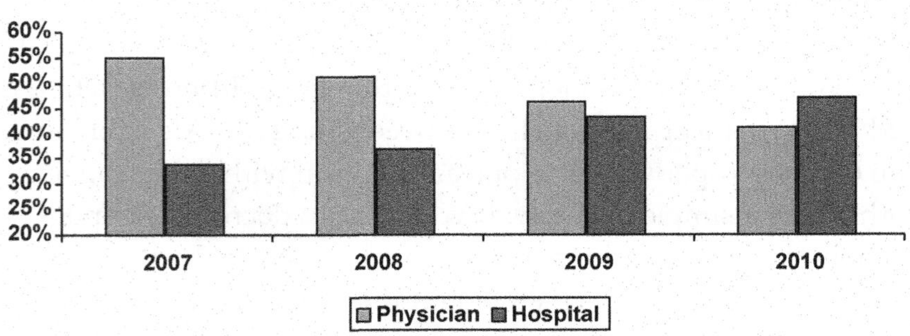


47 In a truly random sample, which the MGMA is not, a sample as small as 30 or 32 drawn from a population can be statistically relevant to one extent or another, depending upon the presence of outliers. What the MGMA *does* tell us is how the physician population included in that data fares from year to year.

The data are then broken down by single specialty and multispecialty practices. A single-specialty practice would represent a group practice reporting to MGMA that employs only physicians of a specific specialty, such as hematology and oncology or cardiology. The multispecialty groups include the physicians of more than one specialty—how many more, we do not know. Multispecialty practices could simply include cardiology and gastroenterology, for example. The combination of these two types of groups should equal the data contained in the combined data.

The data by geographic section or region breaks the combined data down into East, West, South, and Midwest. Looking at the tables, you should note that the sample size is, of course, smaller for each region than the total. The regional data are then broken down by single specialty and multispecialty practices, with even smaller sample sizes. There may be as few as only several dozen sample items, and perhaps fewer.

The problem is even more pronounced in the cost survey for specific physician practice specialties. The sample sizes for each of these practice types are quite small—and remember that those are number of physicians, not numbers of reporting practices. The data for multispecialty practices, which constitute a large sample size, are more meaningful. Nonetheless, this data are commonly cited and are the best available. They are most wisely used when their limitations are understood.

## Accounts Receivable

In many valuation engagements, the valuation analyst may not need to be overly concerned with intangible value but may need to reach a conclusion of value on such assets as accounts receivable. Many small businesses and virtually all professional practices use the cash method of accounting. Under this method, accounts receivable are not reflected on the tax returns (or financial statements, if they exist), and the valuation analyst will need to obtain the necessary reports and compute the collectible value.

### Introduction

In the absence of accrual accounting, measuring the accounts receivable becomes in large part the responsibility of the valuation analyst. (And even if accrual accounting is in place, the accounts receivable warrant careful attention.) In many medical practice valuation engagements, it may be the largest single asset. Some common examples include:

- A divorce where intangible assets such as goodwill are not marital property;
- A hospital-based practice where the patient base and other intangibles are owned by the hospital and not by the practice;

- A practice buy-in where goodwill is being excluded;
- Any practice where the intangible value is small; and
- In a liquidation scenario.

Like many aspects of valuation, valuing medical accounts receivable is perceived to be as much an art as it is a science. However, a number of key factors must be evaluated if the valuation analyst is to generate a meaningful estimate of value. The considerable expertise necessary to value this asset accurately is often greatly underestimated.

#### Characteristics of Medical Accounts Receivable

Unlike manufacturing or most service businesses, medical accounts receivable tend to consist of a large number of accounts with relatively small balances. Oil dealerships[48] are analogous in some ways, but they typically are selling a single product—oil—and perhaps some service and repair contracts.

Although some medical specialties, such as cardiac surgery, may have relatively large balances from a particular patient for procedures, there are typically additional smaller balances for office visits and similar services. In an internal medicine or family medicine practice, the typical charge may consist of a $100 office visit plus additional small charges such as $15 to draw blood and $20 for a rapid strep test. Each of the charges that originate with a single visit must be separately billed and accounted for. When (if) it is paid, the payment, if made by an insurer, will specify both the date the service was provided and the specific service that is being paid: There is a specific matching of service date and procedure with the payment. Not all of the services will necessarily be paid and the percentage that is paid will not necessarily be the same for each service—and it is a rare instance indeed where 100% of the charge for any service is paid. Note: If, in fact, 100% of an insured charge is being paid, it typically suggests the practice is charging less than the insurer is willing to pay!

The payment of medical charges raises another significant issue: The majority of such charges are not paid for by the patient individually, but rather by the third-party insurance company that provides the patient's insurance or by a government program, such as Medicare or Medicaid (hereinafter collectively referred to as payors). Further, these payors typically pay by a fee schedule that they set and that often bears little or no resemblance to the fee that the physician charges. As a result, each charge that is processed by the physician's billing department reflects both a payment and an *adjustment* or *contractual allowance*. There may be multiple payments for a particular service,

48 At least before the $145 a barrel prices seen in 2008!

such as when the patient has a deductible or co-pay due after the insurer pays its share or where the patient has a secondary insurance that covers any balance not paid by the primary insurance. The term "write-off" is generally limited to those situations involving a bad debt from an uninsured patient or where a payor refuses to pay for a service due to any of a host of reasons described below.

#### Situations in Which Write-Offs May Occur

The following is a nonexhaustive listing of the causes of write-offs or bad debts in a medical practice. These factors are also significant for normalizing revenue and determining the specific risk premium.

1. Uninsured patient fails to pay.

2. Office personnel fail to collect co-pays at the time of treatment.

3. Practice fails to meet payor's contractual deadline for submitting a "clean claim." A clean claim is one in which all of the necessary information appears on the claim, including the patient's name, insurance number, the procedure provided by Current Procedural Terminology (CPT) code, the diagnosis by International Classification of Disease (ICD) code, consistency of the CPT and ICD codes, the date of service, and other requirements specified by the payor. Typical periods for submission of clean claims are 45 to 60 days; thereafter, the payor is not obligated to pay the claim (although a denial can be appealed).

4. Failure to meet any requirements for preauthorization of the service by the insurer or a primary care physician, for example.

5. Failure to obtain correct insurance information from the patient.

6. Failure to submit additional information with the claims, such as operative reports for certain surgical procedures.

7. Failure to timely appeal denial of claims.

8. Billing for uncovered services (those that are not covered by the patient's insurance).

9. Billing incorrectly for services, which are considered part of a package or "bundle" of services, such as preoperative and post-operative visits considered part of the global fee paid for the surgery.

There are a host of others. One conclusion the valuation analyst should draw from this discussion is that the billing process in a medical practice is very complex, both in generating the charges and in recording the payment and adjustments for write-offs.

This complexity leads to a variety of errors in all but the best-run practices. These errors result in otherwise collectible balances not being collected, uncollectible balances not being written off, uncovered services being paid, and the same service being paid more than once (a credit balance). Office staff involved in the process may be poorly educated, inadequately assisted or supervised, overwhelmed, or simply irresponsible.

### The Process of Valuing Accounts Receivable

Generally speaking, the valuation of accounts receivable consists of two distinct components: identification of those charges that include *some* collectible amount and determination of the portion of those charges that is ultimately collectible. We will examine each of these two components in the paragraphs that follow.

### Identification of (Partially) Collectible Balances Versus Uncollectible Balances

The first step is to obtain an aged accounts receivable by payor. This report typically consists of a listing of the various payors that the practice does business with and the total due from each of those payors by aging category: current, greater than 30 days, greater than 60 days, greater than 90 days, and greater than 120 days. The "# Days" is the number of days gross charges in accounts receivable. (See Exhibit 11.)

**Exhibit 11. Total Due for Each Payer by Aging Category**

| Payor | Current | > 30 | > 60 | >90 | >120 | Total | # Days |
|---|---|---|---|---|---|---|---|
| A | $7,000 | $8,000 | $5,000 | $5,000 | $15,000 | $40,000 | 72 |
| B | 1,000 | 4,000 | 5,000 | 10,000 | 20,000 | 40,000 | 144 |
| Total | $8,000 | $12,000 | $10,000 | $15,000 | $35,000 | $80,000 | 96 |
| | 10.0% | 15.0% | 12.5% | 18.8% | 43.7% | 100.0% | |

Analysis of this report provides the valuation analyst with a significant amount of the information necessary needed to determine what steps will be necessary to properly measure the accounts receivable. The first step is to compare the percentage of receivables in each aging category to statistical norms or to the valuation analyst's own experience. (Statistical norms are typically obtained from the Medical Group Management Association's Cost Survey). If the aging falls within accepted parameters, the valuation analyst may employ simple "short-cut" computations to estimate the collectible value. If not, a more complex computation may be required.

The most common indicator that a short-cut approach will not work is where the percentage of receivables in the greater than 90- or 120-day category is more than the expected level. The larger the variance, the more complex the computation required to determine the true collectible value.

***Insight and Analysis***

What is the expected level of receivables in the greater-than-120-day category, or in any category for that matter? One primary determinant is the whether or not and to what extent the practice uses electronic claims submission. This is the norm in most markets and can result in a clean claim being paid in less than 25 days. Depending upon the electronic sophistication of a given market and the practice, accounts receivable agings may be under 25 days or as low as 15 days! Another factor is the presence of a "prompt pay" statute in the state in which the practice operates. These statutes generally *require* an insurer to pay a clean claim within 30 to 45 days of receipt. Medicare generally requires all physicians except those with fewer than 10 full-time equivalent employees to bill electronically.

**Example**

Assume that the MGMA norm for the greater-than-120-days category is 20% and the valuation subject has 44% of its receivables in that category. This is an almost certain indication that uncollectible balances are not being written off. These balances more often than not consist of the unpaid portion of a charge representing the contractual allowance—that being the amount the payor is not obligated to pay under the terms of its contract with the physician. Another common component is uncollectible "self-pay," or uninsured balances. These balances accumulate because identifying such balances and getting approval for having them written off often take a lot of work. In the typical medical office, time tends to be spent on collecting collectible balances rather than on writing-off uncollectible ones.

The fact pattern of the example will require, at a minimum, that the valuation analyst separate the aged accounts receivable into two distinct groups: those greater than 90 or 120 days old and those less than 90 or 120 days old. Each of the two groups will then need to be valued separately.

The balances should be analyzed by payor if the data are available and the amount is material. For example, certain payors may have unusual aging distributions while others do not. Another common occurrence is where the practice's *largest* payor has an aging distribution different than that of the remaining payors.

**Examples**

In a valuation of a large healthcare facility where the cost approach was important, the entity's single largest payor was in serious financial difficulty. The aging of receivables from that payor was significantly worse than for the balance of the receivables. Although there was an audited financial statement, it was on the income tax method of accounting and therefore did not reflect an allowance for uncollectible accounts. A substantial reduction in the audited accounts receivable balance was required to reach fair market value of the receivables.

In a litigation matter, an opposing expert blindly accepted the calculation of collectible accounts receivable appearing in a practice consultant's report without undertaking a collectibility analysis. The consultant testified that the amount was, in fact, overstated by 20%. The error resulted in the expert's value of receivables being overstated and a working capital deficit being missed.

#### Measuring the Portion of Charges That Are Collectible

A standard analysis that should be done in any medical practice valuation is to compute charges, collections (payments), and adjustments for each of the practices principal insurers. Perform this analysis by payor is important because the contractual payment rate is likely to vary (and often significantly) for each payor that the practice contracts with.

#### Example

For simplicity, assume that a practice has contracts with two payors. Data from the billing system indicate that Payor A reimburses the practice at a rate equal to 50% of charges, while Payor B reimburses at a rate equal to 60% of charges, as shown in Exhibit 12.

**Exhibit 12. Rate of Reimbursement by Payor**

| Payor | Charges | Payments | Adjustments | Collection Rate | Realization Rate |
|---|---|---|---|---|---|
| A | $200,000 | $100,000 | $100,000 | 50% | 50% |
| B | $100,000 | $60,000 | $36,000 | 60% | 62.5% |

*The* collection rate *is equal to current payments divided by current charges.*

*The* realization rate *is equal to current payments divided by current payments plus current adjustments.*

If the billing system is working properly and adjustments are being recorded properly at the time payments are received, the realization rate is the best measure of the true collectible value. This is due to the fact that it reflects *both* elements of the charge relief activity: the payment and the contractual allowance or adjustment. If the adjustments are not being recorded properly however, the realization rate is inaccurate and the collection rate may be a better measure. The collection rate may understate collectibility when unpaid claims are inadequately reviewed and overstate collectibility when, for example, charges to a payor in the current period decline from prior periods.

A "short-cut" valuation of receivables would appear as follows (see Exhibit 13):

**Exhibit 13. 'Short-Cut' Valuation of Receivables**

| Payor | Receivable | Collection Rate | Collectible |
|---|---|---|---|
| A | $40,000 | 50% | $20,000 |
| B | $40,000 | 60% | $24,000 |
| | $80,000 | 55% | $44,000 |

Or using the realization rate approach (see Exhibit 14.):

**Exhibit 14. Valuation Using the Realization Rate Approach**

| Payor | Receivable | Realization Rate | Collectible |
|---|---|---|---|
| A | $40,000 | 50.00% | $20,000 |
| B | $40,000 | 62.50% | $25,000 |
| | $80,000 | 56.25% | $45,000 |

The problem with either of these approaches should be obvious: Payor B constitutes only 33% of charges, while it constitutes 50% of receivables. This is a clear clue that something may be "wrong" with the Payor B receivables. A further analysis is likely to reveal one of several generic causes: Payor B pays more slowly than Payor A, there are completely uncollectible balances included in the Payor B receivables meeting one or more of the criteria discussed earlier, there has been a contract issue or termination, or an unusual decline in charges to Payor B patients.

If the valuation analyst suspects or determines that the collection rate and realization rate approach are inaccurate, the earlier approach described of dividing receivables into two distinct groups of those greater than 90 days old (the sum of the greater-than-90-days and greater-than-120-days categories) and those less than 90 days old should be followed. (Refer to this approach as the "detailed" method.) In Exhibit 15 below, the valuation analyst determines that the Payor B receivables greater than 90 days will yield only 40 cents on the dollar rather than the collection rate of 60 cents. (It should not be seen as unusual for insured receivables in the greater-than-90-day category to be worth substantially less than the historical collection rate for a particular payor.)

**Exhibit 15. Yield on Receivables Great Than and Less Than 90 Days, by Payor**

| Payor | <90 Days | Factor | Collectible | >90 Days | Factor | Collectible | Total |
|---|---|---|---|---|---|---|---|
| A | $20,000 | 50% | $10,000 | $20,000 | 50% | $10,000 | $20,000 |
| B | $10,000 | 60% | $6,000 | $30,000 | 40% | $12,000 | $18,000 |
| | $30,000 | | $16,000 | $50,000 | | $22,000 | $38,000 |

**Exhibit 16. Recap of Methodologies**

| | Collection Rate | Realization Rate | Detail |
|---|---|---|---|
| Value | $44,000 | $45,000 | $38,000 |

The recap in Exhibit 16 indicates that the choice of approach to valuing receivables can generate very different results. If you are not convinced, multiply each of the values in the recap by 10.

### Gaining Insight Into the Aging

Depending upon the sophistication of the practice's billing software, the importance of the receivables to the overall valuation, and the budget for the engagement, it may be desirable to obtain a *detailed aging by individual account* of the greater-than-90-day balances.

#### *Insight and Analysis*

In a litigation engagement, the greater-than-90-day balances were 3.5 times the MGMA norm. My investigation indicated that a host of problems existed in the recording (or lack thereof) of contractual allowances. The review, for example, of several annual detailed agings demonstrated that the same balances appeared year after year and there was a clear failure to write them off. Inquiries of management disclosed that the largest payor had negotiated a fixed weekly payment (or capitated arrangement) for services and that the difference between the practice's charges to that payor and the capitated payment were never written off. The uncollectible balances in this case amounted to multiple seven figures and resulted in a dramatic reduction in the valuation.

### Credit Balances

This is one of the most difficult potential problems to identify and resolve when valuing medical accounts receivables. Credit balances *may* represent overpayments on a particular account or they may be payments posted to an account that could not be matched with a particular service and service date. For example, assume that a patient has four distinct services recorded. A check is received from the patient's insurer that does not specify which services are being paid. The data entry person posts the payment to the patient's account but does not apply it to any particular service. The detailed aging will typically reflect the credit separately from the individual charges. In this case, the credit balance is not a true credit, but rather requires a journal entry. As another example, assume that the insurer mistakenly pays the claim twice, creating a true credit balance. Finally, a common source of credit balances exists where the patient has insurance, but the practice has not contracted to accept direct payment from the insurer. As a courtesy, the practice may submit a bill to the insurer for the patient but expects the patient to pay the bill directly. If the insurer subsequently pays the practice as well, a true credit balance will result.

Because credit balances are generally considered lost property under most states' law and must be "escheated"[49] back to the state, the seriousness of this problem should not be overlooked. Further, failure to refund overpayments from government programs may subject the practice to civil or criminal sanctions. Certain state laws may provide for civil or criminal sanctions for nongovernmental payors as well.

#### Tax Affecting

The question frequently arises whether "zero basis" accounts receivable (as they are known for tax purposes where the taxpayer uses the cash method) should be tax-affected, or reduced for the estimated income taxes that will be due when they are collected. If the standard of value is fair market, many valuation analysts believe the adjustment is appropriate; some jurisdictions would not allow tax-affecting if the tax would never, in fact, be paid. This is of particular significance if the ultimate value of the business will be offset against property received by the other spouse in a divorce. For example, if the spouse is to receive cash of $100,000 (previously taxed by definition) and the business owner is to receive a like amount of accounts receivable that have not yet been taxed, there will clearly be an inequitable result.

In valuing a corporate professional practice with zero basis receivables, they would typically be offset by a claim for future compensation due to the owner. Arguably, therefore, the balance sheet accounts receivable and liability for deferred compensation would offset and reflect no increase in equity. However, the deferred compensation would be an individual asset of the practice owner. This asset should, again arguably, be offset for the taxes expected to be paid when the receivables are paid out of the corporation as salary. In addition, it should be considered whether these same receivables, when collected, will be subject to a claim for alimony and whether there should not be some adjustment for this as well. Because receivables are the source of future income typically

49 The term is commonly believed to be based on the fact that the '**S**'tate ['**Es**'] "cheats" the consumer or business out of the money but actually is a term originating in feudal England and Wales when land was owned by the king and granted in "fiefs" to royalty and would revert to the king upon certain occurrences.

subject to alimony, counting them as both an asset and as income is seen as "double counting" in some courts and by some valuation experts.

#### *Insight and Analysis*

If the standard of value for divorce in your state is fair market value on a going concern basis, reducing the receivables by collection costs is likely an inappropriate modification to collectible value. Going concern means that after the valuation date (hypothetical sale date) the practice will continue to operate in the ordinary course. If the standard of value were liquidation value, collection costs would be considered.

#### Conclusion

To properly measure accounts receivable of a medical practice, the valuation analyst requires a considerable knowledge of what information to request and how to interpret and use it. Even if relying primarily on an income approach or market approach, failure to properly estimate net working capital can expose the valuation to a serious possibility of overstatement. If the valuation engagement is to measure asset value, the individual components thereof—fixed assets, net working capital, and intangible value—must be known to compute the tax benefit from depreciation of fixed assets and amortization of the intangible value. It is difficult to escape the need to apply the cost approach in valuing a medical practice, at least as far as net working capital is concerned.

### An In-Depth Review of the Correct Use of the Excess Earnings Method

#### *Insight and Analysis*

This section is based upon material I use in my continuing education courses for both basic business valuation and medical practice valuation. The premise is that the excess earnings method is a very useful tool, but one that has been maligned due to its misuse, rather than any inherent weakness in the method itself. Be certain to read this *entire* section to avoid drawing incorrect conclusions about the examples (the initial example contains a deliberate error). Bear in mind that "when weighted capitalization rates for tangible- and intangible-asset cash flows are used to derive a single capitalization rate for all cash flows, capitalized excess earnings (CEE) will generate the same result as capitalization of cash flows (CCF)."[50]

The appropriateness of the excess earnings method, notwithstanding the many valuation analysts who are apparently unfamiliar with the basic accounting equation, can be seen in that assets equals liabilities plus equity, the right-hand side of that equation

50 "Medical Practices: A BV Rx," *Journal of Accountancy*, November 2005 by the author.

being capital. As such, the weighted average cost of capital for assets must be equal to the WACC for capital, or else our valuation balance sheet will not balance! This was explored earlier in the chapter on WACC. The concept is presented visually in Exhibit 17.

**Exhibit 17. Weighted Average Cost of Capital for Assets Equal WACC for Capital**

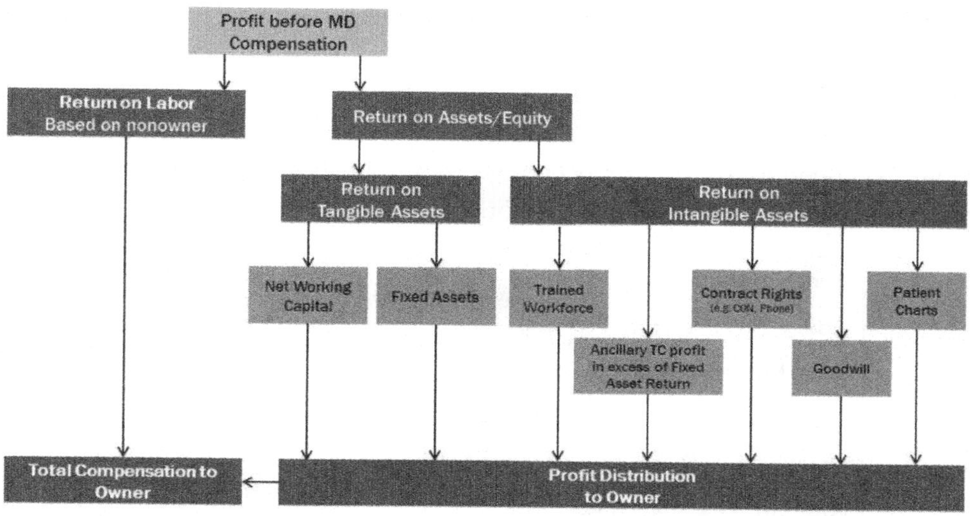


### Net Tangible Assets

Though there is no uniform agreement as to what the term "net tangible assets" means, it is important that the choice of a return on those net assets, however defined, is consistent (i.e., properly paired) with the definition being used—and there is no disagreement about that.

One definition of net tangible assets is the sum of net working capital and fixed assets (See Example 1. Historical Balance Sheet, Option 1). These values should be stated at fair market value, although typically the book value of fixed assets is used unless the valuation analyst is comfortable *estimating* his or her fair market value or has a separate appraisal.

| Example 1. Historical Balance Sheet | |
|---|---|
| Net working capital | $80,000 |
| Fixed assets | $290,000 |
| **Net tangible assets—Option 1** | $370,000 |
| Long-term debt | $300,000 |
| | |
| **Equity or net tangible assets—Option 2** | $70,000 |

The correct computation of the required return on net tangible assets using this definition is shown in Example 1: Weighted Average Cost of Capital. Here, we have assumed that the pretax cost of debt is 6%, based upon a borrowing rate of 9% less long-term growth rate of 3%. The cap rate for equity is 34%, determined by the 37% pretax discount rate less long-term growth rate of 3%. We know from the Historical Balance Sheet that there is $300,000 of debt and that the equity is equal to the net tangible assets of $70,000. Doing the calculations results in a required return on net tangible assets of 11.3%.

***Valuation Tip***

The components of the build-up of a discount rate below are hypotheticals for a valuation date. You need to use the correct components based upon the *actual* valuation date from Morningstar's SBBI Yearbook and other sources.

| | |
|---|---|
| Long Treasury Bond | 5.8% |
| Equity Risk Premium, S&P 500 | 7.5% |
| Base Equity Rate | 13.3% |
| 10th Decile Risk Premium, S&P 500 | 4.6% |
| Practice Risk Premium | 5.5% |
| **After-Tax Discount Rate** | 23.4% |
| Less: Growth Rate | -3.0% |
| **Capitalization Rate, Subsequent Year** | **20.4%** |
| **Pre-Tax Cap Rate** | **34.0%** |
| Plus: Growth Rate | **3.0%** |
| **Pre-Tax Discount Rate** | **37.0%** |

**Example 1. Cap Rate From the Weighted Average Cost of Capital**

| | | | | |
|---|---|---|---|---|
| Debt | 6% | $300,000 | 81.08% | 4.86% |
| Equity | 34% | 70,000 | 18.92 | 6.43 |
| | | $370,000 | 100.00% | 11.30% |

In the next portion of Example 1, we illustrate the calculation of the value of the business enterprise using the excess earnings method. Normalized 2002 earnings are based upon cash flows to invested capital (debt-free cash flows), which includes both long-term debt and equity, as should be clear from Example 1—Option 1.[51] The fair market value of the owner and employee physician's services is $270,000. For simplicity, we assume

51 Read this two or three times. It is the key to understanding how to do the calculation correctly!

that the required return on intangibles is equivalent to the required return on equity of 34%. In an actual engagement, the valuation analyst should, of course, consider whether the intangibles require a higher rate of return than the "generic" return on equity.[52]

| Example 1. Net Tangible Assets Based on Net Working Capital (NWC) Plus Fixed Assets | | | |
|---|---|---|---|
| Normalized 2002 earnings | | | $375,000 |
| Fair market earnings | | | -270,000 |
| Excess earnings | | | 105,000 |
| "Net tangible assets" | $370,000 | 11.3% | -41,800 |
| Excess earnings attributable to intangibles | | | 63,200 |
| Capitalization rate | | | 34% |
| **Intangible Value** | | | **$185,882** |
| **Practice Tangibles** | | | **$370,000** |
| **Business Enterprise Value** | | | **$555,882** |

The second definition of net tangible assets (Example 2. Historical Balance Sheet, Option 2) is the sum of net working capital and fixed assets, less long-term debt. If book values are used for all of these factors, net tangible assets in this circumstance will equal stockholders' equity, unless there are excluded assets or liabilities.[53]

| Example 2. Historical Balance Sheet | |
|---|---|
| Net working capital | $80,000 |
| Fixed assets | $290,000 |
| **Net tangible assets—Option 1** | **$370,000** |
| Long-term debt | $300,000 |
| **Equity or net tangible assets— Option 2** | **$70,000** |

Recall that normalized 2002 earnings are based upon cash flows to invested capital (debt-free cash flows), which includes both long-term debt and equity. There are two critical aspects of correctly performing the calculation when using this (Option 2) definition of net tangible assets. The first is to recognize that the return on the $300,000 of debt ($18,000) must be subtracted from the normalized 2002 earnings. This is necessary because the $18,000 is not available to equity.

52 In fact, the return on equity of the entire business should be a separate weighted average of the required equity rates of return on tangibles partially financed by debt and intangibles financed by equity.

53 An example of excluded assets in valuing the business enterprise would be marketable securities not part of required working capital that are considered a nonoperating asset. Another example would typically be a loan receivable from an officer of the company.

The second critical aspect is that there is no need to compute a weighted average return because the net tangibles assets are equal to equity only. As such, the required return on the $70,000 is 34%, or $23,800.

| Example 2. Net Tangible Assets Based on NWC Plus Fixed Assets Less Long-Term Debt | | | |
|---|---|---|---|
| Normalized 2002 earnings | | | $375,000 |
| Interest on debt | | | -18,000 |
| Fair market earnings | | | -270,000 |
| Excess earnings | | | 87,000 |
| Net tangible assets | $70,000 | 34.0% | 23,800 |
| Excess earnings attributable to intangibles | | | 63,200 |
| Capitalization rate | | | 34% |
| **Intangible Value** | | | **$185,882** |
| **Practice Tangibles** | | | **370,000** |
| **Business Enterprise Value** | | | **$555,882** |

The proof that the two calculations have been handled correctly is that the valuation result—*$555,882*—is exactly the same in both options! I highly recommend that valuation analysts using the excess earnings method structure their spreadsheet models to perform the calculation using both Option 1 and Option 2. In this manner, you have an automatic proof of the correct application of the method.

The balance sheet based upon the fair market value calculation is shown below. The business enterprise value of $555,882 would be the price a buyer would pay for the assets, while the $255,883 would be the value of the equity (stock) of the company.[54]

| Fair Market Balance Sheet | | | |
|---|---|---|---|
| | Historical Cost | Adjust | Fair Market |
| Net working capital | $80,000 | | $80,000 |
| Fixed assets | 290,000 | | 290,000 |
| | 370,000 | | 370,000 |
| Intangibles | | $185,882 | 185,882 |
| Business enterprise value | 370,000 | 185,882 | 555,882 |
| Long-term debt | 300,000 | | 300,000 |
| | | | |
| Equity | $70,000 | $185,882 | $255,882 |

54 If the goal of the valuation is to value assets, the valuator should consider adding the present value of the tax benefit of amortizing the intangible value under Internal Revenue Code 197.

***Insight and Analysis***

Bear in mind that the above example contains (what may be) a deliberate error in the concluded value. See the discussion under the caption Cost of Capital later in this chapter.

## The Use of the Capitalization of Cash Flows in Conjunction With the Excess Earnings Method

A common user error is the failure to consider or properly assess whether the *overall* (weighted average) capitalization rate that results from the *separate* rates on tangibles and intangibles is reasonable. Computing the weighted average capitalization rate and using it to determine the practice's value under the capitalization of cash flows method can prevent this pitfall.

Exhibit 18 revisits the example from the previous section. In Exhibit 19, we have determined that the *pretax*[55] cost of debt is 6% and the pretax cost of equity is 34%. The cost of equity will apply to the tangibles not financed by debt as well as to the intangibles.[56]

**Exhibit 18. Historical Balance Sheet**

| | |
|---|---|
| Net working capital | $80,000 |
| Fixed assets | $290,000 |
| Net tangible assets | $370,000 |
| Long-term debt | $300,000 |
| | |
| Equity or net tangible assets | $70,000 |

**Exhibit 19. WACC Cap Rate for Tangible Assets**

| | | | | |
|---|---|---|---|---|
| Debt | 6% | $300,000 | 81.08% | 4.86% |
| Equity | 34% | 70,000 | 18.92 | 6.43 |
| | | $370,000 | 100.00% | 11.30% |

Exhibit 20 is the calculation of the value of the practice using the excess earnings method from the previous section. The return on the tangibles of 11.3% is based upon the weighted average of the return on debt and the return on equity reflected in Exhibit 19 above.

55 We use pretax rates of return since that is what is commonly done for medical practices.

56 It is (also) correct to have a *higher* cost of equity for the intangibles and a *lower* cost of equity for the tangibles under the theory that intangibles are more risky and therefore, demand a higher rate of return.

**Exhibit 20. Excess Earnings Method**

| | | | |
|---|---|---|---|
| Normalized 2002 earnings | | | $375,000 |
| Fair market earnings | | | $(270,000) |
| Excess earnings | | | $105,000 |
| "Net tangible assets" | $370,000 | 11.3% | $(41,800) |
| Excess earnings attributable to intangibles | | | $63,200 |
| Capitalization rate | | | 34% |
| **Intangible value** | | | **$185,882** |
| **Practice tangibles** | | | **$370,000** |
| **Business enterprise value** | | | **$555,882** |

It is important to understand that the excess earnings method is nothing more (or less) than a *two-stage* capitalization of cash flows: The first stage is "reversed" in that we determine the value of the tangible assets *first*[57] and then apply a predetermined rate of return to that value. In the second stage, we determine the value of the intangible assets by capitalizing the remaining cash flow by the predetermined rate of return for intangibles. In effect, the excess earnings method says that there are two returns on equity to the owner of the practice: one on tangibles and one on intangibles. The reasonable compensation is a return on labor.

How do we know that the rate of return on the earnings after reasonable compensation—earnings attributable to both tangibles and intangibles—is itself reasonable? The only way to confirm this is to compute the weighted average return based upon the values determined in the excess earnings method and then apply it to the total earnings in excess of reasonable compensation. This computation is shown in Exhibit 21.

**Exhibit 21. WACC Cap Rate for Entire Practice**

| | | | | |
|---|---|---|---|---|
| Tangibles | $370,000 | 66.56% | 11.30% | 7.52% |
| Practice Intangibles | 185,882 | 33.44 | 34.00 | 11.37 |
| Weighted Average Cost Of Capital | $555,882 | 100.00% | | 18.89% |

Thus, we see that the choice of a 6% pretax cap rate for debt and a 34% pretax cap rate for equity results in a WACC cap rate of 18.89% applied to the pretax earnings or cash

57 This is why the method is thought of as a hybrid method: In effect, you have to use the cost approach to determine the value of the tangibles.

flow of the practice, after the payment of reasonable compensation for labor. The analysis of whether or not this is reasonable requires the valuation analyst's assessment of the reasonableness of the separate costs of equity (34%) and debt (6%). It can also be viewed in the conventional fashion of the weights of equity and debt, rather than the weights of tangibles and intangibles, as shown in Exhibit 22.

**Exhibit 22. Conventional WACC Cap Rate for Entire Practice**

| | | | | |
|---|---|---|---|---|
| Debt | 6% | $300,000 | 53.97% | 3.24% |
| Equity | 34% | 255,882 | 46.03 | 15.65 |
| | | $555,882 | 100.00% | 18.89% |

What Exhibit 22 demonstrates is that the high percentage of debt is making the WACC quite low. The valuation analyst should consider whether this is a reasonable degree of debt for an engagement to value a controlling interest—the excess earnings method should only be used to value a controlling interest.

Finally, we can "prove" the computation of the WACC for the entire practice and the excess earnings method by valuing the practice using the traditional capitalization of cash flows method. This proof does not confirm the reasonableness of the 18.89% cap rate, only that it has been computed correctly.

**Exhibit 23. Capitalization of Cash Flows**

| | |
|---|---|
| Normalized 2002 Earnings | $375,000 |
| Fair Market Earnings | (270,000) |
| | |
| Cash Flow After Reasonable Compensation | $105,000 |
| Capitalization Rate | 18.89% |
| | |
| | $555,882 |

The value is exactly the same, as it should be!

Exhibit 24 indicates the most common mistake: assuming that all of the tangible assets can be financed with debt or at a low rate of return, based upon the IRS excess earnings method. Exhibit 25 is the calculation of the value under the excess earnings method. This silly result is based upon a case study presented in my course on business valuation.[58]

58 This is a case study based upon actual mistakes I have seen made by other "experts."

**Exhibit 24. WACC Cap Rate for Tangible Assets**

| | | | | |
|---|---|---|---|---|
| Debt | 0% | $0 | 0% | 0% |
| Equity—Tangibles | 10% | 1,000,000 | 100 | 10 |
| | | $1,000,000 | 100% | 10% |

**Exhibit 25. Excess Earnings Method**

| | | | |
|---|---|---|---|
| Normalized 2002 earnings | | | $375,000 |
| Fair market earnings | | | (270,000) |
| Excess earnings | | | 105,000 |
| Net tangible assets | $1,000,000 | 10% | (100,000) |
| Excess earnings attributable to intangibles | | | $5,000 |
| Capitalization rate | | | 34% |
| **Intangible value** | | | **$14,706** |
| **Practice tangibles** | | | **$1,000,000** |
| **Business enterprise value** | | | **$1,014,706** |

Exhibit 26 will clue the valuation analyst in to the *fact* that a mistake has been made: A pretax return of 10.35% for a medical practice is not reasonable in any event! If we do a short-cut conversion of this rate to an after-tax rate by multiplying by 1 minus the tax rate (40%), or 60%, we get a return we can compare to standard costs of equity from Morningstar. 10.35% times 60% equals 6.21% (a cap rate). Adding the growth rate of 3% gives us an after-tax discount rate of 9.21%. This is *less than* the required rate of return on the S&P 500, which represents the risk of an equity investment in the broad market, the standard of comparison. Simply put, it is ridiculous.

**Exhibit 26. Conventional WACC Cap Rate for Entire Practice**

| | | | | |
|---|---|---|---|---|
| Tangibles | $1,000,000 | 98.55% | 10% | 9.86% |
| Practice intangibles | 14,706 | 1.45 | 34 | 0.49 |
| Weighted average cost of capital | $1,014,706 | 100.00% | | 10.35% |

Notwithstanding the mistake in the selection of the return on the $1 million of tangibles, Exhibit 27 demonstrates that this method agrees with Exhibit 23's excess earnings method.

**Exhibit 27. Capitalization of Cash Flows**

| | |
|---|---|
| Normalized 2002 earnings | $375,000 |
| Fair market earnings | (270,000) |
| Cash flow after reasonable compensation | $105,000 |
| Capitalization rate | 10.35% |
| | |
| | $1,014,706 |

### Conclusion

Failure to test the reasonableness of the two rates of return used in the excess earnings method by computing a single rate of return for the cash flow attributable to both tangibles and intangibles (capitalization of cash flows method) can lead to serious mistakes, such as that shown in Exhibits 22 to 25. The valuation analyst should structure spreadsheets to perform this test *automatically*. The key element is whether the combined pretax cap rate (or the return in the practice's assets) is reasonable when compared to proper external benchmarks, such as those developed from Morningstar data under the capital asset pricing model or build-up method.

## Control Adjustments to the Excess Earnings Valuation Model?

### Introduction

The excess earnings method generally produces a control value. The technical reason for this is that the tangible asset measurement requires the cost approach, which always produces a control value. It *is* mathematically possible to adjust the assumptions in an excess earnings model to generate a noncontrol value, just as it is possible—and common —to vary the assumptions in a capitalization of cash flows model to produce a control or a noncontrol value. Medical practices are somewhat unusual in that the excess earnings method—properly applied, of course—could be used to determine a noncontrol value. This is in large part because the distribution of cash is generally governed by employment contracts and other ownership rights via a stockholders agreement and because the tangible assets are not typically material when compared to the intangible assets.

### Control Adjustments

To apply control premiums to reach a control value, you must first have used a method that determines a *noncontrol* value. In addition, the valuation community has moved toward the position that most "control" premiums actually represent strategic considerations not consistent with fair market value. Use of control premiums when using the excess earnings method is therefore inappropriate, or stated more frankly, *wrong*.

Equally risky is use of the excess earnings method to determine a *non*control value. Lack of control or minority discounts should be *considered* when the excess earnings method is used to produce a noncontrol value. Better yet, *eliminate the control adjustments*. Perhaps the most frequently overlooked fact of medical practice valuation is that if all cash distribution is contractual, i.e., via a compensation plan and employment contracts, and the tangible value is low, using the excess earnings method for a physician practice buy-in is acceptable (and common), providing the noncontrol elements are properly considered.

#### Reasonable Compensation

In valuing medical practices using the excess earnings method, the most important adjustment is the one for reasonable compensation. As noted earlier in the chapter, determining the reasonable compensation for a physician requires more than merely looking at a statistical source and choosing the mean or median. The valuation analyst needs to first compare the physician's productivity or work effort to statistical norms and then base the reasonable compensation on that productivity. You cannot expect to pay a hypothetical buyer of the practice a 35-hour wage for 50 hours of work.[59]

It is equally important to focus on where the income in the practice is coming from. Practices that own laboratories or imaging equipment, e.g., x-ray, ultrasound, CT scan or MRI, may have significant profits from such operations. These profits need to be determined to correctly perform the valuation. They are not part of the physician work effort. Moreover, they may not be part of personal or professional goodwill in a divorce context and should be factored out of that debate in those jurisdictions where personal goodwill is not a divisible asset. Here is the same chart we looked at earlier in the chapter in the discussion of the weighted average cost of capital for the asset side of the balance sheet, now presented to show how the profit paid out as compensation in the typical physician practice consists both of a return on labor and a return on assets or capital.

The "compensation" needs to be considered in its broader sense of fringe benefits, retirement plan contributions and other perquisites. For example, the compensation in the MGMA data includes only W-2 (and equivalent[60]) compensation; retirement plan benefits are reported separately. As such, when figuring reasonable compensation in a

59 See, e.g., "Medical Practices: A Bv Rx," *Journal of Accountancy*, November 2005 by the author. This is not to say that anomalous situations do not exist where P.T. Barnum's rule is in effect.

60 Bonuses, a partner's or S stockholder's share of income, etc.

valuation model, if the valuation analyst adds back the retirement plan contribution to available earnings, he or she then needs to add the MGMA retirement plan contribution to whatever (W-2) earnings are selected from the MGMA data.

**Exhibit 28. Profit Paid Out as Compensation Consists of Return on Labor and a Return on Capital**

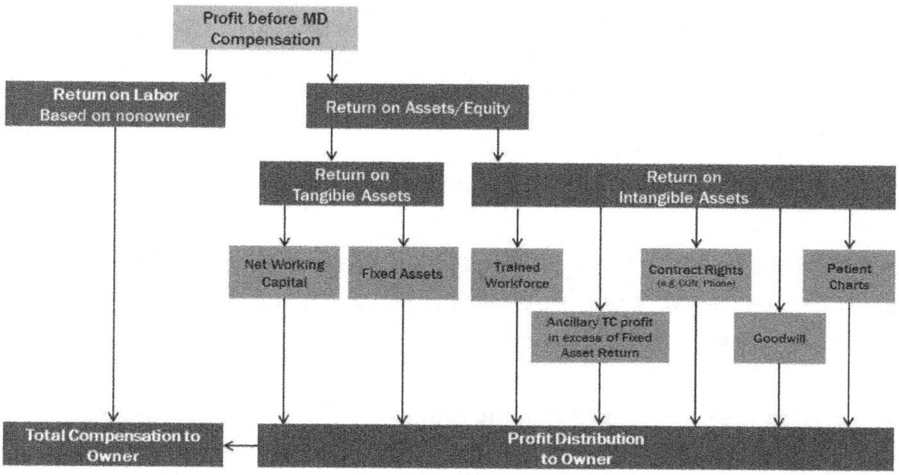


### *Insight and Analysis*

In my experience, there is a cyclical pattern of the use of high contribution retirement plans by physicians and dentists with high incomes—typically solo practitioners or two- or three-partner practices. Defined benefit plans, target benefit plans and cash balance plans became highly attractive again during the George W. Bush administration due to a relaxation in the rules. Annual contributions for a high-income beneficiary over age 50 can be $150,000 per year or more, *plus* a 401(k) contribution and even a profit-sharing contribution of up to 6% of the Section 415 compensation limit. These add up to more than $200,000 per annum. Thus, it is critical to normalize compensation to take into account retirement contributions.

### Cost of Capital

In the first part of this section, we saw that there was substantial debt in the practice used to finance tangible assets. This debt drove down the required rate of return on the tangibles, which in turn increased the amount of excess earnings available for intangible assets. This, of course, apparently increases the value of the practice. In short, the more debt one adds to the capital structure, the lower the cost of capital goes and the higher the value goes—*unless* one understands the CAPM and betas! This suggests that the analysis of the percentage of debt in the capital structure is critical to a correct valuation, although simply adding debt to lower the cost of capital is not acceptable since increased debt also increases the cost of equity.

Variations in the percentages of debt and equity that a hypothetical control owner of a practice would make need to be thought through carefully. In the real world, the debt of a medical practice is limited to some portion of the fixed assets and the accounts receivable in the practice. Rarely does one see the intangible value financed with debt. As such, it would generally be inaccurate to assume that the intangible value would be financed with debt in the absence of some peculiar set of circumstances.

Exhibit 29 is the computation of the pretax cap rate and discount rate for this example.

***Insight and Analysis***

The components of the build-up of a discount rate are *hypotheticals* for a valuation date. You need to use the correct components based upon the actual valuation date from Ibbotson's *Yearbook* and other sources.

**Exhibit 29. Computation of the Pretax Cap Rate and Discount Rate**

| | |
|---|---|
| Long Treasury Bond | 5.8% |
| Equity Risk Premium, S&P 500 | 7.5% |
| Base Equity Rate | 13.3% |
| 10th Decile Risk Premium, S&P 500 | 4.6% |
| Practice Risk Premium | 5.5% |
| **After-Tax Discount Rate** | 23.4% |
| Less: Growth Rate | -3.0% |
| **Capitalization Rate, Subsequent Year** | **20.4%** |
| **Pre-Tax Cap Rate** | **34.0%** |
| Plus: Growth Rate | **3.0%** |
| **Pre-Tax Discount Rate** | **37.0%** |

Exhibit 30 highlights the hypothetical optimal mix of debt and equity used for the (same) practice that was presented in the first two parts of this article.

**Exhibit 30. WACC Cap Rate for Tangible Assets**

| | | | |
|---|---|---|---|
| Pretax discount rate | | 37.00% | |
| Equity percentage | | 75.00% | |
| | | | 27.75% |
| Cost of debt | 9.00% | | |
| Tax rate | 0.00% | | |
| After-tax cost of debt | | 9.00% | |
| Debt percentage | | 25.00% | |
| | | | 2.25% |
| Weighted average cost of capital | | | 30.00% |
| Less: growth rate | | | -3.00% |
| Cap rate, subsequent year | | | 27.00% |

Exhibit 31 is the calculation of the value of the practice using the excess earnings method from the previous section.

**Exhibit 31. Excess Earnings Method**

| | | | |
|---|---|---|---|
| Normalized 2002 earnings | | | $375,000 |
| Interest on debt | | | (5,550) |
| Fair market earnings | | | (270,000) |
| Excess earnings | | | 99,450 |
| Net tangible assets | $277,500 | 34.00% | (94,350) |
| Excess earnings attributable to intangibles | | | $5,100 |
| Capitalization rate | | | 34.00% |
| **Intangible value** | | | **$15,000** |
| **Practice tangibles** | | | **$370,000** |
| **Business enterprise value** | | | **$385,000** |

Exhibit 32 is the cap rate determined in the earlier example, followed by the cap rate based on Exhibit 33.

**Exhibit 32. WACC Cap Rate for Tangible Assets**

| | | | | |
|---|---|---|---|---|
| Old Debt | 6.% | $300,000 | 53.97% | 3.24% |
| Equity | 34% | 255,882 | 46.03 | 15.65 |
| | | $555,882 | 100.00% | 18.89% |

**Exhibit 33. WACC Cap Rate for Tangible Assets—New**

| Here, debt is 25% of the tangible assets of $385,000, or $92,500. | | | | |
|---|---|---|---|---|
| Debt | 6% | $92,500 | 24.03% | 1.44% |
| Equity | 34% | 292,500 | 75.97 | 25.83 |
| | | $385,000 | 100.00% | 27.27% |

***Insight and Analysis***

Note the substantial difference in the weighted average cost of capital when the debt level is adjusted to 24% from the nearly 54% in the original example. Since "the lower the cap rate, the higher the value," we know that the value of the practice with 25% debt (Exhibit 34) will be much less than with 54% debt (Exhibit 35).

**Exhibit 34. Capitalization of Cash Flows—New**

| | |
|---|---|
| Normalized 2002 earnings | $375,000 |
| Fair market earnings | (270,000) |
| Cash flow after reasonable compensation | $105,000 |
| Capitalization rate | 27.27% |
| Asset value | $385,000 |
| Less: long-term debt | 300,000 |
| Equity value | $85,000 |

**Exhibit 35. Capitalization of Cash Flows—Old**

| | |
|---|---|
| Normalized 2002 earnings | $375,000 |
| Fair market earnings | (270,000) |
| Cash flow after reasonable compensation | $105,000 |
| Capitalization rate | 18.89% |
| Asset value | $555,882 |
| Less: long-term debt | $300,000 |
| Equity value | $255,882 |

Which of these two answers is correct? This decision requires that most difficult of skills: judgment. Part of the answer lays in the conversion of the two cap rates to after-tax discounts rates (Exhibit 36) that can be compared to Morningstar's return on capital. Bear in mind that the cap rates are being applied to *invested capital* whereas the Morningstar data determine a cost of *equity* that then needs to be used in a computation of a weighted average cost of capital capitalization rate. The valuation analyst needs to ask the question: Is 19.36% (14.33%) a reasonable return[61] on invested capital for a medical practice? In point of fact, 14.33% would be quite low by both current and historical standards. At the peak of acquisition activity in the mid-1990s, when perceived risk was lowest, the weighted average cost of capital for the best physician practices was rarely less than 16%. Today, practices are considered much more risky. The 19.36% is a more reasonable rate of return.

**Exhibit 36. Conversion of the Two Cap Rates to After-Tax Discounts Rates**

| | | |
|---|---|---|
| Cap rate—pretax | 27.27% | 18.89% |
| 1 less the tax rate | 60.00 | 60.00 |
| Cap rate—after-tax | 16.36 | 11.33 |
| Growth rate | 3.00 | 3.00 |
| Discount rate—after-tax | 19.36% | 14.33% |

### *Insight and Analysis*

One question I have often been asked: If using a hypothetical mix of debt and equity in the WACC, what is subtracted from the result to determine the actual equity of the practice, actual debt or hypothetical debt? The answer, of course, is the actual debt. The assumption is that the hypothetical owner would use an optimal mix of debt and equity, which in turn is what drives the enterprise value in the valuation. From the *seller's* standpoint, it gets the entire enterprise value and then pays off *whatever debt it has, if any*. Think about a scenario in which the optimal debt-equity mix is 25% to 75%, but the seller has 50% debt Clearly, the equity is less than if it had 25% debt. It is useful to prepare a pro forma FMV balance sheet[62]—allocating to working capital, fixed assets and intangibles—from the model so you can see what the actual assets, debt, and equity look like.

### What About a Noncontrol Value?

Lawyers, judges, and some valuation analysts[63] like the excess earnings method for valuing physician practices. Many of the members of that subset of professionals do not really understand how it works, however. The most frequent mistake in a transactional setting is using the excess earnings method to inappropriately value a *non*control interest.

For example, let's assume that the practice in Figures 3 and 6 consisted of one owner and one employee physician. The owner is paid $250,000 per year, and the employee is

61 Net of growth.
62 And beware what you call it if subject to SSVS and SSARS.
63 Including the author for physician to physician transactions.

paid $125,000. The valuation analyst determines that reasonable compensation for the owner is $140,000 and for the employee, $130,000. The employee is going to buy 50% of the practice. Since the value is a control value and you do not get control with 50%, this should be your first clue that the value of the 50% interest is *not* one-half of $385,000, or $192,500. Since the employee does not get control, he or she cannot reduce the current owner's salary to $140,000 per year and therefore cannot get 50% of the excess earnings of $105,000. If he or she doesn't get that 50%, what is the practice worth? It is only worth the excess earnings that the employee receives, capitalized at 27.27%. If the owner continues to get paid $250,000, there are not any excess earnings *and the practice is worth nothing to the employee.*

In point of fact, valuing a practice for buy-in purposes really requires that the terms of the buy-in be known. The 2008 *Derby* tax court case indicates that the actual terms must be known for a sale to a hospital. As can be seen from the simple example above, *the value to the buyer depends upon what the buyer's income will be after the purchase.* If it doesn't change, there is no value. If the income does not change for a number of years, the excess earnings method (or CCF method) is not a correct choice, as both of these methods assume that there is level cash flow throughout the period of ownership that grows at a fixed rate each year. The correct method in such a circumstance is the discounted cash flow (DCF) method, which permits the valuation analyst to specifically match the year of the cash flow with the appropriate discount factor for that year.

A noncontrol owner could not alter the cost of capital, either. Therefore, one generally would not make this adjustment in determining a value for noncontrol purposes. However, if the capital structure contains *excessive* debt, the noncontrol buyer should not be willing to pay the inflated value resulting from the apparently lower WACC—since the lower WACC likely does not accurately reflect the true cost of equity. *Remember that fair market value will generally not exceed the amount determined on a control basis for the hypothetical buyer.* If the level of debt exceeds that hypothetical amount, the value will exceed fair market value. If fair market is the standard of value, then a lower level of debt would have to be assumed in the valuation model.

## Chapter Summary

In this chapter, we reviewed the nuts and bolts of applying the commonly accepted valuation methods to physician practices. The key points for most readers are as follows.

The discount rate for a valuation measures the expected return on investment based upon the risk involved. The greater the risk, the higher the discount rate a hypothetical investor will demand. The discount rate consists of a risk-free rate, a large company equity risk premium, a small company equity risk premium plus a specific practice risk premium. The latter is subjective and highly contingent upon the skill, knowledge, and experience of the valuation analyst. The capitalization rate is derived from the discount rate by subtracting the expected growth rate in cash flows during the terminal period from the discount rate.

The discounted cash flow method is the most commonly accepted valuation method for physician practices subject to regulatory scrutiny and should be used with after-tax earnings. It measures enterprise value (EV), which includes tangible assets such as equipment and working capital plus intangible assets. Use of the method requires considerable effort and skill on the part of the valuation consultant.

Physician compensation expense in the valuation model should be based upon what is to be paid if the transaction takes place because a hypothetical investor would not pay for a cash flow return that was, in fact, being paid out to a physician employee. Valuation analysts may wish to advise clients that actual compensation negotiated in a transaction that differs from that used in the valuation suggests revisiting the valuation.

The excess earnings method is, in the author's opinion, the best method for small-scale transactions between physicians and can be performed using pretax or after-tax cash earnings, as long as the discount and capitalization rates are adjusted appropriately.

For experienced valuation consultants new to physician practice valuation, the factors for selecting the specific practice risk premium should be considered, along with the requirements of regulatory authority outlined in this chapter and throughout this guide.

*This chapter was edited by Carol Carden, CPA/ABV, ASA of PYA.*

*The Thornton letter on the following pages is a 1992 response on valuing physician practices.*

**The Thornton Letter**

*This letter is one of the seminal events in physician practice valuation "lore and legend." Although it is generally accepted, nearly 20 years later, that a physician practice may be valued based upon its own internal revenue streams, there are still those who feel—or fear—that the letter is relevant.*

November 2, 1993
John E. Steiner, Jr., Esquire
Assistant General Counsel
American Hospital Association
840 North Lake Shore Drive
Chicago, IL 60611

Dear John:

I am responding to your letter of July 20, 1993, requesting assistance in interpreting the scope of prohibited referrals under the Medicare and Medicaid anti-kickback statute with respect to the acquisition of physician practices. The focus of your inquiry was the position taken in my Dec. 22, 1992 letter to T. J. Sullivan at the Internal Revenue Service that payments for intangible assets or goodwill were open to question under the anti-kickback statute, and my subsequent oral comments on this issue.

In particular, in your letter you presented two specific situations involving the acquisition of a physician's practice. The first situation involved the purchase of a physician practice by another physician or a group practice. I have assumed the acquiring practice is not in a position to benefit from referrals by the acquired practice. After reaching agreement on the price for the hard assets, the parties proceed to value the remainder of the practice and assign a value for the expectation of future patronage by patients to the practice being acquired. The total price negotiated for the practice includes an amount for both the hard assets and the intangible assets. You described this situation as involving a "one-step" referral, a situation where the patients "self-refer" because of word of mouth about the physician or because another unrelated physician refers to the practice.

The second situation involves the acquisition of the same or a similar physician practice, except that the purchaser is a hospital, which is in a position to benefit from referrals by the acquired practice. The same valuation method is used to determine the purchase price. Even though the hospital can be expected to receive admissions and referrals from the practice, the value of these referrals are not used in the valuation of the practice. Only the expected future patronage to the practice is included and the hospital does not pay more for the practice than would another physician. This situation is described as involving a "two-step" referral process, one to the practice and a second one to the hospital.

You sought an opinion clarifying whether the payments made in either or both of these situations would be allowable under the anti-kickback statute. As you know, the Medicare and Medicaid anti-kickback statute, Section 1128B(b) of the Social Security Act, 42 U.S.C. 1320a-7b(b), makes it a criminal offense to knowingly and willfully offer, pay, solicit, or receive remuneration to induce, or in return for, the referral of business covered by Medicare or Medicaid.

For a number of reasons, we are not in a position to issue advisory or interpretive opinions on whether a particular practice or arrangement violates the anti-kickback statute. One reason is that since Section 1128B(b) is a criminal statute, the Department of Justice has exclusive authority to initiate a criminal prosecution or decline to do so under the statute. Another reason is that the statute requires proof of knowing and willful intent, and it is generally impossible to evaluate intent on the basis of a paper submission. Finally, in reviewing a particular arrangement, we cannot be sure that we have all the necessary information concerning the nature of the arrangement or practice and how it operates to make a proper decision concerning its legality or illegality.

I would like to emphasize that the position I articulated in the Dec. 22, 1992 letter to T. J. Sullivan remains the same. I did not state that payments for intangible assets are illegal per se. Nor have I indicated approval of any particular acquisition practices or valuation methodologies. Since payments for items other than the hard assets of a physician practice could be a payment to induce referrals or could be in return for future referrals, any such payments are subject to scrutiny to determine whether they violate the anti-kickback statute. The fact that the parties may identify the purpose of the payment as something other than a payment for referrals is not determinative.

Similarly, the fact that two different parties may offer to pay the same price for a particular or a comparable physician practice or may use a similar approach in "valuing" the practice does not mean that both will be afforded the same treatment under the anti-kickback statute. The intent of the parties is the critical element in the determination of a violation under the anti-kickback statute, and different parties may have different purposes and reasons for seeking to acquire a particular physician practice and for paying a particular price. Finally, the facts and circumstances involved in each situation are likely to be different as will be the nature of the relationship between the parties. Consequently, each particular situation must be judged on its own merits and based on its own facts and circumstances.

Turning to the two situations described above, we believe the first situation is far less problematic than the second. However, either situation could constitute a violation of the anti-kickback statute, depending on the intent of the parties, the nature of the intangible assets, the amounts paid for the intangible assets, and the past and future relationship of the parties, etc. One major factor is where the seller becomes or remains affiliated with the buyer. In such a case, the terms of that continued affiliation as well as the remuneration paid to the seller for services rendered would also need to be taken into account in determining whether a violation exists.

With respect to the second situation involving the purchase of the practice by a hospital, anytime an entity is acquiring a practice where the entity is in a position to benefit from referrals from the practice, there is always a question that a portion of the amount paid for the practice is attributable to the future referrals. As indicated above, it is the intent of the parties and the facts and circumstances of the particular acquisition that are relevant. Accordingly, the fact that a hospital purchases a physician practice for the same amount that another physician might pay does not insulate the hospital from liability under the anti-kickback statute. For example, another physician may offer a high price based on the savings in administrative costs and overhead which could be realized by combining practices. However, a hospital may not have that motivation at all; its offer of the same price could be motivated by a desire to pay for future referrals.

We hope this information is helpful and regret that we are unable to provide further guidance. Thank you for your interest in this matter.

Sincerely,

/s/
D. McCarty Thornton
Associate General Counsel
Inspector General Division

Chapter 15

# Sample Table of Contents for a Physician Practice Valuation Report

TABLE OF CONTENTS

**ANALYSIS AND SUMMARY OF OUTLOOK FOR THE PRACTICE AT THE VALUATION DATE**

- Practice Positives
- Practice Risk Areas
- Summary

**OVERVIEW OF VALUATION APPROACHES AND ISSUES**

- Introduction
  - Income Approach
  - Market Approach
  - Asset Accumulation (Cost) Approach
  - Workforce-in-Place
  - Other Intangible Assets of a Business Enterprise
  - Revenue Ruling 59-60
- Discussion of Market Approach
  - Internal Revenue Service
  - Goodwill Registry
  - Pratt's Stats
  - Differences in Geographic Market Areas
  - Market Activity in General
  - Chosen Approaches

**VALUATION DISCUSSION**

- Income Statement Normalization Adjustments: For Valuation Purposes
  - Depreciation
  - Rent
- Balance Sheet Normalization Adjustments: For Valuation Purposes
  - Accounts Receivable
  - Prepaid Rent
  - Fixed Assets
  - Prepaids
  - S Corporation Distributions
  - Reasonable Compensation for Services

**VALUATION METHODS UTILIZED**

- Working Capital Assumption
- Capital Cost Assumption
- Working Capital
- Rates of increase

Chapter 16

# A Healthcare Appraiser Reviews a Judge-Appraiser's 'Report'

*By Mark O. Dietrich, CPA/ABV*

The decision in *Delaware Open MRI Radiology Associates, PA (majority) v. Kessler, et al. (minority)*[1] has created a great deal of commotion in the valuation community for a variety of reasons. Not the least of these is that Vice Chancellor Strine (Judge) of the Delaware Chancery Court adopted an S corporation tax-effecting scheme based on the difference between the after-tax dividend cash flow in the hands of an S shareholder versus that of a C shareholder, the latter taxed at 15%. There is also a replication of a discounted cash flow (DCF) model based upon the Judge's changes in the underlying assumptions and an often scathing critique of the majority's valuation expert. This article does not focus on those issues but rather on the failures in the application of the income approach, including a discussion of the use of the industry risk premium in lieu of the *capital asset pricing model*'s (CAPM) beta in the buildup method.

When using the income approach in any business valuation engagement, the appraiser's most critical task is to perform a reasoned analysis of the future revenue and profit prospects for the valuation subject. Industry expertise is required for many valuation engagements in various industries. In the valuation of healthcare entities in general and the MRI facilities that were the subject of this case in particular, studying industry trends commonly used by the peer group of healthcare industry valuation specialists is required. As will be seen from the analysis that follows, either the experts failed to

1 Since the case involved suit and countersuit, "majority" and "minority" is more descriptive than plaintiff and defendant.

address known industry trends in their reports, legal counsel failed to bring them out in testimony, or the Judge ignored it. Healthcare industry knowledge can be readily obtained from sources such as the Medicare Payment Advisory Commission (MedPAC) described below.

### Time Line of the Case

The merger giving rise to the lawsuit in this matter occurred in January 2004. This date is critical because the MedPAC had already identified high-tech imaging such as MRI as a problem spending area in 2003. The first lawsuit was filed in February 2004.

The court's findings on revenue growth are directly contradictory to foreseeable changes—foreseen by the majority expert (Mr. Reed), whose testimony was dismissed in the following extract from the opinion. If, in fact, Mr. Reed failed to cite external sources to give his revenue reduction forecast credibility, it is indeed unfortunate since he had it right.

> I also find that Mitchell (minority expert) made reasonable assumptions regarding the revenues that Delaware Radiology would receive for doing scans. Mitchell began by using the same base reimbursement rates as Reed for Delaware I ($601 per scan) and Delaware II ($571 per scan). Mitchell used those reimbursement rates because they were the numbers the Broder Group provided to Reed for the purpose of performing a valuation, and Mitchell found them reasonable. *Mitchell held these rates constant throughout his projection period.* Reed, by contrast, assumed reductions in reimbursement rates of 9% for Delaware I and II in Year 2, or 2005, and then increased them at 3%, the rate of inflation, annually. Essentially, the basis for Reed's reduction was speculation by Carr and Reed's own opinion that Delaware reimbursement rates were high relative to neighboring states and that they were likely to fall. But the record is devoid of information from more objective sources to substantiate that viewpoint, which, like other elements of Reed and Carr's testimony, fits within the self-interest of the Broder Group.

### History of MedPAC's Identification of High-Tech Imaging Expense Trends

"The Medicare Payment Advisory Commission (MedPAC) is an independent federal body established by the Balanced Budget Act of 1997 to advise the U.S. Congress on issues affecting the Medicare program."[2] This is the most easily identifiable and readily obtainable source of insight into future healthcare industry reimbursement. Although it

2 2003 Report to Congress.

applies specifically to Medicare payments to healthcare providers, many health insurers link their payment levels to Medicare.

Revenue, of course, is a function of the number of units of service provided and the rate per unit paid. Consider the following from the March 2003 MedPAC Report to Congress, highlighting the rapid growth in MRI services provided to the Medicare population.

> Relatively high growth rates for imaging services were concentrated in several specific categories, all of which involve technology of one kind or another. For instance, nuclear medicine grew by 13%, computerized automated tomography (CAT) of parts of the body other than the head grew by 15.3%, *magnetic resonance imaging (MRI) of parts of the body other than the brain grew by 15.9%, and MRI of the brain grew by 14.6%.* It is noteworthy, however, that none of these technologies are new. Instead, *it appears that use of well-established technologies is increasing.* CAT, for example, was introduced in the 1970s. MRI began to diffuse as a new technology in the 1980s. Thus, the indications for use of these technologies may be changing. (*Emphasis added*)

The March 2004 MedPAC Report to Congress repeated the observation.

> Among broad categories of services—major procedures, evaluation and management, other procedures, imaging, and tests—growth rates vary, but all are positive. Imaging and tests grew the most. *From 2001 to 2002, the imaging growth rate was 9.4%,* and the growth rate for tests was 11.1%.
>
> Within these categories, some services grew much faster than others (see Exhibit 1). From 2001 to 2002, we see the highest growth in volume—*approaching 20%*—of nuclear medicine, computed tomography, *magnetic resonance imaging*, laboratory tests, and minor procedures, which include outpatient rehabilitation. (*Emphasis added*)

And yet again the observation was repeated in the March 2005 MedPAC Report to Congress (see Exhibit 2) At this time, MedPAC formally advised Congress to implement strategies for reducing the volume of MRI and other high-tech imaging. These reductions were announced in August 2005 by CMS[3] and were scheduled to be implemented over two years starting in January 2006. The Deficit Reduction Act, signed in 2006, brought further dramatic reductions to MRI reimbursement in 2007.

> Imaging services have been growing much more rapidly than other services paid

3 Centers for Medicare and Medicaid Services of the Department of Health and Human Services.

### Exhibit 1. Change in Per Capita Use of Physician Services by Beneficiaries in Traditional Medicare, by Selected Type of Service, 1999-2002

| | Per capita service use | | | | | | |
|---|---|---|---|---|---|---|---|
| | | | | | Average annual percent change | | Percent of total service use |
| Type of service | 1999 | 2000 | 2001 | 2002 | 1999-2001 | 2001-2002 | |
| All services | 663.4 | 691.8 | 707.9 | 738.5 | 3.3% | 4.3% | 100.0% |
| Evaluation and management | 353.6 | 359.4 | 361.9 | 372.5 | 1.2 | 2.9 | 50.4 |
| Office visits—established patient | 127.6 | 131.2 | 130.3 | 133.3 | 1.1 | 2.3 | 18.1 |
| Hospital visit—subsequent | 65.0 | 64.6 | 64.7 | 66.7 | -0.2 | 3.1 | 9.0 |
| Consultations | 39.8 | 41.5 | 42.6 | 44.5 | 3.5 | 4.4 | 6.0 |
| Emergency room visit | 18.1 | 19.0 | 20.1 | 21.4 | 5.3 | 6.5 | 2.9 |
| Specialist—psychiatry | 18.5 | 18.3 | 18.2 | 18.5 | -1.0 | 2.1 | 2.5 |
| Specialist—ophthalmology | 15.9 | 16.8 | 17.5 | 18.1 | 4.9 | 3.5 | 2.4 |
| Hospital visit—initial | 17.6 | 17.4 | 17.2 | 17.2 | -1.2 | 0.3 | 2.3 |
| Office visits—new patient | 15.4 | 15.5 | 14.9 | 14.9 | -1.4 | -0.2 | 2.0 |
| Imaging | 81.1 | 88.2 | 96.1 | 105.1 | 8.9 | 9.4 | 14.2 |
| Echography—heart | 12.6 | 13.8 | 14.9 | 16.5 | 8.8 | 10.8 | 2.2 |
| Standard—nuclear medicine | 10.0 | 11.7 | 13.6 | 15.4 | 16.5 | 13.0 | 2.1 |
| Advanced—CAT: other | 9.3 | 10.7 | 12.3 | 14.1 | 14.8 | 15.3 | 1.9 |
| Advanced—MRI: other | 6.4 | 7.9 | 9.4 | 10.9 | 21.3 | 15.9 | 1.5 |
| Standard—musculoskeletal | 8.5 | 8.8 | 9.2 | 9.5 | 3.9 | 2.9 | 1.3 |
| Advanced—MRI: brain | 5.1 | 5.8 | 6.5 | 7.4 | 12.6 | 14.6 | 1.0 |
| Standard—chest | 6.7 | 6.5 | 6.3 | 6.3 | -3.3 | 0.4 | 0.9 |
| Advanced—CAT: head | 2.7 | 2.8 | 2.9 | 3.0 | 3.2 | 4.5 | 0.4 |
| Imaging/procedure—heart, including cardiac catheterization | 1.9 | 2.1 | 2.4 | 2.4 | 10.4 | -0.4 | 0.3 |

### Exhibit 2. Use of Physician Services in Fee-for-Service Medicare, for Selected Services, 1999-2002

| | Percent change in units of service per beneficiary | | Percent change in volume per beneficiary | | |
|---|---|---|---|---|---|
| Type of service | Average annual 1999-2001 | 2001-2002 | Average annual 1999-2001 | 2001-2002 | Percent of total volume |
| All services | 3.8% | 5.1% | 4.9% | 5.6% | 100.0% |
| Evaluation and management | | | | | |
| Office visit—established patient | 2.2 | 2.8 | 2.7 | 4.0 | 18.3 |
| Hospital visit—subsequent | 1.9 | 2.6 | 2.1 | 4.0 | 8.5 |
| Consultation | 4.6 | 4.2 | 5.8 | 6.0 | 5.9 |
| Emergency room visit | 4.1 | 2.8 | 6.9 | 6.6 | 2.7 |
| Hospital visit—initial | 0.3 | 1.1 | 0.4 | 1.8 | 2.2 |
| Office visit—new patient | 0.4 | 1.2 | 0.1 | 0.9 | 2.1 |
| Nursing home visit | -0.8 | 1.2 | 0.3 | 3.5 | 1.8 |
| Imaging | | | | | |
| Echography—heart | 9.2 | 9.8 | 11.0 | 13.1 | 2.0 |
| Standard—nuclear medicine | 14.7 | 12.1 | 18.0 | 17.1 | 1.9 |
| Advanced—CT: other | 14.5 | 13.8 | 16.4 | 16.5 | 1.8 |
| Advanced—MRI: other | 18.5 | 15.3 | 22.3 | 17.4 | 1.5 |
| Standard—musculoskeletal | 3.5 | 3.7 | 5.5 | 6.5 | 1.2 |
| Advanced—MRI: brain | 19.2 | 12.3 | 16.1 | 13.8 | 1.0 |
| Standard—chest | -0.4 | 1.9 | -1.1 | 1.2 | 0.8 |
| Advanced—CT: head | 5.6 | 5.6 | 4.9 | 5.3 | 0.4 |
| Imaging and procedure—heart, including cardiac catheterization | 6.9 | 3.2 | 8.8 | 6.4 | 0.3 |

under the physician fee schedule. We examined per-beneficiary growth in the volume and intensity, or complexity, of fee schedule services. Between 1999 and 2002, the per-beneficiary average annual growth rate in the use of fee schedule imaging services was twice as high as the growth rate for all fee schedule services (10.1% versus 5.2%) (See Exhibit 3). Use of the following types of imaging services increased by 15% to 20% per year: MRI of parts of the body other than the brain, nuclear medicine, computed tomography (CT) of parts of the body other than the head, and MRI of the brain.

**Exhibit 3. Use of Selected Physician Services Per Beneficiary in Fee-for-Service Medicare, 1999-2003**

| Type of service | Percent change in units of service per beneficiary: Average annual 1999–2002 | Percent change in units of service per beneficiary: 2002–2003 | Percent change in volume per beneficiary*: Average annual 1999–2002 | Percent change in volume per beneficiary*: 2002–2003 | Percent of total volume* |
|---|---|---|---|---|---|
| **All services** | **4.3%** | **3.6%** | **5.2%** | **4.9%** | **100.0%** |
| **Evaluation and management** | **2.3** | **2.2** | **3.4** | **3.9** | **42.1** |
| Office visit—established patient | 2.4 | 2.5 | 3.2 | 3.9 | 18.1 |
| Hospital visit—subsequent | 2.2 | 1.8 | 2.8 | 3.5 | 8.4 |
| Consultation | 4.5 | 3.3 | 5.9 | 5.0 | 5.9 |
| Emergency room visit | 3.7 | 1.9 | 6.8 | 4.8 | 2.7 |
| Hospital visit—initial | 0.6 | 1.3 | 0.9 | 2.1 | 2.1 |
| Office visit—new patient | 0.7 | –1.9 | 0.4 | –1.2 | 2.0 |
| Nursing home visit | –0.1 | 1.8 | 1.4 | 4.0 | 1.8 |
| **Imaging** | **5.4** | **4.2** | **10.1** | **8.6** | **14.8** |
| Echography—heart | 9.4 | 6.2 | 11.8 | 7.6 | 2.1 |
| Standard—nuclear medicine | 13.8 | 9.1 | 17.8 | 13.2 | 2.2 |
| Advanced—CT: other | 14.3 | 12.9 | 16.6 | 14.6 | 2.0 |
| Advanced—MRI: other | 17.4 | 15.9 | 19.5 | 16.5 | 1.6 |
| Standard—musculoskeletal | 3.6 | 3.6 | 5.9 | 4.5 | 1.3 |
| Advanced—MRI: brain | 16.9 | 8.0 | 15.5 | 8.6 | 1.0 |
| Standard—chest | 0.4 | 0.5 | –0.3 | 0.1 | 0.7 |
| Advanced—CT: head | 5.6 | 4.6 | 5.1 | 4.2 | 0.4 |
| Imaging/procedure—heart, including cardiac catheterization | 5.6 | 1.6 | 8.0 | 4.6 | 0.3 |

Between 2002 and 2003, the per-beneficiary growth rate for imaging services moderated to 8.6% but was still much higher than the growth rate of all fee schedule services (4.9%). Although imaging services paid under the fee schedule have been shifting from facilities, such as hospitals, to physician offices, about 80% of the increase in the volume and intensity of these services between 1999 and 2002 was unrelated to this shift in setting (MedPAC 2004a).

The secretary should improve Medicare's coding edits that detect unbundled diagnostic imaging services *and reduce the technical component payment for multiple imaging services performed on contiguous body parts. (Emphasis added)*

To reiterate, *one place valuation analysts are sure to find insight into future changes in Medicare reimbursement is in the annual MedPAC report released in March of each year.*

## The Medicare Conversion Factor

Valuation firms have work codes and rates per hour (unit of service) for their services. Similarly, healthcare providers have work codes (current procedural terminology,[4] or CPT, codes) for their services. The Medicare program and most health insurers pay for services included in Medicare Part B based upon a unit of service called a relative value unit, or RVU (see discussion later herein) assigned to services under the resource-based relative value scale (RBRVS). The rate per RVU from Medicare is known as the Medicare conversion factor.

The lack of growth in the Medicare conversion factor is separate and distinct from this foreseeable response to the enormous growth in imaging utilization and expenditures, which has risen from $36.69 in 1998 to $37.90 in 2007—a compound growth rate of virtually zero. For non-Medicare services, the compound rate of growth for the last 11 years based upon the Bureau of Labor Statistics' producer price index for physician services is 1.85%.

The Gordon growth model used in the discounted cash flow models of the two experts and the Judge assumed perpetual growth in cash flow to equity (3% for one the majority expert and 4% for the minority expert, the Judge choosing 4%). Cash flow to equity is revenue *less* expenses! There is no evidence in available industry data to suggest that a 4% perpetual growth rate could be sustained.

The recent history of the relationship between physician practice expenses and the physician producer price index demonstrates that practice expenses are rising much more rapidly than fees (Centers for Medicare & Medicaid Services, or CMS, data).

As the facts demonstrate, expenses were and are rising more rapidly than per unit costs. This is called an eroding profit margin. The only way to maintain an overall profit would be to do more services at a lower margin—*precisely* what the MedPAC analysis from 2003 forward indicated was happening and precisely what the government moved to put an end to in 2005!

Exhibit 4 shows the recent history of Medicare payments for an MRI scan of the chest (CPT code 71552), one of the most frequently performed MRI services. Note that the bottom drops out in 2007. No future increases could be expected to offset such a dramatic drop so as to generate a 4% terminal growth rate.

4 Copyrighted by the American Medical Association.

The decreases in another common MRI procedure were less dramatic, but nonetheless wholly inconsistent with a 4% terminal growth rate.

Exhibits 4 and 5 are the *per unit* of service payments only. They do *not* illustrate the effect of the implemented recommendation from MedPAC in its 2005 report that the *"payment for multiple imaging services performed on contiguous body parts"* be reduced, which had a dramatic effect on many MRI providers.[5]

**Exhibit 4. Medicare Payment for Chest MRI**

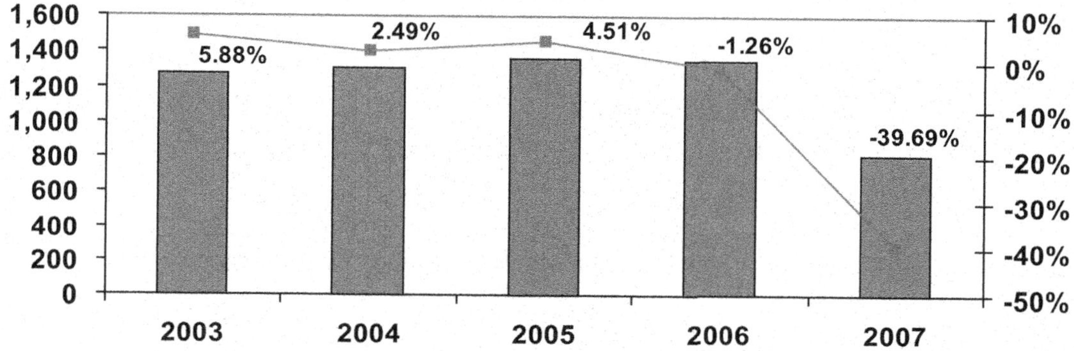


**Exhibit 5. Medicare Payment for Brain MRI**

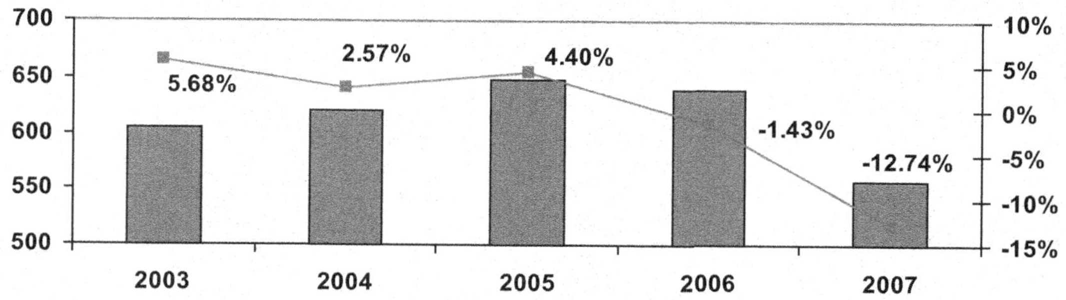


## Reduction in the Relative Value of MRI Services

As if this is not compelling enough evidence that explosive growth in service volume leads to forceful counter-measures, on June 29, 2006, CMS published in the *Federal Register* notice of a plan to revalue physician services under the resource-based relative value scale; the plan was adopted in August 2006. Less one think this only affects Medicare, many insurers follow Medicare's lead—particularly when it gives them an excuse to cut expenses. The changes followed closely on the heels of a suggestion by

5 Medicare estimated the cuts at 8% of revenue for the affected scanning procedures.

MedPAC in its March 2006 report that evaluation and management services (typically, face-to-face physician-patient encounters) had declined in value, in large part to the benefit of high-tech imaging services. The changes would cut radiology reimbursement 5% as of January 2007.

### A Quantitative Analysis of the Court's Excessive Terminal Growth Rate

Returning to the court's conclusion that the terminal growth in cash flow (profit) should be pegged at 4%, the following sort of quantitative analysis must have been missing from the experts' reports.

Exhibit 6 presents a "base case" scenario with no growth in volume of services. A "profit margin" of 44% (close to that determined by the court) is used in the illustration. Note that the compound growth rate in cash flow continues to decline at an ever increasing amount.

**Exhibit 6. 'Base Case' Scenario With No Growth in Volume of Services**

| Year | 0 | 1 | 2 | 3 | 4 | 5 |
|---|---|---|---|---|---|---|
| Revenue | $100 | $101 | $102 | $103 | $104 | 105 |
| Expense | 56 | 58 | 60 | 62 | 64 | 67 |
| Cash flow | 44 | 43 | 42 | 41 | 40 | 39 |
| Compound growth in cash flow | | -2.18% | -2.27% | -2.37% | -2.48% | -2.59% |
| Revenue growth | | 1.00% | 1.00% | 1.00% | 1.00% | 1.00% |
| Expense growth | | 3.50% | 3.50% | 3.50% | 3.50% | 3.50% |

Exhibit 7 presents what the growth in annual volume would have had to have been to maintain the constant 4% growth rate in cash flow through the fifth year as determined by the court. The key assumption is that total unit expenses grow as rapidly as the units provided. The lower the profit margin, the greater the annual growth in units of service to maintain the 4% cash flow growth rate. By Year 5, growth in units of service would have to be 7.26%. By Year 15, to maintain a constant growth rate of 4%, the units of service would have to grow more than 13% per annum—and that rate would *increase* in each subsequent year *into perpetuity*. Clearly, this is an unrealistic assumption that violates professional standards as well as common sense.

**Exhibit 7. Annual Volume With Constant 4% Growth Rate**

| Year | 0 | 1 | 2 | 3 | 4 | 5 |
|---|---|---|---|---|---|---|
| Revenue | $100 | $107 | $116 | $125 | $135 | $146 |
| Expense | 56 | 62 | 68 | 75 | 83 | 92 |
| Cash flow | 44 | 46 | 48 | 49 | 51 | 54 |
| Compound growth in cash flow | | 4.00% | 4.00% | 4.00% | 4.00% | 4.00% |
| | | | | | | |
| Revenue growth per unit | | 1.00% | 1.00% | 1.00% | 1.00% | 1.00% |
| Revenue growth units | | 6.32% | 6.52% | 6.74% | 6.99% | 7.26% |
| Expense growth per unit | | 3.50% | 3.50% | 3.50% | 3.50% | 3.50% |
| Expense growth units | | 6.32% | 6.52% | 6.74% | 6.99% | 7.26% |
| | | | | | | |
| Constant growth per court | | 4.00% | 4.00% | 4.00% | 4.00% | 4.00% |
| Target growth in cash flow | | 46 | 48 | 49 | 51 | 54 |

## The Broader Revenue Picture in the Healthcare Industry

*The cutback in imaging is not an isolated occurrence.* The same thing happened with outpatient physical, occupational, and speech therapy, on which Medicare has imposed an annual limitation per beneficiary of only $1,790 (with some limited exceptions). This was done to rein in explosive growth in the cost of outpatient physical therapy in particular, as noted in this quote from a Dec. 30, 2004 MedPAC letter to the vice president of the United States.

> **Amount of medically unnecessary PT services**
>
> The Office of Inspector General (OIG) of the Department of Health and Human Services examined the provision of outpatient physical and occupational therapy services provided in skilled nursing facilities (SNFs) and found considerable and widely varying shares of medically unnecessary services. One study found that from 5% to 26% of services was unnecessary, depending on the patient diagnosis. Another OIG study found that three-quarters of the contractors hired to review and process claims for payment commonly found medically unnecessary and excessive therapy claims. The services were medically unnecessary because:
>
> - the services were not skilled,
> - the treatment goals were too ambitious for the patient's condition, and
> - the frequency of the service provision was excessive given the patient's condition.

> The appropriateness of care provided at CORFs[6] and ORFs[7] has also prompted examination. In its study of ORFs, the OIG found that about 40% of the claims reviewed were for services that were not reasonable and medically necessary for the conditions of the patient. The Government Accountability Office (GAO) examined CORFs in Florida and found that on a per-patient basis, Florida CORFs' payments were two to three times higher than payments to other facility-based therapy providers and that the differences were not explained by patient characteristics, such as diagnosis. These studies indicate that unnecessary therapy is frequently provided and that the current requirements alone do not eliminate unnecessary service provision, even in settings supervised by physicians, such as SNFs and CORFs. The studies may also reflect low levels of physician oversight provided in some institutional settings. It is possible that unnecessary services are provided more frequently in settings where there even less physician supervision. Finally, the findings may illustrate a poor understanding of Medicare coverage by physicians and physical therapists.

Another recent case of significance in the healthcare valuation arena—*Caracci*—found the Fifth Circuit[8] throwing out the tax court's decision that a home healthcare agency that had never made a profit had an asset value well in excess of its liabilities. The tax court had acknowledged that the government was planning a changeover to a prospective payment system (PPS)[9] at the time the *Caracci* case arose, but rather than focusing on the income approach to value the taxpayer, the tax court used the IRS's expert's *market* approach, primarily based upon guideline public companies that were in dissimilar lines of business. The changeover to the PPS resulted in total Medicare spending on home health falling by 52% in two years! It is difficult indeed to see how a business losing money (i.e., expenses in excess of revenues) could make more money if revenues dropped by 52%.

There are numerous examples across all sectors of the healthcare industry to conclusively prove that the government and private insurers will move to defeat excessive utilization and cost. In the hospital sector, outlier payments for inpatient services—those where the patient's length of stay exceeded a defined limit for the underlying diagnosis-related group (DRG)—were a major cost problem for the government. In a June 29, 2006 press release, the Department of Justice Civil Division and U.S. Attorney for the Central District of California in Los Angeles announced that Tenet Healthcare Corporation, the nation's second largest hospital chain, had agreed to pay a fine of

6 Comprehensive outpatient rehabilitation facility.
7 Outpatient rehabilitation facility.
8 Correctly in the author's view.
9 Simply stated, a PPS establishes a standard fee schedule for services, rather than basing the fee on a retrospective settlement, such as one based upon the actual cost of providing those services.

more than $900 million for "alleged unlawful billing practices." "Of the $900 million settlement amount, the agreement requires Tenet to pay more than $788 million to resolve claims arising from Tenet's receipt of excessive "outlier" payments (payments that are intended to be limited to situations involving extraordinarily costly episodes of care) resulting from the hospitals' inflating their charges substantially in excess of any increase in the costs." A fine of nearly $250 million was levied against the University of Medicine and Dentistry in New Jersey for similar outlier issues—and that is a tax-exempt, state-owned institution.

## An Observation on the Industry Risk Premium

An analysis of *Ibbotson Stocks Bonds Bill and Inflation Industry Premia Company List Report for 2003* would indicate that the companies used in the determination of the industry risk premium are not comparable to an MRI operator. The Standard Industrial Classification (SIC) codes of some of these companies were likely assigned at a point in their history when they were engaged in some other line of business (see Exhibit 8).

**Exhibit 8. SIC Code 801**

| | |
|---|---|
| Amsurg Corp. | Surgery center operator |
| Coventry Health Care | Managed care products |
| Health Grades Inc. | Provides ratings of hospitals, physicians, etc. |
| Integramed America | National network of fertility/infertility clinics |
| Metropolitan Hlth Ntwrks Inc. | Provides healthcare benefits to Medicare Advantage members in Florida |
| Novamed Eyecare Inc. | Surgery center operator |
| Sight Resource Corp. | Manufactures, distributes, sells eyewear and related products |

An analysis of *Ibbotson Stocks Bonds Bill and Inflation Industry Premia Company List Report for 2004*[10] in SIC Code 807 would indicate that only three of the companies (Alliance, Primedex, and Miracor) used in the determination of the industry risk premium is arguably comparable to an MRI operator (see Exhibit 9). The betas of these stocks would have been a better indicator of industry risk.[11]

10 The only match for the -4.51% negative risk premium cited in the case is SIC 807 in Ibbotson's 2004 yearbook, which post-dates the merger-valuation date of January 2004.

11 An interesting exercise is to plot the prices of these stocks against the S&P 500 in this time period; they are quite volatile!

**Exhibit 9. SIC Code 807**

| | |
|---|---|
| Alliance Imaging Inc. | Medical diagnostic imaging |
| Array Biopharma Inc. | Biopharmaceutical company |
| Bio Imaging Technologies Inc. | Medical image management for clinical trials |
| Bio Reference Labs | Clinical laboratory in the greater New York |
| Enzo Biochem Inc. | R&D, MFR, biotechnology, and molecular biology |
| Labone Inc. | Medical laboratory operator (now part of Quest) |
| Laboratory Cp. of Amer. | Medical laboratory operator |
| Medcath Corp. | Cardiac hospital operator |
| Medtox Scientific Inc. | Specialty laboratory testing services |
| Miracor Diagnostics Inc. | Medical diagnostic imaging |
| National Dentex Corp. | Dental laboratory operator |
| Orchid Biosciences Inc. | DNA testing |
| Primedex Health Systems Inc. | (Now part of Radnet: diagnostic imaging services) |
| Psychemedics Corp. | Detection of abused substances |
| Quest Diagnostics Inc. | Medical laboratory operator |
| Sagemark Companies Ltd.* | Management and operation of PET imaging |
| Specialty Laboratories Inc. | Medical laboratory (now part of Ameripath) |
| *Unlike MRI, positron emission tomography (PET) was not covered by the Stark laws at this time (although it now is) giving it a much different cash flow profile. | |

Outside the community of healthcare appraisers, there seems to be an assumption that all providers are paid in a similar fashion. Nothing could be more factually inaccurate. This leads to such errors as the use of inappropriate and irrelevant comparables for obtaining betas and market transactions. Physicians, nonhospital-based imaging providers, such as Delaware Open MRI, podiatrists, and a host of others, for example, are paid from Medicare Care Part B using the RBRVS as described above. Hospitals are paid from Medicare Part A using a methodology based upon DRGs, which bundle hospital services based upon an expected length of stay for the patient's diagnosis. Home healthcare agencies are paid in yet another fashion, as are surgery centers and skilled nursing facilities. Most private health insurers follow a similar construct, but the rates of payments vary radically from state to state and even market areas within states.

Perhaps the most fundamental valuation mistake in the healthcare industry is failure to differentiate the risk of a small entity operating in a single state (Delaware) in a single line of business (MRI) with a few dominant health insurers[12] from the risk of large

12 See, e.g., Government Accounting Office *Private Health Insurance: Number and Market Share of Carriers in the Small Group Health Insurance Market.*

public entities operating in multiple states in multiple lines of business with multiple health insurers paying for the cost of services. Use of the industry risk premium in the buildup method compounds this typical error.

## Conclusions

As valuation experts, we can only fault the court if a) we do not provide adequate compelling evidence, b) legal counsel does a poor job on direct and cross-examination, or c) the court decides to ignore the evidence and rule on some other basis, the expert testimony notwithstanding. Like newspaper reporters trying to write stories on complex economic matters without adequate research, judges need lots of input in understandable terms that must be coupled with a desire and willingness to be educated when making decisions on healthcare valuation. Most of the traditional valuation rules fail in healthcare because of the substantive and repetitive interference by government regulators that make historical performance nothing more than yesterday's news.

A unit growth analysis is a critical part of the determination of the reasonableness of a perpetual growth rate for a healthcare entity. Due to the statutory construct of Medicare Part B reimbursement, providers drawing revenue from that program face fixed or declining per-unit revenue even as costs increase more rapidly than the generic rate of inflation. Entities limited to a single service line—such as *Delaware Open MRI*—have no ability to respond by expanding services, unlike large healthcare entities, which operate in multiple lines of business. Even those large entities face numerous problems, as witnessed by the fines levied against Tenet.

*This article first appeared in the Summer 2007 Edition of* Business Valuation Review. *Reprinted with permission.*

Chapter 17

# Critical Condition—A Coding Analysis for a Physician Practice Valuation

*By Mark O. Dietrich, CPA/ABV, and Frank Cohen, CMPA*

At the outset, we should emphasize that a coding analysis is not always feasible. In a number of circumstances, the data may not be available because of poor information systems or a refusal to provide the data. Depending upon the nature of the engagement, the analyst may want to consider the implications of the lack of availability or a refusal to supply data. That said, this article focuses on the significance of a coding analysis. Basic coding analysis is within the reach of the valuation analyst using the approaches and tools described herein.

## Established Patient Office Visits

The most commonly used codes in the Medicare database are the established patient office visits, which are designated 99211 through 99215. The codes are copyrighted by the American Medical Association (AMA). Of these five codes, 99212, 99213, and 99214 are the most frequently used; 99214 pays about 60% more than a 99213 and more than 220% of 99212. Clearly, incorrect or improper coding can dramatically affect the normalized revenues of a practice. For this reason alone, a coding analysis is critical.

In the last five years, there has been a steady, rightward shift of the historical bell curve coding pattern, with a decrease in 99212 codes and an increase in the 99214 codes. (See Exhibit 1.)

**Exhibit 1. Internal Medicine Coding**

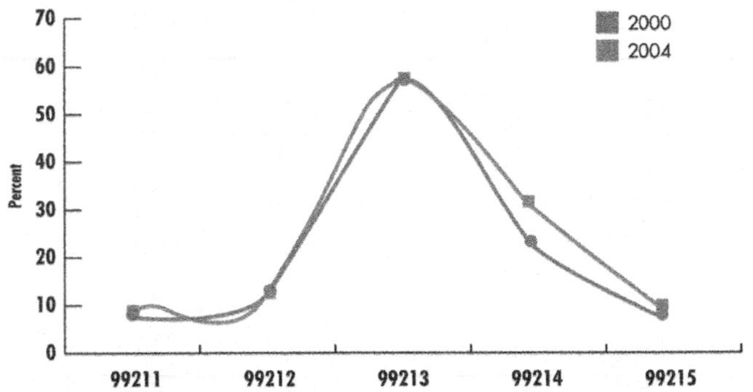


This shift has not gone unnoticed. The Department of Health and Human Services (DHHS), Office of Inspector General (OIG) produced Medicare fee for service (FFS) error rates from 1996 to 2002. This process, known as the comprehensive error rate testing (CERT) program revealed that payers were reimbursing practices erroneously for procedures that were not documented properly and did not meet medical necessity tests. A focus of this study has been a select group of procedure codes that have historically had very high levels of improper payment, the least of which has been the aforementioned code 99214. Medical reviews of 4,436 lines for the period between Jan. 1, 2004, and Dec. 31, 2004, disclosed that 648 lines, or 14.6%, were in error. Based on the application of these results, Centers for Medicare & Medicaid Services (CMS) estimates that improper payments of $234,489,004 were made to physicians for this code alone. For medical practices, this means that these codes are under greater scrutiny from payers and other outside investigative agencies.

Evaluation and management (EM) coding in particular is dependent on a series of guidelines that require the physician to consider 1,600 unique decision points during a typical patient visit. In determining the code to be assigned, there are two major players with respect to validating the use of the EM code, namely, documentation and medical necessity.

*Documentation* is simply the process of recording or writing down a detailed summary of the visit, including the chief complaint, past family and social history, results of the physical exam, and information that would indicate the level of complexity of decision-making during the examination. This process is analogous to the working papers of the valuation analyst or certified public accountant (CPA).

*Medical necessity* is a process used by Medicare and private payers to determine whether they should pay for goods or services billed by the physician. Medical necessity is defined as including that which is reasonable and necessary to diagnose or treat illness or injury or improve the function of a malformed body member. Medicare has a number of policies, including national coverage determinations (NCDs) and local medical review policy (LMRP), also known as local coverage determinations (LCDs), that outline what is and is not covered. In a small number of cases, Medicare may even determine whether a method of treating a patient should be covered on a case-by-case basis. Even if a service is accepted as reasonable and necessary, coverage may be limited if the service is provided more frequently than allowed under standard policies or standards of care.

In almost every case, these two tests dominate the decision to reimburse the provider for the procedure submitted on the claim. It is a complicated process because there is no effective relationship between documentation and medical necessity even though both medical necessity and documentation are tied to the procedure code. Submitting a claim for a service or procedure binds the practice to a highly complex and complicated series of laws, policies, rules, and regulations, any violation of which could result in substantial civil and criminal penalties.

## Other Examples

Many medical specialists, such as cardiologists, infectious disease specialists, and pulmonologists, earn a substantial amount of their income from consultations. A consultation is specifically defined as a request from another physician. The AMA's current procedural terminology defines a consultation as "a type of service provided by a physician whose opinion or advice regarding evaluation and management of a specific problem is requested by another physician or other appropriate source." There are four parts to a consultation, namely, a request for review and an opinion; the rendering of the opinion; the documentation in the patient's chart; and the report provided to the referring physician. A recent OIG study suggests that billions of dollars in improper consultations were being billed to Medicare, placing these procedures, along with established office visits and subsequent hospital visits, high on the OIG's hit list.

## Sources Of Data

Certain data can be downloaded from the CMS Web site, at www.cms.hhs.gov/PhysicianFeeSched/01_Overview.asp#TopOfPage.

Copies of the CERT report, updated definitional information on consults, the physician fee schedule database (PFSDB), and other files related to this article may be downloaded for free by going to www.cpahealth.com and clicking on the download tab.

## Identifying Problematic Coding

A major area of utilization analysis involves the use of the EM codes. This kind of analysis involves looking at the use of codes within specific categories and between specific categories and comparing the utilization of each category to the global use of EM codes. Performing a complete EM utilization analysis can be complex and time-consuming; however, it is the category that most frequently accounts for the resource utilization and financial revenue of the practice. The use of EM codes is under considerable scrutiny from outside reviewers and special attention should be paid to this area.

In the valuation practice of Mark Dietrich, one of the co-authors of this article, the top 50 code spreadsheets by specialty are used extensively to identify potential issues that warrant further inquiry. (See Exhibit 2.) These data are extracted from the Medicare master database and summarized by CPT code and frequency of use. A complete set of tables for all specialties can be purchased by contacting info@cpahealth.com.

**Exhibit 2. Ranking of Codes Within Top 50**

| Rank in Top 50 | CPT Code | Service Description | Count | Percent of Inpatient Consults |
|---|---|---|---|---|
| 7 | 99254 | Initial inpatient consult | 337,300 | 52.31% |
| 13 | 99255 | Initial inpatient consult | 204,283 | 31.68% |
| 21 | 99253 | Initial inpatient consult | 103,218 | 16.01% |
| | | | | 100.00% |

| Rank in Top 50 | CPT Code | Service Description | Count | Percent of Top 50 |
|---|---|---|---|---|
| 35 | 99291 | Critical care, first hour | 37,849 | 0.68% |
| 45 | 99238 | Hospital discharge day | 24,241 | 0.44% |
| 26 | 99262 | Followup inpatient consult | 61,413 | 1.11% |
| 34 | 99263 | Followup inpatient consult | 39,668 | 0.71% |
| 39 | 99223 | Initial hospital care | 26,367 | 0.48% |
| 7 | 99254 | Initial inpatient consult | 337,300 | 6.08% |
| 13 | 99255 | Initial inpatient consult | 204,283 | 3.68% |
| 21 | 99253 | Initial inpatient consult | 103,218 | 1.86% |
| 33 | 99312 | Nursing fac care, subsequent | 40,830 | 0.74% |
| 43 | 99311 | Nursing fac care, subsequent | 24,467 | 0.44% |
| 46 | 99244 | Office consultation | 22,299 | 0.40% |
| 6 | 99213 | Office/outpatient visit, established | 339,957 | 6.13% |
| 10 | 99214 | Office/outpatient visit, established | 247,192 | 4.45% |
| 24 | 99212 | Office/outpatient visit, established | 67,810 | 1.22% |
| 29 | 99215 | Office/outpatient visit, established | 49,383 | 0.89% |
| 31 | 99211 | Office/outpatient visit, established | 47,594 | 0.86% |
| 2 | 99232 | Subsequent hospital care | 2,367,869 | 42.67% |
| 3 | 99231 | Subsequent hospital care | 840,012 | 15.14% |
| 4 | 99233 | Subsequent hospital care | 704,910 | 12.70% |
| | | | 5,586,662 | 100.00% |

For example, the spreadsheet for infectious disease (ID) indicates that the most frequently billed consult code is 99254, initial inpatient consult, which is 52% of all inpatient consults. The most frequently billed code is 99232, subsequent hospital care. The ratio of all consultations (both office and hospital) to all patient visits is 12%.

Note that the remaining Top 50 services in this subspecialty represent injections or tests. In reviewing the coding of an infectious diseases (ID) practice as part of a valuation, the Medicare data can easily be compared to those of the practice.

Another benchmark is to statistically analyze the incidence of related procedures, such as office visits and outpatient consults. In performing this intercategory analysis, we could take the total number of outpatient consults (99241 to 99245) compared to the total volume of new office visits (99201 to 99205). For example, the ratio of office consults to new office visits for cardiology is 4.3-to-1, meaning that for every new patient office visit, the average cardiovascular (CV) doctor or cardiologist reports about four consults. In our example, let's say that, for the practice, the ratio was 2-to-1. This might indicate that the practice is shifting what should be consults to new office visits. These kinds of aberrant practices could result in financial and compliance problems.

For example, significant excessive numbers of consults, no matter how they are measured, can help frame the interview questions used to assess whether there is something particular to the practice. The interview of an ID doctor might take place as follows:

Analyst:

*Dr. Smith, I noted in my review of your coding data that the volume of office consultations you report is significantly higher than that of your peer group. I generally see physicians in your specialty seeing consults in the hospital. Can you tell me about the unique aspects of your practice that might explain the difference?*

Dr. Smith:

*Answer A: Since my office is here on campus, many patients simply come here rather than wait for me to see them in the hospital.*

*Answer B: You'll note that many of my patients have communicable diseases, and, in this area, I receive most of the referrals to confirm or rule out a particular diagnosis.*

*Answer C: I didn't realize there was a difference.*

*Answer D: When I see patients for the first time, I charge for a consult. It pays more than a new patient visit.*

### Analysis

Answer A would require the analyst to know whether a particular medical condition typically requires hospitalization before an ID consult. Answer B might be a perfectly acceptable answer if, for example, Dr. Smith practices in an inner city, where tuberculosis is often a public health problem. Answer D is a red flag and a tacit admission of incorrect coding. Obviously, Answer C is of no assistance to the analyst.

### Modifiers

The same sort of analysis applies to the use of modifiers. Over- or underuse of certain modifiers may raise a flag with carriers, payers, and other outside reviewing agencies. For example, if modifier 25 (used to describe *separate, distinctly identifiable* services from other services or procedures rendered during the same visit) is used at a level greater than 10% of a particular EM category, it may cause a carrier to perform a review of the practice's billing and coding patterns. These flags are most often the source of focused reviews and audits. Most recently, OIG published two separate reports, one on modifier 59 and one on modifier 25. According to the reports, violations in the way these codes are reported by providers resulted in hundreds of millions of dollars in inappropriate payments. These reports are also available at www.cpahealth.com by clicking on the download tab.

### Utilization of Tests

One process is the ranking of procedure codes within the practice compared to national averages. For example, we might rank the codes within our practice by frequency and dollar volume, and compare this result with the top 50 codes for that specific specialty based upon the national average. This analysis identifies areas in which there may be patterns of over- or underuse. A subset of this analysis is the utilization of tests in the physician's office, and many of the top 50 CPT codes consist of such tests. Some of this variation can be traced to the ancillary capabilities of the practice, such as whether it has a blood chemistry lab, X-ray, or other imaging technology. Comparisons between the practices with and without this equipment are not possible; therefore, it is important to ascertain the practice's capabilities before attempting a utilization analysis.

### Surgical Practices

For surgical practices, the utilization of procedure codes is more complex and can involve a number of different kinds of analysis, many of which are likely beyond the purview of the valuation analyst. However, certain simple analyses can rule out or identify common problems. It may also be helpful to identify the revenue potential associated with procedures that are not being provided by the practice but that are being performed or reported by other practices within the same specialty. In specialty practices, such as ophthalmology, physicians trained in the most recently developed surgical techniques may have greater earning power than the current practitioners, who are relying on less-advanced techniques.

Another utilization issue concerns the use and reporting of the post-operative code 99024. Medicare pays for all surgery on the basis of a global fee that includes *both* pre-operative and post-operative care. For example, a practice reports 5,250 global surgical procedures that have either a 10- or 90-day follow-up period. In performing a utilization analysis, it is found that they reported the 99024 code (surgical follow-up) 1,025 times. The resulting ratio of 0.195-to-1 indicates that only one in five surgical procedures was followed! This conclusion could raise troubling questions about the quality of care, as well as compliance and *the potential for reimbursement*. Even though the relevant codes are considered bundled codes for Medicare, it is important to ensure that all post-operative visits that fall within the global period, i.e., are recorded for reasons relating to the global procedure, and accurately documented as such. For each global surgical code, there is a preservice, intraservice, and post-service component that represents both the resource consumption and fee allocation for that procedure. For example, for procedure code 28190 (the removal of a foreign body from the foot), the preoperative portion is 10%, the surgical portion is 80%, and the post-operative portion is 10%. If adequate follow-up is not reported, the insurer could reduce the post-service payment portion (by 10%), indicating that the follow-up portion was not satisfied based upon the utilization statistics.

The use of global fees for surgery is a critical consideration in valuation or litigation. For example, assume a surgeon has left the group practice and the geographic area and is seeking additional compensation or other benefits. The group practice has the responsibility and lost revenue associated with providing post-operative care, including the repair of complications, for any patients of that departed surgeon. This must be considered in any damages calculation.

### Beware Changes in the Value of Codes

For example, in June 2006, CMS announced its intent to increase the relative values of EM services in 2007, following closely on the heels of a suggestion by MedPAC in its March 2006 report that these services had declined in value, in large part to the benefit of high-tech imaging services.

*The work component for RVUs [Relative Value Units] associated with an intermediate office visit [99213], the most commonly billed physician's service, will increase by 37%. The work component for RVUs for an office visit requiring moderately complex decisionmaking and for a hospital visit also requiring moderately complex decisionmaking will increase by 29% and 31%, respectively. Both of these services rank in the top 10 most frequently billed physicians' services out of more than 7,000 types of services paid under the physician fee schedule.*

The 99213 code presently has a fully implemented work RVU value of 0.67. Under this proposal, the value would rise to approximately 0.92 RVUs. With a conversion factor of $37.90, this would represent an increase in the fee of nearly $10, or 18%, to about $62.15 from the present level of $52.68 on the National Physician Fee Schedule.

Significantly, because of the budget-neutrality provisions of the existing Part B system, the increased cost associated with the increased RVUs has to come from a reduction in the value of other services and CMS proposes "to establish a budget-neutrality adjustor that would reduce all work RVUs by an estimated 10% to meet the budget-neutrality provisions." For example, CMS estimated that the proposed changes would increase reimbursement for internal medicine by 5% in 2007 while decreasing the reimbursement for radiologists by the same amount. The *Federal Register* notice contains the details of estimated changes for all specialties.

CMS is also proposing changes to the practice expense component of the RVUs to be phased in over four years through 2010, which will result in further revenue shifts.

## Conclusion

Valuation analysts are not coding consultants. Nevertheless, given regulatory issues and the impact of coding on the future cash flow being valued, it is necessary that analysts have some basic knowledge of the subject and conduct a basic review. Relatively simple processes can be implemented using readily available data from the Internet or vendors such as MIT Solutions Inc. (www.mitsi.org) to incorporate a basic assessment of coding into the valuation process. This results in a valuation conclusion that reflects the risk, if any, of unusual coding patterns and may identify potential lost revenues available to a hypothetical or other owner of the practice. In the latter instance, the analyst can bring additional value to the valuation.

*This article first appeared in the Fall 2006 Edition of* CPA Expert. *Reprinted with permission.*

Chapter 18

# Understanding and Using the Technical and Professional Component of Ancillary Revenue When Valuing Medical Practices

*By Mark O. Dietrich, CPA/ABV, and Kathie L. Wilson, CPA, CVA*

Valuing any business requires an understanding of how revenue is generated: what products or services are sold, how much revenue comes from each, competing products or services, and competing sellers. Valuing a medical practice is no different in that regard. It is important to understand that services sold by medical practices are commonly specified by current procedural terminology (CPT) codes and healthcare common coding procedure system (HCPCS or "Hickpicks") codes. For example, CPT code 99213 is a Level 3 office visit for an established patient. HCPCS codes can denote "products" such as certain injectible drugs or chemotherapy that are specified by J codes or services and procedures that are specified by G codes. The HCPCS codes are alphanumeric and start with a letter. For example, J0133 is the code for an acyclovir injection; G0202 is the code for screening mammography. Thus, considerable background is required by an appraiser to understand the revenue lines in the variety of medical practice specialties.

Many of the more common specialties require more expertise than simply being familiar with the codes for seeing patients in the office. Of particular note is the differentiation between the technical component and professional component of ancillary services for practices such as radiology, cardiology, neurology, and others. The technical component is paid in connection with ownership of equipment, provision of a technologist to operate the equipment, supplies, and general overhead. The professional component is paid to the physician specifically for interpreting the results of the test or study, e.g., an imaging study such as an X-ray or MRI. Revenue from the technical component, therefore, is related to the equipment investment of the practice, not the efforts of the physician.

This can be seen in the following quotes from the Centers for Medicare and Medicaid Services' Medicare Physician Fee Schedule 2010 Final Rule:[1]

> Services with technical components (TCs) and professional components (PCs). Diagnostic services are generally comprised of two components: a professional component (PC) and a technical component (TC), both of which may be performed independently or by different providers. When services have TCs, PCs, and global components that can be billed separately, the payment for the global component equals the sum of the payment for the TC and PC. This is a result of using a weighted average of the ratio of indirect to direct costs across all the specialties that furnish the global components, TCs, and PCs; that is, we apply the same weighted average indirect percentage factor to allocate indirect expenses to the global components, PCs, and TCs for a service. (The direct PE RVUs for the TC and PC sum to the global under the bottom-up methodology.)
>
> Modifier. A modifier is shown if there is a technical component (modifier TC) and a professional component (PC) (modifier -26) for the service. If there is a PC and a TC for the service, Addendum B contains three entries for the code. A code for: the global values (both professional and technical); modifier -26 (PC); and, modifier TC. The global service is not designated by a modifier, and physicians must bill using the code without a modifier if the physician furnishes both the PC and the TC of the service.

Within the relative value unit (RVU) allocations are components for physician work, practice expense, and malpractice insurance. As you might expect, the largest element in the TC is for practice expense, whereas the largest element in the PC is typically for physician work, known as wRVUs. In some circumstances, these can be important in measuring the productivity for reasonable compensation purposes as defined later herein.[2]

## Some Common Mistakes

Most appraisers determine reasonable compensation when valuing a medical practice by reference to the physician's (or physicians' aggregate) productivity benchmarked against statistical norms such as those from the Medical Group Management Association (MGMA). The definition of collected revenue in the MGMA data is with the technical

1 CMS-1413-FC.

2 Not all, or even many, practices track wRVUs, however.

component of ancillary services excluded! MGMA does have some data that include the technical component and nonphysician providers at two levels, greater than 10% or less than 10%, but that differentiation is generally not specific enough to be useful for reasonable compensation purposes.[3] Thus, to use the data appropriately, it is necessary for the appraiser to separate the revenues associated with the professional component (related to the efforts of the physician) from those of the ancillary or technical component (related to the equipment investment).

### Example

While valuing a four-physician neurology practice with a single owner, the appraiser notes that the owner has collected revenue credited to him of more than twice the 90th percentile of MGMA. Upon investigation of the practice's reports of productivity by CPT (including HCPCS) code and the list of fixed assets, he determines that the practice owns an MRI unit in addition to other ancillary equipment. The technical component of the MRI services representing approximately 85% of the global (or total) collected revenue has been credited to the owner-physician as well as the professional component. To determine the owner's productivity consistent with the MGMA definition, the technical component of the MRI and other ancillaries will have to be backed out. This has a dramatic effect on the reasonable compensation determination: After the appropriate modifications are made, the owner-physician's collections are only at the 75th percentile of MGMA. Failure to identify and appropriately adjust for the technical component collected revenue would have resulted in a dramatic understatement of the practice's value due to an overstatement of reasonable compensation for the services of the owner-physician.

### Jurisdictional Issues

Aside from the obvious effect on the reasonable compensation determination, the source of profit in a practice can be quite significant from a jurisdictional standpoint. For example, in marital dissolution valuation, many jurisdictions distinguish between personal goodwill and enterprise goodwill. In many circumstances, the revenue, profit, and value resulting from the technical component of ancillary services may be included in enterprise goodwill and therefore, considered marital property subject to division, again, because it is not related to the personal efforts of the physician, but to the investment in the equipment of the practice. In other circumstances, even the technical component element may be considered nondivisible if a noncompete agreement is required from the seller to maintain the related revenue and profit in the hands of

3 See the Rhode Island example later herein for an important exception.

a buyer. Absent a jurisdictional rule, that portion of the practice value connected to technical component revenue that would be present absent the seller is perhaps the clearest element of enterprise goodwill.

### Transactions

In the current transaction market, differentiating reasonable compensation along with enterprise and personal goodwill can be equally important. After a physician practice is acquired by a hospital, a number of employment settings are possible, including employment by the hospital, a hospital-controlled group practice, or the physician practice itself, if the hospital purchases the stock. The Stark laws have different permitted compensation rules depending on the nature of the employment setting, which can impact how profits from the technical component of ancillaries are handled. This should, in turn, influence precisely what is being valued and how reasonable compensation is determined.

One of the most important practice types from a valuation and transaction standpoint in the present market is cardiology. Cardiologists employ a variety of ancillary testing equipment including single photon emission computed tomography (SPECT),[4] used for myocardial perfusion, ultrasound (echocardiogram as distinct from an electrocardiogram, or EKG), coronary computed tomography angiogram, and cardiac MRI. Despite some fairly dramatic cuts for SPECT and other nuclear medicine in the 2010 Medicare Physician Fee Schedule, these practices remain attractive for the technical component of tests as well as for the highly profitable admissions they generate for hospitals.

### Example

CPT code 78465,[5] heart image (3rd) multiple, is a SPECT code for myocardial infusion and represented a staggering 10.3% ($2,072,176,147) of charges for cardiovascular physicians billing Medicare in 2007, the highest single code in terms of charges as well as frequency of billing. CPT code 78465 also represented 10.4% ($2,017,599,660) of charges in 2006 and 10.4% ($1,863,154,763) of charges in 2005. Exhibits 1 and 2 are taken from the indicated proposed and final rules and show the global, technical, and professional component breakdown by RVU.

---

4 Due to its ability to generate true three-dimensional images, it is gradually replacing traditional gamma (ray) cameras.

5 Codes are Copyright, American Medical Association. This code was "cross-walked," or changed to 78452 in the period between the 2010 proposed and final rules. This illustrates one more complication that emphasizes the import of understanding CPT codes.

**Exhibit 1. 2010 Final Rule**

| CPT[1]/ HCPCS | Mod | Status | Description | Physician Work RVUs[2,3,4] | Fully Implemented Non-Facility PE RVUs[2,4] | Year 2010 Transitional Non-Facility PE RVUs[2,4] | Fully Implemented Facility PE RVUs[2,4] | Year 2010 Transitional Facility PE RVUs[2,4] | Mal-Practice RVUs[2,4] | CPT[1]/ HCPCS |
|---|---|---|---|---|---|---|---|---|---|---|
| 78452 | | A | Ht muscle image spect, mult | 1.62 | 8.84 | 8.84 | NA | NA | 0.06 | XXX |
| 78452 | TC | A | Ht muscle image spect, mult | 0.00 | 8.32 | 8.32 | NA | NA | 0.01 | XXX |
| 78452 | 26 | A | Ht muscle image spect, mult | 1.62 | 0.52 | 0.52 | 0.52 | 0.52 | 0.05 | XXX |

**Exhibit 2. 2009 Final Rule**

| CPT[1]/ ICPCS | Mod | Status | Description | Physician Work RVUs[2] | Fully Implemented Non-Facility PE RVUs[2] | Year 2009 Transitional Non-Facility PE RVUs[2] | Fully Implemented Facility PE RVUs[2] | Year 2009 Transitional Facility PE RVUs[2] | Mal-Practice RVUs[2] | Global |
|---|---|---|---|---|---|---|---|---|---|---|
| 8465 | | A | Heart image (3d), multiple | 1.46 | 10.96 | 11.32 | NA | NA | 0.67 | XXX |
| 8465 | TC | A | Heart image (3d), multiple | 0.00 | 10.23 | 10.64 | NA | NA | 0.62 | XXX |
| 8465 | 26 | A | Heart image (3d), multiple | 1.46 | 0.73 | 0.68 | 0.73 | 0.68 | 0.05 | XXX |

Exhibit 3 is sample data from a cardiology group practice with numerous subspecialties (service codes in addition to those for SPECT also shown). Net revenue (expected collections) from SPECT nuclear medicine tests is $2.8 million. Assuming for the sake of illustration that all payors use an 85% TC and 15% PC split, nearly $2.4 million of net revenue has to be excluded from individual physician production to be comparable to MGMA data.

**Exhibit 3. Sample Data From a Cardiology Group Practice With Numerous Subspecialties**

| STRESS LAB (P-K counted once) | | UNITS | PERCENT | NET REVENUE | PERCENT |
|---|---|---|---|---|---|
| SPECT MYOCARDIAL PERF | 78465 | 1,353 | 5.82% | 1,488,000 | 24.00% |
| MYOCARDIAL PERFUSION | 78478 | 1,143 | 4.92% | 248,000 | 4.00% |
| MYOCARDIAL PERFUSION | 78480-78481 | 517 | 2.22% | 310,000 | 5.00% |
| MYOCARDIAL PERFUSION | 78483 | 860 | 3.70% | 744,000 | 12.00% |
| GENERATION AUTODATA-P | 78490 | 1,240 | 5.33% | 248,000 | 4.00% |
| INFUSION | 90765 | 559 | 2.40% | 248,000 | 4.00% |
| STRESS | 93015 | 1,488 | 6.40% | 372,000 | 6.00% |
| OTHER | | 4,960 | 21.33% | 248,000 | 4.00% |
| SUBTOTAL | | 12,119 | 52.12% | 3,906,000 | 63.00% |

In some practices the professional component and technical component may be billed separately either because of payor rules or because the practice, in fact, only provides one or the other. In this case, a modifier is used for billing and should appear in the billing system reports: "26" is the modifier used for the professional component only and "TC" is the modifier used for the technical component only. If the billing is global (has no modifier), it is necessary to separate the professional component and technical component. The accompanying checklist provides detail on how to accomplish this.

### Professional and Technical Component Analysis Checklist

1. What is the practice's specialty?

   Note: Certain specialties may include technical component revenue (neurology, cardiology), while other specialties (family practice, pediatrics) would probably not include technical component revenue.

2. Does the practice own ancillary equipment that has a technical component?

   Note: Look through the depreciation schedule for expensive pieces of equipment. Technical equipment purchases typically stand out from the routine office equipment and furnishings.

3. Identify expected technical component CPT codes for equipment identified in Step 2.

   Discuss with provider and billing staff. Inquire as to whether ancillary revenues are billed globally separately for professional and technical component, or both; this may be payor-specific.

   Some practices may bill globally for in-office ancillary services and professional only for hospital-based services when the hospital owns the equipment. This is common for cardiology practices where the physician may interpret the result of hospital-based stress tests, for example.

4. Request production data by provider and CPT code for your period of analysis. If available, request both charges and receipts by CPT code.

   Review services by CPT code; professional component only income is denoted with a "26"; technical component income is typically denoted with "TC," but other acronyms may be used. Global is typically not specified, but assumed by default if no modifier is present.

5. Calculate production, by provider, preferably using receipts, excluding technical component receipts

   Receipts are used because best MGMA data is based upon collections. Because payment rates are set by insurers, the amount a practice charges has little significance except to an uninsured patient or noncontracted insurer.

   For globally billed ancillary tests, it is necessary to separate out the professional component. Download the Medicare Physician Fee Schedule for the years the data related to, state, and region in which the practice is located. www.cms.hhs.gov/PhysicianFeeSched/PFSCSF/list.asp#TopOfPage

## Individual Market Idiosyncrasies

In some poorly reimbursed markets, it may, in fact, be necessary for the technical component income to supplement reasonable compensation for the physicians. For example,

For example, these are codes for certain imaging procedures from the Massachusetts Medicare fee schedule, with the modifier:

**Codes for Imaging Procedures From Massachusetts Medicare Fee Schedule**

| CPT Code | Modifier | Fee Nonfacility | Fee Facility | Percent |
|---|---|---|---|---|
| 70490 | | $309.59 | $309.59 | 100.0% |
| 70490 | 26 | 70.80 | 70.80 | 22.9 |
| 70490 | TC | 238.79 | 238.79 | 77.1 |
| 70491 | | 373.21 | 373.21 | 100.0 |
| 70491 | 26 | 76.19 | 76.19 | 20.4 |
| 70491 | TC | 297.02 | 297.02 | 79.6 |

Not all payors use the same split between professional and technical component, so make inquiries of the practice.

Consider alternative measures of productivity including wRVUs or collections including TC revenue depending upon data available from client.

For forecasting purposes, the values of CPT codes may change dramatically from year to year, particularly when ancillary testing is involved. You may want to look at the subsequent year's fee schedule, for example, if using 2009 data as a basis for forecasting 2010 results.

6. Compare calculated production to applicable statistical data to determine reasonable compensation.

   Subtract reasonable compensation from the practice's precompensation profit to determine cash flow to capital and equity.

   (Alternatively, add difference between actual compensation and reasonable compensation to the practice profit and loss.)

7. Isolate the cash flow attributable to the technical component production. Be sure to identify expenses associated with technical equipment.

   Note: Examples include billing and collection, technician wages and benefits, insurance, maintenance contracts, certifications, and so on.

8. Compare the cash flow profit in Step 7 to the practice's profit in Step 6.

   Consider Jurisdictional rules as to determination of personal and enterprise goodwill.

   E.g., if a noncompete agreement is nondivisible in a marital dissolution, calculate the impact on TC profit due to a noncompete.

Rhode Island is notorious for the low levels of fees paid to physicians. This is due in large part to the fact that two insurers control nearly all of the health insurance market in that state and rates are artificially low as a result. As such, to attract and retain physicians, many practices have profitable ancillaries in place. In such a circumstance, it may be necessary to test the reasonable compensation analysis against an alternative measure of production, such as compensation per RVU, wRVUs, or annual encounters. This is an example where the productivity data *including* technical component revenue may need to be evaluated as well.

## What Is 'Incident to' Billing?

Many medical practices increase revenue through the use of nonphysician providers (NPPs). These are employees who provide separately billable services to patients, but are not physicians. Physician assistants (PAs), nurse practitioners (NPs) and midwives are examples of NPPs.

Although they provide separately billable services, there are options for how to bill these services. The services can be billed directly and, because they are not physicians, the reimbursement for these services is a portion of the physician's fee schedule (Medicare sets the rate for many services at 85% of the rate for a physician; non-Medicare payors may have different rules). Another option is to bill the services as "incident to" the services of a physician. If the requirements for incident to billing are met, the services are billed under the physician's provider number and reimbursement is at the full physician's fee schedule. The physician is required to participate in the services provided by the NPP (e.g., supervision, chart review, physical presence in the office suite when the services are provided, among others), but the bulk of the effort is provided by the NPP.

This becomes an issue in valuation because, like the technical component billing, the productivity related to the nonphysician providers' services could be included in the physician's productivity. Without identifying and segregating the production unrelated to the efforts of the physician from the productivity related to the efforts of the physician, the valuation analyst can end up with an inconsistent reasonable compensation calculation.

In addition to understanding technical component revenue, understanding the use of nonphysician providers and the methodology for billing their services is important to developing reasoned valuation conclusions.

## Conclusion

Valuing medical practices requires an in-depth understanding of the individual practice and the healthcare industry. This article highlights just one aspect of a myriad of issues unique to medical practice valuation and the determination of reasonable compensation (see sidebar, What Is "Incident to" Billing?). The environment that physicians work in, dominated by the Medicare system, changes frequently. Some of these changes can be anticipated, such as the annual Medicare fee schedule modifications. Other changes are less predictable but can have a far greater impact, such as legislation. As any other highly regulated industry, it is critical that valuators remain current. The goal is always to have your valuation upheld, be it in court or in a settlement conference. Failure to understand the industry and its related terminology can undermine your authority as a valuation analyst and reduce the value of your opinion.

Chapter 19

# Identifying and Measuring Personal Goodwill in a Professional Practice:[1] *Part I—Basic Concepts*

*By Mark O. Dietrich, CPA/ABV*

In many situations, most notably valuation for marital dissolution and allocation of purchase price for tax or financial reporting purposes, distinguishing personal goodwill from enterprise goodwill is a critical undertaking.

In the marital arena, personal goodwill is not a divisible asset in some jurisdictions, and the status is uncertain in many and therefore, cannot be awarded by the court. Given this norm, it is curious that many valuation analysts fail to provide evidence as to the separate values of personal and enterprise goodwill.

In tax planning, particularly for C corporations, allocating the proceeds of a sale of a business to personal goodwill and a noncompete agreement can reduce or eliminate the amount recognized as corporate gain and the related corporate-level tax. In valuation for purposes of a sale of a business, properly attributing value to different intangible assets may be critical to both buyer and seller in obtaining the proper measure of the bargain.

There are two fundamental issues in differentiating personal from enterprise goodwill:

1. Identifying which portions of cash flow are attributable directly to the individual's characteristics; and

---

1 Copyright 2005 by AICPA, reproduced with permission. Opinions of the authors are their own and do not necessarily reflect policies of the AICPA.

2. Identifying which cash flows attributable to otherwise enterprise-level tangibles and intangibles would be lost if the individual competed.

### Illustrative Examples

1. Personal goodwill flowing from individual characteristics:
   - A physician at a renowned medical center is well-known for his skill in diagnosing complex diseases. His ability to do so is due to his intellectual skills, knowledge base, and experience in similar cases.
   - An attorney has won several high-profile cases because of her ability to relate to the jury and make complex issues understandable. In her current firm, she is also the principal "rainmaker."
2. Enterprise goodwill flowing from individual characteristics:
   - The same physician is part of a group practice. Subsequent to the diagnosis, other group physicians, some of whom are employed, may treat the patient. The employed physicians generate a profit in excess of their compensation that the practice owners share.
   - The same attorney has attracted dozens of new cases and is unable to handle most of them, which are assigned to other partners or members of the growing staff. The "points system" in the law firm allocates profits based in large part upon who generated the underlying business.

*Observation: The second set of examples is perhaps subject to some dispute in jurisdictions that treat personal goodwill as a nondivisible asset in marital dissolution. Some judges may treat any profit resulting from the personal goodwill of a marital litigant as nondivisible. For example, in a Florida appellate case (*Weinstock *v.* Weinstock 634 So. 2d at 777*), the court ruled that a dental practice had no divisible goodwill because the expert testified that a noncompete agreement would be required in any sale of the practice as well as the dentist's continued presence for a six-month patient transition period. Valuation analysts need to obtain a clear understanding from legal counsel as to the proper interpretation of state law or precedent.*

Personal goodwill, then, is the asset that generates cash profits of the enterprise that are attributed to the business generating characteristics of the individual, and may include any profits that would be lost if the individual were not present.[2] The value of a noncompete with that individual is the value of those cash profits, adjusted for the probability of the individual competing in each future year where the potential of competition exists. Thus, the noncompete is a portion of the value of personal goodwill and cannot exceed that value. Unless the probability of competition is 100%, the personal goodwill will always exceed the value of the noncompete.

### Enforceability of Noncompetes

How much is an unenforceable promise to pay worth? Or, better yet, how much will the hypothetical buyer pay for an unenforceable contract with a hypothetical seller? "Not much" would seem to be the answer. To illustrate the concepts involved in factoring enforceability into the value of a noncompete, the following section looks at the statutes and precedents of several states.

> *Observation: The enforceability of noncompetes is a volatile area of law. Courts in many states have moved to restrict enforceability when public policy is an issue, such as noncompetes that by their nature restrict the free access of a patient to his or her physician. Other states have liberally interpreted noncompetes, finding that separate consideration is not necessary.*

### Representative State: Texas

The Texas Business and Commercial Code §§15.50 provides that for a noncompete to be enforceable, it must be "ancillary to or part of an otherwise enforceable agreement at the time the agreement is made." If there is only an at-will employment relationship, the covenant is not enforceable. The term "at-will" appears to be interpreted as one in which the agreement has no specific term. If the relationship is other than at-will, the limitations of the covenant in time, scope, and geographic area must be no more than necessary to protect the goodwill of the employer or other entity.

Noncompetes among physicians are subject to a special set of provisions. To be enforceable, the agreement must conform to the statutory provisions, including not denying the physician access to a list of his or her patients whom he or she had seen or treated within one year of termination of the contract or employment and the covenant must provide for a buy out of the covenant by the physician at a reasonable price.

2 Subject to jurisdictional precedents.

Therefore, the value of the covenant must exclude the value of that patient list.[3] The provision in subparagraph (C) would appear to require that the covenantor receive an electronic copy of medical records if they are kept in that fashion. As a logical consequence, the enterprise value of a medical practice in Texas is different from an identical practice located in another state that has no limitations on the enforceability of a noncompete and does not require that the physician be given a patient list! When fair market value is the standard, hypothetical buyers and sellers must be assumed to be familiar with the law in the state in which the transaction takes place—as should valuation analysts.

### Representative State: Pennsylvania

It is likely that a November 2002 Pennsylvania Supreme Court decision has significantly altered the law as it applies to the transfer of a business, including employment contracts. The case, *Hess v. Gebhard & Co., Inc.*, involved the sale of an insurance agency. As an employee of the agency, Hess' employment contract contained a covenant not to compete within a 25-mile radius for a five-year post-employment term. Significantly, the contract contained no language regarding the transferability of the contract.

The related purchase and sale agreement allocated no value to the Hess employment contract. Hess did not continue employment with the purchaser[4] and sought a position with another insurance agency. In the process, Hess solicited a customer of his former agency. As a result of threatened legal action, the new agency did not hire Hess. Hess then sued for interference with contractual relations.

The Pennsylvania Supreme Court ultimately held that the noncompete was not transferable to a subsequent purchaser absent a specific transferability provision: "We hold that a restrictive covenant not to compete, contained in an employment agreement, is not assignable to the purchasing business entity, in the absence of a specific assignability provision, where the covenant is included in a sale of assets." Perhaps a different result would have been reached if a sale of stock had been at issue.[5] It seems that, in Pennsylvania at least, when valuing the assets of a business, the analyst should read any employment contracts to see whether the noncompete is transferable.

3 Always ask: Would the hypothetical buyer pay for something it already own?
4 He was not offered a position he was interested in.
5 And may I further add that this is but one dramatic difference between asset sales and stock sales, suggesting that a hypothetical buyer should pay a different price for assets than for stock.

> *Observation: Valuators should be aware that the various states might have one standard for enforcing covenants not to compete in an employment setting and another for enforcing a covenant in a purchase and sale of a business.*

## Reasonable Compensation

In the typical valuation of any professional practice or small business, the analyst's key assumption relates to reasonable compensation for services—there will not be any excess earnings to capitalize or any cash profit to discount if the professional does not earn more than "reasonable compensation." The higher the reasonable compensation relative to the total compensation earned, (of course) the lower the value of any goodwill.

Arguably, if there is no business or practice profit before normalization of the income statements, then some portion of the compensation earned must be coming from the return on tangible assets of the enterprise, namely net working capital and fixed assets. Later in this article, in the section titled "Mechanics of Valuation," we address the importance of this analysis. The analyst must understand not only how much compensation is earned, but also what the sources of that compensation are.

The other critical aspect of determining reasonable compensation is the work effort of the individual, typically referred to as "productivity." Many analysts determine reasonable compensation for their valuation models by taking the median or mean (average) compensation for a particular position, without considering the individual's productivity compared with the median or mean.

For example, the Medical Group Management Association (MGMA) data are commonly used for valuing physician practices. MGMA reports not only median and mean compensation, but also the 25th, 75th, and 90th percentiles of compensation. It reports the same percentiles for productivity, as to both charges and collections for professional services. The analyst should ask: "Can I hire a replacement physician for this practice at a median salary if the practice owner is producing at the 75th percentile?"[6] Given that most medical practices, as well as accounting and law practices, compensate their senior associates and partners at a percentage of production, the answer is almost surely *"no."* For those practices and businesses in which compensation is a function of piecework (patients seen, hours billed and collected, and so on), reasonable compensation must be a function of productivity.

6 Certainly, if one looks at tax court cases involving reasonable compensation, the court always focuses on hours worked, responsibilities, and so on. Why should it be any different in "regular" valuation engagements?

Proper compensation analysis is critical to the overall quest to value goodwill because an understatement of reasonable compensation will result in an overstatement of goodwill. To the extent that reasonable compensation is understated, the amount of personal goodwill included in total goodwill will be greater. Alternatively stated, some portion of the personal goodwill issue can often be minimized by properly addressing reasonable compensation.

### Categories of Intangibles

Perhaps the most easily identified discreet intangible in a professional practice is the value of a trained workforce, or workforce-in-place. This asset is also one of the easiest to measure, typically being based upon a percentage of payroll reflecting longevity and skill, along with training and recruiting costs.[7] An initial analysis should be considered to determine whether the practice-owners can leverage junior or support staff, such as associates (as in a law firm) and staff (as in an accounting firm). For example, one of the reasons dental practices are readily saleable and at significant prices is that they afford the owner an opportunity to profit from providing cleaning (prophylaxis) through hygienists. Workforce-in-place should thus be divided into two components: one for direct revenue producers, such as dental hygienists or staff accountants, and another for support personnel, such as medical assistants, secretaries, and the like. Direct revenue producers can be valued similar to any other intangible using their associated profit stream, while support personnel can be valued in the conventional manner, based upon costs of recruiting and training, as a percentage of payroll.

### A Simplified Example[8]

The analyst determines that $45,000 of annual free cash flow is derived from profits on nonpartner professional staff who are direct revenue producers and that this profit stream will continue to grow at a constant rate.

| | |
|---|---|
| Free cash flow from direct revenue producers | 45,000 |
| Cap rate from weighted average cost of capital | 16.17% |
| Value | 278,336 |

Often missed in the analysis of personal goodwill is the potential impact of the presence or lack of a nonsolicitation provision. Such a provision would preclude the signer from seeking to employ the practice's personnel after terminating. As such, a portion

7 See, for example, "Financial Valuation," Hitchner, et al.; Medical Practice Valuation Guidebook, Mark O. Dietrich.

8 I use capitalization of cash flows here assuming the profit stream qualifies for capitalization.

of the value of workforce-in-place can be attributable to the noncompete if it contains a nonsolicitation provision and the analyst believes that certain employees would leave if the covenantor were no longer with the business. This could result from the covenantor operating a competing business or simply no longer being associated with the sold enterprise. A standard purchase and sales document would typically contain both a noncompete and a nonsolicitation provision. Nonsolicitation provisions may also apply to the business's clients, patients, and customers.

## Mechanics of Valuation

It is critical that the analyst consider the three principal categories of assets included in business enterprise value (BEV) when assessing the profits attributable to the seller: net working capital (NWC), fixed assets, and intangible assets. Just as the right-hand side of the BEV equation has a rate of return or discount rate for each of equity and debt, the left-hand side has a return on each of the assets. It does not seem reasonable for the return on NWC or fixed assets to be attributed in its entirety to a seller and therefore, the noncompete.

Once the BEV is known, it is typically possible to calculate the value of NWC using the historical balance sheets; certainly, if a discounted cash flow (DCF) is used, the working capital requirement needs to be estimated. Fixed assets can be valued by an appraisal. Once these two values are known, they are subtracted from the BEV to determine the aggregate value of the intangibles.

Constructing a noncompete DCF is best accomplished after estimating the value of each of the asset categories; it may also require calculating the value of certain individual components for each category, such as the workforce-in-place described above. This assists the analyst in gauging a reasonable total value for the noncompete. The analyst should also consider whether any portion of the value of fixed assets or working capital is attributable to the covenantor.

One approach to making this determination is to differentiate between the going concern value of these two categories of assets—which requires, to one degree or another, the continued presence or forbearance of the seller—and their liquidation or other value. For example, fixed assets are likely to have a significantly greater value in use as part of a going concern than as an assemblage not in a going concern or in liquidation. In liquidation, a buyer will not pay for the in-use value and is likely to consider the cost to transport and a markup to resell. The value of working capital may or may not be different in a going concern context depending upon the collectibility of receivables, for example.

Estimating that value may also require establishing a discount rate for each asset and allocating the cash flow based upon the discount rate.[9] The weighted average of those discount rates must, of course, be equal to the weighted average cost of capital (WACC) determined from the right-hand side of the BEV equation. Therefore, the analyst must also consider the portion of the value of each category that would be financed with debt.

*Observation: Notwithstanding the disdain with which some in the valuation community regard the excess earnings method, it is the classic example of a left-hand side of the equation approach to capitalization rates, and, by adding the appropriate long-term growth rate, deriving discount rates. Unfortunately, users of the method rarely calculate the capitalization rate derived by weighting the respective returns on tangibles and intangibles and comparing it to the traditional WACC approach for reasonableness.*

Note: *The weighted average cap rate based on assets should then be used in the capitalization of cash flows method.*

Exhibit 1 shows the result of a DCF valuation along with an allocation of fair market to the three major categories of assets and their percentage of total BEV.

Exhibit 2 is the calculation of the WACC used in the DCF model; note that the WACC is based upon the fair market value of debt and equity, not book values.

**Exhibit 1. Result of DCF Valuation**

| | Value | % of Value |
|---|---|---|
| Fixed assets | $975,000 | 34.97% |
| Net working capital | 1,064,217 | 38.17 |
| Intangible value | 749,141 | 26.87 |
| | 2,788,358 | 100.00 |

**Exhibit 2. Calculation of WACC**

| | Weight | Capital | Discount rate | WACC |
|---|---|---|---|---|
| Debt | 25% | $697,089 | 3.54% | 0.89% |
| Equity | 75 | 2,091,268 | 23.71 | 17.78 |
| | | 2,788,358 | | 18.67 |

9 This process is described in Financial Valuation as well as Valuation for Financial Reporting, Mark, Hitchner, Hyden, Zyla.

Exhibit 3 is the computation of the WACC, based on returns for the individual categories of assets. Fixed assets are financed with 50% debt (the pretax rate is 6%, the after-tax rate is 3.54%, using a 41% tax rate) and 50% equity; net working capital is financed with the remainder of the debt and the balance with equity. Intangible assets are financed entirely with equity.

**Exhibit 3. Computation of WACC**

| Category (Cat) | Value | % | Debt | Cost of Debt | Equity | Cost of Equity | Cat WACC | Return | Total WACC |
|---|---|---|---|---|---|---|---|---|---|
| Fixed assets | $975,000 | 34.97% | $487,500 | 3.54% | $487,500 | 17.25% | 10.40% | $101,351 | 3.63% |
| Net working capital | 1,064,217 | 38.17 | 209,589 | 3.54% | 854,628 | 17.50 | 14.75 | 156,979 | 5.63 |
| Intangible Value | 749,141 | 26.87 | | | 749,141 | 35.00 | 35.00 | 262,199 | 9.40 |
| | 2,788,358 | 100.00% | 697,089 | | 2,091,268 | | | 520,530 | 18.67 |

The analyst determines equity returns for each asset category. The aggregate weighting should agree with the WACC used in the original DCF.[10] The appropriate discount rates will vary from industry to industry and subject to subject. Bear in mind that intangible assets are generally the most risky and therefore, have the highest expected rates of return.

Exhibit 4 is a condensed version of the DCF from which the Exhibit 4 values are determined.[11] The analyst has concluded that a net of 55% of the free cash flow is attributable to the seller and would be lost to the buyer in the event of competition.[12] This is approximately equal to that percentage of the total return represented by the intangibles as reflected in Exhibit 4. This does not suggest, however, that only intangible value is relevant to the determination of cash flows attributable to the seller, since some of the workforce-in-place value might not be lost in the event of competition and some of the fixed asset value might be lost. For example, if the valuation subject was a medical practice using equipment for diagnostic testing, the departure of a physician might lower

10 This is easier said than done using a DCF and individual WACCs for each asset category because discount rates (WACCs) are different for each category and there is not a linear relationship between discount rates and present value; the solution can only be found iteratively. It is comparatively easy to do using capitalization rates since the cash flow is fixed in the first period.

11 Note that the free cash flow in any year is not equal to the "return" shown in Exhibit 4. As noted earlier, an iterative process is required in the actual reconciliation of the individual WACCs with the entity WACC, in part because year-to-year cash flows are, in fact, variable, as shown in Exhibit 5.

12 As more fully explained in the original article, there may be a difference between the gross profits attributable to the sellers and what profits the buyer would lose if the sellers competed. This gives recognition to such intangibles as location.

the volume of tests and therefore, the value in use of the equipment.[13] The analyst can also utilize these allocated cash flows to assess the reasonableness of the annual cash payment for a noncompete.

**Exhibit 4. Discounted Cash Flow**

| Year | | 1 | 2 | 3 | 4 | 5 | Terminal |
|---|---|---|---|---|---|---|---|
| Base valuation | | | | | | | |
| Free cash flow | $3,002,869 | $489,819 | $552,804 | $580,024 | $577,724 | $450,838 | $351,660 |
| Present value | 2,788,358 | 449,645 | 427,635 | 378,109 | 317,365 | 208,702 | 1,006,901 |
| Gross % attributed to seller | | 50.00% | 50.00% | 50.00% | 50.00% | 50.00% | 50.00% |
| Attributed to seller | 1,394,179 | 224,822 | 213,818 | 189,054 | 158,683 | 104,351 | 503,451 |
| Net % attributed to sellers | | 55.00% | 55.00% | 55.00% | 55.00% | 55.00% | 55.00% |
| PV sellers free cash flow | 766,798 | 123,652 | 117,600 | 103,980 | 87,275 | 57,393 | 276,898 |

Exhibits 5, 6, and 7 show the calculation of the probability-adjusted lost cash profits assuming that competition begins in Year 1 (Exhibit 5), Year 2 (Exhibit 6), and Year 3 (Exhibit 7). In this example, if competition does not commence before the end of Year 3, it is assumed never to commence.

**Exhibit 5. Competition Begins in Year 1**

| Year | 1 | 2 | 3 | 4 | 5 | Terminal |
|---|---|---|---|---|---|---|
| PV net profits attributed to sellers | $224,822 | $213,818 | $189,054 | $158,683 | $104,351 | $503,451 |
| Net % attributed to seller | 55% | 55% | 55% | 55% | 55% | 55% |
| Net profit attributed to seller | $123,652 | $117,600 | $103,980 | $87,275 | $57,393 | $276,898 |
| Probability of competing | 10% | 10% | 10% | 10% | 10% | 10% |
| PV of lost profits by year | $12,365 | $11,760 | $10,398 | $8,728 | $5,739 | $27,690 |
| PV of Year 1 lost profits | **$76,680** | | | | | |

13 The analyst could isolate the profit on the equipment and determine that profit's present value.

**Exhibit 6. Competition Begins in Year 2**

| Year | 1 | 2 | 3 | 4 | 5 | Terminal |
|---|---|---|---|---|---|---|
| PV net profits attributed to sellers | | $213,818 | $189,054 | $158,683 | $104,351 | $503,451 |
| Net % attributed to seller | | 55% | 55% | 55% | 55% | 55% |
| Net profit attributed to seller | | $117,600 | $103,980 | $87,275 | $57,393 | $276,898 |
| Probability of competing | | 18% | 18% | 18% | 18% | 18% |
| PV of lost profits | | **$21,168** | **$18,716** | **$15,710** | **$10,331** | **$49,842** |
| PV of Year 2 lost profits | **$115,766** | | | | | |

**Exhibit 7. Competition Begins in Year 3**

| Year | 1 | 2 | 3 | 4 | 5 | Terminal |
|---|---|---|---|---|---|---|
| PV net profits attributed to sellers | | | $189,054 | $158,683 | $104,351 | $503,451 |
| Net % attributed to seller | | | 55% | 55% | 55% | 55% |
| Net profit attributed to seller | | | $103,980 | $87,275 | $57,393 | $276,898 |
| Probability of competing | | | 21.6% | 21.6% | 21.6% | 21.6% |
| PV of lost profits | | | **$22,460** | **$18,851** | **$12,397** | **$59,810** |
| PV of Year 3 lost profits | **$113,518** | | | | | |
| | | | | | | |
| Total: **$305,964** | | | | | | |

At first glance, Exhibit 5, 6, and 7 may appear to count the same cash flows multiple times.[14] The way to be certain that there is no double counting is to check the joint probability table (see Exhibit 8). The probability of possible outcomes must total exactly 100%. For example, adding the probability-adjusted present value of lost profits for Year 3 from Exhibit 5, 6, and 7 totals $51,574, less than the total present value of Year 3's profits attributable to the sellers of $103,980. Assuming the rest of the model is properly constructed, the probability check assures that there is no double counting.[15]

If the probability of competing were 100% at the beginning of Year 1, the value of the noncompete (see Exhibit 4) would be $766,798, slightly more than the total intangible value. This value could be compared to the value of workforce-in-place and any other discretely measured intangibles while considering the probability that the sellers would

14 As noted by one reviewer, thereby prompting this explanation.

15 The second test, as discussed in the following paragraph, is to determine the value of the noncompete if the probability of competition is 100%; any probability less than 100% in Year 1 should result in a lower value for the noncompete.

take some portion of the value of those intangibles with them if they competed, as well as any diminution in the value in use of fixed assets. The $766,798 represents all of the present value of future profits attributable to the seller and is therefore also the value of personal goodwill.[16]

**Exhibit 8. Joint Probability**

| | Year 1 | | Year 2 | | Year 3 | | |
|---|---|---|---|---|---|---|---|
| | Compete | Don't Compete | Compete | Don't Compete | Compete | Don't Compete | Joint Probability |
| Compete Year 1 | 10% | | | | | | 10.0% |
| Compete Year 2 | | 90% | 20% | | | | 18.0 |
| Compete Year 3 | | 90 | | 80% | 30% | | 21.6 |
| Never compete | | 90 | | 80 | | 70% | 50.4 |
| | | | | | | | 100.0 |

The distinction between the value of personal goodwill and the value of a noncompete is less important in equitable distribution than for tax purposes. For the latter, the noncompete is ordinary income to the covenantor, while personal goodwill should be long-term capital gain.[17] It is prudent for the analyst to value both the noncompete and the personal goodwill when tax considerations are important.

In the following article, a single period capitalization model is explained and the author summarizes the key tasks for the valuation analyst.

The author expresses his gratitude to Kevin R. Yeanoplos, CPA/ABV, ASA, for his thoughtful critique of the concepts explored in this article, as well as for his corrections to my use of English language grammar.

16 I caution that the example has personal goodwill in excess of total intangible value. I do not mean to imply or suggest that this is, or is not, the norm or that the analyst should not carefully note the implications.

17 With respect to tax issues, see, e.g., Martin Ice Cream 110 TC 189 (1998) and *Norwalk v. Commissioner* TC Memo 1998-279. The full-text court opinion of Martin is included online.

## Chapter 20

# Identifying and Measuring Personal Goodwill in a Professional Practice: *Part II—Using the Single Period Capitalization Model*[1]

*By Mark O. Dietrich, CPA/ABV*

As noted in the footnotes to the discounted cash flow (DCF) model used in Part I of this article, it is very difficult to devise a weighted average cost of capital (WACC) for each asset category, allocate the cash flow to each category, and get a net present value that agrees to the enterprise-level cash flow discounted to present value. Although a single-period capitalization model is not appropriate for those circumstances in which the future growth rate is not the same for all years, it is much easier to use and understand.

In this example, which might be representative of an approach in many jurisdictions for marital dissolution purposes, the data in Exhibit 1 were used.

The WACC cap rate[2] is based upon the fair market value (FMV) of the business enterprise. From the right-hand side of the balance sheet—debt and equity—the weighted average cap rate is based upon $30,000 of debt costing 4%, net of growth at 2.5%, with the balance of the capital structure consisting of equity. From the left-hand side of the balance sheet, the weighted average cap rate is based upon the pretax cap rates applicable to tangibles and intangibles. The result must be the same in both cases.

1 Copyright 2005 by AICPA, reproduced with permission. Opinions of the authors are their own and do not necessarily reflect policies of the AICPA.

2 Technically, it is the capitalization rate derived from the WACC, the latter being the discount rate.

**Exhibit 1. Calculation of WACC Cap Rate**

| | WACC | Equity Only |
|---|---|---|
| Discount rate | 41.86% | 49.04% |
| Growth rate | 2.50 | 2.50% |
| Capitalization rate | **39.36** | **46.54** |

| | | FMV | Percent | Return | Weighted |
|---|---|---|---|---|---|
| Debt | 4.00% | $30,000 | 24.49% | 0.98% | |
| Equity | 46.54 | 92,500 | 75.51 | 35.14 | |
| Cap rate: tangibles | | **122,500** | **100.00** | **36.12** | |
| | | | | | |
| Practice intangibles | | $55,341 | 31.12% | 46.54% | 14.48% |
| Practice tangibles | | 122,500 | 68.88 | 36.12 | 24.88 |
| Cap rate—weighted average cost of capital | | **177,841** | **100.00** | | **39.36** |
| | | | | | |
| Debt | | $30,000 | 16.87% | 4.00% | 0.67% |
| Equity | | 147,841 | 83.13 | 46.54 | 38.69 |

The capitalization of cash flows method reflects all pretax cash earnings in excess of reasonable compensation capitalized at the cap rate derived from the WACC of 39.36%. The excess earnings method capitalizes excess earnings on tangibles at the rates of return applicable to the portion financed with debt, $30,000, and the portion financed with equity, $92,500. These may be based upon the actual balance sheet of the valuation subject or upon optimal mix of debt and equity, depending upon the analyst's assessment. (See Exhibit 2.)

**Exhibit 2. Capitalization of Cash Flows**

| | |
|---|---|
| Normalized 2002 earnings | $460,000 |
| Fair market earnings | $390,000 |
| Cash flow after reasonable compensation | $70,000 |
| Capitalization rate | 39.36% |
| Business enterprise value | $177,841 |

Note that the two methods produce exactly the same value. If used correctly, the WACC cap rate derived from either the left- or right-hand side of the balance sheet when applied to all enterprise cash flows will yield the same value as the excess earnings method, which splits those cash flows into two components. (See Exhibit 3.)

**Exhibit 3. Capitalization of Excess Earnings**

| | | | |
|---|---|---|---|
| Normalized 2002 earnings | | | $460,000 |
| Fair market earnings | | | 390,000 |
| Excess earnings | | | 70,000 |
| Return on practice tangible value: debt capital | $30,000 | 4.00% | (1,200) |
| Return on practice tangible value: equity capital | 92,500 | 46.54 | (43,046) |
| | 122,500 | | |
| Excess earnings attributable to intangibles | | | 25,754 |
| Capitalization rate | | | 46.54% |
| Practice intangible value | | | 55,341 |
| Practice tangibles | | | 122,500 |
| Business enterprise value | | | 177,841 |

The excess earnings grow at a constant rate of 2.5% into perpetuity. Exhibit 4 values the noncompete assuming that the probability of competition is 100%, as it may be in many valuations for marital dissolution purposes. The base valuation reflects a DCF model with a uniform growth rate of 2.5%. Note that this DCF produces exactly the same value as the capitalization of cash flows and capitalization of excess earnings method.[3]

The section of Exhibit 4 titled "Noncompete Valuation—Using WACC" values the cash flows attributable to the seller using the WACC of 41.86%. This is less than the cost of equity, of 49.04%, and therefore, results in a higher value. Use of the WACC would be appropriate if the analyst concludes that the cash flows attributable to the seller are a uniform blend of enterprise-level cash flows from both tangibles and intangibles. The section of Exhibit 4 titled "Noncompete Valuation–Using Equity Discount Rate" values the cash flows attributable to the seller using the equity discount rate of 49.04% and results in a lower value. This would be appropriate if the analyst concludes that the cash flows attributable to the seller are limited to those associated with intangibles. The value is identical to the value of intangibles previously determined. This is due to the probability of competition being 100%.

### Probability of Competition

In addition to the factors discussed in the first part of this article, the analyst should consider how the noncompete is paid for. Payments are often made annually over the period of time that the covenant is in place as part of the inducement to the covenantor not to compete. Such a payment structure is likely to reduce the probability of competition.

3 Using end-of-period cash flows. It will not produce the same result if the midperiod convention is used, since that convention results in a higher value.

**Exhibit 4. Valuation of Noncompete**

| | | 1 | 2 | 3 | 4 | 5 | Terminal |
|---|---|---|---|---|---|---|---|
| **Base valuation, constant growth** | | | | | | | |
| Free cash flow | | $70,000 | $71,750 | $73,544 | $75,382 | $77,267 | $201,210 |
| Present value | $177,841 | $49,344 | $35,653 | $25,761 | $18,613 | $13,449 | $35,021 |
| **Noncompete valuation—using WACC** | | | | | | | |
| % profits attributed to seller | | 36.79% | 36.79% | 36.79% | 36.79% | 36.79% | 36.79% |
| Free cash flow | | $25,754 | $26,397 | $27,057 | $27,734 | $28,427 | $74,027 |
| PV sellers free cash flow | $65,429 | $18,154 | $13,117 | $9,478 | $6,848 | $4,948 | $12,885 |
| Probability of competing | | 100.00% | 100.00% | 100.00% | 100.00% | 100.00% | 100.00% |
| Present value | $65,429 | $18,154 | $13,117 | $9,478 | $6,848 | $4,948 | $12,885 |
| **Noncompete valuation—using equity discount rate** | | | | | | | |
| Free cash flow—sellers | | $25,754 | $26,397 | $27,057 | $27,734 | $28,427 | $62,613 |
| PV sellers free cash flow | $55,341 | $17,280 | $11,884 | $8,173 | $5,621 | $3,866 | $8,515 |
| Probability of competing | | 100.00% | 100.00% | 100.00% | 100.00% | 100.00% | 100.00% |
| Present value | $55,341 | $17,280 | $11,884 | $8,173 | $5,621 | $3,866 | $8,515 |

## Key Conclusions

Personal goodwill is the asset that generates cash profits of the enterprise that are attributed to the business generating characteristics of the individual and may include any profits that would be lost if the individual was not present.

Tasks for the analyst:

- Identify which portions of cash flow are attributable directly to the individual's characteristics and which cash flows attributable to otherwise enterprise-level intangibles would be lost if the individual competed.
- Have a clear understanding from legal counsel of the proper interpretation of state law or precedent as to the value of a noncompete—and, therefore, the business itself. An unenforceable contract has little if any value. Even enforceable agreements are subject to "the hazards of litigation."[4] Similarly, the analyst should read all contracts between the valuation subject and its employees or others that may have a bearing on who owns what and obtain clarification from counsel as appropriate.

4 A term of art used to explain why unwinnable cases are won and unlosable cases are lost.

- Conduct a proper reasonable compensation analysis because an understatement of reasonable compensation will result in an overstatement of goodwill.
- Estimate the fair market value of the three principal categories of assets included in BEV: NWC, fixed assets, and intangible assets.
- Consider the need to value individual intangible assets, such as workforce in place. Recognize that a portion of the value of the workforce in place could be attributable to the noncompete if the agreement contains a nonsolicitation provision.
- Construct a joint probability table to be certain that the sum of the probability of competing and not competing is exactly 100%.

Chapter 21

# Valuation Solutions for Special Situations With Medical Practices

*By Mark O. Dietrich, CPA/ABV*

## SECTION I: PRACTICE BUY-INS, BUYOUTS, AND MERGERS

One of the most common situations confronting a physician practice is the need to assign equity interests in a practice buy-in or merger. As the healthcare market experiences renewed consolidation, those practices that choose not to sell to hospitals or other buyers will invariably choose to merge into larger entities or expand through the addition of new owners via buy-ins. Many specialists, rarely afforded the opportunity of a hospital purchase, look to merging to maintain their competitive position in an era dominated by a focus on primary care. Many of these mergers do not involve the payment of cash by one of the merging parties to the other but accurately measuring the value of the merging units rationally is important in the allocation of equity. This segment of the chapter first addresses practice buy-ins, then mergers.

### A Series of Group Practice Buy-In Considerations

#### *Author's Insight and Analysis*

*Group practice buy-ins and mergers are typically a matter of negotiation between the parties, guided by professional advisors if necessary, and not necessarily a conventional exercise in "fair market value," as appraisers might see it. Notwithstanding what an appraiser without direct transaction experience might think when looking at a practice, large buy-in prices in an era of physician shortages, hospital recruitment alternatives, and high post-medical school debt are a barrier to obtaining good physician partners and a source of considerable friction in the practice. Supply and demand is critical in determining what the fair market value of an interest in a practice is, just as it is in any other industry's services or products. It is part of the market that needs to be understood to arrive at fair market value.*

#### Overview of Transactional Valuation

In transactional valuation, it is critical that the appraiser look at the actual documents that will govern the transaction price. This is not strategic value! The documents determine the precise nature of the interests being transferred, which in turn, determines how much they are worth. "Terms make the deal" is a common cliché in transactions, but it is not an indicia of strategic value. As a simple example, consider the value of a noncompete agreement as part of the enterprise value of a given medical practice. Assume that the seller has the ability and intent to compete post-transaction absent a contractual provision precluding that competition. A hypothetical buyer would pay less for the business—if it pays anything at all—absent the noncompete, while a hypothetical seller expects to be paid for not competing in addition to the value of the other assets being sold. Thus, the noncompete has an identifiable value—that can be determined through a "with and without" analysis, as described elsewhere in this guide—and two different fair market value prices would be determined for the enterprise based upon the terms of the deal. The question is not whether the presence or lack of a covenant represents strategic value—it does not—but what purchase price the hypothetical buyer and seller would reach for the business with and without the noncompete.

The analysis doesn't end there. The terms of the noncompete itself determine its value. Thus, a noncompete with a geographic restriction of 10 miles might be expected to have a value less than one with a geographic restriction of 25 miles, assuming that the catchment area of the medical practice extended beyond 10 miles. The sale of the practice with a 10-mile noncompete provision versus one with a 25-mile noncompete provision would have two different fair market values! Nothing about the geographic range of the noncompete term represents strategic value as long as the appraiser focuses his or her attention on what a hypothetical buyer and seller would agree to as a transaction price.

One of the important lessons learned from the professional literature on FAS 141/142 and the focus on valuing the left—asset—side of the valuation equation is that the market value of invested capital (MVIC) is the aggregate of the assets of the business. If the transaction documents pull out certain of those assets—such as accounts receivable net of payables, which is a common exclusion in a medical practice sale—a hypothetical buyer and seller would and, in fact, must adjust the actual transaction price, notwithstanding any conclusion of MVIC.

The 2008 tax court case Derby makes it very clear that the appraiser of a practice for a hospital purchase must—read that must—review the actual transaction documents specifically with respect to the post-transaction compensation and terms of the non-compete to determine the value of what was transferred. If the actual documents are not available, key assumptions such as post-transaction compensation and noncompete terms must be obtained from the client, and they should be 1) specified in the report and 2) considered for a representation letter. This is a left-hand-side, or asset, approach to valuing transaction, which is in contrast to the simpler, default right-hand-side, or invested capital, approach. Assets have a fair market value just as invested capital does, and due to the terms of the deal, the two may not always be equivalent because either 1) some element of the invested capital is not transferred, such as working capital, or 2) the terms of the transaction transfer more or less value than what the appraiser's generic concept of the transaction might be, such as a noncompete with a 10-mile versus a 25-mile radius.

In healthcare transactions in general and medical practices in particular, we encounter these nuances more often than not. We are expected under the regulatory standard of practice to assign value to these nuances, otherwise the transacting parties and the appraiser risk regulatory review.

As a final thought, real estate appraisal and transaction are no different. If a hypothetical buyer makes an offer on a home and the building inspection determines that the heating system is about to fail and will cost $10,000 to replace, one expects that the hypothetical buyer and seller will make an adjustment to the offer price—or else a transaction will not take place. Simpler still, if there are two otherwise identical four-bedroom homes located in the same neighborhood and one has been recently renovated with new kitchen cabinets, bathroom fixtures, and a deck and the other requires updating, they will have two different prices. The reason is that the condition of the underlying component assets being transferred differs. The reduced utility and the present value of expected future outlays by the owner to maintain House 2 are greater than those for House 1, making House 1 more valuable today.

#### Documents to be Considered

Medical practices typically have at least two core documents that have a substantial impact on the value of the practice: the stockholders' agreement or other document establishing the arrangement amongst equity owners, such as an LLC Operating Agreement or Partnership Agreement, and the employment contract. The employment contract may—and should—contain or refer to a compensation plan that determines how the available income in the practice is divided among the owner-employees. That compensation plan represents the most critical document for the appraiser to be familiar with in most circumstances. As discussed later in the chapter in "Defending Against Unwarranted Damage Claims in a Practice Dissolution," income in productivity-based compensation schemes is not allocated based on equity, but rather according to who generated it. As such, the "excess earnings" available to one new owner may be very different than that to another new owner—and two owners may pay different prices for the same equity interest.

#### Minimum Buy-In

For an employee physician coming into a partner or shareholder status within a group, the minimum buy-in generally would consist of the accounts receivable resulting from services he or she performed through the date of buy-in along with those related to any ancillaries or other profit centers that might be shared, plus a pro-rated share of the fair value of fixed assets—what appraisers would call tangible assets. Fixed assets are typically valued by using adjusted book value, adjusting for any Section 179 deductions and considering extended useful lives as compared to tax lives. Salvage value may also be considered. As examples, a dental operatory or an ophthalmic "lane" (the chair and basic surrounding equipment) may be in service for 15 or 20 years if properly maintained and perhaps rehabbed at some point along the way. The same is true for basic X-ray machines.

The accounts receivable portion of this price is generally paid via reduction of the new partner's compensation otherwise payable, spread over a period of 12 to 36 months. The portion related to fixed assets may be paid in cash for shares of stock or other equity ownership position. Attention should be given to trade payables and outstanding loans for the purchase of fixed assets, of course.

#### Compensation-Shifting Strategies

Many practices accomplish buy-ins via compensation shifts. The rationale is that senior members contribute more in the way of compensable activity and that the value of an equity investment (dividends and capital appreciation) is comparatively minor. This is sometimes termed a "senior disparity" allocation. A simple form of this shift involves crediting a portion of the new partner's productivity in terms of receipts (or net income) to the existing partners, generally for a period not exceeding three years. Often, the new partner will have a minimum salary during this period, pegged to productivity in terms of number of hours or sessions worked,[1] charges generated, or some other standard to which the parties agree.

1 Pediatric practices often use sessions, such as a day session, afternoon session or evening session.

Sometimes, the use of a compensation shift in lieu of an outright stock purchase will be "grossed up" to account for the tax benefit to the buyer and tax detriment to the seller. Other times, it is not. It is important for the valuation analyst to determine this when looking at the practice's historical transactions under the market approach.

#### *Author's Insight and Analysis*

*Internal buy-ins should be based upon the excess earnings the new partner or stockholder will receive by virtue of the buy-in, valued at some multiple or cap rate and adjusted for discounts for minority shares and marketability, if appropriate. For example, if an employee physician is earning $120,000 per year and will earn $150,000 per year after becoming a stockholder, the excess earnings are $30,000. This $30,000 would be capitalized or discounted to determine the value of the interest.*

#### Deferred Compensation Approach

Another far less common version of a compensation-shifting strategy is to accrue a liability for deferred compensation to the seller equal to all or some portion of the intangible value. The normalized balance sheet would then include an intangible asset for the value of services contributed by the seller to the practice that have not yet been compensated, offset by a liability to pay for those services in the future. All things being equal, this enables a buyer to acquire an interest at a substantially lower price, but will likely obligate him or her to be responsible for what may be a significant payment to the seller when the deferred compensation obligation matures.

Among other downsides to this approach is that the Internal Revenue Code (§3121(v)) requires FICA and Medicare tax to be paid on deferred compensation at the time it is earned and becomes nonforfeitable. The amount subject to tax is based upon the present value of the deferred benefit; as such, if the amount is payable in the future and does not bear interest, the present value will be less than the total obligation. Of course, the accrual should be equal to the present value, not the total obligation, if the recording of the liability is handled consistently. Valuators should be aware that Section 409A of the Internal Revenue Code could also present an issue and any such arrangement should be carefully structured by an attorney or other individual with tax expertise in this area.

**Exhibit 1. Compensation-Shifting Strategy: Deferred Compensation Equals Intangible Value**

| | | | | |
|---|---|---|---|---|
| Tangibles | $20,000 | | Tangibles | $20,000 |
| Intangibles | 300,000 | | Intangibles | 300,000 |
| Total assets | 320,000 | | Total assets | 320,000 |
| Deferred comp | -0- | | Deferred comp | 300,000 |
| Net worth | $320,000 | | Net worth | $20,000 |

#### Economic-Equivalence When Buy-In Prices Are Significant

Substantial buy-in prices require, or should require, substantial buy-outs at the time of departure from the practice. Physicians who are ready to accept their share of buy-in proceeds may be reluctant to forgo income when it comes to buying out a retiring partner.

In terms of potential IRS attacks on unreasonable compensation and a lack of return on equity investment—a cyclical occurrence of which appraisers should be aware—large buy-ins represent a potential problem, especially in C corporations. If, for example, a physician pays $100,000 for a stock interest in a practice, basic economics, to say nothing of valuation theory, dictates that he or she should receive a market rate of return on that investment. Returns on equity investments are paid via either dividends or capital appreciation. The former, of course, are not tax deductible by C corporations—and are rarely paid for that reason. Equity returns are far less problematic in S corporations or LLCs, the latter having the greatest degree of flexibility since there is no one class of stock required if they are taxed as partnerships. Partnerships can use "guaranteed payments" under Section 707 to pay a return on capital. Capital appreciation should drive the need for an ever-increasing buy-out price over the term of the investment if dividends are not paid, since the present value of the future payment in retirement or redemption of the stock needs to be equal to the price paid today for that stock.

#### Purchasing a Retiring Equity Holder's Minority Interest

In the best of circumstances, a medical practice will have a stockholders' (or similar) agreement that provides a mechanism for buying out retiring members as well as a valuation method. Unfortunately, this is frequently not the case. If there has previously been a substantial buy-in price, a substantial buy-out at the time of departure from the practice is typically in order. Nonetheless, physicians who are ready to accept their share of buy-in proceeds may be reluctant to forgo income when it comes to buying out a retiring partner.

***Author's Insight and Analysis***

*In my experience, one of two things happens at buy-out time when a large sum of money is involved: (1) The amount is paid to the first individual to retire and the remaining partners then realize the plan is unworkable and terminate it.—"first man out wins"or (2) the remaining partners cannot or will not pay it, and a lawsuit results.*

#### Sale or Retirement Versus Continued Employment Post-Transaction

Another critical factor is the difference in transferability of goodwill between a sale or retirement and a sale with continued employment. In a retirement setting, the buyer has the opportunity to obtain the intangible value of the seller. In a setting where the seller continues in employment, typical of a practice management company, hospital, or integrated delivery system transaction, the buyer cannot separate the personal and professional goodwill from the practice goodwill, and therefore, an employment contract containing an enforceable covenant not to compete is necessary. One also needs to distinguish going-concern value to a physician-buyer from that of a hospital-buyer, which many valuators unfamiliar or deliberately ignorant of the Stark law and anti-kickback statute fail to do. A hospital-buyer that employs the selling physicians post-transaction at a rate of compensation that results in no positive cash flow from the practice would not be expected to pay for going concern value because to do so may, and likely does, implicate buying proscribed referrals.

#### Goodwill and Other Intangibles

A factor compounding buy-ins is the often apparent confusion in the business community at large between intangible value and goodwill. *Intangible value* includes, of course, a variety of assets beyond goodwill, including such things as workforce-in-place and going-concern value. Here, we use "going concern value" to describe an asset representing the value of the positive cash flow of an established business. (That term also, of course, refers to a premise of value.) In a medical practice, it can include patient charts, a phone number, payer contracts, and other items. *Goodwill* typically includes everything not separated out after all other intangibles have been measured. The residual allocation method under §338[2] of the Internal Revenue Code allocates to goodwill only that value left after all other assets have been identified and valued. Note that intangibles require a cash flow to demonstrate value to a buyer.

#### Personal Versus Practice Goodwill

In any professional practice, goodwill may be a significant asset. Goodwill is often a catchall term that encompasses a range of intangible assets that includes the income-generating ability of the underlying client or patient base and other items, including personal skills. This goodwill may be *personal* and nontransferable, *practice*-related and subject to transfer, or *both* personal and practice-related. A buy-out from a departing physician in excess of the tangible value of the underlying practice assets presumes the transferability of the goodwill. To accomplish this transfer to the buyer, buyers and sellers usually bargain at arm's length for a noncompetition agreement to prevent the seller from being paid for the *practice* goodwill and simultaneously taking that goodwill and using it in a competing practice. If the goodwill is both paid for and used in a competing practice, the "seller" is double-dipping.

An alternative argument might be made that a portion of the goodwill is personal and a portion of the transferable practice goodwill, with the latter representing the

2 See Form 8594.

asset purchased by the buyer. However, the compelling transaction evidence is that practice goodwill cannot be purchased if the seller simultaneously competes. The two are inextricably linked, and the hypothetical informed buyer would not pay anything for goodwill without a noncompete. A good example of this transaction fact is the SEC filings and press releases for publicly traded physician practice management companies, such as Mednax, a buyer of anesthesia practices.

#### Impact of Noncompete Agreements

In addition to statutory prohibitions against physician noncompetes in some states such as Massachusetts and Delaware, there is a line of case law around the doctrine of "contravention of public policy." In medical practices, this doctrine provides that agreements among providers, or their employing entities, should not be permitted to interfere with the physician-patient relationship. In some states, agreements found to violate this doctrine, or otherwise found to be unconscionable, may be thrown out in their entirety by courts. More common is a modification by the court to something reasonable. The status of a noncompete in the state in which the practice is located is a factor to consider in the risk premium, the discount for lack of control or minority discount, and the lack of marketability—or as an intangible to be valued separately (see Chapter 12).

#### Example of a Noncompete's Impact on a Buyout Agreement

A noncompete agreement basically transfers some portion of a physician's personal goodwill to the employing entity, based upon the terms of that noncompete agreement, including duration and geographic scope. Not all goodwill in a practice will necessarily be personal, and some portion of it may therefore be a corporate asset.

At least if one follows the logic of the tax court in the *Martin Ice Cream* and *Norwalk* cases, along with the *Howard*[3] case, whether or not the stockholders have entered into a noncompete agreement with their employing entity determines to a large extent who owns the practice's goodwill. For tax purposes, the physician-stockholders selling their corporate practice can negotiate to have the buyer pay them directly for their *personal* goodwill, as properly valued, and then report it on their personal returns at favorable capital gain rates, avoiding double taxation if the practice is a C corporation. This tax-legal analysis is consistent with the underlying economics and should be considered in doing buyout and buy-in valuations.

3 *Larry E. Howard and Joan M. Howard, Plaintiffs v. United States of America, Defendant,* U.S. District Court, E.D. Washington, 2010-2 U.S.T.C.

To illustrate the concept for buy-in and buyout purposes, assume one stockholder-physician departs a corporation and opens another practice in the same area. It would seem irrefutable that if the goodwill is used in a new practice by the departing physician and also paid for by the stockholder's former colleagues in a buyout, the seller has been compensated twice for the same asset. Careful drafting of stockholder agreements should address this possibility.

#### *Author's Insight and Analysis*

*Here are several cases that indicate the contravention of public policy trend in certain states in noncompetition agreements. Before valuing a practice, the valuation consultant should be aware of the status of the law in the state the practice is located in. If covenants are unenforceable, certain intangible assets can be acquired, but the risk associated with maintaining them will be higher.*

##### Massachusetts: Ell Pond Medical Associates v. Lipski, MD

Massachusetts has a statute that makes unenforceable any contractual term that restricts the right of a physician to practice medicine in any geographic area after termination of employment. Several years ago in a case called *Abisla v. Falmouth Ob/Gyn*, a Massachusetts trial court ruled that a financial penalty imposed on an employed physician who left a practice and opened a competing office was unenforceable. In 1998, Judge Hiller Zobel expended the interpretation of the statute to preclude an employer from limiting a former employee-physician's solicitation of patients, or suggesting that patients have their medical records transferred to the new practice.

##### Alabama: Michael B. Kline, MD v. Anniston Urologic Associates, PC

Alabama has a statute that voids any contractual provision that restrains the practice of a profession, citing contravention of public policy. In this case, Dr. Kline was a shareholder in Anniston Urologic (Anniston). The stock redemption agreement had two provisions that were the subject of the proceeding.

The first provision reduced the buyout price for the stock by $20,000 in the event the shareholder terminated employment voluntarily with less than nine months' notice. The second provision reduced the buyout price by $75,000 if the shareholder voluntarily terminated and engaged in a competing practice during the first year post-termination within a 25-mile radius of Anniston's office.

The Alabama Supreme Court, on appeal, ruled that the first provision did not restrict the physician's right to practice. The second provision, however, was found to violate the statute. Noting that a similar argument was made and rejected in *Associated Surgeons, PA v. Watwood*, where Associated argued that it was not a restraint of practice, but compensation for the benefit received by Watwood by his having been associated with

Associated, the court rejected Anniston's argument that the provision did not restrict Kline's right to practice.

**Tennessee: Murfreesboro Medical Clinic, P.A. v. Udom**

Although a noncompete agreement between a physician and a hospital, for example, was then enforceable in Tennessee, in the above 2005 case, the Tennessee Supreme Court banned noncompete agreements between physicians and their private physician practice employers. The court cited the right of a patient to choose his or her physician in its decision.

The legislature followed in 2008 by almost entirely undoing the court's decision with Tenn. Code Ann. §63-1-148 and expanded the allowability of noncompetes beyond physicians to healthcare providers, such as chiropractors, dentists, optometrists, and psychologists. At that time, noncompetes effectively expired after the healthcare provider had been employed for six years. More significant from a valuation standpoint, Tenn. Code Ann. §63-1-148(a)(2) effectively exempts noncompetes in connection with a sale of a practice from the six-year term, allowing the noncompete to be enforced if it is otherwise reasonable.

In 2010, the legislature acted again to allow enforcement beyond six years but required that the noncompete be reaffirmed with consideration, amending TCA 63-1-148(a)(2) to read:

> The healthcare provider and the employing or contracting entity may agree to an unlimited number of extensions of the six (6) year period so long as the extension is in writing, is supported by consideration, and each extension does not exceed a term of six (6) years. Any agreement to extend the six (6) year time period must be accomplished through subsequent negotiations and cannot be extended by an automatic renewal provision in an employment contract. Refusal by either party to extend or enter into a new employment contract shall not be considered grounds for terminating an existing employment contract so long as the employment term of the contract then in effect is a term longer than month- to-month.

The legislature, yet again, modified the noncompete rules on May 20, 2011, effective Jan. 1, 2012, removing the above-described limitations on enforcing a noncompete that had been in place for more than six years.

Physicians who are employed as a result of their practice being acquired are subject to a different provision than physicians who are employed without a practice acquisition.

A "reasonable"[4] geographic noncompete may be imposed that cannot exceed a 10-mile radius from the primary practice site; the noncompete cannot exceed two years in length unless the parties agree to a longer term, and that term cannot exceed five years. Further, the physician has to have the right to reacquire the practice at either the original purchase price or fair market value at the time it is repurchased. Finally, the physician need only give 30 days' notice to exercise the option to repurchase.

#### Texas: Valley Diagnostic Clinic, P.A. v. Dougherty

This Texas Court of Appeals case found a noncompete provision in a deferred compensation contract to be unenforceable The relevant provision contained a 50-mile radius around the practice location of Harlingen and lasted for four years. Texas law contains a Covenants Not to Compete Act (CNCA).

> Covenants not to compete are generally considered restraints of trade and are disfavored in law. See Tex. Bus. & Com. Code Ann. § 15.05(a) (Vernon Supp. 2008) ("Every contract, combination, or conspiracy in restraint of trade or commerce is unlawful."); see also *Travel Masters, Inc. v. Star Tours, Inc.*, 827 S.W.2d 830, 832 (Tex. 1991). However, the Covenants Not to Compete Act (CNCA) sets forth certain circumstances under which such covenants are enforceable.
>
> Notwithstanding Section 15.05 of this code, and subject to any applicable provision of Subsection (b), a covenant not to compete is enforceable if it is ancillary to or part of an otherwise enforceable agreement at the time the agreement is made to the extent that it contains limitations as to time, geographical area, and scope of activity to be restrained that are reasonable and does not impose a greater restraint than is necessary to protect the goodwill or other business interest of the promisee.
>
> Section 15.50(b) of the CNCA provides additional requirements for a covenant not to compete to be enforceable against a physician licensed by the Texas State Board of Medical Examiners. Specifically, the statute provides that:
>
> (1) the covenant must:
>
> (A) not deny the physician access to a list of his patients whom he had seen or treated within one year of termination of the contract or employment;
>
> (B) provide access to medical records of the physician's patients upon authorization of the patient and any copies of medical records for a reasonable fee as established by the Texas State Board of Medical Examiners under Section 159.008, Occupations Code; and

4 Tenn. Code Ann. § 63-1-148 (2011).

> (C) provide that any access to a list of patients or to patients' medical records after termination of the contract or employment shall not require such list or records to be provided in a format different than that by which such records are maintained except by mutual consent of the parties to the contract;
>
> (2) the covenant must provide for a buyout of the covenant by the physician at a reasonable price or, at the option of either party, as determined by a mutually agreed upon arbitrator or, in the case of an inability to agree, an arbitrator of the court whose decision shall be binding on the parties; and
>
> (3) the covenant must provide that the physician will not be prohibited from providing continuing care and treatment to a specific patient or patients during the course of an acute illness even after the contract or employment has been terminated.

To be enforceable, a covenant must comply with the terms of the statute, which require that any such covenant be "ancillary to or part of" another enforceable agreement, and as the court noted, "satisfy a two-pronged test: "(1) the consideration given by the employer in the otherwise enforceable agreement must give rise to the employer's interest in restraining the employee from competing and (2) the covenant must be designed to enforce the employee's consideration or return promise in the otherwise enforceable agreement."

The court concluded that the agreement failed to satisfy the second prong of the test:

> To satisfy the second prong, the forfeiture clause must have been "designed to enforce" Dr. Dougherty's "consideration or return promise" made in the deferred compensation provision. See id. Here, the only "consideration or return promise [s]" that Dr. Dougherty could be said to have provided under the deferred compensation provision were: (1) that he not compete with VDC after departing the practice, as detailed in the forfeiture provision, or (2) that he continue to practice with VDC. To the extent VDC claims that the consideration for its deferred compensation promise was a reciprocal promise by Dr. Dougherty not to compete, the forfeiture clause fails, because there would be no otherwise enforceable agreement—that is, there would be no agreement that is enforceable wholly separate from the covenant not to compete."

#### Indiana: Central Indiana Podiatry, P.C. v. Krueger

In Indiana, noncompetition agreements may be allowed to the extent deemed reasonable. Central Indiana was a multilocation podiatry practice that employed noncompete agreements with the providers staffing its various locations.

> To be geographically reasonable, the agreement may restrict only that area in which the physician developed patient relationships using the practice group's resources.

Dr. Krueger in this case worked for Central Indiana in Clinton, Marion, Howard, Tippecanoe, and Hamilton counties at one time or another during his nine-year relationship. His noncompete clause was described as follows:

> For two years after leaving CIP's employ, Krueger would be prohibited from divulging the names of patients, contacting patients to provide podiatric services, and soliciting CIP employees. Krueger also would be prohibited from practicing podiatry for two years within a geographic area defined as 14 listed central Indiana counties and "any other county where [CIP] maintained an office during the term of this contract or in any county adjacent to any of the foregoing counties.

The court observed that employer's have a protectable interest in their customer relationships:

> Indiana courts have held that "the advantageous familiarity and personal contact which employees derive from dealing with an employer's customers are elements of an employer's 'goodwill' and are a protectible interest which may justify a restraint...." E.g., Licocci, 445 N.E.2d at 561–62 (Ind. 1983) (citations omitted). CIP asserts that the noncompetition agreement serves its legitimate interest of protecting its goodwill and investment in developing its patient base."

After leaving Central Indiana, Krueger entered into an employment agreement with Meridian Health to work in Hamilton County, which was north of Marion County and subject to his noncompete clause. The court observed that:

> The record does not support any inference that Krueger used CIP's resources to establish relationships throughout the approximately 40 counties the agreement identifies by name or description. Because that is the area sought to be restricted by the agreement, the agreement is clearly overbroad. If a noncompetition agreement is overbroad and it is feasible to strike the unreasonable portions and leave only reasonable portions, the court may apply the blue pencil doctrine to permit enforcement of the reasonable portions.

In determining whether the geographic scope of the noncompete was reasonable, the court recorded the following analysis:

> "However, the geographic scope is unreasonable to the extent it reaches contiguous counties. The Nora office in northern Marion County is nearly 40 miles from parts of contiguous Johnson County.... Similarly, because CIP selected entire counties as the building blocks of its agreement, even more proximate Hamilton County includes an

area too broad to be reasonable.... Accordingly, the contiguous county restriction is unreasonable, and the restriction applies only to Marion, Tippecanoe, and Howard counties.

#### When a Third-Party Sale Is Likely or Possible

In a circumstance where associate physicians are negotiating to become partners in a market where a sale of the entire practice to a third party is possible in the near future, additional consideration is necessary. For example, primary care physician groups may have significant value in an ACO setting as described elsewhere in this guide, whereas such values do not exist and are therefore not economically appropriate in a traditional buy-in.

States require at least a simple majority vote for approval of a corporate sale or liquidation, while many states require super-majorities. Corporate documents may also influence the required vote, so they need to be studied carefully before addressing discounts. Minority discounts are intended to reflect the *difference* in future economic benefit from a control interest. Such a discount may be appropriate in a market where there is third-party sales activity. If no sale is contemplated, then the future economic benefit will be governed by the compensation system used by the practice and the buy-out agreement, if any, among the partners or stockholders. If a third-party sale is a significant possibility, a new minority owner will not be able independently sell his or her interest; a discount for lack of marketability may also be indicated in such a circumstance.

### Reality Checks

It is a basic principle of valuation that the valuator conduct "reality checks" on the value to ascertain whether it is reasonable. In a transaction between one physician and another, such as the sale of a solo practice or the purchase of a partial interest in a solo or group practice, a useful check is the debt service analysis below. This represents an actual proposal received by a client to buy a 50% interest in a subspecialty practice. The seller's representatives had valued the practice at $650,000 and asked for $325,000 for a 50% interest, payable over 36 months at 10% interest. The buyer had alternative income opportunities as an employee of $225,000 per year.

The monthly payment is $10,487 (see Exhibit 2) and, of course, nearly $110,000 of principal (on average) must be repaid in each of three years, leading to what proves to be impossible tax consequences resulting from paying off the debt with after-tax dollars. *Alternative earnings* are those available to the physician by remaining in his or her present circumstance as an employee. *Taxable debt service* is the annual payment, less interest and the amortization deduction for intangible value allowed. The amortization deduction is $325,000 divided by 15 years, or $21,667 per year, assuming that the entire purchase price is for intangible assets and that the entity structure permits the buyer to claim this deduction. The *disposable income* line indicates that the physician attempting to execute this transaction would be in an impossible circumstance. (The tax rate of 37% was estimated based upon federal, state, and Social Security taxes after a reasonable level of itemized deductions.)

**Key Valuation Tip**

**Example 1: Buy-In to a Solo Practice**

**Exhibit 2. Compensation-Shifting Strategy: Deferred Compensation Equals Intangible Value**

| | |
|---|---|
| Purchase price | $325,000 |
| Term | 36 |
| Rate | 10% |
| Monthly payment | $10,487 |
| Annual payment | $125,842 |
| Total payments | $377,526 |
| Total interest on debt | $52,526 |

| | | 1 | 2 | 3 | 4 | 5 | Totals |
|---|---|---|---|---|---|---|---|
| Earnings before taxes | | $225,000 | $225,000 | $225,000 | $225,000 | $225,000 | $1,125,000 |
| Annual debt service | | 125,842 | 125,842 | 125,842 | 0 | 0 | 377,526 |
| Net cash flow | | 99,158 | 99,158 | 99,158 | 225,000 | 225,000 | 747,474 |
| Income taxes on principal | | -28,148 | -31,934 | -36,118 | 8,017 | 8,017 | -80,167 |
| Earnings less tax on principal | | 71,010 | 67,223 | 63,040 | 233,017 | 233,017 | 677,307 |
| Alternative earnings | | 150,000 | 160,000 | 170,000 | 185,000 | 200,000 | 865,000 |
| Difference | | -78,990 | -92,777 | -106,960 | 48,017 | 33,017 | -197,693 |
| Earnings before taxes | | 225,000 | 225,000 | 225,000 | 225,000 | 225,000 | 1,125,000 |
| Interest on debt | | 28,101 | 17,866 | 6,559 | 0 | 0 | 52,526 |
| Amortization deduction | | 21,667 | 21,667 | 21,667 | 21,667 | 21,667 | 108,333 |
| Taxable adj. gross income | | 175,233 | 185,467 | 196,774 | 203,333 | 203,333 | 964,141 |
| Income/FICA taxes | 37% | 64,836 | 68,623 | 72,806 | 75,233 | 75,233 | 356,732 |
| Taxable debt service | | 76,075 | 86,309 | 97,616 | -21,667 | -21,667 | 216,667 |
| Taxes on debt service | 37% | 28,148 | 31,934 | 36,118 | -8,017 | -8,017 | 80,167 |
| Net cash flow | | 99,158 | 99,158 | 99,158 | 225,000 | 225,000 | 747,474 |
| Income taxes | | 64,836 | 68,623 | 72,806 | 75,233 | 75,233 | 356,732 |
| Disposable income | | 34,322 | 30,535 | 26,352 | 149,767 | 149,767 | 390,742 |

***Author's Insight and Analysis***

*In this particular case, I found the practice seriously overvalued. Though it was a very profitable practice, the buyer was purchasing, in effect, only a right to "hang his hat" in a successful practice and would have to develop his own income stream—he was not purchasing the seller's income stream. The practice had been valued as a 100% controlling interest, with no thought given to the lack of control inherent in a 50-50 arrangement. In addition, the payment terms—as noted above—were draconian in their financial implication for the buyer, who had a family to support as well. The deal could be made viable by a combination of decreasing the purchase price and perhaps extending the payment period, though buy-ins extending beyond three years are problematic from an internal relations standpoint. Ultimately, the deal was done on a highly simplified basis, with the buyer agreeing to pay the seller a fixed percentage of his net from the practice for a period of years via an income reallocation. The transaction proved to be highly successful for both buyer and seller from a financial standpoint.*

#### Example 2: Buyout of a Retiring Solo Practice by Management Company With Employed Physician

The second series of examples represents an actual offer for a specialty practice where the prospective buyer intended to hire a physician to work in the practice and (hoped to) earn a return from the investment. The valuation was prepared by a nonaccredited valuation consultant on a discounted free cash flow basis using what were wildly unrealistic growth assumptions, a marginal federal tax rate of 15%, and appeared to be designed to return a value of 100% of annual gross receipts or *$700,000*. The author suggested to the buyer that the maximum payable would be *$448,000*, based upon a cash flow break-even in the first five years (see Exhibit 3). The valuation model assumed that revenues would increase over the forecast period with a greater increase in the compensation paid to the employee physician, which accounts for the decline in *earnings before taxes*.

***Author's Insight and Analysis***

*I thought the practice was worth no more than $350,000, however, due to the flaws in the valuation model.*

## Solving the Two-Person Practice Buyout Dilemma

#### Background

One of the most difficult engagements an advisor or appraiser can encounter is devising a plan for one physician (or dentist) of a two-physician practice to buy out the other. Generally speaking, if both physicians are busy, the continuing physician (or survivor) will be unable to absorb the workload of the retiree. This, in turn, leads to a circumstance in which the survivor is confronted with working long additional hours

**Exhibit 3. Buyout Analysis**

| | |
|---|---|
| Purchase price | $700,000 |
| Term | 60 |
| Rate | 10.00% |
| Monthly payment | $14,873 |
| Annual payment | $178,475 |
| Total payments | $892,376 |

| | | 1 | 2 | 3 | 4 | 5 | Totals |
|---|---|---|---|---|---|---|---|
| Earnings before taxes | | $180,000 | $165,000 | $155,000 | 4145,000 | $125,000 | $770,000 |
| Annual debt service | | 178,475 | 178,475 | 178,475 | 178,475 | 178,475 | 892,376 |
| Net cash flow | | 1,525 | -13,475 | -23,475 | -33,475 | -53,475 | -122,376 |
| Income taxes (next chart) | | -27,378 | -26,136 | -27,392 | -29,198 | -27,612 | -137,716 |
| Cash out of pocket | | -25,854 | -39,611 | -50,867 | -62,673 | -81,087 | -260,092 |
| Tax computation | | | | | | | |
| Earnings before taxes | | 180,000 | 165,000 | 155,000 | 145,000 | 125,000 | 770,000 |
| Interest on debt | | 64,887 | 52,993 | 39,854 | 25,338 | 9,303 | 192,376 |
| Amortization deduction | | 46,667 | 46,667 | 46,667 | 46,667 | 46,667 | 233,333 |
| Taxable income | | 68,446 | 65,340 | 68,480 | 72,995 | 69,030 | 344,291 |
| Income taxes | 40% | 27,378 | 26,136 | 27,392 | 29,198 | 27,612 | 137,716 |

| | |
|---|---|
| Purchase price | $448,000 |
| Term | 60 |
| Rate | 10.00% |
| Monthly payment | $9,519 |
| Annual payment | $114,224 |
| Total payments | $571,121 |

| | | 1 | 2 | 3 | 4 | 5 | Totals |
|---|---|---|---|---|---|---|---|
| Earnings before paxes | | $180,000 | $165,000 | $155,000 | $145,000 | $125,000 | $770,000 |
| Annual debt service | | 114,224 | 114,224 | 114,224 | 114,224 | 114,224 | 571,121 |
| Net cash flow | | 65,776 | 50,776 | 40,776 | 30,776 | 10,776 | 198,879 |
| Income taxes (next chart) | | -43,442 | -40,487 | -39,851 | -39,567 | -35,672 | -199,018 |
| Cash out of pocket | | 22,334 | 10,289 | 925 | -8,791 | -24,896 | -139 |
| | | | | | | | |
| Earnings before taxes | | 180,000 | 165,000 | 155,000 | 145,000 | 125,000 | 770,000 |
| Interest on debt | | 41,528 | 33,916 | 25,506 | 16,217 | 5,954 | 123,121 |
| Amortization deduction | | 29,867 | 29,867 | 29,867 | 29,867 | 29,867 | 149,333 |
| Taxable income | | 108,605 | 101,218 | 99,627 | 98,917 | 89,179 | 497,546 |
| Income taxes | 40% | 43,442 | 40,487 | 39,851 | 39,567 | 35,672 | 199,018 |

for no additional income, and perhaps less income, trying to generate the cash to fund the buyout.

#### Origin of the Problem

This problem is typically encountered either (1) when a sole proprietor is negotiating to bring in a new partner or (2) at or near the retirement of one partner. In the latter circumstance, there may be a buyout agreement in place with or without a formula or requirement of appraisal or there may be no prior agreement.

#### New Partner

Buying into a practice is complicated. There is often a dispute between buyer and seller as to whether or not any saleable goodwill (using the term broadly to encompass all intangibles) exists between physician-buyers and -sellers. Most small practices do, in fact, have some intangible value that is not attributable to the personal goodwill of the physicians, such as the value of a trained workforce, providing there is a positive cash flow from that goodwill. The following is a list of practice intangibles commonly present in a small practice, representing a list of tasks necessary to establish a practice:

1. Conduct a feasibility analysis;
2. Retain advisors;
3. Prepare a business plan;
4. Obtain financing;
5. Identify a location;
6. Negotiate the lease;
7. Choose and order furniture, equipment, billing system;
8. Hire employees;
9. Develop employment policies;
10. Develop a filing system;
11. Develop marketing materials;
12. Advertise for patients;
13. Develop coding and compliance policies;
14. Develop an encounter form;
15. Develop a general ledger system;
16. Develop a compensation system in a group practice;
17. Establish professional relationships;

18. Recruit patients;
19. Prepare patient charts; and
20. Register patients in the billing system (database).

In some circumstances, the advisor can move the transaction along by deemphasizing personal goodwill—which physicians are loath to pay for—and emphasizing the presence of practice intangibles. The use of the term "goodwill" should, in fact, be avoided.

#### Example

Dr. Smith has been working in Dr. Jones' ophthalmology practice for three years. He is paid 35% of his collections, and the practice has an overhead of about 50%, leaving Dr. Jones with a 15% profit. Dr. Smith is 41 years old, and Dr. Jones is 55 years old. If Dr. Smith does not buy into the practice, he plans on leaving and starting his own practice.

Dr. Jones has offered Dr. Smith an opportunity to buy an equal interest in the practice. After the elimination of various "senior doctor rights" that Dr. Jones wished to retain but which would have made Dr. Smith's "50%" share worth substantially less than 50%, the parties agree on a price to be paid over three years. Dr. Jones also wishes to come to an agreement on the amount he will be paid at retirement. When the buy-in is completed, he will be 58. He is reluctant to commit to waiting until age 65 to retire and may want to retire at age 62. In contrast, Dr. Smith is reluctant to finish his buy-in and have only four years of "full" earnings before he has to start working to pay Dr. Jones again. In addition, Dr. Smith does not see how he could possibly carry the workload of both physicians, even if he were inclined to do so—which he is not.

#### Analysis

All other things being equal, once the value of the 50% share being acquired by the new partner is established, it should serve as the measure of what the other 50% share is worth. The value is particularly important since it serves as a reference point for two transactions. If Dr. Smith is unwilling or unable to start his own practice—because of an enforceable covenant not to compete, for example—his options are limited and his negotiating position will be substantially undermined.

Physician buy-ins are often accomplished by income shifts, except for that portion of the buy-in related to fixed assets and existing cash balances. Using after-tax dollars to purchase the intangible value of a practice as part of the stock would make the cost prohibitive. In addition, in a small practice, it can be difficult to argue that there is a true return on investment from the intangibles as opposed to a return on labor, given that the physician must work in the practice to recognize the benefit.[5] After the buy-in period is complete, the physician expects to be earning a salary equivalent to what another partner in the practice would earn, based upon whatever compensation plan is in place.

#### Senior Doctor Rights

Senior doctor rights (SDRs) refer to a basket of special privileges that senior physicians try to retain when bringing in a new partner. From a valuation standpoint, these constitute factors leading to a minority discount or discount for lack of control for the buyer. It is quite common for individuals inexperienced with valuation to ignore SDRs, senior shareholder's protection, and similar restrictions on the ownership of stock that substantially diminishes its value.

Note: The presence of SDRs during the buy-in is not uncommon. The disposition of the payments made toward the buy-in if the seller terminates the deal needs to be negotiated, however. Following are some of the options:

1. If the buyer engages in a competing practice, the income shift payments are forfeited.
2. If the buyer engages in another practice outside the service area, a portion of the payments may be forfeited or they may all be returned.
3. If the buyer chooses to terminate, a portion or all of the payments may be forfeited.

You should never pay 50% of the entire value of an entity if the interest you are acquiring does not have the same rights as the other 50% interest. For example, assume that the buyer's stock is subject to a repurchase option held by the seller. The seller can repurchase the buyer's stock if he or she (the seller) decides that the arrangement is not working out, using the original purchase price. Any payments made via the income shift are not returned. In addition, the seller retains all of the intangible practice assets, including the employees, phone number, location, and other items included in the list above. It should be easy to see that the buyer's "50% share" does not constitute anything close to 50%.

The most critical factor reflected in this discount is the difference in future economic benefit from that of a control interest. Particularly in a small practice, such as where an employee physician is buying into an existing solo practice, a minority discount can be

5 Practices with profitable ancillary services and mid-level providers can have "profits" more in the nature of a return on capital or equity.

considerable. Some common instances indicating a need for a minority discount include: where the interest acquired is less than 50%; where the present owner's spouse works in the practice; where certain SDRs are reserved to the seller; where the buyer has an inferior claim on certain practice assets in the event of a dissolution, such as the phone number, location, employment of staff, and possession of patient charts; and where the senior doctor has a tiebreaker vote or veto in a practice with more than two doctors. The following examples are intended to demonstrate that certain of these preferences can be directly valued, rather than being rolled up into an arbitrary percentage discount, which is frequently the subject of controversy. This chapter also considers techniques for valuing preferences within the context of a buy-in.

**Key Valuation Tip**

**Examples: Valuing Senior Doctor Rights (SDRs)**

Managing partner: As part of a buy-in, the senior doctor is granted managing partner status in the practice for a period of 10 years at an annual salary of $40,000 in a two-person practice. The true value of these services, assuming they are performed and performed competently, is $12,000. The difference of $28,000 can be discounted to a present value for the 10-year period of time. Assume that the 100% control value of the practice is $500,000, using a discount rate of 20% on pre-tax earnings. The present value of $28,000 at 20% for 10 years is $117,000, which must be subtracted from the $500,000 to reach a value of $383,000, since the salary strips out a portion of the value. One-half of $383,000 is $191,500, placing a ceiling on the value of the 50% interest considered for purchase. Additional discounts may apply, depending upon the compensation formula, stockholders' agreement, and other factors.

Call schedule preference: A frequent and very contentious SDR is reduced or "no call," the term used to describe evening and weekend coverage of the practice. As one would expect, one of the least desirable aspects of practicing medicine is getting called in the middle of the night or on a weekend afternoon. Exclusion from the call schedule has a significant value that should not be overlooked. Even if the physicians who must take the additional call get credited with the revenue for any services provided, they probably won't care (except in those specialties, such as plastic surgery, where taking an emergency room call is a common method for the young surgeon to demonstrate his or her skill in repairing injuries, particularly facial lacerations). In many specialties, the cost of coverage can be quantified by reference to market prices for locum tenens, or a per diem physician to provide the service. This is very common in radiology, for example, with costs in the vicinity of $1,200 to $1,500 for an overnight session where the radiologist is physically present (with residents receiving 20% to 30% less). Another reference source might be the cost of coverage from a company such as NightHawk/VRC that provides night and weekend coverage to practices via phone lines, now common in pediatrics (staffed with nurse practitioners) as well as radiology. (Imaging industry consulting expert Douglas Smith of the Barrington Lakes Group observes that many larger practices now provide their own night and weekend call as part of their schedule and that some practices hire radiologists solely to take night coverage.)

Assume that the senior doctor is taking a half-share of night call in a four-doctor pediatric practice, commencing at age 60 with expected retirement at age 65. There are 1,300 (52 weeks × five days × five years) nights in five years, with a value of $200 per night ($260,000 total). An equal share of night call would be worth $65,000, and half of that is $32,500, as computed in Exhibit 4. The half-share of weekend call would be worth another $26,000. This might be considered a pre-payment of any retirement benefit.

**Exhibit 4**

| | |
|---|---|
| Number of Years in Preference | 5 |
| Weeks per Year | 52 |
| Call Nights per Week per M.D. | 1.25 |
| Total Days | 325 |
| Share of Call | 50.00% |
| Preference Nights (rounded) | 163 |
| Value per Night | $200 |
| Value | $32,600 |

Governance: It is much more difficult to quantify an SDR discount for practice governance. Clearly, having veto authority in one individual can impact the ultimate flow of cash, even if the compensation arrangement is specified in employment contracts and is otherwise fair. The veto could be used to block acquisition of a potentially profitable item of equipment; a move to a better and potentially more profitable location; hiring, retaining, or firing key, or more often nonkey, employees; or generally creating a nuisance. Each of these circumstances needs to be carefully evaluated, with the initial focus on the compensation allocation plan and the employment contract. The adviser has to identify those areas where the veto might influence the cash distributable to a prospective owner.

***Author's Insight and Analysis***

*The medical world is full of these SDRs, some silent and some explicit. Advisers routinely overlook or ignore them, leading to preposterous results from a valuation standpoint. I recall one situation involving two surgeons where an overly aggressive (in polite terms) advocate on behalf of the seller loaded up the proposal deal with SDRs, including a one-way noncompete for the buyer, a permanent management salary for the seller, a job for the seller's spouse, and a deferred compensation plan for the seller that would have choked the proverbial horse—an annual accrual for the seller equal to about 40% of current earnings. To top it all off, the potential buyer was outproducing the seller by 40%, but net income was to be split equally. The buyer decided to open her own practice—and lived happily ever after.*

#### Impact of Compensation and Stockholder Agreements

Many practices provide rules for distribution of income and resolution of conflicts through employment contracts or stockholder agreements that may substantially mitigate against a minority discount. The larger the number of shareholders and the more comprehensive the employment contracts and stockholder agreements, the less likely a minority discount is indicated. Centralized control via management is common in large group practices, as government by committee doesn't work well. Management, however, should serve at the discretion of ownership, just as in any other business.

#### *Author's Insight and Analysis*

*General business valuators may not agree with the above discussion. In my experience, physician practices arrange for distribution of the net income of the practice via compensation formulas, eliminating the most significant factor—control over distribution of cash—indicating a minority discount. Historically, practices tend to have equal shareholders, with no one individual or few individuals controlling the majority of the stock. However, when there is disproportionate control, minority discounts should be considered.*

#### Length of Service by Seller

The buyer's principal goal is to obtain an income stream commensurate with that of an owner in the practice. The longer the buy-in period lasts, the longer the period before that goal is reached. If the seller retires and expects a second wave of buy-out payments to begin, it may be many years before the buyer obtains the benefit of what he or she has bargained for.

#### Buyout

Once the parties have agreed on a buy-in price and terms, they can proceed to the buyout negotiation. It is difficult to reconcile the competing needs of buyer and seller in this regard. In addition to the buyer's legitimate concerns about becoming a full partner, the seller does not wish to be in a position where the new partner will be unable to fulfill the obligation of buying out the other half of the practice when the seller retires. Practically speaking, both buyer and seller need to cooperate to effectively arrange for the seller's retirement. One strategy is to develop the practice to the point where it will partially sustain a third individual and gradually transfer the senior physician's practice to that person. If the practice is inadequate in size, the replacement physician will need to be recruited no later than the year prior to the intended retirement. This may entail some loss of profit in the practice due to excess capacity, but this is a cost that must be incurred by the typical small practice to arrange for an orderly transition.

### Sample Language

**The following is not legal advice and should not be construed as same. Competent legal advice should be sought.**

"A party to this agreement desiring to retire shall notify the corporation no later than September 1 of the second year preceding the July 1 on which he intends to retire. For illustrative purposes, if a party desires to retire on July 1, 2012, he shall notify the corporation in writing no later than Sept. 1, 2010. (These dates are consistent with the recruiting period for physicians leaving residency programs, and the parties recognize that these periods are critical to the ability of the practice to recruit a replacement.) Both parties agree to contribute their best efforts to identifying and recruiting a qualified individual to take the place of the retiring party."

#### *Author's Insight and Analysis*

*There is a nearly two-year window in this version, which is probably more favorable to the buyer, although it may contribute to the ultimate success of the buyout for the seller.*

"In the event that the recruited individual or some other appropriately qualified individual should be invited to purchase an interest in the practice, the parties agree that any compensation differential negotiated in connection therewith shall be allocated to the retiring party to the extent of the fair market value of the deferred compensation owing to that party. In the event that the parties cannot agree on the amount of deferred compensation, an appraisal shall be conducted by an individual qualified specializing in the healthcare industry and qualified in such matters and holding a valuation designation from one or more of the following: the American Institute of Certified Public Accountants, the American Society of Appraisers, the Institute of Business Appraisers, or the National Association of Certified Valuation Analysts. Notwithstanding the appraisal, the deferred compensation shall not exceed any compensation differential negotiated in connection with the purchase of an interest in the practice." (As a reminder, Section 409A has to be addressed in such an agreement.)

#### *Author's Insight and Analysis*

*Buyouts are often structured in the form of deferred compensation payments.*

"In the event that the retiring party retires due to death or disability, a qualified appraisal, if necessary, shall be conducted as described above to determine the deferred compensation liability. The continuing party shall promptly use his or her best efforts to identify and recruit a qualified individual to take the place of the retiring party, if the practice's existing staffing is insufficient to do so. The deferred compensation liability shall be paid as follows: The net income available for payment of deferred compensation shall be determined after providing for the compensation negotiated with any non-owner physician and an amount to any owner not to exceed his annual salary for the calendar year immediately preceding the death or disability of the retiring party. Practice income in excess of these amounts shall be applied in full to pay the deferred compensation liability, until it is reduced to zero."

#### *Author's Insight and Analysis*

*It is also common to express the maximum payments as a percentage of net income before physician compensation, as a percentage of net collections, or as a maximum fixed dollar amount.*

#### Summary

One of the most difficult tasks confronting an advisor is to develop a fair and rational approach to buying out one person of a two-person professional practice. Arrangements that place an unmanageable burden on the buyer often fail and lead to legal actions. The author has found the approach suggested in the sample language above to be a valuable tool in resolving this issue.

## Strategies for Creating Merger Value

The healthcare industry is once again experiencing an historic period of consolidation. Many physicians are selling their practices outright to hospitals, integrated delivery systems, or for certain specialties such as anesthesia and practice management companies. Others are merging their practices with those of colleagues, hoping to stay independent and gain sufficient size to effectively compete in a marketplace of giants. Below, some of the strategies for successful formation of a group practice are explored.

#### Economies of Scale

One of the commonly cited synergies of a merger is cost reductions from economies of scale. The hoped-for reductions are in areas such as the billing function and information systems costs, including electronic medical records (EMR).[6] Often overlooked are the significant increases in costs resulting from the need for professional administration,

6 Starting in 2015, physicians who fail to "meaningfully use" EMR are subject to a reduction in Medicare reimbursement that starts at 1% and increases to 5% in 2019 and beyond.

a human resources department, and the cost of legal, accounting, and benefit plan consultants necessary to accomplish the transaction. Significant commitment of time is always required from the physicians as well. Many mergers simply result in a break-even scenario at best from a cost standpoint.

#### *Author's Insight and Analysis*

*Mergers should not be undertaken unless both cost savings and significant revenue enhancement opportunities are available from capitation, accountable care organizations, expansion of services, or at least, conservation of existing revenues. Ideally, mergers should be offensive, not defensive, in nature, although for many specialists in an era focused on primary care, defense may be the most plausible strategy.*

*Valuation may be important in the allocation of equity among the physicians or if an opinion is desired as to the value of the post-merger entity to demonstrate the strategic value of the transaction. In general, value added or synergistic effects are expected from merger and acquisition transactions in industries, such as healthcare, undergoing consolidation. Appraisers need to differentiate strategic opportunities available to most or all merger candidates in a given timeframe versus those available to only a limited number of such candidates if the standard is a strict fair market value.*

#### Actuarial Stability

Historically, capitation was used in the market as a means for creating financial incentives to control utilization of expensive services, such as ancillary testing and referrals to specialists. Actuarial factors create a significant issue for group practices looking to accept capitation. The eventual likelihood of one or more catastrophic cases, even when stop-loss insurance is in place, can have a severe adverse impact on the group's financial performance. Only if this risk is spread out among a large number of covered lives can the group have a reasonable expectation of successfully managing care. As an example, a client with approximately 1,000 patients in a full-risk commercial capitation contract had a catastrophic "out of area" case. The hospital where the patient was treated did not have a contract for allowed charges with the insurer, and as a result, 100% of the hospital charges were paid, with no discount. The patient developed severe complications and spent several months in the hospital. Even with a $100,000 stop loss, this one case increased costs by more than $4 per member, per month, in a total budget of under $200 per member, per month. This was an example of poor contract structure by the network with which the practice was affiliated. At least 10,000 lives are probably necessary (in this instance) for a reasonable balancing of actuarial risk, although the accountable care organization (ACO) regulations from the federal healthcare reform legislation start at 5,000—and that is a unmanaged system with substantial out-referral risk.

In another instance, a client with a panel of approximately 3,500 patients experienced six catastrophic cases in a single six-month period, each with a $50,000 stop loss. The insurer paying the capitation also had a marketplace strategy that tended to attract unhealthy patients and was suffering ongoing losses. This $300,000 of cost increased costs by more than $7 per member, per month in a budget of $110 per member, per month. In addition, this practice was located in an area with extremely unfavorable socioeconomics, including a high incidence of substance abuse among the insured population and a generally older, unhealthy population.

These two examples are intended to illustrate the serious risk inherent in taking capitation for small panels or more so, getting involved in a small ACO. Reducing or spreading this risk over a large number of lives is one of the principal goals of practice mergers. The latter example also illustrates the potential for "arbitrage" profits in a market where the competing insurance companies do not have uniform distribution of health status among their insureds. Arguably, the best place to begin a capitation strategy is with an insurer with positive rather than adverse selection.

(*Arbitrage* refers to the strategy of taking advantage of price differences in two different markets for the same thing. The insurer is presumed to set a price high enough to cover the costs [plus profit] of its insureds. Rates historically were typically only age and gender adjusted, not for severity of illness. A capitated group that succeeded in attracting healthy patients could obtain capitation rates based upon the higher costs of a sicker population.)

In markets employing capitation, premiums and, therefore, capitation rates will likely reflect health status differences in the underlying insured population. In early time periods, the insurers may have had less sophisticated approaches to health status determination. Further influencing this process is experience rating of (notably) the small employer and self-employed or individual markets and requiring community rating. These laws preclude insurers from increasing premiums to particular classes of insureds based upon prior claims experience. The ability of the insurer to selectively attract a healthier population through its marketing, advertising, and sales efforts historically created enormous differences in costs. Practices might be able to attract healthier patients through their own characteristics, such as location, age of providers, presence of female physicians, inclusion of pediatricians, and other factors. The 2010 federal healthcare reform legislation, however, has as one of its principal aims eliminating this type of arbitrage opportunity. Health status adjustments and uniform rating across a combination of the small group and individual markets will severely restrict this profit area and place a premium on medical management rather than demographic and health status selection.

A larger practice is more attractive to an insurer for negotiating purposes since a number of providers can be bound with a single contract, along with their underlying patient panels. Clinical protocols and medical management can be adopted more easily. Of course, the group obtains both efficiencies and leverage in its negotiations if it presents a plausible, integrated practice.

#### Addition of Ancillaries

This strategy can be successful in those increasingly fewer markets with little or no capitation or managed care and much fee-for-service reimbursement.

The Stark laws are critical in evaluating and executing this strategy and prohibit anything amounting to a payment in exchange for referrals among medical providers. Specifically, physician group practices must meet a qualifying definition under Stark to avoid liability for referrals among the members of the group.

As an example, assume a group practice of eight physicians includes the subspecialties of cardiology, invasive cardiology, and hematology. As a result, they own echocardiography equipment as well as a full lab with blood chemistry capability. Maintaining specialty referrals from primary care physicians becomes increasingly difficult. Certain insurers no longer permit the practice to perform laboratory tests on their patients but require the tests to be done by an outside reference lab with which the insurer has contracted. The practice will likely experience a steady decline in profitability.

This situation can be the foundation for a successful expansion of the group practice by adding primary care physicians and perhaps solo specialists who do not have the investment in equipment. A Stark qualifying group practice could provide laboratory and cardiac services to its new members' patients, as well as lock up the referrals that might otherwise go to specialists outside the group. The net income from the ancillary services would have to be allocated among the physicians in a manner permitted by Stark, basically one that does not reward a provider for the value or volume of referrals made. The simplest allocation would divide the ancillary profits up equally among the physician-owners of the group, but other methodologies are permitted.

Note that the two revenue strategies reviewed—gaining actuarial stability and negotiating leverage for capitation, and expansion of ancillary services—are enhancement or offensive strategies, not defensive strategies. Successfully executing either strategy is difficult, but more value is placed on growth and expansion than on operating efficiency in a practice of a given size. An expanding revenue base usually offers growing profit opportunities to the hypothetical buyer, where a fixed revenue base offers fixed profit once efficiencies are maximized. Nonetheless, revenue growth, in reality, does not always translate to profit growth due to such factors as payor pushback and poor management, but it remains the "Holy Grail" of value, since normalized profit assumes competent management.

## Structures for Successful Mergers

There are a variety of issues besides value and allocation of equity involved in a merger of medical practices. Many of these issues, however, impact on the standard of value and the valuation approach chosen. *Failure to understand the nonvaluation issues can result in the valuation advisor killing, rather than aiding, a merger.*

### Identifying Group Strategic Goals

With consolidation running rampant in the healthcare industry again, many physicians seek larger organizations simply because everyone else is doing it, without understanding the underlying market pressures or plotting a post-merger course. If the market dictates a larger physician practice for negotiating leverage and risk-taking, for example, the physicians then need to decide what they plan to do with the practice three, five, and 10 years out.

### One Man, One Vote

Most physician groups historically developed around the concept that each equity holder should play an equal role in the governance of the entity, at least as far as voting power is concerned. In a small practice, quality physicians will not be subservient to other physicians with larger equity positions for extended periods; they will seek to establish their own practices instead. In larger practices, voting will lead to the creating of an executive committee, which then elects a managing physician and hires professional, nonphysician management.

The equality of voting can be established through a number of mechanisms without necessarily affecting the allocation of financial equity. Voting common stock can be allocated per physician, with individual physician equity in the practice—based upon general valuation principles—settled through preferred stock or a second class of common. Similarly, an LLC can have provisions that give the same result in conjunction with tax provisions under Section 704 of the code.

### Financial Equity Versus Voting Equity

Financial, as opposed to voting, equity is a function of the market and the long-term strategies of the physicians. When physician practices are the target of third-party acquirers, resale in a control transaction of a recently acquired minority interest may be a very real possibility. Limited liability companies (LLCs) have thus increasingly become the vehicle of choice for accomplishing practice mergers since they are typically taxed as partnerships,[7] eliminating the double taxation problem of personal service corporations. From a federal tax standpoint, partnerships offer significant variability in the permitted manner of allocating income and expense, gains, and losses to the partners. It is perfectly acceptable for each partner to have an equal vote in practice governance, but very different shares in practice value. In contrast, a corporation with a single class of common stock would be compelled to have both voting and equity equivalent.

Due to the flexibility inherent in LLCs taxed as partnerships, it is possible to value each physician's interest *at the time of a third-party sale,* for example, rather than at the time the practice forms. Particularly for younger physicians, this mitigates the likelihood that the practice value will be determined by their success during the 15 or 20 years after a formation of a larger group by having that value allocated to another physician near retirement or, in fact, already retired. If the third-party sale does not occur during the career of the older physicians, they need to rely upon the buyout provisions in the agreement, coupled with the "lookback" provision described below.

**Key Valuation Tip**

The lookback provision: An active market for practice acquisition by physician practice management companies (such as now exists for anesthesia practices) or other buyers creates a substantial impediment to the orderly retirement of senior practice members who may fear being left out of the windfall that can result from such a sale. The character of a windfall generally accrues to those who will retire soon, while the burden associated with producing the future income stream necessary to support the value falls to the junior members who enter into long-term agreements for services with the acquirer. A common problem in group practices confronted with the "opportunity" for such a sale is the conflict between junior (in terms of age) and senior members. Due to income taxes and lack of capital, it will virtually never be practical or wise for the juniors to buy out the seniors at anything approaching third-party value—which may or may not represent fair market value in a physician-to-physician transaction. Experienced appraisers familiar with cost of capital will no doubt recognize that a public company will have a lower cost of capital and therefore a higher cap rate applied to earnings—another example of arbitrage between the public and private sector that can drive consolidation transactions.

7 See IRS Publication 541 for a simplified discussion of the workings of distributions between partnerships and partners.

By the same token, junior members should not be in the position of vetoing a sale, forcing senior members to retire at less than third-party value, and then selling the practice thereafter and collecting the windfall for themselves, even if they must enter into the long-term agreements customarily required to consummate such a transaction.

The lookback provision basically phases out the equity ownership for a retiring member of the practice and provides that if the practice sells to a third party within, say, three years after the retirement, the retiree will be entitled to some portion of the sales proceeds. The following is a sample: "Assume Dr. Jones held 10% of the equity and retired. The group sells to a third party two years later. His 10% would phase down at the rate of 20% of the total (or 2%) per year, or have a value of 6% at the sale date."

## SECTION II: OTHER SPECIAL CIRCUMSTANCES

Although much of the "action" in medical practice valuation is for "transactional" purposes, where a hospital is buying the practice, there continues to be a number of routine valuation scenarios involving medical practices. This segment will review the additional factors to be considered in a variety of valuation engagements.

### Divorce

Divorce proceedings are a common source of valuations. The values of practices may vary from state to state, and even court to court within a state, based upon case law and the presence of *professional* versus *practice* goodwill (see Chapters 18 and 19 for detailed discussions). Although the standard of value is not the same in all jurisdictions, the valuation methods typically employed assume that a hypothetical seller will depart and leave the practice with the buyer. If the physician-spouse continues to work in the practice and the earnings are the subject of alimony or child support, a substantive question arises (or should arise) as to whether or not the practice has any value as marital property. The double-dip argument suggests that if an excess earnings method is employed, only the base earnings should be considered for alimony, while the excess earnings are considered property. The next paragraph looks at a common situation encountered by valuators.

#### Separating Professional From Practice Goodwill

*Professional goodwill* is that future income-producing capacity that attaches to the individual practitioner, while *practice goodwill* is that which attaches to location, workforce-in-place, phone number, and perhaps other intangibles that may be sold to a third party or considered an asset of the marital estate subject to division. Depending upon the jurisdiction, professional goodwill should be addressed in a marital dissolution through support payments based upon future income since the practitioner will be unable to sell it and maintain his or her income stream. Notwithstanding, state laws and local judges may have different views of which elements of intangible value are allocated to professional or practice goodwill.

It is common among dentists, for example, to find arrangements where a general dentist has excess office capacity and "rents" the space to one or more specialists who can provide services compatible with but not in conflict with his or her own; alternatively stated, the renter is a subcontractor to the general dentist or physician with the office and patient base. A typical arrangement would be to have the practice pay the "renter" specialist 40% to 50% of the receipts generated from such services. (Note: Valuators should be aware of the anti-kickback and Stark laws that regulate relationships among healthcare providers when applying this method to physician practices. Any affected rent or subcontractor payment has to meet a fair market value standard.) Several examples follow: a general dentist who rents space to a periodontist or endodontist, an ophthalmologist who rents space to another ophthalmologist who is a retina specialist, and a dermatologist who rents to a plastic surgeon who perhaps does liposuction or removes large skin growths outside the skill of the dermatologist.

### Example

While it may be true that the ability to recruit other physicians into the office and then direct patients to them is tied to the professional's reputation, the rent payments represent a separate source of income not directly tied to the professional's services. How can this revenue stream be valued? Assume facts in Exhibit 5.

**Exhibit 5**

| | | |
|---|---|---|
| Owner receipts | $600,000 | 75.0% |
| Renter receipts | 200,000 | 25.0 |
| Total receipts | 800,000 | 100.0 |
| | | |
| Variable expenses | 240,000 | 30.0 |
| Fixed expenses | 60,000 | 7.5 |
| Renter direct expense | 100,000 | 12.5 |
| Total expense | 400,000 | 50.0 |
| | | |
| Owner's net income | 400,000 | 50.0 |

Several approaches may be taken to determine the income attributable to the renter payments. The simplest approach on the surface would be to conclude that the income netted from the renter is $100,000 and that this is the income stream subject to valuation.

This approach implies that all of the operating expenses would have existed without the renter and that the 50% of the renter's receipts retained is "pure" profit. Depending upon the risk associated with the future use of the location by the renter and with income for the particular specialty, a capitalization rate might range from 25% to 40%, or more. For the sake of illustration, assume that the cap rate is 33.3% and the value of this practice goodwill is therefore $300,000.

Another approach would be to argue that all the fixed costs are attributable to the owner and that the true profit from the renter is total revenue less variable cost less than the renter payment, as illustrated in Exhibit 6.

**Exhibit 6**

| | Without | Renter | With |
|---|---|---|---|
| Owner receipts | $600,000 | $200,000 | $800,000 |
| Fixed expenses | 60,000 | | 60,000 |
| Variable expenses | 180,000 | 60,000 | 240,000 |
| Renter direct expense | | 100,000 | 100,000 |
| Total expense | 240,000 | 160,000 | 400,000 |
| Net income | 360,000 | 40,000 | 400,000 |

This clearly will yield a very different result. Using the same 33.3% cap rate from above, a value of $120,000 is generated.

The final approach to look at (although infinite variations are possible) is that of fully allocating costs to both the owner and the renter, as illustrated in Exhibit 7.

**Exhibit 7**

| | Without | Renter | With |
|---|---|---|---|
| Owner receipts | $600,000 | $200,000 | $800,000 |
| Fixed expenses | 45,000 | 15,000 | 60,000 |
| Variable expenses | 180,000 | 60,000 | 240,000 |
| Renter direct expense | | 100,000 | 100,000 |
| Total expense | 225,000 | 175,000 | 400,000 |
| Net income | 375,000 | 25,000 | 400,000 |

The difference is striking. Using the same 33.3% cap rate from above, a value of $75,000 is generated, one-fourth of the $300,000 derived from the "pure profit" approach.

Which method is most accurate, if any? The pure profit approach seems highly unlikely, unless the renter is bringing all the supplies, staff, and other items normally part of variable expense (which should, or course, be ascertained) and the owner has excess physical space that would be paid for in any event. The latter argument might be considered as being akin to strategic value since taking advantage of excess capacity in a buyer or seller is often seen as a synergistic adjustment. It is, of course, virtually impossible to perform additional services in any business with absolutely no increase in marginal costs.

#### Summary

The second approach is defensible on a contribution-margin basis, although some may find this to have synergistic overtones as well. An analysis of historical results may indicate that all fixed costs are, in fact, fixed for the indicated range of volumes with and without the renter, and the owner's compensation increased by $40,000 due to the rental arrangement. If the historical analysis points to a conclusion, it should be followed.

The third approach is the most conservative and reflects the normal view of fully allocating costs to income-producing divisions within a business. It can certainly be defended on conceptual grounds, although it seems unlikely that a historical analysis would support it unless the owner had expanded the physical plant to accommodate renters. As in all valuation engagement, the extent of the valuator's investigation is critical to reaching the correct valuation conclusion.

### Valuing Independent Practice Associations (IPAs)

IPAs are commonplace in the practice of medicine. On the West Coast, they have been the norm for decades. Although they may not view it this way, physicians who join IPAs may create value in it that can then be sold to a third party. The value depends in large part on the ability of the IPA to bind the physicians to the insurer contracts it negotiates via the participating provider agreement the physicians sign when joining it. (IPAs may also be called or be analogous to physician networks, for example, and the discussion herein applies to both.)

Although fee arrangements for IPAs vary, the standard structure is a percentage of the budget, typically capitation (see Chapter 2, Section II), plus a share of profits if the IPA is investor-owned. Exhibit 8 illustrates this structure.

The annual budget for the IPA is generally fixed each year based upon the contract with the health plan. Since the IPA is allocated 5% of this budget, this portion of the revenue stream is predictable, or known in advance. It is necessary to carefully evaluate the

**Exhibit 8. Illustration of IPA Revenue**

| | | PMPM | Total | |
|---|---|---|---|---|
| Insured members | | 20,000 | | |
| Months | | 12 | | |
| Member months | | 240,000 | | |
| Capitation rate PMPM | | 100 | | |
| Annual revenue | | | $24,000,000 | |
| IPA fee | 5% | | | |
| IPA share of revenue | | 5 | | $1,200,000 |

trends in the market to know whether the current year's budget makes a reasonable basis for establishing a forecast to use the DCF model (Chapter 5) and whether subsequent budgets will increase or decrease.

#### IPA or Network Contracts With Payors

For anti-trust reasons, IPA contracts with HMOs and other payors are generally *risk-based*, meaning that a portion of the compensation in the contract is contingent upon the physicians in the IPA meeting certain defined performance standards, such as keeping the total cost of services within a predetermined budget. In limited instances, an IPA may have the exclusive right to provide services to an HMO's patients within its service area. An IPA may receive a higher budget from the HMO if it is exclusive with respect to that plan, meaning that it does not contract with any other HMO. This may occur when an HMO is attempting to develop market share or to keep other HMOs out of the market.

#### IPA or Network Contracts With Physicians

Contracts between an IPA and its participating physicians will generally fall into two categories: exclusive and nonexclusive. Under an exclusive contract, the IPA has the right to contract with HMOs and other payors on behalf of the physician, and the physician is generally bound to accept the contract and cannot contract directly with that HMO or via another entity, such as a physician hospital organization.

Under a nonexclusive contract, the physicians may accept or reject a proposal from the IPA. If rejected, the physician is generally free to contract with the HMO directly or through a different entity.

Within these two general categories, there are, predictably, infinite variations. A common example is an opt-out provision, where even though the contract is exclusive, the physician may choose not to participate. If the physician opts out, he or she may be permitted to maintain an existing relationship with that HMO, but not to enter into a new contract. Opt-outs may be structured to require the IPA to bring a "market best" contract to the physician to require participation.

Such contracts may also contain a "right of first opportunity" provision requiring a physician to bring any new proposals to the IPA for evaluation.

***Author's Insight and Analysis***

*I have frequently used precisely this opt-out strategy in negotiating on behalf of IPA clients. Physician members need to expect that if they join an IPA and grant it exclusive contracting rights, they will be better off than if they did not join.*

*One method employed for potential IPA or network members or physicians considering joining another network is the so-called "black box" analysis. In this case, a neutral subject to a confidentiality agreement receives fee schedule information from each party and compares the fees for a number of CPT codes and payors deemed necessary to generate a meaningful conclusion to the neutral. The report back to the parties however, is very broad and contains only general statements, such as the new network fee schedule is 0% to 10% better than the physician's existing fee schedule.*

#### Issues in Forecasting Revenue and Profit

The IPA's share of the profit shown above is much less predictable. Historical experience is critical to forecasting future profits, in addition to the market analysis. Profits in an IPA result from two general factors: the success of the physicians in controlling utilization of services by and on behalf of their patients and the IPA's success in negotiating good contracts, whether with an HMO or other insurer or for discounted prices for the services of non-IPA specialists or ancillary service providers the IPA utilizes. Experience in these areas is, in fact, one good predictor of future experience, but certainly not the only predictor. Utilization control is a learned skill. Obtaining good contracts is a function of negotiating skill and experience as well as market clout.

What cannot be forecasted with any certainty, particularly in small IPAs, is adverse actuarial experience, as is described elsewhere in this chapter.

#### Events Triggering a Need for Valuation

Although valuation of an IPA can arise at any time and for any reason, a common event triggering a valuation request is the need to decide whether to sell the IPA to a third party, perhaps a hospital network or a private equity firm, the latter of which would ultimately look to sell to a public entity or go public itself.

## Defending Against Unwarranted Damage Claims in a Practice Dissolution[8]

Not all marriages are made in heaven, and neither are all business partnerships. Inevitably, the practitioner will encounter a breakup of a client medical practice or be asked to serve as an expert in assessing damage claims. This section highlights some of the typical goodwill and damage claim issues, how to identify their weaknesses, the importance of regulatory review, and how to defeat the claim in appropriate circumstances. It draws on information and facts presented in various sections of the book.

### Loss of Goodwill

A typical damage claim involves a claim against one party for loss of goodwill by the other. One measure of this goodwill is accomplished through an "excess earnings" or capitalization of cash flows[9] approach, as illustrated below for simplicity, although a discounted cash flow methodology might be appropriate. Practitioners should also be aware of the relevant definition of "damages" as used in the statutes and the case law in the state in which the damage case is filed.

**Exhibit 9. Three-person practice, one partner expelled**

| | |
|---|---|
| Earnings of entire practice | $900,000 |
| Statistical earnings (e.g., from MGMA) | 600,000 |
| Excess earnings | 300,000 |
| Cap rate | 20.00% |
| Claimed goodwill value | 1,500,000 |
| Plaintiff's interest | 33.33% |
| Value to plaintiff | $500,000 |

When presented with such an "analysis," the first thing to ask is: "Who among the doctors was earning the $900,000?" (See Exhibit 9.) What was the compensation formula? What do the employment contracts say? How many services did each physician provide by CPT code (technical versus professional)? Did the practice provide any ancillary services? Were these services a source of profits? Were there any physician extenders? If so, were they profitable? What are values of the practice intangibles and related returns?

Is there a buy-sell agreement? Buy-sell agreements might treat accounts receivable as a compensation offset to permit entry and exit with much lower cash amounts than would be the case if accounts receivables were being purchased.

8 An earlier version of this material, co-authored by John J. Mayerhofer, CPA, FACHE, FHFMA, appeared in *CPA Expert*.

9 The EEM and CCF should generate equivalent results if the discount rates applied to assets and capital are equivalent—which they should be.

***Author's Insight and Analysis***

*Whether partnership interests or stock shares, the practice should annually ratify the value of each unit of ownership, although few do, despite the old adage that "an ounce of prevention is worth a pound of cure."*

Assume that the $900,000 of the income in the example was earned $400,000 by Dr. Allday, $300,000 by Dr. Begood, and $200,000 by Dr. DoLittle (see Exhibit 10). Dr. DoLittle is the plaintiff. The damage claim presented effectively redistributes $200,000 of Dr. Allday's "excess earnings" to the entire practice and accounts for $1 million of the valuation. If Dr. Allday is producing that income through a disproportionate number of total encounters, it will be difficult to convince a court that Dr. DoLittle is entitled to the fruits of Dr. Allday's labor. In fact, Dr. DoLittle is earning only $200,000 and contributing no excess earnings to the practice. Dr. Allday's counsel might ask Dr. DoLittle whether he was ever paid any portion of Dr. Allday's income or whether he ever expected to be paid a portion.

**Exhibit 10**

| | Allday | Begood | DoLittle |
|---|---|---|---|
| Earnings | $400,000 | $300,000 | $200,000 |
| MGMA norm | $200,000 | $200,000 | $200,000 |
| Excess earnings | $200,000 | $100,000 | $0 |
| Cap factor | 20% | 20% | 20% |
| Value | $1,000,000 | $500,000 | $0 |

If the doctors in the example were, in fact, dividing income equally, Dr. DoLittle might have a better argument, since, as the lowest producer, he would be getting the fruits of someone else's labor. Whether the damages are for loss of equity or earnings would still be open to question. (See the discussion of Stark anti-referral issues, below, regarding the dangers of distributing the technical component of referred procedures on the basis of production.)

#### Wrongful Discharge

Another line of inquiry involves whether the damage claim is for loss of an asset—goodwill—or whether it is for loss of income due to wrongful discharge from employment. These are two different claims. If the plaintiff presents expert testimony as to the loss of an asset, it may be possible to defeat that claim, whereas an improper discharge claim may be more difficult to defeat.

It is important to analyze the underlying intent of the parties with respect to any excess earnings and whether the value of same was to be considered equity or a liability to the producer of that excess for compensation. Perhaps the first inquiry should be whether any prior buy-in transaction included accounts receivable (AR) as part of equity or whether the AR is reallocated via the compensation system and employment contracts.

The typical employment contract in a small practice will provide that upon retirement or other termination of employment for defined reasons the physician will be entitled to receive his or her share of AR as collected or over a period of time. (A cost of collection may be charged against the receivables to determine the amount due.) Paying the specific receivables of a physician to him or her at retirement or other termination clearly puts the offsetting credit on the right side of the balance sheet in the liability class, not equity. On the other hand, if the total AR were included in the buyback of stock under the shareholder's agreement, equity could clearly be indicated. If the retiring shareholder were entitled to a pro rata share of the AR regardless of who produced them, this would enhance Dr. DoLittle's claim of loss of equity if he did not get paid out.

Is there any (business) goodwill value in a practice that allocates all compensation on a productivity basis and at retirement pays receivables on the basis of who produced them? There may well be, but it will certainly not be determinable by lumping all the excess earnings into a single bucket. Some portion of the excess earnings may well be attributable to economies of scale resulting from the three doctors practicing together or return on enterprise intangibles such as workforce in place or going-concern value. This is where the "left-hand," or asset, side of the valuation balance sheet and related assignment of discount rates can be important. Note that the compensation values in common sources of data used to establish reasonable compensation such as MGMA likely include profit distributions as well as payment for services.

To measure economies of scale, the valuator might compare the overhead expense per physician in a hypothetical solo practice to that in the contested practice. For example, assume that overhead per physician in a hypothetical solo practice is $150,000 per physician. In the example above, it is $375,000, or $125,000 per physician, assuming expenses are shared equally. It may be possible for the plaintiff to successfully argue that $25,000 of each physician's earnings are attributable to being in a group, for a total of $75,000. Applying a 20% cap rate yields a total practice intangible value of $375,000. (We ignore a return on tangible assets for simplicity.)

#### Federal Anti-Referral Legislation

There are two principal statutes regulating the referral of Medicare and Medicaid patients for health services: the fraud and abuse law, also known as the anti-kickback statute (AKS), and the Stark laws (named for the California Congressman who introduced them). The fraud and abuse laws (criminal) are broad in scope and prohibit, generally, payments in exchange for referral of Medicare, Medicaid, and other patients covered by federal programs. The most feared penalty is to exclude offenders from participation in the Medicare and Medicaid programs, even in the absence of possible criminal conviction.

The Stark laws are civil statute and prohibit payments for referrals of designated health services. Basically, a referral is any request by a physician for designated health services that are reimbursable under Medicare Part A or B, whether or not Medicare actually pays for the service. Designated health services include clinical laboratory services, radiology and other diagnostic services, and inpatient hospital services, in addition to a number of others. A physician can violate the law and regulations by referring Medicare or Medicaid patients to their group practice for designated health services, unless the group meets the qualifying definition of a "group" and is excepted from the provision.

Any valuation must take these laws into account. It is conceivable that a settlement negotiated outside of a court with respect to damage claims may ignore these laws, leaving the parties with uncertain exposure, particularly if a whistleblower gets hold of the documents. A valuation methodology that takes into account referrals and allocates value upon dissolution in exchange for past referrals would appear to run a clear risk of violating the statutes.

In performing a valuation, the valuator must first assess the liability employment contracts imposed on the underlying net assets of the practice. Next, compliance of the compensation system with the various statutes and regulations must be determined, i.e., is the obligation valid under those laws? Assuming the system is found compliant, the valuator must utilize assumptions in constructing the valuation model that respect both the contracts and the regulatory environment.

#### Example

Assume the productivity-based compensation system in a multispecialty practice properly allocates certain income from cardiac echo exams to the cardiologist who performs the procedure, resulting in a disproportionately high income for the cardiologist. Many, but not all, of the referrals come from his partners in the practice, such as general internists, who do not perform such tests. One of these internists is forced out of the practice and seeks damages. Use of an excess earnings method with respect to the cardiologist's earnings to determine the value to the internist (1) contravenes the productivity-based compensation system and (2) may violate the prohibition against referral payments, depending upon whether the income is from designated health services (DHS). Generally, a test that has a technical component to the payment is subject to Stark, while the professional component to the physician for interpreting the test is *not* subject to Stark. An analysis of certain relevant provisions of the Stark law follows.

> The prohibition on referrals set forth in §411.353 does not apply to the following types of services:
>
> (a) Physician services.
>
> (1) Physician services as defined in §410.20(a) of this chapter that are furnished -
>
> (i) Personally by another physician who is a member of the referring physician's group practice or is a physician in the same group practice (as defined in §411.351) as the referring physician;[10]

Thus, one member of a group practice may refer patients for DHS to another member of the group practice.

> Referral does not include any designated health service personally performed or provided by the referring physician. A designated health service is not personally performed or provided by the referring physician if it is performed or provided by any other person, including, but not limited to, the referring physician's employees, independent contractors, or group practice members.'[11]

This is critical. A cardiac echo exam has both a professional component and a technical component. If the cardiologist both orders and does the test himself or herself (as opposed to having a tech do the test which is the norm), then all the *technical* component revenue can be allocated to him or her in the compensation plan.

> (i) Special rule for productivity bonuses and profit shares. (1) A physician in a group practice may be paid a share of overall profits of the group or a productivity bonus based on services that he or she has personally performed (including services "incident to" those personally performed services as defined in §411.351), provided that the share or bonus is not determined in any manner that is directly related to the volume or value of referrals of DHS by the physician."[12]

A group practice compensation plan must also meet specific requirements under Stark, including the distribution of income from the technical component of ancillary services. To the extent that other group practice members refer their patients to the cardiologist for echo exams, the technical component income is subject to Stark's rule

10 § 411.353.
11 § 411.352.
12 § 411.352.

that the compensation plan cannot incent the volume or value of services. Thus, for example, the referring internist could not be credited with a share of that technical component net income based upon how many referrals he made to the cardiologist. (See "Understanding and Using the Technical and Professional Component of Ancillary Revenue when Valuing Medical Practices.")

Now, it should be clear that the use of an excess earnings method to compute damages, as described in the example of Dr. DoLittle, risks running afoul of the anti-referral rules. Remember that the valuator must first understand the existing compensation system and then assess the system's compliance with the regulatory environment. Obviously, the valuator must have some basis for assuming that the existing compensation arrangements among the parties are to be ignored for purposes of the valuation. Having passed that threshold, if the valuation method chosen for purposes of the damages calculation changes the allocation of compensation or earnings among the parties—as could be the case with the typical application of the excess earnings method—the valuator must (again) assess the compliance of his or her new compensation system with the regulations. If the procedure is also compensated with a facility fee, a separate and distinct analysis is required with respect to those fees. Clearly, performing this assessment requires the valuator to have an intimate knowledge of the various laws and regulations.

If the existing compensation system passed muster, the "valuator-installed" new compensation system for purposes of damages calculation must also pass muster and withstand the clear challenge that it is an attempt on behalf of the plaintiff (Dr. DoLittle) to obtain value for past referrals, which could also be a violation of the anti-referral legislation. Again, defendant's (respondent's) counsel might ask the valuation expert whether the changes to the compensation system are based on assumptions that attempt to reallocate historical results to compensate Dr. DoLittle for past referrals. It is not difficult to imagine the unfamiliar expert answering yes to that question.

Valuators should recognize as well that use of market approaches, such as actual control acquisitions of private group practices by publicly traded companies or private equity firms, may not be relevant to valuing a minority interest in a dissolution. There are separate considerations under the anti-referral laws when a third party controls the practice and sets or approves compensation agreements that may be irrelevant to the private control setting where the parties control compensation arrangements among themselves. There is the obvious difference between a nonmarketable minority interest in a private company and a nonmarketable controlling interest in a private company. There is also a valuation difference between a nonmarketable controlling interest in a private company and the marketable controlling interest represented by the acquisition of a practice by a publicly traded company.

More importantly, most of the practice management transactions provide that the acquirer will retain 15% to 20% of what would otherwise be physician compensation (or pre-distribution earnings), a typical structure used by the practice management industry, for example. Unless this same 15% to 20% of the earnings is reallocated in the valuation method applied to the group practice and such reallocation is valid under the regulations, it is easy to misuse the data. Given the structure of such transactions, it is multiples of earnings actually purchased from the physicians, and not revenue or other multiples, that are driving the value.

#### Ancillary Income

If a portion of the excess earnings arises from ancillary services (imaging, laboratory, and other testing), a going concern valuation analysis should be done, with the addition of the inquiry as to compliance with the Stark and Medicare fraud and abuse laws and regulations. The professional component of income from supervised tests—those requiring the presence and participation of the physician (e.g., colonoscopy and cardiac echoes)—should be considered separate from those that do not (e.g., blood chemistry panels). In fact, the final Stark II regulations recognize this distinction. Another important analysis is that of the professional and technical component in imaging studies, or the facility fee for certain outpatient procedures in a licensed facility setting. Supervised tests will tend to generate income more in line with personal goodwill if the compensation system is based on productivity (compliant with the Stark law as previously discussed), while unsupervised tests tend to generate income in line with business goodwill. Neither is an absolute. Under the anti-kickback statute, a wholly owned and controlled technical component is treated as an extension of the physician's office practice. If a single physician with a different specialty becomes a partner or stockholder, however, then the 60-40 rule described above may well be applicable.

In a radiology practice, the professional component of reimbursement is designed to compensate the radiologist for reading the film or study. The technical component compensates for the use of equipment, supplies, staff, and other costs to perform the study. If business goodwill exists, it will likely come from two sources: net income on the technical side and any profit from paying radiologists less than the professional component. The latter needs to be evaluated in light of the standard of value. Under fair market value, the hypothetical buyer or seller may not be able to sustain a pattern of paying less than the professional component for the services of radiologists.

#### Impact of Noncompete

The *Norwalk, Derby,* and *Howard* cases highlight the proposition that goodwill cannot exist at the entity level unless enforceable noncompetes are in place with the owner-employees, at least as far as the tax court is concerned. (This likely could extend to key nonowner employees' inclusion as part of the workforce in place.) Any damages measure should therefore make some assessment of the enforceability of noncompetes under local law and any relevant shareholder or employment agreements.

#### Conclusion

In a professional practice, much of the goodwill may attach to the individual professional, and excess earnings are often the result of longer hours, more procedures, and special skills. In a practice split-up or dissolution, valuation or damages methods that measure undifferentiated intangible value as part of business enterprise value are generally inaccurate with respect to the intangible value owned by the individual versus the entity. If an enforceable covenant not to compete exists between the individual professional and the entity, the professional may have assigned some portion of his or her goodwill to the entity. However, even in that case, only that portion of the individual's intangible value that inures to the benefit of the other professional in the entity should be the basis for valuation of damages. Practices in which the earnings are allocated on the basis of production—to whomever did the work—inherently have lower enterprise intangible value. Measuring intangibles value through non-earnings-based approaches, such as the going-concern analysis (really, a cost approach), seems to avoid the anti-referral problem. Treating a portion of the compensation received by each physician—an equal amount, if equal equity interests are held—as described in the earlier reduced-overhead scenario, also seems to avoid the issue.

Medical practices offer a unique valuation challenge since there is a federal statutory ban against paying for referrals of Medicare or Medicaid patients. Many states have analogous and more expansive statutes. Unlike a law firm or accounting firm, rainmaking (for others) may or may not legally be a direct factor in setting a physician's compensation. A number of common assumptions in methods used to compute damages, or goodwill for division in a breakup of a medical practice, may implicate federal anti-referral (Stark) and fraud and abuse law. The knowledgeable practitioner should be alert to point out these apparent violations and in so doing, assist legal counsel to appropriately limit claims for damages.

## Chapter Summary

This chapter dealt with a variety of special circumstances that may arise in the context of a medical practice valuation.

The actual transaction documents in a medical practice purchase and sell determine precisely what is being bought and sold and therefore, need to be reviewed for consistency with the valuation. When a physician buys into an existing practice, the advisor and valuator should be certain that the economic return on the equity investment is reasonable. The greater the amount of the purchase price allocated to stock, the greater the direct return on that stock should be, either in the form of dividends or as a part of the buy*out* price. It is perhaps more common for buy-ins to be structured as some form of compensation shift to the existing owners.

Noncompetition agreements are typically included in a transfer of a physician practice and in buyout agreements among physicians. It is critical that the valuator understand the applicable state law with respect to the enforceability of such agreements when valuing a practice or testifying as an expert witness in a claim for damages. The author believes courts will increasingly be reluctant to enforce such agreements involving physicians as being in contravention of public policy—the right of the medical patient to have free access to the physician of his or her own choosing.

Any valuation result should be subject to a reality check. A reasonable standard for an internal buy-in is that the price must be payable in no more than five years, with the purchaser earning a reasonable after-tax income in excess of the purchase payments during the buy-in period.

Merger transactions, which may require valuations, should be evaluated based upon their potential for increased profitability, preferably from revenue enhancements, actuarial stability in capitated settings, negotiating leverage, and cost reductions. Strategic value plays an important role in such mergers, but valuators should assess whether the strategic opportunities are available to most market participants.

Damage claims among physicians and their acquirers are likely to increase as failed transactions start to unwind. Some damage concepts explored in this chapter include loss of workforce-in-place value, loss of goodwill, and loss of value from increased competition.

Chapter 22

# Why Transaction Structure Affects Value and Other Nuances of Valuing Medical Practices

*By Mark O. Dietrich, CPA/ABV*

## A Review of Complex Tax Issues

Defining the standard and premise of value, such as fair market value, on a going concern basis; the interest being valued, such as market value of invested vapital (MVIC) or equity; and the level of value, control or noncontrol, is not the end of the story. Substantial differences in the concluded value of an interest should result when the transaction contemplated by the engagement is an asset transaction or a stock transaction. Further, some apparent stock transactions should be treated as if they were asset transactions due to requirements of the Internal Revenue Code, and a variety of other code provisions influence the ultimate valuation result. Finally, the cost approach for the valuation of intangible assets is not appropriate for the valuation of a medical practice for transfer to a tax-exempt hospital if the intangible have less or no value under the income approach.

## Fair Market Value?

Many times, appraisers feel that the specifics of a transaction are outside the scope of their assignment, citing the "hypothetical" buyer and seller as a rationale such that looking at the specific terms of the transaction would represent strategic value. This represents a misunderstanding of the term "hypothetical" within the context of an actual transaction. The hypothetical refers to the buyer and seller and their price motivations being consistent with fair market value. It does *not* refer to the specific interest being valued. For example, a hypothetical buyer and seller would pay two different prices for a business where one contemplated transaction included a noncompete from a seller capable of competing post-transaction and the other excluded such a noncompete. Thus, the specific transaction terms for a business result in different values under the fair market value standard.

In healthcare appraisal and transaction, fair market value is modified by the statutory and regulatory constraints of the Stark laws, the anti-kickback statute, anti-inurement provisions of the Internal Revenue Code, and, as described below, other tax statutes and regulations. Proper application of the government restrictions on the underlying motivations of the buyer and seller and the resultant price that can be paid for a business must of necessity be part of the consideration of Fair Market Value; the law always trumps *perceived* differences with appraisal standards. Certainly, a hypothetical buyer subject to fair market value would not pay anything for an illegal cocaine dealership, recognizing that law enforcement officials could confiscate not only all the assets of the business but also any assets acquired from income generated by the business—to say nothing of sending the owner to prison. The anti-kickback statute, coupled with the False Claims Act, works in much the same way.

### Stock and Asset Transactions

The principal difference between an asset transaction and a stock transaction, of course, is that in an asset transaction, the buyer obtains a basis step-up in fixed assets and if intangible value is present, a code section 197 asset that can be amortized over 15 years. These added depreciation and amortization deductions create additional value[1] in an asset transaction because they reduce future taxable income and taxes, thus making after-tax cash flow higher. In contrast, when valuing an equity interest, only the pre-existing basis of depreciable and any intangible assets is used for purposes of computing future depreciation and amortization deductions. Thus, after-tax cash flow and value are lower.

Unlike the generic market value of invested capital, or right-hand side of the balance sheet approach to valuation, medical practices and other healthcare enterprises should also be viewed from the asset, or left-hand, side.[2] In structuring a discounted cash flow model for an asset transaction, it is advisable for the appraiser to, at least, estimate the value of underlying assets using the residual method of allocation under Section 338; otherwise, the necessary depreciation and amortization deductions cannot be

1 Generally, pretax proceeds are higher to both buyer and seller, but not after-tax for the seller; for the buyer, individual asset components must be analyzed to determine the difference between pre- and after-tax value.
2 See the 5th Circuit of Appeals decision in *Caracci/Sta-Home* for a good explanation of why.

incorporated into the valuation model. This method first allocates value to cash, then receivables and inventory, fixed assets, various intangibles, and finally, goodwill. It is comparatively easy to estimate the value of cash and receivables, of course. An appraiser with industry experience can often obtain sufficient knowledge of the fixed assets from studying the depreciation schedule and other records of historic acquisitions and inquiries of management to estimate that value. Good examples of where this is possible include ophthalmology and optometry practices, imaging centers, and dental practices.

For tax purposes, code section 1060 requires buyer and seller to file a statement with their tax returns for the year of sale (Form 8594) indicating the allocation of the transaction value to the underlying assets. Many times this may seem outside the scope of the typical asset transaction appraisal, but to reiterate, the depreciation and amortization deductions directly affect the concluded value, creating the equivalent of an algebraic simultaneous equation: The total value of the assets cannot be known until allocation of that value to each class of assets is known.

## Healthcare Transactions, in Particular

"Where ignorance is bliss, 'tis folly to be wise"[3] seemingly defines the state of appraisal engagements in the healthcare industry, with methodologies debunked in the 1990s reappearing and lessons learned then forgotten or overlooked.

### *Cash-Basis Taxpayers*

One advantage that CPAs often have over competing appraisers is their familiarity with tax law as a result of providing tax services in addition to performing business valuations. Medical practices are a peculiar beast in this regard.

IRC section 441 permits "qualified personal service corporations" (PSCs) of practically any size to utilize the cash method of accounting. The price paid for this flexibility is that PSCs are subject to a flat 35% federal corporate tax rate and cannot use the graduated rates available to other (small) businesses. For CPAs or other appraisers unfamiliar with cash-basis taxpayers, the cash method creates some interesting issues to be addressed in valuation, particularly when addressing "normal" working capital.

### *Year-End Tax Planning*

Many valuations take place at the end of a company's fiscal year. For a closely held accrual method taxpayer, IRC section 267 may require any bonuses to stockholder-management

3 *Ode on a Distant Prospect of Eton College,* Thomas Gray's poem, 1742

and family members, as well as related entity transaction, to be settled via a cash payment, but unrelated trade payables and (many[4]) accrued expenses can be deducted irrespective of whether they have been paid in cash.

For a cash-method taxpayer, virtually all expenses have to have been paid in cash by the end of the year to be deducted in computing taxable income for that year. The primary exception is the deduction for qualified retirement plan contributions, which can be deducted for a given year if paid over to the plan before the due date (including extensions) of the tax return—which is the 15th day of the third month after the tax year closes, or if a valid extension is filed, the 15th day of the ninth month after the tax year closes.

As a result of the differences in tax planning between a cash-method and accrual-method taxpayer, there may be significant differences in the historical working capital levels for a cash-basis taxpayer at the end of a taxable year versus an accrual-method taxpayer. One thing that is common to cash-basis medical practices is paying all available trade payables at year end, before paying out "bonuses" as part of "zeroing out" taxable income. Many practices, in fact, pay bonuses only once a year at year-end such that during the year, there may be significant accumulations of cash—resulting in *apparent* excess working capital when looking at a cash-basis balance sheet since accrued bonuses will not be reflected. Depending upon the reason for the valuation, this excess can be addressed in several different ways.

1. Treat as excess working capital and add back to operating asset value.
2. Accrue a bonus to extent of apparent excess cash less outstanding trade payables, based upon historic practice.
3. Normalize working capital to industry levels for an accrual taxpayer and reassess the presence of excess working capital.

***Observation***

When preparing a discounted cashflow method valuation under the income approach, there is likely to be a significant difference between the historical working capital and the "normal" working capital for a hypothetical nonphysician practice buyer. As such, if possible, a thorough analysis of current and prior years' balance sheets should be made, and each year should be converted to a "full" accrual basis. Besides obvious accruals that are typically made for accounts receivable, there may be inventories and

4 Accruals treated as "deferred compensation" such as those for uncompensated absences are one troublesome aspect.

prepaid items on the asset side that the valuation analyst or appraiser will have to identify through inquiry or analysis.[5] On the liability side, there are often little readily available historical data for payables or accruals. The lack of historical data can make conversion of prior-year balance sheets problematic.

Working capital is, of course, equal to current assets less current liabilities. If accruals for inventories and prepaids are not made, current assets will be understated and existing working capital understated.[6] This could, in turn, lead to a failure to properly calculate any excess working capital. Similarly, if accounts payable or accrued items are not reflected—considered in light of cash balances not reduced by early payment of these items—working capital could be overstated along with any excess working capital—or a deficit in working capital could be understated. In the assessment of normal working capital, cash balances and accounts payable are closely tied for the typical medical practice.

### *Section 448*

Less well-known than the nuances of cash-basis tax planning and working capital is the requirement under section 448 that the acquisition of 80% or more of the stock of a cash-method taxpayer by an accrual method taxpayer requires the cash-method taxpayer to convert to the accrual method as of the transaction date if the combined entities' receipts exceed $5 million. For purposes of section 448, the two entities are treated as one under Section 448(c)(2)'s aggregation rules. This typically occurs because the acquirer (a hospital or related entity, private equity entity, or public company) is not eligible for PSC status, and the cash-basis of accounting is only available generally to entities with less than $5 million in gross receipts.

### *Section 337*

Prior to the Tax Reform Act of 1986, C corporations could liquidate and not incur a tax at the corporate level on any appreciated assets distributed in the liquidation. Since that legislation, any liquidation of a C corporation generally subjects the liquidating corporation to tax on the difference between the fair market value of its assets and their tax basis. An election is available to avoid any tax by the acquiring entity electing to take a carryover tax basis in the assets.

Since many hospital-buyers of physician practices are tax-exempt, this may appear not to be an issue. However, hospital buyers of the stock of a physician practice in jurisdictions

5 Privately held companies typically focus on tax minimization in their bookkeeping and tax filings. As such, "product" inventories, such as chemotherapy drugs, could be understated, and supplies inventories, such as X-ray film or MRI and CT contrast, may not even be recorded.

6 This also has implications for the net asset value or asset accumulation approach.

where the corporate practice of medicine doctrine[7] permits same often plan to convert the for-profit practice to tax exempt status. *Section 337(d)(4) specifically treats the conversion to tax-exempt status as if an asset sale had taken place, resulting in a gain at the corporate level.* The IRS has long taken[8] two significant positions with respect to acquisition of a taxable healthcare corporation's stock by a tax-exempt entity: 1) that continuing to operate the acquired corporation as a taxable entity is not an efficient use of the acquirer's tax-exempt status and 2) that the conversion tax must be taken into account by the appraiser in opining on the fair market value of the stock. It is directly analogous to the built-in gains tax in valuing S corporations. Whether and to what extent the tax can be discounted may be open to question in the appraisal community, but it is not clear that the IRS would entertain such a discount if the conversion is contemplated at the time of the sale of the stock.

> If the hospital purchases the C corporation's stock, the corporate level tax is borne while the corporation is owned by the exempt hospital, and does not reduce the proceeds available to the selling physician-shareholders. However, in an arm's-length purchase, the buyer would pay less for the stock than it would for the net assets because the buyer assumes the burden of the corporate level tax on the assets built-in appreciation. Thus, the hospital's failure to make a downward adjustment to the fair market value of the stock, as determined by an independent appraisal, to reflect the corporate level tax might be viewed as a private benefit to the selling physicians.
>
> Under Reg. 1.337(d)-4, a taxable corporation that transfers substantially all its assets to a tax-exempt organization must recognize gain or loss at the time of the transaction. The corporate tax is imposed on the taxable corporation. The act of transferring is referred to as the Asset Sale Rule under Reg. 1.337(d)-4(a)(1). It is very important to understand that transferring assets includes liquidating the corporation's assets, which was previously a taxable event to the taxable corporation, *as well as transferring the taxable corporation's stock, which is considered an asset under IRC 1.337(d)-4.*" [to wit, Reg. 1.337(d)-4(a)(2) states: "For example, if a state, a political subdivision thereof, or an entity any portion of whose income is excluded from gross income under section 115 acquires the stock of a taxable corporation and thereafter any of the taxable corporation's income is excluded from gross income under section 115, the taxable

7 An excellent if perhaps dated discussion is in the IRS Exempt Organizations CPE Text *Corporate Practice of Medicine* by Charles Kaiser III and Marvin Friedlander; another source is *Corporate Practice of Medicine Doctrine 50 State Survey Summary* by the firm Boerner Van Deuren s.c. in conjunction with the National Hospice and Palliative Care Organization (NHPCO) and the Center to Advance Palliative Care (CAPC)

8 2000 Exempt Organizations CPE Text *Treas. Reg. Section 1.337(d)-4 and Exempt Organizations* by Charles Kaiser III and Thomas Miller

corporation will be treated as if it transferred all of its assets to a tax-exempt entity immediately before the stock acquisition." (Note: The meaning of the italicized portion of this statement is not clear; however, it appears that the statement would be incorrect if the intent was to make the mere transfer of the stock an asset gain recognition event in the selling corporation. It is possible it refers to a subsequent transfer of the stock by the acquirer.)

Under Reg. 1.337(d)-4, if a taxable corporation converts to a tax-exempt organization, the taxable corporation must pay the corporate taxes. The act of conversion is referred to as the Change in Status Rule under Reg. 1.337(d)-4(a)(2). Thus, the corporate level tax is borne while the taxable corporation's stock is owned by the selling physician/ stockholders, which ultimately reduces their available proceeds.

Reg. 1.337(d)-4(a)(4)(b) provides that if an asset will be used partly or wholly in an exempt entity's IRC 511(a) activity, the taxable corporation will recognize an amount of gain or loss that bears the same ratio to the asset's built-in gain or loss as 100% reduced by the percentage of use in the IRC 511(a) activity bears to 100%.

A taxable professional medical corporation, C, merges with a tax-exempt affiliate of hospital A or medical foundation B, created by A to operate C. After Jan. 28, 1999, this A reorganization is subject to gain or loss recognition by C, and payment of corporate tax on gain by C.[9]

When valuing a medical practice for acquisition by an exempt entity, it is wise to consider whether section 337 has an impact similar to that of the rules for estate tax valuation (Chapter 14) and ESOP valuations. If, however, one ignores the statutory and regulatory construct, this raises two issues for the appraiser:

- Would the hypothetical buyer of the subject—whether it be a C corporation, a tax-exempt, or some other form of business enterprise—liquidate the target to obtain a basis step-up in the underlying assets to fair market value; and

- Would that hypothetical buyer insist on a discount equal to the tax incurred on liquidation.

If the answer to the first question is yes, then the expected basis step-up to be obtained in the liquidation has to be taken into account in the appraisal via the higher depreciation and amortization deductions described above! This will result in higher sales

9 *Treas. Reg. Section 1.337(d)-4 and Exempt Organizations,* ibid.

proceeds to the seller, partially compensating it for the loss of capital gains treatment. Thus, employing the proper approach to the appraisal—assets versus stock—is necessary.

If the answer to the first question is an unqualified no, the second question may be evaluated in the more traditional built-in gains tax approach. Typically, one would not expect a hypothetical buyer of a going concern operating company to insist on any built-in gain discount for the underlying operating assets inside a corporation. By the same token, a properly undertaken appraisal would not reflect any of the value associated with an asset acquisition, effectively building the discount into the price.

If the specific tax-exempt buyer does, in fact, intend to convert the target corporation to exempt status, buyer and seller may have an issue independent of the appraisal, depending upon the appraiser's assessment of the hypothetical buyer and seller. This requires a more complex assessment of hypothetical buyer and seller driven by local market conditions and jurisdictional rules. For example, if a medical practice transaction takes place in a state where only a licensed physician or another professional corporation can own the stock, an asset transaction may effectively be the only way to consummate the sale. A variant on this circumstance may occur if the state permits the stock to be held through a so-called friendly PC, where a physician employed by the acquiring entity is the nominal owner of the stock, but all the rights of that stock are effectively held by the acquirer. This suggests that an asset transaction is not mandated.

Another consideration for the appraiser is the use of the cost approach or asset accumulation method to determine net asset value and the impact on the conclusion of value. If net asset value is the concluded value, the appraiser will have to evaluate whether the hypothetical buyer would liquidate the target to acquire the assets or is motivated by avoiding replication cost on a going-concern basis. This may involve consideration of the premise of value and highest and best use of the assets.

#### *Use of the Cost Approach*

As enumerated in the CPE texts cited above, the long-standing IRS position is that the use of the cost approach in valuing *intangible* assets of a medical practice is only appropriate if intangible value is first found to be present under the income approach. The 1996 CPE Text explains:

> The value of goodwill can be allocated to specific intangible assets; the value of the latter is limited to the value of the former, as calculated under the income approach. For example, if the total value of the individual intangible assets exceeds the total value of the medical practice net of the aggregate fair market value of the tangible assets, the amount of value that can be allocated among the intangible assets is more

> limited. Also, it is important to note that intangible value may not always be present in a medical practice. Thus, ascribing value to intangible assets is a matter of allocating value derived using the income approach to specific intangible assets.[10]

In other words, the total value of the individual intangible assets cannot exceed the total value of the medical practice under the income approach, net of the aggregate fair market value of the tangible assets.

The 2008 Tax Court case *Derby*[11] specifically mentions the 1994 CPE Text having to do with integrated delivery systems and how institutions might acquire the assets of a physician practice, including outright purchase, donation, or a combination of both. Irrespective of the means of transfer, the entire transaction is subject to fair market value. Thus, the court's commentary in the *Derby* opinion applies to fair market value in general, not solely to the specific means of transfer present in the *Derby* matter, namely a charitable donation.

In the following extracts from the opinion, the court highlights what are general principles of transactions: Specific contractual rights are obtained in the exchange, and those rights are subject to valuation.

> More fundamentally, the Dutcher appraisal takes no account of the various contractual rights and other intangible benefits that petitioners and the other SWMG physicians sought and obtained in the transaction with SMF, such as avoiding signing noncompete agreements and obtaining preferred working conditions. Because it does not fully account for the benefits that petitioners received in the transaction with SMF, the Dutcher appraisal does not establish that petitioners contributed property to SMF that exceeded the values of the benefits they received in return.
>
> But when petitioners were offered the opportunity to affiliate with foundation (and receive an outright cash payment for their intangibles), they collectively rejected the prospect in favor of an acquirer that offered them working conditions they preferred, greater economic security through multiple sources of payment, a "free to compete" provision whereby any of them could essentially "unwind" the transaction and retrieve his or her patients if he or she desired to terminate the relationship with the acquirer, a role in management, and other intangible benefits that were negotiated between the SWMG physicians and SMF. Viewed in this light, it is apparent that the

10 Charles F. Kaiser and Amy Henchey, IRS Exempt Organizations Continuing Professional Education Text for FY 1996, Topic Q, "Valuation of Medical Practices" (1996 EO CPE Text), available at www.irs.gov/pub/irs-tege/eotopicq96.pdf

11 *Derby et al v. Commissioner*, T.C. Memo. 2008-45

> intangible benefits that petitioners received in the transaction with SMF were of substantial value to them. Petitioners spurned a cash payment for their medical practice intangibles in order to obtain these benefits in a different transaction.[12]

Where the *Derby* court states "... the Dutcher appraisal does not establish that petitioners contributed property to SMF that exceeded the values of the benefits they received in return," it is easy to foresee a circumstance in which a court would similarly state: "The cost approach appraisal of intangible assets does not establish that the sellers transferred property to the buyer that exceeded the value of the tangible assets transferred by the sellers and the contractual employment benefits that the sellers received."

## Conclusion

The wave of transactions in healthcare today mirrors that which took place during the 1990s, providing evidence that my late mentor, Jim Rigby, CPA/ABV, ASA was correct when he advised that consolidation trends are cyclical every 10 years or so. It is wise for those new to healthcare appraisal as well as those who have been practicing in the sector since the last consolidation to review the lessons and rules learned in the 1900s.

*A version of this material originally appeared in the Spring 2010 (final) edition of the AICPA's* CPA Expert.

12 Ibid.

Chapter 23

# Physician Compensation and Financial Statement Benchmarks: Using MGMA Data

*By David Fein, MBA*

Valuation of a medical practice, as with any valuation, consists of quantifying earnings and risk. The drivers of earnings and risk in a medical practice, however, are unique. There is a tremendous amount of diversity in medical practices, with over 700,000 physicians in the United States and over 470,000 working in over 40,000 group practices. There are single-specialty, multispecialty, hospital-affiliated, non-hospital-affiliated, for-profit, not-for-profit, and academic practices. Specifically, on the revenue side of a medical practice, the valuator must understand how encounters, procedures, and surgeries (physician production per RVUs) drive gross charges and billings and how the collection process (which can be complicated in a medical practice) drives gross revenue. In addition, many medical practices operate on a cash basis and pay out dollars to physician-owners before year-end earnings.

On the expenses side, a medical practice has significant physician and staff (e.g. business, front office, clinical, ancillary, contracted, and so on) costs as well as a number of unique general operating costs (e.g., medical supply, drug supply, lab, radiology and imaging, and so on). It's also very important to evaluate physician compensation in relationship to production, whereas in most businesses, the relationship between compensation and production is disregarded. A medical practice can be managed by physician owners, a hospital, a health maintenance organization (HMO) or management service organization (MSO). Medical practices also exist within a complex regulatory environment that must also be evaluated in relationship to revenue and risk.

Exhibit 1 shows some of the revenue and expense drivers in a medical practice.

To accurately value a medical practice, the valuator must understand these distinct characteristics. Medical Group Management Association's (MGMA) data provide excellent information professional valuators rely on to normalize physician compensation and benchmark financial performance. It is also important to understand that valuation of physician compensation arrangements (particularly when paid by tax-exempt hospitals) is becoming an increasing focus of the Internal Revenue Service (IRS) and the Office of Inspector General scrutiny.

**Exhibit 1. Medical Practice Revenue and Expense Drivers**

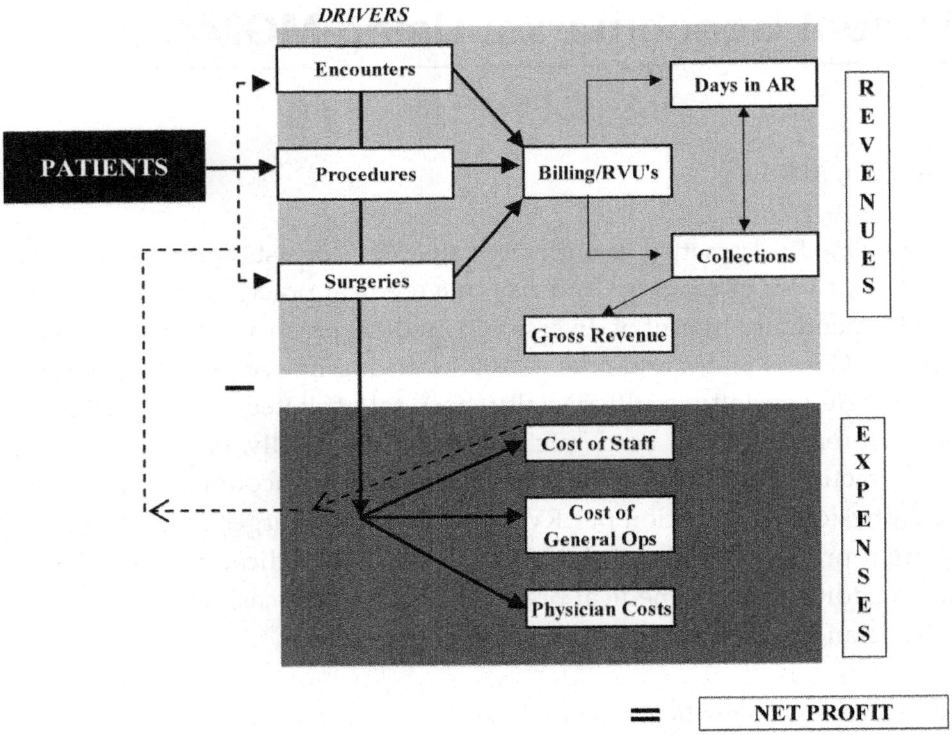


Founded in 1926, MGMA has nearly 21,000 members who manage and lead 12,500 practice organizations, representing 270,000 physicians. MGMA's survey *Interactive Reports* provides the valuator with statistically robust data, as well as sophisticated, easy-to-use tools.

The MGMA is a premier source of benchmarking data, but valuators should consider other sources, as well. You can find benchmarking data from the following:

- MGMA offers a number of benchmarking tools as well as the comparative data;
- The Centers for Medicare & Medicaid Services (CMS) and state governments can provide some external data, but they may be limited;
- Some specialty groups offer data, but they also may be limited;
- Physician Compensation and Production Survey reports that can be used include:
    - Medical Group Management Association's *Physician Compensation and Production Survey Report;*
    - Sullivan-Cotter & Associates' *Physician Compensation and Productivity Survey Report;*
    - Hay Group's *Physician's Compensation Survey Report;*
    - Hospital and Healthcare Compensation Services' *Physician Salary Survey Report;*
    - ECS Watson Wyatt's *Hospital and Health Care Management Compensation Report;*
    - American Medical Group Association's *Medical Group Compensation & Financial Survey; and*
    - American Medical Association's publications on physician statistics.

MGMA data are specifically useful for valuators because:

- MGMA has conducted physician practice surveys for over 50 years;
- Data are derived from group practices of all sizes, types, and specialties (with major reporting categories separately portrayed);
- The *2007 Report on Physician Compensation* observes more than 50,000 providers;
- Distinguishes private and academic physicians;
- The *2007 Cost Survey* observes more than 1,200 single- and multispecialty practices;

- Cost surveys are individualized for some of the larger specialties;
- Both tools use a census-style approach; and
- Built-in benchmarking tools are provided.

As with any data, MGMA data have limitations you should understand. One limitation is the data may not be representative of all practices. Because participation in MGMA surveys is voluntary and all practices do not complete and return the survey questionnaires, respondents represent only a sample of medical practices. It's difficult, therefore, to determine whether a sample is biased. Bias could occur if more professionally managed practices participate, with differences in region and size, with a lack of responses, and other characteristics.

It's important to use statistics correctly and understand both their strengths and weaknesses. There are a number of things to keep in mind when using statistics, including MGMA's:

- *Benjamin Disraeli* once said, *"Lies, damn lies, and statistics."* It's important to understand the data, how they were collected, what they truly represent, their strengths, limitations, and appropriate application to avoid both misusing and misinterpreting statistics.
- Understand medians versus means. Means include every data point; the median is the middle data point. Medians remove the impact of outliers and are a better representation of the midpoint than the mean.
- *Skewness.* The shape (or skewness) of sample can have a large impact on how you interpret the data. Understand not only the specific data points, but also the overall response curve, as well. The shape of the curve is represented by the standard deviation, but having a good visual picture of what this represents can be very useful.
- Exercise your judgment. Understand the limitations of the data and do not read more into them than is warranted.
- Talk to your peers. They can validate your thinking, and you can learn from them.
- Know the practice! Understand that MGMA data may not represent a particular practice due to specific characteristics of the practice.
- Consult other sources of information, such as specialty societies.

## The Three Ps of Benchmarking

Before delving into the specifics of MGMA data, it's important to have a general feel for the kind of data the survey represents. MGMA data are best understood as a function of the three "Ps" of medical practice benchmarking. The three "Ps" are based on what the survey is observing or the "unit of observation." MGMA develops its survey products by sending out questionnaires to its members and asks questions about various aspects of physician and medical practice performance. The three major areas the surveys observe are the physician, the practice, and the procedure. MGMA produces surveys covering each of these areas.

The first "P" is for "physician." Individual physicians are the focus of MGMA's *Physician Compensation and Production Survey*, which has over 50,000 responses from more than 100 specialties. This survey includes compensation and productivity (compensation; relative value units, or RVUs; collections; gross charges; and so on). This survey, in other words, revolves around what the physician is paid and what he or she produces. As a valuator, it's crucial to understand the relationship between physician compensation and production and to normalize physician compensation in relationship to both of these metrics.

The second "P" represents the practice. Based on the entire practice, the MGMA *Cost Survey* measures more than 700 practicewide variables, such as revenue, costs, staffing, and accounts receivable (AR).

The third "P" is procedures. This survey is based on measuring individual procedures. Physicians can perform more than 10,000 procedures, and each has a unique current procedural terminology (CPT) code. Think of procedures as the unique (mostly billable) tasks a physician performs when he or she sees a patient. The CPT procedure codes are the basis for all medical practice billing and also are the basis for computing physician work RVUs (more information RVUs to follow). Although you can perform a great number of complex analyses using procedure-based data, one of the most useful is understanding how physicians are coding (i.e., what CPT code they assign) office visits (CPT codes 99201 to 99205 and 99211 to 99215). Although this advanced benchmarking topic will not be covered in this chapter, it's a very useful analysis we encourage valuators to understand. The survey pertaining to procedures is the MGMA *Coding Profiles Sourcebook*.

The data we are going to examine in this chapter come from two following MGMA interactive reports:

- *Physician Compensation and Production Survey;* and
- *Cost Survey.*

This chapter will cover both compensation normalization and financial statement benchmarking, and how each of the interactive reports data and tools can be used effectively. The chapter is organized around some of the important steps in the valuation process and concepts unique to medical practice valuation. As these topics are discussed, I will explain more about the available data and relevant tools that provide the valuator a strong quantitative approach.

### Benchmarking Basics

It's important to understand benchmarking basics to best use the MGMA interactive reports. Benchmarking means comparing the data from a practice to either internal or external standards. Internal standards can be based on either comparing to physicians within the practice or comparing to data from a different time period (i.e., this quarter versus last quarter). This chapter will focus on external benchmarking using the MGMA data as the external standard.

### Benchmarking Checklist

To understand the general concepts and steps in benchmarking, let's review the benchmarking checklist from Consulting Training Institute's "Health Care Boot Camp." This checklist applies to both the interactive reports as well as the printed reports. The checklist takes you step by step through the benchmarking process:

Step 1: Determine what you are benchmarking (i.e., RVUs, compensation, A/R aging, cost per full-time equivalent—FTE—and so on).

Step 2: Determine what is the benchmark (i.e., the specific number you are benchmarking against). For example, median RVUs for family practice would be 4,073).

Step 3: What is the practice data? (If you are benchmarking RVUs, determine the physician's RVU data.)

Step 4: Determine how you compare to the benchmark.

- Is your performance better than the benchmark? ❐ Yes ❐ No
- Is your performance in an acceptable range? ❐ Yes ❐ No

- Is your performance worse than the benchmark? ❒ Yes ❒ No
- Is there any action we need to take? ❒ Yes ❒ No (This step can be ignored for valuation.)

Step 5: If the benchmark is not acceptable, estimate the economic benefit derived if the benchmark were achievable and quantify best-case potential. (This is a very valuable step for valuators to take.)

*Note: Steps 6 to 9 can be ignored for valuation but are included to provide the full benchmarking process.*

Step 6: Assess potential changes if action needs to be taken.

Step 7: Quantify potential cost and estimate potential cost benefit of action and changes.

Step 8: What are the action items and responsibilities for the above action?

Step 9: How often will you review this benchmark and what progress do you expect?

Exhibit 2 is a diagram of the full benchmarking process. For the purposes of valuation, focus on the "assess" phase of the process. If you consult with medical practices as well, you can provide a tremendous service to your clients by understanding and using the full benchmarking process.

**Exhibit 2. The Benchmarking Process**

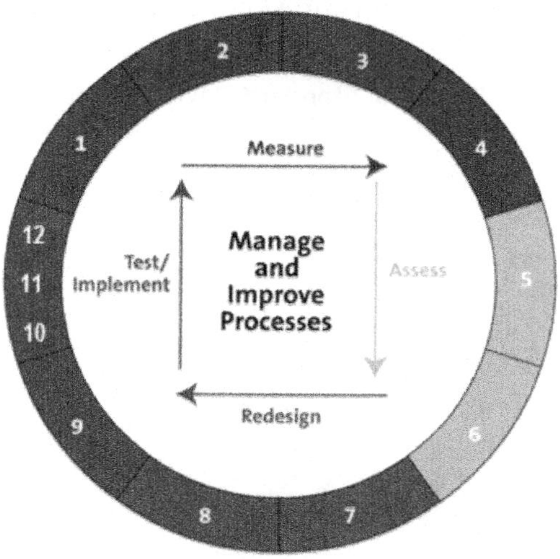

***How MGMA Interactive Report Can Help You Benchmark More Precisely***

One important concept to understand is the difference between benchmarking against medians and using rankings. Medians (also called the 50th percentile) represent the midpoint of the data and are commonly used as the key measure to benchmark against. For example, the median compensation for a family practice physician (without obstetrics) is $164,000. If the physician you are benchmarking is making $185,000, you would determine the difference as a percentage and use that as your benchmark. In this case, $185,000 is 13% greater than the median. If you have access to the entire curve of responses as you do in the interactive reports, however, you can quickly determine that $185,000 represents the 64th percentile. In other words, the compensation of $185,000 is larger than 64% of what the survey respondents reported as their compensation. Determining that your physician ranks at the 64th percentile is more precise than saying their compensation is 13% greater than the median.

Since response curves can have small or large standard deviations (i.e., be steep or shallow), it's difficult to quickly determine whether the magnitude of the variation from the median is significant. MGMA interactive reports allow you to easily understand the shape of the response curve and exactly where your data are ranked.

Exhibit 3 shows two different response curves: one with a standard deviation of one and the other with a standard deviation of two. You can see that the number "2" on the x-axis represents the 99th percentile for the curve with a standard deviation of one and the 62nd percentile for the curve with a standard deviation of two. The numerical difference from the median of zero is two for both curves, but this really represents vastly different situations. For the steeper curve, the data point 2 is extremely high, but for the flatter curve, the data point represents being slightly higher than the median.

**Exhibit 3. Standard Deviation Curves**

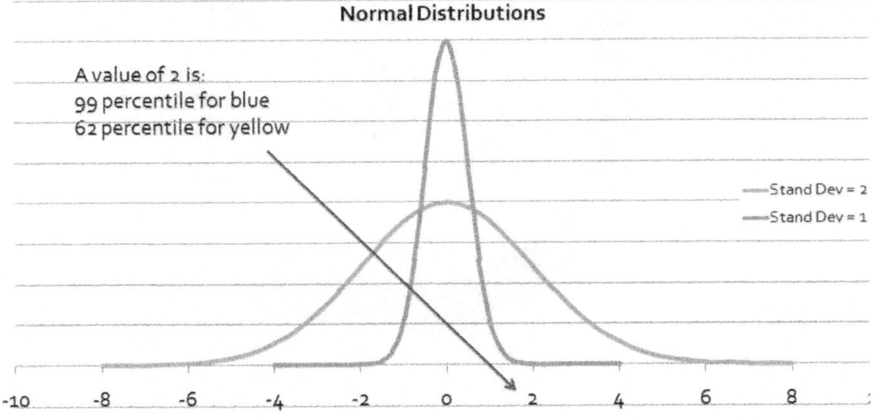

## Normalizing Physician Compensation

MGMA's *Physician Compensation and Production Survey* interactive report provides a wide variety of data and tools to assist you in normalizing physician compensation for a medical practice valuation. The goal in normalizing physician compensation is to determine what is fair compensation for all owner-shareholder physicians and make an adjustment (normalize) for the excess compensation. For example, if there are three owner physicians in a family practice with each of them receiving more than fair compensation, you would make the following adjustments as shown in Exhibit 4.

**Exhibit 4. Compensation Normalization Example**

| | Actual Compensation | Fair Compensation | Adjustment |
|---|---|---|---|
| Physician 1 | 190,000 | 174,000 | 16,000 |
| Physician 2 | 209,000 | 174,000 | 35,000 |
| Physician 3 | 234,000 | 174,000 | 60,000 |
| Total | 633,000 | 522,000 | 111,000 |

This example is simplified to show the concept of making adjustments for each physician based on fair compensation. However, in reality, each physician's "fair compensation" will probably be different based on a number of factors, including years in specialty, production, and so on.

Your task in normalizing compensation is to develop a practicewide compensation adjustment that will normalize the physician's compensation; it represents what owners would be earning if they were paid as nonowners. This means looking at each owner in a practice and determining the fair market compensation for each of them. To accomplish this, you will have to look at each individual physician, taking into account all the various conditions that impact fair compensation, including specialty, years in the practice, production levels, and so on.

It is possible to develop a practicewide compensation adjustment by using metrics, such as overall compensation, as a percentage of revenue or average compensation on a per-FTE basis. Using these practicewide adjustments, however, is just an approximation and not nearly as accurate as evaluating each physician and making individual adjustments. It is recommended you develop normalization adjustments for each individual physician.

To understand physician compensation, you have to understand physician production. To understand production, you have to understand specific production metrics, including:

- **RVUs:** relative value units, the value the Centers for Medicare and Medicaid Services (CMS) assigns to physician procedures;
- **Encounters:** number of patients the physician treats;
- **Procedures:** number of procedures the physician performs;
- **Gross charges:** how much the physician bills;
- **Collections:** how much the physician actually collects; and
- **Hours worked:** wow many hours per week the physician works.

Many valuators feel RVUs are the most appropriate measure for gauging production, but collections and charges are commonly used, as well. When using something other than RVUs as a productivity measure, you should compare RVU productivity to the measure being used. If both measures lead to the same conclusion about productivity, you can be more confident in the productivity measure. On the other hand, if RVUs provide a different productivity benchmark, you need to understand why. Collections can be used as a productivity measure, but a practice's billing procedures, payer mix, and other variables make it more challenging to isolate physician production from collections data. Encounters are a very weak indicator of production because they measure how many patients a doctor sees, rather than how much work they are performing. Therefore, attempting to gauge the amount of "work" a physician does based on encounters is not feasible. Gross charges can be a useful measure of productivity, but because there is wide variation in fee schedules, it's once again difficult to isolate physician productivity from the data.

The relationship between compensation and production is an area where medical practice valuation is significantly different from general business valuation. In general business valuation, there is no standardized method to gauge "productivity," therefore compensation is analyzed without regard to productivity. An easy way to think about this is to consider physician compensation as based on the amount of work performed. The more work a physician performs, the more he or she is compensated. A physician who is making 50% more than another physician may be fairly compensated if he or she is working twice as hard (however you measure "work"). That is why only looking at compensation data without considering production data is not recommended for normalizing physician compensation.

## What is an RVU?

Now that we understand that an RVU is a good measure of physician productivity, let us review what an RVU is and how it is calculated. There are a number of complexities in understanding RVUs, but this chapter will provide only the basics so you can use them as productivity measures to normalize physician compensation. For a fuller understanding of RVUs, we recommend *RVUs: Applications for Medical Practice Success*, 2nd edition, by Kathryn P. Glass, MBA, MSHA, PMP, available through the MGMA store.

RVUs were developed by CMS to provide a standardized method to measure the work performed by physicians, as well as provide the basis to reimburse physicians. RVUs were constructed to represent the relative intensity of resources required to care for a broad range of diseases and conditions and are associated with CPT codes. An RVU contains three components: malpractice, physician work (work RVU, or wRVU), and practice expenses. For our purposes, we will only use wRVUs.

## How are RVUs and CPT Codes Related?

When a physician provides any type of service to a patient, he or she must provide a billing code associated with that service to get paid. There are over 10,000 different CPT codes representing every possible service a physician can provide, from an office visit to brain surgery. Each CPT code has a corresponding RVU assigned to it; these values are the basis to determine how many RVUs a physician produces in a period of time.

Let's look at an example to see how this works. The CPT for a new patient office visit is 99201; the associated work RVU is 0.45. The CPT code for removal of a brain lesion (brain surgery) is 61510; the associated work RVU is 28.41. This makes sense, because brain surgery requires more "work" from a physician than an office visit. The beauty of the RVU system is that for most specialties, it is a very reliable indicator of how hard a physician is working. However, if you are working with radiologists, anesthesiologists, pathologists or emergency room physicians, you will need to find a different productivity measure than RVUs, because they do not accurately reflect the amount of work physicians in these specialties are performing.

For our neurosurgeon, let us take a very simple example calculating his RVU production for the year. We will assume he does only two procedures (new patient office visits and brain surgery). We need to determine how many of each of these procedures he performs, then calculate his total work RVU number for the year, shown in Exhibit 5.

**Exhibit 5. Calculating RVU Production**

| CPT Code | Frequency | Description | RVU Value | Total |
|---|---|---|---|---|
| 99201 | 500 | New patient office visit | 0.45 | 225 |
| 61510 | 100 | Removal of brain lesion | 28.41 | 2,841 |
| Total | | | | 3,066 |

Although this is a simplified example, the concept is exactly how you would calculate a physician's total wRVUs for a period of time. Take every procedure (i.e., CPT code) he or she performs, how many times he or she performs the procedure, and multiply that frequency by the wRVU value. Do this for every procedure, add them up, and you have calculated the total number of work RVUs for the physician.

Remember, the MGMA data is based on annual data, so make sure your data also represent a full year. The MGMA data also represent a full-time physician, so make sure you normalize your physician data to one FTE. For example, if you have a physician that is working half-time (i.e., 0.5 FTE), you will need to multiply his or her wRVUs by two, to calculate a one FTE equivalent.

Luckily, most practice management systems have a built-in report that computes RVUs; just ask someone in the practice for the wRVU report. Make certain you specify "work RVUs" or you may get total RVUs, making your benchmarks meaningless because you will be comparing apples to oranges.

### Using the Physicians Compensation and Production Interactive Report

The interactive report provides access to both data and tools to assist you in developing reasonable and defendable normalization adjustments for physician compensation. It also offers a wealth of data on more than 100 specialties and breaks the data down into a number of categories, including:

- By all providers;
- Group type;
- Region of the country;
- Method of compensation; and
- Ownership

The metrics the survey reports on are in Exhibit 6:

**Exhibit 6. Metrics of Survey Reports**

| | |
|---|---|
| Compensation | Total compensation<br>Retirement contribution |
| Productivity | Collections<br>Gross charges<br>Work RVUs<br>Total RVUs<br>Encounters<br>Surgical cases<br>Hours worked per week<br>Weeks worked per year |
| Relationship of compensation to productivity | Compensation per $ of collections<br>Compensation per $ of gross charges<br>Compensation per work RVU<br>Compensation per total RVU |

The interactive report also includes data based on individual characteristics:

- Specialty;
- Years of experience;
- Gender; and
- Partner or shareholder status.

And organizational characteristics:

- Ownership;
- Geographic location;
- Percentage of capitation contracts;
- Compensation method; and
- Group type.

There are two basic tasks the interactive reports will be used for: opening tables and using the built-in benchmarking tools. When the interactive report starts, you'll see this startup dialog box in Exhibit 7.

From this dialog, you can perform all the major functions of the interactive report. We encourage you to read the MGMA documentation, particularly the Survey Data Definitions, for a clear understanding of each metric in the survey. When you are collecting data from a practice, it is crucial you explain exactly what you are looking for. Otherwise, you may be provided data that do not match the MGMA definitions and

**Exhibit 7. Startup Dialog in the Interactive Report**

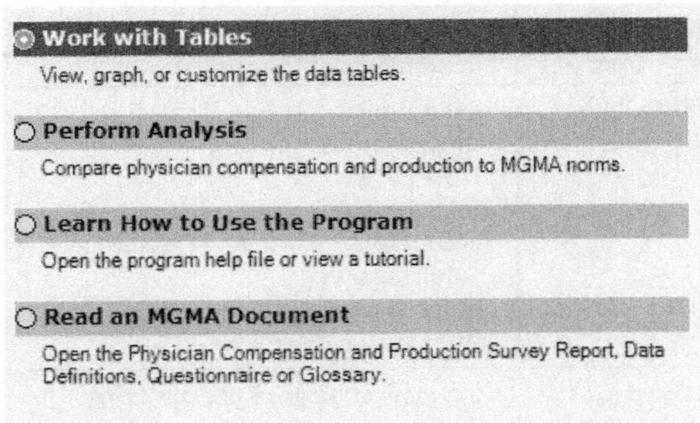


your comparisons will be meaningless. For example, if you are seeking encounters, be sure the practice is not providing procedures.

To open a table, select the "Work with Tables" option or the "Open Tables" toolbar button from the main menu. You will see the following dialog (advanced mode is shown) in Exhibit 8.

**Exhibit 8. Table Open Dialog in the Interactive Report**

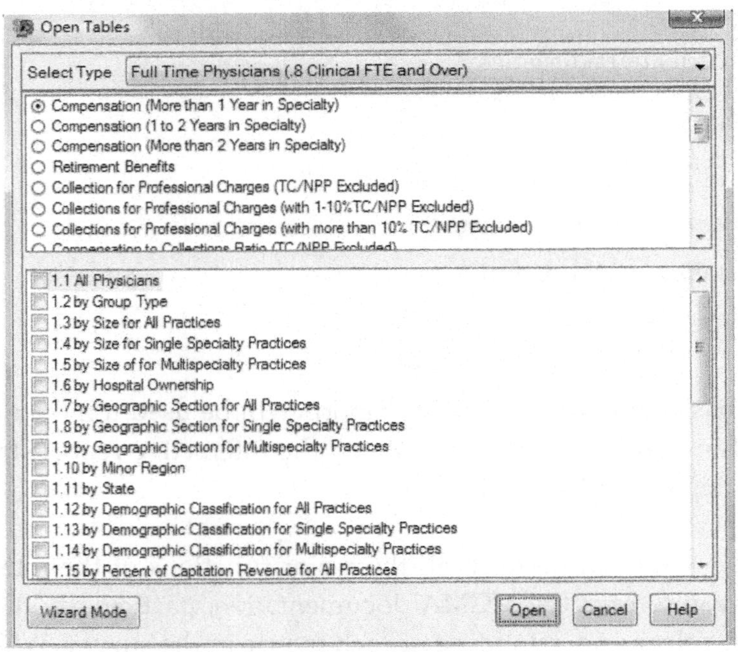

This dialog allows you to open any table on the interactive report. Note that for every metric (compensation, retirement benefits, collections, and so on) there are a number of tables available for view. Select the metric, then choose the table to open. For example, the Compensation for All Physicians appears in Exhibit 9.

**Exhibit 9. Table 1.1**

| Specialty | Providers | Practices | Mean | Std. Dev. | 25th %tile | Median | 75th %tile | 90th %tile |
|---|---|---|---|---|---|---|---|---|
| Allergy/Immunology | 175 | 85 | $295,873 | $136,255 | $208,263 | $267,688 | $340,967 | $539,160 |
| Anesthesiology | 3,903 | 184 | [illegible] | [illegible] | [illegible] | [illegible] | [illegible] | [illegible] |
| Anesthesiology: Pain Management | 191 | 62 | [illegible] | [illegible] | [illegible] | [illegible] | [illegible] | [illegible] |
| Anesthesiology: Pediatric | 105 | 10 | [illegible] | [illegible] | [illegible] | [illegible] | [illegible] | [illegible] |
| Cardiology: Electrophysiology | 203 | 96 | [illegible] | [illegible] | [illegible] | [illegible] | [illegible] | [illegible] |
| Cardiology: Invasive | 528 | 139 | [illegible] | [illegible] | [illegible] | [illegible] | [illegible] | [illegible] |
| Cardiology: Inv-Intvl | 627 | 161 | [illegible] | [illegible] | [illegible] | [illegible] | [illegible] | [illegible] |
| Cardiology: Noninvasive | 516 | 138 | [illegible] | [illegible] | [illegible] | [illegible] | [illegible] | [illegible] |
| Critical Care: Intensivist | 97 | 20 | [illegible] | [illegible] | [illegible] | [illegible] | [illegible] | [illegible] |
| Dentistry | 58 | 18 | [illegible] | [illegible] | [illegible] | [illegible] | [illegible] | [illegible] |

Specialties are displayed on the left, with statistics shown in the columns. Be aware the interactive report will not display data unless there are at least 10 providers (physicians) and three unique practices. If you see blanks or stars in the data, it's because there are insufficient physicians or practices.

Since the interactive report contains every percentile from 10 to 90, you can customize the display to show more of the data. This is helpful to get a feel for what the entire MGMA curve looks like. The same table expanded to show deciles appears as below in Exhibit 10.

**Exhibit 10. Table 1.1 Expanded to Show Deciles**

| Specialty | Providers | Practices | Mean | Std. Dev. | 10th %tile | 20th %tile | 30th %tile | 40th %tile | Median | 60th %tile | 70th %tile | 80th %tile | 90th %tile |
|---|---|---|---|---|---|---|---|---|---|---|---|---|---|
| Allergy/Immunology | 175 | 85 | $295,873 | $136,255 | $161,674 | $196,748 | $218,202 | $239,055 | $267,688 | $284,229 | $320,976 | $374,534 | $539,160 |
| Anesthesiology | 3,903 | 184 | [illegible] | [illegible] | [illegible] | [illegible] | [illegible] | [illegible] | [illegible] | [illegible] | [illegible] | [illegible] | [illegible] |
| Anesthesiology: Pain Management | 191 | 62 | [illegible] | [illegible] | [illegible] | [illegible] | [illegible] | [illegible] | [illegible] | [illegible] | [illegible] | [illegible] | [illegible] |
| Anesthesiology: Pediatric | 105 | 10 | [illegible] | [illegible] | [illegible] | [illegible] | [illegible] | [illegible] | [illegible] | [illegible] | [illegible] | [illegible] | [illegible] |
| Cardiology: Electrophysiology | 203 | 96 | [illegible] | [illegible] | [illegible] | [illegible] | [illegible] | [illegible] | [illegible] | [illegible] | [illegible] | [illegible] | [illegible] |
| Cardiology: Invasive | 528 | 139 | [illegible] | [illegible] | [illegible] | [illegible] | [illegible] | [illegible] | [illegible] | [illegible] | [illegible] | [illegible] | [illegible] |
| Cardiology: Inv-Intvl | 627 | 161 | [illegible] | [illegible] | [illegible] | [illegible] | [illegible] | [illegible] | [illegible] | [illegible] | [illegible] | [illegible] | [illegible] |
| Cardiology: Noninvasive | 516 | 138 | [illegible] | [illegible] | [illegible] | [illegible] | [illegible] | [illegible] | [illegible] | [illegible] | [illegible] | [illegible] | [illegible] |
| Critical Care: Intensivist | 97 | 20 | [illegible] | [illegible] | [illegible] | [illegible] | [illegible] | [illegible] | [illegible] | [illegible] | [illegible] | [illegible] | [illegible] |
| Dentistry | 58 | 18 | [illegible] | [illegible] | [illegible] | [illegible] | [illegible] | [illegible] | [illegible] | [illegible] | [illegible] | [illegible] | [illegible] |
| Dermatology | 361 | 128 | [illegible] | [illegible] | [illegible] | [illegible] | [illegible] | [illegible] | [illegible] | [illegible] | [illegible] | [illegible] | [illegible] |

You can set the program defaults to always show more data so you do not have to customize each table. The interactive report allows you to open many tables at the same time to view multiple metrics or slices of the same table. All of the tables can be easily exported to Excel for custom analysis and charting. You also can chart any table by selecting the chart toolbar buttons.

## Benchmarking Tools

One of the most important functions of the interactive report is the seven built-in benchmarking tools, which allow you to input data from a practice and have the benchmarks performed automatically.

## Physician Benchmarking Tool

This comprehensive benchmarking tool provides both internal (i.e., physician against physician) and external (i.e., against MGMA norms) benchmarking. You can input data monthly, quarterly, or annually. It provides a ranking report both in table and graphic formats. You can automatically load data from a practice's IT system into this tool, without having to manually input data. This tool also produces a number of tables and charts, including the ranking report below in Exhibit 11, which you can export to Excel for custom analysis. Note each physician is ranked for each metric benchmarked; the rankings show exactly where the physician lies on the curve.

**Exhibit 11. Ranking Report Section of the Physician Benchmarking Tool**

Physician Ranking
Compared to MGMA Data for Specialty Cardiology: Invasive

| | MGMA | Tyler Jones | Michael Cane | Sample Practice |
|---|---|---|---|---|
| **Compensation** | Median | 3 to 7 years in Specialty | 8 to 17 years in Specialty | Practice Average |
| Physician Compensation | $431,533 | <10th %tile | 68th %tile | 30th %tile |
| Physician Retirement Benefits | $29,500 | 18th %tile | 70th %tile | 32nd %tile |
| **Production** | | | | |
| Physician Collection for Professional Charges | $629,195 | 42nd %tile | 45th %tile | 42nd %tile |
| Physician Gross Charges | $1,497,479 | 13th %tile | 58th %tile | 34th %tile |
| Physician Total RVUs | 18,419 | 12th %tile | 31st %tile | 20th %tile |
| Physician Work RVUs | 9,256 | 27th %tile | 48th %tile | 38th %tile |
| Physician Ambulatory Encounters | 2,257 | 31st %tile | 43rd %tile | 36th %tile |
| Physician Hospital Encounters | 1,264 | 34th %tile | 52nd %tile | 43rd %tile |
| Physician Surgery/Anesthesia Cases | 82 | 61st %tile | 82nd %tile | 71st %tile |
| Physician Clinical Hours Worked per Week | 40 | 54th %tile | 23th %tile | 53rd %tile |
| Physician Weeks Worked per Year | 46 | 11th %tile | 11th %tile | 11th %tile |

## Physician Compensation Analysis Tool

This tool offers a quick method to determine compensation based on data from a number of tables. The output (see Exhibit 12) is a weighted average compensation that allows you to change the default weights and recalculate the weighted average compensation level.

## Physician Compensation Estimator Tool

This tool provides a predictive statistical model based on the most significant compensation drivers. Note: This tool should not be used to normalize physician compensation.

**Exhibit 12. Compensation Analysis Tool**

| Data Source | Compensation | Weight |
|---|---|---|
| **Physician Compensation by All Physicians** | | |
| All Physicians | 187,393 | 1 |
| **By Years in Specialty:** | | |
| 1 to 2 years | - | 0 |
| **By Method of Compensation:** | | |
| 1-99% prod less allocated overhead | - | 0 |
| **By Group Type:** | | |
| Single Specialty | 187,396 | 1 |
| **By Geographic Location:** | | |
| Midwest | 251,518 | 1 |
| **By Gender:** | | |
| Male | 201,148 | 1 |
| **By Size of Practice:** | | |
| 10 FTE or fewer | 212,785 | 1 |
| **Weighted Average Compensation Level** | $ 208,048 | |

## Physician Pay-to-Production Plotter Tool

This is the single best (and statistically valid) method to get a comprehensive picture of how physician compensation and production (RVUs and collections) are related. You can input the compensation and production values for your physicians, and they are plotted against the MGMA data. This is the only tool that allows you to see individual MGMA responses rather than statistics based on the responses. The Pay-to-Production

**Exhibit 13. Pay-to-Production Plotter**

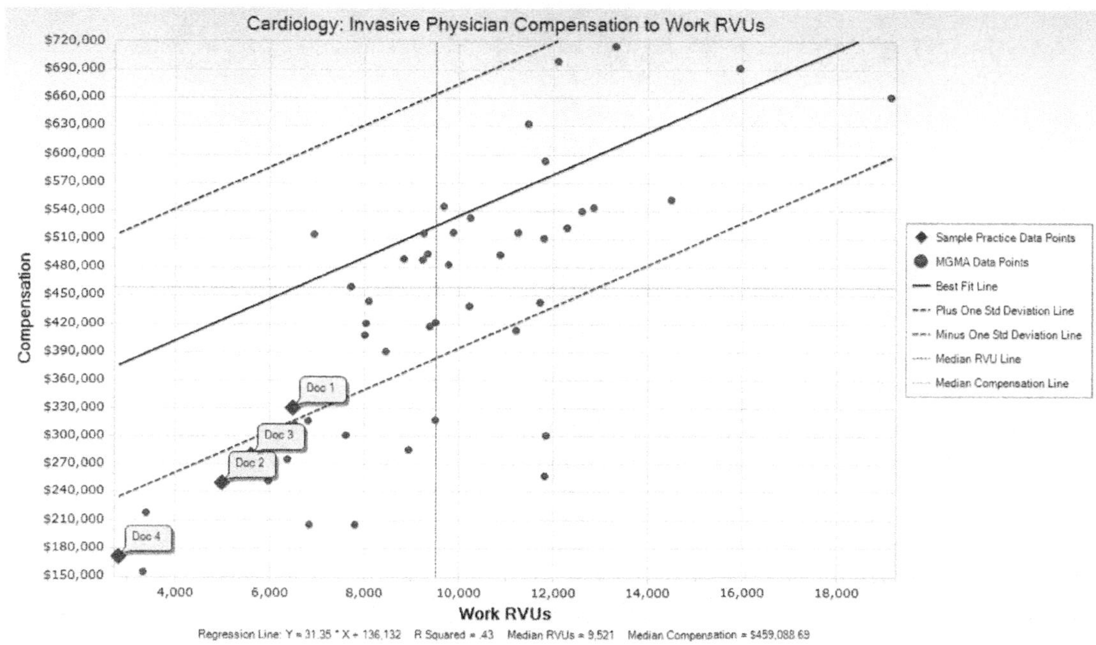

Plotter Tool offers a significant advantage to using compensation and production tables to correlate compensation and production, because the data are based on a sample population that responded to both the compensation and production questions. In this case, RVUs are along the x-axis, with compensation along the y-axis. You will see your physicians plotted as diamonds against the MGMA data (circles) in Exhibit 13.

### Physician Dashboard Report Tool

This tool provides a 50,000-foot view of physician compensation and production in a dashboard format. The dashboard gauges provide rankings for compensation, charges, collections, RVUs, ambulatory encounters, and hospital encounters. Because the dashboard presents the data in an easy-to-understand, green-yellow-red gauge format, the "benchmarking story" the gauges tell can be communicated to those who do not understand statistics, benchmarks, or MGMA data. Exhibit 14 shows the dashboard.

**Exhibit 14. Physician Compensation and Production Dashboard**

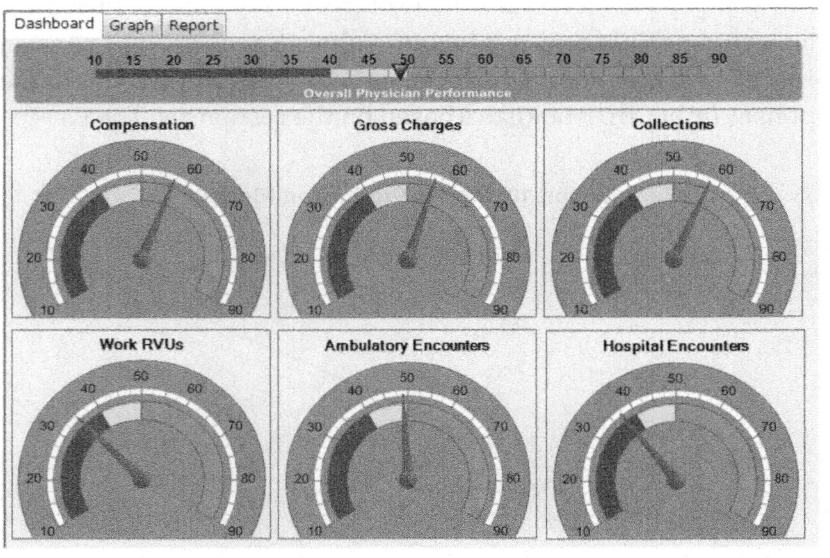


### Management Summary Analysis Tables Tool

Provides summary tables for the management data that are included in an expanded version of the *Physicians Compensation* interactive report.

### RVU 06-08 Conversion Utility Tool

This tool allows you to convert wRVUs from one year's values to another year's values. RVU values changed substantially between 2006 and 2007 and a little between 2007 and 2008. It's important that the data you input into the benchmarking tools and the comparisons you make are based on the same year's RVU scale.

## Financial Statement Benchmarking

In the normal course of valuing a company, a financial statement benchmark often is performed to better understand how the company performs against industry norms. Performing this analysis assists the valuator in assessing ongoing cash flows, company risk, and sustainable growth. One of the challenges of financial statement benchmarking, however, is there is no direct correlation between the results of benchmarking and drivers of business value (cash flows, risk, and growth). In other words, there is no accepted valuation standard that allows the valuator to apply a formula or method to translate the results of financial statement benchmarking into something directly related to company value. Financial statement benchmarking will provide you a better understanding of the practice's financial and operational dynamics and give you a quantitative approach to assist you in developing and defending your assumptions relating to value drivers.

## Finding Financial Statement Benchmarking Data

In looking for financial statement benchmarking data for medical practices, the industry has relied on sources such as Risk Management Association (RMA), Integra, and other general sources of benchmarking data. Although this general data provide some insight into how a medical practice is performing, a medical practice is substantially different from a general business. For example, in RMA data, you'll find common size statements and general financial ratios for physician practices, but the underlying financial and operational drivers that are unique to a medical practice are ignored.

This is where the MGMA data provide a far superior set of data and tools to benchmark a medical practice. RMA provides approximately 45 metrics (i.e., data points); MGMA's *Cost Survey* has more than 700.

## Medical Practice Benchmarking Basics

To understand financial statement benchmarking for medical practices, you have to understand some of the value drivers in the practice. To understand these drivers, you have to understand the fundamental categories of group practice metrics including:

- **AR:** Accounts receivable should be broken down per physician, as well as a percentage of total medical revenue. You should also review a standard AR aging.

- **Gross charges by payer type:** A practice's revenue can be significantly impacted by its payer mix (i.e., insurance companies).
- **Charges and revenue:** Physician charges and revenue should be broken down per physician and as a percentage of total medical revenue.
- **Operating cost:** General operating costs should be broken down per physician, as well as a percentage of total medical revenue.
- **Provider cost:** Provider costs (i.e., cost for anyone providing billable services, including physicians, physician's assistants, registered nurses, and so on) should be broken down per physician, per provider along with as a percentage of total medical revenue.
- **Staff FTE levels and costs:** Staff costs should be broken down by FTE (i.e., how many FTEs per position) and their associated costs. The data should be also broken down on a per-FTE basis as well as a percentage of total medical revenue.
- **Procedures:** Procedures are broken down on a per-FTE basis.

This data, as you can see, delve deeper into the dynamics of value in a medical practice than a general data set such as RMA. As with the *Physician Compensation* data, it's important to understand the exact definition of each metric you use to obtain and interpret the data correctly. The *Cost Interactive Report* includes a definitions document we strongly encourage you read to be sure you are collecting data based on the same definitions that MGMA uses to collect it. There also are a number of complex formulas that go into calculating some of these metrics. By using the benchmarking tools in the interactive report, you are assured the calculations are performed correctly.

### Using the Cost Interactive Report

The cost interactive report is based on observing organizations, not individuals. The data are presented in 30 tables that cover the 700-plus metrics. Each "slice" of data contains the exact same 30 tables. The 30 tables include the following:

### Staffing and Practice Data

- AR data, collection percentages, and financial ratios;
- Breakout of total gross charges by type of payer;
- Staffing, RVUs, patients, procedures, and square footage per FTE physician;

- Charges and revenue per FTE physician;
- Operating cost per FTE physician;
- Provider cost per FTE physician;
- Net income or loss per FTE physician;
- Charges and revenue as a percentage of total medical revenue;
- Operating cost as a percentage of total medical revenue;
- Provider cost as a percentage of total medical revenue;
- Net income or loss as a percentage of total medical revenue;
- Staffing, RVUs, patients, procedures, and square footage per FTE provider;
- Charges, revenue, and cost per FTE provider;
- Staffing, RVUs, patients, and procedures per 10,000 square foot;
- Charges, revenue, and cost per square feet;
- Staffing, patients, procedures and square footage per 10,000 total RVU;
- Charges, revenue, and cost per total RVUs;
- Staffing, patients, procedures, and square footage per 10,000 wRVU;
- Charges, revenue, and cost per wRVUs;
- Staffing, patients, procedures, and square footage per 10,000 patients;
- Charges, revenue, and cost per patient;
- Activity charges to total gross charges ratios;
- Medical procedure data (inside the practice);
- Medical procedure data (outside the practice);
- Surgery and anesthesia procedure data (inside the practice);
- Surgery and anesthesia procedure data (outside the practice);
- Clinical laboratory and pathology procedure data;
- Diagnostic radiology and imaging procedure data; and
- Nonprocedural gross charge data.

The data is broken down by:

- Per FTE physician;
- Per FTE provider;
- Expense as a percentage of total medical revenue;
- Per square foot;
- Per total RVU;
- Per wRVU; and
- Per patient.

The key indicators for medical group are included in Exhibit 15.

**Exhibit 15. Key Indicators for Medical Group Practices**

| | |
|---|---|
| Financial | **Revenue** - Medical revenue, ancillaries, other revenue<br>**Expense** - Support staff, general operating and provider expense |
| Operational | **Staffing**<br>**Process efficiency and quality**<br>**Resource utilization**<br>**Contracting**<br>**Relationship management** – referrals/marketing |
| Clinical | **Profile**<br>**Quality** – outcomes, adverse events<br>**Patient satisfaction**<br>**Compliance** |
| Individual | **Productivity** – work effort<br>**Income/Cost**<br>**Clinical Profile** – quality, procedure mix<br>**Job Performance** |
| Environmental | **Population**<br>**Other Medical Groups** – partners/competitors<br>**Payer Market**<br>**Hospital Market**<br>**Vendors** |

Depending on the nature of the engagement, you may have to understand and review one or more of these areas. The interactive report provides a robust benchmarking tool that allows you to quickly and easily perform a financial and operational benchmark.

The two basic tasks you will use the interactive report for are opening tables and using the built-in benchmarking tools. When the interactive report begins, you'll see the startup dialog box in Exhibit 16.

**Exhibit 16. Startup Dialog in the Interactive Report**

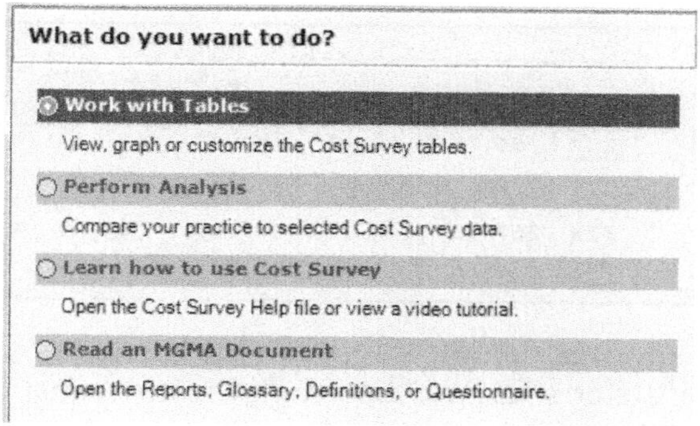


To open a table, select the "Work with Tables" option or the "Open Tables" toolbar button from the main menu. You will see the dialog (advanced mode is shown) in Exhibit 17.

**Exhibit 17. Table Open Dialog in the Interactive Report**

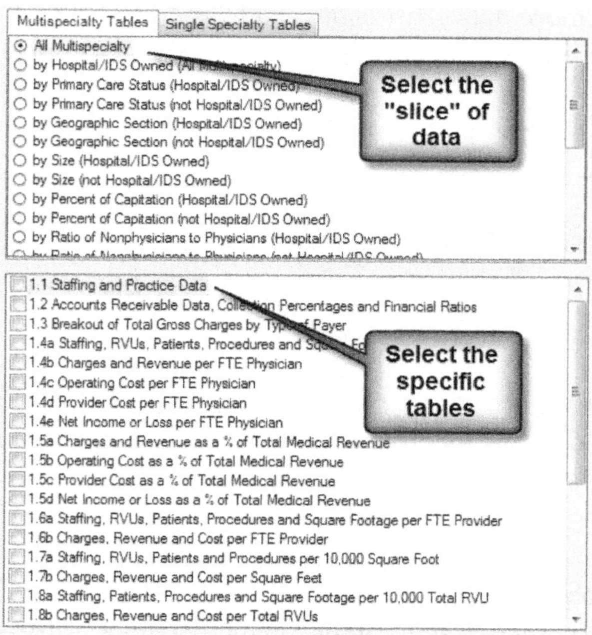


The interactive report consists of both multispecialty and single-specialty tables. In each of these categories, you may select from a number of different data "slices," including all, hospital-owned, geographic section, and so on. The next step is to pick one of the tables to display the specific data you are interested in. For all multispecialty, staffing, and practice data, the table appears in Exhibit 18.

**Exhibit 18. Table 1.1**

| Staffing and Practice Data | Practice Type | | | | | | | |
|---|---|---|---|---|---|---|---|---|
| | All Multispecialty | | | | | | | |
| | Count | Mean | Std. Dev. | 10th %tile | 25th %tile | Median | 75th %tile | 90th %tile |
| **Total provider FTE** | **282** | **69.76** | **86.47** | **9.45** | **18.37** | **45.51** | **89.79** | **160.93** |
| Total physician FTE | 325 | 52.90 | [illegible] | [illegible] | [illegible] | [illegible] | [illegible] | [illegible] |
| Total nonphysician provider FTE | 283 | 13.95 | [illegible] | [illegible] | [illegible] | [illegible] | [illegible] | [illegible] |
| **Total support staff FTE** | **325** | **257.65** | [illegible] | [illegible] | [illegible] | [illegible] | [illegible] | [illegible] |
| Number of branch clinics | 315 | 8.95 | [illegible] | [illegible] | [illegible] | [illegible] | [illegible] | [illegible] |
| Square footage of all facilities | 279 | 110,946 | [illegible] | [illegible] | [illegible] | [illegible] | [illegible] | [illegible] |

Metrics are on the left; statistics are shown in the columns. As with the *Physician Compensation and Production* interactive report, the program will not show data unless there are at least 10 providers (physicians) and three unique practices. If there are blanks or stars in the data, it is because there are insufficient physicians or practices.

Since the interactive report contains every percentile from 10 to 90, you can customize the display to show more data. This is helpful to get a feel for what the entire MGMA curve looks like. The same table expanded to show deciles appears in Exhibit 19.

**Exhibit 19. Table 1.1 Expanded to Show Deciles**

| Staffing and Practice Data | Practice Type | | | | | | | | | | | |
|---|---|---|---|---|---|---|---|---|---|---|---|---|
| | All Multispecialty | | | | | | | | | | | |
| | Count | Mean | Std. Dev. | 10th %tile | 20th %tile | 30th %tile | 40th %tile | Median | 60th %tile | 70th %tile | 80th %tile | 90th %tile |
| **Total provider FTE** | **282** | **69.76** | **86.47** | **9.45** | **15.84** | **21.95** | **29.12** | **45.51** | **55.48** | **71.42** | **102.78** | **160.93** |
| Total physician FTE | 325 | 52.90 | [illegible] | [illegible] | [illegible] | [illegible] | [illegible] | [illegible] | [illegible] | [illegible] | [illegible] | [illegible] |
| Total nonphysician provider FTE | 283 | 13.95 | [illegible] | [illegible] | [illegible] | [illegible] | [illegible] | [illegible] | [illegible] | [illegible] | [illegible] | [illegible] |
| **Total support staff FTE** | **325** | **257.65** | [illegible] | [illegible] | [illegible] | [illegible] | [illegible] | [illegible] | [illegible] | [illegible] | [illegible] | [illegible] |
| Number of branch clinics | 315 | 8.95 | [illegible] | [illegible] | [illegible] | [illegible] | [illegible] | [illegible] | [illegible] | [illegible] | [illegible] | [illegible] |
| Square footage of all facilities | 279 | 110,946 | [illegible] | [illegible] | [illegible] | [illegible] | [illegible] | [illegible] | [illegible] | [illegible] | [illegible] | [illegible] |

In the cost interactive report, data are available for multispecialty and 18 single-specialty practices. If your specialty is not provided, you will either have to use the multispecialty data or select a single specialty you feel is representative of the specialty.

## Benchmarking Tools

One of the most important functions of the interactive report is three built-in benchmarking tools, which allow you to input practice data and have the benchmarks performed automatically.

## Dashboard Report Tool

This tool provides a 50,000-foot view of a medical group in a dashboard format. The dashboard gauges provide rankings for total medical revenue per physician, total AR per physician, total operating cost per physician, total general operating cost per physician, total support staff cost per physician, and total medical revenue after operating cost per physician. Once again, because the dashboard presents the data in an easy-to-understand, green-yellow-red gauge format, the "benchmarking story" can be communicated to those who do not understand statistics, benchmarks, or MGMA data. The following screen shows the dashboard in Exhibit 20.

**Exhibit 20. Cost Dashboard**

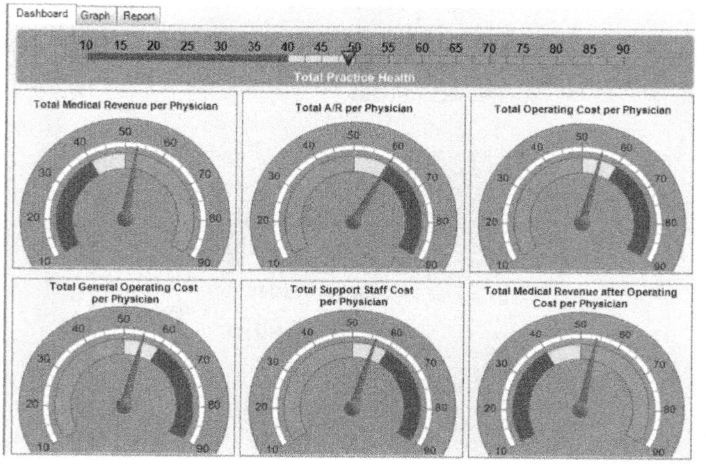


## Practice Performance Report Tool

This is the tool you want to use if you are a valuator. Once data are collected, you can perform a comprehensive income statement, staffing, AR, and ratio analysis in under an hour. As with all benchmarking tools, select the areas you want to benchmark and ignore the rest. Unless you have the background to interpret staffing data (FTEs and costs), stick with the other sections of this tool. Staffing levels and costs, however, are a significant driver of value in a medical practice; we encourage you to learn how this area impacts both financial performance and value. This tool is Excel-based, so you can export the entire tool to perform detailed analysis, roll-ups, and other custom analyses. It is also possible to prepopulate the tool with data, so you do not have to type in each engagement's data. Exhibit 21 shows the first input screen from the tool.

Once you input data, the tool performs the rest of the calculations and benchmarks, including a ranking report. The following schedule shows the revenue and cost as a percentage of total medical revenue, which is calculated based on the input screen. The last three columns show MGMA data, the differences between the practice and MGMA data, and the ranking of the practice. The ranking gives you a precise picture of how your practice compares to MGMA data, shown in Exhibit 22.

**Exhibit 21. Practice Performance Report Input Screen**

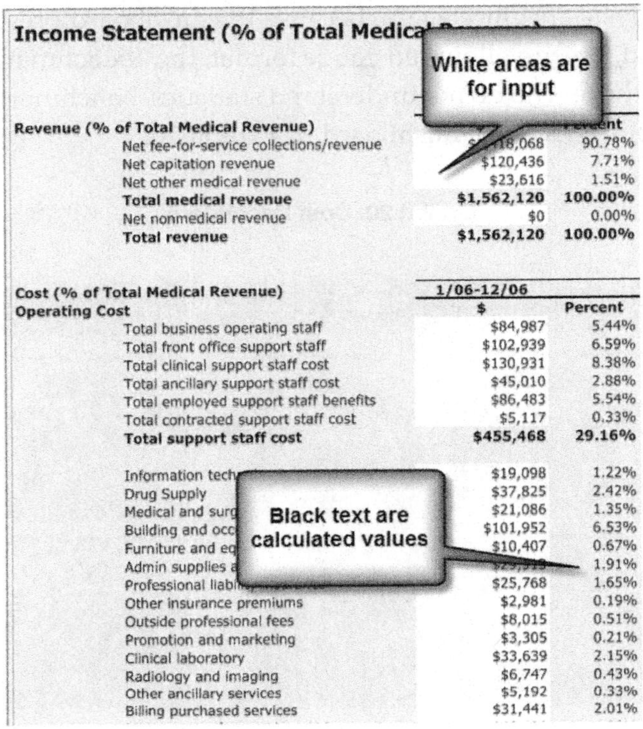


**Income Statement (% of Total Medica…**

| Revenue (% of Total Medical Revenue) | [illegible] | Percent |
|---|---|---|
| Net fee-for-service collections/revenue | [illegible] | 90.78% |
| Net capitation revenue | $120,436 | 7.71% |
| Net other medical revenue | $23,616 | 1.51% |
| **Total medical revenue** | **$1,562,120** | **100.00%** |
| Net nonmedical revenue | $0 | 0.00% |
| **Total revenue** | **$1,562,120** | **100.00%** |

| Cost (% of Total Medical Revenue) | 1/06-12/06 | |
|---|---|---|
| **Operating Cost** | **$** | **Percent** |
| Total business operating staff | $84,987 | 5.44% |
| Total front office support staff | $102,939 | 6.59% |
| Total clinical support staff cost | $130,931 | 8.38% |
| Total ancillary support staff cost | $45,010 | 2.88% |
| Total employed support staff benefits | $86,483 | 5.54% |
| Total contracted support staff cost | $5,117 | 0.33% |
| **Total support staff cost** | **$455,468** | **29.16%** |
| Information tech… | $19,098 | 1.22% |
| Drug Supply | $37,825 | 2.42% |
| Medical and surg… | $21,086 | 1.35% |
| Building and occ… | $101,952 | 6.53% |
| Furniture and eq… | $10,407 | 0.67% |
| Admin supplies a… | [illegible] | 1.91% |
| Professional liab… | $25,768 | 1.65% |
| Other insurance premiums | $2,981 | 0.19% |
| Outside professional fees | $8,015 | 0.51% |
| Promotion and marketing | $3,305 | 0.21% |
| Clinical laboratory | $33,639 | 2.15% |
| Radiology and imaging | $6,747 | 0.43% |
| Other ancillary services | $5,192 | 0.33% |
| Billing purchased services | $31,441 | 2.01% |

**Exhibit 22. Practice Performance Report Benchmark Screen**

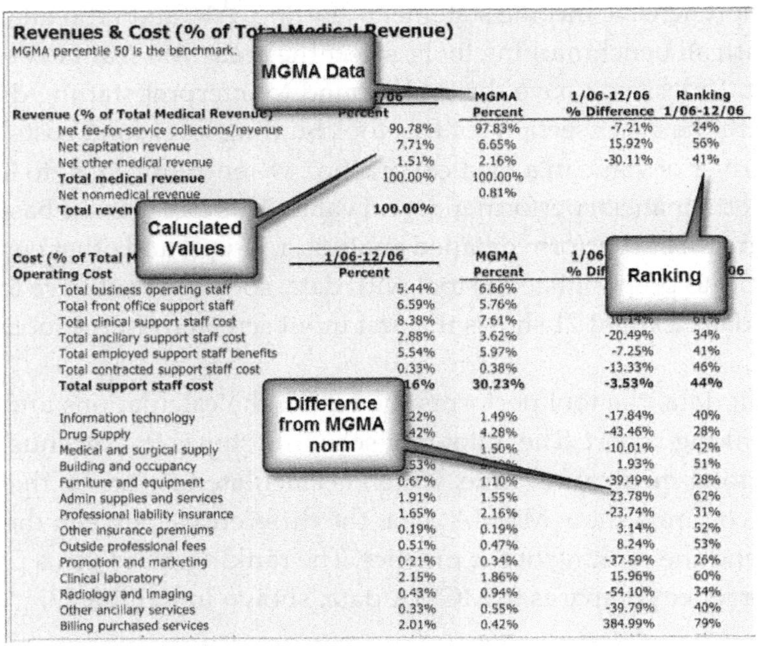


**Revenues & Cost (% of To… Revenue)**

MGMA percentile 50 is the benchmark.

| Revenue (% of Total Medical Revenue) | Percent | MGMA Percent | 1/06-12/06 % Difference | Ranking 1/06-12/06 |
|---|---|---|---|---|
| Net fee-for-service collections/revenue | 90.78% | 97.83% | -7.21% | 24% |
| Net capitation revenue | 7.71% | 6.65% | 15.92% | 56% |
| Net other medical revenue | 1.51% | 2.16% | -30.11% | 41% |
| **Total medical revenue** | 100.00% | 100.00% | | |
| Net nonmedical revenue | | 0.81% | | |
| **Total reven…** | **100.00%** | | | |

| Cost (% of Total M… | 1/06-12/06 | MGMA | 1/06… | |
|---|---|---|---|---|
| **Operating Cost** | **Percent** | **Percent** | **% Dif…** | **…06** |
| Total business operating staff | 5.44% | 6.66% | [illegible] | [illegible] |
| Total front office support staff | 6.59% | 5.76% | [illegible] | [illegible] |
| Total clinical support staff cost | 8.38% | 7.61% | [illegible] | [illegible] |
| Total ancillary support staff cost | 2.88% | 3.62% | -20.49% | 34% |
| Total employed support staff benefits | 5.54% | 5.97% | -7.25% | 41% |
| Total contracted support staff cost | 0.33% | 0.38% | -13.33% | 46% |
| **Total support staff cost** | [illegible] | **30.23%** | **-3.53%** | **44%** |
| Information technology | [illegible] | 1.49% | -17.84% | 40% |
| Drug Supply | [illegible] | 4.28% | -43.46% | 28% |
| Medical and surgical supply | [illegible] | 1.50% | -10.01% | 42% |
| Building and occupancy | [illegible] | [illegible] | 1.93% | 51% |
| Furniture and equipment | 0.67% | 1.10% | -39.49% | 28% |
| Admin supplies and services | 1.91% | 1.55% | 23.78% | 62% |
| Professional liability insurance | 1.65% | 2.16% | -23.74% | 31% |
| Other insurance premiums | 0.19% | 0.19% | 3.14% | 52% |
| Outside professional fees | 0.51% | 0.47% | 8.24% | 53% |
| Promotion and marketing | 0.21% | 0.34% | -37.59% | 26% |
| Clinical laboratory | 2.15% | 1.86% | 15.96% | 60% |
| Radiology and imaging | 0.43% | 0.94% | -54.10% | 34% |
| Other ancillary services | 0.33% | 0.55% | -39.79% | 40% |
| Billing purchased services | 2.01% | 0.42% | 384.99% | 79% |

### Advanced Benchmarking Report Tool

The practice performance report provides an easy-to-input financial statement format benchmark report. However, it only provides benchmarking for a subset of the *Cost Survey*'s 700-plus metrics. If you need to benchmark anything that is not contained in the practice performance report, use the advanced benchmarking report. This tool will allow you to customize the report for exactly the metrics you are interested in benchmarking.

### Summary

Since medical practices are unique, using MGMA and other medically based data will help you understand the unique drivers of value in a medical practice. This chapter was developed as a brief look at using MGMA data for valuing a medical practice; it does not provide a comprehensive discussion of these topics. If you are interested in getting more detailed information, we encourage you to check out the following resources:

- Join the MGMA (www.mgma.com);
- MGMA *Physicians Compensation and Production Survey* interactive report;
- MGMA *Cost Survey* interactive report;
- *RVUs: Applications for Medical Practice Success*, 2nd edition by Kathryn P. Glass, MBA, MSHA, PMP;
- *Benchmarking Success: The Essential Guide for Group Practices* by Gregory Feltenberger, MBA, FACMPE, FACHE, CPHIMS, and David Gans, MHSA, FACMPE;
- Arrange a custom training session with ValuSource on these topics. You can reach ValuSource at 800-825-8763 or email sales@valusourcesoftware.com or visit its Web site at www.valusourcesoftware.com;
- Participate in the Consulting Training Institute's (CTI) five-day healthcare boot camp (www.nacva.com); and
- Read books and take webinars on these topics.

### Thanks

I would like to thank the MGMA, Laurie Foote, Bill Sipes, and Robert Cimasi for their time, numerous conversations, and outstanding comments and suggestions regarding material in this chapter.

Chapter 24

# Benchmarking Practice Performance

*By Gregory S. Feltenberger, MBA, CACMPE, FACHE, CPHIMS, and David N. Gans, MSHA, FACMPE*

Why benchmark? There are many reasons for benchmarking, and most are related to a specific purpose (usually improvement). For example, a practice may want to determine how the billing office performance or physician productivity compares to other like practices. But in general, practices benchmark to gain a deeper understanding of where they are, where they want to go, and how to get there.

However, benchmarking when used in conjunction with trending—comparison to a standard over time—can be a powerful tool for assessing the past and present. And although the past cannot predict the future, it can be used to "suggest" the future. Therefore, benchmarking and trending can provide numerical insights into the past, present, and future "value" of an organization. And since the current state of healthcare—constantly changing and growing in complexity—dictates more elaborate and accurate methods of measurement, analysis, comparison, and improvement, long-term success has become directly related to a practice's ability to identify, predict, and adjust for changes.

Two key principles of benchmarking are: (1) If you don't measure it, you can't manage it and (2) if you don't value it, you won't change it. These principles have been applied to nonhealthcare industries for many years and are ideally suited for use in healthcare. It has been said that healthcare is the only service industry that doesn't treat itself like one. And although the healthcare industry appears to have gone to great lengths to separate itself from other business sectors, there are many more similarities than differences.

### If You Don't Measure It, You Can't Manage It

To manage something, it's necessary to know what it is (description), where it is (comparison), and how it got there (context). This can be accomplished through measurement and benchmarking. Proper practice management requires the use of subjective and objective measurement, analysis, comparison, and improvement.

### If You Don't Value It, You Won't Change It

Driving change in a practice will affect every member of the organization and many will resist; therefore, the value (benefit) of instituting a change must outweigh the status quo, or leaving things as is. Measurement and benchmarking are not the final step in the process—they simply enable the process to evolve toward action. It is completely appropriate to measure and benchmark; however, this activity is in vain if something isn't done with the findings. Ideally, the results should be used to support change; however, they may be used to validate past changes or support the current status. And once a benchmarking process is finished, the practice can pick and choose the areas in which to focus its efforts, create buy-in (sell the change), and start the process of improvement (or repeat the entire benchmarking exercise—that is, continuous process improvement).

What can be done with the findings? There are many options: (1) drive and support change, (2) educate staff, (3) validate the past, (4) build buy-in, (5) conduct performance reviews, and (6) plan for the future.

When using the key benchmarking principles—"if you don't measure it, you can't manage it" and "if you don't value it, you won't change it," it is imperative to understand the interrelationship. First, proper management requires some degree of measurement to ensure the attribute of interest if fully understood (for example, is a full-time equivalent (FTE) clearly defined?). Second, once measurement has taken place, management must decide whether the value of pursuing change is worth disrupting the practice in the quest for improvement. And third, if management feels the measures dictate a need to change and value can be realized by making the change, the most important step is to instill a sense of value in making the change with physicians and staff—without buy-in, the value (benefit) of change will never be fully realized.

Of special note, processes can easily be changed, but it's only with the support and buy-in of physicians and staff that real improvement can be achieved. It has been said, "If you take care of your people, your people will take care of you, but if you don't take care of your people, your people will take care of you."

What is benchmarking? Simply put, benchmarking is measurement and comparison for the purpose of improvement. In particular, medical practice benchmarking is a systematic, logical, and common-sense approach to measurement, analysis, comparison, and improvement (see Exhibit 1). Therefore, benchmarking is comparison to a standard. Benchmarking improves understanding of processes and clinical and administrative characteristics at a single point in time (snapshot) or over time (trend).[1] In addition, benchmarking is the continuous process of measuring and comparing performance internally (over time) and externally (against other organizations and industries). And finally, benchmarking is determining how the best-in-class achieve their performance levels. This consists of analyzing and comparing best practices to uncover what they did, how they did it, and what must be done to adopt it for your practice (process benchmarking).

**Exhibit 1. What Is Benchmarking?**

- A systematic, logical, and common-sense approach to measurement, comparison, and improvement.
- Copying the best, closing gaps and differences, and achieving superiority.
- "A positive, proactive process to change operations in a structured fashion to achieve superior performance. The purpose is to gain a competitive advantage."
- Comparing organizational performance to the performance of other organizations.
- Continuous process of comparison with the best or "the toughest competitors or companies renowned as leaders."
- A method for identifying processes to new goals with full support of management.

## The 'Value' of Benchmarking

Proper benchmarking consists of more than simple comparison of two numbers. The true value of benchmarking lies in the numbers and through an understanding of the current state of the practice, calculation of a difference between the current state and a new value or benchmark, knowing the context and background of the practice values when interpreting the results, deciding on a course of action and goal, and determining when the goal is achieved. For example, a comparison of average number of procedures per patient visit per physician to a known benchmark will only permit a mathematical analysis. However, what if one physician in the practice has been focusing on patients with simple medical issues that don't generate multiple procedures? The numbers alone would indicate this physician is underperforming and is below the others in procedural productivity; whereas, knowing the background, context, or other measures permit for a more detailed analysis. Perhaps this physician's focus is on acute care services and

1 E.W. Woodcock, "Practice Benchmarking," in *Physician Practice Management: Essential Operations and Financial Knowledge* (Sudbury, MA: Jones and Bartlett Publishers, 2005).

his or her average number of patient encounters per day is almost twice that of other physicians in the practice?

### How to Benchmark

There are several methods of benchmarking. A simple 10-step process might consist of the following:

1. Determine what is critical to your organization's success;
2. Identify metrics that measure the critical factors;
3. Identify a source for internal and external benchmarking data;
4. Measure your practice's performance;
5. Compare your practice's performance to the benchmark;
6. Determine whether action is necessary based on the comparison;
7. If action is needed, identify the best practice and process used to implement it;
8. Adapt the process used by others in the context of your practice;
9. Implement new process, reassess objectives, evaluate benchmarking standards, and recalibrate measures; and
10. Do it again—benchmarking is an ongoing process and tracking over time allows for continuous improvement.

### Standardizing Data for Comparison

Since the primary purpose of benchmarking is comparison, it is necessary to standardize data so organizations of different sizes can be compared. A common method for standardizing data is to convert measures to percentages, per unit of input, or per unit of output. For example, per unit of input can be presented as per FTE physician, per FTE provider, or per square foot, whereas per unit of output can be presented on a per-patient, per-RBRVS unit, or per-procedure level.

### What's Our Baseline?

Benchmarking, like any activity involving comparison, requires an understanding of "where you are"—this is known as your baseline. The baseline represents where you are today or where you've been and provides a point of origin or starting point. In addition, a baseline is an initial state that forms a logical basis for comparison. For example, to determine whether physicians have increased the average number of procedures per patient visit, it is necessary to have two measurements: the old value or baseline and the new value. To calculate the delta (or difference) between the two values, a simple formula can be used: new value minus old value. Without the baseline, it would not be possible to perform this or many other calculations like percentage change.

## How Are We Doing?

This question can be answered by asking the question, "What is the difference between the baseline and current state (or where we are today)?" The baseline can be an internal benchmark (historical measure) from inside the practice, a benchmark across like practices from a Medical Group Management Association (MGMA) *Survey Report*, or a benchmark from outside the industries such as Disney or Wal-Mart. Additional insights can also be assessed by calculating the difference between current state and an established benchmark or industry average or median. To determine the difference, there are several methods and statistical tools. For instance, the mathematical difference, or delta, consists of subtracting the baseline value from the current value, whereas percentage change is a method for assessing changes over time or the proportion of one value in comparison to another. In addition to these methods, there are more statistically intense methods to determine difference that can be generalized across a group (see Exhibit 2).

**Exhibit 2. What Is the Difference?**

- Mathematical difference (delta)
- New value minus old value
- Current state minus Initial state
- Benchmark and industry value minus current state
- Percentage change
- Difference between three or more average

Interpretation of the difference is dependent on the method used. When using the delta, the difference will be a raw number, since the method consists of simple subtraction. Determining whether the difference is good or bad depends on the context, background, and what the values represent. For example, if medical revenue after operating cost per FTE family practice physician is $145,000 and the MGMA benchmark indicates a median of $214,377, then the delta is $69,377 ($214,377 minus $145,000). A delta of $69,377 may suggest poor practice performance, reduced physician productivity, a capital investment, or other practice deficiencies or large expenses, Whereas the percentage change method indicates this practice is only generating 67% of the median for similar types of practices (see Exhibit 3). Therefore, the result is different between delta and percentage change, and the interpretation may also be different.

**Exhibit 3. Difference Between Delta and Percentage Change**

| Is the result positive or negative? | Delta | Percentage Change |
|---|---|---|
| Positive value | New value (or benchmark) is greater than the old value. For example, $214,377 minus $145,000 equals a delta of $69,377 | New value has increased. For example, $145,000 divided by $214,377 equals 0.67. This when multiplied by 100 equals 67%. |
| Negative value | New value is less. | New value has decreased. |

## Methods and Checklists

Failing to plan, it has been said, is planning to fail. Therefore, an integral component of the benchmarking process is the proper use of systematic methods, checklists, scales, and comparable measures. Systematic methods consist of formulas and ratios as found in this chapter. Checklists are a planning tool to ensure all variables and methods are used and considered—checklists ensure attention to detail and minimize the chance of missing steps in a process (see Exhibit 4). Scales provide the measuring stick—meaning they indicate whether your measures are high or low, good or bad, or where they are in comparison to others. And comparable measures are key to the heart and soul of benchmarking and provide a means for determining how your practice compares to others.

**Exhibit 4. Example Checklist[2]**

The following checklist items can be used to increase the likelihood that a claim will be processed and paid when first submitted:

- ❒ Patient information is complete.
- ❒ Patient's name and address matches the insurer's records.
- ❒ Patient's group number and subscriber number is correct.
- ❒ Physician's Social Security number, provider number, or tax identification number is completed and correct.
- ❒ Claim is signed by the physician.
- ❒ All necessary dates are completed.
- ❒ Dates for care given are chronological and correct—for example, is the discharge date listed as before the admission date?
- ❒ Dates for care given are in agreement with the claims information from other providers, such as the hospital, etc.
- ❒ Diagnosis is complete.
- ❒ Diagnosis is correct for the services or procedures provided.
- ❒ Diagnostic codes are correct for the services or procedures provided.
- ❒ CPT and ICD-9 codes are accurate.
- ❒ Diagnosis is coded using ICD-9-CM to the highest level of specificity.
- ❒ Fee column is itemized and totaled.
- ❒ All necessary information about prescription drugs or durable medical equipment prescribed by the physician is included.
- ❒ The claim is legible.

2 DecisionHealth, "A/R Benchmarks," Part B News 20, no. 40 (Oct. 16, 2006).

## Small and Solo Practice Benchmarking

Small and solo practices share many similarities with their larger counterparts; however, the benefits and risks associated with the differences can have significant impact on a small practice's longevity and financial success.

## Similarities With Larger Practices

Small and solo practices share many similarities with larger organizations. For instance, all medical practices must operate in the same healthcare environment and deal with the same healthcare legislation, malpractice insurance, payers, collection challenges, patient needs and expectations, delivery and standards of care, and processes—just to name a few.

Also, the benchmarking methods used by large organizations are identical to those used by small and solo practices (see Exhibit 5). And the use of normalized metrics permits comparison regardless of organizational size. Common examples available in most benchmarking datasets consist of measures per FTE physician or provider, per square foot, per patient, per procedure, and per RVU.

**Exhibit 5. Similarities Regardless of Size or Type[3]**

- Legislation can change payment (for example, Medicare and Medicaid reimbursement rates are determined through legislation).
- Costs are increasing greater than inflation (for example, medical supplies and equipment costs are increasing at a greater percentage than reimbursement rates).
- Expenses change.
- Increases in physician compensation are from production (for example, much of physician compensation is based on physician production or the number of patients seen and the procedures performed).
- Health savings accounts will change patient behavior (for example, patients will treat medical care more like a product or service they pay for using the funds in their account).
- Hospitals are purchasing physician practices (again).
- Advances in medical care are changing care delivery.
- Physicians are publicly rated for quality and outcomes.
- Physicians are publicly rated for patient satisfaction.

## What's the Difference?

Small and solo practices are different from larger groups in several ways, some of which are beneficial, while others are not. For instance, smaller organizations are generally more flexible, can adapt or change quickly and in general, tend to be more efficient. However, small and solo practices are more sensitive to the risks associated with costly

3 E.J. Pavlock, *Financial Management for Medical Groups*, 2nd ed. (Englewood, Col.: MGMA, 2000).

mistakes, lack of alternative revenue-generating methods, and the absence of (or antiquated condition of) robust information systems. For example, with only one or two physicians in a practice, what impact would a poor decision or loss of a physician (due to sickness or some other unforeseen event) have on the practice? Can a small practice afford to retain adequate earnings for contingencies? Does the existing information system compliment and add to the efficiency of the practice? And does it interface (communicate) with the information systems used by payers, hospitals, and other medical practices such as referring practices and physicians?

Ultimately, the goals of smaller practices mirror those of larger groups—to have more satisfied patients, more fulfilling work environments for physicians and staff, and better economic outcomes. However, the additional sensitivities of small and solo practices must be considered to ensure surprise events don't adversely impact the practice.

### Practice Measurement

Measurement is the collection and organization of data. In many cases, measurement is a method of converting an array, group, list, or set of data into a single variable that describes the entire dataset. A mean or average is a calculation that summarizes the central tendency or mathematical center of many data points, provided all data are of the same unit of measurement. In general, an average is the most common calculation used to analyze and compare data. It's the most common, since most people understand the concept of an average and how to calculate it. For example, if we count the number of patients seen per month for the last 10 months for an eight-provider family medical practice located in the suburbs, we have an array of data with 10 data points—one data point for each month (see Exhibit 6). If we also have a list with the number of patients seen per month for the last 10 months for an eight-provider family medical practice located in a rural community, how can we easily compare these two practices? We can line up and organize the data points in ascending order, but what does this tell us? We might conclude the suburban practice sees a greater number of patients per month, but we can't accurately describe the difference or make a comparison. All we've done so far is arrange the data and guessed there was a difference by looking at or "eyeballing" the data—not the most accurate method. However, by calculating the average number of patients seen per month for the last 10 months for each practice, a single and accurate measure can be used to describe and compare the two groups.

**Exhibit 6. Example of Measurement: Number of Patients Seen Per Month**

| Month | Suburban Practice | Rural Practice |
|---|---|---|
| January | 2,620 | 2,650 |
| February | 2,231 | 2,660 |
| March | 2,264 | 2,266 |
| April | 2,650 | 2,067 |
| May | 2,657 | 1,687 |
| June | 2,670 | 3,690 |
| July | 3,067 | 3,070 |
| August | 2,690 | 2,071 |
| September | 3,171 | 2,731 |
| October | 3,710 | 3,730 |
| **Sum of patients seen** | **27,730** | **26,622** |
| Number of data points (months) | 10 | 10 |
| **Average patients seen per month** | **2,773** | **2,662** |

Comparing these practices, the suburban practice, on average, sees more patients per month than the rural practice—111 more (average number of patients seen per month in the suburban practice minus average number of patients seen per month in the rural practice; 2,773 minus 2,662 equals 111).

## Art and Science of Benchmarking

Benchmarking, as it's related to measurement, is the art and science of comparison. The "art" takes place during the data gathering and interpretation phases and requires a method with some common sense, whereas the "science" is the systematic and logical process of analysis. Once interpretation and analysis have occurred, data are considered transformed into information that can be used for comparison and decisionmaking. That is, it is possible to determine whether the data are similar or different and by how much. Exhibit 7 represents several examples of metrics and associated benchmarks.

**Exhibit 7. Examples of Benchmarks**

| | | | | | | |
|---|---|---|---|---|---|---|
| Encounters per FTE* physician | Mean | 3,006 | 4,759 | 5,891 | 7,612 | 9,159 |
| Total procedures per FTE physician | 6,341 | 3,006 | 4,759 | 5,891 | 7,612 | 9,159 |
| Physician work RVUs per FTE physician | 4,751 | 4,412 | 7,506 | 5,123 | 5,622 | 6,809 |
| Physician compensation | $4,751 | $1,426 | $3,684 | $5,123 | $5,622 | $6,809 |

Other topics associated with benchmarking are: (1) continuous improvement and (2) evaluation and assessment. Continuous improvement refers to the need for repeated analysis using the same measures over time (trend). An evaluation is a subjective, personal judgment of the value (or worth) of something, whereas an assessment is objective and quantifiable (or assigned a numeric value).

## Benchmarking Methods

Effective benchmarking consists of a systematic process; therefore, several methods have been developed to ensure the process is efficient (see Exhibit 8).

Proper measurement begins with selecting the right practice attribute, characteristic, property, dimension, or variable to be assessed. In other words, what do we want to measure? For example, encounters per FTE physician, total procedures per FTE physician, and physician work RVUs per FTE physician are common examples of benchmarks and practice measures. This book presents many practice attributes that have been operationally defined, that is, the attribute and measurement process have been clearly described in practice and literature as generally accepted. However, there may be practice attributes that are not typically measured or found in the literature. In these cases, it would be necessary to fully explore the characteristic before moving to the next step—this type of attribute could be called "homegrown." Of note, there are probably few instances when "homegrown" attributes are needed since the healthcare management field is sufficiently mature to have identified most, if not all, key practice characteristics.

Once a practice variable is selected, the next step is to decide on the appropriate method of measurement (or what metric should be used) and the intended purpose. There are two general categories of metrics: (1) informational and (2) actionable. Informational metrics provide a simple description and unlike actionable metrics, they don't clearly suggest ways of affecting change. For example, if we decide to measure the average number of patients seen per month in a suburban practice as a metric to describe monthly practice productivity, then this metric simply tells us the arithmetic mean—it doesn't suggest anything more, whereas, actionable metrics are usually more complex, require an understanding of the context, and are compared to a benchmark or baseline. For instance, the formula to calculate average number of patients seen per month (for the last 10 months) per provider for an eight-provider family medical practice is the sum of the number of patients seen per month for the last 10 months divided by the number of months divided by the number of providers. If we use this formula as a metric to assess monthly practice productivity per provider and want to improve productivity per provider, then this metric used in this context suggests, for example, we can affect change by working with individual providers whose average is below the practice's overall average to increase the number of patients seen per month by the provider of interest.

**Exhibit 8. Methods of Benchmarking**

| Transfer Model | Five Stages of Benchmarking | 5 Steps of Benchmarking | 10 Steps to Benchmarking |
|---|---|---|---|
| 1. Identification and documentation of best practices.<br>2. Validation and consensus of what to focus on and what are true best practices.<br>3. Transfer and develop buy-in; sell ideas to management and get commitment to performance assessments, identify priorities, and establish a plan.<br>4. Implementation using team champions, selection of critical practices to support strategic initiatives. | 1. Planning, selecting the processes to benchmark, and identifying customer expectations and critical success factors.<br>2. Form the benchmarking team from across the organization.<br>3. Collect the data from best practice organizations and identify own processes.<br>4. Analyze data for gaps.<br>5. Take action, identify what needs to be done to match best practice, and implement change. | 1. Planning what to benchmark and what organization to benchmark against.<br>2. Analyze performance gaps and project future performance.<br>3. Set targets for change and communicate to all levels.<br>4. Develop action plans, implement plans, and adjust as necessary.<br>5. Achieve a state of maturity by integrating best practices into organization. | 1. Determine what is critical to your organization's success.<br>2. Identify metrics that measure the critical factors.<br>3. Identify a source for internal and external benchmarking data.<br>4. Measure your practice's performance.<br>5. Compare your practice's performance to the benchmark.<br>6. Determine whether action is necessary based on the comparison.<br>7. If action is needed, identify the best practice and process to use to implement it.<br>8. Adapt the process used by others in the context of your practice.<br>9. Implement new process, reassess objectives, evaluate benchmarking standards, and recalibrate measures<br>10. Do it again—benchmarking is an ongoing process and tracking over time allows for continuous improvement. |

Several questions should be asked as part of preliminary measurement steps. For instance, what do you want to measure? Is it a generally accepted practice characteristic (typical practice factor) or is it a homegrown practice attribute (custom or self-defined factor or metric)? What metric should be used? What is the appropriate method for measurement? And finally, what type of metric do you want to use and what is your intended purpose (information or action)?

### Interpretation Pitfalls

Reliability is defined as repeatability and consistency. If given the same dataset and using the same measure, someone else should be able to calculate, describe, and compare the data in the same way. For instance, if given the number of patients seen per month for the last 10 months in a suburban and rural practice and asked for the average number of patients seen per month for both practices, you would find the same average with the same comparison for each practice. Note that the same unit of measurement must be used, that is, all the data in your data set or data array should be the same unit of measurement (in the example above, all numbers are based on number of patients seen). Reliability cannot be achieved if the unit of measurement is different in any of the data used in the measurement. For example, you cannot calculate an average using 2,650 patients seen in January, 2,264 seen in February, 3,265 seen in March, 2,166 seen in April, 3,167 seen in May, 1,869 seen in June, 2,771 seen in July, and 3,171 appointments booked in August without first changing appointments booked to the number of patients seen in August.

Validity is meaningfulness within a generally accepted theoretical basis (see Exhibit 9). Or simply stated, does it really mean what it's expected to mean or is it being interpreted accurately? How you interpret your data and measurements are as important as ensuring you have used a highly reliable method. Understanding what a particular measure is meant to describe is paramount to using data properly to support good decisions. For instance, averages (means) represent the mathematical center of an array of data or central tendency, whereas the median is the 'actual' center of the array. In some cases, the average and median can be the same, but often, there is a difference. Therefore, knowing how a measure is used, collected, and calculated will assist in supporting your decisions, that is, your conclusions and analysis will be more valid and meaningful. This is particularly important when presenting your findings to others since the better you understand the measures, why you selected them, and how to explain them to others, the value and usefulness of your results will add significant credibility to your recommendations and decisions.

Another pitfall to avoid that is a common mistake is averaging averages, for example, which presents a danger during measurement. Since any array of data points can be averaged (or measured using other methods), it's important to understand the limitations or implications of measuring calculated measures. The validity of the interpretation may be suspect.

The extremely low and high values in all the practices are minimized or diluted (their effect is almost eliminated). The effects of the low- and high-productivity practices almost eliminate one another, which is why the average of the averages is near the

**Exhibit 9. Example of Meaningfulness**

It is important to understand the formulas used for measurement and how the measurement is collected and calculated. Using the data array from the previous example of number of patients seen per month [suburban practice: 2,620 (January), 2,231 (February), 2,264 (March), 2,650 (April), 2,657 (May), 2,670 (June), 3,067 (July), 2,690 (August), 3,171 (September), 3,710 (October)]:

- Average (mean) = Sum of all data divided by the number of data points
- Sum of all data = 27,730
- Number of data points = 10
- Average = 2,773
- Median = The data point in the center of the array (when arranged in order)
- Data array = 2,231, 2,264, 2,620, 2,650, 2,657, 2,670, 2,690, 3,067, 3,171, 3,710
- Center of array are two data points = 2,657 and 2,670
- Median = 2,657 + 2,670 divided by 2 = 2,664
- Note: If the data array consisted of an odd number of data points, the median would be the true center data point.

average of the more balanced array (Family Practice 1).

Strength is related to validity and is the power, magnitude, or accuracy of your interpretation or how confident you are in your interpretation. For instance, if you want to describe the number of patients seen per month for three months (2,231, 2,264, and 2,620), a mean is an ideal descriptive statistic (mean = 2,372). This figure is somewhat descriptive of the lower months of 2,231 and 2,264, but a mean of 2,372 is not descriptive of the higher months when 2,620 patients were seen. Therefore, your confidence in a mean of 2,372 patients seen per month provides a less accurate description of the average number of patients seen per month. However, if this array consisted of a large number of months, that is, a large dataset with many data points, the accuracy of this metric and your confidence in the descriptive power of the mean is much higher.

A final interpretation issue is related to the mutually exclusive and exhaustive nature of data. Mutually exclusive refers to a data point fitting into only one category. For example, we decide months with 3,600 patients or more are categorized as high productivity, months with between 2,401 and 3,599 patients are medium or normal, and months with 2,400 patients or less are low. Therefore, each month fits into only one category—that's mutually exclusive—a single month cannot be categorized as "high" and "medium." If a single month could be assigned to multiple categories, it would be difficult to accurately describe each month or interpret your findings. Exhaustive refers to the description of the attribute, that is, does the definition encompass all collected attributes? For example, since all the measurements taken consisted of the number of patients seen per month, this attribute was defined to be actual patient encounters with a provider and all collected measures were based on this definition. That is, patients seen only by a nurse were not included since these encounters didn't fit the definition (or criteria).

Management can use numbers to diagnose and treat practice deficiencies, plan improvements, and examine practice activities and processes. And because numbers are less susceptible to the effects of human variation (feelings and emotions), they are more appropriate for decisionmaking. The beauty of numbers comes from their brevity, clarity, and precision. For example, using the example array (list) that shows the number of no-shows per day from last month, it is possible to quickly summarize the week or entire month regarding no-show activity. These averages and totals provide a brief, clear, and precise picture describing no-show activity during each week or the entire month. There's little room for misinterpretation or confusion, provided a no-show is clearly defined, that is, a no-show is a patient who fails to show up within 15 minutes of an appointment, rather than someone who fails to cancel 24 hours prior to his or her appointment.

Organizing a group of numbers is the cornerstone in the benchmarking process. An array or group of numbers only becomes valuable once it is organized, whereas statistical methods and proper interpretation of the findings are necessary to uncover the useful information behind the numbers. A systematic approach is necessary and has been established through the use of averages (or means), medians, standard deviations, percentiles, quartiles, and percentage change. These techniques can be used to measure and benchmark all practice attributes. In addition, these methods are easy to use, understand, and communicate—most people are familiar with some, if not all methods.

There are a handful of key financial performance indicators understood and used by the majority of practices to measure financial operations. Many of these formulas are presented in this chapter as a comprehensive "starter set" of key performance indicators and financial metrics for benchmarking.

## Key Financial Indicators

Benchmarks for many of the following formulas are available in the MGMA *Cost Survey and Performance and Practices of Successful Medical Groups* reports.

#### Total net collections

Net fee-for-service revenue + capitation revenue – provision for bad debt

#### Gross (unadjusted) collection ratio

Definition: Indicates how much of what is being charged is actually collected.

Goal: The higher, the better

$$\frac{\text{Total net collections}}{\text{Total gross charges}}$$

Note: In general, the goal of this measure is "the higher, the better"; however, this metric will vary significantly depending on the fee schedule of the practice. For instance, a practice with a high fee schedule will have a lower gross collection ratio than a practice with a low fee schedule (setting a fee schedule too low can have a negative effect on net revenue). This metric is often used to measure billing office performance.

#### Gross collection ratio

Definition: Indicates a ratio of the amount of revenue "actually" collected over the amount charged.

Goal: The higher, the better

$$\frac{\text{Net FFS revenue or collections}}{\text{Gross FFS charges}}$$

#### Adjusted (net) collection ratio

Definition: Indicates how much of what is being charged (gross FFS charges) is actually collected after total adjustments to charges; does not include funds the practice should not receive (e.g., contractual allowances) and funds it will not receive (e.g., bad debt).

Goal: The higher, the better

$$\frac{\text{Net fee-for-service collections}}{\text{Net fee-for-service charges}}$$

#### Average adjusted revenue per day

Definition: Indicates the average amount of revenue generated per business day.

Goal: The higher, the better

$$\frac{\text{Adjusted charges for the last three months}}{\text{Number of business days for the same time period}}$$

Note: It isn't required that the time period be three months; rather, it should be a recent period of time.

**Days revenue outstanding**

Definition: Indicates how long it takes before claims and charges are paid.

Goal: The lower, the better

Step 1: Calculate "days revenue"

$$\frac{\text{Total revenue for the last three months}}{\text{Number of business days in the last three months}}$$

Step 2: Calculate "days revenue outstanding"

$$\frac{\text{Outstanding net AR}}{\text{Days revenue}}$$

**Days in AR**

Definition: Indicates how long it takes before claims and charges are paid.

Goal: A net collection ratio (NCR) of 96% to 99% and 40 to 50 days in AR (a days in AR of 45 or less is ideal) indicate your practice is functioning efficiently and doing very well. If NCR is 93% to 95% and 50 to 60 days in AR, there is some (little) room for improvement. And if 92% or less and 70 days or more in AR, there is significant room for improvement in billing operations.

$$\frac{\text{Outstanding AR}}{\text{(Average monthly charge /30)}}$$

Note: Include at least the last three months to calculate the average monthly charges

**Days in AR (alternate calculation)**

Definition: Indicates how long it takes before claims and charges are paid.

Goal: The lower, the better

$$\frac{\text{Outstanding net AR}}{\text{Average adjusted revenue per day}}$$

#### Months revenue in AR

Definition: Indicates the average number of months charges are outstanding for collection.

Goal: The lower, the better

$$\frac{\text{Total AR}}{(\text{Annual adjusted FFS charges} * 1/12)}$$

#### Expense to earnings

Definition: Indicates the ratio of overhead (expenses) to revenue (collections).

Goal: The lower, the better

$$\frac{\text{Total operating expenses}}{\text{Total collections}}$$

#### Average revenue per patient

Definition: Indicates the average amount of revenue generated per patient seen. In addition, it can be used to determine the number of patients that must be treated to receive a predetermined amount of revenue (collections).

Goal: The higher, the better

$$\frac{\text{Total monthly collections for last month}}{\text{Total patient visits last month}}$$

#### Average cost per patient

Definition: Indicates the average cost of providing treatment per patient visit.

Goal: The lower, the better

$$\frac{\text{Total operating expenses}}{\text{Total patient visits}}$$

#### Departmental or service ratio

Definition: Indicates the expenses to revenues ratio for a specific department or service.

Goal: The lower, the better

$$\frac{\text{Total expenses for ancillary service for the last three months}}{\text{Total net charges for all CPT codes related to ancillary service}}$$

#### Collections rate by payer

Definition: Indicates different rates of reimbursement by payer.

Goal: Depends on many practice factors; should be proportional to the percentage of patients covered by each payer.

$$\frac{\text{Net collections by payer}}{\text{Total gross charges by payer}}$$

Note: Reimbursement received from a payer is based on the specific fee schedule established with a payer and is on a per-procedure basis. Net collections is the sum of all reimbursement received from a payer, whereas gross charges is what the practice billed the payer.

#### Volume and reimbursement by service line

Definition: Indicates workload volume and revenue generated by service line; provides a method for identifying the relative contribution of each service line.

Goal: Depends on many practice factors; in most cases, volume should be directly related to revenue generated by service line.

Volume by service line:

$$\frac{\text{Volume measurement (encounters/visits, RVUs, etc.) by service line}}{\text{Volume measurement for total practice}}$$

Reimbursement by service line:

$$\frac{\text{Revenue by service line}}{\text{Total practice revenue}}$$

#### Surgical yield

Definition: Indicates relative contribution of revenue generated from surgical or procedural workload to total practice revenue.

Goal: Depends on many practice factors; in most cases, volume should be directly related to revenue generated by service line.

$$\frac{\text{Revenue derived from surgeries or procedures}}{\text{Total practice revenue}}$$

**Reimbursement per procedure code**

Definition: Indicates average amount of revenue generated from procedures provided to patients.

Goal: Depends on many practice factors; in general, it will be higher if the procedures provided to patients are higher RVU procedures.

$$\frac{\text{Net collections}}{\text{Total number of procedures}}$$

Note: This metric can be adapted to show average reimbursement per procedure by payer using net collections by payer divided by total number of procedures charged to a payer.

In conclusion, benchmarking provides a means to measure performance in relation to a standard like the odometer (total mileage) in a car is used as one of many measures to assess value (future performance). For example, a car with 100,000 miles is probably worth less than the same type of car with 50,000 miles. And this can be determined by comparison (benchmarking) against a standard like the Kelly Blue Book values for a car or the MGMA surveys for medical practice performance. Trending, as it's related to benchmarking, can be used to compare practice measures against a standard over a period of time—this increases the "value" benchmarking by displaying past and present performance. And once benchmarks are complimented with trended data, it is possible to extend the measures into the future, thereby predicting the future. However, like any measure of a complex system or organization, a single measure studied in a vacuum only provides a narrow view that's prone to error. Therefore, multiple benchmarks and trends should be evaluated to gain a richer, fuller, and more rewarding picture of the performance landscape and associated value of the organization.

Chapter 25

# Designing a Chart of Accounts to Meet the Needs of Physician Practices

*By David N. Gans, MSHA, FACMPE, and Steven Andes, Ph.D., CPA*

The chart of accounts is the basis for an organization's accounting system. Whether the organization is a public entity or a private business, it needs a set of statements to record its financial condition. The chart of accounts is the starting point for every organization's financial records because it is the list of accounts used to record the organization's expenses and revenues as well as its assets and liabilities.

Businesses use accounting to record, monitor, and report their financial condition to managers, owners or shareholders, creditors, and governmental bodies. Accounting records describe an organization's current financial position as well as any changes. Managers require accurate and consistent financial information for both short-term and strategic decisionmaking. Creditors need the same information to decide the level of lending risk that is the basis for the amount of the loan and the interest rate that the organization is qualified to receive. Financial statements are also the basis for the tax return and other financial documents required by local, state, and federal agencies.

To be useful to all the various users, accounting records need to reliable, relevant, and consistent. Reliable means that the records are free from bias or error, faithfully represent the financial status of the organization, and must be verifiable, after the fact. Reliability means that financial records are neutral in their nature and can be verified by different accountants using the same objective data and measurement techniques. Accounting records must also be relevant, meaning that the records have the information that decisionmakers need and are sufficiently prepared and distributed in a timely manner. Additionally, accounting records should show consistency, meaning that there is comparability across organizations and with previous time periods.[1]

Financial accounting has standard rules, terms, and procedures that have been developed over time. These rules, terms, and procedures are classified as "generally accepted accounting practices," or GAAP. Until recently, a nongovernmental agency, the Financial Accounting Standards Board, was the ultimate authority for GAAP. Since the Sarbanes-Oxley Law of 2002 (Public Company Accounting and Investor Protection Act), the Public Company Accounting Oversight Board (PCAOB, www.pcaob.org) is now the final authority for GAAP, at least as it relates to publicly traded corporations. While the PCAOB is also technically not a government agency, the Security and Exchange Commission, which is a government agency, appoints the chair and the members and approves the budget.[2]

As stated before, the chart of accounts forms the basis for all accounting information recorded in the financial records. The chart of accounts lists each account with a corresponding number for the accounting system to track. The accounts in the chart of accounts determine the detail that financial transactions are recorded. Without a designated accounting code stated in the chart of accounts, it is impossible to track a revenue or expense item in the accounting records.

Therefore, the designation of an account code from the chart of accounts determines how an expense or revenue can be recorded into the financial records and from there, into the financial reports prepared for the organization.

All business and public entities have similar legal requirements to maintain accurate, representative accounting records that accurately show the financial status of the organization. All business and public entities have similar needs for reliable, relevant, and consistent accounting information for managerial decisionmaking. Healthcare organizations, in particular, have unique business requirements that dictate how financial information should be categorized. Healthcare entities need to understand their sources of revenue, how discounts and contracts are applied, how expenses are incurred and a detailed understanding of the costs incurred to provide services. These complexities make it necessary that healthcare organizations use a chart of accounts developed to meet their specific needs.

A healthcare manager must ensure that the chart of accounts has an account for every revenue and expense it needs to track. The number of separate accounts an organization

1 Chart of Accounts for Health Care Organizations. Neill F. Piland, Dr. P.H. and Kathryn P. Glass, MBA, MSHA, Center for Research in Ambulatory Health Care Administration, Englewood, Colo. p. 2-3.

2 Wolper chapter. "Accounting and Budgeting for Medical Practice Managers," Gans and Andes. P.

needs in its chart of accounts depends somewhat on its size and organizational complexity. Generally, larger and more complex organizations need more accounts than smaller, less-sophisticated entities. Managers need input from their organization's financial and legal advisors, as well as their creditors, to identify particular revenues or expenses that must be tracked to meet specific legal and other reporting needs.

As stated earlier, a medical practice cannot track any revenue or expenses not listed in the chart of accounts. However, the more the accounts listed for recording various revenues and expenses, the more costly it is to maintain an accounting system. Additionally, if the accounting system records information in too much detail, the managerial uses of the information are handicapped by the inability to easily interpret financial records. The selection of the level of detail is an important aspect in the design of the organization's chart of accounts. Managers need to designate the accounts needed to generate the financial reports required for decisionmaking, for lenders, and to meet the legal reporting and tax filing requirements of government. In general, smaller organizations usually need fewer accounts than larger ones, and all organizations will usually expand the number of accounts they use as managers find the need for more detailed accounting and financial recordkeeping.

To set up a chart of accounts, a manager needs to define the various financial accounts the organization will need. Each account will be given a unique number, and similar financial activities should have numbers that have closely associated digits. Smaller, less-complex organizations may find that all of their accounting needs can be accommodated using only three digits (potentially yielding 999 separate accounts). However, more digits may be needed to simplify how accounts are categorized and provide room to add new accounts in the future. Complex organizations may have a chart of accounts with hundreds of categories with each category having multiple subclassifications. The chart of accounts for a large, complex organization can have thousands of different account numbers. Additionally, a chart of accounts can be set up to have multiple fields, allowing the organization to use the same accounting system for various legal entities and subordinates or to track the specific revenues or expenses for various responsibility centers within each entity.

Every chart of accounts is divided into five major categories:

1. assets,
2. liabilities,
3. equity, net assets, or fund balances,
4. revenues, and
5. expenses.

Each category will have a block of numbers assigned to it to show the general classification of each financial account and are generally presented in a standard order, beginning with the accounts presented in the balance sheet (also called the "statement of financial position") and then the accounts that build the "statement of income" for the organization.

Assets are resources owned by the organization such as accounts receivable, equipment, and property. Assets may be tangible, such as land, buildings, and equipment; a direct right to tangible property, such as amounts due from patient or insurance company payers, or assets can be intangible, such as goodwill, patents owned by the organization, licenses, and leaseholds. The chart of accounts will usually list assets in descending order of liquidity. Cash and other assets that are easily converted to cash are listed first, fixed assets such as property and equipment are listed next, and intangible assets are listed last. Asset accounts usually start with the number "1" and will be the first accounts listed in the chart of accounts.

Liabilities are debts or obligations owed by the organization to creditors, such as loans and accounts payable. These obligations come from the purchase of goods or services on credit or by obtaining a loan from a financial institution to finance the purchase of equipment or buildings. Current liabilities, the obligations that are due to be paid within one year, are generally listed first in the chart of accounts, with accounts payable, bank overdrafts payable, and payroll obligations (tax, insurance, and retirement plan withholdings and accrued payroll amounts) will be listed before other payables such as rent or insurance. Long-term liabilities, such as construction loans, long-term notes, and capital leases, follow current liabilities. Deferred revenue, deferred compensation, and severance plan obligations will be listed last. Liability accounts usually start with the number "2."

Equity accounts (sometimes called "fund balance" in some nonprofit organizations) reflect the financial worth of the organization and represent the residual value of an entity's assets after deducting its liabilities. In a for-profit business enterprise, the equity will be the ownership interest and in a not-for-profit, will represent the net financial worth of the organization. In for-profit organizations, equity generally is derived from two sources: contributed capital by the owners or shareholders and retained earnings, the accumulated value of income, less expenses and owner's withdrawals. Typical equity accounts are contributed capital, preferred and common stock, dividends and distributions (unique to for-profit corporations), and not-for-profit equity accounts, such as unrestricted assets, restricted assets, and endowments. Net asset accounts usually start with the number "3."

The accounts used to create the income statement accounts follow the statement of position accounts. While there is general agreement in the general numbering system for the accounts used to create the statement of position, there is no such convention for the income statement accounts. Generally the accounts used to describe revenue will precede the expense accounts and the last accounts will reflect nonoperating revenue, expenses, and income taxes paid. This sequence enables the chart of accounts to follow the same sequence as the statement of position, with account numbers that start with a "4" reflecting revenue, operating expenses will start with a "5," "6," "7," or "8," and nonoperating revenue and expenses starting with a "9."

In 1979, the Medical Group Management Association (MGMA) published a chart of accounts that was specifically designed to record the financial information needed to manage a medical group practice. The MGMA Chart of Accounts is structured to accurately describe the revenue and expenses associated with a healthcare organization, and its accounts flow logically into the financial statements a medical group practice has to produce. It classifies financial transactions into eight major categories and assigns a four-digit coding number to each.[3]

The eight major categories used by the MGMA Chart of Accounts are ordered in the way they appear on the practice's financial statements. The major categories and their corresponding codes appear in Exhibit 1.

**Exhibit 1. Major Categories and Their Corresponding Codes That Appear on the MGMA Chart of Accounts**

| Account numbers | Description |
|---|---|
| 1000 | Assets |
| 2000 | Liabilities |
| 3000 | Owner's equity |
| 4000 | Revenues and adjustments to revenue |
| 5000 | Operating expenses—support staff salaries and fringe benefits |
| 6000 | Operating expenses—general and administrative |
| 7000 | Operating expenses—clinical and ancillary services |
| 8000 | Operating expenses—physician and nonphysician provider salaries and fringe benefits |
| 9000 | Nonoperating revenue and expenses |

3 Chart of Accounts for Health Care Organizations. Neill F. Piland, Dr. P.H. and Kathryn P. Glass, MBA, MSHA, Center for Research in Ambulatory Health Care Administration, Englewood, Colo. p. 2.

The first three categories relate to the balance sheet, or statement of financial position. The remaining categories relate to the statement of income and to the order in which they appear on the statement of income.

Two unique aspects of the MGMA Chart of Accounts differ from most other charts of accounts. "Adjustments and allowances" is categorized as a 4000 series, the category for revenues, rather than a 6000 series expense, because allowances and adjustments must be treated as offsets to revenue rather than as expenses to understand the effect of the discounts required by government and insurance payers and to easily gauge the net revenue associated with operations. Another difference is to categorize provider salaries and fringe benefits as an 8000 series account. The majority of medical groups are owned and operated by the physicians who practice in the medical group. The compensation of the physicians-owners is based on the amount that remains from total net revenue after all expenses are subtracted. By organizing the MGMA Chart of Accounts with physician compensation and benefits as the last series of accounts, the logical flow of financial information is maintained. This sequence also allows management to logically present the financial situation of the practice in the same sequence as the chart of accounts.

The chart of accounts structure should allow the user to add subcategories in the future and to logically associate expenses with like costs. If the chart of accounts utilizes a four-digit accounting system, it can use the second digit of the account for a subcategories of the eight major categories and can use the last two digits of the coding number to reflect specific elements. Using this logic, a chart of accounts subdivides each major category into as many as nine subcategories. The subcategories can each have nine more minor classifications. Each category can be "rolled up" to equal the total for that category, usually reflecting the "0" account in the series. For example, if account 7000 is used to reflect "clinical expense," account 7100 can address "clinical Equipment, Supplies, and Services", account 7110 will record "Drugs and Medications," and 7111 will be "vaccines," and 7112 will be used for "chemotherapy drugs." In this example, the general ledger for the organization will provide both detailed information (71111 shows only the cost of vaccines). While 7110 shows the costs of all drugs and medications for the organization, 7100 is the sum of all the subaccounts related to clinical equipment, supplies, and services, and 7000 will have the total costs of all clinical expenses for the organization.

A chart of accounts can also establish codes for specific revenues and expenses that relate to more than one of the categories. For example, the employee benefits section can categorize payroll taxes paid for employees as 5710 and payroll taxes—state unemployment insurance—as 5713. The same chart of accounts can classify physician benefits as 8200 and nonphysician provider (nurse practitioner, physician assistants, and so on) benefits as 8400. In this organization, the cost of state unemployment insurance for physicians would be categorized as 8213 and the cost of state unemployment insurance for nonphysician-providers would be categorized as 8413.

Different business types need to structure their chart of accounts using different sequences that, ideally, will meet their individual needs. However, this may not always be the situation for healthcare organizations. Often a healthcare organization is a legal subset of a government entity, university, or private business. In these instances, the healthcare organization may be required to use the chart of accounts of its parent organization, so its financial performance can easily be aggregated into the parent organization's financial records.

When a healthcare organization has the flexibility to design a chart of accounts that can meet its specific information requirements, it has options well beyond the "basic field" of three or four digits that describe the specific asset, liability, revenue, or expense.

Through the use of additional single and multidigit fields, the chart of accounts can be expanded to allow the reporting of financial information from multiple legal entities, to track revenues or expenses to a specific responsibility center, or to identify the revenue or costs attributed to a specific physician or nonphysician provider. Using a multitiered chart of accounts enables the organization to easily customize the information collected in its financial information system to meet management's need for accurate information for its major units or to allow a medical group practice to track the productivity of each of its physicians.

A complex healthcare organization often has separate legal entities that integrate their functions in what externally appears to be a seamless organization but require separate financial statements. For example, an ambulatory care center may be part of a larger hospital-owned integrated delivery system, with a separate imaging center and ambulatory surgery center.[4] If each organization uses the same chart of accounts, expenses can be easily tracked for each organization as can patient revenues. Using an "entity field" as the first digit of the chart of accounts allows each entity to use the same "basic field" that describes the actual asset, liability, entity, revenue, and expense accounts, while keeping a separate set of financial records. The use of the same accounts with a different entity field allows the parent organization to easily roll up the financial performance of its subordinate organizations to evaluate the performance of the entire enterprise.

4 Management Accounting for Fee-for-Service/Prepaid Medical Groups, Eldon L. Schafer, Ph.D., CPA; Dwight J. Zulauf, Ph.D., CPA; Michael E. Gocke, MBA, CPA, Center for Research in Ambulatory Health Care Administration, Englewood, Colo., 1985, pp. 5-17.

Another often-used field allows the organization to track costs by responsibility center, organizational units within the organization that have responsibility to generate revenue and expenses. Such a "responsibility center field" simplifies the accumulation of revenue and expenses for a specific department or location. By tracking revenue and direct costs to each specific responsibility center, management can understand the relative contribution of the responsibility center to the organization. Additionally, if direct costs can be easily traced to a responsibility center, the organization can also allocate a fair share of the indirect costs incurred by other parts of the organization.

Some healthcare organizations need to track the amount of revenue produced by individual physicians and nonphysician providers or the expenses associated with their use of fringe benefits, such as continuing education tuition, travel, and lodging costs. Using a separate field that identifies each physician or nonphysician provider can enable the organization to easily prepare financial reports for each healthcare provider. Use of a provider field can be limited to recording only revenue or to record revenue and only certain expenses, such as fringe benefits.

The use of multiple tiers or fields allows the organization the greatest flexibility in its accounting records. Simultaneously, the organization can record revenue or expenses for specific locations or clinics (responsibility centers) and for each physician practicing in the location or clinic (provider field).

To decide what to include in a chart of accounts, a manager needs to evaluate several issues:

- What reports does the organization want to prepare?
- What financial decisions, evaluations, and assessments will be made regularly?
- What level of detail is required in the financial reports?
- Will the organization compare its financial performance to other organizations and therefore, need to collect financial data using agreed-upon definitions?
- Does the organization report financial performance to national, state, or local governmental agencies?
- Does the accounting software used by the organization limit the design?

Designing a chart of accounts that meets all the needs of a health organization can be a complex task. While complex, the task is not impossible, and the benefits that the organization will obtain from a well-designed chart of accounts and financial information system will far outweigh the costs associated with its design and implementation.

Chapter 26

# When the Marriage Is Over, What Is the Practice Worth?

*By Stacey D. Udell, CPA/ABV/CFF, ASA, CVA*

When a physician gets divorced, the value of his or her ownership interest in the practice is likely to be included as an asset for property distribution purposes. Additionally, the income generated from the practice is likely to be utilized in the determination of support.

Valuation is an art, not a science, which makes the task of valuing a medical practice more difficult (and more likely to be disputed) than valuing the marital residence or a spouse's retirement plan. The value of a practice is based on the valuator's judgment applied to the specific facts and circumstances. Different assumptions lead to different conclusions of value, any of which may be reasonable.

Some of the major issues that must be considered are:

- Standard of value;
- Premise of value;
- Valuation dates;
- Buy and sell agreements;
- Goodwill; and
- Double dip.

### Standard of Value

The valuator must determine the appropriate standard of value applicable in the state or jurisdiction of the divorce. Standards of value differ among the various states and jurisdictions. Often, the family law attorney can inform the valuator of the appropriate standard of value. This standard may be based on state statute or case law. Reliance on an incorrect standard of value could lead to an incorrect value conclusion, your report and testimony being excluded as evidence and more significantly, becoming the basis of a malpractice suit.

Arkansas[1] and Louisiana[2] have statutes precisely defining the standard of value to be used in divorce. In other states, the standard of value is often left undefined. To confuse matters even more, many state statutes refer to "value" or "net value" without any further clarification or definition. To take it even further, many states inconsistently apply standards of value to arrive at an equitable result. We are not aware of any case law or statutes in Alabama or Georgia discussing the standard of value to be used in matrimonial litigation. Therefore, determining the appropriate standard of value can be a perplexing problem for the valuation expert to resolve.

The standards of value utilized in the valuation arena are fair market value, fair value, intrinsic value, and investment value.

*Fair market value,* which is used for estate and gift tax purposes, is defined as:

> the price, expressed in terms of cash equivalents, at which property would change hands between a *hypothetical* [emphasis added] willing and able buyer and a *hypothetical* [emphasis added] willing and able seller, acting at arms length in an open and unrestricted market, when neither is under compulsion to buy or sell and when both have reasonable knowledge of the relevant facts.[3]

While the foundation of fair market value considers a hypothetical sale, fair market value could be viewed as not contemplating one sale but a blend of potential sales.

In a marital dissolution, an actual sale of the practice is not usually contemplated. Often in divorce, the term "fair market value" is used but the court's definition may not conform to the definition for tax purposes as quoted above. Frequently, in application, a different standard of value is actually used, even though it is termed fair market value.

1 Arkansas Statute § 9-12-315 (4).
2 La. R.S. 9:2801.
3 *International Glossary of Business Valuation Terms*, 2001.

One derivation of fair market value is "net value," which is defined as the fair market value of the business minus any debts, liens, liabilities, or encumbrances. Net value is the standard of value used in Alaska,[4] Michigan,[5] Nevada,[6] North Carolina,[7] and West Virginia.[8]

Exhibit 1 reflects the states that are considered fair market value states, either explicitly or by application. States that have utilized fair market value in addition to another standard of value are reflected in Exhibit 2.

*Discounts.* As part of the determination of fair market value, it may be appropriate to apply discounts for lack of control and marketability. These discounts have historically been allowed in Alaska, Arkansas, Connecticut, Iowa, New Hampshire, New York, Oregon, Vermont, West Virginia, and Wisconsin.[9]

*Fair value* is a statutorily or judicially defined standard of value. Frequently used in oppressed minority shareholder actions, this standard assumes one owner is an unwilling participant in the transaction, generally the seller. To compensate, discounts (for lack of control and marketability) are often not applied or applied only under extraordinary circumstances.

As reflected in the New Jersey case of *Brown v. Brown*, 348 N.J. Super. 466 (App. Div. 2002), New Jersey's standard of value for divorce purposes is fair value. In New Jersey, fair value reflects fair market value without discounts (for lack of control or marketability), barring extraordinary circumstances.[10] Unfortunately, what constitutes an extraordinary circumstance is undefined. Case law indicates that Indiana,[11] North Dakota,[12] Virginia,[13] and Massachusetts[14] are also considered fair value states. North Dakota has also utilized fair market value, as reflected in *Heggen v. Heggen*, 452 N.W.2d 96, 99 (1990).

*Intrinsic value* is defined in the *International Glossary of Business Valuation Terms* as "the value that an investor considers, on the basis of an evaluation or available facts, to be the 'true' or 'real' value that will become the market value when other investors reach

4 *McQueary v. McQueary*, 902 P.2d 1326, 1327 (Alaska 1995).
5 *Kowaleski v. Kowaleski*, 148 Mich. App. 151; 384 N.W.2d 112; 1986 Mich. App. LEXIS 2380.
6 *Robison v. Robison*, 691 P.2d 451, 455 (Nev. 1984).
7 *Walker v. Walker*, No. COA03-998, 2004 LEXIS 1319, at 7-9 (N.C. Ct. App. July 20, 2004) (unpublished).
8 *Alley v. Alley*, No. COA02-594, 2003 LEXIS 1986, at 8-10; *Durnell v. Durnell*, 460 S.E.2d 710, 717-18 (W. Va. 1995).
9 Fishman, Jay *Standards of Value: Theory and Applications* (Hoboken, NJ: John Wiley & Sons, Inc., 2007), 218.
10 *Brown v. Brown*, 348 N.J. Super. 466 (App. Div. 2002).
11 *Bobrow v. Bobrow*, 711 N.E.2d 1265:1999.
12 *Fisher v. Fisher*, 568 N.W.2d 728, 732-33 (N.D. 1997).
13 *Gardner v. Gardner*, No. 0468-04-03, 2005 LEXIS 10, at *15 (Va. Ct. App. Jan. 11, 2005) (unpublished).
14 *Judith E. Bernier v. Stephen A. Bernier*, SJC-09836, Sept. 14, 2007.

**Exhibit 1. Fair Market Value States—Explicitly or by Application**

| | |
|---|---|
| Arizona | *Sample v. Sample*, 731 P.2d 604, 606 (Ariz. Ct. App. 1986) |
| Arkansas | Ark. Code Ann. § 9-12-315 (2005) |
| Connecticut | *Eslami v. Eslami*, 591 A.2d 411, 416 (Conn. 1991) |
| Delaware | *E.E.C. v. E.J.C.*, 457 A.2d 688, 694 (Del. 1983); |
| District of Columbia | *McDiarmid v. McDiarmid*, App. D.C., 649 A.2d 810 (1994) |
| Florida | *Thompson v. Thompson*, 576 So. 2d 267 (Fla. 1991) |
| Hawaii | *Antolik v. Harvey*, 761 P.2d 305, 319 (Haw. Ct. App. 1988); |
| Idaho | *McAffee v. McAffee*, 971 P.2d 734, 740 (Idaho Ct. App. 1994); |
| Illinois | *In re Marriage of Grunsten*, 709 N.E.2d 597, 602 (Ill. App. Ct. 1999); |
| Indiana | *Trost-Steffen v. Steffen*, 772 N.E.2d 500 (Ind. Ct. App. 2002); |
| Iowa | *In re Marriage of Frett*, No. 4-083/03-1305, 2004 LEXIS 694, at 7 (Iowa Ct. App. May 14, 2004) (unpublished); |
| Kansas | *Bohl v. Bohl*, 232 Kan. 557; 657 P.2d 1106; 1983 Kan. LEXIS 236 |
| Maine | *Dargie v. Dargie*, 778 A.2d 353, 357 (Me. 2001); |
| Maryland | *Long v. Long*, 743 A.2d 281, 291 (Md. Ct. Spec. App. 2000); |
| Massachusetts | *Champion v. Champion*, 764 N.E.2d 898, 901 (Mass. App. Ct. 2002); now replaced by *Bernier* |
| Minnesota | *In re the Marriage of Berenberg*, 474 N.W.2d 843 (Minn. Ct. App. 1991); |
| Mississippi | *Singley v. Singley*, No. 1999-CT-00754-SCT, 2003 LEXIS 283, at 20 (Miss. June 12, 2003); |
| Missouri | *L.R.M v. R.K.M.*, 46 S.W.3d 24, 29 (Mo. Ct. App. 2001); |
| Montana | *In re Marriage of Ortiz*, 938 P.2d 1308, 1310 (Mont. 1997); |
| Nebraska | *Gohl v. Gohl*, 13 Neb. App. 685 (Ct. App. 2005), No. A-03-1102, 2005 LEXIS 143, at 30-31 (Neb. Ct. App. July 5, 2005); |
| New Hampshire | *Rattee v. Rattee*, 767 A.2d 415, 421 (N.H. 2001). |
| New Mexico | *Trego v. Scott*, 961 P.2d 168, 172-73 (N.M. Ct. App. 1998); |
| Oklahoma | *Bond v. Bond*, 916 P.2d 272, 275 (Okla. Ct. App. 1996); |
| Oregon | *I/M/O the Marriage of Hanson*, 86 P.3d 94, 98 (Or. Ct. App. 2004); |
| Pennsylvania | *Traczyk v. Traczyk*, No. 78435. 891 P.2d 1277. 1995 OK 22 |
| Rhode Island | *Moretti v. Moretti*, 766 A.2d 925, 928 (R.I. 2001); |
| South Carolina | *Dixon v. Dixon*, 512 S.E.2d 539, 549 (S.C. Ct. App. 1999); |
| South Dakota | *Fausch v. Fausch*, 697 N.W.2d 748 (S.D. 2005), No. 23316, 2005 LEXIS 63, at 11, 13-14 (S.D. May 18, 2005); |
| Tennessee | *Barbara Lee Bunce Kerce v. Stephen Paul Kerce*, No. M2002-01744-COA-R3-CV (Tenn. Ct. App. August 29, 2003) |
| Texas | *Zeptner v. Zeptner*, 111 S.W.3d 727, 738 (Tex. Ct. App. 2003); |
| Utah | *Sorenson v. Sorenson*, 769 P.2d 820 (Utah App. 1989) |
| Vermont | *Goodrich v. Goodrich*, 613 A.2d 203 (Vt. 1992), 158 Vt. 587, 591-92 (1992); |
| Wisconsin | *Frawley v. Frawley*, 693 N.W.2d 146 (Wis. Ct. App. 2005), No. 03-2550, 2005 LEXIS 7, at 4 (Wis. Ct. App. Jan. 6, 2005); |
| Wyoming | *Neuman v. Neuman*, 842 P.2d 575, 581-82 (Wyo. 1992). |
| Primary source of data: Vuotto, Charles F., Jr., Esquire. "Fair Market Value— Everyone Else Is Doing It, So Why Can't We?" *New Jersey Law Journal: Family Law Supplement* (2005), www.vuotto.com/new-jersey-divorce-articles/fairmarket-value.htm | |

**Exhibit 2. States Utilizing More Than One Standard of Value**

| State | Fair Market Value Case Law | Additional Standard of Value | Additional Standard Case Law |
|---|---|---|---|
| California | *In re Cream*, 16 Cal. Rptr. 2d 575, 579 (Ct. App. 1993) | Investment value | *In re Marriage of Hewitson*, 142 Cal. App. 3d 874 (Ct. App. 1983). |
| Michigan | *Golden v. Golden*, No. 218106, 2001 LEXIS 1057 (Mich. Ct. App. Mar. 20, 2001) (unpublished) | Investment value | *Sutherland v. Sutherland*, No. 240158, 2004 LEXIS 174, at 9 (Mich. Ct. App. Jan. 20, 2004) (unpublished) |
| New York | *Morse v. Morse*, 784 N.Y.S.2d 590, 591 (App. Div. 2004); | Investment value | *O'Brien v. O'Brien*, 66 N.Y.2d 576; 489 N.E.2d 712; 498 N.Y.S.2d 743 |
| North Dakota | *Heggen v. Heggen*, 452 N.W.2d 96, 99 (N.D. 1990), | Fair Value | *In Fisher v. Fisher*, 568 N.W.2d 728, 732-33 (N.D. 1997). |
| Ohio | *Cronin v. Cronin*, 2005 Ohio 301 (Ct. App. 2005), No. 02-CA-110, 03-CA75, 2005 LEXIS 268, at 5-6 (Ohio Ct. App. Jan. 28, 2005). | Intrinsic Value | *Brookhart v Brookhart*, No. 93 CA 1569, 1993 LEXIS 5586 (Ohio Ct. app. Nov. 18, 1003) (unpublished) |

Primary source of data: Vuotto, Charles F., Jr., Esquire. "Fair Market Value—Everyone Else Is Doing It, So Why Can't We?" *New Jersey Law Journal: Family Law Supplement* (2005), www.vuotto.com/new-jersey-divorce-articles/fairmarket-value.htm

the same conclusion." In other words, for valuation purposes, intrinsic value represents the value that a securities analyst places on the investment based on his or her perception of the risk and returns inherent in the investment.

The term "intrinsic value" has been used rather liberally by the courts and appears to be defined by the facts and circumstances of the particular case. The only state specifically requiring the use of the intrinsic value standard is Virginia. In the Virginia case of *Howell v. Howell*, 31 Va. App. 332, 345-46, 523 S.E. 2d 514, 521 (2000), Mr. Howell was an owner in a family business started by his father. Mr. Howell's two sons worked in the business, with one likely to operate the business after him. The court determined that since the sale of the business to a third party was not contemplated, no discount for lack of marketability should be taken from the value of the stock. In its decision, the court defined intrinsic value as "the value of the business interest to its current owner given the owner's current use of the interest, current resources, and current capabilities for economically exploiting the business interest." By application, this appears to be a fair value standard even though it is specifically identified as intrinsic value by the Virginia court.

*Investment value* represents the value to a specific buyer, as opposed to the hypothetical buyer contemplated in the fair market standard of value. In his book *Standards of Value: Theory and Applications*, Jay Fishman aptly states that "fair market value is impersonal, but investment value reflects the unique situation of a particular person or company."[15]

15 Fishman, Jay *Standards of Value: Theory and Applications* (Hoboken, NJ: John Wiley & Sons, Inc., 2007), 218.

This standard of value allows the consideration of synergies available to the potential buyer. In the California case of *Golden v. Golden*, 270 Cal. App. 2d 401, 75 Cal. Rptr. 735, 1969 Cal. App. LEXIS 1538, the court recognized the similarities between value to the holder and investment value. [Editor's note: California divorce cases are discussed in Chapter 17 of this guide.]

Particularly in divorce matters, investment value is often referred to as "value to the holder" or "divorce value" because it recognizes that, in the context of a divorce, there is no hypothetical or actual sale of the practice and the physician owner will continue to receive benefits based on his or her ownership in the practice. Courts in California, Colorado,[16] Michigan, New York, and Washington[17] have adopted the investment value standard of value for marital dissolution purposes.

### Premise of Value

The *International Glossary of Business Valuation Terms* defines premise of value as "an assumption regarding the most likely set of transactional circumstances that may be applicable to the subject valuation."[18] The two recognized premises of value are going concern and liquidation.

The going concern value assumes the business will continue operating into the future. This results from having such things as "a trained work force, an operational plant, and the necessary licenses, systems, and procedures in place."[19] Unless otherwise excluded from the marital estate (by statute, for example), goodwill is included under the going concern premise of value.

Liquidation value can be defined as the amount that would be realized if the business were terminated. Liquidation can be either "orderly" or "forced." An orderly liquidation would generate higher proceeds and results when the business is terminated and the assets are sold piecemeal. In a forced liquidation, the assets are sold as quickly as possible and lower proceeds are usually generated. Liquidation value is applicable when a controlling interest is being valued because a minority (noncontrolling) owner may not compel the sale of the business. Furthermore, the liquidation value would be pertinent only if it is greater than the value determined by an income or market approach.

16 *In re marriage of Huff*, 834 P.2d 244, 254 (Colo. 1992).
17 *Matter of Marriage of Fleege*, 588 P.2d 1136 (1979).
18 *International Glossary of Business Valuation Terms*, 2001.
19 *International Glossary of Business Valuation Terms*, 2001.

In the North Dakota case of *Sommers v. Sommers* , 2003 N.D. 77, 660 N.W. 2d 586 (2003), when valuing an orthodontics practice, the court stated "liquidation value is the least favored method of valuing any type of marital property in a divorce."

## Valuation Date

State law reflects the appropriate date to value the practice for divorce purposes. Fourteen states require the use of a date as close as possible to the date of trial. Fifteen states and the District of Columbia require the use of the date of complaint. Nineteen states suggest using the date of divorce. Two states mandate the use of the date of separation. When the use of a trial date or dissolution date is required, often the state laws suggest the use of a current date. Exhibit 3 reflects each state's requirement.

**Exhibit 3. Property Valuation Date**

| Trial | Complaint | Divorce | Separation |
|---|---|---|---|
| Alabama | Arizona | Arkansas | Hawaii |
| Alaska | Dist. of Columbia | Connecticut | North Carolina |
| California | Florida | Georgia | |
| Colorado | Indiana | Idaho | |
| Delaware | Kansas | Illinois | |
| Iowa | Maine | Kentucky | |
| Missouri | Michigan | Louisiana | |
| North Dakota | Mississippi | Maryland | |
| Oregon | New Hampshire | Massachusetts | |
| Pennsylvania | New Jersey | Minnesota | |
| Rhode Island | New York | Montana | |
| Tennessee | Ohio | Nebraska | |
| Vermont | Oklahoma | Nevada | |
| Virginia | South Carolina | New Mexico | |
| | West Virginia | South Dakota | |
| | Wyoming | Texas | |
| | | Utah | |
| | | Washington | |
| | | Wisconsin | |

## Appreciation

What happens when a physician gets married and then divorced, all while owning a medical practice? Depending on the state, the appreciation in the value of the practice during the marriage may need to be determined. The appraiser must determine the value of the practice at the date of marriage and the date of complaint.

*In re Marriage of Ackerman,* 146 Cal. App. 4th 191 (Cal. App. *2006*), the husband was board certified in plastic and reconstructive surgery. He began his practice in 1987 and was married in 1991. The husband and wife signed a premarital agreement in which they stipulated to a value of the practice as of the date of marriage. In 2001, the couple separated. Therefore, only the increase in value from the date of marriage to the date of complaint was deemed community property subject to equitable distribution.

Clearly, when a value is not determined at the beginning of the marriage, the valuator has a difficult task ahead because often a significant amount of time has passed and records may not be available.

## Buy and Sell Agreements

Often physicians are party to a buy or sell agreement. These agreements are typically utilized in situations of death, disability, retirement, or withdrawal of a partner. While these agreements may set a value and be binding for transfers of an ownership interest, disagreements exist as to the use of these values or formulas in the context of marital dissolution because the nonphysician spouse is not party to the agreement and no change in ownership is occurring.

The courts have recognized that often values included in these agreements contain artificially low values. However, some states consider the agreement value the sole indicator of value, concluding that the amount in the agreement is the only amount the owner will ever receive and it would be inequitable for the nonowner-spouse to receive more than the owner-spouse.

In the New Mexico case of *Hertz v. Hertz*, 99 N.M. 320, 325, 657 P.2d 1169, 1174 (N.M. 1983), the spouse was bound by the $1 value contained in the attorney husband's Restrictive Stock Agreement because, as the court stated, "We hold that a nonshareholder spouse is bound to the same terms of a shareholder valuation agreement, which affects the shareholder spouse. This insures that the nonshareholder spouse does not receive a *greater* value than that of the shareholder." The State Supreme Court, overturning the local district court's decision, noted that if the husband terminated his employment with the law firm, he would never realize the value of the goodwill that was awarded to the wife by the district court.

The New York case of *McDiarmid v. McDiarmid*, 649 A.2d 810, 815 (D.C. App. 1994) referenced the *Hertz* case and stated that goodwill of the medical practice was not includable as marital property since the buy or sell agreement specifically excluded it.

In *Weaver v. Weaver*, 72 N.C. App. 409, 324 S.E.2d 915 (1985) and *Stern v. Stern*, 66 N.J. 340, 331 A.2d 257 (1975), the courts indicated that when the terms of a partnership agreement are followed, the value of the interest calculated is only a presumptive value, which can be attacked by either plaintiff or defendant as not reflective of the true value. In *Stern v. Stern*, the Supreme Court of New Jersey stated that the value of a partnership interest determined by use of the partnership agreement should only be used "once it is established that the books of the firm are well-kept and that the value of the partners' interests are in fact periodically and carefully reviewed . . ."

The majority of states follow West Virginia's ruling in the case of *Bettinger v. Bettinger*, 396 S.E.2d 709, 714 (W.Va. 1990), wherein the court opined that the value pursuant to the buy or sell Agreement should be considered along with any other relevant evidence regarding the value and weighted accordingly.

Additionally, the physician's age may be a consideration. A value set by an agreement may be more relevant in the case of a 58-year-old physician subject to mandatory retirement at age 60 who is nearing the end of his professional career than the case of a 38-year-old physician subject to the same agreement when sale or retirement is not imminent.

**Valuation approaches.** Generally, the preferred approach for valuing a medical practice, like any other service business, is an income approach. This method considers the expected long-term earnings stream that the physician can reasonably expect to receive until retirement.

In valuing medical practices, asset approaches are generally not favored because there is often value beyond the physical assets.

The market approaches, particularly the comparable transactions method, are often utilized, but many times sufficient details regarding the transactions are unknown, and the valuator may not be comparing apples to apples. Specifically, a valuator would not be aware of any synergies or other investment value characteristics that influenced the transaction.

There are situations where the market approach may be considered an indicator of value. For example, in recent years, AmSurg, a publicly traded hospital management company, has purchased a number of ambulatory surgical centers. The multiples used by AmSurg have been relatively consistent, so their application to the subject practice may be appropriate. The weakness in this approach, of course, is knowledge of the underlying characteristics of the comparable companies and the subject company. [Editor's note: See Chapter 2, "Healthcare Market Structure and Its Implication for Valuation of Privately Held Provider Entities."]

The question arises as to whether it is fair to use a market approach when a transaction is not likely to occur. A market approach is often better used as a reasonableness check, rather than a primary or even secondary indicator of value.

## Goodwill

In addition to the value of the tangible assets owned by a medical practice, the value is also comprised of intangible assets such as goodwill, patient lists, medical records, and covenants not to compete. The value of the intangible component is often greater than the value of the tangible component.

Goodwill is defined as "that intangible asset arising as a result of name, reputation, customer loyalty, location, products, and similar factors not separately identified."[20] It can be viewed as the ability to earn a return over and above the return earned on the tangible assets.

Once it has been determined that goodwill exists, it must be valued. Goodwill is often valued to compensate the nonphysician spouse for his or her marital contribution.

Two types of goodwill may be associated with the value of a medical practice. Personal (or professional) goodwill is attached to the individual and his or her unique abilities and characteristics. Practice (or entity) goodwill is attached to the medical practice and is not associated with the physician's unique abilities and characteristics.

Personal goodwill presumes that a practice has a higher value as a result of the particular professional's knowledge, experience, and reputation. "Personal goodwill is that which would make a doctor's patients follow him even if he changed his location, staff, and phone number."[21] As such, personal goodwill is difficult to transfer, but it

20 *International Glossary of Business Valuation Terms*, 2001.
21 Fishman, Jay E. *Standards of Value: Theory and Applications* (Hoboken, NJ: John Wiley & Sons, Inc., 2007), 203.

**Exhibit 4. Practice Goodwill is a Divisible Marital Asset**
**Personal Goodwill is not a Divisible Marital Asset**

| | |
|---|---|
| Alaska | *Fortson v. Fortson*, 131 P.3d 451 (Alaska 2006) |
| Arkansas | *Wilson v. Wilson*, 294 Ark. 194 (1987) |
| Connecticut | *Eslami v. Eslami*, 218 Conn. 801, 591 A.2d 411 (1991) |
| Delaware | *E.E.C. v. E.J.C.*, 457 A.2d 688 (Del. 1983) (Law Practice) |
| District Of Columbia | *McDiarmid v. McDiarmid*, 594 A.2d 79 (D.C. 1991 (Law practice) |
| Florida | *Young v. Young*, 600 So.2d 1140 (Fla. App. 5 Dist. 1992). |
| Georgia | *Miller v. Miller*, 2010 WL 4704326(Ga.)(Nov. 22, 2010) |
| Hawaii | *Antolik v. Harvey*, 761 P.2d 305, 319 (Haw. Ct. App. 1988) |
| Illinois | *In re Marriage of Head*, 273 Ill. App.3d 404, 652 N.E.2d 1246, 210 Ill. Dec. 270 (1995) |
| Indiana | *Yoon v. Yoon*, 711 N.E.2d 1265 (Ind. 1999) |
| Kentucky | *Gaskill v.Robbins*, 2009 WL 425619 (Ky.) (Feb 19, 2009) |
| Maine | *Ahern v. Ahern*, 2008 ME 1, (January 3, 2008) |
| Maryland | *Skrabak v. Strabak*, 108 Md. App. 633, 673 A.2d 732, 1996 Md. App. LEXIS 39 |
| Massachusetts* | *Goldman v. Goldman*, 28 Mass. App. Ct. 603, 554 N.E.2d 860 (1990) |
| Minnesota | *In re Marriage of Baker*, 2007 Minn. App. A06-1252 |
| Missouri | *Hanson v. Hanson*, 738 S.W.2d 429 (Mo. 1987) |
| Nebraska | *Taylor v. Taylor*, 222 Neb. 721, 386 N.W.2d 851 (1986) |
| New Hampshire | *In re Watterworth*, 149 N.H. 442, 821 A.2d 1107 (2003) |
| Oklahoma | *Traczyk v. Traczyk*, No. 78435. 891 P.2d 1277, 1995 OK 22 |
| Oregon | *Matter of the Dissolution of the Marriage of Goger*, 27 Or. App. 729 (1976) |
| Pennsylvania | *Gaydos v. Gaydos*, 693 A.2d 1368 (Pa. Super. 1997) |
| Rhode Island | *Gibbons v. Gibbons*, 619 A.2d 432 (R.I. 1993)) |
| Texas | *Nail v. Nail*, 486 S.W.2d 761 (Tex. 1972) |
| Utah | *Sorenson v. Sorenson*, 769 P.2d 820 (Utah Ct. App. 1989) |
| Vermont | *Mills v. Mills*, 167 Vt. 567 (1997) |
| Virginia | *Hoebelheinrich v. Hoebelheinrich*, 2004 Va. App. LEXIS 376 |
| West Virginia | May v. May, 214 W.Va. 394, 589 S.E.2d 536 (2003) |
| Wisconsin | Holbrook v. Holbrook, 103 Wis.2d 327, 309 N.W.2d 343 (1981) |
| Wyoming | Root v. Root, 2003 WY 36, 65 P.3d 41 (2003) |

*Although *Goldman* is oft-cited as suggesting that personal goodwill is nondivisible, it has little sway in that it involved a neurosurgery practice where transferable enterprise goodwill would be hard to find. The sole statement in this Appellate decision is "The judge was warranted in accepting the husband's accountant's opinion that there was no goodwill in this one-man professional corporation." As a result of *Sampson* (62 Mass . App. Ct. 366 (2004), Massachusetts now considers the extent of any "Double Dip" in what is equitable; Double Dipping is not precluded, however, as it may be in other jurisdictions.

**Exhibit 5. Goodwill is a Divisible Marital Asset - Whether Personal or Practice**

| | |
|---|---|
| Arizona* | *Wisner v. Wisner*, 129 Ariz. 333, 631 P.2d 115 (Ariz. Ap. 1981) |
| California* | *In re Marriage of Foster*, 42 Cal.App.3d 577 (1974) |
| Colorado | *In re Marriage of Nichols*, 43 Colo. App. 383 (1979) |
| Kentucky | *Clark v. Clark*, Ky. App., 782 S.W.2d 56 (1990) |
| Michigan | *Kowalesky v. Kowalesky*, 148 Mich. App. 151, 384 N.W.2d 12 (1986) |
| Montana | *Marriage of Hull*, 219 Mont. 480 (1986) |
| Nevada* | *Ford v. Ford*, 105 Nev. 672, 782 P.2d 1304 (1989) |
| New Jersey | *Stern v. Stern*, 66 N.J. 340, 331 A.2d 257 (1975) (Law practice) |
| New Mexico* | *Hurley v. Hurley*, 94 N.M. 641, 615 P. 2d 256 (1980) |
| New York | *Nehorayoff v. Nehorayoff*, 08 Misc. 2d 311; 437 N.Y.S.2d 584 (1981) |
| North Carolina | *Poore v. Poore*, 75 N.C. App. 414, 331 S.E.2d 266 (1985) |
| North Dakota | *Sommers v. Sommers*, 2003 ND 77, 660 N.W.2d 596 (2003) |
| Ohio | *Kahn v. Kahn*, 42 Ohio App.3d 61 (1987) |
| Washington* | *In re Marriage of Fleege*, 91 Wn.2d 324 (1979) |
| * Community Property State | |

**Exhibit 6. Goodwill is Never a Divisible Marital Asset**

| | |
|---|---|
| Kansas | *Powell v. Powell*, 231 Kan. 456, 648 P.2d 218 (1982) |
| Louisiana | *Chance v. Chance*, 694 So. 2d 613 (La. App. 1997) |
| Mississippi | *Singley v. Singley*, 1999-CT-00754-SCT (Miss. 6-12-2003) |
| South Carolina | *Donahue v. Donahue*, 299 S.C. 353, 384 S.E.2d 741 (1989) |
| Tennessee | *Hazard v. Hazard*, 833 S.W.2d 911 (Tenn.App. 1991) |

may be done with advance planning and cooperation between the buyer and the seller. However, would a hypothetical buyer pay anything for personal goodwill (under the fair market value standard of value)?

Practice goodwill is associated with the practice as a unit, including its location, systems, operating procedures and policies, staff, an established client base, and patient records. Another indicator of practice goodwill is a telephone number. Assume a family practice has a telephone number of 808-555-1212. As a patient of that practice needing an appointment, you will call that number and ask for an appointment with Dr. A. If Dr. A is not there, you still are likely to see whatever doctor is available at that telephone number.

A distinction must be made between personal goodwill and practice goodwill because the majority of states do not consider personal goodwill a marital asset (Exhibit 4).

A minority of states have ruled that goodwill is never marital property, whether it is personal goodwill or practice goodwill (Exhibit 5). Then, there are states that have ruled that all goodwill is marital property (Exhibit 6). These three exhibits reflect cases specifically related to medical practices, unless noted otherwise. Of course, there are some states (Alabama, Idaho, Iowa, and South Dakota) that are undecided in this matter.

In Indiana, enterprise goodwill is marital; personal goodwill *may* be. The party wishing to exclude personal goodwill must submit evidence of its value to the trial court.[22]

Many court cases have detailed factors to consider in determining professional goodwill. *In re Marriage of Lopez*, 38 Cal.App.3d 93 (1974) identifies the following factors:

1. Practitioner's age and health;
2. Demonstrated earning power;
3. Reputation for judgment, skill, and knowledge;
4. Comparative professional success;
5. Nature and duration of practice, either as sole practitioner or as a contributing member of a partnership or professional corporation.

The Pennsylvania case *Fexa v. Fexa*, 396 Pa. Super. 481, 578 A.2d 1314 (1990) addressed the distinction between personal goodwill and practice goodwill. The court reasoned that since:

> . . . partners have bought in and been bought out and the practice has been maintained, there is a clear basis upon which to determine that the goodwill enjoyed by the practice was not entirely personal to the individual professionals involved. Likewise, where the professionals share clients within the corporation or partnership, there is a basis upon which to conclude that the goodwill is not purely personal.

In valuing a medical practice, many factors, such as those described below, must be evaluated that contribute to goodwill, whether it is personal or practice goodwill.

*Age and health of practitioner.* There is likely less goodwill in the case of an older or unhealthy practitioner, since expected future earnings are not expected to continue for a long period of time.

*Ancillary services.* A medical practice that has a laboratory attached or is in close proximity is likely to have greater practice goodwill and receive a greater return on its investment.

22 *Balicki v. Balicki*, 837N.E.2d 532 (Ind. App. 2005)

Alternatively, however, a primary care physician with a single X-ray machine is not likely to earn excess profits by having that single machine.

*Area of specialization.* A cardiologist or neurologist is likely to have personal goodwill, while a radiologist is more likely to have practice goodwill, particularly because the patient may not even see the radiologist.

*Cash flow and earnings ability.* A physician's cash flow or earnings ability as compared to his or her partners is likely an indicator of personal goodwill, while the earning ability of the practice compared to its peers is likely an indicator of practice goodwill.

*Changes in ownership.* When physicians are entering and leaving the practice regularly and there is little or no impact on the practice, it likely is an indicator of practice goodwill. On the other hand, if the practice disbands or suffers economically upon the termination of an individual, it was likely personal goodwill creating the value.

*Location and competition.* If the subject is the only local practice, it is likely that practice goodwill exists. However, if there are many physicians in town, personal goodwill is likely the driver.

*Patient base.* Where a practice has a large, established patient base that requires recurring care, practice goodwill is likely to exist. This could be the case with practices specializing in primary care, internal medicine, pediatrics, and family medicine, for example.

*Patient visits.* If a patient is shared among practice physicians, it likely represents the existence of practice goodwill. For example, in a group obstetrics practice, a pregnant woman is likely to visit various physicians. If she returns to the practice, she is likely continuing due to practice goodwill.

*Referral base.* Referrals made to the individual physician would likely indicate personal goodwill, while referrals to the practice in general would indicate practice goodwill. Some examples are that a patient is likely to get a referral to a specific cardiologist (personal goodwill) or may be referred to a certain radiology practice for X-rays (practice goodwill).

*Relationships.* Example: A pulmonologist is an owner of a group medical practice that provides inpatient services to various hospitals under contract. The physician also sees patients in the office one or two days per week, which are primarily follow-up visits from hospital patients. This pulmonologist is likely to have practice goodwill because the practice receives the majority of its patients due to the follow-up visits required as a result of the physician's relationship with the hospital, rather than the physician's individual reputation. However, one could argue that if a patient continues to visit this same pulmonologist after the initial follow-up visit, then personal goodwill exists. [Editor's note: Appraisers should also consider the underlying contracts with the hospitals as part of this practice and personal goodwill analysis.]

*Tangible assets and equipment owned.* A practice with a significant investment in equipment is likely to have more practice goodwill than a physician, such as a family practitioner, that does not require the use of highly technical and expensive equipment.

*Work habits.* When comparing two physicians working the same amount of hours in the same specialty, for example, the physician that works more efficiently is likely to have more personal goodwill. Increased time spent per patient is also likely an indicator of personal goodwill.

*Years in profession.* The longer a physician has been in practice, the more likely he or she is to have personal goodwill.

## Double Dip

The "double dip" dilemma exists when the same income stream is used for multiple purposes—for example, when the income stream of a business is utilized to value a practice and that same earnings stream is used as the basis for support.

Normalized compensation is utilized in determining the value of a practice. It represents what the owner physician would have to pay another physician to come in and perform the same function as the owner-physician, distinguishing between the return on labor and the return on equity.This is the key task for the appraiser of a professional practice. Often, the determination of reasonable compensation is the most disputed part of the valuation. Further discussion of reasonable compensation is located at the end of this chapter.

The actual compensation, which is usually greater than the normalized compensation, often includes discretionary personal expenses that are paid by the business, such as automobile expenses, dues and subscriptions, household expenses, meals and entertainment, retirement plan contributions, telephone, and travel. The use of normalized compensation for valuation purposes increases the value of the practice. At the same time, actual compensation is often used as the basis for support.

For example, assume the information in Exhibit 7 for Dr. A.

**Exhibit 7. Information for Dr. A**

| | Actual | Normalized |
|---|---|---|
| Revenue | $800,000 | $800,000 |
| Operating expenses | 300,000 | 300,000 |
| Operating Income before physician compensation | 500,000 | 500,000 |
| Physician compensation | 490,000 | 200,000 |
| Pretax income | 10,000 | 300,000 |
| Income taxes | 4,000 | 120,000 |
| Net income | $6,000 | $180,000 |

Assuming a capitalization rate for net income of 20%, the value of the practice using normalized compensation is $900,000. The spouse's alimony is going to be calculated based on the physician's compensation of $490,000. Therefore, the spouse is receiving the double benefit from the normalized earnings utilized in determining the value of the practice and the actual compensation taken by the physician.

As is the case with determining the applicable standard of value, the states' treatment of the double dip varies.

Michigan[23] and New Jersey have implied that the double dip dilemma does not exist. In 2005, the New Jersey Supreme Court ruled in *Steneken v. Steneken*, 183 N.J. 290 (App. Div. 2005):

> The interplay between an alimony award and equitable distribution is subject to an overarching concept of fairness.... The goal of a proper alimony award is to assist the supported spouse in achieving a lifestyle reasonably comparable to the one enjoyed during the marriage....Much of the controversy inherent in this appeal stems from the unspoken premise that because alimony and equitable distribution are interrelated, a credit on one side of the ledger must perforce require a debit on the other side; otherwise, defendant claims, the interplay between alimony and equitable distribution results in "double counting." We disagree...

In other words, in Michigan and New Jersey, it is acceptable to use a normalized compensation for purposes of valuing the business but actual compensation for determining support.

23 *McGregor v. McGregor*, 2004 Mich. App. Lexis 2560.

On the other side of the coin, in *Holbrook v. Holbrook*, 103 Wis. 2d 327, 309 N.W. 2nd 343 (Ct. App. 1981), a Wisconsin Appellate Court disallowed the double dip and stated that Mr. Holbrook's actual earnings could not be utilized for purposes of determining the value of the practice's goodwill.

New Hampshire[24] and New York have taken it a step further, by stating that the double dip is not allowed for alimony but is allowable for child support. In *Holterman v. Holterman*, 3 N.Y. 3d 1; 814 N.E. 2d 765; 781 N.Y.S. 2d 458 (2004), the state reiterated that there is a value to a physician's medical license (or other advanced degrees, certifications, or celebrity status) for equitable distribution purposes. The court also opined that the income stream utilized in valuing the license may not be used to determine spousal support but is allowed to be used in the determination of child support.

**Reasonable compensation.** The reasonable compensation adjustment is likely the biggest bone of contention in marital litigation because it is often the largest adjustment in terms of dollars. While this section is not designed to discuss the topic in its entirety, this discussion will provide an overview specifically for the purposes of medical practice valuation.

Often, surveys provide the best data for use in determining reasonable compensation, also called normalized compensation. Some of the most commonly referenced surveys are the following:

- American Medical Association's *Physician's Socioeconomic Statistics* surveys;
- Medical Group Management Association *Physician Compensation and Production Survey;*
- Merritt Hawkins *Physician Compensation* surveys; and
- Sullivan Cotter and Associates Inc. *Physician Compensation Survey.*

Additionally, the Economic Research Institute has a database that provides compensation figures based on numerous classifications.

Rather than relying on any of the survey data blindly, as the appraiser or valuation analyst, you must know and understand how and where the data are obtained. While the data themselves may be reliable, common sense must also be utilized. In the California case of *In re Marriage of Ackerman* (2006), Cal. App. 4th, at issue was the reasonable compensation of a plastic surgeon located in Newport Beach. The experts utilized

24 *Rattee v. Rattee*, 767 A.2d, 415 (Sup. Ct. New Hampshire 2001).

information contained in the Medical Group Management Association surveys and the American Medical Association surveys. The court requested the husband's expert survey local plastic surgeons. In this particular case, the survey of local practitioners was given the greatest weight by the court. The court reasoned that plastic surgery used discretionary income, which is more available in Newport Beach than other areas that would have been included in the survey data. [Editor's note: See also Chapter 18.]

In addition to the specialty and geographic area of a physician, the appraiser must consider, at a minimum, the duties, experience, efficiency, productivity, and hours worked. Often, the size of the practice has an impact on compensation, as does the profit distribution method. In addition to a physician's patient care duties, any administrative duties or hospital board duties should be evaluated.

### Summation

Successful valuation engagements require sound judgment. You must be confident that the conclusions reached are reasonable based on the unique facts and circumstances of the case and that your value is reasonably defensible. With the majority of the issues discussed in this chapter, the courts have looked to previous decisions not only in their own state, but also in other states. As valuators, knowledge of the relevant case law would likely increase the value of your services to referring attorneys.

Chapter 27

# Jurisdictional Issues in Physician Practice Divorce Valuation: California

*By Kathie Wilson, CPA, CVA, and Tracy Farryl Katz, Esq., CPA*

Family law courts are "courts of equity," and as such, they can define and redefine concepts to achieve just results. The result in California has been a very fluid body of family law. A significant amount of the medical practice valuation methodology is not found in the Family Code or prior court cases but is entirely up to the discretion of the court. In recognition of this, the organization of this chapter is based upon the stability of the concepts. It starts with some concepts right from the Family Code and ends with an analysis of four recent court cases involving professional practice valuation issues. The discussion here is limited to concepts that appear to be unique to California. As you read through this chapter, you will get a flavor for the concepts that are routinely accepted by the courts and those that are more situationally accepted. The fluidity of family law means that the effects of the four recent significant court cases are still not completely known.

## Family Code §771, Earnings and accumulations after date of separation are separate property

It is a relatively simple concept: What you earn after the date of separation, you get to keep. Once the community is irreparably broken, it no longer has an interest in either spouse's earned income or accumulations related to that earned income. This general rule impacts physician practice valuations in two key ways: date of value and permissible valuation methods.

### Family Code §2552, Valuation date of assets and liabilities

The valuation date for the assets and liabilities of the community, under Family Code §2552, is "as near as practicable to the time of trial." As a general rule, this makes sense; the community retains its interest in the assets and liabilities until they are legally divided. Certainly a clear example of this is the valuation of a brokerage or retirement account that has no activity subsequent to the date of separation and nothing affecting its value other than market forces. In this instance, the community either bears the risk or shares in the reward when the asset is ultimately divided at the time of trial.

It is the reconciliation of these two code sections that can affect the date of value of a physician's practice because the value of the practice is typically impacted by the efforts of the physician. If he or she is working less after the date of separation, all things being equal, the value of the practice would be expected to decrease. By the same token, an increase in efforts after the date of separation, all things being equal, should result in an increase in practice value. In both of these examples, the rise or fall in value after the date of separation is due to the efforts of the doctor. When post-separation efforts affect the practice value, an alternate valuation date (i.e., date of separation) may be available. An alternate valuation date is only available if it is requested and approved by the court. It does not apply automatically.

It follows that the community's interest in the physician practice is correctly determined at the date of separation as earnings and *accumulations* after the date of separation are separate property. This is not to say that all physician practices are greatly impacted by the efforts of the individual doctor. A large group practice or one with significant ancillary income, nonphysician providers, large capital investment, and a compensation system less determined by individual productivity could arguably be correctly valued near the time of trial as an individual physician's efforts may not have a great impact on the practice value. In the case of *Aufmuth v. Aufmuth*, 89 Cal.App.3d 446 (1979), valuation at the date of separation was denied because the court determined that the efforts of the spouse, a young attorney with a 5% ownership interest in his firm, were not the reason for the increase in the value of the law firm between date of separation and time of trial. The court concluded that the increase in the value of the law firm was related to the increase in the accounts receivable and that Mr. Aufmuth's efforts were not responsible for the increase in the accounts receivable.

The concept that earnings after the date of separation are separate property can also impact the valuation methodology. In the case of *Foster v. Foster*, 42 Cal.App.3d 577 (1974), the court summarized permissible valuation methods for goodwill as follows:

> In sum, we conclude the applicable rule in evaluating community goodwill to be that such goodwill *may not be valued by any method that takes into account the post-marital efforts of either spouse* but that a proper means of arriving at the value of such goodwill contemplates any legitimate method of evaluation that measures its present value by taking into account some past result. Insofar as the professional practice is concerned, it is assumed that it will continue in the future. [emphasis added]

The above quote seems to prohibit the use of any method of valuation that involves projecting income or cash flow into future periods, such as a discounted cash flow model. In practice, although discounted cash flow models are not used, capitalized excess earnings models are permitted (see Exhibit 1). The growth rate used in a capitalization rate buildup would seem to violate the prohibition against looking into the future. One can only surmise that the courts accept this form of projection because the long-term growth rate is often presented and defended based on the expected rate of inflation, not actual practice growth, and the efforts of the physician could hardly be deemed to influence rates of inflation. That being said, the use of buildup models to achieve capitalization rates for medical practice valuations is less common in California than the use of rounded capitalization rates, such as 40% or 50% (or the reciprocal multipliers, 2.5 or 2), which have not been built up.

### Premise of value

Investment value seems to be the premise of value for medical practice valuations in marital dissolutions in California. Investment value here means "value to the holder," as contrasted with fair market value, which is the "willing buyer" standard. This principle does not come directly from the Family Code but has been accepted and reaffirmed throughout the years. Numerous cases have used investment value rather than fair market value for professional practices, each making the statement slightly differently. For example, in 1962, *Brawman v. Brawman*, 199 Cal.App.2d 876 (1962), the court said:

> In considering this value, consideration must be given to the fact that, on divorce and dissolution of the community, a professional practice goes automatically to the spouse licensed to practice it. He or she is not selling out or liquidating but continuing the business. Effectually, it is the case of a silent partner withdrawing from a going business. And if such partner is to receive fair compensation for his or her share on his or her enforced retirement, it should be evaluated.

Another California case, *Golden v. Golden*, 270 Cal.App.2d 401 (1969), stated it slightly differently and contrasted divorce with the dissolution of a partnership:

> We believe the better rule is that, in a divorce case, the goodwill of the husband's professional practice as a sole practitioner should be taken into consideration in determining the award to the wife. Where as in *Lyon* (*Lyon v. Lyon*, 246 Cal.App.2d 519 (1966)), the firm is being dissolved, it is understandable that a court cannot determine what, if any, of the goodwill of the firm will go to either partner. But, in a matrimonial matter, the practice of the sole practitioner husband will continue, with the same intangible value as it had during the marriage. (case citation added)

In 1974, in *Foster*, the court confirmed again:

> The value of community goodwill is not necessarily the specified amount of money that a willing buyer would pay for such goodwill. In view of exigencies that are ordinarily attendant in a marriage dissolution, the amount obtainable in the marketplace might well be less than the true value of the goodwill. Community goodwill is a portion of the community value of the professional practice as a going concern on the date of dissolution of the marriage.

**Property can be characterized as separate, community, quasi-community, or a combination**

California is a community property state. The rebuttable presumption is that property acquired during marriage is community. This means that the court presumes that all property acquired during marriage is community property unless that presumption is contested and proven otherwise. In the case of a medical practice started or joined during marriage, the value of the practice on the date of separation (or trial depending on whether the factors discussed above exist) is generally the value that will be divided. An interesting issue regarding the character of the practice arises when a practice is started or joined *before* marriage. Arguably, this practice would be both community and separate in nature. A portion of the value of the medical practice is the separate property of the spouse that owned it prior to marriage, and it therefore, is not subject to division by the community. The portion of the practice fostered during marriage belongs to the community. Remember that earnings and accumulations after the date of separation are separate. Family Code §760 states: "Except as otherwise provided by statute, all property, real or personal, wherever situated, acquired by a married person during the marriage while domiciled in this state is community property." The physician's efforts during marriage that increase the value of the practice benefit the community via his or her earned income and the increase in practice value.

How to apportion value between separate and community estates is the subject of two very old, yet very significant, court cases, *Pereira v. Pereira*, 156 Ca.1, 103 (1909) and

*Van Camp v. Van Camp*, 53 Cal.App 17 (1921). In the case of a typical medical practice, *Pereira*, decided in 1909, is the case most applicable. Under the *Pereira* methodology, as applied to a medical practice, valuations are performed as of the date of marriage and the date of separation. The value calculated as of date of marriage, which is the value of the separate property interest, is treated as if it had been "invested" during the marriage and earning interest. That value, grown by the interest factor, represents the separate property component of the valuation as of either the date of separation or trial. To derive the community's interest in the practice, the value as of date of marriage, grown by the interest factor, is subtracted from the value calculated as of either the date of separation or trial. The court described this concept as follows:

> It appears, however, that the decision of the court was made upon the theory that all of his or her gains received after marriage, from whatever sources, were to be classed as community property and that no allowance was made in favor of his or her separate estate on account of interest or profit on the$15, 500 invested in the business at the time of the marriage. This capital was undoubtedly his separate estate. The fund remained in the business after marriage and was used by him in carrying it on. The separate property should have been credited with some amount as profit on this capital.

Conversely, the *Van Camp* decision, in 1921, typically applies when the efforts of the spouse are farther removed from the overall success of a business. In other words, the business grew in value, but it did so as a result of the capital invested rather than the efforts of the owner-spouse. The types of businesses that would be vulnerable to a *Van Camp* argument would be capital-intensive with more than one investor, perhaps manufacturing concerns or very large companies. This is usually not an arguable case with medical practices, even large medical practices.

You can compare the courts' statements in *Pereira* and *Van Camp* to understand the different views of the circumstances. In *Pereira*, where the husband owned and operated a saloon and cigar business, the court states:

> It is true that it is very clearly shown that the principal part of the large income was due to the personal character, energy, ability, and capacity of the husband. This share of the earnings was, of course, community property. But without capital he could have not carried on the business.

In *Van Camp*, where the husband was president of Van Camp Sea Food Co., the court states:

> While it may be true that the success of the corporation of which the defendant was president and manager was to a large extent due to his capacity and ability,

> nevertheless without the investment of his and other capital in the corporation, he could not have conducted the business, and while he devoted his energies and personal efforts to making it a success, he was by the corporation paid what the evidence shows was an adequate salary, and for which another than himself with equal capacity could have been secured.

The significant difference between *Pereira* and *Van Camp* is that *Pereira* allows the community to obtain an interest in an otherwise separate property business. *Van Camp* does not. Even if the spouse in a *Van Camp*-type business receives inadequate compensation (i.e., below-market salary), all that the community can get is the value of the services provided. The community does not gain an interest in the separate property business.

### Current Case Analysis

*Rosen v. Rosen,* 105 Cal.App.4th 808 (2002)

In 2002, in the *Rosen* case, the court once again affirmed the use of excess earnings in the calculation of professional goodwill, but also concluded that Mr. Rosen did not have any professional goodwill. The court had interesting discussions about a variety of issues surrounding goodwill calculations in the context of divorce. One of the primary issues was that Mrs. Rosen's expert used one year's net income to calculate goodwill. That single year was the most recent full calendar year at the time the valuation was performed, but it was also a high income year. The court said:

> Further, it is obvious that using one year's net income (not coincidentally a high-income year) is not illustrative of Bruce's volatile income over a period of several years.... Picking one year's net income, where income rises or falls from year to year, is not a reasonable basis for determining value.... Pat's expert admitted that had he averaged Bruce's income over any period of years he considered, goodwill value would be nominal or nothing.

The court was also displeased with Mrs. Rosen's expert's use of national surveys for the calculation of reasonable compensation without applying the survey results against some kind of local measure:

> Pat's expert testified he did not have any particular knowledge of lawyer compensation, other than what he had learned from valuations he had performed. He admitted he was not familiar with a law practice such as Bruce's. He did not conduct a survey or perform any kind of study of lawyer compensation in Southern California. Rather, he relied entirely upon two surveys of compensation (the Altman Weil survey and the

> Robert Morris survey), neither of which dealt with a sole-practitioner lawyer handling state-funded criminal appeals. The expert did not attempt to relate the information in the surveys to Bruce's law practice.

The surveys were deemed, by the court, not representative of law practices such as Mr. Rosen's. The court also disliked the fact that Mrs. Rosen's expert used his own judgment in determining which reasonable compensation numbers to use. Her expert stated that he had no experience in the area of attorney reasonable compensation outside of preparing law practice valuations in the context of divorce.

> Pat's expert then used his own judgment to come up with a compensation figure based upon the numbers in these two surveys, even though he admitted he did not have any particular knowledge about lawyer compensation and did not know of any attorney with a law practice such as Bruce's. In essence, Pat's expert did nothing more than pick $100,000 because it was about halfway between $125,000 and $67,000. Those two numbers bear no particular materiality to the issue of reasonable compensation in this case.
>
> Our concern is that the surveys relied upon by Pat's expert were not relevant to Bruce's law practice and therefore were not useful in establishing compensation under either the "average salaried person" standard of *In re Marriage of Garrity* and *Bishton* (181 Cal. App.3d 675) or the "similarly situated professional" standard. We are also troubled by the fact that Pat's expert ultimately reached his determination of compensation by exercising his judgment when the expert admitted he did not have any knowledge of a law practice such as Bruce's (citation added).

In the end, the court determined that Mr. Rosen's law practice had no goodwill without any expert testimony being offered by Mr. Rosen.

*Iredale v. Cates,* 121 Cal.App.4th 321 (2004)

Two years later, the court affirmed and expanded a concept used in *Nichols v. Nichols,* 27 Cal.App.4th 661 (1994) that allowed a stock purchase agreement to determine the value of the community's interest in a corporate law firm. In *Nichols,* the court allowed the limited use of the stock purchase agreement where the stockholder did not purchase accounts receivable or work in process upon joining and did not own any accounts receivable or work in process upon withdrawing. The court was persuaded because the agreement was arm's length: was entered into for an independent business purpose, not entered into in contemplation of divorce: and resulted in a value similar to the value derived from other approaches. Although the stock purchase agreement also addressed the value of goodwill, the court did not discuss goodwill valuation in the context of goodwill in the law firm as opposed to personal goodwill of the attorney, but ultimately decided that the attorney had personal goodwill. In *Iredale*, the court followed the partnership agreement, which stated that the partner (and therefore, the community) had no interest in certain assets (e.g., accounts receivable, work in progress, and goodwill of the firm). The *Iredale* court, while using *Nichols* as a basis to accept the values from the partnership agreement, took it one step further by discussing the partnership agreement's limitation on Ms. Iredale's interest in the firm's goodwill. The court opined:

> Thus, the trial court was not evaluating Iredale's interest in PHJW at liquidation value rather than as a going concern as Cates claims, but instead was looking at the specific interest that Iredale holds in PHJW. That interest does not include an entitlement, at any time, to collect a portion of the accounts receivable, work in progress, or goodwill of the law firm. The trial court reasonably concluded that Iredale's interest was limited to the value of her capital account, which reflected the value of her interest in the hard assets of the firm, but not the firm's accounts receivable, work in progress, or goodwill.

The court did find goodwill for Ms. Iredale—not goodwill in her law firm, but personal goodwill.

> After concluding that Iredale did not have an interest in a proportionate share of the goodwill of her law firm, the court determined that Iredale herself possessed goodwill and accepted the value of that goodwill offered by her expert, $42,318, finding her goodwill to be "partially a community asset."

In reviewing the goodwill calculation, the court revisited the reasonable compensation issue. It adopted the "similarly situated professional" standard over the "average salaried person" standard. The court stated:

> We conclude that the trial court's use of the "similarly situated professional" standard to calculate goodwill was entirely reasonable and supported by substantial evidence. Cates' own expert had to concede that his method of comparing Iredale's compensation number to what it would cost to hire an associate (actually 1.4 associates) did not account for the nonbillable hours expended by Iredale, nor would an associate be likely to have a client base comparable to Iredale's. Comparing Iredale's compensation to that of similarly situated professionals, rather than to a salaried employee, was indeed a more rational and reasonable method by which to calculate the value of Iredale's goodwill in this case.

*Iredale* marks the end of using an "average salaried employee" in the calculation of reasonable compensation in favor of the "similarly situated professional." Use of the "similarly situated professional" usually means a lesser value for goodwill; e.g., there are zero excess earnings when reasonable compensation mirrors actual compensation. Further, when relying on national surveys to obtain reasonable compensation, the valuator must consider adjustments to the compensation of the "similarly situated professional" that make the national survey data more relevant and applicable to their subject—i.e., for excessive hours worked. It also solidifies the use of agreements to limit the community's interest in a law firm's (or, logically, medical practice's) goodwill in certain situations.

*McTiernan v. Dubrow,* 133 Cal.App.4th 1090 (2005)

California's celebrity goodwill case was *McTiernan,* and, unlike New Jersey, it was decided that celebrities do not generate divisible goodwill. The court focused on the definition of goodwill found in the Business and Professions Code at §14102: "The goodwill of a business is property and is transferable." The court also focused on the definition of a business, determining that it is "...professional commercial or industrial enterprise with assets, i.e., an entity other than a natural person." The court stated:

> Endowing "a person doing business" with the capacity to create goodwill, as opposed to limiting goodwill to "a business," has wide ramifications.... all such persons who would have the "expectation of continued public patronage" would possess goodwill. This would create a substantial liability, as in this case, without a guaranty that the liability would be funded. It is clear that, from an economic perspective, the goodwill in this case is based on earnings and that goodwill is an expression of a husband's earning capacity.[1] However, there is no guaranty, especially in the arts that earnings will not decline or even dry up, even though expectations were to the contrary. In such an event, a person would find himself or herself saddled with a massive liability without the means of satisfying it. Putting it another way, endowing directly persons with the ability to create goodwill would create an "asset" predicated on nothing more than predictions about earning capacity.

The court makes the observation, more than once, that Mr. McTiernan's business activity is unlike doctors' or lawyers' practices.

1 While we acknowledge that the "excess earning" method of valuing goodwill in a professional corporation is generally accepted, it is true that this method is not far removed from a prediction about future earnings. For good and sufficient reasons, the expectancy of future earnings may not be considered in determining goodwill. (See generally 11 Sitkin, Summary of Cal.Law, Community Property, §71.) Whether categorized as "excess earnings" or "future earnings," the point is that this type of goodwill is an expression of earnings that have not yet been paid. Thus, when, as here, a person doing business is found to have goodwill and it is measured by the excess earnings approach, the "asset" that is credited is a prediction, not a fact. This is quite a distance from an established business enterprise with assets, and a clientele, that has generated goodwill in the traditional sense.

> The fact that the husband's "elite professional standing" is not transferable effectively refutes the trial court's conclusion that the husband's practice as a motion picture director is like the practice of an attorney or physician. The practice of an attorney, physician, dentist, or accountant is transferable, but the husband's "elite professional standing" is his alone, and not susceptible to being transferred or sold.

*McTiernan* opened the door for all professionals to craft arguments grounded in the case's dicta to try to subvert the traditional calculations of goodwill. Although the case specifically states that a film director is different from a doctor or lawyer, in stating that "'elite professional standing' is not a property interest," it has opened the door for any professional to make a claim of "elite professional standing." If a medical practice has to be transferable to generate goodwill, what about psychiatrists' practices? The characteristics of a physician that would allow the generation of significant excess earnings are the same characteristics that would allow a claim of "elite professional standing" and the corresponding claim that the practice is not transferable.

Judge Cooper concurred with the court on all issues except the determination of goodwill. In his concurring and dissenting opinion, he states:

> The lead opinion's effort to limit goodwill to a business as opposed to an individual is semantic. Any professional who independently practices his or her profession, for profit—be it lawyer, doctor, computer consultant, or film director—thereby conducts a business, with the lead opinion's own unattributed definition, as well as more traditional ones.

In discussing the issue of transferability, he says:

> As for whether this goodwill is transferable and therefore qualifies as property, the short answer is that the law has determined both question. Business and Professional Code Section 14102 establishes, as a matter of law, that "the goodwill of a business is property and is transferable." That includes the goodwill of the husband's business as a director. Whether or not a third party is willing to buy it is not material.

Judge Cooper's final statement on the case:

> In this case, the trial court properly determined the existence and extent of the husband's goodwill, in accord with substantial evidence and with California law, as consistently expounded for half a century. Even under the majority's refashioning of that law, those determinations remain sustainable. I respectfully dissent.

The ramifications will become clear when *McTiernan*-type arguments wind their way through the courts. So far, California has not distinguished between personal or professional goodwill and enterprise (practice) goodwill. *McTiernan* appears to identify a type of personal goodwill that is not owned by the community. If McTiernan's excluded personal goodwill is combined with an *Iredale* agreement that excludes enterprise goodwill, it leads to a conclusion that the "court of equity" might not favor.

*Ackerman v. Ackerman*, 146 Cal.App.4th 191 (2006)

*Ackerman* follows *Rosen* regarding the use of national surveys and their applicability locally to determine reasonable compensation. The addition in *Ackerman* was that Dr. Ackerman's attorney compared survey data from the American Medical Association to an informal local survey that he performed. In the end, the court determined the reasonable compensation for Dr. Ackerman, using neither expert's numbers, and applied the excess earnings method to determine goodwill.

The trial court once again rejected the "average salaried person" for the "similarly situated professional" standard saying:

> . . . it just boggles the mind to think anyone making as much money as the husband would work for an employer and receive a third of what he is actually making.

The above quote seems to indicate that using compensation statistics that do not correspond to productivity statistics would generate incorrect reasonable compensation assumptions.

Although *Ackerman* was decided after *McTiernan*, its proximity in date to *McTiernan*, meant that Dr. Ackerman, a plastic surgeon, would not have been able to make a claim of "elite professional standing." Future cases involving professional practices will be important in determining where California goes from here.

## Conclusion

California's family law principles come from both the Family Code and court cases, but court decisions are the primary sources for most of the business valuation issues (see Exhibit 1). The concrete concepts, such as earnings after date of separation are separate, fairly easily understood and have an impact on both the date of valuation and the methodology allowed. California, over the years, has recognized practice value using the "value to the holder" or investment value premise, rather than the "willing buyer" or fair market value premise, although the *McTiernan* case could possibly signal a change in this area. A medical practice can consist of both community and separate property, necessitating multiple valuations. The date of marriage and date of separation are two of the most important pieces of information that are needed for any case. Finally, the valuation case decisions over the last few years signal that the court may be changing its direction in the future. We await the first professional practice valuation case in the post-*McTiernan* period to see what that future holds.

**Exhibit 1. Selected California Dissolution Cases Timeline**

| Year | Case Name and Citation | Valuation Issues |
|---|---|---|
| 1909 | *Pereira v. Pereira* 156 Ca. 1, 103 | Cigar store owner, separate and community property valuation and apportionment; theory based on efforts. |
| 1921 | *Van Camp v. Van Camp* 53 Cal.App 17 | President of large seafood company, separate and community property valuation and apportionment; theory based on capital. |
| 1969 | *Golden v. Golden* 270 Cal.App.2d 401 | Physician, goodwill exists in professional practice, valuation methodology not addressed. |
| 1974 | *Lopez v. Lopez* 38 Cal.App3d 93 | Attorney, trial court erred in not determining the value of any goodwill in law practice. Discusses factors to be considered in determination of goodwill. |
| 1974 | *Foster v. Foster* 42 Cal.App.3d 577 | Physician, goodwill value upheld, valuation methodology not specifically identified. |
| 1976 | *Fonstein v. Fonstein* 17 Cal.3d 738 | Attorney, value determined by partnership agreement that called for compensation payments upon withdrawal from firm. Improper to take into account tax consequences in determining value unless the taxable event occurred during marriage or will occur as a result of the division of property. To be taken into account, a tax liability must be "immediate and specific," not speculative. |
| 1979 | *Aufmuth v. Aufmuth* 89 Cal.App.3d 446 | Attorney, date of valuation should be date of trial because spouse's efforts were not responsible for increase in value after date of separation. |
| 1986 | *Garrity v. Bishton* 181 Cal.App.3d 675 | Attorney, excess earnings method not sufficient to calculate practice value if it fails to take into account fixed assets, accounts receivable, costs advanced, and work in process. |
| 1986 | *Slivka v. Slivka* 183 Cal.App.3d 159 | Physician, no goodwill in case of partnership that services only Kaiser patients. Situation deemed similar to an employee with no ownership interest. |
| 2002 | *Rosen v. Rosen* 105 Cal.App.4th 808 | Attorney, use of a single year's income in the excess earning method to calculate goodwill when historical income is highly volatile is incorrect. Reasonable compensation based on national surveys is incorrect unless related to local data. |
| 2004 | *Iredale v. Cates* 121 Cal.App.4th 321 | Attorney, upheld use of partnership agreement to limit value of accounts receivable, work in process, and partnership goodwill. Calculated personal goodwill using excess earnings. |
| 2005 | *McTiernan v. Dubrow* 133 Cal.App.4th 1090 | Movie director, no goodwill, despite excess earnings. Elite professional standing deemed not transferable and therefore could not generate divisible goodwill. |
| 2006 | *Ackerman v. Ackerman* 146 Cal. App.4th 191 | Physician, goodwill calculated using excess earnings method. Discussion of national surveys to determine reasonable compensation. |

Chapter 28

# The CPA's Role in M&A Due Diligence Assistance to PPMCs and Private Equity Firms

*By Ronald D. Finkelstein, CPA/ABV, and Lydia M. Glatz, CPA*

*Editor's Note:* Many of the approaches and techniques described in this chapter are appropriate to a regular valuation engagement as opposed to a due diligence engagement. The discussion of the reports to obtain from the medical practice's billing system, how to use them, and the nuances thereof is of particular value. Portions of the checklist can be adapted for a standard valuation engagement.

Caveat emptor—let the buyer beware—and the term "due diligence" go hand in hand. Due diligence, or the process of investigating and providing financial analysis and assistance, can prove to be an invaluable tool during mergers and acquisitions (M&A) when planned and carried out properly. CPAs can assist their physician practice management company (PPMC) and private equity firm (PEF) clients to properly structure M&A transactions to reach optimum financial results for both the acquiring and acquirer entity. This chapter will address the various types of due diligence assistance the CPA can provide as well as provide insightful information and guidance on carrying out the engagement.

## Professional Reporting Standards

The first step in the M&A due diligence assistance process is for the CPA to determine the scope of the work and the type of reporting desired by the PPMC/PEF. Due diligence services performed by the CPA generally fall under the following professional engagement and reporting standards promulgated by the American Institute of

Certified Public Accountants (AICPA) and the Financial Accounting Standards Board (FASB):

- Audit of financial statements—rendering an independent audit opinion in accordance with the Statement on Auditing Standards (SAS) by adhering to generally accepted auditing standards (GAAS) and applying generally accepted accounting principles (GAAP);
- Agreed-upon procedures—performing specific analytical testing agreed upon by the PPMC/PEF and the CPA and rendering a findings report in accordance with the Statement on Standards for Attestation Engagements (SSAE),
- Forecasts and projections—reporting on an entity's forecasted or projected financial position and operating results in accordance with the SSAE;
- Pro forma financial information—reporting on the effects a M&A transaction (proposed or consummated) would have on the historical financial information of an entity in accordance with the SSAE;
- Financial analytics—review and analysis of key financial areas of a target entity that PPMC/PEF requests the CPA to perform in accordance with the Statement on Standards for Consulting Services (SSCS);
- Calculating the value of intangible assets—rendering a report on the calculated value of the intangible assets in an M&A transaction in accordance with the Statement on Standards for Valuation Services (SSVS).

### Engagement Planning

After the PPMC/PEF and CPA have agreed upon the scope and extent of the M&A work, the next important step is to develop a due diligence assistance program and related detailed document request list. The document request list is a very useful tool in planning any due diligence engagement; it should be tailored to request sufficient information that the PPMC/PEF needs for the M&A transaction. The document request list should include requests for documentation that can be utilized to perform analytical procedures on the operational statistics of the target practice. The list should be sent to the target practice well in advance of any due diligence field work to provide the target practice ample time to gather the requested information.

A sample document request list is attached in Appendix A.

For larger transactions that require a significant exchange of documents, the latest trend in due diligence document management is for the PPMC/PEF to set up a Web-based data site, where designated parties to the M&A transaction can access and share stored information.

A critical step the CPA must perform at the initial stage of engagement planning is to obtain and read the memorandum of understanding or, as it is commonly referred to, the letter of intent (LOI). The LOI will provide the CPA with information on the purchase price, the type of purchase for tax purposes (stock or asset purchase), the calculation of the purchase price, and any related purchase price adjustments agreed upon by the parties. To the extent the purchase price is based on a multiple of earnings before interest, taxes, depreciation, and amortization (EBITDA), the CPA may be required to report on EBITDA and calculate an adjusted or normalized EBITDA, as defined in the LOI.

### Operating Statistics

Physician practices maintain a plethora of historical data that can assist the CPA in analyzing the operational statistics of the practice. Historical data containing operational statistics may consist of:

- Reports produced from electronic databases containing patient billing information;
- Insurance company contracts;
- Contracts for the provision of professional medical services with hospitals, ambulatory facilities, diagnostic facilities, and third-party and related party contracts;
- Audited, compiled, and internally produced financial statements;
- Filed tax returns; and
- Monthly bank statements.

Historical data from these sources can be utilized to extract and analyze various operational aspects of target practices, such as information relative to the number of patient encounters, types of procedures performed, charges billed, charges collected, accounts receivable, and reimbursement rates. Further, historical productivity data can be utilized to compare and analyze the operational results of the target practice with the operational results of other practices of similar specialty and size in the same geographic area. The target's historical performance measures can also be benchmarked to performance measures contained in published industrywide data, and various analytics and pro forma calculations can be performed to compare the target's productivity to the performance measures of the PPMC/PEF.

The information gathered can prove to be invaluable in yielding answers to past and future trends, which in turn may be utilized by the acquiring and selling practices to arrive at mutually agreeable buy and sell transactions.

### Patient Volume

When comparing a practice's operational results, patient volume is by far one of the leading indicators of revenue trends. Patient volume can be measured in terms of the number of patients seen by the physician providers in the office, inpatient hospital consults, and in the number of cases and procedures performed at outpatient diagnostic testing facilities. Patient volume also bears a direct relationship to practice size, number of physicians in the practice, number of midlevel providers, employees, and number of practice locations. In other words, when comparing patient volume, the CPA should not just look at medical billing reports but should compare the medical billing reports with other practice variables to verify the accuracy and reliability of the reports.

The CPA should request that billing reports be generated, by date of service, and, at the very least, for two concurrent periods, such as for the immediate and previous calendar year. Comparing similar reports of differing periods can also prove to be invaluable at yielding answers to past and future trends.

Some sample patient volume comparisons may include comparing the number of patients seen in total by the practice and by the individual providers in the office, hospitals, diagnostic centers, and outpatient facilities during the current and prior year. Testing the reliability of the billing reports may include comparing the number of patients listed on the billing reports to the patient sign-in sheets and hospital admission or operating room case records.

Trends generated through this exercise can assist and provide the PPMC/PEF with an understanding of the productivity of the practice and of individual physicians within the group. It will also assist in addressing areas for improvement, pinpointing profitable and nonprofitable practice centers, and determining the size of the personnel pool required to run and maintain the practice efficiently. Further inquiry into this flux analysis will most certainly generate answers to questions that could improve physician productivity post-acquisition and assist in crafting an incentive-based productivity compensation arrangement. A sample table comparing daily and weekly patient volume by provider could be fashioned as follows:

**Patient Volume Analysis**

| Physician | Average Number of Office Visits | | Average Number of Surgeries | |
|---|---|---|---|---|
| | Daily | Weekly | Daily | Weekly |
| Dr. 1 | 13 | 38 | 3 | 12 |
| Dr. 2 | 31 | 94 | 4 | 12 |
| Dr. 3 | 21 | 41 | 3 | 14 |
| Dr. 4 | 38 | 76 | 6 | 19 |
| Dr. 5 | 20 | 61 | 5 | 15 |
| Dr. 6 | 20 | 61 | 3 | 11 |
| Dr. 7 | 9 | 19 | 2 | 7 |
| **Total** | **152** | **390** | **26** | **90** |

## Charges and Collections

Medical billing reports can be generated to provide historical physician practice productivity data related to charges billed and collections received. These reports can be customized to include numerous variables, such as total charges billed and collections received by provider, CPT code, payor source, and practice location. And, as a caveat, the CPA should be cognizant during this exercise that medical billing systems have the capability of producing reports that match collections to actual charges based on date of service (accrual basis reporting)[1] or, in the alternative, that simply track collections received in a period to charges posted in the same period (cash basis reporting). Reports that match collections to actual charges by date of service are comparable to accrual financial statements, and reports that match collections to charges posted in a period are comparable to cash basis financial statements. Both types of reports contain valuable information, but must be read with caution, as the data contained in each of the two reports may be misleading when not interpreted and applied to analytical procedures correctly.

The PPMC/PEF would be interested in the historical information these medical billing reports contain. For instance, the PPMC/PEF would want to know information such as the types of procedures the physicians perform, reimbursement rates, total charges and collections during specific periods, and the productivity of the various practice locations. Numerous analytical procedures can be performed utilizing the data contained

1 Editor's note: When looking at charges and matched collections for a fixed period, such as 12 months, the collections will reflect *less than* 12 months' volume, because of the lag between billing a charge and collecting it. To see the total collections against charges specified by date of service, it is necessary to use what auditors call a cutoff period, of at least 90 days and perhaps 180 days, depending upon the efficiency of the billing and collection effort, state prompt-pay statutes, and similar factors.

in the medical billing reports. Analytical procedures may include summarizing and comparing total charges and collections received by procedure (CPT) code during the current year and comparing them to the previous year's total charges and collections, calculating gross and net collection percentages, calculating average charge and average collections by type of practice specialty, and determining the significance the practice's fee schedule plays on these calculations.

This type of information can be presented in the form of a table that highlights total charges and collections by CPT code, location, and provider. The table could also be expanded to include information relative to gross and net collection percentages. The CPA should utilize the "accrual"-type billing reports for this exercise to compare actual collections applied to actual charges. Utilizing the "cash"-type billing reports could skew the true collection percentage results.

Physician fee schedules play an important role in comparing a physician practice collection ratio to another practice of similar size and specialty. Since fee schedules can be fashioned utilizing numerous variables, prior to calculating a practice's gross and net collection percentages, the CPA should obtain the group's fee schedule and inquire about how the fee schedule was developed and whether there were any changes to the fee schedule during the reporting periods. Was it based on Medicare allowable rates, a multiple of Medicare allowable, or some other benchmark? Lower fee schedules will produce higher gross collection percentages than will higher fee schedules. Preparing a chart that compares the practice's fee schedule to other fee schedules will assist the PPMC/PEF with its gross and net collection analysis. The table that follows demonstrates the role a practice fee schedule plays when calculating gross and net collection percentages.

Assuming a Medicare reimbursement rate of $50, the following gross collection percentages can be calculated.

**Fee Schedule Comparison**

| | Physician Fee Schedule | CPT Code 99242 | Gross % |
|---|---|---|---|
| Medicare x 2 | 100 | 50 | 50% |
| Medicare x 3 | 150 | 50 | 33% |

Total collections during specific periods can be verified to the total deposits per the bank statements. Further inquiry and analysis can be performed utilizing the "cash" basis billing reports to verify the validity of the receipts by tracing a sample of individual deposits from the bank statement to the supporting back-up documentation. This exercise could be taken one step further by reconciling the previous year's net collections to financial statements and to the net revenues reported on the federal income tax returns.

Appendix B contains a list of the more commonly used ratios, including formulas for calculating gross collection and net collection ratios.

## Payor Mix

A payor mix analysis can provide valuable insight into understanding the target practice's reimbursement rates and who its key payors are. This type of analysis will highlight profitable and nonprofitable payors. A payor mix analysis will assist the PPMC/PEF in planning and projecting future revenue growth trends and highlighting nonprofitable payors whose contracts the PPMC/PEF may want to renegotiate.

Medical billing reports generated on the "accrual" basis to include total charges, collections and adjustments by payor will contain the information required to perform this analysis. Most medical billing software can export reports into Excel-formatted files, which allow data to be sorted to achieve various results. The data should be sorted by total charges in descending order to segregate payor billings from largest to smallest. This type of analysis can be presented in the form of a table that highlights the top 10 payors, along with charges, collections, adjustments, and gross and net collection percentages by payor.

A payor mix analysis could also be utilized by the PPMC/PEF to compare the practice's collection percentages with those of published industrywide benchmarks and with its own collection percentages.

## CPT Code Analysis

A practice's total charges and collections are a function of the number and type of procedures performed. CPT codes can be compared with payor reimbursement rates. For instance, a payor reimbursement matrix could be prepared to compare the fee charged by the practice for its top 10 procedures to the reimbursement rate of its top 10 payors.

A sample matrix of five payors is presented in Exhibit 1.

**Exhibit 1. Payor Reimbursement Matrix**

| Top CPT Code | Fee Schedule | Payor 1 | Payor 2 | Payor 3 | Payor 4 | Payor 5 |
|---|---|---|---|---|---|---|
| 64483 | $ 374 | $ 77 | $130 | $104 | $ 86 | $271 |
| 64484 | 267 | 50 | 135 | 69 | 94 | 149 |
| 77003 | 120 | 27 | 19 | 40 | 23 | 21 |
| 99214 | 220 | 43 | 62 | 64 | 72 | 64 |
| 99215 | 355 | 73 | 92 | 95 | 97 | 91 |
| | $ 1,336 | $ 270 | $438 | $372 | $372 | $596 |
| Collection % | | 20% | 33% | 28% | 28% | 45% |

This type of analysis highlights reimbursement and collection percentages by payor and can lead to PPMC/PEF contract renegotiation and follow-up.

### Accounts Receivable

Accounts receivable play a vital role in the determination of a practice's cash flow. How quickly charges are collected is determined by the efficiency and accuracy with which the practice's billing and collection department processes claims and makes subsequent timely collection follow-up. The practice's accounts receivable can be benchmarked with the Medical Group Management Association (MGMA) annual publications, which provide statistical comparisons for different specialty and size practices by geographic regions. Ratio analysis can also be performed to calculate the number of days the practice takes to collect its receivables. Accounts receivable at the beginning of a period can be compared to those at the end of the period, and cash collections can be analyzed to determine whether significant differences have occurred as a result of increases or decreases in accounts receivable.

### Cash to Accrual Conversion

Generally, most medical practices and other healthcare providers maintain their accounting records and financial statements on the cash basis of accounting. The PPMC/PEF usually requests the CPA to convert the financial statements from the cash to the accrual basis of accounting. This conversion process requires revenue and expense cutoff information for both the beginning and ending reporting periods to properly measure EBITDA under GAAP.

The following financial information can assist the CPA in preparing cash to accrual accounting conversion adjustments:

- Accounts receivable aging reports;
- Charges, adjustments, and collections—by date of service;
- Accounts payable and accruals;
- Cash disbursements cutoff data;
- Payroll register for payroll period ending reporting; and
- For risk based providers—IBNR lag analysis.

### EBITDA Measurement

The LOI may define how the purchase price is calculated and specify certain agreed-upon purchase price adjustments to EBITDA. The PPMC/PEF may request the CPA to report on EBITDA as of a certain period. The period(s) can be as of the most recent year and a subsequent stub period through the closing date of the transaction or a trailing 12-month period. EBITDA measurements for purposes of the LOI are generally calculated as follows:

GAAP EBITDA

Purchase price adjustments for:

- Nonrecurring revenue and expenses;
- Owner compensation and fringe benefits;
- Assumption of certain debt;
- Related party transactions; and
- Other agreed-upon post-acquisition expenses.

### Acquisition Accounting

The PPMC/PEF may also require assistance early in the due diligence process to properly account for the fair value of the assets acquired and liabilities assumed as part of a business combination in accordance with ASC Topic 805, Accounting for Business Combinations (formerly FASB 141R). Identifying and understanding the target's operations can assist in addressing some of the post-deal accounting impacts and decrease the risk of restating financial statements.

A challenging area in meeting the requirements of ASC 805 is measuring the fair value and reporting contingent consideration or "earnouts" paid as part of the M&A. ASC 805 requires contingent consideration be reported at fair value as part of the acquisition or be expensed as part compensation expense. Assistance with projections and forecasts may be helpful in forecasting future earnings, structuring post-acquisition incentives by tying payouts to future performance, and avoiding earnings volatility.

### Tax Matters

Depending upon the type of M&A tax structure, the PPMC/PEF may request the CPA to assist in computing the tax consequences to both the buyer and seller. Typically the PPMC/PEF buyer prefers an asset purchase: The purchased assets are allocated on a tax basis equal to the purchase price, and there is no assumption of seller-related liabilities. Conversely, the selling entity owners prefer a sale of stock because this form of transaction maximizes the after-tax sale proceeds by taking advantage of the lower capital gains tax rates, eliminates the 35% built-in gain (BIG) tax for S corporations with unrecognized built-in gain still within the recognition period, and avoids sales tax on the sale of tangible personal property for corporations residing in states imposing such tax.

Whether structured as an asset sale or a stock sale, the recognized total net gain may be the same.[2] However, the character of the gain is different. An asset sale will trigger ordinary income while a stock sale will trigger capital gain. A common tax strategy that may be agreed upon by both the buyer and seller is the Internal Revenue Code Section 338(h)(10) election. This code section is intended to make the tax benefits neutral with respect to acquisitions of corporate assets and acquisitions of corporate stock. Following a qualified stock purchase and depending on the circumstances, the purchasing corporation could elect under Section 338(g) to step up the basis of the underlying acquired assets to their adjusted grossed-up basis (generally equal to FMV). In this scenario, the buyer obtains a tax benefit on depreciation and amortization deductions on the acquired tangible and intangible assets. To the extent the seller recognizes an incremental tax liability on the difference between the tax liability incurred on the sale of stock versus the tax liability incurred on the theoretical sale of assets, the CPA can assist the parties by computing the incremental gross up in income taxes required to be reported in the purchase agreement.

Since this is only a deemed sale of assets for tax purposes, a Section 338(h)(10) election does not relieve the buyer of the target's corporate liabilities (known and unknown). Buyers should obtain legal advice from an attorney specializing in this area so a thorough due diligence is performed.

2 *Editor's Note:* There are circumstances where the "inside" and "outside" basis of a stock interest differ from the underlying basis of the corporate assets; this in turn can lead to a difference in the gain realized between a stock and an asset sale. One example is where are previous purchase of stock by a current holder of same reflected a higher value than the amount paid by stockholders at the time the corporation was formed.

## Reverse Triangular Merger

Unique structural considerations relating to healthcare entity buyouts include those designed to minimize the possibility that the transactions will constitute a change in ownership (CHOW) for licensure or certification purposes or trigger anti-assignment provisions in professional service or managed care contracts (which should be avoided, if possible, because the counterparties often use the consent process to renegotiate or extract additional consideration).

One way to minimize the regulatory and contractual approvals required is through a reverse triangular merger structure under Internal Revenue Code Section 368(a)(2)(D) in which a newly formed subsidiary of the acquirer merges with and into the parent of the target holding company. Often the providers and facilities are organized as subsidiaries of the target holding company, and in many cases, CHOW approvals will not be required using this approach. Similarly, this structure may limit (but not eliminate) the managed care and provider contract consents required. See Exhibit 2.

**Exhibit 2. Reverse Triangular Merger Code Section 368(a) (2) (D)**

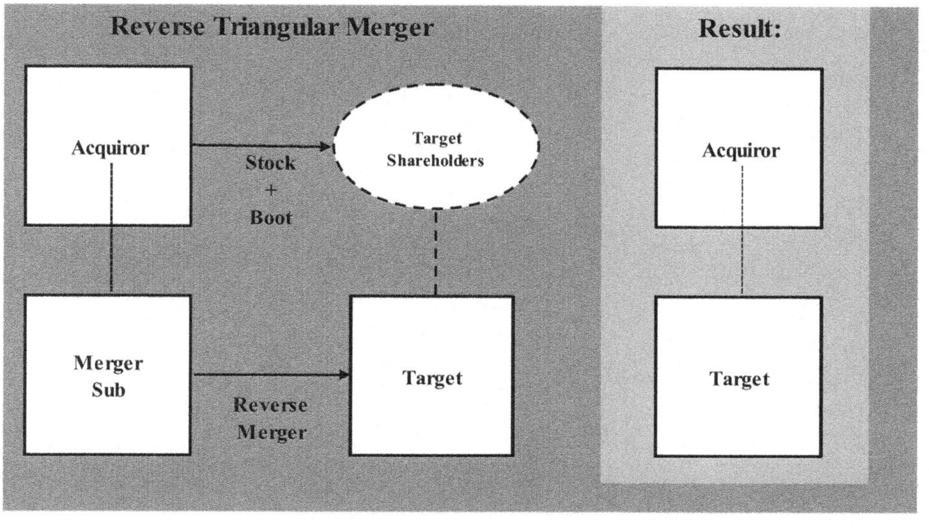


## Conclusion

The CPA's role in providing M&A assistance should be guided by the professional standards promulgated by the AICPA and the FASB. The professional standard hierarchy to be utilized will be dependent on the scope and type of reporting required. Understanding the transaction and properly planning the engagement will lead to efficiencies during the process.

A wide range of information, documentation, reports, and other data is available to physician practices to assist the CPA in quantifying results and performing numerous analytics. The information obtained can be utilized to obtain insight into the practice's operational aspects (historical and future), benchmark the target's performance to similar targets, and obtain information about the target's historical and future revenue streams.

Most physician practices maintain their accounting records on the cash basis of accounting, and the CPA may be requested to provide assistance in converting cash-basis financial statements to accrual-basis financial statements. This type of assistance can provide the PPMC/PEF with a full understanding of the target's economic cash flow and a more accurate measurement of EBITDA.

The due diligence assistance engagement plays an important role in M&A transactions and can assist not only the PPMC/PEF prospective buyer, but also the selling target entity in reaching optimum financial results.

## Appendix A: Sample Document Request

### Due Diligence and Document Request

For the Acquisition of: ______________________________

*If you feel that any of the requested information does not apply or exist, please provide a statement to that effect for the applicable section.*

### Financial Data: Comments

______ 1. Audited or compiled financial statements for six months ended June 30, 200_ and for the year ended December 31, 200_ and supporting detailed general ledger reports for both periods. ____________

______ 2. Accounts receivable aging report run at June 30, 200_ month-end closing and at December 31, 200_ month-end closing by patient and payor source, detailing charges, payments, adjustments, and credit balances. ____________

______ 3. All bank statements for the six month period ended June 30, 200_ and for the 12 months ended 200_. ____________

______ 4. Description of intercompany transactions, if any. ____________

______ 5. List of related parties and transactions with related parties. ____________

______ 6. List of suppliers and vendors and copies of any written purchase agreements or other contractual agreements. ____________

______ 7. Copies of debt or line of credit arrangements. ____________

______ 8. Copy of any operating budgets or forecasts of the Companies. ____________

______ 9. Income tax returns filed for federal, state, city and county for prior 3 years. ____________

______ 10. Copies of 200_ Form 940—Employer Annual Federal Unemployment Tax Return, Forms W-2 and W-3, and most recent federal and state quarterly payroll tax filings, Form 941. ____________

______ 11. Tangible personal property tax returns for prior three years. ____________

### Corporate Documents:

______ 1. Articles of Incorporation of the entities. ____________

______ 2. Bylaws of the entities and any other shareholder/partnership agreements. ____________

______ 3. Minutes of Board of Directors. ______

______ 4. Copies of stock certificates including both sides and copy of stock transfer ledger. ______

______ 5. Copies of any D/B/A and fictitious name filings. ______

______ 6. Corporate organizational chart of entities and ownership. ______

______ 7. List of states in which Company is qualified to do business and evidence that Company is qualified to do business in each state. ______

**Physical Plant, Real Property and Other Property:**

______ 1. List of all real estate (owned and leased). ______

______ 2. Instruments evidencing title to such real estate (e.g., deeds, title papers, title insurance policies and binders, title opinions, appraisals, and surveys). ______

______ 3. Real property office leases. ______

______ 4. Personal property leases, for example; copier lease, telephone equipment lease, computer equipment and software, etc. ______

______ 5. Description of any property which is collateral under financing arrangements. ______

______ 6. Detailed listing of furniture, fixtures, and medical equipment, and a general description of condition. ______

**Environmental Matters:**

______ 1. Biomedical hazardous waste permits. ______

______ 2. Description of the Company's generation, storage, handling, and disposal of all hazardous and infectious waste, including asbestos, chlordane, medical related waste and radioactive materials. ______

______ 3. Copy of written agreement with any contracted waste disposal service. ______

**Risk Management:**

______ 1. Complete copies of professional liability insurance policies (malpractice) and commercial liability policies (property and office). Malpractice insurance policy and loss history (loss runs) as provided by malpractice insurance carrier, including claims status reports from the insurance carrier. Include status on any physicians for which there are no claims. Description of any claims or events which have not been reported to the insurance carrier. ______

______ 2. Copies of letters from Company's outside legal counsel to independent accountants for the past three years regarding litigation in which the Company or an employed physician was involved. ______

______ 3. Copies of correspondence relating to any federal or state governmental investigations or proceedings before any federal, state, or municipal department, board, bureau, agency, or other instrumentality and any citations received. ______

______ 4. Copies of any documents related to payment denials, appeals, or other payment controversies between the Company and a nongovernmental third-party payor. ______

______ 5. A description of any settled, pending, or threatened claim or action against the Company arising from its participation in a government program, including, without limitation, investigations or legal action arising under the federal healthcare program fraud and abuse laws. ______

______ 6. Copies of internal investigation memoranda, assessment or audit reports, correspondence, review letters, or other documents relating to healthcare regulatory compliance audits and other activities. ______

______ 7. Any correspondence regarding employees or personnel policies from any regulatory agency such as: ______
The Department of Immigration and Naturalization
Department of Labor
National Labor Relations Board
Internal Revenue Service ______

______ 8. Identify any employment related claims, lawsuits, arbitrations, or other proceedings (including administrative and arbitrage proceedings and government agency investigations) which are pending or threatened. Furnish copies of any related documentation. ______

______ 9. List all discrimination complaints against the Company or any predecessor during the last 5 years. Show date of claims, persons involved and actual or expected outcome. ______

______ 10. Description of workers' compensation program and copies of certificates of insurance. ______

**Human Resources:**

______ 1. Copies of all employment or employment-related contracts, agreements, or understandings with current employees (inclusive of officers, directors, managers, physicians, nurses, technicians and any other allied healthcare professionals). Include agreements with former employees if employment-related commitments exist. ______

______ 2. Listing of all current personnel, including title, date of hire, site location, classification (full-time, part-time, per diem), experience, certifications and education, compensation, bonus targets, and accrued benefits. Description of any special compensation arrangements or incentive programs and accrued but unpaid benefits. ______

______ 3. Copies of all consulting agreements currently in effect. ______

______ 4. Most recent payroll register. ______

______ 5. Current internal organizational chart of officers and key management. ______

______ 6. Provide a description of any of the following programs: bonus, company car or auto expense allowances, cellular phone, housing and relocation, deferred compensation arrangements, jury duty, bereavement leave, personal time off, educational assistance, tuition reimbursement, employee recognition, community service programs, service awards, and executive perquisites. Provide copies of all relevant documentation, including plan documents/ communication to employees. If you have programs other than those listed above, please include. ______

______ 7. Copies of employer policy manuals or statements. ______

______ 8. To the extent not provided above, describe all vacation, sick pay, paid time off, and holidays. ______

______ 9. Description of any employee loans or loans to directors or officers. ______

______ 10. Description of group employee benefit plans, for example: (i) group health, (ii) pension and profit sharing, (iii) disability, (iv) life insurance, and (v) cafeteria plan and copies of invoices. ______

______ 11. Employee benefit plan documents for the above and 5500 filings for 200_ and 200_ for both 401k, money purchase pension plans, and cafeteria plans. The original adoption agreements, the plan document and any amendments, the summary plan descriptions, copies of fidelity bonds, most recent nondiscrimination testing results, external audit report if required, trust agreements, recent plan statements, any cafeteria plan documents, and IRS determination letters. ______

**Contractual:**

______ 1. All hospital, ambulatory facility, diagnostic facility, or other contracts related to the provision of professional services. ______

______ 2. Copies of operating policy and procedure manuals. ______

______ 3. All written contracts and agreements, for example; postal meter agreements, biomedical waste agreements, maintenance agreements, telephone equipment, etc. ______

**Billing and Collections:**

______ 1. Copies of current billing fee schedules. ______

______ 2. Schedule of major payor contract rates. ______

______ 3. All contracts, agreements and understandings with any party regarding the provision of medical services to patients, including all provider agreements with HMOs, PPOs, third party payors, IPAs, PHOs, MSOs, etc. Include all supporting schedules, amendments, addendums, referenced documents, etc. ______

______ 4. Describe global or special arrangements with facility/providers (written and verbal). Provide copies of agreements. ______

______ 5. Describe self-pay arrangements (written and verbal). ______

______ 6. Description of any outsourced billing services and copies of agreements. ______

______ 7. Medical Billing Systems generated reports (by date of service) for the six months ended June 30, 200_ and for the year ended December 31, 200_ detailing unit volume, charges, adjustments, and collections by:
   a. CPT Code
   b. CPT Code for major managed care providers
   c. Provider
   d. Location
   e. Payor source ______

**Credentialing:**

______ 1. Licensing and credentialing information for all physicians, other allied healthcare providers, and the P.A. These include medical licensure, curriculum vitae, occupational licenses, radiological licenses, bio-medical hazardous waste permits, and CLIA licenses. Note: Please see grid provided (Provider Information). ______

______ 2. Listing of health care facilities in which good standing staff memberships are maintained by physicians ('privileges'). Note: This should be indicated on the grid above. ______

______ 3. Listing of Medicare and Medicaid group and individual provider numbers and any other billing numbers pertinent to claim submission. Note: Please see grid provided (Government Plan Information). ______

**Other:**

______ 1. Software and computer hardware licenses and agreements for services (please specify function software is used for, i.e. accounting, billing, payroll, etc). ______

______ 2. Listing of other business interests of any owners, partners, or employees that represent a potential conflict of interest. ______

______ 3. Provide copies of all government permits, clearances, and approvals for each clinic(s) held by the Company or its employees necessary to conduct business (e.g. HCC Clinic License for the State of ______). ______

## Appendix B: Commonly Used Physician Practice Ratios

$$\text{Gross Collection Ratio} = \frac{\text{Gross Collections}}{\text{Gross Charges}}$$

$$\text{Net Collection Ratio} = \frac{\text{Gross Collections}}{\text{Gross Charges} - \text{Adjustments} + \text{Refunds}}$$

$$\text{Days in Accounts Receivable} = \frac{\text{Average AR for the year x 365 days}}{\text{Net Collections for the year}}$$

$$\text{Overhead Expense \%} = \frac{\text{Operational (nonphysician expenses)}}{\text{Net Collections}}$$

$$\text{Current Ratio} = \frac{\text{Current Assets}}{\text{Current Liabilities}}$$

$$\text{Debt Ratio} = \frac{\text{Total Liabilities}}{\text{Total Assets}}$$

$$\text{Total Asset Turnover} = \frac{\text{Total Net Medical Revenue}}{\text{Total Assets}}$$

Chapter 29

# Lost Profits for Physician Practices

*By Mark O. Dietrich, CPA/ABV*

Unlike lost profits pertaining to other businesses, claims for lost profits in connection with physician practices are typically defined in terms of loss of compensation. As such, for the typical small practice, a lost profits analysis might look much the same as a physician's claim for lost earnings in a personal injury case, although the loss period is likely to be different.

Larger practices and those with ancillary testing capability, such as imaging and laboratory services, may have more traditional lost profits damages claims, as might those practices with greater leverage over nonowner physicians or physician extenders such as nurse practitioners and physician assistants. A good example would be a medical practice's claim for damages resulting from the alleged violation of a noncompete or nonsolicitation agreement by a former employee. In this situation, the practice could lose profits related to ancillary testing revenues and from losing the violator's patients. It could also incur recruiting and training costs for replacing the lost employees and losses due to the unabsorbed overhead that revenues from the violator formerly covered.[1]

## Basic Factors to Consider

### *Basic compensation analysis*

Physician profits and compensation are in large part driven by individual productivity and the rate-per-unit-of-service paid for the various services. Thus, any claim for lost

1 Note: Financial aspects of medical and physician practices involve unique terms and statutory regulations; for the reader's convenience, a glossary of such terms and legislative references is set forth in the final section (*Section G*) of this chapter.

profits should consider the historical pattern of work by the physicians and the local market area. A proper analysis would require, at a minimum, consideration of the following factors:

- Plaintiff's work hours in the office, hospital, or other venue;
- Number of patients seen, surgeries performed, images read, and so on;
- Use of physician billing codes;
- Trends in reimbursement rates for the services provided;
- Staffing and overhead rates for the practice;
- Age of the physicians;
- Historical earnings of the physicians;
- Presence of physician extenders;
- Ancillary testing income, if any;
- Ancillary-driven differences in physician compensation;
- Regional, localized, or practice-specific differences in payments by insurers for physician services;
- Regional differences in physician compensation due to:
  - Supply and demand effects of a surplus (unlikely) or shortage of physicians;
  - Cost of living;
  - Utilization (clinical practice styles);[2]
- Collection rate for services performed versus charges for those services;
- Payor mix; e.g., percentage of revenue generated from Medicare, Medicaid, private insurance plans, self-pay, and so on;
- Training and skill of the physician, such as surgical skills for a surgeon;[3]
- Malpractice claim history;
- Activities in developing the practice; and
- Competing practices.

Of course, undertaking the analysis requires that the financial expert (through efforts by the attorney) successfully obtains the necessary data during the discovery process. Thus,

2 For example, certain areas of the country have high incidences of Caesarean deliveries, use of advanced imaging such as MRI, or surgical versus interventional treatment of coronary artery disease.

3 A decline in physician's income could be traced to failure to train in current surgical or clinical techniques, for example.

it is wise to retain an expert early in such litigation to be certain the document request contains the appropriate information. Furthermore, review of *initial* documents produced invariably leads to additional requests for other documents, making early retention in the discovery phase even more critical.

#### Example

A member of a hospital medical staff brings a claim for lost income against the hospital after it terminated her staff privileges. In valuing her claim, the plaintiff's financial expert uses Medical Group Management Association (MGMA)[4] national data for median physician earnings as a basis for the "but-for" earnings calculation (the income the physician would have earned, but for the defendant's alleged wrongful termination). The following are the particular areas that the expert should review for purposes of analyzing potential lost earnings.

#### *General measures of productivity*

Productivity measures in a physician practice include hours worked, patients seen, physician extenders (such as nurse practitioners and physician assistants) supervised, as well as charges and collections for services.

Hours worked is an important element to assess in conjunction with the number of patients seen during those hours. Industry sources such as MGMA, for example, provide data on the number of patients seen and hours worked. Looking at the relationship between the two can offer insight into the efficiency of the practice, an important driver of income.

Nurse practitioners and physician assistants (referred to as nonphysician providers, or NPPs, in the MGMA data) are frequently billed under the physician's provider number if the physician supervises their services, including reviewing the charts of patients seen.[5] In some instances, these extenders can also bill directly for their services without physician supervision. If extenders are included in the individual physician's productivity, then the analyst will need to separately identify the work that the particular physician actually performed versus the work that extenders did when using the MGMA benchmark data. *Tip*: All the MGMA data exclude the productivity associated with physician extenders. Thus, one all-too-frequent misuse of MGMA data is failing to adjust for physician extender revenues.

4 Medical Group Management Association; www.mgma.com.

5 Medicare allows this under the so-called "incident to" rules; other insurers may or may not follow Medicare guidelines.

### *Physician Billing Codes*

One of the most challenging aspects of measuring damages relative to a physician practice is to understand the revenue cycle, including CPT[6] codes for billing. These are a series of five-digit billing codes used for the vast majority of physician services, although there are also HCPCS (Healthcare Common Procedure Coding System) codes for certain testing, G[7] codes and J[8] codes, and a host of other esoteric terms that may be relevant in a particular engagement.

#### Example 1

An orthopedic surgeon specializing in knee and shoulder arthroscopy brings a claim for lost wages against a practice for wrongful discharge. During his employment, the CPT™ codes associated with arthroscopy permitted the practice to use multiple codes to bill for certain procedures, resulting in enhanced payments. Subsequent to the alleged discharge and damaging event, these codes were combined into a required G code for billing, resulting in significantly lower payment levels for the same arthroscopic services. As a result, part of the physician's decline in income could be traced to specific reductions in payment for the services he provided, and the expected "but for" earnings could be lower.

#### Example 2

A primary care physician brings a claim for loss of income due to unlawful discharge from a medical practice. Prior to the discharge, she was earning $150,000 per year and her use of billing codes was subject to review by the practice manager and compliance officer before their submission to insurance companies for payment; the physician did not properly educate herself in the use of codes.

**Exhibit 1. Coding Distribution**

| Code Level | Distribution | Visits | Fee | Revenue |
|---|---|---|---|---|
| 99211 | 5% | 250 | $20 | $5,000 |
| 99212 | 10. | 500 | 40 | 20,000 |
| 99213 | 50 | 2,500 | 60 | 150,000 |
| 99214 | 30 | 1,500 | 80 | 120,000 |
| 99215 | 5 | 250 | 110 | 27,500 |
| | 100 | 5,000 | | 322,500 |

6 Current Procedural Terminology, trademarked by the American Medical Association.

7 G codes apply to professional healthcare procedures and services that would be coded as CPT but for which no CPT code exists; insurers sometimes combine services that have separate CPT codes into a single G code resulting in reduced payment. See, e.g., www.reimbursementcodes.com/hcpcs_codes_d.html.

8 J codes are used for injections and pharmaceuticals.

In her new practice, an inexperienced individual who does not understand physician codes manages the billing, and is concerned that patients may be overcharged. Although the physician sees the same number of patients with a similar set of clinical problems in the new practice as in the old, her income has dropped to $100,000.

**Exhibit 2. Drop in Income Due to Incorrect Coding of Services**

| Code Level | Distribution | Visits | Fee | Revenue |
|---|---|---|---|---|
| 1 | 15% | 750 | $20 | $15,000 |
| 2 | 20 | 1,000 | 40 | 40,000 |
| 3 | 50 | 2,500 | 60 | 150,000 |
| 4 | 10 | 500 | 80 | 40,000 |
| 5 | 5 | 250 | 110 | 27,500 |
| | 100 | 5,000 | | 272,500 |

As Exhibits 1 and 2 indicate, the entire $50,000 drop in income *could* be due to incorrect coding of services.

### *Physician Supply and Demand*

The relevance of local-versus-national data on physician compensation depends on many factors, including supply and demand and the recruiting market. A nationwide shortage of a particular specialty can lead to relative equivalence in compensation expectation from one area to the next. Other factors are rates paid by particular insurers for services, cost of living differentials, and local factors such as the relationship between a physician with significant influence and his or her hospital. The latter is a particularly important factor in hospital-based practice, such as radiology, pathology, and anesthesia.

### *Ancillary testing income*

This item refers to physician practice profits or compensation contributed by testing equipment owned or leased by the practice. (The MGMA data refer to this revenue as "TC," or the technical component.[9] Clearly, if the practice does not have such equipment, the physician cannot partake in any such profits or compensation.

### *Collections for Services*

Charges are generally considered a poor measure of productivity because the payment system controlled by health insurers is often indifferent to charges. Charges may be

9 For an excellent discussion of technical component revenue and its implications in physician compensation see BVR's *Guide to Physician Practice Valuation*.

relevant as *one* productivity measure in a practice with little or no insured patients, such as a cosmetic plastic surgery practice or a walk-in clinic that does not accept insurance.

Exhibit 3 shows the representative data for collections available from the MGMA survey. Note that "NPP Excluded" is part of each subset of the sample data. Collections for practices with over 10% TC are significantly higher than those with less than 10% TC. The sample sizes also vary significantly.[10]

**Exhibit 3. Data for Collections**

| | Providers | Practices | Mean | Std. Dev. | 25th %tile | Median | 75th %tile | 90th %tile |
|---|---|---|---|---|---|---|---|---|
| Overall TC/NPP excluded | 1,569 | 182 | $345,779 | $140,449 | $258,320 | $329,767 | $403,896 | $501,279 |
| Eastern region TC/NPP excluded | 369 | 40 | 354,056 | 133,686 | 275,169 | 346,302 | 421,846 | 514,994 |
| Overall NPP excluded, with 1%-10% TC | 601 | 85 | 410,983 | 166,632 | 313,776 | 386,401 | 476,962 | 564,883 |
| Overall NPP excluded, with over 10% TC | 164 | 38 | 474,743 | 212,399 | 344,813 | 441,338 | 582,429 | 727,105 |

*Data from Eastern Region are representative; other regions are reported*[11]

***Payor mix***

Perhaps the most critical factor affecting a physician's income after productivity and coding is the practice's revenue per procedure, which is significantly influenced by the underlying payor mix. There is no uniformity among the ways that various government and private insurers pay for services. Although Medicare[12] might pay 60% of a particular charge, Medicaid[13] might pay only 25% and Blue Cross might pay 70%. Data from a Medicaid plan in one state will usually have no relationship to data from another, and the many Blue Cross and Blue Shield plans in the United States do not value physician services the same way. Medicare actually adjusts the fee schedule for each state to account for geographic differentials such as cost of living and wages.

The payor mix therefore constitutes a limitation on using national data, and an analysis of the mix is critical to assessing a plaintiff's future income prospects in a "but-for"

10 MGMA bases its data on a survey of medical group members as opposed to a random sample from a population; it includes more private practice groups than other surveys, something to consider.
11 *Medical Group Management Association Physician Compensation and Production Survey*, 2006 Report Based on 2005 Data.
12 A federal program primarily for the elderly with a generally uniform benefit package but vastly different pay rates from area to area. Local coverage determinations by Medicare intermediaries can affect the benefit package.
13 A state-specific program of benefits that is funded partially by each of the state and federal government; which government pays what depends in part on state decisions as to benefits.

earnings analysis. Financial experts should also bear in mind that the payor mix may have changed during the loss period, which could impact the "but-for" damages analysis. In a given circumstance, assessing the payor mix over several years should be considered to see how any changes may impact the measurement of damages.

#### Example

A financial expert reviews the physician's productivity in terms of hours worked, patient encounters, and gross charges and finds that each figure is at or near the MGMA mean value. In examining the collections, however, the value is near the 25th percentile. Analysis of the payor mix indicates that the practice has a large Medicaid patient base and Medicaid is paying only 30% of the practice's charges. Conclusion: The "but-for" earnings prospects of this practice are not comparable to a mean MGMA value.

### *Compensation*

One of the difficulties with MGMA compensation surveys is that they do not present the data in the same categories as the collections data, i.e., there are no categories for compensation with NPP excluded or for TC included. Therefore, the financial expert must exercise judgment and adjust the compensation data as necessary to account for differences in the degree of NPP and TC (ancillary) revenues.

### *Competition*

The financial expert should also assess the extent to which the alleged damages might be due to some factor other than the cause alleged by the plaintiff. This prescription applies regardless of which party, plaintiff or defendant, engages the expert.

Physicians compete on many factors. An adage among doctors says that practice success is driven by "availability, affability, and ability," in that order. Although the saying may be trite, this discussion has already identified hours as a key element in compensation. If at the time the alleged damages occurred, a competing practice extended its hours to evenings and weekends, this might have been a contributing factor in the plaintiff's loss of income. A financial expert would have to consider and measure the impact of this and other factors, since the plaintiff must prove that the defendant's actions proximately caused the damages.

Affability may be difficult to assess other than from a personal interview, which an expert for the defendant may not have access to; a change in affability contributing to a decline in the physician's income is also difficult to assess, if not altogether unusual. To the extent possible, legal counsel should make inquiries about the plaintiff's reputation with patients and colleagues as well as personal difficulties contributing to demeanor, such as a divorce or death in the family. Financial experts should expect cross-examination questions such as, "If Dr. Smith were known to raise his voice with employees, how would this affect your conclusion?" or "If patients had lodged complaints about Dr. Smith's hostile attitude during examinations, how would this affect your conclusion?" Defense counsel may very well depose various fact witnesses to assess a physician's comportment and professional as well as patient relationships. In addition to the physician's affability, that of the office staff, particularly the front desk and reception personnel, may also be critical. If a key employee was replaced at or near the time of the alleged damages, the financial expert should also consider its potential impact on the claimed damages. Public records, such as the state Boards of Registration in Medicine, are generally good sources of information regarding prior complaints or disciplinary action involving the physician.

Ability is another factor that the attorney and financial expert should consider, particularly when the case involves specialists such as surgeons; however, assessing a physician's ability may require another expert with clinical expertise. Medicine is a dynamic practice area and new techniques and procedures are always being developed. These technical and procedural innovations can have consequences on the physician's income. If competing surgeons at a hospital, for example, have trained in a new, less invasive procedure with a lower complications rate and the plaintiff-surgeon failed to train in it, then this lapse could lead to a gradual decline in referrals from other physicians, with a concomitant loss of income. An excellent example is the current rise of using interventional radiology in breast cancer biopsy. Certain gynecological surgeries versus traditional surgical intervention are another. Another example is the shifting tide of opinion about the effectiveness of coronary stents[14] placed by interventional cardiologists versus traditional coronary bypass surgery done by cardiac surgeons. The advent of drug-eluting coronary stents[15] and their approval by Medicare led to dramatic declines in cardiac surgeon incomes and dramatic increases in interventional cardiologists incomes.

Other factors that financial experts may commonly overlook in their lost profits analysis include:

- An increase in the number of physicians practicing a particular specialty in a service area (known as a "catchment" area), resulting in decreased volume for existing physicians;
- A decline or increase in population;

14 Another area under current debate is drug-eluting stents versus standard stents.

15 See 67 *Fed. Reg.* 49,983, 50,004 (Aug. 1, 2002) for advance approval of drug-eluting stents by CMS even before its approval by the FDA.

- Poor economic conditions contributing to a rise in bad debts and a drop in patient insurance coverage, such as those present in 2008 through 2010;
- Changes in health insurance that reduce a patient's benefits;[16]
- Decreases (or increases) in the fee schedule paid by health insurers to the physician;
- Competition among hospitals that affect the incomes of physicians on the staff of those hospitals, particularly when a hospital system is able to negotiate contracts superior to that of competing hospitals (common in many market areas);
- Failure of the physician practice billing department to collect all otherwise collectible amounts (an absolute must-review in any damages analysis); and Poor quality medical billing software or a failed attempt at changing to a new software program.

In short, dozens of factors can contribute to an observed change in physician income that both parties' financial experts should consider in assessing causality.

## In-Depth Look at Special Issues in Identifying Damages

### *Physician compensation systems*

#### Unallocated Overhead

A physician who quits a group practice in violation of a noncompete agreement or a fiduciary responsibility may leave his former colleagues with a large amount of fixed overhead to pay out of what otherwise would have been their income. Physicians often share variable expenses based upon productivity; e.g., if one doctor produces 30% of the revenues, then he or she will be allocated 30% of the variable expenses.

#### Example 1: fixed expense

A two-owner medical practice with four physicians relocates to new office space designed for the four physicians. But the two employed physicians leave the practice in violation of their noncompete agreements and open a competing practice nearby. Each physician's share of the rent was $50,000 per year, such that the remaining two physician-owners

16 This factor will be exacerbated by the 2010 federal healthcare reform, for example, which increases the economic burden of healthcare on insured patients, thereby discouraging utilization even as it expands coverage to the uninsured, trying to make room for them in the system.

now face an additional out-of-pocket cost of $50,000 a piece. The expert's "but-for" lost profits analysis should consider fixed and variable expenses projected separately for the relevant period of time, depending upon the circumstances. Generally, one would expect variable expenses to trend down sooner as part of the mitigation process, and the fixed expenses to remain fairly constant for a longer period of time. Experts should, however, consider that even for fixed expenses, plaintiffs will likely be expected to mitigate their losses within a reasonable period of time.

#### Example 2: variable expense

Assume further that this same practice spends $800,000 per year on staff wages and benefits, representing 25% of annual revenues of $3.2 million. The competing physicians recruited staff with a cost of $200,000. As part of their attempt to mitigate damages, the owners reduced staff by an additional $100,000. On a per-capita basis, the two owners now have $50,000 of additional payroll costs to contend with, but depending on the compensation system, each may suffer a different degree of harm.

For example, if Owner 1 generates 55% of the collections and Owner 2 generates 45%, Owner 1 suffers a loss of $55,000, while Owner 2 suffers a loss of $45,000. This can be important if the financial expert is required to allocate the damages among the injured parties.

### *Large practices and integrated providers*

Depending on the type of entity claiming the damages—e.g., a hospital or a large, integrated group practice with significant ancillary capability—the magnitude of the loss-types can be substantial. One ready source for assessing the magnitude of these potential revenue losses is the survey by Merritt Hawkins & Associates of hospital chief financial officers (CFOs), although data specific to the litigation should be used in a damages calculation, if available:

> The 2010 survey indicates that average net inpatient and outpatient revenue generated by physicians for their affiliated hospitals differed from the 2007 survey based upon specialty. Average revenue generated by primary care physicians declined from $1,433,532 in 2007 to $1,385,775 in 2010. Specialist physician revenue increased from $1,509,910 in 2007 to $1,577,764 in 2010. Neurosurgery was the single largest contributor followed by invasive [invasive is generally considered a cardiologist who performs cardiac catheterization, while interventional is a cardiologist who inserts coronary stents] cardiology, orthopedics, and general surgery.[17]

17 *2010 Physician Inpatient/Outpatient Revenue Survey*, Merritt Hawkins & Associates (Irving, Texas); www.merritthawkins.com.

Surgical specialties tend to generate the largest revenues. The largest and most profitable lines of business in the typical acute care hospital are cardiology and orthopedics. For example, an orthopedic surgeon who leaves a hospital position in violation of a noncompete and goes to work for a competing organization may cause the hospital to lose significant inpatient and outpatient surgery revenues. Orthopedic surgeons are large users of MRI and CT scans, both of which represent significant revenue sources. Similarly, if the orthopedic surgeon leaves a position with a medical practice that provides an outpatient surgery center along with MRI and CT services, damages well in excess of the surgeon's annual income can result.

### *Growth rates in "but-for" and future earnings calculations*

In the author's experience, this is the most common and serious error that occurs in physician damages calculations. In general, there are a variety of broad economic and Medicare-specific limitations on physician incomes.

#### General price per-unit of service[18]

What about increases in fees per-unit of service? From 1994 to 2009—or for 15 years, the compound rate of increase for all physician services was only 1.94%, based on data from the Bureau of Labor Statistics Producer Price Index for Physician Services (see Exhibit 4).

**Exhibit 4. BLS PPI-Physician Services, Annual**

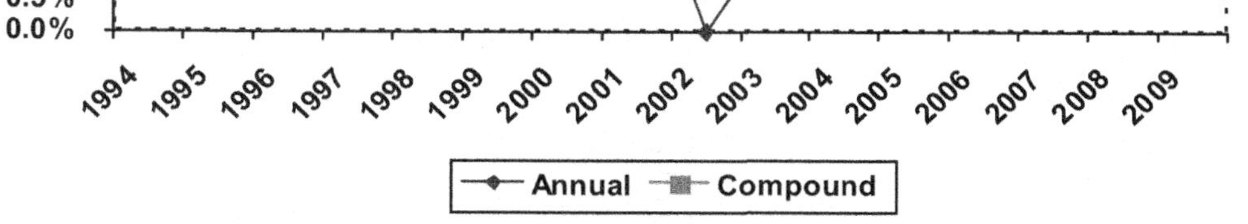

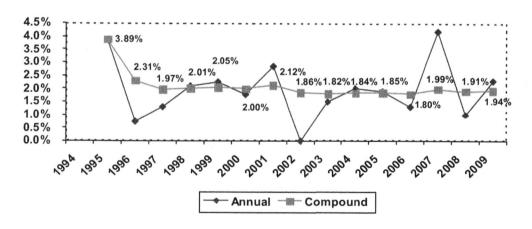


18 Mark Dietrich, "Choosing and Using the Right Valuation Methods for Physician Practices," BVR's *Guide to Healthcare Valuation*, Business Valuation Resources (2009).

### Medicare Price Per Unit of Service[19]

Clearly, there is no evidence that per-unit reimbursement rates are growing at the gross domestic product (GDP) rate or the Consumer Price Index rate, and a small practice's capacity to provide units of service is limited. Under the federal Medicare sustainable growth rate (SGR) formula, Medicare expenditures for physician services are limited by a complex formula that considers the change in fees, the number of beneficiaries, growth in GDP per capita, and the impact of new laws. The SGR is then applied to the Medicare Economic Index (MEI), which measures the weighted average price change in physician services. The MEI is a physician practice-specific measure of inflation and generally is in the range of 3.5%. The Medicare Payment Advisory Commission (MedPAC) Web site publishes the updated, annual data each March.[20]

The pattern since 2006 has been for Congress belatedly to suspend the statutory cutbacks in the conversion factor. The 2007 conversion factor of $35.9848 initially reflected a decrease of 5% and was subsequently overturned by Congress and left equal to the 2006 factor. The 2008 factor was scheduled to drop by 10.1% until the end of December 2007, when the Medicare, Medicaid, and SCHIP Extension Act of 2007 legislation updated the conversion factor by 0.5%, to $38.0870. In July 2008, Congress extended the $38.09 conversion factor for the balance of 2008 over the president's veto and put a 1.1% increase in place for 2009. Since November 2009, Congress has acted several times to delay the scheduled cut for 2010 to $28.41, having failed to include a fix in the healthcare reform legislation. *Note*: The 2009 Medicare physician fee schedule final rule on Oct. 30, 2008 provided for the statutorily mandated 1.1% update for calendar year 2009; *however*, the budget-neutrality adjustment to the conversion factor associated with the review and reallocation of relative value units (RVUs) was a negative 6.41%, resulting in a rate of *$36.07*. The budget-neutrality adjustment is now included in the conversion factor where historically it was applied to a reduction of RVUs for each CPT code. As such, the 2009 rate and the precipitous drop in the 2010 rate shown in Exhibit 5 are not entirely comparable to the prior years.

**Exhibit 5. Medicare Conversion Factor**

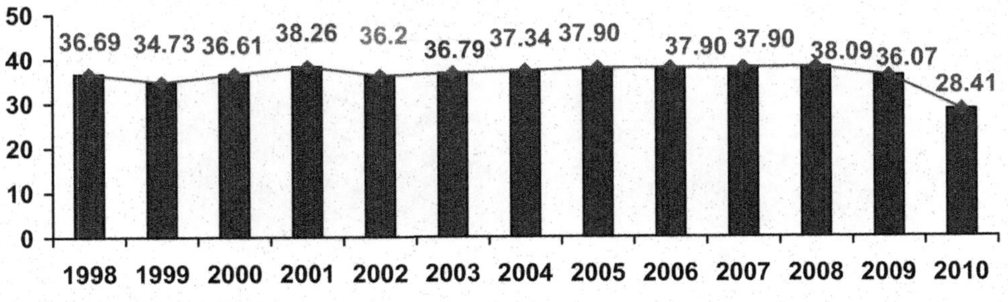


19 Ibid.
20 www.medpac.gov.

These two items represent the broad picture for physician practices in general. For a physician practice of a specific specialty, an in-depth analysis of that particular specialty's income growth opportunities is necessary.

**Example**

Larger physician practices including cardiology, neurology, and orthopedics as well as multispecialty practices frequently invest in high-tech imaging equipment, such as MRI and CT scanners. A lost profits analysis that involves a practice with such equipment should account for the impact of the Deficit Reduction Act of 2005 on the payment for these services;[21] the changes in independent diagnostic testing facilities qualification;[22] and the Stark IV regulations adopted as part of the 2009 inpatient payment system final rule.[23] MRI, CT, and PET were all further negatively impacted by provisions of the federal 2010 healthcare reform legislation, with the utilization assumption[24] increased from 50% to 75% for diagnostic imaging equipment, costing more than $1 million. This significantly reduces the technical component of Medicare revenue and will spread to other payors.

### *Regulatory considerations*

Healthcare may well be the most regulated industry in the country. Since it also represents the largest sector of the economy (+/-17%) and drives federal and state budget concerns, regulatory and other government agencies conduct extensive enforcement activities in the healthcare sector. Many of the more common claims for damages may, in fact, be irrelevant in a physician practice analysis because the underlying rationale for the claim violates one or more federal or state laws. As such, the financial expert should make a threshold determination whether the conduct of the allegedly damaged entity is consistent with the law. Cases in which the plaintiff and defense counsel may be experienced in civil litigation but unfamiliar with healthcare law can create considerable challenges for the expert.

Violations of noncompete agreements are one area that results in frequent litigation. In these cases, financial experts must carefully scrutinize the assumptions related to expected profit contributions from the covenanter.

---

21 Pub.L. 109-171, 120 Stat. 4, Feb. 8, 2006; see, e.g., Mark Dietrich, "A Healthcare Appraiser Reviews a Judge-Appraiser's 'Report,'" *Business Valuation Review* (Summer 2007); Douglas Smith, "Valuation Considerations Specific to Diagnostic Imaging Entities," BVR's *Guide to Healthcare Valuation* (2009).

22 See generally 42 CFR 410.33, Independent Diagnostic Testing Facility (December 2005); cfr.vlex.com/vid/410-independent-diagnostic-testing-19805522.

23 42 CFR Part 412, Medicare Program; Inpatient Rehabilitation Facility Prospective Payment System for Federal Fiscal Year 2009; Final Rule, *Federal Register*, Vol. 73, No. 154 (Friday, Aug. 8, 2008); edocket.access.gpo.gov/2008/pdf/E8-17797.pdf.

24 The utilization assumption determines the expected number of units of service over which fixed expenses of operation are spread in establishing the fee that Medicare will pay. The higher the utilization assumption, the lower the expected fixed expense per unit of service and as a result, the lower the fee Medicare will pay.

**Example**

Assume that a hospital claims lost profits against a former physician employee (cardiologist) who violated a noncompete agreement by joining a competing practice. During the course of his former employment, the physician referred patients to the hospital for services such as catheterization and angioplasty as well as lab tests, CT scans, stress testing, and cardiac ultrasound (collectively considered "ancillaries" for this example). After leaving the hospital, the physician's new practice has the same testing capabilities, so he refers his patients there. The physician also joins the medical staff of a competing hospital to admit his patients.

Because federal law prohibits payment for patient referrals, there could be some concern that the hospital could not claim damages against the physician based on his historic referrals. Although this appears unlikely.[25] the financial expert needs to carefully examine the physician's historical utilization patterns for compliance with applicable laws before using these as the basis for the damages calculation. Even if otherwise permissible, the type of "hockey stick" assumptions seen in many damage claims are unlikely to pass regulatory muster, because they will likely be difficult to construct a permissible rationale for the physician referring ever-increasing amounts of business to the hospital.

Another common but perhaps fatal approach to calculating damages in this example would be to use the physician's *post*-employment utilization in his new practice as a basis for measuring the hospital's losses. If the physician becomes an owner in his new practice and shares in the profits generated by ancillary referrals, then utilization is likely to be higher than the physician historically incurred as an employee in the hospital, where the Stark laws precluded him from receiving a part of the ancillary profit.[26] A proper analysis would differentiate between growth in referrals due to an increase in the number of patients seen by the physician, which might have been foreseeable had he remained with the hospital, as opposed to growth motivated by his ability to profit from those referrals. Plaintiff's counsel could use the latter, of course, to attack the credibility of the defendant and his motives to violate the noncompete.

From the standpoint of the physician-defendant, the scrutiny of the previous relationship may yield potential defenses and counterclaims. So-called *qui tam* or whistleblower cases in healthcare, along with their astounding fines—in which the whistleblowers

25 "A requirement to refer to a specific provider is different from an agreement not to establish a competing business. In other words, a covenant not to compete might prevent a physician from setting up a private practice or offering services that compete with the entity that purchases his or her practice. If an agreement also included the requirement that the physician refer business to the purchaser, it would be suspect under the anti-kickback statute." 66 Fed. Reg. 879 (Jan. 4, 2001).

26 See generally 420 CFR 411.

often share—frequently result from wrongful termination or other lawsuits that the informants may have instigated against the *qui tam* defendants.[27] Surprisingly, perhaps, informants often escape penalties for whatever part they played in the alleged schemes because the government has a vested interest in whistleblowers coming forward.[28]

From the standpoint of the plaintiff, the discovery process directed against the new practice unit could uncover regulatory violations that would lead to settlement.

### *Typical physician practice claims that do not 'fly'*

A typical claim for lost profits generally arises from the proximity of the parties to one another in a business relationship and the resulting strategic advantages that they each enjoyed prior to a breach. For example, a small donut store located in a strip mall next to a major consumer retailer such as Home Depot or Loews would benefit from the customer flow to those stores. If the donut shop brings a claim against the landlord for failure to deliver the lease, for example, then a financial expert would certainly look at both the historical and future customer traffic flow to the home goods retailer as one basis for measuring the donut shop's lost profits.

By contrast, the Stark laws specifically prohibit market value from being based on the ability of strategic parties to refer patients to one another; similarly, the anti-kickback statute prohibits payment for referrals.[29] Assume that the physician-owners of a medical office building lease space to a tenant who plans to construct an imaging center; assume further that the physicians-owners decide to construct their own center and force out the tenant. If one accepts the premise that claimed damages cannot be based on a possible violation of the law, then it would be incorrect to base the tenant's future profits on the potential referrals that would have been available from all physicians in the building. Further, with respect to referrals from the physician-owners, although they likely would have referred all of their business to their own center, they likely would not have referred all of their business to a tenant's independent center. Of course, the tenant may have alternative damages claims available, to preclude the physician-owners from unjustly profiting from their actions.

27 The University of Medicine and Dentistry in New Jersey (UMDNJ) investigation is an excellent case in point. In December 2005, the DOJ entered into an agreement with UMDNJ, by which UMDNJ paid back nearly $5 million in double-billings to Medicaid and undertook certain operational reforms in return for deferred charges of healthcare fraud; see www.usdoj.gov/usao/nj/press/files/pdffiles/UMDNJFINALDPA.pdf.

28 *McLeod Regional Medical Center to Pay U.S. Over $15 Million to Resolve False Claims Act Allegations,* DOJ Press Release (Nov. 1, 2002); www.usdoj.gov/opa/pr/2002/November/02_civ_634.htm.

29 Arguably, even if the standard of value in physician lost profits is not fair market value, the outright prohibition on paying for referrals likely precludes the use of "strategic value" assumptions.

## Conclusion

After reading this chapter, one might conclude that it focused primarily on factors that tend to reduce potential claims for lost profits related to physician practices. In fact, a host of potential damages theories can apply to these and related cases, but because physician practices are one of the economy's most heavily regulated sectors, calculating damages based on these damages theories requires a body of knowledge that the typical damages expert may not generally have. More importantly, in litigation of this type, the opposing party is more likely to retain an expert to refute any damages claim, and any plaintiff's expert who does not appropriately consider the factors discussed in this chapter will likely be subject to attack. Accordingly, it is critical that any financial expert retained in this area of practice consider the following *areas of inquiry and evaluation for potential damage claims:*

1. Loss of physician income in general;
2. Loss of nonphysician support staff;
3. Loss of nonphysician provider staff who perform billable services;
4. Loss of physician staff (e.g., to a hospital);
5. Loss of practice value;
6. Loss of ancillary revenue from laboratory, imaging, and cardiac testing;
7. Loss of inpatient admissions;
8. Loss of skilled nursing facility admissions;
9. Loss of outpatient surgical facility fees;
10. Loss of home health agency revenue; and
11. Loss of durable medical equipment revenue.

In an era when hospitals and larger practice entities are fiercely competing for physician specialties—including cardiology, cardiac surgery, and orthopedics—events giving rise to potential damages claims are on the increase. Analysis of the expansive revenue and profit opportunities that plaintiffs have lost in such circumstances is where financial and damages experts should focus their attention.

## Glossary of Terms

In many ways, the financial aspects of medical practices have a unique vocabulary. The following definitions will be helpful to financial experts and attorneys who may be new to the area.

- Ancillary—refers to a collection of testing equipment such as imaging (CT, MRI, ultrasound, stress testing, and so on).
- Payor—An industry term for the source of payment for services, such as Blue Cross, Medicare, Medicaid, an HMO, and so on.
- Payor mix—the percentage of business done with various payors.
- Stark laws—Federal civil legislation comprised of three separate statutory provisions governing physician self-referral for Medicare and Medicaid patients.[30] Stark regulations contain an outright prohibition on physicians referring certain services to entities in which they have defined financial interests, for example. The statute is enforced with draconian fines.
- Anti-kickback statute—Federal criminal legislation that prohibits payment of anything of value to a healthcare provider for referring services provided to beneficiaries of federal programs including Medicare, Medicaid, and Civilian Health and Medical Program of the Uniformed Services (CHAMPUS).[31]
- Integrated provider—An entity that engages in a variety of services in the "continuum of care." For example, a large physician practice may have both primary care and specialist physicians, broad-based radiology and imaging capability, a freestanding ambulatory surgery center, and a laboratory.
- Integrated delivery system—An entity with hospital and physician components, usually both primary care and specialist care, in addition to such services as radiology and imaging, laboratory, skilled nursing facility, and home health care.
- Professional component (PC or "26")—The portion of a payment for a test or imaging (e.g., cardiac stress or a CT scan) that compensates the physician for interpreting the results of the test.
- Revenue cycle—the process commencing with the preparation of a charge or bill (claim) for a service through the collection of all the payments for it. In

30 Stark legislation is codified at 42 U.S.C.S. §1395nn (§1877 of the Social Security Act) and 42 C.F.R. §411.350 through §411.389.

31 See Criminal Penalties for Acts Involving Federal Health Care Programs, 42 U.S.C. § 1320a-7b(b)(2000).

healthcare, the process is complicated by different rates for the same service by different payors, partial payments by one or more payors for the same service, and the need to collect from the patient after all insurance and government payors have weighed in on a claim. There are also complex documentation and coding rules as well as retrospective review of charges for claims already paid.

- Technical component (TC)—The portion of a payment for a test or imaging (e.g., a cardiac stress test or a CT scan) that compensates the physician practice for owning the equipment, employing the technician (if any), providing supplies, and so on (See also Professional Component, above).
- Global—The combination of the PC and TC for a service.

# Part IV
# Valuing Physician Services and Relationships with Hospitals

Chapter 30

# Valuing Physician Employment Arrangements in Five Parts: Economics, the Market, Cost and Income Approaches, and Valuation Synthesis

*By Timothy R. Smith, CPA/ABV*

## PART I. INTRODUCTION TO THE ECONOMICS OF PHYSICIAN SERVICES

The employment of physicians by nonphysician-owned healthcare entities, particularly hospitals and health systems, is becoming more commonplace in today's healthcare marketplace. As discussed later in this chapter, many believe that physician employment by hospitals and health systems will become the prevailing physician practice paradigm within the next 10 years or less. Yet, such employment by hospitals and health systems is subject to various healthcare regulations, including the requirement that the compensation paid under such arrangements be consistent with fair market value (FMV). As a result, these employers generally pursue various programs or approaches for ensuring that employed physicians are paid FMV compensation for their services. Typical FMV compliance efforts include internal review processes, use of survey data, and engaging outside consultants to determine FMV compensation.

From the standpoint of the professional practice of appraisal, the key to valuing services of any kind, including those provided under employment agreements, is matching the appropriate compensation with the services provided under the terms of the arrangement. It is essential, therefore, that the valuation of physician employment arrangements be based on a sound understanding of the economics and market dynamics of physician services. Unfortunately, many players in the healthcare industry fail to understand the broad scope and complexity of factors affecting the value of physician services in the marketplace and thereby in employment arrangements. The purpose of Part I, therefore, is to provide an introduction to the fundamental economic and marketplace dynamics that should be understood and considered by those seeking to value the compensation paid to employed physicians.

## 1.0 Introduction to Physician Services

Since the key to valuing service agreements is matching the compensation paid for services rendered, it is essential for an appraiser to have a solid grasp and understanding of the key characteristics of the services provided by physicians. Failure to comprehend these characteristics can lead to appraisals of physician services that do not reflect the fundamental economics of the underlying services, and consequently, that are not consistent with the standard of FMV. The following sections discuss important aspects of physician services that can affect the FMV analysis of employment arrangements.

### *1.1 Types of Physician Services*

Physicians provide a variety of services in the healthcare industry for which they can receive compensation. The most common type of service for a physician to provide is patient care or clinical services. Patient care or clinical services, however, can generally be broken down into two major categories: professional component services and technical component services. These services can be described as follows.

#### Professional Component Services

Professional component services encompass procedures generally performed directly or personally by the physician in examining, diagnosing, or treating patients. Office visits, surgical procedures, or interpretations of diagnostic imaging exams are common examples of professional services performed by physicians. The type of procedures performed by a physician will tend to vary according to specialty and practice focus. The place of service for these services can also vary, but most services are provided in either a physician practice or facility setting, such as a hospital. One type of procedure that is common to most physician specialties is an office visit, which is a basic evaluation and management procedure performed in a physician practice. Other services that can be broadly placed under the heading of professional services are so called "incident to" services that are performed by other medical personnel, such as nonphysician providers. A physician supervises such personnel in the provision of these services, which are typically billed under and credited to the supervising physician.

#### Technical Component Services

Technical component services, which are also frequently referred to as ancillary services, on the other hand, are not typically provided directly or personally by the physician, but by technicians, nurses, or medical assistants working under the supervision of the physician in the physician's practice. Such services are generally provided to patients under the direction of a physician and are part of the patients' overall diagnosis and treatment. These services usually include the use of various medical technologies and may involve pharmaceuticals that are also used in the examinations or procedures. Examples of technical component or ancillary services include lab tests, diagnostic imaging procedures, immunizations, radiation therapy treatments, chemotherapy, infusion, and physical therapy. Historically, these services have been provided in the physician practice setting, with the attending physician referring the patient to undergo them as part of diagnosis or treatment. As a result, they are included in the broad categories of physician services and patient care or clinical services because of their provision to patients in the physician practice setting. In addition, technical component services generally require the supervision or oversight of a physician. In the case of diagnostic imaging and other testing procedures, a physician is also required to provide an interpretation of the results of the exam. These factors are additional reasons for including technical component services under the general category of physician services.

Physicians also provide other types of services in the healthcare marketplace. These nonclinical services may be broadly outlined as follows.

#### On-Call Services

Physicians provide two key forms of on-call services in the healthcare marketplace. First, physicians regularly provide hospitals and other healthcare facilities with immediate availability or access to their clinical services on an as-needed basis. Typically, the physician provides call coverage for the physician's specialty to a hospital's emergency department (ED) or to unassigned inpatients in the hospital. A second form of on-call services is provided to the patients in a physician's practice. Physicians provide their patients with access to them or their designated substitutes to address issues and questions that arise outside of general office hours at night and on weekends. Such "practice call" is generally considered part of the physician-patient relationship and should be distinguished from "hospital call." Unhappily, many in the healthcare arena fail to distinguish between practice and hospital call coverage, not recognizing the varying economics and market dynamics related to each type.

#### Administrative

Physicians provide various forms of administrative services to healthcare facilities and entities. While these services may be administrative in nature, they are often based on a physician's clinical expertise and knowledge and cannot be performed by nonphysicians. A prime example of physician administrative services is hospital medical directorships. Physicians may also serve in executive roles within organizations either part-time or full-time. Again, some positions may require the skills and acumen of an experienced clinician to perform the duties of the position, such as chief medical officer. For other positions, however, the physician's clinical background may play an important but not necessarily required role in the job duties of the position. Many physicians become chief executive officers or fill other executive or managerial positions within healthcare entities, where being a physician is not a requirement.

#### Clinical Co-Management or Service Line Management

The recent emergence of so-called clinical co-management or service line management arrangements has given rise to a new hybrid form of services that combine administrative and clinical duties and tasks. In these arrangements, physicians provide management services to healthcare organizations, using their clinical knowledge and expertise to help such entities improve clinical and operational processes to improve clinical quality or operational outcomes. The physicians are also typically participants in these processes through their practice at the facility for which they provide the services.

#### Educational or Academic

Educational services provided by physicians can range from teaching positions at medical schools and residency programs to specialized training programs for healthcare facilities and organizations.

#### Research and Development

Physicians can provide an array of research and development services to healthcare organizations, particularly in life sciences. They can also perform research as part of an academic position.

#### Business Management

When physicians are the owners of their practices, they often provide business management services to their practices. They make key operational and planning decisions and may be involved in the daily supervision of practice support staff. Owner-physicians may negotiate with vendors, landlords, and commercial payers. They may be directly involved in employee hiring and firing decisions and actions. While services such as these are common for physicians to provide in physician-owned groups, they should be distinguished from clinical or patient care services.

#### Entrepreneurial and Investor

Perhaps one of the least recognized forms of service provided by physicians are the entrepreneurial or owner services that physicians provide to their practices. In cases where physicians own their practices, they invest in their practices, often providing capital to their businesses in the form of reduced compensation that is used to finance operations and asset purchases for the practice, such as working capital, equipment, and business expansions. In essence, physician-owners provide financial services to their practices in the form of equity capital financing. Even when physicians use debt to finance capital and operating needs of their practices, the debt payments serve to reduce the earnings or cash flow available for physician compensation. In addition, physicians often give personal guarantees when borrowing money to use in their practices.

It is important to distinguish among these various forms of physician services because each type of service has its own unique characteristics and economics. More importantly, the marketplace tends to compensate for each type of service differently based on its unique characteristics and economics. Thus, the valuation tools and techniques employed to determine FMV compensation often vary by type of service. Since the key to compensation valuation for service agreements is matching the appropriate level of compensation to the services provided, valuations of physician services should be grounded in a thorough understanding of the key types of services provided by physicians and the fundamental economics of such services.

### *1.2 The Scope of Services for a Physician's Specialty*

The nature and scope of services provided by a physician are generally a function of the physician's specialty or subspecialty. The physician's specialty denotes his or her training and clinical expertise and the types of procedures performed for clinical patient care. *The scope of services for a specialty is important because various clinical as well as other types of physician services are frequently compensated at different levels in the healthcare marketplace.* As a result, market trends and key economic factors affecting a specialty are critical considerations in the valuation process for physician services. Important trends and factors include reimbursement, physician shortages, procedural and patient care innovations, technology use and innovations, and prevailing practice paradigms for the specialty. It should also be noted that a physician's specialty can define the range of administrative, management, and education services that he or she is qualified to provide in the healthcare marketplace.

Since most physicians receive the majority of their compensation from providing clinical patient-care services, it is essential to have a basic knowledge of the top clinical procedures for a given specialty when attempting to value these clinical services. Such knowledge is important for understanding the essential aspects of a physician's practice, including the nature and scope of services provided to patients and the revenues and costs associated with the practice. In addition, it facilitates benchmarking analysis in comparison to peer group data, such as that found in the various publicly available physician compensation and productivity surveys. Knowledge of the prevailing practice paradigm and most common procedures can illuminate the causes of variances from such data. Major procedures often define key productivity measures for a physician.

Examples would include office visits for primary care physicians, certain types of surgical cases in the various surgical specialties, stents for interventional cardiology, and lesion removals for dermatology.

It is important to note that common procedures for a given specialty may include various technical component services. For certain specialties, such services represent a significant portion of the procedures performed in the practice and are important sources of practice revenue and earnings. Examples include diagnostic imaging for cardiology and orthopedic surgery, radiation therapy treatments in radiation oncology, and chemotherapy for medical oncology. Many of these ancillary procedures are technology-driven, and these technologies can be costly, with equipment ranging from tens of thousands to millions of dollars to acquire. At the same time, the reimbursement for such procedures may produce significant operating margins for the practice, affording higher levels of practice earnings that may be available for distribution to physicians as compensation. Such reimbursement may also be subject to downward market pressures, especially from Medicare and those payers whose rates are tied to Medicare reimbursement levels, making long-term returns from investments in such technology unpredictable over its useful life. Moreover, low utilization rates for such high-cost technology can create losses for physicians from technical service lines. Thus, ancillary services can be both a source of incremental or reduced earnings for a physician practice, depending upon the facts and circumstances.

Another important element to consider in evaluating the prevailing practice paradigm for a given specialty is ownership in nonpractice entities, facilities, and business ventures. In certain specialties, physicians are often owners in ventures other than their practices and ownership in these ventures can represent a significant source of income to the physicians. Surgical specialists, notably orthopedic surgeons and gastroenterologists, are frequently owners in ambulatory surgical centers (ASCs), from which they receive periodic cash distributions. Many urologists have historically been owners in ventures that lease equipment or provide equipment-related services for procedures used in hospital or ASC settings for urologic patient care, such as lithotripsy. In such cases, the urologist provides the professional service for the urologic procedure, but also indirectly provides a component of the technical component or ancillary service through ownership in such leasing or service ventures. Understanding such practice paradigms for a specialty is important in evaluating total compensation data for a specialty and in matching compensation for the services provided by a physician in that specialty.[1]

1 In the author's experience, physician ownership in ASCs and other ventures, such as those mentioned relative to urologists, is often held at the individual physician level and not by the physician practice entity. Thus, the distributions received from such entities would not flow through the physician practice. As a result, such compensation may not be necessarily included in the physician compensation survey data.

### *1.3 Distinguishing Between Office-Based and Hospital-Based Physician Specialties*

Physician specialties are typically divided into the four major specialty categories of primary care, surgical, medical, and hospital-based. These categories are widely used to denote general similarities in practice patterns among the various specialties that fall under each category. When looking at physician compensation issues, however, there is another way to categorize and think about physician specialties that can be helpful. One can group most specialties into two basic classifications based on certain operating and practice-setting characteristics and tendencies that are common to the specialties in each group. These two major categories of specialties can be labeled as office-based physicians (OBPs) and hospital-based physicians (HBPs). Examples of HBPs include anesthesiologists, hospitalists, trauma surgeons, radiologists, transplant surgeons, and critical care physicians. Examples of OBPs include primary care physicians as well as most surgical and medical specialties.[2]

The essential operating characteristics that distinguish OBPs from HBPs can include the following areas:

- Source of the patient base for the physician:
- Setting in which the physician provides clinical services;
- Productivity or workload measures; and
- Relationship between physician efforts and physician productivity outcomes.

For each major area, OBPs tend to work in settings and service environments that can differ materially from HBPs. While not absolutely distinguishable in all cases, recognizing these differences can be useful in identifying important operating, productivity, and economic dynamics for specialty. Such factors can also affect the structure and level of compensation afforded to physicians in the marketplace. As will be discussed in subsequent chapters on valuing employment arrangements, this distinction between OBPs and HBPs can affect the methods and techniques used to value compensation. In the following sections, the distinctions in each area between OBPs and HBPs are discussed and analyzed.

#### Source of Patient Base

For HBPs, the source of patients for the physician is generally the hospital or other healthcare facility, such as an ASC, at which the physician provides clinical services.

2 It should be noted that surgical specialties are included with OBPs, despite many to most procedures being performed in a facility setting. As will be shown in the subsequent discussion, surgical specialties are included with OBPs based on their key operating characteristics.

Patients are typically admitted to such facilities based on referrals from physicians. These referrals are generally made to the facility and not to an individual HBP. In other words, the patient is typically not referred to the facility for the sole reason of being treated by a specific HBP. Rather, the referring physician generally has a relationship and practice pattern with the facility that drives the referral to a facility. Thus, HBPs are usually dependent upon referrals to the facility for patients, rather than direct referrals from other specialists. Highlighting this referral pattern does not imply that the HBPs do not have an impact on referrals to the facility. Quality patient care by HBPs at a facility can be an important factor in referrals, but HBPs are generally not the primary or specific determining factor in such referrals. Contrast this situation to that of OBPs. Patients come to the OBPs for healthcare services based on either patient selection of the physician or referrals from other specialists. Generally, choice of OBPs is based on the attributes of the individual physician or the group in which the physician practices. In other words, there is a greater relationship between the reputation, skill, and personal efforts of OBPs and their patient volumes than is found for HBPs.

#### Service Context

For HBPs, the primary reason the hospital or facility is the source of patients is that the physician provides services in the context of staffing a hospital or facility unit, function or service line. The physician is a resource input to a larger service. Consider, for example, the role of an anesthesiologist in an inpatient surgical procedure. An inpatient surgical procedure requires various facility and staffing resources and inputs. Facility resources include operating, recovery, and inpatient stay rooms that are appropriately equipped and maintained, while staffing includes a surgeons, an anesthesiologist, nursing staff, and other hospital support staff. While the anesthesiologist is critical to the procedure, he or she is not the only critical requirement for the total service. Each resource plays a vital role.

Another key aspect of the practice setting for HBPs is that they usually provide shift-based coverage for the facility with respect to their clinical services. Facilities often require physician coverage for certain specialties to staff their units or service lines, whether in the form of unrestricted or on-site coverage. Such coverage is tied to the facility's operating schedule and needs, which in the case of hospitals, can be continuous coverage 365 days a year.

For OBPs, physician services are usually the primary element of patient care. Patients go to OBPs primarily to obtain clinical services related to a physician's particular specialty. Even when OBPs perform the majority of their clinical services in a hospital or facility setting, such as in the case of the various surgical specialties, patients generally come to the OBP first. The OBP usually selects the facility at which to perform the procedure. In other words, the patient initially seeks physician clinical services; facility-based services are the setting in which the physician services are provided. Because physician services are the primary driver of patient care considerations for office-based specialties, the schedules of OBPs are generally centered around pre-set office hours or procedure days at facilities that correspond to the normal work-week cycle. In short, OBPs usually have more control over their working hours and days.

#### Productivity Measures

Because HBPs are generally dependent for their patient base on hospitals or facilities, the productivity of HBPs is necessarily limited by the volumes and case acuities coming into the facility. An HBP may be quite capable of handling significant patient volumes and skilled at treating high acuity cases, but if the patient base of a facility does not provide such volumes and cases, the HBP's actual productivity will not reflect his capability and skill. In addition, the professional collections of an HBP may also be dependent on the payer mix for the facility at which the physician practices. Since the HBP does not have an independent practice and referral base and works to provide coverage for a facility, she is not able to pick and choose among health plans and payers when treating patients. Even when an HBP goes "out of network" for various health plans and payers, the HBP is still affected by the essential demographics of the referral base to the facility. Patients with low reimbursement health plans may not necessarily yield better collections under out-of-network billing practices, especially when high levels of government payer, self-pay or charity are prevalent at a facility. Moreover, because HBPs often provide shift-based coverage for hospital or facility operations, they may be required to cover shifts in which there are minimal patient volumes. HBPs, therefore, tend to have less control over their day-to-day productivity levels. Outside of changing facilities, the individual efforts of HBPs may have little bearing on their productivity and on the revenues and earnings associated with their practice. In summary, HBPs have limited control over key factors that affect their compensation vis-à-vis the economics of their services.

OBPs, by contrast, have a much greater level of influence and impact on their productivity levels and the economics that relate to their compensation. The more skilled and efficient that an OBP becomes in performing procedures and providing patient care, the more patients he or she can treat within a given period of time. Moreover, the physician may be able to treat more complicated cases. The OBP may also choose to work more hours to treat higher patient volumes and case acuities. As a result, individual efforts by OBPs can directly impact productivity levels. OBPs, moreover, generally have greater flexibility with respect to the choice of health plans and payers that they will accept in their practices. They have, therefore, much more control over the economics of their services and corresponding relation to their compensation.[3]

### *1.4 The Impact of Physician Practice Organizational Characteristics*

The scope of services provided by a physician and his or her corresponding level of compensation can be influenced by the type of practice in which the provider works. Thus, knowledge of how various practice characteristics can affect physician compensation levels is useful in establishing FMV for physician services, and especially employed physicians. Three types of practice characteristics are germane for understanding the operational and economic dynamics of the physician practice:

1. Practice size;

2. Practice specialty mix; and

3. Practice ownership.

The following sections discuss the dynamics for each characteristic that can affect the scope of services and corresponding compensation for physicians in such practices.

#### Practice Size

In general, larger physician practices are in a better position to offer an expanded scope of services to patients in terms of subspecialty care, access, and ancillary services. Larger practices may provide the critical mass of patients necessary for physicians within the group to develop subspecialty practices or areas of particular expertise. It may also provide for the effective use of nonphysician providers (NPPs) in the provision of patient care. Such critical mass may also allow larger practices to provide expanded levels of technical component services to patients. Unless a sufficient patient base is achieved, the acquisition cost for various forms of ancillaries is too high to justify offering such services to patients. Larger groups may also be able to achieve economies of scale with respect to various resources and costs, such as utilization of space and staff.[4] As discussed in more detail in "The Variability of Physician Reimbursement Across Markets" below, larger groups can also have more leverage in reimbursement

3 There are certainly cases in which OBPs may have reduced control over such factors. Employed OBPs may have less control over payer mix and volumes as a result of conditions imposed by an employer. OBPs in less populated or in low payer-mix markets may also be limited. The relevant point, however, in the distinction between HBPs and OBPs for the current discussion is that the operating profile of hospital-based specialties is structurally different than that for OBPs. This structural difference generally gives rise to fundamental dissimilarities in the ways that such physicians can impact their productivity and practice economic performance.

4 It is possible that larger groups also achieve diseconomies of scale with respect to other costs. Solo physicians often do not provide market-level benefits to staff. Larger organizations tend to offer such benefits, thereby increasing their staffing costs.

negotiations with commercial payers due to their size. This leverage can translate into higher reimbursement levels for the practice.

If managed properly, the economies of larger groups can increase the level of practice earnings available for physician compensation. Increase ancillary revenues, higher acuity cases, effective use of NPPs, higher reimbursement, and economized costs can all serve to increase the total earnings pool for physicians. As with all group practices, however, a critical compensation issue for the group is how these earnings are distributed to the physicians. Such distributions can be influenced by factors that may relate more to group dynamics and "politics" than to the fundamental economics of the group and the physician services it provides in the marketplace. They may not be related strictly to issues of physician productivity and contribution to net earnings. Often, larger groups experience greater levels of organizational politics in determining compensation, because the economics of multiple locations, subspecialization, and "too many cooks in the kitchen" play out within the group.

Large group practices, moreover, may actually experience diseconomies of scale relative to groups of smaller sizes. Larger practices often require more layers of middle management, more specialized support staff, and more expensive management due to complexity of managing a sizeable organization. Larger groups can be more bureaucratic, formal, and structured, resulting in physicians being more removed from directly affecting cost-effectiveness. They may also develop compliance and other programs that add to the overhead burden. Staff benefits may also be higher as groups compete in the corporate marketplace for professional and experienced personnel.

#### Practice Specialty Mix

Physician group practices are either based on a single specialty or include multiple specialties. Each type of group has unique operating characteristics and economics that affect both the types of services offered and the compensation of physicians in the group. Single-specialty practices are generally organized in terms of a broadly defined specialty, such as cardiology or orthopedic surgery. Within such practices, there may be varying degrees of subspecialty physicians and services represented in group. For certain types of specialties, the physicians may implement a division-of-labor approach, in which certain physicians perform specific types of procedures to increase overall group productivity. For example, certain physicians focus on in-office or diagnostic work, while others concentrate on major procedural services. Many cardiology groups function in this manner. Noninvasive cardiologists in the group feed their invasive and invasive-interventional colleagues, allowing the latter to remain focused on cath lab-based procedures.

Multispecialty groups are generally organized in terms of primary care physicians (PCPs) and specialists. The spectrum of specialists present in a multispecialty practice can vary. An important operational feature of the multispecialty group model is the cross-referrals that occur within the group along a continuum of care that can be provided to patients on a coordinated basis within the group. Another key aspect of multispecialty groups is that they can often achieve the critical patient mass necessary for a variety of technical component services. Various specialties often utilize the same technologies for ancillary services. The concentration of such specialties under a single group generally creates the opportunity for significant diversification and support of ancillary services.

As noted previously in the discussion of group size, the distribution of group practice earnings to group physicians is a challenging area. When groups integrate their services and increase group productivity and earnings through specialized care within the group, they often implement models in which all group physicians share in the earnings from such integrated services. Such models can afford higher levels of compensation for physicians in comparison to physicians of similar specialties who practice in different settings. If the integration model is not economically efficient, however, the opposite compensation outcome may be true. In short, group practice dynamics can add new variables into the physician compensation equation.

#### Practice Ownership

In the current marketplace, there are two major types of ownership for physician practices: physician owned and hospital or health system owned. Practice ownership can have an impact on the operations and economics of physician practices. As a general matter in physician-owned practices, the physician-owners are at risk for the overall profitability of the practice. Since such profitability is the basis for the levels of compensation that may be paid to these physicians, physician-owned practices generally make decisions based upon considerations related to the economic viability of the practice. Decisionmaking with respect to locations, the number of physicians, ancillary services, overhead, and other key practice variables are made from the perspective of the group and its clinical and economic optimization.

Hospital or health-system owned practices often operate out of a different planning horizon. Such practices function as part of a larger integrated delivery system (IDS) for healthcare services. Decisions related to the practice can be based on larger considerations related to the IDS and not the practice on an isolated basis. For example, a practice may be operated in a particular service market as part of meeting community need for physician services. Thus, a hospital or health system may operate a practice at a loss in this market as part of its mission to provide healthcare services in the community. Another example relates to practice costs and operational requirements. Hospitals and health systems often have greater levels of healthcare regulations that affect their operations, requiring them to implement significant compliance programs. Such programs can increase the costs of operating physician practices. As a result, physician compensation in hospital or health system owned practices may be based on considerations that are different from those affecting physician-owned practices. Indeed, such considerations may be foreign with respect to the fundamental operations and economics of the practice as a physician practice.

## 2.0 The Economics of Physician Services

### *2.1 Understanding the Economics of Physician Services and Physician Practices*

As with having knowledge of clinical and other types of services provided by physicians, it is essential to have a sound understanding of the economics of physician services for valuation purposes. The appropriate implementation and interpretation of various appraisal methods and techniques are contingent on the valuation analyst having a fundamental grasp of the economics related to physician services in the marketplace. Indeed, one of the most common causes of misapplications of appraisal methods in the healthcare sector arises from a lack of understanding of marketplace factors that are necessarily embedded in various data used to establish FMV compensation for physician services. To use such data appropriately, one must understand the economic dynamics that affect the characteristics and outcomes of market data as well as information sources used in the valuation process.

There are two key economic factors to consider when evaluating physician services. First, physician services are generally compensated in accordance with the type of services provided. The healthcare marketplace pays physicians differently for varying kinds of services. Second, physicians generally incur costs and utilize various resources when providing these services. Thus, the revenues and fees that physicians receive for their services do not necessarily flow through as cash compensation to the physician. Rather, such revenues and fees are offset by various costs incurred by the physician in generating such cash inflows. As a result, an appraiser should consider the impact of both revenues and expenses when evaluating the appropriate level of physician compensation for a service. The following sections outline some of the key considerations in assessing the revenues and expenses of physician services.

### *2.2 Clinical or Patient Care Revenues*

The core revenue base for clinically practicing physicians comes from the fees generated from patient care or clinical services. As discussed above, these revenues can be further broken down into professional component and technical component services. Such services are generally detailed in terms of the specific procedures performed as denominated by current procedural terminology (CPT) or healthcare common procedure coding system (HCPCS) procedure codes. Clinical services may be paid for through a variety of reimbursement mechanisms, including fee-for-service, capitation, or episodic-care reimbursement models. Fee-for-service is by far the predominant reimbursement model in the current physician marketplace. Yet, efforts at healthcare reform are seeking to move the healthcare industry, including physicians, away from this model, toward payment for quality outcomes, patient disease management, and bundled payments for episodes of care. The extent and the speed at which the physician market migrates to these new models have yet to be determined.

It should be noted that each reimbursement mechanism has its own unique economics. Fee-for-service presents a direct correlation between revenues and services: the more services provided, the more revenue received. Capitation models, on the other hand, reflect a fixed amount of revenue for patient care. Depending on the utilization of services required by the patient base or covered lives included in the capitation payments, a practice may achieve more or less total capitation revenue. Greater levels of service per patient mean that fewer patients can be cared for on a per-physician basis. A smaller number of covered lives results in lower total capitation revenues and comparatively lower practice net earnings than could be achieved when patient care services were lower, per covered life.

Whatever the reimbursement model, the revenues received represent what the local marketplace is willing to pay for physician services on a "gross" basis, including both physician compensation and practice expense. Practice revenues may also include sales of drugs, pharmaceuticals, and durable medical equipment, some of which may be used as part of technical services for diagnostic testing, while others are provided to patients as part of treatment regimens. For some specialties such as oncology or cardiology, sales or usage of these items can represent a significant proportion of the practice's revenues. Indeed, revenues in a medical oncology practice from chemotherapy drugs can dwarf revenues from professional component services, although profitability from such drugs may be limited based on their reimbursement levels relative to cost.

One should not fail to note the potential for state-level restrictions that limit the scope of services provided by a physician practice. Maryland, for example, bars nonradiology physician practices from owning and providing MRI and CT services to patients.[5] For

5 See the Jan. 24, 2011, Maryland Court of Appeals ruling that the state's self-referral prohibition applies to orthopedic surgeons who refer patients for MRI and CT scans in their practices.

orthopedic surgery groups, this prohibition creates a significant limitation of the technical component services available in the practice, and thereby, on the available earnings for physician compensation. MRI services are typical in orthopedic groups of sufficient size. State certificate of need considerations as well as local market dynamics may also limit the scope of services provided by a physician practice. In addition, reimbursement and regulatory changes can also affect the scope of services. In the mid-2000s, many practices were involved in so-called under-arrangements, or block leasing of diagnostic testing facilities, until federal healthcare regulations effectively ended such practices. These restrictions point out the need for appraisers to research and understand regulatory matters as part of valuation assignments involving technical component services.

### 2.3 The Variability of Physician Reimbursement Across Markets

A recent study by the Center for Studying Health System Change (HSC) indicates a wide range of commercial reimbursement rates across various local markets in the United States and within those local markets.[6] The study noted that local market dynamics play a significant role in the reimbursement levels paid to physicians. Commercial payers establish a standard fee schedule, often based on the framework of the Medicare Physician Fee Schedule (MPFS) and its resource-based relative value system (RBRVS), that reflects the network goals of the insurer along with local physician supply considerations. Groups with leverage in the marketplace, however, are generally able to negotiate rates that are higher than the standard fee schedule. Small practices with little bargaining power are typically faced with accepting the standard fee schedule or not participating in the network or insurance plan.

The study selected eight markets for research because they were thought to have a wide range of payment rates, based on government studies. Exhibit 1 below presents a summary of the study's findings for the standard fee schedule and the 75th percentile rate for specific practices in selected specialties. The data from this study show a wide variation in commercial payer rates across markets and within markets, particularly by specialty. The data indicate that groups with bargaining power are able to negotiate significantly higher rates than the standard fee schedule.

6 See *Wide Variation in Hospital and Physician Payment Rates Evidence of Provider Market Power*, Research Brief, No. 16, November 2010. Center for Studying Health System Change. www.hschange.org.

**Exhibit 1. Commercial Rates as a Percentage of Medicare[7]**

| | | 75th Percentile Rates | | | | | |
|---|---|---|---|---|---|---|---|
| Market | Standard Rates | Internal Medicine / Family Medicine | Cardiology | Orthopedics | Anesthesiology | Radiology | Oncology - Physician Services |
| Cleveland | 101% | 112% | 155% | 124% | 251% | 166% | 138% |
| Indianapolis | 110 | 117 | 156 | 140 | 217 | 147 | 138 |
| Los Angeles | 92 | - | - | - | 177 | - | - |
| Miami | 82 | 89 | 110 | 101 | - | 134 | 116 |
| Milwaukee | 166 | 175 | 223 | 212 | - | 238 | 204 |
| Richmond, VA | 112 | 128 | 145 | 144 | - | 153 | 132 |
| San Francisco | 108 | - | - | - | 177 | - | - |
| Rural Wisconsin | 176 | 169 | 234 | 195 | - | 240 | 195 |

The potential impact of such variations in commercial reimbursement on local-market physician compensation should not be ignored. Revenue levels can have a significant impact on the earnings available in a practice for physician compensation. The impact of commercial reimbursement on physician compensation was first noted by Dietrich and Anderson in a groundbreaking analysis published in *Health Lawyers Weekly* in November 2008.[8] Their analysis, based on their first-hand experience in the market, showed how commercial rates can significantly affect compensation on a per-wRVU (work relative value unit) basis. To test and evaluate their seminal work further, I have used the HSC data to develop a comparative model for a hypothetical cardiology group. The purpose of the model was to show the impact of varying commercial reimbursement rates on physician compensation. Since there is also material variation in Medicare rates, the model also reflects the variation in Medicare reimbursement from market to market. Significant variations in the practice expense geographic practice cost index (GPCI) and the malpractice GPCI produced notable differences in revenues for Medicare.

The model was based on 2010 relative value unit (RVU) values for an actual nine-physician cardiology group to compute reimbursement using Medicare rates. A simplified payer mix of 46% Medicare and 54% commercial was also used in the computation of revenues. Commercial reimbursement was calculated using the data provided in the HSC study, including the standard fee schedule rates and the 75th percentile rates, noted as "Premium." A national average was added based on the rates as reported by Medicare and an assumed commercial reimbursement ratio of 125% of Medicare.[9]

7 See Table 3 from study.

8 "Evaluating RVU-Based Compensation Arrangements," *Health Lawyers Weekly*, Nov. 14, 2008, Mark O. Dietrich, CPA/ABV, and Gregory D. Anderson, CPA/ABV, CVA

9 Report to the Congress: Medicare Payment Policy, MedPAC, March 15, 2011, p. 8. Medicare pays approximately 80% of private insurer rates.

Exhibit 2 shows the revenue rates per wRVU for Medicare, commercial, and then the blended rate based on the payer mix assumption for the model.

**Exhibit 2. Revenue Per wRVU**

| Market / Rate Level | Market Commercial to Medicare Ratio | Medicare Revenue per WRVU | Commercial Revenue per WRVU | Blended Revenue per WRVU |
|---|---|---|---|---|
| Milwaukee, WI - Premium | 223% | $73.57 | $164.06 | $122.44 |
| Milwaukee, WI - Standard | 166 | 73.57 | 122.13 | 99.79 |
| Cleveland, OH - Premium | 155 | 76.04 | 117.86 | 98.62 |
| San Francisco, CA - Standard | 108 | 93.50 | 100.98 | 97.54 |
| Indianapolis, IN - Premium | 156 | 74.07 | 115.55 | 96.47 |
| Richmond, VA - Premium | 145 | 74.68 | 108.29 | 92.83 |
| Miami, FL - Premium | 110 | 85.46 | 94.01 | 90.07 |
| National Average | 125 | 76.70 | 95.88 | 87.05 |
| Los Angeles, CA - Standard | 92 | 85.97 | 79.09 | 82.26 |
| Richmond, VA - Standard | 112 | 74.68 | 83.64 | 79.52 |
| Indianapolis, IN - Standard | 110 | 74.07 | 81.48 | 78.07 |
| Miami, FL - Standard | 82 | 85.46 | 70.08 | 77.15 |
| Cleveland, OH - Standard | 101 | 76.04 | 76.80 | 76.45 |

As illustrated in Exhibit 2, reimbursement can varying significantly across and within markets, with commercial rates yielding the greatest differences in comparison to Medicare. It should be noted that differences within a market or from practice to practice could also result from payer-mix differences, which were not accounted for in the model's assumptions. In short, *the model indicates that reimbursement for the same level of productivity can vary widely from market to market and from practice to practice within a market.*

To isolate the potential impact of these differences in reimbursement on physician compensation, the model was expanded to include a computation of compensation based on a standard cost assumption applied to all markets. The computation included the following assumptions. HCPCS Level II codes were held constant over all markets. The median overhead and physician benefits per full-time equivalent (FTE) physician from the *2011 MGMA Cost Survey* for cardiology practices were used to estimate operating expenses and benefits for the hypothetical group. Physician compensation was computed as available earnings in the practice after deducting for overhead and physician benefits. The compensation results of the model are presented in Exhibit 3.

**Exhibit 3. Compensation for Hypothetical Cardiology Group**

| Market / Rate Level | Market Commercial to Medicare Ratio | Revenue per WRVU | Compensation per WRVU | Compensation to Revenue |
|---|---|---|---|---|
| Milwaukee, WI - Premium | 223% | $122.44 | $80.40 | 65.7% |
| Milwaukee, WI - Standard | 166 | 99.79 | 57.75 | 57.9 |
| Cleveland, OH - Premium | 155 | 98.62 | 56.58 | 57.4 |
| San Francisco, CA - Standard | 108 | 97.54 | 55.50 | 56.9 |
| Indianapolis, IN - Premium | 156 | 96.47 | 54.43 | 56.4 |
| Richmond, VA - Premium | 145 | 92.83 | 50.79 | 54.7 |
| Miami, FL - Premium | 110 | 90.07 | 48.03 | 53.3 |
| National Average | 125 | 87.05 | 45.01 | 51.7 |
| Los Angeles, CA - Standard | 92 | 82.26 | 40.22 | 48.9 |
| Richmond, VA - Standard | 112 | 79.52 | 37.48 | 47.1 |
| Indianapolis, IN - Standard | 110 | 78.07 | 36.03 | 46.1 |
| Miami, FL - Standard | 82 | 77.15 | 35.11 | 45.5 |
| Cleveland, OH - Standard | 101 | 76.45 | 34.41 | 45.0 |

It should be noted that, while the model shows the impact of varying commercial and Medicare reimbursement rates, its results are not necessarily reflective of expected compensation levels in each market; variances in cost among markets were not accounted for in the model. Cost variances were not considered because the focus of the model was to highlight the impact of reimbursement rates on compensation, all things being equal. Adjusting for cost-of-living differences among the markets would most likely reduce compensation in higher cost markets, such as those in California.[10] Notwithstanding this potential adjustment, the model illustrates how commercial reimbursement can materially affect physician compensation levels.

### *2.4 Payer Mix Considerations in Practice Revenues*

In addition to the reimbursement rates reflected in the local market, payer mix can also affect the level of revenues in a physician practice. Low or poor payers can reduce the revenues received per unit of service, e.g. patient counter, RVU, or surgical case. High payers can increase such revenues. Thus, the relative mix of low- and high-reimbursement payers can have a significant impact on the revenues of a physician practice, and thereby, on the practice's net earnings available for physician compensation. Government programs, such as Medicare and Medicaid, are generally considered to be low payers. As shown in the previous section, however, Medicare may not always be the lowest payer in all markets. Medicare pays better than commercial payers in Miami and Los

10 The amount of any adjustment would depend on the market from which the median was derived.

Angeles. Moreover, in a few states, Medicaid reimbursement exceeds that of Medicare.[11] Thus, one needs to evaluate the dynamics of a local market before determining whether a practice has a poor payer mix. High and low payers may be relative to unique factors in the market.

Another key consideration in the assessment of a practice's payer mix is whether it is reflective of the local service market or the practice's positioning within this market. In certain locales, the demographics of the service area may only lend itself to a certain payer mix; practices in this service area will not be able to achieve a different mix. Thus, one must evaluate patient volumes and physician productivity in these service markets as yielding revenues that may not be subject to improvement. Moreover, the payer mix in these service areas may not be affected by whether the practice is owned by a physician or a health system. Appraisers should be careful about summarily attributing poor-payer-mix issues to be the natural operating by-product of nonprofit health systems. The payer mix of a physician practice may be a function of the service market, not the practice's charity-care policies. On the other hand, a practice's payer mix be may the result of its marketing (or lack thereof), network participation strategy, or physician referral patterns. In such cases, an improved or more financially viable payer mix may be possible.

### *2.5 Other Sources of Revenue*

As touched on earlier in this chapter, physicians often provide other types of services in the healthcare marketplace, such as call coverage, administrative, research, and educational services. These services often provide supplemental revenue streams and fees for physicians. The impact of revenue sources on physician compensation should not be ignored in evaluating the economics of a specific physician or practice. Stipends for hospital call coverage and medical directorships can provide a substantial amount of income for an individual physician or a physician group. Indeed, the potential impact of such revenue sources creates a difficulty for application of the market approach in valuing physician services under employment because the effect of such revenue on compensation is not gathered and reported separately in the various physician compensation surveys.

In addition, some physicians and practices provide certain types of clinical services that are indirectly provided to patients and billed to payers through another healthcare provider. Many physicians subcontract with hospitals, other facility-based healthcare providers, or other physician practices to provide professional interpretations of diagnostic testing. In such cases, the other provider or practice performs the technical component

11 Based on the 2008 Medicaid-to-Medicare Fee Index, from www.statehealthfacts.org.

of the test, while the physician performs the professional component or interpretation of the examination results. The other provider or practice bills the patient or payer globally for the test and then pays the physician separately for the interpretation based on a preset fee. For some physicians and practices, the revenue streams from these types of subcontracted professional services may constitute a material source of revenue.

As also discussed previously, the physician marketplace has witnessed the proliferation of so-called clinical co-management or service line management arrangements, in which physician-related entities or physicians are engaged to manage hospital or health system service lines. The physicians involved in these arrangements provide various management and quality-improvement services and functions in exchange for fees, a majority of which are usually based on performance and quality measures. The revenues generated by these arrangements can be in the hundreds of thousands to millions of dollars. Clinical co-management or service line management fees are becoming important and material sources of revenues and income for practices and individual physicians. The first versions of these arrangements were typically structured using separate legal entities in which the physicians were owners. Thus, the compensation for these arrangements was usually paid outside physician practice entities.

Some physicians and practices receive revenues from various nonoperating activities, such as space or equipment rentals, expense sharing agreements, investments, and ownership in other entities. Depending on the facts and circumstances, the revenues from these nonoperating activities can be material. The critical point to remember about these revenues is that they are not generally associated with the physician professional services. Thus, the compensation impact of such revenue streams should be excluded from the FMV analysis of a compensation for a physician's professional services.

### *2.6 Practice Overhead*

Practice overhead represents the cost of those economic resources that are necessary to provide patient care services in a physician practice, apart from the cost of a physician's services. For office-based physicians, two key practice costs are nonphysician staffing and office space. These two resources often represent the two largest cost items in a practice's overhead structure. More importantly, they often represent the areas in which practices either run efficiently or inefficiently. For practices that benchmark relatively high for cost or overhead rates, staffing and space tend to be the culprits. Physicians will often overstaff their practices or lease more offices or square footage than is optimal for their practices. (Indeed, physicians are notorious for doing bad real estate deals.) With respect to staffing costs, benefits are an area in which practices can vary. Smaller practices often provide below-market benefits in comparison to larger groups or to corporate-owned entities. On the other hand, physician-owned groups with physicians nearing retirement may provide rich retirement benefits to support staff in order for the group to meet ERISA requirements for tax-free treatment of the practice retirement plans.

Two other key areas for costs are equipment and supplies. Some physician specialties, such as cardiology or radiation oncology, are very technology- or equipment-driven. The cost of such equipment, whether in the form of leasing or capital expenditures and the resulting depreciation expense, can run in the hundreds of thousands to millions of dollars. Drug and pharmaceutical supplies may be another area for significant overhead, especially for medical oncology practices. Finally, malpractice insurance can be another significant cost item for certain specialties, such as obstetrics and various surgical specialties.

It is also important to understand the cost behavior pattern for key resources in a practice. Some costs, such as drugs and pharmaceuticals, are variable and correlate directly with volume. Other costs do not necessarily fluctuate directly with patient or procedure volumes. Examples of such cost can often include staffing, space, and equipment. It is often assumed that these resources remain fixed over any level of patient or procedure volume. Such resources, however, are more accurately characterized as step costs, rather than fixed. Such costs can remain fixed up to a certain level of volume at which the practice must expand its facilities and staffing to accommodate the increased patient demand. Such expansion of resources may not always be achievable or practicable in the specific increment needed, e.g., hiring a 0.20 FTE or leasing an extra 500 square feet of adjacent or continuous space. Rather, resources are typically obtained in larger increments that create significant resource capacity for volume growth in the practice. Medical Group Management Association (MGMA) studies of highly productive practices over the years have frequently noted higher costs per unit of service in many of these practices, pointing to the "stair step" characteristics of many practice costs.[12]

Ultimately, resource utilization and overhead levels are an indication of the economic efficiency of the physicians in a practice vis-à-vis their volumes levels. Physicians may be highly productive from a volume or procedural standpoint, while economically inefficient because they incur excessive levels of overhead to sustain these high volume levels. Other physicians may be less productive, but more economically efficient, because they utilize lower levels of resources than their peers in generating these volumes. Such differences in economic efficiency can affect physician compensation levels in the marketplace. All things being equal, the economically efficient physician creates a larger

12 I am thankful to my colleague Dana Boatman, a long-time practice manager and MGMA member, for sharing this insight with me.

pool of available practice net earnings out of which physician compensation can be paid.[13]

Different specialties tend to have varying cost structures based on the manner in which they utilize resources in the provision of patient care services. Some specialties are more capital intensive than others, based on the technologies that are used in the typical bundle of services provided by practices of the specialty. Examples include cardiology and orthopedic surgery for various diagnostic imaging modalities and radiation oncology for cost of linear accelerators and other radiation therapy equipment. As a result, these specialties tend to have higher fixed cost ratios. One should not fail to include the depreciation expense on capital equipment in a practice's overhead structure. The cost of such equipment, allocated over its useful life, is necessary for the production of practice revenues and should be included in the computation of practice net earnings.

Supply-intensive specialties, on the other hand, may have significantly higher variable costs. The prime example of a supply-intensive specialty is medical oncology practice, where the revenues and costs associated with chemotherapy and other drugs are usually in the millions of dollars. Cardiology practices can have significant variable costs for the radiopharmaceuticals used in nuclear imaging, while pediatric practice may have material supply expenses for vaccines and other injectibles. By contrast, the overhead ratios of various surgical specialties may be relatively lower than other specialties because they perform a majority of their procedures in healthcare facilities. Only a limited amount of office space, support staff, and overhead are needed to support pre- and post-operative patient encounters performed in an office setting. Surgical procedures, moreover, tend to generate higher revenues per patient in comparison to other specialties, such as primary care and certain medical specialties, in which the primary procedures are office visits and exams. Primary care physicians have significant fixed costs related to support staff and space, since their key services consist of office encounters.

### *2.7 Cost of Capital and Practice Owner Return*

Another important distinction in evaluating physician compensation is the extent to which compensation is derived from physician services versus compensation associated with ownership of the practice. When a physician provides patient care or serves as a medical director, the payment for such services should be classified as compensation for professional services. This type of compensation should be distinguished from income that a physician receives from being an owner of a business enterprise, such as a physician practice. As an owner in a practice, a physician is *taking risk* based on the level

13 My former HCA colleague, Ed Richardson, CPA/ABV, introduced me to this concept of the economic efficiency of a physician relative to productivity.

of investment the physician has made in the business, including working capital and other assets, such as capital equipment. He or she may also be responsible for certain liabilities of the practice, such as leases and loans. From an economic perspective, the total payment that an owner-physician receives from the practice necessarily incorporates the income (or loss) associated with his or her investment and willingness to take risk. In other words, the earnings paid to owner-physicians include payment for the cost of capital provided by the physician to the practice, in addition to compensation for physician services. Physicians may also receive owner-related compensation that derives from the profitability of other nonowner providers in the practice, such as employed physicians or mid-level providers.

### *2.8 The Economics of Nonphysician Providers*

NPPs constitute a broad category that can include an array of various types of specialized providers, ranging from audiologists to social workers. The most common type of NPP used in the physician marketplace, however, is either a nurse practitioner (NP) or a physician assistant (PA). These types of NPPs can be used to provide a much more expansive scope of patient care services than the other types of NPPs, who tend to provide only a limited specialized set of services. Depending on state regulations, NPs and PAs can have more or less independent capacity from physicians for providing patient care services, including examinations and diagnosis, implementation of treatment plans, and prescribing of drugs and medications. In most jurisdictions, however, NPs and PAs are generally required to have some level of physician supervision.

Physician practices generally utilize NPs and PAs in two basic clinical modes or a combination of the two: as physician extenders or as practice providers. In the physician-extender mode, NPs and PAs assist physicians in patient encounters and procedures. The NPPs perform certain preparation and data-gathering activities before the patient sees the physician. The NPPs may also wrap up the office encounter with the patient, after the physician portion of the encounter is completed. If any in-office procedures are performed, the NPP is used in a similar way, including potential assistance in the procedure. This "extender" use of the NPPs increases the overall productivity of the physicians in the practice by minimizing their contact time with the patient and assigning the more routine and less clinically demanding portions of the office encounter or procedure to the NPP. The physician, therefore, is able to see more patients. NPPs may be used in a similar way for hospital patient encounters. Some practices will also use NPPs in the hospital setting as a way to minimize physician hospital call coverage response burdens. NPs or PAs placed in the hospital prescreen emergent or inpatient events for the practice to ensure that physicians are only called for clinically necessary cases. In the extender mode, NPPs do not typically generate independent procedural volume and revenue. Rather, they are used to leverage the productivity of the physicians they support in the practice.

In their use as practice providers, by contrast, NPs and PAs perform independent office encounters and procedures with patients. These encounters are not provided on a shared or "tag team" basis with physicians; patients do not see the physicians as part of the office visit or procedure. Under a typical arrangement, the physician sees the patient in the initial visit to the practice and develops a course of treatment for the patient. The NPP performs subsequent visits that are part of the treatment plan, including various pre- and post-procedural or -operative visits in certain medical and surgical specialty practices. Used as practice providers, NPPs usually create procedural volume and revenue that is separate from the physicians in the practice.

How the services of the NPP are billed to payers is a function of the payer's rules with respect to reimbursement of NPP services. Medicare affords three different billing options for the services of NPPs: incident to billing, direct billing, and shared or split encounter billing. There are specific criteria and regulations for each billing mode. Other payers besides Medicare, including Medicaid, can have different criteria and billing options for the services of NPPs. Discussing these billing criteria is beyond the scope of this chapter. Appraisers, however, should have a general understanding of these billing rules so as to understand the revenue cycle dynamics of a subject physician practice as part of an employment valuation assignment.

Either use of NPPs in a physician practice, whether as extender or provider, has an economic impact on the net earnings of a physician practice that are available for distribution to physicians. Used as extenders, NPPs provide for increased productivity by physicians, resulting in higher patient care revenues. These revenues come, however, at a cost equal to the compensation and benefits related to the NPP, along with any other incremental costs related to the use of the NPP. Thus, the net earnings from NPPs used as extenders would result from the increased revenues less NPP compensation, benefits, and incremental costs. Where NPPs are used as practice providers, the net earnings attributable to the use of NPPs would be equal to the collections generated by the NPP less compensation, benefits, and incremental costs. The key to incremental practice earnings from NPPs is ultimately their productivity, whether in terms of increased physician productivity or production attributable to the NPPs. It should also be noted that the utilization of NPPs may represent a lifestyle or convenience choice by physician practices. As noted earlier, physicians may use NPPs in the hospital setting as a means of limiting the burden associated with hospital call coverage.

One critical question that arises from the use of NPPs is whether the net earnings from their use should be treated as compensation for professional services or as a form of owner compensation. In reality, the net earnings may represent or include both forms of compensation. In most states, NPPs cannot practice medicine without the supervision of a physician. This supervision can include chart reviews as well as discussions between the supervising physician and the NPP. Since such supervision requires time and effort on the part of the physician, NPP supervision constitutes an administrative service provided to the practice. The value of these supervision services should not be underestimated. The success and ultimate productivity levels of NPPs can be greatly affected by the nature of this supervision relationship. In physician-owned practices, these administrative NPP supervision services may be compensated by distributing the net earnings from NPPs to their supervising physicians. Strictly speaking, however, not all of these earnings would appear to relate to supervision.

The ability of the NPP to generate net earnings is also a function of the practice's economics in terms of its capacity for attracting a patient base large enough to warrant the effective use of NPPs. Thus, some portion of these earnings would appear to accrue to the benefit of the owners of the practice. In cases of employed physicians providing such supervision, an argument can be made that supervision compensation should not be tied to net earnings from the NPP. The physician incurred time and effort supervising the other physician at the request of the employer, regardless of whether the NPP generated net earnings for the employer. Ultimately, the determination of compensation for supervision services and for ownership would need to be based on the facts and circumstances of the underlying arrangement.

### *2.9 The Economics of Startup and Newly Hired Physicians*

It is important to understand the economics of startup and newly hired physicians because appraisers are frequently presented with a valuation assignment that involved such physicians. Startup physicians are those doctors placed in newly formed practices. Newly hired physicians are those providers that are added to an existing practice. They can be added as a replacement for a retiring or exiting physician in the practice, as an expansion of the practice, or as the addition of a new specialty or subspecialty to an existing practice. A key economic question for startup and newly hired physicians is how quickly they can "ramp up" to a normalized level of production. This normalized level will determine the expected revenues and expenses associated with the new physician. These economics are a function of the intersection of basic supply and demand as denominated in the currency of physician practices.

On the supply side of the supply-demand equation, one first considers the productive capacity of the new physician. If the physician has recently completed residency, fellowship, or other training, there is a general expectation that he or she will not ramp up as quickly to a normalized level of productivity in comparison to an experienced physician. Such "baby docs," as they are often affectionately called within the industry, are new to the practice of medicine and, thus, have a basic learning curve with respect to patient care and to the fundamentals of working in a practice. In addition, the actual level of normalized productivity for a specific newly matriculated physician is unknown. Such physicians have no track record to indicate their productive capacities. An experienced physician, on the other hand, will have a track record of historical productivity that can serve as an indication of the potential normalized level of production for which he or she is capable. For newly hired physicians coming into an established group, one should not fail to consider the typical productivity levels for physicians in the group. Generally, there can be an expectation that newly hired physicians will ramp up to a production level that is commensurate with their peers. Otherwise, the physician's continued practicing with the group may be jeopardized.

For the demand side of the equation, one must evaluate the potential for patient volumes from the four basic sources for such volumes within a local service market: 1) unmet patient demand or an underserved market, 2) increased market share or taking existing volumes from other providers in the market, 3) redistributed or "cannibalized" volumes from within the existing practice, or 4) population growth or demographic changes within a population, e.g., the aging of a population base. A new physician must draw a patient base from these four basic sources. Depending on the facts and circumstances, a new physician may have more or less favorable conditions for building a patient base. For example, a physician hired to replace a retiring physician may be more likely to have higher initial patient volumes than a physician starting up a practice in a community. A new physician in a multispecialty group can immediately benefit from group referrals, whereas a solo physician must become established in the local medical community to gain referrals from other physicians.

The cost economics of startup and newly hired physicians can also vary depending on the facts and circumstances. A solo physician is generally at risk for the fixed or step costs in a practice during the initial ramp-up period. Depending on the duration of the ramp-up period, significant startup losses can be incurred. A newly hired physician in an existing group, on the other hand, may be able to utilize excess resources or economies of scale from the existing group such that the startup losses are reduced or minimized. Typically, physicians incur startup losses during the initial one to two years of practice. Ultimately, the level of startup losses and the level of earnings available for physician compensation in a practice will be a function of the supply-and-demand curve for physician services vis-à-vis the local market demand and the physician's productivity capacity along with the dynamics of startup costs.

### *2.10 The Economic 'Margin' on Physician Services*

One factor that should be noted in analyzing the economics of physician practices is that there is frequently little to no margin on physician services, after compensating physicians for providing those services. Physician practices contrast with other professional practices in which there tends to be billing margins on staff in the provision of professional services. In law, accounting, and consulting firms, the fees generated from the work of the professional staff are usually based on a graduated fee scale. Less experienced staff are billed at rates that are lower than more senior staff. The billing rates are intended to reflect varying levels of professional services provided to clients. Yet, professional staff who are not shareholders or partners in the firm are typically billed at rates that provide not only an allowance for overhead, but also include a margin that creates an earnings pool that is shared among the firm's owners. The higher the billing rates and the greater the economic realization and utilization of staff within such firms, the greater the compensation pool for owners.

The margin billing for junior staff is not generally present in physician practices. Physicians, whether baby docs or experienced and renowned, are paid at the same reimbursement rate for each procedure by payers. Physician professional services are compensated equally by payers under the assumption that the same level of service is provided by each physician.[14] Moreover, physicians have an expectation to be paid at rates commensurate with other physicians for their productivity. There is no graduated pay scale for physicians that is comparable to the typical graduated staffing levels and pay scales in other professional practices that are based on experience. Thus, available earnings streams in these professional practices are generally higher than those of physician practices, where there is an expectation that such earnings are paid to the physicians as compensation for professional services.[15] It should be noted that there are practices in which nonowner physicians do generate net earnings for owner physicians. In the author's experience, however, such practices are generally the exception and not the rule, primarily because physicians with sufficient productivity usually become owners in their practices. Most physicians tend to be recruited into private practice groups with an expectation that they will become owners after an initial ramp-up period. It should also be noted that there can be significant margin on NPP staffing, where such providers are highly productive. The use of NPPs reflects the general patterns for margin observed in other professional practices.

14 As discussed previously, commercial payers may pay certain groups or physicians more than others within a market, but this is a function of bargaining power rather than of experience per se.

15 One exception to this general trend is a practice staffed by physicians on work visas. One often observes practices staffed by nonresident physicians seeking U.S. residency who are paid at compensation rates relative to their production that generate margins. In this specific pattern, part of the consideration for services would appear to be a pathway to U.S. citizenship or residency status.

### *2.10 The Economics of Health System and Integrated Delivery System Practices*

The ownership and operation of physician practices by hospitals, health systems, IDS, insurance plans, or other large healthcare organizations can affect the underlying services and economics of physician practices in ways that are distinct from physician-owned practices. The reason for this difference is that ownership by other types of healthcare entities can introduce business and operational considerations that are not intrinsic or related to the economic and operational efficiency or optimization of a physician practice. The larger concerns and objectives of the healthcare organization can override goals and plans that would maximize physician practice outcomes. As part of a larger healthcare organization, physician practices become one resource or service line within a larger continuum of services and product lines. Optimization of the organization takes precedence over that of the practice in terms of the healthcare entity's goals, strategies, and priorities. In addition, the practice becomes a participant in the owner healthcare entity's economics in terms of access to contracts, resources, policies, practices, and corporate culture.

Ownership by a larger healthcare organization can affect nearly every aspect of the operations and economics of physician practices in ways that are both favorable and unfavorable from the singular or solitary perspective of the practice. It can affect the revenues of the practice in many ways, including the following:

- *Participation in payer contracts:* Larger health systems or organizations may have greater leverage on commercial payers in a local market, providing a practice with higher reimbursement on commercial patients. Various studies indicate that health system power in the local market generally yields higher reimbursement for its physicians.[16] On the other hand, some health systems lack the acumen and experience in negotiating physician fee schedule rates or they may sacrifice physician rates for gains in other areas for the system. Thus, a health system may not always achieve improved reimbursement for a physician practice.

- *Centralized billing and collections:* When a practice becomes part of a larger health system, the billing and collections are often moved to a centralized office or absorbed into the hospital's billing and collection function. This move could negatively affect the practice's revenue cycle if the centralized function is inefficient or inexperienced with respect to physician practices. One of the lessons of the 1990s' wave of physician practice acquisitions and employment

16 "Unchecked Provider Clout in California Foreshadows Challenges to Health Reform," Robert A. Berenson, Paul B. Ginsburg, and Nicole Kemper, *Health Affairs*, Vol. 29, No. 4, 2010. "Rising Hospital Employment of Physicians: Better Quality, Higher Costs?" Ann S. O'Malley, Amelia M. Bond, and Robert A. Berenson, *Issue Brief*, No. 136, August 2011, Center for Studying Health System Change, www.hschange.org.

by hospitals was that hospital systems frequently did not understand physician billing and collection issues and performed poorly in this area in comparison to the pre-acquisition practice.

- *Payer mix:* Hospital-oriented health systems, especially those with a charitable mission, have a focus on serving community need that directs them to provide services or products in areas that may not be self-sustaining. Because these systems have access to larger resources outside of these areas, they are able to provide these services despite significant losses that occur from doing so. Physician-owned practices, by contrast, do not generally have access to such resources. Thus, they are not economically able to provide services in all areas and to all payer groups. When a physician practice is owned by a health system, it may be required to expand its payer mix to less favorable payers, thereby decreasing practice revenues on a per-unit-of-service basis.
- *Technical component and ancillary services:* The economics of technical or ancillary services in a physician practice change once the practice is owned by a health system or IDS. The health system may seek to move or consolidate such services into existing IDS facilities to maximize reimbursement. Generally, hospital or provider-based rates for certain ancillary services are higher than those for services provided in a physician practice setting. A health system or IDS may also seek to eliminate duplicative services, thereby reducing overhead and increasing the utilization of existing facilities and resources.
- *Hospital call coverage:* As will be discussed in a subsequent section, one reason that health systems are employing physicians is to ensure adequate coverage of hospital emergency departments and inpatient care. There is usually a reason that health systems are attempting to secure such coverage: Private practice physicians may be averse to such coverage for lifestyle and economic reasons. Physician practice opportunities and outcomes can be affected by such coverage.

Health system and larger healthcare organization considerations can also influence decisions related to issues such as the number of providers, the type and specialty or subspecialty of providers, and the locations of physician practices in ways that may not optimize the economies of the specific physician practice or group. These decisions can have an impact on both the revenues and overhead of a practice.

The cost and overhead structure of a practice can also be affected by health system or healthcare organization factors that may or may not benefit a physician group from the sole perspective of the practice. Such factors can include the following:

- *Corporate pay grades for support staff:* Health systems and large healthcare organizations often have formal, structured pay grades for employees. Frequently, these rates exceed those paid by smaller physician groups or solo physicians.

- *Employee benefits:* Frequently, smaller physician-owned practices do not offer benefit packages that are comparable to larger, corporate organizations in the employment marketplace. This disparity is often the result of company size: Smaller companies are usually at a competitive disadvantage in the pricing of employee benefits, such as health insurance or group life or disability policies. As noted previously, the benefits offered by physician-owned groups can also be a function of the retirement and other fringe benefit goals of the owner-physicians. Thus, ownership of a health system or healthcare organization can mean a significant change in employee benefits costs to a physician practice. For most small to medium-size physician-owned groups, this change usually entails an increase in such costs.

- *Supply and resource costs:* It is easy to assume that large organizations have bargaining power with vendors that would enable them to achieve discounts and improved pricing for supplies, equipment, and third-party services. Yet, this is not always the case. Larger organizations often have priorities in negotiating with vendors that do not always produce the cheapest pricing for goods and services. They may look at quality and delivery considerations that may create the best value, but not necessarily the least expensive cost. Large organizations with a broad spectrum of supply-chain needs may also negotiate to get reduced pricing on high-volume or high-dollar-value goods and services for the overall system, while conceding higher pricing for less used items. In the case of physician practices, many of the quality, delivery, and volume and value considerations that are considered by a health system are not applicable to the needs of the practice. Thus, health system supply and resource costs can often be higher than those experienced by a stand-alone physician practice.

- *Corporate management and support resources:* Health systems and large organizations often have multiple layers of management and support functions that are allocated to various departments and entities within the system or organization. Because of the complexity involved in managing large organizations, management and support functions may be more expensive than they would otherwise be for the effective operating of a physician practice. Larger healthcare organizations, moreover, often perceive higher levels of risk and compliance for their operations, and thus, initiate critical and extensive risk-avoidance and compliance programs. These programs, however, are not implemented without significant costs. Thus, health systems and larger healthcare organizations can have higher administrative and corporate overhead costs than physician-owned practices.

In summary, ownership of physician practices by health systems and large healthcare organizations can introduce factors and considerations that add complexity to the operations and economics of these practices. Discussion of these factors should not necessarily lead to the universal conclusion that such ownership leads to suboptimized physician practice economics in all cases. Further study and data research would be needed to establish general trends and findings. Appraisers valuing physician services, however, should be aware of the potential impact of these factors.

## 3.0 Physician Compensation in the Marketplace

The following sections discuss how the economics of physician services and practices can affect physician compensation.

### *3.1 Sources and Types of Physician Compensation*

As touched upon in earlier sections, physician compensation is a function of the services provided by the physician. The level of compensation and the factors that affect it relate to the type of service provided. Different services have varying economics and dynamics that have an impact on the compensation paid for the services. Moreover, physicians provide an array of services in the marketplace. The following list provides a summary of many of the services that physicians can provide in the healthcare marketplace:

- Patient care or clinical:
  - Professional component services performed personally by the physician,
  - Technical component services supervised by a physician, and
  - "Incident to" services supervised by a physician:
- On-call;
- Administrative;
- Educational or academic;
- Supervision of nonphysician providers;
- Clinical or service line management;
- Research and development;

- Business management;
- Entrepreneurial and investor;
- Executive; and
- Managerial.

To evaluate and analyze physician compensation, therefore, one must identify the scope of services provided by the physician and essentially compile and aggregate a series of specific compensation analyses based on the services provided. Moreover, the total earnings received by a physician from a practice or other healthcare organization should not be summarily taken as compensation for clinical services. A physician's total compensation may be the result of a variety of different services provided on an employee, independent-contractor, or business-owner basis.

Since the predominant form of services provided by physicians in the marketplace is clinical or patient care services, and such services are typically the subject of employment valuations prepared for healthcare clients, the remaining subsections will discuss marketplace compensation trends for clinical services. Readers may consult other chapters in the guide for discussions of compensation trends and factors related to other forms of physician services.

### 3.2 General Market Trends and Factors for Clinical Services

There are several general market trends that affect the overall national marketplace for physician clinical or patient care services and compensation. Many of these trends will have an impact on local market dynamics for these services. Appraisers should be aware of these trends and stay informed as the physician and healthcare marketplaces evolve in the coming years. Some of the top key trends include the following:

- *Physician shortages:* The long-term outlook for the demand for physician services is that such demand will exceed the projected supply of physicians. This shortage is forecasted across nearly all specialties, and indeed, shortages among some specialties are already arising in certain markets.[17] The expected higher demand for physician services stems from the aging of the baby-boom generation as well as the increased access to health insurance through various healthcare reform initiatives. On the supply side, the limits placed on medical school entrance rates during the past two decades have served to reduce or cap the number of U.S.-trained physicians.

17 Currently, there appear to be shortages as well as excesses for selected specialties in certain markets around the United States.

- *Healthcare cost containment:* While the limited supply of physicians indicates the need for rising physician compensation according to classical economic theory for supply and demand, healthcare cost containment concerns are bringing market pressures to limit physician compensation levels. The increasing cost of healthcare services, including physician services, is viewed as unsustainable economically. Thus, insurers will seek limit reimbursement for services.

- *Medicare's sustainable growth rate formula:* Beginning in the late 1990s, Medicare reimbursement was tied to a sustainable growth rate (SGR) formula that sought to limit the growth in Medicare spending for healthcare services. The SGR formula began to require reductions in Medicare reimbursement to physicians beginning in the early 2000s. Since that time, Congress and the president have intervened with a series of legislative acts that temporarily stayed the SGR reductions and replaced the cuts with modest increases. The current SGR adjustment calls for a reduction of over 25% in physician fees, which was factored into the computation of purported budget neutrality of the recently passed federal healthcare reform legislation. Odds are, however, that this reduction will not be enacted at its current level.

- *Reductions in reimbursement for technical component services:* Cost-containment efforts have also focused on the issue of ancillary services utilization by physicians, particularly in the area of diagnostic imaging. Many healthcare analysts think that overutilization of such services by physicians is one of the causes of increasing healthcare costs. Medicare recently changed the utilization assumptions for equipment in practice expense RVUs—particularly for imaging modalities—such that reimbursement declined for many technical component services. The recent Phase III Stark regulations also placed certain restrictions on the provision and billing of many technical component services that further limited physician practices for ancillaries. These reductions, as well as the potential for further reductions in technical service revenues, have placed or are expected to place limiting pressures on physician compensation levels, especially for specialties that derive a significant amount of compensation from technical component services.

- *Changes in reimbursement mechanisms:* The recent string of healthcare reform initiatives include a movement away from the current fee-for-service payment system toward other payment mechanisms. One key trend is toward pay-for-performance programs, in which payment for healthcare services is linked to quality and clinical outcomes and performance. A related trend is toward payment for disease management through medical homes and other structures, rather than for disease treatment procedures. Other reimbursement innovations include payment bundling, in which hospitals or other healthcare facilities and physicians receive a single payment for certain types of cases or episodes of care. The various providers are expected to split these payments among themselves, rather than each provider billing separately for its portion of the care related to the case or episode of care. The end goal of these various reimbursement innovations is cost containment. In other words, these initiatives will tend toward limiting or reducing reimbursement for physician services.

- *Physician employment by health systems:* For a variety of reasons, many think the recent trend toward health system employment of physicians is generally expected to sustain or provide increases to current physician compensation levels in the marketplace.

The interplay of these various market forces on physician compensation present something of an economic theory conundrum. Basic economic theory for supply and demand predicts that physician compensation for clinical services needs to rise for the supply of physicians to increase to meet the demand for services. Thus, the general market prognostication would appear to be that physician compensation will be rising in future years. Yet, cost containment efforts are seeking to limit such increases. Which forces will ultimately prevail? This question will be taken up in Section 4 below in the discussion of physician employment trends by health systems.

### 3.3 Practice Ownership Factors

The ownership of a physician practice can have a critical impact on the level of physician compensation for clinical services. Physician-owned practices are necessarily limited in their total or overall compensation to the net earnings of the practice as calculated using the basic formula of revenues less expenses. In other words, total group compensation in physician-owned practices is based on the "eat what you catch" or "eat what you treat" paradigm.[18] It is true that physician-owned groups may borrow money in the short run to supplement physician incomes, but such borrowing cannot be sustained over the long run. Physician compensation for private practice groups is essentially a by-product of the revenues and expense outcomes of the physicians in the group.

Physician compensation in practices owned and operated by health systems or other healthcare organizations is not necessarily limited to the economics of practice revenues less expenses. These types of owners may be willing and able to underwrite practice losses, where physician groups provide essential services relative to the larger system

18 This paradigm is also known as "eat what you kill." For obvious reasons, this metaphor may not be the best choice for thinking about compensation for physician services.

or organization. The health system or organization is able to draw on funding from other sources, including the total earnings from operations within the organization.[19] In addition, the genesis of such practice losses may not necessarily relate to revenue and expense outcomes inherent to the physician practice as such, but rather to operational and economic decisions made in the context of IDS or organizational objectives. Notwithstanding such considerations, health systems and healthcare organizations can often afford to pay more for physician services, due to the earnings derived from other operations. Since the reasons and justification for such underwriting of physician compensation may not be intrinsic to the economics of physician practices, a certain level of "noise" is introduced into the physician compensation marketplace by health systems and other healthcare organizations employing physicians.

### *3.4 Local Service Market Factors*

Physician compensation for clinical services is generally affected by a variety of local service market factors and considerations. As discussed previously, commercial, Medicare, and Medicaid reimbursement vary from market to market across the United States. Commercial reimbursement levels are the result of the supply and demand of physicians in the local market, payer objectives and goals, and available health insurance premium dollars, among other local market dynamics. Medicare reimbursement rates, on the other hand, are determined based on GPCIs related to cost of living and wage differentials in the local service area in comparison to the other service areas in the United States. Medicaid rates are set based on state budgets. These key payer reimbursement rates establish the horizon for practice revenues in the local service market and thereby, have an impact on physician compensation levels.

The payer mix of the local service market is another factor that affects the determination of physician compensation. The demographics of the local population frame the boundaries of the payer mix that is possible in a given service area. For example, a large retirement population in a community necessarily implies a significant mix of Medicare patients for a practice in this community. Service markets that include low-income areas generally have higher levels of Medicaid patients. In general, a physician practice will have a patient base that reflects the local service market's demographics. The revenue base of the practice will necessarily be circumscribed by this payer mix, and physician compensation will also be affected.

Local population and demographic factors may also determine the level of market demand for physician services of a given specialty in the local service market. Areas

19 The funding sources referenced here do not contemplate the volume or value of referrals, but rather the overall earnings from the health system or integrated delivery system.

with younger populations will have higher demand for pediatrics and obstetrics than retirement communities. Likewise, service markets with older populations may have greater need for cardiology, orthopedics, and geriatrics. Population size also determines the level of market demand for services. Rural areas, along with smaller cities, often cannot support a full-time physician in a given specialty, resulting in many service markets not having local access to certain types of physician services. Large population areas, by contrast, generally provide sufficient demand for a cornucopia of physician specialties, subspecialties, and highly specialized subspecialties, such as pediatric cardiovascular surgery.

The cost of resources used in a practice may also be affected by cost-of-living and wage-level factors in a local service markets. Labor costs for support staff and office rental rates are determined by the prevailing rates in a given location. These costs can vary widely across the United States and tend to be higher in large urban areas and in specific states and regions. Malpractice insurance premiums are another practice cost that is unique to state or local market dynamics. These premiums are generally tied to state insurance and malpractice considerations, but certain local markets may have claims histories and tendencies that may also affect such premiums. The cost of other resources and services used by practices can also vary based on local cost of living and expense factors. Certain practice resources, however, are not as indicative of local cost-of-living indexes. Technologically advanced equipment as well as major drugs and medical supplies are generally priced at national levels rather than varying significantly by local markets. The supply and demand for these resources is measured in national rather than local terms.

These various local market economic factors necessarily affect the total net earnings from practice operations that are available for physician compensation. They establish certain boundaries for the physician compensation pool for a practice based on the practice's fundamental economics. As discussed in the following subsection, a practice may optimize its specific operations and economics. Yet, this optimization can only occur within the horizon of what is possible in the given local service market context. For physician-owned groups, this horizon circumscribes the potential total compensation for the group. Whatever the local market economics allow is what the physician can ultimately make. This circumscription may not be as direct in the case of groups owned by health systems and other healthcare organizations. As noted previously, such organizations have a larger operational framework and pool of resources from which physician compensation levels can be established. Nonetheless, these entities are affected by local market dynamics. There is only so much in operating losses that such organizations can underwrite as part of their larger objectives and strategies.

In certain instances, local market economics are such that health systems or larger healthcare organizations tend to be the owners and operators of physician practices, at least on a significant scale. Patient demand, reimbursement rates, and payer mix in many rural areas or smaller population centers may be such that they do not afford competitive or attractive economics for physicians in private practice. For example, a rural community may only need the services of a given physician specialty at a production level equal to the 35th percentile of the major physician compensation and production surveys such as MGMA. This level of demand does not lend itself to compensation that is competitive in the physician recruiting arena. In such cases, a health system may step in and essentially subsidize or underwrite physician compensation to make practice in this smaller market competitive to potential physician candidates. Health systems are willing to make these types of funding commitments as part of their overall goals of serving community need, once the system has determined that the services of a given specialty are needed in the local community. Health systems are able to make these funding requirements for physician compensation because they have a larger pool of resources to use for such endeavors related to community need.

### 3.5 Practice and Physician Specific Factors

Within the larger framework of national and local market economic factors, physician practices and individual physicians can position themselves to optimize their compensation levels. The unique characteristics and attributes of practices and physicians determine physician compensation levels achieved within this framework. Practices and physicians can be highly productive from a volume or procedural standpoint and thereby increase their total compensation. If they have leverage in the local market, they can negotiate for reimbursement rates above the standard fee schedule with commercial payers. They can attempt to optimize their payer mix to the extent possible given the demographics of the service area. Practices can seek to improve their total revenues with the addition of technical component services, as allowed by federal and state healthcare regulations, as well as with other revenue sources, such as compensated hospital call coverage, medical directorships, diagnostic testing interpretations, and other professional services. The efficiency and effectiveness of the practice's resource utilization and overhead structure will also affect the available pool of net earnings for the practice. For physician-owned groups, these endeavors will necessarily have a direct impact on physician compensation levels, while they may have a direct or indirect effect on the compensation in nonphysician-owned practices.

### 3.6 Group Practice Compensation Plans

When physicians are part of a group practice, their individual compensation is generally a function of the group's compensation plan. The group compensation plan establishes the basic structure for how physicians are compensated within the group. It may also set out the specific compensation amounts or rates for particular areas or measures that are part of the basic structure. Compensation structures and specific incentive measures can vary widely from group to group.[20] A survey of the measures used by groups reporting in the MGMA and American Medical Group Association (AMGA) surveys indicates that for compensation methodologies based on productivity measures, RVUs and professional collections are the two top measures used.[21] For incentive pay and bonuses, the most frequently used incentives are based on patient satisfaction, quality, peer review, specific goals and objectives related to financial and productivity concerns, administrative duties, call coverage, and citizenship.[22] Use of base salaries is also a common structure among group practices.[23]

Group practice compensation plans can be more or less reflective of individual physician performance and outcomes. They can also be based on group performance or a combination of group and individual physician measures. Some smaller groups opt for pure egalitarian or communitarian compensation models in which group physicians share equally in group practice earnings. Other groups may elect a "silo" model in which costs are allocated individually to each physician along with the physician's professional revenues and a share of technical component service earnings. Each physician is then paid on an "eat what you catch" basis. Some groups establish a groupwide or specialty by specialty compensation per unit of productivity rate by which individual physicians are paid. In summary, individual compensation paid to physicians in groups can be based on an array of varying performance and economic factors.

20 Indeed, the complexity and potential permutations of various compensation plan options is evidenced by an over 500-page tome devoted to this singular topic. See *Physician Compensation Plans: State-of-the-Art Strategies*, by Bruce A. Johnson and Deborah Walker Keegan, MGMA, 2006, for a comprehensive and in-depth discussion of group compensation plans.

21 See Table 17 in the *Demographics—Physician Practice* section of MGMA for the 2010 and 2011 surveys and Figure 7 in the 2010 and 2011 AMGA surveys.

22 See Table 18 in MGMA and Figure 8 in AMGA for the 2010 and 2011 surveys.

23 See Figure 8 in AMGA.

# PART II. INTRODUCTION TO VALUING PHYSICIAN EMPLOYMENT ARRANGEMENTS

## 1.0 Recent Trends Toward Physician Employment

### *1.1 Typical Employers in the Marketplace*

There are a number of different types of healthcare organizations employing physicians to provide clinical services in the current marketplace. They include:

- Physician-owned groups;
- Hospitals and health systems;
- Physician practice management companies;
- Health plans; and
- Government agencies or departments.

Excluding employment by governmental entities, the vast majority of physicians are employed either by hospitals and health systems or by physician-owned groups. Since most physicians in physician-owned groups are actually employee-owners, hospitals and health systems are by far the predominant employers of physicians in true private practice employment arrangements in the United States. Various market forces are converging to accelerate this current market trend.

### *1.2 Hospital Employment: Wave of the Future?*

In the past several years, employment of physicians has been increasing. Two recent studies noted that the proportion of physicians with ownership in their practices has declined from 61.6% in 1996-97 to 56.3% in 2008.[1] Employment by hospital or health systems has been a major contributor to this market shift, which has been accelerated in the past few years. Indeed, the president and chief executive officer (CEO) of the Medical Group Management Association (MGMA) recently predicted that within five years, the majority of physicians will work for hospitals.[2] A Health Management Academy reports that 88% of responding health system CEOs and chief marketing offiers (CMOs) believe physician employment will become the dominant and permanent model for medical

1 "Physicians Moving to Mid-Sized, Single-Specialty Practices," Center for Studying Health System Change, *Tracking Report* No. 18, August 2007. "A Snapshot of U.S. Physicians: Key Findings From the 2008 Health Tracking Physician Survey," Center for Studying Health System Change, *Data Bulletin* No. 35, September 2009. www.hschange.com.

2 "Become a Partner or Remain an Employee?," Kenneth J. Terry, 5-19-09. Medscape Business of Medicine: www.medscape.com/viewarticle/702784_print, accessed June 4, 2009.

staff relationships.[3] This recent trend in physician employment is especially common with specialists. In April 2010, a spokesperson for the American College of Cardiology indicated that roughly half of all cardiology practices had migrated to health system employment.[4] This percentage has surely risen since that time. Cardiology, primary care, neurosurgery, and orthopedics comprise the top specialties pursued by hospital-health systems for employment.[5]

A convergence of various market forces has created the context in which hospital or health systems and physicians are increasingly seeking to align through an employment relationship.[6]

For hospital or health systems, the motivations for employing physicians are varied, but systemic in relation to developments in the healthcare arena:

- Hospital competition and expansion into a new markets.
- Staffing profitable service lines and providing for physician-leaders to "brand" the service.
- Ensuring hospital call coverage and inpatient care.
- Filling shortages of particular specialties in the service area of a facility.
- Gaining cooperation with quality improvement efforts as part of pay-for-performance and public reporting programs.
- Increasing acceptance by hospitals and physicians of the employment model.
- Disappointing results from other, less-integrated models of physician-hospital alignment.
- Seeking the potential benefits of actualized integration: better quality, coordination of care, and increased efficiency; anticipation of bundled payment approaches.
- Healthcare regulatory climate that favors employment over other types of physician arrangements.

---

3 "Physician Alignment in Health Systems: Building Infrastructure," *The Academy*, December 2008, hmacademy.com/latestIssue.html, accessed Oct. 30, 2011.

4 "Independent Medical Practice: Does Healthcare Reform Mark the Beginning of the End?," Barbara Kircheimer, April 22, 2010. *Becker's ASC Review*, www.beckersasc.com, accessed June 21, 2010.

5 "3 Medical Specialties Most Pursued for Employment by Hospitals," Catlin LeValley and Lindsey Dunn, Sept. 27, 2010. *Becker's Hospital Review*, www.beckershospitalreview.com, accessed Oct. 1, 2010.

6 The following section is a summary of salient points from various articles and studies on recent employment trends in the healthcare marketplace. The specific articles and studies are cited in the bibliography for this part.

For physicians, the motivations for employment also stem from major healthcare trends, but also from changes in the lifestyle attitudes of younger physicians:

- Declining physician incomes resulting from downward reimbursement trends, high malpractice costs, and restrictions on income from under arrangements, specialty hospitals, and similar arrangements.
- Complexity of running a physician practice.
- Uncertainty in the healthcare arena.
- Gaining more regular work hours.
- Reducing call coverage responsibilities.
- Aligning with one or another hospital or health system in a highly consolidated market.

The meeting of these forces has created a strong trend toward employment of physicians, especially specialists, by hospital or health systems.

### *1.3 Physician Employment Structures and Terms*

Physicians can be employed through a variety of contractual structures. The most common employment arrangements are those in which the employer entity is a subsidiary or affiliate of a hospital in the larger corporate entity structure of a health system. This employer entity is generally a physician practice entity that employs other physicians as well. Some hospitals and health systems will employ physicians of the same or similar specialties in a single group; others will employ physicians in a single multispecialty group. Employer entity practices may also be denominated by locations or by affiliation with particular hospitals. In some cases, physicians are employed directly by hospital entities. Generally, state laws and billing considerations, such as the so-called 72-hour rule related to what prehospital admission outpatient services can be billed separately from hospital services to Medicare, can affect the legal organization of physician practice entities within a larger hospital or health system.

Some states prohibit the so-called corporate practice of medicine by barring nonphysician-owned entities from employing physicians. Thus, hospitals or health systems are proscribed from direct employment of physicians by subsidiaries or affiliates. In some of these states, corporate entities are allowed exceptions to these prohibitions through use of certain nonprofit legal entities or foundations. The two notable exceptions are Texas and California.[7]

7 The discussion of the Texas and California exceptions is intended to be general summaries of the requirements for each. Readers should consult alternative materials or legal counsel for the precise statutory requirements for each exception.

*Texas "501a" entities:* Texas allows physicians to be employed by so-called 501a entities that meet certain requirements. These requirements include, without limitation, that the entity have a board of directors comprised of physicians and be nonprofit. These entities are allowed to have corporate members who retain certain reserve powers over key decisions of the 501a entity.

*California foundation model:* California affords a narrow exception to its corporate practice prohibition through use of a so-called foundation model. A charitable foundation is permitted to enter into an independent-contractor arrangement with a physician practice to provide professional services to its clinical patients, subject to certain specific conditions. Among these requirements, the foundation must be a nonprofit entity organized for the purpose of providing both medical care and research, and the physician practice must meet certain size, specialty, and full-time practice requirements for its physicians.

Other states with the corporate practice prohibition may have similar exceptions that allow indirect employment or professional services contracting with physicians or physician groups by health systems.

Recently, a new market model has emerged that is a variation or adaptation of the foundation model. Often called a foundation or "synthetic employment" model, it is used in states where employment of physicians by corporate entities is permitted. The structure of the model can be described as follows:

- Physicians remain in their current group entity (Group) as owners or employees.
- Group entity sells or leases its assets to the health system's (HS) new practice entity (HS Practice).
- HS Practice hires Group's support staff as employees (or leases from Group).
- HS Practice assumes leases and operations of the practice.
- HS Practice contracts with payers and bills and collects for all patient care provided by practice.
- HS Practice enters into a professional services agreement with Group to provide clinical patient care services.
- HS Practice compensates Group for services based on a compensation model that includes an allowance for benefits and professional liability insurance (PLI) of Group's physicians.

- Group determines how compensation received from HS Practice is paid to physicians within the group.
- Group determines and pays for the benefits provided to its physicians and nonphysician providers.
- Group maintains and pays for its PLI.
- Group manages its own internal affairs.

This new foundation or synthetic employment model has benefits for both physician groups and hospital and health systems. From the physician side, this model allows the physicians to retain a certain level of internal autonomy in terms of compensation and benefits. Physician groups determine how the compensation paid by the health system practice is distributed among the group's providers, provided such allocations are within the bounds of applicable healthcare regulations. Physician groups may also determine the level of benefits provided and paid for by the group, and since only physicians or providers are employees of the group, many of the Employee Retirement Income Security Act (ERISA) and nondiscrimination requirements related to benefits for highly compensated employees may be avoided.[8]

This autonomy feature is also a key benefit for the health systems in managing their practices. They can avoid the "herding cats" issues commonly associated with employing physicians, especially with respect to individual physician compensation and benefit issues. Synthetic employment can also represent an intermediate pathway to hospital-physician integration that allows for clinical integration, but organizational independence with respect to group practice matters among the physicians. Some physicians and health systems find the foundation model attractive for its exit strategy implications. If the relationship does not work out, the arrangement can more easily unwind with the physician group remaining intact and ready for business on its own. One might metaphorically say that synthetic employment is the "live-together-before-getting-married" approach to hospital-physician integration.

Another factor that affects the structure of the current employment arrangements is the status of technical component services within hospital or health system practices. Many hospital and health systems are transferring or converting the ancillary services

8 Editor's note. This is a complex area of the tax law that involves the affiliated service group provisions of IRC §414(m) and the leased employee provisions of §414(n). The Patient Protection and Affordable Care Act (PPACA) introduced nondiscrimination requirements in the provision of health insurance under §105, although implementing regulations have been deferred by the IRS. The "Copperweld Doctrine" may also apply to permit otherwise related entities to stand alone and not be treated as an integrated entity for fringe benefit purposes.

formerly provided by physician practices to hospital-based outpatient department (HOPD) or provider-based status. As a result, the net earnings from these technical component services are moved out of the legal entity housing the physician practice and over to the hospital. The reason for this transference or conversion is that these services receive a higher level of reimbursement when provided as part of an HOPD rather than a physician practice. Hospital and health systems can increase overall system earnings by making this conversion.

### *1.4 Popular Compensation Plans Under Employment*

Typical compensation plans offered under hospital and health system employment include a variety of structures and characteristics. In today's market, most tend to be productivity-based. By far, the most popular plan is the compensation per work relative value unit (wRVU) model. The following provides an overview of this model as well as other commonly used compensation plans observed in the current physician employment marketplace.

- *Compensation per wRVU:* Under this model, the physician or group is paid a set rate of compensation per wRVU generated by the physician or group. The compensation rate may be set as single amount or based on a graduated scale.
- *Base Salary and Incentive and Productivity Bonus:* It is common for physicians in startup practices or in new positions to receive a base level of compensation during the initial years of an employment arrangement. Frequently, these salaries are coupled with productivity bonuses or incentive compensation based on a variety of measures. One popular formula includes compensation based on the greater of a base compensation level or compensation per wRVU.
- *Percentage of revenue:* While not as common, some employers may compensate physicians based on the collections or revenues generated in the practice. There are various healthcare regulations that must be satisfied to compensate physicians legally based on practice collections or revenues, particularly those relating to the prohibition on being compensated for the volume or value of referrals for technical component services.
- *Percentage of practice precompensation earnings:* Precompensation earnings (PCE) are defined as practice revenues less expenses, excluding physician compensation. Often thought of as the "Phycor" model because of its relation to the former physician practice management giant of the 1990s, the PCE model compensates physicians based on a percentage of the practice PCE. This model also must meet certain healthcare regulatory requirements because it involves the earnings from ancillary services.

- *Hybrid and mix-and-match models:* Many hospital and health systems are developing hybrid compensation models that address various organizational or transactional objectives for the physician employment arrangement. For example, one variation on the compensation per wRVU model places a portion of the wRVU compensation rate into a quality or clinical outcomes pool. Physicians must reach various quality targets to receive a graduated percentage of this pool. In a similar move, a portion of the compensation per wRVU rate may be placed into a retention bonus pool. Monies from this pool are paid to physicians based on their tenure with the employer. Sign-on bonuses are also common in physician employment arrangements.

Physician compensation models under employment are often applied at the individual physician level. They are also applied at the specialty or group level in some employment arrangements. In the group or specialty level models, a compensation pool is determined first at a collective level based on group or specialty performance and productivity. Individual physicians are then paid a pro rata share of this group or specialty compensation pools based on various criteria or measures.

Another frequently observed compensation trend is so-called compensation "stacking," in which physicians are required to provide multiple levels or types of services under employment. Commonly observed stacking services include medical directorships, extensive hospital call coverage, or clinical or service line management of hospital service lines or departments. These services are required of a physician *in addition to* his or her clinical services that are provided to practice patients. Consequently, a physician is paid incrementally for these services *over and above* the compensation for clinical patient care services. So-called stacking arrangements can yield significant levels of additional compensation such that, when aggregated with clinical compensation, the physician's total compensation benchmarks in the upper percentiles of survey data. The potential difficulties or issues that can arise in so-called stacking arrangements include whether a physician is 1) being overpaid in the aggregate for the totality of services, 2) being compensated twice for the same work, or 3) realistically capable of providing the totality of services. (Note: The valuation issues associated with compensation stacking are discussed in Part V.)

### 1.5 Typical Benefits Packages for Employed Physicians

It should be noted that most hospital or health system employment arrangements will include the typical basket of employee benefits that one observes in corporate and larger organizations. Frequently, the employee benefits offered under employment will exceed the benefits physicians were receiving in their own practices, especially when the physician practiced on a solo basis or with a small to medium-size group. The one exception may be where a group was comprised of physicians nearing retirement and who had implemented a rich retirement plan. Most market-based retirement plans will not match the retirement benefits that physicians could pay themselves under various tax-free retirement benefit plans. Finally, physicians under employment are not able to expense or have reimbursed various "perks" that commonly run through the expenses of a physician-owned practice.

## 2.0 Healthcare Regulatory Requirements for Physician Compensation and Employment

### *2.1 Understanding Healthcare and Tax Laws and Regulations Governing Physician Compensation and Employment*

There are a series of healthcare and tax laws and regulations that have a bearing on physician compensation and particularly on physician compensation in the employment setting. Appraisers working in the discipline of healthcare compensation valuations should have general familiarity with these laws and regulations. They establish parameters for how compensation can be structured for physicians, but more importantly, they promulgate requirements for physician compensation. In general, these laws and regulations mandate that physician compensation:

- Not include compensation for the volume or value of referrals for certain healthcare services.
- Be consistent with fair market value (FMV).
- Be consistent with reasonable compensation.
- Be commercially reasonable.

It is essential for appraiser to have a solid working knowledge of the requirements for FMV under these laws and regulations because most appraisal engagements will have as their task the determination of FMV compensation for an employed physician. Many hospital and health systems will engage appraisers to value the compensation in physician employment arrangements as part of a healthcare regulatory compliance program. In fact, obtaining an independent appraisal has become a best practice in recent years for many large systems. An assessment of the commercial reasonableness of the employment arrangement may also be an objective of the valuation assignment. As a result, appraisers practicing in the healthcare space need to be aware of the issues involved in FMV and commercial reasonableness for healthcare regulatory purposes.

It is also helpful for an appraiser to have a basic understanding of the parameters placed on physician compensation by these healthcare regulatory and tax rules to navigate through potential issues and pitfalls in valuing compensation plans. While the appraiser does not provide legal, tax, and regulatory advice in a transaction, a working knowledge of these rules will help ensure that the valuation is generally consistent with regulatory requirements. It will also allow the appraiser to identify potential issues or areas where legal or tax counsel will need to provide specific direction and guidance relative to the compensation structure and the scope of the valuation engagement. Appraisers should seek to familiarize themselves with the overall framework of applicable healthcare and tax regulations. The following subsections provide an overview of the key regulatory matters. An in-depth analysis of these areas is beyond the scope of this chapter. Appraisers seeking a more detailed discussion of healthcare and tax regulations should consult the appropriate chapter within the *BVR/AHLA Guide to Healthcare Valuation* as well as other resources.[9]

### 2.2 The Federal Anti-Kickback Statute and Stark Regulations

Two key sets of regulatory requirements are the federal anti-kickback statute (AKS) and the so-called Stark laws and regulations (Stark). Both AKS and Stark have highly specific requirements and related compliances issues that are not discussed here. There are, however, common elements between the two sets of regulations. First, AKS and Stark proscribe payment for the referral of certain healthcare services. Second, they require that transactions between parties with referral relationships should include remuneration that is consistent with FMV. Third, AKS and Stark specifically address physician employment arrangements where the employer is a provider of healthcare services referred by the employed physician. As part of its regulations for "in-office ancillaries" and the definition of a "group practice," Stark has an array of specific requirements related to how physicians may be compensated for technical component services that are generated within practices.

### 2.3 Tax Law Issues for Physician Compensation and Employment Arrangements

The tax considerations that can affect physician compensation in employment arrangements relate to the legal form and status of the employer entity. First, the legal form of the employer entity can raise the issue of how compensation paid to physicians is characterized for tax purposes. Specifically, C and S corporations are subject to rules related to whether amounts paid to physician-owners should be classified as compensation for services provided as employees or as ownership distributions or dividends in the case of C corporations. These classification issues affect the taxation of the amounts

9 See Chapter 9 of *Physician Compensation Plans: State-of-the-Art Strategies,* by Bruce A. Johnson and Deborah Walker Keegan, MGMA (2006), for a well-written and accessible discussion of healthcare and tax regulatory issues.

distributed. Second, tax-exempt organizations face a series of requirements related to compensation paid to employees. In particular, such compensation is subject to the standard of reasonable compensation as defined by tax regulations. It must also be based on methods that are consistent with the mission of the exempt organization.

### *2.4 State Laws and Regulations*

Many states have their own so-called "mini" Stark laws and regulations addressing the referrals of healthcare services. As discussed previously, some states have prohibitions on the "corporate practice of medicine" that bar nonphysician-owned entities from employing physicians to provide clinical and patient care services. States may also prohibit physician practices from providing certain types of ancillary services or have certificate-of-need requirements for such services. An overview and discussion of the myriad of state laws and regulations in these areas is clearly beyond the scope of this chapter, but appraisers should be aware that such regulations may have a bearing on their engagements to value physician employment arrangements. It is advisable for appraisers to inquire with clients and legal counsel involved in transactions as to whether any such laws and regulations are applicable to the subject arrangement.

## 3.0 Key Issues in Valuing Physician Employment Arrangements

### *3.1 Matching Compensation to Employment Services Provided*

Since the key to the valuation of service arrangements is matching compensation to the services provided, it is essential to delineate the services being provided by the physician under a proposed employment arrangement. Compensation should be set in accordance with the services rendered to the employer by the employed physician. The first step in the valuation process for an employment agreement, therefore, is to identify the specific scope of services that the physician will provide. The scope of services can include clinical, administrative, or other types of services. Part of the process for identifying the scope of services is not only distinguishing among the types of services, but also the work requirements for each type of service. Key duties and work requirements can include the following, without limitation:

- Weekly required clinical hours;
- Required weeks worked per year;
- For physicians who are providing shift coverage (such as hospital-based physicians), shifts worked per week, month, and the required hours per shift;
- Required hospital call coverage, including type of coverage (restricted or unrestricted), shifts worked per month, and duration of shifts;

- Administrative duties, such as a medical directorship, including the specific duties and the required or estimated hours for performing these duties; and
- Supervision duties, including supervision of NPPs and technical component services.

The next step in the appraisal process is to determine the appraisal methods and techniques that are relevant and applicable to the valuation of the specific services. Since physician services are usually compensated based on the economic characteristics of the service, different valuation methods may need to be applied to each of service. The data sources for each type of service may also vary. Engagement planning, therefore, is built around an evaluation of the scope of services under employment and the economics characteristics of each service. A comprehensive assessment of total compensation may also be required as part of the valuation assignment. Many clients seek valuation opinions that address the total compensation paid for all services under an employment arrangement, not just the clinical services. When appraisal of the total compensation is included in the assignment, an appraiser will also need to prepare a "stacking" or total compensation analysis that assesses whether there is any overlap in compensation for the same service provided by the physician.

#### *3.2 The Determination of FMV for Healthcare Regulatory Purposes*

Since the predominant employer of physicians are hospital and health systems, independent appraisals of the compensation paid in employment arrangements are usually obtained for purposes of healthcare regulatory compliance. The reason for obtaining valuations of employment compensation is that physicians are referral sources for certain types of healthcare services provided by hospital and health systems. As a result, physicians and hospital and health systems are subject to AKS and Stark. Both AKS and Stark have highly specific requirements and related compliances issues that are not discussed in detail here. One common requirement for both sets of regulatory requirements, however, is that transactions between parties with referral relationships should include remuneration that is consistent with FMV.

While appraisal professionals are familiar with the standard definition of FMV promulgated by Revenue Ruling 59-60 or the International Glossary of Business Valuation Terms, both Stark and AKS advance their own definitions of FMV. The definition of FMV for Stark purposes is formulated as follows:

> Fair market value means the value in arm's-length transactions, consistent with the general market value. "General market value" means the price that an asset would bring, as the result of bona fide bargaining between well-informed buyers and sellers

> who are not otherwise in a position to generate business for the other party; or the compensation that would be included in a service agreement, as the result of bona fide bargaining between well-informed parties to the agreement who are not otherwise in a position to generate business for the other party, on the date of acquisition of the asset or at the time of the service agreement. Usually, the fair market price is the price at which bona fide sales have been consummated for assets of like type, quality, and quantity in a particular market at the time of acquisition, or the compensation that has been included in bona fide service agreements with comparable terms at the time of the agreement.[10]

The AKS definition of FMV is similar to that found in Stark.[11] What appears to be critical to the regulatory definition of FMV is that the valuation excludes the volume or value of referrals for certain healthcare services. The impetus of both AKS and Stark are to prevent and penalize the payment of referral sources for referring to providers of these services. Hence, the regulatory definition of FMV seeks to establish a standard of value that not only excludes consideration of such referrals but also seeks to place the parties in a hypothetical or assumed context in which a referral relationship does not exist. FMV is defined as the price for a transaction between parties where the focus of the compensation relates solely and exclusively to the economics of the subject transaction.

In addition to providing its own definition of FMV, Stark contains some discussion of valuation methodology. This guidance is noteworthy and should be considered in appraisals prepared for healthcare regulatory compliance purposes. First, Stark states that the definition of FMV "differs depending on the type of transaction." Second, Stark posits that valuation methodologies consistent with its definition of FMV may deviate from those of standard appraisal practice.[12] The specific example given by Stark for such divergence is the prohibition on using market data based on transactions from parties in a position to refer certain healthcare services. Parties in such a position are not considered by Stark to be at arm's-length or independent. As a result, the transaction pricing between such parties is not considered to be an indication of FMV. Stark instructs parties to seek other methods, such as the cost approach, to determine FMV when only such related-party transactions are available under the market approach. [13] Second, Stark allows for FMV to be determined by "any method that is commercially reasonable."[14] Yet, it provides no systematic guidance or criteria for assessing what is commercially reasonable with respect to valuation methodology. Stark does characterize

10 42 CFR §411.351.
11 42 U.S.C. §1320a-7b.
12 *69 F.R. 16107 (March 26, 2004).*
13 *66 F.R. 876-77, 919, 941, 944 (Jan. 4, 2001).* See also *69 F.R. 16107 (March 26, 2004).*
14 *66 F.R. 944 (Jan. 4, 2001).*

the use of physician compensation surveys as a "prudent practice" but does specify the valuation techniques by which one could apply the survey data to a subject physician.[15] In addition, Stark does indicate that FMV does depend on "the nature of the transaction, its location, and other factors."[16] Nonetheless, Stark provides no systematic or conceptual guidance that can serve as the basis of a distinct valuation framework or methodology for determining FMV for healthcare regulatory purposes. Similarly, AKS provides no conceptual or practical guidance for determining FMV consistent with its own definition of this standard of value.

In summary, Stark and AKS provide distinct meanings for FMV in the healthcare regulatory context, but little to no guidance on its determination using various valuation methods and techniques. The question of appraisal methodology is, in general, left unresolved and uncertain. This silence with respect to appraisal methodology presents an appraiser who has been engaged to prepare a valuation of a healthcare transaction subject to AKS or Stark with a *conundrum*. Since the purpose of the valuation is healthcare regulatory compliance, the appraiser must look to the applicable regulations to understand the definition of value and valuation considerations that should be taken into account in the appraisal process. Yet, there is a noted absence of guidance as to what methodologies are consistent with this regulatory determination of FMV. Moreover, Stark posits that regulatory compliant methods can reflect a departure from standard appraisal procedures. As a result, an appraiser enters a kind of regulatory "no man's land."

Added to this conundrum is the regulatory requirement that employment agreements be commercially reasonable. Appraisers are often requested to provide an analysis of commercial reasonableness along with an opinion of FMV when valuing physician employment arrangements with hospital- or health system-affiliated entities. Healthcare regulations provide even less guidance as to what is and is not commercially reasonable. While there is no formal definition in the regulations, Stark provides the following formulation of potential criteria that could be taken into account in determining commercial reasonableness:

> An arrangement will be considered "commercially reasonable" in the absence of referrals if the arrangement would make commercial sense if entered into by a reasonable entity of similar type and size and a reasonable physician (or family member or group practice) of similar scope and specialty, even if there were no potential DHS referrals.[17]

15 *72 F.R. 5015 (Sept. 5, 2007).*

16 *69 F.R. 16107 (March 26, 2004).* CMS reiterated these criteria in *72 F.R. 5015 (Sept. 5, 2007).*

17 *69 F.R. 16093 (March 26, 2004).* This formulation is consistent with the OIG's guidance found in the "OIG Supplemental Compliance Program Guidance for Hospitals" at *70 F.R. 4866 (Jan. 31, 2005).*

Added to the difficulty of determining what is commercially reasonable is the fact that there is no standard concept or definition of commercial reasonableness in the appraisal body of knowledge. Commercial reasonableness is not a standard of value to which professional appraisers are trained to provide analyses and opinions. There is no formal body of knowledge or professional standards for the determination of commercial reasonableness. Thus, valuation assignments that include this determination require professional appraisers to engage in original thinking and analysis, outside of any established methodology or definitions coming from the profession.

In summary, valuations assignments for healthcare regulatory compliance purposes present appraisers with a series of challenges and difficulties in attempting to apply standard appraisal methods and techniques to subject transactions. There is a lack of regulatory guidance with respect to FMV methodology, especially in light of the fact that the healthcare regulations posit a departure from standard appraisal methodology.

### 3.3 FMV and Appraisal Methodology as Understood by the Appraisal Profession

In evaluating valuation methods and techniques that can be used in valuations prepared for healthcare regulatory purposes, it is helpful to consider valuation methodology and the definition of FMV as understood by the appraisal profession. The classical definition of FMV for business appraisal purposes was promulgated by Revenue Ruling 59-60:

> The price at which the property would change hands between a willing buyer and a willing seller when the former is not under any compulsion to buy and the latter is not under any compulsion to sell, both parties having reasonable knowledge of relevant facts.

This definition was modified and enhanced slightly in the definition promulgated in the *International Glossary of Business Valuation Terms*:[18]

> The price, expressed in terms of cash equivalents, at which property would change hands between a hypothetical willing and able buyer and a hypothetical willing and able seller, acting at arm's length in an open and unrestricted market, when neither is under compulsion to buy or sell and when both have reasonable knowledge of the relevant facts.

18 *The International Glossary* was developed and adopted by the four major U.S. business appraisal professional societies (American Society of Appraisers, American Institute of Certified Public Accountants, Institute of Business Appraisal, and the National Association of Certified Valuation Analysts) along with their Canadian counterpart (Canadian Institute of Chartered Business Valuators).

What is key in both definitions is the idea of two parties to a transaction who are willing parties with no compulsion to act and who both have a reasonable knowledge of information that would be germane to their transaction. The *International Glossary* definition goes further, to add the idea of an arm's-length transaction in an "open and unrestricted market."

A corollary to the business valuation definition of FMV is the concept that it entails a transaction by a hypothetical-*typical* buyer. Business appraisers use the notion of a hypothetical-typical buyer when applying various valuation methods and techniques to a subject transaction. To the extent that such methods employ inputs and assumptions about the buyer's operation and economic capacity of a subject business, this concept circumscribes the nature and characteristics of these inputs and assumptions to those that are consistent with the hypothetical-typical buyer in the marketplace, not taking into account the particular attributes and resources of the specific buyer to the transaction. In other words, valuation inputs and assumptions are based on what the hypothetical-typical buyer could do in operating the subject business. The synergies, resource and competitive advantages, and business opportunities available to the specific buyer are not used as inputs or assumptions in valuation models and techniques. Appraisals prepared using such inputs and assumptions are considered to be prepared on an investment- or synergistic-value basis, rather than being consistent with FMV. In business appraisal, investment value is the value definition that takes into account the properties of a specific buyer in applying valuation methods and techniques.

With regard to valuation methodology, the professional practice of appraisal looks to consideration of the three approaches to value: the cost, market, and income approaches. The major appraisal disciplines, whether from real estate to business valuation, begin with this fundamental point of departure. Consideration of these three approaches is one of the fundamental concepts in the body of knowledge that is common to the professional practice of appraisal. The reason for this commonality is that each approach provides a different, but critical, perspective on the value of a subject entity or service contract. Each approach looks at the economics of the subject from a different point of view, providing a unique focus on value from a given vantage point. For example, the market approach may take into account the valuation principle of substitution, while the cost approach may utilize the principle of alternatives. Generally, each approach will entail relative strengths and weaknesses in valuing a subject. Use of the three approaches can serve to offset and mitigate the weaknesses of a single approach, while providing for greater strength in the synthesis of multiple approaches. Within each appraisal discipline, standard definitions are formulated for each approach so that practitioners have a common framework for using the various approaches in valuation assignments.

It should be noted that consideration of the three approaches does not necessitate the application and completion of each approach in a specific valuation assignment. The implementation of an approach is a function of available and relevant data as well as the capacity of the approach to address the fundamental economics of the subject arrangement and services. Lack of available and relevant data may inhibit the effective use of an approach. In addition, an approach may not encompass or account for key economic factors in a transaction. As a result, an appraiser may not always use an approach in given engagement after considering all the facts and circumstances. In such cases, however, the appraiser should be able to provide the reasons for not implementing an approach. This justification should be based on sound valuation reasoning related the available data or relation of the economics of the transaction or service relative to the available valuation methods or techniques for the approach. Summarily ignoring valuation approaches, however, is not consistent with the professional practice of appraisal. It can lead, moreover, to skewed and misinformed results that do not take into account the totality of the facts and circumstances as well as the fundamental economics of a service.

It should also be noted that multiple appraisal methods and techniques may be available for a given approach to value. Thus, consideration of an approach can also involve the contemplation of multiple methods and techniques. It can also involve evaluation of multiple data sources, such as the numerous physician compensation surveys that are publicly available. As with the consideration of the three approaches to value, assessing the use and application of various valuation methods and data sources should be based on an analysis of the fundamental economics of a subject transaction or arrangement and the quality and extend of available data. The judgment that is exercised in selecting methods and data sources is a key aspect of an appraiser's professional practice. It takes knowledge, experience, and skill to make such determinations as part of the valuation process.

In the professional practice of appraisal, the valuation process culminates in the synthesis of the various value indications arising from those methods and techniques used in the subject assignment. The appraiser evaluates and assesses each value indication and determines the appropriate indication or range of value that is consistent with the standard of value for the appraisal assignment. In the synthesis process, the appraiser analyzes the comparative strengths and weakness of various valuation methods and indications relative to the subject transaction or arrangement. As in the selecting of methods and techniques to use in an appraisal, the synthesis process is a matter of professional judgment. There is no universal formula or equation for synthesizing various value indications. Rather, the appraiser's knowledge, experience, and skill are brought to bear in arriving at a final conclusion of value.

### *3.4 Reconciling of Healthcare Regulatory and Professional Appraisal FMV*

There are two key areas in which standard appraisal practice can be compared and contrasted with healthcare regulatory guidance on the determination of FMV. The first area is in the definition of FMV. The second area relates to appraisal methodology. With regard to the definition of FMV, a comparison of the two definitions shows a general congruence between the two formulations. The healthcare regulatory definition of FMV (healthcare FMV) appears to have a narrower focus than professional appraisal FMV in terms of parties being independent with respect to referrals of healthcare services. It also seems to focus on a definition framed in terms of the market approach. Both definitions, however, refer to well-informed parties, while the professional appraisal definition of FMV focuses on a broader set of economic conditions related to the parties. Both definitions assume independent parties acting in their own self-interest. In summary, the behavior and choices of the parties in the transaction are assumed to be consistent with that of well-informed parties in bona fide negotiations not under compulsion. FMV under the professional appraisal definition adds the concept of an open and unrestricted market to the conditions for the assumed arm's-length negotiations.

A fundamental question arises as to whether these definitions are essentially different and incompatible, or alternatively, if they share a common framework that is harmonious and complementary at a core level. It is also possible that both definitions have areas of agreement and others of divergent implications and applications. One potential approach to addressing this question would be to ask whether sole application of professional appraisal FMV would yield the same or similar results as that of healthcare FMV. The answer to this question would appear to be a function of whether the hypothetical-typical buyer is a provider of healthcare services and the relationship of the buyer and seller is that of parties in a position to refer. (Note: In the case of service agreement valuations, one considers the buyer and seller of a service.) If the answer is no, that the hypothetical-typical buyer is not a service provider with a referral relationship to the seller, then consideration of referrals would appear to be excluded from the valuation analysis under professional appraisal FMV. To take such referrals into account in the valuation would produce a conclusion of value consistent with investment value, but not FMV under the standard appraisal body of knowledge. Even in cases where the only market for services is between physicians and healthcare providers who have referral relationships, one can reconcile healthcare and professional appraisal FMV by adjusting the professional appraisal definition to exclude such referrals and assuming the parties act without regard to such referrals. In other words, the parties act in accordance with their interests solely in regard to the assets or services that are the subject of the proposed transaction. With this one adjustment applied as needed, healthcare and professional appraisal FMV appear to reconcile and converge.

The question of the determination of FMV in terms of methodology presents a more difficult case for attempting a reconciliation between healthcare regulations and the appraisal profession. Healthcare regulations appear to lack the rigor, theoretical coherence, and practical valuation experience that are found in the appraisal profession's methodological framework for valuing subject transactions. This framework considers appraisal methods and techniques under three fundamental approaches to value. The problem with the healthcare regulatory approach in valuation stems from allowing "any commercially reasonable method" to be the sole methodological criterion in determining FMV. As any experienced appraiser will tell you, reasonable and generally accepted methods can sometimes yield a wide range of value indications. As discussed previously, any single method will, in general, have its relative strengths and limitations in yielding results that encompass all the relevant factors in the value of a subject transaction. Conceptually, it is only through consideration of multiple approaches and methods and the synthesis of the indications of value from those relevant and available approaches and methods for a subject transaction that a conclusion of value can be determined that accounts for the broadest scope of factors that can affect value. As a result, the appraisal profession across various disciplines has converged on the conceptual framework of three approaches to value.

In fairness to healthcare regulations, it should be noted that the "any commercially reasonable method" criterion appears to have been a response given in the context of healthcare industry players seeking universal formulas or safe harbors for determining FMV. The reticence on the part of regulators to promulgate such methods is well-founded. The appraisal profession would agree that no singular formula, technique, or method can be said to yield FMV in every context. As Revenue Ruling 59-60 noted in discussing the approach to valuation:

> A determination of fair market value, being a question of fact, will depend upon the circumstances in each case. No formula can be devised that will be generally applicable to the multitude of different valuation issues arising in estate and gift tax cases. Often, an appraiser will find wide differences of opinion as to the fair market value of a particular stock. In resolving such differences, he should maintain a reasonable attitude in recognition of the fact that valuation is not an exact science. A sound valuation will be based upon all the relevant facts, but the elements of common sense, informed judgment, and reasonableness must enter into the process of weighing those facts and determining their aggregate significance.

The specific facts and circumstances should be taken into consideration in each subject transaction, requiring different methods in different contexts. In this sense, the appraisal profession is in conceptual agreement with healthcare regulations as to the variability of methods needed to determine FMV.

It should also be noted that Stark's prime example of where the determination of FMV under healthcare regulations departs from standard appraisal practice may, in fact, not be a deviation at all. While excluding market data would appear to be a fundamental limitation on the use of the market approach, a more careful study of this prohibition can lend a different interpretation. If asked about the use of market data from transactions between family members, related parties, affiliated or parent-subsidiary companies, most appraisers would exclude, discount, or treat cautiously the use of such data as part of the market approach. Such parties or entities would not be considered to be fully at arm's-length, and therefore, any corresponding financial arrangements may not be viewed as being truly independent. Thus, it is not readily apparent that Stark's prohibition on the use of market data between parties in a position to refer healthcare services is a significant departure from the valuation body of knowledge. One is left to wonder whether standard appraisal practice and methodology is really significantly different from what is required to determine FMV under Stark, if this particular proscription illustrates the material divergence of the two definitions.

Because they take into account a larger set of variables and economic factors, valuation conclusions arrived at based on multiple approaches and methods are more robust and comprehensive, and ultimately, more supportable and defensible. As discussed previously, they are less likely to be skewed or lopsided, producing unreasonable value indications that only take into account a narrow set of considerations. On the contrary, use of multiple methods is more likely to produce an opinion of value that is more sustainable and achievable for the buyer of a business or service because a wider array of variables affect value. As a result, valuations based on multiple methods are more likely to reflect the FMV of a subject transaction. Buyers and sellers in the marketplace will frequently take into account a variety of economic and operational factors and considerations in consummating a transaction. Use of multiple methods reflects this wider perspective on value. More importantly, application of multiple methods is more consistent with the idea of informed buyers and sellers acting at arm's length.

Because of the rigor that is produced by valuations using multiple methods, it can be argued that appraisals prepared according to standard appraisal methodology tend to have a higher probability of producing value indications that do not appear to take into account the volume or value of referrals of healthcare services. Valuation conclusions so prepared yield results that can be more readily identified with multiple economic factors apart from referrals. As such, there is less ambiguity as to the economic reasons and rationale for the consideration paid in a transaction. The value can be associated with a broad base of factors, none of which should include the volume of value of referrals. A single variable can often be used to obfuscate or cover other motivations for a transaction. When multiple variables and factors are taken into account, the resulting value adds credence to the claim that the economics do not reflect the volume or value of referrals that may exist between the parties to the transaction.

For the reasons noted above, multiple method valuations have a greater propensity for producing a robust analysis relative to the *commercial reasonableness* of a subject transaction. As noted previously, such valuations are more likely to produce sustainable economic results for a buyer as a result of considering a broad array of economic factors. Sustainable economics, whether from the earnings from a business or the economics of a service contract, can more readily be considered to be commercially reasonable than unsustainable results. A valuation based on a single variable or set of variables has a higher probability or potential to yield an unsustainable price or compensation level because of its narrow focus. The potential for unsustainable results can be magnified or highlighted in service agreements because of their duration over multiple years. In short, a transaction is more likely to be commercially reasonable when it is valued on the basis of multiple economic factors and valuation methods.

### *3.5 The Composite Approach to Healthcare Valuation*

The approach used by most experienced appraisal professionals specializing in healthcare valuation is to follow generally accepted practices consistent with the body of knowledge. They follow general valuation methodology consisting of the consideration of three approaches to value and a conclusion based on the synthesis of all available and relevant valuation approaches or methods. With respect to the definition of FMV, appraisers specializing in healthcare valuation begin with professional appraisal FMV as the primary definition referenced in the valuation process. They then circumscribe or adjust this definition based on the relevant particulars of healthcare FMV. The healthcare regulatory definition of FMV is used to supplement the professional appraisal definition in areas where healthcare FMV does conflict with professional appraisal FMV and where the former has precise or applicable content. In addition, practitioners of healthcare valuation generally apply the idea that FMV entails a transaction by a hypothetical-typical buyer in the marketplace. They think this corollary to the professional appraisal definition of FMV is not only consistent with the healthcare regulatory definition, but also helps ensure consistency with the intent of healthcare regulations to prevent the payment for the volume or value of referrals. Taking into account the synergies and characteristics of physicians and healthcare provider entities to whom physicians refer services, i.e., of a specific hospital or health system buyer, in a transaction may run the risk of including the volume or value of referrals. As discussed previously, even when the hypothetical-typical buyer is a hospital or health system or other type of healthcare facility provider, professional appraisers avoid using characteristics of the buyer in the valuation input and assumptions that would include referrals or give the appearance of including referrals.

Stated in summary terms, professional appraisers specializing in healthcare valuation generally follow the appraisal body of knowledge and professional standards for the determination of FMV in transactions except for where such application would conflict with the healthcare regulatory definition of FMV. In these cases, healthcare laws and regulations clearly supersede and have priority over standard appraisal practices and methodology. The two primary areas where such conflicts arise are 1) including the volume or value of healthcare service referrals, and 2) the use of market data derived from parties who are in a position to refer such services. In both areas, appraisal professionals avoid using such referral-laden economics or data items reflecting referral relationships.

There are certain areas or issues, however, where healthcare regulations are not so clear with respect to the regulatory definition of FMV and specific guidance on appraisal methods. Moreover, there potentially are certain fact patterns in which use of a particular assumption or valuation technique may appear to be inconsistent with healthcare regulations and healthcare FMV. A client or legal counsel for a client may identify certain assumptions or valuation methods as posing a potential regulatory risk for the proposed transaction. These "gray" areas typically involve issues related to technical component services or ancillaries included in a business being sold or in the scope of services being provided in a service contract. A common example is where the physician-sellers of a proposed business or service are also the customer or referral base for the business or service.

In such cases, appraisers may be given explicit instructions by the legal counsel as to the exclusion of certain assumptions or valuation methods from the scope of work completed by the appraiser in a given assignment. *To the extent that such direction is given relative to areas of ambiguity in healthcare regulations and not about matters related to methodology per se, appraisers would be advised to follow direction of legal counsel.* The interpretation and application of healthcare regulations in highly complex, technical, or ambiguous situations is not an area in which appraisers claim expertise. Thus, such direction is followed as clarification by counsel as to the meaning of healthcare FMV, to which the appraisal must conform. It should be noted that this kind of direction should be narrow in focus and selective in scope. The appraiser should not subordinate his or her opinion of what is required for appraising the subject transaction. Rather the guidance should be taken as clarification of the meaning and application of healthcare regulations. Such direction, moreover, should be documented in the appraisal report, with discussion of its impact on the scope of work completed and data assumptions.

On a final note, healthcare valuation appraisers and users alike should be aware that the valuation of compensation in service arrangements is a relatively new appraisal discipline or subdiscipline. There are no formal or specific professional standards for compensation valuations (CV). The *BVR/AHLA Guide to Healthcare Valuation* is the critical first attempt at compiling professional literature on topics related to CV. As a result, the specific application of standard appraisal methodology and practices is primarily based on those found in the discipline of business valuation (BV). BV methodology and practices are usually adjusted or adapted for application to the appraisal of service contracts. Nonetheless CV methodology and practices are consistent with the general methodology and practices found in the various appraisal disciplines, including consideration of the three approaches to value.

## Bibliography

### *Works Cited for Marketplace Trends in Physician Employment*

Darves, Bonnie. "Physician Employment and Compensation Outlook for '07," April 2007. *New England Journal of Medicine*, Career Center Web site: www.nejmjobs.org/career-resources/physician-compensation-trends.aspx, accessed June 15, 2009.

Casalino, Lawrence P., Elizabeth A. November, Robert A. Berenson and Hoangmai H. Pham, "Hospital-Physician Relations: Two Tracks and the Decline of the Voluntary Medical Staff Model." *Health Affairs*, 27, no. 5 (2008): 1305-1314.

Hamilton, James, "Is the Future of Physician Practice Management Changing? Market Indicators Would Say Yes!" Somerset CPAs, Health Care commentaries Web site: www.somersetcpas.com/Newsletters/2007NovemberHCC/HCCarticle3.Print.htm, accessed on May 21, 2009.

Dennis Kennedy, Scott Clay, and Deborah Kolb Collier, "Factors Driving Physician Employment Trend." *hfm Magazine*, April 2009: www.hfma.org/hfm/2009archives/month04/, accessed May 21, 2009.

Liebhaber, Allison and Joy M. Grossman, "Physicians Moving to Mid-Sized, Single-Specialty Practices." Center for Studying Health System Change, *Tracking Report No. 18*, August 2007: www.hschange.com/CONTENT/941/, accessed June 15, 2009.

Merritt Hawkins & Associates, "2008 Review of Physician and CRNA Recruiting Incentives." Physician Salary, Compensation and Practice Surveys: www.merritthawkins.com/pdf/mha-2008-incentive-survey.pdf, accessed June 15, 2009.

Terry, Kenneth J., "Become a Partner or Remain an Employee?" May 5, 2009, Medscape Business of Medicine: www.medscape.com/viewarticle/702784_print, accessed June 4, 2009.

# PART III. THE MARKET APPROACH

### *1.1 The Market Approach Defined*

As defined in the *International Glossary of Business Valuation Terms*, the market approach is "a general way of determining a value indication of a business, business ownership interest, security, or intangible asset by using one or more methods that compare the subject to similar businesses, business ownership interests, securities, or intangible assets that have been sold." In basic terms, the market approach uses comparable sales transactions that have occurred in the marketplace to determine the value of a subject asset or business interest. This approach is based upon the valuation principle of substitution: A buyer will not pay more for a subject asset than it would for a substitute asset that provides the equivalent economic utility.

As applied to service agreements, the market approach seeks to value the subject arrangement by referencing comparable arrangements in the marketplace. *The key to utilizing the market approach for valuing the compensation paid in service agreements is identifying and obtaining information on comparable agreements that can be used to establish the value of the subject contract.* The task of the appraiser, therefore, is first to identify the services to be provided under the subject service arrangement and then to obtain information on comparable service agreements in the marketplace.

### *1.2 Sources of Market Data*

The most widely available and accessible information sources on physician service arrangements are the various physician compensation surveys, which are discussed later in this chapter. These surveys are readily available to the public and can encompass thousands of responding practices and physicians from around the country. They include data from practices in which physicians are employees of health-system owned and operated practices as well as those that are physician-owned. Many of the surveys also include relevant data on physician productivity and other physician characteristics that can be useful in establishing comparability between the subject physician employment arrangement and the market data. Finally, some of the surveys contain data on administrative as well as clinical compensation. There are also surveys that report compensation for specialized types of services such as hospital call coverage and medical directorships. For these reasons, the physician compensation surveys have become a touchstone for establishing market levels of compensation for physicians in employment arrangements.

In contrast to the physician compensation surveys, information on individual employment arrangements in the marketplace is generally difficult to obtain in sufficient detail for use in the valuation analysis. The appraiser needs specific information about the scope of services provided under the agreement for the individual transaction to be useful in the valuation process. Even when such data are available, they are often limited to a few points that may not constitute a sufficient size for extrapolation to the marketplace.

A more detailed discussion of market data sources is included in subsequent sections in Part III.

### *1.3 Limitations on the Use of Market Data Imposed by the Stark regulations*

The Stark regulations place limitations on the usage of certain market data from transactions between parties in a position to refer to one another for determining FMV. The preamble to the Phase II Stark regulations states:

> Moreover, the definition of "fair market value" in the statute and regulation is qualified in ways that do not necessarily comport with the usage of the term in standard valuation techniques and methodologies. For example, the methodology must exclude valuations where the parties to the transactions are at arm's length but in a position to refer to one another.[1]

Thus, market data on physician compensation from service arrangements between doctors and hospitals or other healthcare providers in which there is a referral relationship are generally not allowable for determining fair market value (FMV) for Stark compliance purposes.[2] The Stark regulations argue that such market comparables do not represent arm's-length transactions because the parties are in a position to refer or generate other business between them. Such market data may distort pricing in the marketplace due to the referral relationship or potential for referrals.[3] The regulators acknowledge that this exclusion of market data may prohibit the use of the market approach in valuing compensation arrangements. In those cases, the Stark regulations advise the use of alternative approaches or valuation methods.[4]

1 69 *Federal Register* 16107 (March 26, 2004).

2 There are apparently some valuation consultants, and indeed, attorneys, that take the position that the aforementioned prohibition is not categorical to all types of arrangements. They argue it only applies to the leasing arrangements because the prohibition was made in the section of Stark dealing with leases. Hence, they use information on specific transactions between hospital or health systems and physicians to establish the FMV of employment arrangements. Consultants who take this position should be aware of the regulatory "thin ice" on which they stand. The logic presented in Stark as to why such market comparables should be excluded, i.e., that the parties are not independent and not at arm's length, appears to be categorical in its essential analysis. It is not the type of transaction that is determinative of the exclusion, but the relationship of the parties.

3 66 *Federal Register* 876-77, 919, 941, 944 (Jan. 4, 2001).

4 66 *Federal Register* 876-77, 919, 944 (Jan. 4, 2001).

While many appraisers are quick to criticize this limitation on the use of the market approach, it is important to assess this prohibition within the larger context of the business valuation body of knowledge. Most appraisers would exclude, discount, or treat cautiously any market comparables for transactions between family members, related parties, and affiliated or parent-subsidiary companies. Such parties or entities would not be considered to be fully at arm's length, and therefore, any corresponding financial arrangements would not be viewed as truly independent. In the case of the Stark regulations, however, the potential for referrals is considered significant enough to warrant the *exclusion* of arrangements between physicians and certain healthcare providers as sources of market data for purposes of determining fair market value under Stark.

As a result of this Stark prohibition, appraisers generally look to the physician compensation surveys as the most viable source of market data on compensation for physician services. In should be noted, however, that some of the physician respondents in the surveys are be employed by or receive forms of compensation from entities to which they refer. As a result, such market data would appear to be disqualified under the Stark regulations. Yet, in the Phase III Stark regulations, CMS called use of the surveys a "prudent practice" (72 *Federal Register* at 51015, Sept. 5, 2007). Previously, CMS had provided a safe-harbor calculation using the surveys. While CMS rescinded the safe harbor in the Phase III Stark regulations, the reasons given for this retraction did not relate to the inclusion of physicians from arrangements involving referrals. Thus, one is left to suppose that CMS appears to have validated use of the surveys, despite the inclusion of data from parties in a position to refer.

### *1.4 The Importance of Matching Market Data on Compensation to the Services Provided Under the Subject Employment Arrangement*

For valuations of employment agreements, use of the market approach begins with the identification of the scope of services to be provided under employment:

- Will the services be clinical, administrative, academic, or some combination thereof?
- Will the services be provided part time or full time?
- What scope of duties is required in the subject employment arrangement?

The appraiser should be able to enumerate and differentiate the types of services required under the employment contract as the first step in application of the market approach. Delineating the scope of services allows the appraiser to seek market data that is comparable to the subject arrangement. Market compensation data from arrangements with dissimilar services is not relevant or applicable for valuing a subject service arrangement because it lacks such comparability. It should be noted, however, that an appraiser can often use market information from service arrangements that are not fully similar to the subject arrangement, as long as the appraiser has sufficient information to make the appropriate adjustments to the market data and the subject arrangement to make them comparable for valuation purposes.

### *1.5 The Critical Need to Understand the Details and Nuances of Market Data*

Since the essence of compensation valuation is matching compensation to the services provided, it is essential for the appraiser to have a thorough and studied understanding of the data sources being used for the market approach. Physician service arrangements under employment can often entail a variety of services. Each service may have distinct economics and market dynamics. Moreover, the combination or "stacking" of services may yield the possibility of duplicative payment for the same service or compensation for services or burdens not actually provided by the physician. As a result, the appraiser must be able to navigate through the details and nuances of market data to identify, utilize, apply, or adjust such data for use in valuing a subject employment arrangement. All too often, valuation consultants fail to take the time to understand market data or make unwarranted assumptions about market information without adequate research. Unhappily, their valuation work reflects uncritical and unstudied misapplication of market data.

## 2.0 The Market Transaction Method

While use of physician compensation surveys is the most common source of data for application of the market approach to employment arrangements, the issue of referencing specific employment agreements is often raised, especially by physicians who purport to have such information available to them. Appraisers may also obtain data on specific employment arrangements that they wish to consider in the process of valuing employment-related compensation. The following sections, therefore, provide criteria for utilizing such data under the market approach.

### *2.1 The Market Transaction Method Defined*

The market transaction method uses actual data from individual or specific transactions that have occurred in the market place to establish the value of a subject transaction. As applied to the valuation of employment agreements, the market transaction method utilizes information from specific or individual employment agreements that have transacted to establish a FMV guideline for the compensation in a subject employment arrangement. The method considers the compensation levels paid in other employment agreements as market-based indications of value for what should be paid in similar employment situations.

Under this method, the appraiser completes data gathering on specific employment arrangements that are comparable to the subject arrangement or that can be adjusted for comparability to the subject. The information gathered on the market comparable employment arrangements should be based on data that are accessible to appraisers generally. Use of proprietary data that only a specific appraiser or limited parties can access creates a conflict with the appraisal definition of FMV promulgated in Revenue Ruling 59-60 and the *International Glossary of Business Valuation Terms*. In both formulations of the definition, FMV requires that the buyer and seller have "reasonable knowledge" of the relevant facts. Reliance on proprietary data that are not available to other appraisers or parties raises the question of whether a hypothetical buyer and seller can have such reasonable knowledge. It also raises the question of whether the valuation analysis can be replicated by another appraiser or outside parties. While valuation firms love the business advantages associated with proprietary data, their use can lead to critical objections to the valuation opinion under the appraisal body of knowledge.

### *2.2 Criteria for Using the Market Transaction Method*

An appraiser should consider several key criteria before attempting to use the market transaction method for establishing compensation under a subject employment arrangement:

1. *Are the market transactions between parties in a position to refer under the Stark regulations?* From a strict regulatory compliance perspective, use of market transactions from parties in a position to refer will not be considered valid support for FMV compensation in healthcare valuation practice. If the purpose of the appraisal is healthcare regulatory compliance, the appraiser should not utilize such data for purposes of completing valuation methods under the market approach. An appraiser may elect to present such data as part of the research prepared for the valuation. Reliance on such data, however, appears to be precluded from a regulatory standpoint.

2. *Does the appraiser have actual documentation on market transactions?* Market transaction data should be based on actual transactions accompanied by an appropriate level of documentation from reliable or unbiased sources. Hearsay and oral statements by parties with a bias toward the subject arrangement are generally not reliable for purposes of establishing an objective, reliable, and supportable appraisal.

3. *Does the appraiser have sufficient details and information on the market transaction?* Since the key to using the market approach for compensation valuation is comparability of the services in the subject and the market data, the appraiser should have sufficient detail on the market transactions to determine the scope

of services provided by the physicians in the market employment agreements. In addition, the appraiser should have information on other key aspects of the market transactions to assess their comparability to the subject arrangement. These aspects include local market factors such as commercial reimbursement and payer mix considerations, as well as supply and demand for a specialty. They also include information on the compensation structure or formula in the contract and information on the qualifications and credentials of the subject physician. The reason for obtaining such data is that they have a bearing on the facts and circumstances for the actual transaction. Physician compensation can be set based on consideration of these factors by the parties. To determine whether a market transaction is comparable to a subject, it is important to have some understanding of the factors that affected the subject transaction.

4. *Is the scope of services in the market transactions comparable to the services required under the subject employment arrangement?* The services under the market data should be comparable to the services under the subject employment deal for the data to be considered under the market transaction method. Key service requirements to consider include clinical work hours, hospital call coverage, clinical co-management, and administrative services, such as medical directorships. The compensation in market transactions may have been "stacked", i.e., represents payment for numerous types of services. The compensation payable to a physician providing multiple services to an employer is not comparable to a subject where a physician provides fewer services or a reduced level of services. Where sufficient information is available on the compensation for each type of service, an appraiser may be able to adjust the market data to make the scope of services and corresponding level of compensation comparable to the subject employment services. In addition, comparability of physician specialty or subspecialty should not be overlooked in evaluating market transaction data.

5. *Are the local market conditions and employer profiles of the market transactions comparable to the subject employment arrangement?* Local market factors, such as the supply and demand of physicians for a given specialty, can have a significant impact on the range of compensation for physicians. Commercial reimbursement dynamics can be another significant factor in the range of compensation for a given local market, as noted in the research findings of Dietrich and Anderson.[5] As discussed in Part I, commercial reimbursement varies widely from market to market in the United States. Moreover,

5 "Evaluating RVU-Based Compensation Arrangements," *Health Lawyers Weekly*, Nov. 14, 2008, Mark O. Dietrich, CPA/ABV, and Gregory D. Anderson, CPA/ABV, CVA.

commercial reimbursement can vary significantly within a market based on the relative bargaining power of a physician practice within the local market. Thus, to assess the comparability of market transaction data to a subject employment arrangement, it is important to have some knowledge of these dynamics in both the markets for the subject arrangement and the market transaction data. It is also helpful to know the background on the employer entities in the transaction data. Employer entities may have varying needs for physician services and recruiting histories. Large groups, for example, may have an existing patient base or level of demand for a newly employed physician to service. An existing level of patient demand may affect the compensation structure and rates included in the employment contract. A startup practice, on the other hand, may have different expectations that affect the compensation structure and levels of an employment agreement.

6. *Are the subject physician's qualifications and credentials comparable to the physicians involved in the market transaction data for employment?* A physician's qualifications and credentials can affect the level of compensation in an employment agreement. For example, physicians recently out of residency or fellowship may not receive the same level of compensation as more experienced physicians, for which an employer may have higher productivity expectations. A physician with unique credentials or specialized training, such as robotic surgery, that is in high demand or has national recognition may receive higher compensation than others of the same specialty. If a market transaction data point includes such a physician, the transaction may not be comparable for a physician without such credentials, training, or reputation.

7. *Are there sufficient points in the transaction data set to constitute a reasonable indication of the market?* An appraiser should consider whether the number of transactions for which data are available is adequate for formulating an indication of market compensation levels for comparable services. The question of the sufficiency of the data is generally a matter of judgment based on the facts and circumstances related to the subject arrangement and the data. For example, if the subject employment arrangement involves a highly unique physician specialty or subspecialty or type of services for which there is a limited number of comparable physicians or arrangements in the marketplace, a smaller data set may provide a reasonable basis for formulating an assessment of the market. A subject arrangement for a typical specialty or scope of clinical services would generally warrant a larger number of transactions to establish market trends.

### *2.3 Application of the Market Transaction Method to Valuing a Subject Arrangement*

After addressing the critical issues related to the comparability of the market transactions to the subject employment arrangement, the next step in the application of the market transaction method is adjusting the data for any scope of service or other considerations so that they are comparable for purposes of establishing market-based indications of value. Two key adjustment areas to consider are independent contractor compensation and owner compensation.

1. *Adjustment for Independent Contractor Compensation*

Generally, compensation paid to independent contractors in the marketplaces includes a premium, or "gross-up" amount. This premium is intended to cover benefits costs that are borne by an independent contractor but would otherwise be paid by an employer under an employment arrangement. (Here, we are discussing employer-paid benefit costs, not benefit costs that are paid by employees out of their compensation through payroll deductions.) Market transaction data for independent contractor arrangements that include a benefits premium should be adjusted to eliminate such premiums if the data are being used for a subject employment agreement. Compensation for employment arrangements is generally stated in dollar amounts that do not include the cost of employer-paid benefits.

2. *Adjustment for Owner Compensation*

Market transaction data for employment or other service arrangements in which physicians are both employees and owners of the business entity providing services may include compensation amounts that represent payment for services as well as a payment for owner compensation or a return on investment. In other words, the total amount of compensation received by such physicians includes a payment for the clinical services along with a payment for the owner or management services and a return of and on capital investment. In such cases, it may be necessary to adjust the total compensation for the value of owner compensation to derive the compensation level that relates to the clinical services the physician provided as an employee.

After making any necessary adjustments, the appraiser then analyzes and evaluates the various market data to establish the relevant indication or range of compensation that will serve as the market guideline indication or range. This analysis should consider the relevant facts and circumstances of the subject arrangement and will require judgment on the part of the appraiser.

### *2.4 Benefits and Limitations of the Market Transaction Method*

Where sufficient and comparable data are available, the market transaction method can yield supportable market-based indications of value. The reality surrounding the use of this method, however, is that such data are rarely available or accessible. Private parties are reluctant to provide detailed data on their transactions. Moreover, there is a very limited number of databases available that attempt to provide such data on service transactions and compensation to the public at large. Some attorneys and consultants may maintain proprietary databases with such data, but they are generally not willing or able to make such data widely available for the appraisal profession. There may be cases, however, where the most relevant and applicable data will be found from individual transactions in the marketplace. For subject arrangements involving highly specialized and unique physician services or physicians with highly specialized credentials or national reputations, little data may be available in the physician compensation surveys that are comparable and relevant for valuation purposes. The appraiser may need to attempt to gather transactional data independently to find truly comparable market data.

## 3.0 The Physician Compensation Surveys

### *3.1 Overview of the Major Physician Compensation Surveys*

There are numerous publicly available surveys providing compensation data on physicians for a wide array of services, specialties, and settings. The following list presents *some* of the major surveys.

- Major surveys for clinical and total compensation:
    - Medical Group Management Association (MGMA), *Physician Compensation and Production Survey*
    - MGMA, *Cost Survey*
    - Sullivan, Cotter and Associates Inc. (SCA), *Physician Compensation and Productivity Survey Report*
    - Hospital & Healthcare Compensation Service, *Physician Salary Survey Report*
    - American Medical Group Association (AMGA), *Medical Group Compensation and Financial Survey*
    - Towers Watson Data Services, *Survey Report on Health Care Clinical & Professional Personnel Compensation*
- Survey data for newly hired physicians:
    - MGMA, *Physician Placement Starting Salary Survey*

  - AMGA, *Medical Group Compensation and Financial Survey*

- Major surveys for academic compensation:
  - SCA, *Physician Compensation and Productivity Survey Report*
  - MGMA, *Academic Practice Compensation and Production Survey for Faculty and Management*
  - Association of American Medical Colleges, *Report on Medical School Faculty Salaries*

- Surveys for executive compensation:
  - Cejka Search and the American College of Physician Executives, *Physician Executive Compensation Survey*

As noted, this list is not intended to be exhaustive. Other surveys and compensation data are available from various trade groups, medical specialty groups, and publishers. In addition, surveys are available for specific types of compensation, such as call coverage and medical directorships. Appraisers in the healthcare industry should keep abreast of the available survey data.

#### *3.2 Understanding Survey Methodology and Definitions*

It is important to understand the origins of the data in the physician compensation surveys as well as the spectrum of data available. Unfortunately, many marketplace users of the surveys are often unaware of critical features in the methodology used in compiling the data and in the definitions used for various metrics reported. Such uncritical use tends to promote misunderstandings and misapplications of the data in the market approach. Thus, appraisers should complete a thorough review of the respondent profiles, survey methodology, glossary and definitions, and discussion sections of surveys before using them in valuation practice.

Some of the surveys, such as MGMA, will include a copy of the survey questionnaire and questionnaire guide that was given to respondents to complete the survey. Review of such information is essential for the appraiser to use survey data appropriately as part of the market approach. The appraiser should seek to use survey data that are comparable to the subject service arrangement under valuation, or where necessary, adjust for such comparability. Comparability can only be established *after* an appraiser has an understanding of what is and is not included in survey data.

One key area of the survey methodology that is important to understand is the criteria used for exclusion or inclusion in the report survey data. Does the survey exclude data from respondents meeting certain profiles or criteria? For example, does the survey require a certain full-time equivalent (FTE) level for inclusion? Does the survey exclude respondents who provide only partial responses to the questionnaire? Some surveys exclude apparent anomalies or outliers in their data based on various factors. Knowing such criteria can aid the appraiser in determining the comparability of the data relative to the subject of an employment valuation.

Another example is reviewing the level at which data are collected. For example, MGMA's *Physician Compensation and Production Survey* reports physician work relative value units (wRVUs) and compensation per wRVU based on the wRVUs personally performed by individual physicians. The MGMA *Cost Survey*, by contrast, reports data gathered at the group level, rather than the individual physician level. Moreover, metrics reported on a per-wRVU basis in the *Cost Survey* are based on the total wRVUs reported for a group, including both physician and nonphysician provider wRVUs.

### *3.3 Understanding Available Survey Metrics and Data Subsets*

In addition to providing data on compensation, many of the physician compensation surveys include an array of other relevant metrics related to physician productivity. Key examples include wRVUs, gross charges, and professional collections. They may also include data on various forms of compensation such as base salary or various types of benefits. Many will report compensation and other data based on a variety of respondent characteristics, ranging from the geographical to the demographic. They may also report compensation in terms of ratios or metrics relative to physician productivity, such as compensation per wRVU or the compensation-to-professional-collections ratio.

It should be noted that the number of respondents for the various metrics reported in the surveys generally varies. This variance results from the fact that not all respondents to a survey report data for all requested categories. Generally, the number of respondents for total compensation includes the greatest number of respondents because failure to report compensation is usually one criterion for exclusion from the survey. Failure to include wRVUs or other data items may not exclude a respondent from inclusion in the survey. Thus, users of survey data should be aware of the fact that the respondent base for many metrics is a subset of the total data set. This fact is important in assuming or assessing relationships between compensation and various metrics reported in the surveys.

Some of the surveys provide data based on key characteristics of the respondents. One major characteristic is geographic. Most of the surveys will report selected survey data by geographic region; some will provide these data by state. Another key characteristic by which data can be segregated is physician practice ownership. Some of the surveys will separately report data for physician-owned and hospital and health system practices. Different surveys may offer different ways to "slice and dice" the data. One example is MGMA's CD-ROM version of its *Compensation and Production Survey*. This electronic version of the survey affords multiple selection criteria for organizing and sorting the data from MGMA's flagship survey.

As discussed previously, it is important for appraisers to be aware of the available metrics and survey data breakdowns so that they can gather market data that are relevant and comparable to the subject employment arrangement. In addition, unique facts and circumstances may necessitate seeking highly specialized or selected data from within a survey for comparison purposes. Thus, awareness of the available data selections and tools is essential for appropriate application of the market approach in valuing subject physician employment arrangements.

### 3.4 Comparison of Survey Respondents to the Physician Marketplace

It is important to understand the respondent base to the physician compensation surveys and the extent to which it does and does not reflect the marketplace for physician services. It should be noted that the major physician compensation surveys are not based on statistically valid sampling techniques of physicians in the marketplace. Rather, the surveys are generally produced by trade groups, such as MGMA or AMGA, that obtain data from their members or by survey organizations that solicit information from selected healthcare systems and physician groups. Each survey tends to reflect its members or similar types of physician practice organizations or settings. As a result, the physician compensation surveys tend to represent various segments of the physician marketplace; they individually do not reflect the marketplace as a whole.

Before looking at the various segments of the physician marketplace represented by the surveys, it is helpful to have an understanding of the physician practice landscape in the United States. A nationally representative survey of clinically active physicians is the *Community Tracking Study Physician Survey* compiled by the Center for Studying Health System Change (HSC). This survey has been prepared periodically over the last 15 years. Exhibits 1 and 2 present a summary of the survey results, providing a reasonable picture of the physician practice marketplace. Exhibit 1 shows the distribution of physicians by practice-setting and the percentage of physicians in each type of practice. Exhibit 2 shows the relative percentage of physicians who are owners in their practices in comparison to those employed or practicing as independent contractors.

**Exhibit 1. Physicians by Practice Setting[6,7]**

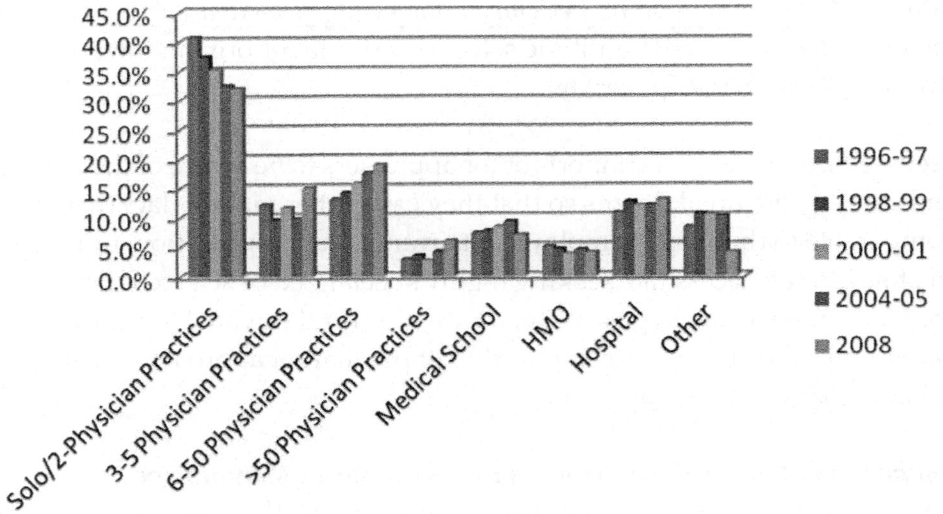


**Exhibit 2. Ownership of Practice[8]**

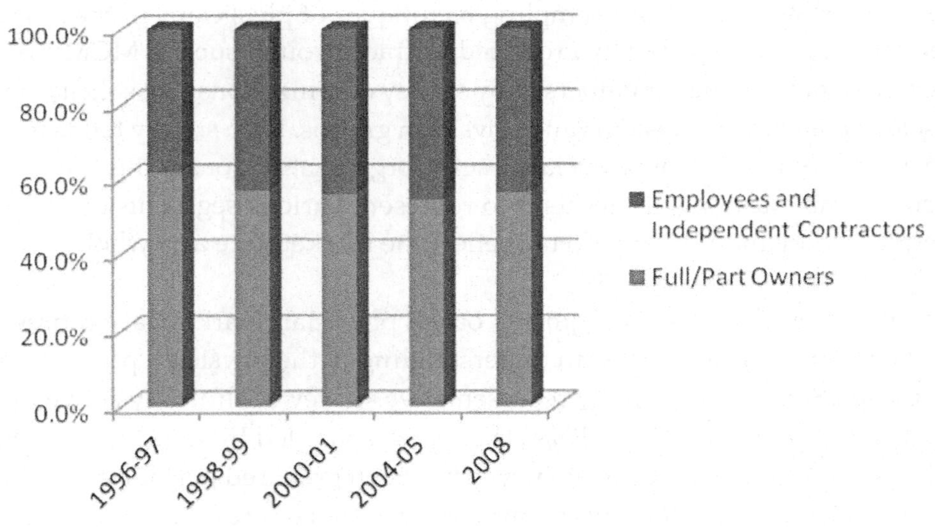


6 Table prepared from *Physicians Moving to Mid-Sized, Single-Specialty Practices, Tracking Report No. 18,* August 2007, and *A Snapshot of U.S. Physicians: Key Findings From the 2008 Health Tracking Physician Survey,* Data Bulletin No. 35, September 2009. See www.hschange.org. While the 2008 study summary indicates that changes in administration of the survey make it not comparable to prior years, the findings for 2008 are included along with prior years for presentation and discussion purposes. This table is intended to provide a broad perspective of the physician marketplace.

7 Per the HSC studies, the hospital category includes hospital-based and office-based physicians employed by hospitals.

8 Table prepared from *Physicians Moving to Mid-Sized, Single-Specialty Practices, Tracking Report No. 18,* August 2007, and *A Snapshot of U.S. Physicians: Key Findings From the 2008 Health Tracking Physician Survey,* Data Bulletin No. 35, September 2009. See www.hschange.org.

The data presented above from the HSC studies do not reflect the recent wave of physician practice acquisition and employment transactions by hospitals and health systems. One will expect the physician ownership percentage to decline significantly in future surveys. In addition, we may see changes in group size as a result of the hospital employment trend and the move toward medical homes and accountable care organizations under the recent healthcare reform legislation. Nonetheless, the picture of the physician marketplace from the HSC studies indicates that the vast majority of physicians practice in groups of less than 50 physicians, with nearly one-third practicing in solo to two-physician groups.

This picture of the physician practice landscape contrasts with the respondent profiles from some of the major physician compensation surveys. The following sections provide overviews of the respondent profiles of MGMA, AMGA, and SCA to illustrate the potential for organizational bias in the survey data.[9]

#### MGMA Data

For the 2010 and 2011 surveys, approximately 63% of the respondent physicians or providers included in the MGMA survey come from physician practices of more than 50 FTE physicians. Approximately 55% of the providers came from groups with total medical revenues in excess of $50 million, while about 72% of providers come from groups with over $20 million in such revenues. Approximately 73% of providers come from multispecialty groups. For 2011, 41% of providers came from physician-owned groups, while in 2010, 46% were from physician-owned groups. The percentage of providers from hospital or integrated delivery system-owned groups was 43% in 2010 and 47% in 2011.[10]

#### AMGA Data

Per AMGA's participant profile summary for the 2010 and 2011 surveys, 97% to 99% of the physicians included in the survey come from multispecialty groups, and 89% to 91% of these physicians are in groups of 100 physicians or more. Physician ownership of groups included in the survey was 40% to 43%, while health system and hospital practices comprised 48% to 51%.[11]

9 MGMA, AMGA, and SCA were selected because they are widely used in the marketplace, but more importantly, because they are the major surveys that include both compensation and productivity data. As discussed later in Part III, matching compensation and productivity is a key valuation method used in the market approach. Thus, surveys without productivity data are generally not used in productivity-matching valuation techniques.

10 See Tables 8, 9, 13, and 23 from the *Demographics—Medical Practice* section of the MGMA surveys for 2010 and 2011.

11 See Table 4 and Figure 2 from the *Participant Profile* section of the 2010 and 2011 surveys.

### SCA Data

The participant data for SCA indicate that approximately 59% of responding organizations in 2010 were from the category of hospital or medical center, while the 2009 percentage for this category was 65%. In 2010, 42% of the participating organizations were teaching institutions. Such institutions constituted 45% of respondents in 2009.[12] The average and median number of employed physicians from survey participants in 2010 was 178 and 54, respectively, and 177 and 80 in 2009.[13]

In comparing the physician practice setting data from the HSC study to the respondent profiles of the major surveys, it is apparent that the surveys are not necessarily reflective of practice patterns found in the United States for most physicians in terms of group size. The surveys tend to be overrepresented by large groups. With respect to practice ownership, some of the surveys, such as MGMA and AMGA, appear to be more representative of the ownership found in the marketplace, in terms of physician ownership. SCA appears to be more representative of hospital or medical center-affiliated groups and significantly reflective of teaching institutions.

It should also be noted that the physician compensation surveys may have limited geographical diversity or may not be reflective of the distribution of physicians in the United States. Review of the number of respondents by state for a given specialty often indicates that certain states will have few to no respondents. In some cases, moreover, respondents may be concentrated in a handful of states. It is possible that in such cases, the respondents for a given state may come from a few groups to a single group, although the data may not be provided in a manner that would allow the user to make such determinations. Minimal to no state representation should also be noted with respect to the regional data presented in the survey. While a state may be included in a given region for geographical categorization, there may be no data for that state in the regional reporting.

### *3.5 The Importance of Understanding Definitions and Terms*

Particular attention should be given to the definitions of various terms and metrics used in the physician compensation survey data. Failure to review and note these definitions can lead to the misapplication of the market approach in the appraisal process. An appraiser may assume that a given term or metric includes certain data, when in fact, the term may exclude such data. Such a misunderstanding can lead to false comparisons and conclusions in the valuation. Most of the surveys provide a general glossary of

12 Note: SCA has multiple response categories in its respondent profile. Thus, teaching institutions may also be included in the category of hospital or medical center.

13 See Section I. "Characteristics of Survey Participants" from the 2009 and 2010 surveys.

terms used in the survey report, and many also provide detailed descriptions of the data included in a given survey metric. These definitions should be studied by the appraiser prior to use of the survey data. Many of the surveys provide contact information if a user has questions about the survey data. When in doubt, an appraiser should make use of this resource to resolve questions about the data.

Notwithstanding the excellent guidance given by a survey's glossary or questionnaire form, appraisers should be aware of the potential for respondents not to follow such guidance when completing the survey. Many experienced healthcare valuation consultants who use the survey data regularly are somewhat dubious about what some groups may be reporting for certain survey metrics. This uncertainty regarding the quality of the data reported reflects the fact that many information systems used by practices often lack the capacities for readily calculating certain data in accordance with survey guidelines or the users of such systems lack the requisite resources to compute the data appropriately. In summary, users of the survey data should understand the complexities involved in the data gathering process for various metrics.

### *3.6 Key Terms and Metrics to Define*

There are certain terms and metrics in the physician compensation surveys whose definitions must be carefully understood for appropriate use of the survey data. An appraiser should ensure that he or she has adequately reviewed the definitions of these terms to ensure that the survey data is not used erroneously. The reason such background research is necessary is that many commonly used terms related to physician services and practices can have highly specific definitions and uses in the surveys. Moreover, surveys may not use certain terms consistently from survey to survey. Finally, there are often data nuances to what may or may not be included in a given metric. The following is a listing of many of the key terms and metrics for which appraisers should ensure a correct understanding.

#### Compensation

The key compensation measures in the surveys generally report total cash compensation from all sources. Some surveys, however, do report data on selected forms of compensation, such as base salary or signing bonuses. To use compensation data in the market approach appropriately, it is essential to use data that are comparable to the compensation for the subject agreement. Thus, use of market data based on total cash compensation for valuing one compensation element in an employment arrangement, such as base compensation, may represent a misapplication of the data, depending on the nature of the other elements. Appraisers should review and be clear on the definitions used for various compensation metrics in the survey data.

#### Physician Specialty

Another critical area for establishing comparability in using market survey data relates to the selection of the relevant physician specialty or subspecialty. To the consternation of many users, the physician compensation surveys do not always use clear or consistent terminology with respect to all physician specialties or subspecialties. Special attention, therefore, should be given to the definitions and terminology used in the surveys. Moreover, appraisers should be aware of the distinction between a physician's training and board certifications and his or her primary practice patterns with respect to specialty or subspecialty designation. Training and board certifications may not always be indicative of a physician's primary clinical focus. Thus, appraisers should not only evaluate the survey definitions and terminology, but also a subject physician's credentials and practice patterns to ensure that the appropriate, comparable specialty in the market data is applied. MGMA, for example, bases specialty classification on the where the physician spends 50% of more of his or her time in providing clinical services.

#### Relative Value Units

Many of the physician compensation surveys provide productivity and other data, including various metrics related to work or total relative value units (RVUs).[14] There are nuances, however, in how such data are reported in the surveys. Most of the surveys report physician wRVUs based on those personally performed by physicians and excluding those performed by nonphysician providers but credited to and billed under physicians. The reason for this exclusion is that the surveys seek to report the personal productivity of physicians. When gathering productivity data on a subject physician, appraisers should ensure that such data are provided on a basis that is consistent with the surveys for accurate comparison purposes. A helpful distinction to make in gathering such data is between rendering or service provider and billing provider. The former represents the provider who actually performed the services, while the latter indicates the provider under which the services were billed to payors.

One exception to this general definition for wRVUs is the MGMA *Cost Survey*. The "physician wRVUs" reported in this survey include all wRVUs for a reporting practice, regardless of the type of provider who performed the services. Thus, they include both physician and nonphysician provider wRVUs.

Total RVUs (tRVUs) is another metric where close attention should be given to the definition in the surveys. The metric of tRVUs in the MGMA *Physician Compensation and Production Survey* includes only RVUs associated with the professional services,

14 RVUs are generally established under the Medicare Physician Fee Schedule.

excluding the technical component of clinical services. The *Cost Survey*, by contrast, includes RVUs from technical component services.

Another key to the definition of RVUs in the surveys is that they generally exclude any adjustments for the geographic practice cost index (GPCI) under Medicare or for weightings based on conversion factors. In addition, RVUs are typically determined based on the Medicare Physician Fee Schedule (MPFS) rates. Where rates are not available for a procedure, the surveys often provide guidance on how to compute RVUs for such services.

#### Professional Charges and Collections

In addition to RVUs, professional charges and collections are frequently reported productivity metrics in the surveys. Like RVUs, these metrics can have precise definitions in the surveys. They generally exclude services performed by nonphysician providers, but billed incident-to a physician. They also exclude technical component services. Other exclusions may also apply in a survey. MGMA, for example, provides specific inclusions and exclusions for professional charges and collections from professional charges as part of the questionnaire guide for respondents completing its survey.

## 4.0 The Market Survey Guideline Method

### *4.1 The Market Survey Guideline Method Defined*

Valuation methods or techniques that use physician compensation surveys to establish the FMV compensation for a subject physician or practice can be categorized under the broad heading of the market survey guideline method. As will be discussed in the following sections, there are a variety of individual methods or techniques that an appraiser can employ to establish a FMV guideline compensation level for the professional services of a physician using survey data. The key to all these techniques is that they attempt, in one manner or another, to establish criteria for comparability between the survey data and the subject physician or practice. The key to using such criteria for the market survey guideline method is identifying those factors that affect compensation in the physician marketplace. In developing individual valuation techniques, the appraiser utilizes the criteria and information available in the surveys to derive relationships between compensation levels and these key factors. The appraiser then evaluates the subject physician or practice according to these criteria and determines an appropriate level or range of compensation using the survey data. In summary, the market survey guideline method is predicated on the concept that physician compensation in the marketplace is not random, but related to key factors that stem from the fundamental economics of physician services and from the market for physician services.

In the healthcare sector today, there are attempts to summarily establish FMV compensation levels based on survey data without any regard to the comparability of a subject physician to the data or to any understanding of the key factors that affect physician compensation in the marketplace. One can observe claims that FMV is consistent with this or that given percentile in a given survey or in multiple surveys without regard to any criteria that establish comparability or an economic relationship between the subject and the market. Such categorical claims should be received incredulously unless substantiated by analysis that is consistent with the appraisal body of knowledge. Indeed, such categorical claims should be viewed as inconsistent with the appraisal body of knowledge because they do not offer any support or analysis related to the market data or the subject in support of such assertions. These categorical claims appear to be nothing more than the uncritical act of simply "pulling numbers out of a book" presented under the guise of the practice of valuation.

The appraisal body of knowledge, which is generally consistent across various appraisal disciplines, looks to rational criteria for relating subject to market in establishing value under the market approach. Think of the claim that the FMV of a given house in a neighborhood is always consistent with the 75th percentile for sales in the neighborhood. Such a claim is dubious. Key real estate value factors, such as square footage, condition, upgrades, and the like, should be considered in looking at real estate market data to establish value. This example from real estate is comparable to claims that the 75th percentile of MGMA is always FMV. Such claims should be viewed similarly as unfounded. Another example from real estate appraisal is instructive on the appropriate use of market data. What would one make of the claim that the FMV price of a home is always national median price per square foot multiplied by the square footage of the subject house? This claim is also questionable. Unfortunately, many in healthcare make a comparable claim that FMV is always and everywhere equal to the MGMA median compensation per wRVU. As has been and will be discussed throughout these chapters on employment valuations, there is wide variability in the factors affecting physician compensation that cannot be adequately encapsulated by the median rate from a single survey.

#### *4.2 Criteria for Applying the Survey Data to a Subject Physician or Practice*

Various criteria can be used to place a subject physician on a comparable basis with the respondents of the survey. Such criteria are considered to have an impact on physician compensation in the marketplace. They can and often vary based on the type and scope of physician services involved in the subject employment arrangement. The following subsections discuss potential criteria for use in establishing comparability between a subject physician and the survey data.

### Academic Physician Compensation

The services, duties, and compensation of academic physicians are generally a function of three factors. The first is the academic position held by the subject physician. Academic positions include such titles as instructor, assistant professor, associate professor, and professor. They can also involve additional duties, such as division chief and department chair. Second, academic physician services and compensation can be affected by the level of clinical practice a physician may engage in as part of a faculty practice plan. Finally, academic compensation can also be affected by the level of research and research funding associated with a physician's faculty activities. Royalties from patents may also be a factor. Certain other administrative duties can be required of academic physicians, such as residency director, chief of hospital services, and clinical ambulatory director.

In view of these factors, a compensation valuation related to academic pay would look to compensation surveys based on academic position as a starting point for gathering comparable market data. Finding comparable academic positions in these surveys and their corresponding levels of compensation would constitute another key step in the process. To the extent that compensation data are available for physicians in an academic clinical practice setting or in faculty practice plans, such data can be related to a subject academic employment arrangement that involved clinical services in an academic setting. Compensation relative to research activities is generally more difficult to obtain. As a result, comparable market data may not be available to the appraiser for this element in academic compensation.

### Executive or Administrative Physician Compensation

The services and compensation of physicians in executive or administrative positions is generally related to the job duties associated with the position. Three key criteria that can reflect the scope of job duties are: 1) job title or position, 2) the type of organization for which the services are provided, and 3) the organization's size. Different job titles can reflect varying areas and levels of responsibility within an organization, and thus, different levels of compensation. An organization's size may also have a significant impact on compensation. All things being equal, the larger the organization, the greater the level of responsibility that is entailed in a given organizational position. Compensation tends to increase with the scope of responsibility. The type of organization may also affect the level of responsibility in terms of the relative degree of organizational complexity. Again, as the scope of responsibility increases, compensation often increases.

### Clinically Practicing Physicians

Most physician employment valuations will focus on physicians who practice full-time or nearly full-time in a clinical setting providing patient care services. Since the nature of the services in this setting is clinical, the criteria used for relating the services should also be clinical in nature. Many potential criteria could be considered by an appraiser in evaluating clinical services. Factors such as training, experience, board certifications, and quality outcomes can affect the type and scope of clinical services provided by a physician.

The most common measure of clinical services used in the marketplace, however, is productivity. Multiple measures of physician productivity abound in the marketplace, and many of the physician compensation surveys include such productivity data. Since the predominant reimbursement mechanism in the current healthcare marketplace is based on fee-for-service, physician productivity is necessarily an important consideration in physician compensation.[15] As a result, physician productivity measures are widely used criteria for applying market compensation data to subject physicians in employment arrangements.

### *4.3 The Concept of Productivity-Matched Compensation*

For clinical physician services, the prevailing techniques for applying physician compensation survey data to subject physicians are predicated on the concept of productivity-matched compensation. Simply stated, the concept seeks to match compensation with productivity: the higher the level of productivity, the higher the level of compensation, and vice versa. Productivity-based compensation presupposes that there is an inherent relationship between compensation and productivity in the survey data, i.e., that compensation correlates with compensation in a fairly consistent fashion. Because of its simplicity and apparent objectivity as a formula for determining physician pay, productivity-based compensation is a widely used concept in valuing compensation for physicians in the healthcare marketplace.

Productivity-matched compensation valuation techniques are generally based on two approaches to applying survey data to a subject physician. In the first approach, a subject physician's productivity can be benchmarked relative to his or her peers in the survey data using productivity metrics. A corresponding level of reasonable compensation can then be determined using the compensation data from the survey. A second approach applies compensation rates per unit of productivity from the surveys to the historical or forecasted level of productivity for the physician and thereby establishes a guideline compensation amount.

The use of productivity measures to apply physician compensation survey data to a subject physician in an employment valuation is analogous and comparable to the

15 It should be noted that quality outcomes may become another critical factor as the healthcare industry focuses more on the quality of services, rather than the mere quantity of services. This pivot to payment for quality, however, appears to be a few years in the making and is not the current paradigm for reimbursement.

guideline public company method in business valuation. Under this business valuation method, various pricing multiples or ratios are derived from the equity markets for publicly traded companies. These multiples or ratios are applied to the subject company being appraised to establish the value or range of value for the subject. Such ratios as price to earnings, price to revenue, or other common-sizing metrics based on market data are considered to reflect a reasonable economic relationship to value in the marketplace. By applying these ratios to key operating metrics of a subject company, a market value can be established. Physician productivity measures are used similarly in valuing physician compensation for clinical service arrangements. Ratios and relationships are derived from the survey data for compensation and productivity. These guidelines are then applied to the subject physician's productivity levels to establish a market-based level of compensation.

#### *4.4 Selecting Productivity Measures*

Several key factors should be considered in selecting productivity measures to serve as the basis for productivity-matched compensation valuation techniques for individual physicians:

1. The measures should be a reflection of an individual physician's productivity and work efforts. Hence, they should generally reflect personally performed services by the physician.

2. Data on the productivity measures need to be available in the survey data, or alternatively, the appraiser should be able to estimate the measure on a reasonable basis relative to the survey data.

3. The measures should have a substantial relationship to the fundamental economics of the clinical services being valued.

4. The measures need to be readily accessible and determinable from the information available in a physician practice. Otherwise, use of a measure may be impracticable for valuation purposes.

5. It is advisable to use measures that are widely accepted or used in physician practices, where such measures meet the other criteria. Obscure or foreign measures may unduly complicate and obfuscate use of the valuation by the parties to the arrangement.

In the following subsections, several commonly used productivity measures are discussed.

#### 4.4.1 Physician Work RVUs

Physician wRVUs are perhaps the most popular measure of physician productivity in the marketplace today. This popularity is not without reason. Physician wRVUs represent a universal scale by which all physicians can be measured because they are calculated using publicly available rates established each year in the Medicare Physician Fee Schedule (MPFS) by CPT and HCPCS procedure code. Thus, wRVUs can be calculated in a consistent and uniform manner from provider to provider. As a result, they provide a highly relevant measure of provider productivity.

There are several important points, however, that appraisers should take into account in using wRVUs as the measure of productivity for physicians:

1. *Personally performed procedures:* As noted previously, the wRVUs used for a provider, whether a physician or a nonphysician provider, should be based on the procedures personally performed by the provider. For physicians, any procedures performed by nonphysician providers that are billed "incident-to" under a supervising physician should not be counted in the calculation of wRVUs for the subject physician.

2. *Modifier adjustments:* The calculation of wRVUs may include an adjustment when procedures are performed subject to the use of certain CPT code modifiers. When these modifier codes are used, adjustment factors should be applied to the wRVU calculations. Each of the relevant modifiers has a separate adjustment factor. Some modifiers reduce the number of wRVUs, while others increase the wRVUs allotted to the procedure. To adjust the wRVUs for the use of modifiers, the adjustment factor for the modifier is multiplied by the wRVU rate for the procedure code and then by the number of procedures performed subject to the use of the modifier. The product of this computation is the adjusted wRVUs for those procedures performed subject to the modifier.[16]

3. *No GPCI adjustment:* Medicare GPCIs should not be used in calculating the wRVUs for physician benchmarking and valuation purposes. The GPCI rates are intended for use in computing Medicare reimbursement for the local market. They are not part of the universal scale for determining how many wRVUs a physician has generated.

16 The reason for this adjustment is that the procedure was performed under circumstances that have a bearing on reimbursement, and thereby, on the RVUs associated with the procedure. It should be noted that there are numerous modifiers related to CPT and HCPCS codes. Not all modifiers will affect the computation of wRVUs.

4. *Annual wRVU scale*: We note that the surveys report wRVUs for responding physicians based on the data from the prior year, e.g., a 2011 report based on 2010 data. Thus, the survey data are based on the wRVU rates from the MPFS for the year of data provided. MPFS wRVUs rates may change from year to year, however, creating potential "noise" for multiyear benchmarking of physicians when using the most recently available survey. To reduce the potential impact of changes in wRVU rates per procedure code when using historical data in comparison to survey data, it is advisable to review the changes in wRVU rates for the relevant years used in benchmarking. An appraiser may need to adjust for any material changes, on a volume-weighted basis, in wRVU rates for the historical years reviewed and the rates used in the reference survey data.

Appraisers should also note the advantages and disadvantages of using wRVUs for measuring an individual physician's productivity level. The advantages of using wRVUs include the fact that they provide a universal and common scale for measuring the productivity of physicians in the same practicing specialty. They are widely used in the healthcare industry for compensation and productivity benchmarking purposes and data for wRVUs is available in many of the surveys. The main disadvantages of using wRVUs as a productivity measure for compensation valuation purposes is that they take into account only one factor that can affect compensation in the physician marketplace. Other key economic factors such as reimbursement in the local market, technical service mix, and cost considerations are not encapsulated in wRVU data.

#### 4.4.2 Professional Collections

Professional collections are the collections received from professional component services and the professional component of global diagnostic testing services provided to patients. The professional component of a global diagnostic testing service represents that portion of a service or procedure that is performed by a physician, which is typically the interpretation of the exam. It is distinguished from the technical component of a global procedure or service, which usually entails the technological aspects of the exam.

Since professional collections are based on the collection efforts of the practice support staff or third-party vendors, one may question why this metric would be used for measuring the individual productivity of a physician. *The critical reason for using professional collections is that they can reflect what the local market is paying for a physician's productivity.* As discussed in Part I, physician services are reimbursed at varying rates by both Medicare and commercial payors. There is wide variability in commercial reimbursement from market to market within the United States and within a market. Moreover, professional collections may reflect local market payer mix conditions that also affect what is paid for a physician's productivity in the local market. Thus, professional collections are a key indicator of the revenue streams generated by a physician's productivity that will ultimately have a significant impact on the level of compensation that can be afforded and sustained by the practice. Professional collections, therefore, adds a local market dynamic to the determination of provider productivity.

Professional collections also reflect the effectiveness of a practice's revenue cycle efforts. Where the billing and collection operations of a practice are reasonable and well-operated, professional collections can provide a window into the revenue value of profession services in the local market. Where a practice has revenue cycle issues, however, the appraiser may need to normalize the collections to reflect what a reasonable operator, or the typical employer (who one would assume is a reasonable operator), would collect for professional services. Normalizing professional collections removes the one aspect of this measure that is not related to the physician's productivity.

The use of professional collections along with wRVUs can provide an appraiser with differing and yet complementary information about a physician's productivity. While wRVUs provide a uniform scale for measuring the productivity across all markets, the amount of professional collections serves as an indication of productivity as measured by local market reimbursement factors. Reimbursement can be a key factor in determining the range of market-based compensation for physicians. Use of professional collections for productivity benchmarking purposes can reflect this market variability and thereby affords an added informational element beyond the uniform productivity scale afforded by using wRVUs. Use of professional collections can provide a more localized indicator of the value of physician compensation in the local market context because they reflect the market reimbursement level for physician services.

#### 4.4.3 Other Measures of Physician Productivity

Other measures can be relevant for assessing the productivity of certain types of physician specialties. For example, patient encounters are a useful productivity measure for primary care physicians, whose main form of clinical services tend to be office and hospital visits. Surgical cases are clearly a relevant measure for surgical physician specialties. Both metrics, however, may not be as informative as wRVUs in that the complexity and level of service may vary by patient encounter or surgical case. Anesthesiologists have created their own RVU-type scale using American Society of Anesthesiologists (ASA) units. These ASA units are based on measures of time established for each anesthesia procedure. In evaluating the use of other measures, the appraiser should consider the utility of such measures based on the previously discussed criteria for evaluating productivity measures.

Some of the surveys report professional charges or gross charge information. While such information may be helpful in certain areas, charge data are not always meaningful for productivity comparison and benchmarking purposes. The difficulty with charges relates to the fact that physician practices establish gross charge levels based on varying formulas. Many practices, for example, set their gross charge rate by procedure based on a percentage of Medicare, but the percentage of Medicare can vary from practice to practice. Thus, comparison of charges across physician practices may not be based on a uniform and standard scale. Gross charges by physician can be relatively higher or lower from practice to practice based solely on varying calculations for establishing gross charge rates. This lack of uniformity in the measuring scale makes the use of gross charges a less meaningful tool for productivity measurement.

#### 4.4.4 Productivity Measures for Hospital-Based Physicians

As noted in Part I, the fundamental economics and service-setting of hospital-based physicians can be significantly different than their office-based peers. These differences may necessitate the use of alternative productivity measures for hospital-based physicians. Moreover, the work requirements and productivity expectations for hospital-based physicians in employment and professional service arrangements often revolve around definitions that are not focused on volumes or maintenance of a weekly office schedule. The workload of hospital-based physicians is commonly denominated in terms of shifts covered at a facility. Often, these shifts are distinguished in terms of the time of day, the day of the week, and the time of year, i.e., holidays. Shifts may be also differentiated in terms of the types of cases that will be covered during the shift. Recognition may be given to the relative workload for a specific shift time or at a given facility. For example, the patient volumes for the emergency department (ED) at one hospital may be substantially higher than the volumes at another facility a few miles away. Similarly, the weekend night shifts for an ED may be busier and more acute when the ED is in close proximity to bars and clubs with histories of closing-time violence. As a result, pay for such shifts may be paid at a premium.

Productivity for hospital-based physicians, therefore, may be better defined or primarily defined in terms of annual hours in comparison to procedure volumes or collections in many circumstances. Annual hours provide a means of converting annuals shifts worked by a physician into a common scale because shift hours and shifts worked per month can vary from facility to facility. One difficulty, however, in attempting to use annual hours as a measure of productivity is that survey data for this metric is not readily available at the level that other productivity measures are. MGMA and SCA had been reporting some data in this area, but in the past couple of years, they have stopped doing so.

#### 4.4.5 Productivity Measures for Physician Practices

An appraiser may want to assess a physician practice's overall productivity in terms of both professional and technical services and thereby look at compensation at the practice level. Such productivity assessment can be helpful in operational evaluations of a practice and in evaluating aggregate or overall compensation at the practice level. Two key productivity metrics that can be used for such measurement are tRVUs and total revenues.[17] Like wRVUs, tRVUs provide a productivity measurement for professional and technical services using a universal scale. Total revenues represent the revenues from both professional and technical services. It may also include other forms of professional service revenues, such as compensated call coverage, medical directorships, special services contracts, and the like. Similar to professional collections, total revenue can provide an indication of the value of a practice's total services in the local marketplace. Since these practice-level measures include technical component services, appraisers should be aware of any potential Stark implications of valuing these services.

### *4.5 Market Survey Guideline Method Techniques*

While there may be a variety of techniques that individual appraisers or appraisal firms have developed over the years, the following section discusses some of the more commonly used or noteworthy methods. In general, the various techniques using market survey data all attempt to relate such data to the subject physician to establish a market-based level of compensation for the subject. They focus on making the subject physician or employment arrangement comparable to the survey data. Each method necessarily has relative strengths and weaknesses and may or may not be applicable to a particular physician or employment arrangement. It is the task of the appraiser using sound valuation thinking and professional judgment to determine what methods are applicable and supportable based on the facts and circumstances. Indeed, such thinking and judgment are the real value-added element that trained and skilled appraisers bring to the healthcare industry in the determination of FMV compensation.

#### 4.5.1 Percentile Matching Technique

The percentile matching technique calculates a compensation level that corresponds to a physician's benchmarked level of productivity based on the reported percentiles of productivity and compensation in the survey data for the subject physician's specialty. For example, a physician who benchmarks at the 65th percentile for productivity is assigned 65$^{th}$-percentile compensation as a market-based guideline for compensation. In benchmarking a physician's productivity and matching level

17 Use of these measures for individual physicians is ill-advised, given the prohibitions on payments for referrals under the Stark regulations. Group-level use of these metrics, however, can be appropriate, where the criteria for sharing in ancillary earnings under Stark are met by the subject arrangement.

of compensation, appraisers generally utilize a linear interpolation computation to determine benchmarked productivity percentile and the corresponding compensation amount. As a result, this technique is also known as the linear interpolation method.[18]

By far, the percentile matching technique is one of the most commonly used methods for appropriating physician compensation survey data and applying them to a subject physician. Its common use is not without reason. First, the method is readily understood and accepted by players in the healthcare marketplace because it directly relates compensation to productivity in a proportional manner. Second, the method is objective in the sense that it is formulaic and applied consistently from physician to physician and from specialty to specialty. Third, the method can be readily replicated by another appraiser using the same input data to the valuation process. Finally, the method appears to be "elegant" in that it provides a simple formula for common-sizing physicians and compensation survey data vis-à-vis productivity.

Users of the technique should be aware, however, of the assumptions inherent in the method as well as its fundamental limitations. The percentile matching technique assumes a one-to-one or directly corresponding relationship between compensation and productivity. Users should note that this is an *assumption* that is not necessarily validated by the underlying data. To use the technique, the user has to reference two sets of data tables, one for compensation and the other for productivity. Generally, the data presented in these tables are not fully consistent. The data set for productivity is usually a subset of the data for compensation. The difference results from the fact that the primary criterion for inclusion in the reported survey data is providing compensation information. Many respondents do not report productivity. Thus, the data set for respondents reporting productivity measures is usually much lower than the number reporting compensation.

In correlating the data set with its subset, the percentile matching technique necessarily assumes that the range and dispersion of productivity for those respondents who reported compensation but not productivity is comparable to those who did report the productivity. Stated alternatively, the respondents who did report productivity are representative of the entire respondent base included in the compensation table. In

18 The linear interpolation method is perhaps the more widely used name for this valuation technique. While this label is descriptive of the mathematical calculations involved in the method, it fails to describe the basic concept and logic entailed in the method. I have therefore relabeled this method in a manner that is more descriptive and user-friendly to the variety of users of valuation reports found in the healthcare market. The invocation of "linear interpolation" unnecessarily complicates the method for the typical user: Most users would rather forget the statistics courses they took in college or graduate school, much less think about how an appraiser applied linear interpolation to survey data.

positing this assumption, the use of a data set and a subset of these data to correlate two variables is not considered to be a fundamental objection to the technique.

A more critical issue related to the percentile matching technique is that the underlying data for compensation and productivity do not generally correspond in the direct relationship presupposed by the method. Conceptually for the technique to hold true, nearly all physicians in the data set would need to be compensated on a productivity basis that is directly variable with the productivity measure and paid at the same effective rate relative to the measure. The reality of the physician marketplace is that physicians are compensated based on a variety of factors, including productivity- and nonproductivity-based factors. Moreover, the variability in market reimbursement, payer mix, service mix, and cost structures in physician practices does not readily lend itself to uniform rates of compensation per unit of productivity.

Moreover, examination of the underlying data from MGMA does not indicate a strong correlation between a productivity measure and compensation. One can measure this correlation using a regression line analysis tool that is included with the CD-ROM version of the MGMA's *Physician Compensation and Productivity Survey*. This tool, labeled as a "physician pay-to-production plotter" under the "Analysis" menu options, allows a user to view a scatter-plot diagram of the actual data points for compensation and a selected productivity measure for a physician specialty. The tool will also provide the user with a regression line analysis, including a regression line formula and the R-squared value for the line. Analysis of these diagrams and particularly the R-squared results for the regression lines for the data indicates a generally weak correlation in the underlying data, i.e., an R-squared value less than 0.50, as presented in Exhibit 3.

*What this regression line analysis may also indicate is that a single productivity measure is insufficient to account for a physician's compensation level.* A multiplicity of productivity factors as well as considerations related to service mix and cost may also affect physician compensation levels. Other noneconomic factors may play a role as well.

Moreover, MGMA has recently starting analyzing the compensation per wRVU rate for physicians in each quartile of productivity based on wRVUs. Their analysis, as detailed in the introductory section of the survey for the past few years, shows that the compensation per wRVU rate is greatest for physicians in the first quartile of production, i.e., up to the 25th percentile. The compensation per wRVU rate is the lowest for physicians in the fourth quartile of production, i.e., for physicians above the 75th percentile. The MGMA data, therefore, appear to present a more complex and less direct relationship between compensation and productivity than is implied through the percentile matching technique.

**Exhibit 3. R-Squared Results for the Regression Lines**

| Specialty | Compensation to Professional Collections | | | | Compensation to wRVUs | | | |
|---|---|---|---|---|---|---|---|---|
| | 2008 | 2009 | 2010 | 2011 | 2008 | 2009 | 2010 | 2011 |
| Anesthesiology | 0.30 | 0.47 | 0.33 | 0.35 | 0.13 | 0.15 | - | - |
| Cardiology: EP | 0.39 | 0.20 | 0.24 | 0.42 | 0.29 | 0.29 | 0.40 | 0.54 |
| Cardiology: Inv-Intvl | 0.58 | 0.38 | 0.42 | 0.19 | 0.25 | 0.38 | 0.49 | 0.31 |
| Cardiology: Noninvasive | 0.30 | 0.12 | 0.24 | 0.47 | 0.17 | 0.25 | 0.43 | 0.45 |
| Critical Care/Intensivist | 0.27 | 0.43 | 0.15 | 0.51 | 0.00 | 0.49 | 0.18 | 0.35 |
| Emergency Medicine | 0.15 | 0.51 | 0.10 | 0.13 | 0.13 | 0.32 | 0.27 | 0.23 |
| Family Practice (without OB) | 0.33 | 0.38 | 0.40 | 0.43 | 0.28 | 0.38 | 0.33 | 0.35 |
| Gastroenterology | 0.40 | 0.41 | 0.32 | 0.40 | 0.33 | 0.45 | 0.36 | 0.26 |
| Hematology/Oncology | 0.06 | 0.01 | 0.02 | 0.21 | 0.21 | 0.27 | 0.35 | 0.38 |
| Hospitalist: IM | 0.17 | 0.44 | 0.29 | 0.27 | 0.24 | 0.43 | 0.29 | 0.30 |
| Internal Medicine: General | 0.40 | 0.50 | 0.33 | 0.32 | 0.40 | 0.45 | 0.41 | 0.44 |
| Nephrology | 0.25 | 0.58 | 0.24 | 0.30 | 0.40 | 0.48 | 0.32 | 0.55 |
| Neurology | 0.39 | 0.46 | 0.39 | 0.38 | 0.43 | 0.44 | 0.28 | 0.54 |
| Ob/Gyn: General | 0.52 | 0.54 | 0.50 | 0.47 | 0.37 | 0.33 | 0.35 | 0.39 |
| Ob/Gyn: Gyn Only | 0.70 | 0.43 | 0.53 | 0.49 | 0.52 | 0.46 | 0.46 | 0.51 |
| Ophthalmology | 0.66 | 0.67 | 0.64 | 0.64 | 0.39 | 0.18 | 0.47 | 0.41 |
| Orthopedic Surgery: General | 0.58 | 0.58 | 0.52 | 0.56 | 0.31 | 0.31 | 0.34 | 0.33 |
| Otorhinolaryngology | 0.64 | 0.65 | 0.66 | 0.74 | 0.39 | 0.39 | 0.42 | 0.36 |
| Pediatrics: General | 0.40 | 0.53 | 0.51 | 0.40 | 0.47 | 0.51 | 0.40 | 0.37 |
| Psychiatry | 0.04 | 0.05 | 0.19 | 0.31 | 0.06 | 0.29 | 0.37 | 0.37 |
| Pulmonary Medicine | 0.42 | 0.41 | 0.31 | 0.38 | 0.27 | 0.41 | 0.38 | 0.53 |
| Radiation Oncology | 0.16 | 0.02 | 0.06 | 0.07 | 0.18 | 0.20 | 0.20 | 0.24 |
| Radiology: Diagnostic-Noninv | 0.04 | 0.33 | 0.09 | 0.03 | 0.07 | 0.19 | 0.02 | 0.12 |
| Surgery: Cardiovascular | 0.08 | 0.16 | 0.16 | 0.29 | 0.03 | 0.20 | 0.14 | 0.21 |
| Surgery: General | 0.40 | 0.49 | 0.40 | 0.40 | 0.37 | 0.41 | 0.36 | 0.46 |
| Surgery: Neurological | 0.62 | 0.69 | 0.60 | 0.51 | 0.46 | 0.44 | 0.56 | 0.37 |
| Surgery: Plastic | 0.56 | 0.51 | 0.58 | 0.49 | 0.11 | 0.24 | 0.33 | 0.34 |
| Surgery: Vascular | 0.24 | 0.29 | 0.18 | 0.14 | 0.15 | 0.16 | 0.08 | 0.33 |
| Urology | 0.52 | 0.61 | 0.40 | 0.50 | 0.49 | 0.31 | 0.50 | 0.48 |

The author notes, however, that the percentile matching technique often yields results that tend to display effective compensation rates consistent with MGMA's compensation by quartile of production data. The author frequently observes that the effective or calculated compensation rate yielded by dividing compensation reported at each major percentile, i.e., 25th, median, 75th, and 90th, by the productivity level at each corresponding percentile frequently declines from the 25th to the 90th percentile. This indicates the effective compensation per unit of productivity rate implied in the percentile matching technique also declines, when one observes this decline in the calculated rates. In short, the percentile matching technique, despite its statistically inadequacies, may yield results that parallel more statistically valid computations in certain cases. The author notes that further study would be needed to determine the overall frequency of this pattern and its relation to actual data.

Observing fundamental conceptual and statistical limitations of the percentile matching technique is not necessarily grounds for rejection of the method. Productivity clearly affects the level of revenue coming into a physician practice, and thereby, the level of net earnings available for physician compensation. Moreover, respondents to the surveys indicate that productivity is one of the key factors in establishing compensation for physicians.[19] In addition, statistical analysis of the MGMA data does show some level of correlation between productivity and compensation. Thus, there is support for the method. The precision and finality of its application to a subject physician, however, should not be viewed in an unqualified or uncritical manner. Recognition of its qualified validity as a method of applying physician compensation survey data to a subject employment arrangement should serve as a governor of uncritical deployment of the method in compensation valuation. Such recognition should also point appraisers away from overreliance or sole use of the method, where other techniques and the required data for these methods are available to the appraiser.

#### 4.5.2 Median Rate Technique

The median rate technique (MRT) uses the median compensation rate per unit of productivity from the physician compensation surveys and a physician's historical productivity level to establish a market-based level of compensation. To compute the guideline compensation level, the median compensation rate for a productivity measure is multiplied by the historical level of productivity. The median rate is used for two reasons. First, the median, as the middle value in a data set, can be viewed as a reasonable or representative proxy for a typical rate within the data set. In addition, some appraisers have observed that the median rate is often fairly consistent with the calculated compensation per unit of productivity rate each reported percentile in the survey data. In other words, compensation at a given percentile divided by the reported productivity level at the same percentile frequently approximates the median rate or is within a reasonable range of the median. The median rate, in such cases, can be viewed as the most explanatory rate for the reported range of compensation and productivity in the survey. Thus, use of the median compensation rate per unit of productivity for a given productivity metric is often employed as technique for establishing market-based compensation guidelines.

Use of the median rate, particularly the median compensation per wRVU rate, has unhappily become a valuation "rule of thumb" for employment compensation. Physician expectations are frequently set for compensation purposes at the median rate from the survey data, especially MGMA. For many in the physician marketplace, the median compensation per wRVU is a categorical imperative: All physicians should receive compensation consistent with their historical productivity multiplied by the median rate. Unfortunately, this market expectation is misinformed.

19 See the respondent profile sections of MGMA, AMGA, and SCA, where methods for compensated physicians are discussed.

Statistically speaking, the median rate represents the middle rate from the data set. Thus, approximately half of the respondents in the data received less than the median, and approximately half received more than the median rate. The claim that every physician should make at least the median compensation per wRVU is just not grounded in sound statistical reasoning and analytics.

MGMA's recent analysis and reporting of the compensation per wRVU rate by quartile production also- provides a reality check on the categorical and unqualified use of the median compensation per wRVU rate to establish FMV compensation for employment arrangements. As noted previously and as will be discussed in more detail in the following section, MGMA has presented data indicating that the compensation per wRVU rate declines as the productivity level of wRVUs increases, and vice versa. The reported median, therefore, may have limited validity at the upper and lower ends of the productivity scale.

Like the percentile matching technique, recognizing the limits and weaknesses of the median rate technique do not necessarily serve as reasons for wholesale jettisoning of the technique. Rather, such acknowledgment can serve to circumscribe, qualify, and limit the use of and reliance on the technique for establishing FMV compensation. Given the availability of survey data and the simplicity of calculation, the median rate technique can be easily calculated when valuing physician employment compensation and used for comparison purposes. Appraisers should be wary, however, of sole reliance, overreliance, and unqualified reliance on the method. As a practical matter, use of the median rate may be the most supportable when a physician's productivity approximates the median level of productivity.

#### 4.5.3 Compensation by Quartile of Production Technique

A new and noteworthy valuation technique has emerged with the publication of certain studies in MGMA that examines the compensation per wRVU rate of physicians by quartile of wRVU production.[20] The compensation by quartile of production technique (CQPT) uses certain median compensation to productivity rates by quartile of production for a given physician specialty to determine a guideline compensation level. The technique is applied as follows. First a physician's productivity level is benchmarked into the appropriate quartile of production based on the survey data for the relevant productivity measure. Next, the applicable median compensation to productivity rate for the quartile of production is multiplied by the physician's productivity level to compute a guideline level of compensation. In general, physician wRVU and professional collections are used as the measure of productivity for this technique.

20 These studies are published in the introductory sections of MGMA.

MGMA is currently the only survey providing these data, and it is available by special order. MGMA has, however, presented limited data from a specialty or two for compensation per wRVU in the "Key Findings" section of its survey in last few years. It has also discussed the implications of these data, noting that the compensation per wRVU generally decreases as productivity increases. Thus, physicians in the fourth or top quartile of productivity generally make less per unit of productivity than those in lower quartiles, although their total compensation is higher.

At its 2010 national conference, MGMA provided the participants with compensation per wRVU data by quartile of production for eight different specialties. Albert "Chip" Hutzler, JD/AVA, prepared a fascinating analysis of these data that is presented in Exhibit 4 and Exhibit 5. Exhibit 4 presents these data and compares them to the reported median for the specialty in the 2010 MGMA survey. Exhibit 5 graphically presents the percentage change between the quartile median and the overall median.[21]

**Exhibit 4. Compensation Per wRVU Data by Quartile of Production for Eight Different Specialties**

| | *Quartile Median* | | | | Overall Median | *Ratio of Quartile to Overall Median* | | | |
|---|---|---|---|---|---|---|---|---|---|
| | 1st | 2nd | 3rd | 4th | | 1st | 2nd | 3rd | 4th |
| Cardiology: Noninvasive | $69.74 | $56.72 | $53.84 | $47.82 | $53.54 | 130.3% | 105.9% | 100.6% | 89.3% |
| Family Practice (without OB) | 45.76 | 39.43 | 36.79 | 36.44 | 39.13 | 116.9 | 100.8 | 94.0 | 93.1 |
| Gastroenterology | 57.37 | 56.10 | 53.40 | 49.28 | 53.93 | 106.4 | 104.0 | 99.0 | 91.4 |
| Internal Medicine: General | 48.91 | 41.85 | 41.67 | 39.08 | 42.50 | 115.1 | 98.5 | 98.1 | 92.0 |
| Obstetrics/Gynecology: General | 49.55 | 42.77 | 41.96 | 41.08 | 43.54 | 113.8 | 98.2 | 96.4 | 94.3 |
| Orthopedic Surgery: General | 67.78 | 59.74 | 58.11 | 55.90 | 60.05 | 112.9 | 99.5 | 96.8 | 93.1 |
| Pediatrics: General | 43.64 | 38.74 | 37.66 | 36.81 | 38.90 | 112.2 | 99.6 | 96.8 | 94.6 |
| Surgery: General | 58.79 | 49.72 | 49.00 | 45.24 | 50.10 | 117.3 | 99.2 | 97.8 | 90.3 |

**Exhibit 5. Compensation Per wRVU—Percentage Difference Between Quartile Median and Overall Median**

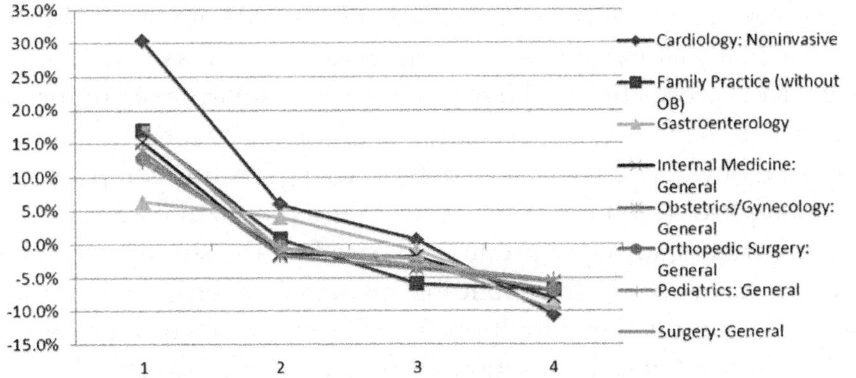


21 My thanks to Chip Hutzler and David Sands of HealthCare Appraisers for the development and preparation of Exhibits 4 and 5.

What is fascinating about the data presented in Exhibits 4 and 5 is the similar patterns in the relationship between the median by quartile to the overall reported median. The author notes that he has observed additional compensation by quartile of production data from MGMA for additional specialties and for the compensation-to-professional-collections ratio. A similar pattern in the compensation per wRVU by quartile was observed for the additional specialties. In the compensation-to-professional-collections ratio data by quartile of production, a comparable pattern was observed in which the ratio was higher for physicians in the first quartile of professional collections production than the reported overall median and then declined throughout the remaining three quartiles of production. A wider variation in the percentage of change between the quartile median and the overall median was observed, however, among the various specialties for these productivity measures.

The appeal and strength of the compensation by quartile of production technique is that it is based on the actual correlation of compensation and productivity within the data. To calculate the median by quartile of production, MGMA segregates individual respondents into quartiles based on their production and then computes the compensation to productivity rate for the respondents in each quartile to derive a median for the quartile. Unlike the percentile matching technique, which assumes that the compensation at a given percentile correlates with the production at the same percentile, these data are based on the actual compensation of respondents within a quartile of production.

In evaluating the CQPT, one should not fail to understand the nature of the data used in the method. The CQPT uses a median for the quartile; the method does not indicate that there are physicians not making more or less than the median for the quartile. Thus, the CQPT should not be taken as a precise value applicable to any physician in the quartile. Once again, there is wider variability in the rates for all respondents within a quartile of production than is indicated by sole consideration of the median rate. A single compensation rate per unit of productivity measure appears to be inadequate to explain the full range of compensation outcomes for physicians. While the CQPT may have more statistical validity and afford greater applicability to varying ranges of productivity, it is not intended to produce an exact and precise determination of market-based compensation. Rather, it provides an indication based on the median for the quartile.

Another area for evaluating the CQPT is analyzing the declining pattern in the compensation by quartile of production data. This pattern is undoubtedly striking and is counterintuitive to many in the healthcare industry. Some would suppose that the compensation rate per wRVU, for example, would increase as wRVUs increase, because the fixed costs of a physician would be spread over a larger volume level, thereby increasing the margin per wRVU. Two characteristics observed in the physician practice marketplace may be conjectured to provide some explanation for this declining compensation rate per unit of productivity phenomenon. First, many physicians are paid using base salaries or base compensation amounts that may not correlate with their productivity. Newly hired physicians, for example, may take a few years to ramp up their productivity to a level commensurate with the compensation level at which they are paid. Physicians in smaller population areas and lower patient volumes may be paid at rates more commensurate with larger markets and higher patient demand to retain them in the community. It is also possible that some physicians are in groups with highly favorable commercial payer contracts and payer mixes, whereby they are able to attain relatively higher revenue levels per wRVU with lower volumes levels, resulting in higher compensation per wRVU.

With respect to highly producing physicians receiving a lower compensation rate per unit, one potential explanation is that key physician practice costs are not fixed over the horizon of the 25th to 90th percentiles of productivity. Rather, practice costs relate to volumes in a step-cost manner, as discussed in Part I. Costs, such as staffing and space, remain fixed up to a certain level of volume at which the practice must expand its facilities and staffing to accommodate the increased patient demand. Such expansion of resources may be not achievable or practicable in small increments, e.g., hiring a 0.25 FTE for a specific function or leasing an extra 500 square feet of adjacent space. MGMA studies of highly productive practices over the years have frequently noted higher costs per unit of service in many of these practices, pointing to the "stair step" characteristics of many practice costs.[22]

While various causes may be conjectured to explain this phenomenon, further study and analysis with the data are surely warranted.

#### 4.5.4 Workload and Hourly Techniques

Another technique for applying physician compensation survey data to a subject employment arrangement focuses on the workload associated with the arrangement in terms of hours worked or on a comparable FTE level. In general, workload and hourly rate techniques use survey data and estimates of annual hours to derive guideline hourly rates. These guideline hourly rates are then applied to shifts or annual hours required by the terms of a subject physician employment arrangement to determine an appropriate level of compensation for the arrangement. As discussed previously,

22 I am thankful to my colleague Dana Boatman, a long-time practice manager and MGMA member, for sharing this insight with me.

this method is highly relevant when valuing employment arrangements for hospital-based physicians in which shifts or annual hours worked may be the primary or critical definition of productivity.

Workload techniques may also be used to assess or adjust salary or base compensation levels when the work requirements of the subject arrangement appear to be above or below market norms for a given specialty. For example, an employment arrangement may provide a physician with eight weeks of leave, including continuing medical education (CME) days. If survey or other market data indicate that the norm for the specialty is five weeks of leave, the appraiser may conclude that the subject arrangement requires a reduced workload in comparison to the market data. As a result, the appraiser will reduce the compensation for the arrangement, when market data from physicians with five weeks of leave or less are used to establish the level of pay for the position. Likewise, a proposed employment agreement requiring 2,400 annual working hours may represent an above-market level of hours for a specialty. The appraiser may increase the compensation level, where the survey data are based on physicians working annual hours substantially below the subject arrangement.

The key factor or analysis point in applying a workload valuation technique is the selection of the annual hours or weeks worked per year that is applied or correlated with survey data to establish an hourly pay rate or the number of weeks of worked expected for a given compensation level. The difficulty for the appraiser in selecting these inputs to the valuation process is the dearth of available data on annual work hours and weeks worked per year. Up until the last couple of survey years, MGMA and SCA reported some data that could be used to make such estimates. SCA had been reporting annual hours by specialty, while MGMA reported weeks worked per year and hours worked per week by specialty. The only metric appearing in the current surveys is MGMA's weeks worked per year.[23]

Exhibit 6 illustrates the potential range of annual hours that can be worked by physicians, based on varying weeks worked and hours worked per week. The level of assumed annual hours is not without consequence for the valuation analysis, since the lower the annual hours, the higher the hourly rate and vice versa.

23 Based on the 2010 MGMA and SCA surveys as well as the 2011 MGMA survey. It should be noted that these data was often reported with few respondents and may not have been meaningful. The frequent use of 40 hours per week or 2,000 hours per year across numerous specialties seemed to indicate respondents were reporting such hours on a pro forma basis.

**Exhibit 6. Annual Hours Worked**

| Weeks Worked per Year | *Weekly Work Hours* | | | | |
|---|---|---|---|---|---|
| | **35** | **40** | **45** | **50** | **55** |
| 50 | 1,750 | 2,000 | 2,250 | 2,500 | 2,750 |
| 49 | 1,715 | 1,960 | 2,205 | 2,450 | 2,695 |
| 48 | 1,680 | 1,920 | 2,160 | 2,400 | 2,640 |
| 47 | 1,645 | 1,880 | 2,115 | 2,350 | 2,585 |
| 46 | 1,610 | 1,840 | 2,070 | 2,300 | 2,530 |
| 45 | 1,575 | 1,800 | 2,025 | 2,250 | 2,475 |
| 44 | 1,540 | 1,760 | 1,980 | 2,200 | 2,420 |

A second challenge in applying workload appraisal techniques is how estimates of annual hours or weeks worked per year should be related to compensation levels reported at the various percentiles in the surveys. Should a normalized or constant number of annual hours or weeks worked per year be used as the divisor for all reported percentiles or should varying levels be used? For example, an appraiser may attempt to rationalize or normalize the compensation data and estimates of annual hours by assuming that compensation levels tend to increase with higher annual hours. Such an assumption can be reflective of certain market realities, where physicians in a fee-for-service reimbursement environment or in productivity-based compensation models can earn more by working longer hours and performing more procedures. To implement this approach, the appraiser associates higher estimated annual hours with higher levels of compensation in the surveys and vice versa. Yet, one cannot be assured of such correlation in the data or meaningful outcomes in utilizing this approach.[24] Another potential assumption is that hourly rates are a function of physician productivity and efficiency within a normalized working year. Higher hourly rates should reflect greater productivity and efficiency achieved per working hour. To utilize this assumption, the appraiser selects a normalized workload of annual hours and divides it into selected compensation levels to derive a range of hourly rates.

In summary, application of workload-based valuation techniques will require appraisers to make estimates, judgments, and assumptions about workload levels and their relation to reported compensation levels in the survey data. Unfortunately, minimal market data are available for physician workloads, and even less data showing the

24 The author recounts his attempt at such correlation using the formerly available workload data. The results did not appear to be meaningful. The use of increasing annual hours divided into reported percentiles of compensation resulted in a wide array of randomly fluctuating hourly rates from percentile to percentile.

relationship between compensation levels and annual hours worked. Given this lack of data and the need for hourly compensation rates in the marketplace, appraisers should strive to make the most of any data that are available and utilize the most supportable estimates and assumptions possible.

#### 4.5.5 Independent Criteria Techniques

In certain circumstances, an appraiser may need to develop criteria independently of the survey data that are then used to apply survey compensation data to a subject physician. The criteria are independent of the survey data in that such criteria are not included in the various reported metrics of the surveys. They are developed and assessed by the appraiser using informed, but subjective judgment. In some cases, alternative data sources may be found to support the criteria as important factors in the determination of physician compensation. Yet, the correlation of these factors with specific percentiles or ranges from the survey data is based on informed but nonetheless subjective judgment on the part of the appraiser.

Because they involve subjective judgment, the use of such methods should only be used when necessitated by a valuation engagement where more objective techniques are not available due to data limitations or unique facts and circumstances rendering alternative methods less relevant and applicable to the subject arrangement. The appraiser should make a concerted effort to document and support the assumptions, estimates, judgments, and reasoning entailed in such subjective techniques. Use of scoring or ratings for various factors used in the judgment process can be a productive way to apply and relate the survey data to the subject arrangement. Such scorings or ratings do not necessarily need to result in a mathematic outcome; they can be used merely to document and present the thought process informing the judgment of the appraiser.

The use of independent criteria techniques based on subjective professional judgments may be analogous to the development of specific company risk premiums in the cost of capital calculation in business valuation. In preparing a cost of capital rate, the appraiser formulates a series of factors that can affect the subject company's risk profile relative to the market and industry and then evaluates the subject using these criteria. The process results in a specific risk premium based on the informed, but subjective judgment of the appraiser. Some appraisers will actually create a scoring formula that assigns a certain number of basis points to the specific company risk premium. Whatever approach is used, the appraiser is expected to support and defend the specific risk premium, notwithstanding the fact that it is ultimately based on professional and informed, but subjective judgment.

Appraisers, who by necessity, utilize subjective valuation techniques in applying the physician compensation survey data to subject employment arrangements should likewise be able to support and defend such methods. The methods should be grounded, to the extent possible, in facts, evidence, research, sound valuation reasoning, and a rigorous understanding of the physician marketplace and the fundamental economics of physician practices. The mere assertion of criteria or relationships between factors and the survey data without clearly articulated support and defense does not constitute the professional practice of appraisal. Users of valuation services should not accept work product that does not meet such professional standards.

### *4.6 Techniques for Academic, Administrative, and Executive Positions*

As discussed previously, academic, administrative, and executive physician services generally relate to position or job title and to other specific criteria or factors. The techniques utilized for these types of physician services in employment arrangements generally focus on matching the subject position and job duties to market survey data for comparable positions. Where compensation survey data are available based on various characteristics of the respondents to the survey, such as organizational size or type, geographic region, compensation structure, and the like, additional factors are considered in the matching process by which the appraiser looks for comparable arrangements in the marketplace.

The key to such matching is comparability to the greatest extent possible given the available breakdowns in the data. Once the appraiser has selected the comparable reference data from the surveys, the next step in the process is selecting the range of compensation from the reported percentiles in a survey that are applicable to the subject physician and arrangement. The appraiser should first look to available data within the survey for factors and techniques to select the applicable range. When such data are not available, the appraiser should consider the use of independent criteria techniques that attempt to relate factors and considerations relative to the subject physician and arrangement to the various percentiles of reported compensation. Selection of an appropriate range of compensation should be based on factors that can be articulated and defended by the appraiser.

## 5.0 Critical Considerations in Using the Physician Compensation Surveys for the Market Approach

The market approach and the use of the physician compensation surveys are, by far, the most commonly used approaches for establishing physician compensation in employment arrangements. For many involved in physician employment deals, they are the only approaches considered. Other approaches, such as the cost and income, are considered foreign and irrelevant to the valuation process. The fundamental question for professional appraisers is whether this sole reliance on the market approach is consistent with the valuation body of knowledge and sound valuation practice. The answer to that question, from a methodological standpoint, is fairly clear: The valuation body of knowledge does not summarily privilege the market approach over and against the other approaches. Rather, it calls for consideration of all three approaches and for the application of methods that are relevant to the valuation of the subject transaction and for which there are reliable and available data. The following sections probe some of the implicit assumptions made about the market data and the market approach in the current healthcare marketplace. The question for professional appraisers is whether these assumptions are valid enough to warrant the market-approach-only orientation that is ubiquitous in the physician employment marketplace.

### 5.1 Understanding the Implications of Using Total Cash Compensation

Many players in the healthcare marketplace commonly mistake the physician compensation surveys to reflect the compensation for clinical patient care services only. As discussed previously, the reality is that the physician compensation surveys generally define physician compensation as total cash compensation from all sources. This definition, therefore, can encompass compensation received not only from clinical patient care services, but also from other types of services as well. It would include compensation from call coverage, medical directorships, clinical co-management arrangements, research, expert witness fees, and other such sources. Compensation may also include net profits earned from nonphysician providers or preferential distributions paid to senior physicians in a group. Earnings from technical services may also be included. As discussed in Part I, a portion of the compensation earned by shareholders or owner-physicians in physician-owned groups can represent owner compensation or a return on investment in the practice.

Recognition of the diversity of sources or types of services contributing to compensation reported in total cash compensation can affect the comparability of survey compensation data under the market approach for employment agreements. To determine comparability, the appraiser must match the services included in the scope of the subject employment arrangement to the scope of services entailed in the survey data. Yet, compensation by type of service or income source is not detailed in the compensation survey data. Thus, the appraiser may not be assured of full or exact comparability between the scope of services included in the subject arrangement and the scope of services provided by the respondents reporting compensation in the surveys. *The inability to fully determine the comparability of a subject arrangement and the survey data in terms of the scope of services represents a notable limitation and weakness in using the market survey data for valuing physician employment.*

One might argue that this limitation on ascertaining the comparability of services only relates to marginal services. The level of compensation for various nonclinical services is not material relative to the total compensation received for patient-care services, given the number of respondents for a specialty in the survey data. In effect, the impact of additional services provided over and above patient care services is diluted with large respondent sizes. Thus, the issue of comparability is merely theoretical, and not a realistic or substantial consideration. This objection certainly has credibility with respect to certain forms of compensation. For example, paid medical directorships at hospitals are common in the healthcare marketplace, but the number of physicians providing these services as a percentage of total physicians is generally small. Expert witness fees or honoraria are also infrequent in the typical physician practice.

There are other nonclinical services, however, where the frequency of such services is not so easily determined, given current market trends. Compensated hospital call coverage is becoming more common in the marketplace and may represent the prevailing staffing model for hospital coverage in many markets. For certain physician specialties, compensation from hospital call coverage can be material relative to the compensation from clinical services. MGMA reports that roughly 75% of the physicians reported in the 2010 and 2011 surveys had on-call duties.[25] Unfortunately, MGMA did not indicate whether such duties were compensated or not. In the 2010 survey, however, MGMA reported significantly higher compensation for specialty care physicians with on-call duties.[26]

The impact of owner compensation may be a diminishing factor in future surveys as the trend toward hospital and health system employment continues in the current round of the healthcare provider consolidation. The percentage of physicians from physician-owned groups has been declining in MGMA and AGMA over the past few years. In addition, owner compensation is often most significant for specialties that are technology-driven or capital-intensive, such as cardiology or radiation oncology. Thus, owner compensation may not warrant significant consideration for all specialties in all cases.

One form of compensation to watch in the next few years is compensation from clinical co-management or service line management agreements. The compensation from such arrangements can be significant. Since compensation for such services was paid through separate or joint venture entities in the initial market iterations of co-management models, such compensation was most likely paid to individual physicians outside of physician

25 See Table 26. "On-Call Duties" from the "Demographics—Medical Practice" section.
26 Page 9 of "Key Findings" section.

practices. Thus, its impact on compensation in the surveys may have been negligible. Trends in co-management agreements, however, are heading toward inclusion of such services as part of physician employment arrangements with hospitals under the new nomenclature of service line management services. This trend may have a significant impact on compensation in the future.

Since the compensation surveys do not report compensation by source or service, the appraiser may be put in the position of making informed judgments or assumptions about what is and is not included in market compensation data or to what extent it is included. For making such determinations, it is essential to know practice norms and trends for a specialty in terms of the expected mix of services and sources for compensation. While one can point to the potential compensation impact of various types of prevalent nonclinical services, quantifying and adjusting the survey data for such compensation can be a highly difficult task. Many variables would need to be determined to attempt to parse the compensation survey data or to adjust it. Thus, it may not be practicable to attempt such quantification and adjustment.

Despite the difficulties in quantitative analysis relative to the issue of compensation from nonclinical services, an appraiser should be aware of such sources of compensation when applying the physician compensation survey data to a subject employment arrangement. This recognition should be factored into the interpretation and analysis of indications of value derived from market approach techniques and in the broader valuation synthesis of the cost, market, and income approaches for a subject employment arrangement. In summary, a qualitative assessment should be included in the valuation process to account for the various forms of compensation included in the survey data.

### *5.2 Do the Surveys Reflect Local Market Conditions?*

Users of the physician compensation surveys tend to assume that national or regional market survey data are readily applicable or comparable to their local market. Indeed, the penchant for using the median compensation per wRVU as a universal benchmark for FMV physician compensation implies the notion that local market conditions, and indeed, specific physician practice patterns and habits, have no material effect on physician compensation. For those that do recognize the impact of local market conditions on physician compensation, regional or state data are often used as a better approximation of local market conditions. Regional data are particularly used since such data are usually available with significant respondent sizes. Moreover, the surveys often publish summaries indicating material differences in regional compensation. Users frequently take these regional analyses and trends to be applicable to their local market.

In Part I, the findings of a recent study were discussed. This study noted wide variability of reimbursement across and within markets for commercial payers.[27] As further discussed in Part I, these findings were included in a model for a hypothetical cardiology group, showing the impact on compensation for these variations in commercial reimbursement. A similar analysis had been prepared by Dietrich and Anderson in 2008. There are two important implications of these various studies for appraisers using physician compensation survey data. First, it is unlikely that the survey data can be applied with any meaningful degree of precision to reflect the dynamics of any one particular market. Variations across the country, region, or even within a state may not allow a reasonable level of specificity to a given market.[28] With regard to state data, there is often a presumption that such data are reflective of the local market. This presumption is not always well-founded. In Texas, for example, there is a material difference in physician reimbursement between Houston and the Dallas-Fort Worth area.[29] There is also a significant variance between reimbursement levels in certain Northern California markets from Southern California.[30] The markets reflected in the survey data represent those of the respondents. Since the respondents are not included based on statistically valid sampling techniques and since the surveys do not report data by individual market, it is indeterminate as to what markets are represented in the survey data.

More importantly, wide variations within a market are possible with respect to commercial payer rates. The HSC study indicated that premium rates were achievable by groups with bargaining power based on size and specialty. *A potential bias may exist in the survey data here.* As discussed in previous sections, the survey respondents are overwhelmingly from large groups, mostly multispecialty groups. Such groups tend to have greater bargaining power within local markets. Thus, the surveys are most likely representative of groups with significant bargaining power in local markets. Where this is the case, the physician compensation for such groups would tend to reflect higher rates of reimbursement than may be achievable by smaller groups in the marketplace. Since large groups are only a small percentage of the physician marketplace, smaller groups and lower reimbursement levels would be the expected norm in most markets. In summary, the tendency of the surveys may be to reflect premium market compensation.

This potential tendency, together with the inability to reflect local market conditions adequately, should give pause to appraisers using the survey data to establish physician

27 See *Wide Variation in Hospital and Physician Payment Rates Evidence of Provider Market Power*, Research Brief, No. 16, November 2010. Center for Studying Health System Change. www.hschange.org.

28 See Chapter 3 of this book, "Healthcare Market Structure and Its Implication for Valuation of Privately Held Provider Entities—An Empirical Analysis," for a detailed analysis of the impact of local market conditions.

29 Based on the author's experience in both markets and on information provided by parties with significant knowledge of these markets.

30 As indicated in the HSC data and based on the author's experience.

compensation levels in employment arrangements. The appraiser should consider the ambiguities and uncertainties of the market data with respect to its relation and reflection of local market dynamics. In addition, the appraiser should consider whether the survey data tend to reflect premium compensation levels that may not be applicable for a given subject physician or practice.

### *5.3 Evaluating the Relationship Between Productivity and Compensation*

A central assumption underlying the exclusive use of the market approach for employment compensation is the belief that productivity is or should be the central, if not *the* critical, factor in establishing FMV physician compensation for clinical services. This belief, moreover, has tended to hold wRVUs as the definitive measure of physician productivity. These assumptions are implicit in one of the most popular methods of establishing market compensation: matching compensation to benchmarked wRVUs. The critical question for the appraiser is: How valid are these assumptions?

From the analysis dealing with the impact of market reimbursement rates on compensation, it should be readily apparent that professional collections are the preferable or more meaningful market indicator for compensation. Professional collections, when such collections are normalized, reflect the dollar value paid for physician productivity. Thus, such payments can indicate key aspects of the local market's dynamics for physician services. Since there is a critical link between the professional component of clinical procedures and wRVUs, professional collections contain information about the physician's work efforts coupled with the local value placed on those efforts. They surpass wRVUs in terms of accounting for a broader mix of compensation factors.

Earlier sections have also shown that compensation and productivity, defined in terms of wRVUs and PCs, have a weak level of correlation in the MGMA data using regression analysis. Use of these productivity measures, especially wRVUs on a solitary basis, seems overly simplistic for addressing all the fundamental economic variables in a physician practice. Physician productivity measures do not address three key factors in generating available earnings for physician compensation in a doctor practice:

1. Level of ancillary services or technical component earnings for the practice.

2. Level of other services provided by the practice, such as compensated call coverage, medical directorships, research, interpretation services for other healthcare providers, and clinical co-management agreements.

3. Cost structure and overhead levels for the practice.

All physicians of a given specialty are not created equal with respect to these factors, nor do they practice equally with respect to these areas. Physician practices can vary widely with regard to each other. One inherent limitation of the physician compensation surveys is that data on these key factors are generally not collected and reported.[31] As a result, use of the compensation surveys under the market approach does not account for all key variables in the economic productivity of a physician or practice, viewed from a comprehensive perspective. The scope of data in the physician compensation surveys lead to a narrow and limited analysis of physician compensation for employment services from a comprehensive economic and valuation perspective.

## 6.0 Determining FMV Compensation Under the Market Approach

### *6.1 Using Multiple Methods, Surveys and Matching Criteria as a Best Practice*

As discussed above, multiple valuation techniques and multiple survey data sources are available to appraisers for determining market-based employment compensation. The case for using multiple methods in the market approach is based on the recognition that each method has its relative strengths and weakness. No single appraisal technique is perfect. Often, a valuation method takes into account a single factor relative to the issue of comparability between the market data and the subject. A singular criterion or consideration, however, is often not fully indicative of the complexity of the physician marketplace relative to compensation. One approach for mitigating the limitations of individual techniques is to use multiple methods and productivity measures. By doing so, a variety of factors and relationships between the subject and the market data are considered in the valuation process. The result of using multiple methods and measures is generally a more balanced and supportable appraisal analysis. One might use this analogy: Each strand of a rope, on its own, may be relatively weak, but bound together, the various strands create strength. This same logic applies to the use of multiple valuation methods as well as multiple criteria or productivity measures for determining comparability.

The use of multiple surveys can also yield a more balanced and supportable analysis. First, use of multiple surveys affords a larger number of reference points in the marketplace. Second, use of multiple surveys can expand the market spectrum considered with respect to the characteristics of the respondents in the data. Wider geographic coverage and diversity of practice types and settings can result from this practice. As

31 The MGMA *Cost Survey* does report information on many of these additional factors. It, however, does not report compensation and productivity data on individual physicians. It reports all data at the collective group practice level, combining productivity from physicians and nonphysician providers. Such collective reporting of data limits the use of the *Cost Survey* for valuing many physician compensation arrangements.

has been discussed previously, each survey tends to represent a segment of the physician marketplace. Using more than one survey is one way to include more market segments in the analysis. It should be noted, however, that the inclusion of more segments may not create a total market data reference set that is reflective of the total physician marketplace or of the relevant marketplace for the subject. Third, use of multiple surveys can serve to dilute or mitigate against anomalies that can sometimes arise in a survey for a particular specialty.

### *6.2 Evaluating the Use of Specific Appraisal Tools and Resources*

That the use of multiple methods, surveys, and comparability measures is a best practice does not mean that an appraiser should summarily use every possible tool and resource in a valuation assignment. Consideration of the relevance and applicability of each tool is still a critical part of the appraisal process. For both practical as well as sound methodologically reasons, an appraiser should go through a systematic process of evaluating the potential tools available for determining FMV compensation for a subject employment arrangement. Based on this assessment, specific methods, surveys, and comparability measures are selected for application in the valuation.

The selection of the relevant and applicable tools for an employment valuation should be based on consideration of various factors related to the subject and the available tools. As noted earlier, employment arrangements should be distinguished between clinical, academic, administrative, and executive services. Different surveys and measures of comparability are relevant for each type of service. When evaluating employment arrangements for clinical services, there are several key factors and criteria one should consider in the selection process. Evaluating these factors relative to valuation resources is often a dynamic process in which the appraiser selects a specific combination of tools based on their combined applicability to the subject. The following subsections outline many of the key considerations in selecting tools.

#### Productivity Data

As discussed previously in Part I, the operating environment and fundamental economics of office-based physicians and hospital-based physicians can be quite different. Hence, the relevant comparability measures, i.e., the definitions of productivity, are often different for physicians in each practice-setting type. The productivity measures used generally determine the available valuation techniques. They can also affect the selection of relevant surveys. For example, some of the surveys do not include physician productivity data on wRVUs or professional collections. Thus, these surveys cannot be readily used for the percentile matching technique based on these metrics. On the other hand, if one is using annual hours as the definition of productivity and assuming 2,000 or 2,080 annual hours as an assumption derived independently of the survey data, one could use all the physician compensation surveys in determining FMV hourly rates. In this case, a survey is not excluded by virtue of not having relevant data for the productivity measure. This measure was independently derived and is applied on a normalizing basis to all market data.

#### Practice Profile and Characteristics

An assignment to value a large multispecialty group may warrant exclusive use of MGMA and AMGA because such surveys are representative of large groups. For valuing compensation in an academic-affiliated group, it may be advisable to exclude MGMA and AMGA and use SCA and other more academically represented surveys.

#### Compensation Structure

Valuation assignments to appraise group-level compensation plans may allow consideration of the MGMA *Cost Survey* data. The group-level compensation formula may be consistent with various compensation-related metrics reported in this survey. AMGA also provides group-level metrics that may be applicable for group-level models in multispecialty groups. It should be noted that the contractual use of a specific metric for compensation in a subject arrangement, such as compensation per wRVU, does not preclude the use of other metrics in applying the market approach. As will be discussed later in Part V, the outcomes of valuation methods can be converted into various compensation formulas and structures. Thus, the contractual compensation formula does not necessarily determine the productivity or comparability measures used in the market approach. For example, if the employment agreement calls for compensation based on a set rate per wRVU, it does not preclude the appraisers from using professional collections as the measure of productivity for application of a given valuation technique. Rather, the valuation indications from methods based on professional collections can be used to establish a compensation per wRVU rate.

#### Data Concerns

Occasionally, one observes anomalies in the survey data. Thus, a best practice is to examine the survey data before using them. If such anomalies are observed, one may choose to exclude a survey or significantly reduce its impact on the valuation based on its relative weighting in the synthesis process. (The use of weighting techniques is discussed in further detail in Part V.) One might also elect to exclude or reduce the weighting on a survey that the appraiser considers to be outdated. As noted previously, the surveys represent data from a prior year; they are published several months after the end of the data year reported. Sometimes, certain surveys are not published for nearly a year after the year for which they publish data. In such circumstances, the current version of a survey may represent data that are nearly two years old. An appraiser may conclude that data from the survey should be excluded or weighted lower when current or future market conditions are thought to be materially different than the year for which data are reported.

#### Available and Relevant Data Considerations

In certain circumstances, data for a subject physician or employment arrangement may not be available. Moreover, available data may not be particularly meaningful or applicable relative to the subject employment arrangement. Examples of such circumstances may include the following, although this listing should not be construed as comprehensive:

- A physician seeking to exit a current employment or work situation may not be able to provide historical productivity data.
- Physicians coming out of residency, fellowship, or other training programs may not have productivity data or productivity data that is relevant or meaningful for a full-time private practice physician.
- A physician coming out of an academic setting may be in a similar position with respect to historical data.
- The historical productivity of a physician moving out of one service market into another may not be indicative of the physician's future productivity. If the physician was in a small, rural market with limited demand for services, the historical productivity may not reflect the physician's skill. In addition, professional collections in one market may not be indicative of productivity in another market.

In circumstances such as these, the appraiser is necessarily limited in terms of the productivity measures, valuation methods, and relevant surveys applicable to the subject physician and arrangement. The appraiser is left with implementing those methods that are available, given the data.

There is one practice tendency in valuation assignments of this type that appraisers should reconsider and view with a critical eye. As discussed previously, there is a tendency to use the median from the surveys representing full-time clinically practicing physicians as the universal benchmark for FMV compensation. The median is often considered to be the best estimate of what a newly hired physician would receive or expect in the marketplace. Essentially, the median compensation level has become a valuation "rule of thumb" for hiring physicians and is essentially treated as a valuation floor for compensation. Examination of the actual recruiting data, however, does not necessarily validate this assumption. A more supportable position with respect to establishing compensation for physicians with little available data is to reference the placement surveys as part of the valuation process.[32] In addition, appraisers should be careful in using a "rule of thumb" as an actual valuation method, as frequently noted in the business valuation body knowledge.

### *6.3 Benchmarking Multiple Metrics as an Indispensable Tool for the Market Approach*

Throughout Part II, questions regarding the comparability of the market survey data to the broad spectrum of physician practices and physicians have been raised in a general manner. One tool for assessing individual comparability between the subject practice or physician and the survey data is the benchmarking of key metrics for the subject against the survey data. By observing benchmarking outcomes and, more importantly, examining such outcomes in tandem, an appraiser can begin to formulate a clearer picture of the comparability of the subject to the data. Once such comparability is examined, the appraiser is in a better position to evaluate the outcomes of the various survey-based valuation techniques under the market approach.

The metrics selected for benchmarking should relate to fundamental productivity and compensation indices. When using MGMA, AGMA, and SCA, the following metrics can be essential to the benchmarking analysis:

1. Productivity: wRVUs, professional collections, and professional collections per wRVU.[33]
2. Compensation: compensation, compensation per wRVU, and the compensation-to-professional-collections ratio.

The benchmarking analysis consists of comparing the subject physician's historical data against the survey data by calculating the subject's approximate percentile ranking for each metric in a given survey. Next, the appraiser compares the percentile rankings across all metrics to examine the relationships among the benchmarking outcomes, looking for variances in productivity and compensation rankings. Such variances can reflect areas in which the subject is and is not comparable to the surveys. For example, do wRVUs and professional collections benchmark differently? Does the benchmarking of professional collections per wRVU help explain this difference? Which productivity measure benchmarks more closely with the percentile ranking of the subject's historical compensation? Examination of such questions can aid the appraiser in assessing comparability of the subject to the survey data and in evaluating the various valuation methods that are based on this data.

32 It is acknowledged that the placement surveys often have a limited number of respondents. Referencing such data in the valuation process, however, is preferable to relying on the median "rule of thumb" as a valuation technique. The median is the middle value in the data set. By definition, it is not a floor.

33 Unfortunately, AMGA does not currently report professional collections per wRVU.

The MGMA, AMGA, and SCA surveys do not include relevant data with regard to certain key factors that can materially affect physician compensation. Overhead levels, ancillary earnings, and other service revenues are data categories that are not collected or reported by these surveys at the physician-specialty level.[34] In many ways, these missing categories of data impede the level of benchmarking that is needed to determine comparability comprehensively. Such supplemental data would also help appraisers better understand the economics of the respondents to whom the subject is being compared and whose compensation levels are being used to establish market-based compensation. Physicians and physician practices are not all equal with respect to these factors.

Use of the MGMA *Cost Survey* can be helpful for benchmarking analysis. Cost, benefits, total revenue, and tRVU metrics can provide useful measures for comparison, along with wRVUs and compensation. Payer mix and staffing ratio benchmarking is also helpful. Even when the *Cost Survey* is not used in a valuation method, benchmarking an array of metrics for the subject physician or practice using it can be useful as part of the valuation process. Such analysis is also useful in applying the cost and income approaches (discussed further in Part IV).

#### *6.4 Critical Use of the Physician Compensation Surveys*

Critical issues and considerations have been raised in the foregoing analysis and discussion of market approach valuation techniques using the physician compensation surveys. These considerations have been raised as part of an examination of the sole use of the market approach using the surveys in valuation practice. What should be apparent from the above discussion of the issue is that exclusive and uncritical use of the market surveys for valuation purposes is beset with imprecision, difficulties, and fundamental limitations. These difficulties and limitations relate to the issue of the comparability of the survey data to specific subject physicians and proposed employment arrangements as well as to the question of the correlation between compensation and physician productivity measures, narrowly defined.

The identification and examination of the relative limitations of the market approach for valuing physician employment compensation is not necessarily an impediment to the use of the approach. Rather, such considerations serve as a cautionary finding relative to the *exclusive* and *uncritical* use of market survey data in establishing physician compensation. In addition, recognition of these issues should affect the interpretation, assessment, and weighting of the outcomes from valuation techniques that rely on the compensation survey market data. It also signals the need for serious consideration of

34 AMGA does provide some data relative to these categories at the group level. MGMA provides an overview of the level of ancillary revenues for all respondents in its introductory practice profile section.

the cost and income approaches in the valuation process. Comparing the indications of value under the market approach with the results of cost and income approaches mitigates the inherent imprecision that arises from use of the market data for establishing physician compensation in employment arrangements. Finally, identifying and critically evaluating relative strengths and weaknesses of valuation data and methods represent the essence of the trade and practice of appraisal! Such evaluation is the kind of professional diligence and analysis that should be expected of trained and skilled appraisal professionals.

Practical considerations should also be noted relative to the market approach and physician compensation survey data. One reason for continuing to use market survey data, however imperfect or unrepresentative such data are relative to the entirety of the physician marketplace, is that the physician compensation surveys are the only readily and publicly available source of market data to use in the valuation process. Practically speaking, the market approach would not be available to appraisers in most cases were it not for the market survey data. It should also be noted that, in certain cases, no other methods and data may be available to an appraiser, save the market approach based on the compensation surveys. When used, however, the market approach should be applied with circumspection and awareness relative to its limitations. Moreover, it should also be noted that areas of potential imprecision and difficulty in the market survey data may not be applicable in every valuation assignment. The critical objections to the application of the survey data should not be taken as categorical. Rather, the claim is that general trends and tendencies of the survey data can make their application to specific employment arrangements and physicians limited and qualified. One should therefore use the market approach based on the surveys, but not to the exclusion of other approaches.

# PART IV. THE COST AND INCOME APPROACHES

## 1.0 Earnings-Based Compensation for Professional Practices

### *1.1 The Concept of Earnings-Based Compensation*

Whereas productivity-matched compensation was a key concept in the application of the market approach to valuing physician employment arrangements for clinical services, the concept of earnings-based compensation is fundamental to the cost and income approaches for these services. The concept of earnings-based compensation is that the net earnings received by a professional are an economic measure of the value for these professional services. It applies not only to physicians, but also to other professionals, such as lawyers, accountants, consultants, and appraisers. Professionals such as these provide services in the marketplace to customers, whether in the form of patients or clients. The revenues received for services less the cost of providing the services (i.e., the net earnings from professional services) represent the value or compensation for the services in the marketplace.

Earnings-based compensation for professional services is grounded in the business valuation body of knowledge with respect to the issue of the value of services provided by owners in closely held and small businesses. In their text, *Reasonable Compensation: Application and Analysis for Appraisal, Tax, and Management Purposes*, Kevin Yeanoplos and Ron Seigneur posit that:

> Professional practices, regardless of the form of organization, primarily do one thing. They provide services that are largely the result of the personal services rendered by the professionals within the enterprise. It is logical to conclude that the net earnings of the professional practice represent the reasonable compensation to those professionals, after an allowance for other ordinary, necessary, and reasonable operating expenses.[1]

They argue that each professional's contribution and corresponding compensation is a function of the excess of what each individual is capable of producing over the cost of production.[2]

Earnings-based compensation is also grounded in various tax court cases that have established the idea that net earnings from services provided by a professional can be considered as reasonable compensation for services rendered.[3] One of these cases

1 *Reasonable Compensation: Application and Analysis for Appraisal, Tax, and Management Purposes*, by Kevin Yeanoplos and Ron Seigneur, Business Valuation Resources, LLC (BVR), 2010, p. 8.

2 Yeanoplos and Seigneur, p. 8.

3 Yeanoplos and Seigneur, pp. 7-10.

dealt directly with the determination of physician compensation. In the 2001 *Pediatric Surgical Associates* case,[4] the court concluded that the value of the services performed by shareholder physicians was related to the earnings from those services only. The distributions the shareholder-physicians received from the net earnings of nonshareholder-physicians in the group were not considered to be reasonable compensation for the services rendered by shareholders.[5] In this case, the court made a distinction between compensation for providing professional services and owner compensation accruing to the ownership of a business.

In general, earnings-based compensation as applied to physicians as professionals looks to the revenues generated by physician services less the cost of providing those services for the value of the services rendered. It includes the revenues, fees, and income generated by the physician in providing the specific scope of services contemplated in the subject service arrangement. These services can include clinical, administrative, hospital call coverage, and other professional services. The cost and expense of providing these various services are then deducted from the revenues or income streams for the services to arrive at a level of net earnings from the professional services rendered. These net earnings are considered the value of the physician's services.

Earnings-based compensation for physician services as a methodology has several conceptual and practical advantages for valuation purposes.

#### Use of Historical and Forecasted Net Earnings

The net earnings used for valuing compensation can be based on both historical and future periods. This ability to use multiple periods affords the appraiser with significant capacity for addressing a broad array of relevant factors related to the appraisal of the services. Expected changes in the marketplace or in the economics of services can be factored into the analysis alongside of the historical economics, thereby allowing the appraiser to assess the impact of trends and forecasts for the services. It also allows the appraiser to evaluate the reasonableness and risk factors associated with projected net earnings.

#### Use of Local Market Conditions and Factors

The net earnings from professional services are generally representative of the local market conditions and factors affecting the value of such services. The revenues for

4 Editor's note: This case warrants a careful reading as to the IRS position, the taxpayer's response, and the court's ultimate decision. The court's changes were comparatively minor compared to the IRS audit results.

5 Yeanoplos and Seigneur, pp. 9-10. The tax issue in this case was the amount of the compensation claimed as a deduction in a C corporation for the shareholder physicians. The IRS claimed some of this compensation should have been treated as dividend income, rather than compensation for services.

such services necessarily reflect the local marketplace in terms of what the subject physician or practice has been able to achieve in the market. While the revenues may not be optimized to the extent possible within this local-market context, they are certainly indicative of it with a level of precision that is not available using physician compensation survey data. As discussed in Part I, local reimbursement levels have a tremendous impact on the net earnings available for compensation in a physician practice. Use of net earnings, therefore, gives a realistic initial picture of local market conditions with respect to reimbursement and payer-mix factors. It may also provide an indication of the demand level for physician services in the local service market. The local cost of resources can also be revealed using net earnings. Critical cost components of a medical practice, such as office rental rates and wage levels, are used in the calculation of net earnings. Such expenses may need to be adjusted or optimized (as discussed in subsequent sections in this chapter), but once revised, they can appropriately reflect the prevailing cost levels in the local market.

#### Use of Practice- or Physician-Specific Patterns and Factors

Medical practices and physicians are not created equal in their clinical practice patterns, patient bases, and utilization of resources. Medical groups and individual doctors can vary in terms of the demographics and diversity of ailments of their patient populations. They may have relatively different service mixes in terms of the specific professional component and technical component services they regularly perform in treating patients. For example, some physicians may elect to limit their inpatient work or may focus on certain types of procedures at a level that is distinguished from their peers within a group or in other practices. Clinical judgments and the case acuity of patient populations can affect the level of ancillary utilization in the practice. These varying clinical practice patterns have different overhead and cost-utilization structures. Moreover, groups and physicians diverge in terms of their economic efficiency in using resources to provide services. Some physicians and practices have lower overhead structures than their peers even though they may have equal or greater productivity levels. Using net earnings from services takes these actual practice patterns and resource-utilization levels into account in valuing these services.

#### Use of Specific Scope-of-Service Adjustments

Earnings-based compensation allows the appraiser to value the specific scope of services contemplated under a proposed arrangement. The revenues and expenses from individual services can be directly included or excluded and calculated in detail as part of determining net earnings. This methodology also provides the appraiser with the ability to analyze so-called "stacking" issues related to duplication of payment for the same service or to overpayments in total compensation for the totality of services provided. Such issues can be evaluated with greater precision, since the particular economics of a service are readily identifiable and quantifiable in the net earnings analysis.

#### Use of Normalization and Optimization Adjustments

As part of the conceptual framework of earnings-based compensation, adjustments can be made to the net earnings from physician services. These adjustments can represent certain normalizations to the net earnings or optimize the net earnings consistent with the hypothetical-typical employer operating a practice on a reasonable basis. (These adjustments will be discussed in greater detail in subsequent sections.) The ability to apply such adjustments affords a greater level of precision or specificity in valuing physician services.

#### Use of Specific Facts and Circumstances Adjustments

Similar to normalization and optimization adjustments, use of net earnings allows the appraiser to make other adjustments that reflect unique facts and circumstances related to the subject arrangement. Such adjustments, however, should only be made consistent with changes or service terms and operations reflective of the typical employer entity. Adjustments made that are unique to a specific employer should move the valuation analysis toward investment value rather than fair market value. (A complete discussion of this issue is provided in a subsequent section.)

These adaptive features and advantages of earnings-based compensation give the cost and income approaches a level of precision that is not available under the various market approach methods and techniques for valuing physician services. As noted in Part III, the market approach is limited and qualified in terms of its precision with respect to various economic aspects of physician services. Generally, the market approach is less effective and exact in accounting for key physician practice economic factors such as local market reimbursement, service mix, clinical practice patterns, resource utilization, and scope of services. Since market data are based on prior periods, the market approach is also limited in its capacity to include actual and anticipated changes in the marketplace that occurred or will occur after publication of survey data. Fundamentally, earnings-based compensation is more precise and exacting than productivity-based compensation, which tends to homogenize physician compensation according to one or two measures of productivity. Earnings-based compensation generally takes into account the whole array of economic factors that can affect physician compensation in the marketplace. Consequently, consideration of earnings-based compensation methods is a critical feature in valuing physician services.

### *1.2 Critical Issues in Earnings-Based Compensation*

When applying the concept of earnings-based compensation to physicians, there can be several critical issues to consider in the application of the methodology. These issues generally revolve around what revenue or net earnings streams are included in the computation of net earnings from professional services. The central issue is whether these revenues or net earnings relate to the professional services of a physician such that they should be considered as a component of physician compensation. Three primary sources of net earnings that can raise challenging issues in the appraisal process are practice ownership, other practice providers, and technical component services. Another source of critical issues can arise from questions related to what costs should be included in the calculation of net earnings. These critical issues may not arise in every context; they tend to become concerns in certain fact patterns. The following sections provide an introduction and evaluation of these issues. These issues arise due to the nature of physician services and medical practices.

### *1.3 Exclusion of Owner Compensation From Net Earnings*

The net earnings from owning and operating a business are distinguished from the net earnings from providing professional services. This distinction may seem misguided, at first glance, because both types of compensation are computed using revenues less expenses. Moreover, professionals tend to own and operate their practices. How, then, are the net earnings from professional services different from the net earnings from owning a professional practice? The difference in the two forms of compensation is found in whether the net earnings are the result of services provided by the professional or from the economics of owning and operating a business. The difference may be stated in the following terms: net earnings from owning a professional practice are what results after deducting the value of professional services from the net earnings from services rendered (see Exhibit 1). Yet, the question remains: How does one distinguish between the two? What portion of the net earnings from services rendered should be allocated to professional services and what portion relates to ownership?

This very same question has arisen in business valuation in the context of determining reasonable compensation for closely held or small businesses. In such entities, owners typically provide functional or operational services to the business that are comparable to those provided by employees of the business. For example, a business-owner may perform functions that would otherwise be provided by managers, accountants, human resource personnel, sales, and the like. The reason that determining compensation for such services is important is that a deduction for the value of such services is critical in the use of the income approach for valuing the business. The net earnings available to the business owner are those remaining after paying for the labor associated with the services necessary to operate the business. Many techniques have been developed to value these services, including use of market survey data for various types of management and executive services. These techniques are comparable to market-approach methods used to value physician services.

**Exhibit 1. Deducting Value of Professional Services From Net Earnings From Services Rendered**

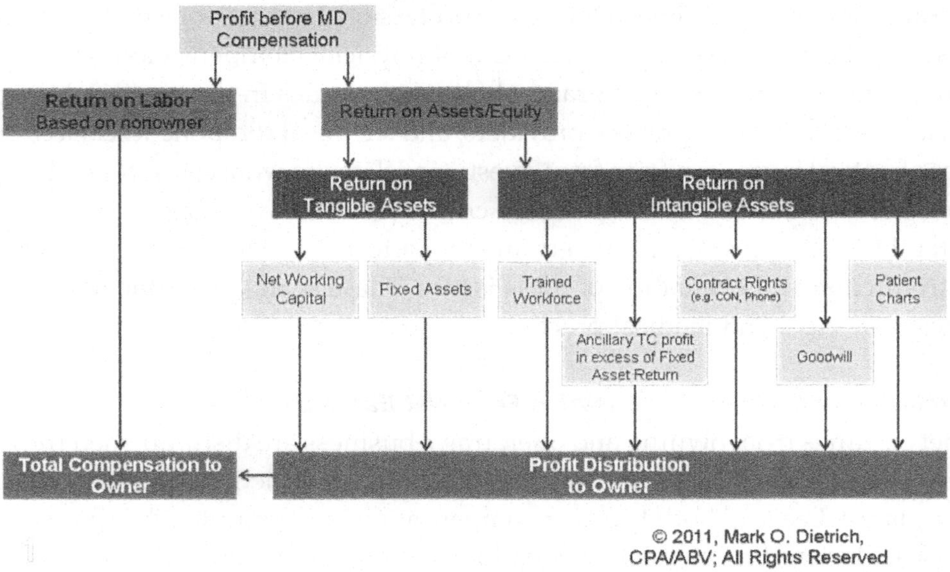


One alternative technique that has been developed in the framework of business valuation, and also in tax matters related to compensation, is the so-called independent-investor test or method. In the independent-investor test, the value of operational services provided by an owner-employee is determined based on the net earnings in the business after providing for an appropriate return on investment in the business. The conceptual framework supporting this method is that owner-employee's compensation for employment-related services is presumed to be reasonable as long as the business owner receives acceptable returns on his or her investment in the enterprise.[6]

As applied to compensation for professional services, the independent investor test would indicate that the value of professional services is the net earnings from those services, where net earnings include a return on assets or investment in the professional services firm. Stated in alternative terms, the net earnings from professional services should include a deduction for the cost of capital necessary to provide the professional services. By adjusting net earnings for the cost of capital, the resulting net earnings should reflect only the value of the professional services rendered. The cost of capital

6 Ronald L. Seigneur, *Closely Held Owner-Employee Compensation*, slide 16-6, AICPA National Business Valuation Conference, Nov. 16, 2009.

represents the compensation for providing capital to the professional practice and for taking risk on this investment. For medical practices, the net earnings from physician services can be determined by deducting a cost of capital for the investment in assets necessary for the operation of the practice.

### *1.4 Inclusion or Exclusion of Net Earnings From Other Practice Providers*

One specific issue that arises in the determination of net earnings from professional services is whether to include or exclude net earnings from other providers in a medical practice. Generally, there are two key types of providers from which physicians can receive earnings distributions as part of a practice:

#### Other Physicians

As shareholders or owners of medical practices, physicians can sometimes receive distributions from the excess net earnings of nonshareholder-physicians practicing in the group.[7] Such distributions should generally be classified as ownership earnings rather than net earnings from physician services. Margins made from nonshareholder-physicians in a group do not relate to the services provided to patients and other healthcare providers by shareholder-physicians. Rather, they relate to being owners in a medical practice, whereby the owners have sufficient patient volume and market position to employ or contract with physicians at compensation levels that generate net earnings or profits for shareholders. In many cases, these net earnings may be temporary because nonshareholder-physicians subsequently become shareholders themselves. These profits may also be returns of and on the underwriting of startup losses by shareholder-physicians during the ramp-up phase of newly hired physicians.[8] At any rate, such margins do not relate to the provision of physician services by the shareholder-physician.

#### Net Earnings From Nonphysician Providers

As discussed in Part I, the issue of how to classify the net earnings from nonphysician providers (NPPs) is a matter to analyze on the basis of the facts and circumstances. Net earnings from NPPs arise from the difference in the revenues generated by the patient procedures personally performed by NPPs and the compensation, benefits, and incremental overhead for the NPPs. Conceptually, NPP net earnings would appear to accrue to the benefit of the employer entity and would not be part of compensation for physician services. There are additional considerations, however, that may lead an appraiser to treat or apportion such net earnings differently in certain circumstances. NPPs in most states require physician supervision, including physician review of patient

7 As noted in Part I, significant or long-term margins from nonshareholder-physicians are not common in the author's experience with medical practices or are not the prevailing practice paradigm.

8 See Part I for further discussion of the economics of this issue.

charts. Such supervision and chart review require the physician's time, which could otherwise be used for personally performed productivity. Some of the net earnings from an NPP, therefore, could be allocable as compensation for supervision services provided by the supervising physician. The amount would depend on the facts and circumstances related to the arrangement.

One such method for apportioning NPP net earnings to physician supervision pay is based on a "subcontractor" model. Under this model, physicians are credited with the work of NPPs that they supervise under an incident-to billing model for purposes of a production bonus or production-based compensation. While a discussion of the various requirements for incident-to billing are beyond the scope of this chapter, it should be noted that the services provided under an incident-to billing model are reimbursed at a higher rate than under a direct billing model. NPP services provided under direct billing are reimbursed at 85% of the level paid to physicians or as incident-to physician services under Medicare. *It should also be noted that certain regulatory requirements must be met for use of this subcontractor model, including those related to Stark.*

In the subcontractor model under employment, the compensation, benefits, and incremental costs of the NPP are deducted from the physician's compensation. Thus, the physician is at risk in these models for the productivity level of the NPP. At lower production levels for the NPP, the physician's compensation can be significantly reduced because the costs for the NPP are greater than the compensation credited to the physician for the production level of the NPP. If the NPP ramps ups, however, the physician is able to retain the net earnings from the NPP as supervision compensation. The conceptual support for such arrangements is that the physician is required to manage the overall productivity of the physician-NPP duo in providing patient care. The physician has downside risk and upside compensation for the NPP's productivity. The physician, in effect, becomes a business owner for compensation purposes relative to the NPP.

In addition, the compensation formula is structured such that the employer makes money from the very first amount of production generated by the NPP because the revenues generated by the NPP exceed the amount credited or paid to the physician for purposes of a production-bonus or productivity-based compensation. (*To use this model, the revenues from the NPP must exceed the amounts credited or paid to the physician.*) Thus, an owner return to the employer is generated by the NPP as part of the structure. A typical example of this structure is where the wRVUs of an NPP are credited to the supervising physician for purposes of calculating compensation based on a compensation-per-wRVU formula. The costs of the NPP, however, are deducted from such compensation as part of the formula. In addition, the collections per wRVU from the NPP's services exceed the compensation-per-wRVU amount that is paid to the physician.

It is possible, therefore, for the net earnings of an NPP to be included in the net earnings from physician services under certain circumstances in terms of supervision pay. Whether such earnings should be included and the amount that should be included requires a specific analysis of the economics of the compensation structure and supervision services provided by the physician. *In addition, Stark issues and requirements may need to be met for such arrangements.* Appraisers should work with legal counsel in such instances to ensure that the valuation is prepared consistent with applicable healthcare regulations.

#### *1.5 Inclusion or Exclusion of Net Earnings From Technical Component Services*

In determining the net earnings derived from physician services, one key question that comes to the fore is whether the net earnings from technical component services *provided in a physician practice setting* (TCS) should be included in the computation of earnings from physician services. Are the net earnings from TCS part of the professional clinical services provided by a physician or are they part of a technical service line offered by a medical practice that accrues to the benefit of the practice owners? From the standpoint of who performs the services, the answer is rather straightforward. TCS are not directly part of physician services because they are not personally provided by a physician. The net earnings from TCS (TCSNE), therefore, would appear to relate to practice ownership rather than physician services. Hence, they should not be included in the calculation of physician compensation for professional services. Yet, an analysis of the historical, economic, and regulatory issues surrounding the provision of TCS in physician practices can give rise to an alternative perspective on including TCSNE in physician compensation.

In thinking about TCSNE and physician compensation, several factors should be considered:

1. TCS generally require the supervision of a physician; they are not procedures that can be performed without some level of general oversight and responsibility by a physician. These oversight requirements may not necessarily entail direct visual observation and immediate, over-the-shoulder supervision of the technicians or nursing staff performing the TCS. Nonetheless, some level of physician supervision is required. As a result, TCS cannot be fully removed from the overall context of physician services.

2. Certain types of TCS have historically been provided as part of the scope of clinical patient care services found in medical practices for selected specialties. For example, diagnostic testing through echocardiograms, EKGs, and nuclear camera studies are routinely provided in cardiology practices are part of the continuum of patient care services. Imaging modalities, such as MRI and CT,

are frequently offered in orthopedic groups, while chemotherapy is part of most medical oncology practices. Primary care practices frequently provide basic lab and radiology (X-ray) services to patients. Most ob/gyn practices provide ultrasound services as part of prenatal care.

3. TCSNE have been part of the historical compensation levels received by physicians in specialties where these services have been provided customarily within a physician practice setting. As a result, such TCSNE are generally included or "baked into" market expectations for physician compensation levels for a given specialty. Moreover, it is highly likely that such TCSNE are included in the compensation amounts reported in the physician compensation surveys. Up until the last couple of years, the majority of respondents to MGMA and AMGA have been from physician-owned practices. Thus, the compensation from these practices would generally include TCSNE. Compensation for hospital and health system-employed physicians is commonly established using such survey data, whether through internal valuation efforts or the use of appraisers or valuation consultants. The referencing of such data by hospital and health systems in establishing compensation for employed physicians is likely to have utilized and perpetuated compensation based on the inclusion of TCSNE.[9] Thus, historical compensation levels, market expectations, and much of the survey data would appear to be inclusive of TCSNE for certain types of TCS in selected specialties.

4. As long as the referring physicians and groups meet various federal and state regulatory requirements, such as the AKS and Stark, they can include certain TCSNE in the computation of physician compensation. Thus, physicians are readily able to refer TCS and be compensated from TCSNE as part of their professional practices and in providing patient care services as long as they are within the bounds of regulatory compliance. (Another condition is that they are not subject to restrictive covenants with respect to TCS that were agreed to as part of acquisition transactions.) The economic reality of this ability is that physicians can readily move their TCS referrals from one practice to another, apart from such restrictive covenants.

5. When the physicians had sold their TCS line to a buyer-employer entity as part of a larger physician practice acquisition and employment transaction, TCSNE

9 The argument that utilization of the market approach allows the appraiser to avoid the issue of TCSNE is somewhat uncritical and superficial. To make such an argument plausible, one would have to make the case that TCSNE were not a factor in establishing historical physician compensation levels and that use of the surveys to establish compensation for hospital and health system physicians was not a prevalent practice in the industry.

necessarily accrue to the benefit of the buyer and would not be included in the resulting compensation for the physicians employed by the buyer. The structure of the acquisition transaction necessarily created a reduction in future compensation to the physicians. In essence, this purchase of the TCS line of the practice is comparable to acquisition patterns in the 1990s, in which physicians gave up future compensation to receive up-front value for their practices.

6. Exclusion of TCSNE may not be consistent with the idea of fair market value (FMV) in the appraisal body of knowledge from the perspective of the typical seller of physician services, i.e., the prospective employee physician. As discussed in Part II, FMV as defined by the appraisal profession looks to what the typical buyer and seller would do, given arm's-length negotiations and full knowledge of the facts. The FMV definition, therefore, poses this fundamental question: Why would a physician become an employee if a material portion of his or her compensation were reduced without a commensurate reduction in the services provided under employment? In short, physicians would not be incentivized to become employees of employers who reduced their compensation for TCSNE, apart from the sale of their practice that contemplated the sale of TCSNE in the purchase price, as discussed above. They would simply remain in their current practices where such net earnings are part of the compensation formula. This analysis from the perspective of the physician, i.e., the seller of physician services, would apply regardless of the potential employer. Whether the potential employer is a hospital or health system, physician-owned practice, physician practice management company, insurance company, or other employer type, the physician would look at his or her alternatives in the marketplace when faced with a significant reduction in compensation. Where alternatives exist in which a physician's compensation includes TCSNE, it is doubtful that a physician acting in accordance with the standard of FMV would choose an arrangement were TCSNE were excluded. Only where other sufficient factors, considerations, and incentives were present would a physician generally make such a choice to forego TCSNE.

In light of these considerations, it is possible to make an economic and valuation argument for the inclusion of certain TCSNE in physician compensation. TCS may not be personally performed professional services, but inclusion of the net earnings from certain types of TCS has become part of the expected compensation for physicians in selected specialties. In addition, such physicians may have marketplace alternatives in which they can readily gain access to TCSNE, as long a regulatory requirements are met. It is hard to contemplate, apart from a separate acquisition of TCS or unique factors specific to a physician, that physicians acting at arm's length would be ready to part with such compensation in employment arrangements. Based on this line of reasoning, a case can be made for the inclusion of TCSNE in physician compensation under a FMV analysis.

On the other hand, TCS fall within the purview of the healthcare services that are the subject of AKS and Stark. Thus, a series of healthcare regulatory concerns are raised in the process of examining the inclusion of TCSNE in the compensation of referring physicians. These concerns may have implications for determining the FMV of physician compensation from a regulatory compliance perspective. Since appraisals are generally obtained for healthcare compliance purposes, the appraiser cannot afford to ignore the potential regulatory implications and issues that can arise as part of a valuation assignment. Guidance of legal counsel as to the impact of such regulations can be an important part of addressing the issues entailed in including TCSNE in physician compensation for valuation purposes.

Since appraisers do not provide legal, regulatory, or investment advice, they would be prudent to seek regulatory guidance from the legal counsel involved in a proposed employment arrangement. As discussed in Part II, such regulatory guidance is not intended to subordinate or supplant the FMV opinion of the appraiser. Rather, regulatory guidance is intended to clarify the definition of FMV for purposes of valuation for the appraiser. Such clarification is appropriate because regulatory compliance is usually the impetus for engagement of the independent appraiser. The healthcare regulatory definition of FMV, moreover, can involve issues and considerations that are legal in nature and beyond the scope of the appraiser's area of expertise and body of knowledge. Legal guidance relative to the standard of value for an engagement is usual and customary in divorce and damages litigation. Legal guidance relative to the healthcare standard of value is similar and comparable to these other areas of appraisal practice.

#### *1.6 Scope of Service Adjustments*

In applying the concept of earnings-based compensation, the appraiser needs to identify the scope of services contemplated under the proposed employment arrangement in terms of the types of services provided. The proposed scope of services can potentially include any of the following:

- Clinical or patient care services, including professional and technical component services;
- Hospital call coverage;
- Other professional services;

- Administrative services;
- NPP supervision services;
- Research services; and
- Other services.

Once the scope of services has been identified, the appraiser uses the revenues and fees earned or collected by the physician or practice for these same services to establish the revenues earned from the services provided. This analysis of revenues from a comparable scope of service eliminates revenues and fees for services or activities that are not part of proposed employment services provided by the practice or physician. For example, fees from a medical directorship that will not be part of the services provided under employment would be excluded. Income from rents, interest, and other nonoperating and nonservice-related items would also be removed from the computation of historical practice net earnings. Next, the appraiser obtains information on the costs and expenses required to produce these same scope of services. The costs associated with the production of the services should be considered comprehensively, including the depreciation or amortization cost of assets such as furniture and equipment, as well as an allowance for a cost of capital on all practice assets. Physician benefits are also included as costs of the practice.

These revenues and expenses are then used to compute the practice net earnings for a physician group or an individual physician. As will be discussed in subsequent sections, the revenues and expenses from services can be based on historical amounts under the cost approach or on projected amounts under the income approach. Use of the earnings-based compensation framework can be applied to historical or expected amounts, thereby providing indications of value that reflect both historical and future operating factors and contexts. The appraiser considers each indication of value derived from the physician's or medical group's practice net earnings—whether based on the past or on the future—in the synthesis process for establishing FMV compensation.

Scope of service adjustments should also look at the services provided at a more granular level to ensure that services are matched in terms of relevant measures for the services. For example, clinical hours worked per week, weeks worked per year, call shifts provided per month, medical director hours, and the like should be established for the subject employment arrangement. Revenues and expenses associated with these services are adjusted so that the quantity or relative measure of the services is consistent between the practice net earnings computation and what will be required under employment. For example, if historical practice net earnings are used, the appraiser should ensure that the annual working hours under the proposed employment arrangement are consistent with the historical working hours. *If historical hours are higher than the required hours under employment, it may not be reasonable to expect a comparable level of practice net earnings to be generated by the physician under employment as in prior years.*[10]

### 1.7 Normalization Adjustments

In determining the amount of practice net earnings, the appraiser may need to make a series of adjustments to the reported or historical revenues and expenses of the subject physician or practice. These adjustments seek to normalize revenues and expenses consistent with what would be expected under the employment arrangement. For revenues, the appraiser considers to what extent historical revenues may reflect volumes and collections that are one-time occurrences, nonrecurring, and not reflective of current productivity levels. Adjustments may be made to historical revenues for such items in an effort to determine a normalized level of historical revenues. Another technique for establishing a normalized level of revenue is to use and evaluate multiple historical periods to determine a normalized base year amount. The adjusted historical revenues are then used as the basis for projecting future revenues from the physician or practice.

For expenses, there are several areas and items for the appraiser to review as part of the normalization of costs for providing professional services.

#### Nonbusiness-Related Expenses

Physician practice expenses often include the costs of items that do not relate to the operation of the practice or to provision of physician services. Some of these items may represent perquisites that are not consistent with typical employment arrangements. In general, such nonbusiness-related expenses should be adjusted out of expenses for purposes of determining practice net earnings.

#### Nonrecurring and Nonoperating Expenses

One time, extraordinary, or nonrecurring expenses should also be removed from historical practice net earnings since they can overstate the normalized costs necessary for the production of physician services. Nonoperating expense should be removed for similar reasons.

#### Related-Party Resource Costs

The cost of resources provided by parties related to the subject physicians may not be reflective of typical or FMV costs for such resources. Examples of such items include rents from physician-owned buildings and the salaries of physician family members.

---

10 Editor's Note: This is a simple fact that is often overlooked in appraisal and was one of the things that led to the failure of the last physician-hospital consolidation in the 1900s.

Such costs may be higher or lower than one could obtain for these resources in the local marketplace. To establish historical practice net earnings that are consistent with FMV, such costs should be normalized using current market rates for such resources.

#### Physician Benefits

The historical level of benefits afforded to a physician in private practice may not be reflective of a market-based level of benefits typically provided in an employment arrangement. Historical benefits may be higher or lower than normalized or market-based benefits. To ensure that practice net earnings are comparable to the compensation to be received under employment, benefits should be adjusted for consistency with market levels. Such benefits can include the following:[11]

- Payroll-related taxes, including FICA, FUTA, SUTA, and workers' compensation;
- Health, dental, life, and disability insurance coverages;
- Employer retirement plan contributions
- Continuing medical education (CME) costs; and
- Dues and licenses.

#### Staff Benefits

As with physician benefits, the benefits provided to the nonphysician staff may not be consistent with market norms for employee benefits. Most small medical practices provide below-market benefits to their employees in comparison to larger groups and those operated by corporate entities. Since the typical buyer-employer entity in the current marketplace is a larger group or corporate entity, adjusting these benefits to a market level may be necessary for practice net earnings to be stated on a normalized basis. As discussed in Part I, some practices provide above-market benefits, primarily in the area of retirement benefits. These benefits are typically above industry norms when the physicians in the group are near retirement age and they have established a rich employer-paid retirement plan. Above-market benefits should generally be reduced to market levels in the same way that below-market benefits are adjusted.

#### Economic Depreciation and Amortization

The costs of a physician practice should include an allocation for the cost of the capitalized assets used in the practice. Capitalized assets are not expensed when purchased because they have a useful life that goes beyond the year in which they are acquired.

11 A best practice for categorizing physician benefits is to use the definition found in the MGMA *Cost Survey*.

Practices will generally depreciate and amortize these assets in their financial statements and tax returns. For purposes of computing net practice earnings, the historical amounts reported for depreciation and amortization may not be relevant indications of the usage costs for these assets. The reason for this disjunction is that financial reporting and tax depreciation methods may not match the true economic life of the assets. Useful lives for tax depreciation, for example, can be much shorter than the expected useful life because they were driven by tax policy. In addition, a practice may have deferred capital expenditures to replace obsolete assets; thus, its depreciation cost is understated. For these reasons, an appraiser should analyze the reported depreciation and amortization amounts along with historical capital expenditures to determine normalized depreciation and amortization levels for the practices. These normalized levels should be reflective of the ongoing capital needs of the practice.

#### Cost of Capital

As discussed in Part I, every business, including a medical practice, has a cost associated with the capital investment that it has in the operating assets of the business. The cost of capital is applicable to for-profit and not-for-profit entities; both require up-front capital investment. A cost of capital should be included in the costs that go into the computation of practice net earnings. The cost of capital is computed using rates of return that are commensurate with the type of operating assets used in the practice. Examples of operating assets include working capital and fixed assets, such as furniture and equipment. (A discussion of intangible assets is included in section "The Cost Approach" below.)

#### Other Normalization Adjustments

Other facts and circumstances may give rise to other normalization adjustments to the historical revenues and expenses of a physician practice. One potential area for adjustment would relate to non-normative or unique activities or costs for a practice. Another area would be operations, activities, and resource utilization that are not consistent with the typical buyer-employer. As discussed in Part I, hospital and health system ownership and operation of medical practices can introduce a series of extrinsic factors into their economics and operations. These factors may place the practice in an operational setting or context that is atypical or not reflective of market norms. It may be appropriate to adjust for such factors in the determination of normalized historical practice net earnings.

### *1.8 Optimization Adjustments*

Many practices are managed and operated at a suboptimized level. They may use unnecessary levels of staff, space, and other resources such that the cost structure of the practice is higher than it otherwise could be if the practice were managed efficiently and effectively. Operational areas, such as billing and collections, may be poorly performing. Since FMV in the appraisal body of knowledge assumes a hypothetical-typical buyer-employer entity, it may be appropriate to optimize the operations of a practice to be consistent with industry norms. The concept supporting such adjustments is that the typical buyer-employer would be expected to operate the practice in a reasonably efficient manner. Moreover, a well-informed seller would also be aware of the sub-optimized level of operations in the practice. Both parties, therefore, would have an expectation that the historical practice net earnings do not represent the potential for the physician or practice. This expectation can be based on how the reasonable operator would run the practice, i.e., based on a reasonable operator standard.

Such adjustments, however, should not be based merely on use of median data from physician compensation and cost surveys. Rather, they should be based on specific analyses relative to the subject practice and its patient base, productivity levels, local market dynamics, and operating profile. The actual facts and circumstances of the practice must be taken into account. The homogenization of practice operations based on the MGMA *Cost Survey* median data as the hypothetical industry norm is not what is contemplated by optimization adjustments that are consistent with the definition of FMV. The reasonable operator standard is not based on a hypothetical practice, but rather on the specific practice as optimized and run as efficiently and effectively as the reasonable operator could realistically achieve.

When looking at areas is which physician practices are not optimized, there are four key areas in which practices can be improved. These areas include the following.

#### Revenue Cycle Operations

Physician practices often have suboptimized revenue cycles. They do not effectively negotiate with commercial payers or attempt to set charge rates that can maximize their commercial reimbursement levels. Practices may also have ineffective and inaccurate coding and billing practices, leading to claim rejections and delays in getting paid. More frequently, practices do poorly at collection efforts including collecting co-pay and deductible amounts from patients. Revenue cycle issues are a frequently observed phenomenon in both physician and hospital- and health system-owned practices and in large groups as well as solo physicians.

#### Support Staff Levels

Physician practices can be overstaffed in various areas, including nursing support, front- and back-office functions, and in technicians used in TCS. This overstaffing can be a function of physicians or practice administrators failing to optimize operations or to downsize as needed by changes in a practice. It can also result from physicians requesting special services and tasks from staff that are not consistent with an efficiently run practice. Where a practice-specific assessment indicates a reasonable operator would adjust staffing levels, it may be appropriate to adjust staffing levels for the determination of practice net earnings. It may also be possible that a practice is understaffed because the physician or physician's family members perform support functions without specific compensation from the practice. Cost increases for understaffing should be treated as part of normalization adjustments.

#### Office Space Utilization and Costs

Unfortunately, physicians are notorious for doing ill-conceived real estate deals. The typical real estate transaction gone bad entails physicians buying or leasing more space than is necessary for the effective operation of their practices. It also tends to include excessive costs incurred in building out space. As a result of such actions, physician practices often have real estate occupancy costs in excess of what a reasonable operator would have incurred to run the practice effectively. The potential optimization adjustment in such a situation involves a facts-and-circumstances specific analysis. In general, adjustments should reflect what is actually achievable with respect to office space utilization and costs. Hypothetical assumptions made in the abstract lack reasonableness in relation to the specific arrangement.

Where the physicians are owners of the real estate, it is easier to assume that the buyer-employer can optimize the space utilization. The new employer would be expected to negotiate a new lease with the physician-landlord that is based on square footage that is commensurate with the operational needs of the practice. Yet, this assumption should be practical. The space should be readily divisible so that the new tenant can actually lease a reduced space level. When such delineation and devising is not practical, it may be necessary to assume that the current square footage is what the new employer would lease, unless alternative space can be effectively obtained for the practice. The cost of such alternative space would need to be factored into the costs for practice net earnings. In addition, rental rates should be based on FMV rates consistent with the local market.

Where the physicians are not the landlords for practice office space, the probability of space optimization is reduced. A new employer-tenant may not be able to negotiate new lease terms and may be required to assume the current lease, if the employer elects to keep the practice in the current location. When this is the case, the suboptimized real estate costs of the practice are generally included in the computation of practice net earnings.

#### Technical Component Service Lines

Many physicians have included technical component service lines in their practices that actually reduce overall practice net earnings. Unfortunately, many physicians only think about TCS in terms of revenue and not net earnings. As a result, they sometimes introduce TCS with high initial investments or fixed costs into their practices without having a sufficient level of volume to make the specific TCS profitable. An appraiser may assume the elimination of such TCS lines as part of the optimization of practice net earnings when such services are not profitable. The basis for this assumption is that the reasonable operator would terminate service lines that are not profitable for the practice. When this assumption is made, the appraiser should remove the revenues and costs associated with the TCS line from the computation of practice net earnings.

### *1.9 Revenue and Cost Allocations to Individual Physicians in Group Practices*

Some employment valuation assignments may require the appraiser to value the compensation of a specific physician who is part of a group practice or to determine compensation individually for physicians in a group. In such engagements, the appraiser may be required to allocate practice net earnings to individual physicians as part of the appraisal process using the framework of earnings-based compensation. An appraisal can use a variety of methods to allocate group practice net earnings to individual physicians. In evaluating allocation methods, an appraiser should consider several issues and factors.

#### Stark Compliance for TCSNE

The allocation of TCSNE should be consistent with the requirements of the Stark regulations. If it is not, the allocation formula for these earnings should be revised for Stark compliance. A fundamental consideration for Stark compliance is that TCSNE must meet the in-office ancillary exception and the group practice compensation rules. These compensation regulations mandate that TCSNE not be directly related to the volume or value of TCS referrals by individual physicians.

#### Using Individual Physician Revenues

Most groups track individual physician revenues in terms of charges and collections. Revenues and fees from other services such as hospital call coverage or medical directorships are also typically tracked by individual physicians. Using individual physician revenues may be preferable when computing practice net earnings by physician, when such information is available and reasonably accurate. There are, however, exceptions to this general preference. A required exception for allocating within a group is exclusion of TCS revenues. To be compliant with Stark, compensation from TCS cannot be determined in a way that directly relates to the volume or value of ancillary service referrals. TCS revenues, in general, should be allocated to Stark-compliant pools in which the TCSNE are computed. In the case of a single physician exiting a group, using total revenues may be appropriate, but such use raises the issues discussed above about the use of TCSNE in the practice net earnings of solo employed physicians.

Sometimes, it may be more appropriate to use an allocation of professional component service revenues and other service revenues, rather than the individual revenues by physicians. Many ob/gyn groups often consider their obstetrics-related revenues to be shared commonly among the group due to equal sharing in delivery call coverage for group patients. Revenues may be credited to the individual physicians based on who delivered a baby rather than on the prenatal services provided to an expectant mother. Some groups may also delegate certain patient bases or cases to individual physicians as a matter of overall group productivity optimization. This organizational pattern may yield results in which certain physicians have higher revenues than others. The physicians may contend, however, that this is not a reflection of individual productivity per se, but rather of how the group has sought to allocate work among group physicians. In summary, there may be cases in which the facts and circumstances warrant an allocation of group revenues rather than use of individual revenues as reported in the group's information systems.

The net effect of using individual physician revenues is that the allocation process becomes a matter of assigning group overhead and costs to individual physicians rather than to group practice net earnings. In these circumstances, the costs allocated should relate to the physicians' professional component services as well as other services provided, excluding TCS. When group revenues are used, the allocation process can become an exercise of allocating group practice net earnings to individual physicians.

#### Matching Services Provided With Allocation Methods

Allocation of net practice earnings or group revenues and overhead should relate to the services provided by group physicians. There are many allocation methods and techniques for achieving reasonable and equitable allocation outcomes.[12] A few simplified methods include allocations based on productivity measures such as wRVUs or professional collections. Productivity measures would appear to be the most relevant when allocating group practice net earnings. When allocating costs, however, there may be an argument for using a hybrid method that allocates costs on a per full-time-equivalent (FTE) basis and on productivity. The concept behind this type of hybrid allocation is that some resources are fixed and relate to supporting a physician, regardless of productivity. On the other hand, the more productive a physician is, the more resources are utilized in the providing services. In summary, the allocation methods used should have a reasonable relation to the services provided.

12 See *Physician Compensation Plans: State-of-the-Art Strategies*, by Bruce A. Johnson and Deborah Walker Keegan, MGMA, 2006, for a comprehensive and in-depth discussion of such methods.

#### Elimination of Ownership Considerations

Allocation methods giving preferences in distributions to shareholders or senior physicians may not relate to the services provided by physicians in the group. Preferential distributions that are not related to physician productivity or physician services are generally reflective of ownership considerations. These considerations do not continue under employment. However, if preferential distributions relate to management or executive services provided by certain senior physicians to the group and these services will continue under employment, it may be appropriate to include additional compensation to these physicians for the specific services provided over and above their clinical services as employees. The value of these services, however, should be factored into the costs used to determine practice net earnings for the group from physician services.

## 2.0 The Cost Approach

### *2.1 The Cost Approach Defined*

The cost approach is defined according to *the International Glossary of Business Valuation Terms* as "a general way of determining a value indication of an individual asset by quantifying the amount of money required to replace the future service capability of that asset." The cost approach looks to the replacement cost of an asset or business interest as the basis for valuing the subject asset or interest. In business valuation, the cost approach is categorized as the asset-based or buildup approach because the appraiser attempts to re-create the value of the subject business by accumulating the values of the individual assets that comprise the subject. The appraisal attempts to re-create the business one asset at a time, building up a business enterprise value based on the value of each asset. The cost approach also illustrates the valuation principle of alternatives: the idea that there are alternatives to acquiring the future service capacity of the subject asset or business interest. One appraisal technique often used under the cost approach is to value an asset based on its adjusted historical cost, where the adjustments to historical cost are intended to reflect the cost to replicate the asset in its current condition and in consideration of relevant marketplace factors related to the re-creation of the asset.

The cost approach as applied to service contracts seeks to value the compensation for the subject arrangement by valuing substitutes or alternatives for those services in the marketplace. Cost approach techniques may also attempt to re-create the cost of the same or comparable scope of services to be provided in the subject arrangement as a method for valuing the subject services. This re-creation of the cost of services may involve a buildup of the costs for various resources or subservices that are part of the subject services. Cost approach methods may also seek alternative sources or providers of a service that is comparable to the services being provided in the subject arrangement. Under these methods, the appraiser may gather market data on the cost of comparable or alternative services with the same utility as the subject services.

Another potential indication of the cost for a service is its historical cost, where past compensation for services was based on arm's-length negotiations between parties who are economically independent of each other, not having other business relationships that might influence the consideration in the historical service contract. Under this analysis, the historical cost for a service is a reflection and indication of the market value for the services because it was negotiated at arm's length by independent parities to the arrangement. This past market value may still be a valid indication of the present and future value of the services. Even when the past marketplace is not a good indication of present or future market conditions, the appraiser may be able to adjust past indications of value to reflect current or prospective conditions.

In the case of employment arrangements, one application of the cost approach is to use the historical compensation of the physician as a measure of the cost to re-create the services provided under employment. For this application of the cost approach, however, the physician's historical compensation should be based on a comparable scope of services to that required under employment. If the scope of services is dissimilar, the compensation may not be indicative of the value of the services in the proposed employment arrangement. In certain circumstances, it may be possible for the appraiser to adjust the historical compensation of the physician to place the past scope of services on a comparable basis with those contemplated under employment. The adjustment process entails a segregation or allocation of the historical compensation for the various types of services for which the physician received income in the past. Past compensation may be payment for services such as patient care, hospital call coverage, medical directorships, and owner compensation.

Once the historical compensation has been allocated to the various services provided by the physician in prior periods, the appraiser adjusts the historical compensation for those past services that are consistent with what is required under employment. Historical compensation may also need to be normalized consistent with various market norms related to benefits and operations. It may also be adjusted to eliminate nonrecurring, one-time, or extraordinary items that are not reflective of the physician's normalized or regular services or the economics of those services.

As noted above, use of historical compensation is predicated on this compensation being the result of arm's-length negotiations between independent parties. This condition generally precludes the use of historical compensation for physicians who were employed by hospital and health systems under the cost approach. The regulatory prohibition on the use of data from parties with referral relationships would appear to be applicable to such historical compensation. The existence of the referral relationship places the independence of the parties into question. As a result, the compensation paid to a referral-source by a hospital or health system employer does not generally meet the criteria for arm's-length negotiations that would be necessary for reliance on such compensation as an indication of value under the concept of fair market value for healthcare regulatory purposes.

### *2.2 The Historical Practice Net Earnings Method*

The historical practice net earnings (HPNE) method is a specific valuation technique that applies the concept of earnings-based compensation to the historical economic outcomes of a physician or medical practice. It uses the revenues from physician services less the costs to produce these services from prior periods to establish historical practice net earnings. These past practice net earnings reflect the historical cost to re-create or reproduce the services. As such, they are in indication of the value of the services under the cost approach. The determination of historical practice net earnings should take into account the scope of service and normalization adjustments discussed above. Optimization adjustments may be considered, but many appraisers find it more practical to include such adjustments under the income approach using forecasted practice net earnings. To apply the historical practice net earnings method, the appraiser needs access to the historical financial statements of the practice along with key details and supplemental information about various revenue and cost items.

The decision to use the HPNE method for an employment valuation when data are available is generally a function of the relevance of past compensation to future conditions under employment. If past operating and market conditions are not indicative of the future circumstances, the method may lack relevance. Even when this disconnect between past and future is present, an appraiser may complete the method as part of preparing the forecasted practice net earnings method that looks to future operating and market conditions under employment. A normalized base year is generally required to prepare a forecast of future practice net earnings. The preparation of a normalized base year can serve as a variation of the historical practice net earnings method.

The HPNE method can be applied to multiple prior periods to derive an indication of the value of physician services. A critical question in using multiple prior periods is whether they are indicative of market and operating conditions that will transpire under the proposed employment arrangement. Changes in reimbursement or operations may render prior periods less relevant and applicable to the value of physician services in future periods. Appraisers should use reasonable and supportable judgment in evaluating whether prior periods are relevant and applicable to future periods. Where practical, it may be helpful to prepare the method using multiple periods as a means of looking at trends and developments in the practice that may have a bearing on future periods. Alternatively, an appraiser may review multiple prior periods of financial information to derive a normalized base year level of practice net earnings that is considered to be relevant and applicable to future periods under employment.

### *2.3 The Adjusted Historical Compensation Method*

The adjusted historical compensation (AHC) method is another cost approach method that employs the concept of earnings-based compensation. It uses similar ideas and adjustments as those included in the HPNE method. The starting point for this method, however, is the actual compensation for the physician in prior years rather than the practice income statement. The historical compensation can be based on W-2 earnings and from K-1 earnings in entities treated as partnerships for tax purposes, *but this compensation needs to be reviewed and adjusted*. Beginning with the historical compensation, the method adjusts this income to reflect the scope of services to be provided under employment. The AHC method also uses normalization adjustment to place the historical compensation on a basis that is consistent with an employment arrangement. In general, the same adjustments made for the HPNE method are applicable to this cost approach method. The AHC method can be summarized as follows. The various adjustments listed are not intended to be exhaustive, but rather illustrative of the types of items for which compensation may need to be adjusted.

+ Reported historical compensation

+/- Scope of service adjustments:

- Changes in clinical services;
- Changes in hospital call coverage services;
- Changes in administrative services;
- Elimination of owner compensation and distributions
- Changes in annual working hours;
- Changes in other professional services.

+/- Normalization adjustments:

- Nonrecurring, nonoperating, and extraordinary revenue and expenses;
- Physician market-level benefits;
- Debt proceeds used to fund physician compensation;
- Prior retained earnings or cash on hand used to fund current-year compensation.
- Adjustments for related-party costs and expenses to market levels;
- Cost of capital; and
- Economic depreciation and amortization.

= Adjusted historical compensation

It should be noted that *the primary use of the AHC method is when historical financial statements are not available for a physician or practice and use of the HPNE method is not available or practical.* This absence of data usually occurs when a physician or number of physicians are seeking to exit their current employment or group practice. The physicians may not have access to such information or may not be able to access it without alerting the current employer to the potential exit. In such cases, the AHC method provides the appraiser with a cost approach technique that takes into account the historical compensation of the subject physician.

*Caution and critical scrutiny should be applied when attempting to use the AHC method when limited data are available.* The appraiser needs to ascertain what scope of services went into the reported compensation and the compensation formula or method used to pay the physician. Without this information, the appraiser cannot be assured that the scope of services and historical compensation are consistent with those contemplated under the proposed employment arrangement. Lack of information with respect to potential normalization adjustments may also limit the appraiser's ability to ensure comparability. Appraisers should be careful and circumspect in using this method.

### 2.4 The Cost to Recruit Method

The cost to recruit method seeks to establish the replacement cost for staffing a physician employment arrangement by recruiting a qualified physician to fill the position. The method looks to the compensation that would be necessary for such a recruitment. Generally, physician compensation survey data are used as the basis for determining the compensation level that would be necessary to recruit a qualified physician. The appraiser selects certain levels of compensation that are believed to be necessary to attract and recruit a physician with qualifications that are required for the subject employment arrangement. An allowance for recruiter fees and costs may also be considered as part of the cost to recruit. The theory behind this method is that it represents the alternative cost for employing the subject physician. While the method uses physician compensation survey data, it is included under the rubric of the cost approach rather than the market approach because it focuses on the replacement cost of hiring an alternative qualified physician.

In applying this method, there are several issues for appraisers to consider. The first issue is determining what data should be used to establish the compensation level that is necessary to attract a qualified candidate. Generally, three options are available for such data: placement and recruiting survey data, general physician compensation survey data, and individual transactions for recently hired physicians. In general, placement and recruiting survey data should be considered first in establishing a range of compensation for a replacement physician (see Part III for a listing of available survey data). The reason for this preference is that these data are taken from actual new-hire transactions. It presents data on the actual compensation amounts that induced a physician to enter into a new employment arrangement. Such data should be distinguished from the general survey data; these data are predominately based on physicians in existing employment and shareholder or owner arrangements. The economic outcomes of an established physician can be significantly different than those of a starting physician. Generally, but not always, a newly hired physician will make less than one with an established practice and a significant level of productivity. An employer will typically pay compensation for an unknown level of service from a newly hired physician.

Use of the general survey data should be used to supplement placement and recruiting survey data. Oftentimes, such supplementation is necessary because the number of respondents to the placement data can be small, giving rise to the potential for skewed and unrepresentative results. For certain subspecialties, placement data may not be available. Practically speaking, therefore, general survey data may be the only basis for establishing the compensation for a replacement physician in certain instances. With respect to the use of individual new-hire transactions, the appraiser should consider the criteria presented in Part III that specifically addresses the use of individual market transactions in appraisal practice.

Once the appropriate market data are selected, the appraiser must use these data to determine the compensation level for the replacement physician. Some of the survey data may have relevant breakdowns that can assist in establishing this compensation level. For example, the placement and recruiting data from MGMA's *Physician Placement Starting Salary Survey* and in the AMGA *Medical Group Compensation and Financial Survey* are segregated between experienced physicians and physician hired out of residency, fellowship, or other training programs. In another example, the general MGMA survey data include compensation by years of experience. Ultimately, however, the appraiser must develop some criteria by which a compensation level is derived from the data for the replacement physician. Attention should also be given to the types of compensation reported in the survey data. Sign-on bonuses and relocation allowances are typical in many new-hire employment arrangements. The appraiser should ensure that the compensation in the survey data is comparable to the compensation assumed for the cost to replace.

Unfortunately, there is a tendency to overuse the median from the general surveys, particularly MGMA, as the universal cost to replace the subject physician. While the gravitation toward the median is understandable, it should not be summarily and universally assumed to be the replacement cost for a new physician. The median means half the data are above this value and the other half are below this value. The median, therefore, should not be misunderstood to be a floor for physician compensation. More importantly, however, the median from the general surveys should not be considered to be the typical compensation level for recruiting a physician because this value is not taken exclusively from newly hired physicians recruited into new positions. Appraisers should use a more informed approach to the survey data than merely assuming the median from the general surveys is the universal compensation floor necessary to recruit a new physician.

### *2.5 The Locum Tenens Cost Method*

Since the cost of locum tenens physicians represents a conceptual alternative to staffing a physician position in a medical practice, its use as an alternative under the cost approach is considered here. In short, use of locum tenens is not a comparable staffing arrangement to the employment of a physician. Locum tenens physicians are intended as temporary staffing to cover services when existing physicians cannot provide them. Because they are used temporarily, the cost of these physicians generally includes a premium and often entails the assumption that the existing practice will bill and collect for services provided by the locums provider. In addition, the cost of locums tenens generally includes a markup for the administrative costs and required return of the locums staffing company. These types of economics and costs are not comparable to an employment arrangement. Thus, use of locum tenens costs as an alternative method under the cost approach is ill-advised at best, and strictly speaking, not comparable from a valuation perspective.

### *2.6 Evaluating the Use and Relevance of the Cost Approach*

In evaluating the potential use of cost approach methods or in assessing the outcomes of cost techniques applied to a subject employment arrangement, it is important to note the relative strengths and weaknesses of the cost approach methods. The advantages of these methods are noteworthy. The HPNE method and the AHC method use the historical performance and actual earned compensation levels of the subject practice or physician in the local market context under independent conditions as the basis for guideline compensation under employment. Local market factors, such as reimbursement, payer mix, and patient demand, are necessarily reflected in the historically earned compensation of the subject, particularly under the HPNE method. Moreover, practice patterns and operating characteristics of the subject are also necessarily reflected in the value indications under the HPNE method. This method is based on the compensation outcomes of these factors on the net earnings of the subject.

The importance of using actual historical compensation outcomes is considerable and significant. Under these methods, the appraiser has a local-market-driven and practice- or physician-specific indication of the value of services that is grounded in actual outcomes and not on an assumed "market" basis using survey data that lack statistical representation of the national, much less a local, market. In very real terms, the HPNE and AHC methods provide specific market indications for the practice or physician in terms of what compensation was, in fact, earned based on arm's-length independent conditions in local service area dynamics. Other methods are not based on this level of realism and factual evidence relative to the subject. Other approaches and methods include levels of speculation, assumptions, projections, and the like. No other valuation methods under the cost approach have this kind of relationship to local market conditions as these two methods.

Moreover, both methods provide indications that reflect the perspective of the seller of the services, i.e., the physician. Since the seller has been receiving this level of compensation for services, it is reasonable for him or her to expect a commensurate level of compensation for those services under employment, unless there are significant changes in market conditions from those in prior periods. In fact, HPNE or adjusted historical compensation reflects the compensation value of the seller's alternative to employment, which is remaining in the current employment or practice arrangement. FMV is intended to reflect the price for services at which both a willing buyer and seller would consummate a transaction. Thus, the alternative price for the same services is highly relevant to determining what the FMV price would be.

The cost to recruit method provides a perspective on one alternative available to the potential buyer-employer through determining the compensation and cost necessary to recruit another physician to provide the services required under the proposed employment arrangement. This alternative cost helps to circumscribe the relevant range of value for these services. All cost approach methods reflect the replacement cost for the services.

The limitations of cost approach methods should be noted as well. These methods are based on past compensation outcomes that resulted from market and operating conditions that may not be indicative of future circumstances. As a result, the cost approach method may not reflect key economic factors and dynamics expected under employment. Past compensation outcomes may not determine future services. The HPNE and AHC methods, moreover, require significant levels of data to be reliably completed. Without this detailed data, the methods may lack the level of precision and accuracy that are part of their appeal. In many valuation assignments, such detailed data are not readily available to allow the appraiser to implement the methods reasonably. In addition, these methods may not be applicable when the subject physician was employed or practicing in an independent or arm's-length arrangement. As more physicians move toward hospital or health system employment, the HPNE and AHC methods will not be available for determining FMV for regulatory purposes. Thus, use of these methods may be limited in many situations.

A major weakness of the cost to recruit method is that it uses general survey data to apply to a specific physician. These general data are not usually reported according to factors that make it easily and accurately comparable to a specific physician. The method provides a general result, rather than a highly specific indication. The cost to get a truly or fully comparable physician can be difficult to determine. Moreover, general survey data may not reflect compensation levels that are relevant for the local service market.

## 3.0 The Income Approach

### *3.1 The Income Approach Defined*

The income approach is defined according to the *International Glossary of Business Valuation Terms* as "a general way of determining a value indication of a business, business ownership interest, security, or intangible asset using one or more methods that convert anticipated economic benefits into a present single amount." The income approach is usually the most difficult of the three standard valuation approaches to apply to the valuation of service arrangements. This difficulty derives from the traditional definition of the income approach in the business valuation body of knowledge. Converting the compensation under a service agreement to a "present single amount" may not produce an indication of value that is meaningful for a service contract.

For valuing service agreements, the income approach may be adapted in terms of the valuation principle of future benefits as the basis for value, but without the conversion to a present value amount. With this adaptation, the income approach can be employed to calculate the future economic benefits to be received by one or both parties to the service agreement.[13] These benefits are then evaluated in terms of investment levels, resources utilized, and services provided in comparison to market rates of return and profitability. Under this reformulation of the income approach, the appraiser seeks to value the services by ensuring that each party receives market returns or margins given the levels of investment, risk, and resource utilization attributable to either party to the service contract.

---

13 Under this adaptation of the income approach, future economic benefits are not intended to include the value or volume of improper referrals. Rather, the appraiser looks exclusively to the revenues, expenses, resources, and investments related to the specific services and service lines provided for in the agreement.

In the case of employment arrangements, the concept of earnings-based compensation can be used in the application of the income approach. A forecast of the practice net earnings is developed as the value indication for physician compensation under employment. This forecast takes into account future conditions for the practice as well as the specific scope of services contemplated under employment. It projects the anticipated compensation to be received by the employed physicians based on anticipated practice net earnings. Earnings-based compensation under the income approach is forward-looking in its measurement of physician compensation. There are two income approach methods that are used by appraisers for valuing compensation under employment agreements: the forecasted practice net earnings method and the adapted discounted cash flow method.

### *3.2 The Forecasted Practice Net Earnings Method*

The forecasted practice net earnings (FPNE) method is essentially the valuation technique used in the HPNE method except that the periods used for purposes of determining practice net earnings are future rather than historical ones. Essentially, the appraiser uses a forecast of revenues and expenses for the practice to compute net earnings from physician services. The forecast is based on the scope of services required under the subject employment arrangement. The projected net earnings are used as the basis for valuing the services under employment. As with the HPNE method, the expenses of the practice include amounts for the cost of capital, economic depreciation and amortization, and market-level physician benefits. Forecasted revenues and expenses may also include normalization and optimization adjustments and assumptions as discussed in the application of the HPNE method. The projected net earnings can also take into account anticipated changes in the marketplace in terms of future volumes, reimbursement, operations, and services.

One key issue in the application of the FPNE method is what future periods should be used to determine earnings-based compensation. At minimum, the future periods included should coincide with the number of years of the employment agreement covered by the FMV opinion of the appraiser. If the appraiser's FMV analysis is effective for the first two years of the employment agreement, then at least the first two years of the contract should be included in the forecasted periods. Taking an average of the PNE from the years covered by the valuation opinion can be appropriate for establishing the value of the physician services, rather than determining a distinct amount for each discrete period. The use of periods outside the effective period of the valuation period for purposes of averaging and determining a compensation level during the valuation period can raise some questions, especially if the compensation in the out years is significantly higher than the initial years covered by the valuation opinion. An appraiser might attempt to defend such out-year inclusion if the out years are consistent with the initial term in the subject employment agreement. The argument would be that the typical buyer-employer is looking at compensation over the term of the employment agreement rather than the effective shelf-life of the appraisal. On the other hand, one might question whether a typical buyer-employer would seek to front-load compensation in a longer-term employment arrangement, given potential future changes in the marketplace. The uncertainty of today's physician marketplace in light of healthcare reform and experimentation in reimbursement structures would appear to mitigate against the economic impetus to front-load compensation.

### *3.3 The Adapted Discounted Cash Flow Method*

Another appraisal technique that can be used to establish earnings-based compensation is an adaptation of the discounted cash flow (DCF) method from business valuation.[14] In this application of the DCF method, the appraiser uses a template to solve for the physician compensation level that makes the net present value of the net cash flows from the practice equal to the value of the assets required to operate the practice.[15] Unlike the HPNE method, however, the adapted DCF (A-DCF) method does not include a deduction for the cost of capital. The cost of capital is reflected in the discount rate applied to the future net cash flows from the practice. Depreciation and capital expenditures are included the A-DCF method consistent with standard business valuation practice. The net cash flows can be tax-effected or not tax-effected, with the requirement that the discount rate reflect market rates consistent with the tax-effecting of the net cash flows.

The valuation theory in support of the A-DCF method is that it is another appraisal technique for determining practice net earnings from physician services using future periods. Under this method, practice net earnings are denominated in terms of net cash flows from the practice, where the costs associated with the total invested capital of the practice are included through capital expenditures and the discount rate. Stated explicitly, the A-DCF method purports to show the compensation level that is available from the practice operations, given the FMV of total invested capital required to own and operate it and a cost of capital that is commensurate with the risk profile of the subject practice. The use of the A-DCF method, as adapted from business valuation practice, separates owner compensation from compensation for physician services by

14 Todd Sorensen, AVA, of VMG Health introduced me to this adaptation of the DCF method for compensation valuation purposes.

15 In business valuation, the DCF is used to determine the value of the assets of the medical practice. Thus, there would appear to be a "chicken and egg" dilemma in using a DCF for business and compensation valuation purposes. For business valuation, a compensation level is needed to determine the net cash flows from the practice, which in turn provides a value indication for the total assets of the practice. Compensation valuation requires the value of the total assets to determine practice net earnings, and thereby compensation for physician services.

determining the latter after accounting for the former. The A-DCF method can also be seen as an adaptation of the independent investor test using a DCF template.

As with the FPNE method, one key issue in the use of the A-DCF method is what periods should be included in the analysis. A corollary but no less important issue is whether a terminal or liquidation value should be used after the discrete period projections. With regard to the number of years used in discrete period analysis of the DCF, the arguments from the same issue in the FPNE method would appear to apply to the A-DCF method. The employment contract term may extend over a longer horizon than the applicable period for the valuation opinion. One might contend that the term of the employment agreement should coincide with the discrete period analysis. The same issue of front-loading compensation can also arise as a potential objection to the use of periods beyond the effective life of the appraisal.

The question of using a terminal or liquidation value raises a potentially more difficult set of issues, especially if normalized compensation is shown to be higher in the terminal value than in the initial years of the DCF analysis. One potential issue is whether an employment arrangement can be considered to continue into perpetuity, as implied by the use of a terminal value. This question is particularly acute, when the subject employment agreement provides for termination without cause. In addition, the experience of the industry from the 1990s provides a cautionary note to the current expectation that physician employment by hospital and health systems is the new permanent paradigm for physicians. A more supportable approach may be to use a liquidation value at the end of the proposed employment term to reflect the uncertainty of future market conditions over the long run.

### *3.4 The Importance of Supportable Projections in the Income Approach*

As noted in the professional literature related to the use of the income approach in business valuation, it is essential to use a forecast that is grounded in supportable and defensible assumptions. Unrealistic projections undermine the credibility of value conclusions arrived at using the income approach. The same requirements for reasonable and realistic forecasts, projections, and assumptions apply in using the income approach in compensation valuation. An unconvincing and unrealistic pro forma for practice revenues and expenses yields a questionable indication of value. To avoid this problem, appraisers should perform sufficient research, data gathering, and analysis on the subject practice, its local service market, the subject physician specialty, reimbursement trends, and the larger physician marketplace. This knowledge base should provide the appraiser with a sound basis for determining reasonable and supportable estimations, projections, and assumptions for application of the income approach in valuing physician employment arrangements.

### *3.5 Determining Asset Values for Use in the Income Approach*

Earnings-based compensation includes economic depreciation and amortization on those assets necessary for the operation of the practice. The cost of capital associated with these assets is also included. These costs are included in the computation of practice net earnings because they are essential elements of the cost of providing services. The net earnings from physician services would be overstated if such capital costs were not included in this calculation. Such costs are required in the production of the services. To exclude these costs misstates practice net earnings because the full cost of providing the services cannot be determined without capital costs. For noncapital-intensive physician specialties, capital costs are generally not that material to the calculation. Capital costs can be significant, however, because those specialties utilize significant levels of technology and equipment in the provision of clinical services, particularly TCS. In addition, the recent requirements for electronic medical records systems (EMRs) have resulted in larger technology costs for all physician practices.

In terms of determining the values to use for determining depreciation and amortization as well as a cost of capital, there are key conceptual and practical issues for the appraiser to consider as part of completing income approach methods. The income approach looks forward to future earnings-based compensation that would arise under the proposed employment arrangement. Where the proposed arrangement includes the purchase of the practice, the FMV of the asset values determined in a business appraisal should be used for the determination of economic depreciation and amortization and for the cost of capital. The reason for this use is that the appraisal has identified and valued those assets, both tangible and intangible, that exist in the practice and have value in accordance with the standard of value. These tangible and intangible assets, therefore, are necessary for the operation of the practice. In addition, the appraisal has determined the value that the typical buyer would pay for those assets in acquiring the practice. These asset values must necessarily be used for determining the capital costs of the practice. *One cannot present a congruent and coherent appraisal analysis by indicating that a typical buyer would pay one value to acquire the assets of a practice and then not use those same values to determine the capital costs associated with operating the practice.*

Moreover, one cannot exclude these capital costs from the determination of practice net earnings. The concept of earnings-based compensation as the measure of value for professional services includes those costs necessary for the production of those services. If tangible as well as intangible assets are necessary for the operation of a physician practice, they are necessarily required for the production of physician services. Otherwise, to what end are these assets needed? They would have to be treated as nonoperational to be excluded from the capital costs of operating the practice. One cannot escape the fundamental economic relationship between the costs of operating a business and the operational asset base needed to run the practice. These costs should be factored into the determination of practice net earnings for establishing the value of the professional services provided in a practice. Excluding these costs would represent a mismatching of revenues and expenses related to the service. It would also provide an undue benefit in determining compensation for services: The compensation does not include an adequate allocation of the costs necessary for the provision of the services. Costs would be understated in computing practice net earnings to use as the value of services, if the costs of all capital needed to operate the practice are excluded. Provision of an undue benefit raises the specter of regulatory exposure.

For those acquisition-employment transactions with high tangible and intangible asset values, the net effect of appropriately burdening practice overhead with the costs associated with all operation assets needed in the practice is to lower physician compensation significantly. Whatever business valuation claim one makes in the debate about the priority in the value indications from the cost and income approaches with respect to appraising physician practices, the implication for compensation valuation is clear. If the practice has significant intangible asset value to a typical buyer under the standard of FMV, the costs associated with these assets should be factored into determination of compensation under the income approach based on a forecast of practice net earnings. To claim otherwise is to present an inconsistent and incoherent valuation methodology that uses one set of economic assumptions and analysis for one purpose, i.e., an acquisition, and subsequently uses a completely different approach for determining compensation.

The reason that one cannot use such a bifurcation in fundamental appraisal analysis is that, under any earnings-based method, professional compensation is a function of the net earnings produced by a professional. These net earnings must reflect the costs, including capital costs, associated with the use of practice assets. As discussed previously, the concept of earnings-based compensation actually arose out of the business valuation body of knowledge in looking at the appropriate level of owner compensation for small business, including professional practices. To posit and successfully defend such a bifurcation, one would have to defeat the conceptual framework developed in the appraisal body of knowledge with regard to the determination of owner compensation and the use of the independent investor test as part of that determination, particularly in relation to professional practices.

Now, the appraisal body of knowledge with respect to the owner compensation does afford other techniques for determining the value of owner services, including the use of market-based compensation data. The claim made here is not that earnings-based compensation is the only method for determining the FMV of physician compensation.

Rather, the point argued here is that the application of earnings-based compensation techniques should be consistent and congruent. Thus, the use of income approach methods for valuing physician compensation should be based on the FMV of assets established based on a business valuation, where such an appraisal was prepared and is available to the compensation valuation analyst. In the absence of such an appraisal, the analyst should use the best available information on practice assets to establish the capital costs associated with the operation of the practice.

### 3.6 Evaluating the Use and Relevance of the Income Approach

The use and application of the income approach has several strong points for the valuation of employment arrangements. First, income approach methods are based on forecasts of future market conditions that will exist under the subject arrangement. This feature is important because market conditions can often change significantly, especially in the area of reimbursement. Second, since income approach methods are based on practice net earnings for the subject practice or physician, the value indications derived from these methods can account for local market dynamics. These indications are also based on the practice and operational patterns of the subject. They can entail normalization and optimization assumptions that adjust net earnings to those consistent with a reasonable operator or a typical buyer of physician services. Income approach methods, therefore, can encompass future conditions along with normalized outcomes at a level of specificity not generally available with the cost and market approach methods. Both the cost and market approaches do not consider future conditions, and the market approach generally lacks precision in looking at local market factors and specific practice or physician operating patterns.

The limitations of income approach methods primarily relate to the validity and supportability of the assumptions used in the forecast of revenues and expenses for the subject practice or physician. The indications of value produced by the income approach are only as relevant and valid as the assumptions used in this forecast. Predictions and prognostications necessarily entail some level of uncertainty, even when they are well-researched and -supported. Another critical drawback of income approach methods is that they can be data-intensive. Significant information is required to prepare a base year pro forma for the practice or physician. Additional detailed information is needed to prepare projections going forward from this base year. Without detailed data, the forecast may be unreliable or uncertain with respect to various key assumptions. Limited data may also give rise to forecasts with various assumptions that cannot be readily research, verified, or supported. A highly assumptionized forecast may lack credibility.

Finally, using the income approach on a hospital or health system practice or employed physician may be difficult if the hospital- or health system-affiliated employer has made significant changes to a practice for reasons extrinsic to the operations of the practice. (See Part I for a discussion of such extrinsic factors.) The hospital or health system may have also converted or moved TCS to HOPD status. Thus, historical data that might be used to prepare a forecast or pro forma for the practice may not reflect economics that are indicative of the typical buyer-employer. It may not be practical or feasible to normalize or adjust the historical financials of a practice to be consistent with the typical buyer-employer.

# PART V. VALUATION SYNTHESIS AND SPECIAL ISSUES

## 1.0 Valuation Synthesis and Conclusion of Value

### *1.1 Synthesis Process Overview*

Valuation synthesis is the process by which an appraiser evaluates the value indications from various valuation approaches, methods, and techniques and concludes with an opinion of value. The synthesis process can yield a single indication of value or a range of value for the subject being appraised. It is used in various appraisal disciplines, ranging from real estate appraisal to business valuation, where multiple approaches and methods were prepared by the appraiser. No specific formula or methodology governs the synthesis process. Sound and rigorous valuation thinking, however, should direct the synthesis process. Ultimately, the synthesis is a matter of professional judgment. Appraisers are expected to support the final outcome of the process and should be able to articulate the reasons and rationale behind the synthesis.

Many appraisers use formal approaches or systematic techniques for synthesizing various value indications. One popular approach is to weight each indication on a relative percentage basis and compute a weighted average value indication. The percentage weightings assigned to each value indication signify the appraiser's assessment of each indication relative to the others. Weightings are assigned based on the appraiser's judgment as to the relative applicability of the value indication to the subject. Such applicability is evaluated in terms of the relative strengths and weaknesses of the methods and the underlying data used in the methods as well as other factors. Appraisers often favor this approach because it provides a ready-made template and framework for synthesizing the results of multiple methods. The use of weightings, however, is not the only pathway to synthesizing multiple value indications. Other valid approaches include the selection of a specific indication or the use of specific indications to serve as lows or highs for a range of value.

Some appraisers prepare a single value indication for each of the three approaches (cost, market, and income). It should be noted, however, that a single indication of value does not necessarily need to be synthesized for each approach, where multiple valuation methods and techniques were completed for a given approach. An appraiser may decide to evaluate and synthesize the value indications from all methods used in a single comprehensive comparison to assess each method relative to all methods used in the valuation process. Depending on the number of value indications, such a process may be more logical or systematic than synthesizing three indications of value from each approach. Moreover, an appraiser may decide to use different evaluation and synthesis approaches from one valuation to the next based on the facts and circumstances. While such divergence in practice or conventions may be subject to scrutiny, doing so may be more rigorous and sound appraisal practice when done for good reasons. Ultimately, the synthesis process is a matter of professional judgment and analysis. To reiterate, however, an appraiser should be able to articulate the reasons and rationale behind the synthesis process used in the particular valuation assignment.

### *1.2 General Criteria for the Synthesis Process*

Whatever the approach for synthesizing value indications, there are general criteria that can aid in the systematic review of relevant factors and issues in evaluating value indications from different valuation issues. These criteria can apply to methods from all three approaches to value, i.e., cost, market, and income. These criteria can include the following.

#### The Relative Strengths and Weaknesses of a Method or Technique

An appraiser should go through a process in which the relative strengths and weaknesses of the various methods completed are evaluated in comparison to each other. Generally, this process begins with a conceptual analysis of each method in which the appraiser evaluates each technique from a methodological standpoint. An appraiser may conclude that some methods have greater applicability in encompassing the fundamental economics and market dynamics of a service than others from a conceptual or methodological point of view. Methods can also be assessed relative to a series of economic factors and market dynamics related to the subject employment arrangement. The appraiser weighs the applicability and relevance of the method with reference to the subject services and practice or physician. These factors can include the following:

- Subject physician specialty;
- Scope of services under employment;
- Compensation structure or formula;
- Key contractual terms and duties; and
- Facts and circumstances related to employment.

Examples of how these factors are applied include the following. For a hospital-based physician, practice net earnings methods may be considered less relevant and applicable because the subject physician covers many night or weekend shifts with low volumes or provides services at a hospital with a poor payer mix. In another example, an appraiser may place significant weight on earnings-based compensation methods in appraising an employment agreement where the physician will be employed in-place with a seamless transition for patients. For recruiting a physician into a new market from out of state, an appraiser may conclude that market-approach-based methods are more relevant to the FMV analysis.

#### The Reliability, Quality, and Quantity of Data Used in the Methods

Data considerations can also play an important role in the synthesis process. Data inputs are a key part of the use of any appraisal method or technique. As a result, valuation methods are dependent on the nature of the data used in their application. To the extent that data are not reliable, questionable, or are lacking in evidence or support, the outcome of those methods using such data is necessarily called into question. The concept of "garbage in, garbage out" applies to the outcomes of valuation methods and their use of data. On the other hand, if clear and well-supported data are used for the implementation of a method, the results of the method should be considered to be relatively strong or supportable from a data-source perspective.

#### The Relative Degree of Assumptions Used in the Methods

Lack of available or reliable data may necessitate the use of assumptions by the appraiser as part of completing a given valuation method. For purposes of this discussion, assumptions here are defined as inputs to appraisal methods, techniques, or models for which there is not actual data or for which the appraiser lacks certitude or material precision, whether quantitative or qualitative, with respect to the inputs. The issue of assumptions in the appraisal process can be significant. Certain appraisal methods and techniques require the appraiser to use assumptions. Income approach methods, for example, require projections of future revenues and expenses. An appraiser may also have to make assumptions about what is and is not included in physician compensation survey data when applying market approach techniques. In general, the extent and defensibility of these assumptions can become a key factor in evaluating the value indication of a method or technique. Highly speculative assumptions or assumptions with little independent support or evidence will generally yield less defensible outcomes than those with more support and less speculation.

#### The Range of Outcomes From the Methods

The relative range in value indications from the various valuation methods prepared can affect the synthesis process. A narrow range may necessitate less comparative evaluation than a broad range of value. When the outcomes are materially disparate, the appraiser will need to complete a more significant comparative assessment of the methods and their divergent indications of value. The appraiser is faced, in such cases, with the necessity of judging between competing ideas, factors, and considerations in arriving at a final conclusion of value.

In addition to these general criteria, specific issues and considerations can go into the assessment and evaluation of methods for each of the three approaches to value. The following sections discuss the specific areas for study and review by appraisers for methods under each approach.

### *1.3 Evaluating the Outcomes of Market Approach Methods*

The examination of value indications from market-approach methods and techniques generally focuses on three key areas: the nature of the market data, the general comparability of the subject to the data, and the measures or criteria used to determine comparability of the subject and market data.

#### Assessing the Relevance of Market Data

As part of the synthesis process, an appraiser should weigh several factors related to the relevance of the market data that were utilized in the market approach. These factors can include the following:

- *The extent and size of the data set:* In general, smaller data sets and those not taken from diverse respondents may be less indicative of the overall marketplace.
- *The representative scope of the data:* Are the data based on respondents or transactions that are representative of the marketplace or on only certain types of respondents and transactions?
- *The relevance of past market data to future conditions:* Has the market changed materially from the time periods reflected in the market data?

In general, less weight or emphasis is placed on methods using data that are considered to be relatively less comparable and applicable to the subject.

#### Assessing the Comparability of the Subject to the Market Data

A critical question in evaluating the outcome of market approach methods is the level and extent of comparability between the subject practice or physician to the market data. Do the operating characteristics, fundamental economics, and marketplace dynamics of respondents or of the parties to transactional data parallel those of the subject practice or physician and the proposed employment arrangement? How similar or dissimilar are they? Relatively less similarity between the subject and the data can reduce the relevance and applicability of a market-approach method.

#### Assessing the Measures or Criteria Used for Establishing Comparability

An appraiser should also weigh the relative importance or priority of the comparability factors, productivity measures, or other criteria used in applying the market data to the subject. Some factors, measures, or criteria may be more determinative than others of compensation in the marketplace for a given type of physician service or physician specialty. In general, such determinants should be given relatively more weight in the synthesis process.

### 1.3.1 Synthesizing Value Indications From Multiple Surveys

In evaluating indications from different surveys for the same basic measures or factors, several considerations can assist the appraiser in the synthesis process:

- The comparability of the subject to the survey in terms of key respondent profile factors and characteristics.
- The relevance of the data, given the year for which data are reported.
- The methodology used in gathering data for the survey.
- The number of respondents to the survey.

Where an appraiser has concerns about a given survey in terms of the above-noted criteria, the appraiser can consider assigning less weight to the value indications of a survey. The appraiser could also consider not using the survey in the synthesis process. When all of the above factors are relatively equal among surveys except for the number of respondents, many appraisers will weight the indications of value derived from different surveys using the same valuation technique and productivity measure based on the number of respondents. This formulaic approach is viewed as bringing some level of objectivity to the weighting process in that it reflects the relative quantity of data in each survey.

### 1.3.2 Synthesizing Outcomes From Multiple Methods Into a Single Value Indication

An appraiser may decide to prepare a single indication of value from the outcomes of various market-approach methods and techniques. When a variety of surveys, measures, and methods have been used in the market approach for physician employment compensation, it can helpful to organize the synthesis process in a logical and relational order. Grouping the various indications by commonalities, such as technique or productivity measure, can narrow the range of issues considered in each step of the synthesis process. Such a protocol can simplify the synthesis process and allow the appraiser to be more systematic in addressing key issues. The following represents a suggested sequencing and organization of the synthesis process for multiple market-approach indications of value:

1. Group indications from each survey based on the same valuation technique and productivity measure, e.g., the percentile matching technique based on wRVUs. Evaluate and synthesize the results into a single indication of value.

2. Group the synthesized indications from each technique using the same productivity measure, e.g., all techniques based on wRVUs. Evaluate and synthesize into a single indication of value.

3. Evaluate and synthesize the indications for each productivity measure as the final step in arriving at a value indication for the market approach.

As discussed previously, a single indication of value that is derived from a synthesis of the various value indications from market-approach methods applied to the subject is not required as part of the synthesis process. An appraiser may choose to synthesize the results of all methods used, regardless of the approach, in a single, but comprehensive synthesis.

### *1.4 Evaluating the Outcomes of Cost Approach Methods*

In assessing the relevance and applicability of the cost approach valuation methods for the conclusion of value, there are several issues for the appraiser to consider:

- *How valid, reliable, and accurate are the historical data provided to the appraiser?* Where the historical data used in the historical practice net earnings (HPNE) or adjusted historical compensation (AHC) methods lack important detail or are limited, the value indications from these methods may be held as less relevant and applicable to the subject.
- *How many assumptions were made in application of cost approach methods?* Value indications based on significant levels of assumptions (as defined above) may be more speculative and less defendable than other methods where fewer assumptions are made.
- *Was sufficient data provided such that the historical compensation could be adjusted for scope of service differences between past practice and the proposed employment arrangement?* Difficulties in adjusting for the scope of service can render past compensation less relevant for a proposed scope of services.
- *Is the past scope of services comparable and applicable to the proposed scope of services?* Historical compensation services that lack comparability with future services may not be a valid indication of value for the proposed services.
- *How relevant and applicable are historical operating and market conditions to the future?* Significant changes in the future can make historical compensation less meaningful to a proposed service arrangement.

- *For the cost to recruit method, how extensive are the market data on newly hired physicians and how relevant are these data to employment in the specific marketplace of the subject?*

### *1.5 Evaluating the Outcomes of Income Approach Methods*

Key questions to assess when reviewing value indications from income approach methods can include the following:

- *How valid, accurate, and reliable are the historical data that were used to establish the base year(s) from which the forecast of revenues and expenses was developed?* Limited and questionable historical data can undermine the credibility of the forecast.
- *To what extent can the assumptions and projections in the forecast be supported and defended by independent research and reliable data gathering?* A forecast based on weakly supported assumptions and estimates can reduce the importance of the income approach in the final synthesis of value.
- *How much uncertainty is there with respect to future changes in the operational and market dynamics of the subject practice, physician, or specialty?* A highly uncertain marketplace can limit the applicability of the income approach to the determination of FMV. In such circumstances, less weight may be placed on future expectations in comparison to historical outcomes.
- *How effectively and accurately is the forecast able to model the economics of the proposed scope of services under employment?* When the forecast is limited in its capacity to reflect the key economics and market dynamics of the proposed services, it may have less relevance in establishing the value of the services.

### *1.6 The Conclusion of Value*

The valuation synthesis process ultimately results in a final conclusion of value for the subject arrangement. To summarize the various key points discussed earlier, this final opinion of value can be in the form of a single value indication or a range of value, depending on the professional judgment of the appraiser. There is no generally accepted formula for making the final determination of value in terms of how the appraiser utilizes the various value indications from those appraisal methods applied to the subject. The final determination is based on the professional judgment of the appraisal given the value indications and the overall facts and circumstances related to the subject arrangement. Above all, the appraiser should be able to articulate the reasons that support and defend the final opinion of value.

## 2.0 Issues in Applying Value Conclusions to Compensation Structures

Depending on how the various valuation methods were applied, it is frequently necessary to convert the conclusion of value into the compensation structure of the proposed employment arrangement. The following sections discuss the issues that can arise when converting conclusions of value into employment compensation structures and potential ways for resolving these issues.

### 2.1 Converting an Opinion of Value Into a Compensation Formula

Compensation plans for employment arrangements often involve productivity models or the combining of various types of compensation elements, such as base compensation amounts, productivity or incentive bonuses, sign-on bonuses, retention bonuses, or payments for quality outcomes. Compensation may also be segregated by type of service. For example, stipends for hospital call coverage may be paid separately per shift. Since many valuation methods yield indications of value for total compensation, it is frequently necessary to convert, translate, or allocate the concluded opinion of value into these compensation elements.

#### 2.1.1 Matching Compensation to Services Provided

In general, the first step in the conversion or allocation process is to match compensation from the opinion of value to the services provided in terms of the proposed compensation structure. The appraiser takes each component of the compensation plan and determines what services are being paid for by the individual element. If compensation was separately calculated by type of service, then the allocation of the conclusion of value can be rather straight forward. One simply takes the buildup of compensation from the valuation analysis and assigns the value of each element to the corresponding service. Some compensation elements, however, may represent payment for the same services. For these cases, the appraiser will need to assign a portion of the FMV compensation for the service to each element.

In matching compensation for services, it is essential for the appraiser to think through what compensation amounts relate to what services. There is a tendency by some in the physician marketplace to treat certain forms of compensation as additive or incremental to the payment for a type of service when in fact these forms of compensation are simply a part of the payment for the same service. For example, sign-on or retention bonuses generally relate to clinic services or the primary type of service for which a physician is being employed. In most cases, these bonuses should be paid out of the total compensation for clinical services; they should not be paid as incremental compensation to total clinical services compensation. The reason for this treatment is that the bonuses relate back to physician services. In the case of sign-on bonuses, they generally represent an advance form of payment for services. Retention bonuses are payments that incentivize the physician to provide the services over a specified period of time; they relate to the duration of the services. Certain forms of compensation, moreover, can overlap and create potential duplications in payment. Thus, the appraiser must carefully analyze various compensation elements to ensure that any duplications are eliminated (see further discussion below in regards to compensation "stacking").

Part of the analysis involved in allocating the opinion of value also takes into account what services were included or not included in the valuation methods and techniques that are used in the appraisal. For example, was compensation for hospital call coverage or for interpretations of diagnostic imaging for a hospital outpatient facility included in the application of the cost and income approaches? If not, then the value indications from the cost and income approach methods would not relate to these services. On the other hand, if they were included, the values from these methods would represent total compensation for multiple types of services. The compensation attributable to each service would need to be calculated when the compensation plan entailed separate payments for these services.

The question of whether compensation for a given type of service is included in a particular valuation method is the most difficult to address when dealing with the use of physician compensation survey data under the market approach. As discussed in Part III, most of the surveys report total compensation from all sources. They do not generally report compensation by type of service. The appraiser, therefore, has to make a judgment as to whether there is a reasonable basis for assuming that compensation for a particular type of service is included in the reported data. This determination requires a solid understanding of the services, economics, and market trends of physician practices as they relate to key characteristics, such as specialty, practice-setting, and ownership. The appraiser must conjecture and estimate based on what is usual and customary in regards to the survey data used.

It may be sometimes necessary for the appraiser to prepare an individual valuation for a specific service that is paid for separately under a compensation plan. The individual valuation would be needed when the compensation indications from valuation methods reflected total compensation from all services. To determine the FMV compensation for the separate service, the appraiser would have to apportion the total compensation using the individual valuation.

#### 2.1.2 Allocating Total Clinical Service Compensation to Individual Elements

Often, an opinion of FMV total compensation for clinical services will need to be allocated among various individual compensation elements included in the proposed employment arrangement. The key to the allocation process is to ensure that the total compensation from all elements is equal and consistent with the FMV total compensation amount. There may be specific issues, however, that the appraiser needs to address in preparing the allocation among the compensation elements:

#### Base or Guaranteed Compensation

Many compensation structures provide the physician with a minimum base or guaranteed amount. Generally, this amount should be used as the minimum payment amount to the physician in computing total compensation payable under the proposed arrangement. Base minimum or guaranteed compensation is usually applicable when a physician's compensation formula includes variable or productivity-based elements. The minimum amount establishes what the physician will be paid regardless of the level of productivity or other variable inputs to the compensation formula. The key valuation issue for such guarantees is whether the appraiser thinks the minimum is consistent with FMV.

#### Sign-On Bonus

As discussed above, sign-on bonuses should generally be treated as part of total clinical compensation. The value of the sign-on bonus should be deducted from the FMV total compensation in the year paid. Many sign-on bonuses, however, include a payback provision if the contract is terminated prior to the term of agreement or some other specified period. In these cases, the amount of the sign-on bonus may be spread out or amortized over the payback period, consistent with the payback terms in the contract. For example, if a $30,000 bonus is subject to a three-year payback period, then $10,000 per year of the bonus could be included in the annual total compensation amount. The reason for this treatment is that the bonus is not effectively earned in total when paid; it is earned economically as each year of service is completed.

#### Retention Bonuses

Retention bonuses are the economic equivalent of a sign-on bonus with a payback provision with one deviation: They are paid out over time, rather than up front. The amount of a retention bonus for a given year should be included in the computation of total compensation for the year in question.

#### Productivity or Incentive Bonus

The total potential amount for a productivity or incentive bonus should be included in the calculation of total compensation for clinical services. For productivity bonuses, the potential should generally be calculated commensurate with the productivity levels used in the valuation analysis to establish the FMV total compensation amount for clinical services.

### *2.1.3 Conversion Into Productivity Models*

The conversion of an FMV analysis into the structure of a productivity-based compensation model can be addressed in two ways. In the first method, the opinion of value for total FMV compensation for clinical services is converted into the compensation rate per unit of measure for productivity. This conversion is calculated by dividing the total FMV compensation amount by the productivity levels used to determine the total FMV compensation. Where different levels of productivity were used in various valuation methods, the appraiser should weight or apply the varying productivity levels consistent with the weighting or application of the value indications from the method used. For the second method, the appraiser computes the compensation rate per unit of productivity for each method and then synthesizes the rates to arrive at a conclusion of value.

### *2.2 Compensation Stacking*

Compensation "stacking" occurs when physicians are hired to provide a variety of services and the proposed compensation for these services is computed based on the cumulatively additive value of each service. In other words, the individual compensation amounts are added up or "stacked" to determine the total compensation under employment.[1] The critical issue arising in such stacking of compensation elements is whether an overpayment for the services occurs when compensation amounts are added together. The overpayment may be the result of duplicative payments for the same service or of payments where the level or scope of service is below that assumed in establishing the compensation. The potential for duplication in compensation typically arises when the compensation for the services is computed individually and then added together for employed physicians. The individual valuations match compensation with the assumed scope of services and duties that are usual and customary for the specific service. Yet, when a physician is employed and required to provide a combination of services, the scope of services can be altered. The purpose of a so-called stacking analysis is to ensure that the potential for such duplication is eliminated. Three key cases can potentially create this kind of compensation duplication.

#### Employed Physician Providing Medical Director Services

A physician may be employed to provide a medical directorship along with patient care and clinical services. In such a case, the required hours for both clinical and administrative duties should be clarified and delineated consistent with the valuation analysis for each to avoid an overpayment for services. For example, assume the clinical compensation was established assuming a clinical workload of 40 hours per week and the medical directorship compensation was based on 10 hours per week. Further,

1 Edward Richardson, CPA/ABV, aptly coined the term "stacking" to describe this market trend.

assume the physician is paid a base salary or a base guaranteed amount. If the employment agreement only requires full-time work without specifying the number of hours or indicates scheduled hours of 40 per week, it is possible that the physician will not provide a level of service that is consistent with the assumed hours in the appraisals used to determine the FMV compensation on a combined basis. The compensation paid may not be consistent with FMV when the level of service provided is below that assumed in the appraisals.

#### Employed Physician Providing Clinical Co-Management Duties

In a recent market development, physicians are being hired by hospital and health systems to provide both clinical patient care services in a physician practice setting and hospital clinical co-management or service line management services for a hospital. This particular stacking of services has a significant potential for overcompensation when the employed physician is paid based on a base salary or a base guaranteed amount. If the scope of duties and workload for each type of service is not clarified or delineated, there is the potential for the physician to provide a lower level of work in one service area to the detriment of the other. As a result, the level of work assumed by the valuations for each service may not be met, and therefore, the compensation paid is not consistent with FMV. Since the compensation for these types of hospital management services can be significant, the potential for a material overpayment for services exists when combining these services.

#### Separate Compensation for Hospital Call Coverage

Perhaps the most ubiquitous case of compensation stacking arises when employed physicians are paid separately for hospital call coverage services. The critical issue in these cases is that the compensation for clinical and call coverage services may be duplicative under certain circumstances. The first instance stems from using the market approach only to establish the base salary or base guaranteed amount for the clinical compensation of an employed physician. The market compensation data may already include payments for hospital call coverage. Thus, when an employer looks to add compensation for call coverage to the clinical compensation, such compensation may be duplicative. To address this potential for double compensation, many appraisers will stipulate that a base salary or guarantee amount includes a normalized level of hospital call coverage. Thus, the physician should only be paid for hospital call coverage shifts worked over and above the normalized level.

A second instance arises when a physician is employed under a productivity or incentive model based on a compensation per wRVU rate. If this model extends to procedures performed while providing hospital call coverage, then the subject physician bears no unfunded care burden associated with providing such coverage. Since hospital call coverage is normally valued including this burden, payment of the typical call coverage stipend amount to such a physician would result in an overpayment for services. The amount paid to the physician for call coverage should be adjusted to eliminate any compensation for unfunded care.

#### Compensation on Independent Contractor Basis

Another critical issue that arises when stacking services is whether the value of the services was computed on an independent-contractor basis. Most medical directorships and hospital call coverage stipends are valued assuming the services are provided by independent-contractor physicians. As a result, most include an allowance or gross-up amount for employer-paid benefits. When employed physicians provide these services, the compensation should not include this allowance or gross-up amount because the employer already pays for and provides these benefits to the employed physicians.[2]

### *2.3 Sensitivity Testing of Compensation Plans Over Varying Productivity Levels*

In dealing with productivity-based models or productivity bonuses, it may be advisable for the appraiser to complete a sensitivity analysis to evaluate the level of compensation produced by the particular model or bonus formula over a range of productivity levels. The purpose of the analysis is to assess whether the productivity rate or formula should be adjusted at varying levels of productivity. As discussed in Part III, the MGMA compensation by quartile of production data indicate that compensation per wRVU or as a percentage of professional collections *declines* as productivity increases. In addition, physician practice can experience step costs as physician productivity ramps up. Because of these factors, an appraiser may want to evaluate the compensation levels at varying productivity levels under the compensation plan in comparison to the outcomes of the valuation methods used to establish the FMV compensation for the subject arrangement. In the sensitivity analysis, the appraiser models compensation under the contractual formula using a range of productivity and then compares the results over the same range of productivity using the valuation methods. The appraiser may recommend changes or adjustments to the FMV compensation amounts and rates based on the results of this analysis.

### *2.4 Qualitative Analysis and Judgments of Compensation Terms*

Appraisers may consider performing qualitative analysis on certain contractual terms and requirements related to compensation and the provision of services in proposed employment arrangements. This analysis focuses on whether the terms are consistent with the definition of FMV, i.e., what arm's-length, independent, and well-informed parties would negotiate apart from referrals. As a corollary assessment, the appraiser

2 Assuming the employer provides a market level of benefits.

may also review whether the terms and requirements of the contract are consistent with the scope of services and service requirements assumed in the valuation. These types of evaluations are not based on numerical models or mathematical techniques. Rather, they are performed on a qualitative analytical basis. The analysis may yield contractual terms or requirements that become opinion qualifications or limiting conditions on the opinion of FMV issued by the appraiser. In the informed judgment of the appraiser, the terms and requirements are needed for the employment arrangement to be consistent with FMV.

Examples of such terms and requirements can include the following facts and circumstances.

#### Productivity Requirement to Maintain Base Compensation

When a physician receives a base salary or a guaranteed minimum amount of compensation, many appraisers require that a minimum level of productivity is maintained for the physician to continue receiving the base amount. Their thinking is that a certain level of productivity is required to support and justify the compensation level paid. Other appraisers think that a physician may be given a guaranteed or minimum amount in the first year or two of a new employment agreement, regardless of productivity outcomes. They base this thinking on the fact that many transition issues can arise in new employment arrangements that can depress the productivity of a physician, but these issues relate to the employer, not the employed physician. As a result, they think that a guarantee for an initial, but limited period is consistent with FMV. They may also require, however, other work measures, such as minimum annual hours and hospital call coverage shifts, as a means to ensure that sufficient work input is provided by the physician to justify the compensation paid.

#### Required Weekly Hours

An appraiser may require that a physician work a minimum number of weekly clinical or work hours as part of the FMV opinion. This requirement may be a function of the appraiser basing the FMV opinion on historical annual work hours or an assumption regarding normalized work hours for physicians in the marketplace. The requirement for work hours consistent with the hours used or assumed in the valuation analysis should not be overlooked by appraisers. If the FMV opinion was based on a certain level of service or work and the contract does not require the physician to provide this level, the compensation paid for services rendered may be inconsistent with the FMV opinion. The physician may not, in fact, provide the level of service or work assumed in the FMV analysis.

#### Required Weeks Worked Per Year

In a similar line of reasoning, an appraiser may require that a physician work a required number of weeks per year as part of maintaining the level of duties necessary to support a base salary or compensation amount. The number of weeks is often based on market survey data or on historical levels for the physician, depending on what methods were used in establishing the base amount.

#### Required Number of Hospital Call Coverage Shifts Per Month

Appraisers will sometimes require that a physician provide a specific minimum level of hospital call coverage or practice call coverage shifts per month as part of the requirements for the FMV compensation amount. Such a requirement would result from assumptions about call coverage made by the appraiser in determining FMV. For example, if a physician historically provided a certain number of shifts per year and the appraiser assumed such coverage in the cost and income approaches along with the accompanying fees from such coverage, the appraiser may require this coverage to continue as part of the FMV opinion. *Appraisers should ensure that scope of service requirements in a subject employment agreement are consistent with the assumptions made in the various valuation techniques used to establish FMV for the arrangement.*

## 3.0 Special Valuation Issues in Employment Arrangements

### *3.1 Evaluating the Impact of Benefits on FMV Compensation*

As discussed in Part II, benefits packages can be an important element in the overall compensation package paid to an employed physician. Thus, the benefits afforded to a physician under an employment arrangement should at least be considered conceptually in evaluating the overall compensation level paid to a physician. Data on certain physician benefits are available through the various physician compensation surveys, allowing for a certain level of comparison with market norms. As discussed in the application of each of the approaches, a market level of benefits is assumed to be paid to physicians in employment arrangements. For the market approach, the reported compensation levels in the physician compensation surveys are assumed to be consistent with market norms. Market-level benefits are calculated into the computations of practice net earnings under the cost and income approach methods based on earnings-based compensation.

When a prospective employer provides more or less benefits than this market level, an adjustment to compensation may be needed. The appraiser should consider local market factors as part of determining whether an adjustment is necessary. Health insurance and other similar benefit costs can vary from market to market. (It should be noted that high and low reimbursement markets tend to correlate with high and low health insurance premiums. Higher premiums are what underwrite higher reimbursement.) The size of the employer entity and whether the entity is self-insured can also affect health insurance premiums. When looking at benefits, therefore, it can be more useful to assess the benefits offered rather than their costs in determining market-level benefits. In addition, payroll and other state-mandated employment taxes can also vary by city and state, causing relatively higher or lower costs in comparison to market data on benefits. Finally, for physicians who have historically received more or less than this market-based level of benefits, the benefits paid under employment may play a role in explaining differences in the compensation under the proposed arrangement in comparison to those received in the past.

### *3.2 Synthetic Employment or Foundation Model Arrangements*

As noted in Part II, so-called synthetic employment or foundation model arrangements are contractual structures in which a physician group provides services on an independent-contractor basis to a hospital or health system physician practice. The physician group is typically responsible for the payment of benefits and professional liability insurance (PLI) for its member physicians and nonphysician providers. As a result, the compensation paid by the practice to the group generally includes an allowance for benefits and PLI. In these arrangements, the benefits are typically established using market data. For PLI, however, it is often difficult to establish a FMV amount for PLI because premiums can be physician-specific based on claims history. In addition, various states have had malpractice crisis or issues in the past that may have adversely affected premium rates. As a result, the actual premiums for the group are frequently used for the PLI allowance. The appraiser, however, may want to review coverage levels to ensure they are reasonable and consistent with market norms.

The compensation paid in synthetic employment deals can be based on productivity-based compensation structures, consistent with regular employment deals. The compensation structure, however, needs to be consistent with healthcare regulatory requirements. The process for determining the rates for the productivity compensation is also consistent with that used in regular employment arrangements, with one exception. The total compensation typically includes amounts for benefits and PLI. Additional sensitivity analysis work may be required to assess the intersection of various productivity levels and the compensation rates vis-à-vis the fixed amounts for benefits and PLI. The rates may need to decline at certain productivity levels, since benefits costs and PLI cost may have been covered at certain threshold levels. On the other hand, an appraiser may conclude that the compensation rate at any level of productivity may be warranted in arrangements where compensation is solely productivity-based. The same rate at higher levels incentivizes the physician to increase productivity over historical outcomes. In addition, the group can have downside risk for covering fixed benefit and PLI costs at lower productivity levels.

### *3.3 Proposed Changes to a Physician's Practice as Part of Employment*

One critical issue that frequently arises in physician employment arrangements is how major changes in the scope of services or operations under employment should affect the determination of FMV compensation. Examples of changes can include those relating to location, service mix, inclusion in commercial contracts, referral patterns from other community physicians, and hospital call coverage at competing hospitals. While each particular change can involve unique considerations related to the facts and circumstances surrounding the change, the general concept followed by experienced appraisers in healthcare valuation is to determine whether the change results from factors related to the specific employer entity or whether they would be made by or would relate to the typical employer. Changes that are a function of the strategies and characteristics of a particular buyer-employer are usually not included in the determination of FMV. Appraisers consider such changes to be reflective of investment or strategic value related to a particular buyer-employer and not FMV. The definition of FMV in the appraisal body of knowledge entails assumptions related to the typical-buyer and seller. This general position, however, is not categorical. The facts and circumstances may warrant consideration of certain changes as being consistent with the definition of FMV.

### *3.4 Caps on Total Compensation*

There is a market trend in which total compensation for a physician is capped at a certain level, often stated in terms of a percentile or a percentage of a percentile from a physician compensation survey. The concept behind these caps is to set an overall limit on the amount of compensation earned by the physician. It appears that regulatory considerations are the impetus behind this trend. Many attorneys and health systems believe that such caps help avoid the potential for regulatory scrutiny with excessive compensation. In addition, these caps may also have operational or business origins, where employers may simply want to limit total compensation. While risk management considerations for regulatory compliance are surely important, it should be noted that, strictly speaking, such total compensation caps do not have their basis in the appraisal body of knowledge. Compensation valuation theory holds that compensation should match the services provided. If a physician provides an array of services and a high volume of services, there is no appraisal reason or economic basis for limiting this compensation at a set total amount, as long as the compensation amounts or rates for each service are established appropriately.

Certainly, the determination of compensation for highly productive physicians should consider the use of stacking and sensitivity analyses to ensure that the compensation is reasonable and consistent with FMV. However, there is no proverbial "Rubicon" level of compensation that serves as a universal or categorical maximum for FMV in terms of standard appraisal methodology. Having made this point from the standpoint of the professional practice of appraisal, there may be sound reasons from a regulatory or compliance risk management standpoint for implementing such caps. Such considerations are important and essential for any healthcare provider in today's regulatory environment.

Chapter 31

# Valuation of Physician On-Call and Coverage Arrangements

*By Gregory D. Anderson, CPA/ABV, CVA*

## Historical Perspectives

Senior physicians in today's market and their predecessors once recognized the importance of emergency department on-call coverage as a community service and as a means for building their practices. Indigent patients, tort system disrepair, and declining reimbursement were not the daily reality for these physicians that they now are. Hospital medical staff bylaws required on-call coverage, and physicians once accepted this in the course of practicing medicine. Compensation for taking calls was not the hotly contested issue that it is in many facilities today.

## Market Forces Affecting Physician Availability

The growth in the trend toward payment for physician on-call services is a function of market factors affecting the need for the service and physician unwillingness to provide the service without separate compensation. These market forces impact physician reimbursement, quality of life, and liability exposure, while hospitals, health systems, and other medical facilities experience increased regulatory requirements and community demands for physician availability in the emergency department.

## Uncompensated Care

The uninsured population in the United States continues to grow at alarming rates. Between 2005 and 2006, an additional 2.1 million people became uninsured.[1] With the

1 "The Uninsured and Their Access to Health Care." *Key Facts: October 2007*. The Henry J. Kaiser Family Foundation, Kaiser Commission on Medicaid and the Uninsured.

growth in the uninsured population, physicians providing emergency and trauma care increasingly provide care to patients who are unable to pay their professional fees.

### Tort Climate

Physicians are reluctant to furnish on-call services in an emergency setting because of the risk of malpractice claims. According to the American College of Surgeons, "a significant number of surgeons have been sued by patients first seen in the emergency department (ED)."[2] This stems from a condition of substantial disrepair that remains in many states. A survey by The Schumacher Group in 2005 identified malpractice concerns as the primary reason that surgeons are being discouraged to provide ED coverage.[3]

### Fewer Emergency Departments and Increasing Utilization

Nationwide hospital closures or closures of emergency rooms have placed additional stresses on those that remain, while increasing problems with limited access to care for many Americans results in over-utilization of the nation's emergency services. This places additional stress on the system and on physicians working in hospital EDs, increases the intensity of on-call services, and negatively impacts payer mix and, consequently, reimbursement for physicians' services.

### Quality of Life for Physicians

Physicians see ED call as a detriment to their quality of life, because most ED calls occur on nights and weekends. Call duties also often interfere with the physician's private practice, requiring more time away from personal or more profitable activities and resulting in greater inconvenience.

### Physician Shortages

Aside from physician shortages resulting from an aging population, other factors such as the following result in a decrease in the number of physicians in the call rotation, magnifying the difficulty and stress of those physicians who remain:

- Shortage of physician residents in certain specialties;
- Desirability of location;

2 "A Growing Crisis in Patient Access to Emergency Surgical Care." American College of Surgeons, Division of Advocacy and Health Policy.
3 *2005 Hospital Emergency Department Administration Survey*, The Schumacher Group.

- General economic factors affecting the ability of many communities to recruit and retain quality physicians;
- Increasing subspecialization of physicians has caused many physicians to limit the patients treated while on call; and
- Increasing numbers of physicians dropping out of call rotation because of age, lack of compensation, and rigorous schedules have exacerbated an already growing problem.

### Other Reasons

In December 2005, the Missouri Hospital Association published a report[4] on the state of ED call coverage, which noted the following additional reasons, among others, for physician resistance to taking call:

- "It's not my responsibility";
- Resentment for not being paid for call; and
- Difficulty in enforcing medical staff bylaw requirements to take call.

Observing this market dynamic in a community can be sobering for a hospital administrator. What begins as a request for on-call compensation by a single physician quickly escalates into broad and costly demands by many specialties, further spreading to other facilities in the market. Physician threats to drop out of the call schedule and demands for higher payment, coupled with hospital concerns about regulatory compliance and fiscal responsibility, create an environment of distrust and emotionally charged tensions.

### Regulatory Environment

Health care is viewed as one of the most heavily regulated industries in the United States, primarily due to the fact that the federal government is the primary consumer of healthcare goods and services through healthcare programs such as Medicare. As such, the federal government controls public policy as it relates to health care and is directly involved in nearly all aspects of the delivery of care. Many laws and regulations directly impact the financial relationships between healthcare providers, bringing compensation arrangements into the spotlight of regulatory agencies.

4 Smith, M. et al., *Emergency Department On-Call Coverage: Issues and Solutions*. Missouri Hospital Association, December 2005.

### Stark Law

Physician self-referral legislation (Stark law) is described in Chapter 7 as a critical regulatory element that must be addressed in most physician compensation arrangements because of its broad, strict liability implications and significant penalty provisions. To avoid violation of its general prohibitions on referrals of designated health services and billing for proscribed referrals, contractual arrangements with physicians for on-call services are generally designed to comply with the provisions of the Stark exceptions for bona fide employment relationships[5] (for employer-employee arrangements) or personal service arrangements[6] (for independent contractor relationships). Among other requirements, the *bona fide* employment relationships exception requires that compensation be consistent with the fair market value (FMV) of the services, while the personal service arrangements requires that compensation not exceed FMV. As such, FMV is an important element of both exceptions, as well as several other Stark exceptions, and critical to compliance with the Stark law's far-reaching scope.

### Anti-Kickback Statute

The federal anti-kickback statute makes it a criminal offense for individuals or entities to knowingly and willfully offer, pay, solicit, or receive remuneration to induce the referral of business reimbursable under a federal health care program.[7]

The anti-kickback statute contains safe harbor provisions to protect legitimate arrangements, including *bona fide* employment relationships[8] and personal services and management contracts.[9]

On Sept. 20, 2007, the Office of Inspector General (OIG) of the Department of Health and Human Services issued Advisory Opinion 07-10[10] in response to a request for an opinion as to whether a physician on-call and uncompensated care arrangement constituted grounds for imposition of sanctions related to acts in violation of the federal anti-kickback statute. This advisory opinion provides useful insight into the mindset of the OIG as it relates to the risk that payments for physician call on-call coverage could result in illegal remuneration and safeguards that the OIG believes reduce the risk that remuneration is intended to generate referrals of items or services reimbursable by federal health care programs.

5 42 C.F.R. §411.357(c).
6 Ibid., §411.357(d).
7 42.C.F.R. §1320a – 7b(b).
8 42.C.F.R. §1001.952(i).
9 42.C.F.R. §1001.952(d).
10 OIG Advisory Opinion 07-10, issued Sept. 20, 2007 and posted Sept. 27, 2007.

In the text of the advisory opinion, the OIG commented on the increasing compensation of physicians for hospital emergency department on-call coverage and the existence of legitimate reasons for such arrangements, including compliance with the Emergency Medical Treatment and Active Labor Act (EMTALA), physician shortages, and access to trauma care. The OIG noted the risk that physicians may demand payment for on-call coverage when neither the services provided nor market conditions warrant payment and that hospitals may misuse payments to entice physicians to generate additional business for the hospital. The OIG further commented that covert kickbacks might take the form of payments in excess of FMV or payments for services not actually provided. Problematic compensation structures noted in the advisory opinion include payments that do not represent *bona fide* lost income, payments when no identifiable services are provided, aggregate payments that exceed the practice's regular medical practice income, and payments for physician services when he or she actually receives separate reimbursement from insurers or patients (essentially double paying the physician).

The OIG noted that the requestor engaged an independent consultant to advise on the reasonableness of the per diem rates paid under the arrangement, the report on which was provided to the OIG. The consultant's analysis incorporated both public and private data on pay rates at dozens of medical facilities, resulting in a set of benchmarks used by the consultant to opine on the FMV of the payment arrangements. The advisory opinion also noted several other features that the OIG considered useful in minimizing the risk of fraud and abuse, which the author believes should be considered by any organization entering into a physician on-call arrangement.

In the advisory opinion, the OIG concluded that it would not subject the requestor to administrative sanctions under the Social Security Act, although it noted that the opinion should not be construed as a requirement for a medical center or other facility to pay for on-call coverage.

## Tax-Exempt Organizations

For organizations exempt from federal income taxes under Internal Revenue Code Section (IRC) 501(c)(3), no part of the net earnings of the organization may inure to the benefit of any private shareholder or individual.[11] Doing so may jeopardize the tax-exempt status of the organization; however, an organization may pay reasonable compensation without violating the prohibition on private inurement. Section 4958 of the IRC also provides for a tax, known as intermediate sanctions penalties, on excess

11 I.R.C. §501(c)(3).

benefit transactions, defined as a transaction in which the economic benefit provided by an exempt organization exceeds the value of the consideration received for such benefit.[12]

Unreasonable compensation contributes to private inurement and to excess benefit transactions, which in the more egregious cases, can jeopardize the organization's exempt status and, in less arrant cases, subject the exempt organization and the compensated individual to intermediate sanctions penalties. Reasonable compensation is the amount that would be ordinarily paid for like services by like organizations in like circumstances. IRC Section 162 guidance on reasonable compensation is often cited as a reference in reasonable compensation cases and examinations of exempt organizations.

### EMTALA

The EMTALA was created by Congress in 1986 to ensure access to care for emergency medical conditions, regardless of an individual's ability to pay. Sections 1866 and 1867 of the Social Security Act impose the requirements of EMTALA on hospitals and critical access hospitals that offer emergency services by imposing civil monetary penalties on hospitals and physicians for failure to appropriately screen or stabilize a patient needing emergency care or negligently transferring a patient.

Section 1866 of the Social Security Act requires that hospitals maintain a listing of on-call physicians to provide treatment to stabilize a patient with an emergency medical condition; however, EMTALA does not specify how frequently a hospital's on-call staff physicians are expected to be available.

In the preamble to the September 2003 final rule, CMS notes, "some physicians have in the past expressed a desire to refuse to be included on a hospital's on-call list but nevertheless take calls selectively. These physicians might, for example, respond to calls for patients with whom they or a colleague at the hospital have established a doctor-patient relationship, while declining calls from other patients, including those whose ability to pay may be in question. Such a practice would clearly be a violation of EMTALA."[13] Because the final rule did not mandate requirements for call coverage, hospitals have lost some leverage in requiring specialists to take calls, a situation that has contributed, at least in part, to the growing demand for on-call compensation.

12 I.R.C. §4958(c)(1).

13 68 *Fed. Reg.* (Sept. 9, 2003) p. 53255.

## Common Structuring of Coverage and Compensation Arrangements

### *Restricted and Unrestricted Arrangements*

As with many physician contractual arrangements, the type of on-call or physician coverage arrangement may vary dramatically from one contract to the next. In some cases, the physician specialty may dictate the type of arrangement. For example, anesthesiologists in a hospital setting are often required to remain in the operating room (OR) department during specified weekday and weekend shifts. This allows for anesthesia coverage for scheduled and unscheduled surgical cases throughout the shift. In other cases, the needs of the facility may dictate the requirements for physician coverage. Consider the example of the cardiovascular surgeon, required by the hospital to remain on-site in a hospital's cardiac catheterization lab during normal operating hours to provide backup services to the cardiologists and their patients in the facility.

*Unrestricted call.* In an unrestricted call arrangement, the physician is not restricted to the facility but obligated to respond timely in accordance with medical staff bylaws or other contractual arrangements. This is essentially known as a "beeper" call, with the physician carrying a pager or cell phone to ensure timely contact. Many arrangements require the physician to respond within 30 minutes. This arrangement is fairly common among a wide range of specialists who provide coverage to a hospital's emergency department and can include primary (first responder) call and secondary (backup) call.

*Restricted call.* In a restricted coverage arrangement, the physician is physically restricted to the facility during the restricted coverage period. This is often called "in-house" call and can apply to many different specialties, although hospital-based specialists are among the most commonly utilized in these agreements.

### *Blended Arrangements*

When circumstances dictate, facilities may contract with physicians for an arrangement that includes more than one type of on-call coverage or service. These may take on the form of arrangements that include both unrestricted and restricted coverage during a specified period, or a blending of on-call and other personal services, such as clinical or administrative services.

*Blended unrestricted call and restricted coverage.* In some situations, the physician will have periods of both unrestricted and restricted call during the same shift. An example of this would include coverage by an independent hospitalist of a hospital's inpatient services, in which the physician is required to be on-site for a 12-hour shift, immediately followed by a 12-hour shift of unrestricted call.

*Blended call with clinical service.* In certain circumstances, the physician will have periods of unrestricted and restricted call, combined with clinical duties and responsibilities. In this arrangement, the physician is also contracted to provide patient care, for which the employer or contracting entity bills for the physician's professional fees. Locum tenens firms often offer these arrangements to hospitals, mixing unrestricted call with two to four hours of patient care within a 24-hour shift. Another example would be a primary care physician who is contracted to work in a weekend community clinic for six hours on Saturday afternoons and remains on unrestricted call for the duration of the weekend.

*Blended call with administrative service.* Under an administrative service arrangement, the physician furnishes administrative or management services, such as a medical directorship, which is often combined with restricted and unrestricted arrangements, such as those found in an outsourcing of a hospital-based physician service. An example of this would be the outsourcing to a physician-owned group practice for ED physician coverage, including medical direction of the ED, restricted coverage (wherein the physician group bills for its professional fees). and unrestricted call.

### Common Payment Arrangements

*Hourly, shift, or daily rates.* Payment rates for physician on-call coverage consist of unrestricted rates, restricted rates, clinical services or administrative rates, and blended rates (such as per diem rates that include an assumed clinical time). Payment arrangements are most often based on hourly, shift, daily, monthly, or annual rates, although many variations and combinations can be found. Among the more creative arrangements include the following:

- Hospital A only pays for shortage specialty ED coverage, such as when the physician is required to cover a call rotation vacated by a departing or retiring physician.
- Hospital B only pays physicians taking call who are otherwise excused from ED call coverage duties by virtue of the medical staff bylaws, such as those who are exempt from call based on age.
- Hospital C only pays for excessive call, basing the payment on the number of days in excess of a threshold number, such as 10 per month.

The appropriate payment mechanism for physician on-call coverage is affected by professional fee billing arrangements and physician compensation plan structure, as will be more fully described later in this chapter.

*Activation fee.* An activity-based payment, or activation fee, usually a flat fee, is initiated when the physician is actually called in while on call. This is often combined with unrestricted call payments. An example of this can be found in a psychiatry weekend coverage arrangement, in which the physician was paid a fixed rate for weekend unrestricted coverage and an additional $200 if the physician was called in during the weekend.

*Group practice "tax" arrangements.* Freestanding, physician-owned groups are not immune from the need to establish the value of physician participation in the on-call rotation. Many groups, faced with aging physicians interested in reducing or eliminating the burden of call coverage, use a variety of means to reduce the compensation of physicians dropping out of the rotation, often with a charge or "tax" levied against the physician, which is then credited to the other members of the group. Examples of this include multispecialty group practices that charge the physician for accepting a reduced call schedule or ob/gyn practices that reallocate compensation to members who elect to drop out of the obstetric call rotation.

*Stipend and subsidy arrangements.* Fixed monthly or annual amounts may be necessary to make physician or group compensation levels representative of market values for services furnished, especially with respect to low- and no-pay care (often effective with hospital-based physician groups and others dramatically impacted by the hospital's payer mix).

*Subsidy for uncompensated care.* Particularly when the physician bills for the professional fee, this is usually in an amount needed to bring net physician compensation to market levels and often based on market reimbursement levels for low- and no-pay care (i.e., Medicare or Medicaid rate). Another example is the malpractice insurance premium subsidy, which serves as a means for providing limited relief toward premium costs incurred by medical staff. Additional examples include payments based on relative value units (RVUs) for uncompensated services and subsidized fee-for-service arrangements, in which the physician assigns his or her benefit under Medicare, Medicaid, or third-party payers to the hospital, the hospital bills and collects the professional fee, and the hospital remits a market-value fee-for-service payment or payment per RVU to the physician.

*Deferred compensation.* A new trend in on-call compensation involves the deferral of pay for on-call compensation until the occurrence of a specified event or certain period of time, such as milestone tenure on the medical staff or for years of participation in the on-call rotation. This method has proven effective in some circumstances in promoting physician loyalty.

## Determining Fair Market Value of On-Call Compensation

The proliferation of health care regulations impacting physician compensation arrangements and the variety of physician on-call arrangements in the market lead to a significant and looming compliance risk for parties to on-call and coverage agreements, particularly when remuneration is exchanged. This necessitates consideration of whether the arrangements are within FMV constraints and the applicable statutory and regulatory exceptions and safe harbors.

## Valuation Theory Applicable to On-Call Compensation

As with most compensation arrangements in the health care industry, there is a limited body of knowledge related to the theory of valuation of compensation for physician availability. While business valuation and asset appraisal standards abound among credentialing organizations, only recently has the American Institute of Certified Public Accountants issued standards[14] related to business valuations, which does not include valuation of compensation arrangements. This absence of published standards on the subject has contributed to inconsistencies in how accountants, appraisers, and consultants approach the valuation of physician compensation arrangements such as on-call payments. The wide range of valuation methods extends from a simple reliance on historical compensation to complex analyses including algorithms and detailed market research.

The following three fundamental principles coexist in the theory of business valuation: the principles of substitution, alternatives, and future benefits, and these can be transferred into the context of valuing service agreements. The principle of substitution states that an investor will pay no more for a service than for a substitute of equivalent economic utility. Under the principle of alternatives, each party to a contemplated contractual arrangement has alternatives to consummating the deal. The principle of future benefits emphasizes that the value of an investment is based on the future benefits the investment will provide. These principles lay the foundation for the application of valuation methodology to developing a conclusion of FMV in compensation for physician availability.

## Valuation Methodology

Several methods exist for determining value in a compensation arrangement. The justification for the use of a particular method or methods will often be dictated by the facts

14 Statement on Standards for Valuation Services Number One. American Institute of Certified Public Accountants.

and circumstances of the contractual arrangement. These methods of valuation can be generally categorized into one of three broad approaches: cost-based, income-based and market-based. Within each valuation approach, numerous methods exist for determining value, the relevance and applicability of each depending on the circumstances and the analyst's considered judgment. Valuation analysts often think of this process as a funnel, with various valuation methods entering the top of the funnel, subsequently yielding a conclusion of value at the bottom.

## Factors Impacting the Value of Call Coverage

The valuation of on-call and coverage compensation is significantly impacted by the specific requirements of the contractual arrangements and factors related to market conditions, physician specialty, and the frequency and intensity of the coverage. To properly analyze FMV, the valuation analyst should consider the following factors, and perhaps others, before employing the valuation methodology necessary to arrive at a conclusion of value.

Before undertaking the analysis of FMV in any on-call or coverage arrangement, it is crucial to understand what makes up the value of these arrangements, as distinct differences lie in whether the valuation results in a conclusion of value related to physician availability, the value of uncompensated care furnished by the physician, or a combination of the two. The burden of physician availability (i.e., the time spent away from family, sleep, and personal activities) carries with it an element of value to the physician as the seller of the service, as does the fact that the physician may be sacrificing time away from the private practice of medicine (clinical disruption) to provide his or her availability to the contracting facility. The physician also experiences foregone earnings from uncompensated care when providing ED coverage, particularly in the case of trauma and indigent care, not only in the facility, but also in follow-up care that may be necessary. Furthermore, the physician subjects himself or herself to heightened risk of malpractice claims in many instances, a situation that is further aggravated by a lack of compensation for that element of risk. In many situations, particularly in trauma center ED coverage, the physician experiences a combination of both inconvenience and uncompensated care. Some facilities address both issues in a single compensation arrangement (i.e., through a single payment for physician on-call shifts or hours) while others separately address the issues (i.e., through a combination of payments for availability only when beyond the norms and with special rates such as a percentage of Medicare or Medicaid allowables for uncompensated care). Understanding these nuances and appropriately considering the elements of risk and reward are key to a comprehensive and accurate analysis and conclusion of value.

*Facility trauma level.* A Level-1 trauma center contracting with the on-call physician will likely have a greater level of intensity, higher acuity, and more frequent call than a facility with a lower trauma level. It is also likely that the facilities with higher trauma designations will have a larger proportion of no-pay or low-pay patients and a higher malpractice risk to the physician. In many cases, this translates into greater stresses and demands on the covering physicians and may result in market conditions that support higher compensation.

*Physician supply and demand.* Markets and facilities with an imbalance between the supply and demand of physicians may see variations in the levels and methods of compensation. For example, some hospitals pay only for on-call coverage when shortage specialties are involved, such as when the number of physicians in the community falls short of a predetermined level of active full-time equivalent (FTE) physicians. Others pay additional compensation to encourage senior physicians to rejoin the call rotation when the medical staff bylaws permit the physician to drop out of call upon reaching a certain age.

*Payer mix.* The payer mix of the community and the hospital can have a dramatic effect on the value of on-call payments. For example, facilities with high indigent-patient volume often find physicians reluctant to participate in the call rotation without separate compensation, because physicians consider the risk of caring for the patient to outweigh the community benefit and professional fees received during the episode of emergency care and any follow-up care required.

*Specialty-specific factors.* The rigors of call coverage vary quite widely among specialties; therefore, the specific physician specialty should be carefully considered. For example, neurosurgery call may be substantially more complex than ear, nose, and throat coverage, necessitating higher compensation for the former to account for complexity and frequency. Most valuation analysts look directly at specialty-specific information when applying methodology to value on-call and coverage arrangements.

*Unrestricted call or restricted coverage.* The value of on-call and coverage arrangements relates to the value of physician availability and the value of care for indigent and low-paying patients. As an important element of value, physician availability increases in value as restrictions on the physician's movement are tightened. Because unrestricted call allows the physician to move about the community while accepting the responsibility to respond timely to calls, it carries a lower value in most cases than restrictions that bind the physician to remaining in the facility while on-call.

*Time of day or week.* It can be said that greater inconvenience for on-call arrangements translates to higher value for compensation, because more intrusive scheduling increases the level of difficulty in finding physicians willing to cover and raises concerns over quality-of-life issues.

*Rotation.* More frequent participation in the call rotation means more time away from practice and personal activities. It is important for the valuation analyst to consider the "normal" level of call for a particular specialty (i.e., one-in-four rotation) and evaluate whether the required rotation results in excessive commitment by the physician beyond the typical level experienced by peers. For example, one proprietary survey of a local market by the author indicated an average rotation of one-in-four for orthopedic surgery and an average of one-in-three for trauma surgery.

*Length of shift.* Clearly, longer hours of on-call time equate to higher value, particularly when considering the value of shifts less than 24 hours paid at per diem rates. More commonly, shift lengths differ among facilities as they relate to weekend coverage, when weekend shifts may range from 48 hours (7:00 p.m. on Friday to 7:00 p.m. on Sunday) to 63 hours (5:00 p.m. on Friday to 8:00 a.m. on Monday), which directly affects the level of shift compensation.

*Intensity.* The intensity level of physician coverage is an essential distinguishing factor in assessing the value of on-call and coverage. Physicians whose coverage results in care for cases of higher acuity experience higher levels of stress, greater risk of malpractice claims, and often an increased likelihood of nonpayment. Intensity can also be measured in terms of the number of interactions during a call shift, such as the number of calls received or the number of times a physician has to physically respond to calls when on unrestricted call.

*Frequencies of calls and call-ins.* Higher call volume and more frequent in-person response to calls generally equates to less time for the physician to spend in his or her practice or personal activities, thus increasing the degree of hardship and, consequently, the degree of resistance of many physicians to accepting the burden of call. In many situations, the sheer intensity of on-call and coverage and the volume of calls and call-ins have driven some physicians and groups to refuse coverage to facilities. Others have used this as rationale for demanding compensation for on-call and coverage arrangements or in demanding higher compensation.

*Concurrent call.* Simultaneous coverage at multiple facilities is becoming a more important factor in determining the FMV of unrestricted on-call arrangements. In many markets, physicians in high-demand specialties agree to cover two facilities or more at the same time. This can become a significant issue, becausee the implications are far-reaching, given the following risks:

- Coverage at multiple facilities can result in a lapse of coverage when the physician is tied up on a case at one facility and another facility calls the physician.
- The need for secondary, or backup, coverage is paramount to avoid the lapse in coverage.
- Some groups have used multifacility unrestricted call as a reason to request payment for secondary coverage when asked to supply a backup physician.
- Spreading physician call coverage across multiple facilities may dilute the value of the service provided to any one facility, yet physicians inevitably feel that each facility should pay the same rate as if exclusive coverage was furnished. However, some valuation analysts believe that some concurrency arrangements result in the diminution of value.

These and other elements pertinent to the specific situation should be given strong consideration when valuing concurrent call arrangements. Further analysis of the specific impact of these characteristics will follow in the discussion of valuation methodology.

**Utilizing the Three Broad Approaches to Valuing On-Call Arrangements**

*Cost-based approach.* Using the cost-based approach, the analyst seeking to reach a conclusion of FMV for compensation related to physician availability, such as an on-call or coverage arrangement, generally considers the cost of an substitute arrangement, such as the avoided cost to replace or re-create the subject service.

*Avoided cost-to-replace method.* In evaluating the avoided cost to replace physician availability with a substitute arrangement, consideration is often given to the costs of *locum tenens,* or physician staffing firm coverage. In most cases, these represent short-term solutions to the problem of physician coverage, and the cost of obtaining this type of coverage can be high. In applying this method, the valuation analyst conducts research of firms to provide the requisite coverage, obtaining information about applicable rates for the level of coverage, considering time and shift requirements, the necessity for unrestricted or restricted coverage, and the appropriate physician specialty, skill set, and experience requirements. It should be noted, however, that rates obtained from firms to provide physician coverage must often be adjusted, or *normalized,* to ensure comparability to the subject arrangement. For example, rates quoted by physician staffing firms most often include some allowance for the cost of malpractice insurance coverage associated with the physician service. However, if a hospital negotiates with an employed physician to assume extra unrestricted call for a shortage specialty, the compensation paid by the hospital (employer) to the physician (employee) does not include reimbursement for the physician's malpractice cost, because this cost is already borne by the hospital as employer. Therefore, a normalizing adjustment would be necessary to remove from the market research on staffing firm rates the portion of the rates attributable to malpractice coverage. Similar circumstances exist with respect to the payment of payroll taxes, employee fringe benefits, and other costs that must be properly matched to the replacement arrangement.

Earlier in this chapter, the quantitative and qualitative elements of on-call and coverage arrangements were discussed. The valuation analyst gives consideration to these traits of an arrangement to arrive at a normalized analysis of the arrangements or data used in the determination of FMV. Using the cost-to-replace method, the analyst must ensure that the substitute arrangement (i.e., physician staffing firm) is comparable in terms of frequency, shift length, intensity, and other factors. Simple comparison of a *per diem* rate to a 12-hour shift would be blatantly unrealistic, as would comparisons that improperly matched the physician specialty, restricted or unrestricted terms, and time of day or week. It is the responsibility of the analyst when performing market research to be certain that the substitute arrangement is comparable to the subject arrangement being valued or to adjust the comparable data accordingly; otherwise, an incorrect result will be obtained.

*Avoided cost-to-re-create method.* Often, the FMV of compensation for physician availability can also be determined through the assessment of the avoided cost to re-create the subject arrangement. One effective use for this method is in the evaluation of avoided costs associated with subsidies tied to hospital-based physician coverage arrangements. In the example of a health system's contract with an anesthesia group to furnish surgery department, obstetrics, and ambulatory surgery center anesthesia coverage, the avoided cost of directly employing anesthesiologists may represent a valid cost-to-re-create method. This analysis is quite complex and incorporates a great deal of assumptions regarding physician professional fees, overhead, and physician costs, and, as a result, can be overly speculative.

This type of analysis is also heavily dependent upon the qualitative and quantitative factors specific to the subject arrangement being valued. For example, physician supply and demand issues, such as community need, will drive the determination of compensation necessary to retain physicians in an employment-alternative analysis, while payer-mix issues have a measurable effect on physician professional fee reimbursement when projecting the expected revenues from the cost-to-re-create service with employed physicians.

*Income-based approach.* In valuing most unrestricted on-call and restricted coverage arrangements, the income-based approach is of little use in the valuation of physician availability. This is primarily attributable to the fact that, in and of itself, physician availability generates no income for the purchaser of the service. However, when considering the value of subsidized arrangements, such as in the case of outsourced anesthesia coverage, the income approach is often one of the most significant methods available to the valuation analyst.

While it is important to consider the economic benefit to both purchaser and seller under income-based approach methodology, it is widely accepted that the economic benefit to the seller of the service—the physician—is measured in the same way as under the market-based approach, using data relevant to evaluate physician earnings associated with the furnishing of availability.

*Subsidy method.* The valuation of subsidy arrangements using a methodology under the income-based approach can be fully applicable and of significant use to the analyst. Consider the example of a hospital-based physician group, paid by a hospital for furnishing 24/7 coverage of a hospital department, such as an emergency physician group's contract with a hospital to furnish complete restricted and unrestricted coverage of the hospital's emergency department. Because a growing number of the group's patient encounters in the ED are unpaid, the hospital subsidizes the operation of the group by payment of a monthly subsidy. The valuation analyst may give strong consideration to a methodology that would quantify the shortfall experienced by the physician group, such as a measurement of the value of unpaid patient visits based on a percentage of Medicare allowables, as a proxy for the FMV of the service provided by the group.

Another method often used in valuing subsidies involves the analysis of compensation deficits experienced by the physician group. This method includes analysis of the financial statements and production information of the physician group for purposes of determining a normalized physician compensation level. Normalizing adjustments necessary for this analysis include, but are not limited to, the following adjustments to the financial statements of the physician group:

- Adjusting nonphysician compensation levels to account for related party arrangements;
- Adjusting occupancy costs to market levels, eliminated related party rental premiums or discounts; and
- Removing one-time or nonrecurring expenses, such as legal fees or nonrecurring physician recruitment costs.

Physician compensation levels should also be adjusted to reflect market levels commensurate with the production levels of physicians in the group. This analysis results from benchmarking comparisons of various production measurements, as more fully described below, including patient encounters, surgical cases, work relative value units (wRVUs), and others. For example, emergency room physician production in a group practice contracted by the hospital for emergency department coverage approximates median levels for emergency physicians in the market, yet actual physician compensation falls below median levels as a result of high indigent and trauma volume in the hospital's ED. The adjustment necessary to reflect market-level compensation is applied to arrive at normalized financial statements for the group, yielding a normalized operating deficit that represents a proxy for the FMV of the hospital subsidy.

*Market-based approach.* In the valuation of on-call and coverage arrangements, methods under the market-based approach are the most often applied, yet most are often misapplied for determining FMV. Methodology under the market-based approach seeks to assess FMV by considering that the buyer of a service will not pay more than, and the seller will not accept less than, the value of a comparable service. Thus, the central focus of the market-based approach and its related valuation methods is to identify comparable services, and to do so within the context of the definition of FMV in the healthcare regulatory environment.

*Published survey method.* As an industry, health care is fortunate to have a plethora of information in the form of published survey data on physician compensation and productivity; however, as a subset of the various types of physician services and the related compensation methods, compensation survey data for on-call and coverage arrangements lag behind other market data in the following ways:

- Lack of surveys committed to obtaining on-call compensation information;
- Low respondent numbers in surveys of on-call compensation;
- Difficulty in comparability; and
- As will be discussed later, concerns that survey data may be tainted by the physician-hospital referral relationship.

Despite these difficulties, competent surveys exist that are gaining in widespread acceptance and in the quality of data presented. An example is the Sullivan, Cotter and Associates, Inc. (SCA) *Physician On-Call Pay Survey Report*, which includes data on physician on-call pay rates and practices of 160 organizations from across the United States. State hospital associations, such as the Florida Hospital Association and the Missouri Hospital Association, also publish survey data on physician on-call market and compensation issues, while private companies and consultants also conduct proprietary surveys of local and regional market for data on compensation and other issues related to the growing need for data on these types of arrangements.

Surveys of physician on-call and coverage payment arrangements bring to light an important limitation when compared to other physician compensation surveys, particularly as it relates to the referral relationship that exists between the parties to the agreement. In the preamble to the Stark II Phase I Interim Final Rule, CMS notes concerns with the use of "comparables or market values involving transactions between entities that are in a position to refer"[15] and in the preamble to the Phase II Interim Final Rule, the Centers for Medicare & Medicaid Services (CMS) notes, "For example, the methodology must exclude valuations where the parties to the transactions are at arm's length but in a position to refer to one another."[16]

Most survey products on physician compensation arrangements include compensation arrangements between hospitals, academic medical centers, and other facilities and the physicians employed or contracted by the health care providers, where the physician has the opportunity to refer federal healthcare program beneficiaries and other business to the employer or contracting facility. However, these surveys also contain compensation data submitted by respondents in solo or physician group practices, where FMV and referral relationships take on less significance. These data, along with what are often large numbers of respondents, help mitigate the effects of any disguised payments for referrals that might be buried in the survey respondent data. On the other hand, physician on-call surveys (published surveys and local and regional surveys) are generally comprised of data furnished by parties to on-call payment arrangements for which at least one party has the ability to refer federal healthcare business to the other. Regardless of whether the payments are truly representative of disguised remuneration for referrals, this fact pattern presents unique challenges in the utilization of the data in determining the FMV of on-call arrangements. For this reason, some valuation analysts do not give consideration to the results of survey methodology.

The market-based approach considers the value of the subject on-call or coverage arrangement based on comparable data as determined through various methods, several of which are described in the paragraphs that follow.

The published survey method considers the value of an on-call or coverage arrangement based on data reported by published surveys. As previously noted, SCA and various

15 66 *Fed. Reg.* (Jan. 4, 2001), p. 944.
16 69 *Fed. Reg.* (March 26, 2004), p. 16107.

state medical associations publish surveys on compensation related to on-call arrangements. The SCA survey reports data on physician compensation in a variety of ways, including the following examples (assuming sufficient respondent data are available):

- By physician specialty;
- Unrestricted and restricted rates;
- Hourly and per diem rates;
- Separate reporting for trauma and nontrauma coverage; and
- Mean, median, quartile, and top decile data.

State medical association reports typically contain less cross-tabulated information about physician payment arrangements, but include good discussions of the market dynamics impacting pay-for-call arrangements in the state. Some surveys include hourly and per diem rates for call coverage, yet only average, median, or high-and-low ranges of data may be reported.

In the application of the published survey methodology, the valuation analyst performs research to gather information from published surveys to determine a broad range of market data on physician compensation, generally from the $10^{th}$ or $25^{th}$ percentile, depending on the survey product, to the $90^{th}$ percentile. It is within this broad range of market rates that the valuation analyst refines the value of the subject arrangement by considering the comparability of the market data and by making normalizing adjustments to the data or by fine-tuning the range of survey data to consider the qualitative and quantitative factors described earlier in this chapter.

At this point in the analysis, it is important to evaluate the quantitative and qualitative elements when valuing call. Some valuation analysts use information such as intensity, acuity, payer mix, frequency, need (i.e., supply and demand), and other defining elements of value to determine where in the spectrum of value the conclusion of FMV should lie. For example, high levels of intensity or frequent participation in the call rotation may contribute a higher value for the on-call arrangement, while a good payer mix and low levels of uncompensated care may partially or completely mitigate the additional value. In many cases, these analysts use professional judgment and experience to determine how these issues impact the value of the arrangement. In one example, the valuation analyst determines that the qualitative and quantitative measures are such that high levels of inconvenience and uncompensated care yield a conclusion of value that ranges between the $75^{th}$ and $90^{th}$ percentile of market survey data, which the analyst concludes as FMV.

Other analysts employ proprietary methods, such as algorithms, to measure the effects on value. In these cases, the analysts input information on qualitative and quantitative measures into the algorithm from which the output aids in narrowing the range of value within the universe of possible values or provides normalizing adjustments to be applied to the survey market data to arrive at a conclusion of FMV. An example of such an algorithm would compute an intensity or severity index for on-call coverage, based on a points structure that awards varying levels of points to each specialty, then using patient admissions and visits data to arrive at the factor representing relative intensity or severity.

*Percentage-of-compensation method.* As valuation theory has been developed by valuation analysts and applied to the area of compensation for on-call arrangements, the percentage-of-compensation method has gained in acceptance and in practice. This method is grounded in the concept that the compensation of most physicians includes an element of compensation attributable to the requirement that physicians make themselves available to their patients and to the community at times other than clinic operating hours. In a more obvious example, in a freestanding, physician-owned group practice of obstetricians and gynecologists, it is understood that most, if not all, physicians in the group must take hospital obstetrics call to handle deliveries that take place at nights and on weekends. Physicians who do not take call, whether because of age or because they have limited their practice to gynecology only, are typically penalized or "taxed" by the group for opting out of the group's call rotation. Hence, a portion of the compensation of those physicians who do take call is made up, to some degree, of compensation for taking call. The same is true for most physician specialties, particularly those with patient care obligations that go beyond the eight-to-five schedule. That said, it is reasonable to apportion some physician compensation to the act of "being available."

Valuation analysts who do a great deal of work in the area of on-call compensation have recognized this fact and have developed methodology to account for the fact that some portion of physician compensation is attributable to on-call duties and responsibilities. This analysis generally involves a review of survey data to compute the relationship of on-call pay to total physician compensation, first by specialty, and then in aggregate. First, the analyst accumulates survey data on on-call pay rates for available physician specialties, using tools such as the SCA survey of physician on-call compensation. From there, the analyst gathers data for those same specialties from surveys on physician compensation, such as the following:

- Medical Group Management Association (MGMA), *Physician Compensation and Production Survey.* The MGMA survey reports national and regional data for more than 2,300 group practices, primarily single specialty practices, representing more than 52,000 physicians and nonphysician providers.

- American Medical Group Association (AMGA), *Medical Group Compensation and Productivity Survey.* The AMGA survey reports national and regional data for more than 220 group practices, primarily multispecialty practices, representing more than 43,000 physicians.

- Sullivan Cotter and Associates, Inc. (SCA), *Physician Compensation and Productivity Survey Report.* The SCA survey reports national and regional data for 263 healthcare organizations and total compensation data for more than 39,000 physicians, Ph.D.s, midlevel providers, residents, and medical group executives.

The data for physician aggregate compensation may be studied individually or as an average of the survey products. Once accumulated, the analyst computes a fraction, the numerator of which is the on-call pay rate and the denominator of which is the total compensation rate (converted to an hourly rate from annual compensation survey data), to arrive at an estimate of the portion of physician compensation attributable to on-call pay. This is most often done using median survey data for both numerator and denominator and, in many cases, results in a nonspecialty-specific estimate of approximately 14% to 15% of physician compensation attributed to unrestricted on-call pay. A similar analysis can also be performed for restricted coverage.

Aside from its usefulness in determining the portion of physician compensation attributed to unrestricted and restricted call for the surveyed specialties, this methodology also has some other very important applications. For example, not all specialties have sufficient respondent volume to permit reporting of on-call pay for unrestricted and restricted arrangements. Using the fraction derived from this analysis on a non-specialty-specific basis allows the valuation analyst to estimate the value of on-call pay for the unreported specialty (although some degree of normalization may be necessary, depending upon the physician specialty).

Another critically important use of this methodology is in addressing the risk of tainting of on-call survey data, due to the referral relationship of parties to arrangements embedded in survey data. In a few cases, valuation analysts have sought to prove that survey data of specialties with referral relationships is not tainted by the possibility that data are corrupted by any respondents that may have a compensation arrangement representing disguised remuneration in exchange for referrals of federal healthcare program business. To accomplish this analysis, valuation analysts have considered only those specialties that are generally considered to not have the ability to refer business to the hospital with which they have an on-call compensation arrangement.[17]

As with the published survey data method, a critical element of analysis considers the quantitative and qualitative elements of the on-call or coverage arrangement. Similar to the previous example, factors such as intensity, acuity, payer mix, frequency, and community need will likely dictate the degree to which the valuation analyst's judgment indicates higher or lower values of compensation. In the percentage-of-compensation method, these elements of risk and intensity are often used in considering the base compensation to which the percentage-of-compensation fraction is applied. As a hypothetical example, trauma surgeons in the community are in short supply, and the market data from the analyst's research indicate compensation between the 75th and 90th percentiles for FMV compensation; thus, the analyst applies a computed fraction of 15% to these levels of compensation to determine the range of FMV compensation for on-call coverage. Additional normalizing adjustments may also be necessary in making determinations under this methodology, as the valuation analyst's research and judgment may indicate that the result obtained should be adjusted to reflect specific market conditions, possibly yielding a premium or discount to be applied to the calculated result to reach the conclusion of FMV.

*Nurse call pay method.* Another method gaining in popularity among valuation analysts is the nurse call pay method, which determines the FMV of physician on-call compensation through the application of a formula based on market rates of compensation for nurses for on-call services. This method is slightly limited in its applicability, because it generally relates only to unrestricted call arrangements and only to the inconvenience and time factor of on-call services, rather than to the uncompensated care element.

The application of this method involves research into the payment arrangements by the subject hospital and other facilities in the market that pay nurses for on-call services. For example, average nurses' salaries are $22 per hour, while the going rate for on-call pay is $3 per hour. The fraction resulting from this data is $3 divided by $22, or 13.6%, which is then applied to the range of compensation for the physician specialty to arrive at the range of comparable physician on-call compensation. This method is particularly useful when considering the FMV of on-call pay for physician-employees, as the element of uncompensated care is absent from the equation. Additionally, this

17 In the author's analysis, the computation of this rate was found to exceed the rate obtained by analyzing all available physician specialties, which supports the theory that the volume of respondent data and other factors mitigate the risk that referral relationships taint the on-call compensation survey data.

methodology is useful in addressing the issue of referral-tainted survey data, because nurses are not considered referral sources for hospitals.

### Methods Not Considered Valid

In the minds of many physicians, the equivalent of private practice earnings, or "opportunity cost," is the value of service in an on-call or coverage arrangement, stating that the foregone practice earnings are representative of the value the physician brings to the on-call arrangement, particularly when the on-call service removes the physician from his or her clinical practice for a time. CMS clearly warns against the consideration of opportunity cost in the preamble to the Stark Phase III regulations when referring specifically to the value of administrative compensation,[18] stating that the two values may differ. Further, the OIG in Advisory Opinion 07-10 identified "lost opportunity" payments as problematic, particularly when they do not reflect *bona fide* lost income.

A significant difference in the value of practice earnings and the value of physician availability is that physician availability is only a small component of a physician's earnings and that the two are not interchangeable.

### Synthesis of Valuation Methods

As in the application of general appraisal theory, valuation of service agreements, including the value of physician availability, is a result of the application of as many methods as are available and reasonably applied. Arriving at a conclusion of value is the result of careful application of all available methods and the synthesis and reconciliation of those methods. As this chapter describes, some methods may be more appropriately applied to the specific circumstances of the subject arrangement, while others may not. The reliability of methods also varies from one to another, as does the degree to which the valuation analyst places considered judgment in weighing the relevance, degree of subjectivity, and overall applicability. The end result, which may be a single point value or a range, is the result of the analyst's judgment as to the relative weight of each method in contrast to the others available, or as to the methods that create the lower and upper boundaries of FMV.

### Capping Physician Compensation

It is important with many physician compensation arrangements to ensure that variable compensation arrangements contain an aggregate limit, or cap, to avoid runaway

18 72 *Fed. Reg.* (Sept. 5, 2007), p. 51016.

compensation. In the area of compensation for physician unrestricted on-call and restricted coverage, the cap is quite often a function of the *per diem,* or hourly rate, and the maximum expected number of hours or days of coverage. However, determining a cap for stipend or subsidy arrangements may be exceedingly complex. In those cases, the upper end of the FMV range is most likely the level at which the valuation analyst will establish the cap. For example, the valuation analyst involved in an analysis of FMV for anesthesia coverage found that the range of stipend compensation for an anesthesiologist to furnish unrestricted on-call coverage to a hospital's obstetrical unit was $150,000 to $175,000, based on cost-, income-, and market-approach methodology applicable to the proposed subsidy arrangement. In that instance, the upper limit or cap on physician compensation was determined to be $175,000.

## Other Considerations

### Stacked Arrangements

Ensuring that compensation for physician services represents FMV, both separately and in the aggregate, can be difficult when a physician is performing separate tasks under separate, or "stacked," agreements. In some situations, a physician may not only receive compensation for clinical services under an employment agreement, but also receive compensation for providing on-call coverage or other services. To accurately determine FMV for each service provided, careful consideration must be given to the data and methods used to determine FMV to ensure that compensation under each agreement accurately reflects compensation for the type and level of service actually provided.

When reviewing the FMV of each agreement as related to the services being provided, it is important to understand how the compensation for each was determined, including the sources and methodology considered to arrive at FMV for each agreement or component thereof. As already noted, one method of establishing the FMV of compensation for physician services is through the use of market data, including the use of published surveys. Due care must be taken in considering the types of payments likely included in compensation figures presented in physician compensation surveys.

Paying employed physicians for on-call availability presents its own unique challenges. For employed physicians, it is important for the analyst to consider the fact that compensation for call is likely included in the physician's compensation structure. In certain circumstances, it may be appropriate to pay an employed physician with an additional layer of compensation for call, but only when the call responsibility exceeds a level generally expected for the specialty. For example, to fill vacancies left by a departing physician, a specialist may be asked to temporarily assume an additional slot in the

ED call rotation, essentially doubling his or her current call responsibilities. Further, a physician already taking call for the hospital-owned clinic in which he or she practices may also be asked to cover call for another hospital-owned clinic or other facility run by the hospital. In these and other situations, considering additional compensation means considering the additional value the services bring, how much beyond the norm the on-call services are, and how long the additional services will be required.

If a physician is employed and the employer is billing and collecting for the physician's professional services and the physician's compensation is not dependent on collections, the burden of uncompensated care falls on the employer, not the physician. In such a situation, incorporating compensation for uncompensated care into the call coverage arrangement (through the failure to consider its inclusion in survey data) results in a twofold problem, as the employer ends up taking a loss on the care and compensates the physician for the loss, essentially doubling the loss to the employer and overpaying the physician.

## Conclusion

To conclude, economic and market forces not experienced by earlier generations of physicians have caused today's physicians to rethink the former practice of accepting on-call responsibilities as an obligation to the community and a requirement of the active medical staff. This environment has resulted in reluctance on the part of physicians to take call and in demands for compensation associated with physician availability and for the risks assumed by physicians in caring for indigent and low-paying patients.

The uniqueness of the various types of on-call and coverage arrangements, along with the implications of violating important statutory and regulatory requirements applicable to tax-exempt entities and to providers caring for federal healthcare program beneficiaries, makes payment for physician availability a costly and risky venture for many facilities. Crucial to this process is the valuation of the compensation arrangements, yet no formal guidance exists as to how to determine the FMV of these payments. The various types of coverage arrangements and the difficulty in obtaining truly comparable data make the science of valuating physician availability difficult at best. Regardless of the approaches and methods used by the valuation analyst, determining the FMV of these types of agreements is a complex task. Only through a complete understanding of the specifics of the subject arrangement and in the proper application of widely accepted methodology and analyst judgment can a reliable and defensible conclusion of value be reached.

## Bibliography

"A Growing Crisis in Patient Access to Emergency Surgical Care," *American College of Surgeons* (June 2006) www.facs.org.

O'Malley, Ann, Debra A. Draper and Laurie E. Felland. "Hospital Emergency On-Call Coverage: Is There a Doctor in the House?" *Center for Studying Health System Change* No.115 (November 2007): 1.

"Availability of On-Call Specialists," *American College of Emergency Physicians* (May 2005), www.acep.org.

Henzke, Leonard J., findarticles.com/p/articles/mi_m3257/is_1_61/ai_n17114335/. [Internet accessed May 9, 2008].

Rowland, Robert G. and Leonard J. Henzke. "What Boards Should Know About the Emerging Call Coverage Crisis," *American Governance Leader* Vol 3, no.4 (July 2003): 1.

"Report of the Board of Trustees: Report 14-I-06," *American Medical Association.*

www.ama-assn.org/ama1/pub/upload/mm/475/bot14i06.doc. [Internet accessed on May 9, 2008].

Trugman, Gary R. CPA/ABV, MCBA, ASA, MVS. *Understanding Business Valuation* Second Edition. American Institute of Certified Public Accountants Inc., 2002.

Broccolo, Bernadette M. Esq., et al. *Fundamentals of Health Law* Third Edition. American Health Lawyers Association. July 2004.

Chapter 32

# Evaluating RVU-Based Compensation Arrangements

*By Mark O. Dietrich, CPA/ABV, and Gregory D. Anderson, CPA/ABV, CVA*

Compensation arrangements based on relative value units (RVUs) are increasingly popular for compensating physicians. Where collected revenue-based systems—historically common in group practice, for example—reflect the individual physician's underlying payor mix, RVU systems are payor-mix neutral. A RVU system[1] is therefore attractive to a physician employed by a hospital that treats patients regardless of their ability to pay. However, RVU systems may be tainted by payor mix and other market conditions, requiring that the analyst understand and examine the effects of this issue when using compensation survey data to establish fair market value incentive compensation based on RVUs.

There are several RVU measurement systems associated with physician billing codes (current procedural terminology, or CPT™), but the most commonly used is the resource-based relative value scale (RBRVS), which is also used by the Medicare program for establishing its physician fee schedule (MPFS). The RBRVS allocates RVUs to each procedure or service in the CPT™ based upon the amount of physician work, the cost of delivering the service, and the cost of malpractice insurance associated with the service. These RVUs are then multiplied by an amount known as a conversion factor and adjusted for geographic differences (the GPCI) to arrive at the fee for the service.

1 It is important to note that most compensation systems focus on the physician work RVU component (wRVU), which is but one component of the RBRVS measuring of total RVU values; the other two are practice expense and malpractice insurance cost. This allows for measurement of physician productivity using a tool that essentially measures those areas of productivity that are under the control of the physician.

RBRVS has its weaknesses. The Medicare conversion factor suffers from a statutory construct, which attempts to peg overall Medicare physician spending to an annual limit that would seem to make that measurement unit meaningless in the present environment. Sitting at around $38 per RVU before geographic adjustment, the rate has been virtually flat for many years and does not maintain pace with inflation, which the Medicare Payment Advisory Commission (MedPAC) estimates at approximately 3% per annum in physician practices. Nonetheless, the vast majority of physicians continue to accept Medicare patients, suggesting, at least to government agencies such as MedPAC, that payment rate has some relevance in assessing value. RBRVS is also subject to government manipulation that manifests itself in instability. For example, legislative intervention into the formula used to account for the practice expense formula and statutory five-year adjustments to the physician work component of the RVU affect how RBRVS impacts physician payment.

Payment rates per RVU vary significantly from region to region, as well as from payor contract to contract. Providers and, particularly, provider-systems with negotiating strength may have payment rates per RVU well in excess of their competitors. Evaluating reasonable compensation for a physician therefore requires knowledge of the specific contract rates being paid for that physician's services, as well as knowledge of the underlying payor mix. Consider the following example of how contract rates and payor mix impact physician compensation:

**Exhibit 1. How Contract Rates and Payor Mix Affect Compensation**

| Payor Mix | 40% | 10% | | |
|---|---|---|---|---|
| Payor | Medicare | Best | Non-Medicare Avg. Including Best | Weighted Average |
| Total RVUs | 10,000 | 10,000 | 10,000 | 10,000 |
| Rate | $38 | $55 | $48 | $44 |
| | | | | |
| Collections | 380,000 | 550,000 | 480,000 | 440,000 |
| Practice Expenses | 250,000 | 250,000 | 250,000 | 250,000 |
| | | | | |
| Physician Income | 130,000 | 300,000 | 230,000 | 190,000 |
| Compensation per total RVU | 13 | 30 | 23 | 19 |

Note: Payor mix weights are used to determine the weighted average rate per RVU. Each column indicates what the physician would have earned if 100% of the services provided were for each of the payor columns shown. For purposes of the example, assume that none of the total RVUs include Stark or other prohibited incentives.

In the example, the physician is earning $190,000 per year on collected revenue of $440,000. The physician's earnings would vary from $130,000 if the practice were entirely Medicare to $300,000 if it was entirely "market-best," a difference of 230%. The key observation to be taken from the example is that because expenses are fixed for a given volume of services in each scenario, all of the additional revenue from better contracts drops to the bottom line as physician compensation. That in turn suggests that "reasonable compensation" for 10,000 RVUs of services could range from $130,000 to $300,000, depending upon the mix and strength of the underlying payor contracts.

Lest that seem unrealistic on its face, consider the view from the physician working in a private practice holding only "market-best" contracts. Certainly, he or she would not be willing to work for $130,000 per year seeing only Medicare patients. Similarly, a physician employed by a hospital or integrated delivery system (IDS) with strong contracts for physician services would expect to be compensated at a commensurate rate, rather than have the employing institution retain the excess as profit. Similarly, it is unlikely that the managed care companies and other payors would be paying premium rates per RVU, unless market conditions warranted it and made it necessary to attract physician providers into their networks.

The non-Medicare average value per RVU of $48 is an initial reference point for what "market" value for physician services is in this particular circumstance, assuming the weighted average conversion factor, as described in the following paragraph. The Medicare conversion factor is not negotiated but is rather a legislatively imposed *force majeure* disconnected from market forces. As such, it has limited worth in assessing "market" value.

The compensation reported in survey data such as that of the Medical Group Management Association will reflect the "weighted average" compensation or rate per RVU of only those entities participating in the survey. In the example, this compensation would be $190,000. The actual rate per RVU in a given practice may be more or less than the survey result. If practices participating in the survey have a better payor and rate mix than all practices in a given area, the compensation will be higher and conversely, if the participating practices have poorer rates, the survey compensation will be less.

This type of analysis is critical in assessing the fair market value of compensation for hospitals employing physicians. In many markets, integrated provider networks that include both physicians and hospitals succeed in obtaining superior reimbursement from payors, which in turn results in superior compensation. The contracts may be a function of enhanced clinical quality from integration, market-based negotiating leverage, reduced administrative costs to payors due to single-signature contracting, or shifting of contract administration. Traditional analysis focusing solely on compensation surveys to determine fair market value may well fall short of the market value of services based upon actual negotiated contracts for providers with a strong market position.

Returning to Exhibit 1, assume that an IDS has managed care and other payor agreements that result in the following Payor Distribution and Revenue for a physician practice.

**Exhibit 2. Payor Mix**

| Payor Mix | 35% | 30% | 35% | 100% |
|---|---|---|---|---|
| | Medicare | Best | Other Payors | Weighted Average |
| Total RVUs | 3,500 | 3,000 | 3,500 | 10,000 |
| Rate | $38.00 | $55.00 | $48.00 | $46.60 |
| | | | | |
| Collections | 133,000 | 165,000 | 168,000 | 466,000 |
| Practice expenses | 87,500 | 75,000 | 87,500 | 250,000 |
| | | | | |
| Physician income | 45,500 | 90,000 | 80,500 | 216,000 |
| Compensation per total RVU | 13.00 | 30.00 | 23.00 | 21.60 |

Note: Exhibit 2 differs from the first in that the payor mix has been applied to the total RVUs of services performed to arrive at the actual compensation earned based upon the given payor mix.

In this case, the actual contracts in place generate physician compensation of $216,000 as compared to the "market" compensation described in the first example of $190,000, or about 14% greater. Solely relying on the survey result would seem to understate what is "reasonable compensation" for a physician employed in this particular provider entity. The determination of what is reasonable requires the valuation analyst and the employing provider to have keen insight into market conditions to arrive at an appropriate conclusion.

An appropriate alternative to sole reliance on survey data is to measure the value of compensation per RVU based on data from the practice on revenues and RVUs produced by major payor or payor group. Some analysts will benchmark the physician practice on a more global scale, analyzing collections per RVU to get an overall sense of favorable or unfavorable payor arrangements when the practice is compared against survey data. After this initial "litmus test" is interpreted, exploration of data by payor group, drilling down to compensation per RVU as in Exhibit 2, can give an indication as to whether and to what extent favorable or unfavorable payor contracts impact physician compensation. This, essentially the use of the income-based approach in analyzing physician compensation value, supplements the market-based approach conclusions derived from an interpretation of raw survey data.

What becomes clear to the analyst is that simple reliance on single survey data is not enough to yield a completely defensible conclusion of value for compensation under a RVU arrangement. Use of as many independently published surveys and as many different valuation methods as are reasonably available is certainly a prudent practice for those with the responsibility for determining compensation that must be defended as fair market value. Not only should the use of RVUs be considered, but other physician productivity benchmarks (i.e., encounters and visits for primary care and surgical cases for surgeons) may also be appropriate.

Finally, as an observation, physician practice acquisition value is often considered simultaneously with an employment decision and reasonable compensation analysis. In the practice valuation model, it is *not* appropriate to consider payor contracts held by a *particular* purchasing provider entity unless such contracts are common to the universe of potential purchasing entities in the market. This is because such an adjustment would be inconsistent with fair market value's requirement for "*any* willing buyer."

In contrast, compensation is a function of who employs you and what your services are worth at the time they are performed. From the standpoint of the hypothetical seller of services—i.e., the employed physician—being employed at a rate less than what the market is paying his or her employer currently for the physician's services would be inconsistent with the expected result in arm's-length negotiation where reasonable knowledge is present. Thus, a physician practice may have a low value because there is little profit once the physician receives reasonable compensation for services based upon the practice's existing contracts. However, the physician may be better compensated in the future because his or her new employer holds better payor contracts.

Chapter 33

# Valuation of Clinical Co-Management Arrangements

*By Gregory D. Anderson, CPA/ABV, CVA, and Scott Safriet, AVA, MBA*

## Origin of the Co-Management Arrangement

Even before health care reform took center stage, most healthcare organizations found themselves caught in an era of increasing competition, changing reimbursement structures, and shifting operational paradigms. Benchmarks and key clinical performance indicators have taken on even greater importance as carrot-and-stick reforms in government reimbursement now join existing pay-for-performance initiatives in the private payer community. Technological advances allowing less invasive interventions and improved outcomes offer the promise of revolutionizing the way medicine is practiced. These market forces demand a shift in the healthcare industry toward collaborative care and aligned incentives, yet collaborative relationships among healthcare providers trigger compliance and business strategies that have not yet been fully played out in the marketplace and the healthcare regulatory environment. These market forces and compliance risks lead physicians and hospitals to create relationships that concentrate on patient outcomes, safety, and satisfaction, while yielding incentives that reward positive behavioral changes by both parties.

### *Increasing Competition*

"Hospitals and physicians care for the same patients. Both feel squeezed by stagnating payment, rising expenses, proliferating regulations, and rising consumer expectations."[1]

1 Cohn, "Making Hospital-Physician Collaboration Work," Healthcare Financial Management Association, October 2005

Hospitals also face pressures from consumers for the latest technology, shortages of hospital personnel, increased regulation, rising cost of liability premiums, and the obligation for providing care to the uninsured.[2] Yet, the American Hospital Association recognizes that "the integration of clinical care across providers, across settings, and over time" is needed to reduce fragmentation in healthcare delivery and improve the quality and efficiency of care.[3]

#### *Changing Landscape of Where Services Are Performed*

Advances in technology have transformed the delivery of health care in more ways than could have been imagined just a few decades ago. Many procedures that were exclusively performed in an inpatient setting are now furnished in hospital outpatient settings, specialty hospitals, and ambulatory surgery centers, significantly altering the landscape in the industry and raising the element of competition between physicians and hospitals. These surgical and diagnostic facilities represent viable alternatives to acute care hospitals, as patient and physician convenience, cost, and comfort lure insured patients away, leaving hospitals with an ever increasing mix of indigent and low-pay patients. In increasing numbers, hospitals are entering into clinical co-management arrangements (CCMAs) with physicians who once operated competing facilities (e.g., in most instances, a hospital acquires a physician-owned entity, integrates it into the hospital infrastructure, and considers a CCMA with the physician owners). The competitive environment and reimbursement reforms led hospitals to place even more emphasis on achieving better outcomes, higher patient satisfaction scores, and more cost-effective care. Capitalizing on the physician clinical expertise is invaluable to hospitals in reaching these objectives.

#### *Difficulty in Securing Robust Medical Directorships*

Healthcare regulatory enforcement activity by the federal government continues to spotlight medical directorships as highly susceptible to abuse, with examples of arrangements alleged to be disguised payments for referrals of federal healthcare program beneficiaries. Many of these suspect arrangements lack substantiation of duties and fail to implement appropriate systems for tracking and documenting hours worked in providing these services. Further, because commercial reasonableness has received much attention in fraud and abuse enforcement of late, many hospitals and their healthcare legal counsel are rightfully scrutinizing traditional medical directorships.

---

2 "Improving Health Care: A Dose of Competition," U.S. Department of Justice and the Federal Trade Commission, July 2004

3 Am. Hosp. Ass'n., *Aligning Hospital and Physician Interests: Broadening the Concept of Gainsharing to Allow Care Improvement Incentives*, 2005

### *Need for Increased Efficiencies and Quality in Patient Care*

In response to American's costly, sometimes unsafe, and often inefficient healthcare system, momentum built for a shift to a pay-for-performance (P4P) system that correlated financial rewards with improved outcomes in patient care. The Centers for Medicare and Medicaid Services (CMS) and many commercial payers implemented pay-for-performance programs that promoted quality patient care through financial rewards. These pay-for-performance programs each include the following elements:

- A set of targets or objectives that define what will be evaluated;
- Measures and performance standards for establishing the target criteria; and
- At-risk financial rewards and a method for allocating payments among individuals who meet or exceed the target criteria.[4]

Furthermore, the core measures of pay-for-performance programs were often quite similar in that they were driven by evidence-based medicine and intended to increase the quality of care and reduce costs by reducing readmissions and limiting medical errors.[5] However, pay-for-performance programs often varied in their development, design, and financial rewards. By the beginning of 2008, 160 pay-for-performance programs had been implemented in the United States,[6] and in March 2010, the United States passed the Patient Protection and Affordable Care Act (PPACA), establishing several healthcare delivery system reforms intended to increase quality and patient satisfaction, and reduce costs. Reform provisions focused on reducing hospital-acquired infections and preventable 30-day readmissions, as well as implementing hospital value-based purchasing and bundled payments, and established accountable care organizations ("ACOs").[7] However, although the final rule on ACOs was released in November 2011, the full impact of ACOs on the delivery of health care is yet to be determined because many have not embraced this as the primary vehicle through which integrated care will be delivered in the future. What the ACO rules have shown the industry is that other viable means of delivering collaborative care, such as medical home models or vertically integrated care models, may thrive as long as physicians and hospitals work together toward the common triple-aim of quality gains, cost savings, and better outcomes.

4 Congressional Research Service, *Pay-for-Performance in Health Care.*

5 Rosenthal, M., Fernandopulle, R., Song, H., & Landon, B. (2004, March/April). "Paying For Quality: Providers' Incentives for Quality Improvement". *Health Affairs*, pp. 127-141.

6 Francois, S. de Brantes, MBA and B. Guy D'Andrea, MBA. "Physicians Respond to Pay-for-Performance Incentives: Larger Incentives Yield Greater Participation." (2009) *The American Journal of Managed Care*. Vol. 15, No. 5. Pg 305 – 310.

7 Clarke, Richard L. "Impact of Healthcare Reform: A Conversation With HFMA's Dick Clarke." Healthcare Financial Management Association. March 31, 2010.

### Government and Payer Recognition of Core Measures of Quality

Common measures of quality performance allow physicians to receive feedback and tie performance to financial and other incentives through P4P and public quality reporting. Several types of systems have gained traction in the past few years, particularly with the introduction of quality-reporting initiatives by professional organizations, accrediting agencies, and the Medicare Physician Quality Reporting System (PQRS, former PQRI) that provided in 2011 a 1% physician quality reporting incentive to physician groups based on their total Medicare Part B allowed charges. These programs contribute to physicians' acknowledgement that other stakeholders have the right to monitor their behavior and hold them accountable.[8]

### Opportunities for Increased Hospital-Physician Alignment

Long-standing hospital-physician integration strategies that remain in the current market include direct employment of physicians by hospitals, development of clinically integrated hospital and physician entities, formation of community health information networks, and various hybrids and permutations of provider integration strategies. Physician engagement is essential for many cultural and behavioral changes to be successful at the hospital level. Compensation under these plans is increasingly tied to success with varying measurements that align financial incentives among the provider groups.

It is within this environment of interrelated priorities that the CCMA has emerged as an increasingly popular option. In fact, the realization that hospitals and physicians need to work together to achieve desired outcomes has fueled the rapid increase in the number and structural diversity of CCMAs because they represent an effective way to integrate hospital and physician management of clinical services and generally exist between physicians and hospitals. Physicians in a CCMA provide management services to a hospital that go beyond traditional medical director roles, and the CCMA involves physicians as participants in the day-to-day management of the hospital's clinical service line operations. The primary advantage of the CCMA is the significant operational input of the physicians and the alignment of physician and hospital interests to achieve improvements in the overall efficiency and quality of patient care.

8 Pham and Ginsburg, *Unhealthy Trends: The Future of Physician Services*, Health Affairs 26(6):1586-1598, November/December 2007

## Structure of Co-Management Arrangements

### *Rationale for Formation*

**Competition.** As described above, competitive market forces are primary drivers in the creation of the CCMA. Below is a hypothetical example of a community hospital's struggle to remain competitive by aligning with physicians:

> Healthy Regional Hospital (one of two hospitals in its community) and one of the local cardiology groups reached an impasse when the cardiology group announced its intent to open a cardiac catheterization lab (cath lab) in its own clinic facility. When the cath lab became operational, Healthy Regional saw a substantial decline in commercial patients in its own cath lab, and revenues immediately began a sharp downward trend. As tensions grew, the cardiology group began demanding payment for emergency department call coverage and one of the cardiologists, the medical director for cardiology at Healthy Regional, elected not to renew his administrative contract.
>
> Healthy Regional's new CEO entered into discussions with the cardiology group to form a CCMA. This endeavor would be a joint venture, which would acquire and operate the cardiologists' cath lab and enter into a management agreement with Healthy Regional to manage the its entire cardiology service line (i.e., inclusive of the cath lab) in the creation of a cardiovascular center of excellence. The end result was an immediate change in the competitive landscape in the community for cardiac care and an integration of the hospital and cardiology group in the operation of the joint venture CCMA.

**Alignment with payer interests and participation in payer incentive programs.** Many payers, including Congress, the Medicare Payment Advisory Commission (MedPAC) and CMS, all recognize the benefits to patients and the healthcare system as a whole through enhanced quality care, better outcomes, and more efficient care.

CMS has implemented various projects over the years to promote quality and efficiency by rewarding healthcare providers and suppliers for the quality of care they provide by tying a portion of Medicare payments to performance on quality indicators. These projects included demonstration and quality reporting programs applied in settings such as physician practices, ambulatory care facilities, hospitals, nursing homes, home health agencies, and dialysis facilities. CMS's goal has been to transform Medicare from a passive payer to an active purchaser of quality health care for its beneficiaries.

In 2010, section 3001 of PPACA established a budget-neutral hospital valued-based purchasing (VBP) program to compensate hospitals for performance against certain quality measures. The program is scheduled to begin in fiscal year 2013, applicable to payments for discharges occurring on or after Oct. 1, 2012. The hospital VBP program generally applies to acute-care prospective payment system hospitals with certain exceptions for hospitals and those with few applicable measures. The quality measures used in the hospital VBP program will be similar to those used in the Medicare pay-for-reporting program. The hospital VBP program will receive its funding from a reduction in Medicare severity diagnosis-related group (MS-DRG) inpatient prospective payment system (IPPS) reimbursement to hospitals to which the hospital VBP program applies. VBP incentive payments will be made with respect to discharges occurring during fiscal year 2013, and the quality measures will include those applicable to the following conditions:

- Acute myocardial infarction;
- Heart failure;
- Pneumonia;
- Surgeries, as measured by the surgical care improvement project; and
- Healthcare-associated infections, as measured by the HHS Action Plan to Prevent Healthcare-Associated Infections.[9]

Additionally, measures of patients' satisfaction with the level of care will be measured.

The following continues the hypothetical example of Healthy Regional Hospital and its cardiology CCMA:

> In addition to a robust set of day-to-day management services, Healthy Regional and its cardiology group partner developed a set of quality measurements that paralleled those of a significant local payer. The payer's program resulted in bonuses to the hospital for attainment of the payer's targets in quality care. The CCMA agreement for Healthy Regional's cardiac service line included financial incentives for reaching these quality measures, which effectively aligned the interests of the joint venture and the hospital with those of the payer.

9 Department of Health and Human Services, "HHS Action Plan to Prevent Healthcare-Associated Infections: Incentives and Oversight," www.hhs.gov/ash/initiatives/hai/incentives.html.

**Consolidate medical directorship duties.** With physicians as partners in clinical quality, the CCMA affords hospitals with opportunities to develop more robust duties and responsibilities for physician administrative positions over the managed service line. CCMA agreements provide for significant enhancements in administrative requirements for clinicians, to which a portion of the compensation is related (often referred to as the base management fee), and often allows for a consolidation of multiple, and sometimes duplicative, directorships. The hypothetical example of Healthy Regional's CCMA continues below:

> In developing the CCMA, Healthy Regional's legal counsel recommended termination of the hospital's separate cardiology and cath lab medical directorship agreements, in favor of inclusion of the duties of both in the administrative responsibilities of the CCMA. The previous medical directorship agreements contained no requirements for contemporaneous documentation of physician administrative time and were paid in fixed monthly amounts, representing a significant compliance risk. Legal counsel also recommended additional requirements related to physician participation in quality assurance meetings, attendance at quality assurance training conferences and additional duties as medical staff liaison to address quality concerns with staff physicians. As will be discussed in detail further in this chapter, such medical director duties were "folded into" the CCMA and paid out of the negotiated management fee.

**Consolidate other physician duties.** With broader ties to physicians in hospital service line management, hospitals can use CCMAs to address other service deficiencies and staffing needs. The Healthy Regional Hospital example continues as follows:

> Prior to the CCMA joint venture, a rift developed between the hospital and cardiology group, and the hospital found itself in a position of seeking sporadic (and expensive) emergency department on-call coverage for the specialty of cardiology. Through negotiations with the cardiology group to enter into the CCMA with the hospital, Healthy Regional was able to gain physician commitment to cover emergency call on a 24-hours-a-day, 7-days-a-week, 365-days-a-year basis. This embedded call arrangement saved Healthy Regional nearly $200,000 in annual call coverage compensation paid to other local physicians and physician staffing companies, resulting in dependable cardiology coverage and improved patient quality outcomes.

### *Applicable Specialties*

CCMAs apply to many physician specialties, particularly when there is a relationship between the physician's administrative and clinical skills and the success of the hospital in meeting quality measures within the related service line. Some of the more common specialties, in no particular order, include the following:

- Cardiology /cardiovascular surgery;
- Orthopedic surgery;
- General surgery;
- Oncology;
- Neurosciences; and
- Gastroenterology.

#### *Ownership*

In some circumstances, CCMAs are formed and operated as joint ventures between hospitals and physicians in what is commonly known as the joint venture or equity model CCMA. While typically done on a 50-50 basis, it is not uncommon to see many different variations. For example, while a hospital may want to have good alignment with its physicians, it may still want to retain ultimate control, and therefore, a 60-40 split (i.e., in favor of hospital) may be the preferred outcome. The impact of this issue will be discussed in more detail later in this chapter. Because some CCMAs have ownership in healthcare facilities (e.g., cath lab or outpatient imaging center), these are also structured as joint ventures, although usually with a significant requirement for capital infusion to accommodate the acquisition and operation of the outpatient facility, and subject to applicable fair market value analysis.

Another variant of the CCMA is the contractual model CCMA, which is, in the vast majority of cases, owned by individual physicians, physician groups, or combinations of the two. The contractual model CCMA is generally thought of as less capital intensive and less structurally complex than an equity model CCMA; however, despite some misinformation, contractual model CCMAs are generally no more or no less favorable to physicians than equity model CCMAs, as will be described more fully later in this chapter.

#### *Organizational Structure*

The CCMA entity is typically established as a limited liability company. This entity enters into a management services arrangement with the hospital for purposes of managing the hospital's designated service line. In general, the equity model CCMA can be somewhat more complex than the contractual model CCMA because the introduction of joint venture partners and multiple classes of ownership can result in a complicated legal structure of the entity.

### *Regulatory Compliance*

Designing a CCMA requires the guidance of experienced healthcare legal counsel to avoid missteps that could cause the venture to run afoul of federal and state healthcare laws and regulations that govern hospital and physician relationships. Although not discussed in depth in this chapter, compliance with the terms of applicable exceptions to the Stark physician self-referral legislation is critical, as well as applicable anti-kickback statute safe harbors, such as the one for personal services and management contracts. Such violations are also often "bootstrapped" with federal false claims act penalties, which can significantly increase the government's claims. Additionally, because some CCMAs focus on efficiency, care should be taken to avoid incentives that induce physicians to reduce or limit services to Medicare or Medicaid beneficiaries, or hospitals and physicians face civil monetary penalties. Tax-exempt hospitals, as parties to CCMAs, should also be careful to avoid private inurement or excessive private benefit. Intermediate sanctions penalties allow the IRS to levy excise taxes against organization managers and parties to a transaction, thus requiring that tax-exempt hospitals focus on payment of reasonable compensation to physicians.

### *Fee Structure—Base Plus Incentive*

CCMAs ordinarily maintain management service agreements with the hospital for the service line management, with a multistage compensation structure. The first stage is base compensation associated with the day-to-day medical direction, management, and administrative duties and responsibilities under the contract, and such services are paid for out of the base management fee, as further discussed in our chapter. While this level of compensation is often paid out on a flat "monthly" basis (with an annual true-up based on the percent completion of the assigned management services), more hospitals are electing to inject an additional degree of conservatism into their arrangements by electing to administer the base management fee in the form of an hourly rate applied to the documented hours spent by the physicians furnishing the administrative services. This amount generally does not vary depending on the performance of the manager or the success in meeting the quality objectives of the arrangement. However, it is important to note that should a hospital elect to disburse the base management fee on an hourly basis, the hospital also needs to ensure that it carefully tracks the performance of the management services, as payout of the entire base management fee (whether paid on a flat fee or hourly basis) is only appropriate if the management services have been performed in their entirety.

The second component of compensation is the P4P incentive compensation, which is based on the attainment of clinical quality objectives and other factors such as patient satisfaction and budgetary compliance. P4P incentives are calculated and paid in a variety of ways, the more common of which will be described below.

### *Incentive Metrics and Pay-for-Performance*

Core measures developed by CMS, the Joint Commission, and third-party payers are often referred to as organizations develop quality standards for incentive pay under CCMAs.

Exhibit 1 summarizes core measures from CMS and the Joint Commission for heart failure:

**Exhibit 1. Heart Failure Core Measures**

| Medicare Short Name | Description |
|---|---|
| Discharge instructions | Heart failure patients discharged home with written instructions or education material given to the patient or caregiver at discharge or during the hospital stay addressing all of the following: activity level, diet, discharge medications, follow-up appointment, weight monitoring, and what to do if symptoms worsen. |
| Evaluation of LVS function | Heart failure patients with documentation in the hospital record that left ventricular systolic (LVS) function was evaluated before arrival, during hospitalization, or is planned for after discharge. |
| ACEI or ARB for LVSD | Heart failure patients with left ventricular systolic dysfunction (LVSD) and without both angiontensin converting enzyme inhibitor (ACEI) and angiontensin receptor blocker (ARB) contraindications who are prescribed an ACEI or ARB at hospital discharge. For purposes of this measure, LVSD is defined as chart documentation of a left ventricular ejection fraction (LVEF) less than 40% or a narrative of left ventricular systolic (LVS) function consistent with moderate or severe systolic dysfunction. |
| Adult smoking cessation advice and counseling | Heart failure patients with a history of smoking cigarettes, who are giving smoking cessation advice or counseling during the hospital stay. For purposes of this measure, a smoker is defined as someone who has smoked cigarettes anytime during the year prior to hospital arrival. |

Quality measures like those above for heart failure are used as measurements in CCMAs to assess the level of quality attained through the management of the hospital service line. For example, a cardiac CCMA would likely measure quality for AMI, heart failure, and cardiac artery bypass graft (CABG), comparing the actual quality scores with expected or target scores. In the case of the Discharge Instructions core measure, the quality score is a fraction, the numerator of which is the number of patients discharged home that were given discharge instructions or educational materials that included all of the required instructions (i.e., activity level, diet, discharge medications, follow-up appointment, weight monitoring, and what to do if symptoms worsen) and the denominator of which is the total number of heart failure patients discharged home.

One of the key distinctions between a CCMA and a traditional management agreement is the P4P component, which provides for incentive compensation to the manager of an incentive above and beyond the base compensation. The incentive compensation component is often based on attainment of quality scores such as the one described above for heart failure. In the example of discharge instructions to heart failure patients, 78% may be the target score for discharge instructions. Reaching or exceeding this level would result in incentive bonus credit or payment to the CCMA manager. CCMAs vary in the application of bonus methodology, as some examples include specific amounts of bonus payment upon attainment of target scores or credit in the form of points to the manager, which are accumulated for purposes of determining payment under the CCMA incentive bonus formula.

## Determination of FMV

In the context of a CCMA, determining the FMV of management fees is critical not only for compliance with existing laws, but is also important to the ultimate success of the project. Therefore, before any hospital undertakes the implementation of a co-management arrangement, it is critical to determine the FMV of the management fee, including both the base and incentive components (these two components were discussed earlier in the chapter), to maintain compliance with existing laws and regulations.[10] However, there is little valuation theory for an appraiser to rely upon in assessing performance-based incentive or pay-for-performance programs because these arrangements are still relatively new and, therefore, vary widely in their structure.

In theory, the FMV of the management fee could be established by assessing the required number of work hours needed to provide the management services, multiplied by a FMV hourly rate. However, as with most management services and service arrangements, the exact number of required work hours cannot reasonably be determined in advance. Most management arrangements observed in the marketplace are not based upon actual underlying time to establish the management fee.

### *Valuation Theory Applicable to CCMAs*

The following three fundamental principles co-exist in the theory of business valuation: (1) the Principle of Substitution, (2) the Principle of Alternatives, and (3) the Principle of Future Benefits; each of these can be transferred into the context of valuing service agreements. For example, the Principle of Substitution states that an investor will pay no more for a service than for a substitute of equivalent economic utility. Under the Principle of Alternatives, each party to a contemplated contractual arrangement has

10 In addition, it should be noted that according to Rev. Proc. 97-13, certain not-for-profit entities with public bond financed property may also face additional Internal Revenue Service scrutiny regarding the split of the management fee. The authors would recommend that any hospital considering a co-management arrangement involve outside counsel in the process.

alternatives to consummating the deal. The Principle of Future Benefits emphasizes that the value of an investment is based on the future benefits the investment will provide. These principles lay the foundation for the application of valuation methodology to developing a conclusion of fair market value in compensation arrangements as well, including CCMA compensation arrangements.

#### *Valuation Methodology*

Several methods exist for determining value in a compensation arrangement. The justification for the use of a particular method or methods will often be dictated by the facts and circumstances of the contractual arrangement. These methods of valuation can be generally categorized into three broad approaches: cost-based, income-based, and market-based. Within the each valuation approach, one or more methods exist for determining value, with the relevance and applicability of each depending on the circumstances and the analyst's judgment.

In considering the value of payments under a CCMA, it is important to consider the value of the individual components of compensation (base compensation and incentive compensation), as well as aggregate compensation under the arrangement. A key consideration that must not be overlooked is that the methodology (and application thereof) that considers the fair market value of the individual components of compensation may differ from methodology that considers the value of aggregate compensation. The valuator should consider the merits and applicability of all three valuation approaches in developing an appropriate FMV range.

#### *Income-Based Approach*

Valuation of a CCMA under the income-based approach considers the economic benefits enjoyed by the hospital from the management services furnished by the manager.

Revenues earned by achieving or reporting quality target attainment under governmental and private payer programs result in bonus reimbursement, and income from these programs represent a "proxy" for the fair market value of the attainment of quality metrics within the boundaries of the CCMA. In many cases, these quality, outcomes, and efficiency measures mirror or closely resemble those of the CCMA and therefore represent an income stream associated with the same quality variables with which the CCMA measures its own success. Payers often use a point structure to determine the level of qualifying reimbursement, and scoring information can be made available by the payer to the hospital for use in determining hospital reimbursement and value of the incentive program. For example, some states' Blue Cross programs offer hospital performance or quality improvement programs, based on quality, efficiency, safety, and outcomes. When these measures can be attributed to the service line managed under the CCMA, they represent a stream of economic benefit directly associated with the attainment of quality and other metrics that can sometimes be closely associated with those of the CCMA and therefore represent a proxy for the value of CCMA quality attainment. Not all CCMA valuations present opportunities for valuation in such a manner for a number of reasons. First, payer incentive programs may not be directly measurable in a way that can be related to the management services furnished by the manager in a CCMA. Second, payer incentive programs may not facilitate direct correlation to a specific service line, such as that of an oncology program managed under an oncology CCMA.

#### *Cost-Based Approach*

**Discussion of applicable service lines.** While the income approach certainly has applicability in many instances, the two more prevalent valuation approaches utilized in the marketplace appear to be the cost and market approaches. In considering the cost approach (or "replacement cost" methodology), a possible alternative to the implementation of an agreement is a hospital's opportunity to engage (either as employees or as independent contractors) various medical directors to manage its identified service line offerings.

However, in this approach, it is important to note that the exact number of required work hours typically cannot reasonably be determined in advance. Furthermore, most management arrangements we have observed in the marketplace are not based upon actual underlying time to establish the management fee. Notwithstanding the foregoing, however, we believe that an approach wherein a valuator reviews benchmark data for hypothetical medical directorship positions is reasonable in establishing an alternative means to determine the FMV of the management services.

As an example, if a valuator was engaged to determine the FMV of a cardiovascular co-management arrangement, such service line offerings for consideration would likely include, but not be limited to: medical cardiology, interventional cardiology, cardio and thoracic surgery, cardiac rehabilitation, cardiac intensive care, and outpatient programs and services. Giving consideration to the number of medical directors that might reasonably be required to provide physician management to hospital's service lines, the valuator could then consider the following key factors:

- What is the projected net revenue of the service line? Since most co-management arrangements are implemented for the management of existing service line offerings, looking at the most recent 12-month period of historical collections would be advisable. Alternatively, if the service line in question is a new division of a hospital, for example, a cardiovascular center of excellence, relying on the hospital's annual projected net revenue for purposes of an analysis would be acceptable..

- How diverse are the service offerings? The diversity of service offerings in combination with the complexity of clinical operations and the volume of procedures, including both inpatient and outpatient services, requires significant coordination among numerous physicians, associated hospital services, and a myriad of operational details. For example, for hospital-specific reasons, a proposed orthopedic co-management arrangement might *exclude* outpatient rehabilitation services. In this instance, all other things being equal, the resulting range from methodology employed under the cost approach would likely be less than an arrangement that was all encompassing.

- How many subservice lines are contemplated? For example, in a cardiovascular services CCMA, the analysis is likely more complicated (and thus, the upper end of supportable FMV likely higher) if the arrangement includes general cardiology, interventional cardiology, cardiovascular surgery, and electrophysiology, as compared to a CCMA that solely contemplates invasive cardiology.

**Determination of comparable positions.** Once the scope of the service line is discussed and agreed upon, the determination of the particular physicians and the corresponding amount of time required to provide medical director services is dependent upon a variety of factors including (1) the size of the hospital, (2) the complexity of services being provided, and (3) the annual number of procedures performed. In consideration of these factors, the initial step would be to develop an expectation for the number of medical director positions that could have reasonably been supported in the absence of the co-management arrangement. The valuation analyst can either develop this guidance based on his or her own experience and informed judgment with similar arrangements or can engage the services of an independent staffing expert (most typically, an independent physician with previous department head experience). By evaluating the applicable service lines through probative inquiry and comparison to comparative data from similar facilities, the valuator should be in a good position to identify the relevant medical director positions, ensuring that there is no overlap and redundancy in the identification of such positions.

For example, as referenced above, if the valuator were analyzing a co-management arrangement for a comprehensive cardiovascular center of excellence, by evaluating each potential service line component, it would not be unreasonable to conclude that Exhibit 2 contains the six part-time medical director positions that might have been engaged. Such positions would have been engaged on an independent contractor basis, in the absence of a co-management arrangement, to manage daily operations and provide needed oversight to hospital's service line.

**Exhibit 2. Identified Service Line Medical Directorships**

| |
|---|
| Medical cardiology |
| Interventional/invasive cardiology |
| Cardiovascular and cardiothoracic surgery |
| Cardiac rehabilitation and recovery |
| Cardiac intensive care (CCU) |
| Outpatient programs and services |

**Determination of appropriate compensation rate.** To determine the appropriate compensation for each identified medical director position, it is important to note that compensation earned by a physician in his or her specialty practice of medicine may not be directly comparable to the compensation for medical directorship duties. However, the valuator should recognize that with regard to a medical director position, a hospital would need to identify not only an appropriately experienced clinician, but also an individual with the skills and experience necessary to perform required administrative duties. At this point in the analysis, the valuator should also give recognition to the size of the hospital. For example, a 500-bed trauma facility, given its size and focus, would likely need the support for a more diverse community of both inpatients and outpatients than a 150-bed regional hospital. The implication here is that there is likely support for higher compensation and allowable monthly hours for the 500-bed trauma facility arrangement.

Given the above, the valuator should review available compensation levels expected to be earned by a physician in his or her specialty practice of medicine as a reasonable starting point.[11] However, in most instances, such compensation values are likely *not* comparable to the FMV of compensation for medical directorship duties as described above. As stated above, in valuing administrative positions, a FMV analysis is not intended to establish an "opportunity cost" related to professional services. Therefore,

11 A good resource for cash compensation values can be obtained from the *MGMA Physician Compensation and Production Survey* because it is a commonly used benchmark percentile in the determination of appropriate FMV compensation values.

to develop the most appropriate compensation range, the valuator should review and consider available, published sources of administrative compensation data, such as publicly available administrative compensation surveys. In developing compensation ranges, as *general* guidance, the valuator should consider benchmark compensation values up to 90th percentile values, as physicians with the ability to operate a significant clinical practice, coupled with the time-consuming administrative responsibilities of the CCMA, generally command compensation in ranges higher than those experienced in a more traditional medical directorship role. However, as will be discussed below in detail, depending on the specific facts and circumstances of the arrangement, it may be reasonable to limit the upper end of the compensation range to the 75th percentile (e.g., in those instances where there are multiple medical director positions, relatively low program revenue, and so on).

**Determination of appropriate hours.** Once a compensation range is identified, the next step in the cost approach would be to identify the applicable hours attributable to each identified position. For ease of calculation, the typical convention would be to identify an annual number of hours. This number would then be multiplied by the hourly compensation range identified above to determine the annual compensation attributable to the position. To identify the appropriate range of expected monthly hours, the valuator should consider the following questions:

- How large is the hospital's service line to be managed (as measured by net revenue)?
- How large is the hospital, as measured by licensed bed count?
- Are both inpatient and outpatient services included in the arrangement?
- Does the co-management arrangement contemplate the management of a single campus or multiple campuses?[12]

As with the development of the compensation range, the valuator should review and consider available, published sources of administrative data regarding ranges of hours for respective administrative positions. This is an area where a significant amount of analysis and valuator judgment should come into play. Based on a review of the particular aspects of the arrangement (i.e., scope of the subservice lines, whether inpatient and outpatient services are included, whether there are multiple sites of services, and so on), the determination of annual hours will likely range between the 25th and 75th

12 In the authors' experience, it is not uncommon to see co-management arrangements covering multiple campuses for a hospital, particularly if certain services (i.e., rehabilitation) are handled in a distinct location. This dynamic increases the complexity of the management arrangement and would likely warrant an adjustment to the hourly and rate ranges.

percentiles However, as with the derivation of the hourly compensation, specific facts and circumstances might warrant exceeding this upper range in certain instances. For example, using a hypothetical cardiovascular center of excellence, co-management arrangements relate to unique cardiovascular surgery services in that these services are also provided to a hospital's patients that are transferred in from smaller regional hospitals where such services are not provided. In recognition of the added complexity of this relationship between hospitals, it may have been reasonable to utilize benchmark data for the 90th percentile to determine the number of hours required by the applicable cardiovascular surgery medical director positions.

Once these two market data points are identified, this data would then be used in conjunction with the appropriate staffing breakdown as detailed from Exhibit 2 to determine the total FMV range as determined under a cost approach. Exhibit 3 provides a simple summary of a hypothetical analysis used to determine the FMV range, under a cost approach, associated with the management of a hospital's cardiovascular center of excellence.

**Exhibit 3. Summary of Cost Approach**

| Service Offering | Hours Worked Per Year | 50th Percentile | | 90th Percentile | |
|---|---|---|---|---|---|
| | | Hourly Rate | Annual Compensation[1] | Hourly Rate | Annual Compensation |
| Medical cardiology | 215 | $134 | $28,810 | $174 | $37,410 |
| Interventional and invasive cardiology | 150 | $141 | $21,150 | $184 | $27,600 |
| Cardiovascular and cardiothoracic surgery | 856 | $186 | $159,216 | $256 | $219,136 |
| Cardiac rehabilitation and recovery | 174 | $150 | $26,100 | $173 | $30,102 |
| Cardiac intensive care (CCU) | 220 | $164 | $36,080 | $200 | $44,000 |
| Outpatient programs and services | 220 | $164 | $36,080 | $200 | $44,000 |
| TOTAL | 1,835 | | ≈ $308,000 | | ≈ $402,000 |

***Market-Based Approach***

The market approach to valuation provides an effective methodology to determine a FMV range while eliminating the constraints of a time-based analysis as required under a cost approach. However, the uniqueness of each co-management arrangement precludes *direct* market comparisons of the subject arrangement to other arrangements in the marketplace. Therefore, a critical part of the valuation process involves breaking down the co-management arrangement into its individual components. Once individual tasks, objectives, and performance metrics are identified, the arrangement can be compared to other arrangements with similar elements.[13] By comparing specific elements item by item, the valuator is able to assess the relative worth of each metric,[14] and determine the presence or absence of each metric in comparison to the comparable arrangements. Then, with reasonable objectivity, the valuator is able to assess the overall relative value of the identified arrangement by comparing it to other available market arrangements.

**Identification of services performed**. To compare the management services to be provided by a manager against market comparables where the management fees are known (i.e., a review of ASC management agreements), the valuator should consider the creation of a "scoring grid," whereby a weighting factor and point value are assigned to each specific identified task contemplated under the arrangement. The services to be included in the arrangement can usually be found in the draft agreement provided by counsel (usually as an exhibit to the body of the agreement), but often such services are also either contained within the body of the agreement or not addressed in detail at all. In these latter two examples, the valuator should be certain to have a detailed discussion with counsel with regard to the detail and "breadth" of the contemplated management services because the accurate identification of the specific services to be performed is the main driver within the market approach. For example, will the management company simply "assist" with the credentialing function by coordinating the necessary paperwork or will the management company be responsible for handling the credentialing function? Once these services are identified, the valuator will have a grid comprised of up to 40 specific services. This comprehensive listing of services that are typically provided by management companies will be a "baseline" listing from which the valuator can then begin to make a series of "normalizing" adjustments to the available management fee percentages in developing a range applicable to the agreement.

**Identification of baseline market comparables**. One common type of management arrangement whereby significant market data are available involves the management of ambulatory surgery centers (ASC) by professional management companies. Generally, ASC management companies provide comprehensive management services, with recognition that the services do not include those that typically require the involvement of physicians.

13 In the case of co-management arrangements, in the authors' experience, similar tasks and objectives might be found in ASC arrangements, which are readily available in the marketplace.
14 For example, metrics can be focused around tasks, objectives, or performance outcomes.

Some companies survey ASCs for operating statistics, and this information is readily available. Data on public ASC operating companies, such as AmSurg Inc. (AMSG), and available data from transactions involving privately held companies, such as Symbion Inc., may provide additional information, Additionally, the valuator can conduct a survey of identified national or regional ASC management companies, identifying the management fee ranges, stated as a percentage of collections (or net revenue). In the authors' experience, management fees range from approximately 3% to 6% of collections; however, the vast majority of such arrangements involve the existence of a full-time on-site manager who is compensated by the ASC, thereby effectively raising the total management fees to levels higher than 6%. If there is not enough available marketplace data on such arrangements, the valuator can also attempt to identify other management arrangements involving programs such as substance abuse, respiratory therapy, and physical therapy.[15] In considering the applicability of these arrangements to the agreement, however, the valuator should be careful to ensure that such arrangements do not include clinical staffing services because they would report a higher-than-expected management fee and result in a skewed analysis. As a result, a review of such arrangements may be helpful from a comparison perspective but may not be as reliable as information gleaned from more "typical" management company arrangements.

**Adjustments given scope of services**. Armed with the data developed in steps 1 and 2 above, the valuator is now in a position to utilize the developed "grid" to evaluate and score each task under the agreement. Some aspects to consider in the creation of a grid would be the following:

- Task importance—Develop a point system that values the complexity and anticipated time commitment required by each identified task, possibly ranging from 1 to 5. For example, "arranging for the purchase of liability insurance, paid for by the hospital" is a much complicated and time-intensive task compared to "developing community relationships that result in a satisfied referral base." As such, the scoring grid should be able to effectively distinguish between the two, and in this example, the latter task may be scored a "5," whereas the former task may be scored as a "3."

- Task—In management agreements, it is common to see tasks identified in an agreement that are meant to be more "supportive" in nature as compared to the management company having sole responsibility for the task. As referenced in the hypothetical example above, will the management company

15 Such arrangements may not be based upon designated percentages of net revenue. As such, to ensure an accurate comparison, it will be essential for the valuator to convert each arrangement to a percentage of net revenue equivalent basis to facilitate comparisons.

simply assist with the credentialing function by coordinating the necessary paperwork or will it be responsible for handling the credentialing function? The grid should be able to delineate between the two because the former task is certainly more limited in nature.

- Weighting factor—A weighting factor is recommended to be developed and applied to each task based on the above identified categories. As an example, a limited task may receive a weighting of 1, whereas a full task may receive a weighting of 3. Similarly, those tasks not included in the proposed agreement would receive a weighting of 0.

As a result of the above calculations, the analysis will yield a total point value, calculated as the sum of the various point values assigned in the above *task importance* section. In addition, the grid would have produced a weighted point value, which would be the product of each specific point value, multiplied by the identified weighting factor. As an example, if there were 30 tasks, resulting in a total score of 110 possible points, the weighted score might have totaled 80 points, resulting in a final score of 73% (i.e., 80 divided by 110). To determine a comparable value for the management services, the results of the above-described scoring grid (i.e., 73%), would be applied to the identified market range for management fees. In this example, the result would be a *preliminary* fee range for the management services, under a market approach, of from 2.2%[16] to 4.4%[17] of net revenue.

**Adjustments given revenue size**. Depending on the specific facts and circumstances of the arrangement, the valuator should also give consideration to the application of a discount of the preliminary range. While this may not appear to be intuitive, it is logical for a number of reasons. First, although the management services contemplated by the co-management agreement are likely comprehensive in nature, the hospital likely has the ability to rely upon many aspects of its infrastructure.[18] This is a significant point to consider, in that it reduces the hospital's required degree of dependence upon the management company. Second, in most instances, the revenue size of a service line subject to a co-management agreement is significantly higher than the typical ASC that is subject to an outside management arrangement, thereby warranting a lower fee as a percentage of net revenue.[19] Third, research indicates that as revenue sizes grow, there

16 0.03 times 73%

17 0.06 times 73%

18 Even if the agreement is not a traditional co-management agreement (i.e., it is not uncommon to have such management companies solely owned by the physicians), the authors believe that the participating hospital will still be in a position to leverage aspects of its infrastructure.

19 In the authors' general experience, the "typical" revenue size of a co-managed service line might be in the $30 million-to-$70 million range, whereas the typical ASC has revenues in the range of $10 million or less.

is an increased likelihood that a management organization would discount its normal management fees in recognition of the fact that it is able to achieve certain economies in the arrangement. Furthermore, once net revenue exceeds a certain threshold, the correlation between net revenue and the cost to manage the services is significantly reduced. Therefore, in recognition of this disconnect and to apply a certain degree of conservatism to the analysis, the valuator should consider the application of a discount to the initially calculated fee range, with a reasonable range of discounts being from 10% to 30%.

**Reconciliation of the approaches.** In considering the outcomes of the valuation approaches, the market approach is generally preferable in valuing management services. However, the market approach can be subject to certain limitations since, as discussed above, there are no directly comparable market values. The income approach contains some element of speculation in the projection of LOS and readmission impact and may sometimes yield inconclusive results; therefore, the valuation analyst must weigh these factors in determining the degree of reliance placed upon these methods. With respect to the cost approach, the build-up of the medical director time requirements does not necessarily value the services that will be contributed by a hospital partner in the management company. As such, a common approach would be to give each methodology equal weighting and take a simple average of the calculated values. In other instances, however, there may be a need to provide a double weighting of one approach or the other, in recognition of additional arrangement dynamics. As an example, if the valuator were analyzing a relatively "light" management arrangement (i.e., a small service line such as ENT at a regional hospital), given the relatively scaled down services contemplated under that type of arrangement, an equal weighting may not necessarily accurately capture the essence of the arrangement.[20] In this instance, the valuator might elect to normalize the valuation by giving a *double weighting* to the results of the cost approach.

## Valuing the Total Fee

Within the framework of co-management arrangements, a reliable and comprehensive valuation approach should provide a fair market value range that encompasses the total management fee (i.e., both the base management fee *and* the incentive management fee). In addition, each co-management arrangement is unique and reflects specific market and operational factors, which are singular to the specific setting. Therefore, the valuator should generally provide a FMV range that encompasses the *total* management fee, providing the hospital with the opportunity to establish the proportion of the management

20 In other words, the results of the market approach would likely understate the value of the services being provided by sole virtue of its reliance on the net revenue of the service line.

fee payable as a base management fee versus the incentive management fee (which will be based upon achievement of the predetermined measures). That said, although the hospital should have significant discretion in establishing the relative value of the base management fee as compared to the incentive management fee, certain regulatory and market-based constraints should be observed. In particular, regulatory considerations may affect the maximum percentage of the total fee that can be incentive based.[21]

However, within those constraints, it is not likely beneficial to set the incentive management fee too low as a percentage of the total management fee (since such an overemphasis on the base fee would seem to diminish the ideals of achieving the pre-established performance objectives). As general guidance, the base management fee should generally be no higher than 60% and no lower than 25% of the total management fee. These constraints are based upon observations in the marketplace of similar arrangements and, in the authors' opinion, preserve the general intent of the hospital with respect to the desired outcome of the co-managed services.

#### *Issues Impacting the FMV Analysis*

Once the FMV range of the management agreement is identified, it is important that the valuator recognize that each management arrangement is completely unique, and as with most arrangements, these unique attributes can have a significant impact on the resulting FMV of the arrangement. This section of the chapter will focus on some of the common areas for discussion amongst the parties, each of which should be thoroughly explored by the valuator.

**The use of medical director positions**. A very commonly used practice within co-management arrangements is to utilize medical directorships for select physician participants. While the intent of the arrangements typically is to have the management company perform all of the management services, it is not uncommon to find that certain of the management services are intended to be provided through a medical director arrangement provided by a qualified physician associated with the management company. While this is an acceptable practice, the valuator should ensure the following:

- Such medical director arrangements are to be paid as an expense from the identified base portion of management fee. Since the FMV build-up of the management fee as discussed above in the cost approach section already contemplates the use of such positions, paying for them outside of

21 According to Rev. Proc. 97-13, certain not-for-profit entities with public bond financed property must ensure that the incentive portion of the management fee is not set too high as compared to the base fee, depending on the length of the contract term and other terms of the arrangement. Therefore, parties considering such arrangements are advised to seek the advice of experienced legal counsel prior to entering into any such arrangements.

the management fee would be considered redundant. However, there are instances in which such positions would be allowed in a manner consistent with FMV, such as when the medical directorship was for a specific subset service line, which was now going to be carved out from the management company (e.g., in a cardiac co-management arrangement, the parties might agree to carve cardiac rehabilitation out of the arrangement). In this instance, the valuator should ensure that the net revenue provided for the analysis specifically excludes any revenue attributable to the cardiac rehabilitation so as to not allow for redundancy of payment.

- If all parties agree on the treatment of revenues and positions, it is important that the valuator ensure that such medical director arrangements will be for a number of monthly hours and rate that is *consistent with FMV.* As an example, and as a good rule of thumb, the valuator should ensure that the proposed hours and rate are equal to or below the upper end of the values provided in Table 3 (of course tailored to the specific analysis in question).

- Since the intent of a co-management arrangement is that there are no "passive investors," the valuator should also give consideration to the magnitude of the total monies being allocated toward medical directorships. As discussed above, the base management fee is meant to compensate the management company for handling the day-to-day management services, which are expected to be handled in a proportional manner to each party's ownership. Therefore, assuming a 50-50 ownership (as is typical), it would not be reasonable to have a disproportionate share of the base management fee paid out as medical directorships. While there is latitude in the ultimate percentage "ceiling" that can be approved, another good rule of thumb is that *no more than* 25% of the base fee should be allocated to medical director positions. By doing so, the valuator can avoid any possible interpretation that this management company is simply a vehicle under which a hospital intends to distribute monies to the physicians while allowing them to perform less than the required share of the overall duties. This is especially critical when the medical directorships are going to be with physician owners.

**Provision/purchase of administrative services.** It is not uncommon in many arrangements for the management company, whether jointly owned or not, to need certain administrative services. In the case of a physician-owned management company, given the "loose" structure of the arrangement and since there is no need for dedicated building space and staff, the physician owners simply do have the requisite infrastructure necessary to manage their operation. Such needed administrative support services may include, but not be limited to, the following: accounting, financial statement preparation, tax return preparation, payroll processing, and legal support and clerical support. In most instances, the hospital is more than willing to provide such services to the management company. By doing so, however, the hospital has just unintentionally (or intentionally as the case may be) created a fair market value implication by providing additional services that have a defined market worth. The valuator should ensure that such services are independently negotiated and implemented at a rate that is FMV between the parties.[22]

**Ensuring equitable division of responsibilities.** As has been stated numerous times throughout this chapter, the co-management structure is intended to be a vehicle that ensures that hospital and physician members both actively participate in the provision of the management services (i.e., there are no passive investors in a management company). Furthermore, a key representation in most management company analyses is that the resulting division of responsibilities within the management company (i.e., the management contribution of each party related to providing the management services) will be in approximate proportion to the ownership percentages determined. However, under most arrangements, assuming a 50-50 ownership structure, it would be virtually impossible to ensure that all of the required duties are handled on an exact 50-50 basis. That said, if the parties each own 50% of the management company and will thus receive 50% of the management fee, the valuator should ensure that (1) each party takes an active role in the management duties and (2) each party will manage efforts in approximate proportion to their ownership.

**Ensuring no overlap of responsibilities.** Similar to the discussion above related to a medical director position, a service line administrator is often engaged to perform services in conjunction with a CCMA. As with the medical director, if the service line administrator is responsible for performing tasks similar to those required of the co-management company, then the administrator must be compensated as an expense from the base management fee. Notwithstanding, in an increasing number of management arrangements, the administrator is an employee of the hospital and is responsible for overseeing the hospital's interests in terms of service line management (i.e., purely providing oversight), rather than *actually providing* any of the management services. In these cases, since the administrator does not have any responsibility for actually performing any of the specified management services, there is no duplication of activities, and therefore, the administrator would not be required to be compensated from the base management fee.

22 In many instances, the valuator is not asked to analyze and determine the FMV of such services. It is therefore acceptable to rely on the party's representation and to list such a governing assumption in the valuation report, i.e., that any such services will be subject to an appropriate FMV analysis.

As an additional example, in arrangements that are structured as straight "management arrangements," (i.e., there is no hospital ownership in the management company, only physician owners), it is very common for an operational committee to be established, with the members comprised of both management company (i.e., physician) and hospital participants. In this case, the committee would typically meet monthly to review operational issues and other issues related to the service line and the management arrangement. While this is acceptable from an operational and structural standpoint, from a FMV standpoint, it is key to ensure that any hospital appointed members of the committee do not perform any of the management services that are the sole responsibility of the management company as set forth in the applicable agreement (i.e., any hospital appointed members function solely in an oversight capacity).

### Developing and Implementing a Compliance Program

As discussed throughout this chapter, a fundamental assumption in the determination of the FMV of CCMAs involves the "actual performance" of the base management tasks and the "achievement" of specific performance metrics. Since the authors have hopefully made clear the fact that these arrangements are not passive in nature, the lack of an effective compliance plan, coupled with a reliable mechanism to track and document both base management task performance and the achievement of the identified performance metrics, will be an area of great concern in helping to ensure that you have a supportable arrangement.

Since the calculated FMV range is based on the completion of very specific management tasks, it is not sufficient to simply identify the management tasks to be performed by the management company and document them in an agreement, never to be looked at again until contract renewal time. Most importantly, the hospital needs to track and document task completion, including receipt of associated deliverables, to demonstrate that the tasks have actually been performed and the performance metrics have been met.

Therefore, any organization undertaking a CCMA should take care to "define" each base management task (i.e., in the context of your specific hospital and arrangement), and determine the required deliverables (e.g., training programs, development of staffing plans, creation of protocols and standards, and so on). In addition, take the time to ensure that the identified performance metrics include measurable goals. Furthermore, while it is acceptable to provide for a certain portion of the incentive management fee to be based on "maintenance" of certain performance levels (and even in these cases, maintenance should only be allowed for metrics whose performance is equal to or above national benchmarks), the majority of the metrics should only allow for 100% payout in the event that significant improvement above "baseline" levels is achieved.

Lastly, a hospital should establish a mechanism to track the progress made toward the completion of each base management task and performance goal annually and ensure that, as appropriate, an annual "rebasing" of the performance metrics is undertaken.

## Summary

The emergence of incentive-based models for the delivery of healthcare services has contributed to the development of a broad range of new opportunities for hospital and physician partnerships. One of the most common forms of these partnerships involves the establishment of a physician-owned or hospital and physician-owned co-management company for the purpose of managing a specific hospital service line. This type of arrangement offers significant value propositions to patients, who have improved access to needed services; to hospitals, which realize improved patient satisfaction, operational efficiencies, financial controls, and enhanced clinical quality; and to physicians, who are incented to effectively and efficiently manage the service line and facilitate the achievement of identified performance-based metrics.

However, the uniqueness of each co-management arrangement precludes direct market comparisons of the subject arrangement to other arrangements in the marketplace. Therefore, a critical part of the valuation process involves breaking down the co-management arrangement into its individual components. Once individual tasks, objectives, and performance metrics are identified, the arrangement can be compared to other arrangements with similar elements and analyzed by completing a build-up of comparable positions that would be required in the absence of such an arrangement. Regardless of the approach undertaken, determining the fair market value of these types of management agreements is of paramount importance, and by incorporating the above elements into a valuation repertoire, one can be assured that a thorough analysis will result.

## Bibliography

Specifications Manual for National Hospital Quality Measures, The Joint Commission and Centers for Medicare and Medicaid Services

Callender, Arianne N. et al., "Corporate Responsibility and Health Care Quality: A Resource for Health Care Boards of Directors", Office of Inspector General

oig.hhs.gov/fraud/docs/complianceguidance/CorporateResponsibilityFinal%209-4-07.pdf. (September 2007).

Lindenauer, Peter K. et al., "Public Reporting and Pay for Performance in Hospital Quality Improvement" *New England Journal of Medicine* Vol. 356, no. 5 (February 2007): 486-96.

Rosenthal, Meredith B. et al., "Paying For Quality: Providers' Incentives for Quality Improvement" *Health Affairs* Vol. 23, no. 2. (March /April 2004): 127.

Williams, Jeni. "Making the Grade With Pay for Performance: 7 Lessons From Best-Performing Hospitals" *Healthcare Financial Management* (December 2006): 79.

"Improving Acute Myocardial Infarction Reliability and Outcomes", Institute for Healthcare Improvement http://www.ihi.org. [Internet accessed on Jan. 24, 2008].

"Keeping 'Pay' in Pay-For-Performance ("P4P") for Anesthesiologists: A Strategic Analysis of the Opportunities and Threats to Anesthesia Related to the Emerging P4P Trend" Smith Anderson Blount Dorsett Mitchell & Jernigan, LLP (September 2005).

"Testimony Before House of Representatives Committee on Ways and Means, Subcommittee on Health: Promoting Quality and Efficiency of Care for Medicare Beneficiaries" Pacific Business Group on Health www.pbgh.org (March 2005).

Chapter 34

# Next Generation Clinical Co-Management Agreements: The Challenges of Valuing 'Value'

*By Mark Browne, M.D., David McMillan, CPA, and Burl Stamp, FACHE*

*"Price is what you pay. Value is what you get."* – *Warren Buffet*

Although there is no doubt the healthcare industry is journeying ever closer to a model based on the value, not the quantity, of care delivered, the path to get there is at best a confusing one. The idea of aligned incentives between hospitals and physicians is an easy one to agree with, but a very difficult one to implement in reality. The clinical co-management model (CCM) is one tactic used by many health systems to begin to aligning the existing disparate financial incentives for hospitals and physicians. Valuation experts are often called upon to provide opinions of value related to the compensation paid to the participating physicians. To comply with federal regulations, participants in these models must ensure that compensation received by physicians is at fair market value (FMV) to prevent overpayment to physicians based on the value or volume of referrals.

To properly evaluate the FMV compensation associated with CCMs, valuators must have a thorough understanding of the components of a co-management agreement and must provide analytics supporting the basis of their valuation. This can be difficult given that many of the "value-based" concepts underpinning these agreements (such as specialty-specific quality and outcomes metrics):

- Are highly subjective;
- Are not yet recognized in a definitive manner within the available regulatory guidance; and,
- Do not correlate easily to widely circulated benchmark materials.

In addition to these challenges, valuators are now faced with second-generation CCMs whose scope of services managed, number of facilities managed, and scope of geographic regions served are expanding. For example, hospitals and health systems are exploring concepts such as:

- Whole-hospital clinical co-management agreements;
- Multiple facility or single service line co-management agreements; and
- Multiple facility or multiple service line co-management agreements.

The emergence of these newer, more expansive models, understanding their construct, and evaluating various valuation issues they present are the topics of conversation among hospitals, physicians, attorneys, healthcare leaders, consultants, and valuators. To explore the unique valuation challenges associated with these second-generation CCMs, it is imperative to first ensure an understanding of the construct and valuation principles underpinning traditional models.

### Understanding Traditional Co-Management Models

Significant attention and professional guidance have been given to the valuation challenges and approaches related to CCMs. Our purpose is not to present a comprehensive overview of the valuation issues inherent in the determination of FMV compensation associated with these more traditional models. However, a brief narrative on the subject is included below to provide appropriate context for the reader when considering the implications of second-generation CCMs.

Historically, co-management agreements have been designed around a single, hospital-based service line. Common service lines considered include orthopedics, cardiology, and neurosurgery. When valuing the compensation associated with CCMs, the approaches utilized by the valuator are consistent with the valuation approaches used for any form of compensation methodology: the income approach, the cost approach, and the market approach.

- Income approach—This approach measures the economic benefit accruing to the contracting organization (typically a hospital or health system) as a result of the management services rendered by the parties to the CCM. Additionally, the income approach may attempt to also measure the economic benefit accruing to the contracting organization from the achievement of certain quality or outcome metrics. Measuring the economic benefits of these services or outcomes, however, involves certain potential risks, such as the implication of valuing volume or referrals, and the perception that the agreements might result in compensation to physicians that is generated more directly from the energies of existing hospital management functions. Despite those concerns, many valuators continue to employ this approach when valuing the compensation associated with CCMs.

- Valuing the economic benefits accruing to the hospital from the achievement of quality and outcome metrics prior to the implementation of the Centers for Medicare and Medicaid Services (CMS) value-based purchasing program (VBP) and other similar reimbursement structures sponsored by private insurers was, at best, subjective. However, the emergence of these defined VBP programs provides today's valuator with discernible economic risks and benefits associated with these metrics. While this clarity is certainly helpful, the introduction of metrics that are increasingly difficult to measure and report, as discussed below, introduce new challenges to the valuator when employing the income approach.

- Cost approach—This approach evaluates the alternative to the proposed structure, i.e., what it would cost the hospital to hire or provide for the management and other services within the CCM. As with all approaches, the valuator must ensure a thorough understanding of the components of the CCM agreement to properly evaluate the merits and usefulness of this approach. Often, due to the inability to match desired services with internal resources, this approach requires significant judgment by the valuator. When making these judgments and assumptions, the valuator may have to access expertise from experts in clinical and operational matters to have an appropriate degree of understanding of the issues and factors contributing to the application of this approach. As a result, the use of multiple approaches, when applicable, will provide a more comprehensive basis for the opinion of value related to the compensation component of the CCM.

- Market approach—A powerful tool in the valuator's arsenal is the ability of the valuator to draw upon experience with other CCM arrangements and analyses. Having an experienced valuation team adds significant value for the hospital seeking assistance. While each CCM is unique in its construct and purpose, various components within the CCM often have characteristics and specific elements common to other CCMs. Once the valuator has gained a thorough understanding of the components of the CCM, he or she can then draw upon his or her experience with other, similar components in assigning an indication of value using this approach.

Ultimately, the valuator's opinion of value will likely be the result of a combination of multiple approaches and judgment.

Traditional CCMs often result in compensation being awarded for the defined services (fixed fee) and the ability to earn additional compensation based on the achievement of predetermined metrics (variable fee). Evaluating the valuation issues presented by these traditional models include:

- Defining the fixed fee component—Careful consideration should be given to the construct of this component of compensation. Hospitals and physicians should collaborate to define these services, whose purposes are to improve the quality of care provided and improve the outcomes of the patients treated. Simply assigning traditional medical directorship services, which are often administrative in nature, is not a substitute for the work and analysis necessary to define the services and duties that will positively impact the care provided to patients.

That is not to say, however, that administrative functions have no place in a co-management agreement. Many co-management agreements include management functions performed by physicians and nonphysician personnel. These functions can be important toward the goals of improved care. However, the valuator must be cognizant of Stark regulations that expressly limit compensation paid to physicians for administrative functions to administrative rates. Having qualified clinical professionals, such as physicians, nurses, and other experienced operational executives, evaluate the duties outlined in the fixed fee component of the co-management agreement is critical to ensure the valuator understands the basis for opining upon this portion of the compensation.

- Defining the variable ("at risk") fee component—The more substantive challenge facing those designing and valuing traditional co-management models is the definition of the metrics and parameters of the components composing the variable compensation portion of the agreement. These components typically consist of quality and outcome metrics, performance metrics, and satisfaction metrics. Regulatory bodies such as the Centers for Medicare and Medicaid Services (CMS) and the Office of Inspector General (OIG) have provided guidance on the construct and measurement of these components. Such guidance should be carefully evaluated by qualified legal counsel when constructing the co-management agreement. Valuators must have an understanding of these regulations, because the valuator's ability to ensure there is a basis for measuring these metrics is dependent upon such.

Despite these efforts, however, the healthcare industry continues to refine its ability to track and measure many quality measurements. As a result, there is not always unanimity among participants as to how these metrics are measured.

- Defining the structure to house the co-management functions—Typically, the traditional co-management companies have been structured in one of three ways:
  - As a contract between a hospital and physicians;
  - Within a joint venture company owned by physician-participants and the hospital; or,
  - Within a joint venture company owned by physician participants.

When housed within a joint venture company, the valuator is often called upon to value equity interests in the company often associated with changes in ownership.

### Next Generation Co-Management Models

As organizations continue the simultaneous journeys of new care model development, many are searching for ways to further build on the foundation of existing clinical co-management arrangements. Leveraging the investments made in the infrastructure, operational improvement, and relationships necessary for these existing co-managements arrangements can provide a framework for systems to move closer to the ultimate goal of consistent high quality care delivery rewarded through a value-based payment system. To that end, health systems that have clinical co-management agreements in place are beginning to move toward more complex, integrated types of arrangements as a vehicle to ease the transition to a fully value-based model of care.

These new arrangements often share the same basic tenets of traditional co-management agreements, i.e., a structure that includes an hourly rate for management-related activities and a variable or at-risk component. However, in the more contemporary clinical co-management models, variables constituting the at-risk component emphasize activities related to quality, outcomes, and efficiency.

### New Model Structures

In response to these new challenges, hospitals, healthcare systems, and their physician partners have developed new CCM models whose scope and reach extend beyond the traditional structure. Whole-hospital agreements, multihospital service line agreements, and other model constructs continue to emerge. The scope of services or expanded geographies can present unique challenges to the valuator. Of particular concern to the valuator, when multiple service lines or geographies are involved, is the need to perform additional analyses and due diligence to gain an understanding of the multiplicity of agreements outside the scope of the CCM that may exist. Call arrangements, medical directorships, consulting agreements and other similar contracts must all be considered for the evaluator to accurately estimate the cost of services (application of the cost approach) and the resulting compensation.[1]

While many of the mechanics of compensation (fixed base compensation and variable compensation earned through the achievement of predetermined metrics) are expanded in these second-generation models, the concepts remain fairly similar to traditional CCM models. The challenges faced by the valuators are often associated with the expanded clinical metrics and quality standards incorporated in the models and the leadership and governance structures that can have an impact on roles, responsibilities, and compensation.

### Second-Generation Quality and Outcome Metrics

The traditional co-management model design is quite effective in managing costs and improving quality within the hospital but does little to address issues beyond the acute care continuum such as readmission, outpatient imaging, rehabilitative care, or other clinical issues presented by patients outside of the service line. These other clinical issues, such as diabetes, heart failure, and so on, have a significant impact on the total cost and quality of care delivered. Additionally the traditional co-management models have been limited as to the type of quality metrics typically defined and measured as part of an arrangement. Many hospitals are limited in the quality of data that are readily available for use in these arrangements. As a result, many of the co-management agreements previously executed have reverted to the frequent use of process metrics as opposed to true outcome-based metrics. Measures of performance in this type of model begin to evolve from process-based measures to more sophisticated outcome types of metrics. Measures within the specific service line are transformed to focus more on clinical performance (i.e., infection rates and complication rates) as well as incorporating more subjective measures, such as patient and physician satisfaction. Also in these newer models, a larger percentage of total compensation is placed at risk

1 Although not considered within the scope of this discussion, these expanded models and the potential for a multiplicity of agreements may present commercial reasonableness issues and concerns. A thorough evaluation of commercial reasonableness is an important consideration for valuators, consultants, counsel, and providers when contemplating the compliance standards to be addressed.

for performance on quality metrics, typically in the 25%-to-30% range and sometimes as high as 50%.[2]

**Exhibit 1. Examples of Process and Outcome Metrics**

| Process Metrics | Outcome Metrics |
|---|---|
| Did the heart attack patient receive an aspirin? | Mortality rate for heart attack |
| Did the congestive heart failure patient receive discharge instructions? | Percentage of patients with congestive heart failure readmitted within 30 days of hospital discharge |

The valuator's ability to effectively apply the income, cost and market approaches with respect to quality and outcome metrics was often limited in the past because the economic return to the hospital resulting from the achievement of these metrics was limited. As providers have increasingly provided enhanced reimbursement for proven improvements in quality (or, conversely, penalties to reimbursement for quality or outcome deficiencies), the ability of the valuator to confidently utilize the income approach has improved. Of particular note, the initiation of the value-based payment program by CMS provides significant guidance for measuring the potential economic return to hospitals resulting from increased quality and enhanced outcomes. Contemporary valuators should understand the basic tenants and construct of CMS's value-based reimbursement system because this methodology will likely be prevalent, in some form or fashion, within many privately sponsored value-based reimbursement programs.

### *Understanding CMS's Value-Based Program Construct*

As the name suggests, the new VBP regulations are designed to reward those healthcare institutions that offer superior *value* to Medicare patients. The VBP program provides a structured mechanism to level the playing field across healthcare institutions that deliver varying levels of quality. Simply, institutions providing measurably higher quality can justify higher cost and reimbursement, while institutions with lower scores on quality metrics should be paid less to balance the value equation. It is important for staff and physicians at all levels of the organization to understand this dynamic and why paying attention to VBP factors is so critical.

2 At-risk or variable compensation amounts may be subject to certain limitations depending upon factors such as the presence of tax-exempt debt within the financing structure of the participating hospital or health system. For example, IRS Revenue Procedure 97-13 outlines certain safe harbors that apply to agreements of this type to ensure that the tax-exempt entity does not use bond-financed assets for private business. Valuators and consultants should work closely with tax professionals and counsel when defining the compensation structure for these newer models.

**Exhibit 2. FY2012 Metrics**

| | | |
|---|---|---|
| • Fibronolytic therapy received within 30 minutes<br>• Primary PCI received within 90 minutes<br>• Discharge instructions for CHF<br>• Blood cultures performed in Emergency Department for pneumonia<br>• Initial antibiotic selection for Community Acquired Pneumonia | • Prophylactic antibiotic received within one hour prior to incision<br>• Surgery patients with appropriate selection of prophylactic antibiotics<br>• Surgery patients with appropriate discontinuation of prophylactic antibiotics<br>• Cardiac surgery patient with controlled post-operative serum glucose | • Surgery patients with recommended venous thromboembolism prophylaxis ordered<br>• Surgery patients who received appropriate venous thromboembolism prophylaxis before and after surgery<br>• Appropriate beta blocker use in surgical patients |
| • Communication with Nurses<br>• Communication with Doctors<br>• Hospital Staff Responsiveness | • Pain Management<br>• Communication about Medicine<br>• Hospital Cleanliness & Quietness | • Discharge Information<br>• Overall Hospital Rating |

While the new value-based purchasing methodology was designed to be revenue- or cost-neutral in aggregate, the funding and incentive payment design forces individual winners and losers. Approximately 50% of participating hospitals will lose money, while the other half will benefit from higher reimbursement for Medicare services. This is particularly important to consider in the context of valuing compensation associated with these next-generation CCMs; achieving the ability to earn reimbursement in the CMS value-based program is not necessarily solely dependent upon achieving certain scores but is also dependent upon how a particular hospital or organization scores *relative to other hospitals and organizations.* This concept is not often found in the CCM construct. The ability to earn compensation relative to the achievement of quality and outcome metrics is usually defined. As value-based reimbursement systems evolve, valuators need to be aware of these market forces when applying the market approach to compensation considerations.

#### *Paying for the Value-Based Program*

To fund incentive payments, base diagnosis-related group (DRG) rates for hospitals reimbursed under the prospective payment system (PPS) will be reduced by 1% beginning Oct. 1, 2012 (see Exhibit 3). For each of the next four years, rates will drop an additional 0.25% until payments are reduced a full 2% in fiscal year 2017.

Although DRG rates are being cut, remember that the regulations today require that all reduced reimbursement—estimated to be approximately $850 million in the first year of the program—be redistributed to providers. CMS estimates that the mean redistributed value-based incentive payments will range from 48% to 155% of an institutions' reduction in DRG reimbursement.

### *Value-Based Program Metrics—Scoring and Awarding Reimbursement*

The metrics that matter under the new value-based purchasing program are grouped into two broad categories that should be very familiar to hospitals. Clinical Processes of Care Measures were first introduced on CMS's Hospital Compare Web site (www.hospitalcompare.hhs.gov) in 2005 and Hospital Consumer Assessment of Healthcare Providers and Systems (H-CAHPS) measures of patient experience followed in 2007. The 12 process of care measures determine 70% of a hospital's incentive score, with the H-CAHPS survey results accounting for 30%. CMS has committed to additional new measures being available on the Hospital Compare Web site for at least one year before they are added to the incentive formula under VBP.

For both clinical processes of care and H-CAHPS measures, there are two ways for a hospital to earn its performance score in a range from 0 to 10 points: 1) by hitting achievement targets based on its performance as compared to all hospitals across the country or 2) by improving results compared against its own performance during the benchmark period.

**Exhibit 3. Reduction Timeline**

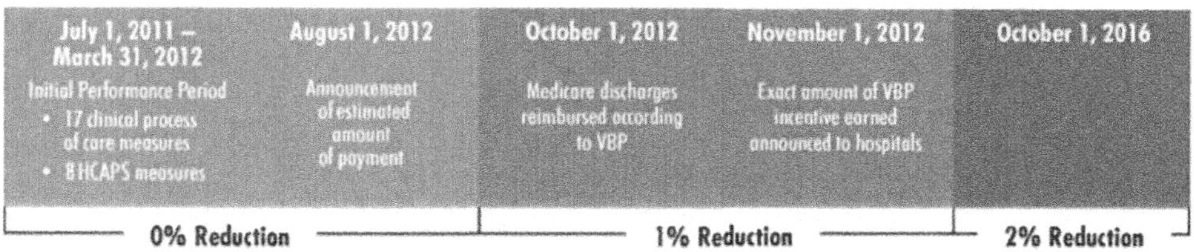


*Achievement scores* are awarded for each individual care process and H-CAHPS measure on an incremental scale from a "threshold" up to the "benchmark" for that performance component, where:

- Threshold = median ($50^{th}$ percentile) of all participating hospitals' performance during baseline period (July 2009 to March 2010) and
- Benchmark = mean of the top 10% of all hospitals' performance during the baseline period.

*Improvement scores* are awarded on a similar scale, but the organization's lower threshold is set at its own actual performance on each dimension during the baseline period. The improvement score methodology makes it possible for a hospital to receive points when it is making progress on a clinical process or H-CAHPS measure even when its score is still below the median for all hospitals.

In Exhibit 4, this hospital scored 0.43 during the baseline period on one of the VBP dimensions. Its score improved significantly during the 2012 performance period, to 0.82, putting it above the achievement threshold of 0.65 on this measure. Its achievement score on this measure would be approximately 7.2 and rounded to 7. But note that its improvement score would be slightly higher and rounded up to 8. On this measure, it would be awarded the higher improvement score.

For clinical processes of care and H-CAHPS measures, CMS will calculate both the achievement and improvement score and give the hospital the higher of the two scores, rounded to the nearest whole number (see Exhibit 4).

**Exhibit 4. Example Scoring Model**

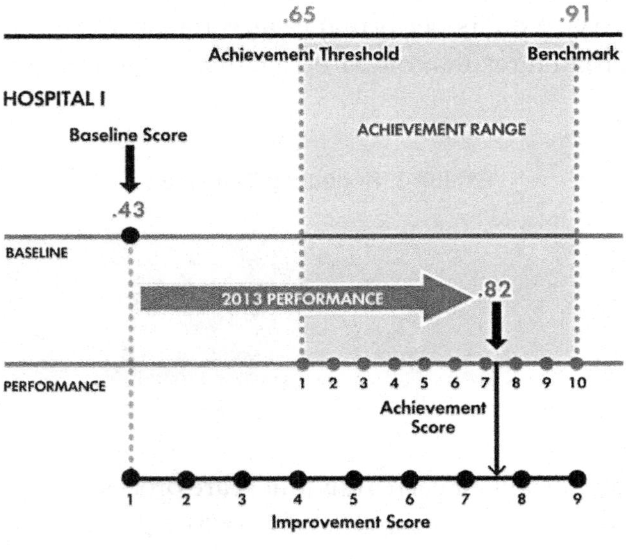


For the patient experience component of value-based purchasing, CMS also wants to reward hospitals for achieving consistency across the various H-CAHPS dimensions. The consistency score, which will comprise 20% of the total H-CAHPS score, will be awarded in a range of 0 to 20 points if a hospital makes improvement across all eight components. If a hospital's scores on all eight of the H-CAHPS dimensions are above the achievement threshold, it will receive the maximum, 20 points.

Actual incentive payments will be calculated at the end of each CMS fiscal year using a hospital's individual scores as compared to performance scores of all other participating hospitals. Again, CMS estimates that the mean redistributed value-based incentive payments will range from 48% to 155% of an institutions' reduction in DRG reimbursement.

As demonstrated above, there is much to learn from CMS's example for hospitals in the design and implementation of contemporary CCM models. An experienced valuator, well-versed in contemporary reimbursement models, will be a valuable member of the team, working to define and implement these next-generation models.

Because CMS is the single largest payor in healthcare, the quality metrics utilized in its value-based program deserve careful consideration and study. However, providers and payors are continually developing new and unique ways to measure quality and outcome metrics, and these concepts are continually finding their way into CCMs.

One such concept being incorporated is that of the "trigger metric." In this model, physicians must overcome a defined performance hurdle (i.e., top decile performance in all relevant core measures) to access any quality-related bonus at all, independent of their performance on the other defined quality metrics. No compensation is directly tied to the achievement of the trigger metric. It is simply the minimum threshold necessary to participate in any quality-related compensation. This model is closely aligned with models currently being employed by CMS in its shared savings program (ACOs) as well as the bundled payment initiative pilot. Structuring the quality portion of co-management agreements in this way allows physicians and hospitals to mutually define clinical priorities and begins to align incentives, leading to a greater focus for all in achieving the desired quality and efficiency outcomes.

Another contemporary quality metric being considered in contemporary CCMs is the composite metric. In this type of metric, efficiency or cost components are married with clinical outcome metrics into a single composite score. This type of metric is frequently used as a trigger metric to remove it from any direct association with the value or volume of referrals. This type of metric must obviously be carefully designed to be compliant with Stark and anti-kickback statutes but can lead to significant improvements in both cost and quality if well-designed.

A third quality concept differentiating this type of alignment model from traditional models is the introduction of shared quality metrics. In this model, "all ships rise, and all ships sink" together. In other words, if all physicians in each individual service line agreement do not achieve the goal outlined by the shared quality metrics, no physician is rewarded for his or her individual performance. Incentive compensation is only rewarded if all physicians in each arrangement achieve a defined goal. This style of metric can be used at the individual service line level as well as at a higher governance level, such as the clinical coordination integration listed above. A good example of a metric to be used in this way is patient satisfaction measures. Each service line will have different satisfaction-related opportunities to address, but it is a measure that is common to all service lines and has direct impact for the system as well.

As the valuator is charged with the task of assigning value to the compensation associated with these new and more comprehensive metrics, he or she may be faced with metrics to measure and value that are unique to the situation being studied, for which other examples (market approaches) are not readily available. To assign an economic "value" to the "value" provided by the accomplishments of these newer, more comprehensive metrics, the valuator must have access to significant expertise in healthcare operations and to qualified clinical resources that can provide expertise and perspective to the activities that may result in compensation to council members. Once again, coordination across a multidisciplinary team of professionals, including the valuator, is required to properly measure the value of compensation and services associated with these newer models of care. Valuators must be actively seeking these resources if they are to continue serving the healthcare industry associated with newer care delivery models. Those who recognize the necessity of such a multidisciplinary approach will be in high demand and will provide a defensible, value-added service for their clients. Those who do not prepare themselves nor recognize the need for these resources may ultimately place both themselves and the clients they serve at risk with regards to defending the compensation associated with these models as being consistent with the standard of FMV.

### Clinical Leadership and Governance

As mentioned previously, historical agreements of this type have typically been focused on a single service line. Model participants are now exploring new designs to begin to address care across the continuum of care. One way this is being accomplished is through the creation of a multidisciplinary clinical advisory or integration council (see Exhibit 5). As it relates to clinical co-management models, this council might be the contracting or governing body for agreements for multiple service lines (necessitating the inclusion of multiple specialties among the council's membership.) Alternatively, this group may function as a complementary committee focused on coordinating the efforts of existing clinical co-management agreements. In this capacity, the council provides oversight to ensure consistent, standardized care delivery across multiple specialties.

This council may also manage other types of agreements (i.e., professional services agreements) to ensure consistency of a value-based design of all physician and hospital arrangements across a system. Physicians on this committee are chosen specifically for their ability to lead and manage care across the continuum and are not necessarily chosen on a representative basis. In other words, they need not be a representative from each existing co-management agreement on the council for it to be a successful model. Physicians invited to participate in the council may also have defined requirements for participation that lead to a more integrated care delivery system. As an example, one system with this type of arrangement requires the physicians to actively participate as members of the statewide Healthcare Information Exchange to assure the necessary collection and analysis of data for value-based payment models.

Physicians serving on this council may receive compensation for their service. While providing hourly compensation is an option, the nature and purpose of these councils are often more in keeping with an at-risk or performance-based compensation construct. To the extent council members may also be a party to other, specialty-specific co-management agreements or contracts, the construct of the council compensation must take into account the risk of compensating a physician member twice for the same achievement of value. The valuator must be particularly attuned to the compensation methodology and the complex flow of funds that can accompany these types of relationships.

Comprehensive approaches to value-based healthcare, such as the council described above, present attorneys, consultants, providers, and valuators with new and often unexplored issues for clarification. While the maintenance of independence is fundamental to the valuator's professional standards, models such as this present the valuator with an even greater need to coordinate and collaborate with other experts to render a defensible opinion of value. Thus, we find that the goal of coordinating care in the clinical aspects of healthcare also requires enhanced coordination among the professionals assigned with designing, valuing, and operating those same models.

**Exhibit 5. Makeup of Clinical Integration Council**

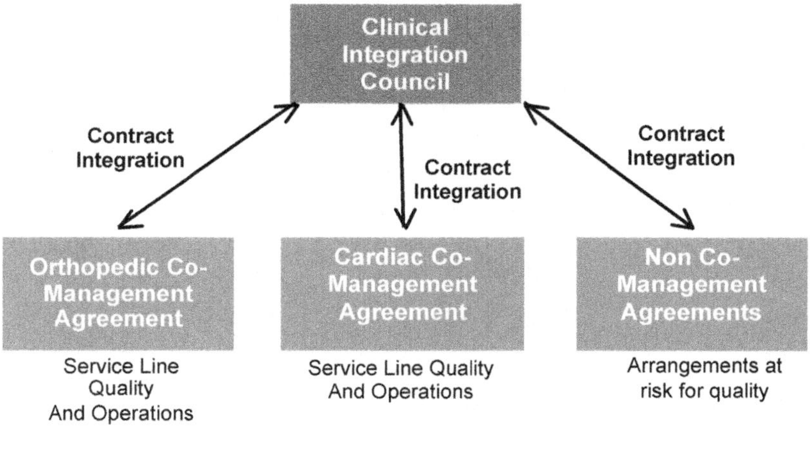

## Conclusion

As mentioned at the outset, the road to value-based models of care is not yet fully defined, and we will certainly take many different paths to get there. For those organizations that have clinical CCMs in place, transitioning to this next-generation style of model will create an excellent place to learn about value-based reimbursement, allow your organization to work within this type of model and identify any gaps in abilities or resources, and will ultimately provide a vehicle to help navigate toward a more fully developed value-based model of care, no matter which model it may be. Making certain the experts employed by organizations to assist in the construct of these models (such as attorneys, consultants, and valuators) are aware and capable of working in a multidisciplinary setting will be crucial to the hospital's or health system's ability to manage the complex compliance and risk issues that accompany these models.

Chapter 35

# Fair Market Value: Ensuring Compliance Within the Life Sciences Industry

*By Ann S. Brandt, Ph.D., Jason Ruchaber, CFA, ASA, and Timothy R. Smith, CPA/ABV*

The "life sciences industry," as it is frequently termed, encompasses a broad range of healthcare-related industries, including the pharmaceutical, medical device, medical supplies, medical equipment, and biotechnology industries. Two practices that are common in these industries are (i) contracting with physicians to provide speaking, consulting, and or research services and (ii) licensing various forms of intellectual property (IP) from physicians. Because physicians can also be referral sources for the products and services sold by companies in these industries, transactions between life science companies (LSCs) and physicians are subject to federal healthcare regulations that seek to prohibit payments for referrals of healthcare services and products. Such regulations require arrangements between referral-source physicians and LSCs to be commercially reasonable and consistent with fair market value. In recent years, federal regulators have significantly stepped up enforcement actions within the life sciences industry, and this industry is now experiencing the same fair market value compliance scrutiny that the hospital sector experienced over the past two decades. Most recently, under the Physician Payments Sunshine Act, which was included as Section 6002 of the Patient Protection and Affordable Care Act of 2010 (ACA), manufacturers of drugs, biological products, medical devices, and medical supplies must track and report to the U.S. Department of Health and Human Services (HHS) all payments and other transfers of value that they provide to physicians and teaching hospitals. This will be a yearly reporting requirement, commencing March 31, 2013. However, payment tracking by such companies commenced Jan. 1, 2012.[1] As a result, companies in the life sciences industry are seeking to employ widely recognized valuation approaches to ensure compliance and are increasingly turning to appraisal professionals for valuations of services provided by physicians.

This chapter will address issues in determining fair market value within the life sciences industry. It provides an overview of the regulatory context for this industry and an introduction to the service and IP licensing arrangements that are commonly entered into by LSCs and physicians. The chapter discusses key valuation issues and considerations to be addressed by the healthcare appraisal profession in appraising both types of compensation arrangements. Since the valuation of IP has a considerable, established body of knowledge within the business valuation community, discussion of IP licensing in the life sciences industry is presented in a summary manner. The valuation of service arrangements, on the other hand, receives a more detailed and comprehensive account in an effort to provide healthcare valuation analysts with the theoretical framework for appraising these unique services.

## Regulatory Issues in the Life Sciences Industry

Physicians who provide services or IP licensing to LSCs may also be referral sources for the healthcare goods and services provided by LSCs. They may be in a position to purchase or prescribe the products marketed by LSCs with whom they have compensation arrangements. As a result of this potential referral relationship, transactions and arrangements between physicians and LSCs may be subject to both federal and state healthcare laws and regulations. These healthcare laws and regulations, among other things, prohibit providers of certain healthcare goods and services from paying for referrals for these goods and services, particularly if the provider entities derive revenue from federal healthcare programs. Therefore, whenever such entities wish to enter into transactions or arrangements for other legitimate goods and services, the requirement that the compensation paid must be consistent with fair market value is a fundamental regulatory tool for ensuring that such exchanges do not entail payments for referrals among the parties. LSCs frequently engage appraisal firms to establish fair market value in these arrangements for regulatory compliance purposes.

As a consequence, understanding the application of healthcare laws and regulations to compensation arrangements is critical for establishing the scope of work for appraisal

1 The law applies to cash and noncash items received by physicians for consulting, speaking engagements, advisory board services, travel, food, gifts, research, royalty payments, clinical research, and other transfers of value designated by the secretary of HHS. Physician investment interests and ownership (other than publicly traded securities and mutual funds) must also be reported.

assignments within the life sciences industry.[2] Healthcare laws and regulations will often dictate the intended use of the appraisal opinion as well as the definition of value to be used for the assignment. In addition, they require that certain types of agreements comply with specialized definitions of value that may differ from those used outside of the healthcare industry. For this reason and others, LSCs and other clients related to the life sciences industry who engage appraisers to value compensation arrangements with physicians will generally need the appraiser to understand the legal and regulatory context in which the arrangement is being entered, as well as any guidance from regulators concerning appropriate methods for valuing the subject services. Otherwise, the appraiser may provide a client with a value that is later found to be in violation of healthcare laws and regulations. The penalties for such violations can be significant and costly to LSCs and other providers related to the life sciences industry. Appraisers should note that federal healthcare regulators do not consider independent valuations to be the definitive basis for determining fair market value in a given arrangement. In fact, in the commentary to the Stark regulations,[3] the Centers for Medicare & Medicaid Services (CMS) stated, "While good-faith reliance on a proper valuation may be relevant to a party's intent, it does not establish the ultimate issue of the accuracy of the valuation figure itself."[4] Appraisals prepared for regulatory compliance purposes, therefore, must seek to follow any promulgated regulatory guidance on valuation methodology.

Since healthcare laws and regulations may be complex and voluminous, it is advisable for appraisers to consult with the client and the client's legal counsel to ensure that the applicable regulations are followed when determining the value of service and IP licensing arrangements. These laws and regulations may be subject to varying and complex interpretations. As such, regulatory interpretation and guidance most often require the expertise of legal counsel rather than that of the appraiser. Consequently, the appraiser may need to seek clarification from a client's legal counsel as to the regulatory definition of value that is applicable to the assignment. Such regulatory guidance is comparable to the legal direction given in litigation-related valuation assignments with respect to specialized, state-law-based definitions of value, such as fair value in shareholder lawsuits or personal goodwill in divorce proceedings. The appraiser, however, should not subvert his or her judgment to that of the client or the client's counsel

2 While the Uniform Standards of Professional Appraisal Practice (USPAP) do not formally apply to the valuation of compensation amounts under service arrangements, appraisers would do well to follow the broad outlines of USPAP's Scope of Work Rule in appraising such arrangements. Identifying key assignment elements, such as intended use and users of the appraisal opinion, definition of value, and so on are useful tools in providing clients with appraisal reports that meet their needs, especially in the healthcare regulatory context.

3 The "Stark" law is the common term for the "physician self-referral law" (42 USC § 1395nn).

4 Taken from the Stark Phase II commentary on the definition of fair market value; *69 F.R. 16107 (March 26, 2004)*. However, despite this statement, CMS has indicated a slight preference for independent appraisals over nonindependent ones; see Stark Phase I commentary where CMS indicated that internally generated surveys may be "subject to more intensive scrutiny" than independent ones; *66 F.R. 945 (Jan. 4, 2001)*.

for matters that are properly the domain of the appraisal professional.[5] Disclosing any such client-provided regulatory guidance in the appraisal report is a useful means for communicating to intended users of a report how such regulatory and valuation issues were addressed as part of the scope of work for the assignment.

Generally, there are three major areas of federal healthcare laws and regulations that govern compensation arrangements with referral-source physicians in the life sciences industry:

- The Patient Protection and Affordable Care Act of 2010 (PPACA);
- The federal anti-kickback statute and related regulations and advisory opinions (collectively, FAKS); and
- The Stark law and accompanying Stark regulations (Stark).

### *PPACA*

The Patient Protection and Affordable Care Act,[6] signed into law on March 23, 2010, includes provisions from the Physician Payment Sunshine Act (the Sunshine Act).[7] Following the enactment of PPACA, H.R. 4872, the Health Care and Education Reconciliation Act of 2010, was enacted into law on March 30, 2010, "reconciling" and revising portions of PPACA.

The Sunshine Act requires "applicable manufacturers," which are manufacturers of a "covered drug, device, biological, or medical supply," to report annually certain "payments or other transfers of value" provided to a "covered recipient." "Covered drug, device, biological, or medical supply" is defined as a product "for which payment is available under [Social Security Act] title XVIII or a state plan under title XIX or XXI (or a waiver of such plan)." "Covered recipients" are defined as physicians and teaching hospitals. The first report from applicable manufacturers is due to the secretary of Health and Human Services (the Secretary) by March 31, 2013.[8]

5 Unfortunately, the distinction between legal issues related to regulatory matters and valuation issues may not always be clear. This lack of clarity frequently poses one of the more significant challenges for appraisal professionals in healthcare valuation.

6 H.R. 3590.

7 The Sunshine Act was introduced in 2009 by Senators Charles Grassley (R-Iowa) and Herb Kohl (D-Wis.).

8 At the time of this publication, the final rule has not yet been published, and CMS noted that a final rule will not be published in time for applicable manufacturers and applicable GPOs to begin collecting the information required in Section 1128G of the act on Jan. 1, 2012, as indicated in the statute. Therefore, CMS *will not* require applicable manufacturers and applicable GPOs to begin collecting the required information until after the publication of the final rule.

For each payment or transfer of value, the manufacturer must report the following information:

- Name, business address, specialty, and Medicare billing number for the covered recipient;
- Amount of the payment or transfer of value;
- Date of the payment or transfer of value;
- Description of the form of the payment (e.g., cash, cash equivalents, in-kind items or services, stock, stock options, other ownerships interests, and dividends);
- Description of the nature of the payment (e.g., consulting fees, compensation for services other than consulting, honoraria, gifts, entertainment, food, travel, education, research, charitable contributions, royalties, licenses, ownership or investment interests, direct compensation for serving as faculty or as a speaker for a medical education program and grants);
- Name of the covered drug, device, biological, or medical supply, if the payment or other transfer of value related to marketing, education, or research of a covered drug, device, biological, or medical supply; and
- Any other categories of information required by the secretary.

The Sunshine Act excludes from the definition of "payment or other transfer of value" anything with a value of less than $10. However, items under $10 may not be excluded from reporting if the aggregate amount to a covered recipient exceeds $100 per calendar year. Furthermore, after providing opportunity for review, the secretary must make the reported information publicly available in a searchable format by Sept. 30, 2013, and on June 30 of each year thereafter.

The Sunshine Act provides civil monetary penalties for noncompliance. Manufacturers that fail to report "in a timely manner in accordance with rules or regulations" are subject to a civil monetary penalty of $1,000 to $10,000 for each payment or other transfer of value not reported as required. The limit on this provision for each annual submission is $150,000. Similarly, manufacturers that "knowingly"[9] fail to report "in a timely manner in accordance with rules or regulations" are subject to a civil monetary penalty of

9 "Knowingly" is defined as "a person, with respect to information, [who] (i) has actual knowledge of the information; (ii) acts in deliberate ignorance of the truth or falsity of the information; or (iii) acts in reckless disregard of the truth or falsity of the information, and no proof of specific intent to defraud is required."

$10,000 to $100,000 for each payment or other transfer of value with an annual maximum of $1 million.[10] Manufacturers also may be subject to other penalties for noncompliance

### *FAKS*

The federal anti-kickback statute[11] provides that *anyone who knowingly and willfully pays or receives anything of value to influence the referral of business, which is reimbursable in whole or in part by a federal healthcare program, can be charged with criminal penalties, civil monetary sanctions, and even exclusion from federal healthcare programs.*[12] Prosecution under FAKS requires the government to prove that the parties possessed the intent to induce referrals at the time they entered into the arrangement. As a practical matter, the requirement to prove intent often limits prosecution and enforcement actions under FAKS. FAKS provides for certain safe harbors and outlines requirements that help establish that a given arrangement is not structured to be payment for referrals. One critical requirement is that the compensation paid in an arrangement with a referral source for other legitimate goods or services must be at fair market value. It is important to note, however, that under FAKS, an arrangement is illegal even if only one of the intended purposes of the arrangement is to generate referrals between the parties. Such an arrangement violates the statute regardless of whether the compensation paid is fair market value.[13]

There have been several recent well-publicized enforcement actions for alleged illegal conduct under FAKS for consulting arrangements within the life sciences industry, some of which are discussed below. Many pharmaceutical companies and medical device companies have settled the allegations by entering into a deferred prosecution agreement[14] (DPA) with the U.S. Department of Justice and simultaneously executing a corporate integrity agreement (CIA) with the Office of Inspector General (OIG). DPAs and CIAs are intended to cause the offending organization to develop a plan of self-improvement and self-monitoring, coupled with independent outside review to insure that the risk of future violations is minimized. One element of a number of DPAs and CIAs that have been executed with the government is the requirement that independent third-party fair market value analyses be performed for all physician compensation arrangements over a certain dollar value threshold. (In the recent case of five of the country's largest medical device companies, this threshold was identified to be compensation exceeding $500 per hour.) These specific requirements imposed by certain DPAs and CIAs signal

10 Manufacturers also may be subject to other penalties for noncompliance.

11 42 U.S.C. §1320a-7b.

12 Section 1128B(b) of the act (42 U.S.C. 1320a–7b(b))(2003).

13 *United States v. Kats*, 871 F.2d 105 (9th Cir. 1989); *United States v. Greber*, 760 F.2d 68 (3d Cir.), cert. denied, 474 U.S. 988 (1985).

14 In some cases, the Department of Justice will enter into a "nonprosecution agreement" instead of a DPA, which differs in that the case cannot be later reopened if the agreement is breached by the defendant. This article refers to both types of agreements as DPAs.

the government's concern when physicians receive "high" rates of compensation. The following section presents highlights from some of these enforcement actions.

In July, 2006, Medtronic signed a DPA with the U.S. Department of Justice in which it agreed to pay $40 million to the United States and participating states to settle allegations stemming from two qui tam lawsuits.[15] These lawsuits, which were brought under the federal False Claims Act (FCA), allege that Medtronic made illegal payments to physicians to promote its spinal products in violation of the federal healthcare program anti-kickback statute. The alleged illegal payments included (i) consulting and royalty agreements for which little or no work was performed and (ii) all-expenses-paid trips to lavish venues. In addition to the $40 million payment, Medtronic was required to enter into a five-year CIA with the OIG.

In another well-publicized case, to resolve allegations under the FCA, four major medical device manufacturers[16] entered into civil settlement agreements with the government for a combined total of $311 million. The government alleged that the companies provided financial incentives to physicians, including consulting agreements and lavish trips, to persuade physicians to use their joint replacement products. The government alleged that by offering illegal inducements, the identified companies violated the FCA by causing hospitals to seek and obtain reimbursement from Medicare. To avoid criminal prosecution, each of the identified companies entered into an 18-month DPA with the Department of Justice, under which they agreed to multiple remedies, including the posting on their Web sites of the names of consultants, along with the amount of payments to these consultants. In addition, each of the identified companies entered into a five-year CIA with the OIG.

Another case involves a physician who accepted kickbacks from a medical device company in return for using the company's products. Even though criminal prosecutors have rarely directly targeted physicians, a physician who accepts a kickback in return for using a product can be as culpable as the company that provided the kickback. Dr. Patrick Chan, a neurologist in Arkansas, paid a $1.5 million civil settlement in January 2008 and pled guilty to soliciting and accepting kickbacks from Blackstone Medical. The kickbacks included gifts and payments for sham consulting agreements and fake research studies.

15 Qui tam lawsuits are initiated by a third party on behalf of the government. These actions are generally brought by whistleblowers under the federal False Claims Act.

16 Biomet Inc., DePuy Orthopedics Inc., Smith & Nephew Inc., Zimmer Inc.

In another recent case, Lincare Holdings, a provider of respiratory care, infusion therapy, and medical equipment to patients in the home, paid $10 million and entered into a five-year CIA for allegedly providing kickback payments to physicians in the form of sporting and entertainment tickets, rounds of golf, golf equipment, fishing trips, meals, office expenses, and medical equipment, all of which were intended to induce the physicians to refer patients to the company. The government also alleged that Lincare provided kickbacks in the form of purported consulting arrangements that had no basis or foundation for payment. In addition, the government alleged that Lincare violated the Stark .law by accepting referrals from parties to the consulting agreements.

***Stark***

The federal physician self-referral ban (commonly referred to as the Stark law[17]) prohibits referrals by a physician or an immediate family member[18] to an entity for "designated health services"[19] if the physician has a financial relationship with the entity receiving the referral. Within the framework of the Stark law, (i) the physician may not make a referral to the entity for the furnishing of designated health services for which payment may be made under Medicare or Medicaid and (ii) the entity may not bill for designated health services furnished pursuant to such referral. A physician who has a financial relationship with an entity cannot make a referral to the entity for the furnishing of designated health services unless it is demonstrated that the financial arrangement qualified for one of the identified exceptions.[20] Unlike FAKS, Stark is a *strict liability* statute. As such, enforcement of Stark does not require the government to prove any intent by the parties to induce referrals. A physician making a referral with a financial relationship that is not exempted by one of the exceptions violates the law, regardless of intent. Violations of Stark, however, are considered to be civil infractions rather than criminal. Monetary penalties and exclusion from federal healthcare program participation (i.e., Medicare and so on), as opposed to criminal penalties, are the proscribed sanctions for Stark violations.

17 The physician Self Referral Law (the Stark law) is codified at 42 U.S.C.S. §1395nn.

18 The term "immediate family member" includes a husband or wife, birth or adoptive parent, child or sibling, father-in-law, mother-in-law, brother in-law, sister-in-law, grandparent, or grandchild.

19 Designated health services include: radiology and other imaging services (MRI, CT, and ultrasound); physical therapy; occupational therapy; radiation therapy; durable medical equipment; parenteral and enteral nutrients, equipment, and supplies; prosthetics, orthotics, and prosthetic devices and supplies; home health services; outpatient prescription drugs; and inpatient and outpatient hospital services. *Note that this listing of designated health services is not intended to be exhaustive, as the government has expanded the list on several occasions.*

20 Stark exceptions can be either statutory or regulatory, and exceptions exist for personal services provided by physicians (e.g., LSC consulting arrangements) and for other goods and services provided by physician (e.g., IP license arrangements); the key features of both exceptions are that the compensation must be consistent with fair market value.

### *The Regulatory Definition of Fair Market Value*

In their current form, FAKS and Stark generally prohibit payments to physicians for referrals of healthcare good and services.[21] To ensure that remuneration flowing between physicians and providers of healthcare services are not disguised payments for referrals, FAKS and Stark generally require all arrangements between such physicians and providers of such goods and services to be *commercially reasonable* and consistent with *fair market value*. Appraisers need to be aware that fair market value for purposes of complying with healthcare laws and regulations differs in some respects from the standard formulation of fair market value as understood by the appraisal profession. For example, as defined by the *International Glossary of Business Valuation Terms*, the term *fair market value* is defined as the price, expressed in terms of cash equivalents, at which property would exchange hands between a hypothetical willing and able seller, acting at arm's length in an open and unrestricted market, when neither is under a compulsion to buy or sell and when both have reasonable knowledge of the relevant facts. In the context of healthcare transactions, *fair market value* is generally defined as the value in arm's-length transactions, consistent with the general market value, where "general market value" means the compensation that would be included in a service arrangement as the result of bona fide bargaining between well-informed parties to an arrangement when neither party is otherwise in a position to generate business for the other party.[22] Thus, the primary difference between the two definitions is that financial consideration cannot be given to the ability of two parties to generate referral business between them.

#### Stark Exclusion of Market Comparables Between Parties in a Position to Refer

Over the years and through various phases of the Stark regulations, CMS and its predecessor agencies have provided guidance and commentary on the definition and determination of fair market value for purposes of complying with Stark. CMS has explicitly noted that fair market value as defined by Stark may differ from fair market value as determined through standard appraisal practices. One example of an *apparent* difference in the valuation methodology prescribed by Stark and the valuation methodologies used in standard appraisal practice is that compliance with Stark requires certain limitations on the use of a market approach. *[Editor's note: A critical point made in numerous other places in this guide.]* That is, the determination of fair market value for Stark purposes should not be based on market comparable transactions between

21 Note that a wide variety of state legislation exists which is similar to Stark and FAKS, and some require additional considerations, depending on the particular state.

22 This is the Stark definition, set forth in 42 CFR §411.351. This definition is also consistent with similar fair market value guidance related to FAKS (codified at 42 U.S.C. §1320a-7b) and with the definition relied upon by the Internal Revenue Service (see, for example, Treas. Reg. 53.4958 et seq.).

referral-source physicians and providers of designated health services (DHS).[23]

This restriction has been promulgated by CMS because it believes that transactions between parties who are in a position to refer or generate other business for each other are not "arm's-length" transactions. The prevalence of transactions between referral-source physicians and providers of health care goods and services may distort pricing in the marketplace since, consciously or otherwise, the parties to such transactions may tend toward compensation that rewards referrals.[24] CMS has acknowledged that exclusion of such market comparables may prohibit the use of the market approach in valuing compensation arrangements in certain cases. In these cases, CMS advises the use of alternative approaches or valuation methods.[25] Applying this prohibition to the valuation of service and IP licensing arrangements may have critical consequences.[26] Market information from the life sciences industry between referral-source physicians and LSCs may need to be excluded from the determination of fair market value for Stark compliance purposes. As a result, appraisers may be significantly limited in the market information that can be used to establish fair market value for compensation arrangements in the life sciences industry.

It is not uncommon for appraisers to take exception with this limitation on the use of the market approach at first glance. Yet, it is important to assess this prohibition within the larger context of business valuation body of knowledge. Most appraisers would exclude, discount, or treat cautiously any market comparables for transactions between family members, related parties, affiliated or sister companies, or parent-subsidiary companies. Such parties or entities would not be considered to be fully at arm's length, and therefore, any corresponding financial arrangements would also be viewed as not fully arm's length. In the case of the Stark regulations, the potential for referrals is considered significant enough to warrant the required exclusion of arrangements between physicians and certain healthcare providers as sources of market data for purposes of determining fair market value under Stark. Appraisal professionals may disagree with the conclusion reached by Stark as to the effect of referral relationships

23 CMS has stated, "... the definition of 'fair market value' in the [Stark] statute . . . is qualified in ways that do not necessarily comport with the usage of the term in standard valuation techniques and methodologies. For example, the methodology must exclude valuations where the parties to the transactions are at arm's length but in a position to refer to one another." 69 *FR 16107 (March 24, 2004).*

24 66 *FR* 876-77, 919, 941, 944 (Jan. 4, 2001).

25 66 *FR* 876-77, 919, 944 (Jan. 4, 2001).

26 We should also note that some attorneys argue that the above limitation on the market approach is applicable only to the office space and equipment lease exception under Stark. They argue for this qualification because the limitation on the use of market comparables between referring physicians and DHS providers is discussed under the rubric of the space and equipment lease exception. On this exclusion, therefore, an appraiser may be given conflicting guidance from different clients. Appraisers should therefore obtain clarification from the client and the client's legal counsel as to the interpretation of Stark that is required for the particular appraisal assignment.

on whether transactions are arm's length. Such a disagreement, however, is a question of fact rather than methodology. In general, the business valuation body of knowledge suggests excluding or adjusting transactions not considered to be arm's length for use of the market approach.

#### Stark Distinction Between Clinical Services and Administrative Services

In Stark regulations issued in September 2007 (the Stark Phase III Regulations), CMS made an important distinction between the clinical and administrative work provided by physicians and the determination of fair market value for physician services. In its commentary to responses, CMS stated:

> A fair market value hourly rate may be used to compensate physicians for both administrative and clinical work, provided that the rate paid for clinical work is fair market value for the clinical work performed and the rate paid for administrative work is fair market value for the administrative work performed. We note that the fair market value of administrative services may differ from the fair market value of clinical services.[27]

Given this guidance, an appraiser who is engaged to value a service arrangement for Stark compliance purposes should consider the distinction between clinical and administrative duties when appraising the physician services.

### Service Arrangements in the Life Sciences Industry

In valuing the compensation provided under a service arrangement, it is essential for the appraiser to understand the nature and scope of the services provided under the subject arrangement. The types, level, and extent of services provided are key factors in arriving at the compensation paid under a service contract. Another critical element in determining the compensation is the required qualifications of the service provider. This relationship between the services provided and amount of compensation should be self-evident to appraisers, who establish appraisal fees routinely with clients based on the scope of the particular appraisal assignment. The level and extent of valuation services coupled with the qualifications of the appraisers providing those services generally determine the fees. In a similar manner, the scope of services and the required qualifications of the individual providing those services are fundamental factors in determining the compensation for service arrangements between physicians and LSCs. The beginning point for valuing such service arrangements, therefore, is cataloging and analyzing the scope of services and the qualifications necessary for providing these services.

27 *72 F.R.* 51016.

In general, physicians provide three types of services in the life sciences industry: consulting, research, and speaking and education (which will be considered as a subset of consulting services within this chapter). LSCs seek such services because experienced physicians offer a level of expertise that often cannot be duplicated by any other group of professionals. As a result, physician (i) input into product design and development, (ii) insight into market requirements, and (iii) expertise in the use of products and services are invaluable to LSCs. Within the life sciences industry, physicians with varying levels of expertise and experience can provide these types of services, ranging from local-level practitioners to internationally acclaimed "thought leaders." Thus, establishing the fair market value of consulting, research, or speaking and educational services provided by varying "levels" of physicians is a central issue for healthcare valuation in the life sciences.

From a regulatory standpoint, the government's concern with these types of service arrangements focuses on whether they are being used as a vehicle to induce physicians to purchase or prescribe a given LSC's products. Therefore, regulators have been focusing their attention on various types of service arrangements to determine whether they are tied to prescribing practices or to usage patterns involving the company's products. Of obvious importance in this scrutiny is whether the fees for these services appear to be in excess of fair market value for actual services rendered. Similarly, medical device companies are being targeted for investigation when there is doubt as to the legitimate need for the particular consulting services or when there is a lack of documentation of the services rendered.

### *Types of Consulting Services*

LSCs contract with physicians to provide an array of consulting services related to the products offered by such companies. These consulting services include:

- product development;
- product design;
- product research activities;
- advisory services;
- marketing; and
- physician education and training.

Such consulting services are provided to LSCs that market drugs and medications, medical devices, medical instruments and equipment, and medical supplies. In today's marketplace, LSCs engage legions of physician consultants and advisors to conduct research and development as well as marketing activities on behalf of their products. Payments to these physician advisors and consultants, which often total millions of dollars per year, have become routine expenses for LSCs.

Why do LSCs contract with so many physicians to provide such consulting services? As noted previously, experienced physicians offer a level of expertise that often cannot be duplicated by any other group of professionals. Their knowledge and experience in treating patients with diseases, illnesses, and sundry healthcare problems is vital to the effective use of life sciences products in the healthcare marketplace. This knowledge base can be tapped to provide important considerations in the development and marketing of products that improve patient care and disease treatment. Such first-hand knowledge of patient care is not always readily available in database or informational formats. It is also essential for marketing such products to the primary decisionmakers in the healthcare arena—physicians.

Physicians must be very knowledgeable about the drugs and devices they recommend to their patients. Thus, physician education is of paramount importance to the marketing and distribution of these products. This need for education is especially necessary for new drugs and devices that are introduced in the marketplace. Physicians and other healthcare providers need to be educated about the unique properties and medical efficacy of these newer, potentially more effective (and often more costly) products. Yet, physicians may have little time to meet with manufacturers' representatives, who are often forced to compete with patients for the physician's limited time.

In an effort to inform physicians about newly developed products, it is common practice for pharmaceutical companies to engage the services of a broad range of physicians to serve as advisors and consultants to other physicians practicing medicine in their targeted markets. Marketplace trends indicate that physicians are more willing to listen to and change their prescribing patterns after obtaining information regarding the relative benefits of new products from other well-credentialed physicians. With respect to medical device companies, physician input is required to ensure that products are designed, implanted, and used appropriately. LSCs have found that physician consulting services are a necessary and integral part of the product development and marketing life cycle.

The scope of services in consulting arrangements can vary widely within the life sciences industry. In valuing consulting arrangements, it is essential to analyze the specific duties and responsibilities provided by a physician consultant to an LSC under a proposed service agreement. A useful framework for identifying and evaluating the scope of services includes the following considerations:

- Number of hours associated with each duty and responsibility.
- The specific duties and responsibilities of the position.
- The complexity of each duty and responsibility.
- Level of physician expertise required for the duties.
- Specific objectives and deliverables.
- Potential impact of thought leader on organizational and product success, in terms of visibility and credibility within the medical community or particular physician specialty.

The physician qualifications for consulting arrangements will also vary. Since LSCs generally seek higher credentialed and experienced physicians for consulting services, it is critical to identify, analyze, and categorize qualifications that are required of the physicians who will provide consulting services under an arrangement. These qualifications typically include:

- Educational credentials and specialized training.
- Professional certifications.
- Leadership experience.
- Academic appointments.
- Research experience and funding history.
- Invited presentations.
- Publication history.
- Other professional leadership activities and reputation in the healthcare community.

In the life sciences industry, it is not uncommon to observe interdependencies between the duties and responsibilities and the qualification requirements of a consulting arrangement. Basic consulting services, for example, may not require the skill and experience of a uniquely qualified or specialized physician or a physician with high visibility and credibility within the medical community or a physician specialty. More advanced responsibilities and services, on the other hand, may only be performed by physicians with specific qualifications and credentials, as well as peer acknowledgement of a certain degree of expertise. Such interdependencies can become important considerations in determining the fair market value compensation for consulting services in the life sciences industry.

### *Types of Research Services*

In addition to consulting arrangements with physicians, LSCs frequently enter into compensated arrangements with physicians involving clinical trials or research studies. Clinical trials (or studies) are treatment protocols that are coordinated by pharmaceutical companies, biotechnology companies, or medical device manufacturers (commonly referred to as "sponsors") to obtain clinical data involving the use of its drugs or devices in the course of actual patient treatments. Clinical trials are classified as Phase I, II, III, or IV. Briefly described, Phase I and II trials are early-stage studies that are intended to establish the safety and the apparent efficacy of a new drug or device that is not yet FDA-approved. Phase III clinical trials involve much larger groups of human subjects, and the results of Phase III testing are used by sponsors in support of their applications for FDA approval. Phase IV studies entail additional research that is conducted on a post-FDA-approval basis. Sometimes referred to as "market studies," Phase IV trials are intended to establish additional information concerning a drug that may, for example, lead to new indications or improvements in dosing guidelines.

These studies often involve compensation agreements by and among the sponsors, physicians, and other third parties, such as hospitals or ambulatory treatment facilities. As these types of trials involve compensation payable to parties who are in a position to refer to one another, compliance with the fair market value standard is required to demonstrate compliance with applicable federal and state healthcare regulations.

The clinical trials process is complex, and each trial requires the designation of a physician who serves as the principal investigator (PI) of the trial. There are a number of compensable arrangements inherent in clinical trials that must be consistent with fair market value. First, the overall financial arrangement between the sponsor and the PI must be consistent with fair market value. Typically, fees paid by a sponsor to a PI are based upon a study budget and include a fixed payment and a variable payment based upon the number of patients. The fixed payment includes compensation for overall initiation of the study, as well as costs that may be assessed by third parties. For example, clinical studies involving hospital care must generally be approved by the hospital's governing body called the institutional review board, or the IRB. The *per-patient* fees can range from $1,000 per patient or less to $25,000 per patient or more. From the *per-patient* fees, the PI may be responsible for purchasing certain services from third parties, such as diagnostic imaging studies from a hospital or an imaging center. In some cases, the study budget may also contemplate payment to a study participant (i.e., a patient). Thus, when analyzing the services provided under a research arrangement between a sponsor and a PI, an appraiser may want to give consideration to the PI's overall duties and responsibilities in terms of the following categories:

- The intellectual process of identifying desired clinical trials in which to participate;
- The investment in one or more research nurses and required research infrastructure and resources; and
- The assumption of the overall responsibility and liability for the conduct of such trials.

Identifying responsibilities of the PI in terms of these three major functions allows the appraiser to evaluate the level and scope of services provided in the subject clinical study arrangement.

In determining the value of research services in the life sciences industry, it is important to note that clinical studies frequently require services beyond a physician's time and expertise. Other resources of a physician's practice may be used to perform the research, including nursing staff, space, medical records, equipment, and supplies. In certain circumstances, the conduct of clinical trials may be more comparable to an ancillary service as opposed to a professional service when evaluating the use of physician practice resources. A physician practice may assume certain levels of liability under the terms of some research arrangements. Such liability may require changes in malpractice or other types of liability coverage. In general, research services contrast with consulting services in that the latter typically entail only the provision of a physician's time and expertise, rather than the assembled or turnkey resources of a physician practice.

As described above, many clinical studies reflect financial arrangements negotiated between sponsors and PIs. In other instances, organizations, such as hospitals, may be the party that attracts and negotiates the financial arrangement with the sponsor. Since a PI is still required for the study, a hospital may engage and compensate a physician to serve as the PI. Under this type of arrangement, the PI's services and involvement are significantly different than if the PI assumed the full risk for the study. Accordingly, the valuation methodology used in this case should focus on the more value of the physician's personally performed services.

### Consideration of the Three Approaches to Value in Service Arrangements

While the conceptual framework for generally accepted appraisal practice was developed to value assets and business interests, the valuation principles and concepts supporting the three approaches to value can also be applied to the appraisal of compensation in services agreements, including the valuation of physician consulting and research services. At the foundation of the three approaches to value are the fundamental appraisal principles of substitution, alternatives, and future benefits. The following section of this chapter seeks to demonstrate how these principles can generally be applied in valuing compensation in service arrangements. It specifically employs concepts from the business valuation body of knowledge to derive principles applicable to the valuation of service contracts. This section also explains various general considerations that confront the appraiser in valuing physician service arrangements. The theoretical and general concepts discussed are then applied to the valuation of physician consulting and research services in the life sciences industry.

#### *The Market Approach*

The *International Glossary of Business Valuation Terms* (the *International Glossary*), defines the market approach as *"a general way of determining a value indication of a business, business ownership interest, security, or intangible asset by using one or more methods that compare the subject to similar businesses, business ownership interests, securities, or intangible assets that have been sold."* In basic terms, the market approach uses comparable sales transactions that have occurred in the marketplace to determine the value of a subject asset or business interest. The valuation principle of substitution is employed in the market approach as the concept that a buyer will not pay more for a subject asset than for a substitute asset that provides the equivalent economic utility. As applied to service agreements, the market approach seeks to value the subject arrangement by referencing comparable arrangements in the marketplace.

The key to utilizing the market approach for valuing the compensation paid in service agreements is identifying and obtaining information on comparable agreements that can be used to establish the value of the subject contract. Yet, finding such information on comparable agreements with sufficient detail is often the greatest difficulty an appraiser experiences in applying the market approach to the valuation of service agreements. It should be noted, however, that an appraiser can often use market information from arrangements that are not fully similar to the subject arrangement, as long as the appraiser has sufficient information to make the appropriate adjustments to the market data and the subject arrangement to make them comparable for valuation purposes.

Use of the market approach in valuing service arrangements underscores the need for the appraiser to identify and understand the scope of services provided in both the subject arrangement and the market comparables. Without such information, the appraiser may treat as comparable service arrangements that are essentially different as to the services provided and the qualifications required of the service provider. As a result, the appraiser may arrive at a range of value for the subject arrangement based on a fundamentally dissimilar mix of services or qualifications. In addition, any unique facts and circumstances related to the subject service arrangement should be carefully analyzed and factored into the valuation. As noted previously, there is often an interdependency between the scope of services and the qualifications required to provide those services in a physician consulting or research arrangement in the life sciences arena. A comprehensive understanding of the subject arrangement, therefore, is crucial to identifying appropriate market comparables for valuing physician consulting services in the life sciences industry.

In utilizing the market approach to value physician service arrangements in the life sciences industry, the appraiser performs market research to accumulate information on comparable arrangements, including the scope of services provided, the required qualifications of the physicians providing such services, and the level of compensation paid. Unfortunately, such market information is not readily accessible. Few sources of data are specific to physician compensation for specialized nonclinical services, such as consulting, research, or administration (e.g., medical directorships).[28] By contrast, multiple sources of published data exist relating to physician compensation for clinical services or compensation from all sources, such as the Medical Group Management Association (MGMA), American Medical Group Association (AMGA), or Sullivan, Cotter and Associates Inc. (SCA) physician compensation surveys described in the following section. Appraisers attempting to create such market data "from scratch" may encounter LSCs or physicians who are unwilling to share information about existing service arrangements for confidentiality or proprietary reasons.

Appraisers attempting to accumulate market data on physician consulting and research service arrangements or using published or proprietary sources of market data should be aware of the issues and limitations that may be encountered in using such market information. It is preferable to obtain and use highly detailed market information to establish market comparables for specialized physician services. Differences in the detailed scope of services and the required qualifications for providing those services may have a material impact on the comparability of services and the valuation analysis.

28 We have elected to treat use of the general physician compensation surveys (e.g., MGMA, AMGA, SCA, and so on) under the cost approach for purposes of valuing physician consulting and research services in the life sciences industry. Because such surveys are based primarily on clinical services and frequently report compensation from all sources (clinical, administrative, consulting, research, call coverage, business owner, ancillary income, and so on), we would argue that such surveys do not represent pure market data on compensation for specialized services, such as physician consulting and clinical trials, in the life sciences industry. Under the cost approach, however, such general information on physician compensation levels from all sources may be utilized to estimate the cost to re-create such specialized services.

The valuation analyst should use caution in making comparisons when limited information is available on other service arrangements in the marketplace. Unhappily, limited market information may be all that the appraiser is able to obtain on physician consulting and research contracts in the life sciences industry.

A second layer of difficulty may be encountered in using market comparables to establish the value of physician consulting and research services for LSCs. It is highly probable that market information on such services will come from physicians and LSCs who have potential referral relationships that implicate Stark or the FAKS. When, as is often the case, the valuation is requested for purposes of complying with healthcare laws and regulations, market comparables derived from physicians and providers with referral or potential referral relationships may need to be excluded from consideration. Compensation to physicians under these types of arrangements may be skewed by the potential for referrals between the parties and as such, may not be an appropriate benchmark for fair market value in these types of transactions under the regulatory definition of fair market value. Even when the Stark limitation on the use of market comparables is not part of the valuation assignment scope of work, it may be advisable not to rely solely on market data to establish the fair market value of physician services in the life sciences industry. While some market data points may represent arm's-length transactions, others may not. Sorting out which transactions are independent may not be possible or practicable.

One line of research that may yield potential market comparables for physician consulting services in the life sciences industry is identifying comparable consulting services provided outside of the healthcare context by comparably qualified professionals. Under this valuation technique, the appraiser obtains compensation rates paid to comparably qualified professionals providing comparable services in other nonhealthcare industries and "crosswalks" these rates to the subject arrangement in the life sciences industry. This technique may be derived from an analysis of the consulting services provided by physicians and their qualifications to provide those services. While physicians tend to be among the nation's most highly educated and experienced professionals, the consulting services they provide to LSCs have considerable financial as well as operational implications for these companies. These financial and operational characteristics of physician consulting services can provide a range of comparability with services performed by comparably qualified consultants and specialists in various industries. Compensation rates for attorneys may also provide market guidance. Legal advice and consulting may be comparable in some circumstances to consulting provided by physicians, while legal education and licensing requirements may also provide a certain level of comparability with regard to the educational and licensing qualifications of physicians. Nonetheless, establishing compatibility for valuation purposes may be quite difficult in pursuing this line of research.[29]

### The Cost Approach

The *International Glossary* defines the cost approach as "a general way of determining a value indication of an individual asset by quantifying the amount of money required to replace the future service capability of that asset." The cost approach looks to the replacement cost of an asset or business interest as the basis for valuing the subject asset or interest. In business valuation, the cost approach is categorized as the asset-based or buildup approach because the appraiser attempts to re-create the value of the subject business by accumulating the values of the individual assets that comprise the subject. The appraisal attempts to re-create the business one asset at a time, building up a business enterprise value based on the value of each asset. The cost, asset-based, and buildup approach illustrates the valuation principle of alternatives: the idea that there are alternatives to acquiring the future service capacity of the subject asset or business interest.[30]

The cost approach as applied to service contracts seeks to value the compensation for the subject arrangement by looking to the value of alternatives for those services in the marketplace. The value of alternatives may be determined under a buildup technique in which the cost of each component or resource utilized in a service is calculated separately. The accumulated cost of all elements provides the value of the alternative for those services. Since resources are not provided in the marketplace without an appropriate return, a profit margin or rate of return is generally a component of the cost buildup technique for valuing service arrangements. Such rates should be based on market data for comparable services. There are two generally used methods for applying market-based margins or returns in the buildup approach. The first method uses a margin or return for the service considered as a whole. In other words, an overall margin or return is computed on the total cost for the resources employed in the service. The alternative method applies a margin or return to each resource included in the service. A market-based margin or return is calculated for each type of resource and is accumulated along with the costs of the resource in deriving the value of the alternative. Appraisers often use this latter method because market information on margins or returns may be more

29 Editor's note: The SEC filings of publicly held Huron Consulting Group Inc., FTI Consulting Inc., Navigant Consulting Inc. and Charles River Associates (CRA International Inc.) may provide some insight.

30 One can also argue that the cost approach is derived from the principle of substitution in that the individual assets separately valued are substituted for the subject business. Conversely, it can be argued that the market approach illustrates the principle of alternatives: Market comparables indicate the existence of alternatives to the subject in the marketplace. Such lines of reasoning illustrate the integral relationship among the fundamental principles of valuation and the three approaches to value. They also indicate the difficulty in assigning a given principle to only one approach to value. The principles may be found in more than one approach.

readily available for each type of resource employed in a service, rather than for the service as a whole or viewed on a turnkey or assembled basis.

As applied to valuing physician services in the life sciences industry, the cost approach seeks to value an arrangement between a LSC and a physician by considering the LSC's costs in the alternative to contracting with a physician. For example, such alternate cost might be based upon the employment of one or more physicians to provide the required services. For research services, the alternative cost may require ownership and operation of a physician practice, including employment of a physician. As a practical matter, however, the appraiser should keep in mind that most consulting or research arrangements in the life sciences industry are structured as independent contractor arrangements. Such consulting or research services require variable and often limited hours. As such, securing these services through an employment or ownership arrangement is generally less practical than through an independent contractor arrangement. Application of the cost approach, therefore, generally represents a hypothetical alternative to obtaining physician services in the life sciences industry.

Because clinical studies may require resources beyond a physician's time and expertise, application of the cost approach to research services involves additional considerations over and above the value of the services provided by an individual physician. Use of the cost approach for research services, therefore, requires a separate analysis for each type of resource used in research studies. Since the value of a physician's time and expertise is a component of both consulting as well as research services, it may be helpful to begin with a discussion of the application of the cost approach to consulting services. Many, if not all, of the issues and considerations in valuing physician consulting services are also applicable to valuing research services in that a physician's time and expertise are critical resources in the latter. Research services include physician services as well as other services and resources.

#### Application of the Cost Approach to Valuing Consulting Services

In following the valuation principle of alternatives, an appraiser may look to physician compensation levels in the marketplace, whether from employment or private practice, as a hypothetical basis for the alternative cost to procuring the physician services provided in physician consulting and research arrangements. There are several reliable and readily available sources of survey data for physician compensation in the marketplace. These sources include:

1. Medical Group Management Association (MGMA), *Physician Compensation and Production Survey*. This is an annually published survey that typically reports compensation data from over 2,800 physician practices (predominantly

independent physician-owned organizations representing over 59,000 physicians and midlevel providers).

2. Sullivan, Cotter and Associates Inc. (SCA), *Physician Compensation and Productivity Survey Report* (SCA). This is a compendium of data reported by 351 healthcare organizations (including medical centers, group practices, integrated delivery systems, and health maintenance organizations, or HMOs). The 2011 edition represents responses from 58,626 MDs, PhDs, midlevel providers, residents, and medical group executives.
3. Client & Healthcare Compensation Service (HCS), *Physician Salary Survey Report* and *Client Salary & Benefits Report.* The *Physician Salary* report incorporates data from 333 healthcare organizations (including group practice facilities and HMOs). The 2011 edition represents responses from 28,295 physicians. The "Client Salary" report incorporates data from 539 HCS clients, including responses from various client executives, administrators, and nonphysician and midlevel providers.
4. American Medical Group Association (AMGA), *Medical Group Compensation and Financial Survey.* The AMGA report discloses salary survey data obtained from medical groups, (predominantly large multispecialty group practices). Second in size to only the MGMA survey, the AMGA survey is one of the most reliable sources of physician clinical compensation data. The 2011 edition incorporates data from 239 medical groups, predominantly large multispecialty group practices, representing approximately 51,700 physicians and midlevel providers.
5. Towers Watson Data Services (TW), *Health Care Clinical and Professional Compensation Survey Report.* The TW report incorporates data from 368 healthcare organizations representing 652,352 physicians, midlevel providers, and healthcare executives.

It is essential that appraisers understand how these various physician compensation surveys gather and report financial information on physician compensation. Such knowledge is needed for the valid use of the survey data to determine physician compensation rates. An appraiser will need to address five critical issues in using the survey data to establish the fair market value of physician compensation for purposes of medical director services. These issues include:

1. The distinction between clinical services and nonclinical services, such as consulting, research, and administrative, and any corresponding differentiation in compensation levels for clinical versus other specialized work.

2. The relative comparability of physician qualifications as well as job duties and responsibilities in the various surveys relative to the subject consulting arrangement.

3. The distinction between compensation for physician services and business owner compensation.

4. Determining the appropriate level of annual hours worked for purposes of computing an hourly rate for physician services.

5. Adjustment of employment compensation hourly rate to an independent-contractor basis.

The appraiser's analysis and resolution of these critical issues may have a material impact on the valuation opinion for a subject physician service arrangement.

#### Compensation for Clinical Versus Administrative Services

At noted in the section on the regulatory context for valuing physician services in the life sciences industry, CMS recently indicated that it recognizes a distinction between clinical and administrative services with regard to physician compensation. According to the regulators, the fair market value for physician clinical services may differ from the fair market value of administrative services provided by a physician for Stark compliance purposes. Appraisers valuing physician consulting and research services for Stark compliance purposes should address this distinction between clinical and administrative duties when determining the fair market value of those services. The salient point to this distinction appears to be that the value of clinical work may be greater or less than the value of nonclinical work in certain instances. On the one hand, clinical services may warrant higher levels of compensation than administrative or other forms of nonclinical services. Under this line of reasoning, clinical work is deemed to involve a higher degree of complexity and risk than administrative or consulting work. Clinical procedures involve the immediate health and well-being of patients and in some specialties and cases, the literal difference between life and death. While consulting services may require a skill set only found in physicians of a given specialty, these functions and duties do not generally entail the same level of complexity or risk as the provision of healthcare services to patients. As a result, the level of compensation paid for administrative or consulting services may be less than the compensation paid for the same amount of time spent performing clinical procedures.

An alternative line of reasoning derived from an opportunity cost analysis argues against the opinion that administrative services should be compensated at a level different from clinical work. It contends that physicians would not agree to provide services at a lower rate because of the opportunity cost for providing administrative or consulting services in comparison to clinical services. Compensation levels for clinical procedures are the indicator of the value of a physician's time. Physicians should be paid at clinical levels for them to agree to provide nonclinical types of services. Otherwise, physicians have no incentive to provide administrative or consulting services.

A third line of reasoning argues that consulting services may entail a higher degree of risk or complexity than a physician encounters in a patient care environment. The risk in product design and development may be greater than a physician experiences in daily practice due to the sheer number of patients that may be affected by flaws in a medical device or instrument. The financial risk inherent in development and marketing plans for some pharmaceuticals and medical equipment can potentially include hundreds of millions of dollars. The services of a physician providing marketing consultations and advice for such products may have a financial impact beyond any malpractice claim or decline in practice profitability resulting from clinical procedures. It is possible, therefore, to determine that levels of physician compensation for consulting services should exceed levels for clinical services.

In considering the idea that the risk and complexity of consulting arrangements for an LSC may exceed that found in a clinical setting, it is interesting to note the terms of recent government settlements with medical device and pharmaceutical manufacturers concerning payments to physician-consultants. While the settlements are not applicable to other companies and their physician-consultant arrangements, they may provide some insight into the areas of concern for healthcare regulators. These settlement agreements reiterated that compensation for such arrangements must be within fair market value, and further, certain settlements require the manufacturers to seek *independent third-party opinions* to establish fair market value for any physician-consultant compensation in excess of $500 per hour.[31] In a striking contrast, Hospital Corporation of America's (HCA) corporate integrity agreement from December 2000 required that it obtain an independent third-party opinion for any physician compensation in excess of $150 per hour. Such disparities in hourly rates may be an indication that regulators perceive a difference in the consulting services provided in the life sciences industry in contrast to physician services provided to hospital systems. It would be problematic, however, to cite these disparate rates as establishing the range of fair market value for physician services.

31 See article titled "Artificial-Joint Makers Settle Kickback Case," *New York Times*, Sept. 28, 2007, and the agreements between the U.S. Department of Justice and Biomet, DePuy Orthopedics, Zimmer Holdings, Stryker Orthopedics, and Smith and Nephew.

Whatever position an appraiser takes on the issue of clinical and consulting and administrative compensation, appraisal opinions prepared for Stark compliance purposes should address the distinction and provide support and defense for the position taken on the issue. Failure to consider this question may constitute an inadequate scope of work for such appraisal assignments. In addition, appraisers may be given regulatory guidance by the client and the client's legal counsel that determines the approach to be taken by the appraiser in valuing consulting services. In such cases, the appraiser should document this regulatory guidance as part of definition of value applicable to the assignment.

The approach taken in comparing compensation for clinical and administrative work is critical in determining how physician compensation survey information is used in valuing physician consulting and research services. Physician compensation surveys generally report compensation from all sources. The primary source of income for a physician outside of an academic practice setting or a purely administrative role is clinical services. As a result, the compensation in most of the published surveys primarily represents clinical compensation. If an appraiser takes the position that administrative services should be compensated at a lower rate than clinical services, he or she may need to adjust the survey compensation levels or choose the lower percentiles from the survey to derive hourly physician compensation rates applicable to medical director services. On the other hand, appraisers who argue in favor of the opportunity cost basis for valuing nonclinical services will tend to use compensation levels from the published surveys without such adjustment or consideration of the lower percentiles.

#### Relative Comparability of Qualifications and Responsibilities in Using Survey Data

As noted in detail above, the published physician compensation surveys generally represent compensation from clinical services. These services are essentially different from consulting services provided to LSCs. Because the economics of clinical services differ from that of consulting services, the compensation levels indicated by the published surveys may not be an exact indicator of fair market value for consulting arrangements in the life sciences industry. In using these surveys to establish general levels of physician compensation, however, an appraiser may find that certain surveys contain physician respondents whose qualifications and current job functions are relatively more comparable to those of physician consultants to LSCs than the respondents of other surveys. For example, an appraiser may determine that physicians in an academic practice setting may be relatively more comparable to physician-consultants than physicians in private practice. In such a case, the appraiser may weight compensation levels from one or more surveys, and even one or more job descriptions within a survey, more heavily than others for purposes of establishing a general range of physician compensation to use as a guideline for consulting services.

### Compensation for Physician Services Versus Business-Owner Compensation

The various published physician compensation surveys gather and publish data from a variety of physicians who practice in diverse settings. The surveys report compensation information in varying levels of detail corresponding to these diverse practice settings. The key compensation measures, however, tend to report total compensation received by the physician from all sources. This reporting of compensation from all sources may obscure the fact that certain forms of compensation received by the physician may not relate to services provided directly or personally by the physician. Income received from ancillaries, employment of midlevel providers or physician extenders, leasing of space or equipment, or sharing in group practice earnings may relate more to ownership of a medical practice rather to physician services. In other words, business-owner compensation is often reported along with compensation from physician services in the physician compensation tables in published surveys. Other forms of nonclinical income such as on-call pay stipends, medical directorship payments, expert testimony fees, and other forms may also be included in the physician compensation tables.

Appraisers seeking to find market information on the value of physician services may need to adjust reported compensation levels to eliminate forms of compensation not related to physician services, such as business-owner compensation. Quantifying these amounts, however, may be extremely difficult. Analysis of various financial, production, and operational metrics, ratios, and benchmarks reported in the surveys may be required for the appraiser to attempt to adjust for business-owner compensation that is included in the survey-reported physician compensation tables. While there are clear practical difficulties to addressing this issue, appraisers valuing physician consulting and research services should be aware of disparate forms of income or compensation that are included in the published surveys and make adjustments to the valuation analysis where they deem appropriate and practicable.

### The Annual Hours for Use in Computing Hourly Physician Compensation Rates

In using published survey data on physician compensation to arrive at hourly rates for valuing physician services, appraisers must select the number of annual hours to be used as the divisor for the published annual compensation amounts. Many appraisers use 2,000 or 2,080 hours as the best approximation of typical hours worked by physicians. While this convention may be appropriate and valid, appraisers should be aware of the reported levels of annual physician work hours as provided by certain surveys. For those surveys that do report physician work-hour levels, reported levels may indicate a continuum of annual hours worked that deviates from the standard 40-hour workweek less 10 holidays (i.e., 2,000 hours). Indicated hours may be below or above the typical annual hours. The assumption of standard annual hours may have the greatest valuation impact when an appraiser uses the upper percentiles of the reported compensation levels to determine an hourly rate. In reality, physicians at these higher compensation levels may be working more annual hours than assumed in the standard rates for annual hours worked. As a result, appraisers may need to perform additional research and analysis using survey information to arrive at the appropriate amount of annual hours used for determine hourly physician compensation rates when relying on the upper percentiles of the compensation surveys.

#### Adjustment of Hourly Physician Compensation to an Independent-Contractor Basis

Because most physicians providing consulting or research services to LSCs are independent contractors, many appraisers argue that the hourly rates derived from physician compensation surveys should be grossed-up to include a provision for benefits. The theory supporting such gross-up is that independent contractors across all industries are generally paid at higher rates than employees. Such premium rates are intended to cover benefits and other costs incurred by contractors providing services. In the area of physician services, it is argued that one can observe such premiums in the rates paid to locum tenens physicians. Appraisers who value physician consulting and research services should be aware of this issue and provide the support and defense in the appraisal report for the position taken.

#### Application of the Cost Approach to Valuing Research Services

In addition to valuing the physician component included in research services, an appraiser using the cost approach must attempt to value the cost of the additional resources employed in providing such services to LSCs. Such resources may include nursing and other practice staff, equipment, supplies, space, and various services. How does the appraiser establish the appropriate cost basis for such resources? Generally, there are two sources for such cost information: 1) the subject physician practice that will provide the research services and 2) market information obtained through the research efforts of the appraiser. In practice, an appraiser may experience difficulties in obtaining cost information from either source. Such data may not be available or obtainable in a feasible or cost-effective manner.

Yet, there is an important conceptual issue that the appraiser must address in choosing between the two sources of cost information. If the standard of value for the appraisal assignment is fair market value, the appraiser must determine whether specific cost information from the subject physician practice represents the cost to the hypothetical willing buyer and seller in a service arrangement. Many appraisers would argue that only normalized or market-based costs should be used in the buildup method. Using the actual costs of the subject service provider may be more consistent with investment value than fair market value because it takes into account the cost structure and economies of a particular seller rather than the hypothetical-typical seller of such services in the marketplace.

Arriving at the appropriate cost basis of resources is only one difficulty in applying the cost approach to valuing research services. Since some of these resources are utilized partially or on a limited basis in performing clinical studies, the appraiser must determine an appropriate allocation or apportionment basis in the cost buildup analysis. Such allocations can be difficult or cumbersome to compute. Appraisers may need to exercise judgment in such calculations with a view to the materiality and cost and benefit of complex allocation formulas. Such judgment may also be necessary in determining the level of detail that is necessary for identifying and valuing the various resources used to provide clinical research studies to LSCs.

***The Income Approach***

The income approach may be the most difficult of the three approaches to value to apply to the valuation of service arrangements. This difficulty derives from the traditional definition in the business valuation body of knowledge. As defined by the *International Glossary*, the income approach is a "a general way of determining a value indication of a business, business ownership interest, security, or intangible asset using one or more methods that convert anticipated economic benefits into a present single amount." Converting the compensation under a service agreement to a "present single amount" often represents a conundrum for appraisers. How can such a statement of value be meaningful for a service contract? For valuing service agreements, the definition of the income approach may need to be adapted in terms of the valuation principle of future benefits as the basis for value, but without the conversion to a present value amount. With this adaptation, the income approach can be employed to calculate the future economic benefits to be received by each party to the service agreement.[32] These benefits are then evaluated in terms of investment levels, resources utilized, and services provided in comparison to market rates of return and profitability.[33] Under this reformulation of the

32 Under this adaptation of the income approach, future economic benefits are not intended to include the value or volume of referrals. Rather, the appraiser looks exclusively to the revenues, expenses, and resources investments related to the specific services and service lines provided for in the agreement. For example, in applying the income approach to physician employment arrangements, the appraiser would project future economic benefits derived from the physician practice only. The value or volume or referrals to other business lines of the employer or the employer's parent or affiliated companies is not included in the projection. In some cases, future benefits may not be separately attributable to the subject agreement. In other cases, the future benefits may indirectly or unintentionally include certain ancillaries or other revenues that arise out of referral relationships. In these cases, the appraiser may be prevented from using the income approach to value the future benefits to one or both parties to a service arrangement.

33 This reformulation of the income approach appears to converge with the cost buildup approach discussed previously. For certain types of compensation valuation assignments, the two approaches may be identical. In other types, however, the income approach may entail use of adaptations of the excess earnings or discounted cash flow methods found in business valuation that are distinguishable from the cost buildup technique.

income approach, the appraiser seeks to value the services by ensuring that each party receives market returns or margins given the levels of investment, risk, and resource utilization attributable to either party to the service contract.

For valuing physician consulting and research services in the life sciences industry, use of the income approach may be limited or impracticable. Evaluating future benefits under these service arrangements requires the appraiser to access market rates of compensation for physician services and other resources employed in clinical studies. This evaluation returns the appraiser to the analyses of the market or cost approaches. In general, the income approach appears to be the least relevant and applicable of the three approaches available for valuing consulting and research services.

#### *Formulation of the Opinion of Value*

After completing the applicable approaches to value, the appraiser engages in an evaluation and reconciliation process to determine the fair market value of the subject arrangement for consulting or research services. This process is ultimately based on the independent and professional judgment of the appraiser. Weight may given to a greater or lesser degree to the results of any particular valuation method or technique based on a variety of considerations, such as the reliability of data, extent of comparability, scope of information, regulatory guidance, and facts and circumstances unique to the subject arrangement. The opinion of value may be stated as a specific dollar amount or a range. Whatever the conclusion of value determined, the appraiser should be prepared to support and defend the conclusion based on the relevant information and sound valuation methodology.

### Valuing IP Licensing Arrangements Within the Life Sciences Industry

The pharmaceutical industry was one of the first industries in the United States to routinely use licensing programs as a means for identifying and commercializing new drugs. Prior to the rapid advances made over the last 30 to 40 years in computing and the development of sophisticated methods for mapping chemical paths, the process of finding and developing new drugs was arduous and exceptionally expensive, and the probability of successfully commercializing new pharmaceutical applications was extremely low. To combat these hurdles, pharmaceutical companies began licensing the right to screen the chemical libraries of industrial companies for pharmacological properties. This proved to be highly effective in reducing the cost of up-front research and development and allowed existing discoveries to be further exploited through commercialization in previously unconsidered applications.

Today, intellectual capital has become a central focus of business strategy across all industries, and licensing activity for patents alone is estimated to account for more than $100 billion in revenue for U.S. firms. The healthcare industry continues to play a key role in this market. In the medical devices sector of the life sciences industry, it is not uncommon to find physicians who own patents that are licensed to medical device companies. Other types of LSCs may also license various forms of IP from physicians. Thus, an understanding of the basic tenets of IP licensing is critical for appraisal professionals providing valuation services in the life sciences.

### *Definition of Licensing*

Licensing is the act of granting another person or entity the right to make use of a particular asset in a specific context or application for a specific length of time and within a specific geographical area. A license does not typically carry the full rights of ownership, and therefore, license agreements must be defined narrowly to prevent conflicts of interest between the owner of the asset (licensor) and the user of the asset (the licensee). This is particularly important when the licensor is exploiting the asset in other commercial uses such as in its own products or through additional licenses.

Why do owners of property find it advantageous to enter licensing arrangements? The basic conceptual framework of the license is to create a symbiotic relationship whereby both the owner of the property and the licensee share in the commercial success of the end product. An example of this type of situation might include an inventor who does not have the resources to successfully commercialize the invention or an owner of property who does not have the necessary expertise to commercialize the product in a new area.

### *Asset Types*

A licensing arrangement can be entered into for virtually any type of asset, but licensing activity generally centers on intellectual property, such as patents, trademarks, copyrights, and technologies.

#### Patents

The United States Patent & Trademark Office (USPTO) is the governing body that issues patents and trademarks in the United States. The USPTO defines a patent as "the right to exclude others from making, using, offering for sale, or selling" the invention in the United States or "importing" the invention into the United States. Patent grants have a finite life typically defined as 20 years from the original date of the patent application. There are three distinct types of patents:

1. *Utility patents*—granted for "the invention or discovery of a new and useful process, machine, article of manufacture, or composition of matter or any new and useful improvement thereof."

2. *Design patents*—granted for the invention of a "new, original, and ornamental design for an article of manufacture."

3. *Plant patents*—granted "to anyone who invents or discovers and asexually reproduces any distinct and new variety of plant."

4. Within the life sciences industry, most patents fall under the category of utility patents and include chemical compounds, medical devices, and medical equipment.

#### Trademarks

Trademarks, or service marks, were established by the Lanham Act, and are described by the USPTO as "a word, name, symbol, or device that is used in trade with goods to indicate the source of the goods and to distinguish them from the goods of others. A service mark is the same as a trademark except that it identifies and distinguishes the source of a service rather than a product." Trademarks need not be registered to enjoy protection under the act; however, most commercially used trademarks are registered with the USPTO. Trademarks registered after November 1989 are valid for a period of 10 years and may be renewed for successive 10-year periods. Nearly every branded product with name recognition enjoys protection under the Lanham Act, but the most commonly observed trademarks in the life sciences are name-brand pharmaceuticals and medical devices.

#### Copyrights

A copyright is a form of protection for original works of authorship (literary, artistic, musical, and so on) established by the Copyright Act of 1976. A copyright generally establishes the exclusive right to print, publish, reproduce, perform in public, and create derivative works of the material. In the United States, copyrights are issued and registered with Copyright Office of the Library of Congress and have a term equal to the lifetime of the author plus 50 years. In some instances, the copyright may be valid for a period of 75 years from the date of first publication. Within the life sciences industry, copyrights may include medical texts, manuals, research papers, articles, diagrams, photos, and the like.

### *Royalties*

Compensation under a licensing agreement typically includes the payment of a royalty by the licensee to the owner-licensor for the use of the property. Royalties can take many forms but are most frequently set as an up-front lump-sum, an annual fee, a percentage of revenue on products sold, a dollar amount per unit sold, or a combination thereof. Royalties paid on ongoing revenue or units of sales are referred to as running royalties. It is also common to see royalty arrangements whereby an annual minimum and annual maximum fee applies, the royalty rate decreases with volumes in a stair-step pattern, or royalties decline over time. These types of arrangements are appealing to licensees, because they attempt to match the economic life of the licensed asset with the commercial success of the end product.

Royalty rates vary significantly from one licensing arrangement to the next, and many factors must be considered when attempting to establish a reasonable royalty rate within the context of a specific licensing agreement. Frequently there is no single right answer, and royalty rates for seemingly similar technologies may vary widely. In the landmark case *Georgia Pacific Corporation v. United States Plywood Corp.,*[34] the court set out 15 factors that parties to a hypothetical negotiation would likely consider in determining a reasonable royalty. Though the case dealt specifically with reasonable royalties within the context of patent infringement damages, the context the court used was a hypothetical royalty arrangement that would have been negotiated had the parties negotiated immediately prior to the infringement. This is very similar to the hypothetical negotiation contemplated in the definition of fair market value,[35] and the factors the court used are applicable in assessing reasonable royalties for licenses outside the construct of patent infringement.

The 15 factors identified by the court are listed (in generic form to remove the patent infringement context) and briefly discussed below:

1. The royalty rates received by the owner of the property in other licensing arrangements for the same property, proving or tending to prove an established royalty.

   Existing licensing arrangements for the subject property would tend to establish a reasonable royalty rate. However, it is important to consider relevance of prior licenses within the context of the contemplated license. Differences in the terms of the license (such as Factor 3 below), the remaining life of the property (such as Factor 7 below), and other factors presented in this list may limit the relevance of prior agreements.

34 *Georgia Pacific Corporation v. United States Plywood Corp.*, 318 F. Supp. 1116, 166 U.S.P.Q. 235, May 28, 1970.

35 Fair market value is defined in the *International Glossary of Business Valuation Terms* as "the price, expressed in terms of cash equivalents, at which property would change hands between a hypothetical willing and able buyer and a hypothetical willing and able seller, acting at arms length in an open and unrestricted market, when neither is under compulsion to buy or sell and when both have reasonable knowledge of the relevant facts."

2. The royalty rates paid by the licensee for the use of other property rights comparable to the property (for which a license is being contemplated).

   Established rates paid by the licensee for similar properties in agreements with comparable terms may serve to establish the reasonable royalty rate. As with Factor 1, however, terms of the license agreements should be carefully examined for comparability to the contemplated arrangement.

3. The nature and scope of the license, as exclusive or nonexclusive; or as restricted or nonrestricted in terms of territory or with respect to whom the manufactured product may be sold.

   Exclusivity—A license granting an exclusive right to use a property would generally demand a higher royalty rate than one that is nonexclusive (i.e., allows additional licenses to be granted).

   Geography—The geographical limitations of the license grant will influence the appropriate royalty rate. A worldwide license would typically demand a higher royalty rate than a license limiting use to a specific territory or boundary.

   Use—The use of the license may influence the royalty rate. A license granting unrestricted use of a property would generally demand a much higher royalty rate than one that is defined narrowly—for example, a chemical compound to be used only in drug-coated stents.

4. The licensor's established policy on licensing, either by not licensing to others the use of the property to maintain a monopoly or by granting licenses under special conditions.

   An owner who is highly protective of his or her property rights or has an established policy of not licensing its properties may justify a higher royalty rate. Such a rate would be necessary to induce the owner to deviate from his or her established policy. This is especially pertinent in infringement cases but may be less so in the normal course of establishing a reasonable royalty rate between two willing parties. The absence of a history of licensing or policy restricting licensing should not be used as justification for a higher royalty rate in and of itself.

5. The commercial relationship between the licensor and licensee, such as whether they are competitors in the same territory in the same line of business or whether they are inventor and promoter.

   License agreements between competitors tend to justify higher royalty rates than those of noncompetitors. Even when the license is structured to limit the use of the product or if the product's application is in a market where there is no competitive threat, licensors are reluctant to allow competitors to gain information or profits that would advance their competitive position.

6. The effect of selling the licensed property in promoting sales of other products of the licensee, the existing value of the invention to the licensor as a generator of sales of his nonpatented items, and the extent of such derivative (or convoyed) sales.

   Licenses that allow the licensee to gain sales in other nonlicensed products tend to justify higher royalty rates. For example, Bausch and Lomb may pay a higher royalty for new contact lens technology if it believes sales of the licensed product will lead to gains in sales of related products, such as saline solution, and so on. Higher royalty rates may also be justified if the license agreement allows the licensee to gain access to new commercial channels, new customers, appeal to a new population demographic, or augment its current commercial presence.

7. The economic or functional life of the property (i.e., expiration date of a patent) and the term of the license.

   A product nearing the end of its life cycle will generally demand a lower royalty rate due to economic obsolescence, increased competition, and design around considerations. This may also be true for new technologies that are expected to have a short, useful life.

   In some instances, the license is written as a perpetual license. This might be seen in the context of a trademark license agreement, where the name brand is expected to continue indefinitely. In these situations, additional analysis may be required to evaluate the life of the economic benefit associated with the licensed property.

8. The established profitability of the property or products embodying the property, its commercial success, and its current popularity.

   It follows logic that royalty rates for highly popular and profitable products are also high. As the popularity and profitability of the product diminishes, so does the appropriate royalty rate.

9. The utility and advantages of the subject property over the old modes or devices, if any, that had been used previously for achieving similar results.

   Products that have significant advantages over currently existing technologies justify higher royalty rates. This is due to the simple fact that products with significant utility advantages also enjoy significant profit advantages.

10. The nature of the subject property, the character of the commercial embodiment of it as owned and produced by the licensor, and the benefits to others who have used the invention.

11. The extent to which the infringer has made use of the subject property and any evidence probative of the value of that use. (*Outside the context of infringement, the intended use of the subject property may be a substitute.*)

12. The portion of the profit or of the selling price that may be customary in the particular business or in comparable businesses to allow for the use of the subject property or comparable properties.

    A common rule of thumb, referred to as the Goldscheider rule,[36] suggests that a reasonable royalty represents 25% of the preprofit expected to be made through the use of the licensed asset. Many databases can also be used to search for comparable license transactions within a given industry. In some cases, these databases can provide insight into the royalty rates being paid for similar properties. However, these should be referenced cautiously, because a truly comparable license transaction may be difficult to identify and overgeneralization may miss many of the nuances of the particular license arrangement.

13. The portion of the realizable profit that should be credited to the invention as distinguished from other elements of the end product, such as the manufacturing process, business risks, or significant features or improvements added by the infringer.

    Understanding the relative contribution of the licensed property to the overall utility of the end product may be helpful to the determination of a reasonable royalty. A license arrangement whereby both parties contribute technologies that equally support the end product may justify a profit split of 50-50. An example of this might be an owner of a medical laser device licensing sophisticated positioning and tracking software to control the movement of the laser.

14. The opinion of qualified experts.

    Frequently professionals in the licensing industry will have experience and expertise that can be helpful in establishing the reasonable royalty.

15. The amount that a licensor and a licensee would have agreed upon if both had been reasonably and voluntarily trying to reach an agreement; that is, the amount that a prudent licensee—who desired, as a business proposition, to obtain a license to manufacture and sell a particular article embodying the subject property—would have been willing to pay as a royalty and still be able to make a reasonable profit and the amount that would have been acceptable by a prudent patentee who was willing to grant a license.

36 Robert Goldscheider is a specialist and recognized authority on licensing. His calculations performed in the 1950s laid the ground work for the "25% rule" now frequently referred to as the Goldscheider rule.

Though this list is fairly comprehensive, additional factors should be considered in determining a reasonable royalty rate. These may include cost to design around the subject property (re-creating the asset versus licensing) and availability and preponderance of nonprotected alternatives. It stands to reason that a licensee would not reasonably pay a royalty rate in excess of the cost to design or develop its own property with the same functionality (assuming it was possible to do so). Royalty rates will also be limited by the availability of acceptable alternatives. A licensee may prefer to have the subject property but will not likely pay a high royalty rate if there are acceptable alternatives with the same or similar attributes available for license at a lower rate.

### *Valuation of Royalty Agreements*

In some instances, it may be necessary to determine the value of a license agreement. Situations when this might be necessary include purchase price allocations, formation of a new entity (such as a joint venture) where the license agreement is assigned by one of the parties as its initial contribution, bankruptcy, termination of a licensing agreement, or sale of the licensing rights, among others. Though a complete discussion of valuation methodologies is beyond the scope of this chapter, the following is a high-level overview of some of the more common methodologies to valuation and key considerations therein.

#### Income Approach

Any income-producing asset can be valued with respect to its income-generating capacity. Because royalty agreements have a fairly predictable royalty stream and a finite life, an income approach to valuation is generally used. Under the simplest variation of this approach, expected future royalties over the remaining life of the agreement are discounted to their present value using a risk-adjusted rate of return or discount rate. This rate of return is set at a level commensurate with the risk of realizing the projected royalty stream. Uncertain royalty streams will have a higher discount rate, and reasonably certain royalty streams will have a lower discount rate.

To demonstrate the mechanics of this approach, assume a royalty arrangement calling for a royalty rate of 10% on sales of a specific product payable at year end over the next three years. Assume further that sales of the product are expected to total $1 million in each of the next three years. Based on the risk profile of the projected sales, a qualified appraiser has determined that a 25% rate of return is appropriate.

**Exhibit 1. Calculating the Value of a Royalty Agreement**

| | Year 1 | Year 2 | Year 3 |
|---|---|---|---|
| Expected Product Revenue (000s) | $ 1,000.0 | $ 1,000.0 | $ 1,000.0 |
| Royalty Rate | 10% | 10% | 10% |
| Royalty Income | 100.0 | 100.0 | 100.0 |
| Taxes @ 40% | (40.0) | (40.0) | (40.0) |
| After Tax Royalty Income | 60.0 | 60.0 | 60.0 |
| | | | |
| Present Value Factor @ 25% | 0.800 | 0.640 | 0.512 |
| Present Value of Royalty Income | 48.0 | 38.4 | 30.7 |
| **Value of Royalty Agreement (sum of above)** | **$ 117.1** | | |

In Exhibit 1, the present value factor is calculated as 1/(1 + rate of return)^(time), where time equals the number of years in the future (i.e., Year 2 = 1/(1.25)^2). Excluding consideration of any additional factors, the value of the royalty agreement in this example is $117,100. As suggested, this is an oversimplified example, and each royalty agreement must be valued in context, giving proper consideration to all elements that contribute to value.

#### Market Approach

The market approach is premised on the idea that the value of an asset can be estimated by drawing reference to the prices paid for other assets with similar characteristics. The challenge to this approach and especially with intellectual property assets, is finding truly comparable assets. Transactional data related to the prices paid for licensing agreements are somewhat limited, and even when a sufficient volume of data are available, it is highly unlikely that the underlying license agreement contains substantially all of the provisions of the subject agreement or an underlying asset of substantially the same nature.

#### Cost (or Asset) Approach

The cost approach is rooted in the concept of replication. Value under this approach is estimated with reference to the actual cost to create the asset or by estimating the cost of reproduction or replacement of the asset. For license agreements, the cost approach has limited application because the primary cost consideration pertains to the underlying asset subject to the license, not the license itself. Additionally, the rights associated with a license are generally less than those associated with full ownership of an asset, and the cost approach may significantly overstate value. However, there are circumstances when the value of the license may be determined in this manner. The question the appraiser must ask is: "But for the license, what would it cost the licensee to develop its own noninfringing alternative to the licensed asset?" Assuming a noninfringing alternative is feasible, the appraiser would then attempt to estimate the indirect costs (man-hours, overhead costs, and so on), direct costs (materials, equipment, lab costs, and so on), and the opportunity costs (time to re-create the asset versus licensing it now).

## Bibliography

Licensing Executive Society International, *The LESI Guide to Licensing Best Practices, Strategic Issues and Contemporary Realities*, Robert Goldscheider, Ed., May 2002.

Anson, Weston. *Intellectual Property Valuation Primer*, [DRAFT]. Available on www.lesi.org.

Reilly, Schweihs. *Valuing Intangible Assets*. McGraw-Hill, 1999.

Smith, Parr. *Valuation of Intellectual Property and Intangible Assets*, 3rd Edition. Wiley, March 31, 2000.

Sullivan and Fradkin, "A Primer on Benchmarking a Licensing Operation," September 2001, available on www.lesi.org.

Porter, Mills and Weinstein, "Industry Norms and Reasonable Royalty Rate Determination," March 2008, available on www.lesi.org.

Wendt, Jeffrey, "Medical Devices: New License Issues for Single Use Devices," *les Nouvelles*. September 2003.

Chapter 36

# Valuing Medical Director Services

*By Andrea M. Ferrari, JD, MPH and Timothy R. Smith, CPA/ABV*

A wide variety of healthcare providers, including hospitals, long-term care facilities, and pharmaceutical and device manufacturers, routinely engage physicians to provide administrative services. These arrangements are most commonly termed "medical directorships," although other descriptions, such as "thought leader arrangement," are common as well. Although medical directorships have been a staple of the healthcare industry for many years, regulatory activity over the last several years has increased the attention being given to these types of arrangements.

This chapter explores the various, sometimes complex issues that should be considered when valuing medical directorships in the current regulatory environment. It covers topics in the following order:

1. Legal and regulatory issues to consider when determining compensation for medical directorships.
2. Identifying and analyzing the scope of services covered by a medical directorship arrangement.
3. Selecting and applying the appropriate valuation methodology to determine the fair market value (FMV) of medical director services.
4. Arriving at an FMV range based on consideration of all relevant facts and circumstances.

### Regulatory Issues to Consider When Valuing Medical Directorships

An understanding of the regulatory environment that is the backdrop for most requests for medical directorship valuations is important before undertaking one. Generally, when healthcare providers request the valuation of medical directorship agreements, at least one purpose in doing so (and, typically, an important purpose) is to establish FMV for the services being provided and thereby, ensure that the arrangement will not implicate Medicare fraud and abuse laws, such as the Stark and anti-kickback statutes. The definition of "fair market value" as it relates to the Stark and anti-kickback statutes is somewhat different from the definition that most valuators know. Therefore, it is generally advisable that valuators have some understanding of the regulatory issues that are implicated by a medical directorship.

The maze of laws and regulations that may have bearing on a medical directorship is complex and may differ from one arrangement to another. As such, valuators are advised to consult with the client or the client's legal counsel to ensure an appropriate understanding of the applicable legal and regulatory issues prior to undertaking the valuation of medical director services. Regulatory guidance given by a client or client's counsel should not interfere with the appraiser's independent judgment but rather should be a helpful aid for determining the scope of work for the appraisal assignment by, for example, identifying the appropriate definition of value for the appraiser. We generally think that it is good practice for valuators to disclose and discuss the regulatory considerations that influenced the appraisal somewhere in the report, usually in the context of the considerations that went into determining the scope of work for the assignment.

There are two major categories of laws and regulations that may be implicated by medical directorships:

- The federal anti-kickback statute and its related regulations and advisory opinions (AKS).
- The Stark law and its related regulations and government guidance (Stark).

A third category may be implicated when an entity has not-for-profit status: provisions of the Internal Revenue Code that prohibit private inurement in transactions with tax-exempt entities (tax regulations). Since the effect of tax regulations for tax-exempt entities is often similar to and superseded by the effect of concerns related to Stark and AKS, we are not providing a detailed discussion of the tax regulations in this chapter.

AKS prohibits individuals from knowingly and willfully offering, paying, soliciting, or receiving any remuneration, in cash or in kind, to induce referrals of items or services that are covered by a federally funded healthcare program, such as Medicare or Medicaid. The courts have interpreted AKS to prohibit any arrangement for which it is established that even *one* purpose is to induce referrals of healthcare items or services.[1] Medical directorship arrangements may implicate AKS if the physician is in a position to order or recommend goods or services that are offered by the party engaging the physician, the goods or services are covered by a federally funded healthcare program, and the compensation paid to the physician under the arrangement exceeds the FMV of the services that are provided by the physician or of the services that are legitimately needed to accomplish the purposes of the arrangement (other than generation of referrals). The Office of the Inspector General of the United States Department of Health and Human Services (OIG), which is the entity that is responsible for monitoring enforcement of AKS, has created certain "safe harbors" for activities that pose a low risk for abuse and overuse of federal healthcare funds. To fit within a safe harbor, an arrangement must meet all the requirements that have been set forth by OIG. The safe harbor that is potentially applicable to most medical directorship arrangements is the one for personal services and management contracts, which has the following requirements:

- The arrangement is set out in writing and is for a term of at least one year.
- The agreement covers all of the services to be provided during the term of the agreement.
- The agreement specifies the services to be rendered and if services are to be provided on a periodic, sporadic, or part-time basis, the agreement specifies the schedule of intervals, their precise length, and the exact charge for such intervals.
- The aggregate compensation that is to be paid over the term of the agreement is set in advance, consistent with FMV in arm's-length transactions, and not determined in a manner that takes into account the volume or value of any referrals or business otherwise generated between the parties that is covered by Medicare or a state healthcare program.
- The services performed under the agreement do not involve the promotion or counseling of an activity or business arrangement that violates any state or federal law.
- The aggregate services do not exceed those that are reasonably necessary to accomplish the commercially reasonable business purpose of the agreement.

1 *United States v. Kats*, 871 F.2d 105 (9th Cir. 1989); *United States v. Greber*, 760 F.2d 68 (3d Cir.), cert. denied, 474 U.S. 988 (1985).

- Most requests for valuation of medical directorship services are, at least in part, to allow the parties to establish compliance with requirements for the safe harbor for personal services and management contracts.

In the most simple terms, Stark prohibits a physician's referral to an entity for a designated health service (DHS) when the physician or a member of the physician's immediate family has a financial relationship with the entity (such as a compensation arrangement), *unless* the arrangement meets one of several enumerated exceptions. Stark broadly defines a referral to include a physician's request for, ordering of, or certifying or recertifying the need for, any DHS that is paid for by Medicare, including a request for a consultation with another physician and any test or procedure that is ordered by or to be performed by that other physician or under that other physician's supervision, and any request for a plan of care that includes DHS. DHS is defined to include:

- clinical laboratory services;
- physical therapy services;
- occupational therapy and speech-language pathology services;
- radiology services, including nuclear medicine, MRI, CT, and ultrasound services;
- radiation therapy services and supplies;
- durable medical equipment and supplies;
- parenteral and enteral nutrients, equipment, and supplies;
- prosthetics, orthotics, and prosthetic devices and supplies;
- home health services;
- outpatient prescription drugs; and
- inpatient and outpatient hospitalization services.

Stark provides for stiff fines and possible exclusion from participation in federal healthcare programs for violators. Hence, although Stark is not a criminal prohibition like AKS, violations of Stark are a significant concern for entities that provide DHS to Medicare patients, including most hospitals, long-term care centers, durable medical equipment suppliers, and home health and pharmaceutical suppliers. The Stark exceptions include an exception for personal services arrangements, which may be applicable to medical directorship arrangements if the following requirements are met:

- The arrangement is set out in writing, is signed by the parties, and specifies the services covered by the arrangement.
- The arrangement covers all of the services to be furnished by the physician under the arrangement.
- The aggregate services do not exceed those that are reasonable and necessary for the legitimate business purposes of the arrangement.
- The term of the arrangement is for at least one year.
- The compensation to be paid under the arrangement is set in advance, does not exceed FMV, and is not determined in a manner that takes into account the volume or value of any referrals or other business generated between the parties.
- The services to be furnished under the arrangement do not involve the counseling or promotion of a business arrangement or other activity that violates AKS or any state or federal law.

The reader will note that the criteria for the Stark exception for personal services arrangements and the AKS safe harbor for personal services and management contracts are very similar. In addition, both the Stark exception and the AKS safe harbor for personal services require that compensation is set in advance, does not exceed FMV, and is not determined in a manner that takes into consideration that volume or value of any referrals or other business generated between the parties.

It is important for valuators to be aware that Stark and AKS define FMV somewhat differently than it has traditionally been understood by the valuation profession. As defined by the *International Glossary of Business Valuation Terms*, the term "fair market value" means the price, expressed in terms of cash equivalents, at which property would exchange hands between a hypothetical willing and able buyer and seller, acting at arms' length in an open and unrestricted market, when neither is under a compulsion to buy or sell and when both have reasonable knowledge of the relevant facts. For purposes of complying with AKS and Stark, FMV means the value in arm's-length transactions, consistent with the general market value, where "general market value" means the compensation that would be included in a service arrangement as the result of bona fide bargaining between well-informed parties when neither party is otherwise in a position to generate business for the other party.[2]

2 This is the Stark definition, set forth in 42 CFR §411.351. This definition is also consistent with similar fair market value guidance related to AKS (codified at 42 U.S.C. §1320a-7b) and with the definition relied upon by the Internal Revenue Service (See, for example, Treas. Reg. 53.4958 et seq.)

Over the years and through various phases of the Stark regulations, the government has provided a fair amount of guidance and commentary regarding the meaning of FMV for purposes of complying with Stark, including explicitly noting that its definition for purposes of meeting a Stark exception may differ from the one commonly understood by appraisers.[3] One critical difference arises from Stark regulatory text that states that FMV compensation is compensation that is consistent with the compensation that would result from bargaining between parties who are not otherwise in a position to generate business for each other. This difference warrants attention by valuators because it may necessitate limits on the use of a market approach when valuing medical directorship arrangements. An opinion of value for medical directorship compensation should, perhaps, not be based in whole or substantial part on market comparable transactions unless it is clearly known that the market-comparable transactions are not between providers of DHS and referral-source physicians. Valuators should also consider the possibility that a high prevalence of medical directorship arrangements between entities that are in a position to refer or otherwise generate business for each other may "taint" nearly all medical director survey data, thereby eliminating the market approach as a valid valuation methodology for medical directorships. The government itself has noted that potential tainting may preclude the use of the market approach for valuing certain physician compensation arrangements and has recommended alternative approaches for these cases.[4] We note, however, that some counsel and Stark experts purport that the government's discouraging of the market approach is applicable only with respect to the Stark exception for office space and equipment leases (which is the context for the relevant government language). As such, there are differing schools of thought on the use of the market approach to value medical directorship arrangements.

In Stark regulations issued in September 2007 (the "Stark Phase III regulations") the government distinguished between clinical and administrative work by physicians and stated:

> A fair market value hourly rate may be used to compensate physicians for both administrative and clinical work, provided that the rate paid for clinical work is fair market value for the clinical work performed and the rate paid for administrative work is fair market value for the administrative work performed. We note that the fair market value of administrative services may differ from the fair market value of clinical services.[5]

3 CMS has stated: "... the definition of "fair market value" in the [Stark] statute ... is qualified in ways that do not necessarily comport with the usage of the term in standard valuation techniques and methodologies. For example, the methodology must exclude valuations where the parties to the transactions are at arm's length but in a position to refer to one another." 69 *F.R.* 16107 (March 24, 2004).

4 66 *F.R.* 876-77, 919, 944 (Jan. 4, 2001).

5 72 *F.R.* 51016.

Given this guidance, an appraiser who is engaged to provide an opinion of value for medical directorship services should probably take care to distinguish between clinical and administrative duties when assigning value to the services to that the physician will provide in the arrangement. Although most medical directorships consist wholly of administrative services, we are increasingly seeing arrangements that are labeled "medical director" arrangements but consist of a mix of clinical and administrative duties. Often, the proposed compensation in these hybrid arrangements is somewhat higher than in traditional (wholly administrative) medical director arrangements. Such compensation may be appropriate based on proper consideration of the existence and proportion of clinical duties in the services to be performed and the fact that market rates for clinical services compensation often range higher than market rates for administrative services compensation.[6]

We also note that, for arrangements that are intended to fit the Stark exception for personal services arrangements and the AKS safe harbor for personal services and management contracts, the requirement that the aggregate services do not exceed those necessary for the "commercially reasonable" purposes of the arrangement may have implications for an appraisal of the FMV of such services. Although not specifically defined anywhere in Stark or AKS, government commentary suggests that, in the context of a medical directorship, the term "commercially reasonable" describes an arrangement that would make commercial sense if entered into by a reasonable entity of similar type and size to the engaging party and a reasonable physician of similar scope and specialty to the engaged physician, even if there were no potential business referrals between such parties.[7] Generally, an entity will not, in the absence of a potential referral relationship, provide compensation for performance of services that are:

- Already sufficiently performed by another party (i.e., redundant services, unless there is a legitimate reason for redundancy).
- Services for which the performing physician already receives compensation from another source (i.e., for which the physician is already "made whole").
- Services that add no value to the entity's operations.
- Services that are to be performed during physician time that an entity has already "purchased" (i.e., medical director services that are performed during hours when a physician is being paid hourly to be onsite at the hospital to provide clinical care but has downtime in the clinical schedule).

6 Based on comparisons of hourly rates derived from the general physician compensation surveys to hourly rates in compensation surveys for administrative services.

7 This definition is based on text set forth in the preamble to the Stark II Phase II regulations at 69 *F.R.* 16093 (March 26, 2004). It is also consistent with guidance provided in the "OIG Supplemental Compliance Program Guidance for Hospitals" at 70 *F.R.* 4866 (Jan. 31, 2005).

As such, the value of certain service components should be carved out of an appraisal and the market data used to determine value should be adjusted to ensure that the appraiser's conclusion of value excludes any services that may be in excess of those that are reasonably needed to achieve the commercially reasonable business purposes of the arrangement.

## Understanding the Types of Services Provided by a Physician Medical Director

The type, level, and extent of services provided are key factors for establishing a defensible opinion of value for a service contract. Another key factor is the qualifications that are required to perform the services. The starting point for valuing medical directorship services is, therefore, cataloging and analyzing both the scope of services and the qualifications necessary for providing such services.

Many types of arrangements fall into the category of medical directorships. These arrangements do not always come with a label that clearly identifies the arrangement as a medical directorship. A medical directorship arrangement may be inked on a generic form agreement that is titled "Professional Services Agreement" or may be a component of a complex management services arrangement, employment arrangement, or other service arrangement. Likewise, arrangements that are labeled "Medical Director" or "Medical Directorship" do not always fit an easily definable mold. The duties that are included under this label vary widely and are increasingly a mix of administrative and sometimes clinical duties that may require various special qualifications.

Given that medical directorship arrangements are diverse, comparison of medical directorship arrangements for purposes of either identification or valuation is not an easy task. That being said, most medical directorship arrangements share at least a few common characteristics. To identify and appropriately appraise a medical directorship arrangement, a valuator should understand the typical as well as distinguishing characteristics of the subject arrangement.

### *Medical Directorships Frequently Involve Specialized Physician Services*

In basic terms, a medical directorship is an arrangement by which a physician is engaged to provide leadership, oversight, and planning services for a clinical program or department. Generally, medical directorship services consist of duties that are most appropriately performed by a physician and often, by a physician of a particular specialty. Many medical director duties require the professional training, experience, and peer-to-peer communication skills that only a physician (or in some cases, a physician of a particular specialty) is likely to possess. Examples of common medical directorship duties are:

- Developing, leading, and managing quality and efficiency initiatives for a particular clinical unit, department, or program, including developing clinical quality assessment and improvement programs; providing direct oversight of the care that is provided to patients by the clinical practitioners in the department or program; and selecting, procuring, and directly providing clinical education for practitioners in the department or program.

- Identifying clinical equipment needs and selecting appropriate equipment to purchase to meet those needs and to ensure that the department or program is able to maximize the quality, efficiency, and safety of care.

- Communicating and securing buy-in for operational initiatives from clinical staff that are reluctant to take directives from nonphysician managers.

The training, knowledge, and peer-to-peer communication capability of a physician are assets—if not requirements—in effectively performing these types of tasks. As such, general training as a physician is a requisite qualification for almost all medical directorships.

Training and experience in a particular medical or surgical specialty or subspecialty is an additional qualification for some types of medical directorships. For example, an internal medicine physician who does not regularly perform or participate in cardiac surgeries would not reasonably be expected to develop clinical quality assessment and improvement programs, to anticipate the equipment and staffing needs, or to secure clinical practitioner buy-in for operational initiatives in a cardiovascular surgery program. In short, there are a number of reasons why training and advanced practice experience in a specific medical or surgical specialty or subspecialty may be required to perform the duties of a specific medical director position, and a valuator should be tuned in to these when assigning value to a particular set of duties.

#### *Understanding the Duties to be Performed by the Medical Director*

A valuator should carefully assess the nature of medical directorship duties when assigning value to those duties, including asking the fundamental questions of Who? What? When? Where? and How? Although the details of a specific arrangement may warrant that specific, pointed questions be asked by the valuator, questions may generally be similar to those posed here:

- Who will perform the duties required by the arrangement?
  - Do the duties require the expertise of a physician?
  - Do the duties require the expertise of a physician of a particular specialty (e.g., pediatrics, cardiology, neurology, or surgery)?

  - Do the duties require the expertise of a physician of a particular subspecialty (e.g., pediatric cardiology, stroke, or sports medicine)?
  - Do the duties require the expertise of a physician with highly specialized training, experience, or expertise (e.g., joint replacement, fetal surgery, or neuroradiology)?
- What are the specific duties to be performed under the arrangement?
  - Is the physician providing oversight of a department or program?
  - Is the physician developing or administering quality assessment or improvement programs for a particular department or program?
  - Is the physician assessing need for, selecting, developing, and personally delivering education programs for staff in a department or program?
  - Is the physician selecting, purchasing, testing, or developing protocols for the use of new equipment or supplies in a department or program?
  - Is the physician performing other duties related to leadership, oversight, or planning of specific services, departments, facilities or clinical units?
- When are the duties to be performed?
  - What is the term of the agreement under which the duties are to be performed?
  - What is the specific schedule or time interval over which the duties are to be performed (e.g., a fixed or maximum number of hours per month, year, or week)?
  - Can the duties be performed during regular work hours (i.e., Monday through Friday during regular business hours)?
  - Does the physician have a greater or lesser burden as a result of the schedule (or lack thereof) for performing the duties?
- Where will the duties be performed?
  - What is the geographic region where the services and related duties will be performed?
  - In which facility or service location will the physician perform the duties?
  - What is the specific service center or unit within a facility where the physician will perform the duties?

- How will the physician be compensated for performing the duties?
  - Will payment be hourly, based on hours worked and documented?
  - Will payment be a fixed fee or salary?
  - If compensation is with a fixed fee or salary payment, the valuator should discern whether the payment is based on one of the following:
    - The estimated time (hours) required to perform the duties.
    - The completion of discrete tasks or work products that have a measurable and discernible value.
    - Other measurable and discernible measures of value.

Detailed answers to the questions of Who? What? When? Where? and How? assist the valuator to identify the scope and level of contemplated medical director services. The valuator may use this information to determine the value of these services with greater accuracy and precision.

#### *Medical Director Compensation: Hourly Rate or Fixed Fee Arrangements*

Medical director services are often provided through independent contractor agreements that provide for hourly compensation based on time worked and documented. However, some medical directorships are components of other agreements, such as employment agreements, management arrangements, or other agreements under which compensation is fixed and paid at regular intervals (e.g., weekly, monthly, or yearly). When a physician is compensated for medical director duties with a fixed fee, the appraiser must carefully consider: 1) the nature of the administrative duties that the physician performs, 2) the range of reasonable hourly compensation for performing such duties, and 3) the hours that are reasonably required and likely to be spent actually performing such duties. A more detailed discussion of valuation considerations for fixed fee arrangements is provided later in this chapter.

### Application of the Three Approaches to Value

The same approaches to value that are generally accepted for valuing assets and business interests may also be used to value compensation in services agreements and medical directorship agreements. At the foundation of the three generally accepted approaches to value are the fundamental appraisal principles of substitution, alternatives, and future benefits. The following section of this chapter seeks to demonstrate how these principles may be applied in valuing medical director services.

### *The Market Approach*

The *International Glossary of Business Valuation Terms* (*International Glossary*) defines the market approach as "a general way of determining a value indication of a business, business ownership interest, security, or intangible asset by using one or more methods that compare the subject to similar businesses, business ownership interests, securities, or intangible assets that have been sold." In basic terms, the market approach uses comparable sales transactions that have occurred in the marketplace to determine the value of a subject asset or business interest. The market approach relies on the concept that a buyer will not pay more for a subject asset than for a substitute asset that provides the equivalent economic utility. As applied to service agreements, the market approach assigns value to the subject arrangement by referencing comparable arrangements in the marketplace.

The key to utilizing the market approach for valuing the compensation paid in service agreements is identifying and obtaining information on comparable agreements. Identifying and obtaining such information with sufficient detail to allow for valid comparisons is often the greatest difficulty an appraiser experiences in applying the market approach to the valuation of service agreements. However, an appraiser can often use marketplace information relating to arrangements that are not fully similar to the subject arrangement as long as he or she has sufficient information to make the appropriate adjustments to the market data and the subject arrangement to make them comparable for valuation purposes.

Use of the market approach in valuing medical directorship arrangements necessitates that the appraiser identify and understand the scope of services provided in both the subject arrangement and the market comparables. Without such information, the appraiser may treat as comparable service arrangements that are materially different as to the services provided and the qualifications required to perform them. As a result, the appraiser may arrive at a conclusion of value that is based on a materially dissimilar mix of services or qualifications. In addition, the specific facts and circumstances of the service arrangement, such as the geographic locality and other characteristics of the local market in which the services are being provided, should be carefully analyzed and factored into the valuation, to whatever extent that such information is available. The specific facts and circumstances of an arrangement are crucial considerations when identifying appropriate market comparables, and identifying appropriate market comparables is a key step in valuing the services using a market approach.

#### Applying the Market Approach

When utilizing the market approach to value medical director services, the appraiser performs market research to accumulate information on medical director arrangements, including the scope of services provided, the required qualifications of the physician director, and the level of compensation paid. There are multiple sources of data relating to physician compensation in the marketplace. These include the general physician compensation surveys described below. Few sources of published survey data are specific to physician compensation for specialized services such as medical directorships.[8] One potential source of market data for medical directorship compensation is the *Medical Director Survey*, which is published annually by Integrated Healthcare Strategies. The *Medical Director Survey* reports data for a comprehensive list of specialty medical directorships. It sorts the universe of medical directorships into a large number of specialty categories and reports compensation levels by hospital size. Other medical director surveys, such as one published by MGMA, may also be available to a valuator.

Valuators should be aware of several issues and limitations that may be encountered in using medical director compensation surveys or other medical director data. These sources generally do not present survey compensation results in ways that allow identification of the specific duties or services that are related to the compensation. As a result, comparisons between the subject medical directorship and those referenced in the published data may be difficult. In addition, labels and descriptors that are assigned to the categories of medical directorships for which data are reported in surveys often lack precision and uniform definition. Therefore, a valuator should use caution in making comparisons based solely on such labels and descriptors.

Since the essence of the market approach is using comparable transactions from the marketplace to establish the value of the subject arrangement, sole or unqualified use of medical director surveys or other published data to establish the FMV of medical director services is problematic. Differences in details distinguish medical directorships, even though agreements may appear to be similar on the surface. Significant differences in the who, what, when, where and how of the medical director's duties may have a material impact on the comparability of services and the appropriate outcome of the valuation analysis. The valuation of medical directorships is not a "one size fits all" analysis. Unless sufficient appropriate information is available for the appraiser to determine comparability, survey results reported in a general or summary manner may not be adequate for establishing the value of medical director services. As stated

8 We have elected to treat medical director compensation surveys under the rubric of the market approach and the more general physician compensation surveys (e.g., MGMA, AMGA, SCA, and so on) under the cost approach. Some appraisers conversely place use of the general compensation surveys under the market approach and directorship surveys under the cost approach. Either categorization system has merit and validity. Regardless of how one categorizes the use of the surveys under an approach to value, the analytic and regulatory difficulties discussed in this section apply to the use of such surveys.

previously, FMV is ultimately a function of the specific facts and circumstances of the arrangement being analyzed.

As also noted previously in this chapter, much of the available market data concerning medical directorships comes from physicians and healthcare providers who have referral relationships that may implicate Stark or AKS. Hence, the available market data may be tainted by the potential for referrals between the parties and as such, may not be an appropriate benchmark data for determining FMV, even when comparability among arrangements is established. Simply put, some market data points may not represent arm's-length transactions.

Compensation paid in medical directorship arrangements that are *not* between parties in a position to make or receive referrals or other business for each other are less likely to be tainted. Accordingly, to the extent available, data concerning compensation paid by (as an example) an automotive manufacturing company to a physician who oversees the company's cardiovascular health program for its employees may be a reliable supporting benchmark for valuation of a hospital-based cardiovascular health medical directorship, assuming that the duties of the medical director in the company and hospital-based programs are comparable.

When utilizing the market approach, comparability issues may arise when service contracts for medical director duties are included in larger service arrangements between the parties. Increasingly, we observe situations in which a candidate for a medical directorship is party to other existing or contemplated compensated service agreements with the contracting healthcare entity. The existing or contemplated arrangements may include other services in addition to medical director services. When this situation occurs, the appraiser must be attuned to possible overlapping duties in the various arrangements to which the physician and healthcare entity are parties. If appropriate, the appraiser should demonstrate that the physician is not compensated for the same duties through different arrangements, since multiple payments for a single set of duties may result in compensation that is in excess of FMV for the overall bundle of services.

#### *The Cost Approach*

The *International Glossary* defines the cost approach as "a general way of determining a value indication of an individual asset by quantifying the amount of money required to replace the future service capability of that asset." The cost approach looks to the replacement cost of an asset or business interest as the basis for valuing the subject asset or interest. In business valuation, the cost approach is categorized as the asset-based or buildup approach because the appraiser attempts to re-create the value of the subject business by accumulating the values of the individual assets that comprise the subject. The appraisal attempts to re-create the business one asset at a time, building up a business enterprise value based on the value of each asset. The cost, asset-based, or buildup approach illustrates the valuation principle of alternatives—i.e., the idea that there are alternatives to acquiring the future service capacity of the subject asset or business interest.[9]

The cost approach as applied to service contracts values the compensation for the subject arrangement by looking at the value of alternatives for those services in the marketplace. As applied to medical directorship arrangements, the cost approach arrives at an opinion of value based on consideration of the engaging entity's costs to secure similar benefits by an alternative means to the medical directorship arrangement. For example, the cost approach may entail consideration of the cost of employing one or more physicians to perform the duties that are otherwise to be performed under the medical directorship agreement. As a practical matter, a valuator should consider that most medical directorships are structured as independent-contractor arrangements because the duties of the medical director require variable and often limited hours. As such, securing medical director services through an employment arrangement is generally less practical than through an independent contractor arrangement.

#### Applying the Cost Approach

The valuator may look to establish physician compensation levels in the marketplace, whether from employment or private practice, as a basis for the alternative cost to procuring the physician services provided in medical directorship arrangements. There are several reliable and readily available sources of survey data for physician compensation in the marketplace. These sources include:

1. American Medical Group Association, *Medical Group Compensation and Financial Survey.*
2. Hospital & Healthcare Compensation Service, *Physician Salary Survey Report* and *Hospital Salary & Benefits Report.*
3. Medical Group Management Association, *Physician Compensation and Production Survey.*

9 One can also argue that the cost approach is derived from the principle of substitution in that the individual assets separately valued are substituted for the subject business. Conversely, it can be argued that the market approach illustrates the principle of alternatives: Market comparables indicate the existence of alternatives to the subject in the marketplace. Such lines of reasoning illustrate the integral relationship among the fundamental principles of valuation and the three approaches to value. They also indicate the difficulty in assigning a given principle to only one approach to value. The principles may be found in more than one approach.

4. Sullivan, Cotter and Associates Inc., *Physician Compensation and Productivity Survey Report.*

5. Towers Watson Data Services, *Health Care Clinical and Professional Compensation Survey Report—U.S.*

It is important that appraisers understand how these various physician compensation surveys gather and report financial information. Such knowledge is needed for the valid use of the survey data to determine physician compensation rates. An appraiser will need to address four critical issues when using the survey data to establish the FMV of physician compensation as it may apply to medical directorship duties. These issues include:

1. The distinction between clinical services and administrative services and any corresponding differentiation in compensation levels for clinical versus administrative work.

2. The distinction between compensation for physician services and business owner compensation.

3. The value of annual hours worked (for purposes of computing an hourly rate for physician services).

4. Adjustments of employment compensation to achieve hourly rates that are applicable to independent contractor services.

The appraiser's analysis and resolution of these critical issues will have a material affect on the valuation opinion.

#### Compensation for Clinical Versus Administrative Services

As noted previously in this chapter, the government has indicated that it recognizes a distinction in FMV compensation for a physician's clinical and administrative services. Given that most valuations of medical directorship arrangements are, at least in part, to assist in compliance with government regulations, a valuator should be mindful of the distinction between clinical and administrative duties when assigning value to the duties to be performed in a particular medical directorship arrangement. The salient point is that, generally, the value of clinical work is somewhat greater than the value of administrative work because, generally, clinical work involves a higher degree of complexity and risk than administrative work. Indeed, clinical work may involve responsibility for the immediate health and well-being of patients and in some specialties and cases, the literal difference between life and death. Although administrative duties may require a skill set that is unique to physicians of a particular specialty, these functions and duties do not generally entail the same level of complexity or risk as clinical services. Since medical directorships have historically entailed only *administrative* duties, FMV for medical director duties is, on an hourly basis, generally less than the hourly rate that comparably qualified physicians would receive for their clinical services. We note, however, that recent trends suggest a move toward more hybrid arrangements with physicians (i.e., arrangements that require a mix of clinical and administrative duties by the physician, perhaps owing to increased efforts at clinical integration). These hybrid arrangements may be presented to the valuator with the label of a medical directorship, but with proposed compensation that is higher than may have been paid under similarly termed arrangements in the past. As such, valuators should carefully assess the duties that are required by new medical directorship agreements to determine and appropriately factor into the valuation the existence and relative proportion of clinical versus administrative functions.

Some argue that there should not be a difference in compensation between administrative and clinical work because there is an "opportunity cost" to the physician's time. Opportunity cost proponents argue against the government's purported position that administrative services have a different value than clinical work. They contend that physicians may not agree to provide services for an outside entity for lower hourly compensation than they would expect to receive performing services in their own office. Moreover, the compensation received for clinical services is the best indicator of the value of a physician's time. Regardless of the merits of these arguments, valuation opinions that are prepared for Stark compliance purposes should address the distinction between clinical and administrative services and provide support and defense for the value indications that were ultimately selected by the valuator.

We note that physician compensation surveys generally report compensation from all sources. The primary source of income for a physician who is not in an academic setting or a purely administrative role is clinical services. As a result, the compensation values that are reported in most published surveys are most representative of clinical compensation. If a valuator takes the position that administrative services should be compensated at a lower rate than clinical services, he or she should consider whether survey compensation data should be adjusted to account for the administrative nature of the medical directorship duties and whether lower percentiles are the appropriate reference points from the survey data.

#### Compensation for Physician Services Versus Other Forms of Compensation

Publishers of physician compensation surveys gather and publish data from a variety of physicians who practice in a variety of settings. The surveys report compensation information in varying levels of detail. However, the key compensation measures generally reflect total compensation received by the physician from all sources, including compensation that may not relate to services provided directly or personally by the physician. Income received from ancillary services, employment of physician extenders, leasing of space or equipment, or sharing in group practice earnings may be included in the reported compensation values. In other words, business owner compensation may skew the values reported by the surveys, as may other forms of nonclinical income, such as on-call pay stipends, medical directorship payments, and expert testimony fees.

As such, the valuator should consider whether compensation survey data should be selected or adjusted to weed out the effect of compensation not related to physician services. Although there are obvious practical difficulties in doing this, a reasoned attempt is preferable to using data from the surveys in an uncritical, unqualified manner, which may lead to an overstatement of the cost of physician services when assigning a value to the relevant medical directorship duties.

#### The Annual Hours for Use in Computing Hourly Physician Compensation Rates

When using published survey data that relate to annual physician compensation, a valuator must frequently translate the annual values to hourly amounts. This requires selection of an appropriate denominator for division of the annual values. As a matter of convention, many valuators select 2,000 or 2,080 hours as an approximation of annual physician work hours. Although these denominator values are generally both reasonable and defensible, specific data on annual work hours by specialty are preferable to generic annual work hours. Unfortunately, however, there is little publicly available, current data on physician work hours. The valuator's assumption of "standard" annual hours may have the greatest valuation impact with respect to physicians' earning compensation at the highest percentiles, as physicians earning compensation that is consistent with the highest compensation levels may be working high numbers of annual hours.

#### Adjustment of Hourly Physician Compensation to an Independent-Contractor Basis

Because most medical directors serve as independent contractors to healthcare facilities, many appraisers argue that the hourly rates derived from physician compensation surveys should be grossed-up to include a provision for benefits. The theory supporting such gross-up is that independent contractors across all industries are generally paid at higher rates than employees to account for the fact that independent contractors incur costs that employees do not, such as payment of health and liability insurance premiums.

### *The Income Approach*

The income approach may be the least desirable approach for valuing physician service arrangements. As defined by the *International Glossary*, the income approach is a "a general way of determining a value indication of a business, business ownership interest, security, or intangible asset using one or more methods that convert anticipated economic benefits into a present single amount." Converting the compensation under a service agreement to a "present single amount" often represents a conundrum for appraisers. When valuing service agreements, the income approach may need to be adapted to allow for use of future benefits as the basis for value, but without the conversion to a present value amount. With this adaptation, the income approach can be employed to calculate the future economic benefits to be received by each party to the service agreement.[10] These benefits are then evaluated in terms of investment levels, resources utilized, and services provided in comparison to market rates of return and profitability. Under this reformulation of the income approach, the appraiser values the services by ensuring that each party receives market returns or margins given the levels of investment, risk, and resource utilization attributable to either party to the service contract.

Given the regulatory context for most valuations of medical directorship arrangements, use of the income approach may be limited or impracticable. An appraiser might attempt to isolate such benefits by borrowing the with-and-without competition technique commonly used in business valuation to arrive at the value of a covenant not to compete. Under such a method, the appraiser would attempt to place a value on medical director services by showing the decrement in net cash flow to the healthcare entity by not contracting with a medical director. Isolating the specific amount of future benefits attributable to contracting with a medical director, however, is a difficult task. In addition, the appraiser would need to prepare projections of revenues and expenses related to the entity or service line in question. The cost of preparing such a pro forma statement appears to outweigh its benefit. Applying the income approach to the other party to the arrangement, i.e., the physician, would require the appraiser to assess the future benefits to the physician in terms of market rates of compensation for physician services. This evaluation returns the appraiser to the analyses of the market and cost approaches. In general, the income approach appears to be the least relevant and applicable of the three approaches available for valuing medical director services.

10 Under this adaptation of the income approach, future economic benefits are not intended to include the value or volume of referrals. Rather, the appraiser looks exclusively to the revenues, expenses, and resources investments related to the specific services and service lines provided for in the agreement. For example, in applying the income approach to physician employment arrangements, the appraiser would project future economic benefits deriving from the physician practice only. The value or volume or referrals to other business lines of the employer or the employer's parent or affiliated companies is not included in the projection. In some cases, future benefits may not be separately attributable to the subject agreement. In other cases, the future benefits may indirectly or unintentionally include certain ancillaries or other revenues that arise out of referral relationships. In these cases, the appraiser may be prevented from using the income approach to value the future benefits to one or both parties to a service arrangement.

### *Formulation of the Opinion of Value*

After completing the applicable approaches to value, the valuator engages in an evaluation and reconciliation process to determine the FMV of the subject arrangement for medical director services. This process is ultimately based on the independent and professional judgment of the valuator. Greater or lesser weight may be assigned to the results of any particular valuation method or technique based on a variety of considerations, such as the reliability of data, extent of comparability, scope of information, regulatory guidance, and facts and circumstances unique to the subject arrangement. The opinion of value may be stated as a specific dollar amount or a range. Whatever the conclusion of value, the appraiser should be prepared to support and defend the conclusion based on the relevant information and sound valuation methodology.

## Evaluating the Method of Compensation: Hourly Versus Fixed Fee Arrangements

Medical directorships may be independent contractors or employment relationships. In either case, the method of compensation for medical director services is most often hourly and paid in accordance with the number of hours actually worked and recorded by the physician. The alternative compensation structure is a fixed fee paid in weekly, monthly, or other time intervals, or upon the achievement of certain milestones or the completion of certain tasks.

Regardless of whether an arrangement provides for hourly or fixed fee payments, all payments should be based on a FMV hourly rate. Accordingly, to evaluate fixed fee payments, the valuator should determine the hours reasonably required to perform the required services and calculate an underlying hourly rate. Unfortunately, there is rarely appropriate benchmark data to allow estimation of the time requirements for specific medical directorship duties; thus, the valuator must rely upon his or her best judgment, the client's representations, or the requirements specified in the arrangement.

To appraise and validate the FMV of an arrangement involving a fixed fee payment for medical director services, a valuator should be able to compare the compensation derived from the arrangement to benchmark data from the marketplace. To permit such comparisons, values must be in comparable units (i.e., they must have the same denominator). If all compensation values are reduced to and expressed in terms of dollars *per hour*, the valuator can readily make comparisons to benchmark data as required to validate an appraisal using market data.

When asked to value a medical director arrangement that provides for fixed fee payments, the valuator may tie the fixed fee payment to an hourly rate using the following four-step process:

1. As specifically as possible, identify the duties that the medical director is required to perform.
2. Determine (from benchmark data) reasonable hourly compensation for performing such duties.
3. Determine the hours that are reasonably necessary (based on any available benchmark data, client representations, or the valuator's independent judgment) or that will actually be required under the arrangement to perform the duties.
4. Multiply the reasonable hourly compensation for performing the duties by the hours that are reasonably necessary or that will actually be required to perform the duties.

After applying this four-step process, the fixed fee should reflect reasonable hourly compensation for the duties, based on a reasonable estimate of the time to be spent performing the duties as required under the arrangement.

## Conclusion

Valuing medical directorship arrangements requires careful consideration and analysis of the applicable facts and circumstances, including the nature of the services and the qualifications necessary to perform them, the available market data to perform valuation analysis using one of the three accepted valuation approaches, the regulatory context for the valuation request, and the applicable definition and considerations for determining FMV and any unique aspects of the arrangement that warrant adjustment of the valuation approach or reference data. The valuator should take care to validate the conclusion of value by comparing it to marketplace benchmarks and ensuring that the conclusion of value seems reasonable and defensible in light of general marketplace practices.

Chapter 37

# Valuing Management Services Contracts Between Physicians and Hospitals

*By Randy A. Biernat, CPA/ABV/CFF*

This chapter presents a brief overview of the physician-hospital relationship present in management services contracts (MSCs) and then provides an analytical framework and some tools to prepare a credible fair market value appraisal.

Appraisers typically prepare an appraisal report at the request of a hospital or its counsel to analyze the contractual compensation and certify that the compensation component of a particular arrangement is consistent with fair market value. The resulting appraisal, or "fair market value (FMV) opinion," is then utilized in an attorney's legal opinion regarding the arrangement's compliance with the applicable laws and regulations governing the transaction.

This chapter briefly describes the what and why of management services contract appraisal and more extensively presents the how of executing the various analyses for this type of engagement.

## I. BACKGROUND AND OVERVIEW

### Management Services Contracts—The Basics

One nonscientific observation of the healthcare marketplace is an increasing tendency for hospitals to contract directly with physicians to provide management services, either exclusively or in combination with its internal managers, as an alternative to providing management services exclusively with employed nonphysician staff. The result is MSCs, which require FMV opinions to comply with the hospital's and physicians' legal obligations.

MSCs come in all shapes and sizes. Some are little more than slightly expanded medical directorships, while others provide for the virtual outsourcing of nearly every permissible service required to run a department of a hospital. This chapter presumes that the MSC terms will call for a modest scope of services.

A discussion of appraisal techniques for MSCs that call for the provision of the majority of services necessary to provide the technical component of a hospital service is outside the scope of this chapter, although some of the techniques discussed in Part 3 may be applicable. For instance, some management agreements will actually call for the MSC to provide the staffing, equipment, supplies, and management necessary to provide the technical component of outpatient surgery, cardiac catheterizations, imaging services, and so on. These types of arrangements require the application of analyses not presented in this chapter.

### Hospital Motivation for Purchase of Physician Management Services

The core purpose of engaging a physician or physician management company is to create operating synergies through the alignment of hospital and physician goals. Establishing an understanding of the background and genesis of the contemplated arrangement with management will help the appraiser clearly capture the expected mutual benefits and will likely result in a better FMV opinion. Reasons that a hospital would enter into an agreement with a physician management company include the following:

- To obtain management expertise, including the integration of clinical leadership from the physician community to provide excellent patient care;
- To develop and implement best practices with respect to the delivery of clinical services; and
- To expand and improve the clinical services offered to patients and the community served by hospitals.

### Motivation for Physicians' Provision of Management Services

Physicians generally seek management opportunities for two reasons. First, engaging management services are a means to enhance personal income for physicians struggling in the present era of flat or declining reimbursement. Second, the ability to influence one's workplace entices a number of physicians to participate.

The intersection of the goals of hospitals and physicians often result in the formation of new physician–owned entities to contract with hospitals to provide management services. These entities are referred to in this chapter as MSCs, which can be presumed to be physician-owned and -operated unless otherwise stated.

## II. MSC APPRAISAL CONSIDERATIONS

The task of an appraiser of an MSC is to provide a FMV opinion regarding the proposed compensation. The appraiser balances the facts and circumstances surrounding an arrangement and determines whether the price to the hospital and the income to the physicians are reasonable and consistent with market levels of compensation for comparable services. The MSC appraisal process will result in a better end product if two questions are repeatedly considered: "Is it reasonable?" and "Can it be supported?" Every step along the path of analysis should be anchored by these two questions.

### Appraisal Objective

The FMV analysis is intended to result in the appraiser gathering sufficient evidence to support a professional judgment as to whether or not the proposed compensation is consistent with FMV. Therefore, as with other arrangements between physicians and hospitals, the appraiser must systematically measure the expected benefits and costs to gather sufficient evidence to support an opinion regarding the contractual compensation.

### Appraisal Process

It is important not to overlook the small details of a report. Very good financial analyses can be hindered by a poor explanation of the purpose of the agreement or confused by the reader due to too little narrative explaining the relationship of the parties. Therefore, this section starts with a summary of important considerations in preparing a strong MSC appraisal.

*Overview*—For purposes of determining whether the MSC compensation is reasonable and within the range of FMV, an appraiser should consider and document the following, when possible:

1. Identify the requirements for FMV;

2. Discuss the jurisdictional exceptions to FMV (Stark, and so on);

3. Identify the parties to the agreement;

4. Discuss the purpose of the agreement;
5. Discuss the method of compensation;
6. Present the valuation methodologies available and appropriate to the analysis of compensation;
7. Evaluate the transaction from the MSO's perspective;
8. Evaluate the transaction from the hospital's perspective;
9. Reconcile the findings from different methodologies; and
10. State a conclusion.

Depending on the engagement, appraisers may perform and present some or all of the steps identified above. However, the above list can serve as a starting point for the contents of a solid FMV opinion.

*Gather information*—For many engagements, the art of the appraisal process is to maximize the utility of the information made available to the appraiser. Different circumstances and relationships among the parties yield differing mixtures of data available for analysis on a given project. Below is a short list of the items typically requested at the outset of a FMV opinion engagement related to management services:

- The management services contract;
- Financial statements for the relevant department of the hospital for a representative period of time prior to the engagement of the physician management company;
- A financial forecast for the hospital department, including the expected management fee;
- A written summary of the clinical and administrative benefits expected to be gained through the engagement of the physician management company; and
- A forecast of financial results for the physician management company.

*Review information*—The information provided must be sufficient to perform one or more procedures that will provide the appraiser with a suitable basis for expressing a FMV opinion. Appraisers would do well to be wary of accepting engagements when there is a very limited set of data. It may be necessary to expand the scope of the engagement or have the hospital or management company engage a third party to prepare the necessary projections or other relevant schedules.

*Discussions with management*—It would be difficult to capture the intent of management without interviewing the parties responsible for the particular initiative under consideration. These individuals may be hospital executives, consultants to the hospital, hospital's counsel, or some combination thereof. Limited contact with the appropriate parties can impact the credibility of the FMV opinion. Appraisers should clearly state their need to work with hospital management or their representatives very early in the appraisal process.

*Management approval of facts and data*—Ultimately, management is responsible for reading, understanding, and accepting an appraiser's FMV opinion, either on a stand-alone basis or in conjunction with a legal opinion. Therefore, before finalizing any project, management should be given sufficient opportunity to review draft report language and related exhibits. This allows management the opportunity to review and comment on the report's contents. This process can be an important quality measure because the key parties to the arrangement typically have additional insight into the analyses once presented in the context of an appraisal.

## III. APPRAISAL METHODOLOGIES

This section is devoted to the mechanics of preparing FMV opinion analyses. These four subsections discuss the procedures often used to prepare FMV opinions. However, there are other valid methodologies to determine whether MSC compensation is within the range of FMV.

### Salary Survey Benchmarking

In a basic management services agreement, the management company is paid for providing physician management services to a hospital department. In this arrangement, physician compensation represents virtually all of the management company's costs. Applying the cost approach in this case involves making a comparison between the proposed compensation and the range of compensation presented in market survey data.

The appraiser must study the agreement and work with management and counsel to ensure a good understanding of the expected efforts of the physicians. For example, the management company may commit to providing an average of 10 hours per week of physician management services every week of the year. In this case, the expected "physician management efforts" would be 520 hours (52 weeks times 10 hours per week). If, for example, the stated compensation for such service was $85,000, it can be inferred that the physician compensation is approximately $163 per hour, according to the terms of the agreement.

Once the contractual hourly compensation is identified, the appraiser must then analyze the available salary survey data to determine the market level compensation and whether the proposed compensation fits within the identified range.

*Physician management market data*—Typically, medical director market data are utilized as a proxy for market levels of physician management compensation. Except in vary narrow circumstances, appraisers should avoid the use of compensation for medical services (e.g., vascular surgeon compensation data for a medical director whose training is in vascular surgery) for medical director compensation. Doing so can limit the validity of a FMV opinion, since the riskiness and expertise required for clinical services does not translate directly to management services.

Medical director market data for compensation can come from multiple sources. The following are three annual surveys often used: the Medical Group Management Association (MGMA) *Management Compensation Survey*, the American Medical Group Association (AMGA) *Compensation and Production Survey*, and the Hospital & Healthcare Compensation Service (HHCS) *Physician Salary Survey Report*.

Based on the available set of relevant survey data, the appraiser must use professional judgment to determine a range of applicable market data. Typically, the data are presented in the surveys at the 25th, 50th (median), 75th, and 90th percentiles. The appraiser might also consider making an adjustment for the fact that the survey data are based on a prior year, while the contractual compensation under consideration is for work being performed in the present. How to make this adjustment is a matter of professional judgment. Options for making this adjustment include using an inflation benchmark, trends in historical data, or other observable market measures.

*Conversion of annual salaries to hourly rates*—The market data available are typically presented on an annual basis. To compare this annual data to the hourly data implied in the management services contract, the data must be converted to an equivalent basis. However, doing so presents a challenge since the surveys generally do not provide an "annual hours worked" metric. The compiled survey data is presented as a full-time equivalent (FTE) medical director, which is the number of hours "FTE" means to each organization submitting the data. That is, the FTE metric is not uniform but is instead defined according to each submitting organization's standards.

Therefore, the appraiser must estimate the number of hours worked per year to determine an effective hourly rate for a medical director. Again, reasonable estimates are in order. Options for appraisers include: estimating a 40-hour week for 48 weeks a year, considering the terms of full-time medical directorships in place for the hospital engaging the management company, or surveying hospitals to inquire about trends in relevant market data.

Once an annual hours commitment is assigned to a medical director FTE, an hourly management services rate can be calculated. However, this rate will likely not be suitable for comparison to the contractual rate since the services will, in virtually all cases, be provided on an independent-contractor basis. Review of the survey instructions will likely indicate that the data are presented for employed medical directors.

*Premium for independent contractor status*—Since most, if not all, market data for medical director compensation consist of gross W-2 wages, employment costs such as benefits are excluded. Also worthy of consideration is the cost an employer must bear to replace the productivity of vacationing employees. This is particularly true if management services are to be rendered continuously. A hospital will be financially indifferent to hiring a medical director versus contracting with a nonemployee medical director if the costs are equivalent. Therefore, the appraiser must identify and account for the "hidden" costs of employment to carefully compare the implied contractual compensation to the survey data.

An appraiser should consider applying a premium to the survey compensation to account for those items that are not included in the survey data but are standard costs of employment, including vacation pay, health insurance, retirement benefits, employer paid taxes, and other benefits. To calculate the premium, an appraiser can look to additional data in the identified surveys and other sources that will help validate the estimated costs of the foregone employee-type benefits. This data can be corroborated through an analysis of the benefit packages of local medical directors, if available. The adjustment for independent-contractor status will create the "apples-to-apples" comparison necessary for analyzing the proposed management compensation.

*Salary survey benchmarking: conclusion*—By carefully analyzing and utilizing available market surveys, an appraiser can determine a range of physician management costs relevant for comparison to an implied hourly management fee in a subject contract. The key to a successful benchmarking analysis is to ensure that the market data and the proposed compensation are modified, as necessary, to be stated on an equivalent basis.

In some agreements, the management company will provide services to a hospital in addition to physician management. Even in these expanded arrangements, an analysis of the underlying compensation to physicians for their efforts can be an important component of the overall FMV analysis.

### Profit Margin Analysis

When a management services agreement calls for the physician management company to provide other services, such as nonphysician staff, the purchase and management of supplies, or billing and collections services, an entity-level application of the cost approach can be utilized when considering the compensation's FMV status. In the case of this expanded arrangement, an appraiser can analyze the underlying costs in a similar manner to the benchmarking approach identified in the previous section. However, in most circumstances, an aggregate analysis of the expected revenue and expense should be undertaken to compare the physician management company to similar businesses. One indication that the aggregate compensation under a management services agreement is within the range of FMV is when the overall profit margin of the management company is consistent with market data for similar businesses.

To determine the reasonableness of the compensation to be paid according to the subject agreement, an appraiser can compare the expected future profit margins of the physician management company to profit margins of other management services organizations. Unfortunately, there is not a great deal of reported data for small medical management services companies. However, one source appraisers can use is the data compiled by Risk Management Association (RMA). RMA reports profit margin data in a number of ways. Accordingly, the appraiser should work to gain a thorough understanding of the underlying data and use professional judgment to select an incisive metric for comparison to their subject.

*Profit margin comparison data*—Although the RMA data are not specific to medical industry data, the included companies do provide management services. The appraiser should demonstrate that the service nature of the business is similar enough to management services specific to the healthcare industry to warrant a meaningful comparison.

*RMA statement studies*—*The RMA Annual Statement Studies: Financial Ratio Benchmarks 2007-2008* is a collection of financial information provided by RMA members, including banks of all sizes as well as nonbank institutions. The "Valuation Edition" classifies the underlying data by asset size and revenue size and allows the appraiser to view the results in deciles, which is useful for presenting a range of values. The ability to access deciles is only available on CD-ROM.

Appraisers can consider utilizing the data reported for "Administrative Management and General Management Consulting Services," which is comprised of businesses primarily engaged in providing operating advice and assistance to businesses and other organizations on administrative management, records management, office planning, strategic and organization planning, site selection, new business startup, and business process improvement.

While certainly not identical to the services to be provided by an MSO, the identified set of services provided by the companies included in the RMA data are similar in nature and may be suitable for comparison. Analyzing the RMA data is certainly a place to start, but other sets of data may apply or better apply to the particular agreement being appraised.

*Considerations for the analysis of profit margin data*—Appraisers should be comfortable that the underlying data can be reasonably compared to the management company data. Issues such as the dates of published information, company asset and revenue size, as well as geography should be considered for reasonableness.

*Profit margin comparison: conclusion*—The analysis of overall profit margins for physician management companies that provide expanded services to a hospital can assist in determining whether the proposed compensation results in a profit margin consistent with similar firms in the marketplace. Profit margins within the identified range can be a useful determinant for a conclusion of FMV.

### Relative Profit Margin Comparison

This approach views the agreement from the hospital's perspective, before and after implementation of the MSC. To complete this analysis, an appraiser can assess a hospital's historical income and expenses to determine whether the additional costs associated with contracting with an MSO to provide management services have a material impact on a hospital's margin for that particular reporting unit.

By outsourcing management duties to an MSO, a hospital frequently acquires an increased scope of services but incurs higher labor costs due to a physician management company's use of physician managers. This drives an expectation of some type of financial impact to the hospital. The question then becomes whether a rational relationship exists between the margins of a hospital department before and after entering into the agreement. If there is a material impact to a hospital's margins, it may be an indicator that compensation is excessive. That is, a comparison of "before-and-after" profit margins can help determine whether a hospital's payment to an MSO for services under the subject agreement is consistent with FMV.

*Before and after analysis*—A meaningful before and after analysis can provide valuable insight into the financial significance of entering into an outsourcing agreement for management services. An appraiser should prepare this type of analysis to measure the reasonableness of the financial impact of a hospital's decision to outsource services.

Several different profitability measures can be used on a before-and-after basis, including EBIT, EBITDA, net income, and so on. Because it is difficult and often subjective to assign indirect costs to hospital departments, appraisers might utilize a metric such as "contribution margin," which is generally defined as net revenue less direct expenses. This limits the appraiser's need to focus on whether or not the correct level of overhead is being allocated into the hospital department. This is irrelevant to the before and after analysis as long as the complete set of management costs are included in the analyzed expense data.

An appraiser should be able to work with hospital management to determine expected future margins for the hospital department by estimating the likely financial results on an as-is basis. That is, the before scenario would be based on current conditions and expected trends for the hospital department. The after scenario is based on the expected financial results of entering into the management agreement.

The results of this analysis should be discussed with management to ensure a good understanding of the underlying differences between the two scenarios. The results of the appraiser's analysis coupled with management's input will help drive the report narrative critical in describing the value of the analysis as it relates to FMV.

The before and after analysis is intended to detect unreasonable changes in the relative margins of a hospital department. If the expected difference in the contribution margin percentages under the before and after scenarios is relatively minor, it may indicate that the fee arrangement would not materially impact the hospitals ability to earn net margin or other comparison metric for the relevant department If there is a large variance in contribution margins, in the absence of extenuating circumstances, further scrutiny would be required to determine whether the services to be provided by the physician management company are necessary and reasonable.

Critical to the analysis of a MSC is a thorough analysis of the nonfinancial benefits of the proposed arrangement. Benefits to the hospital could include items such as: improved clinical quality through protocol review and development, improved patient satisfaction, and increased efficiencies with respect to supply usage and patient flow.

It is often unclear at the time of the appraisal the extent to which nonfinancial benefits of a proposed transaction will be realized. If a management company has been in place, these values may be quantifiable. For example, the value of improved clinical quality could be measured through the reduction of "never events" (where the patient or insurer does not pay for complications). The associated savings could also be calculated through a documented reduction in the unit's average length of stay, and so on.

When reconciling a before and after analysis, it is important for an appraiser to document all of the financial and nonfinancial benefits expected to be received in the engagement. There can be circumstances under which a hospital's contribution margin goes down significantly, but the payment per the contract is at FMV due to the expected benefits of the arrangement, which are not quantifiable at the time of appraisal.

If, in considering all of the relevant facts and circumstances, an appraiser believes that a reasonable balance is maintained between contribution margins, the before and after analysis can provide an indication that the proposed compensation is consistent with FMV. That is, if increased management costs associated with an arrangement are not unreasonable when considering the benefits expected to be accrued to a hospital, the appraiser's analysis can support the notion that the proposed compensation is within the range of FMV.

### Management Fee Benchmarking

As a secondary method to analyze the reasonableness of the fees to be paid by a hospital to a physician management company, appraisers can use a procedure consistent with the market approach. This procedure consists of comparing the fees to be paid to a physician management company as a percentage of a hospital's net revenue and comparing this percentage to the fees paid by other healthcare entities for management services.

There are only a limited number of sources for this type of data. Large national hospital management companies will not contract with a hospital to provide management services to a single department of a hospital. These companies, such as MedCath Corporation and Health Management Associates Inc., typically own and operate hospitals and the level of detail in their public filings is insufficient to isolate the financial activity related specifically to management services. Therefore, as a substitute, an appraiser might consider turning to ambulatory surgery center (ASC) benchmarking information to analyze management services provided to a hospital surgery department.

While it is clear that a hospital's surgery department is not the same as an ASC, the skill set required of its managers is similar to that required by an ASC in terms of scheduling, personnel management, equipment selection, budgeting, marketing, quality assurance, utilization review, and general regulatory compliance. A fair number of surgery center managers also have hospital backgrounds. Therefore, an argument can be constructed that supports drawing a comparison between the management of an ASC versus the management of a surgery department of a hospital as a procedure to test the FMV status of MSC compensation.

One of the available ASC surveys is published by MGMA, the *Ambulatory Surgery Center Performance Survey*. By using the different stratifications of data in this survey and potentially others, an appraiser can identify a relevant range of management services expense as a percentage of revenue. This particular survey has good information for benchmarking purposes but has historically not had high levels of participation. As always, appraisers should be cautious when applying and relying on surveys with small data sets. A second data source to consider is Intellimarker's *Ambulatory Surgical Center Financial and Operating Benchmarking Study*, which also presents management fee data.

The appraiser must be aware that a hospital's surgery department might generate net revenue in excess of the 90$^{th}$ percentile of ASC survey data. However, given that a hospital surgery department, in isolation from the rest of the hospital, may have a similar cost structure to an ASC with respect to management expenses, the appraiser must be cognizant of two limiting factors:

- Hospitals are more regulated than ASCs. The additional burdens of regulatory compliance are either the direct or indirect responsibility of management. This would tend to make management services to a hospital service line more costly and more valuable.
- Because net revenue may be high compared to ASC revenue, the appraiser must be sure that management fee percentages are congruent with the actual expenses of the physician management company. There is risk that a percentage applied to a hospital's surgery department revenue would overstate the amount that a management company would need to cover its costs and achieve a reasonable profit. Therefore, this analysis of survey data cannot be conducted without a corresponding analysis of the costs associated with providing the services, which would need to be included elsewhere in the report.

*Management fee benchmarking: conclusion*—The market cost of acquiring management services can be determined either by securing comparative pricing for the desired services or by assessing the market for similar services through benchmark surveys. Because competitive market data may not available for management services provided to a single service line of a hospital, appraisers may consider the use of cost surveys for a variety of healthcare entities as a proxy for market-level hospital expense. This can assist the appraiser in determining whether the costs of purchasing management services are reasonable. It is not uncommon for appraisal reports to specifically state that a particular procedure was not relied upon as a primary means of analyzing the FMV of the proposed compensation. Instead, reports often indicate the performance of this type of analysis is a secondary measure of the reasonableness of the conclusions drawn from the consideration of other methodologies. There are circumstances in which an appraiser may rely upon this methodology as a primary determinant of FMV, but this, of course, should be decided by an appraiser on a case-by-case basis.

## IV. SPECIAL TOPICS IN MSC APPRAISAL

### 'At Risk' Compensation

One of the variables seen in some MSC compensation formulas is the inclusion of an "at-risk" component. This creates a situation where MSC compensation is variable. From an appraisal point of view, appraisers must turn to management for guidance as to the expected outcome in terms of paid compensation to the MSO.

Once the expected compensation has been quantified, the appraiser can then consider the impact of volatility in compensation outcomes. In certain scenarios, compensation may be in excess of the appraiser's initial range of FMV. In this situation, the appraiser should consult with management and legal counsel to determine whether this is an acceptable risk or whether the agreement can be modified to include some type of cap at the high end of the range of FMV.

Appraisers do not have the capacity to independently judge the likeliness of achieving a given performance benchmark. Therefore, the appraiser must rely on management to develop a sound understanding of the benchmarks and then consider whether or not management's estimates appear reasonable. The goal of the appraiser should be to collaborate with hospital management to ensure that the best possible estimates are used in the FMV opinion. In some cases, there will be insufficient data to make a judgment. In these instances, there will often be contractual clauses that trigger a reassessment of FMV when compensation falls outside of an expected range.

### Return on Investment (ROI) Analysis

One topic worth considering is the use of return on investment analyses with respect to the appraisal of MSCs. The general theory is that a physician's investment in an MSO selling services to a hospital should produce a return on investment similar to the return of an arm's-length investment. While an analysis can be performed in which the MSO's expected ROI is compared to market data, its probative value may be limited.

General market theory provides that investors will invest in businesses that generate the highest return commensurate with their tolerable level of risk. As a corollary, the greater the risk of an investment, the greater the return an investor would require to invest in the business. When reviewing ROI market data for management companies, as compared to a projected ROI for an MSC, it is very difficult to compare the risks of publicly traded companies to those of the management company under consideration. In addition, the capital investment required to run a publicly traded management company is significantly different than a one-off management company that may not even have its own separate office.

When the ROI definition of [income divided by investment] can change so significantly by the level of underlying investment, the usefulness of the entire ROI measure is suspect. For instance, if an appraiser determined a 10% to 75% ROI to be the range of FMV, it seems unreasonable that investors of the management company (20, for example) could achieve FMV status by each contributing an additional $5,000. The following two exhibits illustrate how unnecessary capital could distort the FMV analysis:

**Exhibit 1.**

| |
|---|
| Range of FMV—10% to 75% |
| Initial expected investment—$100,000 |
| Initial startup costs and working capital needs—$50,000 |
| Capital reserve—$50,000 |
| Expected annual return—$85,000 |
| ROI = 85% ($85,000 divided $100,000) |
| Conclusion: not consistent with FMV |

**Exhibit 2.**

| |
|---|
| Range of FMV—10% to 75% |
| Initial expected investment—$200,000 |
| Initial startup costs and working capital needs—$50,000 |
| Capital reserve—$150,000 |
| Expected annual return—$85,000 |
| ROI = 42.5% ($85,000 divided by $200,000) |
| Conclusion: consistent with FMV |

It does not stand to reason that holding $150,000 in capital reserve versus $50,000 in capital reserve for a non-asset-intensive firm is a good measure of FMV. [Editor's note: In a business valuation engagement, this would be considered "excess working capital" and a nonoperating asset.] While analyzing the adequacy of the capitalization of a management company is certainly a reasonable inquiry for an appraiser, the ability to depress ROI to be within a given range does not lend much credence to an ROI analysis.

Also of concern with respect to an ROI analysis is the selection of market data and the development of a comprehensive framework upon which to benchmark the characteristics of the management company for indicators of where in the range of identified ROIs the subject company should fall. Limiting factors include differences in size, services provided, differences in capital structure (publicly traded companies typically carry more debt than private MSCs), which make comparisons more complicated.

While this type of analysis cannot be relied upon as a primary measure of the FMV of this type of contractual arrangement, attorneys sometimes request that this procedure be considered by an appraiser.

## CONCLUSION

This chapter was designed to provide appraisers with an introduction to physician–hospital relationships in the management services context, an overview of the appraisal process, detailed descriptions of FMV analyses, and an introduction to select special topics related to MSCs.

The goal of the chapter is not to establish a right and wrong way of analyzing MSC compensation, but to provide a framework for analyzing FMV in the context of these types of arrangements. Ultimately, an appraiser must collaborate with all of the interested parties to gather sufficient evidence to certify that the MSC compensation is reasonable and consistent with FMV.

# Part V
# Valuation of Healthcare Enterprises

Chapter 38

# A Valuation Model for the Formation of ACOs

*By Carol W. Carden, CPA/ABV, ASA, CFE and Mark O. Dietrich, CPA/ABV*

This material was initially written in early 2011 prior to the release of the proposed and final regulations implementing the ACO provisions of the 2010 reform legislation and published in AHLA's *Health Lawyer's Weekly*. The authors have modified the content based on their understanding of the final regulations and added a detailed example illustrating their model.

## Part I

The movement toward accountable care organizations (ACOs) harkens back to the integrated delivery system models of the early 1990s that drove hospital-physician transactions throughout that decade. The healthcare provider community and the specialized healthcare industry appraisers that provide valuation opinions are confronted with the need to develop new valuation models that conform to the Stark law and anti-kickback statute, as well as anti-trust law—all as modified by the ACO final regulations—and recognize the underlying economic reality of the ACO model. These models will involve both determining the value of the ACO participants' investments into the entity and the fair market value compensation for their services.[1] The development of a fair market value fee schedule that guides the ACO in making payments to its various providers as a component of the ACO's operations will also be necessary for those ACOs that want to break away from the fee-for-service incentives inherent in

1 Over and above those of the various Medicare prospective payment systems.

using existing RBRVS-based fee schedules. It is not possible to forecast the operations of the ACO necessary for valuing asset contributions without knowing what the expenses of providers will be, of course.

Under the language of the Patient Protection and Affordable Care Act (PPACA) legislation, ACOs can take a number of different forms:

1. IN GENERAL.—Subject to the succeeding provisions of this subsection, as determined appropriate by the secretary, the following groups of providers of services and suppliers that have established a mechanism for shared governance are eligible to participate as ACOs under the program under this section:

    A. ACO professionals in group practice arrangements.

    B. Networks of individual practices of ACO professionals.

    C. Partnerships or joint venture arrangements between hospitals and ACO professionals.

    D. Hospitals employing ACO professionals.[2]

    E. Such other groups of providers of services and suppliers as the secretary determines appropriate.

ACO professionals are defined to include physicians (doctors of medicine or osteopathy) or practitioners, including physician assistants, nurse practitioners, and clinical nurse specialists. The final regulations also permit federally qualified health clinics and rural health clinics to form ACOs. Although only certain entities can actually form or sponsor an ACO, other types of providers and suppliers may be ACO participants under the auspices of a qualified ACO sponsor.

That said, given the lessons of the 1990s and the type of organizations successfully engaged in accountable-type arrangements today, such as capitation, it is clear that more integrated providers must emerge and this trend is already fully engaged in late 2011. In addition to superior physician medical directors with strong clinically based utilization controls, a successful ACO will require sophisticated information systems to

2 Critical access hospitals (CAH) were included as eligible in the final regulations if they submit bills for both facility and the professional services of physicians and practitioners to their Medicare fiscal intermediary (known as Method II).

both manage costs, particularly those of high-risk beneficiaries with multiple chronic conditions, and file the necessary reports with the Medicare program and other payors, as well as binding three-year contracts among its participants that permit the ACO to enter into entitywide contracts on a single-signature basis. A mechanism for identifying the minimum 5,000 Medicare beneficiaries receiving care from the ACO points once again to the use of primary care physicians (PCPs) as a means of capturing a defined patient base, particularly in light of the legislation's emphasis on the importance of primary care.

> (D) The ACO shall include *primary care ACO professionals* that are sufficient for the number of Medicare fee-for-service beneficiaries assigned to the ACO under subsection (c). At a minimum, the ACO shall have at least 5,000 such beneficiaries assigned to it under subsection (c) in order to be eligible to participate in the ACO program.[3] (Emphasis added.)

Medical homes are another significant aspect of the form of care contemplated by the ACO, and it is difficult to conceive a medical home model that does not have a primary care physician at its center.

2. Support patient-centered medical homes, defined as a mode of care that includes:

    A. personal physicians;

    B. whole person orientation;

    C. coordinated and integrated care;

    D. safe and high-quality care through evidence-informed medicine, appropriate use of health information technology, and continuous quality improvements;

    E. expanded access to care; and

    F. payment that recognizes added value from additional components of patient-centered care.[4]

3 Patient Protection and Affordable Care Act.
4 Ibid.

### *Lessons From the Risk-Based Models of the 1990s*

An important lesson from Medicare risk contracts of the 1990s, which continues into the current decade with certain forms of Medicare Advantage contracts, is that financial risk for the cost of care is a key element in driving success. Too much financial risk on any one segment of the entity bearing that risk, however, can lead to catastrophic failure and poor clinical results as well. Thus, a blend of risk and commensurate reward is an integral part of ACO structure—just as risk and reward are critical to developing a valuation model.

Authoritative guidance from the Centers for Medicare & Medicaid Services (CMS) came in the final regulations released in October 2011 as to the types of structures that qualify for ACO status. ACOs driving integration transactions have the following elements:

1. Need for significant capital to develop and contract the organization and to acquire information systems.
2. Need to contract a sufficient quantity of PCPs to have at least 5,000 Medicare beneficiaries in the ACO panel. Due to the significant actuarial risk of small risk-taking, fee-for-service panels, larger populations are desirable for so-called two-sided ACOs. (This is true even in light of CMS's minimum savings rate based on confidence intervals modeled using Monte Carlo simulations and the "stop-loss" coverage at roughly $100,000 of claims per beneficiary.)
3. Need for strong medical directors with experience in clinically based utilization management.
4. Need for sufficient coverage in the panel to prevent "leakage" to providers not part of the ACO. If non-ACO providers are utilized by panel members, the financial incentives are not properly aligned because the non-ACO providers do not have a vested interest in the success of the ACO. The proposed regulations cited extensive leakage of primary care visits approximating 25% in the Physician Group Practice Demonstration Project that is the basis for the ACO model.
5. Need for sophisticated management with experience in risk-based contracting.[5]

### *Primary Care Physicians*

Perhaps the most dramatic physician shortages are among primary care physicians, including general internal medicine, family medicine, and others collectively referred to as generalists.

5 So-called one-sided ACOs have no downside risk during the allowed three-year period; two-sided ACOs have both upside and downside risk.

> If the 2002–2005 rate of decline continues through 2008, the supply of generalists to provide adult care in 2025 will be only 2% above 2005 levels. . . . In the face of a 29% increase in workload, the adjusted supply figures point to a 20% shortage of adult care generalists in 2025, or 27% if graduate declines continue through 2008. These translate into shortfalls of 35,000 to 44,000 adult care generalists, assuming that generalists maintain current numbers of visits.[6]

Supply and demand have a substantial influence on the value of anything, including a primary care physician. Thus, the ACO movement coupled with the already well-established shortage of adult PCPs will drive up the compensation expectations of those physicians and the dollars ACOs and other competing organizations will need to pay to hire or contract adult PCPs. Further, a premium on midlevel providers has already emerged and will be a key element of ACO provider participation. The importance of PCPs drives the valuation model presented in the second part of this article.

### The Actual Transaction Must be Valued

One of the lessons of the tax court decision in *Derby*[7]—involving an integration transaction from the 1990s—is that appraisers *must* value the actual transaction; fair market value contemplates the price that would take place between a hypothetical buyer and seller of a specific interest or item of property. The transaction itself is not a "hypothetical," and failure to recognize that point makes many valuations inaccurate. Thus, contrary to the view held by many appraisers who are not familiar with the regulatory structure of the healthcare industry, any valuation of an ACO requires the appraiser to be intimately familiar with the transaction documents. If those documents change after the valuation is completed, the valuation should be reconciled to the final version of the documents.

As appraisers in the healthcare industry, it is also important to bear in mind the Covenant Medical Center settlement from 2009. In this particular settlement, even though the hospital obtained fair market compensation opinions, the regulators rejected the opinions. Therefore, it is critical to not only do valuations for ACO transactions, but to also do them using sound methodologies and assumptions.

The most common barrier to physician participation in capital-intensive undertakings is the lack of desire or ability to put up cash to match that contributed by the hospital,

6 "Will Generalist Physician Supply Meet Demands of an Increasing and Aging Population?" Jack M. Colwill, James M. Cultice, and Robin L. Kruse; *Health Affairs*, 29 April 2008.

7 T.C. Memo. 2008-45, involving a tax-exempt hospital system and private practice physicians.

health system, or similar co-venturer. This is also the most common source of potential overvaluation of goodwill and other intangibles leading to regulatory concerns under Stark, the anti-kickback statute (AKS), and the anti-inurement provisions of the Internal Revenue Code.

The structure of the ACO and distribution of the (hoped for) profits therefrom can be used to ameliorate both the capital concern of the physician and the regulatory risk associated with lack of physician capital. Appraisers as well as ACO participants should keep in mind, however, the following requirements for tax-exempt hospitals participating in an ACO:

1. The tax-exempt organization's share of the ACO's losses (including its share of Multipurpose Senior Services Program, or MSSP, losses) does not exceed the share of ACO economic benefits to which the tax-exempt organization is entitled.

2. All contracts and transactions entered into by the tax-exempt organization with the ACO and the ACO's participants and by the ACO with the ACO's participants and any other parties are at fair market value."[8]

It will be incumbent upon the appraiser to conduct the engagement in such a manner that the "ACO's losses [do] not exceed economic benefits to which the tax-exempt organization is entitled."

### Areas for Valuation Consideration

There are two primary areas where valuation services may come into play for ACO arrangements. A valuation will be needed for purposes of determining the equity investment of the respective owners of the ACO. Additionally, a methodology for payment of the services delivered by the various members of the ACO (i.e., hospital, PCP, specialists, and ancillary providers, such as imaging centers) will need to be developed if existing fee-for-service incentives that undercut reduced utilization goals are to be eliminated.[9] It is likely that this fee payment methodology, given the regulatory risks of splitting reimbursement among various, otherwise unrelated, referral sources, will require the opinion of an appraiser. Therefore, the business valuation professional will need to understand the relative intensity of the various services included in the ACO bundled payment if that option is chosen to appropriately develop a fee schedule that the ACO

8 Notice 2011-20.

9 Based on present regulations, Medicare will pay providers under the various existing prospective payment system (PPS) models.

can use to pay providers on a regular, ongoing basis, outside of any payments to the ACO providers related to their equity investment. We will address valuation issues related to appraisal of the ACO participants' equity contributions in the following section with development of the fair market value fee schedule to follow later in this chapter.

## Valuation of the ACO Participants' Equity Investment

### *Assigning Valuation Risk Rates to the ACO*

Most appraisers focus their development of the risk of a transaction or business on the right-hand side of the balance sheet consisting of debt and equity. However, as the term suggests, a balance sheet has an *equal and offsetting* quantity on the *left*-hand side: the assets. As such, *the risk of a specified transaction can be determined by assigning risk-based rates of return to the assets of the ACO.*[10] This calculation is then tested for the required equality with the traditional debt and equity-based determination of risk rates.

In addition to the common risk factors considered in traditional debt and equity-based risk rates, the following are some of the additional factors that should be considered for an ACO:

- Actuarial risk, including stop-loss level (set at approximately $100,000 in the final regulations);
- Inability to control out-referrals and utilization due to lack of a gatekeeper model;
- Heightened uncertainty regarding projections;
- Intensity of coding by physicians and specialists in particular;
- Intensity of ancillary utilization;
- Utilization of hospital in-patient and outpatient services where less expensive service venues are available;
- ACO providers are not required by the final regulations to stay in the ACO for the full three-year minimum term required. This places a premium on contracting language for the ACO with respect to its participating providers;
- What entity or entities are forming and sponsoring the ACO? The risk factors

10 This is the underlying basis of valuation for the Financial Accounting Standards 164 testing of goodwill and other intangibles for impairment.

for a physician-only ACO will be different from a hospital-only ACO or one formed by both physicians and hospitals; and

- What entity or entities are participating in the ACO even though they may not have an ownership interest? The presence or lack of aligned incentives is critical to risk determination.

This approach is consistent with the concepts employed in valuations done for fair value financial reporting purposes where rates of return are assigned to the various asset categories as the preliminary valuation approach. Then, as a testing to the results achieved, the weighted average of the various asset risks are compared to the weighted average cost of capital for the entity to ensure that the risks assigned to the bundle of assets "reconciles" to the appraiser's overall assessment of the risk of the organization. A similar methodology could be employed in the valuation of the participants' asset contributions into the ACO.

Assets have a risk gradient from low to high that starts with cash and working capital (accounts receivable and inventory) then moves to fixed assets (equipment and furniture) then certain intangible assets, and finally goodwill. The greater the risk, the higher the expected return. *Thus, contributions of cash to purchase fixed assets for an ACO would have a relatively low rate of return assigned, while the contribution of intangible assets would have a higher rate of return assigned.*[11] Exhibit 1 depicts the relative risk gradient of various categories of assets.

**Exhibit 1. Risk and Rate of Return for Types of Assets**

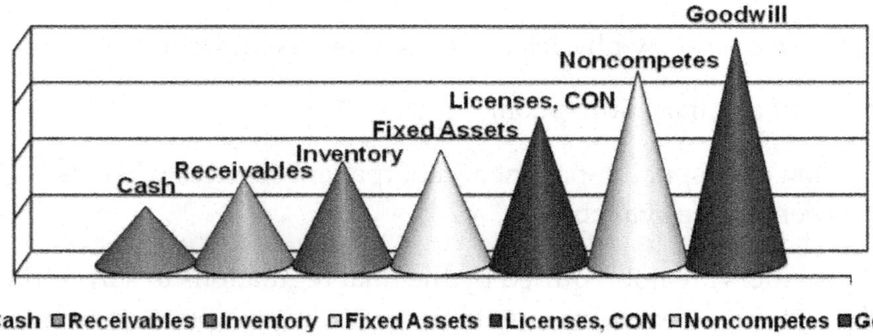


11 Conversely, high rates of return translate to low valuation multiples, such that intangible assets have a lower value per dollar of cash profit generated.

In the structure of cash and liquidating distributions, the risk needs to be considered not only from an expected rate of return standpoint, but also from a risk of failure standpoint. Thus, distribution priority typically is assigned based on the asset risk gradient such that contributions of cash to acquire fixed assets would receive their return out of profit first before higher risk contributions were paid. Similarly, liquidating distributions would give priority to cash contributions or the assets acquired with them with contributions of intangible assets—such as a patient base—returned to their contributor as well. *To the extent that a contribution by one party to the venture has a priority claim on distributions versus that of another party, the priority claim has a lower risk and lower expected rate of return associated with it.*

Although often missed, the term of a contract has a significant impact on the underlying risk, and therefore, the expected rate of return. For simplicity and because business valuation generally assumes perpetual life for the business, appraisers typically use a single expected rate of return to account for all future periods and those periods' cash returns. In fact, the nearer years have less uncertainty associated with them than do the later years: It is more difficult to forecast what will happen in five years than it is to forecast what will happen in six months, although both can be challenging. As a technical matter, this term risk can be seen by examining the yields on various United States Treasury securities. For example, Treasury bills with a 90-day term have a dramatically lower yield than Treasury bonds, which have a 30-year term at issue. In valuation, the difference between the two is known as the horizon [risk] premium. *Shorter terms have less risk than longer terms.*[12]

In addition to the difference in the rates of return on different assets, there is also a difference in the return on the capital used to acquire those assets versus the return on labor for individuals working with those assets. A PCP contracting with an ACO thus would look to two potential sources of return: a return on capital associated with any assets he or she contributes to the ACO and a return on labor associated with any services provided to the ACO. Later herein, we describe how this allocation affects valuation of the medical practice in the event of a contemplated sale.

Exhibit 2 illustrates how a physician practice generates both a return on labor and a return on the assets utilized in the practice and by extension, the need to differentiate the two.

12 There are times when the so-called "yield curve" for interest-bearing securities is inverted, leading to short-term rates being higher than long-term rates.

**Exhibit 2. Generating Both a Return on Labor and a Return on Assets**

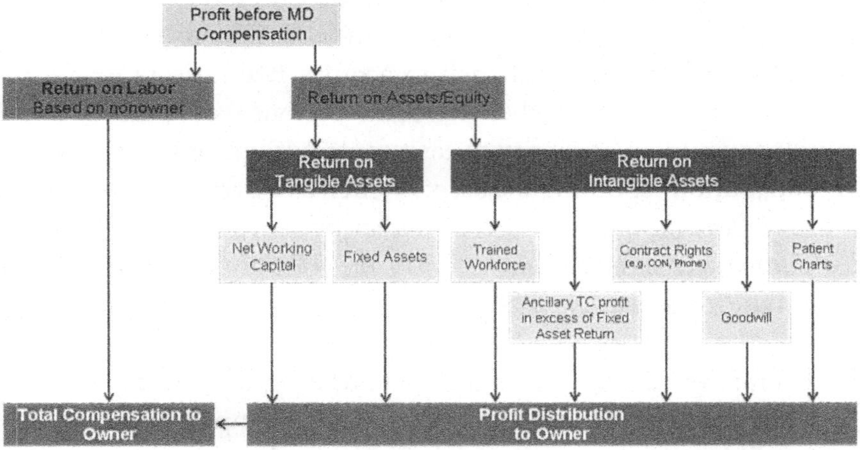




In summary, within the context of an actual ACO transaction, the appraiser must consider the risk of the asset (as outlined in Exhibit 1), the contractual documents of the ACO as to the priority and amount of return on the assets invested, which participants bear the risk of loss if the ACO fails to generate profits, and finally, how to compensate participants for the labor (as opposed to capital) they provide to the ACO.

***Developing the Rate of Return***

Contribution of cash or tangible equipment into the ACO is a fairly straightforward exercise from a valuator's standpoint due to the relative risk characteristics just discussed. The real challenge to the business appraiser is the assignment of equity contribution for the intangible assets contributed by the various ACO owners. The principal intangible asset a PCP is likely to contribute to an ACO is a patient base. As indicated above, the PCP will also be compensated for care[13] (labor) provided to the patients in that patient base, but these are two distinct cash return streams: one associated with an asset that an ACO cannot exist without and the other associated with labor that the PCP will be compensated for, whether in the ACO or not. Thus, this should not be seen as a double count. The PCP joining an ACO will be foregoing other opportunities for deploying this patient base, perhaps to a competing ACO.

In its Nov. 22, 2010 letter to CMS Administrator Daniel Berwick, the Medicare Payment

13 Typically, on a fee-for-service basis, primary care capitation, or a combination of the two.

Advisory Commission (MedPAC) argued vigorously for a requirement that beneficiaries be notified of their assignment to an ACO, a position adopted to a large extent in the final regulations released in October 2011. MedPAC cited many of the issues that arose with gatekeeper models in the 1990s, the backlash against which contributed to the ever-expanding growth rate in healthcare spending. In light of this suggestion and the import of PCPs in defining a "patient base," we will focus on the contribution of the patient base because this will be a common intangible asset required by most ACOs. To develop an appropriate rate of return for the patient base, the appraiser needs to look at asset risk and term risk, as described earlier, along with the actual ACO documents. The patient base asset is an intangible so it will have a relatively high risk and therefore, high expected rate of return. Conversely, the patient base would have a relatively low value per expected dollar of cash flow from profit because high risk translates to a low valuation multiple.

It is important to note that the value of any business, commodity, or intangible asset depends upon the market conditions that exist at the date of valuation. For example, due to economic uncertainty not seen since the late 1970s, the price of gold is at historical highs. Similarly, primary care practices were in high demand and very valuable in the 1990s relative to specialty practices and are yet again. In the run-up to the reform legislation, cardiology practices had been in high demand due to cutbacks in nuclear medicine and consultation fees paid to physicians and the importance of cardiovascular admissions to acute care hospitals. Unlike the supply and demand-based valuation of commodities such as gold, the valuation of physician practices and their assets must consider anti-referral and anti-kickback issues, a particular problem for cardiology practices.

The determination of risk and return for any of the ACO assets will be dependent upon the earnings stream available from the ACO that can, in turn, be attributed to the various assets to provide the return. To determine the available earnings stream, management and the appraiser will need to develop a forecast of expected shared savings for Medicare (and perhaps other participating payors) that will lead to profits for the ACO. These profits will then need to be allocated to the various assets of the ACO based upon the assessment of risk of those assets. This exercise also assists potential ACO participants in assessing the desirability of participation. In other words, is the available earnings stream sufficient to appropriately reward the participant for the risk of investing his or her asset?

Once the determination is made that the economics of the ACO makes sense to participants (at least based upon management's preliminary analysis), management needs to ensure the participation of providers who bring to the table at least 5,000 Medicare beneficiaries.

Although purchasing primary care practices is one option, one potential alternative may be contracting the PCP's patient base to the ACO via a licensing agreement.[14] This method is similar to that which might be employed by a facility requiring a certificate of need, or CON. CONs are typically valued on a "relief from royalty" basis. The royalty is based upon a percentage of net revenue that, importantly, is compared to the expected profits of the entity associated with the licensing. The royalty or licensing fee as a percentage of net revenue would typically be in the range of 1% to no more than 5% and not exceed 20% of expected profit and may be much less than that. This royalty also needs to be tested against the returns required for other assets contributed to the ACO. Again, valuation in such a circumstance requires appraiser consideration of the expected returns of all assets of the ACO as opposed to just the patient base and undertaking that consideration within the context of the documents establishing the ACO.

### Development of the ACO Fee Schedule

Once a determination is made relative to the fair market value of the various assets needed to operationalize the ACO, the next challenge to the appraiser will generally be assisting ACO management in developing a fee schedule, assuming that something other than the existing payor fee schedule will be used as a means of compensating providers on an interim basis.[15] This fee schedule will be used on a regular, at least monthly and probably more frequently than that, basis to compensate providers for the labor portion of their contribution to the ACO.

To illustrate the necessity for the development of a fee schedule, consider that, in the current fee-for-service environment, a PCP treats a patient in his or her office. Following delivery of this service, the PCP sends a bill to a non-Medicare payor. Two weeks or so after delivering the bill, the PCP receives payment of the agreed-upon fee for delivery of the patient care service. This routine process happens daily (or at least weekly for smaller practices) and provides the cash flows necessary for the PCP to pay normal operating expenses, such as staff salaries, rent, supplies, and to provide for the PCP's compensation. When the PCP's services are contracted and not employed and payments are not made directly to the PCP, the ACO needs a mechanism by which to provide this routine cash flow to the PCP rather than the PCP waiting for cash distributions related to the investment in the ACO. It may also be that given the simplicity of fee-for-service payments on a current basis from both Medicare and other payors, *retroactive*

14 Recognizing that many of the relationships contemplated by ACOs require the regulatory waivers including preparticipation waivers, such as paying for a primary care physician patient base on other than a purchase basis.
15 Medicare fee schedule payments will continue in Medicare shared savings models. At least at the outset, the prevailing Medicare fee schedule is likely to be used for all ACO participants. This translates into a higher degree of risk for realization of shared savings.

re-valuation of services for purposes of ACO shared savings or shared loss distributions may be employed.

In developing such a fee schedule or other interim payment mechanism, the appraiser must take into the consideration the complement of services contemplated to come from Medicare (or other payors) in the form of the ACO bundled payment, a separate feature of the reform legislation for Medicare that may be adopted by those in ACOs as well. The challenge to the appraiser will be to evaluate the relative intensity of the services included in the ACO bundle as well as the expected frequency of the various types of services to be delivered. It will be critical for the appraiser to gain an understanding of the payment methodology stipulated in the ACO documents. In other words, does the ACO plan to compensate providers on some type of fee schedule basis or is the payment methodology intended to be a form of capitation either on a per-patient basis or by a flat monthly payment for services delivered? By the same token, if the ACO is to share downside risk for failure to meet budget, the payment mechanism should take account that risk and provide for some form of retention, such as a withhold of a portion of the fee-for-service payment or reduced capitation.

#### *Evaluating Benchmarks for Fees*

Once an understanding has been gained relative to the payment methodology and relative intensity and frequency of services to be delivered by ACO providers, the appraisers must then settle on a valuation methodology by which to assign value to the various services to be delivered. A starting point for this analysis could be the Medicare fee schedule[16] for services delivered on a fee-for-service basis. Of course, if the ACO encompasses more than Medicare beneficiaries, the appraiser will have to gain an understanding of the reimbursement rates for the commercial payors relative to Medicare.

An important consideration to be made in the determination of the ACO fee schedule using Medicare as a basis[17] is that for the ACO to be profitable, it will have to reduce costs from those currently incurred by Medicare. In absence of these cost reductions, the ACO will have no operating profits and could very well incur losses that would need to be funded by its owners. Therefore, when using Medicare as the basis for the fee schedule, one of two assumptions must be made. Either the fees on a per-procedure basis must be reduced or the volume of services delivered must be reduced. Otherwise, the cost to the ACO will be identical to what Medicare is incurring and the ACO model will fail. For the ACO to succeed, some "failure" of revenue must occur amongst the

16 Or given the limitations of the sustainable growth rate (SGR) formula, the relative value units (RVUs) assigned by the resource-based relative value scale employed by Medicare at some market-based conversion factor.
17 The SGR-driven limitations of the Medicare fee schedule described in the previous footnote complicate the establishment of an ACO fee schedule.

providers who treat the beneficiaries. This may affect which providers the ACO sponsor permits to become ACO participants.

#### *Determining the Impact of Other Factors on the Fee Schedule*

In addition to gaining an understanding of the services included in the ACO bundled payment and the relative frequency and intensity of services to be delivered by ACO providers, other factors must be considered in the development of the ACO fee schedule. These factors include: 1) costs associated with administering the ACO; 2) the impact (i.e., costs) of "leakage" if non-ACO providers are utilized to provide a portion of the bundled service; and 3) the profit retention policy of the ACO.[18] In essence, the ACO must be able to meet all of its obligations in addition to paying providers for their labor contributions. For consideration to be made for all of the ACO obligations, the appraiser must gain an understanding of the operations of the ACO in its entirety when developing the ACO fee schedule to avoid creating a fee schedule that results in unintended financial losses.

#### *Implications if the Fee Schedule Is Too High*

If the other obligations of the ACO are not factored into the ACO fee schedule, the unintended consequence is that the fee schedule is too high and the ACO providers will be overpaid. There are two significant implications of a fee schedule that is too high and therefore, exceeds fair market value. One consequence is that the ACO owners will not receive an appropriate return on their investment commensurate with the risks assumed as discussed previously in this article. The second implication, and one that has significant ramifications for both the ACO and the individual ACO providers, is that payment of fees that exceed fair market value could result in a violation of the AKS, as well as the Stark law, if the provider has equity ownership in the ACO. There are many regulatory considerations to be made in the structure of an ACO, and ACO management would be well-advised to engage competent legal counsel experienced in healthcare regulations. That said, the waivers available under the final rule are quite broad and may be sufficient to protect compensation that arguably exceeds fair market value. (Note that the IRS position for exempt organizations may not be so flexible: See Notice 2011-20.)

### Summary of Part I

ACOs are extremely complex from an organizational, infrastructure, and operational standpoint. From the perspective of appraisers, ACOs should generate a fair amount of

---

18 This raises a technical valuation question because standard appraisal practice uses a midyear assumption as to cash distributions as opposed to an end-of-year assumption, the former yielding a higher value. The midyear assumption may be inappropriate if transaction documents call for end-of-year distributions or no distributions for several years.

valuation and financial consulting work. However, due to the complexity of the ACO structure as well as the healthcare regulations that govern ACOs, it is critical that the appraiser has the relevant background and experience to provide valuation services to ACOs. The consequences of a valuation that is outside the scope of the waivers of Stark, the AKS, and the civil monetary penalty (CMP) provisions are dire and far-reaching to the owners and providers associated with the ACO.

## Part II—Building the ACO Valuation Model

In Part I, we provided an overview of both the ACO as well as the issues to be considered in valuation engagements. In Part II, we look more in-depth at structuring the actual valuation model and assumptions, as well as valuing a physician practice[19] patient base.

As discussed earlier, the ACO documents are keys to the valuation engagement because they will provide the data necessary to develop the risk or discount rates to be used by the valuation analyst. The following is a list of factors described in Part I as well as other factors the appraiser should consider in the discount rate development.

### *Summary of Factors Influencing the Discount Rate*

1. Nature of assets contributed:
    a. Cash;
    b. Fixed assets; and
    c. Intangible assets such as a patient base;
2. Return of capital distributions;
3. Priority of profit distributions, if any;
4. Priority of claims in liquidation, if any;
5. Need for liquidity; particularly important for Track 2 or risk-taking ACOs that must provide CMS with the means by which they will pay any shared losses;
6. Liquidity of contributed assets;
7. Leakage or out-referral risk;
8. Existing utilization patterns and coding intensity; and
9. Equity classes, e.g., single class, multiple classes, voting rights, and so on.

19 Here we will be talking specifically about primary care practices.

## Example[20]

For ease of presentation, the fact pattern in Exhibit 3 is kept simple. In reality, the ability of the ACO to reasonably forecast shared savings will be complicated by the resetting of its benchmark or budget over the term of the ACO agreement. CMS contemplates a number of factors that may affect future benchmark setting, in addition to the actual performance of the ACO itself.

There are three classes of ACO participants and equity holders: hospital, PCPs, and specialists. The hospital contributes cash of $4 million and $750,000 of furniture and equipment. PCPs contribute $1,000 per physician plus the value[21] of their Medicare patient base. Specialists contribute $10,000 per physician. (See Exhibit 3.)

**Exhibit 3. Sample ACO Assets**

| Assets Contributed | Hospital | PCPs | Specialists | Totals |
|---|---|---|---|---|
| Cash | 4,000,000 | 32,000 | 420,000 | 4,452,000 |
| Furniture | 100,000 | | | 100,000 |
| Computer Equipment | 150,000 | | | 150,000 |
| Electronic Health Records System | 500,000 | | | 500,000 |
| Patient Base | | 929,000 | | 929,000 |
| | 4,750,000 | 961,000 | 420,000 | 6,131,000 |
| **Equity Allocation** | 77.5% | 15.7% | 6.9% | 100.0% |
| *ACO Professional Count* | | *21* | *42* | |

The appraiser estimates the average number of Medicare patients for each of the 21 participating PCP practices at approximately 715, resulting in anticipated beneficiaries to be assigned to the ACO of 15,000. As a cross-check of this calculation, the appraiser finds that the PCPs experienced an aggregate 30,000 annual visits from Medicare beneficiaries based on CMS-supplied data and that the expected rate of PCP visits per beneficiary per annum is two. (See Exhibit 4.)

20 All values have been rounded, so individual totals may not calculate precisely.

21 The expectation is that the payment for this patient base would qualify for a shared savings waiver as an incentive to attract primary care physicians.

**Exhibit 4. Anticipated Beneficiaries**

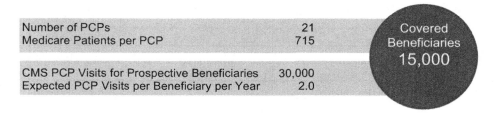

| | |
|---|---|
| Number of PCPs | 21 |
| Medicare Patients per PCP | 715 |
| CMS PCP Visits for Prospective Beneficiaries | 30,000 |
| Expected PCP Visits per Beneficiary per Year | 2.0 |

Covered Beneficiaries
15,000

Three sources of potential savings are identified: reduction in average length of stay (ALOS), reduction in admissions, and reduction in coding intensity by specialists. The reduction in average length of stay is a savings that comes out of operating costs rather than from reduction in fee-for-service revenue from the Medicare program, thus the Medicare program does not participate in those savings. (See Exhibit 5.)

**Exhibit 5. Estimated ACO Shared Savings**

| Estimated ACO Shared Savings | | |
|---|---|---|
| *Fact Pattern* | | |
| Covered Beneficiaries | | 15,000 |
| Cost per Beneficiary Year | | 10,800 |
| ACO Budget | | 162,000,000 |
| Existing ALOS per 1000 | | 6.5 |
| Reduction in ALOS | 10% | 0.65 |
| Case-Weighted Average MS-DRG | | 14,000 |
| Admissions per 1000 | | 340 |
| Expected admissions | | 5,100 |
| Average cost per Day 3 and later in LOS | | 1,400 |
| Reduction in Admissions | 5% | 255 |
| MD Visits per Beneficiary | | 8.0 |
| MD Visits | | 120,000 |
| Reduction in coding intensity $ from correct coding initiative | | 5 |

Forecasted revenue from Medicare program shared savings and cost savings for the ACO totals $6,911,000, consisting of $3,570,000 from reduced admissions and $600,000 in coding reduction for specialists, totaling $4,170,000, of which the ACO expects to receive the shared savings program maximum 60%, or $2,502,000. Cost reductions resulting from shortened length of stay that are not required to be shared with the Medicare program are $4,409,000. (See Exhibit 6.)

**Exhibit 6. Shared Savings Forecast**

| Shared Savings Forecast | Loss-/Benefit+ | Units | Rate | Savings |
|---|---|---|---|---|
| Reduced admissions | Hospital − | 255 | 14,000 | 3,570,000 |
| Coding intensity reduction | MDs − | 120,000 | 5 | 600,000 |
| Shared Savings | | | | 4,170,000 |
| ACO Share (assume 100% quality score) | | | | 60% |
| Medicare Program Shared Savings | | | | 2,502,000 |
| Reduced Length of Stay | Hospital + | 3,149 | 1,400 | 4,409,000 |
| ACO Revenue | | | | 6,911,000 |
| Rounded | | | | 6,911,000 |

The parties agree to split 50% of any ALOS cost savings 70% to the hospital, 25% to the specialists who will manage the inpatient cases in conjunction with hospitalists, and 5% to the PCPs, subject to the parties each receiving the Tier 1 priority return on their capital contributions described in the next paragraph. The appraiser deems this provision necessary to conform to the IRS's position that "ACO's losses [do] not exceed economic benefits to which the tax-exempt organization is entitled."

The ACO limited liability company (LLC) operating agreement provides that the hospital and physicians will receive a Tier 1 priority return[22] of 4% on their cash investment; the hospital will receive 6% on its fixed assets. The ACO will be taxed as a partnership, and distributions will be in the form of "guaranteed payments" deductible under IRC Section 707(c). (See Exhibit 7.)

**Exhibit 7. Assets Contributed**

| Assets Contributed | Hospital | PCPs | Specialists | Totals | Tier 1 ROI | |
|---|---|---|---|---|---|---|
| Cash | 4,000,000 | 32,000 | 420,000 | 4,452,000 | 4.0% | 178,000 |
| Furniture | 100,000 | | | 100,000 | 6.0% | 6,000 |
| Computer Equipment | 150,000 | | | 150,000 | 6.0% | 9,000 |
| Electronic Health Records System | 500,000 | | | 500,000 | 6.0% | 30,000 |
| Patient Base | | 929,000 | | 929,000 | | |
| | 4,750,000 | 961,000 | 420,000 | 6,131,000 | | 223,000 |
| **Equity Allocation** | 77.5% | 15.7% | 6.9% | 100.0% | | |

The hospital and physicians have a (ratable) priority claim on any assets in liquidation of the ACO should it fail equal to their cash contributions. Liquidating distributions in excess of cash contributed then go to a return of capital contributed for fixed assets and then based upon remaining capital account balances. PCPs receive their Medicare

22 ROI equals return on investment.

patient base in liquidation, subject to sharing in any deficit remaining to the extent of their percentage equity interest.

The appraisal of the value of the contribution of the PCP patient base is based upon the ACO having a potential revenue base of $6,911,000, including the savings from reduction in length of stay. The valuation is based upon the relief from royalty method, looking both to the potential revenue and the potential profits, with a ceiling on the potential royalty of 20% of forecasted profit. The appraiser believes that 15% of forecasted profit or 5% of revenue is an appropriate measure of the royalty value of the patient base, given the priority claims of the cash capital contributions and other market-related research. This results in an expected royalty payment of $323,000. Since this is a guaranteed payment deductible by the ACO, it is "pretax."

To determine the value of the patient base as a contribution to capital, the appraiser selects a discount rate of 25%.[23] Since the ACO is taxed as a pass-through entity, the royalty payment is tax-effected at 28%, which the appraiser determines represents the effective tax rate for a pass-through, rather than the 40% rate that might be used for a regular C corporation. Capitalizing the resulting after-tax royalty stream of $232,000 at 25% results in a value of the patient base of $929,000. Should the hospital desire to acquire the PCP practices to create an employment model ACO, the $929,000 (or approximately $44,000 per PCP, or $62 per patient) would be one element of intangible value, all other things being equal.

The ACO expects to incur $2,150,000 of operating costs in generating $6,911,000 of shared savings and cost reductions. Note: Absent the ALOS cost savings, the Medicare shared savings would be insufficient to cause the ACO to go forward. (See Exhibit 8.)

**Exhibit 8. ACO Forecasted Profit and Loss**

| ACO Forecasted Profit & Loss | |
|---|---|
| Shared Savings | 2,502,000 |
| Cost Savings | 4,409,000 |
| | 6,911,000 |
| Operating Costs | |
| Labor | 1,500,000 |
| Depreciation | 150,000 |
| Other Overhead | 500,000 |
| | 2,150,000 |
| Profit for Distribution | 4,761,000 |

23 Again for simplicity, the discount rate is presumed equal to the cap rate and the commitment of the patient base to the ACO is deemed to be perpetual. If a limited period of the patient base is contemplated, the calculations would have to be modified to reflect that limited period.

Assuming the ACO achieves its forecast, the total profit will be distributed as shown in Exhibit 9. The Tier 1 ROI is based upon cash and fixed asset contributions. The cost savings allocation of $2,205,000 is 50% of $4,409,000 (the savings from the reduction in ALOS). The Tier 2 distribution to the PCPs is $323,000, with the remaining profit of $2,010,000 split based upon equity interests. Exhibit 9 also recaps each class of participant's net result from ACO participation.

Note: The hospital's entire revenue loss from reduced admissions is shown; however, it may also be able to reduce variable costs on a marginal basis to offset this revenue loss, which is not shown. The hospital could also benefit if it owned the skilled nursing facility or home health agency utilized in the length of stay reduction.

**Exhibit 9. Profit for Distribution**

| Profit for Distribution | | | | 4,761,000 |
|---|---|---|---|---|
| Tier 1 ROI | 205,000 | 1,000 | 17,000 | 223,000 |
| Cost Savings Allocation | 1,544,000 | 110,000 | 551,000 | 2,205,000 |
| Tier 2 ROI | | 323,000 | | 323,000 |
| | 1,749,000 | 434,000 | 568,000 | 2,751,000 |
| Equity Shares | 1,557,000 | 315,000 | 138,000 | 2,010,000 |
| Total Distribution | 3,306,000 | 749,000 | 706,000 | 4,761,000 |
| Revenue Loss | (3,570,000) | | (600,000) | (4,170,000) |
| | (264,000) | 749,000 | 106,000 | 591,000 |

## Summary

For the ACO to be successful, it must, of necessity, reduce utilization, since cost, absent a separate bundled payment mechanism, will be based upon existing Medicare PPS and fee-for-service systems. The most readily available utilization reductions are likely to be on the hospital inpatient side, resulting from improvement in such clinical risk factors as management of diabetic, hypertensive, and coronary artery disease patients. Other sources of utilization reduction include better primary care management of patients resulting in fewer specialty referrals along with lower volumes of ancillary services such as imaging. Lower utilization results in less revenue from Medicare to providers treating assigned Medicare beneficiaries, setting up a conflict between providers' desire to maximize Medicare revenue and the ACO's desire to reduce payments from the Medicare system to generate shared savings. ACO participants, particularly hospitals, will only be winners under this model if there is a corresponding cost reduction to offset the loss of fee-for-service revenues.

Chapter 39

# Valuation Considerations Specific to Diagnostic Imaging Entities

*By Douglas G. Smith*

Editor's Introduction: *Appraisers and valuation analysts are often confronted with complex businesses or industries that require detailed study to understand or the retention of an industry expert for assistance. The healthcare industry is a broad example of such an area and the subset involving imaging, particularly high-tech imaging, is more complex still. This chapter is contributed by a leading industry consultant who "talks" to the valuation community about how to approach the development of revenue and expense forecasts that form the underlying basis for a conclusion of value under the income approach.*

There have been a number of significant regulatory, rulemaking, and healthcare landscape changes with material significance to the diagnostic imaging sector since publication of this chapter back in 2009 and the Webinar on this subject in 2011.

These changes in landscape and payment mechanisms continue to highlight the unique considerations related to diagnostic imaging facilities that may not be understood with sufficient specificity by many highly skilled valuation specialists who have not had the opportunity to routinely participate in the diagnostic imaging business space. Diagnostic Imaging is a business sector in which the old adage of "if you've see one valuation", or "If you've performed one valuation," you can be relatively sure the other valuations following will be the same is definitely far from reality; it is more akin to if you've see one valuation, you've seen one valuation. The differences between one facility and another, today, can be quite substantial due to a number of variables in center content and local area influences on the business.

In this section we will provide a detailed understanding of the many unique considerations specific to diagnostic imaging entities. Although a variety of the core elements of a medical practice valuation for other medical specialties can be directly applicable to diagnostic imaging entities, a number of unique elements of revenue and expense requires specific knowledge and experience to assure that an imaging entity valuation is an accurate representation of its value.

We will discuss, explore, and review the following:

1. The unique structure of diagnostic imaging services requiring analysis;

2. The primary influences on diagnostic imaging entity revenue streams; factors for consideration and analysis of historical performance; principal considerations in forecasting future streams of revenue in specific settings and markets;

3. Long-standing, current, recently enacted, and rending regulatory impacts specific to diagnostic imaging entities in certain settings and the analysis required to accurately understand their real and potential impacts to valuations when forecasting future revenue streams;

4. Existing and emerging third-party payor trends and considerations when forecasting diagnostic imaging reimbursement;

5. The primary influences and considerations required when analyzing and forecasting diagnostic imaging infrastructure expense; and

6. Potential landmines and valuation considerations that can come back to haunt you.

To set the stage and make sure we are all using the same language and references, I will list a rather universal set of diagnostic imaging entities you may be engaged to value. The list is not necessarily in any order of interest or importance. There are nuances within the construct of each entity type that need to be taken into consideration when valuing these entities. You should become familiar with each. However, in the interest of time and space available, we will not go into the nuances and subtleties of each entity type with any depth or specificity at this time. The core considerations for all imaging entities discussed will apply to all entity types mentioned here.

- Provider entity- or hospital-owned freestanding imaging center;

- Radiology group-owned "office" imaging center;

- Radiology group- or hospital-owned clinic imaging center;
- Radiology group-hospital independent diagnostic testing facility (IDTF);
- Hospital-radiology group joint venture provider model entity;
- Radiology group, physician group, or hospital freestanding imaging center (IDTF);
- Physician office imaging entity;
- Corporate imaging center(IDTF);
- Mobile diagnostic imaging services;
- Specialty hospital imaging center; and
- OWA (other weird arrangements).

## I. The Unique Structure of Diagnostic Imaging Services Requiring Analysis

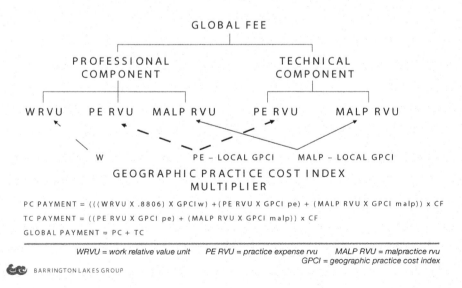

Diagnostic imaging services, unlike medicine services, are billed to third party payors as 1. global services (technical component and professional component together); 2. technical component services only; 3. professional component only services; or, 4. for certain payors, a mix of global, technical, and professional services (see Exhibit 1).

**Exhibit 1. Payment Basis, Diagnostic Imaging Services**

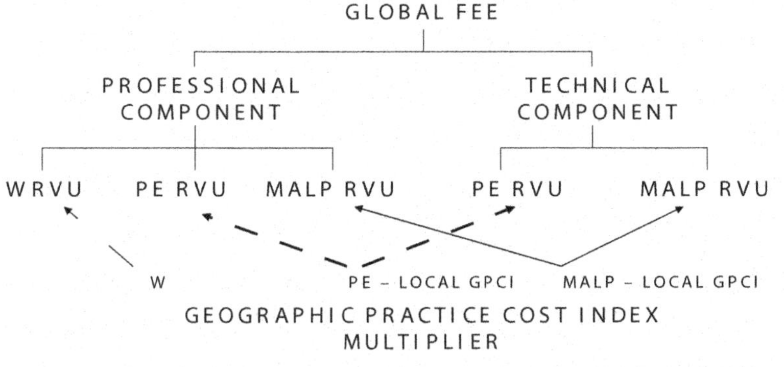


PC PAYMENT = (((WRVU X .8806) X GPCIw) +(PE RVU X GPCI pe) + (MALP RVU X GPCI malp)) x CF

TC PAYMENT = ((PE RVU X GPCI pe) + (MALP RVU X GPCI malp)) x CF

GLOBAL PAYMENT = PC + TC

*WRVU = work relative value unit* *PE RVU = practice expense rvu* *MALP RVU = malpractice rvu* *GPCI = geographic practice cost index*

BARRINGTON LAKES GROUP

Generally, a diagnostic imaging entity will bill global services and receive a global payment from third-party payors. The revenue line in the financial statement will include, by definition, payment for the professional interpretation of the studies performed at the facility as part of the global fee. The entity will then pay a radiologist, radiology group, or other professional services entity for the professional interpretation in accordance with a Professional Services Agreement, and such costs should appear as a line item of expense in the financial statement. The technical component revenue is the principal source of net revenue. The exception to this rule is in the private practice radiology setting, where the professional component is not later expressed as a separate expense to the group.

The importance of understanding the nuances of diagnostic imaging revenue elements is well known to those who have valued diagnostic imaging facilities pre-2005 and post-2005. For those who have not had the experience of doing so, you are in for a real treat when performing an analysis of historical revenue streams, then trying to develop a base year with certain adjustments, and finally springboarding off of this analysis to forecast revenue streams into the future to determine value.

At this point in the chapter, the discussion transitions to the unique considerations and influences on diagnostic imaging revenue streams.

## II. The Primary Influences on Diagnostic Imaging Entity Revenue Streams; Factors for Consideration and Analysis of Historical Performance; Principal Considerations in Forecasting Future Streams of Revenue in Specific Settings and Markets

A watershed event in the diagnostic imaging space occurred in 2005, with the introduction of the Deficit Reduction Act of 2005, which was effective Jan. 1, 2006 (DRA 2005).

DRA 2005 contained two material changes in reimbursement implemented by the Centers for Medicare and Medicaid Services (CMS).

1. Section 5104 of the act froze the national Medicare Physician Fee Schedule (MPFS) conversion factor at the then-current 2005 rate, forgoing the forecast 4.4% decrease budgeted by CMS. That was the good news.

2. Section 5102 of the act introduced two provisions materially effecting reimbursement of the technical component, whether billed separately or global (only the technical component of the global fee is effected—not the professional component)

a. Section 5102(a)—the multiple procedure discount

b. Section 5102(b) payment of the lower of the MPFS or Outpatient Prospective Payment System (OPPS)

Section 5102(a) introduced the multiple procedure discount on 11 families of procedures (CPT codes) (see Exhibit 2). The 11 families included computed tomography (CT), magnetic resonance imaging (MRI), and ultrasound modalities. The act reduced reimbursement for subsequent procedures performed after the first procedure on contiguous body parts on the same patient at the same sitting by 25% of the base value of the procedure.

**Exhibit 2. DRA '11 Family' Discount Illustration 2006 and Beyond**

| | PROCEDURE 1 (CPT 74183) MRI ABDOMEN W/WO | PROCEDURE 2 (CPT 72196) MRI PELVIS W | CURRENT TOTAL PAY | 2006 TOTAL PAY | 2006 PAYMENT CALCULATION |
|---|---|---|---|---|---|
| PC | $ 114.22 | $ 87.70 | $ 201.92 | $ 201.92 | NO REDUCTION |
| TC | $ 857.57 | $ 464.32 | $ 1,321.89 | $1,205.81 | $857.57+ (.75 $464.32) |
| Global | $971.79 | $ 552.02 | $ 1,523.81 | $1,407.73 | $201.92+$857.57+(.75 $464.32) |
| TC VAR 2006 VS 2005 | | | | $ (116.08) | TV VAR 2007 VS 2006 |
| GLOBAL VAR 2006 VS 2005 | | | | ($116.08) | GLOBAL VAR 2007 VS 2006 |
| | | | | -8.8% | TC VAR 2007 VS 2005 |

*BASE RATES AT TEXAS RBRVS GPCI ADJUSTED

Section 5102(a) amounted to a decrease in reimbursement on the technical component of approximately 8% to 11%, depending on the volume and mix of studies performed. However, the net effect on freestanding outpatient services was, on the whole, less than a 1% to 1.5% net decrease, due to Section 5102(a), primarily because these combination of studies performed at the same sitting are more prevalent in the inpatient setting than the outpatient setting .

Section 5102(b) is another story altogether.

Section 5102(b) mandated reimbursement that the technical component, for both federal and state programs, be restricted to the lower of the MPFS) or OPPS level of payment (the hospital outpatient prospective payment rate under Part A Medicare—HOPPS).

The net effect of Section 5102(b) on revenue streams from federal and state payors is, as of 2012, totally complete and evident in all settings. Actual results impacting individual sites of service varied widely depending on the specific mix of billed codes per modality. We saw payments decline, on a per-unit-of-service basis. compared to pre-DRA 2005 as follows:

- CT (12% to 21%);
- MRI (31% to 46%),
- Ultrasound (9% to 11%);
- X-ray (6% to 10%);
- PET and PET/CT (45% to 50%); and
- Dexa Scans (23% to 34%).

At the time, mammography and nuclear medicine were excluded from Section 5102(b). Today, nuclear medicine is now impacted by Section 5102(b), as is breast MRI.

Keep in mind that Section 5102(a) and Section 5102(b) are applicable to federal and state programs. However, many commercial payors link their fee schedules to the MPFS. Therefore, the analysis needs to be performed definitively on studies performed for Medicare, Champus, Medicaid, and other federal program secondary payors, as well as commercial payors with whom the entity contracts and where the payor fee schedule is based upon the MPFS.

Depending on the payor mix and modality mix in the facility, the outcome of these payment policies may be either material to your forecasts or minimal. You need to find out with specificity. The only way to gain specificity is to obtain a report providing count, charges and payments by CPT code by payor for the past two years and the current year (what we call a CPT Frequency Report by Payor). In the absence of such data, you are likely to face a challenge on certain assumptions in your forecast that will quickly become a personality fight instead of a discussion on merit.

The aftershock of DRA 2005, 2008 MPFS, 2009 MPFS, 2010 MPFS, 2011 MPFS, and the 2012 proposed MPFS has been further year-to-year adjustments in payment by certain third-party payor contractual arrangements with diagnostic imaging centers. Certain national payors released new policies on payment for "advanced imaging" services before the ink was dry on DRA 2005, as posted in the *Federal Register*, and have followed suit on every CMS payment policy and rulemaking change ever since. Most national payors have been quick to say "me, too" in their fee schedules, ratcheting down reimbursement for MRI, CT, and PET progressively over the past two to three years.

Following DRA 2005, CMS implemented increased reductions in the multiple procedure discount from 25% to 50%, then reduced the "practice expense" portion of the technical component by recalculating the "advanced imaging" (CT, MRI, PET/CT) medical imaging equipment utilization rate basis from 50% utilization to 62.5% utilization in 2010 and then 75% utilization in 2011 (see Exhibit 3). This technical adjustment significantly reduced payment for the technical component from 2005 through 2012.

**Exhibit 3. Final 2011 Medicare Physician Fee Schedule**

- **Multiple Procedure Discount** Increase 11 Families from 25% to 50% reduction – NOW MOVING TO PC AS WELL.
- **Medical Imaging Equipment Utilization Factor** Increase from 62.5% to 75%
- **OPPS Payment Changes** effecting the "Lower of MPFS/OPPS Determination for TC Payments
- **RVU Changes, PE RVU Changes, Malpractice RVU Changes (PC/TC/Global)**
- **CT Code sets bundled** (Chest Abdomen Pelvis)
  - Some practices forecasting over a million dollar impact – what is impact to valued entity?
- **Budget Neutrality Adjustment Application to CF**
- **GPCI Changes Certain Localities**
- **Commercial Insurance "following" CMS Changes**

In 2011, CMS "bundled" payments for CT chest and CT abdomen resulting in a lower payment than if each study was billed separately. CMS continues to introduce new bundled payments each year. It is important to know what these changes are and how they impact future performance. For example, due to the CT bundled codes, one may easily be fooled by a seeming significant reduction in volume in CT, when in fact, the change in "count" was attributable to bundling of the two codes into one code.

It is important to understand the influences of changes to each payor contract's reimbursement over the retrospective two to three years and fully understand the contracting environment specific to the entity you are valuing. In many cases, we have seen imaging centers maintain a level of "clout" resulting in attractive reimbursement for advanced imaging, while in other markets, we have seen reimbursement follow Medicare in a proportional adjustment to prior contracts—all downward. There are certain states in which some payors refuse to contract with IDTFs or contract with single modality clinic model imaging entities, or in-office imaging entities serving certain medical group practices.

We *strongly suggest* you analyze reimbursement in six-month (or even quarterly) increments rather than in 12-month periods for the preceding years and current year to pick up any changes in contractual reimbursement and trends emerging in the specific market in which the entity operates.

We were recently retained to analyze certain assumptions made by a valuator with respect to forecasted payment for technical component services over the period of the valuation. We discovered a rather material variance between the valuator's payment-per-procedure assumptions for MRI and CT services forecast in Year 1 and the actual current payment per procedure for MRI and CT services by an amount close to 35%—a material difference.

The difference was due to a lack of investigation into actual reimbursement in a defined recent six-month period versus "average reimbursement" for a rolling historical 12-month period resulting in an overstatement of reimbursement. The valuator's analysis did not recognize a major recent shift in reimbursement from all principal payors with whom the facility was contracted for MRI, CT, and ultrasound procedures.

In contrast, we also reviewed a set of assumptions for another party in which the valuator understated current payments per procedure by close to 28% due to a lack of consideration and analysis of changes in payor mix and contract reimbursement following an intense period of contract renegotiations with certain payors in the area.

**Another Important Note:**
If the entity being valued is radiologist-owned and the purchasing entity will not benefit from the professional component revenue, the valuator will need to restate any global revenue as technical component revenue only or make accurate assumptions in the expense lines of the forecast to account for payment of the professional component. With respect to the determination of the professional component, one needs to consider the change in the ratio of PC to global for DRA 2005 technical component impacts for all federal and state program content. The ratio of PC to global is material when the TC is reduced due to Section 5102(b). Using the traditional professional component RVU as a percentage of global RVU is an invalid analysis since the advent of DRA 2005. The MPFS reimburses advanced imaging services at the lower of the HOPPS or MPFS. The only appropriate way to segregate the PC and TC is to express the PC dollars as a percentage of global dollars.

Other considerations to be applied to revenue streams, on a prospective basis, include an understanding of a number of environmental or market-specific forces that may impact future streams of revenue, in addition to the DRA 2005 implications discussed previously.

All or some of the factors illustrated in Exhibit 4 have a significant influence on determining and forecasting the value of future streams of revenue. These influences can arguably be accounted for in risk factors applied to the discount rate used to determine value or what is more accurate, should be reflected through more conservative or aggressive assumptions of volume per modality, reimbursement per modality, or a combination of both in the forecast. Whichever methodology is employed, the valuator should clearly state the assumptions, bases, and rationales used to create the values used in the forecast.

**Exhibit 4. Primary Influence on Future Revenue Streams at Diagnostic Imaging Entities**

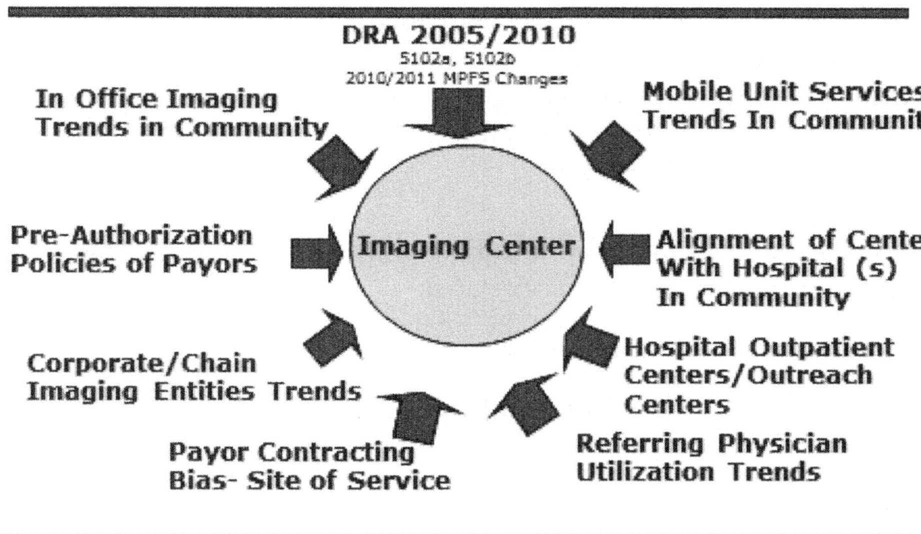


Often, the buyer or seller may attempt, either intentionally or unintentionally, to influence the valuator with respect to the potential effects of each of these factors of influence related to diagnostic imaging entities listed above.

## Emerging Landscape Changes Influence on Valuation Considerations

Over the past year to year and a half, a new consideration hit the imaging center universe we typically did not need to take into consideration: hospital and physician group alignment. Today, this matter is of material concern with respect to the future stream of revenues to be expected at the entity being valued.

Consolidation is *not* coming to healthcare—consolidation is happening with increasing velocity and vector. Physician group practices are being purchased by hospitals at an increasing rate. Groups are merging or finding other affiliation and integration models at an increasing pace.

It is important to understand, with as much specificity as is available at the time of the valuation, existing or emerging trends with respect to competition, regulatory changes affecting revenue and operations, referring physician pattern changes, center alignment in the community, and the other factors listed above. They can make a material difference in the forecasts and ultimate value determination.

These are matters requiring homework to allow you to arrive at your own conclusions with respect to the degree to which the future will follow the documented history of the entity. For example, if the entity being valued is owned by a radiology group or physician group with a historical alignment relationship with a hospital and its medical staff in the community and the relationship with the hospital has changed, then one needs to consider to what extent the change in relationship will affect future streams of revenue—positively or negatively.

Likewise, one needs to examine the historical sources of patients presented to the facility and competitive trends in the service area.

- Are there recent new entrants into the market?
- Is there evidence the new entrant is stealing patients from the entity?
- Is the new entrant a compliment to the entity or a competitor?
- Are the community's referring physicians taking imaging into their practices instead of referring to the entity?
- Are long-standing referring physicians being purchased by the hospital resulting in a shift in referral patterns away from the entity to the hospital-owned facilities?
- Are there emerging regulatory changes to the in-office ancillary services self-referral prohibition exceptions on the horizon that may change the market dynamics?
- Have certain in-office imagers found it financially unattractive to be in the imaging business and plan to return to the market as referring physicians?
- Have certain tightly managed third-party payors entered the area or increased their subscriber populations at the expense of more liberal paying companies?

- Have any major employers in the area changed insurance carriers or covered services benefits for their employees?

You get the idea. *Do the homework.* Do not rely totally upon input from either the buyer or seller.

In diagnostic imaging, due to the high fixed costs associated with the business, a change in volume of as little as two to three procedures per day (260 to 286 days per year) can make a material difference in net revenue. Once break-even is reached (a certain volume at a certain payment per procedure covers all fixed and variable costs), the lion's share of revenue per unit of service will drop straight to the bottom line. Conversely, the loss of two to three procedures per day (260 to 286 days per year) can turn the financial picture upside down in a hurry if the facility is dominated, as most are, by MRI and CT revenue.

## III. Recently Enacted, Current, and Pending Regulatory Impacts Specific to Diagnostic Imaging Entities in Certain Settings and the Considerations Required to Accurately Understand Their Real and Potential Impacts When Forecasting Revenue Streams

We need to closely examine certain documents regarding the structure of the entity to determine what, if any, existing or pending regulatory or policy changes may impact future performance of the entity or exact additional expense on the entity for which we must provide for in the forecast of either revenue or expense if not already experienced by the entity.

Closely examine any existing operating agreements, contracts with outside providers of services, especially management services and professional services. We also urgently need to examine any contracts with third parties related to leasing of the entity infrastructure (slot leases, per-unit-of-service leases, and under arrangement agreements with hospitals to provide technical component services to inpatients) that may need to be eliminated from revenue streams due to the nature of the transaction for which the valuation is being performed on behalf of the seller or buyer. New federal or state policies on these matters may eliminate these streams of revenue (see Exhibit 5). Currently, IDTF sites of service are walking around with targets on their backs due to contracting bias in the payor universe.

**Exhibit 5. Regulatory and Industry Actions to Consider in Valuing Diagnostic Imaging Entities**

- ☐ **Utilization Management Policies (Commercial Payors)**
  - ■ **Pre-Authorization Policies**
    - ☐ Advanced Imaging Modalities
      - ■ CT
        - ▪ CTA, CCTA
      - ■ MRI
        - ▪ MRA
      - ■ PET & PET/CT
- ☐ **IDTF Classification**
  - ■ Compliance with IDTF Rules
- ☐ **Slot Lease and Per Unit Lease Arrangement Legislation and recent actions**
- ☐ **Under Arrangement Legislation**
- ☐ **Anti-Mark-up Legislation**
- ☐ **Accreditation of Diagnostic Imaging Entities.**
- ☐ **OIG and CMS Utilization Audits and Investigations**
- ☐ **CON Laws (State by State)**

Stay tuned to CMS (www.cms.gov) over the next several months as we all see what, if any, of the proposed changes in the 2012 MPFS actually find their way into the regulations, law, and commercial payor policies effecting future reimbursement.

After collecting all of the historical material provided by the client, analyze it by modality, site of service, payor, top 20 to 25 referring physicians, and year. Then, step back and see whether any metric stands out as unreasonable or pops out as a red flag to future performance (see Exhibits 6 and 7).

**Exhibit 6. Revenue Forecasting Considerations: Volume Assumptions**

- ☐ **Volume Assumptions**
  - ■ By Modality (total and Per Day)
    - ☐ Calculate Total Market Demand (Utilization Per Thousand Population in Service Area)
      - ■ Per Year over Forecast Period
    - ☐ Calculate Total Market Supply
    - ☐ Calculate Current Market Share
    - ☐ Calculate Available Market
    - ☐ Determine Assumptions for Market Share Growth/Decline
      - ■ Competitive Landscape
      - ■ Entity Leverage in Market – Specific Contributors

**Exhibit 7. Revenue Forecasting Considerations: Revenue Per Procedure Assumptions**

- ☐ **Revenue Per Procedure Assumptions**
  - By Modality
  - By Payor Category
  - Throughout Period of Forecast (reimbursement do not go up unless there is a significant rationale for Payor Mix Shift based upon evidence available at the time of the forecast)
- ☐ Test Forecast against History for Consistency
  - — does the forecast make sense given the history and facts?
- ☐ Test Volume assumptions against throughput capacity of imaging equipment and staffing to determine:
  - what, if any additional provisions in the forecast need to be made for additional medical imaging equipment, maintenance and repair contracts and additional technician and administrative staff to accommodate additional volume forecast.

Items that should scream out at you also demand you return to the client or source of data and ask probing questions as to potential root causes for results you did not expect. Search for possible errors in data and explanations for variances from expectations not available to you in your client interviews. It is important that you gain a full picture that meets the test of reason before you proceed with a forecast of the future with all of the considerations mentioned herein.

Of special interest today is the trend related to capture of patient-responsible portions of payment, such as co-pays, deductibles, and health savings accounts. If the entity has "forecast" capture of these accounts at full value, the entity is either totally out of touch with reality or misrepresenting the facts. Take a hard look at what, if any, payments are received in these categories of revenue in the 90-day-or-longer accounts receivable. Our experience suggests nothing more than 3% of the charge value will be realized. How does the actual experience of the entity then play into your forecast of revenue over the period of the valuation?

## IV. The Primary Influences and Considerations Required When Analyzing and Forecasting Infrastructure Expense Unique to Diagnostic Imaging Entities

Now let's turn our attention to the expense side of valuation considerations. As with all medical practice settings, there are a number of unique matters to consider when forecasting entity expense. Diagnostic imaging entities have especially unique elements of cost one needs to examine closely. The list provided here may not be totally exhaustive, but points to many material matters that need to be understood (see Exhibits 8, 9, and 10).

**Exhibit 8. Six Primary Influence on Expense at Diagnostic Imaging Entities**

- ☐ FMV of Existing Medical Imaging Equipment
- ☐ Medical Equipment Lease Cost
- ☐ Medical Equipment Depreciation Schedules and status
- ☐ FMV of non-medical imaging assets
- ☐ Medical Imaging Maintenance and Repair Contract Status
- ☐ Technician Staffing and Compensation

**Exhibit 9. Seven Primary Influences on Expense at Diagnostic Imaging Entities**

- ☐ Technician Licensing Status
- ☐ PACS Status and Links to outside images
- ☐ RIS Status
- ☐ Medical Imaging Equipment Technology Relevance to Competitive Community Standard
- ☐ Additional Capacity Forecasts – Medical Imaging Equipment, Space, Personnel, Supply Costs
- ☐ Accreditation Status and investments required
- ☐ Marketing Expense Status and Forecast

**Exhibit 10. 14 Primary Influences on Expense at Diagnostic Imaging Entities**

- ☐ Medical Imaging Equipment Technology
  - ■ Relevance to Competitive Community Standard
- ☐ Additional Capacity Forecasts – Medical Imaging Equipment, Space, Personnel, Supply Costs – Useful Life is not the same as Depreciation Life
- ☐ Technician Licensing Status/Requirements
- ☐ PACS Status and Links to outside images
- ☐ RIS Status
- ☐ Management Fees
- ☐ Medical Director Fees
- ☐ Accounts Receivable Management (Billing) Fees
- ☐ Marketing Expense Status and Forecast
- ☐ Accreditation Status and investments required
- ☐ "Red Flag" Implementation
- ☐ Compliance Program Implementation
- ☐ HIPAA Program Implementation
- ☐ OSHA Compliance Implementation

We often find a certain facility has been prepped for sale by the owners. This means certain normal expense related to equipment maintenance and repair contracts have been deferred or eliminated in favor of "at-risk" expense as required or that certain critical technician and administrative staff has been recently eliminated. It will be important to examine staffing ratios and credentials of certain technicians to determine what, if any, additional adjustments need to be made to the base year and subsequent years.

Another often missing analysis when creating a forecast of expense over the period of the valuation is an analysis of assumptions of volume cross-referenced to each modality of medical imaging equipment's throughput capacity and cross-referenced to staffing requirements to support the volume forecast—technical staff and administrative support staff.

It is very easy, and not unusual, to witness forecasts of volume that exceed the throughput capacity of the existing medical imaging equipment at some point in the out years of the forecast. This is particularly critical not only for revenue but for terminal capital expenditure and depreciation. One must look at the viability of expanding operating hours to absorb the increase in volume in the specific market, but expanding hours of operation may not completely absorb the forecast volume. If throughput capacity is breached, then one must make a provision for the addition of equipment, maintenance, repair of the equipment, and radiologic technicians, with their associated cost of employment to man the facility.

If the entity has a multislice CT unit (32 slice or 64 slice), slot times may be shorter due to the increased scan speed of these devices, thus increasing throughput capacity. Other modifications may need to be made to the times listed above based upon the unique characteristics of the medical imaging device in place. Likewise, a 3Tesla MRI may be faster than a "vintage" 1.5 Tesla MRI or a 0.7 Tesla Open MRI.

In our consulting practice, we always request a document from the client describing its patient scheduling times for each modality. The slot times will include prescan preparation time, actual scan time, and post-scan time escorting the patient from the scanner room. In the case of procedures for which a contrast agent was administered, the total patient time will include the prescan injection time and post-procedure "recovery" time. The actual scan time (time the patient is on the table) is not the true throughput determination—it is the total episode of care time.

If the valuation results in the need for a net asset determination due to lack of excess net profit available to the owners, then the author recommends you retain the services of a qualified and experienced independent medical imaging equipment appraiser to perform a fair market appraisal of the equipment, furniture. and fixtures. To perform such an appraisal, the appraiser will require a comprehensive listing of all assets, noting their purchase date and model number.

Other elements of expense that require examination include general medical supply cost per unit of service (linens, gowns, and general medical supplies) as well as pharmaceutical costs per unit of service, including contrast agents for CT and MRI services performed with and without contrast and radiopharmaceutical costs per dose for PET and PET CT services.

As you forecast volume for these services, you also need to forecast the associated costs for these items on a per-unit-of-service basis. [Editor's Note: Note that per-unit expense is not the same as using a percentage of collected revenue.]

## V. Potential Landmines and Valuation Considerations That Can Come Back to Haunt You

As you enter the forecast stage of the engagement, it is important to do a good deal of homework with respect to very specific conditions on the ground in the specific location of the entity being valued. Although the thought of going back to the basic supply-and-demand calculations that should have preceded the development of the imaging entity could make you lose sleep at night in anticipation, it is almost inevitable that the fight over the results of the valuation will rest primarily in the revenue forecast side and less so on the expense forecast side.

As discussed earlier, diagnostic imaging services are capital-intensive services. Reimbursement for the technical component on a per-unit-of-service basis can either indicate substantial value or certain impending financial death for the entity being valued. A diagnostic imaging entity has several key moving parts impacting revenue streams, which examined individually, may not indicate the true trajectory of the business, but taken together, several factors will definitely paint a brightly colored picture of the entity and its future capacity to generate excess revenue for the owner.

Volume projections will, by definition, be based upon the facts of recent history. If the entity has experienced an erosion of volume in key reimbursing modalities, one will need an impressive and quantitative rationale for a step function increase in volume in the forecast. Likewise, if recent history results in erosion per-unit-payment-dollar amount, then any forecasts of improvement must be directly linked to quantitative explanations for any forecast increases in per-unit-of-service per modality.

We are often asked by an anxious buyer or seller to consider or ignore, in forecasts, past trends in reimbursement and known events. The dilemma for us all is the representation we make as to the fair market value determination. Can we ignore current facts in the forecast? Should we accommodate the probability of such an occurrence in the risk factors instead? That is a question for the valuator.

A simple supply-and-demand analysis for the specific area may be required to test the assumptions of growth. If we know the population demographics of the primary and secondary service area of the entity, then we can, using current, available utilization-per-thousand-population by modality data, estimate the total demand for diagnostic imaging services in the area. If we then know the current market share of the entity, we can forecast with some degree of certainty the available population we should reasonably expect to capture. However, we also need to closely examine the age and sex mix to be more precise and take into consideration known shifts, if any, in the construct of the medical staff in the area.

Are there more physicians who specialize in imaging services coming into the area? Are certain known high users of imaging services fleeing the area? Are high-referring specialist physicians being purchased by a hospital? Do the population metrics support or deny the growth assumptions in the forecast?

If a particular geographic area population is flat or declining, does the natural increase in a certain imaging modality per population fit the forecast? One also needs to test the service area declared by the entity. A quick look at a historical patient population by ZIP code can either confirm or question the assertion of the reach of the entity. It is generally a good idea to at least perform a "back of the envelope" head check on these metrics.

It is important to recognize the source date of the data. Typically, utilization by modality data lag the real world by at least three years. The 2010 data, for example, does not contain effects of utilization management controls put in place by certain national payors, including pre authorization policies and other utilization management policies for advanced imaging. As evidence, the most recent (April 2008) MEDPAC report to Congress noted a slight decrease in utilization due to, in its opinion, DRA 2005 and other CMS policies related to in-office imaging services and utilization controls put in place by commercial insurance companies. There are no "point numbers" upon which we can rely with confidence. Rather we suggest using a range of utilization per thousand as a metric for the purposes described here. If we were performing a feasibility study to examine the viability of establishing an imaging center in a certain locality, then we would need to be significantly more precise.

Both consultant and appraiser are often challenged on the forecast revenue per unit of service per modality—especially for entities with heavy CT and MRI content. The only way revenue per unit of service ever goes up over time is either:

1. a major payor-mix shift to more highly paying third-party payors versus historical payor mix data or
2. if the managed care portfolio has been recently renegotiated to higher-than-historical-aggregate rates.

In today's universe, neither is probable, but the author has experienced situations in which it happens. If evidence can be provided in support of the contention, then we should, by all means, include the evidence and adjust the forecast accordingly.

### Summary

Diagnostic imaging entities, regardless of structure of setting, are in a state of change. Some recent transactions indicate material changes in historical multiples of EBITDA (a metric that drives this author crazy). Some recent transactions have been strategic purchases and sales. Others have been made on the merits. Some diagnostic imaging entities will prosper despite regulatory changes, rulemaking changes, local landscape changes, and other negative impacts. In spite of downward pricing pressures and utilization management directives to reduce access to imaging services, some entities find a way to thrive. Each transaction needs to be assessed at the local level. Valuing these unique entities requires a detailed understanding of the business unit in question.

1. Get into the details. Make a detailed examination of past performance:
   - By modality
   - By payor
   - By site of service
2. Examine referral patterns just as you examine them for other medical practices.
   - Who is coming, who is going, and why?
3. Understand the specifics of certain modalities, such as CT and MRI, as well as other unique modalities.
   - How many studies with contrast are performed?

- How many studies without contrast are performed?
- What effects have code bundling made on the entity?
- How many screening versus diagnostic mammograms are performed—not how many total mammograms are performed?
- How many mammography CAD (computer assisted detection) studies are performed?

4. Do the data make sense, given the patient population demographics and referring physician demographics?
5. Does reimbursement and payor mix suggest the entity is capturing its fair share of better-paying health plans or has it been relegated the low-pay and "self-pay-no-pay population?
6. What events on the horizon do we need to accommodate in the forecast buildup as known facts and how many events on the horizon do we accommodate as risk factors?

Once you have the details and are comfortable that you understand the past with specificity, then employ the same diligence in forecasting the future, based upon past trajectory and known or, reasonable, assumptions of local conditions and their likelihood of continuation, expansion, or contraction. The answers will not come from financial statements and balance sheets alone. The answers will come through the tough drilling down into the details of each modality, payor trends, accounts receivable analysis, payor analysis, denied services analysis, operational efficiency, and expense by line item.

The diagnostic imaging sector is subject to very fast changes. Look for them, understand them, and assess their impact to the entity you are valuing. The devil is clearly in the details.

Do not get caught up in discussions of comparable EBITDA transactions. First, there are not many published sources upon which we can rely that provide us with any of the material facts we would need to know to assure ourselves the transactions are indeed "comparable." Many of the most noted transactions in the press have been strategic acquisitions having little to do with fair market value. The prices and the multiple of earnings paid had little to do with the future stream of revenues any particular unit was expected to spin off to the owners and more to do with the effects of the addition of the business to a larger picture. Many of these transactions have been structured with strings attached to the ultimate payout price based upon certain metrics being achieved in the future.

### A Final Note

An owner of a diagnostic imaging entity considering a sale of the entity at a future date should understand, with specificity, the "factors of influence" to determine value discussed here and take all actions necessary to enhance the value of the entity today. Any new volume coupled with reductions in cost per unit of service will add to net profit—the most influential metric future value by a buyer. Added efforts to "brand" the facility for a potential buyer to leverage will also add to value.

Take action today to enhance value. Actions taken at the time of the valuation will not result in a positive outcome—it will be too late.

Chapter 40

# Ambulatory Surgery Centers

*By Todd J. Sorensen, MBA. AVA*

During the first decade of the new millennium, surgery-center transactions became one of the most popular joint-venture relationships involving both for-profit and not-for-profit healthcare providers and surgeons who perform outpatient surgery. Due to the economic slowdown and the hospital-physician employment phenomenon, the volume of new joint-venture relationships appears to have slowed substantially. However, outside of engagements associated with physician practice transactions, valuation engagements associated with ambulatory surgery center (ASC) transactions continue to represent one of the healthcare segments with the highest volume for our firm. As with most healthcare segments, ensuring that transactions between potential referral source physician owners and healthcare systems occur within the range of fair market value is critical to compliance with the Stark regulations, federal fraud and abuse statutes, and in some cases, state law.

Types of private ASC equity transactions include: (1) controlling interests in stand-alone licensed free-standing surgery centers; (2) minority or noncontrolling equity transactions in free-standing ASCs; and (3) controlling and noncontrolling equity transactions in hospital outpatient departments relicensed as free-standing ambulatory surgery centers. Each of these transactions typically has a different value.

Minority equity interests in private ASCs tend to trade at lower levels than controlling interests in those same ASCs. Surgery centers with little or no physician ownership tend to be valued lower than those with significant ownership. In general, valuations of any equity interest are based not only on external market factors, but also on the facts and circumstances of the particular ASC being valued.

The ASC industry is highly fragmented, composed of several large publicly or privately owned companies and many small, independent operators. Of the 5,876 ASCs operating in the United States, only 1,312 facilities, or approximately 22%, are owned or managed by multifacility chains. AmSurg, United Surgical Partners International (USPI), Surgical Care Affiliates (SCA) and HCA Inc. (HCA) are a few of the largest owners and operators.

This chapter provides an overview of the ASC segment, typical ASC legal structures, ASC financial performance and primary value drivers, and the most common ASC valuation applications.

## Segment Overview

Ambulatory surgery refers to lower-acuity surgical procedures performed on an outpatient basis that do not require an overnight stay. These surgeries can occur in either a hospital outpatient (surgical) department (HOPD) or in a free-standing ASC.

ASCs offer a more productive and comfortable environment for both physicians and patients. A surgeon using an ASC can typically better maintain a schedule with more consistent weekly time blocked to schedule surgeries ("block time") and quicker, more reliable turnaround times. Patients who receive treatment at an ASC benefit from a convenient, less-institutionalized environment; streamlined care; specialized services; and proven lower infection rates.

ASCs provide the surgical equipment and supplies, specialized personnel, and other support services that enable their surgeon-users to perform surgeries. Physicians typically do not pay for these services. Instead, the ASC bills a technical fee, or facility fee, to the patient or payor. The physician bills a professional fee separately. The ASC neither employs nor pays compensation to the surgeon-users. Consequently, an ASC's success or failure relates directly to its ability to provide the necessary technical services to enable its surgeon-users to perform their surgical cases.

## History of ASCs

The idea of performing outpatient surgery first materialized in 1966, in an article in the *Journal of the American Medical Association* (*JAMA*). Shortly thereafter, the health insurance industry began exploring alternatives to the high costs associated with procedures in hospitals, and the U.S. National Advisory Commission on Health Facilities began experimenting with ways to lower them. In 1970, the first ASC opened. In 1971, the American Medical Association (AMA) endorsed ASCs performing surgery under general and local anesthesia for selected procedures and patients. By 1976, 67 ASCs existed around the country.

Although the government, through Medicare, began collaborating with six ASCs in 1974, it wasn't until 1982 that the program approved payment for 200 selected procedures performed in ASCs. Today Medicare, Medicaid, and private insurers allow and pay for more than 3,600 procedures performed in ASCs, and these numbers are expected to grow. Approved procedures generally are those offered in a hospital inpatient setting that also can be performed safely in outpatient facilities. ASC-approved procedures generally require less than 90 minutes of operating-room time, less than four hours of recovery-room time, and no overnight stay.

Expanded acceptance by Medicare and other payors has led to large growth in the number of ASCs and total procedures performed. For example, the number of Medicare-certified ASCs grew at an average annual rate of 8% from 1999 to 2005. During that same period, the Centers for Medicare and Medicaid Services (CMS) noted an annual average of 337 new Medicare-certified ASCs. There are currently close to 5,300 Medicare-certified facilities nationwide. There are an additional 600 ASCs that are not Medicare-certified.

Total Medicare payments for ASC services have continued to grow at a rapid pace. For example, data show that Medicare payments to ASCs more than quadrupled between 1992 and 2005. Payments increased by 15% per year, on average, from 1999 to 2005. Surgery case growth (as a percentage) peaked in 1996 and has slowed to a current rate of near 6%.

### Certificate of need requirements

Some states require a certificate of need (CON) to operate an ASC. A CON is a regulatory review process that evaluates whether a proposed service or facility is actually needed in a specific market. Those subject to CON regulations include hospitals, nursing homes, outpatient surgery centers, and anyone purchasing medical equipment valued above certain state-determined thresholds.

The CON mandate began in response to overwhelming requests for federal funding spurred by the 1946 Hill-Burton Program, which matched grants for the construction of hospitals in medically underserved areas. Congress needed to infuse effective measures to appropriately manage the billions of dollars in federal assistance being requested in response to the program.

In 1974, Congress passed the National Health Planning and Resources Development Act, offering states powerful incentives to enact laws implementing CON programs.

By 1980, all states except Louisiana had one. Congress repealed the federal law in 1986, and many states have since relaxed or eliminated CON laws.

Exhibit 1 illustrates the states that require a CON, those that do not, and the number of Medicare-certified ASCs in the United States in 2007.

**Exhibit 1. CON Regulation by State**

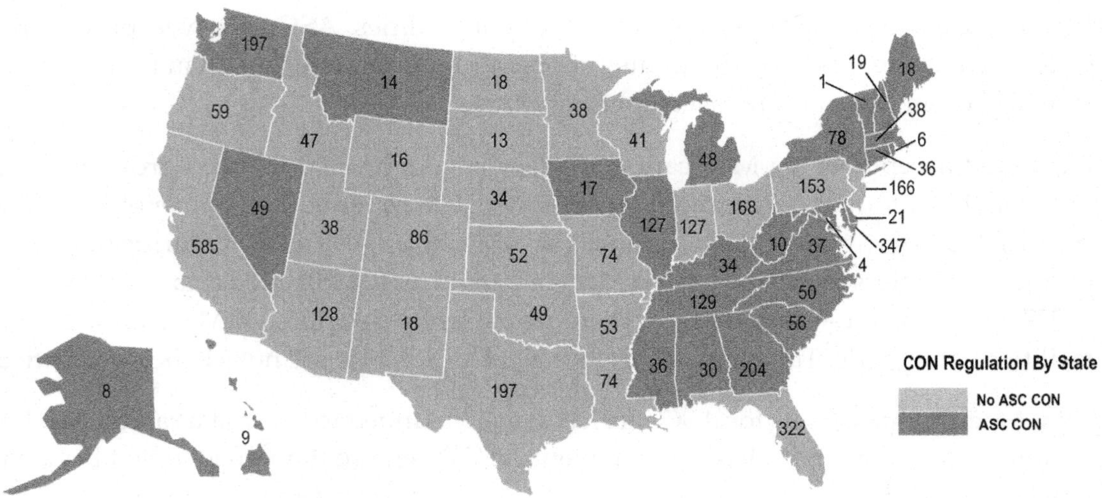


## ASC Growth

That healthcare costs have increased at rates in excess of inflation is considered the primary factor in the development and increased use of surgery centers. Procedures performed in an outpatient setting generally cost between 30% and 60% less than the same procedures performed in a hospital. As a result, Medicare, managed care, and other payors have encouraged moving procedures to ASCs.

While cost containment was the initial driver in the growth of ASCs, current growth in the industry is also driven by advantages to both patients and physicians. In a survey completed by the Office of the Inspector General (OIG), part of the U.S. Department of Health and Human Services (HHS), Medicare beneficiaries who underwent procedures in ASCs strongly preferred the facilities to hospitals.[1] Reasons included less paperwork, lower costs, more convenient locations, better parking, less wait time, better organization, and friendlier staff. The study also determined that ASCs provided safety and post-operative care comparable to a hospital.

1 Richard P. Kusserow, Inspector General: Patient Satisfaction With Outpatient Surgery, A National Survey of Medicare Beneficiaries; December 1989.

For physicians, the benefits of performing surgeries in ASCs go beyond increased patient satisfaction. Not only are their patients happier, but they can also achieve larger volumes and greater economies of scale. Unlike doctors at a hospital that provides a variety of surgical procedures and uses an array of supplies and equipment, doctors at free-standing surgery centers typically focus on a few select procedures. This increases patient turnaround time and decreases time between surgeries because the operating room needs minimal preparation for the next patient.

Physicians who act as partial owners or investors in the venture (by partnering with an ASC management chain such as AmSurg, SCA or USPI, for example), have an additional incentive to prefer the ASC environment: They earn income for the procedures they perform. In other words, physicians capture a portion of a technical fee not accessible to them at a hospital.

Technological developments also have contributed to substantial growth in the ASC segment. Advances in laser, endoscopic, and arthroscopic minimally invasive procedures have allowed for more variance in the array of procedures conducted at ASCs.

Demand for outpatient surgery will continue to increase during the next decade, driven by growth in the 55-plus population, as baby boomers shift into the senior-citizen bracket. This is largely because utilization rates for many outpatient surgical procedures appear to correlate directly with age.

Of all the surgery cases performed in the United States in 2009, approximately 63% were performed in the outpatient setting. Outpatient surgery as a percentage of total surgery has increased significantly from 1980 to 2009. The increase in surgical procedures performed in outpatient settings is primarily linked to both the rise of ASCs as well as innovations in technological and surgical procedures, which have expanded the types of procedures suitable for an outpatient setting. Beginning in the early- to mid-1990s, the shift in surgical volume from inpatient to outpatient began to flatten. Since 2000, the percentage of surgeries performed in the outpatient setting has remained steady at approximately 63% of total surgeries. The lack of growth in outpatient surgery versus inpatient surgery suggests a maturing of the ASC industry.[2]

2 Avelere Health for American Hospital Association: Trendwatch Chartbook 2011.

**Exhibit 2. Total Medicare Payments for ASC Services**

| | 2000 | 2001 | 2002 | 2003 | 2004 | 2005 | 2006 | 2007 | 2008 | 2009 |
|---|---|---|---|---|---|---|---|---|---|---|
| Medicare ASC payments (in billions) | $1.4 | $1.6 | $1.9 | $2.2 | $2.5 | $2.7 | $2.9 | $2.9 | $3.1 | $3.2 |
| Growth | 16.7% | 14.3% | 18.8% | 15.8% | 13.6% | 8.0% | 7.4% | 0.0% | 6.9% | 3.2% |
| Number of Medicare Certified ASCs | 3,028 | 3,302 | 3,545 | 3,848 | 4,140 | 4,441 | 4,711 | 4,991 | 5,174 | 5,260 |
| Growth | 8.7% | 9.0% | 7.4% | 8.5% | 7.6% | 7.3% | 6.1% | 5.9% | 3.7% | 1.7% |
| Medicare Payments per Facility (in thousands) | $462 | $485 | $536 | $572 | $604 | $608 | $616 | $581 | $599 | $608 |
| Growth | 7.3% | 4.8% | 10.6% | 6.7% | 5.6% | 0.7% | 1.3% | -5.6% | 3.1% | 1.5% |

*Source: MedPac March 2011 Report to the Congress*

As Exhibit 2 illustrates, total Medicare payments for ASC services more than doubled between 2000 and 2009. Payments increased approximately 10.9% compounded annually, from approximately $1.4 billion in 2000 to $3.2 billion in 2009. During the same time period, the number of Medicare-certified ASCs grew approximately 7.1% compounded annually, from 3,028 in 2000 to 5,260 in 2009. The growth in Medicare payments to ASCs far outpaced the growth in Medicare certified ASCs during the period prior to 2005. Since 2005, this trend slowed significantly, coinciding with the freeze in Medicare grouper payments to ASCs, which became effective in 2005. Growth in Medicare payments to ASCs has fallen from a high of 16.7% in 2000 to 3.2% in 2009. The reduction in growth in Medicare payments reflects slower annual growth in the number of Medicare-certified ASCs, which has fallen from 9% in 2001 to 1.7% in 2009.[3]

## Changes in Medicare Payment System for ASCs

The Medicare Prescription Drug, Improvement, and Modernization Act of 2003 (MMA) set in motion some much-anticipated changes to the ASC payment system. Through the MMA, CMS eliminated the update for ambulatory surgical center services for fiscal year 2005, changed the update cycle to a calendar year, and eliminated updates for calendar years 2006 through 2009. The MMA also removed the requirement that CMS survey ASCs' costs and charges every five years. It also asked the General Accounting Office (GAO) to study the relative cost of services in ASCs and HOPDs and determine whether the outpatient prospective payment system's (OPPS) procedure groups reflected ASC procedures. The results of this study formed the basis for the 2007 Proposed ASC Rule.

On Aug. 8, 2006, CMS unveiled its proposal for a new ASC payment system. On Jan. 1, 2008, CMS implemented the new system for payments to ASCs for the provision of

3 MedPac: March 2011 Report to Congress.

medical services to Medicare beneficiaries. Exhibit 3 gives a brief description of the major events leading up to the implementation of the new system.

**Exhibit 3. New ASC Payment System Timeline**

| NEW ASC PAYMENT SYSTEM TIMELINE | |
|---|---|
| 1998 | CMS proposes a new ASC payment system and a new hospital outpatient department ("HOPD") payment system. |
| 2000 | CMS Begins paying HOPD using prospectively determined rates for bundles of services, called APCs. Congress prohibits CMS from implementing a new system for ASCs without a new cost survey. |
| 2003 | Congress requires CMS to implement a new ASC payment system by January 1, 2008, and freezes ASC payment rates through 2009. |
| 2005 | Introduction of Ambulatory Surgical Center Medicare Payment Modernization Act of 2005 (legislation) by Congressman Herger (R-CA) and Senator Crapo (R-ID). |
| 2006 | CMS issues proposed rule detailing its recommendations for a new payment system. |
| 2007 | On August 2, 2007, CMS issues a final rule establishing a new payment system for ASCs, including the methodology to be used in determining rates, and proposes rates for 2008. On November 27, 2007, CMS issues final rates for 2008. |

The new payment system is similar to the old Medicare payment system in that CMS pays ASCs a facility fee intended to cover the nonprofessional costs associated with providing a surgical procedure. But instead of categorizing payments into one of nine groupers, the new payment is based on one of 201 ambulatory payment classifications (APCs). Medicare uses the same APCs for ASCs and HOPDs. Each procedure performed is assigned a common procedural terminology (CPT) code, which in turn crosswalks to an APC, and each APC has a specific payment rate. But because CMS will continue to report payment rates by CPT code, ASCs will continue to bill and collect from Medicare using CPT codes.

Though ASCs and HOPDs both use APCs, payment rates vary between the two. The rate paid to an HOPD for each APC is based on relative weight, a measurement that ranks the costs to perform the procedures in one APC compared to the costs of those in another. CMS determines the relative weight for each APC using hospital cost reports. The relative weight is then multiplied by a uniform dollar conversion factor to get the national HOPD payment rate. ASCs payment is a percentage of the national HOPD rate. For 2008, ASCs received, on average, 65% of HOPD payments.

Medicare reimbursed ASCs for providing 3,390 surgical procedures in 2008, 819 more than were reimbursable in 2007. Some of the new procedures realized reimbursement significantly higher than 65% of HOPD rates. For example, for procedures that required the use of a device estimated to cost more than 50% of the procedure's total APC reimbursement, the ASC payment rate included the same dollar value that an HOPD received for the device, without any discount. Forty-five ASC device-intensive procedures are reimbursed in this fashion.

Approximately 44% of the new procedures had reimbursement rates lower than the 65% HOPD conversion factor. For procedures performed in physician offices more than 50% of the time, the ASC payment is the lesser of either the payment rate determined using the HOPD conversion factor or the amount Medicare typically pays the physician for performing the procedures in the office. This payment methodology only applies to new procedures introduced under the new payment system, not to procedures on the list in 2007.

When it comes to multiple procedures, the policy in effect prior to the implementation of the new payment system remained. ASCs earn 100% for the primary procedure (defined as the one with the highest reimbursement rate) and 50% for each additional procedure. Certain procedures are not subject to the multiple-procedure discount; the classification of these procedures hasn't changed.

CMS established a four-year transition period for procedures already on the ASC list, to give individual ASCs more time to adjust to the new payment system. In 2008, Medicare ASC payment rates for these procedures will be based on a blended rate of 75% of the 2007 ASC payment rates and 25% of the amount Medicare would have paid in 2008 under the new system. In 2009, the ASC rate was based 50% on the 2007 rate and 50% on the 2009 rate. In 2010, the payment was made based on 25% and 75% of those respective payment rates, and in 2011, the transition was complete.

The new payment methodology affected surgical specialties differently. Using the 2008 rates, the Federated Ambulatory Surgery Association (FASA), which has since been merged with the American Association of Ambulatory Surgery Center (AAASC) to form the Ambulatory Surgery Center Association (ASCA), estimated a 5% decline for GI rates and a 23% increase for orthopedics. FASA estimated that once fully implemented, the new payment system would cause an overall decline of 19% for GI and an overall increase of 92% for orthopedics. FASA's analysis, detailed in the November/December issue of *Update Magazine*, is summarized in Exhibit 4.

Under the new payment system, Medicare reimbursed nine of the 10 highest-volume procedures performed in ASCs at a lower rate. According to CMS, the overall lower payment rates, taking into consideration the 819 newly covered procedures, resulted in the same total of 2008 Medicare spending on ASCs than if a new payment system had not been adopted.

On Nov. 3, 2010, CMS released the final ruling for 2011 ASC payments. ASCs received a 0.2% across-the-board increase in Medicare payments. For 2011, CMS used a conversion factor of $41.939, up from $41.873 in 2010.

**Exhibit 4. Major Events Leading Up to the Implementation of New ASC System**

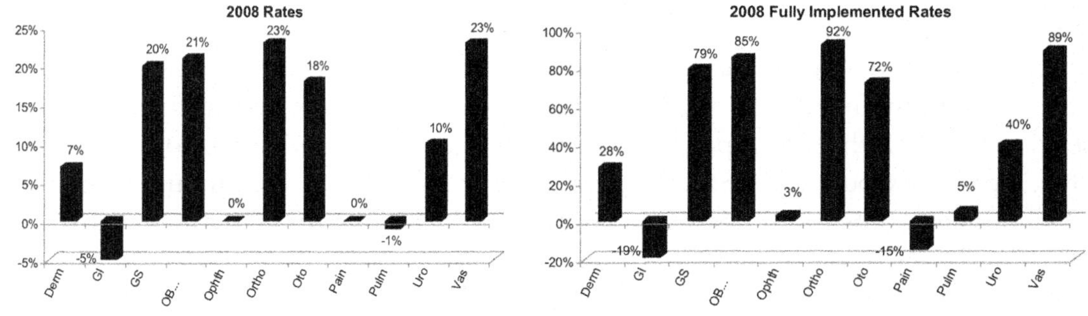


CMS continues to use the prefloor, prereclassified wage index to adjust ASC payments for geographic differences in the relative cost of labor. The differences in some markets starting in 2011 will be particularly pronounced because of a policy in the health reform law that sets the hospital wage index for inpatient and outpatient services in so-called "frontier states" at 1.0. The states affected by the frontier wage index policy include Montana, Wyoming, North Dakota, South Dakota, and Nevada.

CMS updated its estimate of productivity and applied a reduction of 1.3% in 2011, instead of the 1.6% reduction that had been proposed. This is inconsistent with MedPAC's recommended productivity update of 0.6%. Recently, CMS has received criticism from the ASC industry and the hospital industry for an overly aggressive assumption of productivity gains between 2008 and 2010. In the final rule, CMS did respond to the concerns about the productivity calculation and reduced the productivity adjustment by 0.3%.

CMS applies a secondary budget neutrality calculation to the ASC relative weights to ensure that changes to them used to determine HOPD rates do not result in an aggregate increase or decrease in ASC payments. The final rule establishes a scaling factor more favorable to ASC rates of 0.9238 (CMS had originally proposed the factor to be 0.9090 for 2011). Although the final rule was better than the proposed rule, the 2011 factor is lower than the 2010 factor of 0.9567, partly due to the fact that these are the fully transitioned weights and due to increases in the OPPS relative weights for ASC procedures.

The final rule did not require ASCs to report quality data for CY 2011 but did express CMS's intention to implement ASC quality reporting in future rulemaking. In the 2011 final ruling, CMS also added four new quality measures for ASC quality reporting to make a total of 23 measures. CMS suggested that 2012 will be the first year of required quality reporting.[4]

4 CMS: Final Ruling for ASC's 2011.

### Discrepancy in Payments

The discrepancy between ASC payments and hospital outpatient departments continued to grow in 2011. As illustrated in Exhibit 5, ASC reimbursement rates when compared to HOPD reimbursement rates for the same services have decreased since 2003. In 2003, ASCs were reimbursed 87% of what a HOPD would receive for performing the same service. For 2011, this discrepancy in reimbursement increased to 56% of HOPD rates. The discrepancy between ASC reimbursement rates and HOPD reimbursement rates exists because CMS uses different factors to annually update ASC rates and HOPD rates and a process called "secondary rescaling," which ensures that changes to the APC relative weights used to determine HOPD rates do not result in an aggregate increase or decrease in ASC payments. The ASC industry has lobbied to close the discrepancy, but CMS is not expected to change its policy.[5]

**Exhibit 5. ASC Reimbursement as a Percentage of HOPD Reimbursement**

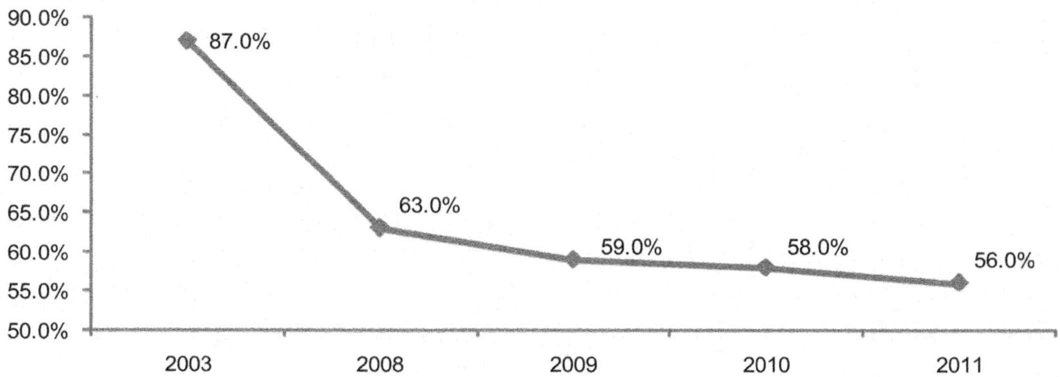


### CY 2012 Proposed Ruling

On July 1, CMS released its 2012 proposed ruling for ASC reimbursement. For CY 2012, CMS proposed a 0.9% increase in payments.

CMS proposed to continue to use the Consumer Price Index for Urban Consumers (CPI-U) to update ASC payments, despite comments from the ASC industry. CMS projected that the CPI-U update will be 2.3% for CY 2012. As required by healthcare reform, CMS proposed to reduce the annual update by a productivity adjustment of 1.4%. Therefore, CMS proposed to apply a 0.9% increase in reimbursement for CY 2012.

CMS also proposed the first Medicare quality reporting system for ASCs. CMS proposed eight quality measures for voluntary reporting beginning in CY 2012 for the CY

5 CMS, ASC Association.

2014 payment determination. The proposed ruling included eight outcome and surgical infection control measures. CMS also proposed two structural measures for reporting in CY 2013 for CY 2015 payment determination. These were a surgery checklist and a volume tracker for specific ASC surgical procedures.[6]

## Typical ASC Legal Structures

Typically, ASC entities are either structured as limited liability corporations (LLCs) or limited partnerships (LPs). In name and in legal form, these entities may differ, but they are similarly governed by the applicable agreement governing operations associated with ASCs, the operating agreement for LLCs, and the partnership agreement for LPs.

The most critical elements that may affect the valuation of assets or an interest in an ASC include:

- Cash distributions;
- Ownership restrictions; and
- Buy-sell provisions.

In particular, these elements in turn have a direct or indirect impact on minority and marketability issues flowing from the valuation of an interest in an ASC.

### *Cash distributions*

Most ASC operating or partnership agreements include detailed provisions that provide for the distribution of virtually all of the discretionary cash on at least a quarterly, and sometimes monthly, basis. Since the cash distributions are normally defined in this manner, this may reduce the impact of any applicable discounts for both lack of control and lack of marketability.

### *Ownership restrictions*

As previously discussed, federal regulations allow physicians who perform surgery and refer patients to ASCs, to maintain ownership in an ASC. To fit in a safe harbor from the federal fraud and abuse statutes, physicians who maintain an ownership interest in an ASC must:

1. Derive one-third of their professional income from outpatient surgery; and
2. Perform one-third of their eligible cases in the ASC in which they invest.

6 Becker's ASC Review: CMS 2012 Proposed Ruling.

Through the relevant operating or partnership agreement, some ASCs require that all physician-owners meet both of these one-third tests to maintain ownership in the ASC, while other ASCs are more flexible and the terms for maintaining ownership are less defined. Not all, but most, ASCs require that physician owners be approved for admission to ownership and that they be redeemed upon their disability, retirement, or move from their service area.

#### *Buy-Sell*

In either case (purchase or redemption), many ASC operating or partnership agreements require that physicians are redeemed, or purchase shares, at either fair market value or an amount based on a formula—often three to four times EBITDA less interest-bearing debt. While occasionally ASC operating or partnership agreements may in effect penalize owners selling an interest, more often than not the buy-sell provisions ensure that the amount received for a redemption is either at or similar to fair market value.

To summarize, the provisions for cash distributions, ownership, and buy-sell arrangements typically included in ASC operating or partnership agreements reduce the impact of lack of control and marketability for noncontrolling equity interests.

### Typical ASC Financial Structure and Performance

All facilities are different. However, VMG Health annually completes benchmarking studies that are free to download at the company's website (www.vmghealth.com). The *Multi-Specialty Intellimarker Study* is based on analyses of actual detailed financial and operating performance information from more than 200 multispecialty surgery centers across the United States. Exhibits 6 through 8 summarize the aggregate statistical analysis of the income statements from the Multi-Specialty *ASC Intellimarker 2011*. Our observations on this data follow.

## Exhibit 6. Median and Standard Income Statement

| *$ in thousands* | Mean | Standard Dev. | 25% | Median 50% | 75% | 90% |
|---|---|---|---|---|---|---|
| **Patient Revenues** | | | | | | |
| Gross Charges | $ 29,979 | $ 18,170 | $ 16,887 | $ 25,688 | $ 40,307 | $ 56,561 |
| Adjustments | (10,288) | (24,763) | (7,716) | (13,014) | (23,653) | (39,734) |
| Net Revenue | 7,736 | 4,530 | 4,479 | 6,957 | 9,710 | 13,260 |
| **Operating Expenses** | | | | | | |
| Employee Salary & Wages | 1,552 | 807 | 1,000 | 1,418 | 1,882 | 2,449 |
| Employee Taxes & Benefits | 359 | 211 | 210 | 332 | 460 | 582 |
| Occupancy Costs | 477 | 299 | 253 | 441 | 621 | 858 |
| Medical & Surgical Supplies | 1,530 | 965 | 818 | 1,365 | 2,018 | 2,682 |
| Other Medical Costs | 111 | 142 | 24 | 67 | 138 | 210 |
| Insurance | 53 | 39 | 28 | 44 | 69 | 98 |
| Depreciation & Amortization | 349 | 253 | 178 | 280 | 4,589 | 682 |
| General & Administrative | | | | 118 | | |
| Bad Debt | 162 | 1,583 | 62 | 322 | 196 | 313 |
| Management Fees | 360 | 235 | 191 | 592 | 462 | 632 |
| Other G & A | 662 | 394 | 396 | 1,006 | 805 | 1,184 |
| Total G & A | 1,123 | 635 | 707 | 774 | 1,384 | 1,870 |
| Total Operating Expenses | 5,222 | 2,485 | 3,497 | 5,235 | 6,475 | 8,311 |
| **Operating Income** | 2,165 | 2,525 | 481 | 1,461 | 3,115 | 5,607 |
| Other Expense (Income) | 86 | 346 | 1 | 5 | 21 | 69 |
| Net Interest Expense | 110 | 130 | 20 | 63 | 144 | 280 |
| **Earnings Before Taxes** | 2,052 | 2,531 | 345 | 1,383 | 3,115 | 5,597 |
| **EBITDA** | $ 2,513 | $ 2,585 | $ 701 | $ 1,807 | $ 3,421 | $ 6,123 |

*VMG HEALTH Multi-Specialty ASC Intellimarker 2011*

## Exhibit 7. Common Size Income Statement

| | Mean | Standard Dev. | 25% | Median 50% | 75% | 90% |
|---|---|---|---|---|---|---|
| **Patient Revenues** | | | | | | |
| Gross Charges | 395.1% | 140.9% | 293.1% | 372.6% | 483.8% | 585.7% |
| Adjustments | -126.4% | -302.7% | -140.0% | -209.8% | -346.5% | -454.6% |
| Net Revenue | 100.0% | 0.0% | 100.0% | 100.0% | 100.0% | 100.0% |
| **Operating Expenses** | | | | | | |
| Employee Salary & Wages | 22.7% | 7.4% | 17.3% | 22.1% | 27.2% | 32.7% |
| Employee Taxes & Benefits | 5.2% | 2.0% | 3.7% | 5.0% | 6.3% | 8.0% |
| Occupancy Costs | 7.5% | 4.8% | 4.2% | 6.7% | 9.7% | 13.1% |
| Medical & Surgical Supplies | 20.8% | 7.1% | 16.6% | 21.3% | 25.3% | 29.6% |
| Other Medical Costs | 1.5% | 1.5% | 0.4% | 1.0% | 1.9% | 3.5% |
| Insurance | 0.8% | 0.6% | 0.4% | 0.7% | 1.0% | 1.3% |
| Depreciation & Amortization | 5.5% | 5.5% | 2.4% | 3.8% | 6.7% | 11.6% |
| General & Administrative | | | | | | |
| Bad Debt | 2.1% | 1.8% | 1.0% | 1.5% | 2.7% | 4.0% |
| Management Fees | 4.8% | 2.5% | 3.7% | 4.9% | 5.9% | 6.8% |
| Other G & A | 9.6% | 4.5% | 6.6% | 8.6% | 11.7% | 14.7% |
| Total G & A | 15.4% | 5.5% | 12.0% | 22.8% | 18.1% | 22.0% |
| Total Operating Expenses | 73.1% | 17.8% | 61.0% | 75.0% | 84.5% | 94.8% |
| **Operating Income** | 21.6% | 20.7% | 10.5% | 22.2% | 34.8% | 47.9% |
| Other Expense (Income) | 1.5% | 5.0% | 0.0% | 0.1% | 0.5% | 1.5% |
| Net Interest Expense | 2.0% | 3.4% | 0.3% | 0.9% | 2.2% | 5.3% |
| **Earnings Before Taxes** | 19.5% | 22.7% | 8.1% | 20.9% | 34.3% | 47.0% |
| **EBITDA** | 26.9% | 17.8% | 15.5% | 27.1% | 39.0% | 51.3% |

*VMG HEALTH Multi-Specialty ASC Intellimarker 2011*

**Exhibit 8. Operating Expense Analysis**

| *as a % of Net Revenue* | Mean | Standard Dev. | 25% | Median 50% | 75% | 90% |
|---|---|---|---|---|---|---|
| Employee Salary & Wages | 22.7% | 7.4% | 17.3% | 22.2% | 27.2% | 32.7% |
| Employee Taxes & Benefits | 5.2% | 2.0% | 3.7% | 5.0% | 6.3% | 8.0% |
| Occupancy Costs | 7.5% | 4.8% | 4.2% | 6.7% | 9.7% | 13.1% |
| Medical & Surgical Supplies | 20.9% | 7.1% | 16.6% | 21.3% | 25.3% | 29.6% |
| Other Medical Costs | 1.5% | 1.6% | 0.4% | 1.0% | 1.9% | 3.5% |
| Insurance | 0.8% | 0.6% | 0.4% | 0.7% | 1.0% | 1.3% |
| General & Administrative | 15.4% | 5.5% | 12.0% | 22.8% | 18.1% | 22.0% |
| Total Operating Expenses | 73.1% | 17.8% | 61.0% | 75.0% | 84.5% | 94.8% |
| ***per Square Foot*** | | | | | | |
| Employee Salary & Wages | $ 108.92 | $ 45.80 | $ 77.28 | $ 103.31 | $ 129.39 | $ 168.92 |
| Employee Taxes & Benefits | 25.24 | 11.62 | 17.45 | 23.58 | 30.95 | 39.09 |
| Occupancy Costs | 34.37 | 12.23 | 26.76 | 34.87 | 41.43 | 48.06 |
| Medical & Surgical Supplies | 103.02 | 58.66 | 63.22 | 94.97 | 125.20 | 175.74 |
| Other Medical Costs | 7.17 | 8.00 | 1.81 | 4.91 | 9.35 | 15.96 |
| Insurance | 3.90 | 3.35 | 1.73 | 2.96 | 4.94 | 7.63 |
| General & Administrative | 81.68 | 61.05 | 47.76 | 68.98 | 96.21 | 136.69 |
| Total Operating Expenses | $ 364.31 | $ 200.70 | $ 236.01 | $ 333.58 | $ 437.47 | $ 592.10 |
| ***per OR ($ in thousands)*** | | | | | | |
| Employee Salary & Wages | $ 421.8 | $ 212.9 | $ 301.1 | $ 394.0 | $ 474.1 | $ 621.4 |
| Employee Taxes & Benefits | 96.7 | 51.7 | 66.7 | 87.5 | 115.1 | 161.8 |
| Occupancy Costs | 129.1 | 69.9 | 91.6 | 120.5 | 161.7 | 206.9 |
| Medical & Surgical Supplies | 401.4 | 230.4 | 259.6 | 375.4 | 499.6 | 639.7 |
| Other Medical Costs | 28.4 | 35.7 | 6.4 | 18.4 | 33.6 | 63.2 |
| Insurance | 14.9 | 13.3 | 7.0 | 11.3 | 18.2 | 28.2 |
| General & Administrative | 325.8 | 255.0 | 185.2 | 259.4 | 387.2 | 586.3 |
| Total Operating Expenses | $ 1,418.1 | $ 868.9 | $ 917.5 | $ 1,266.6 | $ 1,689.5 | $ 2,307.6 |
| ***per Case*** | | | | | | |
| Employee Salary & Wages | $ 358.60 | $ 144.68 | $ 272.85 | $ 337.23 | $ 416.12 | $ 527.76 |
| Employee Taxes & Benefits | 82.62 | 38.93 | 59.59 | 75.42 | 100.23 | 130.75 |
| Occupancy Costs | 122.45 | 94.29 | 63.34 | 107.60 | 152.47 | 230.79 |
| Medical & Surgical Supplies | 353.16 | 191.86 | 233.73 | 323.97 | 463.62 | 563.93 |
| Other Medical Costs | 24.69 | 27.75 | 6.95 | 14.73 | 310.60 | 48.51 |
| Insurance | 12.52 | 11.20 | 7.14 | 10.10 | 14.55 | 20.75 |
| General & Administrative | 282.00 | 204.66 | 162.98 | 237.62 | 339.57 | 496.80 |
| Total Operating Expenses | $1,236.03 | $ 713.36 | $ 806.57 | $1,106.66 | $1,517.62 | $2,019.31 |

*VMG HEALTH Multi-Specialty ASC Intellimarker 2011*

## Income Statement Observations

Median net revenue, or reimbursement for ASCs participating in the *Multi-Specialty ASC Intellimarker 2011,* is $7 million and median earnings before interest taxes depreciation and amortization (EBITDA) is $1.8 million. The single largest expense component is employee cost, including salaries, wages, taxes, and benefits, representing 27% of net revenue. Median medical and surgical supplies costs represent 21% of net revenue. Median EBITDA is 27% of net revenue.

Net revenue for ASCs is driven by volume and specialty mix and varies widely across the spectrum of specialties. Exhibit 9 summarizes the median net revenue per case by specialty from the *Multi-Specialty ASC Intellimarker 2011.*

**Exhibit 9. Multi-Specialty Revenue per Case**

| | Specialty | Gross Charges |
|---|---|---|
| ENT | ENT | $7,433 |
| GI | GI/Endoscopy | $3,517 |
| GEN | General Surgery | $6,058 |
| GYN | OB/GYN | $6,788 |
| OPH | Ophthalmology | $5,708 |
| ORA | Oral Surgery | $3,464 |
| ORT | Orthopedics | $9,398 |
| PM | Pain Management | $4,103 |
| PS | Plastic Surgery | $6,738 |
| POD | Podiatry | $7,574 |
| URO | Urology | $6,484 |

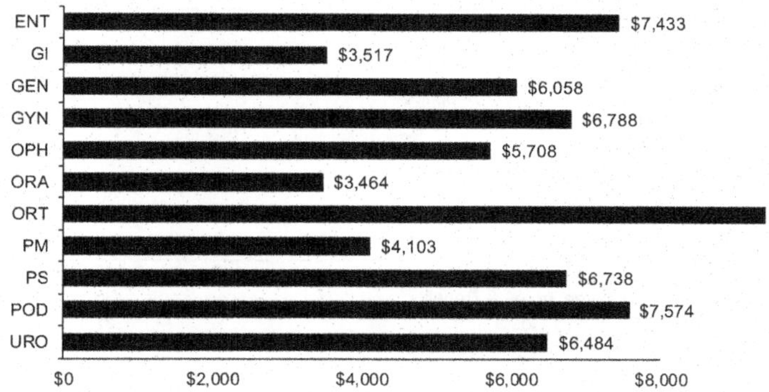


| | Specialty | Net Revenue |
|---|---|---|
| ENT | ENT | $1,761 |
| GI | GI/Endoscopy | $778 |
| GEN | General Surgery | $1,689 |
| GYN | OB/GYN | $1,953 |
| OPH | Ophthalmology | $1,267 |
| ORA | Oral Surgery | $1,078 |
| ORT | Orthopedics | $2,585 |
| PM | Pain Management | $955 |
| PS | Plastic Surgery | $1,516 |
| POD | Podiatry | $1,871 |
| URO | Urology | $1,639 |

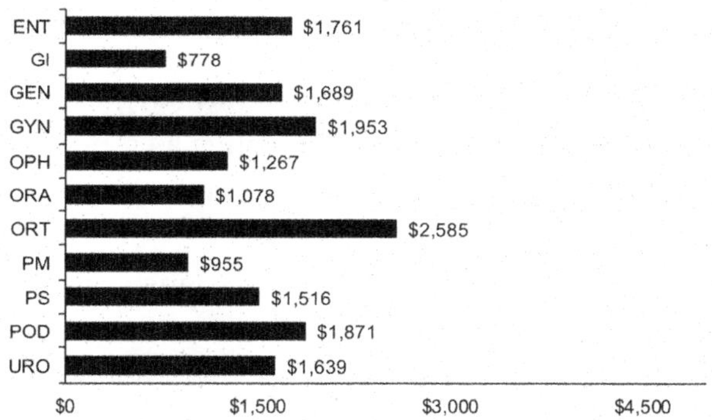


*VMG HEALTH Multi-Specialty ASC Intellimarker 2011*

From the *Multi-Specialty ASC Intellimarker 2011*, net revenue per case ranges from $778 for GI/endoscopy and $955 for pain management on the low end to $2,585 for orthopedics on the high end.

While there is some variability in operating expenses from center to center, the largest components—employee costs and medical and surgical supplies—are both driven primarily by the case specialty mix in an ASC. Generally speaking, less complex cases, such as those procedures for GI/endoscopy and pain, require fewer staffing hours and supplies than more complex cases, such as those in orthopedics. Exhibit 10 contrasts costs per case for all multispecialty ASCs and ASCs with greater than 50% orthopedics.

**Exhibit 10. GI/MS/Ortho Oper Exp % of Net Rev and per Case Comparison**

| | Median | | |
|---|---|---|---|
| *as a % of Net Revenue* | GI | All MS | MS > 50% Ortho |
| Employee Salary & Wages | 22.3% | 22.2% | 19.2% |
| Employee Taxes & Benefits | 5.2% | 5.0% | 4.3% |
| Occupancy Costs | 4.3% | 6.7% | 6.4% |
| Medical & Surgical Supplies | 7.6% | 21.3% | 20.8% |
| Other Medical Costs | 1.8% | 1.0% | 0.7% |
| Insurance | 1.2% | 0.7% | 0.5% |
| General & Administrative | 13.8% | 22.8% | 13.2% |
| Total Operating Expenses | 60.0% | 75.0% | 65.0% |
| *per Case* | | | |
| Employee Salary & Wages | $ 135.92 | $ 337.23 | $ 482.50 |
| Employee Taxes & Benefits | 36.86 | 75.42 | 103.76 |
| Occupancy Costs | 27.14 | 107.60 | 156.46 |
| Medical & Surgical Supplies | 44.63 | 323.97 | 545.27 |
| Other Medical Costs | 10.44 | 14.73 | 22.89 |
| Insurance | 5.94 | 10.10 | 10.16 |
| General & Administrative | 99.37 | 237.62 | 41.42 |
| Total Operating Expenses | $ 368.60 | $1,106.66 | $1,362.46 |

*VMG HEALTH Endoscopy Intellimarker 2007 and Multi-Specialty ASC Intellimarker 2011*

Unlike employee costs and medical and surgical supplies per case, median employee costs and medical and surgical supplies as a percentage of net revenue are fairly consistent across the spectrum of case complexity.

Since the most significant operating expense categories tend to vary somewhat consistently with revenue, the primary driver of surgery-center profitability is relative reimbursement levels. Relative reimbursement levels are, in turn, determined by both the payor mix and an individual center's commercial reimbursement. Government payors such as Medicare and Medicaid tend to reimburse ASCs less than commercial or managed care payors. Local market conditions and the strength of the ASC's commercial and managed-care contracts may affect that ASC's relative commercial reimbursement.

## Balance sheet observations

Median total assets for ASCs participating in the *Multi-Specialty ASC Intellimarker 2011* is $3.1 million and median long-term debt is $1 million. Median total current assets and net property, plant, and equipment represent 43% and 37% of total assets, respectively. Median long-term debt is 31% of total assets. In comparison to the income-statement categories, the standard deviation for balance-sheet categories, and in particular, net property, plant, and equipment and long-term debt, are much higher.

Exhibits 11 and 12 demonstrate the aggregate statistical analysis of the balance sheets from the *Multi-Specialty ASC Intellimarker 2011*.

## Exhibit 11. Multi-Specialty Balance Sheet

| *$ in thousands* | Mean | Standard Dev. | 25% | Median 50% | 75% | 90% |
|---|---|---|---|---|---|---|
| **ASSETS** | | | | | | |
| Cash & Equivalents | $ 744 | $ 783 | $ 242 | $ 511 | $ 924 | $ 1,747 |
| Net Accounts Receivable | 781 | 500 | 427 | 657 | 951 | 1,393 |
| Other Current Assets | 224 | 200 | 100 | 175 | 291 | 439 |
| Total Current Assets | 1,686 | 1,206 | 844 | 1,327 | 2,205 | 3,341 |
| Gross PP&E | 4,100 | 2,699 | 2,103 | 3,328 | 5,597 | 8,321 |
| Accumulated Depreciation | (2,435) | 1,615 | (3,396) | (2,091) | (1,210) | (695) |
| Net PP&E | 1,724 | 1,645 | 551 | 1,132 | 2,513 | 3,902 |
| Other Assets | 1,216 | 3,675 | 17 | 73 | 582 | 2,628 |
| Total Assets | $ 4,071 | $ 3,600 | $ 1,831 | $ 3,100 | $ 5,499 | $ 8,043 |
| **LIABILITIES** | | | | | | |
| Current Liabilities | $ 457 | $ 361 | $ 255 | $ 359 | $ 555 | $ 830 |
| Current Portion of LTD | 276 | 240 | 92 | 212 | 402 | 576 |
| Total Current Liabilites | 599 | 448 | 297 | 501 | 796 | 1,169 |
| Total Long-Term Debt | 1,303 | 1,436 | 172 | 758 | 2,028 | 3,270 |
| Other LT Liabilities | 302 | 862 | 4 | 31 | 245 | 604 |
| Total Liabilities | 1,846 | 1,728 | 578 | 1,257 | 2,667 | 4,007 |
| **EQUITY** | | | | | | |
| Total Shareholders' Equity | 2,264 | 3,030 | 751 | 1,429 | 2,792 | 4,669 |
| Total Liabilities & Equity | $ 4,071 | $ 3,600 | $ 1,831 | $ 3,100 | $ 5,499 | $ 8,043 |

*VMG HEALTH Multi-Specialty ASC Intellimarker 2011*

## Exhibit 12. Multi-Specialty Common Size Balance Sheet

| | Mean | Standard Dev. | 25% | Median 50% | 75% | 90% |
|---|---|---|---|---|---|---|
| **ASSETS** | | | | | | |
| Cash & Equivalents | 18.3% | 21.8% | 13.2% | 16.5% | 16.8% | 21.7% |
| Net Accounts Receivable | 19.2% | 13.9% | 23.3% | 21.2% | 17.3% | 17.3% |
| Other Current Assets | 5.5% | 5.6% | 5.5% | 5.7% | 5.3% | 5.5% |
| Total Current Assets | 41.4% | 33.5% | 46.1% | 42.8% | 40.1% | 41.5% |
| Gross PP&E | 100.7% | 75.0% | 114.8% | 107.4% | 101.8% | 103.5% |
| Accumulated Depreciation | -59.8% | 44.9% | -185.4% | -67.4% | -22.0% | -8.6% |
| Net PP&E | 42.4% | 45.7% | 30.1% | 36.5% | 45.7% | 48.5% |
| Other Assets | 29.9% | 102.1% | 1.0% | 2.4% | 10.6% | 32.7% |
| Total Assets | 100.0% | 100.0% | 100.0% | 100.0% | 100.0% | 100.0% |
| **LIABILITIES** | | | | | | |
| Current Liabilities | 11.3% | 10.0% | 13.9% | 11.6% | 10.1% | 10.3% |
| Current Portion of LTD | 6.8% | 6.7% | 5.0% | 6.9% | 7.3% | 7.2% |
| Total Current Liabilites | 14.7% | 12.5% | 16.3% | 16.2% | 14.5% | 14.6% |
| Total Long-Term Debt | 32.0% | 39.9% | 9.4% | 24.5% | 36.9% | 40.7% |
| Other LT Liabilities | 7.4% | 24.0% | 0.3% | 1.0% | 4.5% | 7.5% |
| Total Liabilities | 45.4% | 48.0% | 31.6% | 40.6% | 48.5% | 49.8% |
| EQUITY | | | | | | |
| Shareholders' Equity | 55.6% | 84.2% | 41.1% | 46.1% | 50.8% | 58.1% |
| **Total Liabilities & Equity** | 100.0% | 100.0% | 100.0% | 100.0% | 100.0% | 100.0% |

*VMG HEALTH Multi-Specialty ASC Intellimarker 2011*

### Does the past tell us anything about the future?

Yes. No. Maybe. Maybe not. It depends. These all could be appropriate answers in a given situation. Whether an appraiser attempts to attach an appropriate market multiple to historical earnings or to develop "most likely case" projections, the future is much more important than the past. ASCs with a substantial portion of out-of-network revenue, (and all other things being equal) the sustainability of maintaining relatively high out-of-network reimbursements is in question. In other words, there is a substantial "risk" in relying on the past to project future performance.

### ASC risk-assessment matrix

It's important to look at the inherent risks of investing in an ASC. To do so, we'll look at a tool developed by Jon O'Sullivan of VMG Health that measures risk along the following lines:

- Contracting;
- service-area growth;
- competition;
- physician ownership;
- nonowner utilization;
- concentration by specialty;
- out-of-network concentration;
- staff and supplies efficiency;
- location; and
- condition of the facility and equipment.

See Exhibit 13 for the complete ASC Risk-Assessment Matrix.

The ASC Risk Assessment Matrix produces a single score but gives different weights to different categories and subcategories based on their relative importance to measuring risk. The weighting may be adjusted based on specific facts and circumstances, but typically, the highest weights are assigned to categories that directly affect volume and reimbursement expectations (e.g., the physician utilization profile, market reimbursement risk analysis, and market competition).

### Exhibit 13. ASC Risk Assessment Matrix – Risk Assessment

| Risk Metric | | Risk Metric: Sub-categories 1 (Highest Risk) to 5 (Lowest Risk) | | | | |
|---|---|---|---|---|---|---|
| Description | Weight | Description | Weight | Rating | Grade | Total |
| **Partnership Operating Agreement** | 3.0% | | | | | |
| | | Buy/Sell Provisions: Voluntary/Involuntary (A1) | 30.0% | 5.0 | | 0.05 |
| | | Covenants Not to Compete (A2) | 30.0% | 5.0 | | 0.05 |
| | | Eligibility Rqmts: Safe Harbors, Active Staff (A3) | 20.0% | 5.0 | | 0.03 |
| | | Governance Structure: GP/LP, LLC, LLP (A4) | 10.0% | 1.0 | | 0.00 |
| | | Partnership Structure Sustainability/Legal Life (A5) | 10.0% | 5.0 | 84% | 0.02 |
| **Partnership Distribution History** | 3.0% | | | | | |
| | | Minority Distribution: Terms and History (A6) | 40.0% | 5.0 | | 0.06 |
| | | 5 year history of distributions (A7) | 30.0% | 5.0 | | 0.05 |
| | | Percentage of Available Cash (A8) | 30.0% | 5.0 | 100% | 0.05 |
| **Partnership Ownership** | 10.0% | | | | | |
| | | Percent of Revenue Produced by Owners (B1) | 30.0% | 5.0 | | 0.15 |
| | | Specialty Mix (B2) | 25.0% | 5.0 | | 0.13 |
| | | Age Dispersion (B3) | 25.0% | 4.0 | | 0.10 |
| | | Number of Physician Owners (B4) | 20.0% | 3.0 | 85% | 0.06 |
| **Concentration of Surgical Specialty** | 5.0% | | | | | |
| | | Volume Concentration by Specialty (D2) | 50.0% | 4.0 | | 0.10 |
| | | Revenue Concentration by Specialty (D3) | 50.0% | 4.0 | 80% | 0.10 |
| **Physician Utilization Profile** | 27.0% | | | | | |
| | | Revenue Dispersion Among Owners (B5) | 30.0% | 2.0 | | 0.16 |
| | | Revenue Dispersion Among Non Owners (C1) | 15.0% | 5.0 | | 0.20 |
| | | Volume Growth History (D1) | 12.5% | 2.0 | | 0.07 |
| | | Ownership by Utilizers in Competing Centers (B6) | 12.5% | 3.0 | | 0.10 |
| | | Individual Physician Volume Retention (B7) | 15.0% | 3.0 | | 0.12 |
| | | Physician Retention Risk (B8) | 15.0% | 2.0 | 57% | 0.08 |
| **Market Reimbursement Risk Analysis** | 25.0% | | | | | |
| | | Revenue Concentration by Payor (E1) | 15.0% | 4.0 | | 0.15 |
| | | Percentage of out of network business (E2) | 60.0% | 2.0 | | 0.30 |
| | | Commercial Reimbursement Relative to Medicare (E3) | 10.0% | 5.0 | | 0.13 |
| | | Pending Legislation Impacting Reimbursement (E4) | 15.0% | 3.0 | 70% | 0.11 |
| **Market Competition Profile** | 15.0% | | | | | |
| | | Health system competition (A13) | 20.0% | 2.0 | | 0.06 |
| | | Freestanding surgery center competition (A14) | 25.0% | 1.0 | | 0.04 |
| | | Potential For New Centers (A15) | 20.0% | 2.0 | | 0.06 |
| | | Market Demographic Growth (A16) | 15.0% | 2.0 | | 0.05 |
| | | Percentage of Physicians with no ASC Investment (A17) | 20.0% | 1.0 | 32% | 0.03 |
| **Barrier to Entry Analysis** | 5.0% | | | | | |
| | | Existence of Certificate of Need (A11) | 50.0% | 5.0 | | 0.13 |
| | | Managed Care Barriers (A12) | 50.0% | 5.0 | 100% | 0.13 |
| **ASC Management/Expense Efficiency** | 2.0% | | | | | |
| | | Relative Staff Efficiency (F1) | 30.0% | 5.0 | | 0.03 |
| | | Relative Supply Cost Efficiency (F2) | 30.0% | 3.0 | | 0.02 |
| | | Existence of Labor Unions (A9) | 20.0% | 5.0 | | 0.02 |
| | | Geographic Cost Index (F3) | 20.0% | 3.0 | 80% | 0.01 |
| **ASC Physical Attributes** | 5.0% | | | | | |
| | | Location in Relation to Affiliated Acute Care Hospital (A10) | 40.0% | 1.0 | | 0.02 |
| | | Age and Condition of Facility (G1) | 20.0% | 4.0 | | 0.04 |
| | | Facility Location Sustainability (G2) | 30.0% | 4.0 | | 0.06 |
| | | Capital Equipment Obsolescence (G3) | 10.0% | 4.0 | 65% | 0.02 |
| **Total Risk Score** | **100.0%** | | | | | **3.05** |

***Note: If any Risk Metric Category has a Grade of less than 60%, a FMV analysis should be conducted***

### *Primary ASC Value Drivers*

An ASC is an accumulation of the practices of the individual surgeons using the facility. Physician practices may be generally characterized as growing, mature, or declining. To assess where an ASC falls on this continuum and the potential for its volume growth, it is critical to analyze the historical case volume by physician and specialty. If, for example, the largest physician utilizers of an ASC are, for the most part, approaching the end of the mature stage of their respective practices, the current volumes and earnings may be relatively strong. However, this may not translate into expectations for growth or a strong future.

Remember, also, that 2008 was the first year of the transition from a payment system based on ASC groupers to one based on a percentage of HOPD APCs. While this move was designed to be neutral overall to Medicare payments, it will result in significant financial losses for GI/endoscopy and pain cases and significant gains for orthopedics and general surgery. For multispecialty ASCs with a balanced case mix, this change may not have affected overall revenues and earnings. However, ASCs with a concentration in one or more of the specialties significantly affected may win or lose big.

In addition, projected reimbursement should take into account out-of-network payments. In many states, large commercial and managed care payors such as Blue Cross have developed statewide fee schedules that apply to all contracted (in-network) ASCs. Rather than simply accepting the relatively low rates, which may range between 110% and 130% of Medicare, ASCs using an out-of-network strategy may collect significantly more based on the usual and customary rates. Because reimbursement may be higher out of network, a large number of ASCs contract with few or no commercial or managed care payors.

However, many commercial and managed care payors have taken steps to eliminate or reduce the level of out-of-network payments. In many markets, commercial and managed care payors have instituted measures in response to the increased costs of out-of-network payments. Examples of these include the following:

- Increased patient responsibility for payment for procedures performed in out-of-network facilities;
- Payment to patients rather than to facilities, requiring ASCs to seek payment for out-of-network services from the patient; and
- Requirement that physicians conduct procedures in contracted facilities to receive professional fees.

Though the efforts of the commercial and managed care payors to curb out-of-network payments have either not been attempted or not been entirely successful, the industry appears to agree that high out-of-network payments are not likely sustainable over the long term. In some cases, the conversion from out-of-network to in-network rates could be immediate; in others, it could take several years.

Regardless of how long the transition takes, it's crucial to look at the potential outcome it will have on volumes. Requiring physicians to do procedures in contracted facilities to receive professional fees may result in movement of those surgeries to hospitals or in-network surgery centers. The increase in volume that often comes with converting an ASC from out of network to in network may partially or entirely offset the reduction in rates.

#### *ASC Valuation Purpose*

As is the case with most valuations in the healthcare industry, the predominant overriding purpose for most ASC valuations is compliance with the fair market value requirements established by the Stark regulations and the federal fraud and abuse and anti-dickback statutes.

While the federal anti-kickback statutes include a safe harbor for surgeons who wish to own an equity interest in an ASC to which they refer patients, pricing for any transaction involving a potential referral source physician must be consistent with fair market value. Whether they are buyers or sellers, hospital systems that have some level of ownership in an ASC are most concerned with ensuring that the purchase of an ownership interest from a physician does not exceed fair market value or the sale of an interest is not less than fair market value. Hence, most ASC valuation engagements happen at the request of a hospital or nonphysician ASC owner-operator for either the hospital system or the ASC owner-operator. The most common specific applications involve:

1. Purchase or sale of controlling equity interest;
2. Purchase or sale of noncontrolling equity interests; and
3. Conversion of a center operated as an HOPD to a free-standing joint venture and simultaneous offering of noncontrolling equity interests in the free-standing joint venture.

### Purchase or sale of controlling equity interest

The most common buyers of a controlling equity interest in an ASC are the national developers and operators of ASCs-hospital systems. Surveys have consistently found that the ASC owner-operators most commonly analyze and price controlling equity interest transactions using a multiple of EBITDA less interest-bearing debt.[7] In light of their talent for recruiting additional physician-owners and improving or maintaining

7 VMG Health: *2011 Value Driver ASC Survey* and HealthCare Appraisers,Inc.: *2008 ASC Valuation Survey* and *2007 ASC Valuation Survey.*

efficient operations, ASC owner-operators are typically less concerned than noncontrolling equity interest holders or hospital systems about the risks associated with potential volume loss.

ASC owner-operators often prefer to own a controlling equity interest to gain control over decisions typically associated with ASC entities such as:

- Deciding which physicians retain or receive equity in the ASC and
- Maintaining the contractual relationship for management of the ASC.

Unlike ASC owner-operators who typically price controlling equity interest transactions using a multiple of EBITDA, most hospital systems rely on the fair market value opinion provided by an independent appraiser to ensure that they meet Stark and fraud and abuse statute requirements and private inurement concerns. Various professional standards require that business appraisers consider all relevant approaches and methods in developing an opinion of value. These other approaches and in particular, the income approach or discounted cash flow method, may provide a superior framework for measuring the impact of the individual facts and circumstances surrounding a subject ASC.

**Cost approach.** Some ASCs are either not profitable or not expected to provide a return greater than the required return on the working capital and fixed assets employed in the operation of the ASC. The key is not historical earnings or cash flows, but instead projected earnings and cash flows under the control of a typical owner-operator.

In a transaction for a controlling interest, an ASC owner-operator is not likely to pay for all, or maybe even any, of the intangible value created through the ownership and management of an ASC. However, in the context of a make-or-buy decision typical of this type of transaction, the buyer may pay for the assembly of all tangible and some intangible assets (e.g., CON, an ASC license, and payor contracts) under the premise of value in continued use, as part of a mass assemblage of assets.

This asset approach provides a "floor," or lowest minimum value, related to a controlling interest in an ASC and may be appropriate when the market and income approaches (which are discussed later) produce lower values.

Surgery centers are an asset-intensive business. The median gross property and equipment plus working capital per operating room from VMG Health's *Multi-Specialty ASC Intellimarker 2011* is approximately $1.3 million. Depending on the age and condition of the furniture and equipment, the costs associated with these assets for an ASC may be substantial. Often, the application of the cost approach is important in situations in which an ASC has been overbuilt in terms of the space (e.g., number of operating and procedure rooms) and equipment required to accommodate the book of business.

**Intangible assets.** Even an ASC that has historically generated operating losses must consider the effect of intangible assets. The intangible assets in this case would be those that almost always have some legal title and are often separately marketable, including:

1. Certificate of need (CON);
2. ASC license; and
3. Payor contracts.

*Certificate of need.* Some states require a CON for an ASC to be licensed by the state and receive reimbursement from public payors, such as Medicare and Medicaid. Again, in the context of the make-or-buy decision, a potential buyer will evaluate the probability of obtaining a CON. In states such as Georgia, Iowa, Kentucky, and Tennessee, for example, many markets are saturated, making it extremely unlikely that a CON for a new surgery center could be obtained.

The valuation methodology for a CON may take the form of a cash-flow comparison under two scenarios: 1) the first assumes the CON is in place; and 2) the second assumes it is not. Using this with-and-without methodology, the value of the CON is quantified as the differential in the present value of the cash flows. In cases where it is likely that a CON might be obtained after legal and consulting costs are incurred and the passage of time, the incremental cash flows simply represent the present value of these incremental costs and cash flows foregone during the time required to obtain a CON. In extreme cases where the perceived probability of getting a CON seems remote, the present value of the incremental cash flows resulting from this analysis approaches the entire unidentified intangible value of the ASC. Since in this case the cash flows without a CON simply reflect the liquidation of the ASC's assets, the present value in the first scenario should be reduced by the value of the working capital, tangible assets, and identified intangible assets. While the probability of getting a CON today may currently be near zero in many markets, the probability likely increases over time. As a result, some discount to the incremental cash flows may also be considered.

Another consideration in the application of the with-and-without methodology is the use of actual and expected versus typical financial performance in the cash-flow projections for the two scenarios. The volumes, reimbursement, and operating expenses assumed in the model should consider whether the buyers' or sellers' expectations reflect their specific circumstances or those of a typical buyer. This assumption is of particular import when either historical operations or future reimbursement expectations reflect the operation of the ASC as a department of a hospital. In particular, if either the historical or projected financial statements provided reflect reimbursement at hospital rates rather than normalized free-standing rates, the rates utilized in the projections for this analysis should reflect normalized free-standing rates.

*ASC license.* An ASC is normally licensed by both the particular state in which it operates and Medicare. It may take two or three months before an ASC receives licensure from both entities. This delay causes a delay in commencing the ramp-up period for operations, and in turn, a delay in reimbursement.

An ASC with a license in place can avoid this period of reduced cash flows. Like with a CON, the valuation methodology normally takes the form of a with-and-without analysis. The value of a CON exceeds that of a license because licenses are much easier to obtain. However, there is still uncertainty surrounding the licensing process. In California, for example, it's unclear how long obtaining an ASC license can take. Some developers believe that it could take more than a year. In states requiring a CON, the value of an ASC license is generally not separated from the value of the CON.

*Payor contracts.* Recent experiences in California also point to the need to consider payor contracts as a potential source of significant value, particularly in cases in which the ASC has contracts with reimbursement in excess of market levels or in which large payors are threatening not to extend contracts to new ASCs. ASC payor contracts that cannot be terminated without cause and multiyear terms are uncommon, but there may be circumstances in which ASCs expect current reimbursement levels to extend beyond the legal term of the contract. Once again, the valuation methodology for payor contracts normally takes the form of a with-and-without analysis.

**Market approach.** ASC developers and operators generally rely on the market approach in pricing transactions. More specifically, they rely on the individual transactions method and use a multiple of EBITDA less interest-bearing debt in pricing a controlling equity interest in an ASC. Surveys have found that most respondents typically observed valuation multiples for controlling equity interests of six to seven times EBITDA or more less interest-bearing debt.[8]

8 VMG Health: *2011 Value Driver ASC Survey* and HealthCare Appraisers Inc.: *2008 ASC Valuation Survey* and *2007 ASC Valuation Survey*.

While ASC developers and operators often reference and use these general-market-guideline multiples, many factors may lead to an adjustment of the historical EBITDA or an ultimate transaction price that resides outside of this range.

In the discussion of the primary ASC value drivers, we detailed the need to consider changes in Medicare and out-of-network reimbursement when analyzing historical information and developing future projections. Based on our experience, the six to seven times or more multiple used to price the purchase of a controlling interest is often applied to prospective or adjusted, rather than raw, historical EBITDA. Accordingly, ASC developers and operators often adjust for changes in reimbursement to estimate the EBITDA to which the multiple is applied. Due to expected changes in the practices of physician utilizers or competitive factors that historical performance might not reflect, prospective or adjusted EBITDA may also reflect case-volume changes.

In addition to adjusting for potential reimbursement and volume changes, historical EBITDA may not reflect the payment of a management fee.

*Valuation impact of management fees.* Virtually all multicenter owner-operators of ASCs charge the centers a fee of between 4% and 7% of net revenues to provide management services. For this fee, the manager typically does the following:

- Manages the ASCs finances and annual operating budgets;
- Administers all accounting, accounts payable, and purchasing functions;
- Manages human resources;
- Oversees information technology;
- Handles public relations;
- Develops plans for facilities and services;
- Maintain all necessary licenses and regulatory compliance;
- Designs, institutes, and supervises the physical and administrative operations of the ASC;
- Prepares and submits all tax returns and cost reports; and
- Negotiates and consummates agreements and third-party contracts.

Incremental costs associated with providing these services are generally fairly minimal. As a result, the contribution margin is very high. In addition, because the owner-operator receives the management fee off the revenue line before operating expenses, the risk associated with the fee is significantly less than the earnings generated by the owner-operator's equity investment in the ASC. Accordingly, when evaluating multiples from guideline transactions, it is particularly critical to understand whether the buyer received a management fee contract pursuant to the transaction.

To illustrate, suppose that an ASC owner-operator pays an amount equal to seven times EBITDA less debt for a 60% interest in the ASC and enters into a long-term management contract at 5% of net revenues. Assuming the subject ASC's revenues are $4 million, its EBITDA is $1 million, and the contribution margin on the management fee is 50%, this seven multiple becomes a six multiple after consideration of the additional $100,000 margin associated with the management contract. If the management fee is greater than 5% or if the assumed contribution margin is greater than 50%, the management contract could play an even greater role. There is a direct relationship between the level of the management fee and the assumed contribution (i.e., the higher the management fee, the higher the assumed contribution margin). We have not discovered any definitive data on the exact level of the contribution margins associated with management fees. While this question should certainly be posed to management for the subject ASC owner-operator, a definitive answer supported with any type of analysis would be the exception rather than the norm. Perhaps this is a function of the fact that many ASC owner-operators do not appear to make an attempt to isolate the costs or perhaps the ASC owner-operators simply do not wish to share this information. In any event, our experience with ASC owner-operators and review of transaction pricing would indicate that the contribution margin is likely in excess of 50% for management fees equal to 5% or higher of net revenues. Exhibit 14 demonstrates this analysis.

**Exhibit 14. Management Fee Impact Example**

| **Subject ASC** | | | |
|---|---|---|---|
| Revenues | | | $ 4,000,000 |
| Operating Expenses (Excluding Depreciation) | | | 3,000,000 |
| EBITDA | | | $ 1,000,000 |
| | Management Fee | 5.0% | $ 200,000 |
| | Contribution Margin | 50.0% | **$ 100,000** |
| **Valuation of 60% Interest (assumes no Long-Term Debt)** | | | |
| EBITDA (60% Interest) | $ 600,000 | **$ 100,000** | $ 700,000 |
| X | X | | X |
| Invested Capital / EBITDA Multiple | 7.0 | ------------------------> | 6.0 |
| Value Indication - 60% Interest | $4,200,000 | | $ 4,200,000 |

Though the existence of the management contract effectively lowers the multiple of EBITDA paid in the previous example, many hospitals and health systems purchasing a controlling interest in an ASC do not receive a management fee. This factor should be considered in utilizing guideline transactions.

*Guideline public company method.* The pricing of these companies, in terms of multiples of revenues or earnings, provides little in the way of guidance regarding the pricing of either a controlling or noncontrolling interest in an individual ASC.

Three of the largest ASC owner-operators moved out of the public sector in 2007 when HealthSouth, USPI and Symbion sold to private equity groups. In addition, though HCA has significant ASC operations, its primary operations fall outside of the ASC segment, in acute care hospitals.

The only pure-play, publicly traded ASC owner-operator is AmSurg, which operates over 220 centers, with a majority of them being single-specialty GI/endoscopy and ophthalmology centers. Exhibit 15 summarizes the key valuation multiples for publicly traded ASC companies. Trailing 12-month EBITDA multiples are approximately 9.3x for AmSurg.

**Exhibit 15. Public Company Multiples**

**$ in Millions** — ***As of December 14, 2011***

| | Market Cap | LTD | MVIC | MVIC / LTM Rev | MVIC / LTM EBITDA |
|---|---|---|---|---|---|
| AmSurg Corp (AMSG) | $ 798.5 | $ 426.8 | $ 1,189.6 | 1.6x | 9.3x |

*Note: LTM EBITDA is less Minority Interest*

*Source: Capital IQ*

Companies such as AmSurg, and until they went private, Symbion and USPI, likely trade at much higher multiples than individual ASCs due to growth achieved through acquisition, access to and lower cost of capital, geographic diversification, and size. There is a fairly substantial spread between acquisition prices and the public company multiples, thereby making it fairly easy for public companies to add substantial value from acquisitions.

Accordingly, while it's necessary to consider the guideline company method, it rarely has a direct application to the valuation of either a controlling or noncontrolling equity interest in an individual ASC.

**Income approach and discounted cash flow method.** In this method, the total equity value is calculated using equity cash flows. Whether the appraiser projects a number of scenarios with a range of applicable discount rates or develops a single most-likely case scenario with a single appropriate discount rate, the mechanics of the projections should be similar.

Volume is the first primary determinant of financial performance. Volume is typically analyzed and projected in terms of number of surgical cases. However, each case may consist of a number of individual procedures. As such, it is important to understand whether the information that has been provided is measured in cases or procedures. As previously discussed, reimbursement varies widely by specialty. In addition, volumes are driven by the sum of individual physician practice expectations. The combination of these factors makes analyzing and developing volume projections by specialty, by physician absolutely essential.

Reimbursement levels are the second primary determinant of financial performance. Like most healthcare services, ASCs maintain a fee schedule consisting of gross charges, by procedure, for services performed and supplies utilized during surgery. Gross charges, though somewhat arbitrary, are often set as a percentage of the Medicare reimbursement for a procedure, say, from 300% to 400%.

Most governmental (including Medicare and Medicaid), commercial, and managed care payors reimburse according to a set fee schedule (either their own or one negotiated during the contracting process). A large share of commercial and managed care payors either directly or indirectly base their fee schedules on Medicare rates, making Medicare reimbursement and reimbursement trends particularly important to future projections.

Except in the fairly rare event that an ASC has a substantial number of payors that reimburse based on a percentage of gross charges, gross charges are somewhat irrelevant.

In addition, employee costs and medical and surgical supplies vary significantly by specialty. To properly accommodate the largely variable component of employee costs, base projections on staffing hours per case and costs per case..Other expenses that typically vary based on volume, specialty mix, or revenues may include contract services, insurance, office supplies, and postage and management fees.

Capital expenditures (CAPEX) are also significant to the discounted cash flow method for ASCs. A surgery center is typically an asset-intensive business. While the dangers of following rules of thumb have been subject to lively debate throughout the history of the valuation profession, we typically look at annual amounts ranging from $50,000 to $100,000 per operating room and slightly less per procedure room as a starting point for maintenance CAPEX. In addition to considering the age and condition of the existing furniture and equipment and the potential maintenance required, CAPEX assumptions should also consider possible growth in volume.

Consistent with the tendencies of ASC owner-operators, we typically execute the indirect convention of the discounted cash flow method whereby the market value of invested capital (MVIC) is calculated using debt-free cash flows and book value of debt is deducted from MVIC to arrive at a total equity value. Use of debt in the capital structure of ASCs varies widely based on the range of long-term debt to total assets from the *Multi-Specialty ASC Intellimarker 2011*. Based on our experience, use of substantial amounts of long-term debt is more prevalent for newer surgery centers and is almost entirely asset-based. While most ASCs typically use long-term debt to fund initial operations, many ASCs fund subsequent furniture and equipment purchases out of cash flows.

ASCs are generally located in either a medical office building or a separate free-standing facility. While it is certainly not uncommon for an ASC to own the land and building, particularly if it is a separate facility, most lease their facilities. This comes into play in the ASC's valuation. If the ASC owns the real estate as well, the business appraiser should consider the potential difference in required returns on the real estate and ASC operations. The preferred solution is to engage a real estate appraiser to value the land and building and to then combine the values of the real estate and the ASC operations. This convention requires an adjustment for the rental rate from the real estate appraisal.

If a separate real estate appraisal cannot be obtained, adjust the discount rate utilized in the discount cash flows to reflect the generally lower expected returns associated with the real estate. An adjustment to account for real estate may be considered when using the market approach (discussed earlier) and is applicable in the valuation of either a controlling interest or noncontrolling interest.

The valuation of a controlling equity interest approaching 100% requires an additional consideration. Under the income and market approaches, the pricing of most controlling interest transactions is for 51% to 60% interest. The same market multiples and rates of return may not apply to the incremental 40% to 49% interest of a 100% equity purchase. Generally the market multiples and implied rates of return reflect the buyer's assumption that the physician utilizers will maintain meaningful ownership. Buyers may not be willing to pay the same premium for ownership in excess of 60%.

## Purchase or sale of noncontrolling equity interests

Generally speaking, ASC owner-operators and healthcare systems are the typical buyers of controlling equity interests. Whether an ASC is a joint venture between a healthcare system and physicians; a three-way joint venture between ASC owner-operators, a healthcare system, and physician utilizers; or wholly owned by physicians, individual physician utilizers are generally the noncontrolling equity interest buyers.

Noncontrolling equity interests in ASCs typically transact at relatively lower values compared to controlling equity interests. The same survey in which a large majority of respondents typically observed valuation multiples for controlling equity interests of six to seven times EBITDA or more less interest-bearing debt found that a large majority of respondents typically observed valuation multiples for noncontrolling equity interests of 2.5 to 4.0 times EBITDA less interest-bearing debt.[9]

While the lower values associated with a noncontrolling interest are consistent with the levels of value framework from general valuation theory in which there may be discounts from the value associated with a controlling interest for both lack of marketability and lack of control, we generally prefer to view the differential outside of this framework. Because the continued success of an ASC depends so much on the continued support of its physician owners, most ASC operating or partnership agreements include provisions that:

1. Provide liquidity to noncontrolling equity interest holders through formulas or requirements for the completion of an independent fair market value opinion; and

2. Clearly define discretionary cash flows but require periodic distributions. ASC operating agreements or partnership agreements typically require monthly or quarterly cash distributions.

Within the levels of value framework from general valuation theory, a premium for control implies an inverse discount for lack of control. However, the difference in values for a controlling equity interest and a noncontrolling equity interest may be more appropriately, and perhaps more specifically, attributed to ASC owner-operators or the typical buyers of a controlling equity interest:

- obtaining a management fee;
- having better access to, and a lower cost of, capital; and
- having the ability to successfully manage and expand ownership.

9 VMG Health: *2011 Value Driver ASC Survey* and HealthCare Appraisers Inc.: *2008 ASC Valuation Survey* and *2007 ASC Valuation Survey*.

Based on these factors and because ASC operating and partnership agreements provide some level of built-in liquidity, we prefer to simply view the valuation of a noncontrolling equity interest as entirely separate, rather than starting with a controlling equity interest valuation and applying marketability and lack-of-control discounts typically utilized in valuations.

**Cost approach.** Like for a controlling equity interest, the application of the cost approach for a noncontrolling equity interest provides a "floor," or lowest minimum value. However, for a noncontrolling equity interest, specific facts and circumstances may ultimately impair the value of any intangible assets.

**Market approach.** ASC owner-operators observed that transactions for noncontrolling equity interests in ASCs occur at 2.5 to 4.0 times EBITDA less interest-bearing debt. Interestingly, for noncontrolling interest buy-ins and buy-outs, more than half of the respondents (eight of 13) rely on a formula to determine pricing, while only four rely on independent fair market value opinions.[10] This is not surprising considering that a large share of ASC operating or partnership agreements typically include formulas in the buy-sell provisions.

Based on our experience, a slightly smaller, but nonetheless large percentage of comprehensive valuations fall above or below the 2.5-to-4.0-times-EBITDA range. In addition, the appropriate multiple to apply may vary widely within the range. Because the range is broad and because of the lack of detailed information from both public and private sources, we typically use the market approach secondarily when valuing a noncontrolling equity interest.

**Discounted cash flow.** The overriding distinguishing feature in the valuation of a noncontrolling interest is that the projected volumes and revenues do not anticipate the change in ownership associated with the potential transaction. For example, if a noncontrolling equity interest is being valued for the purposes of allowing a new physician buy-in, the projections would not include any consideration of the case volumes that the physician would likely perform following the purchase of an interest in the ASC.

Further, while an ASC owner-operator may take into account the potential loss of volumes to either existing or potential competitors, a noncontrolling equity owner, on the other hand, is not in a position to do so. Plus, the typical buyer or seller of a noncontrolling equity interest may have a higher cost of equity in comparison to the typical buyer or seller of a controlling equity interest.

10 HealthCare Appraisers, Inc.: *2008 ASC Valuation Survey* and *2007 ASC Valuation Survey*.

### Conversion of an HOPD

The purpose of the valuation of an ASC being converted from an HOPD to a free-standing center is generally to estimate the fair market value of a noncontrolling equity interest. Though the application of the three approaches to value is generally the same as the application of the approaches to value for a noncontrolling equity interest, modeling the expected financial performance of an ASC that has historically operated as a HOPD can be particularly challenging.

With this in mind, rather than explore the valuation of an ASC converting from a HOPD to a free-standing entity based on the application of the approaches to value, it seems appropriate to expand on the challenges an appraiser faces in modeling this type of center's expected financial performance.

There are three primary challenges, driven by the fact that the financial performance of a HOPD, as presented in the historical accounting for a department of a hospital, bears little resemblance to the financial performance of the operation of the unit as a free-standing entity:

1. Proper volume assumptions;
2. Proper reimbursement assumptions; and
3. Proper operating-expense assumptions

While the cost accounting may be very complex, the historical accounting for a department of a hospital requires a maze of assumptions and allocations that cannot be used in estimating the performance of the business unit as a free-standing entity.

**Volume assumptions.** The level of difficulty in projecting volumes for this type of ASC depends on whether the volumes expected to transition come from the main operating rooms in the hospital or from a separate outpatient unit. As a result, the first consideration in estimating proper volume assumptions involves carving out the outpatient volumes expected to transition to the free-standing entity.

Chapter 41

# Valuing Dialysis Clinics

*By Carol W. Carden, CPA/ABV, ASA, CFE*

## Reasons for Valuation

There are two primary reasons for dialysis clinic valuations: 1) ownership buy-in and buy-out transactions and 2) joint venture transactions between a physician and an operating partner. Although unique considerations apply for each of the above reasons, the underlying valuation approach is generally consistent.

When valuing a clinic for ownership buy-in and buyout purposes, it is critical to understand the control elements associated with the particular interest being transferred as well as any restrictions on transferring the subject interest that could limit the pool of potential future investors.

Noncompetition agreements are often used to help protect the business from departing physicians who try to take part of the business with them. In some cases, noncompetition agreements can have significant value; this value is part of the overall value of the business and represents that portion of the value that would be lost if the departing physician were to compete. However, to have value, the agreement must be enforceable[1] and the departing physician must actually be in a position to compete. For example, a noncompetition agreement may not have much value in connection with physicians who are retiring or relocating to other geographic regions since they are less likely

1 When determining the value of a noncompete agreement, it is necessary to be familiar with local law—both statute and court precedent—to determine the extent of enforceability. For example, Massachusetts General Law 112.12x precludes enforcement of geographic covenants not to compete among physicians.

to compete with the clinic in the future. Even if the noncompetition agreement does not have much value itself, the clinic as a whole may be just as valuable due to the reduced risk of competition. However, if the departing physician can compete and no such agreement exists, the potential impact should be considered when estimating the clinic's future cash flows.

The absence of a noncompetition agreement can be particularly harmful to the value of a dialysis clinic because the lifeblood of the clinic revolves around its relationship with area nephrologists. Additionally, since dialysis clinics are not particularly capital intensive, it is fairly easy for a departing physician to start or join a competing clinic and attract the patients away.

Generally speaking, noncompetition agreements will prohibit the departing physician from having a financial interest (defined as ownership or, more importantly, a compensation agreement, such as a medical directorship) in a competing dialysis clinic within a specified geographic range for a specified time period following his or her departure from the clinic. Given the nature of dialysis services (patients should come three times per week for a three- to four-hour block of time), the geographic limitation tends to be more narrow for dialysis than it might be for other services. Generally speaking, the physician will be prohibited from competing within a 25-mile radius of the current center and a smaller radius for large, metropolitan areas. The rationale for this distance is that it becomes too inconvenient for current patients to follow the physician.

In addition to be prohibited from having a financial relationship, the physician is also generally prohibited from soliciting existing clinic employees for the same time period as the financial interest prohibition. Because patients spend such a significant amount of time at the clinic, they develop relationships with the staff that could be detrimental to patient satisfaction if the experienced staff is recruited away by a departing physician.

A valuation for joint venture purposes can be a much more complicated undertaking. It is critical to understand the nature of the joint venture to ensure that it does not contain unnecessary regulatory risks. In particular, it is important to ensure that the operating agreement does not reward incentives for referrals to the clinic. Also, it is important to understand any medical directorships that are attached to the operating agreement.

A medical directorship is typically awarded to a physician for clinical oversight of the center. If other physicians are in the medical director's group, they will typically be included in any noncompetition and nonsolicitation provisions of the medical director agreement through a joinder. Under the medical director agreement, the physician agrees to head the governing body, provide the supervision of the clinic staff, oversee the safety of the clinic in regards to medical grade purified water, and give input into staffing and capital replenishment. In return, the physician generally receives a fixed amount per year paid monthly. Medical directorship fees can range from $50,000 to $75,000 annually or more, depending on the size of the center. Payment of the medical directorship must be at fair market value to avoid the perception that the payment is being made in exchange for referrals to the clinic (anti-kickback statute—AKS—concern) or, if the clinic is a not-for-profit, the payment must not appear excessive in nature (private inurement and excess benefit concern to the IRS). If a medical directorship exposes the clinic to undue regulatory risks, this factor must be considered when determining its value. This consideration is generally incorporated into the development of the discount rate. A higher discount rate would be attributed to the center, resulting in a lower value than it would otherwise have absent the risky medical director agreement.

## Regulatory Considerations

The following briefly discusses the three main areas of regulatory compliance considerations when appraising a dialysis clinic. A detailed discussion of the myriad of regulatory complications that can arise with healthcare transactions is beyond the scope of this chapter, but interested readers may want to do additional reading from the referenced materials.

### *Stark*

In general, the Stark regulations govern referrals from a provider of designated health services (DHS) to an entity in which the provider has a financial interest, unless the arrangement falls into one of several safe harbor classifications. Dialysis services are not one of the 11 categories of DHS subject to the Stark requirements.[2] Therefore, the Stark restrictions do not generally have much of an impact on dialysis clinic valuations.

### *Anti-Kickback Regulations*

The AKS prohibits the receipt or payment of anything of value to induce referrals of healthcare services.[3] There are 13 established safe harbors; however, even whether the arrangement does not fit squarely into one of them does not necessarily mean it will be per se illegal. In addition to treating patients at the dialysis clinic, any physicians involved in ownership of the clinic also admit patients for a variety of other kidney-related ailments. If a hospital is involved in the transaction, the parties must ensure that the remuneration paid is not impacted by past or future anticipated referral patterns

2 *Federal Register*/Vol. 69 No. 59/Friday, March 26, 2004/Rules & Regulations, XI. Definitions (Section 1877(h) of the Act; Phase I-66 FR 922-49; §411.351).

3 *Federal Anti-Kickback Law and Regulatory Safe Harbors*, Fact Sheet, November 1999,Office of Inspector General, Office of Public Affairs.

to avoid AKS issues. Therefore, any analysis of the proposed dialysis transaction requires careful scrutiny to ensure the value of the interest is not negatively impacted by exposure to criminal, or alternatively, civil monetary penalties.

#### *Private Inurement and Excess Benefit*

The third regulatory area to consider is private inurement and excess benefit transactions, as defined by the Internal Revenue Service (IRS). In general, the IRS is concerned about financial or other arrangements that result in a benefit to private individuals in excess of the benefit supported by arms-length market transactions.[4] These concerns come into play most heavily when valuing joint venture transactions involving a not-for-profit clinic or venture partner. In particular, the IRS is concerned that not-for-profit assets will be transferred in excess amounts to private individuals. If a transaction is determined to contain private inurement or excess benefits, excise taxes may apply to both the organization making the payment as well as the individual receiving the benefit, if that individual is a disqualified person under the excess benefit regulations.

### Reimbursement Models

Before undertaking a valuation of a dialysis clinic, it is important to understand the mechanics and any potential changes in the reimbursement methodology. Patients having end stage renal disease (ESRD) become eligible for Medicare four months after they begin dialysis treatments even if they have not reached the age of 65. Eligibility can begin sooner if the patient elects to train for home-based dialysis. As a result, a significant portion of a dialysis clinic's patient base is covered by Medicare. Commercial insurance companies will cover dialysis services until the patient becomes eligible. Additionally, patients are not required to accept Medicare benefits and can elect to retain their commercial insurance benefits. Even though commercially insured patients do not typically comprise a significant portion of the patient base, they can have a tremendous impact on the profitability of the clinic because the reimbursement from commercial insurance companies is generally significantly greater than Medicare.

Since dialysis services are largely paid for by Medicare, the focus of our reimbursement discussion will be regarding Medicare's payment methodology and any forecasted changes. Historically, outpatient maintenance dialysis treatments (typically done in the free-standing dialysis clinic setting), were paid per treatment using what was referred to as the composite payment rate. The composite payment rate was a partially bundled

4 *Intermediate Sanctions—Excess Benefit Transactions*, Internal Revenue Service at www.irs.gov/charities/charitable/article/0,,id=123303,00.html and Inurement—Section 501 (c)(4), Internal Revenue Service at www.irs.gov/charities/nonprofits/article/0,,id=156404,00.html.

rate that covered dialysis treatments, except for some drug and laboratory costs that were billed and paid for separately on a fee-for-service basis.

Section 153(b) of the Medicare Improvements for Patients and Providers Act of 2008 (MIPPA) replaced the composite rate system with a bundled ESRD payment prospective payment system effective Jan. 1, 2011. There is a four-year transition period, with full implementation by 2014. During the transition period, providers will be paid using a blend of the prospective payment rate and the current payment rate.[5] The MIPPA also mandated an overall decrease in spending for dialysis services of 2%.[6] It will obviously be important to understand how the bundled payment methodology is anticipated to impact specific clinics because some clinics will see increases from the change, while others will see declines in reimbursement. The financial success of a clinic under the bundled payment system primarily depends upon the clinic's ability to manage drug utilization.

## Valuation Approaches

There are three basic approaches utilized for determining the value of any asset. Depending upon the facts and circumstances of the particular clinic being valued, some of the approaches may be more applicable than others.

### *Asset approach*

This approach is generally not used for operating companies, such as dialysis clinics, unless the business is not generating sufficient cash flows to make its operations more valuable than the underlying net assets less any outstanding debt obligations. Because dialysis clinics are not capital-intensive in nature, the net asset value is generally not a good indicator of value for a clinic that is anticipated to produce future cash flows. The exception to this can be a new center under construction where the asset approach can be commonly used to value the clinic.

### *Market approach*

The market approach values a business based upon publicly traded guideline companies or sale transactions of other similar privately held businesses. The challenges of applying this approach are twofold. Due to merger and acquisition activity of recent years, only two publicly traded dialysis companies remain, Fresenius and DaVita. When utilizing the publicly traded guideline method, it is critical to make the necessary adjustments to the public company information so that it is comparable to the private company being

5 www.cms.gov/ESRDPayment/.
6 Ibid.

valued. These adjustments involve an analysis of the balance sheet differences such as levels of debt as well as differences in growth rates. This type of analysis can be quite time-consuming and difficult to accomplish.

When utilizing merger and acquisition transaction data to develop valuation estimates for the subject company, it is important to gather and consider as much information about the sale transactions as possible. If possible, you should ascertain items about the sale such as: 1) was there a noncompete included in the transaction; 2) was the buyer a large, national player or smaller local or regional company; 3) what are the demographics of the market for the sold clinic; 4) the term of the medical director agreement and renewal options; 5) are other physicians in the group bound to the noncompete agreement by a joinder; and 6) are there any significant changes expected in the market demographics or competition in the short term. Unfortunately, these details can be difficult, if not impossible, to obtain. Additionally, sometimes the published transactions include assets (such as real estate) that may or may not be included in your transaction.

Market differences[7] must also be taken into consideration. However, dialysis clinics are typically dominated by Medicare patients (many times as high as 85% of patients). Therefore, individual payor differences between markets do not have the same impact on the use of private transaction multiples for dialysis clinic valuation as they do for other segments of healthcare. Unfortunately, many times the transaction data is limited, making application of the approach difficult.

#### *Income approach*

The income approach values a clinic based upon its ability to generate future cash flows and the anticipated risk associated with those cash flows. Depending upon the circumstances, the income approach can be a single period capitalization of earnings or a discounted cash flow analysis. Many times, an income approach will be stated as a multiple of earnings before interest, taxes, depreciation, and amortization (EBITDA). Publicly traded companies will generally state their acquisition prices as a multiple of EBITDA. The income approach is the most commonly used valuation approach for privately held businesses, such as dialysis clinics.

In applying the income approach, the analyst will need to evaluate potential volume growth and capacity. Clinic volume is stated on a per-patient basis. Dialysis clinics typically run two shifts per day, although a third can be added. Shifts will be run three days a week, and the clinic will operate either three days per week or six days per week,

7 For an extensive discussion of market differences, see Chapter 3, "Healthcare Market Structure and its Implication for Valuation of Privately Held Provider Entities: An Empirical Analysis."

as demand dictates. Generally speaking, for a two-shift clinic, there will be a morning shift that runs from approximately 6 a.m. to 10 a.m. and an afternoon shift that runs from 10 a.m. to 2 p.m. If the clinic runs a third shift, it will run from 2 p.m. to 6 p.m. To calculate capacity, determine the number of stations (each treatment is performed at a station comprised of a recliner and dialyzer machine) multiplied by the number of shifts being run. For volume and future growth to exceed capacity, additional stations or shifts must be added. If there is space in the physical location and the plumbing was planned in advance, adding additional stations is a relatively easy thing to do because the capital requirements are not extensive. However, if the current space is utilized, expansion will require a significant amount of leasehold improvements or build-out costs because the dialyzer machines require medical grade purified water and a substantial amount of plumbing.

In terms of projecting changes in the reimbursement, as previously discussed, beginning in 2011, Medicare moved to a prospective payment system for dialysis treatment that will likely disrupt the normal level of payment adjustment at least until the four-year transition period has ended.

## Value Drivers

There are five primary drivers of value for any dialysis clinic. The following section discusses each of these drivers and their potential impact on value.

### *Demographics of the community*

Senior adults, African-Americans, and Native American adults use dialysis services more heavily than other ethnic groups.[8] Therefore, it is critical to understand the current demographics of the community where the clinic is located as well as the projections for future population growth in the area. Medicare patients often make up as much as 85% of the patient load for many dialysis clinics, although approximately 56% of dialysis patients are under the age of 65.[9] As stated previously, patients can become eligible for Medicare without being seniors. However, generally, on average elderly patients comprise approximately one-fourth of the total population. Therefore, the composition of senior adults in the community as well as the projections for growth of this segment can have a tremendous impact on a clinic's ability to grow. It is also important to consider the geographic placement of the clinic. A location too far from the dominant patient base is vulnerable to competition from another clinic that is more conveniently located.

8 Ibid.
9 *2011 USRDS Annual Data Report*, United States Renal Data System.

### *Relationship with area nephrologists*

For any dialysis clinic to survive long term, it must secure and sustain relationships with area nephrologists. It is important to establish relationships with nephrology groups that have a good reputation in the community and that have a good mix of experienced physicians, preferably some who are still early in their career. Many times, the dialysis clinic will formalize its relationship with a key nephrologist or group by negotiating a medical directorship contract. Medical directorships generally help build the physician's loyalty to the clinic, which reduces the risk of losing revenues to a competing center. However, as stated previously, the terms and compensation of the medical directorship should be carefully evaluated to ensure the agreement does not unduly expose the clinic to regulatory risks.

### *Competition*

The existence and aggressiveness of competitors can have a significant impact on the value of a dialysis clinic just as with any other business. When considering investing in a dialysis clinic, it is important to understand the competitive landscape in the community and any expansion plans that dominant groups may be considering. A community with one or two dominant nephrology groups will be a more difficult competitive environment than one primarily comprised of many independent practices. The value of a clinic can be substantially eroded if the dominant group in a community is planning a competing center in close proximity. Typically, certificate of need (CON) regulations do not govern the establishment of new dialysis clinics because the capital investment is not as significant as with some other healthcare ventures. However, the existence and extent of CON regulations are state-specific so it is important to understand any limitations specific to your community.

### *Merger and acquisition activity*

The dialysis industry has undergone extensive consolidation over the past several years. Currently, a small handful of companies dominate the industry nationally with Fresenius and Davita being the largest players, with a combined 65% market share.[10] When considering the value of a clinic for merger and acquisition purposes, it is critical to understand the status of current consolidation activity taking place, especially in your geographic area. These acquisition transactions could have a substantial impact on what a clinic could be worth in the marketplace.

### *Recent payor initiatives*

A clinic's payor mix can have a substantial impact on its value. However, because dialysis clinics are typically dominated by governmental payors, specifically Medicare, it is very

10 www.wikinvest.com/stock/DaVita_(DVA).

important to stay abreast of any upcoming changes in Medicare reimbursement rates. In March of each year, the Medicare Payment Advisory Committee (MedPac) issues its recommendations for changes in Medicare reimbursement rates for the upcoming year.

The most recent MedPac report (March 2011) did not include any recommendations that would have a significant impact on dialysis treatments specifically. MedPac recommended a payment update of 1% for 2012.[11] However, the MedPac reports generally include recommendations regarding outpatient reimbursements, so it is important to stay abreast of these developments and their potential impact on the clinic's revenues.

11 *Report to Congress*, Medicare Payment Policy, March 2011, Medicare Payment Advisory Commission.

Chapter 42

# Valuing Joint Ventures and 'Under Arrangements'

*By Carol W. Carden, CPA/ABV, ASA, CFE*

As a starting point for a discussion of the value drivers and typical valuation methodologies for joint ventures, it is important to understand the basic forms these joint ventures typically take. The specific characteristics, benefits, and challenges of each structure will be discussed in greater detail later in the chapter, but typically hospital-physician joint ventures come in the form of: 1) equity joint ventures, 2) leases, 3) management agreements, and 4) a more comprehensive form of management agreement called a clinical co-management agreement.

## Reasons for Valuation

The primary drivers for hospital-physician joint ventures are 1) physicians' desire to identify alternative revenue streams to supplement declining professional revenues, 2) changes in regulations that close old avenues of collaboration or open new ones, and 3) management has a desire to involve a higher level of clinical expertise in the management of a particular service.

Any collaboration that occurs between a hospital and physicians is subject to regulatory scrutiny. Therefore, as management contemplates one of the forms of joint venture discussed in this chapter, it will many times decide to enlist a valuation expert to ensure that it can demonstrate its attempt to transact the joint venture at terms that are both fair market value (as defined by both the Internal Revenue Service, or IRS, and for Stark and the Office of Inspector General, or OIG, purposes) and commercially reasonable (as required for regulatory purposes).

## Regulatory Considerations

The following briefly discusses the five main areas of regulatory compliance considered in contemplating a joint venture. The appraiser should have at least a basic understanding of these issues to properly assess the risk of any contemplated joint venture. A detailed discussion of these regulations is beyond the scope of this chapter; however, it is critical that the client has competent legal counsel involved if contemplating a hospital-physician joint venture.

### *Stark*

As discussed previously in this book, the Stark regulations govern referrals from a provider of designated health services (DHS) to an entity in which the provider has a financial interest unless the transaction falls into a safe harbor. More often than not, the contemplated joint venture will involve one of the 11 DHS. Therefore, the Stark implications of a proposed transaction can have a tremendous impact on the valuation of the venture. It is critical when valuing these types of transactions to ensure the historical or anticipated referrals of business are not factored into the value of the venture. That is not to say that historical volume must be eliminated from the valuation analysis, just that the valuation analysis must be structured in such a way as to not specifically give recognition for previous referral patterns or anticipated referral patterns post-transaction.

For example, if after consummation of the joint venture, it is anticipated that, due to the stronger relationship with the hospital, the physicians will move procedures that they currently refer to competitor facilities to the new joint venture, the anticipated volume should not be considered when determining the fair market value of the joint venture during formation. The value of the joint venture should be reflective of the cash flows and risk assessment as it currently exists absent the strengthened relationship that occurs as a result of the joint venture. The analyst must be cognizant of the requirement that the valuation assumptions not reflect the ability of the parties to refer business to one another.

The OIG has recently refocused its concern on the use of referrals in what are otherwise standard valuation methods under the income approach, such as the discounted cash flow method, designed to produce an appropriate measure of fair market value. The so-called Thornton Letter from 1993 has been reinvigorated. (See Chapter 12.) Appraisers and legal counsel need to consider how best to conform to regulatory requirements while still achieving fair market value. One important consideration in using historical volume as the basis for forecasting future volume is to eliminate from both any volume based on a financial incentive to refer or utilize. This can be accomplished by analyzing and comparing referral sources having a financial interest and those not having a financial interest.

Additionally, Stark II, Phase III became effective Dec. 5, 2007.[1] Phase III eliminated the safe harbor for compensation arrangements. Now the parties to the arrangement must be able to demonstrate that the contemplated compensation is stated at fair market value absent authoritative guidance. Phase III does not state that the previous safe harbor methodology cannot be used, just that use of that methodology no longer carries the added benefit of providing safe harbor protection. Compensation comes into play in valuation of management agreements.

Phase III also implemented new rules regarding leases for space and equipment that will be discussed in greater detail later in this chapter.

#### *Anti-kickback regulations*

It is not very likely that the proposed joint venture will fit squarely into one of the 13 AKS safe harbors.[2] Much like the discussion above regarding Stark implications, the valuation analyst must have an understanding of the AKS regulations sufficient to assess any undue risk of the contemplated transaction and the related impact on the value. Consideration of the AKS statute was particularly important when a proposed leasing arrangement was stated on a per-procedure or "per-click" basis. The Centers for Medicare & Medicaid Services (CMS) eliminated per-click leases as discussed in a later section of this chapter.

#### *Deficit Reduction Act (DRA)*

The DRA of 2005 contained provisions that were far-reaching across many facets of the healthcare industry.[3] When providing business valuation services for a contemplated hospital-physician joint venture, it is critical to understand any reimbursement implications that resulted from provisions contained in the DRA. Imaging was the segment hardest hit by reductions implemented as a result of the DRA and, as a result, we saw an increase in divestitures of physician-owned imaging operations.

#### *CMS proposed fee schedule changes*

When CMS issued the Medicare Physician Fee Schedule for 2012, it included a reduction of 27.4% in physician fees across the board. In prior years, Congress has intervened in late December to eliminate proposed reductions of this magnitude across the board. However, as of this writing, the proposed reduction is still an active matter for Congress.

---

1 Department of Health and Human Services, Centers for Medicare & Medicaid Services, 42 CFR Parts 411 and 424, (CMS-1810-F), RIN 0938-AK67, Medicare Program; Physicians' Referrals to Health Care Entities With Which They Have Financial Relationships (Phase III).

2 *Federal Anti-Kickback Law and Regulatory Safe Harbors*, Fact Sheet, November 1999, Office of Inspector General, Office of Public Affairs.

3 Deficit Reduction Act of 2005, Pub. L. No. 109-171, 120 Stat. 4 (Feb. 8, 2006).

It is important for the valuation analyst to understand proposed reductions and monitor "final" changes such as this in light of the contemplated joint venture.

#### *Private inurement and excess benefit*

If the hospital involved in the joint venture is not-for-profit, the transaction must be consummated at fair market value as defined by the IRS (Revenue Ruling 59-60) to ensure no private inurement or excess benefit implications are triggered. In particular, the IRS is concerned that not-for-profit assets will be transferred in excess amounts to private individuals.[4] If a transaction is determined to contain private inurement or excess benefits, excise taxes can apply to both the hospital as well as the physician, if the latter is a disqualified person under the excess benefit transaction regulations.

### Key Features and Typical Valuation Methodologies

It is important to understand the concept of value and in particular, fair market value as defined by regulatory bodies when determining compensation related to any physician-hospital venture. There are valuation methodologies that are more commonly used for particular types of ventures, and having a basic understanding of these will assist you in evaluating the transaction with your client. It is also important to understand the types of information to be considered and the degree to which assumptions should be tested to ensure the valuation will withstand regulatory scrutiny in the event the transaction is selected for review. We will begin our discussion with the simplest form of joint venture and move toward more complex forms.

#### *Equity joint ventures*

Equity joint ventures occur when an existing company or many times a service line of a hospital is contributed into a new entity and an ownership interest in the new entity is offered to physicians. This type of venture is easily understood and has withstood the test of time. For plain, "vanilla" equity joint ventures, an income approach is typically utilized. Generally speaking, equity joint ventures are chosen solely as an investment vehicle making anticipated cash flows the best indicator of value.

As discussed elsewhere in this book, if recent privately held market transactions similar to the entity being joint ventured exist in sufficient number, there are still a number of hurdles to overcome before a market-based approach can be used for these joint ventures. Therefore, the market approach is not widely used for purposes of determining

4 *Intermediate Sanctions—Excess Benefit Transactions*, Internal Revenue Service at www.irs.gov/charities/charitable/article/0,,id=123303,00.html and Inurement—Section 501 (c) (4), Internal Revenue Service at www.irs.gov/charities/nonprofits/article/0,,id=156404,00.html.

the value of equity joint ventures. Typically, the value of the entity to be included in the joint venture is determined from the income approach and the relevant ownership percentage is multiplied by that value. Given the level of ownership contemplated, consideration of discounts related to control and marketability may be warranted.

There are a few challenges to implementing the equity joint venture. Equity joint ventures are prohibited for services comprised of DHS for Stark purposes. The requirement of up-front capital or the incurrence of debt can also make this model less attractive dependent upon the financial goals and risk tolerance of the parties. Finally, equity joint ventures can result in a loss of reimbursement post-transaction due to the DRA discussed previously or other reimbursement differences between hospital-based reimbursement and free-standing entity reimbursement.

***Leases***

Leases typically involve access on a per-block-of-time basis to a piece of equipment or the operations of a service line. Block leases have been commonly used for access to imaging equipment and cardiac cath labs. One of the more attractive features of the leasing option is that it gives access to the equipment or service line even if volume is not sufficient to justify full-time provision of the service.

Typically, an income-based approach is used for leases. In general terms, total costs to be incurred through the lease are accumulated and a fair market return is added. The resulting total is divided by the hours of operation specific to the block desired to determine the lease rate. The rate of return should be commensurate with the risks being assumed and generally speaking, ranges from 10% to 20%.

Alternatively, a market-based approach can be used if the analyst has access to lease rates for similar services in the same geographic market. Given that these leases typically occur between unrelated private companies, this type of market information is not usually readily available.

Leasing arrangements are attractive because they do not require up-front capital and allow for the provision of a service when volume is not sufficient to support a full-time offering. However, leases can be tricky to structure from a regulatory standpoint and are fairly easy for competitors to duplicate.

Under the lease, the billing for the technical component of revenue is generally done by the entity purchasing access to the equipment or service line using its provider identification number.

### *Management agreements*

Traditionally, management agreements have taken the form of physicians providing a stipulated number of hours per month to participate in a somewhat active manner in the management of a service line. Historically, these have been structured as medical directorships. The physician tracks the hours provided and is compensated on an hourly basis for services rendered. The current movement for management agreements is toward what are termed "co-management agreements" or "clinical co-management agreements." These agreements generally have an administrative component with a fixed fee and a quality incentive that allows a bonus payment if certain goals are met.

Typically, co-management agreements are valued using a blend of income and market approaches. The administrative component is generally calculated by multiplying an hourly rate by the number of anticipated hours. With the implementation of Stark Phase III, the safe harbor for determining an hourly rate has been eliminated. The elimination allows for additional flexibility in determining a fair market hourly rate. The flexibility has always been present (as compliance with the safe harbor was never a requirement), but hospitals that previously would have conservatively complied with the safe harbor methodology can now be more creative without stepping outside a comfort zone. The hourly rate analysis will likely now incorporate surveys not previously included in the safe harbor calculation as well as geographic-specific compensation data.

The determination of the quality incentive is a more subjective determination, with little or no regulatory guidance. Generally, the quality incentive is determined based upon either 1) other quality incentive programs, which reward providers for good quality and reporting or penalizes them for bad outcomes or lack of reporting, or 2) the cost the provider would incur absent the quality portion of the agreement. The current direction in the industry is away from paying for reporting and toward paying for outcomes. Therefore, it is important when using an existing quality incentive program criteria as guidance for valuation purposes that the features of the agreement you are appraising match the features present in the existing quality incentive program.

To illustrate the concept of considering the costs the provider would incur absent the quality incentive, consider that if, in the absence of the quality portion of the agreement, the hospital would have to hire a physician or other professional to administer its quality program, the cost of this hire can be used as one indication for the "value" of the quality incentive program.

The attractive features of a co-management agreement are that no change in ownership occurs and no up-front capital is required. The original provider of care remains in place, and the arrangement is virtually seamless to patients. However, the upside reward available to physicians can often be less than in other types of ventures and the payment of the quality incentive can be quite controversial. Additionally, in other industries, fees for management services are typically tied to profitability or performance, but in the healthcare industry, we must ensure that fees are as disconnected from the referral base as possible to ensure the transaction will withstand regulatory scrutiny.

***'Under arrangements' management agreements***

Much touted in prior years, these arrangements were devices to allow a joint venture to provide a hospital with "soup-to-nuts" services (building, equipment, staffing, and day-to-day management of a service) without giving the joint venture an equity stake in the hospital or service line. This type of management agreement is only permitted now for facilities that qualify for a rural exception under the Stark regulations or if the agreement involves nonreferring physicians, such as radiologists.

"Under arrangements" models were frequently used to maximize reimbursement so that services continue to be reimbursed by federal payors at hospital rates, rather than at free-standing rates. The hospital paid the joint venture (in which it might have been a participant) a monthly or per-click fee covering all costs of the delivered services. The hospital maintained oversight and monitored quality standards (the hospital was the provider and remained responsible for service delivery), although on a day-to-day basis, it may have provided very little.

Typically, a new entity was formed that was owned jointly by a hospital and a group of physicians. The physicians could be members of the same group or could have been unrelated physicians in the community normally practicing the same specialty. The new venture had to be capitalized because it typically purchased the equipment necessary to provide the service. Many times, the hospital retained a controlling interest in the new entity for regulatory purposes. Under arrangements joint ventures were used most commonly for outpatient surgery, cardiac catheterization labs, and imaging.

Valuation determinations for under arrangements were generally a blend of the income and market approaches, similar to co-management agreements. Some under arrangements were compensated based upon a flat monthly amount, but more commonly, a fee schedule was developed that compensated the under arrangements service provider on a per-procedure basis.

The attractive features of the under arrangements agreement were that it maintained hospital-based reimbursement, incorporated more in-depth clinical knowledge into management of the service, and freed hospital management time. However, as mentioned previously, this is an option that is only available in very limited circumstances currently.

### Types of Information Utilized and Testing Assumptions

Many of these ventures are complex to model from a valuation standpoint. The valuation analysis is made more difficult due to the fact that hospitals generally only track direct costs by service line, so determining the total costs associated with a given service offering requires in-depth analysis and working closely with management to ensure all costs are captured. Once historical financial performance is developed, projected financial performance must be determined. Once more, it is important to keep the fair market value definitions in mind to ensure that assumptions do not incorporate changes that will come about due to the transaction.

A thorough understanding of historical and projected volumes must be obtained. Often, volume is tracked by hospitals on a per-procedure basis, while the new venture anticipates compensation on a per-case basis. Hospitals typically track volume based on individual charge codes for each procedure performed on a patient. The procedure-based information is transferred electronically to the health information management (HIM) department of a hospital where it is grouped and summarized in a manner that facilitates billing. For outpatient procedures from Medicare and many commercial payors, the hospital receives reimbursement on a per-case basis, rather than on a per-procedure basis. However, absent the coding and grouping performed by the HIM department, it is difficult for the hospital to bridge the gap between procedures and cases. Therefore, the valuation analyst must work with management to ensure accurate adjustments are made to transition from one volume indicator to another. An analysis of historical collections and reimbursement is necessary to ensure that the impact of potential changes post-transaction are understood and accounted for. This analysis can be quite challenging to perform, particularly for inpatient volumes. Hospitals do not track inpatient reimbursement specific to particular departments or service lines because that reimbursement is more traditionally paid to them on a per-admission basis. Therefore, many times outpatient reimbursement is used as a proxy for both inpatient and outpatient volume.

If the Medicare fee schedule is to be used as a proxy under a market-based approach, it will many times require the assistance of outside expertise in coding. To facilitate this analysis, the hospital must be able to produce historical procedure information, including diagnosis codes.

## Chapter 43

# The Valuation of Hospitals

*By G. Don Barbo, CPA/ABV, and Robert M. Mundy, CPA/ABV, CVA*

Valuations of hospitals involve unique circumstances and nuances. It is imperative that an appraiser is mindful of and develops an understanding of these nuances to generate a sound opinion of value. This chapter will focus on these various distinctions from nonhealthcare valuations and will also guide the professional in performing fair market valuations for general acute care hospitals in the context of transactions.

While this chapter will focus solely on general acute care hospitals, the appraiser should also recognize that other "types" of hospitals are present in the market, including:

1. Specialty surgical hospitals, such as heart hospitals;
2. Critical access hospitals (CAH);
3. Rehabilitation hospitals; and
4. Long-term acute care hospitals (LTACs).

Valuations of these types of hospitals are somewhat similar in nature to general acute care hospital valuations, but each has its unique characteristics and trends that must be considered. The appraiser must be aware of the hospital industry, the challenges hospitals face, and trends affecting the values of hospitals.

### Overview of the Hospital Industry

The hospital industry in the United States is highly fragmented. According to the American Hospital Association, there were 5,747 registered hospitals in the United

States in 2006, with the overwhelming majority being community hospitals, at 4,927. Of these community hospitals, over 59% were not-for-profit, 18% were for-profit, and almost 23% were state and local government hospitals.[1]

The industry is highly regulated at the federal level through the Centers for Medicare and Medicaid Services (CMS) and is also regulated by state and local governments. As such, the appraiser needs to be aware not only of the federal regulations affecting hospitals, but also the state and local regulations, which can vary by locality.

Today, hospitals face a number of challenges that can have a significant impact on value. Some of the major challenges are presented below.

#### *Growth in Uninsured Population*

According to the U.S. Census Bureau, there were over 45 million uninsured in the United States as of 2007, up from just over 38 million uninsured in 2000. The uninsured population for 2007 was just over 15% of the total U.S. population.[2] This represents a great challenge to hospitals and their emergency rooms, which cannot refuse care based on insurance status or ability to pay. In fact, according to the American Hospital Association, the cost of uncompensated care has been rising dramatically, from a cost of approximately $3.9 billion in 1980 to $31.2 billion in 2006.[3]

#### *Shortage of Nurses*

According to a 2007 survey of hospital leaders conducted by the American Hospital Association (AHA), hospitals had an estimated 116,000 registered nurse vacancies as of December 2006.[4] This shortage could also increase as demands for health care grow in the future with the aging baby boomer population. The nursing shortages impact the ability of hospitals to attract and retain nurses.

#### *Difficulty in Maintaining Physician ED Coverage*

Hospitals are finding increasing difficulty in providing and maintaining physician on-call coverage for their emergency departments (EDs). According to the AHA 2007 survey, over 55% of the hospital leader respondents experienced gaps in specialty coverage in the ED. Two of the specialties that have been increasingly difficult to staff are orthopedics and neurosurgery. In the past, physicians agreed to provide on-call

1 American Hospital Association Web site—www.aha.org/aha/resource-center/Statistics-and-Studies/fast-facts.html.

2 U.S. Census Bureau Web site—www.census.gov/hhes/www/hlthins/historic/hihistt1.xls.

3 Health Forum, *AHA Annual Survey Data*, 1980-2006.

4 American Hospital Association Web site—www.aha.org/aha/content/2007/PowerPoint/StateofHospitalsChartPack2007.ppt.

coverage to hospitals without charging the hospitals as a way to build their practices (physicians would bill the patients or payers for their professional services rendered). However, with the growing number of uninsured patients visiting hospitals, declining reimbursement, and increasing medical malpractice insurance and operating costs, many physicians are now expecting some sort of payment for on-call coverage, which can be a strain on hospital profitability. In fact, more than one-third of the hospital leader respondents reported some form of hospital payment for physician on-call coverage.[5]

#### *Loss of Patients to ASCs*

Ambulatory surgery centers (ASCs), also known as day surgery centers, are used by doctors to perform a variety of surgical procedures that do not require patients to stay overnight, including eye surgery; orthopedic and hand surgery; plastic surgery; pain management (spinal injections); podiatry; ear, nose, and-throat surgery; endoscopy; laparoscopy; and various other surgical specialties.

The number of ASC facilities has substantially increased in recent years. Between 1991 and 2001, the number of Medicare-certified ambulatory surgical centers increased from 1,460 centers to 3,371, representing an almost 9% compounded annual growth rate.[6] Growth in ASC facilities continues to remain strong. In 2005, there were 4,506 Medicare-certified ASC facilities, which represents a 7.5% compounded annual growth rate.[7]

Since ASCs only provide day surgery services, they are much smaller than general hospitals, which offer a much broader range of medical services. Because of their smaller size and focus on a considerably narrower medical service, they are able to operate with smaller staffs and lower overhead levels. This leads to lower operating costs than larger, full-size hospitals.

Additionally, since the ASC does not provide emergency room services and instead, schedules surgery cases in advance, physician-users prefer to use them. Because of its focus on selected types of surgeries, ASCs typically enjoy the following benefits over full-size hospitals:

- Patients are less at risk of being bumped or losing their scheduled surgery by more critical cases, which can often occur in hospital settings; also, because of the lack of critical trauma cases being treated, the waiting room experience is typically less hectic and more pleasant than in full-service hospitals;

5 Ibid.

6 Report to the Congress: Medicare Payment Policy, Section F; March 2003; MedPAC.

7 *Ambulatory Surgery Centers A Positive Trend in Health Care.* www.ascassociation.org/advocacy/AmbulatorySurgeryCentersPositiveTrendHealthCare.pdf.

- Because of its lower operating cost structure and efficient operating environment, managed care companies and insurance companies look favorably to ASCs and can often negotiate lower payments to ASCs for these medical services;

- Physicians are able to schedule their surgery cases in advance with less risk of being bumped. Also, the nursing staff is familiar and well-trained in supporting the surgeries performed in the ASC. Physicians may also have a greater voice in the equipment and medical supplies being offered in the ASC.

Because of its focus on day surgeries, ASCs can also shift less urgent cases from the hospitals and allow them to treat the more serious and traumatic cases. As a result, many outpatient cases are migrating out of the hospital setting and into ASCs, which can have a significant negative impact on hospital profitability.

### Hospital Transaction Environment

The hospital transaction environment has been active, with a major trend in consolidation and "going-private" transactions. According to *The Health Care Acquisition Report 2008*, as published by Irving Levin Associates Inc., the total number of hospital transactions for 2001 through 2007 appears in Exhibit 1.

**Exhibit 1. Total Transactions (Annual for 2001 to 2007, Including All Transactions)**

| 2001 | 2002 | 2003 | 2004 | 2005 | 2006 | 2007 |
|---|---|---|---|---|---|---|
| 118 | 101 | 56 | 236 | 88 | 249 | 149 |

However, in 2004, 2006, and 2007, the transactions included deals for three major hospital entities. In 2004, the transaction information included 132 Tenet hospitals. In 2006, the total number of 249 transacted hospitals included 176 HCA hospitals (purchase of company to take to private equity). Total transactions for 2007 included the sale of 51 Triad hospitals to Community Health. Eliminating these transactions from the totals, the "adjusted" transaction totals appear in Exhibit 2.

**Exhibit 2. Adjusted Total Transactions**

| 2001 | 2002 | 2003 | 2004 | 2005 | 2006 | 2007 |
|---|---|---|---|---|---|---|
| 118 | 101 | 56 | 104 | 88 | 73 | 98 |

Even with these transactions eliminated, the transaction activity shows an active marketplace. Many of these transactions represent "portfolio shuffling" on the part of the publicly traded and major hospital chain players. An emerging trend in hospital activity is whole-hospital syndication models, where physicians can purchase ownership interests in hospitals.

Knowledge of the hospital industry and its trends is essential for an appraiser. In addition, the appraiser must also have a working knowledge of the hospital value drivers. For general acute care hospitals, the key value drivers typically are: (1) inpatient admissions, (2) outpatient visits, and (3) reimbursement factors affecting both inpatient and outpatient revenues.

## Hospital Value Drivers

### *Inpatient Admissions and Inpatient Reimbursement*

An inpatient is admitted to a hospital when the patient's medical procedure requires an overnight stay at the hospital. Inpatient admissions drive the amount of inpatient revenue that a hospital receives. The total number of days that a patient remains in the hospital after being admitted is called patient days. Patient days also drive another important performance measure for hospitals known as average length of stay (ALOS). ALOS is generally computed as total patient days divided by patient admissions (or patient discharges).

Inpatient services are reimbursed for Medicare patients under the Medicare inpatient prospective payment system (IPPS). Under the IPPS, patients are grouped into Medicare severity diagnosis-related groups (MS-DRGs) based upon the patient's diagnosis and the severity of the diagnosis assigned at the time of discharge. Reimbursement for an MS-DRG is based on the estimated hospital cost for a specific diagnosis. Medicare inpatient payment rates are updated annually based upon market basket updates. The market basket is designed to reflect price inflation by indexing the prices of a mix of goods and services for a certain time period to a base time period.[8]

It is important to note that the MS-DRG is a flat rate, meaning that a hospital is reimbursed the same amount regardless of a particular patient's cost. In other words, a hospital receives the same reimbursement for a diagnosis whether the patient stays one day or three days. Accordingly, under the Medicare MS-DRG system, a hospital has the economic incentive to reduce its ALOS.

8 The Centers for Medicare and Medicaid Services Web site—www.cms.hhs.gov/MedicareProgramRatesStats/downloads/info.pdf.

A hospital's Medicare base reimbursement rate for inpatient services is divided into a labor and nonlabor portion. The labor portion is adjusted by the hospital's local wage index, and the nonlabor portion is adjusted by a cost-of-living adjustment factor.[9] However, a hospital can receive various supplemental payments, for instance, if its costs for treating a patient exceed the usual Medicare reimbursement for that patient's treatment by a certain threshold (referred to as "outlier payments")[10] or if it serves a disproportionately high percentage of low-income patients (referred to as "disproportionate share hospital payments").[11]

Some commercial insurance payers reimburse inpatient services on a per diem basis. Under this method, a hospital will receive reimbursement for an inpatient based on the number of days the patient is hospitalized. Since the first inpatient day is generally the most expensive in terms of the hospital's costs, some per diem structures pay more the first day than for subsequent days. Variations also occur in subsequent days' per diem amounts. This per diem rate can also fluctuate based upon the patient diagnosis and severity. Other payers can pay based upon negotiated rates, such as a percentage of charges billed, or under a capitation plan, which provides a fixed payment per member per month (PMPM) regardless of the hospital services actually provided.

#### *Outpatient Visits and Outpatient Reimbursement*

An outpatient visit is classified as any medical procedure performed in a hospital setting that does not require an overnight stay. Outpatient visits are the volume driver for a hospital's outpatient revenues, which can often be very profitable.

Outpatient services are generally reimbursed for Medicare patients under the Medicare outpatient prospective payment system (OPPS). Under the OPPS, services are classified into ambulatory payment classifications (APCs) based on similar clinical procedures and required resources. Each APC has its own payment rate, which is adjusted based on geographic wage variations.[12]

For non-Medicare payers, reimbursement methods can vary widely from payer to payer (i.e., fee for service, percentage of charges billed, capitation, and so on).

Understanding these value drivers and how they interact with each other is essential for hospital valuations. With these value drivers in mind, it is important for the appraiser

9 Centers for Medicare & Medicaid Services Web site—Overview of the IPPS.

10 Centers for Medicare & Medicaid Services Web site—Press Releases: "CMS Announces Payment Reforms for Inpatient Hospital Services in 2008," August 1, 2007. www.cms.hhs.gov/apps/media/press_releases.asp.

11 Centers for Medicare & Medicaid Services Web site—Overview of the IPPS.

12 Centers for Medicare & Medicaid Services Web site—"Hospital Outpatient PPS Overview." www.cms.hhs.gov/HospitalOutpatientPPS.

to tailor the information request list to the client so that the data received can be useful in identifying trends in these value drivers.

### Information Gathering

The information gathering phase for any valuation is important, and hospital valuations are certainly no exception. It is important to not only receive pertinent financial information, but to also receive the information in a format that allows the appraiser to identify trends and calculate ratios specific to a hospital. With the hospital value drivers in mind, the appraiser should ask for specific information from the client that will enable the appraiser to identify historical trends and provide a basis for reasonable future projections. Some of the specific items unique to hospitals to be requested might include the following:

1. For-profit versus not-for-profit status;
2. Number of patient beds, both licensed and in use;
3. Location of the facility;
4. Current ownership of the hospital (i.e., community board, physician investors, corporate-owned, and so on);
5. Primary services provided and brief history of the hospital;
6. Certificate of need requirements;
7. Detailed financial statements for the last five years, with revenues segregated by inpatient and outpatient revenue, and any other major service lines;
8. Historical inpatient admissions, inpatient days and outpatient visits for the last five years;
9. Other operating statistics of the hospital for the last five years, such as adjusted patient days, average length of stay, occupancy rate, and so on;
10. Client-prepared operating budgets or projections; and
11. An often overlooked source of data and the hospital's position in a given market are the prospectuses required for tax-exempt bond financing by

exempt hospitals. Federal tax law and underwriting standards require far more information in these documents than typically seen in a financial statement or even a Form 990.

Obviously, this list is not exhaustive, but will provide the appraiser with a good starting point for recognizing and analyzing various trends present in the hospital being valued. It is important to be as specific as possible when requesting information and is also a good idea to not request superfluous information so that the client will not be overloaded.

### Analyzing Financial Ratios and Trends

After obtaining the necessary data from the client, the appraiser must now compile this data in a manner useful for identifying trends. An important part of identifying trends is calculating and analyzing various ratios. Hospitals have unique ratios and statistics that need to be considered. The main objective in analyzing ratios is to identify historical trends for projecting future cash flows, although this analysis is also useful in assessing the risks associated with the hospital and potentially could be used as a basis for normalizing adjustments.

Obviously, the appraiser should consider the growth trends in both inpatient and outpatient revenues, inpatient admissions, and outpatient visits. Some other important statistics and ratios to consider are as follows:

1. *Patient Days*–the number of days the patient is in the hospital;
2. *Adjusted patient days (APD)*–patient days plus the calculated outpatient fays. The formula can vary, but may be:<br>(patient days + (outpatient visits × 50%));
3. *Average length of stay (ALOS)*–calculated as the total inpatient days divided by total inpatient admissions;
4. *Average daily census (ADC)*–calculated as inpatient days divided by 365 days per year;
5. *Occupancy rate*–calculated as the ADC divided by the total number of hospital beds in service;
6. *Gross and net inpatient revenue per inpatient day;*
7. *Gross and net outpatient revenue per outpatient visit;*
8. *Total gross and net patient revenue per APD;*

9. *Medical supplies expense per APD;*
10. *Bad debt expense as a percentage of net patient revenue;*
11. *Staff FTEs divided by APD; and*
12. *Salaries, wages, and benefits divided by FTEs.*

Trends in these statistics should be observed and understood, because they will contribute to developing reasonable projections of future cash flows. For example, the ALOS statistic is important in determining how efficiently a hospital is admitting and treating its patients. An increasing ALOS could be negative for a hospital, especially a hospital with a high Medicare patient mix, since Medicare reimburses on a DRG basis, not on a per diem basis. The occupancy rate can give an appraiser an idea of how well the hospital is utilizing its beds and whether the hospital may be facing capacity constraints regarding its future growth potential. The trends in gross and net patient revenues per APD can give some idea of the contracting strength of the hospital. Medical supplies expense per APD can provide insight into how efficiently a hospital is managing its medical supplies. The staffing ratios can also provide insights into how well the hospital is managing its employee costs. The more an appraiser can digest and decipher the reasons for the historical trends, the better basis he or she will have for developing future cash flow projections.

### Normalizing Adjustments

After analyzing the financial trends of the hospital, normalizing adjustments should be made. The primary purpose of the normalizing adjustments is to produce a financial picture that will be used as a basis for future cash flow projections. Hospitals generally have more sophisticated accounting systems than other healthcare businesses. Therefore, normalizing adjustments for hospitals typically entail only eliminating nonrecurring items or adjustments for income taxes. However, historical trends in expenses, especially as a percentage of revenues, should be considered to identify any unusual expenses. One of the largest expenses for a hospital is salaries and wages, so any abnormal trends in terms of salaries per FTE should be discussed with the client and normalized if necessary. Another large expense for hospitals is medical supplies expense. Any significant swings in terms of medical supplies as a percentage of revenue should be understood and, if the trend is not expected to continue in the future, should be normalized. Remember that the primary purpose of normalizing adjustments is to restate the financials in a manner that will be consistent with expected future operations.

### Income Approach

In preparing the income approach value, the client's operating budget or financial projections (if available) should be reviewed for reasonableness by comparing it to observed historical financial trends. If, after review and discussion with the client, the projections appear reasonable, then they could be used as a guide for projecting future cash flows.

In projecting future revenues, growth factors for both volumes and net charges should be considered. For inpatient revenues, the volume driver will be inpatient admissions and days, while the volume driver for outpatient revenues will be outpatient visits. Typically, for a hospital, inpatient admissions are driven by a number of factors, including, but not limited to, the location and attractiveness of the facility, the types of services provided at the hospital, the key physicians practicing at the hospital, the key insurance payer contracts, the competitive environment in the community, the population demographics (including growth, affluence, and age) and the strength of the hospital's medical staff. Outpatient visits will typically be driven by the types of surgeries performed at the hospital, any specialized services provided by the hospital (such as imaging services or cancer treatment), the key insurance payers, the hospital's relationship with area physicians, and the proximity and prevalence of competing physician-owned outpatient facilities (particularly ASCs). The appraiser should discuss these and any other items affecting volume growth with the client and develop a good understanding of how the hospital is affected by these factors. Historical growth trends in inpatient admissions, inpatient days. and outpatient visits should be analyzed and factored into any volume projections. Also, the occupancy rate should be calculated for each projected period to ensure that projected volume growth does not exceed the hospital's capacity.

For projections of the net charge rates of the hospital, analyzing the hospital's payer mix is crucial. For instance, if a hospital has a high Medicare patient mix, its reimbursement will be greatly affected by any reimbursement changes put forth by the CMS. The Medicare reimbursement rates for the IPPS and the OPPS are updated annually and published on the CMS Web site. Likewise, a hospital with a large percentage of commercial payers will be more affected by any changes in negotiated rates or per diems. An appraiser should consider and discuss in detail with the client the contracting strength of the hospital, as well as expectations of any future changes in rates or commercial insurers.

Operating expenses should be projected based upon whether the expense is generally more fixed or variable in nature. For example, facility rent would typically be projected as a fixed expense, with inflationary increases each year. In contrast, bad debt expense or medical supplies expense should probably be projected as a percentage of projected net patient revenues or as a ratio to APD. However, some expenses contain both variable and fixed components, such as salaries and wages. One way to project salaries and wages could be to discuss with the client what level of FTE staffing would be necessary to support any projected volume growth and multiply the projected FTEs by an average salary per FTE employee, with inflationary increases to the average salary per FTE. Whatever method is employed, it is important to ensure that the growth trends in the operating expenses are reasonable compared to the growth trends in the projected volumes and revenues.

Capital expenditures of a hospital can be extremely important in the valuation. The appraiser should discuss with the client any current or planned facility expansions or large equipment purchases, such as highly specialized diagnostic imaging or cancer treatment equipment. The appraiser should also keep in mind that significant capital equipment expenditures can greatly influence the projected inpatient and outpatient volumes. In addition to any planned capital expenditures, the appraiser should also make an allowance for the replacement of the hospital's current facility and equipment.

In developing the weighted average cost of capital (WACC), the appraiser should ensure that it corresponds to the risks associated with the projected earnings stream. Specific company risk factors that either increase or decrease risk should be considered. Some of these factors may include the hospital's operating history (volatile versus stable), status of payer contracts, strength of physician relationships, presence of any certificate of need (CON) requirements, management depth, local competitive environment, and the Medicare reimbursement outlook (particularly if the hospital has a high Medicare patient mix).

### Asset Approach

Under the asset approach, the hospital's assets and liabilities should be adjusted to fair market value. One of the largest assets for a hospital is typically its real estate and related improvements. As with nonhealthcare valuations, the appraiser should consider the need to have the real estate and improvements valued by a qualified real estate appraiser.

The asset approach for a hospital valuation has some unique characteristics that differentiate it from nonhealthcare valuations. There are intangible assets for a hospital that need to be considered and valued that are not typically present for a nonhealthcare valuation. One such intangible asset is a CON.

A CON is a state-regulated license to perform certain medical services. The purpose of the CON is to ensure that health providers and services are correctly matched to the needs for those specific health providers and services in a designated area. Not every state has CON requirements, so the appraiser should research whether the hospital being valued is located in a state that has one. Obtaining a CON can be expensive and time-consuming, and in some cases, the granting of a CON can be uncertain or even impossible (due to an excess supply of providers or a moratorium). A CON is generally valued under one of two methods: (1) cost to re-create method, or (2) relief from royalty method.

Another unique intangible asset that the appraiser should consider is favorable or above-market payer contracts. This scenario may be present if the hospital has particular contracting power or exclusive contracts with payers and is experiencing above-market profits. The appraiser should discuss with the client the nature of any above-market payer contracts, the likelihood of their future status, and the potential financial impact to the hospital.

As with other nonhealthcare valuations, intangible assets such as trade name and trained and assembled workforce should be considered for valuation. However, in assigning values to these intangible assets, the appraiser must remember that patient activity (and therefore, value) for a hospital is primarily driven by factors such as facility location, services provided, insurance coverage, and medical staff.

Typically, patient files are not valued in a hospital setting, since (unlike a medical practice) the likelihood of the patient returning to the hospital for future care is either unlikely or unknown. Also, the costs of maintaining, retrieving, and being a custodian of the patient file may outweigh its future economic benefits (if any).

### Market Approach

Like nonhealthcare valuations, the market approach for a hospital is typically performed under two methods: (1) comparable transactions method and (2) guideline company method.

The best place to find comparable transactions for hospitals is in the 10-K's or 10-Q's of publicly traded hospital corporations. In addition, Irving Levin Associates Inc. publishes an annual report titled *The Healthcare Acquisition Report*, which compiles transaction information for hospitals and other healthcare providers. The appraiser can compile and sort the data based on a number of factors, including, size in terms of revenues and number of beds, geographic location, for-profit versus not-for-profit status, and number of hospital facilities.

The guideline company method can be used as a reasonableness check to the values calculated under the other valuation methods by comparing the pricing multiples (i.e., total invested capital (TIC) to revenue, TIC to EBITDA) for the publicly traded hospitals to the subject hospital's valuation multiples. The reason that this method is generally not the primary indication of value is that the publicly traded hospital corporations generally own dozens of hospitals throughout the United States and even internationally. Therefore, the publicly traded hospitals have distinct advantages over smaller hospitals, including contracting power, geographic diversity, access to capital, and ability to purchase profitable hospitals and divest low-performing hospitals. The guideline company method can also be used to give an appraiser an idea of the hospital industry's growth, EBITDA margin, and capital structure.

Some of the current publicly traded hospital corporations are as follows:

- Health Management Associates Inc. (HMA);
- Community Health Systems (CYH);
- LifePoint Hospital Inc. (LPNT); and
- Tenet Healthcare Corporation (THC).

### Reconciliation of Values

In reconciling or selecting the final value outcome for a subject hospital, the appraiser, based on his or her research, needs to consider the current transaction environment. An important consideration is whether the transaction market is active with many participants and abundant capital. In this type of environment, the most likely buyer of a hospital is another hospital or hospital system that will continue its operations as a hospital. This fact needs to be remembered when reconciling the values under each valuation approach. There could be instances where the asset approach value is higher than the values under the income or market approaches. For example, a hospital could have a large value under the asset approach if its facilities are large complexes that have a high cost to replace. For transaction purposes, the most likely buyer would be a hospital system that would continue to operate the facility as a hospital with the assets currently in place; therefore, more weight should be given to the income approach value, because it encompasses the future cash flows available to an investor from the hospital's operations. While the market approach value is generally not relied upon as a primary indication of value, due to the lack of specific information regarding the transactions (i.e., payer mix, contracting strength, level of competition, and so on), it is important for the appraiser to understand where and why his or her valuation for the subject hospital falls in relation to the observed marketplace transactions.

## Conclusion

Hospital valuations require a thorough understanding of the industry, the current hospital trends, and the various value drivers. The appraiser should stay abreast of the Medicare reimbursement environment, because it can have a significant impact on the profitability of hospitals. The more understanding an appraiser can develop of the hospital industry and its value drivers, the more sound opinion of value can be rendered.

## Resource Materials

The following is a listing of some helpful resources to consider when undertaking a hospital valuation:

- *American Hospital Association—www.aha.org*
- *Centers for Medicare & Medicaid Services—www.cms.hhs.gov*
- *Hospital benchmarking information—www.hospitalbenchmarks.com (subscription site)*
- *Irving Levin Associates Inc.—The Healthcare Acquisition Report*
- *Morningstar Inc.—Cost of Capital Yearbook*
- *IRS Form 990 Finder—www.foundationcenter.org/findfunders/990finder*
- *Merritt Hawkins Physician Inpatient/Outpatient Revenue Survey—www.merritthawkins.com/compensation-surveys.aspx*

Chapter 44

# Home Healthcare Services

*By Alan B. Simons, CPA/ABV, CFF, CMPE, DABFA*

The valuation approaches and methods used to value home healthcare businesses are no different than any other business. However, to competently value these businesses, an appraiser must understand the industry and its associated risks. In addition, a number of home healthcare providers are also nonprofit organizations or they may be sold to a nonprofit organization. Valuing transactions involving nonprofit organizations presents its own subset of issues. As a result, we will focus on what differentiates these businesses from others and what appraisers need to understand to develop a credible business valuation.

### The Industry

Home health and hospice care is a subset of all healthcare providers (such as hospitals, physicians, senior care, and so on) that further breaks down into the following five major service lines:

- Home health—skilled nursing, physical therapy, occupational therapy, speech therapy, aid service, and medical social work provided to patients in their home;
- Home hospice—care provided for terminally ill patients and their families in their homes (can also be provided in a hospice facility);
- Private duty and staffing services—home care that primarily provides home aid services;

- Home medical and respiratory equipment—durable medical equipment such as walkers, beds, wheelchairs, and oxygen concentrators; and
- Home infusion—intravenous therapies such as parenteral nutrition, antibiotics, and chemotherapy.

The goal of home health care is to provide a continuum of services designed to allow disabled or older individuals to stay in their homes for support and treatment as an alternative to assisted living, nursing homes, and hospital facilities. Proponents of home health care believe it is less expensive and a better care alternative for most people.

These services, when combined, might represent a very comprehensive home healthcare business. But, more often than not, the appraiser will be valuing businesses with fewer service lines, and often the business may be comprised of only one service line.

The profitability and risks associated with each of these service lines is driven by a unique set of variables, making it difficult to make global assumptions about the home healthcare business. The appraiser needs to develop an understanding of each service line and how these service lines interact if the subject business operates in two or more.

In some organizations, each service line can stand on its own as an independent, financially viable business. When this is the case, each business has a broad source of patient referrals independent of the other service lines. Under this scenario, each

**Acronyms and Abbreviations Used**

ADC—average daily census

ASP—average sales price

AWP—average wholesale price

CAP—community alternative programs

CBSA—core-based statistical area

CIA—corporate integrity agreement

CMS—Centers for Medicare and Medicaid Services

CON—certificate of need

HHA—home health agencies

HHRG—home health resource groups

HIT—home infusion therapy

HME—home medical equipment funding

LUPA—low utilization patients

MedPAC—Medicare Payment Advisory Commission

OASIS—outcome and assessment information set

OIG—Office of the Inspector General

PPS—prospective payment system

service line and the business as a whole would have more value than when service lines are interdependent upon each other for referrals.

For example, a service line might have no value to a potential buyer if all or most of its business was dependent on a previously related entity. If the service line is sold without the related entity, there is no guarantee that referrals (and therefore, the business) will continue. This can happen when a home health business or service line is a "captive" of a hospital or nursing home. It can also happen when a service line gets most or all of its referrals because of its relationship or proximity to one or more other related service lines. Generally, a home health business will represent the core business or service line having a broad base of referrals, and the other service lines are then added to enhance the profitability of the core business. In this case, most or all of the value may be in the core business.

Appraisers need to understand the relationship among the service lines and referral sources to understand where the value resides. This is particularly important when the business is a captive or when not all of the service lines are being sold together.

### Funding of Home Health Products and Services

Except for private duty services, most home care products and services are funded by government sources, such as Medicare and Medicaid, commercial healthcare insurance, and to a lesser extent, payments from individuals (self-pay or private pay).

Except for reimbursement by Medicare and individuals (because individuals, or "self-pay," would generally pay actual charges), the calculation and method of reimbursement for services can vary for each commercial insurance plan and for each state in the case of Medicaid. As a result, an explanation of each reimbursement system is beyond the scope of this book. However, since Medicare reimbursement is reasonably consistent and is frequently a significant percentage of a provider's total revenue, we will generally explain how Medicare reimbursement works and how it may change as of this writing.

For the calendar year 2006, Medicare paid home health agencies approximately $14.1 billion under Part A and Part B coverage for 103,980,865 visits, covering 3,302,649 patients, which means that for 2006, the average Medicare reimbursement was $135 per visit and $4,254 per patient. These are useful benchmarks in evaluating the relative performance of home health agencies.

It is incumbent upon appraisers to develop an understanding of reimbursement for the payors that drive each service line and those that drive the business being valued. While it is generally assumed that home healthcare services are provided to the elderly, it is not always the case. However, most services provided to the elderly and the disabled will be funded either directly by Medicare or through a commercial (private) payor that is being funded by Medicare Advantage plans. If and when Medicare coverage runs out, reimbursement may come directly from the individual or Medicaid for low-income beneficiaries. Younger patients may be funded through commercial insurance, self-pay, or Medicaid if they meet the requirements. Like Medicare, some states may contract with commercial insurance plans such as a Blue Cross/Blue Shield Plan, Electronic Data Systems (EDS), or other third-party payors to administer some or all of their Medicaid plans. In such cases, the state retains administrative control of allowed services, fee schedules, and other costs, and the administrator focuses on provider payment processing, claim denials, and other administrative functions. In addition, many insurance plans require some contribution (or payment) from the beneficiary.

A general discussion of how Medicare reimburses home health services and products follows.

***How home healthcare services and products are purchased***

Home healthcare treatment plans are prescribed by a patient's physician and provided by a healthcare agency (the provider). Most home healthcare products and services are funded by Medicare, particularly for older or disabled patients. A portion of home health is funded by Medicaid, for lower-income patients; commercial insurance, primarily for patients below Medicare age; and self (or private) pay, for either uninsured patients or for products or services that are not covered by Medicare, Medicaid, or insurance.

During a valuation engagement, appraisers need to understand the mix of payors to evaluate risks and whether normalizing adjustments might be required.

For example, businesses funded primarily by Medicare are at risk for changes in reimbursement (rates and coverage criteria) and age demographics for the market. Businesses funded by commercial insurance may be at risk for the economy and employee layoffs, which would reduce the population covered by commercial insurance. Businesses reliant on payment from individuals (private or self-pay) would also be dependent on the economy. Medicaid rules can be different in every state and are subject to changes in state regulations. Population growth or decline by age and income also need to be considered because it would impact the number of potential patients and how they might pay for these services in the future.

When valuing a controlling interest, the appraiser should consider whether typical normalizing adjustments (for example, owners' compensation and other perquisites or nonrecurring revenues or expenses) need to be made. In addition, normalizing adjustments to revenue might be required if the payor mix being evaluated is not normal for the market, if there are opportunities to add payors, or if the business is not billing properly or is not being reimbursed properly. Assuming these enhancements are available to most buyers in the marketplace, the adjustments would be consistent with the fair market value standard.

## Home Health Funding

### *Medicare*

Since October 2000, Medicare funds the base payment for home heath care under a prospective payment system (PPS). Under PPS, providers are reimbursed a fixed payment for services. Future reimbursement is determined by Congress and is influenced by historical industry results. Medicare pays for home health services in 60-day episodes. Most patients complete their care within 60 days. Additional 60-day episodes may be reimbursed until the patient recovers or moves to an alternative provider, such as a hospital or nursing home, or dies. Often patients are discharged from a "skilled plan of care" and obtain in-home aid, chore, and homemaker services paid for privately (private duty[1]) or possibly using Medicaid funds.

Providers (home health agencies, or HHAs) are paid one fee for each 60-day episode. Medicare adjusts payments to reflect the level of care and services required based on home health resource groups (HHRGs) and the local wage differences. It will also increase the payment for the costliest patients (outliers) and reduce the payment for patients needing significantly less than 60 days of services. If there were less than five visits in the 60-day episode (low utilization patients, or LUPAs), visits are paid on a per-visit basis using a national standard rate that is wage-adjusted based on the core-based statistical area (CBSA) location of the patient.

Medicare implemented the HHRG-153 system on Jan. 1, 2008, which utilizes 153 resource groups and replaces the prior system that used only 80 resource groups. These resource groups establish different payment rates based on patient need (acuity values) that are derived from a standardized national assessment instrument (called outcome and assessment information set, or OASIS).

Appraisers need to be comfortable that historical and forecasted revenues are reasonable based upon the payment system in effect at the time or proposed changes being

1 It is generally paid by the individual or the individual might get reimbursed through private insurance such as Long-term care insurance.

considered and the likelihood that they could become law (either Medicare or a state Medicaid program). In addition, historical and forecasted revenues could be too high or too low if the level of care provided to patients is not properly determined. However, few appraisers could make this determination without using a specialist and most appraisers will consider this outside the scope of their work. Nonetheless, appraisers should become familiar enough with the industry to understand changes in reimbursement and the associated risks so that they can evaluate management's forecast assumptions for reasonableness. Industry surveys and articles that include historical data or assumptions about the impact of future reimbursement changes may be available. Benchmarking the business against similar businesses may help appraisers determine whether historical and forecasted revenue assumptions are reasonable.

## Hospice Funding

### *Medicare*

Hospice services are available to terminally ill patients with less than six months to live. A physician must certify a patient's terminal illness to qualify for the benefit. Benefits are provided in two 90-day increments and an unlimited number of 60-day increments, but payments are subject to the caps discussed below.

Hospice agencies are paid a CBSA wage-adjusted daily rate based on the level of patient care required, which include:

- Routine home care;
- Continuous home care;
- Inpatient respite care; and
- General inpatient care.

The daily rate includes a labor and nonlabor share and is intended to cover all services provided. The payment rates are adjusted annually by a congressionally approved market basket inflation rate to account for both inflation and differences in market wage rates. Currently, the labor share is adjusted based on the hospice wage index and the nonlabor share is adjusted based on the inflation factor approved by Congress.

Total payments to a provider are limited by two caps: 1) inpatient care (for example, in a facility, not home hospice) may not exceed 20% of total patient care days and 2) an aggregate annual payment amount (an amount available to pay all Medicare hospice claims in a given year to control increasing Medicare costs) based on the number of patients electing the hospice benefit for the first time within the cap period. The hospice aggregate cap is adjusted annually by the consumer price index, but the base level of Medicare hospice funding stays constant.

Appraisers should research how these two caps might affect revenue forecasts. Longer average lengths of stay will cause the aggregate payment to be spread among more patients, thereby reducing the benefit available on a per-patient basis. If Medicare runs out of funds to reimburse hospices, providers could be liable for a repayment to Medicare for having exceeded the cap limit. If the payment system becomes inadequate to fund needed services, Medicare legislation may be proposed to change the aggregate base payment or could provide an alternate payment mechanism. The point is that this is a very tricky area, and revenue forecasts and risk rates need to be evaluated based on the facts known at the time of the valuation.

## Private Duty Funding

Private duty home care services are not funded by Medicare but may be funded through self-pay or government-funded through Medicaid and Medicaid Waiver Community Alternative Programs (CAP) and long-term care insurance.

When valuing a private-duty business, appraisers need to consider patient demographics, particularly wealth factors, to determine the potential for services and profitability. Private-duty businesses are generally more profitable in wealthier communities where patients can fund services through self-pay and long-term care insurance. A provider that is heavily dependent on Medicaid funding for in-home aid services has an increased risk of losses or low margins on this service line.

## Home Medical Equipment Funding[2] (HME)

### *Medicare*

Generally, Medicare pays the lower of 1) the average of Medicare's allowed charges for 1986 and 1987 adjusted for the consumer price index for all urban consumers and further adjusted for geographic differences in equipment prices for each state or 2) the provider's charge. State fee schedules are subject to a national floor and ceiling to limit variability. Prosthetics and orthotics are subject to regional limits. The fee is determined based upon where the beneficiary resides and not where the provider is located.

2 Payment basics, Durable Medical Equipment Payment System, Revised: October 2007, published by MedPAC.

In addition, there are the following exceptions to the general Medicare payment rule:

- Customized equipment and medications are paid at rates that are determined item by item, by the regional carrier.
- Prices for most medications used in conjunction with HME are set at 106% of the average sales price (ASP). Drugs used with infusion equipment are paid at 95% of average wholesale price (AWP).
- Prices for home oxygen are based on the median 2002 federal employee health benefit plan price.

Some of these exceptions will be discussed in greater detail in other sections.

A competitive bidding process for HME is being phased in nationwide, starting with 10 CBSAs on July 1, 2008 and expanding to 80 CBSAs by 2009 (unless delayed by Congress in a bill that is not otherwise vetoed by the president). In a demonstration project conducted between 2000 and 2002, competitive bidding lowered HME prices between 17% and 22% without serious quality or access issues. The prices from winning bidders in Round 1 of the initial 10 CBSAs (the winning bidders for the July 1, 2008 effective date) actually averaged 23% lower than the existing Part B fee schedules for HME and respiratory providers in those locales.

Furthermore, Medicare follows a policy referred to as "capped rental" in that many rented items will only be reimbursed for 13 months and the beneficiary must be given a "purchase option" at 10 months. Currently, the capped rental period for oxygen is 36 months; however, there are CMS proposals to lower it to 13 months as with other equipment, such as hospital beds and wheelchairs.

Appraisers will need to evaluate the effect competitive bidding will have on financial forecasts and how it may affect risk-adjusted rates of return. Has management adequately incorporated these changes in their forecasts and, if not, how does that affect the appraiser's key assumptions? Also when using valuation methods under the market approach, consider whether historical transactions are meaningful in evaluating businesses that are subject to a new reimbursement paradigm.

### Home Infusion Therapy (HIT) Funding

This is a very specialized service line and is fraught with regulatory complexities governing coverage and reimbursement. Many infused drugs and biologicals must be "incident to physician services," meaning that the drugs and procedures are administered under the direct supervision of a physician (e.g., drugs administered through implantable pumps). Historically, profit margins in this service line have been the highest of all home care service lines, but payment rates and margins are declining rather dramatically and driving industry consolidation even among large regional and national providers.

Increasingly, hospitals are discharging patients "sicker and quicker." To return home, some patients will require infused drugs or biologicals in their home. Many treatment regimens are of short duration (three to 10 days) and due to this, patients may frequently be discharged from an acute care hospital bed to a skilled nursing facility bed to complete the therapy treatments before being sent home.

Home infusion therapy is covered by Medicare under Part B; however, unlike home health, hospice, and home medical equipment service lines, private insurance (not Medicare) is the major payer of HIT services at this time. Private insurance companies have very competitive pricing and frequently select only a few suppliers in a geographic area for contracting (called "closed panels"). Increasingly, providers must be large in size to compete on rates, and many smaller, independent providers have been exiting the market.

#### *Medicare*

Payment rates are established by each Medicare Part B carrier based on a percentage of the average wholesale price for infusion drugs, related administration supplies, and professional pharmacist fees. As such, these services are subject to Part B coinsurance and deductibles. The Part B benefit does not reimburse for any associated nursing visits for in-home infusion administration; however, there can be additional funding available for the administration of the drug by a nurse if covered under a home health plan of care by a Medicare-certified home health provider or if covered under a state's Medicaid program or the patient's private insurance policy. If the nursing visits are not reimbursable through any of these sources, then the HIT provider can either absorb this cost or attempt to bill and collect from the patient. However, smaller HIT providers may find that charging the patient for the nursing visits could put them at a competitive disadvantage if larger suppliers (especially national providers) do not charge for this as is their standard practice. Additionally, a patient may elect to complete the required infusion therapy in a skilled nursing facility (SNF) bed with the potential for less personal financial liability because third-party coverage would be available. Often, HIT providers contract for HIT nursing services from a local home health agency.

Appraisers must be keenly aware of the service area's demographics and median incomes because collection of coinsurances and deductibles is a significant factor in supporting gross margins in this service line. Also the development, or proposed development, of other competing "locations of care" (such as a new outpatient cancer center operated by local oncologists or the development of a hospital-based or physician-owned ambulatory infusion center) can dramatically reduce a HIT provider's revenue.

### Home Health Industry Information

It is important for appraisers to compare the subject company being valued to industry benchmarks. The comparison can assist the appraiser in reaching a number of conclusions about the subject company. For example:

- Whether the subject company is being run effectively and efficiently relative to its peers;
- Whether the subject company has too much or too little debt;
- Whether the subject company has too much or too little working capital; and
- Whether the subject company is growing faster or slower than other companies, and how growth is being financed.

In addition, it is important for appraisers to understand the outlook for the industry to evaluate growth, risks, and other factors that might affect the subject company.

#### *It's all about labor*

As a service business, labor is the most important resource and cost component for most of the home healthcare service lines (home health, private duty, and hospice). If you understand labor cost and efficiency, you can generally tell how a home healthcare business is performing relative to its peers. First, it's important to know how a company's labor cost per full time equivalent (FTE) employee compares to other home healthcare businesses. Second, you need to know how productive those employees are relative to their peers. For example, according to the *Homecare Salary & Benefits Report 2007-2008* (published by the National Association for Home Care, October 2007), a registered nurse should be compensated $25.50 per hour or $33 per visit (at the median) and average 5.02 visits in an eight-hour day.

It's also important to know the provider mix (for example, registered nurses, licensed practical nurses, home care aids, physical therapists, occupational therapists, and social workers). Provider mix can tell you whether the company is too heavy or too light at various staffing levels and whether it may be missing opportunities to provide additional services.

There may be severe medical personnel labor shortages in many markets. As a result, maintaining low turnover rates is critical and should be carefully assessed during a valuation engagement. Many studies have shown that turnover costs (for example, recruitment, new employee training, and lost productivity) can increase the annual cost of an employee by 33% or more, based on the nature of the position. High turnover rates may result from noncompetitive wages and benefits, poor moral, lack of leadership, and so on.

#### *Except if they sell products*

For those service lines that sell products (home medical and respiratory equipment, and home infusion), gross profit margins are the key benchmarks. Gross profit margins can be positively affected by payor mix on the revenue side or by cost of goods sold on the expense side. By understanding what revenue and margins should be, appraisers can evaluate whether or not there are opportunities available to a hypothetical buyer (under the fair market value standard).

#### *Additional considerations for home hospice*

For home hospice services where per diem (or daily) payments frequently represent the total amount available to care for the patient (that is, there are no separate payments for additional services), it is important to effectively manage the cost of drugs, HME, and continuous care nursing or home health aid expense. Hospice providers with abnormally high costs may be overpaying for these services, and providers that have abnormally low costs may be missing out on necessary services that might attract a better mix of patients for financial success of the service line.

#### *Data sources*

There are a number of standard industry data sources (such as the Risk Management Association and Integra Information Systems) appraisers use, and there may be industry-specific sources, such as surveys developed through trade associations or industry analyses complied by consultants and financial services companies. In addition, sometimes valuable information can be found in trade magazine articles.

For example, the National Association for Home Care & Hospice (www.nahc.org) has valuable industry resources but membership is required to access some of the more substantive information.

For highly regulated industries, such as health care, there is a significant amount of information available from government agencies, think tanks, and advocacy groups.

### *MedPAC*

The Medicare Payment Advisory Commission (MedPAC) is an independent congressional agency established by the Balanced Budget Act of 1997 (P.L. 105-33) to advise the U.S. Congress on issues affecting the Medicare program. The commission's statutory mandate is quite broad: In addition to advising the Congress on payments to private health plans participating in Medicare and providers in Medicare's traditional fee-for-service program, MedPAC is also tasked with analyzing access to care, quality of care, and other issues affecting Medicare.[3]

MedPAC, in its March 2008 report to Congress, projected home health agency margins of 15.4% in 2006 and 11.4% in 2008. However, all hospital-based agencies, which would have significantly lowered these reported margins, were excluded. The report also stated that agencies should be able to absorb cost increases without an increase in base (Medicare) payments. Agencies had profit margins of approximately 9.2% to 16.7% depending on the volume and type of episode mix.

Hospital-based agencies generally have lower profit margins (around 4.9%) because of the allocation of hospitalwide overhead costs. Hospitals usually do a good job allocating direct costs. However, hospital margins would be higher if overhead costs were normalized to reflect a nonhospital agency.[4] This is a critical consideration for the appraiser when valuing a hospital-based agency. In most cases the appraiser will want to recast the agency as non-hospital-based to reflect comparable overhead costs.

CMS plans to reduce Medicare payments to HHAs each year by 2.75% in 2008 through 2010 and by 2.71% in 2011. However, HHAs will receive a 3% "market basket" increase in 2008, resulting in a net increase of 0.25% for the year, *prior to wage adjusting the labor component of the market basket for each CBSA and rural area rate of each state. The labor component is approximately 77% of the total market basket.* A few CBSAs have wage adjustment rates above 1.0, while most CBSAs and state rural areas are far less than 1.0. Thus, many HHAs will actually "net" somewhat reduced payment rates based on the above two regulatory actions. Complicating revenue forecasting even more is that past changes in PPS coding have increased payments overall. MedPAC is also assuming that the change from 80 HHRGs to 153 HHRGs will cause an overall increase in payments of 1.6% in 2008 and 2009. These changes need to be considered by appraisers when evaluating financial forecasts.

3 From MedPAC Web site www.medpac.gov/about.cfm.
4 MedPAC Report to the Congress, March 2008.

As a result, MedPAC is not recommending increases in the Medicare reimbursement rate in the near term. However, Congress will make the ultimate decision on all Medicare home health rate adjustments.

## Valuing Home Healthcare Businesses

### *The income approach*

The income approach, and more specifically the discounted cash flow method, is the valuation approach and method preferred by most appraisers to value profitable operating businesses. This method can be difficult to use for marginally profitable or unprofitable businesses if there is inadequate cash flow to provide a reasonable return on the business' assets. In that case, methods under the market or asset approach may be more appropriate.

Under an income approach, it is important to determine whether the forecasted cash flows are reasonable and achievable. If the appraiser thoroughly understands the business and the industry (as previously discussed), he or she should be able to reasonably make this determination and factor this into the development of a discount rate applicable to the cash flows forecasted for the subject company.

When evaluating forecasted cash flow growth rates, the appraiser needs to consider imminent changes and proposed changes to reimbursement, opportunities for the subject company to expand, population growth, age demographics, and age-cohort specific use rates where data might be available.

Looking at the specific operational issues affecting the company, its historical operations, and by making comparisons to industry data, the appraiser should be able to evaluate the reasonableness of future working capital needs and capital expenditures.

Care must be used in developing an equity discount rate that results in a risk-adjusted rate of return necessary to attract buyers to invest in the subject company. Appraisers need to ensure that they understand the operating characteristics (for example, size, growth rates, margins, product, and service mix) of the business or businesses from which discount rates and equity risk premiums are derived and make appropriate company-specific risk adjustments to reflect differences between the subject company and the source of these rates or premiums. In addition, there could be other changes such as new legislation, proposed or enacted, that was unknown when the market-derived discount rates or premiums were published.

Most home healthcare businesses are not capital intensive. (One exception would be a hospice with an inpatient and residential facility.) As a result, they generally do not incur (or have a need to incur) significant long-term debt. The appraiser must consider this and other factors when determining a debt-to-equity ratio for a weighted average cost of capital (WACC) assumption. Caution should be used in automatically using debt-to-equity ratios derived from publicly traded companies because they may not be "pure plays"[5] and the subject company may have significantly different operating characteristics and growth opportunities. Under the fair market value standard, the debt-to-equity ratio should be one that is reasonably achievable by the subject company and likely to provide the returns anticipated to debt and equity investors, used in the WACC, from the anticipated cash flows used in the forecast.

Appraisers need to ensure that risk-adjusted rates of returns used match the earnings stream being valued. It is generally acknowledged that most discount rates are derived from public company transactions on an after-tax basis. When valuing healthcare businesses for regulatory purposes (for example, under the anti-kickback statute and transactions involving nonprofit IRC 501(c)(3) entities), it is generally accepted that controlling interests must be valued on an after-tax basis (including pass-through entities) under the assumption that the most likely buyer is a commercial C corporation. One rationale for this is that, without having to pay taxes, nonprofit organizations could theoretically afford to pay more than a comparable for-profit organization for the same business. Valuing after-tax cash flows also keeps after-tax discount rates derived from public companies consistent with the subject company's earnings stream. Appraisers need to consider adjustments to the discount rate or methodology that might be required for nonregulatory valuation engagements and for engagements involving minority interests in pass-through entities to maintain consistency between the discount rate and the earnings stream.

#### *The market approach*

Methods under the market approach can be useful but difficult to use correctly when valuing home healthcare businesses because it is always hard to find publicly traded companies and sales transactions for companies that are truly comparable to the subject company. Unless the comparable company is publicly traded, it is almost impossible to adequately evaluate a comparable company's operating characteristics. Some comparable sales transactions may predate current reimbursement levels, economic changes, or not have anticipated proposed legislation, which might result in an erroneous conclusion about a current transaction. Furthermore, a significant number of comparable sales

5 A pure play is a company that is only in one line of business. Many public companies are in multiple lines of business.

transactions represent acquisitions by existing healthcare companies that may realize economic synergies resulting in an investment or synergistic standard of value (not fair market value if that is the standard desired).

Despite these limitations, a thorough analysis of publicly traded companies and comparable sales transactions is extremely useful in developing an understanding of the marketplace, value drivers, who the most likely buyers are, and in determining a reasonable range (low to high) to test values indicated under other approaches.

The market approach can also be useful when operating income and cash flows are indeterminable because of poor records or commingled operations or in the case of the mismanagement of an otherwise sound company. In those cases, market-derived valuation multiples that are not tied to earnings can be useful. Assuming you have reliable revenues and daily census data for the subject company, price-to-revenue multiples, or price-to-average-daily-census multiples from guideline publicly traded companies or comparable sales transactions are useful in estimating an indicated range of potential values.

For example, buyers within the industry will frequently use a multiple of patient average daily census (ADC) data to benchmark the value of these businesses. If the benchmark is $50,000 per ADC and the ADC is 200 patients, the business might be worth $10 million.

However, remember that when choosing a revenue multiple or census multiple, you are implicitly assuming that the subject company has all of the operating characteristics from which the revenue or census multiple was derived. So appraisers must be extremely careful when relying primarily on market multiples.

Developing a significant understanding of the subject company and the industry can go a long way toward overcoming the shortcomings inherent in the market approach. For example, if you can benchmark a company's revenue and direct labor costs relative to its peers, you may become more comfortable in choosing a revenue or daily census multiple.

Methods under the market approach appear simple and intuitive and therefore, have great appeal. But these methods need to be used judiciously and generally in conjunction with other approaches.

Aside from traditional public company research and general sales transaction databases, Irving Levin Associates Inc. (www.levinassociates.com) publishes *The Senior Care Acquisition Report*, which includes information about publicly announced home healthcare transactions.

### *The asset approach*

Methods under the asset approach are rarely used as the primary method to value operating companies such as home health care unless the business is unprofitable or marginally profitable when cash flows do not produce an adequate return on assets. However, methods under the asset approach should still be considered to ensure that values under other approaches (primarily the income approach) exceed values that would be developed under an asset approach, which is usually viewed as the lowest or floor value.

Under an income or market approach, the premise of value is almost always a going concern. When using an asset approach, the premise of value is sometimes more difficult to determine but the valuation methods used must be applied consistent with the premise chosen.

## Special Situations Affecting Home Healthcare Value

### *Management's integrity*

Health care is arguably the most highly regulated industry in the country. Many of the regulations facing providers today were enacted to address years of providers abusing the system and profiting illegally and unethically under government programs, such as Medicare and Medicaid, and private insurance programs.

Today, there are significant fines, penalties and the possibility of prison for violating federal and state regulations governing the healthcare industry and nonprofit organizations. While enforcement has helped to curb abuses, they still exist.

While appraisers generally are not performing due diligence, it is important for them to generally assess management's integrity. Appraisers who understand the home healthcare industry and the associated regulations also understand many of the illegal schemes and can evaluate management's integrity fairly effectively through benchmarking the company against its peers (looking for anomalies) and interviewing management (looking for inconsistencies).

The risk associated with management's integrity can impact whether revenue levels and profitability can be maintained by a hypothetical buyer who may not be willing or able to operate the business illegally or unethically. The appraiser should always require the organization being valued to disclose any and all correspondence and external audit findings that have been conducted by state licensure and Medicare-certifying organizations, Medicare and Medicaid fiscal intermediaries, focused medical review audits and findings, and any past or ongoing notifications from the Office of the Inspector General (OIG) to include past or current corporate integrity agreements (CIAs). Other useful tools to test the operational integrity of the organization is whether there is a compliance plan in place that is modeled after the OIG's suggested format as well as internal audit committee reports and findings that would be a component of the compliance plan.

The appraiser's assessment of management's integrity may create the need for normalizing adjustments and should have a direct effect on risk-adjusted rates of return used under an income approach as well as judgments made by the appraiser using methods under other approaches.

***Certificate of need (CON) states***

States may restrict or limit new home health businesses though CON legislation. Typically, these states limit CON application to service lines that are "skilled in nature" and heavily dependent on Medicare and Medicaid certification and reimbursement such as home health and hospice. However, some states also have CON regulations that govern establishment of new "licensed-only" providers that will not be Medicare-certified but will obtain reimbursements from Medicaid.

To start a new home healthcare business in a CON state, you would need to demonstrate adequate demand and need. Depending on the state, the CON process can be time-consuming and expensive. Generally, home healthcare businesses in CON states will be worth more compared to a similar business in a state without a CON. However, each state's CON rules may be more or less restrictive, and the appraiser should research the state's current plan for home healthcare services to determine whether there is opportunity for new businesses to enter the market. Even if the business is no more profitable in the CON state, the lack of new competition will generally reduce risk compared to businesses in non-CON states.

In states where CONs are very restrictive, the CON alone can be worth a significant amount of money, even without an operating business, and as a result, sometimes CONs are valued independent of the operating business.

Appraisers need to consider the effect on the discount rate when valuing home healthcare businesses in CON states versus non-CON states. When valuing a CON alone (without an operating business), appraisers should generally rely on the income approach (relief from royalty method) or possibly the cost approach, unless comparable transaction data for the CONs in the state are available. If using a relief from royalty method, consider using 25% of the expected operating margin as the pretax royalty rate. For example, if agencies are expected to earn 12% in that market, the pretax royalty rate for the CON valuation calculation would be 3% of the forecasted revenues expected if the CON were used in an operating business.

#### *Valuing provider-based home healthcare businesses*

Home healthcare businesses owned by hospitals or nursing homes are unique because they generally will not have their own financial statements or tax returns and will almost never have a balance sheet. They generally only track costs directly applicable to a department, such as home health services (such as direct supplies, compensation, and benefits) but allocate indirect overhead (such as telephone, security, maintenance, rent, utilities, human resource, and information systems) from the parent entity's total overhead. As a result, operations for provider-based owned home healthcare businesses are generally not comparable to stand-alone businesses.

Without objective financial statements (and particularly balance sheets), it is usually impossible to develop meaningful financial ratios and analysis. However, a number of operational benchmarks, such as revenue per visit, average daily census, or visits per employee, can still be developed and compared to industry benchmarks to evaluate the quality of operations.

Another potential problem in valuing a provider-based home healthcare business is that sometimes they are not motivated by profit. In some cases, the lack of profit motivation may be due to a lack of focused attention on the part of the parent entity's management, particularly if the business is a very small part of overall operations. In other cases, the business may be viewed solely for its contribution to the parent entity's mission or as part of a continuum of care. While profitability is not inconsistent with these views of the business, management sometimes uses them to rationalize underperformance. Appraisers need to understand that marginal profitability or even losses in the hands of management doesn't necessarily mean these businesses cannot be run profitably in the hands of profit-motivated management.

To value provider-based businesses, historical and forecasted operations need to be normalized and made comparable to non-provider-based or stand-alone businesses. Great care must be exercised in doing this to ensure that only controllable costs are adjusted and uncontrollable costs, which may be unique to that marketplace, are not changed. Care must also be exercised to ensure that, under the fair market value standard, adjustments are not unique to a particular buyer.

Appraisers need to develop a reasonable understanding of industry benchmarks for home healthcare businesses to support or evaluate the assumptions that will be necessary to convert the hospital-owned business into a non-hospital-owned business.

Some questions typically asked during these assignments are:

- How much space (square footage) does the business really need?
- Is the rent too high and location too expensive for the needs of the business?
- Is the business sharing management with other departments and how are those costs allocated?
- Are the parent entity's labor costs and benefits comparable to a non-provider-based business?
- Are there cost and other administrative functions that are only required because they are part of the provider-based entity (for example, Joint Commission accreditation)?
- How are patients referred for home healthcare services?

How referrals are made to a provider-based business can have a significant impact on its value—and, of course, referrals are a key regulatory risk area. For example, there is less risk of losing referrals if they come from a variety of physicians as opposed to only physicians employed by or on the staff of the parent entity. While this is a typical risk associated with a concentration of customers, it may be more prevalent for provider-based businesses. In valuing the business under a fair market value standard, the appraiser should evaluate what would change if the business were not part of, or reliant upon, the parent entity.

#### *Real estate and nonoperating assets*

Most home healthcare businesses are not capital-intensive (an exception might be a hospice that has an inpatient or residential facility). As a result, real estate and other nonoperating assets can create special problems in determining value. In particular, cash flows from the operating business often will not provide an adequate return on the real estate and nonoperating assets.

Generally, these assets should be excluded from the value of the operating business and valued separately if they are, in fact, going to be acquired as part of the transaction. These assets should be removed from the balance sheet, and their historical costs should be removed from the income statements. For those assets, such as real estate, that are used in the business, fair market value rent expense (assuming a fair market value standard) should be substituted for the cost of owning and operating the real estate. Fair market value rent for the operating business should be consistent with rents that would be paid by other home care businesses for only the square footage needed to operate a similar business within the subject company's market. Fair market value rent could be more or less than rents paid historically or agreed to prospectively.

If the valuation is being done for regulatory purposes, rent that is below or above fair market value is a potential issue that should be evaluated by a healthcare attorney familiar with applicable regulations. The appraiser should either use the actual rent in the forecasts so that cash flows reflect the positive or negative impact or fair market value rents could be used in the forecast with the incremental increase or decrease in value related to the favorable or unfavorable lease added to or subtracted from the indicated value of the operating business.

## Conclusion

Valuing home healthcare businesses is not unlike valuing other businesses except that appraisers should have a significant understanding of their operating characteristics and the industry. In addition, for any healthcare engagement, appraisers should have a reasonable understanding of regulations affecting healthcare providers and nonprofit organizations and a grasp of the current changes that may be enacted by Congress and state legislatures.

*The author would like to thank Ron Clitherow, MPH and Gary R. Massey, CPA for their significant contributions to this chapter.*

CPSIA information can be obtained at www.ICGtesting.com
Printed in the USA
BVOW08*1133071014

369479BV00003B/3/P

9 781935 081975